Computer Science and Technology

Computer Science and Technology

Proceedings of the International Conference (CST2016)

Shenzhen, China 8 – 10 January 2016

Editor

Ning Cai

Northwest University for Nationalities, China

World Scientific

NEW JERSEY • LONDON • SINGAPORE • BEIJING • SHANGHAI • HONG KONG • TAIPEI • CHENNAI • TOKYO

Published by

World Scientific Publishing Co. Pte. Ltd.
5 Toh Tuck Link, Singapore 596224
USA office: 27 Warren Street, Suite 401-402, Hackensack, NJ 07601
UK office: 57 Shelton Street, Covent Garden, London WC2H 9HE

British Library Cataloguing-in-Publication Data
A catalogue record for this book is available from the British Library.

COMPUTER SCIENCE AND TECHNOLOGY
Proceedings of the International Conference (CST2016)

ISBN 978-981-3146-41-9

Printed in Singapore

Preface

The 2016 International Conference on Computer Science and Technology (CST2016) was held in Shenzhen, Guangdong, China, from January, 8th to January 10th, 2016. CST2016 aims to provide a forum for researchers, engineers, and students to showcase their results, present their finding, and share their views in the area of computer science and technology including big data, computer systems, hardware implementation and applications.

There is a total of 321 submissions, however, only 142 articles were selected by the review committee and included in this proceedings; covering computer systems, computer network, computer security, database and information systems, artificial intelligence, software engineering, and applications.

On behalf of the chair and organizing committee of CST2016, I will like to take this opportunity to thank the keynote speakers, authors, and participants of this conference for their contributions to CST2016. In particularly, I like to express my sincere gratitude to the members of our hard working Organizing Committee, for their time and effort in reviewing and commenting on each of the articles. Without them, we could not have managed to process this vast amount of article and publish this proceedings so soon after our conference.

Hong-zhi Wang
Harbin Institute of Technology
Guest Editor (CST2016)
2016 International Conference on Computer Science and Technology

Committee

Dr. Tian Fan, North China Electric Power University, China

Co-Chair

Dr. Dong Li, North China University of Technology, China

Co-Editor

Dr. Ning Cai, Chair Professor, Discipline of Control, Northwest University for Nationalities, China
Dr. Zhihong Wang, Associate Professor, Harbin Institute of Technology, Harbin, China
Dr. Shaohui Liu, Associate Professor, School of Computer Science and Technology, Harbin Institute of Technology, Harbin, P.R. China

The Technical Program Committee

Prof. Xiaoya Gong, North China University of Technology, China
Prof. Quan Li, Tianjin Polytechnic University, China
Prof. Bingang Xu,The Hong Kong Polytechnic University, Hong Kong
Dr. Yijun Dong, Hebei University of Technology, China
Dr. Zhen Sun, Northwest University, China
Dr. Jun Xu, Northwest University, China
Dr. Huaijin Lv, Northwest University, China
Dr. Ruilin Deng, Hebei University of Technology, China
Dr. Junxi Wang, Taiyuan University of Technology, China
Dr. Qi Shen, Donghua University, China
Dr. Ying Feng, Liaocheng University, China
Dr. Shouxin Luo, Hubei University, China
Dr. Zhi Han, Hubei University, China
Dr. Weiyi Cheng, Guangdong Ocean University, China
Dr. Gang Chen, North China University of Technology, China
Dr. Rulong Li, East China University of Science and Technology, China
Dr. Zhen Zhang, East China University of Science and Technology, China

Dr. Jincai Wang, East China University of Science and Technology, China
Dr. Zijuan Yang, Tianjin Polytechnic University, China
Dr. Shuwen Zhang, Tianjin Polytechnic University, China
Dr. Jun Hu, Northeastern University, China
Dr. Shuting He, Chongqing University of Posts and Telecommunications, China
Dr. Jizheng Zhong, Southwest Jiaotong University, China
Dr. Zhi Fan, Chongqing University of Posts and Telecommunications, China
Dr. He Jiang, Hainan University, China
Dr. Maocai Xia, Northeastern University, China
Dr. Muhan Ding, Northeastern University, China
Dr. Yanshan Zhang, Southwest Jiaotong University, China
Dr. Rudi Zhang, Donghua University, China

Keynote Speech

Professor Ning Cai, PhD

Ning Cai received the B.E. degree in Control Engineering from Tsinghua University in 1996, the M.E. degree in Computer Science from Chinese Academy of Sciences in 1999, and the Ph.D. degree in Control Theory from Tsinghua University in 2010. He was in Tianjin Polytechnic University and Tsinghua University between 2010 to 2011. Since 2011, he took up as the chair professor of the control discipline at Northwest University for Nationalities. His current research interest are in robust simulation and analysis of dynamical complex systems.

Dr. Cai has published over 10 SCI indexed papers published in various international journals. He also serves as the Editor-in-Chief of the journal Equilibrium, Chaos, and Convergence in Dynamical Network, and as a senior member of Chinese Association of Automation. He was awarded the Young Talent for State Ethic Affairs Commission of China in 2013.

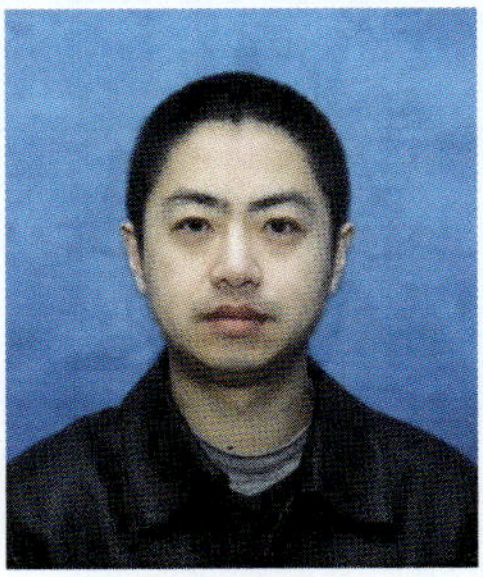

Professor Hong-zhi Wang, PhD

School of Computer Science and Technology, Harbin Institute of Technology, Harbin, China

Prof. Dr Hong-zhi Wang's research interested includes big data management, data quality, graph data management, web data management. Prof Wang have published more than 100 papers and have also been PI of more than 10 projects including three NSFC projects and co-PI of the 973 Research Program, 863 Research Program and other NSFC key projects. Prof Wang was awarded Microsoft fellowship, Chinese Excellent database engineer and IBM PhD fellowship. Dr. Wang's PhD thesis was selected as CCF outstanding PhD thesis.

Working Experiences

2015-now	Harbin Institute of Technology, Professor
2013-now	Harbin Institute of Technology, PHD supervisor
2010-2015	Harbin Institute of Technology, Associate Professor
2012.9-2013.9	UC Irvine Visiting Scholar
2011.4-2011.10	MSRA "Starring Track" Visiting Professor
2008-2010	Harbin Institute of Technology, Asistent Professor
2006.10-2007.4	National University of Singapore, Intern
2004.5-2005.4	University of New South Walses, Visiting Reserach Associate

Awards

2009, CCF Outstanding PhD thesis
2009, Outstanding PhD thesis of Harbin Institute of Technology
2007, IBM PhD Fellowship
2006, The best paper of WISE
2006, Chinese Excellent Database Engineer
2005, Microsoft Fellowship

Professor Shaohui Liu, PhD

School of Computer Science and Technology, Harbin Institute of Technology, Harbin, P.R. China
Multimedia Signal Processing and Analysis, Image/Video Coding and Processing, Supercomputing, Digital Copyright Management, Digital Forensic.
Current research interests
Image Compression in Encrypted Domain
Image Processing and Modeling
Object Detection and Tracking
Image Quality Assessment
Video and Image Encryption
Homepage: http://homepage.hit.edu.cn/pages/liushaohui

Working Experience

Associate Professor from 12/2012 Working
Experience School of Computer Science and Technology,
Harbin Institute of Technology, Harbin, P.R. China

Visiting Scholar 12/2013-12/2014
Department of Computer Science,
University of Missouri-Columbia, Columbia, Missouri, USA

Research Professor 09/2012-02/2013
Department of Computer Sciences and Engineering,
SEJONG University, Seoul, Korea

Assistant Professor 08/2007-11/2012
School of Computer Science and Technology,
Harbin Institute of Technology, Harbin, P.R. China

Contents

Session 4 Databases and Information Systems 451

Session 6: Theory and Software Engineering 971

Session 1

Computer System

Transplantation Research and Implementation of Embedded Linux System Based on S3C2440

Fu-bing WANG[1,†], Jun-ling GAO, Pan-pan LI, Sai WANG and Mei-Hua WANG

College of Electrical and Information Engineering, AnHui University of Science and Technology, HuaiNan, AnHui, China

E-mail: †1078909051@qq.com

An embedded system under the development of the microprocessor is widely applied in the world. The basis of further research and development and application is the question of how to build a small, real-time, good performance of embedded operating system. This research paper describes the methods and process of latest u-boot-2015.07, latest stable version of the linux-4.2.1 kernel, yaffs2 file system and the root file system transplant to the target board based on S3C2440 processor. The results prove that post-transplant Linux runs well on the target board. Embedded system migration not only familiarizes us with in-depth Bootloader, Linux kernel, file system and other software, but also get to know the various hardware resources of the target board.

Keywords: Embedded Linux; Bootloader; Linux kernel; Yaffs2 file system; S3C2440 processor.

1. Introduction

Today, embedded systems have become an important part of the computer field, its various products have entered all aspects of live. Embedded systems are generally defined as: application-centric, computer technology, hard-ware and software can be tailored to meet the special computer system that strictly requires reliability, cost, size, power consumption. S3C2440 with ARM920T core, using 0.13um CMOS standard cell and memory cell macros. Low power consumption, simple, elegant, and fully static design is particularly suitable for cost and power sensitive applications.

Bootloader functions directly related to the CPU and the microprocessor type, so different CPU architectures require different Bootloader. In addition, Bootloader also depends on the specific configuration of the target board related equipment, we need to make the appropriate changes bootloader to use. Linux is

---

[1] Corresponding author.

a free to use and free dissemination of class Unix operating system, is a POSIX and UNIX based multi-user, multi-tasking, multi-threading and multi-CPU supported operating systems, as an embedded operating system is the best choice .

Yaffs2 is the NAND Flash File System developed by engineer Charles Manning Yaffs1 and yaffs2 main difference is that the size of the write PAGE, yaffs2 supports 2K per page, much higher than the yaffs of 512 Bytes, so more advantage for large capacity NAND flash. Since the target board uses the k9f2g08u0c, using yaffs2 as the file system.

This paper aims to transplant the new bootloader, Linux kernel and file system to keep pace with embedded industrial developments. As industrial developments shift towards the operation of embedded user layer application program, the application and function of embedded systems can be realized.

2. Materials Preparation and Compilation Environment Buildings

The latest u-boot-2015.07can be downloaded at http://www.denx.de/wiki/U-Boot, the latest stable version of the linux-4.2.1 kernel can be downloaded at https://www.kernel.org/,yaffs2 file system can be downloaded at www.yaffs.netMajor, Ubuntu12.04 operating system is used as host. After install the arm-linux-gcc-4.3.2 cross compiler, the environment basically be build.

3. Bootloader Function and Transplantation

The first program when the PC power on runs is called BIOS, its role is to initialize the hardware, establishment of memory space map, ready for the final call to the operating system kernel. Similarly, before calling the Linux kernel, it needs to make the appropriate preparations, then transplant u-boot is to carry out the preparatory work.

3.1. *U-boot first stage modification*

The config.mk file in the source of U-boot used "LDFLAGS_u-boot + = -pie" this compiler option , resulting in a larger file code compiler out and more complex, so remove this compile option and locate the u-boot code directly in SDRAM address of 0x33f80000 and change the value of CONFIG_SYS_TEXT_BASE to 0x33f80000 in smdk2410.h file. Remove all the code in the middle of "mov r0,#0 " and "ldr pc,=board_init_r" in crt0.S file.

To make the system start faster, start ICACHE and reset the clock parameters in Start. S file. As the U-boot is not supported from NAND Flash

booting, add code in init. c file for NAND Flash booting support ,function void copy_to_sdram (unsigned char * scr, unsigned char * dest, unsigned int len) call function IsBootFromNorFlash (),determining whether Nor Flash starts, if not, call function nand_read_ll((unsigned int src),dest,len),then jump out to call function void clear_bss() to make sure the global variables can be used. In lowlevel_init.S file, depending on the target board SDRAM model DATASHEET to set 13 registers initialization parameters, then the SDRAM can be used. Start. S file has been re-set PLL before, so delete function correlated with PLL lock time in smdk2440.c files, the purpose is to start the system faster, delete as :writel(0xFFFFFF,&clk_power>locktime);
writel(M_MDIV<<12)+(M_PDIV<<4)+M_SDIV, &clk_power->mpllcon);

After the Start. S file in U-boot copy the entire U-boot code to SDRAM, then set the sp register, making the second stage of the C code can run, the entire U-boot memory usage shown in Figure 1:

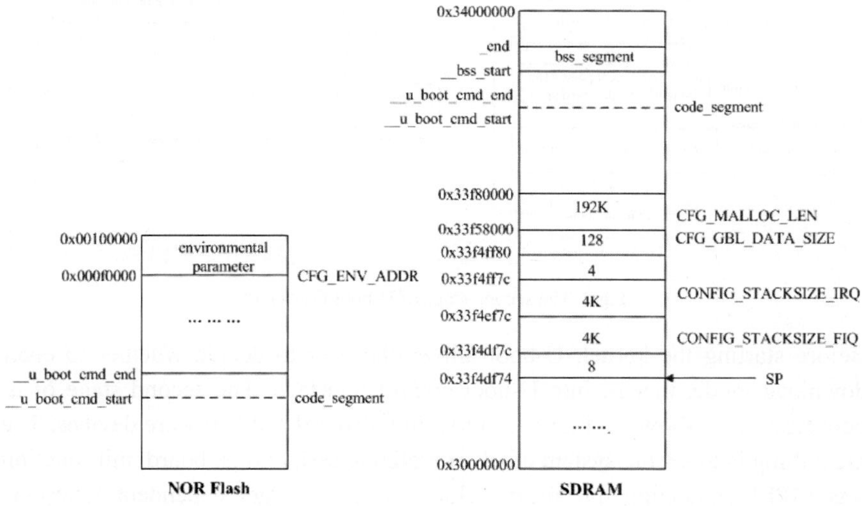

Fig.1. U-boot memory usage

Now, the operating environment of the C function has been completely ready. By the following command"ldr pc,_start_armboot"to jump directly, it calls "start_arm_boot"function in lib_arm / board.c.

3.2. *U-boot second stage modification*

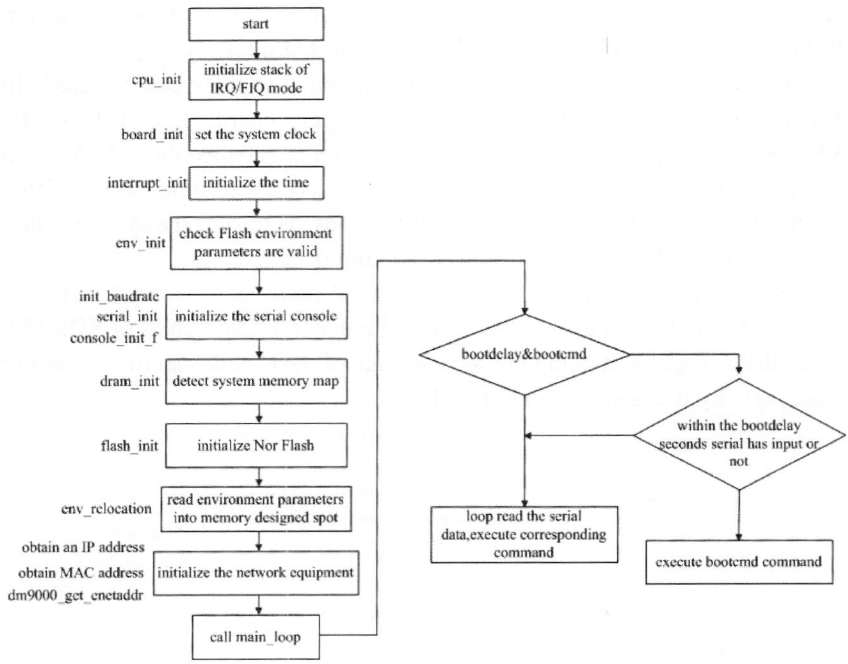

Fig.2. The second stage of U-boot flow chart

Before starting the kernel, U-boot allows the user to decide whether to enter download mode, that is, into U-boot control interface. The second stage of u-boot flow chart shows in Figure 2. First, initialize related hardware devices. The main thing is to set the system clock, initializing serial ports. board_init function sets MPLL , changing the system clock , it is the target dependent function. board_init function also stores machine Type ID : gt -> bd -> bi_arch_number= MACH_TYPE_SMDK2440; Serial port initialization function is mainly serial_ init, it sets UART control register, which is CPU related function. Implemented in the "cup/arm920t/ s3c24x0/ serial. c." Second, detect system memory map. For the target board the memory distribution is clear, set the code is as follows: int dram_ init (void){ gd- >bd->bi_dram[0].start=0x30000000;gd->bd->bi_dram[0]. 0x30000000;gd->bd->bi_dram[0].size=0x4000000;return 0;}. Third, set boot parameter for kernel. U-boot through list of tags pass parameters to kernel,I add the following two configuration items in the configuration file "include/configs/smdk2440.h".as"#defineCONFIG_ETUP_MEMORY_TAGS 1

#define CONFIG_CMDLINE_TAG 1".For the architecture of ARM CPU, by "do_boot_linux" function in the lib_arm/armlinux.c to start the kernel. Finally, the kernel is called by following function "theKernel(0,bd->bi_arch_number,bd->bi_bootparams); " .

4. Linux Kernel Transplantation

Linux boot process can be divided into two parts: architecture/board related boot process, the subsequent common boot process.ARM processor boot Linux kernel process is shown in Figure 3.

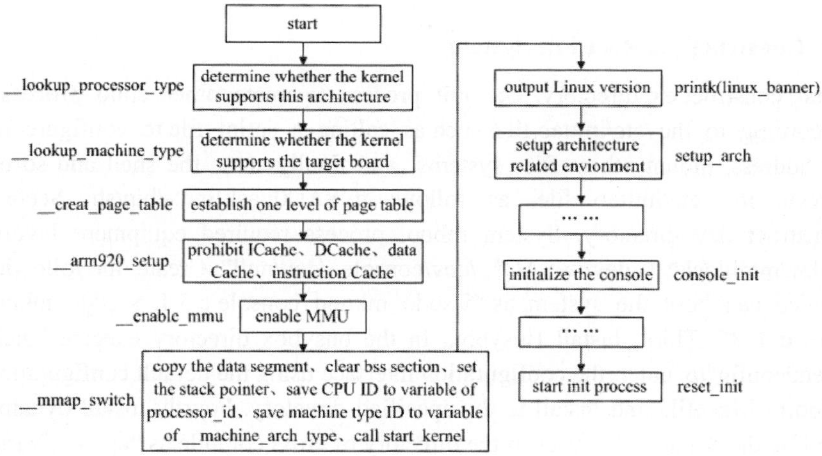

Fig.3. ARM processor boot Linux kernel process

4.1. *Modify MTD partition*

NAND Flash will be divided into four partitions, before 256K is to store the bootloader, next 128KB is for storing params, then store 2M of kernel, finally store rootfs, these are amended in "struct mtd_partition smdk_default_nand_part"

4.2. *Yaffs2 file system migration*

First, join yaffs2code into the kernel. Patch the script file "patch-ker.sh" in the directory of yaffs to the kernel, as follow "./patch-ker.sh c .../linux4.2.1",Second, modify the kernel file of "fs/Kconfig", as " #Patch by YAFFS source fs/ysffs2/

Kconfig ".Third, modify the kernel file of "fs/Makefile", as "#Patch by YAFFS obj-$(CONFIG_YAFFS_FS) +=yaffs2/".

4.3. *Configuring and compile the kernel*

Enter source code of linux-4.2.1 directory, modify the top Makefile, as "ARCH=arm , CROSS_COMPILE ? = arm - linux - ,$ make menuconfig". In the kernel configuration interface select "YAFFS2 file system support", then save default configuration and exit. Finally execute "make uImage" to compile the kernel.

5. Construct the Root File System

First, construct etc directory. The init process to create other child processes according to the /etc/inittab file, such as calling a script file to configure the IP address, mount other file systems and finally start the shell and so on. Create the etc/inittab file, as follow: ttySAC0::askfirst:-/bin/sh. Second, construct dev directory. System reboot process required equipment involve "/dev/mtdblock* *,/dev/ttySAC*, /dev/console, /dev/null". Create the following device can boot the system, as "$ sudo mknod console c 5 1, $ sudo mknod null c 1 3". Third, install Busybox. In the busybox directory execute "make menuconfig"to enter the configuration interface using the default configuration. Modify Makefile and install to the specified directory. Fourth, install dynamic lib.Use the dynamic libraries in the directory of cross compile,as "cp /4.3.2/arm-none-linux-gnueabi/
libc/armv4/lib/*so* /fs/lib -d, cp /4.3.2/arm-none-linux-gnueabi/libc/armv4/usr/lib/*so* /fs/usr/lib -d. Fifth,make yaffs2 image file.Run the following command "$ mkyaffsimage /rootfs yaffs2".

6. Write U-boot, UImage, Rootfs.Yaffs2 to NAND Flash

Through the serial port to print out the following information:

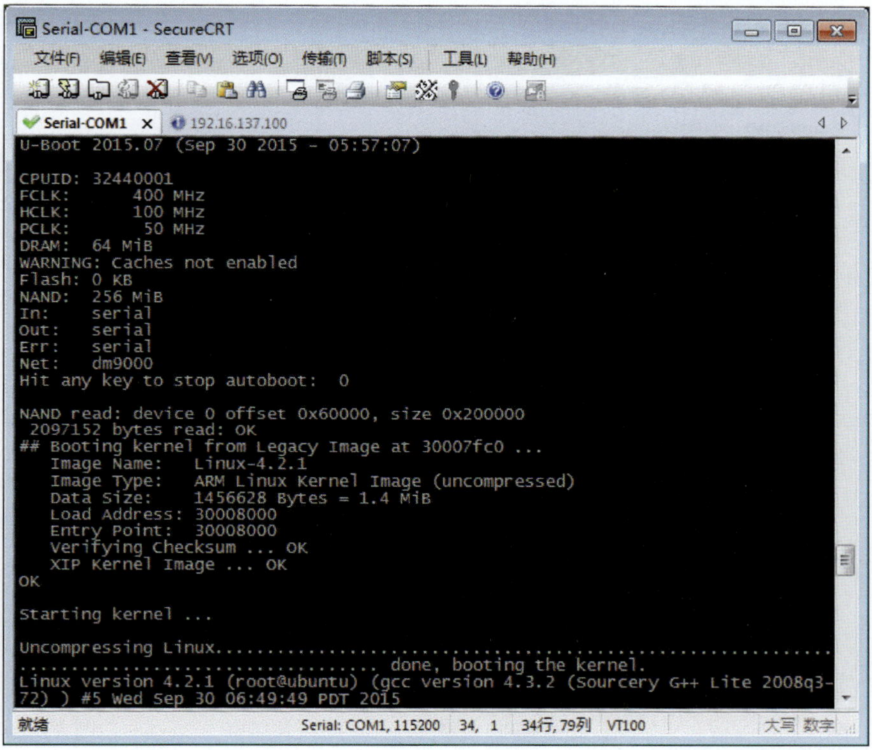

Fig 4. U-boot boot Linux kernel information

As can be seen from Figure 4 the latest u-boot-2015.07 has launched the latest stable version Linux4.2.1 kernel. Figure 5 we can see that Linux has been successfully mounted minimum file system, the entire system is running well.

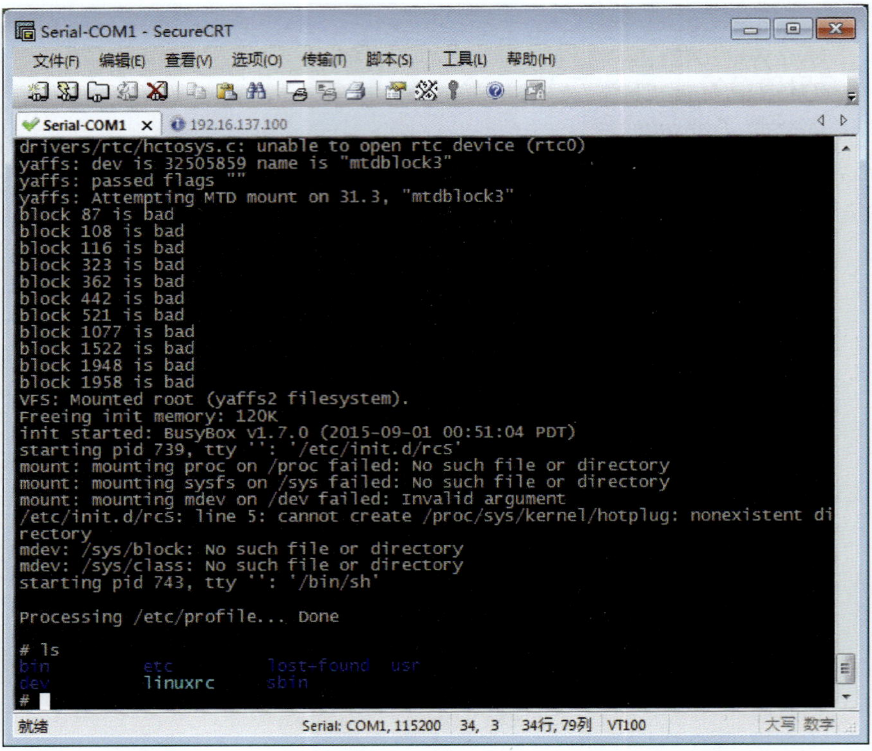

Fig. 5. Linux mounted minimum file system successfully

7. Conclusion

Embedded system migration, not only need to be familiar with in-depth understanding Bootloader, Linux kernel, file system and other software, but also get to know the various hardware resources of the target board. After the completion of building the Linux system, may further write drivers, applications running on it.

References

1. Guo-ling Zheng, Hui Li, Wei Wu, *A Based on S3C2440 transplantation research and implementation of U-boot*, In Chinese.
2. Bing Wei, Yu-tang Guo, Jie Song, Lei Zhang, *with high storage density of the new NAND device management solution* (2014).In Chinese.

3. Yi-qi Xiong, Hua Yan, Yaffs *Construction and Improvement in embedded systems*.(2012) .In Chinese.
4. Dao-qu Geng, Chun Guo, Xiao-long Li, Jun Chai, *ARM9 Embedded Linux System Transplantation Research and QoS functions to achieve*(2014),.In Chinese.
5. Dong-shan Wei, *Embedded Linux application development entirely manual* Beijing. People Post Press, 2009.
6. Jian-ze Zhang, *ARM Embedded Linux transplantation* (2010).In Chinese.
7. Ming Zhao, *Research S3C2440 Embedded Linux system migration and implementation,* (2008), In Chinese.
8. S3C2440 32-BIT CMOS MICROCONTROLLER USER'S MANUAL

The Application Research on the Irrigation Canal System Optimizing the Water Distribution Using Improved Ant Colony Algorithm

Lei-lei DENG[1]

Institute of information technology, Jilin Agricultural University,
Changchun, Jilin Province, China
E-mail: deng_ll@163.com

Bing LIU

School of computer and information technology, Beijing Jiaotong University, Beijing, China
E-mail: 342687048@qq.com

Irrigation and water conservation are an integral aspect of rural infrastructural construction but canal water distribution has a problem of low commonality in most areas of China. For example, the irrigation canal system water distribution was optimized through improved ant colony algorithm, based on the geographic information and remote sensing measurement and control technology in Da an district in Jilin province. People eventually started saving water and its production increased. In irrigation process of northern China, optimization of water distribution is of great importance in the field of agriculture. The improved ant colony algorithm can minimize the water loss of canal water distribution pattern in some constraint conditions to make the limited water resources more useful. The results are more close to reality where it is very worthy of popularizing the improved the ant colony algorithm.

Keywords: Ant colony algorithm; Optimize the water distribution; Optimize the water distribution; Water content; Picture element.

1. Introduction

In China, most region have been irrigated with the canal system except a handful of areas still rely on natural irrigation. Although Canal irrigation are widely used

---

[1] Corresponding author.

in our country, there are still some problems in the actual process of irrigation, most areas still manually operated the irrigation water allocation in canal system, which causes a lot of problems such as longtime of water delivery, invalid abandoning water and wasting water, etc. Government stressed that we should pay attention to the water conservancy project. Irrigation and water conservancy is the most task for the construction of rural infrastructure. We should transform the pattern of economic development strategy by managing the water resources strictly to make the people's livelihood better and to blaze a trail of modern irrigation road with Chinese characteristics. Improving the scheme of water distribution is imperative. Canal system optimization of water distribution consists of the reasonable arrangement of irrigation area water levels, water flow and the number of times to reduce the loss of water and increase the production. Using the improved ant colony algorithm can minimize water loss in canal water distribution pattern under some constraint conditions[2].

Ant colony optimization algorithm is a new type of heuristic search algorithm put forward by Italian scholar Dorigo in the 1990 s. Numerous studies found that the ants leave some chemicals called pheromones in the process of searching food on the places where they have been, and the same ant colony of ants can perceive this kind of material and its strength, leaving and perceiving pheromone material the is the way of communication between this is called a between information ants[3].the more intensity of pheromone trail on the road the higher probability that the ants will track this path, thus the path pheromone trail will be strengthened. A positive information feedback of phenomenon is showed by a large number of ant colony's behavior, namely the more ants passed the path, the higher probability that the other ants will choose the same path. This indirect communication mechanism help ants to cooperatively search food in the shortest path. Ant colony algorithm is widely used to solve the problem of vehicle routes, workshop scheduling problem, quadratic assignment problem and so on. In recent years, ant colony algorithm has gradually been recognized in the process of agricultural irrigation water distribution, in this paper, we used improved ant colony algorithm to achieve the optimization of water distribution in canal irrigation aiming at the low level of canal system generalization.

2. Optimization Mathematical Model of Water Distribution

2.1. *Mathematical model*

2.1.1. *Objective function*

The objective function of biggest yield increase for the irrigation area which contains varieties kinds of crops is below:

$$\Delta Y = \max \left| \sum_{j=1}^{N} \sum_{i=1}^{M} f(E)_j \left| \frac{\ln \left| \frac{\theta_0 + \theta_m - \theta_p}{\theta_f - \theta_P} \right| + 1}{\ln 101} \right|_k^{\lambda_{kj}} - \left| \frac{\ln \left| \frac{\theta_0 - \theta_p}{\theta_f - \theta_P} \right| + 1}{\ln 101} \right|_k^{\lambda_k} \right| . \tag{1}$$

2.1.2. *Constraints*

Minimum of irrigation water :

$$QT\eta_c \geq \sum_{j=1}^{N} \sum_{i=1}^{M} \frac{W_{\min ji}}{\eta} . \tag{2}$$

Supply water:

$$\sum_{j=1}^{N} \sum_{i=1}^{M} \frac{W_{ji}}{\eta} \leq QT\eta_c . \tag{3}$$

The water content of soil:

$$\theta_{\min} \leq \theta_0 \leq \theta_f . \tag{4}$$

The water content of soil after irrigation :

$$\theta_{\min} \leq \theta_0 + \theta_m \leq \theta_f . \tag{5}$$

Other constraints:

$$\theta_0 \geq 0, \theta_m \geq 0 . \tag{6}$$

Where Qis the flow of feeding water(m³/s); $\theta_{\min}$ is The low limit of soil moisture content that suitable for crops; $W_{\min ji}$ is the low limit of irrigation water of pixels of ith of jth crop; η_c is utilization coefficient of a branch of the canal; T is the time of irrigation.

Where N is the total number of the species of the crops; M is the number of pixels the j crops; Hjis the depth of soil wetting layer allowed(m); η is the utilization coefficient of bucket ditches.

3. Data Collection Using Remote Sensing Technology

Farming area is a predominantly agricultural irrigation area. The annual rainfall is 560mm,average time of sunshine is 2078 h annually, the average temperature is 13.2 °C annually, soil is cohesive, the climate is continental warm monsoon, lateral canal is 14 normal water flow allowed through is 2.0 m^2 / s. Remote sensing data is provided by the remote sensing satellite on the ground station, remote sensing image processing consists of geometric correction, radiation correction, graphics enhancement, extracting research area, gaining planting structure and soil moisture content. the degree of drought irrigation area is divided into waterlogging, proper, drought, wilting according to the information of irrigation area of soil moisture content[10-12].

4. The Solution of Improved Ant Colony Algorithm Model

This article adopts multi-objective single species of ant colony algorithm, the advantage of this algorithm is that it has more goals. This kind of algorithm has k pheromone corresponding to k path, τ_i^k is the vector of pheromone, We assume that P_k: $0 \le p_k \le 1, \sum_{k=1}^{k} p_k = 1$

Where P_k is the proportion of k objects at the initial phase of finding the solution by each ant.

A uniformly distributed random variables between o-1 are generated in the ant colony algorithm, there are:

$$P_m(i,j) = \max_{j \in L_m(i)} \left\{ \left| \sum_{k=1}^{k} p_k \tau_m^k(i,j) \right|^{\alpha} \eta_i^{\beta} \right\} (q \le q_0). \tag{7}$$

$$P_m(i,j)=\begin{cases}\dfrac{\left|\sum_{k=1}^{k}p_k\tau_m^k(i,j)\right|^{\alpha}\eta_i^{\beta}}{\sum_{j\in L_m(i)}\left|\sum_{k=1}^{k}p_k\tau_m^k(i,j)\right|^{\alpha}\eta_i^{\beta}} & (i\in L_m(i)) \quad (q>q_0).\\ 0 & j\in L_m(i)\end{cases} \tag{8}$$

Where $P_m(i,j)$ is the probability of choosing j to represent water distribution pixel by ant m in the i step; $L_m(i)$ are all of the water distribution pixels decided by the ant m in the first step I; $\tau_m^k(i,j)$ is pheromone vector of target k of j chosen by the ant m in step i. $\sum_{k=1}^{k}p_k\tau_m^k(i,j)$ is weighted sum of pheromone vector on j ; η_i is the visibility factor; α is a parameter representing the accumulated information when the ants move ; β is a parameter representing the relative importance of inspired information during choosing pixels by ants.

The intensity of pheromone will be partially updated after that an ant completes a search. Assuming pixel(i, j)water distribution pixel chosen by an ant, and the intensity of pheromone updates as follows:

$$\tau^k(i,j)=(1-\rho_0)\tau^k(i,j)+\rho_0\Delta\tau^k(i,j). \tag{9}$$

Where $\rho_0<1$; $(1-\rho_0)\tau^k(i,j)$ is the volatilization level of pheromone; $\Delta\tau^k(i,j)$ is the amount of information of the ant on the path (I, j).

The optimal solution to the current global pheromone When all the ants are completed a search is:

$$\tau^k(i,j)=(1-\rho_1)\tau^k(i,j)+\rho_1\Delta\tau^k(i,j). \tag{10}$$

The global pheromone of other pixel is :

$$\tau^k(i,j)=(1-\rho_1)\tau^k(i,j). \tag{11}$$

We regard remote sensing image pixels as the object of water distribution in the improved process of ant colony algorithm. we make the heuristic information factor α, β and η_i 1 In the process of calculation, taking the ants as pixels for water distribution, and route length is not important, $\tau^1(i,j)$ is pheromone of the increased production target. $\rho_1(0 \le \rho_1 \le 1)$ is the weight of the increased production target decided randomly before construction solution. $\Delta\tau^k(i,j)$ should satisfy.

Where $f_1(m)$ is the objective function value of water distribution scheme chosen by the m ant according to the formula (1).

There are two kinds of selected rule for formula (10):one is the pheromone of the selected path chosen by the maximum number of formula (1) updating the current ant colony algorithm, the pheromone of the selected path chosen by the maximum number of integrated goal in the forefront of improved ant colony algorithm[1].they are below:

$$\Delta\tau^1(i,j) = \frac{1}{\max f_1}. \tag{12}$$

$$\Delta\tau^1(i,j) = \frac{1}{\max I}. \tag{13}$$

$\max f_1$ and $\max I$ are the objective function (11) and a maximum of comprehensive target respectively.

Local and global updating pheromone make the ants opt the optimization yield In the process of improved ant colony algorithm, the solutions received through each iteration are kept into the optimal solution concentration, so as to obtain the optimal algorithm. [3-5]

5. Numerical Analysis to Optimize the Structure with the Aid of Remote Sensing Analysis System

Software was optimized by using improved irrigation requirement, and it will complete water distribution optimization and superposition calculation according to the remote sensing technology to obtain the current situation of irrigation district land figure, soil water content and the lateral canal control boundary figure. this algorithm regarded the soil moisture content and present situation of land use map as matrix, and treated outside of the boundary value as zero, then the model is solved with the improved ant colony algorithm in order to gain the value of all the columns of matrix. the soil moisture content when model reaches its best, then compared with the original map of soil moisture content, calculate net quantity of water used for each pixel using irrigation water and irrigation quota calculation formula combined with the lateral canal control boundary figure to compute statistically to obtain total net water within the scope of the lateral canal.

6. Conclusion

Improved ant colony algorithm optimization of water distribution in irrigation head part of irrigation canal system ultimately achieve the goal of water saving production in northeast China in the process of actual irrigation. This method optimized the irrigation canal system water distribution effectively solved the problem of low generalization degree It is of great significance in irrigation district that is shortage of water

References

1. Zhang Zhitao, Li Yuannong Chen Junying, etc. *And the ant colony algorithm based on 3 s technology of irrigation canal system optimization of water distribution [J].* (Journal of northwest agriculture and forestry university of science and technology: natural science edition, 2010)

2. Zhang Zhitao Huang Zhaoming, Li Yuannong. *Land use remote sensing image method research [J].*(2008)

3. FuYang Meng Lingge, Hu Rong, etc. Improved multi-objective ant colony algorithm in the application of power grid planning [J].(2009)

4. JJ Kattnig. *Use of innovative techniques to optimize the residence time distribution of drinking water contact tanks* (2014).

5. LP Ding,YX Feng,JR Tan,YC Gao. *A new multi-objective ant colony algorithm for solving the disassembly line balancing problem.*(2010)

6. Pan Yongchang, wang jun. Water distribution tree pipe network based on ant colony algorithm optimization arrangement [J]. (2007)

7. Duan Yonggang Wang Zhinong, tiger army, etc. 3 s and its application integration technology in irrigation area information management [J].(2007)

Research of Anti-ship Missile Warfare Simulation System Based on Component

Yong-jie WANG†, Yang SHI, Hui ZHANG and Jun-chao MAO

Scientific Research Department, Navy Submarine College,
QingDao, ShanDong 266000/ GMT+8, China
†E-mail:wyj20080601@sina.com

Our purpose was to improve anti-ship missile warfare simulation models' efficiency. We compartmentalized model component architecture according to anti-ship missile warfare logic. The Paper researched information on the interactivity and design way of model bean. According to JavaEE/EJB architecture, anti-ship missile warfare simulation system was designed as data layer, operation layer and application layer. Hence, we realized simulation system this way. The method improves effective reusability and sharing of anti-ship missile warfare simulation models. It can be applied in all kinds of weapon warfare simulation.

Keywords: Component; Anti-ship missile; Warfare simulation; JavaEE/EJB.

1. Introduction

Software engineering based on component brings forward modularization idea. The idea can be used in anti-ship missile warfare simulation to improve model efficiency. This paper selects EJB technology of JavaEE architecture to achieve distributed anti-ship missile warfare simulation.

JavaEE(Java platform Enterprise Edition) enterprise architecture is criterion of sever port EJB component based java. It can provide transplantable and normal java enterprise sever port deploy platform that is independent of platform. JavaEE carves up sideline of application program and executing base environment. By this way, developers can be absorbed in application program model and logic. At present JavaEE/EJB has been the implement standard of application server.

EJB vessel is the core of simulation model servel. It deploys and manages all kinds of model component, and accepts service request of client, and sends result back to client. So component service can be shared by all clients. Every model is realized once, but they can be used by any client. Models are avoided to explore and deploy repeatedly. Models are accordant in different domain distributed simulation system.

2. Warfare Simulation Model System of Anti-ship Missile Based on Component

2.1. *Model component framework*

At present there are many kinds of anti-ship missile. If we simulate different anti-ship missile warfare, we need establish model system repeatedly. This paper will use uniform model system to establish anti-ship missile warfare simulation system based on component technology.[2] This system will be used by different users.

According to function and logic, anti-ship missile warfare simulation model architecture includes 3: trajectory model, confront model, router planning model, circumstance model, platform model, target model, target indication model, circumstance database, missile parameter database, target parameter database and electron chart database etc. Model architecture is showed in Fig. 1.

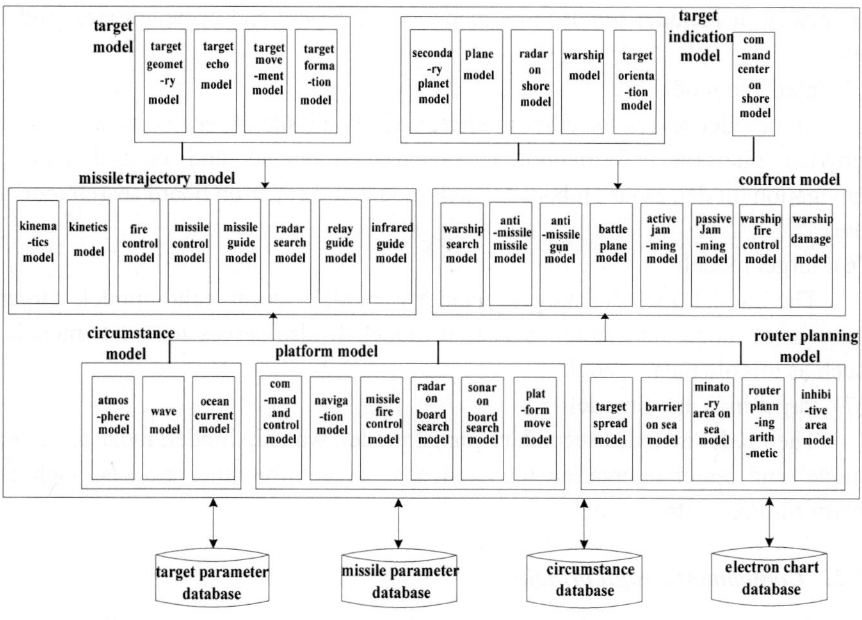

Fig. 1.Anti-ship missile warfare simulation model architecture

In figure 1, every model component's structure and function are as follows:

(1) trajectory model

Trajectory model is the basic model of anti-ship missile warfare simulation, and it is used to research shoot precision. It includes kinematics model, kinetics model, fire control model, missile control, missile guide model, radar search model, relay guide model and infrared guide model etc.

(2) confront model

Confront model is the core model of anti-ship missile warfare simulation, and it is used to research how anti-ship missile breaches kinds of weapon of warship. It includes warship search model, anti-missile missile model, anti-missile gun model, battle plane model, active jamming model, passive jamming model, warship fire control model and warship damage model etc.

(3) router planning model

The model is used to plan router for long-distance anti-ship missile and to calculate inhibitive area of missile. 4It includes target spread model, barrier on sea model, minatory area on sea model, router planning arithmetic and inhibitive area model etc.

(4) circumstance model

The model can calculate nature circumstance parameter for missile trajectory. It includes atmosphere model, wave model and ocean current model etc.

(5) platform model

The model severs for other models, such as missile trajectory model. It can provide platform information. It includes command and control model, navigation model, radar on board search model and sonar on board search model etc.

(6) target model

The model includes target geometry model, target echo model, target movement model and target formation model. It also serves for other models, such as missile radar model.

(7) target indication model

The model includes secondary planet model, warship model, radar on shore model and target orientation model. It also serves for other models, such as platform fire control model.

2.2. *Component design principle*

For the purpose that models can be used repeatedly, anti-ship missile warfare model system must observe two principles.

(1) Model component must be fine-grained for simulation precision.
(2) Connect between components must be loosely coupled for component modularization.

2.3. *Information communion of anti-ship missile warfare model component*

In anti-ship missile warfare model system, models inflect each other by information communion. Information between models is data. Some data is real. For example, the data between missile and platform fire control is actual, so there is data that is sent to missile component from platform fire control component. Some data is fictive. For example, the data between target and missile do not occur, so it is necessary to make up data between target and missile.

Not only actual information but also fictive information must be accordant with data information that occurs between anti-ship missile warfare model components.

3. Component Design of Anti-ship Missile Warfare Simulation Models System

3.1. *Bean design*

Session bean is used to achieve inner operation of anti-ship missile warfare simulation models system. It includes all kinds of bean logic operation and data transfer of different bean.

(1) stateless session bean

Stateless session bean provides stateless operation logic service for entities of anti-ship missile warfare simulation. The service need not save any data in simulation transfer. Circumstance models which have not space-time characteristic should be designed as stateless session bean. The models provide basic calculate service for other models.

(2) state session bean

State session bean's characteristic is that current model state and data are connected with historic state. State session bean's data is should be saved for other models. Trajectory model, confront model and router planning model are should be designed as state session bean.

State session bean packs model of the same type equipment, so as to keep good extensibility and maintenance. For example, different warships have different anti-missile missiles. We can design anti-missile missile model as state session bean, and pack it with ant plus in Netbeans.

3.2. *Bean realization*

(1) stateless session bean realization

In warfare simulation other models will use stateless session beans repeatedly. All entity in operation logic layer will use stateless session bean. The data that has been calculated will accomplish situation recurrence. Stateless session bean must define bean interface.

(2) state session bean realization

State session bean should maintain self-state. Bean can calculate next step self-state according to previous step. Every user has its own instance. State session bean maintains user's information in user life cycles. When user vanishes, user life cycles will be over.

(3) model bean realization

One important characteristic of EJB is that new bean can be accomplished by combination of inner interface. This insures that anti-ship warfare model bean can describe different type equipment entity by different inner bean interface.

3.3. *Bean transfer*

When bean inner operation logic is accomplished, bean should be deployed in server vessel. Client application can transfer operation logic in vessel by interface, and get simulation result.

4. Design and Realization of Anti-ship Warfare Simulation System

4.1. *System composition*

Anti-ship warfare simulation system consists of force/weapon simulation cell, JavaEE sever cell and simulation management cell. Simulation management cell allots force/weapon objects to force/weapon simulation cell dynamically.[5] Every user transfers models to generate different force/weapon.

4.2. *Simulation entity in system*

Entity is unit that behaves independently or under control in simulation environment, such as warship, anti-ship missile, gun, radar and sonar etc. Entity is base of system function, and every entity's static characteristic, dynamic characteristic and intelligent behavior is basic of all simulation actions. In this system, a few fictitious entities are generated by man-in-the-loop. A majority of entities are CGF.

4.3. *Particular design of system*

Anti-ship missile warfare simulation system based on bean adopts three layers separate mode which includes application layer, operation layer and data layer. Application layer achieves client function that includes scene display, simulation surveillance and data analysis etc. Operation logic layer achieves JavaEE sever function that includes pack bean and users requirement disposal. Data layer provides sustain for operation logic layer by circumstance database , missile parameter database, target parameter database and chart database in vessel. Fig. 2 describes bean function transfer in system.

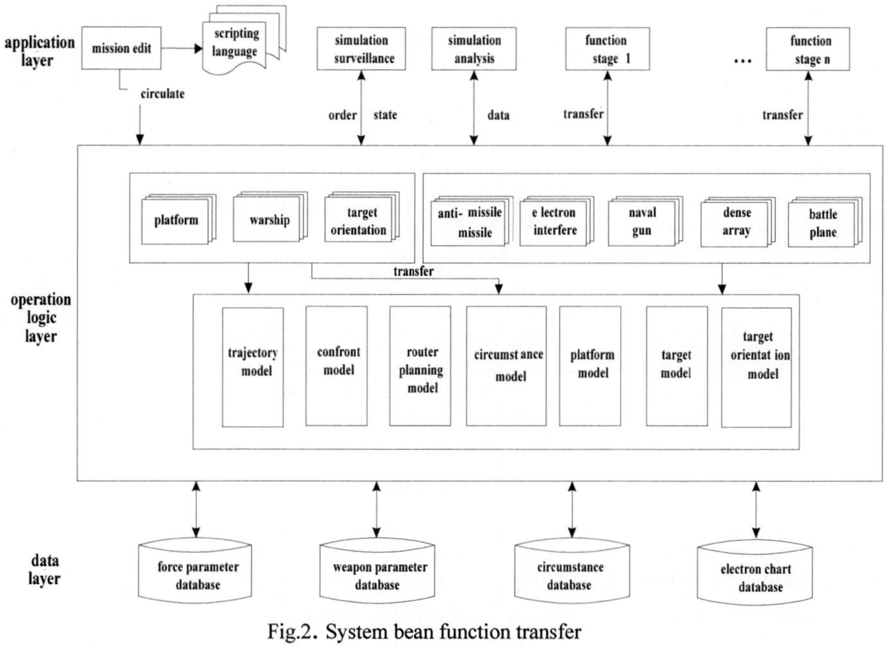

Fig.2. System bean function transfer

4.4. *System warfare simulation flow*

Anti-ship missile warfare simulation system based on bean can achieve particular type equipment entity. For example, anti-missile missile cell can generate “standard-1”, “standard-2” and “sea sparrow” missile. After system begins, user can deploy simulation cell neatly, set parameter and edit scenario.

Then every force/weapon bean user incepts user's information, and feeds back current state and target information. At the same time, "SetTime()" function is transferred to achieve simulation process. Fig.3 describes bean function simulation flow.

4.5. *System realization*

4.5.1. *Application layer realization*

Client application is composed of browser controller interface module, client total control module and client display module. Before simulation glassfish sever starts up. Client program runs, and collects with sever. Then, user sends news order by clicking on option in menu. User transfers correlative bean instance and controls simulation.

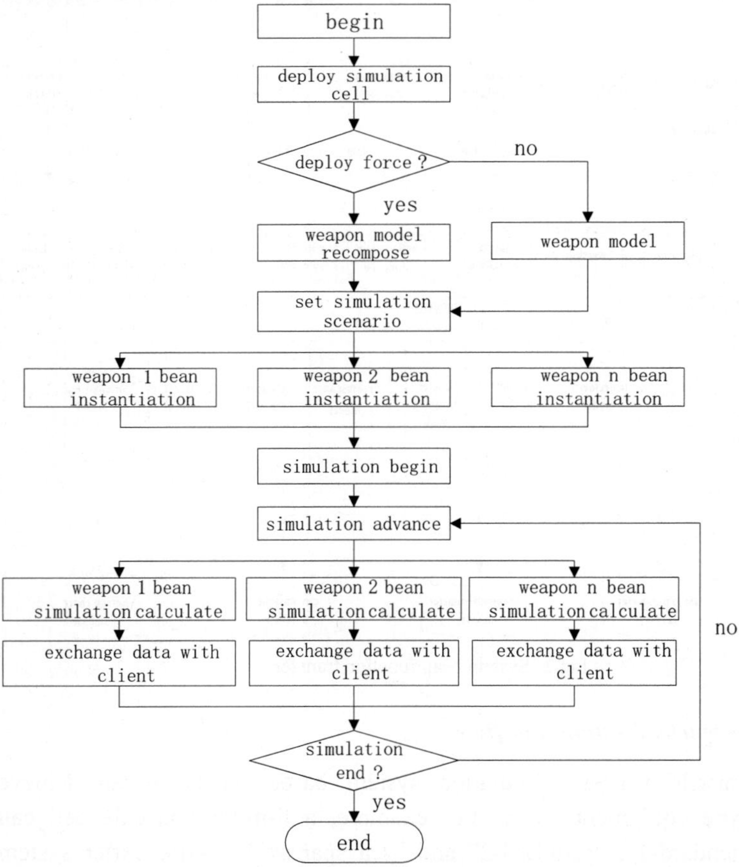

Fig.3. System simulation flow

4.5.2. *Operation logic layer realization*

In system server, there are two kinds of bean service. One is long-distance register service. It achieves simulation sever vessel function. The other provides different simulation service bean for users which is independent with simulation sever vessel. It includes warfare entity models service and management entity models service. Beans that have been designed well are deployed in server vessel. So users can inquire and transfer these beans.

In EJB service structure, users inquire bean service in vessel that they need by JNDI.[6]Bean service instance is established by entity pool interface and gets the bean entity IP. So bean instance is generated to execute corresponding function.

4.5.3. *Data layer realization*

As the base of system, data layer provides data support for beans in vessel. Simulation data is detached with simulation model. Simulation model can get data by connecting with database. For example, trajectory model can get circumstance parameter from circumstance database. We can build database named "ForceData" in MySQL, then build datasheet named ship, submarine, radar and missile etc. Models connect with data by JDBC in NetBeans.

5. Conclusion

JaveEE is new generation distributed simulation structure. Because it applies in anti-ship missile warfare simulation system, reusability and sharing of models are enhanced. In the meanwhile, simulation system can deploy cell flexibly. We need not translate little client program repeatedly, and we can deploy simulation cell client program flexibly according to simulation idiographic request.

References

1. Sun Microsystems J2EE over vie. `http://java.sun.com/j2ee/`.
2. B. Molwler, K. L. Morse, M. Lightner, R. Little, R. Lutz. *HLA Evolved - A Summary of Major Technical Improvements*, 2008.
3. Zhang Gan. Computer and Modernization, 2013, Vol.1,pp.147-148. (In Chinese)
4. Wen-jie Li. Ship Science and Techology,2012, Vol.1,pp.128-129.(In Chinese)

5. Object Management Group. *UML 2.0 Infrastructure Specification*. OMG Adopted Specification ptc.2003.
6. Matthew J. Duftler, *Paul Fremantle eds. Java APIs for WSDL (JWSDL)*, IBM Corp. Mar.21,2003.

Out-of-Band Concealment on Android

Zhi-hao WONG, Jun-sheng WEI and Mary (Rui MA)
Beijing Key Laboratory of Software Security Engineering Technique,
School of Software, BeiJing Institute of Technology,
BeiJing, China
E-mail: wfjr321324@gmail.com

Out-of-band concealment is an effective way of concealing data, but is it feasible on Android? In the paper, we will firstly study the out-of-band concealment and VFS(virtual file system), learn how the file system works, and further figure out whether out-of-band concealment can be implemented on the Android system. After analyzing the process and operations what the file system does when it truncates a file, by a series of experiments, we finally realize the out-of-band concealment on Android system. To improve survivability, we should combine out-of-band concealment with other techniques.

Keywords: Android; VFS; Out-of-band concealment; Truncate.

1. Introduction

As smart devices are more and more popular in the world, Android system, which is the main system of smart devices, is more and more important to the public. So attacks aimed at Android appeared, not only traditional Trojan and virus, but also newer rootkit etc. All these attacks need to conceal themselves to hide from scan and detection of security software, so that they can stay a while in the system. rootkit especially need to do it, as it is a "*kit for maintaining root*" [1], rootkit should make a compromised system works normally as nothing is wrong, so the most important thing for it to do is concealment. Now we want to improve concealed ability of rootkit, so we will study whether we are able to and how to accomplish the out-of-band concealment on Android system.

Out-of-band concealment places data in disk regions that are not described by the file system specification, such that the file system routines don't normally access them. If we can do it, the out-of-band concealment will help rootkit as well as other attacks conceal themselves and sensible data, make it harder to get forensic.

1. Preparation

To realize out-of-band concealment on Android system, we have to know what out-of-band concealment is, and how the file system of Android, the VFS(virtual file system)works as well.

1.1. *Out-of-band concealment*

When it comes to the out-of-band concealment, we will introduce how files are stored in disk. System allocates space for files in terms of clusters, which is a contiguous series of one or more sectors of disk space, and the size of a sector is 512 bytes. Cluster is the smallest unit of storage for a file and the data stored by the file might not always add up to an exact number of clusters, that brings some slack spaces in the disk. In the other way, the space from the logical end of file(EOF) to the end of the cluster is unused, and is useful for us. See figure 1.

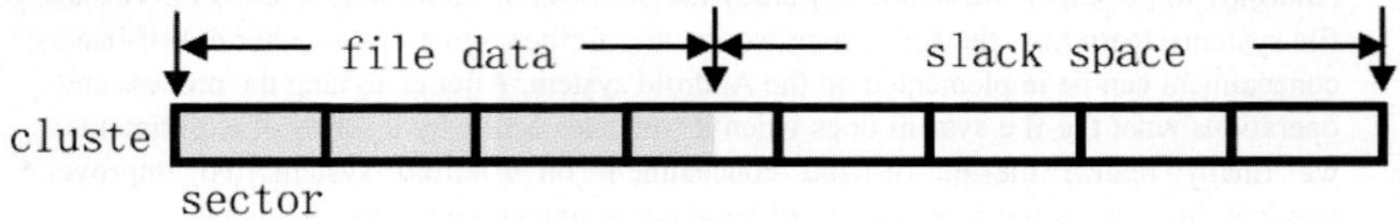

Figure 1. How file is stored in disk

The slack space has three properties that make it proper to store data we want to conceal.

(1) the clusters which contain slack space are already allocated to files, so that the slack space won't be overridden by other files.

(2) since the slack space doesn't belong to any file, the file system won't access the data stored in it, that makes the data invisible to system.

(3) the system have so many files that there are a lot of slack spaces, which are enough to store a plenty of data.

Anyway, if the file we used is always modified, the data will not be safe, so we should make use of file which are hardly modified.

1.2. *VFS*

Android system is built based on Linux kernel, and it uses VFS just like Linux.

VFS manages some actual file systems, which have different operations on data. Besides, VFS control the access and modification to data in disk by a group of objects including file and information node [2]etc. File is expressed as "*struct file*", which is mainly responsible for writing and reading. And information node is expressed as "*struct inode*". which include most information of a file, dictionary or symbolic link. Almost every file has an inode when loaded to memory except some special files such as pipe files. The inode has a member named *i_op* that is a "*structinode_operations*", which has many functions offered by the actual file systems, so they are different when actual file system changes. The inode is quite a low-level data structure, so that the VFS always manage files by operating it.

2. Study and Implementation

2.1. *Target and method*

Out-of-band concealment means that we will write data behind the EOF, and we should *ensure* that the data could be read back from the disk. We separate the concealment into three steps:

(1) open the file and set the file pointer to EOF.
(2) write data into file.
(3) truncate the file nondestructively, so that the data we wrote will be safe in the slack space beyond the EOF.

When we want to read or modify the concealed data, we need to extend the file to the end of concealed data, so that we can access the data just by general read and write operations on the file. After that, we should truncate the file again to conceal the data.

Anyway, truncate the file nondestructively is the key step. There are two functions "*truncate*" and "*ftruncate*" in VFS which can truncate files. But they will clean the data beyond the EOF, that means data we wrote in the slack space will be lost after truncating the file. Though we can't use them directly, we can find the way to conceal data successfully by analyzing the operations and flow of the functions. We will figure it out by some experiments.

2.2. *Study on VFS truncate*

To figure out what the functions "*truncate*" and "*fstruncate*" does, and which part is to alter the size of file and which part is to clean redundant data, we plan to do the operations and call the functions called during the flow directly as well as read the source codes. So firstly, we need the addresses of functions.

2.2.1. *Get addresses of functions*

We got the system source codes in assembly language by disassembling, and found that all of them were compiled as arm assembly language. In arm assembly language, they use "*b*" series instructions including "*b*", "*bl*", "*be*" etc. to call another function. All these instructions are single-operand instructions, with only a operator and a operand. Besides, arm uses RISC, every instruction has the same length, 32 bits [3], so that we can localize the instruction easily, by the address of function and the sequence number of the instruction in the function.

In the "*b*" series instructions, the operator occupies the first 8 bit3, the operand occupies the last 24 bits. The operand is the offset of the target function, coded with complementary code. Because it has just 24 bits, we need some calculation to transform it into an integer.

With the address of the instruction and the offset of the target function, we get the address of the function. See the code in figure 2.

```
unsigned long* get_thefunction(unsigned long* f, int i){
    unsigned long od=f[i];
    unsigned long offset=od;
    offset &= 0x00ffffff;
    if(offset & 0x00800000)
        offset=-((~(offset-1))&0x00ffffff);
    return f+i+offset+2;
}
```

Figure 2. code to get address of function

We have to start from a function which address is already known, so we choose the system call "*sys_fstruncate*". Its address is easily to get from *sys_call_table*, which contains all the system calls of the Android system [4]. We get the address of *sys_call_table* through another way [5].

2.2.2. *Flow and operations of truncate*

As there are different actual file systems in the VFS, such as ext, ext3 and ext4 etc. The flows in different systems are the same while the operations may be different. To simplify our experiment, we choose the ext4 as the target file system and express the flow with its functions.

The VFS do a lot of security checks to protect the system, these checks don't make sense to us, so we will ignore them in the flow, and just list the key operations and functions, as shown in figure 3.

When we truncate a file, we may start from *truncate* or *fstruncate* which will respectively call system calls *sys_truncate* and *sys_ftruncate*, but they will both go to *do_truncate* then, and finally, they will call *truncate_setsize* and *ext4_ext_truncate* of ext4 file system to finish the job. Among them, *truncate_setsize* can alter the page cache of the file, change the value of size attribute in the memory, while *mark_inode_dirty* will submit the inode to the system thread *writeback* after changing the *i_disksize*, which is the size attribute of file in the disk, and then the information of the file will be written back to the disk.

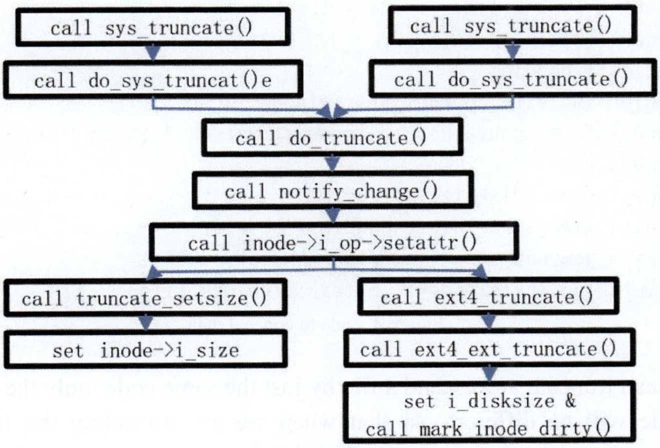

Figure 3. flow chart

Although, *truncate_setsize* will clean the redundant data in the page cache, the only operation to change the EOF is "set inode->i_size", and this is what we are concerned about. Anyway, *mark_inode_dirty* just submits the inode to thread *writeback,* and *writeback* won't clean the redundant data in the disk, so we can directly use it.

2.3. *Implementation*

Through the analysis of the VFS function *truncate*, we have figured out the flow and main operations of it. The keys to conceal data out of band are *i_size*, *i_disksize* and *mark_inode_dirty*, so we can accomplish our target by code shown in figure 4.

```
    //get the addresses of functions that we need
    struct inode* inode = dentry->d_inode;
    struct ext4_inode_info * inode_info;
    my_mutex_lock(&inode->i_mutex);//lock file
    inode->i_size=length;
    handle_t* handle;
    handle = my_ext4_journal_start(inode->i_sb, 3);
    inode_info = (container_of(inode, struct ext4_inode_info,
vfs_inode));
    inode_info->i_disksize = length;
    my_ext4_mark_inode_dirty(handle, inode);
    my_ext4_journal_stop("xxx", 123, handle);
    my_mutex_unlock(&inode->i_mutex);//unlock file
```

Figure 4. code to conceal data

We can truncate and extend a file by just the same code, only the size length set to file will be different, so that when we are truncating the file, we are concealing data, when we are extending the file, we are accessing the concealed data.

We want to simulate the situation as we has attacked the Android system and get root privilege, so we use LKM(loadable kernel module) as carrier as our code, and separate the concealment part and reading part into two LKMs, the results of the code are shown in figure 5.

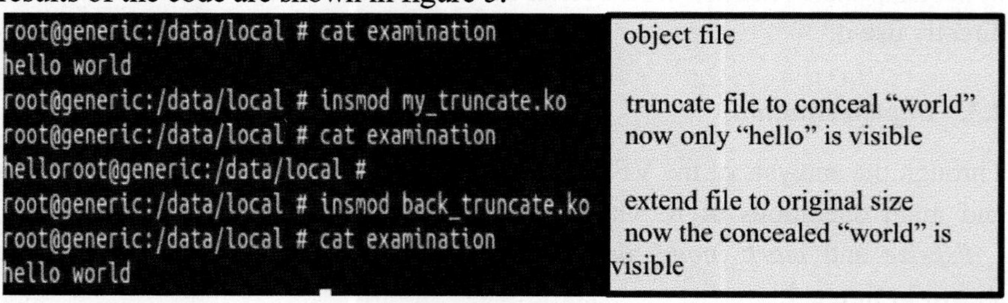

Figure 5. example of tests

As we can see from figure 5, concealing data out of band as well as read the data back is possible. Though the code is simple and deficient, it primarily accomplish the out-of-band concealment.

3. Conclusion

Out-of-band concealment can be accomplished on Android system, and it will improve the concealed ability of the attacks. But this study is defective, for:

(1) we just did experiments on ext4 the actual file system, it may not be representative enough.
(2) we send the task of writing file back to thread *writeback*, so that we can't control everything.

In addition, out-of-band concealment itself is defective too. Since VFS manages files and the disk, it can clean all the out-of-band data regularly to keep potential concealment away. So we should combine out-of-band concealment with other techniques to improve survivability.

Acknowledgments

This paper is supported by the Cultivation and Development Program for Technology Innovation Base of Beijing Municipal Science and Technology Commission under Grant No. Z151100001615034.

References

1. Bill Blundun, *The Rootkit Arsenal Escape and Evasion in the Dark Corners of the System*, 2nd edn. (China Machine Press, 2013).
2. Moshe Bar, *Linux File Systems*.(Tsinghua University Press, 2003).
3. Sloss Andrew N., Symes Dominic and Wright Chris, *ARM system developer's guide: designing and optimizing system software*. (Beihang University Press, 2005)
4. Geng-xin Sun, Chen Bin and Hai-lun Sun, *Linux Kernel Comments* In Chinese. (China Railway Publishing House, 2011).
5. Dong-Hoon You and Bong-Nam Noh, *Android platform based linux kernel rootkit*. (2011 6th International Conference on Malicious and Unwanted Software).

A Method of Fault Detection and Location with Petri Net Process

De-qin SHU[a], Hao FAN[b,*], Liang ZHANG and Cheng-ming ZHANG

College of Information Science and Engineering, Shandong Agricultural University, Tai'an, Shandong, China.

E-mail: [a]shudeqin@126.com, [b]fanhao@sdau.edu.cn

Petri net is an effective tool to analyze the operating rules of the system. Petri net process can reflect the feature of the system fault propagation. Construction and definition method of Petri net fault detection process is presented and the fault performance features in the Petri net process are analyzed. Based on the above research foundation, a method of fault detection and location with Petri net process is presented. Firstly, Petri net model with input and output for fault detection is given. Then fault detection and location method with this model is described in detail. Finally, an example of fault detection in sequential circuit is given to verify the correctness of the method.

Keywords: Petri net process; Fault vector detection; Sequential circuit; Test vector; Fault location.

1. Introduction

For a system, the analysis of its Petri net model can reveal its important information of the static structure properties and dynamic behaviors [1,2]. Based on this information, we can evaluate, improve, or verify the performance of the system. Using Petri net to do the fault detection is one of the hot issues at present. Paper [3], which is aimed at the fault of the discrete system, offered the fault detection model and the detection method of hierarchical Petri net. Paper [4] is aimed at the fault of service composition. It builds on the fault process frame of Petri net. Fault detection and processing of service composition are given. In paper [5,6], Petri net is combined with other technologies. Petri net model and method of fault detection are proposed. The fuzzy Petri net method and its improved method play a prominent role in research and application of fault diagnosis [7,8]. Paper [7] realizes fault diagnosis model and diagnosis decision by using fuzzy Petri net in power grid. Paper [8] realizes the fault diagnosis by using the method of incidence matrix reduction.

* Corresponding author.

However, for these detection models and their detection methods, there are some common features and shortcomings as follows: (1) The fault detection Petri net model only take fault factors from the system as a repository. The model broke away from the simulation system. (2) The established fuzzy Petri net models can not reflect inherent characteristic of fault spreading, and can not accurately locate faults.

Based on the dynamic nature of Petri net process, we propose a Petri net model for fault detection and give the fault description method and fault behavior description method -Petri net fault process and Petri net fault detection process. It realizes fault detection and fault location. Furthermore, this method solves the two shortcomings mentioned above.

2. Petri Net Model with Input/ Output

Here only the basic concepts of Petri net are given. Detailed information about Petri is referred to the document [9]. Petri net with inhibitor arcs (PNI) is a kind of extended Petri net in the basic Petri net introduced with inhibitor arcs.

Definition 2.1.[9] $PNI=(P_1,P_2,T,F,M_0)$ is a Petri net with inhibitor arcs. P_1 is called basic place set; P_2 is called inhibitor place set; T is called transition set; F is called flow relation; M_0 is called initial marking.

Definition 2.2. Petri net with an input /output is a quintuple: $PN/IO=(PNI,IN,OUT,F',M_0')$, where

(1) PNI is Petri net with inhibitor arcs.
(2) $IN=\{in_1,in_2,\cdots,in_m\}=\{0,1\}^m$, which is finite set, is called input table.
(3) $OUT=\{out_1,out_2,\cdots,out_n\}=\{0,1\}^n$, which is finite set, is called output table.
(4) $F'\subseteq(IN\times T)\cup(T\times OUT)$, is called flow relation.
(5) M_0': $IN\rightarrow\{0,1\}^m$, which is an input information for PN/IO net, is called input configuration marking .
(6) M_0 is called state configuration marking (initial state configuration) represents the configuration information in the PNI net.

Description of PN/IO is shown in Fig.1, Block part of which is the structure of $PNI=(P_1,P_2,T,F,M_0)$.

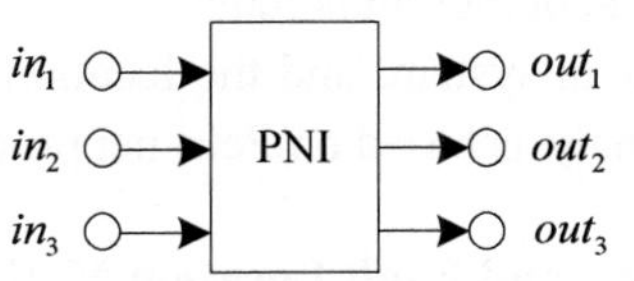

Fig.1. PN/IO description

For $PN/IO=(PNI,IN,OUT,F',M_0')$, after providing an input configuration marking M_0', the net is equivalent to a Petri net with inhibitor arcs. So, the transition initiating regular in Petri with input /output is the same as Petri net with inhibitor arcs.

3. Fault Detection Model of Petri Net

Fault detection is used to determine whether a system fault has occurred or not. Using Petri net to detect the system fault needs to establish two parallel Petri net. Let PN/IO_1 be a no fault model and PN/IO_2 be a fault model, then fault detection model of Petri net is shown in Fig.2.

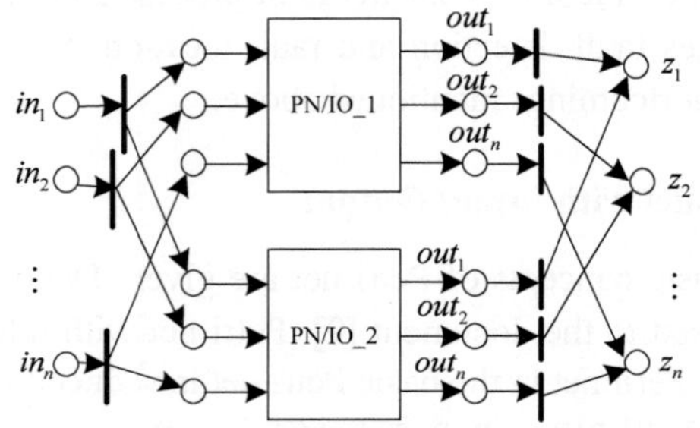

Fig.2. Petri net model of fault detection

The fault detection process is as follows:

(1) $PNI=(P_1,P_2,T,F,M_0)$, in the PN/IO_1 and PN/IO_2, is at state configuration marking (the initial state configuration is determined by M_0).

(2) Configuration information M_0' is used as input to the Petri net model of fault detection and location, that is, give 0 or 1 information to the vector $M_0'=(in_1,in_2,\cdots,in_n)$ .When the system starts running, M_0' is used as input to PN/IO_1 and PN/IO_2 at the same time. (PN/IO_1 and PN/IO_2 have the same configuration information).

(3) After receiving the configuration information M_0', PN/IO_1 and PN/IO_2 respectively run, and form different output of their own.

(4) The output information of PN/IO_1 and PN/IO_2 are concentrated in $(z_1,z_2,\cdots,z_n)$, $\forall z_i \notin (z_1,z_2,\cdots,z_n)$, if $z_i=0$ or $z_i=2$ then the output bit z_i is right, if $z_i=1$ then the output bit is faulty.

For what fault appear in system, and the location of the fault occurred, we need to give a dynamic analysis based on Petri net process.

4. Petri Net Fault Process and Fault Location Method

This section proposed the Petri net fault process and offered fault detection method.

4.1 Petri net fault process

Definition 4.1. Let $PN/IO=(PNI,IN,OUT,F',M_0')$ be Petri net with input/output, where $PNI=(P_1,P_2,T,F,M_0)$. The state configuration marking (initial marking) of PNI is M_0, for a given input configuration marking M_0', the transition in PN/IO fire. After transition fire, PN/IO generates an output while net PNI reach a new state M_1. This is called the net's first run. On this basis, then provide another input configuration marking M_0'. Net PN/IO continue the next run and repeat this run process, forming an occurred net N, which is called a process of PN/IO, noted by $E(N)$. The process of net once run is called basic process.

Definition 4.2. For a process from the beginning to the end of the $PN/IO=(PNI,IN,OUT,F',M_0')$, all input configuration marking formed the vector are called vector model. For the input table $IN=\{in_1,in_2,\cdots in_m\}=\{0,1\}^m$ is an input sequence: $V=a_1,a_2,\cdots,a_m$ that is, an input configuration marking of the PN/IO, of which the input marking width is m ,then the vector model can be expressed: $P=V_1,V_2,\cdots,V_d$, where the number of d is called vector depth. In order to make description convenient, the process is described in the following way:

Initial configuration $M_0 \xrightarrow[\text{vector model } P/\text{output } OUT]{\text{fire transition sequence } \sigma} M_1$ end configuration

Definition 4.3. Let $E(N)$ be the process of $PN/IO=(PNI,IN,OUT,F',M_0')$, if transition fault existed in $E(N)$, so $E(N)$ is called fault process. $E(N)$ is called the basic fault process if the depth of the $E(N)$'s vector model is 1.

Definition 4.4. Let $E(N_1)$ and $E(N_2)$ be the two process of PN/IO. If the two process have same vector model, $E(N_1)$ and $E(N_2)$ is called 2-process. $E(N_1)$ and $E(N_2)$ is called 2-basic-process if depth of vector model is 1. 2-process of $E(N_1)$ and $E(N_2)$ is denoted as: $B=E(N_1)\|E(N_2)$,where "$\|$" represents a parallel operation. The format B can be expressed as follows:

$$\begin{array}{ccc} E(N_1) \text{ states configuration } M_1 & & E(N_1) \text{ end configuration } M_1' \\ \text{vector model} & \xrightarrow[E(N_2)\text{ output sequence}]{E(N_1)\text{ output sequence}} & \\ E(N_2) \text{states configuration } M_2 & & E(N_2) \text{ end configuration } M_2' \end{array}$$

Regulation: $^{\bullet}B=<M_1,M_2>$ and $B^{\bullet}=<M_1',M_2'>$ represent the start state configuration and end state configuration respectively.

4.2 Fault detection method based on Petri net fault process

Based on fault detection model of Petri net in section 3 and Petri net fault process in section 4.1, here we give the method of fault detection and fault location. The steps are as follows:

Step 1. Based on the structure in Fig.2, Petri net with fault detection is established.

Step 2. Based on PN/IO_1 model, by definition 4.1, finding all the basic processes in the model of PN/IO_1 which formed basic process set E.

Step 3. Based on the PN/IO_1 model, for every fault transition, we structured all fault process and formed fault process set $\{A_1, A_2, \cdots, A_k\}$ (k is the number of faults).

Step 4. $\forall a_i \in A_i$ $(1 \le i \le k)$ form $EF = \{a_1, a_2, \cdots, a_k\}$, according to the following steps, for every $a_i \in EF$, we can construct fault detection process.

Step 4.1 For a_i, we can find a process from set E to match definition 4.4. The process can construct a 2-process B_{i1}.

Step 4.2 According to B_{i1}, we find a 2-basic -process B_{i2} that satisfy $B_{i1}^{\bullet} = {}^{\bullet}B_{i2}$ and connect B_{i1} and B_{i2}. That is $B_{i1} = B_{i1} \circ B_{i2}$.

Step 5. For the obtaining of $B_{11}, B_{21}, \cdots, B_{k1}$, we use process connection operation to construct a fault detection process. In this process, vector model is a fault detection sequence, and then we can give a fault diagnosis.

5. Example—Sequential Circuit Fault Detection

Example: Fig.3 is a binary adder which is composed of a D-trigger. Assuming that, we will detect 6 faults. The fault in position a, c, d, the name is s-a-0 fault, in the position b, e, f, the name is s-a-1.

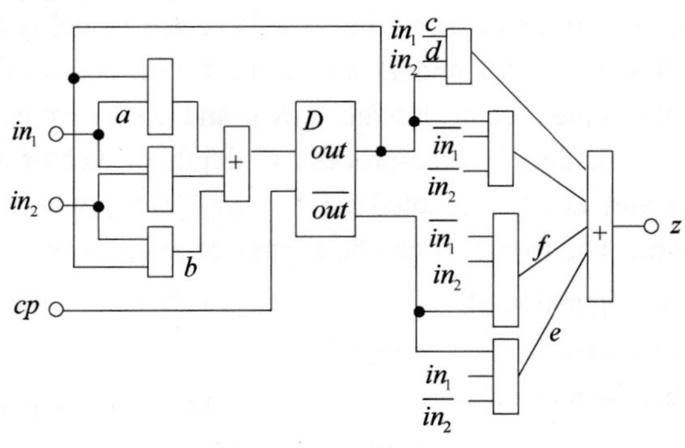

Fig.3. Sequential circuit of D-trigger binary adder

First, we need to convert the sequential circuit into the PN/IO_1 model, and then use fault process to achieve fault detection and location. For Fig.3, we can construct the Petri net model as Fig.4. Where:

(1) $PNI = (P_1, P_2, T, F, M_0)$.

(2) Input table: $IN = \{in_1, in_2\}$.

(3) Output table: $OUT = \{Z\}$.

(4) M_0' : $IN \rightarrow \{0,1\}^*$ is an input information of PN/IO net.

(5) State configuration marking M_0 , there are only two markings of PNI , $out = 0$ or $out = 1$. In order to facilitate the following description, when $out = 0$, it denote as q_0 , when $out = 1$, it denote as q_1 .

(6) t_1, t_3, t_4, t_6, t_7 are all fault transitions.

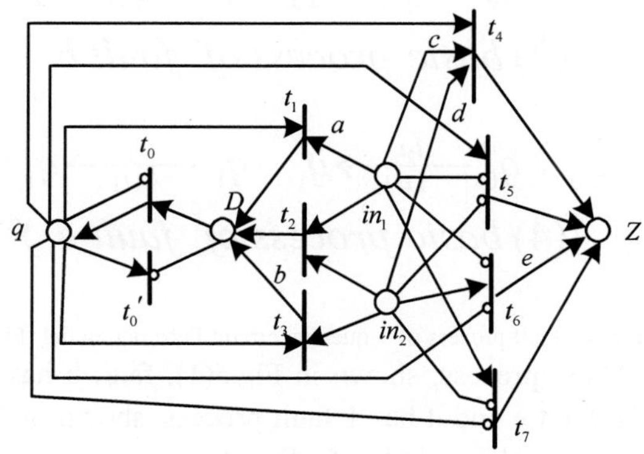

Fig.4. Sequential circuit Petri net model

Explanation: Since the different of PN/IO_1 model and PN/IO_2 model are only in fault transition amount, PN/IO_2 model can be omitted here.

After constructing PN/IO_1 model and PN/IO_2 model, the Petri net of fault detection is constructed based on Fig.2 Based on this model, fault detection and fault location of sequential circuit is as follows:

Step 1. In the model at Fig.4, we can calculate basic process. There are 8 basic processes.

$q_1 \xrightarrow[00/1]{t_5 t_0'} q_0$ *process E* $\quad q_1 \xrightarrow[01/0]{t_3} q_1$ *process F* $\quad q_1 \xrightarrow[10/0]{t_1} q_1$ *process G* $\quad q_1 \xrightarrow[11/1]{t_1 t_2 t_3 t_4} q_1$ *process H*

$q_0 \xrightarrow[00/0]{\varepsilon} q_0$ *process A* $\quad q_0 \xrightarrow[01/1]{t_6} q_0$ *process B* $\quad q_0 \xrightarrow[10/1]{t_7} q_0$ *process C* $\quad q_0 \xrightarrow[11/0]{t_2 t_0} q_1$ *process D*

Step 2. Fault process is constructed (shown in Fig.5).

$$q_0 \xrightarrow[00/0]{\varepsilon} q_0 \qquad\qquad q_1 \xrightarrow[11/0]{t_2 t_4} q_1$$

$$(1)\ basic\ process\ of\ \ fault\ a \qquad (3)\ basic\ process\ of\ \ fault\ c,d$$

$$q_0 \xrightarrow[00/0]{t_0} q_1 \quad q_0 \xrightarrow[01/1]{t_2 t_6} q_0 \quad q_1 \xrightarrow[10/1]{t_0 t_7} q_1 \quad q_1 \xrightarrow[00/1]{t_5} q_1$$

$$(2)\ basic\ process\ of\ \ fault\ b$$

$$q_0 \xrightarrow[00/1]{\varepsilon} q_0 \quad q_0 \xrightarrow[11/1]{t_2 t_0} q_1 \quad q_1 \xrightarrow[01/1]{t_3} q_1 \quad q_1 \xrightarrow[10/1]{t_1} q_1$$

$$(4)\ basic\ process\ of\ \ fault\ e,f$$

Fig.5. basic fault process of sequential circuit Petri net model (Fig.4.)

Fault a has 1fault process, shown in Fig.5(1), fault b has 4 fault process, shown in Fig.5(2), fault c and d has 1 fault process, shown in Fig.5(3), fault e and f has 4 fault process, shown in Fig.5 (4).

Step 3. For each fault, it is to construct fault detection process.

(1)The detection process of fault a is as formula (a):

$$\begin{array}{ccccc} q_1 & & q_1 & & q_1 \\ 10 & \xrightarrow[0]{0} & 11 & \xrightarrow[0]{1} & \\ q_1 & & q_0 & & q_1 \end{array} \qquad (a)$$

The description of this process show that fault a can be detected from configuration state q1 by running the test vector (10) (11).

(2)For fault b, because there are 4 fault processes, we can choose a fault process to design its detection process. Assuming to choose the first fault process, then the detection process is as formula (b):

$$\begin{array}{ccccc} q_0 & & q_0 & & q_1 \\ 00 & \xrightarrow[0]{0} & 11 & \xrightarrow[1]{0} & \\ q_0 & & q_1 & & q_1 \end{array} \qquad (b)$$

The description of this process show that fault b can be detected from configuration state q0 by running the test vector (00) (11).

(3)For fault c and d detection process is as formula (c):

$$\begin{array}{ccc} q_1 & & q_1 \\ 11 & \xrightarrow[0]{1} & \\ q_1 & & q_1 \end{array} \qquad (c)$$

The description of this process show that fault c and d can be detected from configuration state q1 by running the test vector (11).

(4)Fault e and f are similar with fault b, there are 4 fault processes. Assuming that choose the first fault process, then the detection process is as formula (d):

$$\begin{array}{ll} q_1 & q_1 \\ 01 \xrightarrow[1]{0} & \\ q_1 & q_1 \end{array} \qquad (d)$$

The description of this process show that fault e and f can be detected from configuration state q1 by running the test vector (01).

Step 4. We can connect the 4 fault detection process obtained above. We connect $b \circ a \circ c \circ d$ and then form a test vector model which length is 6.

$$\begin{array}{lllllll} q_0 & q_0 & q_1 & q_1 & q_1 & q_1 & q_1 \\ 00 \xrightarrow[0]{0} & 11 \xrightarrow[1]{0} & 10 \xrightarrow[0]{0} & 11 \xrightarrow[0]{1} & 11 \xrightarrow[0]{1} & 01 \xrightarrow[1]{0} & \\ q_0 & q_1 & q_1 & q_0 & q_1 & q_1 & q_1 \end{array} \qquad (e)$$

Test vector mode is : $(00),(11),(10),(11),(11),(01)$, the PNI configuration marking is q_0.

Step 5.The faults detection and location are realized by using formula (e) and test vector model.

The output marking sequence of PN/IO_1 is : 000110(correct output marking).The output marking sequence of PN/IO_2 can express whether there is a fault:

When output is 010110, indicate the presence of fault b;

When output is 000010, indicate the presence of fault a;

When output is 000100, indicate the presence of fault c or d;

When output is 010010, indicate the presence of fault e or f;

When output is 010110, indicate the presence of fault a and b.

Similarly, for other output, we can determine the presence of other combination fault.

6. Conclusions

We use the simulation capability of Petri to analyze the performance characteristics and transferring mechanism of the fault in the Petri net process. Petri net model of fault detection and fault process are proposed. Then a new method of fault detection and location is given. Compared with the previous methods, the outstanding advantages of this method are as follows.

(1)Good detection capability: Fuzzy Petri net fault detection is uncertainly (for some faults may not be detected). The method proposed in this paper, as long as the fault occurred, it can be detected.

(2)Accurate locating: The Petri net process can track propagation path of the fault. The fault source is easy to determined, and the fault can be accurately located.

In addition, the detection model is particularly suitable for system with fault model .The detection model in software fault model detection will be researched further.

Acknowledgments

This work is supported by Science and technology project of colleges and universities in Shandong Province (J11LG26) and Youth Science and Technology Innovation Fund Project of Shandong Agricultural University (23659) and water resources department of Shandong province project of (SDSLKY201503) and department of science & technology of Shandong province project of (2014ZZCX07106).

References

1. Cabasino M P, GIUA A, PAOLI A, et al. Decentralized diagnosis of discrete-event systems using labeled Petri nets [J]. IEEE Transactions on Systems, Man, and Cybernetics, Part A: Systems and Humans, 2013, 43(6): 1477-1485.
2. Cabasino M P, GIUA A, SEATZU C. Diagnosis using labeled Petri nets with silent or undistinguishable fault event [J]. IEEE Trans-actions on System, Man, and Cybernetics, Part A: Systems and Humans, 2013, 43(2): 345-355.
3. Dan-dan YE, Ji-liang LUO. Application of structural information of partially observed Petri net in fault diagnosis [J]. Control Theory & Applications, 2015, 32(3):366-373.
4. Jun GU, Jun-Zhou LUO, et al. Performance Modeling and Analysis for Composite Service Considering Failure Recovery[J]. Journal of Software, 2013, 24(4):696-714(In Chinese).
5. Huan FANG, Yang LU, et al. Research on fault diagnosis method of locomotives dispatching based on partially observed Petri nets[J]. Journal of electronic measurement and instrumentation, 2015, 29(5):722-729(In Chinese).
6. Jiu-fu LIU, Wen-liang LIU, et al. An improved design of online fault diagnosis for partially observed Petri net systems[J]. Control Theory & Applications, 2015, 32(7):866-872.

7. LEFEBVRE D. Online fault diagnosis with partially observed Petri nets [J]. IEEE Transactions on Automatic Control, 2014, 59(7): 1919-1924.
8. Cheng-yan XU, Yan BAI, Ren-shu WANG. The fault diagnosis of the wireless sequence control system based on fuzzy Petri nets[J]. Computer Engineering & Science, 2014, 36(8):1512-1517.
9. Zhe-hui Wu, Brief Introduction of Petri Net [M]. China Machine Press, 2006(In Chinese).

Evaluating Performance and Energy Consumption of Multithreaded Applications in cc-NUMA Multicore Processors

Min CAI, Juan FANG, Shu-ying SONG and Jun-zhong JI

College of Computer Science, Beijing University of Technology,
Beijing, 100124, China
E-mails: min.cai.china@bjut.edu.cn, fangjuan@bjut.edu.cn, songshuying@bjut.edu.cn, jjz01@bjut.edu.cn

Bin LI

Institute of Software, Chinese Academy of Sciences,
Beijing, 100190, China
E-mail: libin@iscas.ac.cn

This paper discusses the methodology used in designing and implementing a full-system cc-NUMA multicore architectural simulator based on the open source gem5 simulation framework. We analyzed the performance and power consumption of multithreaded applications in cc-NUMA multicore processors and the experimental results of the PARSEC benchmark suite demonstrated that fine-tuning cc-NUMA multicore architectural parameters such as shared cache geometry and replacement policies can lead to significant performance improvement and energy reduction of multithreaded applications.

Keywords: cc-NUMA; Multithreaded applications; Multicore processors; Performance; Energy consumption.

1. Introduction

The cache-coherent non-uniform memory access (cc-NUMA) multicore architecture becomes prevalent in high-end servers and large-scale data-center environments, due to its high extensibility and scalability. The cc-NUMA multicore processor is composed of several NUMA nodes, where each node owns its local memory plus a few CPU cores, private L1 caches and a shared L2 cache. All the NUMA nodes are then connected via some on-chip interconnect.

Consequently, accesses to the local memory will be much faster than accesses to remote memories residing in other NUMA nodes. Furthermore, compared to traditional non-NUMA multicore processors, cc-NUMA multicore processors can scale to a few dozens or even hundreds of processor cores, which prevail in the many-core era. However, there is no open source full-system simulator to model and characterize the cc-NUMA multicore architecture in detail. This paper discusses the methodology used in designing and implementing a full-system cc-NUMA multicore architectural simulator based on the open source gem5 simulation framework. Then we analyze the performance and power consumption of multithreaded applications in cc-NUMA multicore processors. Experimental results of the PARSEC benchmark suite verify the correctness of the aforementioned simulator and show that fine-tuning the cc-NUMA multicore architectural parameters can lead to great performance improvement and energy reduction of multithreaded applications.

2. Related Work

The study of the NUMA architecture is mainly focused on the high-end computing environment. Tomasz Bawej etc. [1] proposed NUMA-aware Radix Partitioning (NaRP), which optimizes the performance of shared caches in NUMA nodes to accelerate business intelligence applications. Bellasi Patrick etc. [2] discussed a portable solution to enforce efficient runtime resource management in a NUMA multicore Linux platform. Yi Liu etc. [3] designed an execution-driven full-system simulator to model NUMA systems (SimNUMA). Since the SimNUMA simulator is not open to the public, it could not be used in the experiments presented in this paper. gem5 [4] is a discrete event-driven full-system simulator and is highly configurable in that it supports various ISAs and CPU models, and is popular in use by architectural researchers. Therefore, we choose gem5 to simulate and characterize the cc-NUMA architecture in our work.

3. Methodology

We use Python scripts to extend the gem5 simulator in order to configure and connect all the components in a cc-NUMA multicore architecture. Our simulated cc-NUMA multicore architecture is built up from the multicore architecture, by adding a few caches and buses to construct and link the NUMA nodes. Fig. 1 shows the target cc-NUMA multicore architecture that we use in our work. First, we add the system bus to connect all the NUMA nodes. Then, we add two NUMA caches in each node for sending/receiving downward (D) and upward (U) requests between per-node memory buses and the system bus. In this way, memory requests coming down from per-node memory buses can be forwarded to the local memory controller or via NUMA caches to memory controllers in other nodes. Furthermore, there are I/O bridges and caches in the full system simulation mode, which are not depicted in Fig. 1.

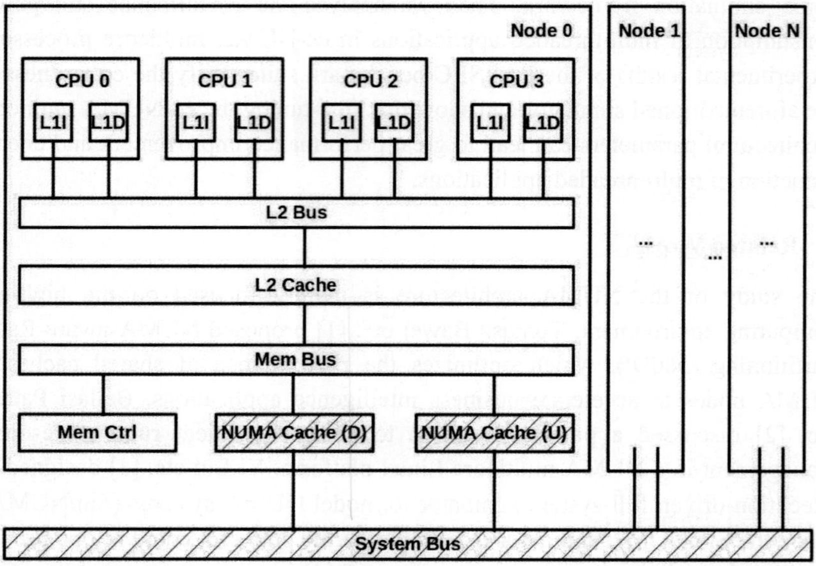

Fig 1. Target cc-NUMA Multicore Architecture

4. Experimental Setup and Results

We use the multithreaded benchmark suite PARSEC[5] to verify the correctness of our proposed cc-NUMA multicore architecture simulator. We choose the following 12 programs from PARSEC for testing: *blackscholes*, *bodytrack*, *canneal*, *dedup*, *facesim*, *ferret*, *fluidanimate*, *freqmine*, *streamcluster*, *swaptions*, *vips*and *x264*. We use the *simsmall* input sets in the PARSEC experiments. Baseline configuration are listed in Table I. To improve the full-system simulation speed, we use the atomic CPU model to boot up the Linux kernel, and then switch to the timing simple CPU model to simulate the running of the benchmark in detail. The McPAT[6] framework is used to compute the energy consumption of the simulated system from gem5 results.

Table 1. Baseline cc-NUMA Multicore System Configuration

Parameter	Value
CPU Model	ALPHA_MESI_Two_Level, TimingSimpleCPU, 2GHz
System Topology	2 NUMA nodes, 2 CPUs in each Node
L1 Caches	32kB, 2 way, LRU
L2 Caches	256kB, 8 way, LRU
NUMA Caches	1kB, 8 way, LRU
Cache Coherence	Bus based MOESI coherence
Memory	DDR3, 256MB per NUMA node

As shown in Fig. 2, we evaluate the performance and energy consumption under the different number of NUMA nodes and CPUs in each node. The total number of CPUs ranges from 2 to 16. For each program, the performance speedup is measured against the case when there are two NUMA nodes and each node has only one CPU (i.e., [2, 1] in the Fig. 2). Among all the programs, the average speedup of up to 3.5x is achieved in the case of two nodes and up to 3.6x in the case of four nodes. Especially for *x264*, its can achieve speedup of up to 14.6x in the case of 4 NUMA nodes and 16 CPUs. The system runtime dynamic energy consumption increases as the number of NUMA nodes and CPUs increase. Specifically, among all the programs, the gaps between the highest and the lowest energy consumption average 82.29%, These results indicate that the number of NUMA nodes and CPUs have great impact on the system performance and energy consumption.

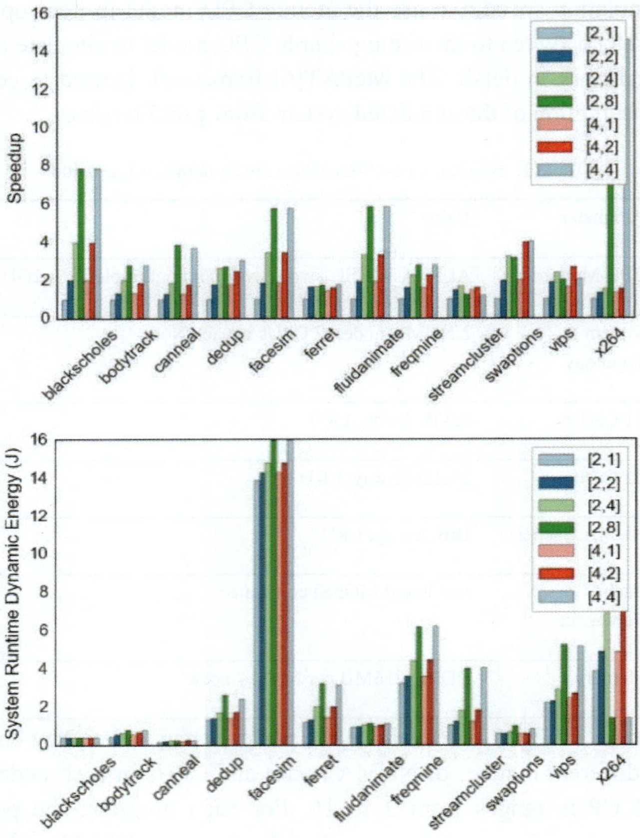

a) System Performance (b) System Energy Consumption

Fig. 2. System Performance and Energy Consumption under Different Number of Nodes and CPUs

Furthermore, we evaluate the L2 cache performance and energy consumption under the different L2 cache sizes, which is depicted in Fig. 3. As we change the L2 cache size from 256kB to 8MB, the L2 cache miss rates of all benchmarks gradually decrease. Though the L2 cache miss rate of *blackscholes* is negligibly low, the average L2 cache miss rate decreases by 25.1% among all the test programs. Especially for *streamcluster*, the L2 cache miss rate is reduced significantly by 57.8%. The energy consumption shows the similar trend, where *facesim* consumes more dynamic energy than other programs.

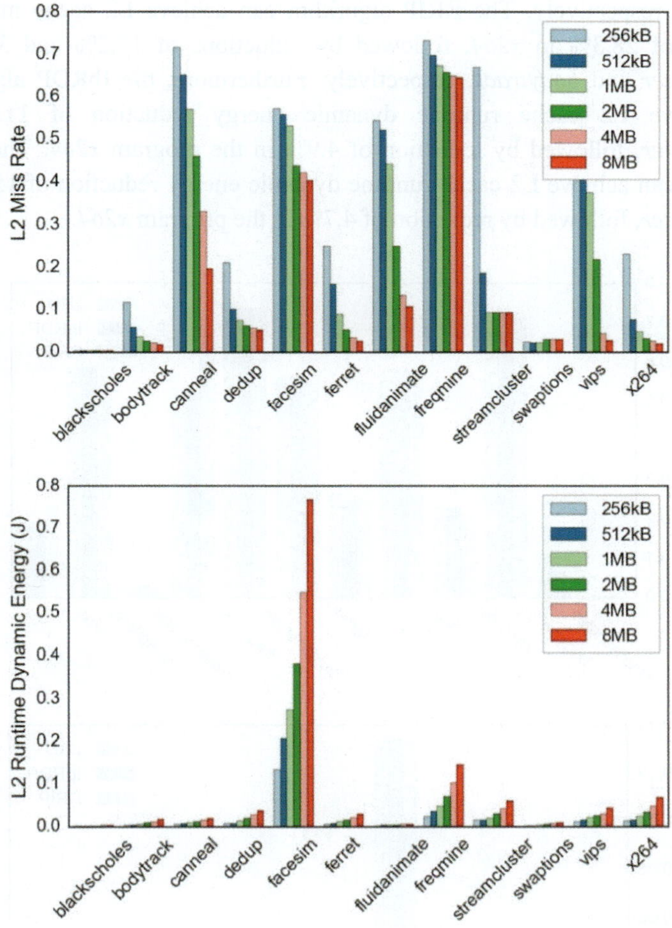

a) L2 Cache Performance(b) L2 Cache Energy Consumption

Fig. 3. Performance and Energy Consumption under Different L2 Cache Sizes

Finally, we evaluate the L2 cache performance and energy consumption when different replacement policies are applied in the L2 cache, as depicted in Fig.4. Here we consider the state-of-the-art IbRDP[7] and RRIP[8] cache replacement policies against the default LRU replacement policy. We can see that, the IbRDP algorithm can achieve L2 cache miss rate reduction of 21.5% in *streamcluster*, followed by reductions of 17.5% and 3.9% in *x264* and *bodytrack*, respectively. The RRIP algorithm can achieve L2 cache miss rate reduction of 28.3% in *x264*, followed by reductions of 17.2% and 3.2% in *streamcluster* and *bodytrack*, respectively. Furthermore, the IbRDP algorithm can achieve L2 cache runtime dynamic energy reduction of 11.6% in *streamcluster*, followed by reduction of 4.9% in the program *x264*. The RRIP algorithm can achieve L2 cache runtime dynamic energy reduction of 15.2% in *streamcluster*, followed by reduction of 4.7% in the program *x264*.

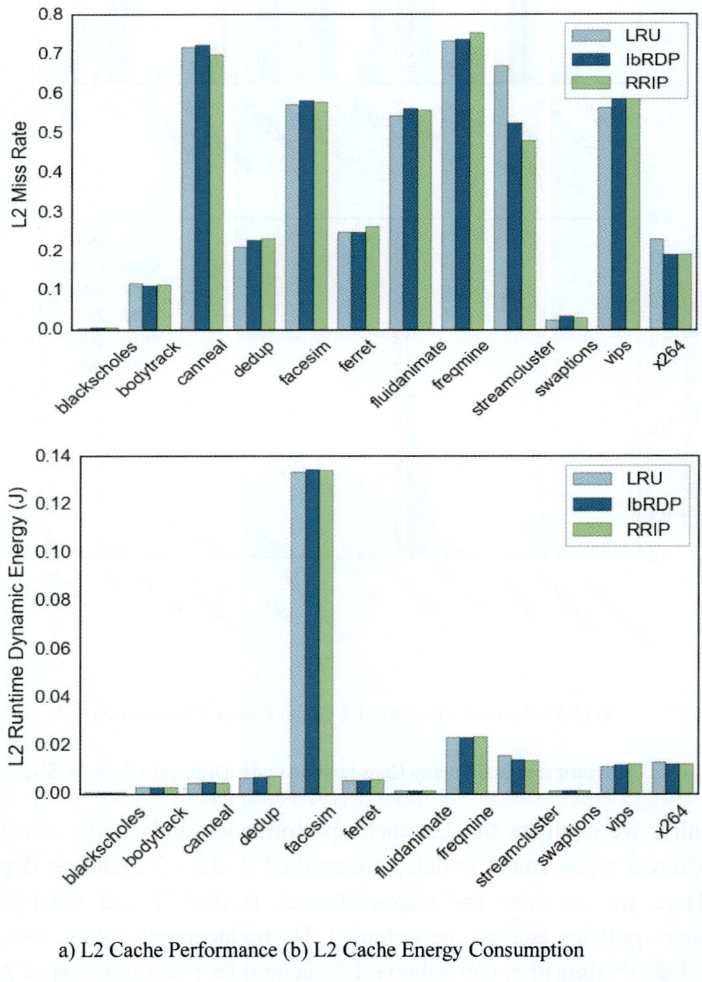

a) L2 Cache Performance (b) L2 Cache Energy Consumption

Fig.4. Performance and Energy Consumption under Different L2 Cache Replacement Policies

5. Conclusion

This paper presents an effective method to simulate the cc-NUMA multicore architecture by extending the popular gem5 architectural simulator, and then analyze the performance and energy consumption of multithreaded applications from PARSEC under different cc-NUMA multicore architecture parameters. The proposed methodology is of significant use to further studies on supporting emerging applications on scalable large-scale multicore architectures.

Acknowledgments

This work is partially supported by the Open Source Operating System Kernel Analysis and Safety Evaluation project under Grant No. 2012ZX01039-004. This research is also supported by the National Natural Science Foundation of China (Grants No. 61202076 and No.61202062).

References

1. L. Wang, M. Zhou, Z. Zhang, M.-C. Shan, and A. Zhou, "Numa-aware scalable and efficient in-memory aggregation on large domains," *IEEE Transactions on Knowledge and Data Engineering*, vol. 27, no. 4, pp. 1071–1084, (April 2015).

2. P. Bellasi, G. Massari, and W. Fornaciari, "Effective runtime resource management using linux control groups with the barbequertrmframework,"*ACM Transactions on Embedded Computing Systems*, vol. 14, no. 2, pp. 39:1–39:17, (Mar. 2015).

3. Y. Liu, Y. Zhu, X. Li, Z. Ni, T. Liu, Y. Chen, and J. Wu, "Simnuma: Simulating numa-architecture multiprocessor systems efficiently," in *Proceedings of 2013 International Conference on Paralleland Distributed Systems (ICPADS)*, (Dec 2013), pp. 341–348.

4. N. Binkert, B. Beckmann, G. Black, S. K. Reinhardt, A. Saidi, A. Basu, J. Hestness, D. R. Hower, T. Krishna, S. Sardashti, R. Sen, K. Sewell,M. Shoaib, N. Vaish, M. D. Hill, and D. A. Wood, "The gem5 simulator," *SIGARCH Computer Architecture News*, vol. 39, no. 2, pp. 1–7, (2011).

5. C. Bienia, S. Kumar, J. P. Singh, and K. Li, “The parsec benchmark suite: Characterization and architectural implications,” in *Proceedings of the17th International Conference on Parallel Architectures and Compilation Techniques*, PACT ’08. (New York, NY, USA: ACM, 2008), pp. 72–81.

6. Sheng Li, Jung HoAhn, R.D. Strong, J.B. Brockman; D.M.Tullsen, N.P.Jouppi, "McPAT: An integrated power, area, and timing modeling framework for multicore and manycore architectures," in *Proceedings of the42nd Annual IEEE/ACM International Symposium on Microarchitecture*, MICRO-42, vol., no., pp.469-480, 12-16,(Dec. 2009)

7. P. Petoumenos, G. Keramidas, and S. Kaxiras, “Instruction-based reuse-distance prediction for effective cache management,” in *Proceedings of the9th International Conference on Systems, Architectures, Modeling and Simulation*, SAMOS’09. (2009), pp. 49–58.

8. A. Jaleel, K. B. Theobald, S. C. Steely, Jr., and J. Emer, “High performance cache replacement using re-reference interval prediction (rrip),” in*Proceedings of the 37th Annual International Symposium on Computer Architecture*,ISCA ’10. (New York, NY, USA: ACM, 2010), pp. 60–71.

Method Realizing both Protocol Performance Evaluation and Validation Based on Petri Net

De-Qin SHU, Hao FAN*, Liang ZHANG and Yue LIU
College of Information Science and Engineering, Shandong Agricultural University, Tai'an, Shandong, China
*E-mail: shudeqin@126.com, *fanhao@sdau.edu.cn*

The Petri net method is a reliable and accurate way of analyzing protocol, albeit with limitations in resolving conflicts between protocol performance evaluation and the protocol validation. A methodology of using original Petri net as a model of protocol verification is proposed to solve this problem. Without changing any part of the structure of the original Petri net, the method introduces protocol performance evaluation by attaching time delay to transition, hence avoiding repeat modeling. Therefore, the model can evaluate the performance of the protocol and validate it at the same time. As an example, the paper validates 0-1 stop and wait for protocol in detail and then evaluates the performance of the protocol by translating original Petri net of 0-1 stop and wait for protocol into timed Petri net.

Keywords: Protocol performance evaluation; Protocol validation; Petri net; Timed Petri net; QoS

1. Introduction

The protocol validation aims to the detection and correction of the protocol errors and defects before its realization [1, 2]. While the protocol performance evaluation mainly aims to evaluate the throughput, data transmission delay which is of vital importance to the qualities of service(QoS) of the protocol[3].

The Petri Net method is a reliable and accurate way of analyzing protocol [4]. In reference [5], the author has made Petri net model of SIP protocol and made consistency analysis to the SIP protocol in mobile networks. And in reference [6,7], The author has made a reach ability analysis to the unsafe state by way of state equation. And in reference[8], the author has made full use of stochastic Petri net to evaluate the service performance quality of VoIP.

Though many results regarding the Petri net analysis method of protocols are already fruitful, there are still conflicts existing between the protocol validation and its performance evaluation. On one hand, the protocol validation model can not make an instant quantitative analysis of the protocol performance;

*Corresponding author.

On the other, the performance evaluation model can not reflect the various static characteristics and dynamic behaviors of the protocol. Based on the above analysis, this paper proposes a method realizing both protocol performance evaluation and protocol validation based on Petri net. It first proposes to establish original Petri net model of the protocol, finishing the protocol validation and then to fulfill protocol performance evaluation by attaching time delay to transition, without changing any part of the model structure. As an example, the paper provides the original Petri net model and timed Petri net model to 0-1 stop and wait for protocol, thus making protocol validation and its performance evaluation for the protocol.

2. The Basic Conception of Petri Net

For the basic concepts of Petri net, please refer to the reference [9].

Definition 1[9] Let $\Sigma = (P,T,F,M_0)$ be a Petri net, $s \in S$, suppose there exists a positive integer B, such that $\forall M \in R(M_0): M(s) \le B$, then the place s is called bounded, and the smallest positive integer B, which meets this condition, is called the bound of place s, marked as $B(s)$. That is, $B(s) = \min\{B \mid \forall M \in R(M_0): M(s) \le B\}$, when $B(s) = 1$, the place s is called safe.

Definition 2[9] Let $\Sigma = (P,T,F,M_0)$ be a Petri net, $t \in T$. Suppose for $\forall M \in R(M_0)$, there exists $\sigma \in T^*$, such that $M[\sigma > M'$ and $M'[t >$, then t is live. If each transition in a Petri net is alive, then the whole net is alive.

Definition 3[9] Let $N = (P,T;F)$ be a Petri net, $P| = m$, $T| = n$, A is the incidence matrix of *N*.

1) If nontrivial m-dimension nonnegative integer vector *Y*, that is satisfied $AY = 0$, then Y is called an $P-$ invariant of the net *N*.

2) If nontrivial n-dimension nonnegative integer vector X, that is satisfied $A^T X = 0$, then X is called an $T-$ invariant of the net N.

Definition 4[9] Timed Petri net is a set with five elements: $TPN = (P,T,F,\tau,M)$, where P,T,F have the same meaning with P,T,F in definition 1. τ is time mapping function $\tau \to 0 \cup Q^+$ (Q^+ is positive rational number), it defines duration time of each transition. If the duration time is 0, it is called instantaneous transition, otherwise (duration time is not 0), it is called timed transition. $M: P \to \{0,1,2,\cdots\}$ is the net marking.

3. Protocol Validation and Protocol Performance Evaluation

3.1. *Protocol validation*

Many specialties of the Petri net can find its actual physical meaning in the protocol(see Table 1).

(1) Static analysis

The static analysis mainly refers to the analysis of the structural characteristics of the protocol: structure-activity, boundedness, P-invariants, T-invariants, etc. For instance, P-invariants mean that the resources (data frame, response frame) of the protocols are safe. By analyzing the topology features of the Petri net, we can analyze many properties of the protocol.

(2) Dynamic analysis

It is to analyze the dynamic features of the protocol, such as action sequences, reachability, etc. The reachability graph of Petri net, can analyze the accessibility (from one state to another), action sequences, the recoverability of the protocol error state, etc.

Table 1 the contents of protocol validity and analyzing methods

the contents of protocol validity	Petri net analyzing property
Accessibility among protocol state	reachability analysis
deadlock	The liveness, deadlock and trap theory of Petri net
Whether some parameters(channels, buffers)in the protocol are bounded	boundedness
Whether some parameters are safe in the course of the running of the protocol	P-invariants
Whether the action sequences of the protocol are sustainable	T-invariants
Whether the action sequences of the protocol are legal	Petri net transition fire sequences

3.2. *Protocol performance evaluation*

The delayed time for the transition definition of the original Petri net can help to realize the protocol performance evaluation. Two points need to be considered when evaluating the protocol performance.

(1) The maximum throughput

The maximum data frames successfully sent out every second is the maximum throughput of the data link, marked as $\lambda_{\max}$.

(2) The average propagation latency

The average time needed for the correctly sent out of the data frames, marked as t_{AV}.

4. A Practical Example: The Protocol Validation and Performance Evaluation for 0-1 Stops and Wait for Protocol

The detailed description of 0-1 stops and wait for protocol see reference [10].

4.1. *The original Petri net model of 0-1 stops and wait for protocol*

The Fig.1 is the Petri net model of 0-1 stops and wait for protocol, with the description of symbols of Fig.1 is shown in table 2.

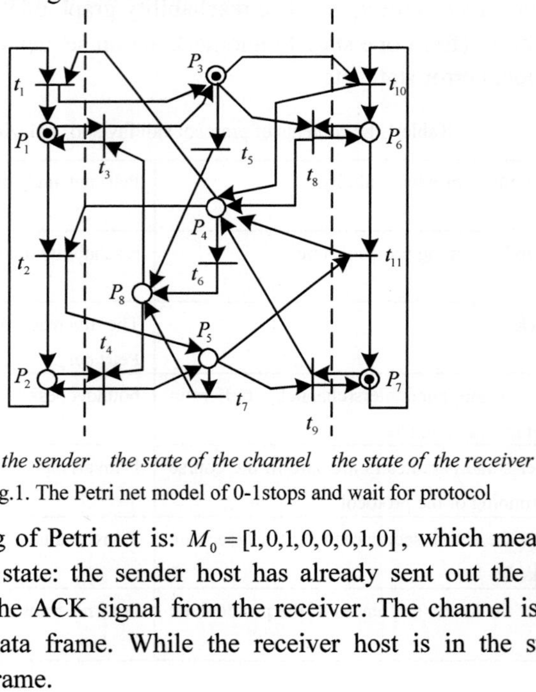

Fig.1. The Petri net model of 0-1stops and wait for protocol

The initial marking of Petri net is: $M_0 = [1,0,1,0,0,0,1,0]$, which means that the protocol is in this state: the sender host has already sent out the [0]data frames of waiting for the ACK signal from the receiver. The channel is in the state of sending [0] data frame. While the receiver host is in the state of expecting the [0] data frame.

Table 2 the description of symbols of 0-1 protocol's Petri net model

Symbols name	Place/Transition Significance	Symbols name	Place/Transition Significance
P_1	Wait ACK	P_8	Lose ACK or data frame
P_2	Wait ACK	t_1	Receive ACK, send [0]
P_3	[0]frame in the channel	t_2	Receive ACK, send [1]
P_4	ACK in the channel	t_3	[0]frame timeout
P_5	[1]frame in the channel	t_4	[1] frame timeout
P_6	Expected receive [1]frame	t_5	Lose [0] frame
P_7	Expected receive [0]frame	t_6	Lose ACK frame
t_7	Lose [1] frame	t_8	Receive duplicate [0] frame, do not send host
t_9	Receive duplicate [1] frame, do not send host	t_{10}	Receive [0] frame, send host
t_{11}	Receive [1] frame, send host		

4.2. *The static analysis of the 0-1 stops and wait for protocol*

(1)The verification of protocol conservativeness by P-invariants

If the protocol is right, the sender host would be in such state: sent the [0]frame wait for ACK or having sent the [1] frame wait for ACK. The receiver host is in such state: expecting the receiving of [0] frame or expecting the receiving of [1] frame. The channel is in such state: in the course of sending [0] frame or in the course of sending ACK or information loss. Corresponding to the Petri net model in Fig.1, if the protocol meets the conditions, $\{p_1, p_2\}$ can express the state of the sender. The state of the receiver is then described as $\{p_6, p_7\}$, the state of the channel is then described as $\{p_3, p_4, p_5, p_8\}$, all of which being the support sets of the P-invariants.

Fig. 2 shows the solution of the equation $AY = 0$. According to the solution, 0-1 wait protocol can be well verified by P-invariants.

$$A=\begin{bmatrix} 1 & -1 & 1 & -1 & 0 & 0 & 0 & 0 \\ -1 & 1 & 0 & -1 & 1 & 0 & 0 & 0 \\ 0 & 0 & 1 & 0 & 0 & 0 & 0 & -1 \\ 0 & 0 & 0 & 0 & 1 & 0 & 0 & -1 \\ 0 & 0 & -1 & 0 & 0 & 0 & 0 & 1 \\ 0 & 0 & 0 & -1 & 0 & 0 & 0 & 1 \\ 0 & 0 & 0 & 0 & -1 & 0 & 0 & 1 \\ 0 & 0 & -1 & 1 & 0 & 0 & 0 & 0 \\ 0 & 0 & 0 & 1 & -1 & 0 & 0 & 0 \\ 0 & 0 & -1 & 1 & 0 & 1 & -1 & 0 \\ 0 & 0 & 0 & 1 & -1 & -1 & 1 & 0 \end{bmatrix} \qquad \begin{bmatrix} Y_1 \\ Y_2 \\ Y_3 \\ Y_4 \\ Y_5 \\ Y_6 \\ Y_7 \\ Y_8 \end{bmatrix} = c_1 \begin{bmatrix} 1 \\ 1 \\ 0 \\ 0 \\ 0 \\ 0 \\ 0 \\ 0 \end{bmatrix} + c_2 \begin{bmatrix} 0 \\ 0 \\ 0 \\ 0 \\ 0 \\ 1 \\ 1 \\ 0 \end{bmatrix} + c_3 \begin{bmatrix} 0 \\ 0 \\ 1 \\ 1 \\ 1 \\ 0 \\ 0 \\ 1 \end{bmatrix}$$

Fig.2. incidence matrix A and solution of equation AY=0

4.3. *The dynamic analysis of 0-1 stop and wait for protocol*

The reachability graph of the Petri model in Fig.1 is introduced, which can conduct the following dynamic analysis and verification to the 0-1 stop and wait for protocol.

(1)the verification of the protocol sending, receiving and channel boundedness

In 0-1 stop and wait for protocol, the data frames use serial number [0]/[1] alternatively, hence the capacity of the send and receive buffers, as well as the channel, should be 1. After the observation of Fig.3, we can know that when the original marking $M_0=[1,0,1,0,0,0,1,0]$ is given, for $\forall s\in S$, $\forall M\in R(M_0): M(s)\leq 1$. The Petri net in fig.1 is then safeness, verifying the fact that the capacity of the send and receive buffers as well as the channel is 1.

(2)the verification of protocol deadlock-free by the liveness of Petri net

According to Fig.3, each transition of the Petri net is alive, namely, the net in the figure is alive, indicating that there is not deadlock in 0-1 stop and wait for protocol.

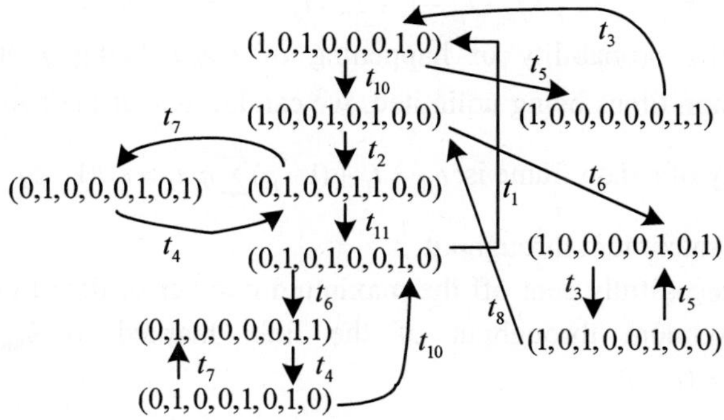

Fig.3. the reachability graph of Petri net

4.4. *The performance evaluations of 0-1stop and wait for protocol*

Adding the following latency, to the transitions of the models in fig.1, the result timed Petri net marked as Σ_2.The latency time of the transition of Σ_2 is as follows:

$t_1 : \tau_1 = t_f + t_{pr} + t_p$, $t_2 : \tau_2 = t_f + t_{pr} + t_p$, $t_3 : \tau_3 = t_{out}$, $t_4 : \tau_4 = t_{out}$, $t_5 : \tau_5 = 0$, $t_6 : \tau_6 = 0$, $t_7 : \tau_7 = 0$, $t_8 : \tau_8 = t_p + t_{pr} + t_a$, $t_9 : \tau_9 = t_p + t_{pr} + t_a$, $t_{10} : \tau_{10} = t_p + t_{pr} + t_a$, $t_{11} : \tau_{11} = t_p + t_{pr} + t_a$.

Explanation of the latency:

t_f : The transmission delay of the data frames

t_a : The transmission delay of response signal

t_p : The propagation delay resulting from the fact that the data frames and ACK propagate along the link

t_{pr} : The processing time after the receiving of data frames and ACK

t_{out} : The setup time of the expiry timer

The meaning of transition t_1 is to receive ACK and send [0] frame. The latency is then defined as $\tau_1 = t_f + t_{pr} + t_p$ .It is the same with the latency of transition t_2 t_8 t_9 t_{10} t_{11}. While the meanings of t_5 t_6 t_7 are all signal loss, the process of that can be viewed as instantaneous, with its latency 0. However, the fact is that not all the signals lose. The probability of its happening is defined as p .We are to make the following evaluations for the 0-1 stop and wait for protocol (see fig. 4).

(1) the average propagation latency

According to the action sequence $M_0[> t_{10}M_1[> t_2M_2$, the least time interval t_T between two successfully sent data frames is:

$t_T = \tau_{10} + \tau_2 = t_p + t_{pr} + t_a + t_{pr} + t_p + t_f = t_f + t_{out} = t_f + 2t_p$

With the probability of happening of t_5, t_6, t_7 being p and the allowed retransmission times being unlimited, we can know that the average time t_{AV} for the correctly of a data frame is: $t_{AV} = t_T + (1-p)\sum_{i=1}^{\infty} ip^i t_T = t_T /(1-p)$

(2) the maximum throughput

The successfully sent off the maximum number of data frame each second is the maximum throughput of the link, marked as $\lambda_{\max}$. Apparently, $\lambda_{\max} = 1/t_{AV} = (1-p)/t_T$.

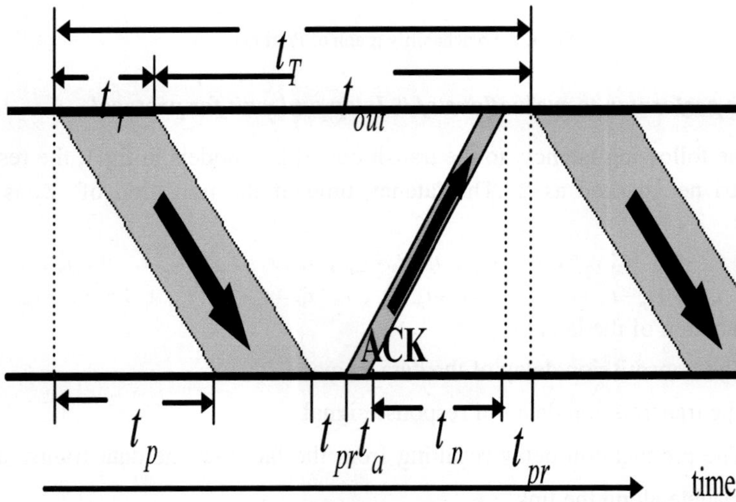

Fig.4. the time relation in stop and wait for protocol

5. Conclusion

Compared with the existing references, the main feature of this paper is to establish the protocol model by original Petri net and to verify the protocol. The time factor is then added to the original Petri net and transformed into timed Petri net, and then we can do the protocol performance evaluation. In this way, when it comes to protocol verification, the existing theories regarding Petri net can be taken well advantage of. When it comes to the protocol performance, it can use Petri net of protocol verification without changing the model. This paper offers a method of protocol verification with original Petri net by providing the case of 0-1 stop and wait for protocol, to which we have made relative complete static and dynamic formal verification. By giving latency time to the transition of original Petri net, we have transformed the original Petri net into timed Petri net and then strictly conducted performance analysis with it, which is one of the main advantages of this paper. And in our later study, we will further study the semantic verification of the protocol, exploiting the language and semantics of Petri net.

Acknowledgments

This work is supported by Science and technology project of colleges and universities in Shandong Province(J11LG26) and Youth Science and Technology Innovation Fund Project of Shandong Agricultural University (23659).

References

1. Jun Xu, Xiaoyu Zhang, Xiuyan Wang, 3GPP Mobile Communication System Standard MAC Layer Design Based on ARM+DSP[J], Computer Measurement & Control. 2015, 23(1):250-253.
2. Kai LI, Hui-chao Ma, Research on unknown label detection protocol based on RFID[J], Application Research of Computers. 2015, 32(3):814-820.
3. Ya-juan Tang, Countermeasures on Application Level Low-Rate Denial-of-Service Attack [J], Information and Communications Security Lecture Notes in Computer Science, 2012, 7618:70-80.
4. Hong-Yue WU, Yu-Yue DU, A Logical Petri Net-Based Approach for Web Service Cluster Composition[J], Chinese Journal of computers, 2015, 38(1):204-217.
5. Dong-min Wang, Research and Implementation of Sip Conformance Testing Suite Based on Petri Net [D], Beijing University of Posts and Telecommunications, 2011(In Chinese).
6. Dong-gin FENG, Jia-jun SHEN, Jian CHU, Analysis of clock synchronization protocol security using colored Petri net[J], Control and Decision, 29(12), 2014, 2144-2150.
7. Guo-Guang Wu, WTIM Modeling and Dynamic Performance Evaluation based on Petri net[J], Journal of the South China University of Technology, 41(9), 2013, 107-111.
8. Shevtekar A, Ansari N. Do Low Rate DoS Attacks Affect QoS Sensitive VoIP Traffic[C]. //Proceedings of IEEE International Conference on Communications. New Jersey, USA, 2006, 5(5):2153 - 2158.
9. Z H Wu. The Introductory Theory of Petri net[M]. Beijing: China, Machine Press, 2006(In Chinese).
10. Yong Wang, longfei Zhang, Computer networks[M]. Beijing: China, Machine Press, 2015(In Chinese).

Prefetch Breakdown for Helper Threading on Shared Cache CMPs

Min CAI

College of Computer Science, Beijing University of Technology,
Beijing, 100124, China
E-mails: min.cai.china@bjut.edu.cn

Zhi-min GU

School of Computer Science and Technology, Beijing Institute of Technology,
Beijing, 100081, China
E-mail: zmgu@x263.net

Jun-zhong JI and Juan FANG

College of Computer Science, Beijing University of Technology,
Beijing, 100124, China
E-mail:jjz01@bjut.edu.cn, fangjuan@bjut.edu.cn

Bin LI

Institute of Software, Chinese Academy of Sciences,
Beijing, 100190, China
E-mail: libin@iscas.ac.cn

This paper proposes the helper thread prefetch request breakdown to differentiate between different performance gains achieved by different helper thread prefetch parameter combinations. Cycle-accurate simulation results of selected benchmarks in Olden and CPU2006 show that, the selection of appropriate helper thread prefetching parameters can maximize the potential of helper thread prefetching, based on the different memory access patterns of target applications.

Keywords: Shared cache chip multiprocessors; Helper thread; Prefetch breakdown.

1. Introduction

The proliferation of shared cache multiprocessors (CMPs) enables helper threads [1, 2] running on the idle cores of CMPs speculatively issue last-level cache (LLC) prefetches [3, 4] to the predicted memory addresses, in order to hide the latencies of subsequent main thread references. Unfortunately, inaccurate and/or untimely LLC requests coming from the helper thread could not contribute to the main thread performance but rather stress and pollute the LLC. Furthermore, effective LLC content management should be used to adapt to the instinct memory access characteristics in the helper thread prefetching applications[5, 6].Three helper thread prefetching parameters are used to control the helper thread's aggressiveness and thus affect its effectiveness: lookahead (L), stride (S) and synchronization period[7]. We extend the open source CMP architectural simulator Archimulator for characterizing helper thread prefetching on CMPs. Furthermore, we propose the helper thread prefetch request breakdown to differentiate between different performance gains achieved by individual helper thread prefetch requests. Experimental results of benchmarks from Olden [8] and CPU2006 [9] show that selection of appropriate parameters can improve helper thread prefetching.

2. Prefetch Breakdown for Helper Threading

The breakdown of helper thread LLC requests are as follows. Firstly, there are four cases based on the relative positions of the helper thread (HT) request and the subsequent main thread (MT) request: (1) *Late*- the MT request to the data H arrives after the HT request to H is initiated but before H is inserted into the LLC. (2) *Timely*- the MT request to H arrives after H is inserted into the LLC but before H is evicted from the LLC. (3) *Bad* - the MT request to the victim data V arrives after H is inserted into the LLC but before H is evicted from the LLC. (4) *Ugly*- the MT request to H arrives after the H is evicted from the LLC. Secondly, there are two more cases based on the relative positions of the MT request and the late HT request: (1) *Redundant_mshr* - the HT request arrives after the MT request is initiated but before the data is inserted into the LLC. (2) *Redundant_cache* - the HT request arrives after the MT data is inserted into the LLC but before the data is evicted from the LLC.

Now we consider the hardware implementation of the proposed breakdown. Firstly, we need to track the event when the LLC receives a request coming from the upper level private cache, whether it is a hit or a miss. Secondly, one field named threadId is added to each LLC line to indicate whether the line is brought in by the MT or the HT or otherwise invalid. Thirdly, an LRU cache named HTRVC is added to maintain the LLC lines that are evicted by HT requests. The HTRVC has the same structure of the LLC, and there is a direct mapping between LLC lines and HTRVC lines. Lastly, in order to measure late HT requests, we need to identify the event when a MT request hits to an LLC line which is being brought by an in-flight HT request.

Besides, when filling an LLC line, we should consider four nontrivial cases as listed below: (1) A HT request fills an INVALID line. A new NULL entry is inserted in the HTRVC. (2) A HT request evicts an LLC line which is previously brought in by a MT request. A new DATA entry is inserted in the HTRVC. (3) A HT request evicts an LLC line which is previously brought by a HT request. The stored HT request tag is updated to the incoming HT request tag in the corresponding victim entry in the HTRVC. (4) A MT request evicts an LLC line which is previously brought by a HT request. The corresponding victim entry found in the HTRVC is invalidated.

When servicing an incoming LLC request, we should consider three nontrivial cases as listed below: (1) If the incoming LLC request is from the HT, we need to first check the contents of LLC and LLC MSHRs in order to determine if the HT request is of either a redundant_mshr or a redundant_cache type. (2) A bad HT request occurs when an incoming MT request hits a victim entry found in the HTRVC, but misses in the LLC. (3) A good HT request, either late or timely, depending on whether the value of inflight ThreadId is valid or not in the involved LLC line, occurs when an incoming MT request hits the data brought by a previous HT request in the LLC but misses in the HTRVC. Furthermore, if a HT request is not identified as non-ugly before evicted, then it is treated as ugly in the end. When an LLC line is invalidated, the LLC line's HT request state is cleared. If the LLC line is brought in by the HT, then the HTRVC entry is invalidated.

3. Experimental Setup and Results

Table 1. Baseline Hardware Configuration

CPU	system-call (SE) emulation mode, MIPS II ISA, 2 cores, 2 threads per core
Caches	Private L1I and D: 32KB, 4-way; Shared L2: 2MB, 8-way; Infinite MSHRs
Cache Coherence	Directory-based MESI coherence
Interconnect	Switch based point-to-point topology, 32B link width
Memory	4GB, 200-cycle fixed latency

Table 2. Target Benchmarks

Benchmark	Input set	Hotspot function
mst	4000	HashLookup
em3d	40000 128 75 1	fill_from_fields
429.mcf	ref	refresh_potential

We used the open source Archimulator multicore simulator in this work. The baseline hardware configuration are listed in Table 1. We conduct the experiments using selected memory-intensive, pointer traversal benchmarks *mst* and *em3d* from Olden and *429.mcf* from CPU2006.Table 2 lists the detailed parameters on the selected benchmarks. To reduce the simulation time, we first fast forward to the *pthread_spawn(..)* function call in the program code, and then run in detail for 200 million instructions on the main thread.

Fig. 1 shows the impact of lookahead and stride on performance and prefetch breakdown for *mst_ht.* The maximum reduction in execution time is achieved in the middle values of lookahead. When lookahead <80, the execution time increases monotonically. When lookahead >= 80, the execution time remains almost constant. However, the execution time increases monotonically again as the value of lookahead becomes even greater. Late, timely and ugly requests dominate the breakdown. There is no bad requests observed. When lookahead is small and the stride is large, there is a large portion of late requests. On the other hand, when the stride is large, timely requests diminishes. When lookahead >= 80, late requests diminishes.

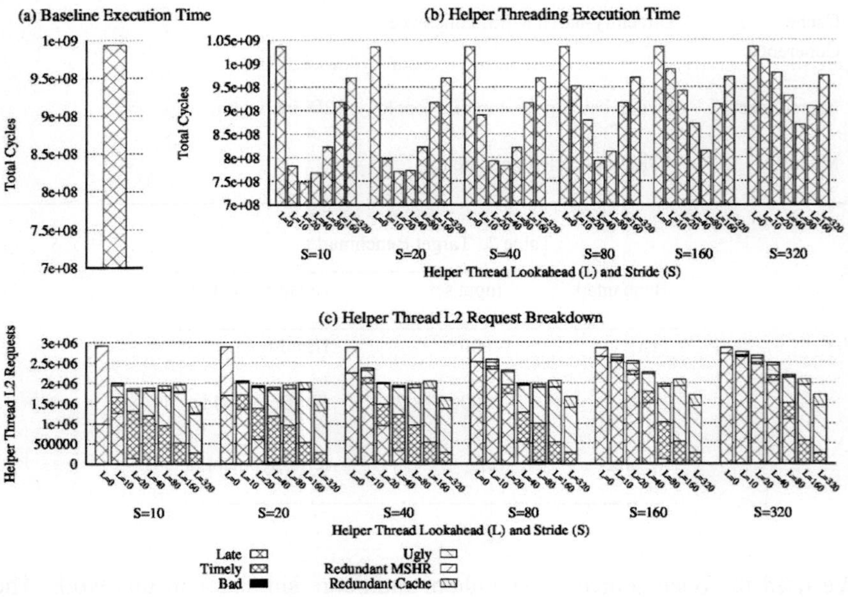

Fig. 1. Impact of Lookahead and Stride, *mst_ht*,L2 Size=1MB, L2 Assoc=8

Fig. 2 shows the impact of lookahead and stride on performance and prefetch breakdown for *em3d_ht*. The minimum reduction of execution time is achieved when stride is 10 and there is no lookahead. Timely requests dominate the breakdown. Few lately requests are observed. No bad requests are observed. There is little variance observed in the breakdown. The total number of timely requests decreases monotonically.

Fig. 3 shows the impact of lookahead and stride on performance and prefetch breakdown for*429.mcf_ht*. The minimal execution time is observed when both stride and lookahead are 20. Timely and ugly requests dominate the breakdown. There are only a few redundant_mshr requests observed. There is no bad requests observed. The amount of timely requests remains almost constant.

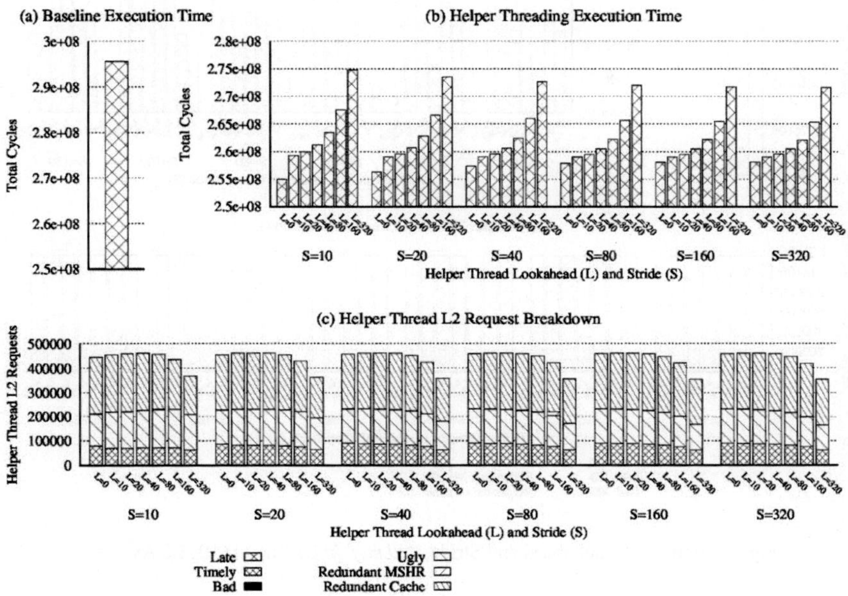

Fig. 2. Impact of Lookahead and Stride, em3d_ht,L2 Size=1MB, L2 Assoc=8

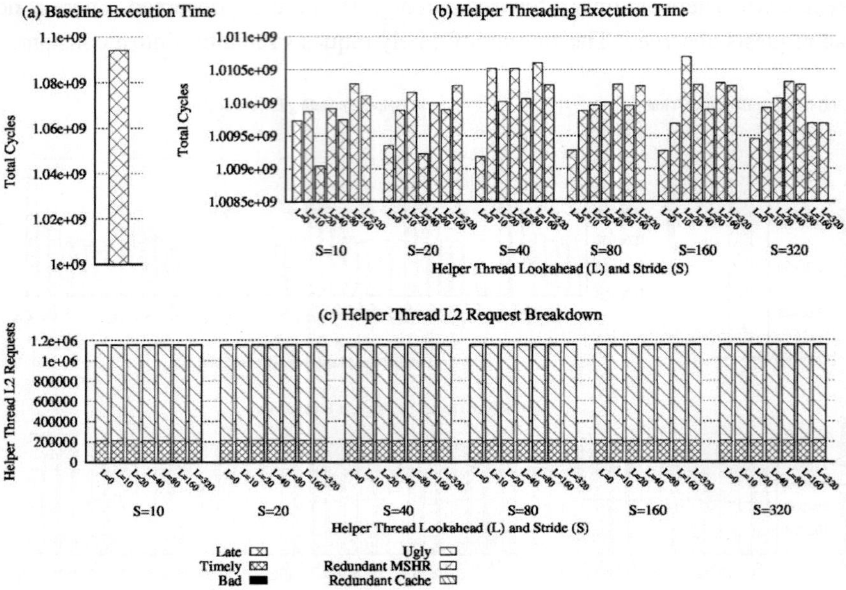

Fig. 3. Impact of Lookahead and Stride, *429.mcf_ht*,L2 Size=1MB, L2 Assoc=8

4. Conclusion

This paper first proposes the breakdown of helper thread prefetches to express helper thread prefetch usefulness, lateness, pollution and redundancy. We then evaluate the breakdown using cycle accurate simulation of benchmarks from Olden and CPU2006. The presented work is indispensable for shedding light on dynamic optimization of helper thread prefetching on CMPs.

Acknowledgments

This work is partially supported by the Open Source Operating System Kernel Analysis and Safety Evaluation project under Grant No. 2012ZX01039-004. This research is also supported by the National Natural Science Foundation of China (Grants No. 61070029,No. 61202076 and No.61202062).

References

1. D. Kim, S.-W. Liao, P. H. Wang, J. d. Cuvillo, X. Tian, X. Zou, H. W. 0003, D. Yeung, M. Girkar, and J. P. Shen, "Physical experimentation with prefetching helper threads on intel's hyper-threaded processors," in *Proceedings of CGO'2004*. (2004), pp. 27–38.

2. Y. Huang, J. Tang, Z. Gu, M. Cai, J. Zhang, and N. Zheng, "The performance optimization of threaded prefetching for linked data structures," *International Journal of Parallel Programming*, vol. 40, no. 2, pp. 141–163, (2012).

3. T. Mowry and A. Gupta, "Tolerating latency through software-controlled prefetching in shared-memory multiprocessors," *Journal of Parallel and Distributed Computing*, vol. 12, no. 2, pp. 87–106, (June 1991).

4. J. Lee, C. Jung, D. Lim, and Y. Solihin, "Prefetching with helper threads for loosely coupled multiprocessor systems," *IEEE Transactions on Parallel and Distributed Systems*, vol. 20, no. 9, pp. 1309–1324, (sep 2009).

5. N. D. E. Jerger, E. L. Hill, and M. H. Lipasti, "Friendly fire: understanding the effects of multiprocessor prefetches," in *Proceedings of ISPASS 2006*. (2006), pp. 177–188.

6. S. Srinath, O. Mutlu, H. Kim, and Y. N. Patt, "Feedback directed prefetching: Improving the performance and bandwidth-efficiency of hardware prefetchers," in *Proceedings of 13th International Conference on High-Performance ComputerArchitecture*, HPCA'07. (2007), pp. 63–74.

7. M. Cai and Z. Gu, "Evaluating the memory system performance of software-initiated inter-core llc prepushing," in *Proceedings of the 2011 Ninth IEEE International Symposium on Parallel and Distributed Processing with ApplicationsWorkshops*, ISPAW '11, (2011), pp. 216–221.

8. A. Rogers, M. C. Carlisle, J. H. Reppy, and L. J. Hendren, “Supporting dynamic data structures on distributed-memory machines,”*ACM Transactions on Programming Languages and Systems*, vol. 17, no. 2, pp. 233–263, (mar 1995).

9. J. L. Henning, “Spec cpu2006 benchmark descriptions,” *ACM SIGARCH Computer Architecture News*, vol. 34, no. 4, pp. 1–17, (2006).

Smart Grid Safe Interactive Strategy Cooperation

Yuan-yuan MA† and Zhi-peng SHAO
State Grid Smart Grid Research Instituteline
Nanjing, 210003, China
†E-mail: mayuanyuan@sgri.sgcc.com.cn

With the continuous development of smart grid technology, the smart grid is moving toward the direction of ubiquitous integration, thus the heterogeneous network elements have different security access techniques. The core of the smart grid information Safe interactive Strategy switch lies in network terminal information awareness, the underlying data of the cooperation decision support. This paper proposes a novel security cooperation framework based on network collaborative, to design a security policy switch decision method. The vertical cooperation security management module can effectively reduce the time delay and energy consumption of information gathering phase of the framework, providing powerful data support for the switching decision method.

Keywords: Smart Grid; Security strategy; Vertical cooperation.

1. Introduction

Based on existing power network, the corresponding network capability is increased and expanded due to the method of network convergence used by smart grid in case to meet new applications with new grid services. To response the information security risks and challenges brought by smart grid, implement the state's requirements for information security work and improve information network security capability, the requests of national information system security protection is combined by the national grid organization and the information security management is further strengthened. As the same time, the company's management information network is divided into information inner and information outer through transformations and implements effective security isolation. Besides, a set of lines of defense have been built from Internet to enterprise information network and then to dispatching data network according to the security policy which is "region dividing, secure access, dynamic perception, comprehensive protection". The following is about the three lines of defense. Secure access is made true mainly through the first line of defense

†Corresponding author.

deploying the interactive platform of the security of outer and universal safety products. Highly strong logical-strong-isolation is made achieved mainly through the second line of defense deploying the information security network isolation device by independent research and development. Quasi physical isolation is made true mainly through the last line of defense deploying network security of pros and cons isolation device. The security of core business and core assets of the power information is effectively guaranteed due to the build of the three lines of defense of company information security. It has already become the cornerstone of the company information security.

The ultimate goal of smart grid terminal safe interactive strategy cooperation is satisfied with “Always Best Connection, ABC” in which “ABC” is meant that the most appropriate and secure access is always chosen by multi-mode terminals to conduct business hosting during the process of moving between different network. However, with the rapid raising of numbers of user terminals and applications and security services with different needs of safe, every application has different needs of safe, such as available bandwidth, delay, BER, shaking and so on. The difficulty of realizing the security management of the smart grid terminal is considered here.

2. Safe Interactive Strategy Vertical Cooperation Framework(SISVC)

As shown in the Fig.1, a SISVC management module based on the original MIH layer is added, which is mainly responsible for the management of safe interactive strategy. The function of the physical /MAC layer is mainly reflected in the mobile terminal, two sub-modules concerning safe interactive strategy cooperation is contained: link management sub-module and interface management sub-module. Turning or closing specified network security interface is mainly in the charge of the interface management sub-module when running the SISVC. Perceiving the quality of link security is mainly in the charge of security link management sub-module and the Link Going Down link case is sent to the upper layer through interface(d) when the quality of link security decline seriously and finally the judgment of whether the sub-module has been finished is done by SISVC management module’s switching. Moreover, establishing new link layer connection to accomplish switching is in the charge of link security management sub-module when executing SISVC.

Three kinds of service are mainly provided by the MIHF sub-layer: MIES, MICS and MIIS. The link quality of the sub-module of SISVC is mainly reported by MIES through interface (d) and (f), which is an important reference factor of the network switch. Controlling the switch of the network interface and the SISVC of networks is mainly in the charge of MICS. Results are sent to MICS through (d) by the sub-module of SISVC and the links in the infrastructure are controlled by MICS through (a) and (b).

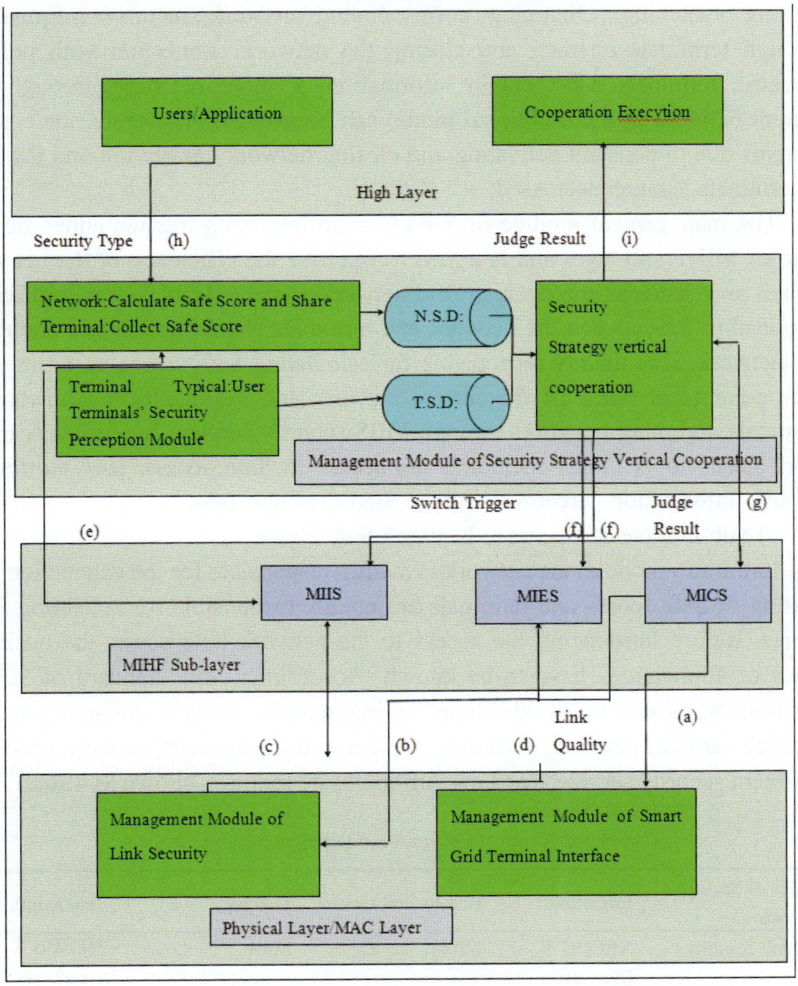

Fig.1SISVC Framework based on MIH

MIIS is modified in this framework and the service about network Safe score on the base of the existing network security information service is increasing. In this framework, network Safe scores is shared with other networks as the base information of network security through terminals. Safe score is got by the calculation of the management module of SISVC in upper layers and sent to MIHF sub-layer through (e). MIH terminals users can directly obtain the Safe scores of the current network and nearly available networks by using information achieving primitive provided by MIH without switching the network interface. The best convenience is provided by MIH: information of nearly safe available network can be obtained through the current network without switching. Obtaining corresponding network security information through terminals opening and closing the network connection with polling (because terminals can't obtain information of other networks through the current network in the traditional mode) can be avoided. Therefore, the cost of systems due to constant activating and closing network connection and the cost of terminals is much decreased.

The management module of SISVC is an important module added on the base of MIHF sub-layer and is aimed to improve the efficiency of the network switch and decrease the delay of the network switch. Besides, much different responsibilities between the network and terminals should be thought about. In the network, it is mainly responsible for calculating Safe scores according the Safe parameters status of the current network and sharing them with mobile terminals and other networks through MIIS security service. In terminals, more work needs to be done, including the access to Safe scores, user terminals' security information perception and the SISVC of networks.

1) Sub-module of Access to Network Safe Score

In the sub-module, the network is mainly responsible for the calculation and sharing of Safe scores and terminals are mainly responsible for collecting Safe scores. Before introducing the access to the network Safe score, the business types of applications have to be known. According to the standard of 3GPP, business types can be divided into calling security service, streaming media security service, interactive security service and background security services. Different security service type have different safe requires, shown as Table1.

Table 1.Safe Parameter Requires of Different Security Service

Types of Security Service	Error Rate	End-to-End Delay	Shaking	Bandwidth
Calling Security	NEEDN'T BE LOW	LOW	LOW	NEEDN'T BE HIGH
Streaming Media Security	NEEDN'T BE LOW	LOW OR MIDDLE	LOW	HIGH
Interactive Security	LOW	MIDDLE OR EQUAL	NEEDN'T BE LOW	NEEDN'T BE HIGH
Background Security	LOW	NEEDN'T BE LOW	NEEDN'T BE LOW	LEAST MIDDLE

After terminals obtaining the Safe scores, they are saved in the network information database to be provided to the module of SISVC. Different security service types need to be distinguished when being recorded and need a time flag to distinguish Safe scores in different time periods. Of course, historical records can be timing deleted and only some recent records can be saved considering the limit of terminals storage. The format of record is similar to the below:

(ID,Network_Id, Security_Type, Safe_Score, Record_Time)

Here, ID is the serial number of the record, Network_Id is the id of the network, SecurityType is the security service type, SafeScore is the Safe score of the responding network and the network of the security service type, and last, RecordTime is the time flag.

2) Sub-module of User Terminals' Security Information Perception

In smart grid, maybe there are much security information of user terminals, but two sides of information are mainly considered: terminals' security situation information and service competence information. Two main parameters are found in security situation information: vulnerability status and defense map information. According to the two parameters and combining the security technology deployment, the safety of terminals in one network is estimated.

3) Sub-module of SISVC

Sub-module of SISVC is a core module and a decision unit. SISVC is finished by this sub-module using security information in the terminal information database and security information in the network information database. Then a safest network is chosen to be the destination network of SISVC and the results are reported to the high layer and the infrastructure to execute the switch. SISVC framework is mainly introduced in the paper and the method of it will be described in another paper.

The high layer module in this framework is a common name of network layer, transmission layer and application layer, there are only two sub-module about SISVC of high layer module: application/user sub-module and SISVC execution sub-module. In the design of the framework, application/user sub-module is in charge of perceiving the types of security professional work of which application the terminal is running now and collect users' preference attributes, convey it to the network Safe score obtaining sub-module of SISVC management module through interface (b), network Safe score obtaining sub-module obtains types of the specified security professional work's network Safe score according to the types of application's security professional work. Switch execution sub-module is mainly in charge of running actual network switch, SISVC's execution, which is normally a cross-layer operation and needs to be finished by the coordination of all layers.

3. Analysis of SISVC Performance

MH-based SISVC framework proposed is to calculate safe score of security networks(net) and collect Safe score of networks(terminal). The security analysis of terminals is decreased much due to the design of calculating Safe score at the network side, and the time of SISVC and the energy of terminals are decreased. Evaluating performance of the framework with quantitative analysis of the switch delay is shown below.

Switch delay is the analysis time costed during the whole period of SISVC, in which the collection of network security information and execution of the SISVC methods are included. Due to the difference of SISVC methods, method is not be an evaluation factor of the framework. Therefore, performance of the framework is depending on the collection delay of network security information. For quantitative analysis of the switch delay, here is the formula of it.

t_l is assumed to be the information delay of the exchange between net and terminal with the length l , then

$$t_l = \frac{l}{\beta} + l_w . \tag{1}$$

In which, β is the available network bandwidth, l_w is the information propagation delay and they are ignored here.

Then, t_h is assumed as switch delay and the formula is as shown below:

$$t_h = \sum_{i=1}^{n} k_i * x_i * t_{li} . \tag{2}$$

Here, k_i is the amount of security networks which are the same net type i, t_{li} is the information delay of terminals exchanging with length l in the network which is type i, n is the number of types of available security network used by terminals, and x_i is the amount of information needed to be exchanged in the ith type of network when executing Safe interactive Strategy switch.

There are three types of access to security network assumed in some segment of the smart grid: UMTS, WiMAX and WiFi, and each type of network only has one available network so here is the conditions which are n=3, $k_1 = 1, k_2 = 1, k_3 = 1$. In the proposed framework, three network Safe scores need to be exchanged with the network when executing Safe interactive Strategy switch which can be finished only through the current network in this framework. The security network of the terminal is assumed as first network and the length of each information is L, so there is $t_{l1} = \frac{L}{\beta_1}$, in which β_1 is the available bandwidth of the current network(the first one) and $x_1 = 3, x_2 = 0, x_3 = 0$, and therefore we get $t_h = 3 * \frac{L}{\beta_1}$.If directly and simply applying the idea of MIH, all Safe parameters of security network can be obtained directly by the current network, but four Safe parameters should be considered in each security network so that twelve parameters need to be exchanged and the formula $t_h = \frac{12L}{\beta_1}$ is got. However, to the traditional methods based on polling, four Safe parameters need to be exchanged with three networks when switching terminals respectively. Therefore, here is $t_h = \frac{4L}{\beta_1} + \frac{4L}{\beta_2} + \frac{4L}{\beta_3}$ and it is assumed that β_1=2048kbps, $\beta_2 = 10000kbps \approx 4.88\beta_1$, $\beta_3 = 11000\text{kbps} \approx 5.37\beta_1$, then the formula $t_h = \frac{4L}{\beta_1} + \frac{4L}{\beta_2} + \frac{4L}{\beta_3} \approx 5.56\frac{L}{\beta_1}$ is got. Thus, compared to the traditional method, the Safe interactive Strategy switch delay is decreased by 75% when using the proposed SISVC framework and the delay can be decreased by 46% with the direct application of MIH.

4. Conclusion

A framework for the MIH-based SISVC is presented in the paper and the function of layers of the framework and information exchanging interface among modules are detailed analyzed. The performance analysis of framework for Safe interactive Strategy switch in the handover decision delay is provided . It is shown that the SISVC framework is considered to have better maneuverability.

Acknowledgments

This work is supported by the Basic and Prospective Project of SGCC SGRIXTKJ[2015]216.

References

1. Xia R, Xu F, Zong CQ, Li QM, Qi Y, Li T, *Dual Sentiment Analysis: Considering Two Sides of One Review*. IEEE Transactions on Knowledge and Data Engineering. 2015, 27(8): 2120-2133.
2. Li QM, Li J. *Rough Outlier Detection Based Security Risk Analysis Methodology*. CHINA COMMUNICATIONS. 2012, 9(7): 14-21.

3. Li QM. *Multiple Safe Constraints Finding Paths Method in TMN.* INFORMATION. 2011, 14(3): 731-737.
4. Li QM, Zhang H. *Information Security Risk Assessment Technology of Cyberspace: a Review*. INFORMATION. 2012, 15(11): 677-683.

Research on Intelligent Irrigation System of Agricultural Base Based on Cloud-Platforms

Tao HUANG

School of Computer Science, Zhaoqing University,
Zhaoqing, Guangdong, China
E-mail: htmouse@qq.com

Li ZHOU†

School of Economics and Management, Zhaoqing University,
Zhaoqing, Guangdong, China
†E-mail: 13322977@163.com

A multi-functional crop intelligent monitoring system, including internet and Arduino micro-controllers, function to upload humiture, soil moisture, light intensity, PM2.5, harmful gas and other real time data. The system's other functions include automatic watering of crops when the humidity data exceeds warning levels, broadcasting the condition of crops by Microblog, remotely controlling the watering and lighting by web and WeChat and remote video monitoring. Data collection of sensor data is conducted by Arduino UNO micro-controller and the data is uploaded real time into the internet by HLK-RM04 WiFi module. Software functions of the system include real time charts by Websocket, JavaScript in PC and mobile internet, and concurrently, the implementation of WeChat control and Microblog broadcast through Tencent micro channel public platform and Sina Microblog.

Keywords: Arduino; Wifi; Web; Microblog; Wechat; Video monitoring; Remote.

1. Introduction

The growth of internet makes intelligent irrigation system of the agricultural base possible. The irrigation system, designed for the original purpose of saving water resources, making it easier for people to manage the agricultural base and promoting the output of agricultural base scientifically, is worth application and popularization [1,2]. So far, there are many intelligent irrigation systems aiming at crops, but not many of them are applied specifically to large scale agricultural base [3,4,5]. The key of the intelligent irrigation system is to ensure the optimal growth state of crops with optimal water consumption. It has considered the water requirement of crops, namely the appropriate water requirement and water quantity; controlling of the irrigation, which means to choose the best way and time for watering [6,7]. With the rapid development of sensor technology, soil moisture sensor becomes the major testing equipment in irrigation system. Most of the existing intelligent irrigation systems collect the information of soil moisture by soil moisture sensor and transfer the data to control systems as feedback information, so as to control the irrigation of irrigation systems [8,9].

Intelligent monitoring system of agricultural base Intelligent monitoring system of agricultural base based on cloud platforms connects the cloud by Wifi gateway, uploading the environmental parameters of crops collected by sensors to the cloud. To a great extent, it saves water and promotes the healthy development of agricultural base. The device takes full account of all important factors of crop irrigation. Combining peripheral temperature sensor, soil moisture metering circuit and water circuit, it realizes the intelligent irrigation of plants according to different soil types, ambient temperatures and soil moisture. It is also equipped with PM2.5 sensor and CO sensor, which can set upper and lower limit of soil moisture and upload it to the cloud, trigger the remind of Weibo or enter the mobile Web or public number of WeChat by scanning the two-dimension code anywhere in real time, also observe through the video monitor window the crop conditions and monitor the growth of agricultural base easily [10,11,12].

2. Design Fundamentals

2.1. *Technical design*

Technologies used in the project include Web application development and wireless transmission. System server is written by mainstream websites developing scripting language ASP. NET and SQL Server database. It communicates with the underlying hardware by API interface to retrieve real time data from hardware and at the same time achieves time continuity of sensor data, relatively constant speed of data inserting and high speed of data retrieving by the efficient performance of SQL Server database. System underlying hardware adopts HLK-RM04 WiFi module, discarding the traditional wired Ethernet module. With HLK-RM04 module, traditional serial device can transfer its own data through the Internet without changing any setting. HLK-

RM04 module provides a complete and fast solution for users' serial devices to transfer data through Internet. As shown in Figure 1.

Figure1. Topological graphs.

In general, the system can be simply divided into four parts as following:

First, sensor hardware and WiFi connect to web. Internet is accessible mainly by combining Arduino, HLK-RM04 WIFI module and other sensors, with the simple configuration. Loop transmission of POST and GET requests is implemented according to the program flow chart above. Arduino encapsulates sensor data according to the custom API standard, orderly uploads it to web port by POST method at regular intervals and uses GET request to retrieve switch state value and judge it so as to achieve remote control.

Second, the real time monitoring carried out in PC and mobile Web. Website is made by ASP.Net MVC4 and the static front page use the latest supported Websocket technology in html5 to send a request to the background, establishing a full-duplex communication connection with server. On one hand, the background returns to the switch data by API response exposing the GET and POST methods, as well as stores sensor data into database. On the other hand, it transfers the correlated parameter of received data to the callback function in the client script by Signal R 2.0 technology and then the callback function realizes the dynamic rendering of chart.

Third, Microblog broadcast and WeChat public platform control. Microblog broadcast, binding web port through API interface of Sina Microblog, is to implement automatic broadcast of the conditions of agricultural production base by setting corresponding triggering events.(For example, when the air temperature is above 30 degree Celsius, Microblog sending is triggered and sending content is specified); Wechat public platform access is to open interface through Tencent micro channel public platform, connecting with web port, so as to collect real time data and implement remote control in personal public platform.

Fourth, equipments carry out the remote video monitoring. The third party household web camera C7823WIP, a mini web camera recently launched by Vstarcam, is used for video monitoring. C7823WIP, with embedded Linux operating system, has a perfect mechanism of video transmission, accessing internet by wireless WiFi or Ethernet, which is equivalent to another cloud platform. This web camera purchased can carry out the second development through official SDK, calling API of Webcam plug-in stalled in the browser through Javascript in the HTML page, so as to implement remote image access and console control toward camera connected to the Internet in the browser. System operation flow chart is as shown in Figure 2.

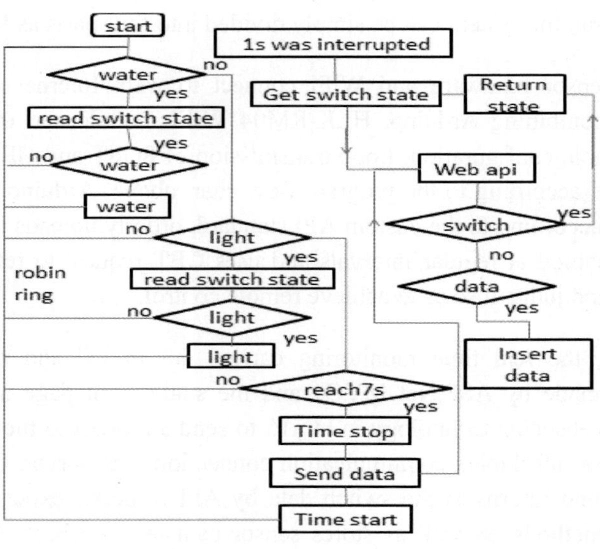

Figure 2. System operation flow chart.

2.2. *Hardware operating principle*

Hardware such as Arduino UNO micro-controller and HLK-RM04WiFi module, and sensors such as soil moisture, DHT11 and MQ-135 are required. As shown in Figure 3.

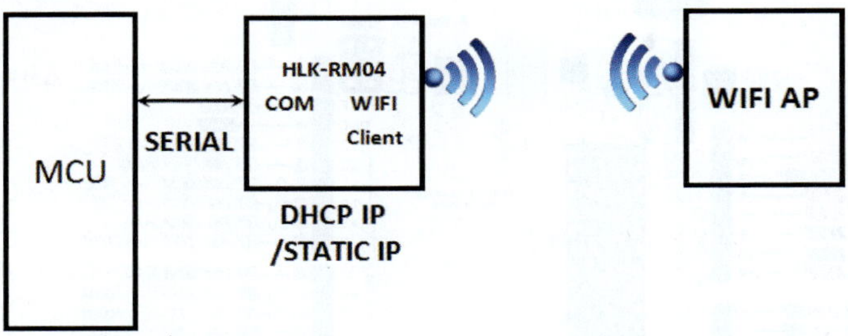

Figure 3. Model of serial interface to WIFI client

The operating principles are as follows:

First, Arduino micro-controller collects sensor data and converts the analog collected by the sensor to the digital via A/D conversion and then converts the digital to data display available to the users with proper formula.

Second, after collecting the sensor data, Arduino micro-controller connects to UART WiFi by the serial and sends the encapsulated data to the configured WiFi module. Then the data is uploaded to the server via routing.

Third, HLK-RM04WiFi module switches to WIFI CLIENT mode in the serial. The principle here is shown in Fig. 3. In this mode, WiFi shuts down ETH1 and ETH2 which can work in the CLIENT mode. With appropriate setting, the data of COM1 can be converted to and from network data of WiFi. To adapt to the external environment, the main control chip and connect components are wrapped in a box.

Hardware schematic diagram is as shown in Figure 4.

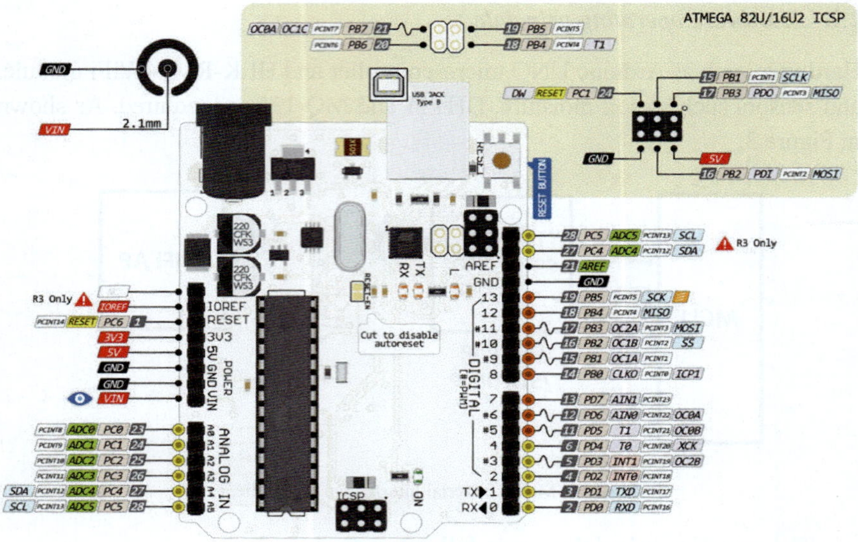

Figure 4. Schematic diagram of Arduino

2.3. *Web interface design*

The real time web data display is constructed by the combination of ASP.NET MVC4, HTML, CSS, Javascript, JQuery and the database SQL server. It provides API interface, with which the hardware are able to submit data using the internet and, at the same time reply the requested data by inserting them into tables of corresponding database. The Web interface is also a connection between web and hardware system. By collecting data from all sensors, it sends the WIFI serial, which is generated by the POST, to the server's web API connection and thus realize remote control by using GET to obtain the status value of the switching.

The main function of Web data display is to obtain latest data of all sensors from the database, and dynamically display the results to users in figures and tables. At the same time the users can also update the data of their table from database through switching control that is provided by the web page. In this way remote control is available. Also, the users can call API that is installed in the web browser for IP camera, and obtain remote images and have control over PTZ.

The real time web data display is constructed by the combination of ASP.NET MVC4, HTML, CSS, JavaScript, JQuery and the database SQL server.

The program execution on PC browser is shown in Figure 5.

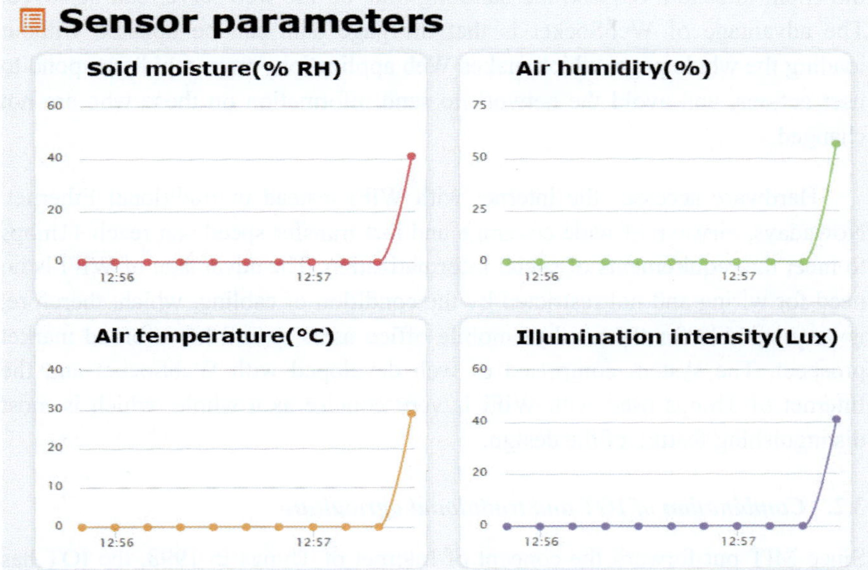

Fig.5 Browser interface

3. Features and Innovation

3.1. *Combination of Web Socket and WiFi transmission*

In terms of the web, the asynchronous update of Web Socket is adopted. Traditional web application is available for the user to fill in a form. When the form is submitted, a request is sent to the web server. The server receives and deals with the form and then returns with a new web page. This way is a waste of much bandwidth because most HTML codes of the front and back pages are frequently the same. For every time the interaction of the applications required a request sent to the server, the application response time depends on the server response time, which results in much slower user interface response than that of that of local application.

Unlike the above, WebSocket application can send data to the server and get back the necessary only, which is a new protocol of HTML5 and realizes the full-duplex between the browser and server. Because of the large re-duction of data exchanged between the browser and server, the application with faster response can be gained. And meanwhile, for much handling can be finished on the client to send a request, the handling time on the web server can be saved. The advantage of WebSocket is that the page data can be updated without loading the whole page, which makes Web applications more rapidly respond to user actions, and avoid the network to send information on those who are not changed.

Hardware accesses the internet with WiFi instead of traditional Ethernet. Nowadays, airwave of wide coverage and fast transfer speed can reach 11mbps to meet the requirements of social informatization. The advantage of WiFi is no need for wiring and not restricted by the condition of cabling, which, therefore, is very suitable for the need of mobile office users to and has a broad market prospect. The system comprised of web developed with WebSocket and the Internet of Things used with WiFi is very concise as a whole, which is most distinguishing feature of the design.

3.2. *Combination of IOT and traditional agriculture*

Since MIT put forward the concept of Internet of Things in 1998, the IOT has gone through more than a decade, from the one equal to RFID to the one with sensor, network and application platform in one place, to today's one represented by smart home and smart city. Internet of Things begins to step out of its application island. At the beginning of the system design, it is conceived according to the development trend of IOT. With the wide IOT, the urgent demand of home and city automation increases rapidly. The IOT appears in many fields and also has a noticeable effect on the modern agriculture. The "Internet plus crop" intelligent system also refers to a series of development and research owing to the demand of smart agriculture[13,14,15]. The main technique that web real time data display is constructed by the combination of ASP.NET MVC4, HTML, CSS, Javascript, JQuery and the cloud server Yeelink.

The core value of IOT through cloud platform is the promoting of the traditional industries through the Internet, and with the depth integration of the IOT and Internet, traditional industries will create new value and new opportunities for new development.

4. Conclusion

With the continuous development of the remote controlling technique, current artificial watering cannot satisfy the needs of large-scale agricultural development. Intelligent irrigation emerges as the times require and will become the primary irrigation tool in agricultural base. Intelligent monitoring system for agricultural production base on cloud platform is available when every sensor is plugged according to the pins of micro-controller and the WiFi parameters are configured. On the software side, deploying the Webpage on the cloud server can realize the most basic function of remote monitoring. There is huge room for improvement of the accuracy of sensor collection and the stability of data upload facing the system, which requires the system of a lot of tests and practices. Experiments have shown that the project is suitable for the automatic watering in agricultural production base. It can realize water resource saving to a great extent and increase the yields of crops at the same time, promising a broad market application prospect.

References

1. Hendrawan, Y. and H. Murase.2011. Neural-Intelligent Water Drops algorithm to select relevant textural features for developing precision irrigation system using machine vision. *Computers and Electronics in Agriculture* 77(2): 214-228.

2. Perera, K. C., A. W. Western, B. George and B. Nawarathna.2015. Multivariate time series modeling of short-term system scale irrigation demand. *Journal of Hydrology*.531(3): 1003-1019.

3. Levidow, L., D. Zaccaria, R. Maia, E. Vivas, M. Todorovic and A. Scardigno.2014. Improving water-efficient irrigation: Prospects and difficulties of innovative practices. *Agricultural Water Management* .146: 84-94.

4. Xu, L., L. Chen, T. Chen and Y. Gao.2011. SOA-based precision irrigation decision support system. Mathematical and Computer Modeling 54(3-4): 944-949.

5. Romero, R., J. L. Muriel, I. García and D. Muoz de la Pea.2012.Research on automatic irrigation control: State of the art and recent results. *Agricultural Water Management* .114: 59-66.

6. Hendrawan, Y. and H. Murase (2011). Neural-Intelligent Water Drops algorithm to select relevant textural features for developing precision

irrigation system using machine vision. *Computers and Electronics in Agriculture* .77(2): 214-228.

7. Zhang Weimin.2009.Cloud Computing Profoundly Changes the Future. Science Press.

8. Chen Lvzhou. 2014.*Basic of Arduino Program Design*. Beihang University Press.pp: 5-6.

9. Xuguang Xing, Ye Liu, Wen' gang Zhao, Duan' gang Kang, Miao Yu, Xiaoyi Ma.2015.Determination of dominant weather parameters on reference evapotranspiration by path analysis theory, *Computers and Electronics in Agriculture,* 120, (1): 10-16.

10. S. Fountas, C.G. Sorensen, Z. Tsiropoulos, C. Cavalaris, V. Liakos, T. Gemtos.2015.Farm machinery management information system, *Computers and Electronics in Agriculture.* 110(1): 131-138.

11. Tamoghna Ojha, Sudip Misra, Narendra Singh Raghuwanshi.2015.Wireless sensor networks for agriculture: The state-of-the-art in practice and future challenges, *Computers and Electronics in Agriculture.* 118(10): 66-84.

12. Mingquan Wu, Chaoyang Wu, Wenjiang Huang, Zheng Niu, Changyao Wang.2015. High-resolution Leaf Area Index estimation from synthetic Landsat data generated by a spatial and temporal data fusion model, *Computers and Electronics in Agriculture.*115(7):1-11.

13. Jing Li, Daniel Rodriguez, Dongqing Zhang, Kaiping Ma.2015. Crop rotation model for contract farming with constraints on similar profits, *Computers and Electronics in Agriculture.*119(11): 12-18.

14. Hatice Citakoglu.2015. Comparison of artificial intelligence techniques via empirical equations for prediction of solar radiation, *Computers and Electronics in Agriculture.* 118(10): 28-37.

15. Mercedes Valdés-Vela, Isabel Abrisqueta, Wenceslao Conejero, Juan Vera, M. Carmen Ruiz-Sánchez.2015. Soft computing applied to stem water potential estimation: A fuzzy rule based approach, *Computers and Electronics in Agriculture.* 115(7): 150-160.

High Efficiency General Memory Allocator

Wen-zhe ZHANG, Kai LU and Xiao-ping WANG

Science and Technology on Parallel and Distributed Processing Laboratory, Collaborative Innovation Center of High Performance Computing, State Key Laboratory of High-end Server & Storage Technology, College of Computer, National University of Defense Technology,
ChangSha, 410072, China
E-mail: zhangwenzhe@nudt.edu.cn, kailu@nudt.edu.cn, xiaopingwang@nudt.edu.cn

Memory allocator is an essential component of a program and it highly determines the overall performance of a program. The current general memory allocator falls short on performance because it is unable to determine the memory allocation information of the upper applications. This paper introduces an optimized mechanism that leverages compiler instrumentation to gather and analyze the upper-level memory allocation patterns. Experiments has shown that our optimized method could achieve better performance (10% increase in performance on average and 18% increase under intense conditions) while incurring low amounts of overhead.

Keywords: Memory allocator; Compiler instrumentation; Performance; Overhead.

1. Introduction

All kinds of applications intensively make dynamic memory allocation, which makes the efficiency of memory allocator very crucial. Research has shown that current general memory allocator [1] is often a bottleneck in a program.

Under this trend, many programmers choose to write their own memory allocator when they need to achieve better performance. The customized memory allocator behaves much better but it needs much programming effort and comprehensive understanding of the memory access pattern of the certain program [2, 5, 8]. Moreover, it is only suitable for certain programs and may introduce large overhead when it is used in other scenarios. Thus, a high efficient and general memory allocator is always an appealing tool.

General memory allocator is usually blind of what happens above it (the memory allocating pattern of the above programs) so that it is outperformed by customized memory allocator. In this paper, we propose an efficient general memory allocator which could collect and leverage some higher-level information to achieve better performance. Our key idea is to focus on the intensive memory allocation and we have made two observations: (1) the intensive memory allocation is usually in a loop and (2) the intensive memory allocation in a loop is usually allocating the same-sized objects. Based on the two findings we can optimize the current general memory allocator to make it perform better.

The rest of this paper is organized as follows: In section 2 we give a brief background of the basic design of a general memory allocator. Section 3 gives the design and implementation of our optimized memory allocator. We show the experiment results in Section 4 and conclude in section 5.

2. Background

The main job of a memory allocator is to ask for large blocks of virtual memory from operating system and then retail small pieces to upper applications. As the memory allocator does not know how many bytes the upper applications will be asking for, it usually organizes the large block of virtual memory into several different sized bins as shown in Figure 1. The super block is allocated from the underlying operating system. The several bins in the super block are for allocating certain bytes objects. For example, if an upper application does malloc(32), it could get a 32-byte-piece from the first bin. If it needs 34 bytes, it will get a 64-byte-piece from the second bin. This organization is simple and widely adopted in many famous memory allocators [2-3].

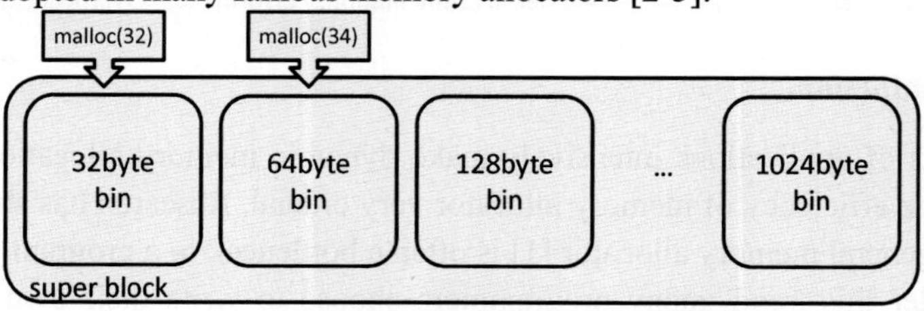

Fig. 1. Basic Design of a Memory Allocator.

3. Design and Implementation

3.1. *Problem of current memory allocator*

A problem of the basic design shown in Figure 1 is the division of the bins. Usually, each bin occupies the same amount of memory. However, for example, if the upper application is always asking for 32-byte object, the 32-byte bin will soon be exhausted and the memory allocator should take further steps to get more memory to serve the following requests, which is an overhead in memory allocator. Thus in this case, if we can know in advance that the upper application will ask for a lot of 32-byte objects, we can enlarge the 32-byte bin at the first place and thus avoid the overhead.

3.2. *Observation and solution*

Our design is based on two observations: (1) the intense memory allocation only happens in loops. (2) the intense memory allocation in a loop is always allocating the same-sized object. The first observation is very natural while the second observation will be tested in our experiment. Based on these two observations, our solution to the above problem is straightforward: (1) firstly, our memory allocator needs to identify the current allocation is in a loop or not. (2) secondly, if the current allocation is in a loop, we get a special super block for all the allocations in this loop. As all the allocations in this loop are likely to be the same sized, using a special super block for them could be very efficient.

3.3. *Loop identification*

We rely on compiler instrumentation to help identify memory allocation in loops. Our idea is shown in Figure 2. Firstly we insert a global variety (the flag in Figure 2) indicating whether current execution is in a loop or not. Then we scan all the code to find loops and insert instructions to change the flag at the beginning and end of the loop. Then in the memory allocation function (malloc) our memory allocator would know whether this allocation is in a loop or not and thus we can optimize the following allocations.

In implementation, we rely on the famous compiler framework LLVM [4] to do the loop identification and instrumentation. In LLVM, the source code of a program would firstly be translated into intermediate code and then be translated into the final binary code. LLVM offers abundant interfaces to help analyze and modify the intermediate code. For loop identification, we just leverage the well-developed loop identification mechanism in LLVM. Basically, any backward jump forms a potential loop.

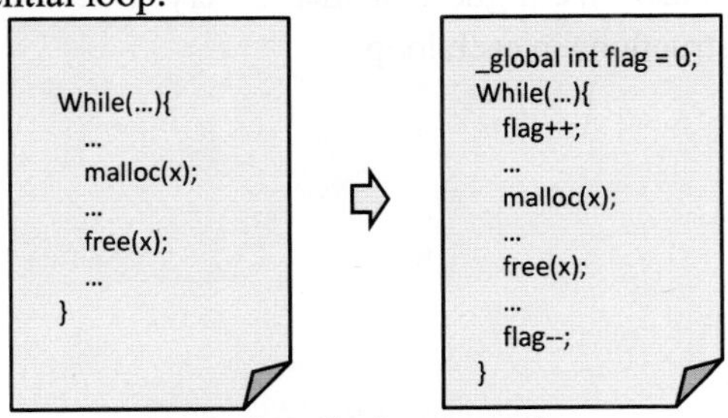

Fig. 2. Compiler Instrumentation.

4. Experiments

As discussed above, we rely on compiler instrumentation to identify whether current memory allocation is in a loop. If so, we will ask for a special super block from operating system to support further memory allocations in this loop. We equip this optimized mechanism to the popular memory allocator Hoard [3]. In this section we will show the improvement of our mechanism compared with the unmodified Hoard (the baseline).

We choose some applications from STAMP [6] benchmark suit which all make intensive memory allocation and are suitable for our experiment. The applications are also for different application domain and thus are representative. Their information are shown in Table 1.

Table 1. Benchmarks.

Benchmark	Input	Number of Objects	Memory Footprint
Baynes	-e-1 -i1 -n4 -p10 -q1 -r32768 -s1 -t1 -v32	48441744	1.46GB
Intruder	-a10 -l32 -n1048576 -s1 -t1	22758600	1.44GB
Vacation	-c1 -n10 -q90 -r 1048576 -t65536 -u80	9691239	0.54GB
Genome	-g32768 -n16777216 -s64 -t1	4288599	1.6GB
Ssca2	-s19	104	2.8GB

Finally, we conduct our experiment on an AMD platform (2.2GHz 12-core CPU and 16GB of physical memory) running Linux 3.11. The LLVM we use to do the compiler instrumentation is versioned 2.9.

4.1. *Results*

Firstly, we show the pure overhead our compiler instrumentation would introduce. Figure 3 shows the result. In this case we just run all applications with unmodified Hoard. The only difference is one set of the applications are instrumented that all loops in the applications are inserted two instructions as shown in Figure 2. As Figure 3 shows, the instrumented application only incurs less than 8% overhead. We argue that this is very little overhead because we only insert two instructions in each loop.

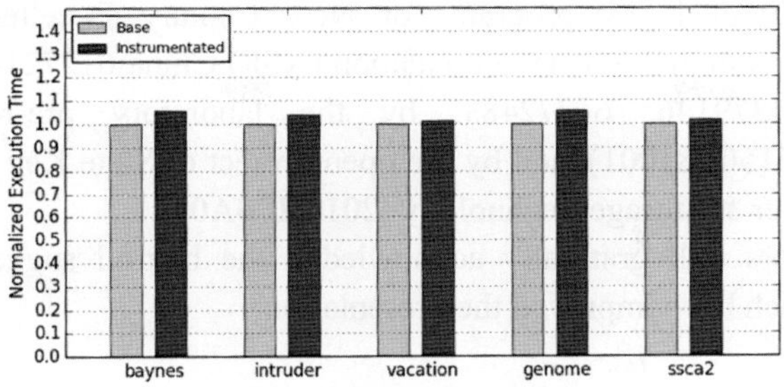

Fig. 3. Instrumentation Overhead.

Figure 4 shows the speedup our optimized memory allocator achieves over the baseline. We can see the speedup we get is positively correlated the number of objects allocated in the certain applications because that naturally much memory allocations are done in the loops. Thus our optimized method can achieve better performance, which is due to we can perfectly guess the further memory allocation pattern in the loop. For the benchmark ssca2, it allocates only a few objects thus we cannot get obvious benefit. Averagely, our optimized memory allocator can achieve around 10% performance improvement.

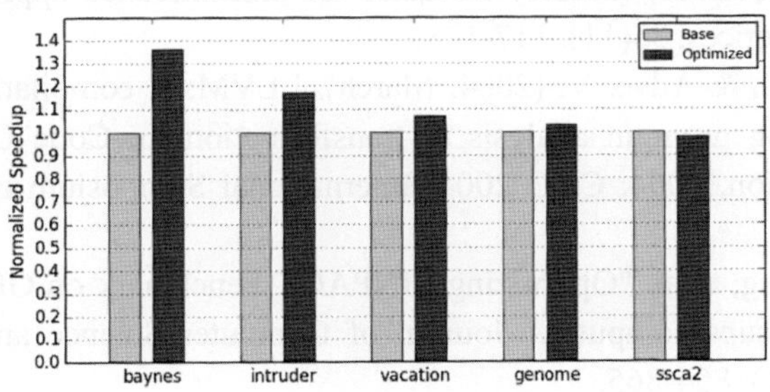

Fig. 4. Speedup over Baseline.

5. Conclusion

Traditional general memory allocator fall short on performance because it does not know the memory allocation patterns in upper applications. This paper propose leveraging compiler instrumentation to get more upper-level information to facilitate memory allocation and thus achieve better performance. Experiments show that our optimized memory allocator would improve performance by average 10% and only introduce ignorable overhead.

Acknowledgments

This work is partially supported by National High-tech R&D Program of China (863 Program) under Grants 2012AA01A301, 2012AA010901, 2012AA010303, and 2015AA01A301, by program for New Century Excellent Talents in University, by National Science Foundation (NSF) China 61272142, 61402492, 61402486, 61379146, 61272483, by the laboratory pre-research fund (9140C810106150C81001), and by the open project of State Key Laboratory of High-end Server & Storage Technology (2014HSSA01).

The authors will gratefully acknowledge the helpful suggestions of the reviewers, which have improved the presentation.

References

1. Krishnan, M. R. (1999). Heap: Pleasures and pains. Microsoft Developer Newsletter.
2. Berger, E. D., Zorn, B. G., & McKinley, K. S. (2000). Building high-performance custom and general-purpose memory allocators. In Proceedings of the SIGPLAN 2001 Conference on Programming Language Design and Implementation (pp. 114-124).
3. Berger, E. D., McKinley, K. S., Blumofe, R. D., & Wilson, P. R. (2000). Hoard: A scalable memory allocator for multithreaded applications. ACM Sigplan Notices, 35(11), 117-128.
4. Lattner, C., & Adve, V. (2004, March). LLVM: A compilation framework for lifelong program analysis & transformation. In Code Generation and Optimization, 2004. CGO 2004. International Symposium on (pp. 75-86). IEEE.
5. Wang, Feng, et al. "Optimizing LINPACK benchmark on GPU-accelerated petascale supercomputer." Journal of Computer Science and Technology 26.5 (2011): 854-865.
6. Minh, C. C., Chung, J., Kozyrakis, C., & Olukotun, K. (2008, September). STAMP: Stanford transactional applications for multi-processing. In Workload Characterization, 2008. IISWC 2008. IEEE International Symposium on (pp. 35-46). IEEE.
7. Smiljkovic, V., Stipic, S., Fetzer, C., Unsal, O., Cristal, A., & Valero, M. R. (2014, October). DeTrans: Deterministic and Parallel execution of Transactions. In Computer Architecture and High Performance Computing (SBAC-PAD), 2014 IEEE 26th International Symposium on (pp. 152-159). IEEE.
8. Lu, Xicheng, et al. "Internet-based virtual computing environment: beyond the data center as a computer." Future Generation Computer Systems 29.1 (2013): 309-322.

Investigations on Simulation Platform for IEEE 1588 Precision Time Synchronization

Yong ZHAO†and Yan-jie GAO

School of Electronic and Information Engineering, Shanghai University of Electric Power, Shanghai 200090, China

†E-mail: jga2008@163.com

A complete simulation platform for master and slave clock synchronization based on IEEE 1588 protocol is presented. Comparisons with the published results from hardware platform have shown that the simulation platform gives a good indication on the level of synchronization performance. It can also be used for choosing the right parameters from both actual hardware devices and IEEE 1588 protocol.

Keywords: Quartz oscillator; Servo clock; Synchronization; IEEE1588; PTP.

1. Introduction

As the adoption of electric power system automation and distributed power networks becomes more widely spread, higher demands are placed on the requirements of time synchronization accuracy. For example, in the application of line fault detection using traveling wave method, time synchronization accuracy required to be less than 1μs [1]. IEEE 1588 protocol [2], also known as precision time protocol (PTP), provides the specifications for precision time synchronization based local area network (LAN), aiming at applications of network based measurements and control. In the standard, master and slave clocks exchanges local clock information through time stamped packets. From these packets, slave clock calculates time and frequency offsets from the reference values of master clock, and achieve synchronization by adjusting its own clock accordingly. Although a large amount of research time and energy has been put to various aspects of the protocol and related applications in network based measurement, control, and telecommunications, relatively few authors [3][4][5] discussed software simulators to the authors' best knowledge.

---

†Corresponding author.

Amongst the published works, [3] and [4] use a network simulator to build simulators using a simplified quartz oscillator model, and have not compared the simulators with hardware platform in terms of synchronization performance.

The aim of this paper is to show a general purpose simulator for the synchronization of master and slave clocks using PTP. The simulator should include all major factors which affect synchronization accuracy, and generate results which are comparable with the published results using hardware based platforms. Built upon the existing research work [5] on modeling of PTP time stamps only, current paper extends to a full synchronization system. Specifically, the well known quartz oscillator model [6] and slave servo clock are included in the simulator. Preliminary tests have shown that the proposed simulator has met its design goals.

The rest of the paper is organized as follows. Firstly, IEEE 1588 synchronization system is analyzed and each of the subsystems is modeled using Matlab/Simulink tool. Secondly, in order to validate the simulation platform, synchronization performance is assessed against those published results using hardware platform. Finally, discussions and conclusions are presented.

2. Synchronization Analysis and Modeling

A complete IEEE 1588 time synchronization system is shown in Fig. 1. It consists of three main subsystems: quartz oscillator, IEEE 1588 protocols, and clock servo subsystem for slave clock. Quartz oscillator provides the nominal frequency plus frequency noise. These values are sent to IEEE 1588 protocol subsystem where time stamps (T_1 to T_4) are generated according to IEEE 1588 specifications. At slave clock side, these time stamps are used to calculated time offset with respect to the time reference of master clock. The offset values are then fed to a clock servo which typically consists of a PI controller. Adjustment is made by the PI controller such that the slave clock follows the reference time by the master clock as closely as possible. This completes one synchronization cycle. The whole process happens at a regular interval which is called synchronization interval as in the standard. In the following, each of the main subsystems and its modeling is discussed in details.

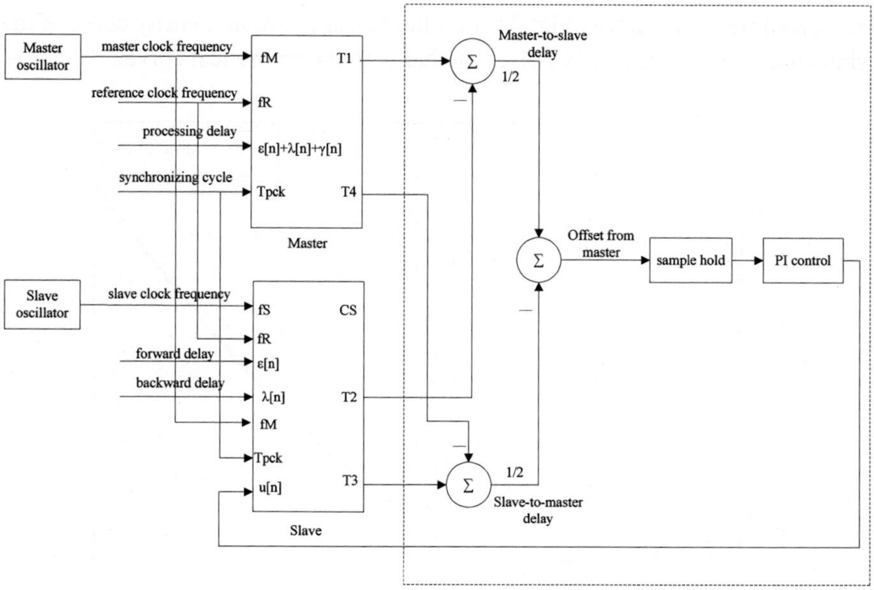

Fig. 1: Complete system model for IEEE 1488 synchronization

2.1. *Quartz oscillator model*

Most of researches on IEEE 1588 protocol use some simplified quartz oscillator model [7]. In order to more accurately reflect the performance of actual hardware, the well known oscillator model [6] is adopted here. Let the nominal frequency f_0 be the reference frequency, and instantaneous frequency denoted by f. Define the instant frequency offset (noise) $y(t) = (f - f_0)/f_0$. According to [6], the power spectrum density of $y(t)$ can be expressed as follows:

$$S_y(f) = h_{-2}f^{-2} + h_{-1}f^{-1} + h_0 + h_1 f + h_2 f^2 . \tag{1}$$

From (1), it can be seen that the total frequency noise spectrum consists of 5 types of noise: white noise, flicker phase noise, white frequency noise, flicker frequency noise, and random walk frequency noise. In the modeling of quartz oscillator, a commonly used technique is to shape white Gaussian noise by a shaping filter whose magnitude square is equal to the desired power spectrum density in order to produce the frequency noise with the desired power spectrum density. Therefore, for each of the 5 types of frequency noise, this technique is used. The outputs of the shaping filters are then summarized to generate the simulated frequency noise. Fig. 2 shows the power spectrum density curve of the simulated random frequency noise together with the theoretical curve.

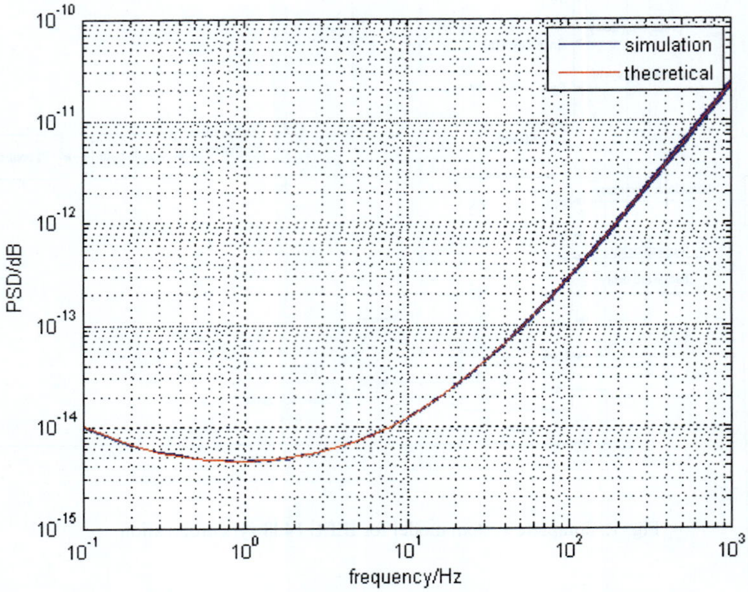

Fig. 2: Power spectrum density of frequency noise of quartz oscillator model

2.2. *IEEE1588 protocol model*

The main function of this model is to generate time stamps (T_1 to T_4) according to IEEE 1588 specifications. In the current research work, the protocol model shown in [5] is used. In the following a brief summary is provided. Further details are obtained from the reference.

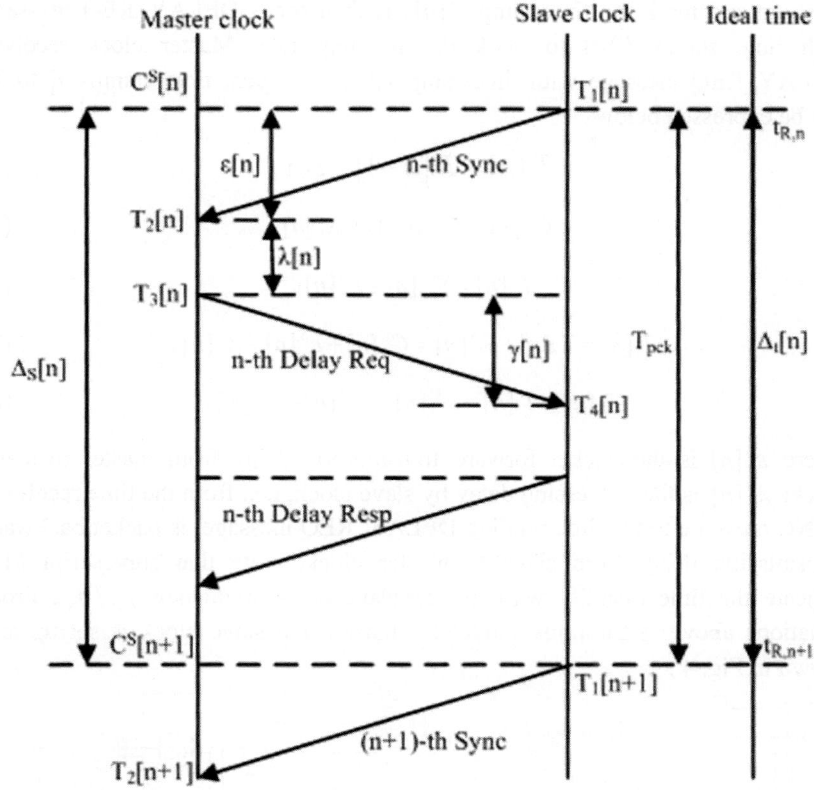

Fig. 3: Synchronization process according to IEEE 1588 protocol

Fig. 3 shows the complete cycle of synchronization process. It should be noted that there are 3 types of time reference which are used in time measurements: master/slave crystal oscillator frequency denoted by f_M / f_S and the nominal frequency by f_R. Master clock sends sync messages at a regular interval T_{pck} w.r.t. f_M . The corresponding values measured w.r.t other frequency references are as follows:

$$\Delta_t[n] = \frac{f_R}{f_M[n]} T_{pck} . \tag{2}$$

$$\Delta_S[n] = \frac{f_S[n]}{f_R} \Delta_t[n] = \frac{f_S[n]}{f_M[n]} T_{pck} . \tag{3}$$

In Fig. 3, a sync message is sent at $T_1[n]$ by the master clock. The corresponding time at slave clock side is $C_S[n]$. Slave clock receives SYNC message and mark the timestamp $T_2[n]$. It then sends DELAY_REQ message with time stamp $T_3[n]$ to mark the sending time. Master clock receives DELAY_REQ message with timestamp $T_4[n]$. As such, time stamps T_1 to T_4 can be expressed below

$$T_1[n] = T_1[n-1] + T_{pck}\,. \tag{4}$$

$$C^S[n] = C^S[n-1] + \Delta_S[n]\,. \tag{5}$$

$$T_2[n] = C^S[n] + \varepsilon^S[n]\,. \tag{6}$$

$$T_3[n] = T_2[n] + \lambda^S[n] = C^S[n] + \varepsilon^S[n] + \lambda^S[n]\,. \tag{7}$$

$$T_4[n] = T_1[n] + \varepsilon^M[n] + \lambda^M[n] + \gamma^M[n]\,. \tag{8}$$

where $\varepsilon^S[n]$ is the packet forward transmission delay from master to slave clock; $\lambda^S[n]$ is the processing delay by slave clock, i.e., from the time receiving SYNC message to the time sending DELAY_REQ message; is packet backward transmission delay from slave to master clock. Note that superscript M/S indicate the time quantity w.r.t. master/slave clock frequency f_M / f_S. From equations above, a Simulink model for master and slave clock is set up and shown in Fig. 4 .

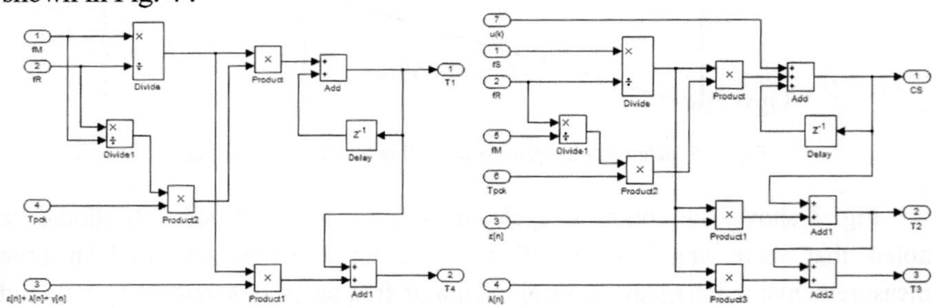

Fig. 4: Simulink model for master and slave clock

2.3. *Clock servo model*

At slave clock side, clock servo adjusts local time according to time offset between master and slave clock. The complete clock servo is shown within the dashed line in Fig. 1. According to IEEE 1588 protocol, assuming transmission delay is symmetric, transmission delay and time offset can be expressed as

$$d_{prop} = \left[(T_1 - T_2) + (T_3 - T_4)\right]/2\,. \tag{9}$$

$$d_{offset} = \left[(T_1 - T_2) - (T_3 - T_4)\right]/2\,. \tag{10}$$

The offset is fed into a PI controller which generates the required amount of time correction to achieve synchronization.

3. Simulation Platform Validation

To validate the effectiveness of the simulation platform as a useful research tool, simulation results generated by the software platform are compared with the published results based on hardware platforms [8][9], using the parameters setup as close to that of the hardware as possible.

In the first comparison, the main parameters are set up according to [8]: Nominal master and slave crystal oscillator frequency is 50 MHz with frequency drift within ±50 ppm, synchronization interval $T_{pck} = 125$ ms; Since reference [8] does not provide line delay parameters, these values are set according to [11], where forward, backward path delay has uniform distribution $U(1602,1608)$ ns, and processing delay has normal distribution with the mean (2 μs) and standard deviation(0.5 μs), i.e., $N(2,0.5)$ μs

Fig. 5 shows the simulated time error of the slave clock and its distribution w.r.t master clock time after convergence. It can be seen that the time error is less than 20 ns. This result is comparable to the performance result of estimated 30 ns shown in [8]

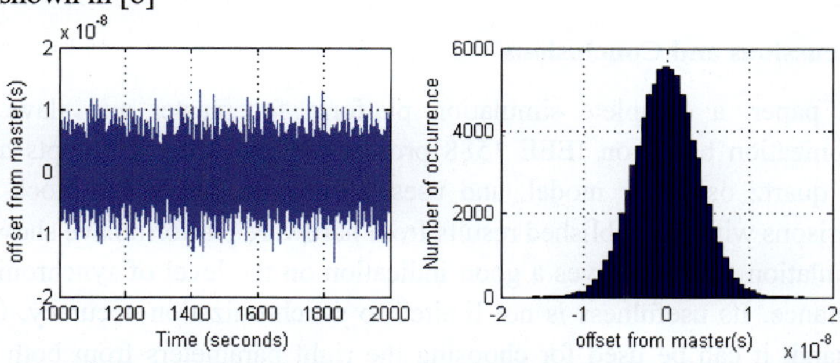

Fig. 5: time error of slave clock, w.r.t master clock(left); distribution of error (right)

In the second comparison, the key parameters according to [9] are: the nominal frequencies for both local clocks are the same at 50 MHz; frequency drift is within ±50 ppm; forward, backward line delay has uniform distribution $U(1602,1608)$ ns, and processing delay has the same normal distribution $N(2,0.5)$ μs. Note the total transmission path in [9] also includes a switch. According to [11], the delay caused by the switch is modeled by Beta(α, β) distribution with $\alpha = 1$ and $\beta = 3$. Further, depending on the traffic on the network, the minimum and maximum delay of the switch is set to10μs and 32.8μs. The setting of the minimum and maximum values corresponds to the average switch delay of 15.7μs which is in line with [9].

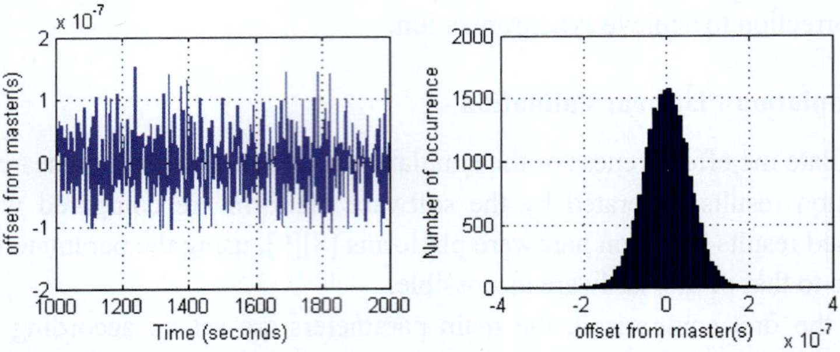

Fig. 6: time error of slave clock, w.r.t master clock(left); distribution of error (right) with normal switch delay beta(1, 3), min. and max. delay are 10us and 32.8 us

Fig. 6 shows the simulated time error of the slave clock. From the results, the distribution is symmetric and the estimated standard deviation of around 53.9 ns. In [9], 3 switches are used for the time measurement. For all switches, the mean error is non-zero, and the standard deviation values are 23 ns, 111 ns, and 142 ns, respectively, depending on the maker of the switches. Clearly, the standard deviation of the simulated results is comparable to that of the measured results.

4. Discussions and Conclusions

In this paper, a complete simulation platform for master and slave clock synchronization based on IEEE 1588 protocol is presented. It adopts a well-known quartz oscillator model, and uses a PI controller as the clock servo. Comparisons with the published results from hardware platform have shown that the simulation platform gives a good indication on the level of synchronization performance. Its usefulness is not limited to synchronization accuracy. On the other hand, it can be used for choosing the right parameters from both actual hardware devices and IEEE 1588 protocol. Future research work will include how these parameters will affect synchronization performance and convergence time.

Acknowledgments

This work is supported by Supported by Innovation Program of Shanghai Municipal Education Commission.

References

1. G.S, Antonova, et al. Standard profile for use of IEEE std 1588-2008 precision time protocol (PTP) in power system applications, *Proc. 2013 66th Annual Conference for Protective Relay Engineers*
2. IEEE Std 1588-2008, IEEE Standard for a precision Clock Synchronization Protocol for Networked Measurement and Control Systems 2008.
3. A. Depari, P. Ferrari, A. Flammini, D. Marioli, A. Taroni., Evaluation of Timing Characteristics of Industrial Ethernet Networks Synchronized by means of IEEE 1588, *IMTC,* 2007
4. G. Giorgi and C. Narduzzi, Modeling and Simulation Analysis of PTP Clock Servo, *ISPCS*, 2007
5. Zdenek Chaloupka, Nayef Alsindi, James Aweya. Efficient and Precise Simulation Model of Synchronization Clocks in Packet Networks *CAMAD*, 2013. pp.79-83.
6. A. Chorti and M. Brookes, A spectral model for RF oscillators with power-law phase noise, *IEEE Transactions on Circuits and Systems I-Regular Papers*, vol. 53, pp. 1989-1999, Sep 2006
7. D. Veitch, S. Babu, and A. Pastor, Robust Synchronization of Software Clocks Across the Internet, *Proc. of the 4th ACMSIGCOMM conf: on Internet measurement*, pp. 219-232, October 2004.
8. Sven Meier, Hans Weibel, Karl Weber. IEEE 1588 Syntonization and Synchronization Functions Completely Realized in Hardware. *ISPCS, 2008.*
9. H. Huckeba, R. Dlugy-Hegwer, Precise Time Synchronization Using IEEE 1588 for LXI Application, pp. 129-135, *Proc. IEEE Autotestcon,* 2006.
10. I. Hadzi, D. R. Morgan, Adaptive Packet Selection for Clock Recovery, in ISPCS, 2010, pp. 42-47.
11. Daniele Fontanelli, David Macii, Stefano Rinaldi. A Servo-Clock Model for Chains of Transparent Clocks Affected by Synchronization Period. *IEEE Trans. on Instru. and Measurement,* pp. 1085-1095, vol. 63, no. 5, May, 2014

Session 2

Computer Network

An Improvement of DV-Hop Localization Algorithm Based on Harmony Search Algorithm

Jing-li YANG† and Qi-shen ZHU

School of Computer and Software, Nanjing Institute of Industry Technology, Nanjing, 210023, China

†E-mail: Jingliy1971@163.com

The conventional range-free positioning DV-Hop algorithm used in wireless sensor networks experience low positioning accuracy due to several factors. An improved algorithm: HSDV-Hop(Harmony Search DV-Hop) was proposed in this paper which provides high convergence speed and outstanding performance in solving global optimization problems as compared to the original DV-Hop algorithm. The improved algorithm establishes the optimization functions by the information of distance between the nodes and the location of beacon nodes, so the locations of unknown nodes are estimated. The results show that the proposed method can significantly improve positioning accuracy as compared to the original DV-Hop algorithm without increasing the sensor nodes hardware.

Keywords: Wireless Sensor Networks; Node Localization; DV-Hop Algorithm; Harmony Search Algorithm.

1. Introduction

With the development of sensor, electronics and radio techniques, low-power and inexpensive wireless sensors have been put into application, then the wireless sensor networks (WSNs) are developing very quickly. For many existent and novel WSN applications, such as vehicle or animal tracking, control of machinery, agriculture, location-aware route selection and environment monitoring, the availability of information about sensor locations is very important in order to collect data [1][2].

Localization technology for wireless sensor network is divided into two categories: range-based and range-free. Range-based algorithms use absolute point-to-point distance or angle information to calculate the location between neighboring sensors. The second class of methods, range-free approach, employs to find the distances from the non-anchor nodes to the anchor nodes. In

† Corresponding author.

the process of location range-free approach needs lower hardware and lower cost. Because of the advantages, this paper focuses the investigation on the range-free algorithms for WSNs[3][4].

DV-hop algorithm is widely used range-free approach. The core idea is that the average distance of each hop is multiplied by minimum hop-count between unknown nodes and anchor nodes and estimates the position of the unknown nodes. But due to some external factors the position accuracy is not high. This paper proposed an improved DV-Hop algorithm based on harmony search algorithm[10][11][12]. Through simulation experiments positioning error of the two algorithms is compared under different node numbers and different communication radius. The results show that the proposed method can significantly reduce positioning error compared with the original DV-Hop algorithm without increasing the hardware overhead of sensor nodes.

2. Improved DV-HOP Location

2.1. *DV-Hop algorithm*

Niculescu and Nath who use the principle of distance vector routing , have proposed the DV-Hop algorithm which is a distributed, hop by hop positioning algorithm. The algorithm implementation is comprised of three steps. In the first step, compute the minimum number of hops. Through this, all nodes in the network get the minimal hop-count to every anchor node. In the second step, compute the distance between unknown nodes and the anchor nodes. In the third step, compute the coordinates of unknown nodes[3][7].

Through the positioning process above-mentioned can be seen that the DV-Hop algorithm uses the average distance per hop between anchor nodes as the distance per hop between unknown nodes and anchor nodes, then the value is multiplied by the corresponding number of hop-count and get the distance d_i between the unknown nodes to anchor nodes. The d_i value estimated must exist large error due to the impact on the environment and communication fact. This will affect the positioning accuracy of the algorithm.

2.2. *Harmony search algorithm*

The basic HS algorithm consists of three basic phases, namely, initialization, improvisation, and updating the harmony memory. First of all, an initial population of harmonies represented by n-dimension real-valued vectors are randomly generated and stored in a harmony memory. Then a new candidate harmony is generated by an improvisation process. Finally, the harmony memory is updated by comparing the generated candidate harmony with the worst harmony in the harmony memory. The above process is repeated until a given termination criterion is reached[5][6][8]. The details of the basic HS algorithm are described as follows.

Step 1: Initialize the algorithm parameters. The optimization problem is defined as Minimize $f(x)$ subject to $x_{iL} \ll x \ll x_{iU}$,(i=1,2, ⋯,N). x_{iL} and x_{iU} are the lower and upper bounds for decision variables, respectively. Parameters of HS algorithm have the harmony memory size (HMS); harmony memory considering rate (HMCR); pitch adjusting date (PAR);and the number of improvisations(K), or stopping criterion.

Step 2: Initialize the harmony memory[9]. The initialize harmony memory (HM) is generated from a uniform distribution in the ranges $[x_{iL}, x_{iU}]$, (j=1,2, ⋯,N), showed as in Eq.(1).

$$HM=\begin{bmatrix} x_1^1 & x_2^1 & \cdots & x_{N-1}^1 & x_N^1 \\ x_1^2 & x_2^2 & \cdots & x_{N-1}^2 & x_N^2 \\ \vdots & \vdots & \vdots & \vdots & \vdots \\ x_1^{HMS-1} & x_2^{HMS-1} & \cdots & x_{N-1}^{HMS-1} & x_N^{HMS-1} \\ x_1^{HMS} & x_2^{HMS} & \cdots & x_{N-1}^{HMS} & x_N^{HMS} \end{bmatrix} \quad (1)$$

where x_j^i are the j-th (j=1,2, ⋯ ,N) harmony component of the i-th (i=1,2, ⋯,HMS) harmony solution vector.

Step 3:Improvise a new harmony. A new harmony vector , $x' = (x_1', x_2', \ldots, x_N')$, is generated based on three rules(1)memory consider,(2)pitch adjustment and (3)random selection.

Step 4:Update harmony memory. If the fitness of the improvised harmony vector x′ is better than that of the worst harmony, replace the worst harmony in the HM with x′.

Step 5:Check the stopping criterion. If the maximal iteration number(K)is satisfied, computation is terminated. Otherwise, Step 3 and 4 are repeated.

2.3. *The computation procedure of improved location algorithm*

In the procedure of searching the optimal solution, the evaluation of the new generated candidate solutions and the update of the harmony memory are performed at each iteration based on fitness function values. To this end, only those harmonies improving the fitness of those from the previous iteration are included in the next harmony memory. Once this has been done, the harmony memory is sorted in ascending order of the fitness values of its compounding melodies. So the setting of fitness function is a vital problem in the optimization process of HS algorithm.

A method of constrain fitness function to obtain the fitness value is proposed in "Constraint particle swarm optimization algorithm for wireless sensor networks localization"[4]and" Improvement of DV-Hop localization based on artificial bee colony algorithm " [3]. We apply this idea to fitness function of HS algorithm. Through the analysis of the positioning process of general DV-Hop algorithm, in step 3, *di* error is larger because of external factors and internal measurement error when the distance between the anchor node and the unknown node is measured. Then computation of unknown nodes coordinates can be converted into the following Eq.(2).

$$\begin{cases} (x-x_1)^2+(y-y_1)^2=r_1^2+\delta_1^2 \\ (x-x_2)^2+(y-y_2)^2=r_n^2+\delta_2^2 \\ \vdots \\ (x-x_n)^2+(y-y_n)^2=r_n^2+\delta_n^2 \end{cases} \tag{2}$$

where $\delta_i(\mathrm{i}=1,2\ \cdots,\mathrm{n})$ is error and $r_i(\mathrm{i}=1,2\ \cdots,\mathrm{n})$ is the actual distance between the unknown nodes and the anchor nodes, so there is $-\delta_i \leqslant r_i - d_i \leqslant \delta_i$. Then the unknown node coordinate (x, y) should satisfy the following formula(3):

$$\begin{cases} d_1^2-\delta_1^2 \leq (x-x_1)^2+(y-y_1)^2 \leq d_1^2+\delta_1^2 \\ d_2^2-\delta_2^2 \leq (x-x_2)^2+(y-y_2)^2 \leq d_2^2+\delta_2^2 \\ \vdots \\ d_n^2-\delta_n^2 \leq (x-x_n)^2+(y-y_n)^2 \leq d_n^2+\delta_n^2 \end{cases} \tag{3}$$

(3)

where f(x,y) is fitness function(4), work out (x, y) which satisfy the minimum value of formula(4).

$$f(x,y)=\sum_{\mathrm{i}}^{\mathrm{n}}\left(\sqrt{(x-x_i)^2+(y-y_i)^2}-d_i\right) \tag{4}$$

So the unknown node coordinate error will be reduced to minimum with the formula(4), and the accuracy is improved. Positioning steps of localization algorithm based on HS algorithm are following:

Step 1: Initialize network and each anchor node broadcasts a beacon throughout the network.

Step 2: Unknown nodes receive the hop-count value from anchors . The main idea is that if it did not receive any information, it will save this information; otherwise it will compare this value with the last value and save the smaller one. Repeat this step until all broadcasts end.

Step 3：Compute average size for one hop and the distance of unknown nodes to anchor nodes.

Step 4：Compute unknown nodes coordinate by HS algorithm.

3. Simulation Results

In this section, simulation results are presented and analyzed. We simulate the DV-Hop algorithm and our proposed algorithm to evaluate location performance.

To compare the performance of the algorithm, we have built three different network topologies by uniformly placing n = 200 nodes in a square region of 1×1. A fraction (10%, hence m = 20) of these nodes corresponds to the anchor nodes set, whose fixed positions are known a priori. In an identified scenario, hop-count value and hop-size between nodes mainly relates to the node communication radius, and the radius is too large or too small to affect the positioning accuracy. So selecting appropriate communication radius is necessary. Different communication radius affects localization accuracy by this algorithm, as is shown in Table 1. In the simulation the value of HCMR,PAR and RSR is respectively set 0.9,0.01 and 0.01.

Table 1. Influence of communication radius on positioning error rate(%)

Initial anchor node number	Node average error rate for different communication radius					
	0.1	0.13	0.15	0.18	0.2	0.25
5	—	—	68.5	51.8	70.3	73.8
10	—	78.9	62.8	46.3	50.8	53.6
15	85.5	69.4	55.3	39.7	42.7	45.7
20	72.5	62.3	48.5	37.1	41.5	42.6

Note：'—' indicates network communication failure

Based on above analysis different connectivity ranges R∈{0.13, 0.15, 0.17} are considered to model different network levels in this algorithm. For each scenario, 20 Monte Carlo runs of the algorithms are executed. Localization error is following as Eq. (5).

$$error=\frac{\sqrt{(x_t-x_e)^2+(y_t-y_e)^2}}{R}\times 100\% \qquad (5)$$

where (x_t, y_t) is real coordinates of unknown node, and (x_e, y_e) is estimated coordinates of unknown node. R is communication radius. In the process of simulation experiment localization error is observed by changing connection radius between nodes, and statistical results are shown table 2. With R=0.13 and a fixed anchor nodes number of m=10, total node numbers are set to 100,150,200,250,300,350 and 400. Other parameters remain unchanged, and the performance is compared and the results are shown in Fig.1.

Table 2. Statistical results of error based on HSDV-HOP and DV-HOP algorithm

R	DV-Hop	HSDV-Hop
0.13	17.12/25.78/16.01	11.55/22.08/10.17
0.15	9.65/25.12/13.31	10.69/17.07/6.08
0.17	6.87/15.93/5.88	7.83/12.33/3.96

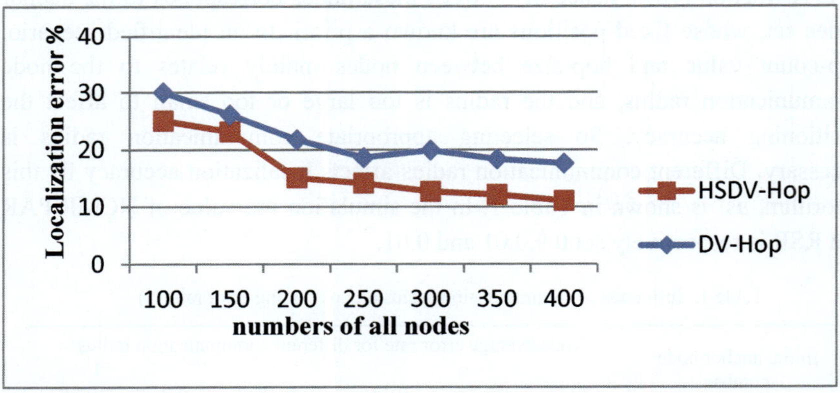

Fig. 1. Location error(R=0.13)

We assess the performance of the proposed HSDV-Hop algorithm over the three network topologies in terms of error defined in Eq. (5), and compare the results with the ones achieved by the DV-Hop algorithm, for the different values of R. Table 2 summarizes the results in the format best/mean/std error value(averaged over 20 experiments). Fig.1 shows error value for two algorithms while the connection radius is 0.13.The first thing to observe is that the mean and standard deviation of the error obtained by the HS-based algorithm are significantly lower with respect to the ones achieved by DV-Hop approach. Furthermore, the respective best error values (i.e., the minimum) are quite similar. In light of these preliminary results, one may conclude that the localization estimation obtained by DV-Hop is on average much less accurate and stable with respect to the one achieved by HSDV-Hop. It is a feasible scheme to apply harmony search algorithm to node localization of wireless sensor network.

4. Conclusion

In this paper, we have analyzed the positioning process using the basic DV-Hop algorithm for the not high accuracy problem because of the environment, distance measurement inaccuracy and other factors. These problems cause large errors when using least square method to compute coordinates of the unknown nodes. The least square method is replaced by harmony search algorithm in the positioning stage based on the analysis of the principle of harmony search algorithm. So we have proposed a HSDV-Hop algorithm based on harmony search algorithm. The simulation results show that the HSDV-Hop algorithm significantly improves the position accuracy compared with the basic DV-Hop algorithm.

Acknowledgments

Work partially supported by grant ZK13-02-06 of the Open Foundation of Intelligent Sensor Network Engineering Technology Research and Development Center of Jiangsu Province.

References

1. A.I.F., W.Su, S. Y, and C. E, A Survey on Sensor Networks, in Proc.IEEE Communications Magazine, Vol.40, pp.102-113, August. 2002.
2. D. Niculescu, B. Nath. Ad Hoc Positioning System (APS) , Proc. of the IEEE GLOBECOM 2001, San Antonio, pp. 2926-2931, 2001.
3. Mu-dong Li , Wei Xiong and Long Guo, Improvement of DV-Hop localization based on artificial bee colony algorithm in Chinese,Computer Science,Vol.40 NO.1, pp 33-36, January 2013.

4. Dan-tong Ouyang, Jin-sheng He and Hong-tao Bai, Constraint particle swarm optimization algorithm for wireless sensor networks localization in Chinese,Computer Science, Vol.38 No.7, pp 46-50, July 2011.
5. Jin Li and Yan Xiong, On harmony search and local search-based nodes localization in wireless sensor networks in Chinese,Computer Applications and Software, Vol.31 NO.9, pp 129-133, September 2014.
6. T. W. Liao,Two Hybrid Differential Evolution Algorithms for Engineering Design Optimization, Applied Soft Computing, Vol. 10, N. 4, pp. 1188-1199, September 2010.
7. Hongyang Chen, Kaoru Sezaki, An improved DV-Hop localization algorithm for wireless sensor networks, in Proc.IEEE Communications Magazine, Vol 38, pp. 101-105, September 2008.
8. Diana Manjarres, Javier Del Ser and Sergio Gill-Lopez, On the application of hybrid harmony search algorithm to node localization in anchor-based wireless sensor nerworks, in Proc. IEEE International Conference on Intelligent Systems Design and Applications, pp. 1014-1019,November 2011.
9. Zhao-hua Cui, Li-qun Gao,Hai-bin Quan, Hong-jun Li, Hybrid differential Evolution harmony search algorithm for numerical optimization problems,25th Chinese Control and Decision Conference, pp.2930-2933,2013.
10. M mahdavi, MFesanghary, E Damangir, An improve harmony search algorithm for solving optimization problems, Applied Mathematics and Computation, Vol.188,No.2,pp.1567-1579,2007.
11. S.Gil-Lopez, J.Del Ser, I.Olabarrieta, A novel heuristicalgorithm for multiuser detection in synchronous CDMA wireless sensor networks, IEEE International Conference on Ultra Modern Communications,pp.1-6, October 2009.
12. J.Del Ser,M.N.Bilbao, S.Gil-Lopez, M.Matinmikko, S.Salcedo-Sanz, Iterative power and Subcarrier allocation in Rate-Constrained orthogonal Multicarrier Downlink systems based on hybrid harmony search heuristics , Engineering Applications of Artificial Intelligence, Vol.24,N.5,pp. 748-756,August 2011.

An Adaptive Refresh Mechanism Based on DTTL Model for DNS

Hua-wei XUE, Bao-sheng WANG, Ning HU and Jing TAO
College of Computer, National University of Defense Technology,
Changsha, Hunan, China
E-mail: huaweicanfly@163.com

Most DNS system apply cache mechanism to improve the efficiency of domain name resolving. Setting up the TTL value of the cache item is the key issue of DNS performance optimization. This paper proposes a dynamic adjustment algorithm for DNS cache item. By using DTTL model, our algorithm dynamically changes the TTL value as the varying of resolving rate. With comparisons to modifying the zone file directly, our algorithm makes a tradeoff between the consistence and hit rate.

Keywords: DNS cache; DTTL; TTL mechanism.

1. Introduction

With the rapid development of the network, DNS is one of the most important infrastructure of Internet[1], mapping the domain name to IP and providing service for client. In order to reduce the network bandwidth and the time of client-perceived lookup delays[2], DNS cache is proposed as a effective way to deal with the problem. The TTL is the time (in seconds) that a resolver will use the data it got from your server before it asks your server again, which is widely used in DNS cache. Lotter M advise that most TTLS should be set to anywhere between a day and a week[3]. However, Barr D says the value is too low except for zones with data that vary regularly and 3 or more days are recommended[4], even 1-2 weeks for some MX, A, PTR records of your mail hosts.

It is crucial that TTLS are set to appropriate values. If you set the value two low, your server will get loaded down with lots of repeat requests. If you set it too high, then information you change will not get distributed in a reasonable amount of time. Although a lot of effort is being spent on improving the weakness, the efficient and effective method has yet to be developed.

Our contributions are as follows: (1) propose the DTTL model in DNS and give the algorithm. (2) DTTL can handle with the changeable DNS request rate and dynamically revise the TTL value according to the request rate. (3) DTTL make a tradeoff between the DNS hit ratio and DNS consistence. (4) DTTL model supports backward compatibility and incremental deployment.

In Section 2 we survey related work. Section 3 analyzes the problem that current DNS TTL mechanism is faced with and proposes DTTL model. Section 4 presents numerical simulations that show that miss of DTTL and ordinal DNS TTL. in Section 5 we evaluate the implement of DTTL in current DNS and then conclude with a summary of our findings in Section 6 .

2. Related Work

The concept of DNS cache was investigated quite intensively in recent years. Many research studies have been carried out on this topic5.

In domain name system, in order to alleviate the load of root servers, the recursive server of DNS caches some resource records. If communication link to root server broke due to network and other reasons, the cache of RR in recursive server decided the quality of resolving services. And the longer TTL acts the better[5]. Zheng Wang analysis the DNS cache effects that occur on query distribution at the CN top-level domain (TLD) server[6]. and concludes that DNS query for the CN TLD server follows Zipf-like distribute. Namely, the load of CN TLD server is dominated by hot domain names. These works indicate that TTL plays an important role in improve the DNS performance.

Jung J, Berger A W, Balakrishnan H rely on a assumption that requests can be modeled as a sequence of independent and identically distributed random variables[7]. They explain the empirical finding of Jung et al. that the cache hit rate for DNS accesses rapidly increases as a function of TTL, exceeding 80% for a TTL of 15minutes. Berger D S, Gland P, Singla S, et al model three kinds of TTL mechanism and presents the hits and memory occupation in theory[8], which can be used in our analysis of DTTL model.

Cohen E, Kaplan H considered a Renewal policy associated with each cached item a renewal credit[9].The credit card is an integer stating the remaining number of renewals and may be updated when the cached item is used. When the item expires and has a positive credit, it is renewed and the credit is decremented. But the research can't deal with the problem that the request turns slow but the credit is so big because of high request just now. apart from this ,when the request is too high, the integer can't express the value because of the size of integer.

3. Motivation and Objective

3.1. *DNS cache*

To begin with, we will provide a brief background on the DNS cache. There are two types of queries defined for DNS systems, Recursive Queries and Iterative Queries. The cache mechanism was introduced in both kinds of the queries. The common of them is that the RRs are cached in servers to improve the performance and the lookup efficiency[10]. We choose Recursive Queries for discussion.

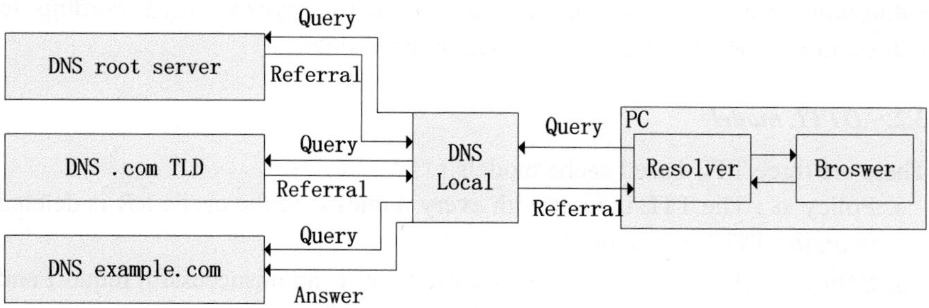

Fig.1.Recursive Query

Fig.1 illustrates the typical recursive resolution procedure. The client's browser is installed with a resolver, and the resolver requests a local recursive server for a name example.com. if the query misses the DNS cache in this recursive server, the server will follow the steps in the figure to obtain the addresses for example.com. requests will begin at the root servers n the DNS hierarchy. If the queried server has delegated its subzone containing the queried name, it returns a referral response. The response conveys the set of servers authoritative for the referral. The recursive server will choose one of these referral servers and repeat its question. This process typically proceeds until the final answer is returned by the authoritative server. And then cache the results.

According to Daniel S. Berger cache modeling analysis. X_i is the time interval between the (i-1)th query for the given data item and the ith. Let N(t) equal the number of queries for the given data item in the interval [0, t] and M(t) be the miss times. So the hit ratio in the time interval [0, t] can be defined as in Eq. (1).

$$H = \lim_{t \to \infty} \left(1 - \frac{M(t)}{N(t)} \right). \tag{1}$$

Passion arrivals for the distribution of inter-request times is assumed. The request rate λ is defined to be the excepted number of requests in a unit duration. So the hit can be expressed as Eq.(2).

$$H = \frac{\lambda T}{\lambda T + 1} . \tag{2}$$

As we can see from Eq.(2), when the request rate is too high, the TTL value should be increased to raise the hit ratio. Otherwise to turn low the value to maintain the consistence because of the small rate and the light load of the authoritative server. In a word, how to turn the TTL dynamically according to request rate is the problem we will solve in this article.

3.2. *DTTL model*

There are three TTL-based cache models.

i. Policy α : The TTL is reset with every request and the cache RR is deleted upon the TTL's expiration.

ii. Policy β : The TTL is reset only when there is an unsuccessful request and the cache RR is deleted upon the TTL's expiration.

iii. Policy $Min(\alpha, \beta)$: Two TTLS are reset in parallel according to the Police α and Police β ,respectively, and the cache RR is deleted upon the expiration of either of them.

Policy α can increase the hit ratio, because popular objects can dwell for much longer, whereas unpopular objects will be deleted quickly from the cache. But it suffer from the lack of consistency. Policy β can achieve weak consistency, but the hit ratio is low. Ordinal DNS TTL mechanism uses the Policy β. Policy Min(α , β) make a tradeoff between the hit ratio and the consistency.

Policy Min(α , β) has two application scenarios :

(1) the flow eviction mechanism in the flow table of SDN[11], idle_timeout and hard_timeout[12].

(2) Amazon Elasticache's mechanism to achieve a good memory tradeoff.

The DTTL model is origin from Policy Min(α , β).

Definition 3.1 *DNS DTTL Model: set two TTLS used in peak and trough period in the zone file of authoritative server,* T_α *and* T_β *separately. When missing, the recursive server get the RR and the two TTLs. Then the actually value of TTL is changed dynamically with the request rate according to the Policy Min(* α *,* β *). We define the value of actually TTL as DTTL, which is the time that the cached item dwell in the memory persistently, namely, DTTL* $\in [T_\alpha, T_\beta]$.

3.3. Algorithm

Let $S_n = X_1 + X_2 + X_3 + ... + X_n$ in the $[0, t_1]$ (0 is the miss time).

(1) if $\forall X_i < T_\alpha (i >= 1), \exists S_n > T_\beta \wedge S_{n-1} <= T_\beta$, then DTTL= T_β.

(2) if $\forall X_i > T_\alpha (i >= 1)$, then DTTL= T_α.

(3) if $\forall X_i > T_\alpha \wedge X_j (i, j >= 1)$, then DTTL $\in [T_\alpha, T_\beta]$.

The specific algorithm is described blow.

```
Timer:
if(aflag==1&&bflag==0){
  if( Tβ==0) remove from the cache;
  if( Tβ==0) remove from the cache;
}
if(aflag==0&&bflag==1){
   Tα--;
   if(Tα==0) remove from the cache;
}
if(aflag==0&&bflag==0){
   Tα--; Tβ--;
   if(Tα==0|| Tβ==0) remove from the cache;
}
//end of timer
Get request with domain name  itemA from client ,record current time ti;
flag=select_from_cache(itemA);
if(flag==0){//not in the cache
   Get response cache _itemA  from  NS;
   insert_cache(cache_itemA);
   if( Tβ==0)  bflag=1;
   if(Tα==0)  aflag=1;
   tempttl=Tα;
}//end of if
else{//in the cache
   if(ti-ti-1< Tα ) Tα= tempttl;
}//end else
```

4. Evaluation

To evaluate the effectiveness and performance of DTTL model, we apply this mechanism to BIND, which is by far the most popular implementation of DNS today[13].

4.1. Experimental design

Bind is used to set up a environment which has a 100 client, as in Fig. 2 . DTTL mechanism is applied to all the DNS server and set two TTLs,10 sec and 360 sec in the zone file of DNS example.com. In contrast , we set TTL value 10 sec in ordinal DNS. The value of DTTL in the DTTL model is tested to verify the dynamically change of TTL. Apart from this ,we also compare the Miss ratio in DTTL model and ordinal DNS TTL model.

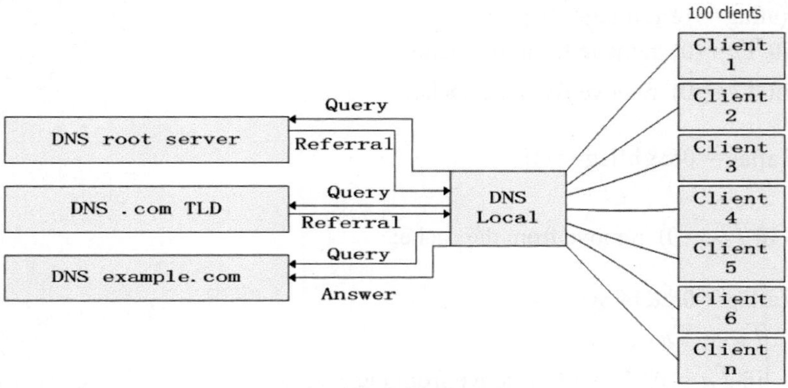

Fig.2. Environment

4.2. Evaluation criterion

We will evaluate our DNS DTTL model from two factors: DTTL value, miss ratio.

We assume N(t) is a renewal process and passion arrivals for the distribute of inter-request times. The request rate λ is defined to be the excepted number of requests in a unit duration.

4.2.1. *DTTL*

We assume k has positive correlation with request λ .

$$DTTL = (1-\mathrm{k})\mathrm{T}_{\alpha} + kT_{\beta}; (\mathrm{k} \in [0,1]) . \tag{3}$$

4.2.2. *Miss ratio*

We define H_{α} be hit ratio of the Police α , H_{β} be the Police β and $H_{Min(\alpha,\beta)}$ be the Police $Min(\alpha,\beta)$. Meanwhile, the γ has positive correlation with request λ .

The hit of Police α is expressed in Eq.(4).

$$H_{\alpha} = P(X < T_{\alpha}) = 1 - e^{-\lambda T_{\alpha}} . \tag{4}$$

The hit of Police β is expressed in Eq.(5).

$$H_{\beta} = \frac{\lambda T_{\beta}}{\lambda T_{\beta} + 1}, M_{\beta} = 1 - H_{\beta} . \tag{5}$$

The hit of Police $H_{Min(\alpha,\beta)}$ is expressed in Eq.(6).

$$H_{Min(\alpha,\beta)} = (1-\gamma)H_{\alpha} + \gamma H_{\beta}; (\gamma \in [0,1]), M_{Min(\alpha,\beta)} = 1 - H_{Min(\alpha,\beta)} . \tag{6}$$

4.3. Analysis

We use 14 samples with different request rate(time interval). Each rate has a 100 requests. Fig.3. illustrates the Miss ratio of DTTL and ordinal DNS of different request rates.

We also sample 100 requests with different time interval to testify that DTTL is dynamically changed by the different time interval.

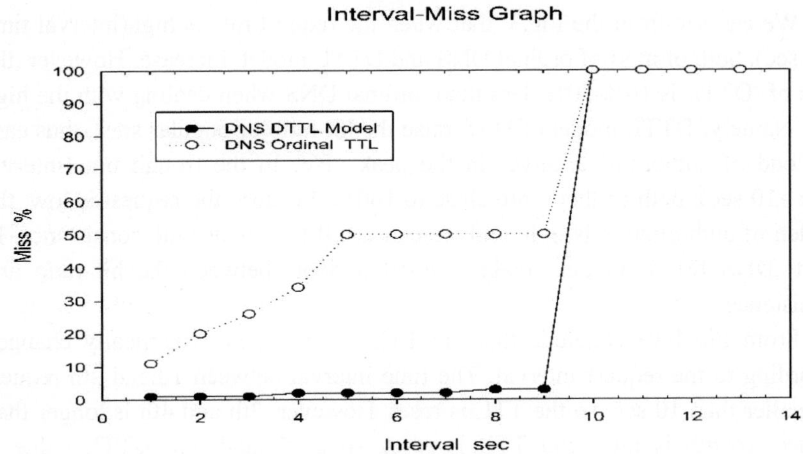

Fig.3. Interval-Miss

In Fig.4. Top-x is the request number. Bottom-x is the request time interval of the request number. We use ten requests in front to analysis the DTTL.

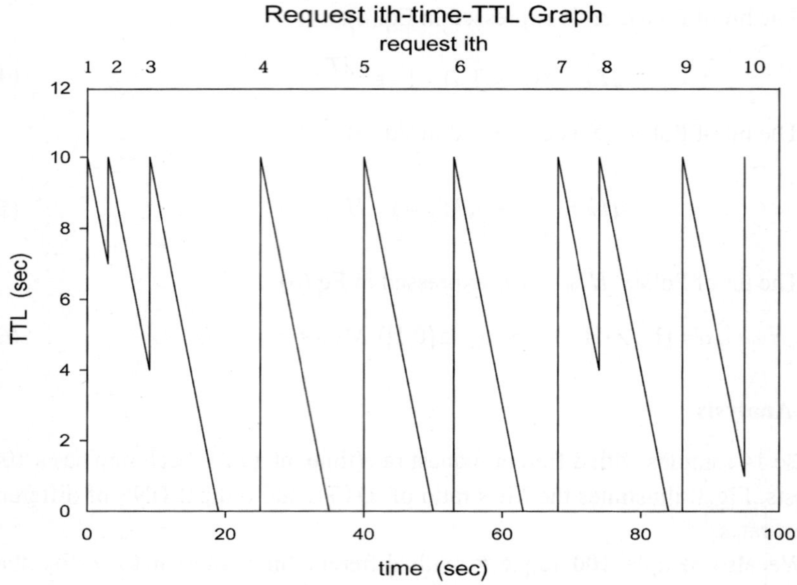

Fig.4. Request ith-time-TTL

We can see from the Fig.3. that when the request rate is high(interval time <10 sec), both of miss of ordinal DNS and DTTL model increase. However ,the miss of DTTL is 10%-50% less than ordinal DNS when dealing with the high rate. Namely, DTTL model of DNS raise the hit ratio of popular sites, thus ease the load of authoritative server in the peak PV. In the trough time(interval time >10 sec), both of them are close to 100%. Because the request is low, the burden of authoritative is light and we can use it to increase the consistence. In short ,DNS DTTL model make a good tradeoff between the hit ratio and consistence.

From Fig.4.we conclude that the TTL of DTTL is dynamically changed according to the request interval. The time interval between 1thand 2th request is smaller than 10 sec, so the TTL is reset. However ,3th and 4th is longer than 10 sec, so 4th is miss and TTL is reset, so as 5thand 6th. DTTL value is X1+X2+10 when request is high and turns 10 sec when request time interval is big. That is to say that DTTL is dynamically changed by the request time interval.

5. Implementation

DTTL can be achieved by set another TTL in the zone file of authoritative and apply the DTTL algorithm to the DNS implement software like Bind.

We can use the additional records and add the additional TTL to the last of Additional records. Fig.5 presents the ordinal and DTTL DNS response message.

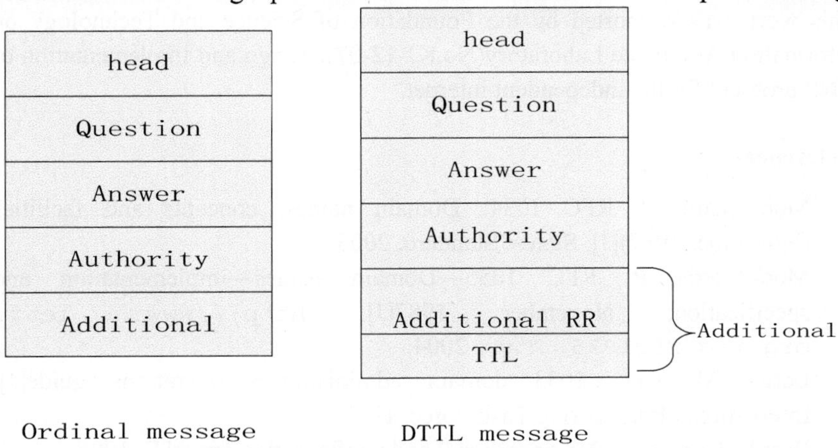

Fig.5. Ordinal and DTTL DNS response message

When the response message containing two TTLs encountered by ordinal DNS, ordinal DNS will think this Additional record only containing TTL is wrong and will delete this Additional record, then deal with the response message as usual. Whereas, if DTTL achieved in DNS, it will cache the two TTLs contained in the Additional record and the Answers or Authoritative name servers and dynamically change the value of DTTL according to request rate. When DNS with implement of DTTL receives the response messages containing not TTL in the Additional records, it will deal with them as ordinal DNS does. Thus, DTTL model supports backward compatibility and incremental deployment.

6. Conclusion

In this paper, we presented an adaptive cache mechanism for DNS. This mechanism is based on DTTL model and can be used to solve the problems of dynamically changing the TTL according to the request time interval. The result of experiment shows DTTL can make a good tradeoff between the hit ratio and consistence. DTTL does not modify the protocol implementation of DNS; it is incrementally deplorable, which means even small groups of DTTL can have immediate benefits from deployment.

Acknowledgments

This work was supported by the Foundation of Science and Technology on Information Assurance Laboratory(No.KJ-12-07),Design and Implementation of DNS protocol for the independent internet.

References

1. Mockapetris P. RFC 1034: Domain names: concepts and facilities (November 1987)[J]. Status: Standard, 2003.
2. Mockapetris P. RFC 1035—Domain names—implementation and specification, November 1987[J]. http://www. ietf. org/rfc/rfc1035. Txt, 2004.
3. Lotter M. RFC 1033 domain administrators operations guide[J]. International Engineering Task Force, 1987.
4. Barr D. Common DNS operational and configuration errors[J]. 1996.
5. Ting Wei, Feng Leng, Dong-yue Zhang,. Study of Resource Record Cache Expiring of DNS Server[J]. Telecommucations Science, 2013, 29(9): 94-97.
6. Wang Z. Analysis of dns cache effects on query distribution[J]. The Scientific World Journal, 2013, 2013.
7. Jung J, Berger A W, Balakrishnan H. Modeling TTL-based Internet caches[C]//INFOCOM 2003. Twenty-Second Annual Joint Conference of the IEEE Computer and Communications. IEEE Societies. IEEE, 2003, 1: 417-426.
8. Berger D S, Gland P, Singla S, et al. Exact analysis of TTL cache networks[J]. Performance Evaluation, 2014, 79: 2-23.
9. Cohen E, Kaplan H. Proactive caching of DNS records: Addressing a performance bottleneck[J]. Computer Networks, 2003, 41(6): 707-726.
10. Lin B, Li S, Liao X, et al. Leach: an automatic learning cache for inline primary deduplication system[J]. Frontiers of Computer Science,2014,8(2).175-183
11. Xie J, Guo D, Hu z, et al. Control Plane of Software Define Networks: A Survey[J]
12. Specification-Version O F S. 1.4. 0[J]. 2013.
13. P. Albitz and C. Liu, DNS and BIND, O'Reilly and Associates, Cambridge, Mass, USA, 1998

A Request Migration Algorithm for Load Balancing in P2P VoD Systems

Gui-min HUANG, Cheng-sen LI, Ping-shan LIU† and Ya ZHOU
Guangxi Key Laboratory of Trusted Software
Guangxi Experiment Center of Information Science
Key Laboratory of Cognitive Radio and Information Processing of Ministry of Education
Guilin University of Electronic Technology, Guilin, China
†*E-mail: liup3@guet.edu.cn*

In a P2P (Peer-to-Peer) VoD (video-on-Demand) streaming system, some nodes may receive too many requests, which leads to overload. On the other hand, some other nodes may receive too few requests, which leads to low utilization. However, existing related studies cannot handle this problem effectively, because they don't have an efficient dynamic load information management mechanism, and they don't distinguish the difference of requests when transfer the nodes' load. In this paper, to manage the dynamic load information efficiently, we design a load information management table for each node. Based on the load information, we propose a load balancing scheme which uses a request migration algorithm (LBRM). Through simulations, our scheme can handle the load imbalance problem effectively and improve the users' playback fluency.

Keywords: Load balance; Peer-to-Peer; Video-on-demand; Request migration.

1. Introduction

In recent years, the P2P VoD streaming systems have been deployed widely. However, due to the arbitrariness behavior of nodes, some nodes may receive too many requests. Thus, in the process of nodes handling these requests, some requests may be delayed or cannot be handled in time, while some other nodes may receive too few requests which leads to low utilization. In this case, the load distribution imbalance problem occurs. Therefore, designing a reasonable load balancing strategy is important. In this paper, we propose a new load balancing scheme which mainly includes the contents as following: (1). We constructed a load information management table of nodes, which can effectively avoid the use of tracker server to manage the nodes' load information. (2). Analyzing the difference of the received requests to ensure

---

†Corresponding author.

users' play fluency. (3). We construct a node's utility function to rational select the nodes with high performance and stability as load receiver.

2. Related Work

At present, many scholars have done a lot of efforts to solve the problem of load balancing in the P2P VoD systems. K. Graffi et al. [1] proposed to use a specific node which called responsible peer to manage the nodes' information, but it may cause the single-point bottleneck problem. literature [2] presented a load balancing algorithm based on partial network information to improve system load balancing speed. Yanming Shen et al. [3] employ SQS policy which chooses the peer with least load to send request so as to avoid some peers receive too many requests. In addition, a self-adaptive load balancing algorithm was proposed in [4], in which nodes would create binary tree back-up node tables for their shared hot files automatically, and transfer extra query request to back-up nodes. Literature [5] proposed a range query approach that also incorporates load balancing, but introduce a large computational overhead.

3. Our Algorithm

3.1. *Node information management*

Table 1. load information management table

<table>
<tr><td rowspan="11">Peer ID</td><td>Type</td><td>Name</td><td>Size</td><td>Number</td><td>Time</td></tr>
<tr><td>1</td><td>Data upload</td><td>32KB</td><td>n_1</td><td>15/06/29/01:02</td></tr>
<tr><td>2</td><td>Confirmation message</td><td>1KB</td><td>n_2</td><td>15/06/30/08:32</td></tr>
<tr><td>3</td><td>Heartbeat message</td><td>12B</td><td>n_3</td><td>...</td></tr>
<tr><td>4</td><td>Request message</td><td>1KB</td><td>n_4</td><td>...</td></tr>
<tr><td colspan="2">Backup peers</td><td colspan="2">Utility value</td><td>Load state</td></tr>
<tr><td colspan="2">ID_1</td><td colspan="2">n_1</td><td>L</td></tr>
<tr><td colspan="2">ID_2</td><td colspan="2">n_2</td><td>N</td></tr>
<tr><td colspan="2">...</td><td colspan="2">...</td><td>...</td></tr>
<tr><td colspan="2">ID_{20}</td><td colspan="2">n_{20}</td><td>O</td></tr>
</table>

In order to manage and disseminate the load information of each node easily, we construct a node information management table. This table save the node and its neighbor nodes' information. We define every twenty neighbor nodes as a node's backup peers, and these nodes are the object of load transfer. This table is divided into two parts: the upper part is mainly used for the judge of load state, the data only depends on the local information of the node itself. The data with the lower half part need to be derived from the network and used to record the load information of the neighbor nodes. Then the parameters of our algorithm mainly come from this table, as show in Table 1.

3.2. *Load definition*

We define the load of nodes firstly. As we know, bandwidth resource is one of the most important index in the P2P system, and the amount of data upload is closely related to the node's load. So we use the amount of data upload by a node to define the load of node, named *loadDegree*. It is calculated as follows:

$$loadDegree = \frac{(\sum_t^{t+T} us + \sum_t^{t+T} ms) * 8}{B * T}. \quad (1)$$

Here, us is the total amount of video data uploaded by the node, which belongs to the type 1 in Table 1. ms is the size of all kinds of message packets sent by the node, which is in response to the type 2 to 4 in Table 1. T is a period of time and B is the total upload bandwidth of the node.

Obviously, design a dynamically changing node load information table is a big challenge because that the load of a node is a time varying value. So we divides the load into three state as shown in Table 1. It is denoted as state O when *loadDegree* is greater than 85%. Similarly, it is denoted as state L when *loadDegree* is less than 30%, the rest is denoted as state N. It is unnecessary to update the load change in real-time after dividing the node state, we just need to pay attention to the state switch of the node. Thus, the judge of the node's load state only depends on the local information and needn't to get other information from the network so as to save cost of the server.

3.3. *Load transfer*

When we transfer the load, if the overload node transfers those requests without screening, some urgent requests may be transferred by mistake. Therefore, we should consider not only the load of the node but also the priority of the transfer requests. We define the request's priority as follows:

$$P_{i,j} = \left[1 - \frac{\sum_{k=1}^{N} \mathrm{BM}[k][j]}{N}\right] * \left[1 - \frac{t_q - t_c}{T}\right]. \quad (2)$$

$P_{i,j}$ means the priority of request j which in node i. $N[i]$ represents a neighbor view of node i, N represents the number of neighbor nodes in the view, BM[k][j] indicates whether the neighbor node k missed data piece j or not, if k does not have the data piece j in its own buffer, then we denote BM[k][j]=0, otherwise BM[k][j]=1. T represents the total duration of the video, and t_q represents the time that corresponding the requested data piece's playback position, t_c represents the node's current playback time. After get the priority, we can gradually transfer the requests with low priority out contrasting to the value of $P_{i,j}$ until the node doesn't overload.

3.4. *Node selection*

We discuss how to select the appropriate low utilization node as the loads' receiver. We use the utility function of the nodes as the basis for the selection. In order not to have additional information exchange, we predict the node's ability by recording the historical maximum upload speed of nodes. Besides, regarding the stability of the node, we use the probability of node's online time to herald it. Literature [6] found that in a P2P VOD system, the probability density distribution function of the online time of nodes obeys lognormal distribution. According to mathematical derivation, we can get:

$$F(t) = \int_{0+}^{t} \frac{1}{\sqrt{2\pi}\sigma t} \exp\left[-\frac{(\ln t-\mu)}{2\sigma^2}\right] dt, t > 0. \quad (3)$$

Here, $F(t)$ represents the online probability starting from the node logging on to moment t, μ represents the average value of the logarithm of the node's online time, σ represents the standard deviation of the μ. The bigger the value of $F(t)$, indicates the longer online time of the node in the future.

For node i, we also consider other factors, here we use S_i to represent the node's maximum upload speed. P_i represents the total amount of the node's upload data pieces. Then, the node's utility functions are as follows:

$$W_i = F(t) * (\alpha S_i + \beta P_i). \quad (4)$$

α and β is the weighting factor. F(t) and P_i indicate the stability of the nodes, when the node is in a low utilization state. The greater the value of W_i, the more the service ability it can provide.

The basic idea of our algorithm is that: when the load state of the node is switching to O , we choose the requests with low priority as the transfer object, and then select a backup node with high utility value to transfer the requests. When the state of the chosen node shifted from L to N due to receiving load continually, we initiate a new round of state updating. The node updates the load information and the utility value of its backup nodes, then we can select a new low utilization node to continue the process of load transfer. If there is no low utilization node in the neighbors, then we select the node in N state for transmission. When the state of the chosen node is transferred from N to O, we should abandon this node and select another node which not overload for load transfer.

4. Performance Evaluation

In order to evaluate the performance of our algorithm LBRM, we do extensive simulations and make comparisons with two other schemes: SQS [3] and a self-adaptive load balancing algorithm(SALB) [4]. In this paper, we mainly analyze the upload bandwidth utilization and the overload proportion.

Our simulation model containing a tracker server, a streaming server and 3000 peers. The tracker server have saved the information of all nodes, meanwhile it is also responsible for returning the original list of the resource nodes. The streaming server have cached all the video resources in the network, the node will ask the streaming server for resources when other nodes in the network don't contain. All videos are divided into pieces with the same size 32K.

4.1. *Simulation results*

In the P2P system, the nodes should contribute their own upload bandwidth resources. We plot the CDF of the upload bandwidth utilization ratio in Fig.1 under three different schemes. From Fig. 1 we can see, in the system using LBRM algorithm, only about 20% of the node's upload bandwidth utilization is less than 0.5, but the proportion has reached 95% and 63% when using SQS and SALB algorithm. The reason can be explained as that SQS algorithm send requests to the low load node preferentially, so most of the nodes' load in the network is in a relatively low level. From the graph, we can see that our algorithm is obviously superior to SQS and SALB.

Then we compared the performance of three algorithms on overload proportion in Fig.2. We measure it by the number of overloaded nodes.

In Fig. 2, we start to record the data of the three algorithms when the number of overloaded nodes accounts for 10% of the total number of nodes in the network, within 0 to 400 seconds, the number of overloaded nodes was significantly declined in the network using LBRM, and the speed of declining in SALB is slower than the first two algorithms. Within 400th to 800th seconds, the number of overloaded nodes in SQS is still more than our algorithm's, it is clearly that our algorithm is better than the other two algorithms in the aspect of reducing the overloaded nodes.

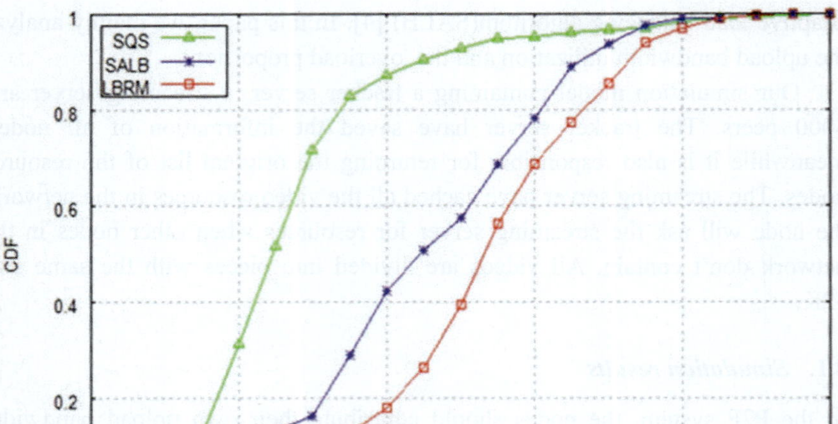

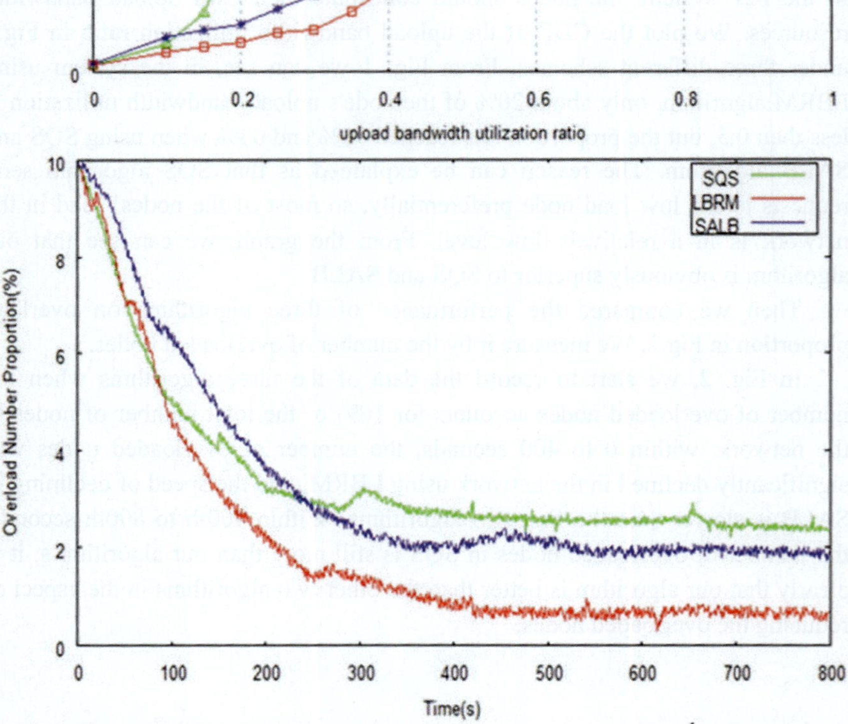

Fig. 1 the upload bandwidth utilization ratio

Fig. 2 overload proportion

5. Conclusion

In this paper, we have proposed a new load balancing scheme which uses a request migration algorithm. First, we constructed a load information management table of the nodes and manage the node's load effectively. Second, we proposed a new algorithm to reasonably transfer the requests from overload nodes to low utilization nodes. In our algorithm, we considered the emergency and the timeliness of requests during load transferring, which can avoid the loss of data caused by the transfer of load. Third, we constructed a node's utility function and then selected the right node as the recipient of the request according to the utility value of the node. Through these measures, we have effectively solved the problem of uneven load in the network. Finally, we demonstrated our scheme through simulations. The simulation results showed that our scheme can effectively balance the load of nodes in the network.

Acknowledgments

This work was supported by the Science and Technology Research Program of Guangxi University (No.KY2015ZD047), the Foundation of Key Laboratory of Guangxi Trusted Software (No. kx201409), the Foundation of Guangxi Experiment Center of Information Science (No. LD13076X), the Foundation of Guangxi Programs for Science and Technology Development (No. GuiKeGong 1598019-3), the Foundation of Key Laboratory of Cognitive Radio and Information Processing, Ministry of Education (GUET, No. CRKL150105).

References

1. K. Graffi, S. Kaune, K. Pussep, *load balancing for multimedia streaming in heterogeneous peer-to-peer systems*, in NOSSDAV, 2008.
2. Yao lei, Guanzhong Dai, *etc*, *load balancing algorithm for P2P systems based on partial network information*, Computer Application, 2007/05. PP:1080-1083.
3. Shiyu Yang, Yanming Shen, *etc*, *a novel On-Demand streaming service based on improved BitTorrent*, Frontier of Computer Science and Technology (FCST), 2010.
4. Naixue Xiong, Kaihua Xu, *etc*, *an effective self-adaptive load balancing algorithm for Peer-to-Peer networks*, IPDPSW, 2012.
5. A. R. Bharambe, M. Agrawal, and S. Seshan, *mercury: supporting scalable multi-attribute range queries*, SIGCOMM Comput. Commun. Rev, 2004.
6. Eveline Veloso, *a hierarchical characterization of a LiveStreaming media workload*[C], MARSEILLE, November, 2006.

A Dynamic Popularity-based Cache Replication Strategy for P2P VoD Systems

Gui-min HUANG, Qian BAI, Ping-shan LIU† and Ya ZHOU

Guangxi Experiment Center of Information Science
Guangxi Key Laboratory of Trusted Software
Key Laboratory of Cognitive Radio and Information Processing of Ministry of Education
Guilin University of Electronic Technology, Guilin, China
†E-mail: liup3@guet.edu.cn

Peer-to-Peer Video-on-Demand (P2P VoD) over Internet has become an effective and popular way to provide video information to users. The knowledge of video popularity is very important for system operation, such as video caching on peer-to-peer network. The video popularity distribution at a given time is quite well understood. However, in this paper, we study how the video popularity changes with time, classifying them into different types, and apply the results to design a novel popularity prediction model, which is derived by analyzing the video's user rating information as well as time-variation. Based on this model, we propose a dynamic popularity-based cache replication strategy (DPCR). The simulation results demonstrate that our proposed algorithm can greatly reduce servers' workload and improve the streaming quality.

Keywords: Cache replication; P2P; VoD; Popularity-based; User rating.

1. Introduction

In a P2P VoD system, the greater the video's popularity is, the greater probability that it could be accessed. However, most of the strategies assume that the popularity is known apriori and don't consider its fluctuation. For videos in a real-world VoD system, the situation is complicated. The trend of popularity often deviates from its fluctuant rule. For example, the popularity of some movies skyrockets during a short time, but it has a quick and prompt decay after the peak due to poor reputation. We classify this change in popularity as type 1; besides, some films usually have a better reputation, but similarly, the popularity can often not reach the expected level because actors are not famous or the releasing time is not appropriate. We classify this trend of the popularity as type 2; Thirdly, a few movies are very popular due to the fascinating plot and actors'

†Corresponding author.

good perform, they have a high popularity which can usually last a long period of time. We classify the fluctuant rule of these movies as type 3. In order to ensure that the number of replicates in the system is reasonable and appropriate, we need a good prediction of video popularity. Thus, we introduce the feedback mechanism of user rating, then we can make a reasonable replication decision.

2. Related Work

Without lowering the quality of streaming media, caching algorithms should be designed cautiously to reduce server load as much as possible. Huang et al. [1] showed the design and implementation of a real P2P-VoD system, PPLIVE. Liu et al. [2] expressed the cache replication as an optimization problem, but they just presented the server workload influenced by the static popularity of the video. As discussed in [3], most of the cache algorithms didn't consider the video popularity's fluctuation, however, the real-world VoD systems have always experiencing a dynamic popularity of movies. Authors in [4] paid close attention to the evolution of the replication during the time-varying video popularity decay, though they just focused on the change in popularity caused by flash crowd. Zhou et al. [5] proposed an adaptive caching replacement algorithm with feedback information, which is similar to our approach, but the evaluation index they relied on was too single, therefore the system performance was often far from satisfactory.

3. Our Algorithm

3.1. *Popularity prediction*

As everyone knows, there are a lot of information in a film, and we should pick and choose the feature related to the popularity among them. In this paper, the attributes related to the film's popularity are the actors, the director and movies' releasing time. And the range of the popularity score is 1 to 10. Then we derive the popularity prediction formula as follows:

$$P_k(t) = (n_1, n_2, n_3)\begin{pmatrix} P_{m_k}(t) \\ V_{a_k} \\ V_{d_k} \end{pmatrix} \quad (t = 0,1,...). \tag{1}$$

$P_k(t)$ is the final value of the k_{th} video's popularity at t moment, $P_{mk}(t)$ is a time-varying value following the fluctuant rule of the popularity. We assume that the initial popularity of each movie is 5, and it will reach the peak value 10 firstly, then the popularity decreases until it stabilizes to a constant value. V_{ak}

and V_{dk} denote the actors' and directors' popularity in the k_{th} movie respectively. At last, we set the value of n_1, n_2, n_3 to 0.5, 0.3, 0.2 separately according to prior knowledge.

3.2. *Cache replication scheme*

Before we start our analysis, we first introduce the notations used in our system model. The summary of the notations are given in Table 1.

Table 1 Summary of the notations

- M is the total number of movies,
- G={G_1,G_2,G_3} is the sets of different kinds of movies, and $M=M_{G1}+M_{G2}+M_{G3}$,
- C_i is the cache capacity of peer I,
- C_{total} is the total capacity of peers in the system, thus $C_{total} = \sum_{i=1}^{N} C_i$
- S_j is the storage space that m_j needs,
- $prop_j$ is the relative frequency of movie j in its corresponding group, so $\sum_{i=1}^{M} prop_i = 1$
- L is the size of movie j,
- R_j is the number of copies that movie j should be replicated in the system.

As is reported by [6], the popularity of the video contents deviates from Zipf distribution. The Zipf-Mandelbrot(MZipf) distribution has been demonstrated to be suitable for the popularity distribution of video objects. Therefore, in this paper, the popularity in streaming videos is assumed to follow MZipf distribution. And the popularity of j_{th} movie can be expressed as follows:

$$prop_{m^y_j} = \frac{[P_{m^y_j}(t)+q]^{-\theta}}{[\sum_{k=1}^{M_y} P_{m^y_k}(t)+q]^{-\theta}} \quad y = 1,2,3. \tag{2}$$

This expression gives the relative frequency of movie j out of M_y videos, where θ is a parameter reflecting the skewness of the distribution curve. In addition, the steepness is decided by the shifting parameter q. When q=0, MZipf distribution will degenerate into Zipf distribution completely.

Now we could classify different movies into different types. Here we define 3 kinds of groups, for example, group 1(namely, G_1) is on behalf of lousy movie; group 2 contains moderate movie(namely, movies that case 2 stated above); similarly, the movies in group 3 are classic movies. By collecting and analyzing the data from IMDb database, we found that the ratio of these three types of films is roughly 2:6:2. However, one thing should be noticed that both lousy and classic movie are usually very hot during some period of time(e.g., at the time movies were newly released), during these periods, the server's workload may dramatically increase due to a sudden surge of demand and inadequate duplicates of the movie that users have required. Thus, these two kinds of movies' cache capacity should be appropriately increased respectively. We did many experiments to obtain the optimal cache ratio of these three kinds of movies, the specific details are omitted here. Eventually, we found that 3:4:3 is the nearest optimal ratio, and we would set the buffer capacity of these three types of movies in the following:

$$C_{G_V} = \begin{cases} 30\% \times C_{total} & v = 1,3 \\ 40\% \times C_{tatal} & v = 2 \end{cases} \tag{3}$$

Then, we can derive the cache storage required by m_j in its corresponding group as below:

$$S_{m\ j}^{\ G_V} = prop_{m\ j}^{\ G_V} \times C_{G_V} \quad v = 1,2,3. \tag{4}$$

Thus, the number of copies of m_j in the system is supposed to be:

$$R_{m\ j}^{\ G_V} = \frac{S_{m\ j}^{\ G_V}}{L} \quad v = 1,2,3. \tag{5}$$

4. Performance Evaluation

In this section, we carry out extensive simulation to evaluate and compare the performance of our proposed cache algorithm with other two typical schemes: LRFU and proportional strategy. The simulation settings and results are specified and analyzed.

4.1. *Simulation settings*

We choose the *PeerSim* simulator to simulate our algorithm. The system model we constructed consists of a tracker server, a media server and many peers. The tracker server manages the information of all nodes in the network. The media server has cached all video resources, and it is mainly served as a back-up when the requests for data resources can not be satisfied. The simulation parameters are described as follows: (1) In this experiment, the number of simulation cycles is 100, the initial size of the network is 200 nodes, 100 nodes are added to the network at each round, and the maximum number of nodes is 5000. The storage space of each peer is 5 movies. (2) The system provides M = 600 kinds of movies. (3) Movie popularity follows *prop(t)* distribution with parameter θ=0.8, q=10. (4) The random scheduling strategy is deployed for partner selection in the simulation. (5) A peer requests a movie at each round, and peers also switch movie channel every round.

4.2. *Simulation results*

In the following, we have chosen server load and cache hitrate as the key indicator of the performance in P2P VoD systems. From Fig. 1 we can see, on the whole, our strategy DPCR is better than the other two caching strategies. Here we define server load as the data quantity that the media server transmit per unit time. We can intuitively find that the server load is smallest when the simulation has just begun, with the increase of the simulation rounds, the server load has also become large, when the simulation rounds is about 18, the server load reached the maximum. The server's average workload is around 200 Mbps using our proposed DPCR algorithm, but is around 300 Mbps using the LRFU algorithm and 360 Mbps using proportional algorithm. Then the load of server begins to fall and eventually stabilizes at a constant value, respectively.

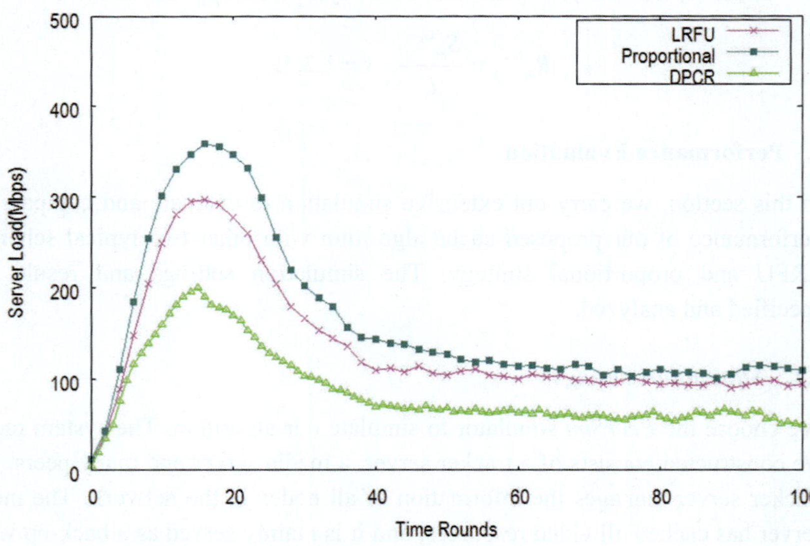

Fig 1. Pressure comparison of the server

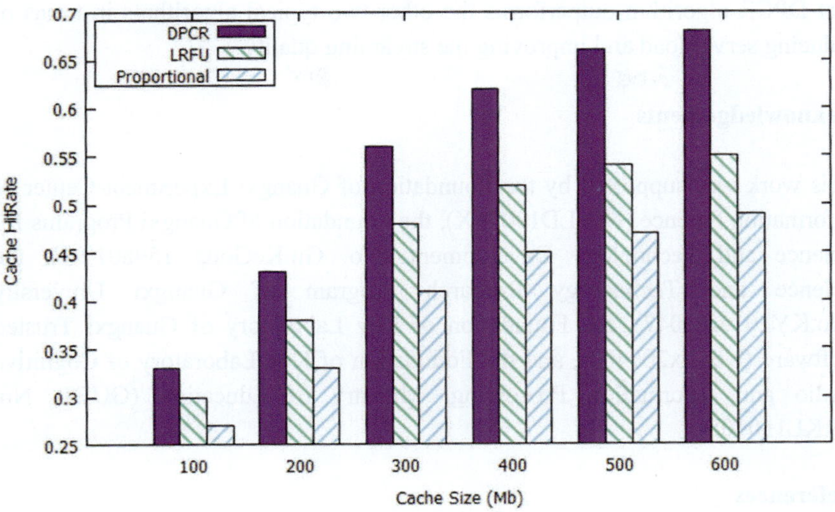

Fig. 2 Relationship between cache size and hitrate

Fig. 2 shows the relationship between cache size and cache hitrate. Cache hitrate is the ratio of the number of requests acquired from neighbors or local cache to the total request number. This indicator reflects the validity of the caching mechanism. It can be seen from the graph that with the increase of the cache space, the hitrate of the three kinds of caching methods also rises. However, in case of the same size of the buffer storage, our DPCR algorithm has a higher hitrate than LRFU and proportional algorithm. Besides, when the node's cache space is increased from 100Mb to 600Mb, the cache hitrate of DPCR will be raised to 68% from the original 33%. At the same time, the cache hitrate of LRFU and proportional scheme are raised to 55% and 49% from 30% and 27%, respectively. This is mainly because our algorithm considers the dynamic of the videos' popularity.

5. Conclusion

In a P2P VoD system, replication is an effective way to reduce servers' workload. In this paper, we have proposed a popularity-based caching replication algorithm, called DPCR algorithm. In DPCR, we have fully considered the volatile nature of the videos' popularity, and make a more reasonable prediction of videos' popularity based on the feedback mechanism of user rating. Then, we classify movies which have various popularities into different types, and the optimal number of video copies has been calculated by our cache replication algorithm DPCR. Through extensive simulations, we show that DPCR algorithm outperforms the other two typical algorithms in terms of reducing server load and improving the streaming quality.

Acknowledgements

This work was supported by the Foundation of Guangxi Experiment Center of Information Science (No. LD13076X), the Foundation of Guangxi Programs for Science and Technology Development (No. GuiKeGong 1598019-3), the Science and Technology Research Program of Guangxi University (No.KY2015ZD047), the Foundation of Key Laboratory of Guangxi Trusted Software (No. kx201409), and the Foundation of Key Laboratory of Cognitive Radio and Information Processing, Ministry of Education (GUET, No. CRKL150105).

References

1. Y. Huang, T. Fu, D. Chiu, J. Lui, and C. Huang, Challenges, design and analysis of a large-scale P2P-VoD system, *In Proc. of ACM SIGCOMM*, 2008.
2. Pingshan Liu, Shengzhong Feng, etc, Bandwidth-Availability-Based Replication Strategy for P2P VoD Systems: C*OMPUTER JOURNAL, vol. 57, no. 8, pp.* 1211-1219, Aug 2014.
3. L. Chang, J. Pan, Towards the optimal caching strategies of peer-assisted VoD systems with HD channels, *in: Proceedings of IEEE ICNP,* 2012.
4. Fei Chen, Haitao Li, Jiangchuan Liu, Popularity decays in peer-to-peer VoD systems: Impact, model, and design implications, *Computer Networks* 60(2014) 75-87.
5. Y. Zhou, T. Z. J. Fu, and D. M. Chiu, "Server-assisted adaptive video replication for P2P VoD," *J. Signal Process., Image Commun., vol. 27, no. 5, pp. 484-495,* 2011.
6. M. Hefeeda and O. Saleh, "Traffic modeling and proportional partial caching for peer-to-peer systems." *IEEE/ACM Transactions on Networking. Vol. 16, no. 6, pp.* 1447-1460. 2008.

MCPP: A High-efficiency Routing Table Lookup Based on NPDK

Jin-li YAN, Lu TANG, Gao-feng LV, Tao LI, Zhi-gang SUN and Jian-biao MAO
College of Computer, National University of Defense Technology, Changsha, P.R. China
E-mail: yan_jinli@126.com

Increasing network traffic requires higher performance in the processing ability of network devices. The routing table lookup based on single thread is not appropriate for usage in general-purpose multi-core processors to achieve parallel processing. Current parallelization of routing table lookup in application layer causes high overhead in data copy, network stack and conflict of shared memory access. Network Processor Development Kit (NPDK) is a development environment for the network processing platform. In this paper, we proposed a routing table lookup mechanism named Multi-copy Parallel Processing (MCPP) provided by NPDK for the purpose of multi-core parallel processing. Based on multi-core parallel processing architecture of NPDK, the overhead of packet copy is eliminated and multi-copy technology efficiently avoids routing table access conflict. Moreover, in order to reduce the number of memory accesses, a lookup algorithm named Configurable Two-Level Operation (CTLO) was implemented. Lastly, we compare the forwarding performance between the MCPP mechanism and the traditional mechanism in NPE platform, which is based on the general-purpose multi-core processor FT1000A. The evaluation results show that the packet forwarding performance based on the MCPP mechanism outperforms that based on the traditional mechanism.

Keywords: Multi-core; Multi-copy; Parallel; Routing table lookup.

1. Introduction

At present, with the network traffic increasing, the packet processing performance could not satisfy people's needs. Nowadays, not only core routers need to process 300,000 routing table entries, but also the frequency of routing table update become higher and higher. These issues put forward higher demands to the design of lookup algorithm, and the key to increase the packet processing performance is to improve the performance of lookup algorithm[1]. Although the general-purposemulti-core processors, depending on strong processing capacity, are widely deployed in network devices, the traditional packet processing applications in general-purpose multi-core processors only use single thread, which lacks multiple threads to implement parallel processing.

Therefore, it has an important significance for the performance improvement of network devices to design and implement a high-efficiency lookup algorithm in multi-core processors.

To implement parallel lookup algorithm, a lot of methods have been proposed in recent years, which involves using MPI message-passing libraries, POSIX multi-threading support library and some new language structure used to implement parallel encoding, and optimizing and accelerating the algorithm in compiling phrase simultaneously[2]. Although using those method can improve the performance of lookup algorithm efficiently, the data copy between kernel space and user space and the high overhead caused by interrupt processing have bad influence on improvement of routing lookup performance[3]. Thus, it has important significance to decrease the overhead of data copy and interrupt processing.

As we know, when conducting parallel lookup, the routing table, as the crucial shared variable, are accessed to get the destination port. In terms of single MCU (Memory Controller Unit), identical memory space can only be accessed by one thread at the same time. Hence, the shared memory access conflict will happen when multiple threads access the same routing entry. Until the current thread releasing the access right, the next thread could access the same resources. The queuing access caused higher latency[4]. So it is critical to improve the lookup performance by decreasing the access latency.

The data plane I/O accelerating software, such as NPDK(Network Process Development Kit) developed by a university in China, DPDK(Data Plane Development Kit) developed by Intel, offers a data plane processing environment with zero interrupt and zero-copy by bypassing Linux kernel. Moreover, using the crucial technology of buffer management and polling mode driver, both of them decrease the overhead caused by traditional NIC driver so that the performance of packet processing has improved a lot[5]. Besides, NPDK provides the development environment, which supports development of various applications. Users not only can implement the function of lookup, matching, split-flow, flow control based on hardware at system level, but also the lookup, matching, forwarding, statistics at user level.

From the perspective of multi-core parallel processing, based on the multi-core parallel processing architecture provided by I/O accelerating software NPDK, we have proposed a routing table lookup mechanism named Multi-Copy Parallel Processing (MCPP). In order to improve the packet processing performance, we create multiple threads in kernel driver, and all of them share the same lookup algorithm, which eliminates the overhead caused by data copy and packet format conversion. Besides, the multi-copy technology in distributed system has been adapted in the design of routing table. The core idea behind multi-copy technology is to store the multiple copies of an object in different subsystem, which can decrease the access latency efficiently[6]. Using this idea for reference, MCPP creates multiple copies of routing table and distributes them in different processing thread, which improves the efficiency of memory access by multiple MCUs accessing different copies simultaneously. It is necessary to keep the information of each copy newest, namely maintain the consistency. Otherwise, errors may appear if the information of each routing table is inconsistent. In order to solve this problem, MCPP creates a specialized manager thread to dispatch update information to every thread.

Based on MCPP mechanism, a lookup algorithm named Configurable Two-Level Operation (CTLO) which evolves from DIR-24-8 algorithm was proposed in this paper. Compared to traditional linear lookup algorithm and binary Trie-tree lookup algorithm, the complexity of lookup is O(1) and the number of memory access is few are the advantages of DIR-24-8. The idea behind DIR-24-8 comes from the background that prefix length of most routing table entries in core routers are less than 24[7,8]. However, as networks grow in size and route aggregation emerged in last decade, on one hand, the prefix length of a large number of routing table entries in core router are more than 24; on the other hand, the number of routing table entries in edge router is less than that of core router and there are great distribution differences in prefix[9]. Thus, the number of memory access is mostly twice when using DIR-24-8 algorithm. In order to make the structure of routing table adapt to different routers better, CTLO algorithm provides configuration interface to programme the structure of routing table dynamically, which improves the efficiency of lookup.

In order to verify the high-efficiency of MCPP mechanism proposed in this paper, we carried out forwarding performance tests in the context of NPE platform developed based on general-purpose multi-core between CTLO lookup algorithm and Hash lookup algorithm in Linux kernel. We observed that the performance of CTLO lookup algorithm is much higher than that of Hash lookup algorithm.

The road map of this paper is as follows. In Section 2, we present an overview of the NPE platform, which involves the development model of NPE and the multi-core parallel processing architecture provided by NPDK. In Section 3, we describe the MCPP mechanism. Section 4 delivers the performance evaluation results. And conclusions are drawn in Section 5.

2. NPE Platform

2.1. *Architecture of NPE*

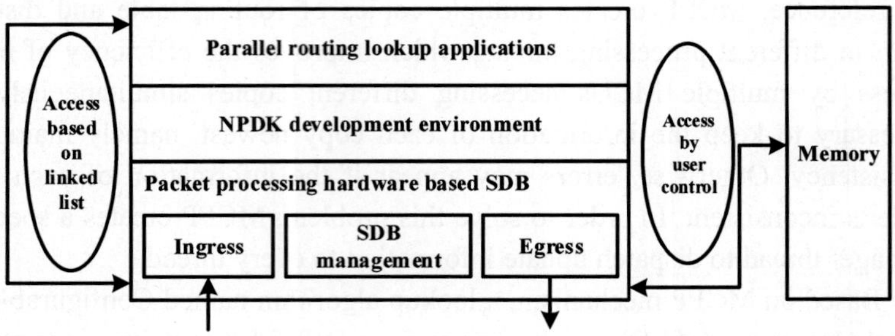

Fig. 1. Software and hardware architecture of NPE.

NPE development platform is composed of packet processing hardware based on SDB, NPDK development environment and parallel lookup applications, as is shown in Figure1. The logic function of SDB can be divided into Ingress process, SDB management and Egress process. We implement the function of packet receiving, packet analysis and revolution, packet multi-thread dispatching and etc. in Ingress. Meanwhile, the Egress is in charge of the function of packet sending, traffic shaping and etc. Besides, SDB management is provided with the function of packet descriptor management, co-processor acceleration, interface management and etc. NPDK development environment, which supports multiple general-purpose multi-core processors like Intel and FT, provides the driver to receive and send packet and application adaptation, and the packet processing development environment at system and user level. Parallel lookup applications utilize the multi-thread technique to implement the lookup algorithm that can be implemented both in kernel and user model.

2.2. *Multi-core parallel processing architecture of NPDK*

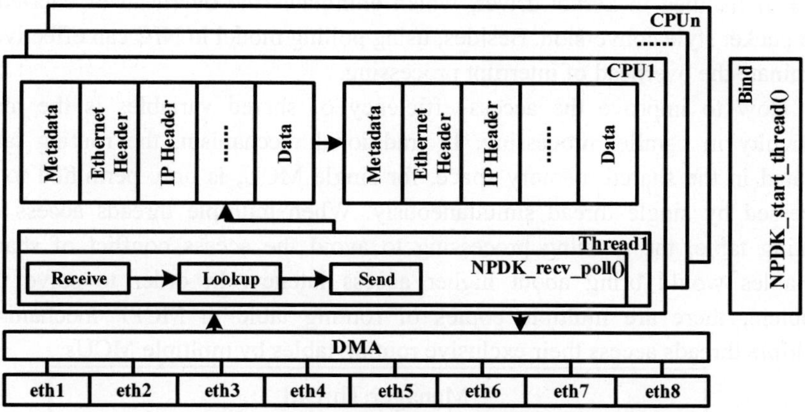

Fig. 2. Multi-core parallel processing architecture of NPDK

After making a detailed study on I/O accelerating software NPDK, we have found that the parallelization of lookup algorithm can be implemented by the multi-core parallel processing architecture of NPDK. As Figure 2 shows, by calling the function named NPDK_start_thread, NPDK can create multiple threads to bind CPU cores separately, and each thread binds the poll processing function named NPDK_recv_poll after the initiation of software and hardware. When NIC receives packets, the DMA controller dispatches them to packet processing threads. The packet buffer can be divided into two parts: one is control area holding metadata information and the other is data buffer for the actual packet data. The polling processing function on each thread consists of three parts that are in charge of receiving packet, routing lookup and sending packet. With this, the parallelization of lookup algorithm is implemented.

3. Multi-copy Parallel Processing Mechanism

3.1. *Introduce of MCPP mechanism*

From the perspective of multi-core parallel processing, based on the multi-core parallel processing architecture provided by I/O accelerating software NPDK, we have proposed a routing table lookup mechanism named Multi-Copy Parallel Processing (MCPP). Based on multi-core parallel processing and multi-copy technology, the high overhead of process in network stack and high access latency of shared variables in traditional mechanism are successfully solved based on MCPP mechanism. The multi-core parallel processing in MCPP is to create multiple threads bound to different CPU cores in kernel driver, and all of them share the same program. Packets do not need being transferred to network stack if handled in kernel driver, which eliminates the overhead of data-copy and packet style conversion. Besides, using polling model in NIC can effectively eliminate the overhead of interrupt processing.

How to improve the access efficiency of shared variables is the main difficulty in parallel processing. In traditional mechanism, the routing table located in the shared memory space, for single MCU, is only permitted to be accessed by single thread simultaneously. When multiple threads access the routing table, the queuing processing to avoid the access conflict of shared variables would bring about higher access latency. In order to solve this problem, there are multiple copies of routing table in MCPP mechanism, multiple threads access their exclusive routing tables by multiple MCUs.

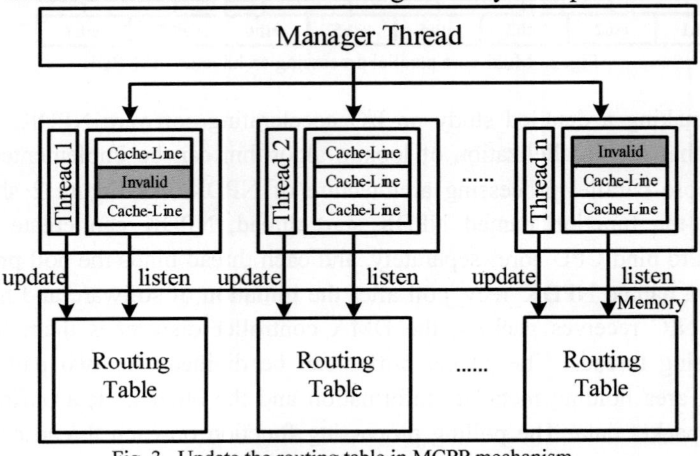

Fig. 3. Update the routing table in MCPP mechanism

However, one issue arising here is how to maintain the consistency. During the update, it is necessary to keep the information in each copy and cache newest. Thus, MCPP creates a specialized manager thread to dispatch update information uniformly based on the multi-thread processing architecture, as is shown in Figure 3. First, when the manager thread receives the entries that need updating, multiple copies of them would be dispatched to every thread. Then, every thread replace the corresponding entries with received entries. Finally, by listening the invalid address on bus, the cache would invalidate the corresponding entries.

3.2. *Configurable two-level operation lookup algorithm*

3.2.1. *Algorithm idea*

Configurable Two-Level Operation (CTLO) lookup algorithm is a tree-structured lookup algorithm, which evolves from DIR-24-8 algorithm. There are two routing tables to store routing information in DIR-24-8 algorithm. The first routing tables stores the routing information whose prefix length is less than or equals to 24, while the second one stores the information whose prefix length is more than 24. The starting point of DIR-24-8 is the fact that the prefix length of most routing table entries in core routers are less than 24 at that time. However, as networks grow in size and route aggregation emerged in last decade, on one hand, the prefix length of a large amount of routing table entries in core router are more than 24; on the other hand, the number of routing table entries in edge router is less than that of core router and there are great distribution differences in prefix. Thus, the number of memory access is mostly twice using DIR-24-8 algorithm. In order to make the structure of routing table adapt to different routers better and decrease the times of memory access, CTLO algorithm provides configuration interface to programme the structure of routing table dynamically, which reduce the number of mostly memory access to one to improves the efficiency of lookup.

3.2.2. *Detailed design*

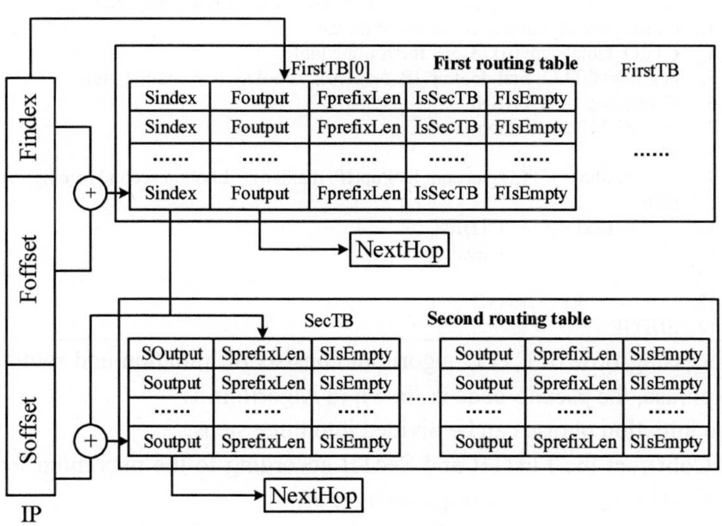

Fig. 4. CTLO algorithm

(i) Data structure

In order to implement the algorithm, the main data structures of CTLO include IP address, first routing table named FirstTB and second routing table named SecTB, as is shown in Figure 4. IP address can be divided into Findex, Foffset and Soffset. The Findex, which is the four bits in front of IP address, is indexed to the first address of FirstTB. Every entry in FirstTB is determined by the starting address and the offset that is indicated by FOffset. Similarly, every entry in SecTB is determined by the starting address and the offset that is indicated by SOffset.

FirstTB entry has 32 bits that can be divided into five parts. SIndex is used to determine the starting address of SecTB. FOutput is result. FPrefixLen indicates the prefix length of first table entry. Its value is greater than 24 only when the prefix length of this entry is greater than 24. IsSecTB is used to judge whether it exists second table or not. FIsEmpty is used to judge whether the entry is empty.

Also, every SecTB has 16 bits that can be divided into three parts. SOutput is result. SPrefixLen indicates the prefix length of this entry, its value is greater than 24. SIsEmpty is used to judge whether the entry is empty.

(ii) Processing flow

Algorithm 1. CTLO

Input: max_len, n, IP
Output: nexthop

```
FirstTB=CTLO_first_init(maxlen);//Initiation of fist routing table
SecTB=CTLO_sec_init(maxlen);// Initiation of second routing table
CTLO_thread_init(n);//Initiation of thread
CTLO_table_copy(n);//Copy the routing table
nexthop=CTLO_first_lookup(IP, maxlen); //Lookup first routing table
IF nexthop != -1 THEN
    RETURN nexthop;
ELSE
    nexthop=CTLO_second_lookup(IP, maxlen);// Lookup second routing table
    IF nexthop != -1 THEN
        RETURN nexthop;
    ELSE
        RETURN -1
END IF
```

The processing flow of CTLO algorithm consists of initiation and routing table lookup phrase, the pseudo-code is shown in Algorithm 1.

The initiation phrase can be divided into three steps:

(a) Construct the FirstTB and SecTB according to the maximum length of FirstTB (max_len) configured by user,

(b) Initiate the thread according to the number of threads (n) configured by user,

(c) Copy the routing table according to the number of threads.

The routing table lookup phrase can be addressed in two steps:

(a) Search in FirstTB to get the next hop according the max_len of destination IP address,

(b) If failed in first step, it searches in SecTB to get the next hop.

4. Experiment

We have made a performance test between CTLO algorithm based on MCPP mechanism and Hash algorithm based on traditional mechanism in NPE platform based on general-purpose multi-core processor FT1000A.

4.1. *Performance test using Hash lookup algorithm*

After loading npe.ko module, the npe driver send the packet to network, stack. Then, Hash lookup algorithm forwards the packet in IP layer. The topology of the experiment is illustrated as in Figure 5. The content of the test involves the packet sending bandwidth and receiving bandwidth over different packet sizes.

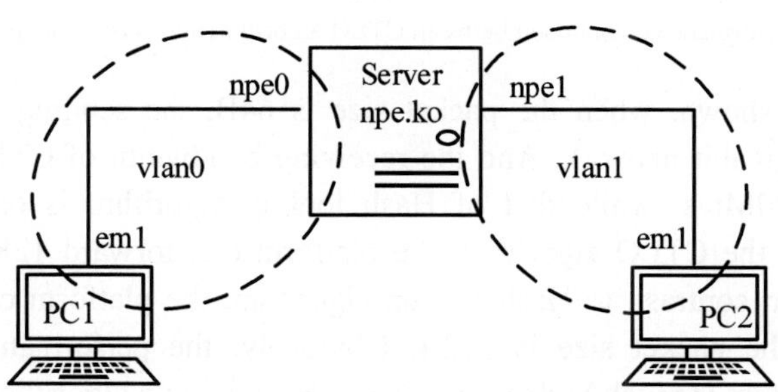

Fig. 5. Topology of experiment

4.2. *Performance test using CTLO lookup algorithm*

The deployment scheme of CTLO lookup algorithm is similar to Hash lookup algorithm. Also, the content of the test contains the packet sending bandwidth and receiving bandwidth over different packet sizes.

4.3. *Performance comparison and analysis*

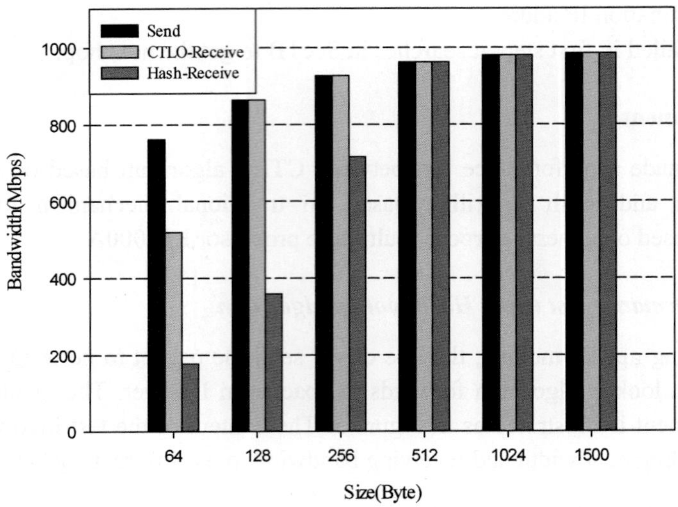

Fig. 6. Performance comparison between CTLO algorithm and Hash lookup algorithm

As Figure 6 shown, when the packet size is 64B, the sending bandwidth is 760Mb/s in gigabit network. And the receiving bandwidth of CTLO algorithm can reach 520Mb/s, while that of Hash lookup algorithm is only 180Mb/s. Moreover, to the CTLO algorithm, the platform can forward 128B packets at wire speed. In contrast, to Hash lookup algorithm, the platform can reach line speed until the packet size is 512B. Obviously, the performance of CTLO lookup algorithm is much higher than that of Hash lookup algorithm.

After analyzing deeply, the reasons why the difference is so large are concluded as follows:

- Hash lookup algorithm only uses single thread, while CTLO lookup algorithm creates multiple threads to process in parallel.
- Hash lookup algorithm passes packet to network stack, which causes overhead of protocol processing; in contrast, CTLO lookup algorithm processes packets in npe driver directly, which eliminates the overhead of protocol processing.
- The number of memory access in Hash lookup algorithm is large, while that in CTLO lookup algorithm is only one in most cases.
- The complexity in Hash lookup algorithm is O(n), while that in CTLO lookup algorithm is only O(1).

5. Conclusions

Considering the background that increasing network flow makes higher requirements to the packet processing performance of network devices, A comprehensive survey on the I/O accelerating software named NPDK and multi-copy technology have been conducted in this paper. Based on the multi-core parallel processing architecture of NPDK, we have proposed a routing table lookup mechanism named Multi-Copy Parallel Processing. On the basis of this, we have designed a lookup algorithm named Configurable Two-Level Operation. After conducting performance test, we observed that the performance of CTLO lookup algorithm is higher than that of Hash lookup algorithm in Linux kernel. To sum up, our MCPP mechanism will be a useful stepping stone in network field. In the future work, the lookup performance might be improved by optimizing the update method of multi-copy technology.

Acknowledgments

This work is supported by National High-tech R&D Program of China (863 Program) (Grant No. 2015AA015603), National Natural Science Foundation of China(Grant No. 61202483 and Grant No. 61202485).

References

1. Kumar S, Crowley P. Segmented Hash: An Efficient Hash Table Implementation for High Performance Subsystem, Princeton: Association for Computing Machinery,(2005).
2. Zhou Qihai, Li Yan. Isomorphic New Parallel Division Methods and Parallel Algorithms for Giant Matrix Transpose.(2010).
3. Mogul C J, Ramakrishman K K. Elimininating receive livelock in an interrupt-driven kernel. ACM Transactions on Computer System, (1997).
4. Medardoni S, Ruggiero M,Bertozzi D. Capturing the interaction of the communication, memory and I/O subsystems in memory-centric industrial MPSoCplatforms. SanJose: EDA Consortium,(2007).
5. High-performance multi-core networking software design options, White Paper, http://www.docin.com/p-601102202.html, (2012).
6. Huang Zhi-bin, Zhu Mingfa, an Xiao Limin. LvtPPP: live-time protected pseudopartitioning of multicore shared caches. IEEE Transactions on Parallel and Distributed Systems, (2013).
7. Pankaj Gupta, Steven Lin, Nick McKeown, Routing Lookups in Hardware at Memory Access Speeds, IEEE INFOCOM, (1998).

8. Marko Zec, Luigi Rizzo, MiljenkoMikuc. DXR: Towards a Billion Routing Lookups per Second in Software. ACM SIGCOM, (2012).
9. F. Baboescu, S. Singh, and G. Varghese. Packet classification for core routers: Is there an alternative to CAMs?. IEEE INFOCOM, (2003).

Automatic Detection of Mind Wandering Using Mobile Device In the Scenario of Online and Mobile Education

Cheng-lu ZHANG† and Rui-min SHEN

SEIEE Department of Computer Science and Engineering, Shanghai JiaoTong University, Shanghai, 200030,China

†*E-mail: ape.chang.1989@gmail.com*

Mind wandering is a state transition from task-related thinking to task-unrelated thinking and it has possible negative effects on learners' performance in online education. The detection of mind wandering can improve learners' performance by signaling, intervening and restoring attention to the process of learning. Traditional methods of detection of mind wandering involve specific devices such as eye gaze or physiologic sensors, tracking movements of eye ball or detecting electro-physiological activities of neurons or skin. This paper presents a new detection method using the camera of a mobile device to detect mind wandering when learners are tasked to watch a teaching video. Through the constant image capturing of the learner's face, his or her eye features can be captured and used to predict the learner's state of mind wandering if any, using methods of computer imagery and supervised machine learning. Through our experiment, we have attained an accuracy of 53%, which exceeded expectations, considering the hardware platform. The performance of the detection system based on the MCPP mechanism outperforms the detection system based on the traditional mechanism.

Keywords: Detection of Mind wandering; Mobile device; Online education.

1. Introduction

With the rapid growth recent years, online and mobile education provides the opportunity for every learner to access teaching materials any place any time[1]. Besides the opportunities, online and mobile education faces some major concerns, including low completion rate[2,3], high in-session interruptions[4], and lack of interactions between teachers and learners. Mind wandering is state transition from task-related thinking to task-unrelated thinking, which is fond more prone to, for a learner, in a non-classroom environment[5]. This is due to external extractions, and the lack of sustained motivation while studying alone. Mind wandering is believed to have negative effects on learners' performance of

†Corresponding author.

online education. There are two fundamental strategies that can be taken into consideration to reduce the negative effects of mind wandering, either by preventing before it occurs, or by signaling once it occurs. Above all, we need find a way to detect or predict mind wandering.

Mind wandering is a mental process, afterall. So the traditional way to detect mind wandering involves specific sensors, to record electro-physiological activities of neurons or skins. Then from theses activities, researchers succeed to find some patterns indicating mind wandering state. Also, mind wandering reflects on eye movements. By using eye gaze, researchers can track movements of eye balls, then to find the patterns related to mind wandering.

Specific sensors and eye gaze, which are not commonly found in learners' learning terminals, can't help in online or mobile education. This paper presents another way around. Almost every terminal, phone or tablet, has a camera. With a camera, we can constantly capture images of learner's face, then analyze these images to find some patterns, mostly focused on locality of eye, using methods of computer vision and supervised machine learning.

2. Related Work

Detection of mind wandering is mostly related to the field of attentional state estimation. And attentional state estimation has been explored in a variety of domains and goals, for example to optimize the position of advertisement on a screen[6], or to monitor drivers' fatigue and distraction[7]. These studies mostly focus on detection of attention using eye gaze. Eye gaze has shown a close relationship between attention state and eye movements[8, 9]. Compared to normal state, mind wandering is associated with longer fixation time, a higher of subsequent fixation on the same area, a higher frequency of blinks, and larger pupil diameters.

Physiology is another direction. Relationship between physiological arousal from the sympathetic nervous system and attentional states[10]. Particularly, a relationship between mind wandering and skin conductance has been found[11]. This document tries to detect mind wandering using galvanic skin response and skin temprature collected with the Affectiva Q sensor[12].

Due to the deficiency of mobile platform, memory limitation and poor computing capability for example, leading to the limited choices researchers own, few researches have been done in the field of mobile education. Phuong Pham and Jingtao Wang present an intelligent mobile learning system, AttentiveLearner, optimized for consuming lecture videos[13]. This system contains a modal to extract learners' heart rate, then to infer their attention state.

The prediction performance of this system is reported to reach 71.22% in accuracy.

3. System Design

3.1. *Overview*

The whole pipeline is shown as follows in Fig-1.

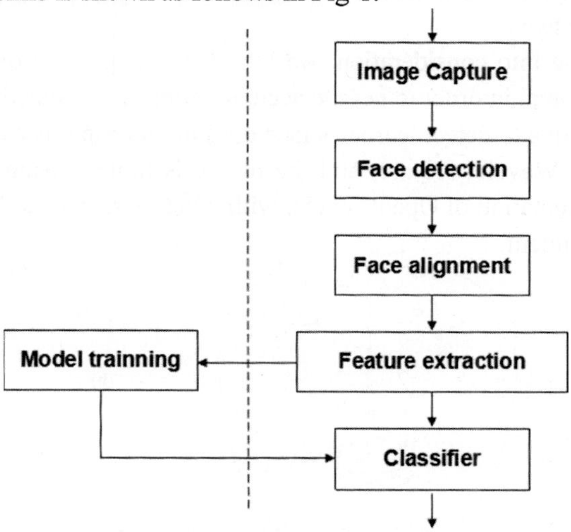

Fig. 1. This figure shows the pipeline of whole system, including 1)image capture 2)face dectection 3)face alignment 4)feature extraction 5)model trainning 6)classifier

3.1.1. *Image capture*

Image capture is base on AVFoundation framework of iOS system[14]. Resolution of camera is set to 320px * 320px, and the capture rate is10 frames per second. Image captured is converted to gray image, dropping the color information. So why low capture resolution and low capture rate? First, this is limited by mobile platform, which has limited memory and computing capability. As we all know, larger resolution and larger capture rate mean more memory and more computing. Second, as we finally find out, the whole system works fine in such a resolution and capture rate. We think this is because distance between learner's face and phone screen is considerably so small that learner's face mostly fill the whole captured image, which means we don't got the need to find the face in a large image. And also, the mind wandering state lasts so long that we can capture it in a few seconds.

3.1.2. *Face detection and face alignment*

What we want is the locality of eye, so why face detection and face alignment? As we find in practice, if we try to detect eye in the first place, two problems will happen:

- Misplacement, the detected area can not match the real position perfectly, there is some pixels transition.
- Error detection, the detected area contains no eye, or the detection finds more eyes than two.

Taken these into consideration, we introduce the process of face detection and face alignment, in order to get the accurate number and position of eyes.

The technique to detect learner's face used in this paper is cascade classifier based on Haar Wavelet feature, and the model is trained using Adaboost. We use the implementation of OpenCV[15], with window size set to 200px * 200px, based on experiment.

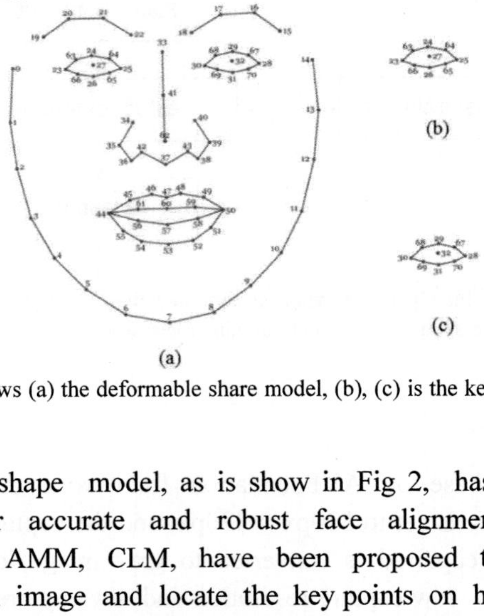

Fig. 2. This figure shows (a) the deformable share model, (b), (c) is the key point we are interested in

Deformable shape model, as is show in Fig 2, has emerged as an excellent tool for accurate and robust face alignment. Many models, including ASM, AMM, CLM, have been proposed to fit a defomable model to a facial image and locate the key points on human face. In this paper, the method propose by Ren and Cao, et al[16] is used. We process every frame and use a subset of key points it output – those describe the positions and deformations of eyes, which our interest lies in , as is shown is Fig 2(b,c). The squared boundary can be achieved using such rectangle defined as

$$\begin{aligned} &[lb, rb] = [\min(x_i), \max(x_i)] \\ &[tb, bb] = [\min(y_i), \max(y_i)] \quad i \in \{locality\ of\ eye\} \end{aligned} . \tag{1}$$

where lb, rb, tb, bb represent left, right, top, bottom boundary. As extracted eyes vary in size, distance, illumination, head pose, etc, we scale these images of eyes to a unified size to eliminate the influence of size, 32px * 32px in this paper, and use histogram equalization to eliminate the influence of illumination.

After such preprocessing, we finally get the locality of eye, which we are interested in. The whole process is illustrated as follows in Fig.3, with a real case.

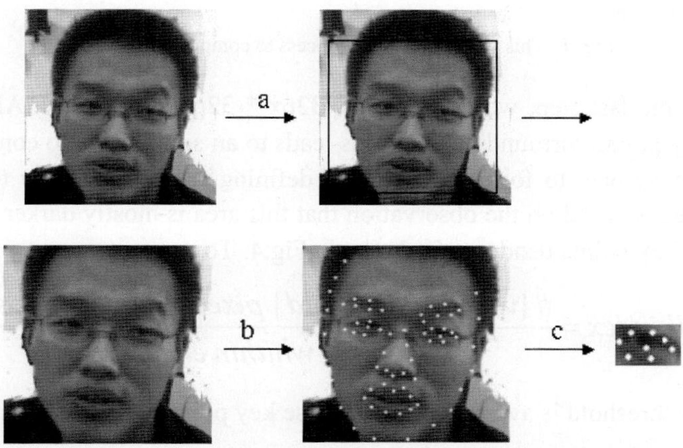

Fig. 3. This figure shows the preprocess of captured iamge, (a) face detection (b) face alignment (c) locate the position of eyes

3.2. *Feature extraction*

Why not feed the raw eye data to a classifier? We tried actually, however, the outcome is not as good as that when we do the feature extraction. Meanwhile, using the raw eye data is too memory and computation intensive, for the dimension of the feature space is too high to be processed within considerable space and time.

3.2.1. *Pupil index*

The first feature we want to extract is the pupil diameter, for people in mind wandering mostly have a larger pupil diameter. However, the size of eye varies in so many ways that people who is not in mind wandering but got a larger eye, may have a larger pupil diameter than those in mind wandering, but got a small eye. Hence, we extract the pupil index, the ratio of pupil's area to eye's area, to eliminate the impact of eye size. We've got the locality of eye, but how can we compute the pupil index?

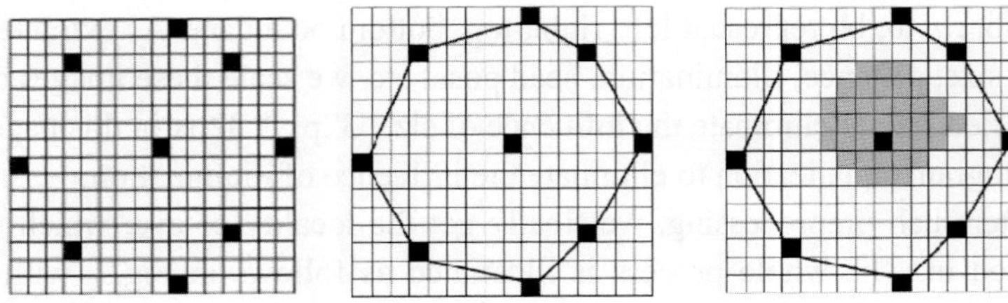

a b c

Fig. 4. This figure shows the process to compute pupil index

From the last step, we have got the 32px * 32px area of eye. Also, we've get the key points surrounding eye. This leads to an simple idea to connect these points one by one, to form an enclosure defining eye's area. How to find the pupil's area is based on the observation that this area is mostly darker than skin, which the key points reside, as is shown in Fig.4. To sum up, we get

$$\text{pupil index} = \frac{\#\{value > threshold \mid pixel\ whithin\ enclosure\}}{\#\{pixel\ whithin\ enclosure\}} \quad .(2)$$

Where the threshold is average value of those key points.

3.2.2. *Eye movement*

Another feature we want to extract is the movement of eye ball, for people in mind wandering mostly have longer fixation time. But how we model this movement? Movement, we must know, is a process, not a state, which means we must have a sequence of images of eye, in order to describe this process. Let's set the window size K. Every k consecutive images are grouped as one observation, and description of movement can be done using the path eye center has passed, in the form of $\{(x_1, y_1), (x_2, y_2), \cdots, (x_k, y_k)\}$. However, this sequence is highly vulnerable to the initial point. So we use the difference sequence, $\{(x_2 - x_1, y_2 - y_1), (x_3 - x_2, y_3 - y_2), \cdots, (x_k - x_{k-1}, y_k - y_{k-1})\}$, which in actual is the motion vector of eye movement, instead of the original sequence, to describe the movement. The whole process is shown as follows in Fig 5.

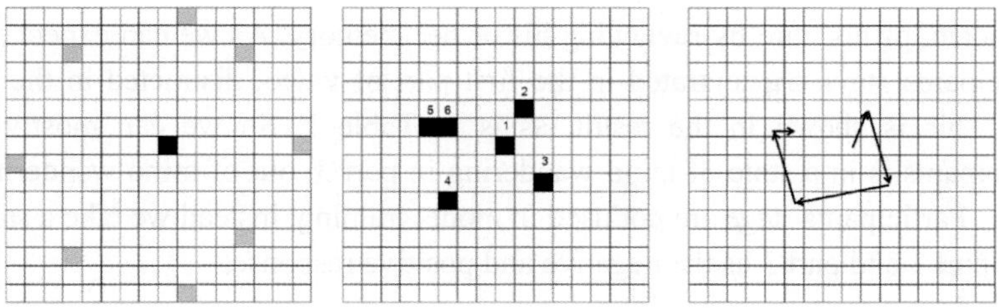

(a) (b) (c)

Fig. 5. This figure shows the process to model eye movement (a) the key point we interested in (b) eye positions of a group of images, in absolute coordinate (c) the motion vector of eye movement

3.3. *Model training*

For a classifier, an observation, in this paper, is consist of eye features extracted from K consecutive images, where K is the window size, and the tag indicating whether in mind wandering or not. Features are composed by two different parts, one is the pupil index, the other is eye movement. Pupil index of K images is the average of each one. Denoted as <Pupil index, eye movement, tag>, these triplets are divided into two parts at a proportion of 9:1, training data set and test data set. While training data set is feed into three different classifiers, LR classifier[17], linear SVM classifier[18], HMM classifier[19], with different window size K. The test data set is feed into these classifiers to evaluate the accuracy. The final result is discussed later.

4. Experiment Design

4.1. *Participants*

All participants are undergraduate students from Shanghai Jiao Tong University, with age from 18 to 22, 19 average. The whole participants include 15 males, and 15 females.

4.2. *Data collection*

Each participant is required to sit in front of a desk, to watch a teaching video of about 10 minutes using iphone. This video is consist of three parts, the first part is normal video, images with sound; the second part, however, is just images, without sound; the third part is just audio, with a blank screen. The participant is required to face the screen as possible as he or she can. The software installed in iphone captures images of the participant at a rate of 10 frames per second. The participant is required to tag each of captured images concentrated or distracted, or not sure by reviewing his or her memory. As we can expect, most participants stays concentrated in the first part of video, distracted in the third part. This is shown in the result, as is in Table 1. So we can mostly say, participants is in a state of mind wandering in part 3, out of mind wandering in part 1. Participants' tags are not used in model training, instead we take a sample from part 1 and part 3 as the negative and positive response.

Table 1. This table shows composition of participants' tag in each part of the video

	Part 1	Part 2	Part 3
Concentrated	89%	31%	8%
Distracted	1%	44%	87%
Not sure	10%	23%	5%

5. Model Training and Evaluation

For each participant, we gather two parts of information. One is positive response, which is mind wandering, and the other is negative. For each part, we extract the middle part, 1000 frames, of totally ~1800 frames as the input to the system. So we get 30000 frames in total. These frames are converted to image streams of eye, after passing through face detection and face alignment. These streams, grouped with a size of K, are then sent to feature extraction module. Observations are divided into two parts, training set and test set, with a proportion of 9:1. Training set is passed to three different classifiers, LR classifier, linear SVM classifier, HMM classifier, to train the model. The test set is then used to evaluate the accuracy of these model. The final result is shown as in Table 2.

Table 2. This table shows the accuracy of different classifier with different window size

	LR	Linear SVM	HMM
2	34%	41%	31%
8	41%	53%	39%
16	37%	45%	35%

From table 2, we can find linear SVM classifier works best with the window size set to be 8, reaching 53% in accuracy.

6. Conclusions

In this paper, we have presented a system of automatic detection of mind wandering. This system uses face detection and face alignment techniques to locate the locality of eye, and with this locality, the system automatic extract eye features, and with these features, the system managed to detect the state of mind wandering. Experiment has shown a promising accuracy. Our effort shows that, even without specific sensors or eye gaze, we can make the detection of mind wandering using the camera of mobile platform.

Our future work focuses on two aspects, one for optimization of mobile platform, the other for more feature extraction. As the development of hardware of mobile platform, limitation of memory and computing resource may relax. So we can use bigger images, faster capture rate, thus more features to improve the accuracy. Meanwhile, more and more physiological sensors are built into mobile phone, which means we can detect physiological signals to help the automatic detection process. That is a huge enrichment of feature set, I believe.

Acknowledgments

The authors would like to thank all reviewers for their helpful suggestions and constructive comments. This work is fully supported by National Science & Technology Pillar Program during the Eleventh Five-year Plan Period(No. 2012BAH55F02). This work is supported by National Science & Technology Pillar Program during the Eleventh Five-year Plan Period(2012BAH55F02).

References

1. Kop, R., Fournier, H.: New Dimensions to Self-Directed Learning in an Open Networked Learning Environment[J]. International Journal of Self-Directed Learning 7(2), 2 - 20 (2011).
2. Fowler, G.A.: An Early Report Card on Massive Open Online Courses. The Wall Street Journal (2013).
3. Parr, C.: Not Staying the Course, Times Higher Education (2013).
4. Guo, P.J., Kim, J., Rubin, R.: How video production affects student engagement: an empir-ical study of MOOC videos. In: Proceedings of the First ACM Conference on Learning@ Scale Conference, pp. 41 - 50. ACM, New York (2014) .
5. Risko, E., Buchanan, D., Medimorec, S., Kingstone, A.: Everyday attention: Mind wander-ing and computer use during lectures. Computers & Education 68, 275 - 283 (2013).
6. Navalpakkam, V. et al. Attention and Selection in Online Choice Tasks. User Modeling, Adaptation, and Personalization. J. Masthoff et al., eds. Springer Berlin Heidelberg. 200 - 211(2012)..
7. Just, M.A. and Carpenter, P.A. A Theory of Reading: From Eye Fixations to Comprehension. Psychological Review. 87, 4, 329(1980).

8. Dong, Y. et al. Driver Inattention Monitoring System for Intelligent Vehicles: A Review. IEEE Transactions on Intelligent Transportation Systems. 12, 2, 596 – 614. (2011.)
9. Rayner, K. Eye Movements in Reading and Information Processing: 20 Years of Research. Psychological bulletin. 124, 3, 372(1988).
10. Andreassi, J.L. Psychophysiology Human Behavior & Physiological Response. Psychology Press.(2013)
11. Smallwood, J. et al. Subjective Experience and the Attentional Lapse: Task Engagement and Disengagement During Sustained Attention. Consciousness and Cognition. 13, 4, 657 – 690(2004).
12. Blanchard, N. et al. Automated Physiological-Based Detection of Mind Wandering During Learning. Intelligent Tutoring Systems, 55 – 60(2014).
13. Xiang Xiao, Phuong Pham, Jingtao Wang: AttentiveLearner: AdaptiveMobile MOOC Learning via Implicit Cognitive States Inference[C], Proceedings of the 2015 ACM on International Conference on Multimodal Interaction, 373-374 (2015).
14. https://developer.apple.com/library/prerelease/ios/documentation/AudioVideo/Conceptual/AVFoundationPG/.
15. http://docs.opencv.org/2.4/doc/tutorials/objdetect/cascade_classifier/cascade_classifier.html.
16. Shaoqing Ren, Xudong Cao, Yichen Wei, Jian Sun: Face Alignment at 3000 FPS via Regressing Local Binary Features[C], Computer Vision and Pattern Recognition, IEEE, 1685-1692(2014).
17. https://www.csie.ntu.edu.tw/~cjlin/liblinear/
18. https://www.csie.ntu.edu.tw/~cjlin/libsvm/
19. https://github.com/KorfLab/StochHMM

An Offloading Mechanism Based on User Satisfaction Oriented for LTE Networks

Kuo-Chih CHU and Tzu-Chi HUANG
Department of Electronic Engineering, Lunghwa University of Science and Technology, Taoyuan, Taiwan
E-mail: kcchu@mail.lhu.edu.tw

The rapid deployment of LTE networks in recent years has lead to the issue of LTE networks being unable to satisfy user requirements with the available bandwidth. This is also compounded by the appearance of various new services and the increase of client numbers. Wi-Fi offloading is the popular technology to ease LTE network congestion. In this paper, we propose the User Satisfaction Oriented Data Offloading (USODO), which is capable of offloading certain users' traffic from LTE networks to Wi-Fi networks according to user duration in Wi-Fi networks and the scheduling result. Through simulations, we can confirm that USODO decreases LTE network traffic and improves user experiences in networking.

Keywords: Wi-Fi offloading; LTE networks; User satisfaction.

1. Introduction

Wi-Fi offloading is designed to decrease the traffic in LTE core networks and increase data transmission speed by transmitting data through Wi-Fi networks instead of LTE networks, when a client enters an area covered by both LTE and Wi-Fi networks. Currently, most telecommunication companies do not enable Wi-Fi offloading; even though certain telecommunication companies enable it, they use very simple policies. The existing simple policies merely detect whether clients enter the area covered by Wi-Fi networks of the telecommunication company or not. If it is positive, the client is switched from LTE networks to Wi-Fi networks and then switched back to LTE networks when the client leaves the area covered by Wi-Fi networks. The existing simple policies do not consider the traffic in both LTE and Wi-Fi networks, so the client maybe is switched from free LTE networks to busy Wi-Fi networks, which increases the data transmission delay of the client. Accordingly, we propose the User Satisfaction Oriented Data Offloading (USODO) in this paper. USODO locates clients who have bad LTE network signal quality and bad user experiences of scheduling, and switches them to free Wi-Fi networks in order to improve user experiences in networking.

2. Introduction of LTE Networks and Wi-Fi Offloading

A LTE network is composed of Evolved Packet Core (EPC), User Equipment (UE) and Evolved Universal Terrestrial Radio Access (E-UTRAN). A EPC includes the LTE core network and management devices. A UE is a client device. A E-UTRAN has the evolved NodeB (eNB) where eNB has one side connected to a UE via the RF signal and another side connected to the EPC via wire networks. A LTE network schedules network accesses inside the eNB to allocate bandwidth to a UE in units of RB (short for Resource Block). A LTE network uses SC-FDMA in its upside channel in order to decrease the Peak to Average Power Ratio (PAPR) and the power consumption of the UE. When SC-FDMA is used, the eNB has to allocate more than 1 RB to the UE and the RBs have to be conjoint, which complicates the design of upside scheduling.

Currently, many scheduling policies are proposed for the upside channel in LTE networks. According to [1], Wi-Fi offloading can be classified into the AP-based offloading infrastructure [2,3] and the Terminal-to-Terminal (T2T) offloading infrastructure [4]. In the AP-based offloading infrastructure, base stations (BSs) of LTE networks and Wi-Fi networks are connected to each other. When a UE enters the area covered by Wi-Fi networks, the BS of LTE networks transmits data through Wi-Fi networks. In the T2T offloading infrastructure, UEs can transmit data to each other directly without the BS of LTE networks. In this paper, we focus on the AP-based offloading infrastructure in Wi-Fi offloading. In this paper, we design a Wi-Fi offloading. Because Wi-Fi networks mostly use ISM channels that easily suffer interference, it is difficult to avoid a delay in transmitting real-time data. Accordingly, we only target our Wi-Fi offloading at the non-real-time data of a UE. Besides, because most clients access the Internet through indoor Wi-Fi networks, we can predict which clients will long stay in Wi-Fi networks and offload their data in order to decrease the traffic of LTE networks. Furthermore, our Wi-Fi offloading can transmit data through Wi-Fi networks when LTE networks have bad signal quality. Moreover, we transmit data through Wi-Fi networks for clients that cannot get enough bandwidth in the scheduling result of eNB, in order to improve throughputs of the clients.

3. USODO Mechanism

In this paper, we propose an offloading policy working in the eNB. The proposed policy mainly predicts the time of a UE staying in Wi-Fi networks and determines whether offloading its data from LTE networks to Wi-Fi networks according to the type of data transmitted by the UE, the scheduling result of the upside channel and the signal quality of LTE networks. The proposed policy is named User Satisfaction Oriented Data Offloading (USODO) that utilizes the upside channel scheduling of USO [5] proposed in our previous paper and adds algorithms to determine when to enable Wi-Fi offloading. The detail of the new offloading mechanism of USODO is presented as follows.

(1) Building Transmission Matrix: The step is intended to build a transmission matrix that maps the bandwidth of UEs to RBs. We assume that 5 UEs want to transmit data and their data type, stay time and data transmission rate are shown in Table 1. Real-time data cannot be delayed but non-real-time data can be delayed. The stay time is the time of a UE staying in a Wi-Fi network. The data transmission rate is the quantity of data transmitted per second by a UE. Because each UE has different signal quality between it and the eNB, a UE may get different bandwidth in a RB. The eNB can build the transmission matrix according to the messages returned by UEs. We assume that the scheduling process is intended to allocate 6 RBs to 5 UEs in Table 2. We take the UEs that use RB_1 to transmit data for example. In RB_1, UE_1 has 20bps bandwidth, UE_2 has 40bps bandwidth, UE_3 has 30bps bandwidth, UE_4 has 30bps bandwidth and UE_5 has 20bps bandwidth.

(2) Calculating User Satisfaction: In the step, we define the User Satisfaction Index (USI) as the matrix to evaluate user satisfaction (i.e. user experience in networking) as shown in Eq. (1). In Eq. (1), $alloc_i$ is the bandwidth allocated to the ith UE in the scheduling process, req_i is the bandwidth requested by the ith UE, and USI_i is user satisfaction of the ith UE.

$$USI_i=(alloc_i/req_i). \tag{1}$$

Next, we use data in Table 1 and Eq. (1) to calculate the USI between a UE and a RB as shown in Table 3. We observe that the USI of UE_1 is 1 if UE_1 uses RB_6, which implies that the bandwidth requirement of UE_1 can be satisfied with RB_6. After that, we calculate the average USI of each UE to get UE_1=0.78, UE_2=0.65, UE_3=0.54, UE_4=0.54 and UE_5=0.16 respectively.

(3) Determining and Executing Procedure of Offloading: USODO determines whether should offload data of a UE or not according to the following considerations. First, we only offload non-real-time data of a UE from LTE

networks to Wi-Fi networks, because Wi-Fi networks cannot guarantee that real-time data will not be delayed. Second, we only offload data for a UE staying long in Wi-Fi networks, because a UE staying short in Wi-Fi networks cannot get much effect from the help of Wi-Fi offloading. Third, we offload data for a UE with higher priority if the UE is covered by bad signal quality of LTE networks and cannot get enough bandwidth in LTE networks.

USODO executes the offloading procedure in Figure 1. First, we define $t_{offload}$ as the threshold of the offloading time. Status offloading in Figure 1 indicates that data of a UE will be offloaded when it stays in Wi-Fi networks longer than $t_{offload}$. Status immediate offloading in Figure 1 indicates that data of a UE will be offloaded immediately once it enters Wi-Fi networks without staying longer than $t_{offload}$. A UE is always at Status immediate offloading until it enters Wi-Fi networks twice without staying longer than $t_{offload}$. After that, data of the UE will be offloaded again if it stays in Wi-Fi networks longer than $t_{offload}$.

Besides, a UE connected to a eNB through bad signal quality may transmit more data accidentally if we offload data of the UE from LTE networks to Wi-Fi networks. Accordingly, we define three thresholds, i.e. L_H, L_M and USI_{low}. The traffic of a Wi-Fi network reaches Threshold L_H, which implies that the Wi-Fi network has high traffic. Threshold L_M defines the middle traffic of a Wi-Fi network. Besides, a USI between a UE and a RB is less than USI_{low}, which implies that the proportion of bandwidth quantity to data transmission quality is low. Accordingly, when a USI of a UE is less than USI_{low}, which implies that the UE has bad signal quality or transmits much data because of the insufficient bandwidth in LTE networks, we can alleviate the situation by offloading data of the UE to Wi-Fi networks. To avoid offloading data of a UE to congested Wi-Fi networks to suffer a data transmission delay, USODO enables Wi-Fi offloading only when the traffic of a Wi-Fi network is less than Threshold L_H. Table 4 presents the rules of deciding when to offload data of a UE from LTE networks to Wi-Fi networks.

According to Table 1, for example, we assume that $t_{offload}$ is equal to 60 (seconds), USI_{low} is equal to 0.3 and current traffic of a Wi-Fi network is less than L_M. Because UE_1 and UE_2 both transmit real-time data, their data will not be offloaded from LTE networks to Wi-Fi networks. Data of UE_4 will be offloaded to Wi-Fi networks because it stays in Wi-Fi networks longer than $t_{offload}$. Although UE_5 stays in Wi-Fi networks shorter than $t_{offload}$, data of UE_5 will be offloaded to a Wi-Fi network too, because its USI is less than USI_{low} and current traffic of a Wi-Fi network is less than L_M. Data of UE_3 will not be offloaded to Wi-Fi networks because it does not meet any rule in Table 4. When the offloading procedure is ended, data of UE_4 and UE_5 both will be offloaded to Wi-Fi networks with the CSMA/CA access control and they will not enter the scheduling phase of LTE networks. However, UE_1, UE_2 and UE_3 will use USO algorithm [5] to schedule of LTE networks.

Table 1. Transmission Data Type.

	Data Type	Stay time (s)	Data Rate (bps)
UE_1	Real-Time	20	45
UE_2	Real-Time	120	50
UE_3	Non-Real-Ttime	30	60
UE_4	Non-Real-Ttime	500	70
UE_5	Non-Real-Ttime	50	100

Table 2. Transmission Matrix.

	RB_1	RB_2	RB_3	RB_4	RB_5	RB_6
UE_1	20	30	40	35	40	45
UE_2	40	35	25	35	30	35
UE_3	30	30	35	30	35	35
UE_4	30	40	50	40	35	30
UE_5	20	15	10	15	20	15

Table 3. USI for all UEs and RBs.

	RB_1	RB_2	RB_3	RB_4	RB_5	RB_6
UE_1	0.44	0.67	0.89	0.78	0.89	1
UE_2	0.8	0.7	0.5	0.6	0.6	0.7
UE_3	0.5	0.5	0.58 0.5	0.58	0.58	
UE_4	0.43	0.57	0.71	0.57	0.5	0.43
UE_5	0.2	0.15	0.1	0.15	0.2	0.15

Table 4. Rules of Deciding When to Offload Data.

<table>
<tr><th colspan="3">Data Type</th><th>Wi-Fi load≧L_H</th><th>Wi-Fi load <L_H</th><th>Wi-Fi load <L_M</th></tr>
<tr><td colspan="3">Real-Time</td><td>×</td><td>×</td><td>×</td></tr>
<tr><td rowspan="3">Non-Real-Time</td><td colspan="2">Stay Time ≧ $t_{offload}$</td><td>×</td><td>○</td><td>○</td></tr>
<tr><td rowspan="2">Average USI ≧ USI_{low}</td><td>×</td><td>×</td><td>×</td><td></td></tr>
<tr><td>Average USI < USI_{low}</td><td>×</td><td>×</td><td>○</td></tr>
</table>

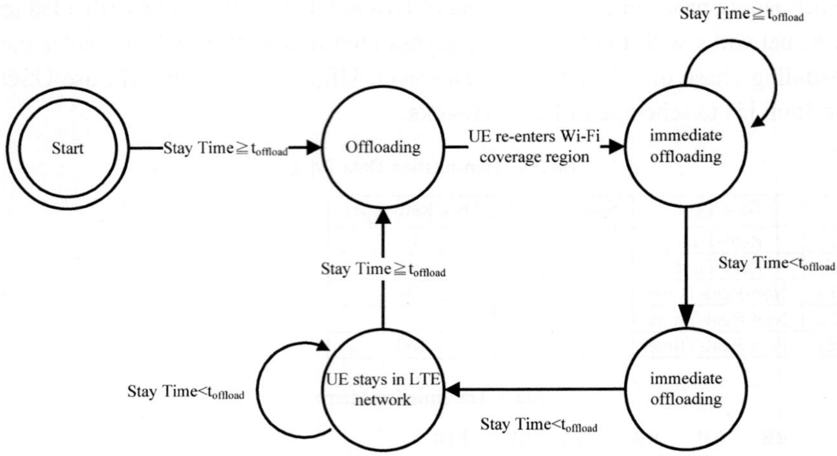

Fig. 1. Offloading Procedure.

4. Simulation and Analysis

In the section, we use simulations to compare user satisfaction of USO and that of USODO by using UEs to transmit different quantities of data. Because USO does not support Wi-Fi offloading, we assume that UEs in USO randomly choose LTE or Wi-Fi networks to transmit their data. In simulations, we assume that each UE transmits 30% real-time data and 70% non-real-time data, and we assume that 50% UEs stay in Wi-Fi networks longer than $t_{offload}$. Besides, we set L_H to 0.8 and L_M to 0.5.

Figure 2 shows user satisfaction of a UE when it transmits different quantities of data in a Wi-Fi where the traffic is less than L_M. Because there is not much traffic in the Wi-Fi, the UE does not suffer a serious delay when data is offloaded from the LTE network to the Wi-Fi network. When the UE transmits more data, the LTE network cannot give the UE enough bandwidth with the allocated RBs, so user satisfaction of the UE is decreased. However, both USO and USODO still can give a UE more than 80% user satisfaction. Because USODO can offload data of a UE to the Wi-Fi network when the LTE network has bad signal quality, it gives the UE more user satisfaction than USO.

Figure 3 presents user satisfaction of a UE when it transmits different quantities of data in a Wi-Fi network where the traffic is equal or more than L_M but less than L_H. Because the Wi-Fi network has middle traffic, offloading too much data of the UE to it may alleviate overheads of the LTE network but congests the Wi-Fi network to accidentally decrease user satisfaction. Even so,

USODO still outperforms USO because it can limit the number of UEs whose data is offloaded to the Wi-Fi network.

Figure 4 presents user satisfaction of a UE when it transmits different quantities of data in a Wi-Fi network where the traffic is equal or more than L_H. When the Wi-Fi network has high traffic, USODO does not offload data of the UE to the Wi-Fi network to congest it. Meanwhile, the admission control of USODO limits the number of UEs when the traffic of the LTE network increases. Accordingly, USODO can keep user satisfaction at a certain level. Conversely, USO does not stop offloading data to the Wi-Fi network even when the Wi-Fi network is congested. Accordingly, the congestion in the Wi-Fi network degrades user satisfaction of USO much more than that of USODO.

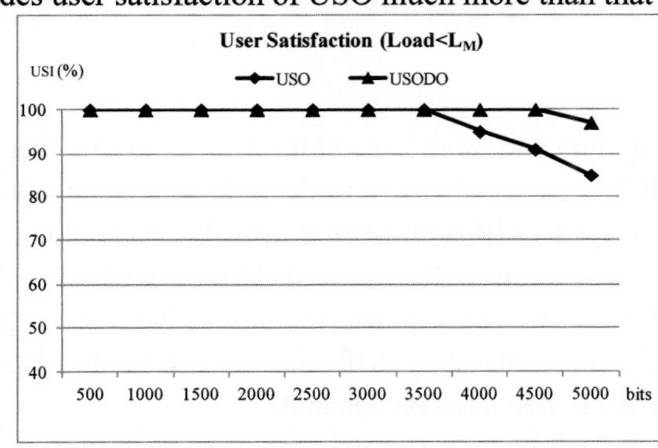

Fig. 2. User Satisfaction Comparison between USO and USODO (Load<L_M).

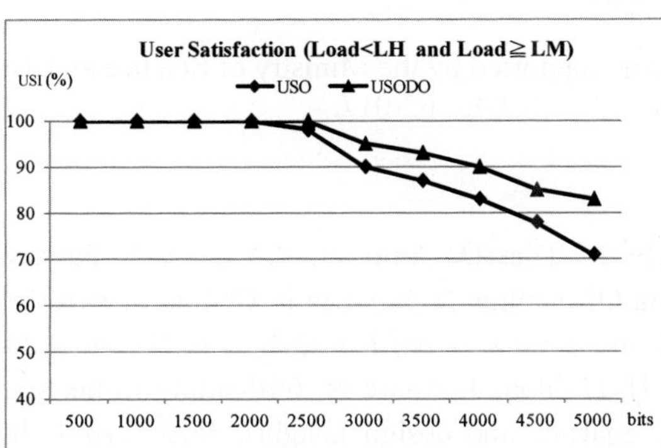

Fig. 3. User Satisfaction Comparison between USO and USODO (Load<L_H and Load≧L_M).

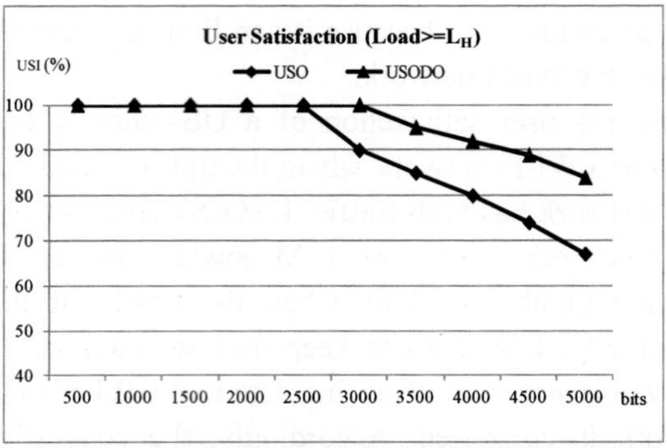

Fig. 4. User Satisfaction Comparison between USO and USODO (Load$\geqq L_H$).

5. Conclusion

Since clients need more and more bandwidth, we can expect that LTE networks in the future will be congested easily to degrade user satisfaction. Against the problem, Wi-Fi networks offloading is a practicable technology. We propose a Wi-Fi networks offloading policy named User Satisfaction Oriented Data Offloading (USODO). In simulations, we show that the proposed USODO indeed can greatly increase user satisfaction by offloading data of UEs from LTE networks to Wi-Fi networks on demand.

Acknowledgments

This research was supported by the Ministry of Science and Technology under contract: MOST 103-2221-E-262-017.

References

1. F. Rebecchi, M. Dias De Amorim, V. Conan, A. Passarella, R. Bruno, M. Conti, Data Offloading Techniques in Cellular Networks: A Survey, *IEEE Communications Surveys and Tutorials*, Vol. 17, no. 2 (2015), pp.580-603.
2. S. Singh, H. Dhillon, J. Andrews, Offloading in heterogeneous networks: Modeling, analysis and design insights, *IEEE Trans. Wireless Commun.*, Vol. 12, no. 5, (May 2013), pp. 2484–2497.
3. A. de la Oliva, C. Bernardos, M. Calderon, T. Melia, J. Zuniga, IP flow mobility: Smart traffic offload for future wireless networks, *IEEE Commun. Mag.*, Vol. 49, no. 10 (2011), pp. 124–132.

4. B. Han et al., Mobile Data Offloading through Opportunistic Communications and Social Participation, *IEEE Trans. Mobile Comput.*, Vol. 11, no. 5, (May 2012) pp. 821–834.
5. K.-C. Chu, T.-C. Huang, S.-H. Cheng and W.-C. Tsai, An Uplink Scheduling Mechanism Based on User Satisfaction in LTE Networks, in *Proc. International Conference on Consumer Electronics, Communications and Networks*, (Beijing, China, 2014).

10 Gigabit Ethernet Data Frame Reconstruction Based on FPGA

Yi-chen WANG and Yue-yang CHEN†
Beijing Institute of Technology
Beijing, 100081, P.R. China
†E-mail: wangyichenwychen@sina.com

Improving network transmission efficiency is an important issue in 10 Gigabit Ethernet (10GigE) transmission. FPGA functions by receiving, sorting, combining and repacking required UDP protocol frames, before sending them to the downstream receiver. This design has high efficiency and low delay through FPGA hardcore programming. The start, stop and necessary parameters for the frame reconstruction are controlled and configured by the upper computer software, providing easy modification and good adaptation. The design can effectively improve the utilization of 10GigE transmission link, optimize the network environment, and enhance the processing efficiency of downstream receiving device.

Keywords: FPGA; 10GigE; Frame reconstruction; UDP.

1. Introduction

10-Gigabit-Ethernet (10GbE) has characters of reducing the complexity of the network and good compatibility, etc. Recently, with the gradual improvement of the standards-making and pursuit of the commercial achievements' utilization, 10GbE has already been used to enterprises' and telecom operators' networks and the data center networks [1]. Using FPGA to optimize the design of 10GbE reduces the chips and the chip interfaces in quantity, increasing the stability of the system [2].

The data frame transmitted data in accordance with the TCP/IP consists of the header of the Protocol and the data item. When the number of the transmitted data is fixed and the data item is short, more headers of the Protocol will be included in the data frame to reduce the utilization of the communication link of the network. In practice, when multiple collecting sources of HSCSD transmit data to the same receiving terminal and the length of the data frame is relatively short, the multiple headers of the Protocol will reconfigure these data frames, combining the multiple data frames to one data frame, and that can raise

† Corresponding author.

the utilization of the communication link, optimize the environment of the network transmission, reduce the overheads of the receiving devices and improve the processing efficiency of the receiving terminal hardware devices.

2. System Design

2.1. *System framework*

Outside UDP data frame passes the 10-Gigabit fiber-optical module (adopt the AFBR-703SDZ 10Gps fiber-optical module of Avago Company) [3-4], the interface of the 10GbE, and enters the FPGA system. Then, it goes on to pass the PHY module (transform the differential signal to the 64-bit identifiable digital signal), the GMAC module (the module for checking the effectiveness of the data frame), the data sorting module, the data merging module, the data sending module, and through the interface of the Ethernet and the fiber-optical module to the user receiving terminal [5-6].

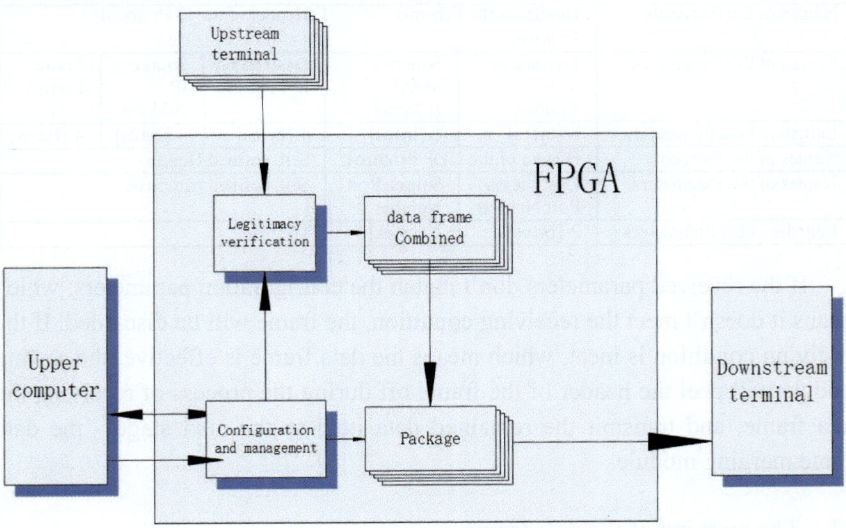

Fig. 1. Block Diagram of the data frame reconfiguration system

2.2. *Design scheme*

After the data enter the FPGA system, the data receiving module will analyze its header, defining whether the frame is that the device should receive. If it doesn't meet the receiving condition, it will be discarded; whereas, the header will be peeled off and the data item of the frame enter the data merging module. When the mergence is completed and the condition of packaging into frame is meat, the merged data item will enter the data sending module. Then the module will add fitted UDP header to the item to complete a data frame and send the frame to the downstream receiving node. The UDP header and the needed parameter in the process of the frame reconfiguration dispose the whole system in advance through the upper-computer software [7].

3. Key Problems & Solutions

3.1. *The sorting and analysis of the data frame*

The sorting module will extract the parameters in the corresponding positions in the frame and contrast them with the configuration parameters. In view of the actually needs of the engineering, in applications, there is a 16-byte self-defined header added to the existing protocol after the header of the UDP and before the user data item. The main parameters in it are as follows:

Table 1. Main Configuration Parameters

Names of the Protocols	Header of the Ethernet Protocol		Header of the IP Protocol		
Names of the Parameters	Destination MAC Address	Source MAC Address	Destination IP Address	Source IP Address	Frame Length
Lengths of the Parameters	6 [bytes]	6 [bytes]	4 [bytes]	4 [bytes]	4 [bytes]
Names of the Protocols	Header of the UDP Protocol		Self-defined Header		
Names of the Parameters	Destination Port Number	Source Port Number	Self-defined parameter		
Lengths of the Parameters	2 [bytes]	2 [bytes]	16 [bytes]		

If the received parameters don't match the configuration parameters, which means it doesn't meet the receiving condition, the frame will be discarded. If the receiving condition is meat, which means the data frame is effective, the sorting module will peel the header of the frame off during the process of receiving the data frame, and transmit the remained data item to the next stage - the data frame merging module.

3.2. *The merging of the date frame*

Because the whole system works under the 10GbE environment, the clock frequency the system adopted is 156.25MHz and the data width is 64 bits(8 bytes), which means the system processes 8-byte data per clock cycle. As the key part of the design scheme, the main role of the module is to merge the data items of the multiple data frames into one, and the most important role is to concatenate multiple independent data items into an integral whole.

According to the UDP data frame format, after the header of the data frame(42 bytes) is peeled off, the initiation structure of the data item is relatively fixed, which is as shown below:

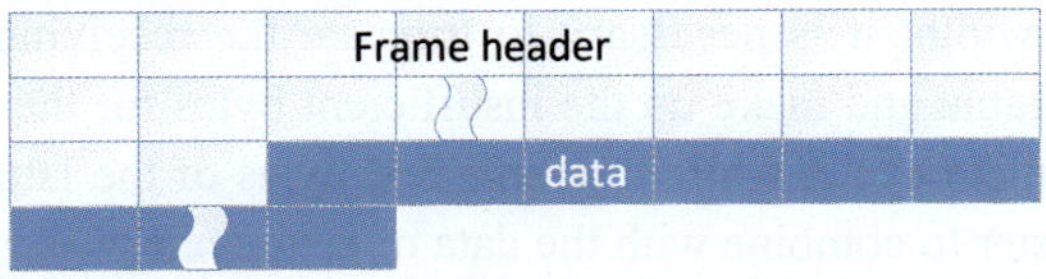

Fig. 2. Diagram of the concatenation of the header and the data item of the frame

But, according to the different lengths of the frames, the trailer structure of the data item, based on the results of the complementary operations of eight, will have 8 kinds of situations which can be generalized to the following 3 kinds of situations in accordance with different processing methods:

2 bytes remained at the trailer: this kind of situation is the easiest to process, because the trailer of the former frame (2 bytes remained) and the header of the latter frame (6 bytes remained) can just compose a complete cycle width (8 bytes). The processing method is to directly pad the header of the latter frame to the blank part at the trailer of the former frame.

The operating principle is as follows:

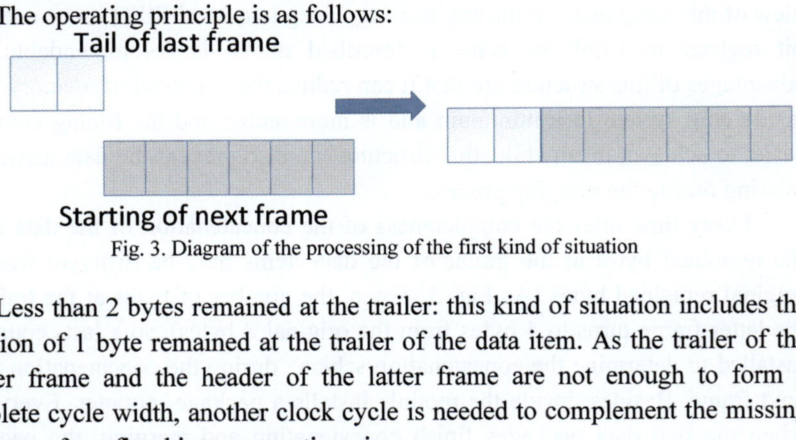

Fig. 3. Diagram of the processing of the first kind of situation

Less than 2 bytes remained at the trailer: this kind of situation includes the situation of 1 byte remained at the trailer of the data item. As the trailer of the former frame and the header of the latter frame are not enough to form a complete cycle width, another clock cycle is needed to complement the missing data items for a fitted interconnecting piece.

The operating principle is as follows:

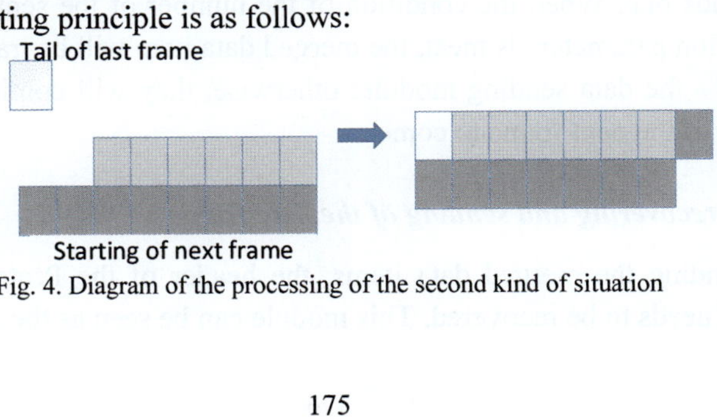

Fig. 4. Diagram of the processing of the second kind of situation

More than 2 bytes remained at the trailer: such kind of situation includes situations of 3 bytes remained to 8 bytes remained at the trailer of the data item. As the trailer of the former frame and the header of the latter frame are over a complete cycle width, it is necessary to truncate the receiving data per cycle from the latter frame and make up the insufficient bytes for the former frame to compose a complete cycle, while the remained bytes of the latter frame will be cached in a register to combine with the data of next cycle.

Taking the situation of 4 bytes remained at the trailer as an example, the operating principle is as follows:

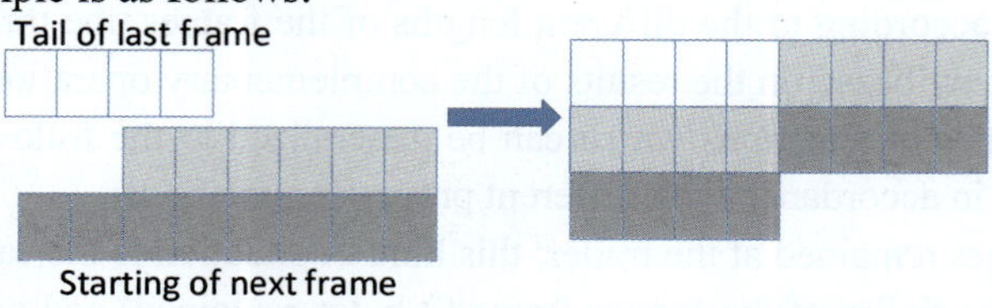

Fig. 5. Diagram of the processing of the third kind of situation

Thus it can be seen that, in most cases, the completeness of the concatenation of the data items needs several cycles and data-caching, so in view of the complexity of the engineering, using two-level FIFO cache and a 64-bit register to fulfil the scheme described above is recommendable. The advantages of this structure are that it can reduce the overhead of memory in the inside chip system to a minimum and is more stable and the timing control is easier to achieve; meanwhile, this structure can also prevent the data items from missing during the merging process.

Every time after the completeness of the concatenation of the data items, the remained bytes at the trailer of the data items may be different from the original remained bytes (As Fig. 5 shown, the number of bytes at the trailer of the latter frame turns to 4 bytes from the original 8 bytes), so a last- counter is installed to determine the concatenation scheme during the concatenation to the next frame. Besides, inside the module installs a package- counter. Every time when the two data packages finish concatenating and merging, the package-counter adds one. When the condition of the number of the sent packets in the configuration parameters is meat, the merged data item will be transmitted to the next stage - the data sending module; otherwise, they will continue to wait for data items of the next frame to come.

3.3. *The recovering and sending of the data frame*

Before sending the merged data items, the header of the Protocol previously peeled off needs to be recovered. This module can be seen as the inverse process of the data sorting module, which adds the header of the Protocol to the data item in accordance with the parameters disposed by the upper computer. The concatenation of multiple data items will not affect the position of the initial byte in the head of the data item of the first frame, so when adding the header of the Protocol, directly loading the data item is enough.

4. Test & Verification

4.1. *Test environment*

The test system mainly includes the HSCSD source, 10-Gb switch, frame reconstruction prototype system, the upper computer and the user-target receiving terminal. The data source and the test prototype system both adopt the hardware platform which based on the FPGA(use the XC6VLX24OT of the Xilinx Company); the 10Gb switch is H3C S5800-32C-PWR; the upper computer and the downstream receiving node adopt the general computer system(Windows operating system of the desktop computer).

4.2. *Test results*

The relationship between the network utilization and the length of the data frame can be denoted as follows:

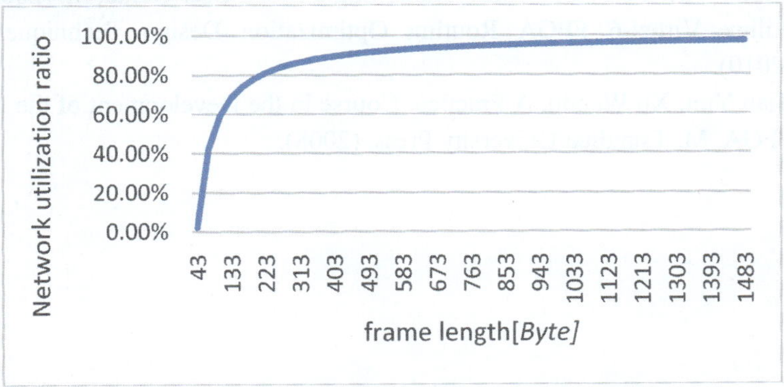

Fig. 6. The relationship between frame length and network utilization

If the test results and the theoretical value are same and the data are accurate, it can be sure that the design scheme is feasible and correct. The network link has been more sufficiently used.

5. Conclusion

This paper uses the hardware platform based on the FPGA and adopts the general TCP/IP to fit all kinds of communication devices worked in the general network environment. Merging and reconfiguring the UDP data, merging the shorter data frame in length into the longer one improves the utilization of the network link. Using the upper computer to configure the FPGA system in advance makes it more flexible and adaptable.

References

1. Zeng Li, Tang Yong, 10GbE Technology and its Application Prospect, J. Agricultural Network Information. 6 (2009) 97-99.
2. Liu Jichuan, Li Dongmei, Research and Implementation of the 10GbE Technology, J, Radio Engineering. 42 (2012) 7-9, 45.
3. Chen Changlin, Qiu Zhaokun, RocketIO and its Application in the HSCSD Transmission, J, Application of the SCM and the Embedded System. 11 (2010) 2528.
4. Hu Jinxian, Zhang Yingbo, Li Rengang, Verification of the Optical Transmission Scheme Based on the Aurora Protocol, J, Science Technology and Engineering. 30 (2012) 8038-8041.
5. Xilinx Virtex-6 FPGA Configurable Logic Block User Guide, M. (2009).
6. Xilinx Virtex-6 FPGA Routing Optimization Design Techniques, M. (2010).
7. Tian Yun, Xu Wendu. A Practical Course in the Development of the Xilinx FPGA, M. Tsinghua University Press. (2008).

Methods for the Improvement of Computer Network Reliability

Zong-zhe NIE, Dong-dong WU and Ruo-peng YANG†
Academy of National Defense Information
Wuhan, Hubei, China
†*E-mail:jiandao2000 @sina.com*

With the popularization of computer network technology, people are becoming increasingly dependent on computer networks, thus the reliability problem of computer network systems has become an important and pressing issue. This paper has identified and analyzed four influential factors of reliability and discusses the four effective methods to improve the reliability of computer network based on the connotation of computer network reliability.

Keywords: Computer network; Reliability; Computer network reliability; Factors; Methods.

1. Reliability for Computer Network System

The computer network reliability is the ability and probability of the network to complete the specified function in the condition of the provision[1]. It represents the ability to transmit information of the computer network in a certain period of time, and highlighting the effectiveness of computer network system. Its connotation mainly includes three aspects: condition, time and task. In theory, computer network reliability is that the computer network can provide the required time and conditions, the network system is connected, no abnormal situation occurs, and can provide the required network capacity within the normal operation of the network system[2]. Now, the measure of computer network reliability can be divided into four categories: the connectivity of computer network, the survivability of computer network, the anti-destructive of computer network, and the effectiveness of computer network components in multi-mode. Reliability is an important indicator and the most fundamental standards to judge whether the security of the network.

2. Factors Affecting the Reliability of Computer Networks

2.1. *Network equipment factor*

2.1.1. *User equipment factor*

The connection of the computer network needs to use the user terminal to realize, its reliability is very important, also is the key of the computer network reliability. In process of the computer network operation daily maintenance, ensuring the reliability of the user terminal is the major thing. Ability to interact with the user terminal is higher, and the network reliability is much higher.

The server is the information center and service provider of the whole computer network. It usually includes the database server, the file server, the print server, the mail server, the event server, the Web server, etc. These sub servers are reliable and directly affect the reliability and operating efficiency of computer networks. Generally speaking, the error resilience and the response time of the server are proportional to its reliability.

2.1.2. *Transmission switching equipment factor*

Through the analysis of a large number of network construction practices, the following conclusions can be drawn: Generally, the malfunction of computer network caused by the wiring system is the most difficult to find, and the price paid is the biggest. This phenomenon indicates that if we want to strengthen the computer network reliability, we should use the standard communication circuit and the wiring system in the process of network construction.

Router can not only realize the interconnection of the same type local area network, but also realize the interconnection between LAN and WAN[3]. When analyzing the reliability of the router, the first problem is to choose a protocol, which has the flexibility to choose as possible. Secondly, it is the most insurance method to improve the reliability of the router. Then, when the main router fails, the router can automatically replace the work, so as to ensure the normal operation of the computer network.

2.2. *Network topological structure factor*

The interconnection network topology is the main connection between the components in the computer network, which belongs to the computer network planning problem, and also a factor affecting the reliability of computer networks[4]. Different application fields and different scales of computer networks have different network topologies, and different topological structures have different effects on the accuracy of information transmission.

With the increase of the computer network topology structure, the cost of the network topology is increased. The design of network topology is unreasonable, which makes some problems in the application, and directly leads to the computer network reliability. In order to guarantee the reliability of the network information transmission, we need to focus on the network topology, so that we can choose the reasonable and reliable network topology based on the different degree and different range of network reliability.

With the in-depth study and analysis of the computer network topology, computer network designers put forward many new concepts such as fault tolerance, wide diameter, restricted connectivity, restricted edge connectivity, restricted fault tolerance and so on. These parameters can measure the reliability and fault tolerance of computer networks more accurately, and provide scientific basis for computer network planning and design.

2.3. *Network management factor*

Typically, a large computer network is made up of different network products and devices from different manufacturers, which are large and complex[5]. The result in the overall installation of the computer system is not deterministic. This computer network system once the construction is completed and running, easy to cause data loss. When the loss of data, the network will produce a series of errors, computer equipment will produce quality problems. The safety and reliability of computer network system will be greatly reduced. To ensure the integrity of information transmission, reduce the incidence of failure, reduce the loss of information, reduce the BER and error, and improve the reliability of computer network, we should use the advanced network management technology, carry out the real-time collection of network operation parameters and statistical network information, monitor the network operation state, find fault and troubleshoot timely.

2.4. *Network security factor*

At present, many users do not have enough safety awareness in the computer. In the process of using the computer, they lack of basic prevention of network security, inadvertently because of an operation and the destruction of the computer's security features[6]. In the course of using computer, they lack the basic prevention of network security, even inadvertently destroyed the computer's security features for a certain operation.

At the same time, the computer virus invasion also has brought the challenge to the computer network reliability. Because of the design of the computer network, there are some problems which will inevitably be affected by the virus. So the vast majority of computer network system in order to strengthen the reliability of the computer, have installed anti-virus software or set up a virus firewall. However, in the presence of a wide variety of viruses, anti-virus software is lagging behind, unable to identify the new virus, and thus easy to have a new virus to take the opportunity to infringe, endangering the safety of the system, and thus reduce the reliability.

3. Effective Methods to Improve the Reliability of Computer Network

3.1. *Scientific design of fault-tolerant computer network program*

Scientific design of computer networks for fault tolerance, which can effectively guarantee the normal operation of the computer network when the network system fails. It is mainly based on the analysis of common failures in computer network equipment, and the fault tolerance design is enhanced. Ultimately improve the ability to solve the network failure, reduce the network failure when the user cannot use the phenomenon of the network. And then reduce the error of the generation or failure to bring the loss, improve the reliability of computer network system.

Firstly, using related computer networks and computer redundant data parallel manner, connect different network centers to servers and users when a network center failure occurs to automatically switch to other network center.

Secondly, we should expand the scope of the computer network connection. The router, LAN, WAN and the corresponding data is effectively connected, and then can effectively ensure that the data link failure will not cause a substantial impact on the entire computer network.

3.2. *Actively take double network structure design*

Dual structure design, calculate the original network redundancy in the current computer network, and improving the fault tolerance of the network system and add a layer of backup network for the computer network operation[7]. When the main network failures occur in the computer network, the backup network will replace the existing network system. The new network uses the new network internal structure to realize the network data and information continue to transmit, to ensure the smooth operation of the computer network. Compared with the computer network fault tolerance design, double network structure design is the high cost. But it easier to find the fault point and the reason, and be able to timely troubleshooting, ensures security and stability of the entire network. In terms of topology can be choose binary N-dimensional BF network, is shown in Fig. 1. With flexible regional distribution, it makes the network upgrade and expend more convenient, and also less network construction and maintenance costs. Because there are more independent network nodes, those play great role for improvement of network reliability.

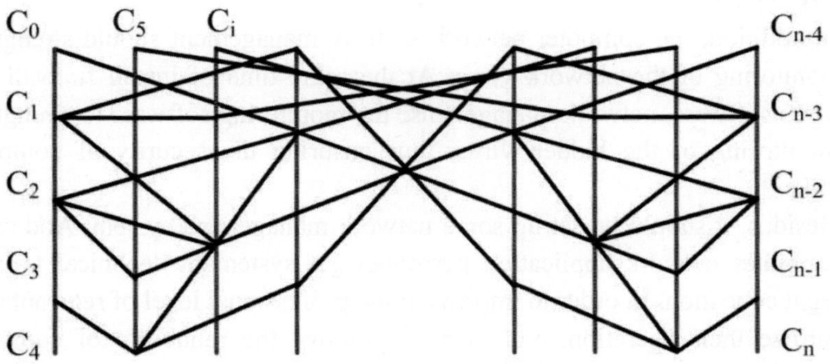

Fig. 1. BF network topological structure

3.3. *Design scheme of whole network system*

With the increasing demand of users, the use of decentralized network structure design has become more important. This design can replace the centralized network architecture design, complete the network internal structure of continuous development, solve the user operation of a series of problems, and ultimately enhance the safety and reliability of computer networks[8]. At the same time, the design method of the system structure of computer network is reasonable upgrades and improvement, which solves the existing problems and the insufficiency effectively.

Network topology can choose N * M - dimensional mesh network. N * M - dimensional mesh network is a kind of topological structure in many of the more important network system application. In this kind of topological network, any node damage will not have larger overall impact on the network, and more won't produce similar to the significant loss of entire network paralysis. It will play a greater role for improving the reliability of the network.

3.4. *Strengthen the monitoring of network management*

The implementation of computer network design is not enough to completely avoid the occurrence of computer network failure. To improve the reliability of the computer network, it is also need to strengthen the management and control in the daily use of computer network, and strengthen the maintenance of the whole network. Monitoring and management of the reliability of network operation in real time, and strengthening the security and reliability of computer network system.

In addition, the computer network security management should strengthen the monitoring of the network virus. At the same time of install firewall and anti-virus software, network managers use the monitoring software to strengthen the monitoring of the hidden virus, thus ensuring the security of computer networks.

Besides, it should be set up some network management system. And make the computer network application personnel get systematic technical training and legal education. In order to improving the professional level of relevant staff, standardize their operation, and then to improve the reliability of computer network to make a good foundation.

4. Conclusion

In summary, the reliability of computer network is very important for the safe and stable operation of computer networks. The development of the social economy has a profound impact. In order to improve the reliability of computer network, we should pay more attention to the use of advanced network equipment and network design scheme, from the factors that affect the reliability of the system, and take measures to promote the reliability of computer network system.

References

1. Bo Gong, Wen Zhang, Hongxia Yang. Basic Knowledge of Network. Publishing House of Electronics, 2003(In Chinese)
2. Wen Zhang, Hongxia Yang. Network Interconnection Equipment. Publishing House of Electronics,2003(In Chinese)
3. Liang Wei. Routers Principle and Application. The People's Posts and Telecommunications Press .2005(In Chinese)
4. Kcnncth D.Rccd. Network Design. Publishing House of Electronics,2003

5. Wenyuan Dong. Methods to Enhance the Reliability of Computer Network. Network Security Technology and Application, 2014(22):194-195. (In Chinese)
6. Weihua Li. The Reliability of Computer Network Optimization Strategy. Information of China,2013(06):116-116. (In Chinese)
7. Siyuan Zhang. The Reliability of Computer Network and Optimization Analysis. File, 2014 (04): 383-383. (In Chinese)
8. Zhiyi Wu, Xiaohong Mao. Explore the Security of Computer Network and Maintenance Measures. Science and Technology Transmission, 2014(10):131-132. (In Chinese)

Data-based Sensor Similarity Matching Algorithm for IoT Search

Lun LI†, Bi-hua TANG, Fan WU, Chao WU and Wen-hao FAN
School of Electronic Engineering, Beijing University of Posts and Telecommunications
Beijing, 100876, China
†E-mail: lun2baobao@bupt.edu.cn

The traditional search engines show incompatibility and inefficiency in the search in the Internet of Things (IoT). To improve the effectiveness and efficiency of IoT search, we constructed a new search framework for IoT that supports searching for entities and the entity information featured by multidimensional dynamic data and status. We proposed and explained the MAMS (Matching Analytical Mechanism in Searching) system, in addition to the similarity matching method based on multidimensional sensory data to fulfil the search framework. Furthermore, we designed a set of reasonable experimental environment with real world data gathered by the Smart Lab to verify the validity and efficiency of the framework and algorithm. The experimental results demonstrates the efficiency and suitability of the search framework, MAMS and the similarity matching method for IoT search.

Keywords: IoT (Internet of Things); Support Vector Machine (SVM); Data matching; Sensor network; Entity search.

1. Introduction

Since the number keeps increasing of sensor nodes connecting to Internet, diversity and richness have been enhanced of the data-query provided by various sensor nodes and of the comprehensive service by integrating heterogeneous multidimensional sensor terminals[1-3]. It is critical in IoT to locate some interesting sensors and obtain useful sensory information from large-scaled dynamic and comprehensive information resources.

In traditional search systems, the targets of search are static files, figures, music and so on, and the search method of which focuses on describing the captured data and files by metadata and analyzing the metadata next. The searching is done by matching keywords with the metadata analyzed. However, this method is inappropriate for IoT search, because the entity in IoT search is described by multidimensional dynamic sensory data which means the direct

† Corresponding author.

features (directly represented by the multidimensional sensory data) and the indirect features (derived from the analysis of the multidimensional sensory data) of the entity described by multidimensional sensors cannot be thoroughly represented by the traditional search method which is based on describing metadata, while the description using sensory data of the entity can represent the entity information thoroughly. When searching for information about some entity, related entity information can be acquired effectively by matching the sensory data which describes the entity. Therefore, a sensor similarity matching algorithm based on multidimensional data is in demand to match and analyze the multidimensional data which describes the entity in IoT search.

Researchers were trying to solve such problems. Couong Trong and his colleagues have discussed the matching issue of entity information based on sensory data in IoT search in [4-5]. The method proposed is able to match and search for the entity described by single-dimensional sensory data. However, entities and information thereof in IoT are generally featured by multidimensional sensory data instead of single-dimensional sensor nodes. Hence, the existing research cannot fulfill the real demands of IoT search.

In this paper, three issues are discussed:

(1) A search framework of IoT was proposed, which can support the search for entities and information thereof featured by multidimensional and dynamic data and status.

(2) We designed a matching analytical mechanism in searching which is based on multidimensional sensory data and status, and presented a general matching method. Aiming at the key problems of the multidimensional sensory data matching, a sensor similarity matching algorithm based on SVM and multidimensional dynamic data and status.

(3) At last, we verified the feasibility and efficiency of the search method by using the data set derived from our real world.

2. Structure of IoT Search

Involved in IoT search, there are tremendous sensor nodes and procedures like data gathering, data processing, data matching, data indexing and so on. According to the variety, dynamic characteristics and data heterogeneity of sensor entities, we designed the structure of IoT search in Figure 1:

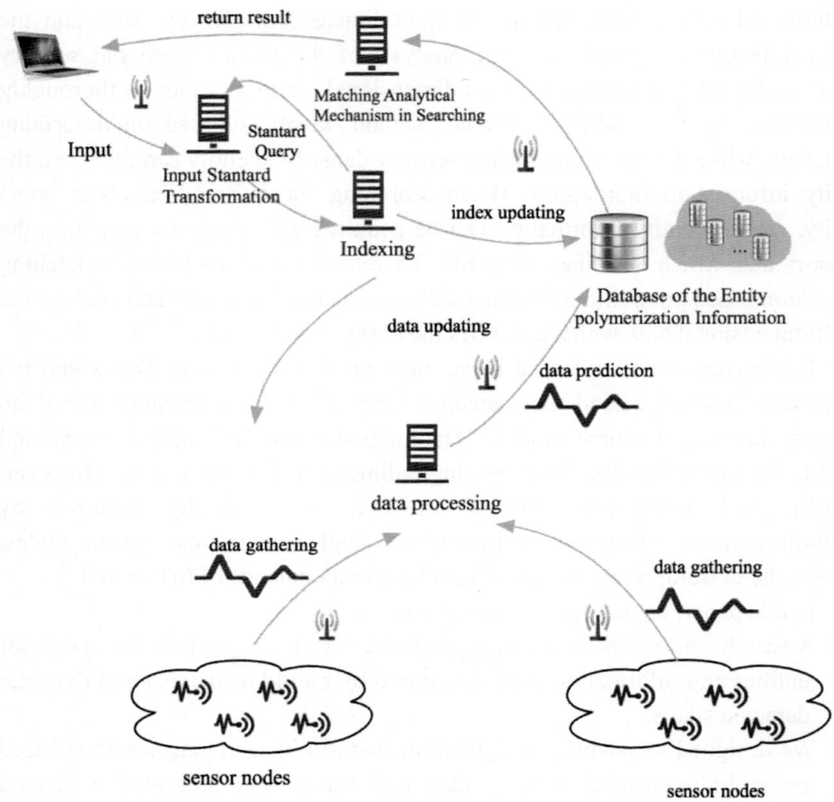

Fig. 1. Structure of IoT search

The data processing center obtains sensory data by connecting to the sensor nodes, and processes the data. Those data make up the processed entity describing data that are stored in the DEPI (database of the entity polymerization information)by the data processing center. The entities are described by multidimensional sensory data. We can get the entity polymerization information based on entities in which each entity contains multidimensional data and status. The indexing mechanism makes it feasible to index the data stored in the DEPI based on entities.

The input of the searching user shall be analyzed through the ISTM (Input Standard Transformation Mechanism). Being different from the traditional search method which is based on key words, the ISTM transforms the input sentence into "entity + key information of the entity + the target of the entity matching + space + time". Then, based on the entity searched by the user, the second step is to find the matching entity polymerization information. By using the MAMS, the search target entity information can be acquired when the multidimensional dynamic polymerization information of the entity is used as the input.

The features of entity mentioned above may refer to the dynamic sensory data or static attributes of the entity represented directly in some dimensions (called direct features) and also can be the dynamic indirect features derived from the analysis of the multidimensional sensory data(called indirect features).

The MAMS based on multidimensional data and status consists of tremendous entity analytical models, each of which takes responsibility for the analysis of some indirect feature in some kind of entity. When user is searching for some indirect feature of a specified kind of entity, the MAMS will correlate the responsible entity analytical model to analyze.

We regard the sought entity as a kind of physical entity with dynamic multidimensional data, which is described by the sensor. The sensor mentioned above is generalized, which means it consists of various kinds of sensors. Therefore, the entity matching can be transformed into the sensor matching with multidimensional data and status.

3. SVM-based Matching Method of Sensor Similarity with Multidimensional Dynamic Data and Status

To solve the sensor matching problem discussed in the last section, we proposed the SMMSS (SVM-based Matching Method of Sensor Similarity). The SMMSS could train corresponding entity analytical model according to the diversity of the entity analytical features, which makes the SMMSS a universal matching method.

As discussed in section 2, information searched by users can be transformed into the pattern consisting of entity, key information of the entity, matching target of the entity and temporal and spatial information. The key information hereof is represented by the multidimensional features of entities. For the analysis of the multidimensional features and the prediction of the target matching of entities, we can represent the entity as:

$$Obj_j^i = \{feature_1, feature_2, \cdots, feature_n, \cdots, feature_N\} N \in Z. \quad (1)$$

In Eq. (1), Obj_j^i represents the i th sought entity in the j th category, $feature_n$ represents the n th multidimensional feature of the entity, and N means the sought entity features N-dimensional sensory dynamic data or status.

In the meanwhile, we represent the matching target as

$$Y \in \{1,2,\cdots m,\cdots,M\} \quad M \in Z. \tag{2}$$

In Eq. (2), Y represents the matching target of the entity, m represents the possible prediction type of the matching target, and M is the amounts of m .

3.1. *Matching method*

Once we have gotten the characteristic data of the i th sought entity in the j th category in the DEPI, which is represented as $X_{(j)}^{(i)} = \{x_1, x_2, \cdots x_N\} \;\; N \in Z$, with the hypothesis that we've already constructed the matching function $S(x)$, we can obtain the prediction represented as $y_{(j)}^{(i)}$ of the matching target of the i th sought entity in the j th category through Eq. 3.

$$y_{(j)}^{(i)} = S(x_j^i). \tag{3}$$

3.2. *Matching function*

In this section, we are going to discuss the matching function $S(x)$ mentioned above.

According to the form of the SVM hypothesis function, we can construct the entity matching function based on multidimensional sensory data and status as:

$$S(x) = \begin{cases} \theta^T f(x) \geq 1 & \forall y = 1 \\ \theta^T f(x) \leq -1 & \forall y = -1 \end{cases}. \tag{4}$$

According to the characteristic of the entity and the distance of correlative entity characteristics in the DEPI, we can get the similarity between the sought entity and the correlative entities which may belong to different categories. The sought entity hereof refers to the entity and information thereof which is derived from the ISTM, and the correlative entity refers to the information we can look up in the DEPI after the entity is transformed through the ISTM. The similarity can be represented as:

$$f(x) = \exp\left(-\frac{\left\| x - l^{(n)} \right\|^2}{2\sigma^2} \right). \tag{5}$$

In the Eq. (5), $\left\| x - l^{(n)} \right\|^2$ can actually be represented as $\sum_{i=1}^{K} (x_i - l_i^{(n)})^2$, in which K denotes the amounts of the training samples of the correlative entity, and $l_i^{(n)}$ denotes the n th dimensional characteristic sample point of the i th sample. $f(x)$ represents the similarity between the characteristic of the sought entity and the one of the training sample.

Assuming that appropriate θ trained and derived from the matching cost function $\cos t(x)$ mentioned in section 3.3 is already obtained, let's substitute the similarity function $f(x)$ of entity $Obj_j^i = \{feature_1, feature_2, \cdots, feature_n, \cdots, feature_N\}$ into the matching function $S(x)$ and get the prediction of the entity matching target.

3.3. *Matching cost function*

In this section, we are going to discuss the details of matching cost function mentioned in the 3.2 section.

According to the constructive method of cost function in the SVM, we construct the matching cost function for Eq. 3 as:

$$\min_{\theta} C\left[\sum_{i=1}^{N} y^{(i)}\left(-\log S_\theta\left(\theta^T f^{(n)}\right)\right) + \left(1 - y^{(n)}\right)\left(\left(-\log\left(1 - S_\theta\left(\theta^T f^{(n)}\right)\right)\right)\right)\right] + \frac{1}{2}\sum_{i=1}^{K} \theta_i^2. \quad (6)$$

In Eq. (6), C is a variable constant, representing the sensitivity of the sensor matching method.

By substituting Eq. (5) into Eq. (6) and using the gradient descent algorithm, θ can be obtained as well as the matching analytical model of the indirect feature within the entity of specific category.

4. Verification and Assessment

4.1. *Envrionment description*

To verify the feasibility of the MAMS and validity of the sensor similarity matching method which is used to train the entity analytical model, we designed the simulation environment for IoT search in which we tried to search for the target entities who have the same behavior as the user and to search for the target groups in the similar activity status as the user. the user input the sentence to be analyzed: "who have the same behavior as me at the moment?"

4.2. *Data preparation*

We use the user behavior data gathered in the real world by the Smart Lab[6] to describe the correlative human (entity) information in the DEPI. These data is generated by triaxial accelerometer, three-axis gyroscopes and other sensors embedded in wearable devices.

4.3. *Experiment process*

The sensor similarity matching method based on the SVM with multidimensional dynamic data and status is a universal method which can train a number of different kinds of characteristic analytical model. In the experimental environment the human-behavior analytical module actually utilizes the matching method mentioned in section 3 to analyze and match features.

We train the human-behavior characteristic analytical module in Matlab with the most popular ls-SVM library. In the simulation, we divide the data sets into two parts, taking the training samples (7165 samples) as the input and train the human-behavior characteristic model according to the sensor similarity matching method based on the SVM with multidimensional dynamic data and status.

4.4. *Experimental assessment*

We designed the formula below to calculate the accuracy and to verify the validity of the sensor similarity matching method based on the SVM with multidimensional dynamic data and status:

$$accuracy = \frac{\sum_{i=1}^{N} y_i^{predict} \odot y_i^{real}}{N}. \tag{7}$$

In Eq. (7), $y_i^{predict}$ denotes the prediction of the i th testing sample. y_i^{real} denotes the actual value of the i th sample. N denotes the total amounts of the samples.

We drew the conclusion by verifying the testing samples derived from the data set in Table 1.

There were 2996 samples in the testing data set, 2898 of which were accurately predicted with 96.7% accuracy.

5. Conclusions

In this paper, we firstly discussed the key issues and features of IoT search and proposed an IoT search structure for searching entities or entity information which can be described by the features of multidimensional dynamic data and status. Then, we elaborated the MAMS of the structure and proposed a sensor similarity matching method based on multidimensional sensory data and status. At last, we verified the validity and accuracy of our algorithms in appropriate experimental environment.

Table 1.Experimental results

Type	Amount of samples	Accuracy
WALKING	496	98.99%
WALKING_UPSTAIRS	471	95.97%
WALKING_DOWNSTAIRS	420	98.10%
SITTING	508	89.96%
STANDING	556	97.48%
LYING	545	99.82%

6. Acknowledgements

This work has been supported by Development Program("863"Program) of China National Natural Science Foundation of China(61170275), National Natural Science Foundation of China(61502050),the National High Technology Research, Beijing Higher Education Young Elite Teacher Project and Technology Project of Guangdong Province and Beijing Key Laboratory of Work Safety Intelligent Monitoring .Moreover, I also thank sincerely my advisor.

References

1. E. Borgia, The Internet of Things Vision: Key Features, Applications and Open Issues, in Computer Communications, Vol.54 (Elsevier B.V. ,2014), pp. 1-31.
2. C.W. Tsai, C.F. Lai, M.C. Chiang and Laurence T. Yang, *Data Mining for Internet of Things: A Survey*, in *IEEE Communications Surveys &Tutorials*, Vol. 16, Issue.1 (IEEE Communications Society, 2014), pp. 77-97.
3. P.N. Zhang, Y. Liu, F. Wu and B.H. Tang, *Matching State Estimation Scheme for Content-based Sensor Search in the Web of Things*, in *International Journal of Distributed Sensor Networks*, Vol.2015 (Hindawi Publishing Corp., New York, 2015), pp. 1-12.

4. C. Truong, K. Römer and K. Chen, Sensor Similarity Search in the Web of Things, in *Proceedings of the 2012 IEEE Int. Symposium on a World of Wireless, Mobile and Multimedia Networks (WoWMoM 2012)*, (San Francisco, USA, 2012).
5. C. Truong, K. Römer, K. Chen, Fuzzy-based Sensor Search in the Web of Things, in *Proceedings of the IEEE2012 3rd International Conference on the Internet of Things (IOT)*, (WuXi, China, 2012).
6. SmartLab, *Smartphone-Based Recognition of Human Activities and Postura l Transitions Data Set*,https://archive.ics.uci.edu/ml/datasets/Smartphone-B asedRecognition of Human Activities and Postural Transitions.

Optimal Placement for Heterogeneous Controllers in SDN Based on Unbalanced Graph Partitioning

Chun-ling DING
Department of Chemistry, Tongji University, Shanghai 200092, China
E-mail: dingcl@tongji.edu.cn

Guo-sun ZENG† and Ye-fu WANG
Department of Computer Science, Tongji University, Shanghai 200092, China
State Key Laboratory of High-end Server & Storage Technology, Jinan 250101, China
†*E-mail: gszeng@tongji.edu.cn*

Software Defined Network (SDN) decouples the control plane from the data plane, yielding a vast flexibility for networks. This paper focuses on the optimal placement for heterogeneous controllers. First, SDN networks are modeled using graph theory. Therefore, the controller placement problem is transformed into a specified graph partitioning problem. Then, an optimal controller placement scheme is proposed based on multi-level graph partitioning. Finally, Simulation experiments are conducted on real network topologies. The results indicate that our scheme can achieve nearly optimal controller load balance and is of application value to wide-area SDN deployments.

Keywords: SDN; Controller; Optimal placement; Graph partitioning.

1. Introduction

In wide area SDN deployment, logically centralized controllers often are placed in a distributed manner to meet reliability and low latency requirements. Thus, how to place these controllers to improve SDN performance is worth investigating. The controller placement problem in SDN was first formulated by Heller et al.[1,2]. Hu et al.[3] introduced a novel placement metric, expected percentage of valid control paths, to quantify SDN's reliability. Beheshti and Zhang[4] investigated the resiliency to failure of SDN network, which is evaluated by the ability of switches to maintain connectivity to their controller using bypass links when link failure occurs. Yao et al.[5]improved the existing latency model and discussed controller placement's impact on transmission and propagation delay. To our best knowledge, most of the existing work on controller placement problem rarely takes controller load balance into account. In this paper, we propose an optimal controller placement scheme to balance controller load distribution based on graph partitioning theory.

2. Controller Placement Problem

Based on the observation of Reference [2], we further describe the general controller placement problem as 3 sub-questions: (1)How many controllers are needed? (2)Where in the topology should they go? (3)What specific switches should each controller controls, or how to define the switch-to-controller mapping scheme? The number of needed controllers depends on the specific application scenario, which is out of the scope of this paper. Hereinafter, we suppose that the number of controllers to be deployed is k, and the controller placement problem refers to sub-question 2 and 3. That is, given the number of controllers to be placed, the computational power of each controller and the network topology, our objective is to determine the locations of the controllers in the topology and the switch-to-controller mapping function, such that one or more placement metrics are optimized. Let $C=(c_1,c_2,\ldots,c_k)$ denote the k controllers to be deployed, $S=(s_1,s_2,\ldots,s_n)$ denote the n switches in the network. A controller placement scheme can be described as a two tuple $D=(P(C), f{:}S\to C)$, where $P(C)=(p_1,p_2,\ldots,p_k)$ is the corresponding locations of the k controllers, and $f{:}S\to C$ is the switch-to-controller mapping function. In this paper, controller load balance and latency are two important metrics used to evaluate network performance.

3. Concepts and Modeling

3.1. *Concepts of related SDN*

Definition 1: A SDN topology graph is defined as graph $G(V, E)$, where vertex set V represents switches in the network and $|V|=n$ is the number of vertices, edge set E represents physical links between switches and edge weights are latencies between associated nodes.

Definition 2: The latency for a controller placement $D=(P(C), f{:}V\to C)$ as follows: $L^{s\text{-}c}_{\text{avg}}=1/n\sum_{s\in V} dist(s,P(f(s)))$, where $dist(x, y)$ represents the sum of edge weights on the shortest path from vertex x to vertex y, $f(s)$ represents the corresponding controller of switch *s*, and $P(f(s))$ is the location of the associated controller of switch *s*.

Definition 3: Computational power distribution vector refers to $A=(\alpha_1,\alpha_2,\ldots,\alpha_k)$, where k is the number of controllers to be deployed, $\Sigma^k_{i=1}\alpha_i=1$, $\alpha_i=CP_i/\Sigma^k_{i=1}CP_i$, where $CP_i(i\in Z$ and $I\in[1, k])$ denotes the computational power of controller i.

Definition 4: Load distribution vector refers to $B=(\beta_1, \beta_2,\ldots, \beta_k)$, where k is the number of controllers to be deployed, $\Sigma^k_{i=1}\beta_i=1$, $\beta_i=CW_i/\Sigma^k_{i=1}CW_i$, where $CW_i(i\in Z$ and $i\in[1, k])$ denotes the load on controller i, that is, the number of switches that controller i manages.

Definition 5: The controller load balance is defined as $LB=AB/|A||B|$, where A is the computational power distribution vector, and B is the load distribution vector.

3.2. *Graph partitioning theory*

Definition 6: Given a graph $G(V, E)$ and vector $A=(\alpha_1,\alpha_2,\ldots,\alpha_k)$, where $|V|=n$, the unbalanced graph partitioning of graph G is defined as partitioning V into k subsets $V_1, V_2,\ldots, V_k$ in such a way that $V_i\cap V_j=\phi$ $(i, j\in Z, i,j\in[1, k]$ and $i\neq j)$, $|V_1|:|V_2|:\ldots:|V_k|=\alpha_1:\alpha_2:\ldots:\alpha_k$.

Moreover, we describe the load-aware controller placement problem as a specified graph partitioning problem. The corresponding formulations are as follows. Given (1)SDN topology graph $G(V, E)$, (2)to-be-deployed controller set, and (3)controllers' computational power distribution vector $A=(\alpha_1,\alpha_2,\ldots,\alpha_k)$, V is partitioned into k subsets $V_1, V_2,\ldots, V_k$ in such a way that $V_i\cap V_j=\phi$ $(i, j\in Z, i,j\in[1,k]$ and $i\neq j)$, $|V_1|:|V_2|:\ldots:|V_k|=\alpha_1:\alpha_2:\ldots:\alpha_k$. The optimal scheme of controller placement is $D=(P(C), f\colon V\to C)$, where $f(V_i)=c_i$ and $P(C)$ minimizes $L^{s\text{-}c}_{\text{avg}}=(D)$ under the constraint of $f\colon V\to C$.

4. Method for Controller Placement

4.1. *Unbalanced partitioning of SDN topology graph*

The main procedure can be divided into three phases: coarsening, initial partitioning and refining. Such three algorithms are described as follows:

Algorithm 1: Coarsening

input: topology graph $G_i(V_i, E_i)$

output: array *map*[] for constructing $G_{i+1}(V_{i+1}, E_{i+1})$

Coarsening (G_i)

{ nodeIndex←1;

```
    while ∃v∈V_i is uncoarsened
      {    v←getAnUnCoarsenedVertex(); //get an uncoarsened vertex randomly
        if ∃u∈adjacentSet(v) is unCoarsened
          {  u←getUnCoarsenedAdjVertex (v); //randomly get adjacent vertex
             map[u]←nodeIndex;
             mark u as coarsened;
          }
        map[v]←nodeIndex;
        mark v as matched;
        nodeIndex←nodeIndex+1;
      }
    return map;
}
```

Algorithm 2: Initial_Partitioning

```
input: G_i(V_i, E_i), A=(α_1,α_2,…,α_k), allowable_err
output: array partition[]
Initial_Partitioning (G_i,)
{  pIndex←0; fIndex←k;     //pIndex for partitions, fIndex for fragment
   initialize queue;
   while pIndex<k ∧ not ∀v∈V_i is partitioned
   {  currentWgt←0;     //reset currentWgt
      v←getAnUnpartitionedVertex(); //randomly get an unpartitioned vertex
      enQueue(queue, v);
      while queue is not empty
      {  v←deQueue(queue);
         currentWgt←currentWgt+weight(v);  //weight(v) is the weight of v
         paritition[v]←pIndex;
         mark v as partitioned;
         if α_pIndex×sNum×(1−allowable_err) ≤ currentWgt
              pIndex←pIndex+1;
              clearQueue(queue);  //partitioning accomplished
         else
              enQueue(queue,u) for ∀u∈adjSet(v) where u is unpartitioned;
         if currentWgt <α_pIndex×sNum×(1−allowable_err)    //if not enough
              partition[v]←fIndex for all v satisfying partition[v]=pIndex;
              fIndex←fIndex+1;
      }
   }
   return partition;
```

```
}
Algorithm 3: Refining
input: array partition, Gi(Vi,Ei), allowable_err
output: refined array partition[]
Refining(partition, Gi, allowable_err)
{  while ∃ unrefined partition
   {  p←getAnUnrefinedPartition();
      if |currentWgt(p)−αp×sNum| < allowable_err×αp×sNum
            mark p as refined;
      else if currentWgt(p)< αp×sNum          //if p's weight is less than ideal
         {    q←getLargestAdjPartition(p); //get p's adjacent partition
              v←getBoundaryVertex(q,p);   //get a boundary vertex in q
              partition[v]←p;             //p gains a vertex
         }
         else
         {    q←getSmallestAdjPartition(p); // get p's adjacent partition
              v←getBoundaryVertex(p,q);   //get a boundary vertex in p
              partition[v]←q;             // p loses a vertex
         }
       if unpartitioned partition number=1 break;
   }
   return partition;
}
```

4.2. *Determining the locations of controller placement*

The next step is determining the locations of controller placement that minimize overall latency. The locating algorithm is described as follows.

```
Algorithm 4: Locating
input: array partition[]
output: controller placement locations
Locating(partition)
{  i←1;
   while i ≤ k
   {  nSet←getN(i);         //getN(Vi)
      latency←INF;          //INF is a number which is large enough
      while ∃v∈nSet is not visited
      {  v←getUnvisitedVertex(nSet); //randomly pick an unvisited vertex in nSet
         vLatency←getLatency(i,v);   // for computing Σs∈V dist(s,v)
         if vLatency < latency
         {  P(ci)←v;
```

```
            latency←vLatency;
        }
        mark v as visited;
    }
    i←i+1;
}
return P;
}
```

So far, controller placement is uniquely determined.

5. Simulation Experiments

We pick 5 networks whose topology statistics are shown in Table 1. In experiments, the initial weight of a vertex or an edge is considered as 1.

Table1 Topology statistics

Network id	Vertex number	Edge number
Network1	243	271
Network2	465	506
Network3	879	1335
Network4	1288	1854
Network5	2133	2849

For Network1 to Network 5, 3 placements are carried out, in which allowable error for initial partitioning is 0.1, allowable error for refining is 0.05. The computational power distribution vectors are A_1=(0.2,0.8), A_2=(0.1,0.2, 0.3,0.4), A_3=(0.05,0.05,0.1,0.1,0.15,0.15,0.2,0.2), respectively. The results are shown in Table 2. It can be discovered that controller load is well balanced. Moreover, latency decreases with the increasing number of deployed controllers as expected.

Table 2 Placement results

Network id	LB(A_1)	LB(A_2)	LB(A_3)	(A_1)	(A_2)	(A_3)
Network1	0.9992	0.9978	0.9828	2.0535	1.8313	1.6049
Network2	0.9983	0.9991	0.9915	1.9484	1.9097	1.8086
Network3	0.9995	0.9999	0.9929	2.2253	1.9545	1.7452
Network4	0.9923	0.9990	0.9994	2.3595	2.2152	1.9977
Network5	0.9982	0.9982	0.9973	2.7084	2.3460	1.9991

6. Conclusions

In this paper, controller placement problem is transformed into a specified graph partitioning problem. A multi-level partitioning technique is adopted to conduct partitioning to SDN topology, and a locating algorithm has been proposed to find optimal placement locations with minimum latency. Nevertheless, placement metrics considered in this work are relatively simple, More complex metrics will be taken into consideration in our further research.

Acknowledgements

This work is supported by the National Natural Science Foundation of China under grant No. 61272107; the Open Foundation of the State Key Laboratory of High-end Server & Storage Technology under grant of 2014HSSA10.

Reference

1. H. Kim, N. Feamster. Improving network management with software defined networking. *IEEE Communications Magazine*, 2013, 51(2): 114-119.
2. B. Heller, R. Sherwood, N. McKeown. The controller placement problem. *Proceedings of HotSDN '12*, 2012, pp7-12.
3. Y. Hu, W. Wang, X. Gong, et al. On reliability-optimized controller placement for software-defined networks. *China Communications*, 2014, 11(2): 38-54.
4. N. Beheshti, Y. Zhang, Fast failover for control traffic in software-defined networks. *Proceedings of IEEE Global Communications Conference (GLOBECOM)*, 2012, pp2665-2670.
5. Y. Yao, Y. Chen, F. Song, et al. Delay-aware controller placement for fast response in software-defined network. *Journal of Electronics & Information Technology*, 2014, 36(12): 2802-2808.

Turbo Equalization Performance Analysis and Application in the HF Communication System

Hua-jun LAI*, Mei WANG and Jie-lin FU

Key Laboratory of Cognitive Radio &Information Processing,
Ministry of Education , Guilin University of Electronic Technology,Guilin,541004,China
**E-mail:laihuajun0227@sina.com*

Science and Technology on Information Transmission and Dissemination in Communication Networks Laboratory, The 54th Research Institute of CETC, Shijiazhuang 050081, China

Data transmission is affected by factors such as multipath effect, noise, time varying and Doppler effect in HF channel. In comparison with traditional equalization, turbo equalization is a better approach to these problems. In this paper, we build a simulation model of turbo equalization in HF communication system based on the characteristics of HF channel, comparatively analyze of the effect of some parameters such as length of interleaver, number of iterations and convolutional encoder. Subsequently the burst waveform in MIL-STD-188-141b and the MMSE-based turbo equalizer was developed, thus providing a reliable basis for the application of Turbo equalization in HF channel. The simulation illustrates that the MMSE-based Turbo equalization can reduce the gap between the simulation BER curve and theoretical curve, alleviating the impact of multipath fading, noise and Doppler effect; providing a high value and extensive application prospect.

Keywords: Turbo equalization; HF channel; Multipath fading; Performance analysis; BER.

1. Introduction

HF communication is an important way of middle and long distance communication. But serious impacts of HF channel such as multipath delay, noise, fading and Doppler effect, and signal through HF channel with ISI (inter symbol interference). At present, there are many ways to solve ISI. Method of mitigating ISI is to use an equalization technology commonly. For instance, equalization used in HF channel mainly includes MLSE(maximum likelihood

* Corresponding author.

sequence estimation),LE(liner equalization) and adaptive equalization etc. But the most effect approach is Turbo equalization[1].

Existing research shows that, compared with the traditional equalization, Turbo equalization can get more performance gain. MAP(maximum a posteriori probability) algorithm[2] has the best performance, but the algorithm has a high complexity in application and not easy to be achieved. There is a minimum mean square error(MMSE)-based equalization[3] that decrease computational complexity significantly. Because the HF channel is imposed on multipath effect, noise, fading effect and Doppler effect, etc. it has a higher demand on the source waveform. The waveform of MIL-STD-188-141B could eliminate Doppler effect and mitigate impact of time-varying characteristics, therefore it has more advantages than any other waveforms[4].

In this paper, we build a simulation model of turbo equalization in HF burst communication system, comparative analysis of the effect of some parameters such as length of interleaver, iterative times, equalization algorithm and different channel conditions. Then combination waveform of MIL-STD-188-141B and MMSE-based turbo equalization. Simulation results indicate that the communication system could mitigate serious influence of multipath delay, noise, fading and Doppler effect, etc.

2. Turbo Equalization System Modeling in HF Communication

2.1. *System structure*

In this paper, transmitting end uses the data frame structure in MIL-STD-188-141B,modulation mapping are BPSK and 8PSK,channel model is Watterson Model. Source waveform after HF channel into the receiver, receiving end is MMSE-based Turbo equalizer structure, include MMSE linear equalizer, interleaver, deinterleaver and SISO(soft in soft out)decoder, decoding algorithm is log-MAP[2].The proposed decoding algorithm convert addition and subtraction into multiplication and division in log-domain, so it reduces complexity and keeps high reliability. Fig. 1depicts a system simulation block.

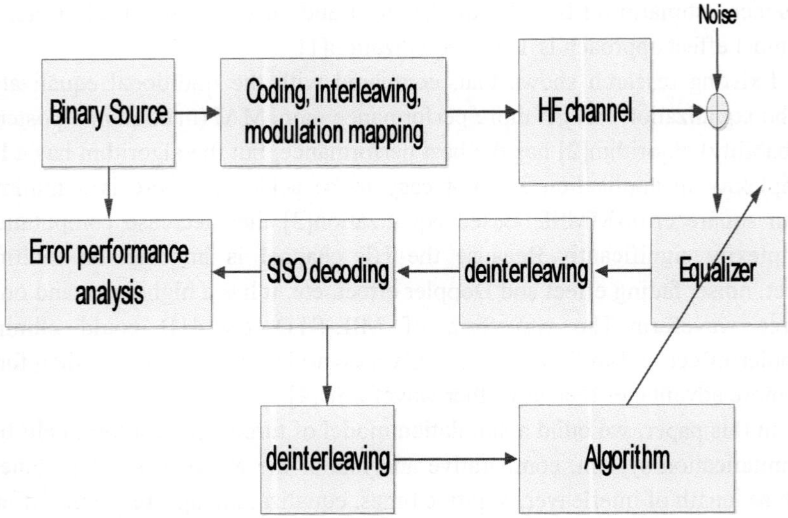

Fig. 1. Application of HF communication using turbo equalization

2.2. *MMSE equalizer*

Applied to Turbo equalization linear MMSE algorithm uses minimum mean square error criterion to determine the estimates of the transmitted signal$\hat{x}_n$:

$$\hat{x}_n = \bar{x} + v_n \cdot \boldsymbol{f}_n^H(z_n - \bar{z}_n).$$

where$\bar{x}$ is the mean, v_n is the variance, both related to the prior information.z_n is channel measurements, $\bar{z}_n = E(\boldsymbol{z})$. Linear filter coefficient$\boldsymbol{f}_n$updated by soft information of each iteration process:

$$f_n = (\sigma_w^2 I_N + H V_n H^H)^{-1} s$$

where$\bar{x}$ is$\mathbf{I}_N$ is the unit vector,$\sigma_w^2$is the noise variance:

$$V_n \triangleq \mathrm{diag}\left[v_{n-M-N_2+1}, \dots, v_{n+N_1}\right]$$

$$s = H\left[0_{1\times(N_2+M-1)}\ 1\ 0_{1\times N_1}\right]^T$$

$$H \triangleq$$

$$\begin{bmatrix} h_{M-1} & h_{M-2} & \dots & h_0 & 0 & \dots & 0 \\ 0 & h_{M-1} & h_{M-2} & \dots & h_0 & 0 & \dots & 0 \\ \vdots & \vdots & \ddots & \ddots & & & \\ 0 & 0 & \dots & 0 & h_{M-1} & h_{M-1} & \dots & h_0 \end{bmatrix}_{N\times(N+M-1)}$$

The parameters $N_1$and N_2specifythe length of the noncausal and the causal part of the estimator filter, respectively, and N is the filter length. $h_M$is the channel impulse response coefficients. Finally, soft demodulate $\hat{x}_n$. Fig. 2 depicts the equalizer structure:

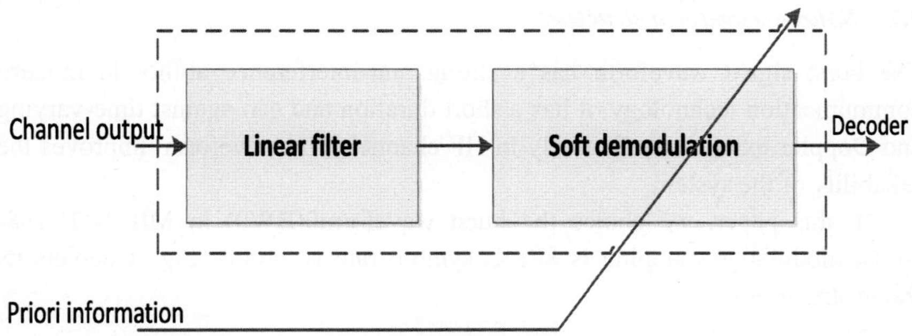

Fig. 2. MMSE-equalizer structure

2.3. *Channel model*

At present, more representative HF channel model is Watterson model[5], it is a narrowband model. In most cases it can be a better response characteristics of HF channel, so is widely used in hardware and software simulation. The time varying frequency domain response of Watterson model can be can be expressed as:

$$H(f,t) = \sum_{i=1}^{n} \exp(-j2\pi\tau_i f) G_i(t)$$

where i is the number of path, τ_i isdelay time of the path i, n is the total number of paths, $G_i(t)$ is stochastic processes.

The power spectrum of Doppler frequency extension of Watterson model can be realize by building low-pass filter of Bigaussion spectrum[6], bandwidth of the filter is decided by Doppler extension .Thus embodies Doppler extension effect on the signal. Moreover, multipath effect, noise and time varying of Watterson model can be realize by Rayleigh fading and white gaussian noise[7].Fig. 3 depicts the Watterson model.

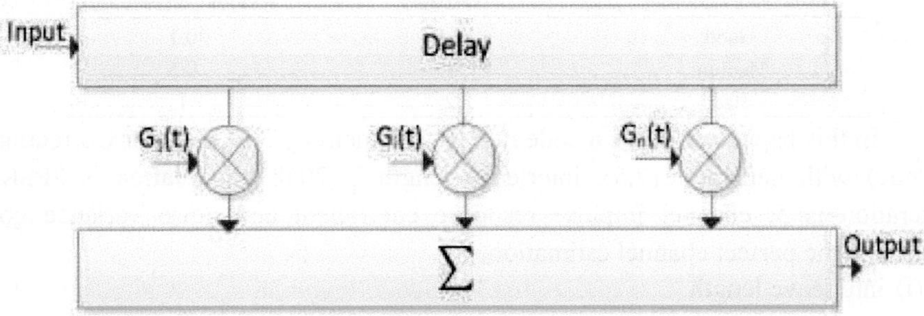

Fig. 3.Watterson model

3. Performance Simulation and Analysis

3.1. *Source waveform structure*

The burst signal waveform has a strong anti-interference ability in modern communication technology, it has a short duration and can against time-varying and Doppler extension effectively in HF channel. The waveform improves the reliability of the system.

In this paper, we choice the burst waveform0(BW0) in MIL-STD-188-141B, modulation mapping is 8PSK, symbol rate is 2400B, Fig. 4 depicts its frame structure.

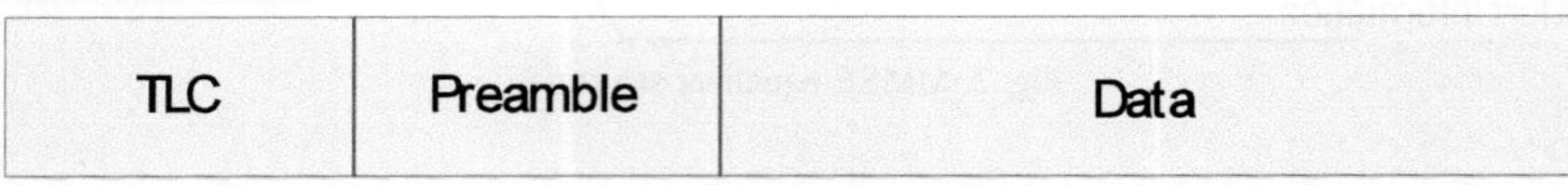

Fig. 4. Frame structure of BW0

T_{TLC}=106.667ms: 256 PSK symbols at 2400 symbols/second
T_{pre}=160.0ms: 384 PSK symbols at 2400 symbols/second
T_{data}=346.667ms: 832 PSK symbols at 2400 symbols/second
T_{BW0}=total duration=613.333ms.

3.2. *Simulation of Turbo equalization performance in HF*

3.2.1. *Simulation of algorithm performance*

In this section, the simulation model of HF channel is constructed by Rayleigh fading and white gaussian noise. Firstly, set the Doppler spectrum for the Bigaussion model, and the related parameters are reasonable[4][6].Then set HF Channel(good, medium, bad) on the basis of ITU-R:

Table 1. HF channel model parameters of ITU-R

Channel condition	Delay(ms)	Doppler spread(Hz)
Good	0.5	0.1
Medium	1	0.5
Bad	2	1

In this paper, we chose a code rate R=1/2 ,memory 3 ECC(Error Correction Code) with generator (7,5), interleave length L=2048, modulation is 8PSK, iteration is 5, channel impulse response coefficient and noise variance got through the perfect channel estimation.

(i) interleave length

Interleave length is the length of the coding bits. The essence of the interleave is maximum changing the structure of a data frame without changing its content, the purpose is to produce in the process of information transmission burst error maximum discretization. Therefore, interleave length is a key factor influencing the performances of Turbo equalization system. Because the processing of the Turbo equalization is a whole, The longer the interleave length, the greater the interleave gain and the closer the system performance theoretical limit. We chose interleave length L=512, 1024, 2048 and 4096, Fig. 5 depicts the BER curve in HF channel(medium).

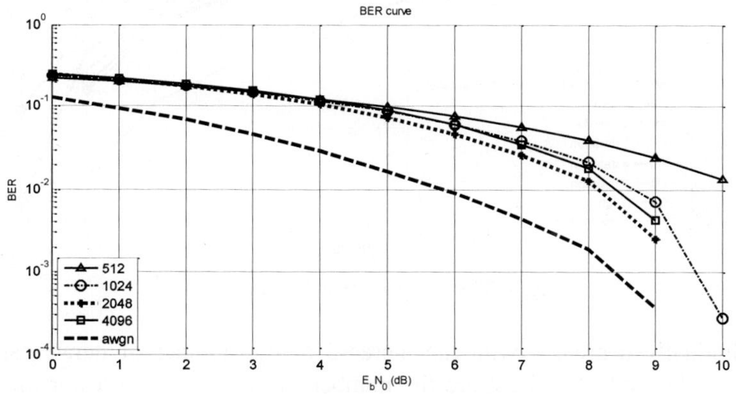

Fig. 5. BER of different interleave length

With the increase of interleave length, the BER curve gradually approaching the theoretical value under the gaussian channel, The BER performance of system is improved, but as the interleave length increasing, the degree of error performance is becoming more and more not obvious, interleave length of 1024 and 2048 are nearly coincidence, the BER curve of performance improvement towards convergence. When interleave length increasing continuously, the reliability is serious decline, such as interleave length 4096 BER curve is worse than 2048,the two differ 0.4dB.So, in the practical application of short-wave communication, it can't use too longer interleave length to improve system performance. Known from the figure, the use of suitable interleave length is 2048 to 4096.

(ii) iterations

Turbo equalization optimizes performance by exchanged outside information between equalizer and decoder, BER decreases with the increase of cyclic number of iterations gradually. With the increase of the number of iterations, equalizer and decoder exchange of soft information continuously strengthen, the relevance of the BER curve gradually convergence. So the number of iterations is also one of the key parameters to determines the performance. We chose the number of iteration 0 to 5, Fig. 6 depicts the BER curve in HF channel(medium).

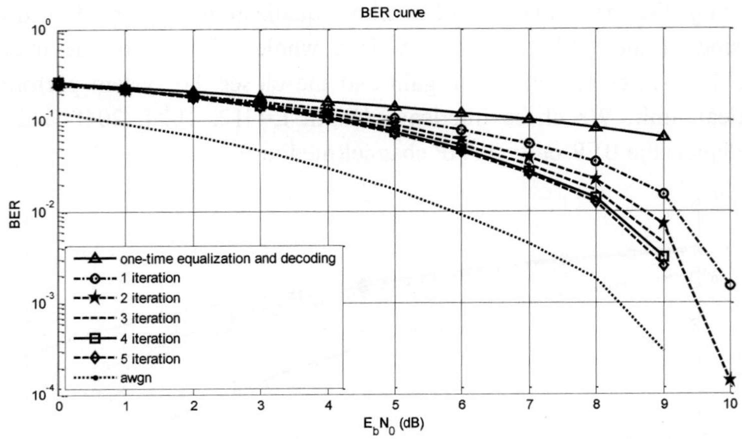

Fig. 6. BER of different number of iteration

Gradually decreases with the increase of the number of iterations, BER curve and leveled off. The more the number of iterations, the lower the BER. The first 3 iterations improve performance of the system obviously, starting from the four iteration, the system tends to convergence, increase the number of iterations is unable to get more gain, BER of the four iteration curve coincide with the fifth. Increase the number of iterations will lead to increase the amount of calculation, when actual application should choose the number of iterations between performance and computational complexity, usually 4 times as appropriate.

(iii) encoder

Encoder also is an important index for Turbo equalization. At present, the encoder uses in Turbo equalization is convolutional code. The constraint degree is an important index of convolution encoder. Constraint degree of different will affect system performance. When positive rate and length are given, with the increase of EbN0, system performance began to form the difference of the constraint degree. Generally, the big convolutional coding performance of constraint degree is better than the small. In this section, we chose constraint degree is 3, generate polynomial convolutional coding for (7, 5), indicate as 3,(7,5),the others are 4,(19,29) and 5,(155,93), Fig. 7 depicts the BER curve in HF channel(good).

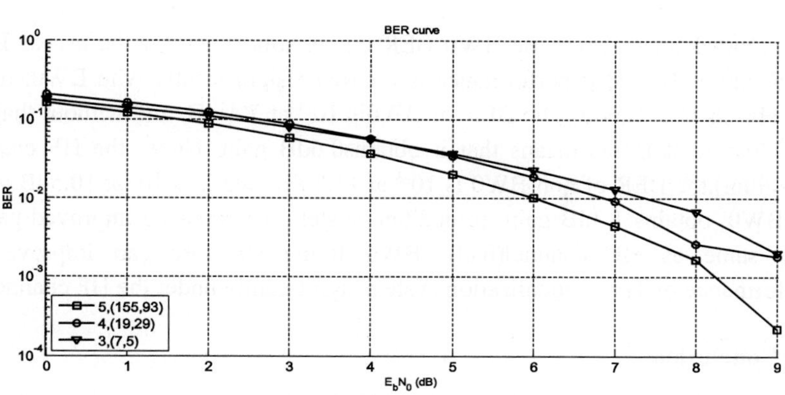

Fig. 7. BER of different encoder

Overall trend point of view, the greater the constraint degree, the better the performance of the system. In the low signal noise ratio (SNR), 3,(7,5) and 4,(19,29) is almost the same performance, With the increase of EbN0, the performance of 4,(19,29) gradually is better than that of 3,(7,5),And 5,(155,93) performance always better than other two kinds of convolution code. As the constraint degree increases, the computational complexity of the receiver decoder also will increase, because the Turbo equalization has been widely applied in the case of low SNR, the advantages of high degree of constraint cannot reflect. Give an overall consideration, the choice of 4,(19,29) convolution code is quite reasonable.

3.2.2. *Simulation of system performance*

In this section, we will show the burst waveform affect in HF channel(good, medium and bad). Fig. 8 depicts the BER curve in HF channel.

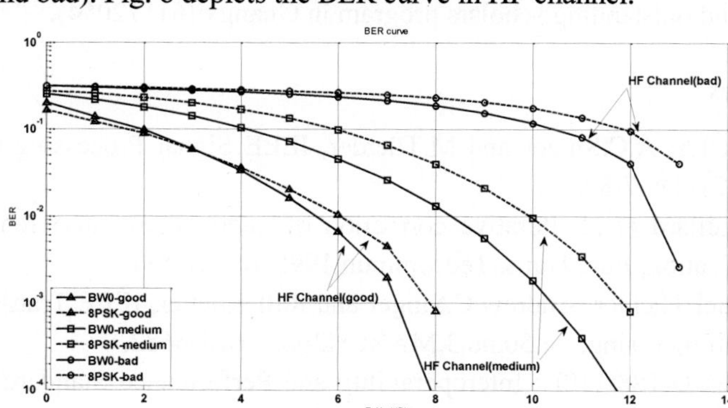

Fig. 8. BER of HF channel

Dotted lines to not use BW0 BER curve, solid lines for the use of BW0 BER curve .The BER performance is improved significantly with BW0: under the HF channel (good), the BER of BW0is 10^{-3} at 7.4 dB, and without that get 10^{-3}close to 8dB,this means that it obtains0.6dB gain. Under the HF channel (medium),the BER of non-BW0 is 10^{-3} at 11.8 dB, and it is 10^{-3}at 10.5dB when useBW0, obtains 1.3dB gain in medium, system performance improved partly. The same as HF channel(bad). BW0 frame structure can improve the performance of Turbo equalization system significantly under the HF channel.

4. Conclusion

In this paper, we construct Turbo equalization simulation model in HF communication, analysis affects with various parameters such as length of interleaver, number of iterations and convolutional encoder under HF channel. Provides reliable parameter selection for the application of Turbo equalization in HF communication. Then combine the frame structure of BW0 with MMSE-based Turbo equalizer, the results show that Turbo equalization with BW0 could counteract impacts of multipath fading, noise, time-varying and Doppler extension, and get more system gain. At the same time, the system has lower complexity and easy to implement, it has broad application foreground in HF communication.

Acknowledgments

This work is supported by Network information transmission and distribution technology key laboratory of colleges and universities cooperation projects(KX142600025). Work partially supported by innovative team of colleges and outstanding scholars program in Guangxi(61172054).

References

1. R.Koetter, A.C.Singer and M.Tüchler, IEEE Signal Processing Magzzine, 2004,21(1):67-80.
2. C.Douillard et al, Iterative correction of intersymbol interference: Turbo equalization, Eur. Trans. Teecommun,1995, 6: 507-511.
3. Michael Tüchler, Andrew C.Singer and Ralf Koetter, IEEE Transactions on SignalProcessing,vol.50,no.3,MARCH2002,p673-p682.
4. MIL-STD-188-110B: Interoperability and Performance Standards for Data Modems, U. S. Department of Defense, 2000.

5. Watterson, C., Juroshek, J. Bensema, W.D., IEEE Transactions on , vol.18, no.6, pp.792-803, December1970 doi: 10.1109/TCOM.1970.1090438.
6. Bing Xia, He Huang, Weizhong Qu.[J].Journal of System Simulation,2009,S2:207-210.(In Chinese)
7. Fangfang Han, Zihao Lin[J].China Radio,2012,05:63-64+69(In Chinese)
8. ITU-R Recommendation 520-2: Use of High Frequency Ionospheric Channel Simulators,1978/1982/1992.

Research on Evaluation of Equipment Support Resource Network Invulnerability

Zhong-guang LI, Ya-dong LIU*, Tian ZHAO and Zheng-ping SHU

Company of Postgraduate Management, Academy of Equipment,
Huairou, Beijing, China
**E-mail: 18622135927@163.com*

Using system break thought as a breakthrough point, the paper clears the connotation of equipment support resource network invulnerability. It discusses the damage model of equipment support resource network from the two sides of attack target and attack strategy. Based on the thought of complex network, it builds the indexes and evaluation arithmetic of equipment support resource network invulnerability, analyzes with samples and verifies the validity of the method, so it can provide technology approach and method for strengthening battlefield construction and equipment support resource defense.

Keywords: Equipment support resource network; Invulnerability; Evaluation.

1. Introduction

Information Warfare is the confrontation between systems and systems, networks and networks. Because of the key elements and mechanisms have been changed from Information Warfare to Mechanization Warfare. The warfare network shows two polarity characteristics between huge power and weak invulnerability. Traditional warfare, such as Annihilation Battle and Attrition Battle, no longer be the single operation pattern, Systems Paralysis, which is satisfying the laws of Information Warfare, has been the fundamental operation pattern in the future.

Equipment support resource network is a pluralistic complexity, whom base on general information/organization network, converge multiple support resource such as people, equipment, facilities and so on, take connection between equipment support resource as the ligament, target on equipment support resource sharing and maximize effects of operations. Meanwhile, the network could evolve with the exchange of military requirement and development of science technology.

---

* Corresponding author.

As the important method of construction and applying effects evaluation for equipment support resource network, it include invulnerability evaluation, fragility evaluation, elasticity evaluation and so on, who take differentiation in the position of studying angle and studying point. For example, fragility evaluation focus on cascading failure resource network and collapsibility dynamics theory, elasticity evaluation focus on the recover abilities under attacked. At modern warfare of Systems Paralysis, under the conditions of inevitably being destroyed to equipment support resource nodes, the problems, such as the how the efficacy of equipment support resource network change and how to increase the robustness of equipment support resource network, belong to the studying scopes of invulnerability evaluation.

2. Connotation

2.1. *Connotation of systems paralysis*

Systems Paralysis is basing on systems superiority, using crack combat powers and multiple combat means, attacking the key nodes of combat systems fast and successively, adopting the operations of establish information superiority, destroying enemy' combat systems, reducing enemy' combat efficiency to complete operation mission. Systems Paralysis has several basic characteristics, such as, targeting on destroying enemy' combat systems and information systems, adopting asymmetric operation pattern, focusing on unitary paralysis and local destroy, coordinating active attack and effective defense.

2.2. *Connotation of equipment support resource network invulnerability*

In the background of Systems Paralysis Operation, who will become primary operation pattern in Information Warfare. Equipment support resource network not only need substance and technology to satisfy network support ability, but also need invulnerability to satisfy equipment support ability.

2.2.1. *Network invulnerability*

The concept of Network Invulnerability comes from Graph Theory. It is a kind of determinacy index for reliability. It can describe the network reliability influence from network topology structure. All network relate to invulnerability. To beneficial network, such as Internet, Electrical Grid and Transport Network, the stronger invulnerability the better. To harmful network, such as Terroristic Organization Network and Viral Infection Network, the weaker invulnerability the better. Up to now, there are two primary concept of network invulnerability.

Concept one/General concept: Network Invulnerability is a network ability to maintain function, in condition of nodes or sides being attacking. Concept two/Restricted concept: Network Invulnerability is an ability for network topology structure keeping connected, in condition of nodes or sides being attacking. It can describe the to destroy a network.

2.2.2. *Equipment support resource network invulnerability*

Equipment support resource network invulnerability is an ability for equipment support resource network keeping persistent support function, when being attacked. Under attacked, because of the attenuation of coordination support, assist support and information support between equipment support resource individualities, the connection of equipment support resource network and the efficacy of network support will reduce. So far, there are two keywords-connection and efficacy, for equipment support resource network invulnerability. The purpose of studying equipment support resource network invulnerability is solving the problems of how the equipment support resource network structure influence support function and support operation. So, increasing equipment support resource network invulnerability can avoid network paralysis, when being attacked.

3. Evaluation

The purpose of equipment support resource network invulnerability evaluation is judging the connection of equipment support resource network and monitoring the efficacy of network support, when getting continually attacked. First of all, we'll analyse the damage pattern of equipment support resource network. Secondly, we'll construct the evaluation index of equipment support resource network invulnerability. Finally, target on evaluation purpose, we'll study an algorithm for equipment support resource network invulnerability.

3.1. *Analysis of damage pattern for equipment support resource network*

3.1.1. *Attack pattern*

There are two kinds of attack patterns- Random Attack and Selective Attack. Random Attack is an operation pattern of nodes been randomly damaged for equipment support resource network. At this pattern, we assume enemy getting none information of equipment support resource network, taking un-relevance attack by random attack pattern. Selective Attack is an operation pattern of nodes been tactically damaged for equipment support resource network. It shows the spirit of Systems Paralysis. At this pattern, we assume enemy getting all information of equipment support resource network, knowing the importance of all nodes and edges of equipment support resource network.

3.1.2. *Attack tactics*

Because of essential factors of equipment support resource network are nodes and edges, there are two kinds of Attack Tactics - Node Attack and Edge Attack. To equipment support resource network, Node Attack means the targets, such as support nodes, information units and command units, will been attacked, and Edge Attack means the targets, such as information flows between support resource units and communication lines between support resource units, will been attacked. Consider equipment support physical condition, this study focus on equipment support resource network invulnerability evaluation of nodes attack.

Initial Degree distribution. As the basic parameter of network topology structure studying, degree can describe the immediate influence of network nodes. The numerial of degree is the sums of immediate connected nodes, as in Eq.(1).

$$k_i = \sum_{j=1}^{N} e_{ij} \cdot \tag{1}$$

Node degree is the basic character of node, it means the importance of node and the interactive with others. Generally speaking, the more node degree, the more important in network. The process of Initial Degree distribution is testing the all nodes' degree numerial of equipment support resource network, making initial degree numerial table, deleting the nodes as degree numerial grade down.

Initial Betweenness distribution. Betweenness can describe the influence of material flow, information flow, energy flow from network nodes. With the increase of material/information/energy flow by way of node, the numerial of betweenness will increase too. So, we can locate overlord nodes and edges by betweenness numerial, as in Eq.(2).N-Sum of nodes; g_{jk}- The number of shortest lines between node j and node k; $g_{jk}(x)$- The number of shortest lines by way of node x between node j and node k.

$$C_b(x) = \sum_{j<k} \frac{g_{jk}(x)}{g_{jk}}. \tag{2}$$

Like Initial Degree distribution, the process of Initial Degree distribution is testing the all nodes' betweenness numerial of equipment support resource network, making initial betweenness numerial table, deleting the nodes as betweenness numerial grade down.

3.2. *Evaluation index of equipment support resource network invulnerability*

We'll construct the evaluation index of network invulnerability in the respects of connectivity and efficacy of network.

3.2.1. *Connectivity of network*

Network connectivity show the connective relationship between nodes with nodes and nodes with environment by connected subgraph number and max connected subgraph.

Connected subgraph number is the number of unconnected subgraph when nodes losing efficacy and network being split. Consider the complication of studying, from equipment support physical condition, we assume that when a node losing efficacy, the edges, who connected with the node, will be deleted. By node deleting, the structure of network will be exchanged. As figure 1 showed, when two nodes are deleted, the shortest lines, between node A and node B, change from 2 to 6, and one network split to 2 connected subgraphs and 3 isolated nodes.

Max connected subgraph is a particular subgraph, who is connecting all nodes by least edges. It is the percentage of the total nodes do the max connected subgraph nodes, when equipment support resource network being attacked, as in Eq.(3).N - Scale of equipment support resource network; N_r- Deleted number of the network; C - Nodes number of max connected subgraph when some nodes been deleted.

$$R = \frac{C}{N - N_r} \,. \tag{3}$$

Max connected subgraph will reduce by nodes been attacked. As Fig. 1 shows, the percentage of max connected subgraph is 68.4%.

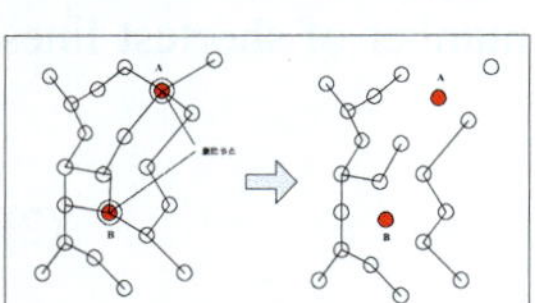

Fig. 1. Influence of nodes deleting for equipment support resource network

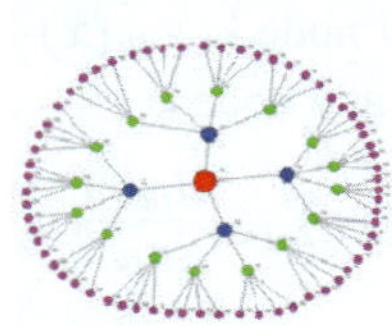

Fig. 2.Tree Structure of Equipment Support Resource Network

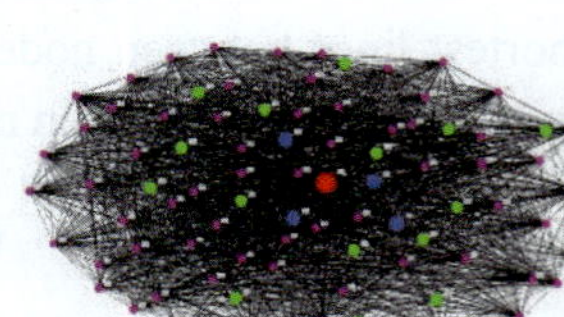

Fig.3.Net Structure of Equipment Support Resource Network

3.2.2. *Efficacy of network*

Using the index of Paolo Crucitti's network efficacy to judge the efficacy of equipment support resource network. The efficacy ε_{ij},which from node *i*to node *j*, is inversely proportionate to the average shortest line l_{ij}. When none line between node *i* and node j,$l_{ij} = +\infty$,$\varepsilon_{ij} = 0$, as in Eq.(4).

$$\varepsilon = \frac{1}{N(N-1)} \sum_{i \neq j} \frac{1}{l_{ij}} . \tag{4}$$

3.3. *Evaluation algorithm of equipment support resource network invulnerability*

According to the principle of step by step, from simple to complex, we assume 3 hypotheses for equipment support resource network invulnerability evaluation. **Hypothesis 1**: Defence ability of all network nodes are equal, once attack, one node or edge been destroyed. **Hypothesis 2**: limitless attack until all nodes and edges of equipment support resource network been destroyed. **Hypothesis 3**: Enemy get all information of equipment support resource network.

The evaluation algorithm of equipment support resource network invulnerability has 6 steps. **Step 1**: Selecting tree structure and net structure of equipment support resource network as evaluation objects. **Step 2**: According to complex network theory, calculating the numerical of all evaluation index for equipment support resource network invulnerability. **Step 3**: Calculating the numerical of degree and betweenness for all nodes, and putting the nodes in numerical grade down order. **Step 4**: According to attack tactics, simulating attack to important nodes. **Step 5**: Calculating the numerical of connected subgraph number, max connected subgraph and network efficacy. **Step 6**: Repeating step three to step five until all nodes been deleted or isolated.

4. Example

4.1. *Evaluation object*

There are 4 levels of support resource noumenon and 85 nodes altogether in equipment support resource network, upper level to lower level ratio is 1 to 4. Here, p means that the connectivity between vertical across level nodes, p_1 means that the connectivity between horizontal same level nodes in same system, p_2 means that the connectivity between horizontal same level nodes in across systems.

When,$p = p_1 = p_2 = 0$,all nodes are isolated. This isolated nodes mean that there are connected nodes, but none vertical across level support nodes and horizontal same level support nodes. It is a classical vertical tree structure network of equipment support resource network. When, $p = 1, p_1 = 0.8, p_2 = 0.5$, the equipment support resource network is a classical net structure network. Fig. 2 and Fig. 3 show the tree structure and net structure of equipment support resource network, by software tools such as Matlab 7.0 and Ucinet.

4.2. *Experimentation design*

Experimentation 1: The studying object is tree structure equipment support resource network. The attack tactics are random attack, initial degree distribution and initial betweenness distribution. Then analyzing the variation of valuation index for equipment support resource network invulnerability.

Experimentation 2: The studying object is net structure equipment support resource network. The attack tactics are random attack, initial degree distribution and initial betweenness distribution. Then taking a contrastive analysis of Experimentation 1 and Experimentation 2.

4.3. *Result analysis*

4.3.1. *Experimentation 1*

Fig. 4, Fig. 5 and Fig. 6 show the experimental data and distribution curve by software tools such as Matlab 7.0 and Ucinet. **Result 1**: Under random attack tactics, index numerical of max connected subgraph and network efficiency show progressively reduction. When number of being attacked nodes up to 60, the efficiency of network is little short to 0, the network structure show a modest invulnerability. **Result 2**:As Figure 4 and Figure 5 show, under initial degree distribution and initial betweenness distribution tactics, when number of being attacked nodes up to 8, the tree structure network split to 15 subgraph, the percentage of max connected subgraph lower to 10%, the efficiency of network is under 0.05. When number of being attacked nodes up to 8, the efficiency of network is 0. So far, the tree structure network show maximum vulnerability under selective attack. The result of Experimentation 1 shows that traditional multi-level support pattern is too inefficiency to satisfy Information Warfare.

4.3.2. *Experimentation 2*

Fig. 7, Fig. 8 and Fig. 9 show the experimental data and distribution curve by software tools such as Matlab 7.0 and Ucinet. No matter using which attack tactics of random attack, initial degree distribution and initial betweenness distribution, the numerical of connected subgraph number and max connected subgraph keep mostly unchangeable, by increasing number of attack nodes. It shows that, to net structure equipment support resource network, even if enemy getting all information of network, the nodes of net structure network keep strong connectivity, it keeps support relationship between each other. When number of being attacked nodes up to 80, the numerical of connected subgraph number and max connected subgraph show rapidly decline, the equipment support resource network almost been destroyed and lose equipment support ability.

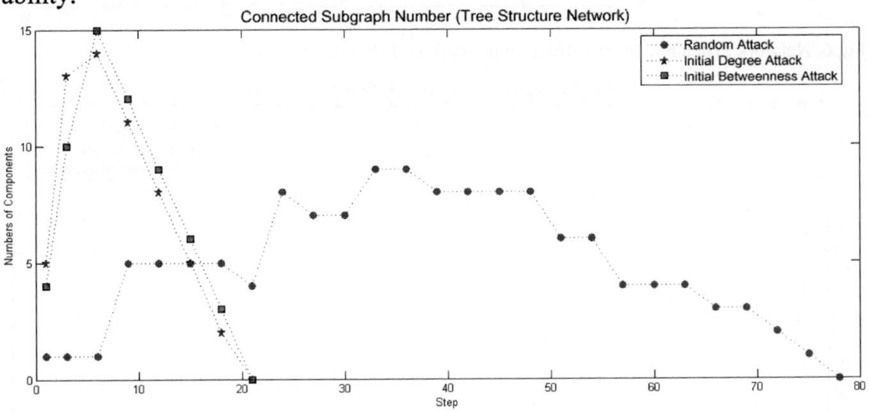

Fig.4. Connected subgraph number of tree structure network in different attack tactics

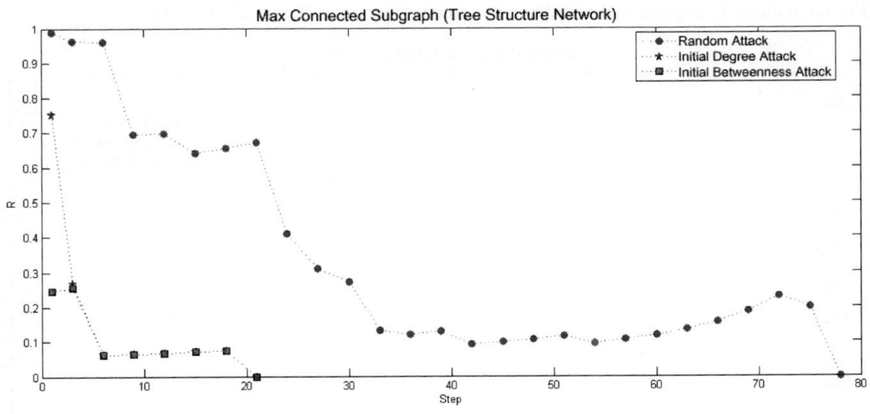

Fig.5. Max connected subgraph of tree structure network in different attack tactics

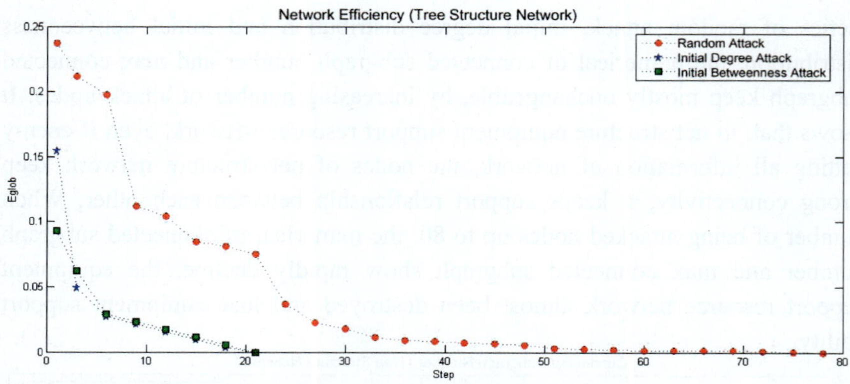

Fig.6. Network efficiency of tree structure network in different attack tactics

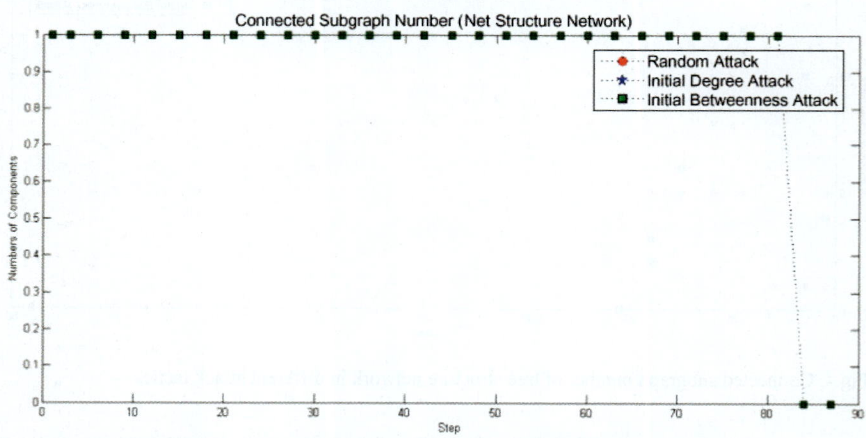

Fig.7. Connected subgraph number of net structure network in different attack tactics

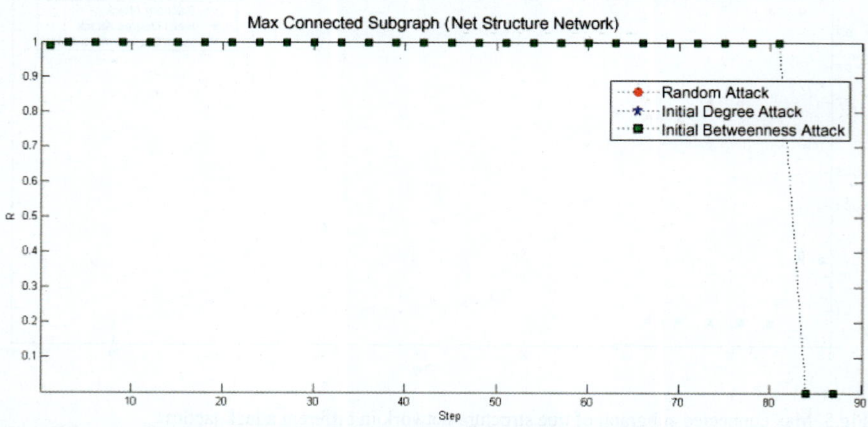

Fig.8. Max connected subgraph of net structure network in different attack tactics

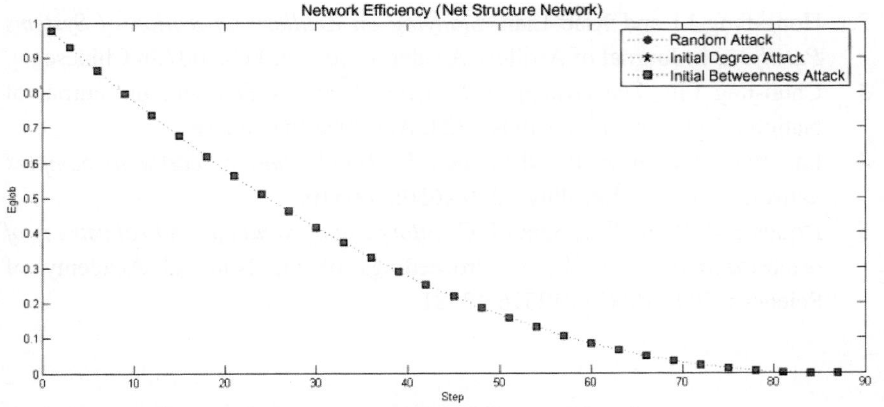

Fig.9. Network efficiency of net structure network in different attack tactics

5. Conclusions

Conclusion 1: The typical vertical tree structure network of equipment support resource is easily breakdown when getting selective attack, especially under the condition of key nodes been destroyed. There for, in future Information Warfare, there are two aspects have to reinforce. One aspect, according to operation preparations and operation environment, in order to avoid the situation of whole network of equipment support resource been destroyed, more equipment support nodes should be increased. The other aspect, in order to optimization structure and enhancement invulnerability for equipment support resource network, infrastructure construction, something like information network, and interconnection interworking nodes of equipment support resource should be enhanced.

Conclusion 2: Enhancement operation risk management, increase invulnerability of equipment support resource network. In equipment support operation, according to risk management theory, something like risk recognition, risk evaluation, risk control, enhancing defence for equipment support resource network key nodes.

Acknowledgments

Work partially supported by grant 2-4570.5 of the Swiss National Science Foundation.

References

1. Zhi-kaiHan, *Studying on Systems Paralysis,* in Journal of National Defence University,No.218, Otc.2007. In Chinese

2. Hong-feng Li and Xiao Lian, *Studying on Artillery Operation of Systems Paralysis,* in Journal of Artillery Academy,No.105, Feb.2007.In Chinese
3. Chun-jing Liu. *The History of Systems Paralysis Thought*, in Journal of National Defence University,No.224, Apr.2008.In Chinese
4. Lai Y C, Motter A E, Nishikawa T. *Attacks and cascades in complex networks* ,in Lect.NotesPhys, 2004,650:299-310.
5. Dodds S P, Watts D J, Sabel F C. *Information exchange and robustness of organizational networks,* in Proceedings of the National Academy of Sciences, 2003,100(21):12516-12521.

A Stackelberg Game-based Incentive Framework for Hybrid Access Macro-Femto Networks

You HAN, Xin CHEN and Zhuo LI

School of Computer Science, Beijing Information Science and Technology University, Beijing, 100101, P.R. China

E-mail: hanyouv@163.com, chenxin@bistu.edu.cn

The hybrid access mode is considered as the most promising access control mechanism for femtocell deployment to enhance mobile service quality and system capacity for cellular networks. However, it is a challenge to encourage femtocell base stations (FBSs) to adopt hybrid access and provide services to roaming unregistered macrocell user equipments (MUEs) in two-tier Macro-Femto networks. In this paper, we propose a novel incentive framework which the wireless service provider (WSP) provides economic compensation to motivate selfish femtocell holders (FHs) to open their resources for MUEs. A Stackelberg game is formulated to maximize the utility functions of both WSP and FHs. The unique Nash Equilibrium for the proposed game is characterized and optimal strategies for both tiers are developed. Simulation results show the utility functions of both WSP and FHs can be improved significantly, which develops the hybrid access mechanism.

Keywords: Macro-Femto networks; Hybrid access; Incentive framework; Stackelberg game.

1. Introduction

With the wide population of mobile terminal devices such as iPhone, iPad, Bambook, and the rapid development of social networks, such as Micro Blog, Facebook, Twitter and so on, wireless mobile communication service has been transformed from traditional short-message and voice services to high-definition image, video and other data-intensive application services[1]. This brings an increasing mobile high-speed data service demand for user[2]. In addition, S. A. Mahmud's survey shows that more than 60% of mobile voice services and 90% of data businesses occur in the interior[3]. In a closed environment, the loss caused by the wall makes the wireless signal coverage poor.

Femtocell is a wireless access point with low power, low cost and small coverage. Its purpose is to solve the problem of poor indoor signal coverage and low quality-of-service (QoS). Femtocell technique offers WSP an exciting and promising market. On the one hand, the enhancement of indoor service quality increases WSP's competition edge by reducing the churn rate (the probability of users leaving the network) of macrocell users. On the other hand, WSP may transfer some traffic from expensive macrocell to low-cost femtocell. In this way, more users can be served with existing macrocell.

However, Spectrum sharing between macrocell and femtocell can bring about high spectral efficiency, but also comes with co-channel interference which may severely degrade the network performance, especially QoS of macrocell users far away from the macrocell base station (MBS) but close to FBS. Such scenario is also known as dead zone. Various techniques have been used in interference management, such as power control, spectrum allocation, and clustering. Femtocell access control mechanism is an efficient approach to mitigate the co-channel interference. There are three categories of access control mechanisms that have been proposed: closed access, open access and hybrid access. In closed access mode, only a few femtocell user equipments (FUEs) who have been authorized by FH can access FBS and strong cross-tier interference caused by dead zone problem may severely impair the network performance yet. Open access allows arbitrary users to access FBS, which is a good solution for dead-zone problem. However, it may result in traffic congestion, putting great pressure on the backhaul and leading to QoS degradation. Hybrid access which can overcome these drawbacks dedicates a limited amount of femtocell resources to MUEs while reserving the rest for FUEs.

Different existing works [4-5] shown that hybrid access outperforms open and closed access by greatly reducing co-channel interference and guaranteeing the QoS of the FUEs. In [4], hybrid access was able to reduce cross-tier interference while guaranteeing a minimum performance to the FUEs. Authors in [5] proposed a refunding framework, in which WSP provides certain refunding to encourage FAPs to adopt hybrid access and open a time portion in each frame to neighboring MUEs. From the perspective of mobile data offloading, authors in [6] investigated the access control mechanism using the Nash bargaining theory. In [7], the author studied power control and time mute scheme via pricing game and [8] studied accessed MUEs' transmission rates pricing along with the interference mitigation problem in hybrid access network. However, all these papers focus on the technical aspects, mainly using information theory to analyze the performance gain.

In this paper, we propose a resource compensation incentive framework that promotes the adoption of hybrid access, considering not only network performance but also individual economic benefit. The main contributions of the paper are as follows.

- A resource compensation incentive framework is designed to motivate both WSP and FHs to be engaged in the hybrid access in Macro-Femto network. Within the incentive framework, WSP provides certain compensation to motivate FHs to open their resource for MUEs. Both WSP and FHs are aimed at maximizing their own utilities by selecting the optimal strategies.
- We formulate the framework as a Stackelberg game, the cooperation and competition relationship between FHs and WSP is analyzed and backward induction is used to obtain the Nash Equilibrium which is also proved unique.
- Numerical simulations show that the utilities of both WSP and FHs are notably enhanced, which provides strong motivation for FHs to adopt hybrid access and implement the proposed framework.

The rest of this paper is organized as follows. First, our system model is described in Section 2. Then, we propose the resource compensation incentive framework in Section 3 and Section 4 uses game theory to analyze the proposed incentive framework. Finally, simulation results are shown in Section 5 and Section 6 concludes this paper.

2. System Model

2.1. *Macro-Femto network architecture*

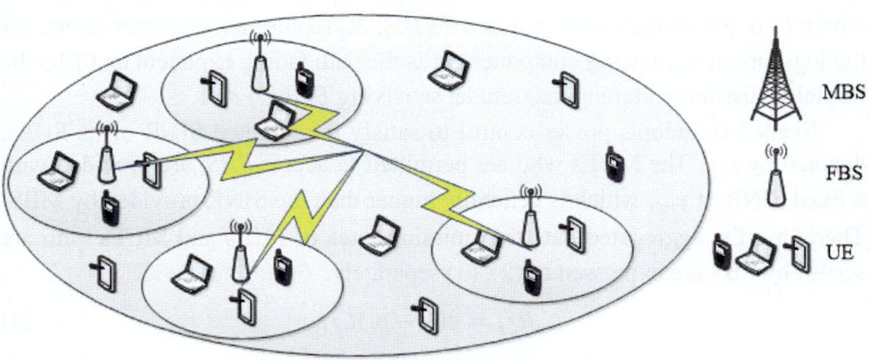

Fig. 1. Two-tier Macro-Femto networks architecture.

As shown in Fig. 1, we consider a two-tier Macro-Femto networks, consisting of one MBS which is deployed by the WSP and a few FBSs which are owned by individual FHs. Assume that there are K FBSs, denoted by $\{FBS_i\}_{i=1}^{K}$, and correspondingly their holders $\{FH_i\}_{i=1}^{K}$. A FBS can provide service for multiple user equipments that have been authorized by the FH and a user can only get access to one FBS. Let $\{FUE_{i,j}\}_{j=1}^{K_{fi}}$ represents the FUEs set, where K_{fi} denotes the number of FUEs supported byFBS_i. In order to guarantee the QoS, the maximum number that a FBS can serve is$K_{fi,max}$, so$K_{fi} \leq K_{fi,max}$. To have higher Signal to Interference plus Noise Ratio (SINR), MUEs who stay in the coverage of a FBS hope to transfer their traffic to that FBS, denoted by$\{MUE_{i,j}\}_{j=1}^{K_{mi}}$. We assume that there are K_{mi}neighboring MUEs who may get permitted to accessFBS_i, and $K_{mi} \leq K_{mi,max}$ is to avoid traffic congestion.

2.2. *Wireless channel model*

We assume that orthogonal spectrum resources are allocated to MBS and FBSs. The available spectrum resources are averaged into multiple sub-channels and each sub-channel's bandwidth is s Hz. The MBS owned by WSP possesses B_m sub-channels, all FHs share B_f sub-channels. Thus, there is no cross-tier interference between macrocell and femtocell, but co-tier interference between femtocells exists. Assume that the co-tier interference received by FBS_i is only determined by the density of FBSs, denoted as $I_i(K)$. When hybrid access is adopted, FBS_i allocates a portion of its spectrum ρ_i, $0 \leq \rho_i \leq 1$, to accessed MUE_i.We model the wireless channel between FBS and FUEs as log-normal distributed shadowing channel[9].Then, the received SINR is expressed as

$$\gamma_i = \left(\frac{P_i}{I_i(K)+N_0}\right) S d^{-n} |h|^2 . \quad (1)$$

where P_i is the transmission power of FBS_i, N_0 represents Gaussian noise, $S$is the log-normal shadowing component, n is the path fading exponent and$|h|$is the Rayleigh distributed fading magnitude, satisfying $E(|h|^2) = 1$.

Every FBS adopts power control to satisfy the targeted SINR of its FUEs, denoted by $\gamma_{f,i}$. The MUEs who are permitted to access FBS_i are provided with a fixed SINR of $\gamma_{m,i}$ which is generally higher than the SINR provided by MBS. Therefore, the aggregated data transmission rates of FUEs and MUEs who are served by FBS are expressed as (2), (3) separately.

$$R_{f,i} = s(1-\rho_i)C_{f,i} . \quad (2)$$

$$R_{m,i} = s\rho_i C_{m,i} . \quad (3)$$

in which $C_{f,i} = log_2(1+\gamma_{f,i})$, $C_{m,i} = log_2(1+\gamma_{m,i})$ are the channel capacities of FUEs and MUEs separately.

3. Resource Compensation Incentive Framework

In this section, we propose a resource compensation incentive framework to motivate FHs to adopt hybrid access and trade spectrum for profit from the

WSP. Specifically, WSP offers certain amount of economic compensation to FHs according to the opening ratios of spectrum they provide for accessed MUEs. To improve their own utilities, FHs also have strong motivation to open resources to neighboring MUEs. Thus, both the WSP and FHs can benefit from this framework.

Both WSP and FHs are selfish and rational. The WSP has strong wish to get support from FHs to aid in MUEs' data transmission, especially when there is great traffic demand from MUEs. Nevertheless, the utility of FHs will diminish if MUEs take up the available spectrum from FUEs. Thus, without any profit, FHs is impossible to be so altruistic as to allow MUEs to access FBSs. A resource compensation incentive framework is designed to solve these problems.

Assume that the WSP puts forward a total economic compensation amount M, which is further distributed among FHswho open their FBSs to MUEs. As the opening ratios of spectrum within FHs are different, it is reasonable to split the economic compensation in the way that the FH who open the most achieves highest compensation from WSP and who contributes the least gets lowest. Therefore, the compensationm_i obtained by each FH can be derived as the total amount of economic compensation multiplies the opening ratio of individual spectrum to the sum of all FBSs.

$$m_i = M \frac{\rho_i}{\sum_{j=1}^{K} \rho_j}. \tag{4}$$

More compensation will stimulate more hybrid access adoption among FHs and yield more benefit for WSP due to capacity expansion and improvement of MUEs' QoS. However, it will be profitable for WSP to carry out such incentive mechanism only when such benefit exceeds the compensation itself. Thus, in order to achieve the optimal incentive mechanism that generates maximum utility for WSP, further analysis should be conducted to determine the quantity of M.

Once the economic compensation amount $M$is broadcast by WSP, FHs react by making decision about whether closed access or hybrid access is more favorable and how much spectrum should be contributed to MUEs for data transmission if hybrid access is chosen. Based on the compensation strategy of WSP, each FH's utility does not only depend on its own behavior but also is affected by the decision of other FHs.

3.1. *The utility function of WSP*

The aim of WSP is to maximize its utility function by deriving the optimal compensation strategy. Therefore, the utility function of WSP consists of two aspects: the benefit from reduced user churn rate and the compensation given to FHs.

$$U_{wsp} = w_m(1 - c) - M \,. \tag{5}$$

where $c \in (0,1)$ represents the churn rate of MUEs and w_m is the equivalent revenue when c decreases by one percent. Poor QoS ends up in user switching WSP for better coverage. The WSP is able to provide better QoS if FHs open their spectrum resources to neighboring MUEs. Therefore, users are willing to stay with the WSP. We use the Sigmoid function to estimate the QoS satisfaction of user.[10] Then the churn rate[5] could be expressed as

$$c = \frac{1}{1+e^{-a(b-\mu)}} \,. \tag{6}$$

In which a denotes the user's sensitivity toward improvement of QoS and b represents the reserved traffic demands of MUEs. μ is the achievable data rate for MUEs. If MUEs get access to FBS for data transmission, the achievable data rate μ_f can be derived as

$$\mu_f = \sum_{i=1}^{K} R_{m,i} + \mu_0 \,. \tag{7}$$

where μ_0 is the channel capacity of MBS. When all FBSs are set to closed access, MUEs can only get access to MBS with a limited capacity. If some FBSs share part of spectrum with MUEs, the achievable data rate increases, resulting in reduced churn rate of MUEs. The Sigmoid function can perfectly capture this trend. It can be easily deduced that the percentage of MUEs who stay with the WSP is $\frac{1}{1+e^{-a(\mu-b)}}$. It is obvious that when the data rate goes up, the more steeper the churn rate falls, the more sensitive users are towards upgraded QoS.

3.2. *The utility function of FH*

The FH is aimed to maximize its utility function by deriving the optimal spectrum opening strategy according to the compensation M offered by the WSP. Then, FH's utility function is defined as the data rate the FUEs have achieved plus the compensation attained from WSP by opening spectrum resources to MUEs. We assume that the utility of FH is linearly increasing with the data rate of FUEs.

$$U_{f,i} = w_f R_{f,i} + m_i \,. \tag{8}$$

where w_f represents equivalent revenue the FH receives on one unit data rate for FUEs.

4. Game Theory Analysis

In this section, we formulate the resource compensation incentive framework as a Stackelberg game, where the WSP is the leader and the FHs act as the followers. We use backward induction method to study Stackelberg game. Then, it proves that a unique Nash Equilibrium exists for this game, which derives the optimal strategies for the WSP and FHs.

Since both WSP and FHs are selfish and rational entities who target to maximize own utilities, it is obvious that Stackelberg game is very appropriate to analyze this problem. In the first stage of Stackelberg game, the WSP hopes to maximize its utility by selecting best economic compensation amount$M$, being aware of the influence of its own decision on the behavior of FHs. In the second stage, every FH determines concurrently which kind of access control mechanism is more favorable and how to allocate spectrum resources between FUEs and accessed MUEs. As FHs are selfish and rational players who make decisions independently and concern about self-interest only, we use non-cooperative game to analyze their behavior.

4.1. *Non-cooperative game of FHs*

By analyzing the decision making process of FHs, we find that the utility of a specific FH not only depends on its own choice but also subjects to the behavior of other FHs. The non-cooperative access control selection game (NACSG) among FHs can be expressed as $G = (\{FH_i\}, \{A_i\}, \{U_i(\cdot)\})$. $\{A_i\}$is the pure strategy space of FH_i, which corresponds to$0 \leq \rho_i \leq 1$. Therefore, the joint set of the strategy space of K FHs is$A = A_1 \times A_2 \times \ldots \times A_K$ .The pure strategy space of FHs that are competitors is denoted by $A_{-i} = A \backslash A_i$.$\{U_i(\cdot)\}$is the set of utility function that FHs want to maximize.

Given the strategy $\rho_{-i}$of all other FHs, FH_i always chooses the strategyρ_i that can maximum utility, namely $\rho_i = arg \max_{0 \leq \rho_i \ll 1} u_i(\rho_i, \rho_{-i})$. In a non-cooperative game, FH has no incentive to deviate from its best strategy because any variation will decrease the utility. If every FH employs the best strategy with regard to other FHs' decisions, no FHs have motivation to alter their strategies unilaterally. In this case, the NACSG reaches the Nash Equilibrium.

Proposition 4.1.*Given ρ_{-i}, the best strategy of FH_i is*

$$\rho_i^* = \begin{cases} 0 & if \ \sum_{j \neq i}^{K} \rho_j > \frac{M}{w_f c_{f,i}} \\ \sqrt{\frac{M \sum_{j \neq i}^{K} \rho_j}{w_f c_{f,i}}} - \sum_{j \neq i}^{K} \rho_j & otherwise \end{cases} . \tag{9}$$

From the upper part of (9) we can see that the best strategy of FH_i is $\rho_i^* = 0$ under certain circumstances, which denotes that FBS_i choose closed access because it can't achieve higher utility by trading spectrum resources for compensation. Thus, the MUEs around FBS_i can only get access to MBS for data transmission. If $\rho_i > 0$, it shows that adopting hybrid access is more profitable forFBS_i. In this case, the best strategy$\rho_i^*$is not only related to the conditionof FBS_ibut also dependent on the decision of other FHs.

Proof. calculating the first and second derivatives of $U_{f,i}$with respecttoρ_i are as follows.

$$\frac{\partial U_{f,i}}{\partial \rho_i} = -w_f C_{f,i} + \frac{\sum_{j\neq i}^{K} \rho_j}{\left(\sum_{j=1}^{K} \rho_j\right)^2} M . \tag{10}$$

$$\frac{\partial^2 U_{f,i}}{\partial \rho_i^2} = -\frac{2\sum_{j\neq i}^{K} \rho_j}{\left(\sum_{j=1}^{K} \rho_j\right)^3} M . \tag{11}$$

We can see from (11) that the second derivative of $U_{f,i}$with respectto ρ_i is less than zero so that utility function $U_{f,i}$ is concave on ρ_i. If satisfying$\sum_{j\neq i}^{K} \rho_j < \frac{M}{w_f C_{f,i}}$, the maximum value of $U_{f,i}$ can be achieved when the first derivative of $U_{f,i}$with respecttoρ_i equals zero. Nevertheless, the $U_{f,i}$monotonically decreases as the opening ratio of spectrum$\rho_i$increaseswhen $\sum_{j\neq i}^{K} \rho_j > \frac{M}{w_f C_{f,i}}$. In this case, the best strategy for FH_i is to let the FBS_i work in closed access mode. □

Proposition 4.2. *A unique Nash Equilibrium for NACSG exists and the optimal opening ratio of spectrum for FH_i is given by (12).*

$$\rho_i^* = \begin{cases} 0 & if\, C_{f,i} > \frac{\sum_{j=1}^{K} C_{f,j}}{K-1} \\ \frac{(K-1)M}{w_f\left(\sum_{j=1}^{K} C_{f,j}\right)^2}\left[\sum_{j=1}^{K} C_{f,j} - (K-1)C_{f,j}\right] & otherwise \end{cases} . \tag{12}$$

Proof. To derive the Nash Equilibrium, every FH must adopt its best strategy. Otherwise, there will be FH who has intention to adjust its strategy for higher utility. Thus, the best strategy for FH_i should be expressed as (13). Then, putting $A^* = \sum_{j=1}^{K} \rho_j^*$ into (13), we can get the equivalentρ_i^* which is shown as (14).

$$\rho_i^* = \sqrt{\frac{M\sum_{j\neq i}^{K} \rho_j^*}{w_f C_{f,i}}} - \sum_{j\neq i}^{K} \rho_j^* . \tag{13}$$

$$\rho_i^* = \frac{A^*(M - A^* w_f C_{f,i})}{M} . \tag{14}$$

Jointly considering the best strategy of every FH, and summing up all the Kequations regarding to each FH, we obtain$A^* = \frac{(K-1)M}{w_f \sum_{j=1}^{K} C_{f,i}}$. Then we can easily calculate$\rho_i^*$for each FH.

In [11], it has proved that the Nash Equilibrium is unique if the best response function is positive, monotonic and scalable. It can be easily proved that ρ_i^* satisfies the above conditions. Thus, there exists a unique Nash Equilibrium for NACSG. □

4.2. *Utility maximization for WSP*

Once the WSP declares the compensation amount M, the FHsreact by choosing access control mechanism and distributing spectrum resources among FUEs and accessed MUEs. As the leader of the game, WSP is aware of the impact of compensation amount M on FHs' behavior. Taking into consideration the possible response of FHs, WSP is able to derive optimal $M$to procure maximum utility.When the NACSG of FHs reaches Nash Equilibrium, the utility of WSP can be further derived as

$$U_{wsp} = w_m \frac{1}{1+e^{-a\left(\mu_f^* - b\right)}} - M . \tag{15}$$

in which $\mu_f^* = \sum_{i=1}^{K} \rho_i^* C_{m,i} + \mu_0$.

Proposition 4.3.*When the following conditions in (16) are satisfied, the WSP maximizes its utility if and only if the compensation amount is set as (17).*

$$\begin{cases} \mu_0 > \frac{\ln 2}{a} + b \\ B > \frac{5}{4} \\ B > \frac{1}{2}(1 + e^{-ab}) \end{cases} . \tag{16}$$

$$M^* = \frac{1}{\sum_{i=1}^{K} C_{m,i}\beta_i} \left[b + \frac{1}{a} \ln\left(B + \sqrt{B^2 - 1}\right) \right]. \tag{17}$$

where

$$\beta_i = \begin{cases} \frac{(K-1)\left[\sum_{j=1}^{K} C_{f,j} - (K-1)C_{f,i}\right]}{w_f\left(\sum_{j=1}^{K} C_{f,j}\right)^2} & if \sum_{j=1}^{K} C_{f,j} < (K-1)C_{f,i} \\ 0 & otherwise \end{cases} .$$

$$B = \frac{w_m a}{2 w_f} \sum_{i=1}^{K} C_{m,i} \beta_i - 1 .$$

Proof. ρ_i^* can be expressed as $\rho_i^* = \beta_i M$. The first and second derivatives of U_{wsp} with respect to M are given as follows.

$$\frac{\partial U_{wsp}}{\partial M} = -1 + w_m \frac{ae^{-a\left(\mu_f^*-b\right)}}{\left[1+e^{-a\left(\mu_f^*-b\right)}\right]^2} \sum_{i=1}^{K} C_{m,i}\,\beta_i\,. \tag{18}$$

$$\frac{\partial^2 U_{wsp}}{\partial M^2} = \frac{-\left(a\sum_{i=1}^{K} C_{m,i}\beta_i\right)^2\left(1-2e^{-a\left(\mu_f^*-b\right)}\right)w_m e^{-a\left(\mu_f^*-b\right)}}{\left[1+e^{-a\left(\mu_f^*-b\right)}\right]^2}\,. \tag{19}$$

From (19) we knows that if $\mu_0 > \frac{ln\,2}{a} + b$, the second derivative of U_{wsp} withrespect to M is always less than zero so that U_{wsp} is concave on M. The optimal M can be obtained by assigning the first derivative of U_{wsp} to be 0. When $\mu_0 < \frac{ln\,2}{a} + b$, we can derive that as M increases, U_{wsp} falls down at the beginning, then reaches a certain point, and it starts to go up afterwards, then becomes a decreasing function at last. In this case, we can get the maximum value of U_{wsp} either in the local maximum point in (17) or the boundary when $M = 0$ which means no FHs are willing to contribute part of spectrum resources to MUEs without charge. □

4.3. *Optimal strategies for WSP and FHs*

According to the game theoretical analysis, the optimal resource compensation for WSP and the choice of access control mechanism for FHs can be summarized as follow.

(1) Each FBS_i periodically collects channel state information of FUEs and MUEs within its coverage. Then they piggyback the gathered channel condition information to WSP via the backhaul link.

(2) Based on the information from FHs, the WSP is able to compute $C_{f,i}$, $C_{m,i}$. Firstly, WSP checks whether conditions in (16) are satisfied. If satisfy, WSP figures out the best compensation amount M^* according to (17). Then it broadcasts M^* to all FHs.

(3) After receiving the aggregated data rate $\sum_{j=1}^{K} C_{f,j}$ and economic compensation amount M^*, FHs choose the access control mechanism. If $\sum_{j=1}^{K} C_{f,j} < (K-1)C_{f,i}$, FH_i chooses closed access. Otherwise, hybrid access is selected.

(4) FHs who have selected hybrid access decide the opening ratios of spectrum resource ρ_i^* for accessed MUEs according to (12).

5. Simulation Results

In this section, we conduct numerous simulations to evaluate the utility gain of hybrid access that is motivated by the resource compensation incentive framework.

The default main system parameters are listed in Table 1. The targeted data rate of FUEs of each FBS follows Normal distribution with mean 10 and variance 1. The data rate of MUEs that are permitted to access FBS follows Normal distribution with mean 5 and variance 1.

The number of FBSs is a highly influential factor as it determines the density of femtocell. From Fig. 2 we can see that the utility of WSP is much higher when hybrid access is promoted by resource compensation incentive policy. In case of closed access, the burden of macrocell traffic is entirely borne by macrocell that has a fixed capacity μ_0. However, the utility of WSP is the highest if open access is somehow forced to be implemented. Although WSP pays FHs for undertaking traffic of MUEs, it gets reciprocated as the MUEs' churn rate decreases, leading to increasing revenue. The utility of WSP goes up along with the number of FBS because there are more FHs who will adopt hybrid access and more macrocell traffic is transferred to femtocell.

Table 1. Simulation parameters setting.

Parameter	Value
The number of FBSs (FHs)K	100
The equivalent revenue for MUEs w_m	5
The equivalent revenue for FUEs w_f	0.1
The user's sensitivity toward QoSa	2
The reserved traffic demand of MUEs b	0.3
The channel capacity of MBS μ_0	0.22

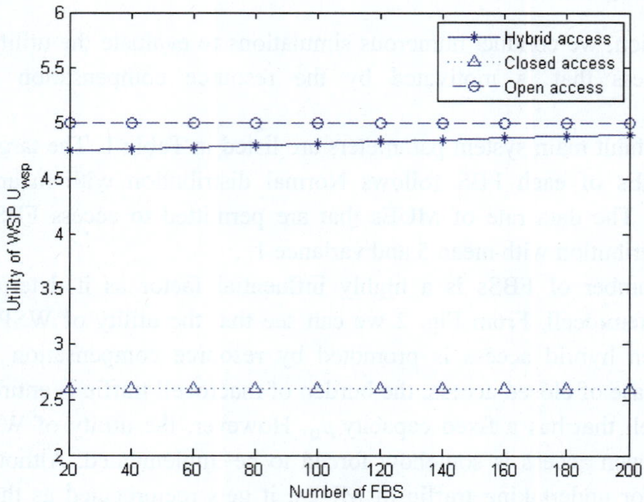

Fig. 2. Utility of WSP U_{wsp} versus number of FBS.

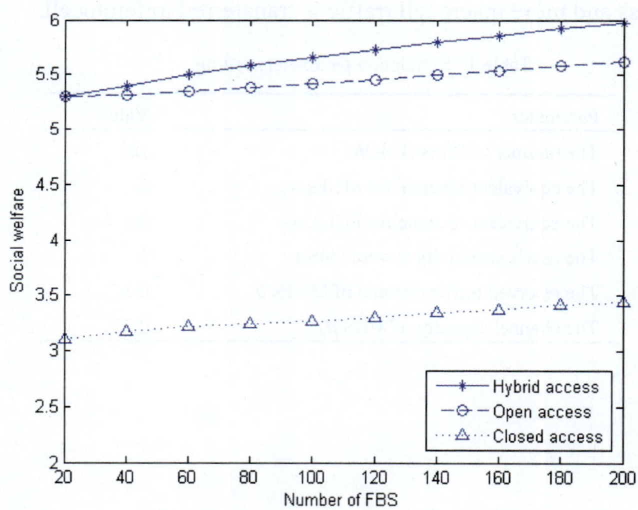

Fig. 3. Social welfare versus number of FBS.

Fig.3 shows social welfare is the highest in case of hybrid access because both the utilities of WSP and FHs are improved compared to closed access. Although WSP can receive higher utility in open access, FHs have to sacrifice considerably without compensation, so they simply will not adopt this access mechanism.

Fig. 4 shows that the compensation amount Mabates when the number of the FBS increases. As the compensation slightly decreases, the spectrum opening ratio of each FBS also declines. However, the growth of number of FBS is so enormous that the aggregated opening ratio still comes up in spite of the low compensation. This indicates that WSP also has the motivation to promote the deployment of more FBSs.

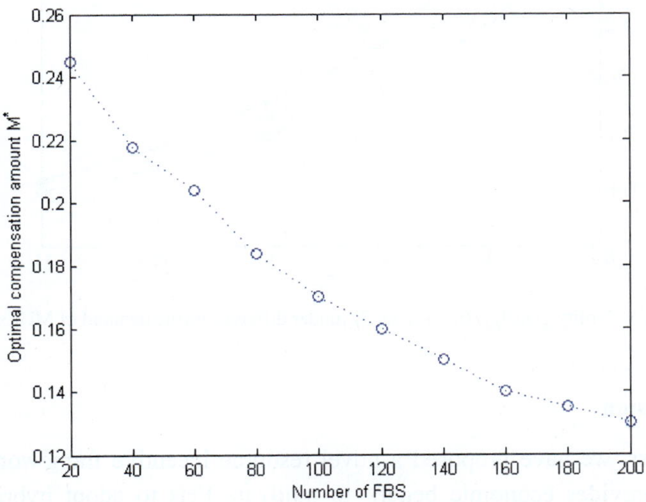

Fig. 4. Optimal compensation amountM^* versus number of FBS.

In order to analyze the utility gain and opening ratio$\rho_i$ofa specificFH_i, we adjust the simulation as follows. There are $K = 6$FBSs in the network. The achievable transmission rate of $FH_j, j \neq i$is held as constant, i.e., $R_{f,j} = 10, j \neq i$. FUEs' targeted data rate $R_{f,i}$is varied to analyze the trend of$U_{f,i}$and ρ_i. Other simulation parameters setting remain unchanged. Let $U_{f,i}$ and $U_{f,io}$ denote the utility of FH_i with and withouthybrid access respectively.

From Fig. 5we can see that the utility gain$U_{f,i}/U_{f,io}$of FH_idecreases as the targeted data rate of FUEs $R_{f,j}$ increases. FH tends to share more of their resources if FUEs demand a lower targeted data rate. As long as the requirement of FUEs is satisfied, FHs are willing to trade spectrum resources for compensation from WSP. It is intuitive that FHs with high-demand FUEs are more likely to choose closed access in order to exclusively serve their FUEs. Therefore, when$R_{f,j}$is low, the utility gain is more appreciable. Also, it is more considerable when MUEs' traffic demand is high since WSP raises the compensation amount Min order to encourage FHs to takeover more macrocell traffic.

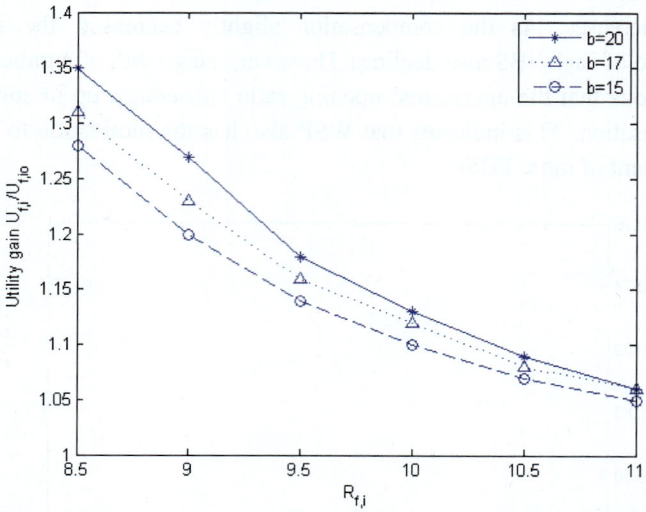

Fig. 5. Utility gain$U_{f,i}/U_{f,io}$versus $R_{f,j}$under different traffic demand of MUEs.

6. Conclusion

In this paper, we have proposed a novel resource incentive framework, which the WSP provides economic benefit to motivate FHs to adopt hybrid access mechanism and guarantee the QoS of accessed MUEs. A Stackelberg game has been formulated to maximize utilities of both tiers, and the corresponding optimal strategies have been obtained. Simulation results verify the efficiency of the proposed framework and show that considerable utility gain for WSP and FHs can be achieved under the resource incentive framework, thus providing strong motivation for FBSs to implement this framework.

Acknowledgments

This work was supported by the National Natural Science Foundation of China(61370065, 61502040), National Science & Technology Pillar in the Twelfth Five-year Plan Project(2015BAK12B03-03) and Program for Excellent Talents in Beijing Municipality (2014000020124G099).

References

1. CISCO SYSTEMS, “Cisco Visual Networking Index: Global Mobile Data Traffic Forecast Update, 2013–2018,” February 5, 2014.

2. Maier M, Verikoukis C. Inside smart FiWi-HetNets and the explosion of mobile data traffic. *Transparent Optical Networks (ICTON), 16th International Conference on. IEEE*, 2014: 1-4(Graz, Austria, 2014).
3. Mahmud S A, Khan G M, Zafar H, et al. *Journal of applied research and technology*, 2013, 11(5): 733-754.
4. Valcarce A, López-Pérez D, De La Roche G, et al. Limited access to OFDMA femtocells. *Personal, Indoor and Mobile Radio Communications, 20th International Symposium on. IEEE*, 2009: 1-5(Tokyo, Japan, 2009).
5. Chen Y, Zhang J, Zhang Q. *Wireless Communications, IEEE Transactions on*, 2012, 11(5): 1688-1697.
6. Gao L, Iosifidis G, Huang J, et al. *Selected Areas in Communications, IEEE Journal on*, 2014, 32(6): 1114-1125.
7. Zhou T, Chen Y, Jiang C, et al. *Wireless Communications, IEEE Transactions on*, 2015, 14(4): 2118-2130.
8. Li L, Wei M, Xu C, et al. *Communications Letters, IEEE*, 2015, 19(9): 1560-1563.
9. Nosratinia A, Hunter T E. *Selected Areas in Communications, IEEE Journal on*, 2007, 25(2): 369-378.
10. Wang L, Kuo G S G S. *Communications Surveys & Tutorials, IEEE*, 2013, 15(1): 271-292.
11. Xie R, Yu F R, Ji H. Energy-efficient spectrum sharing and power allocation in cognitive radio femtocell networks. *INFOCOM, Proceedings IEEE. IEEE*, 2012: 1665-1673(Orlando, FL, 2012).

Session 3

Computer Security

Security Concerns on Cloud Computing from Industry Perspectives

Xiang-dong LI

Computer Systems Technology, New York City College of Technology CUNY
Brooklyn, NY 11201, USA
E-mail: xli@citytech.cuny.edu

The use of cloud computing offers tremendous value to IT business, due to its low cost, agility and rapid elasticity. The commercial public cloud infrastructure can be accessed over the Internet, which offers advantages such as high Return On Investment (ROI) and more efficient purchasing. However it also raises concerns about lack of visibility, security, reliability and regulations. The industry requires cloud service providers to continue providing stronger security and data privacy than ever before. In this paper, we discuss recent security concerns on the cloud from industry perspectives.

Keywords: Cloud computer; Security concern; Industry perspective.

1. Introduction

The virtualization and high-speed Internet have boosted the transformation of compute environments and the computer resources into the cloud. The cloud computing has been attracting more and more industry companies and organizations due to its apparent and prompt evidence of benefits tired to the efficiency, scalability, flexibility and lower cost. The traditional three cloud service models are *Infrastructure as a Service* (IaaS), *Platform as a Service* (PaaS) and *Software as a Service* (SaaS). Recently several new models are defined due to the growing use of their specific services, for example, *Disaster Recovery as a Service* (DRaaS), *Storage as a Service*, *Security as a Service*, etc. The three common deployment models are: *Private cloud, Public cloud,* and *Hybrid cloud,* where the cloud infrastructure contains different type of cloud deployments [1]. The choice of these deployment models depends on the customers' requirements.

2. Standards in Clouds

Cloud computing offers the end users for their applications to utilize centralized infrastructure and capacity on-demand. Because the cloud is self-provisioned and fully automated for many service providers, there is no need for network configuration or server provisioning. As cloud technology has developed, combined with the wide use of bring-your-own-device (BYOD) and "shadow IT" practices (IT solutions deployed without the approval of involvement of the IT department), enable the business truly anywhere, anytime and any-device workforce. However, with the flexibility increased, the risks in security of critical data and business communications are increased too. Processes and policies should encompass physical, network, application, and data-level security, as well as full back-up and disaster recovery. The provider should be compliant with security-oriented laws and auditing programs, including Safe Harbor [2], ISO 27001 [3], and SAS70 Type II [4].

2.1. *New approach to security*

According to an industry survey [5] that a high percent of security decision-makers were confident in the ability of their controls, such as firewalls and VPNs, to protect digital assets in SaaS applications. However, their confidence diminishes significantly when specific aspects such as liability and division of responsibilities are discussed. For example, as SaaS and BYOD are conjoined, new vulnerabilities appear that simplex security tools cannot address. Today, in many area of industry, the security is not just the sole task of IT department; the responsibility should be shared among multiple stakeholder groups, for example, IT security, business stakeholders, cloud providers. As the BYOD practice becomes more and more common in many organizations, it is critical important that BYOD does not bring threats to sensitive data.

Not all cloud providers explain their true competence in security. Recently, many famous providers, like Amazon, Google, and Microsoft teach their cloud users about security and how they approach it. The large data breaches happened in Sony (in 2011), Home Depot and Target (in 2014). Although massive data breaches do not happen in public clouds, but business using public clouds improperly is often seen. The largest threat to security is the lack of qualified cloud developers, engineers, architects, and security experts who understand how to make cloud-based systems secure [6].

2.2. *Cloud security standards*

The biggest challenge for industry to use cloud is the dimness of security standards for cloud provider. This leads to evaluate risk assessment difficultly, because each organization has an applicable standard for security controls. The cloud users want a set of security standards that cloud service providers should implement. In addition, independent third-party firms are required to audit and assess the cloud providers for their security controls policies. The US federal government developed *FedRAMP* standard, which provides a framework that cloud providers must follow in order to do business with government agency. The standard requires independent auditing firms to evaluate cloud provider against the NIST federal standards for security. The UK government developed a similar standard *G-Cloud.*

Those above standards are only applied to governmental agency as cloud users, there is no independent risk program for cloud that fits to all industry organizations internationally. Several programs under the Cloud Security Alliance (CSA) are conceptually similar to *FedRAMP* program, but are maintained by CSA and implemented by a network of independent audit and security firms. These programs include [7]:

- STAR Certification: It relies on an independent third-party assessment of a cloud provider against the ISO 27001 standard, as well as the CSA Cloud Controls Matrix (CCM).
- STAR Attestation: It provides a report via the audit-reporting standard for customer consumption known as the SSAE SOC 2 Report.
- STAR Continuous: It provides a scanning and monitoring console that customers can use to remotely assess cloud providers' control statements using the *CloudAudit* XML-based tag format and the Cloud Trust Protocol (CTP) for data transmission and retention.

Additional cloud risk frameworks and guides are available from the Shared Assessments Program and the European Union Agency for Network and Information Security (ENISA), which breaks down the various areas of risk categorically, aligning more effectively with ISO 27001 and CoBIT standards.

2.3. *Cloud authentication*

Using the user name and password to login clouds is easily to be hacked. In the phishing emails, users follow the instructions and unwittingly give out their usernames and passwords. To enhance user authentication, cloud users are often recommend to adopt approved high standards of authentication. The following lists several recommendations for the authentication from industry [8].

- Fast ID Online (FIDO)is a set of security specifications for providing strong authentication and developed by FIDO Alliance [9];
- Security Assertion Markup Language (SAML) is an Extensible Markup Language (XML) standard that allows a user to log on once for affiliated but separate Web sites, and it is designed for business-to-business and business-to-consumer transactions;
- OpenID is an open specification for authentication and single sign-on, which was first created to allows web sites and authentication services to exchange security information. In 2014, OpenID Connect was built to allow "an end user to log in once and access multiple, disparate resources on and off the Web" [10]. Numerous cloud providers, including Google and Microsoft, support its specification. Industry expects it could replace the on premise identity and access management systems with cloud offerings.

3. Concerns on Virtualization in Clouds

The use of virtualization in cloud brought several security concerns in in industry [11]. In 2006, Blue Pill, a piece of virtual machine-based malware, was demonstrated to take control of a virtual host. The hypervisors are not often updated, the existing vulnerabilities may jeopardize the system when using virtualization in clouds. Furthermore, a cross-virtual-machine attack can happen, in which a hacker is able to attack all other virtual machines on the same host on the network, only when he successfully compromises one virtual machine, because the standard Intrusion Detection Systems (IDS) and Intrusion Prevention Systems (IPS) are not configured to inspect the traffic between the virtual machines on the same network. The attack could happen during migration, the migration channel is not encrypted, which may be sniffed by a hacker performing a man-in-the-middle (MITM) attack in the network.

Another risk is the data leak, which could happen in allocating resource from one virtual machine to another. If a virtual machine is no longer needed and deleted, the new virtual machine receives additional resources and can use "forensic investigation techniques to get an image of the whole physical memory, as well as data storage" [11].

4. Managing Security in Cloud

Several industry vendors provide some tips for cloud users to manage security in clouds [12, 13].

- Encryption – first of all, ensure to encrypt data on clouds and keep encrypting keys safely. The access to the keys should be fully controlled by you or trusted parties. A variety of applicable encryption standards are available in industry.

- Authentication – ensure that only right people can access the cloud. Using only passwords is a weak authentication management. In previous section, we have discussed several industry authentication standards which could be adopted in clouds.

- **Authorization** – ensure to assign correct access permissions to those who can gain the access to clouds. This is so-called the *principle of least privilege*, that "give people only the access they need to do the jobs and not one bit more."
- **Monitoring** – ensure to monitor and record all user activities. This is critical to investigate when data breach occurs. Some concerns include, for example, make sure there is a need to have an audit of service provider; understand how the providers preform auditing and investigation in a shared environment.
- **Legal Compliance** – ensure to understand the legal responsibility and follow all the laws, regulations and guidelines. Today the fast development of IT environment leads industry compliance/privacy laws to change constantly. It is necessary for big enterprise companies to hire a third party consultant to ensure their use of cloud is compliant.
- **Data Ownership** – ensure to understand the ownership of the data on cloud. The law can differ geographically. For example, applying encryption software to data in the cloud may not be permitted in a particular country where you have to deal with.

- **Data Storage** – ensure to understand how the clouds store, backup and recover the data. If you want to remove data from cloud, make sure it is completely deleted on the cloud, not left behind. Ensure that you can retrieve data when you need it and the backup is maintained securely,
- **Service Level Agreements** (SLAs) – ensure to set the SLA as broad as possible and with details covered. For example, how does cloud provider compensate the cost of downtime?
- **Exit Strategy** – ensure to understand if you want to stop the cloud service, the contract with cloud providers should specify the details of exit strategy.
- **Cloud Architecture** – ensure to understand the systems and applications are appropriately and sufficiently isolated. Make sure that security policies are accurately and fully implemented across the cloud architectures
- **Application** – ensure to understand how you can check and manage vulnerabilities in applications. For example, understand how to secure applications in cloud that are□increasingly targeted due to large user population and in the scenario where the patches are not available.

5. Conclusion

While the use of cloud computing is becoming more popular, the concerns about lack of visibility, security, reliability, and regulatory is getting more critical. The legal rules, policies, regulations and industry standards in this area are constantly being developed. Some industry experts have expressed that based on today's regulations/rules/standards the largest threat to security of using clouds is the lack of qualified cloud developers, engineers, architects, and security experts who understand how to make cloud-based systems secure.

References

1. X. Li, The New Trend of Security in Cloud Computing, *Intern. J. Engin.Innov. & Res.*, Vol.1 (2012).

2. S. Dzombeta, V. Stantchev, R. Colomo-Palacios, K. Brandis, and K. Haufe. Governance of cloud computing services for the life sciences. *IT Pro.*, vol. 16 (2014)

3. A. Alebrahim, D. Hatebur, S. Fassbender, L. Goeke, and I. Cote. A pattern-based and tool-supported risk analysis method compliant to ISO 27001 for cloud systems. *Intern. J. Sec. Soft. Engin.*, Vol. 6(2015).

4. S. Srinivasan. Meeting compliance requirement while using cloud services, in *Security, Trust, and Regulatory Aspects of Cloud Computing in Business*. eds. S. Srinivasan (IGI Globa, 2014), pp. 127-144.

5. Forrester, SaaS adoption requires a new approach to information security (Forrester Consulting, 2014), http://www.forrester.com

6. IDG Enterprise, Cloud computing, eGuide. http://resources.idgenterprise.com/original/AST-0146141_cloud-navisite_v4.pdf

7. B. Blevins, How the feds are ramping up security for cloud services, *Information Security*, Insider Edition (2015).

8. R. Shapland, "Are open standards the answer to user authentication in the cloud?".http://searchcloudsecurity.techtarget.com

9. FIDO. https://fidoalliance.org/

10. Techtarget. OpenID (OpenID Connect) (2014), http://techtarget.com/definition/OpenID

11. D. Lukan, How to limit security risks during cloud computing virtualization (2015),http://searchcloudsecurity.techtarget.com/

12. Dell, White paper: 10 Tips for Managing Security in the Cloud(2013), http://www.secureworks.com

13. N. Coleman and M. Borrett, Cloud Security Who do you trust? http://www.ibm.com

The Framework and Implement of Trusted Network Connection Based on Separation of Controlling Flow and Data Flow

Fei WANG*, Yu WANG and Jie QIANG

Equipment Academy, Information Department
Beijing, Huairou District, China
**E-mail: wangfei791009@163.com*

The paper proposes a trusted network connection frame based on the separation of controlling flow and data flow, giving priority to maintaining data stream transmission. This is done through controlling the flow of communication on both sides of the identity authentication and trusted state assessment, and updating the access control policies of both sides, so as to maintain data stream transmission control. On the one hand, it can guarantee the real-time transmission of business data and on the other hand it can improve the efficiency of communication participants' trusted state assessment, which is suitable for the intensive real-time requirements of industrial and business data.

Keywords: Trusted computing; Trusted network connection; Controlling flow; Data flow.

1. Introduction

There is no national safety without safe network. Compared to the traditional security technology, trusted computing technology is an immune computing model, which uses dual architecture based on the parallel computing and defense, to compute and safeguard at the same time [1], it can respond to APT attacks that on behalf of the new information technology offensive effectively.

Compared to the TCG, our trusted computing technology have made some innovations [2]; However, In the network connection level, it is still major in the user authentication and platform-based authentication without checking the state of trusted platform, and usually allows the transmission of traffic flow after the authentication is completed. Under the assumption trusted connections in the process of authentication, platform certification can be allowed, which might cause a decrease in transmission efficiency.

GB <GB / T 29828-2013 Trusted Computing Specification Trusted Connected Architecture>[4] is not given how to achieve the specific trusted framework. The article that on the basis of the ensuring the business real-time industrial control system, designs a trusted framework to separate the controlling

---

* Corresponding author.

flow and data flow, one hand to ensure the high real-time traffic data, on the other hand to complete the trusted network connect under the premise of ensuring efficiency.

2. Trusted Network Connection

There are three entities in trusted network connection architecture: AR (Access Requestor), AC (Access Controller) and PM (Policy Manager). AR requests for the access to protect network; AC controls the requestor to access to the protected network; PM manages the AR and AC. It is divided into three levels from the top to the bottom: integrity measurement layer, trusted platform assessment layer and network access control layer.

AR components include: network access requester, trusted network connection client and integrity collectors

AC components include: network access controller, trusted network connection server and integrity collectors.

PM components include: the service provider of identification strategies, the service provider of assessment strategies and integrity verifier.

3. The Framework of Trusted Network Connection Based on Separation of Controlling Flow and Data Flow, FTNCB-SCD

As far as possible to ensure the real-time, the FTNCB-SCD supports the proof of user identity, the proof of platform identification, status information gathering, and the connection object state assessments after the trusted device is connected to the network, and realizes a trusted network connections and network data stream Fine-grained mandatory access control, the principle is shown in Figure 1.

FTNCB-SCD includes data flow and controlling flow levels. For communication between the two sides data stream can flow directly, in the controlling flow, the trusted connection management component collects the data flow`s platform ID of sender / responder, the identity of the two sides of the platform, trusted state and hand over to PM to evaluate in real-time. Then to notify the sender and responder to control the data flow interruption or released, which based on the assessment results and access policies.

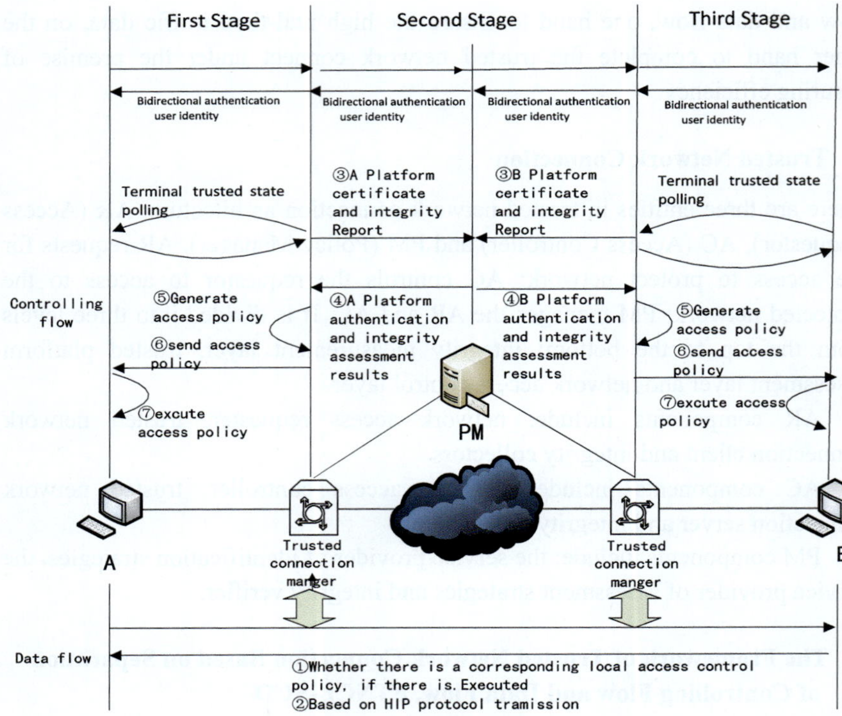

Fig. 1. the principle of FTNCB-SCD

3.1. *Data flow*

In the process of data exchanging, First data sender determines whether there is currently a corresponding access control policy, if there is, send by policy; if not, send directly.

Before data exchanging, the sender gains communication key that communicates with responder through a trusted connection management components, and trusted connection management component pushes the key to the responder at the same time. Communicating parties are based on HIP (Host Identity Protocol) protocol, using the communication key for data transmission.

HIP protocol algorithm uses ESP secure connection for data transmission, data packet format shown in Figure 2.

IP Head	ESP

IP Head	SPI	serial number	Load Data	Filling field	Filling length	Next Head	Verification data

Fig. 2. HIP Protocol data package

3.2. *Controlling flow*

FTNCB-SCD controlling flow logic is shown in Figure 3.

When the system is initialized, each component connects based on the TNCA standards` trusted connection, then the AR and the AC report own device trusted states to the PM regularly or through the instructions, PM always maintain a trusted state that governed by a trusted device.

When the AC intercepts the network communications; AC samples the data packet, according to the IP that is included in packet from AR, to find the corresponding trusted credentials.

AC sends AR`s terminal identification to the PM to verify.

PM returns the authentication results of AC.

AC makes decisions according to the authentication results.

If the authentication results are refused to connect, AC sends the results to AR of the communicating parties.

communicating parties` AR implements data flow control.

4. The Realization of Trusted Network Connection with Separation of Controlling Flow and Data Flow

The realization of FTNCB-SCD, except the trusted computing equipment, there also need trusted network controllers, trusted route switching equipment and trusted front-end processor, which schematically are deployed in Figure 4:

(1) Trusted network controller that corresponds to the PM, realizes a access network trusted (enhanced) equipment to achieve user authentication, platform authentication and platform status assessment; to provide the assessment results for communicating parties, then to configure the network access policies based on the results.

(2) Trusted route switching equipment that corresponds to the AC, on the basis of ensuring itself trusted, can lift complex control functions from the hardware network devices into a unified control layer. So according to PM, it can achieve global deployment and network policy adjustment rapidly.

(3)Trusted front-end processor is to be set up to ensure the business a high real-time, as well as to improve the trusted business server efficiency .It may be deployed independently for incoming / outgoing data flow that encapsulate or decapsulate packets based on the HIP protocol.

In the implementation, after a trusted device and trusted switches have power, both of them submit the user authentication, trusted platform certification and trusted status periodically. Supposing a trusted terminal A want to access trusted server B:

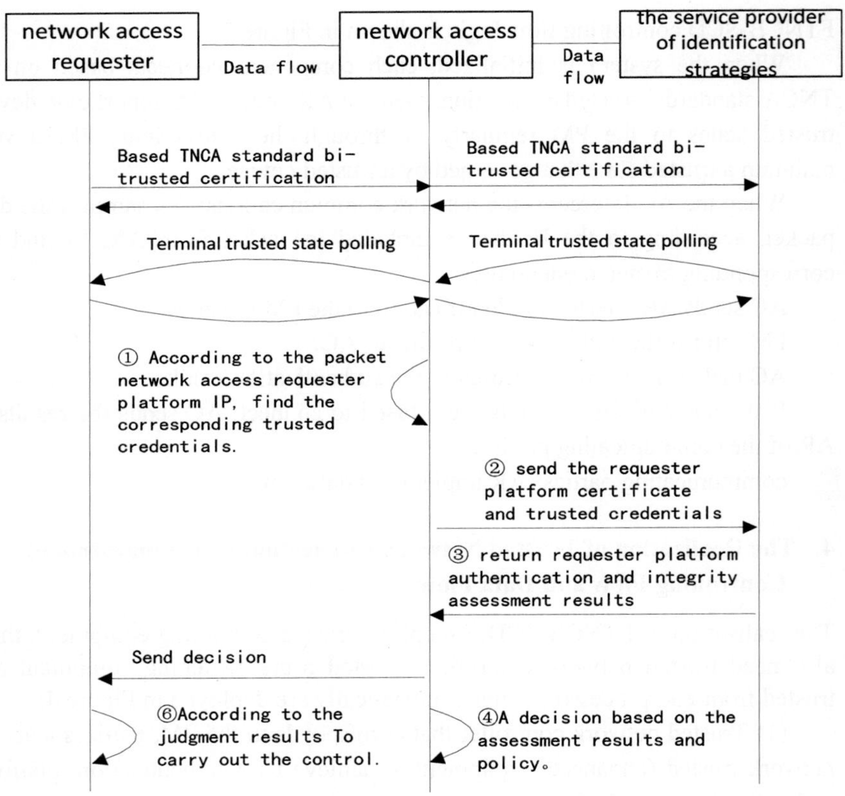

Fig. 3. Controlling flow logic

(1)Data flow level

Trusted terminal A checks its network access control policy whether is allowed to communicate with a trusted server B, if allowed, it can communicate with the B directly;

(2)Controlling flow level

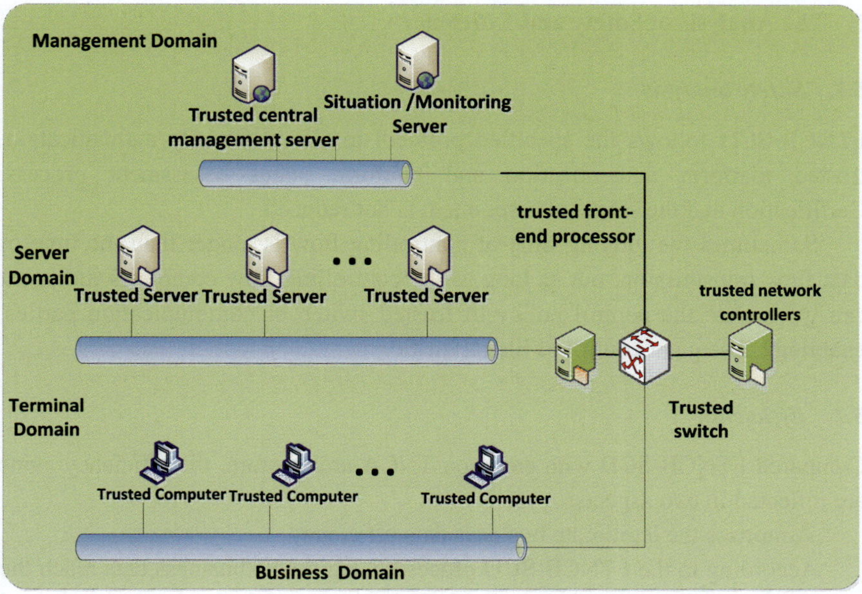

Fig. 4. the implementation of FTNCB-SCD

1)Trusted switch checks the data flow packets from the A to B by sampling, requests trusted network controller to evaluate their identity and trusted state;

2)Trusted network controller which accords to the information that submitted by trusted switch, request credentials and trusted status of A and B; If the trusted state that maintained by trusted network controller is missing the trusted state of A or B, or the trusted state of A or B is not updated beyond a fixed period, then the trusted network controller sends the instruction that submitted from the trusted state to A or B. After the latest trusted state acquisition value of A or B updated, we evaluate.

3)Trusted network controller sends the results of the assessment, namely access control policy, to trusted switches, A and B. Trusted switches, A and B achieve mandatory controls that A connects to and B, according to the latest access policy. That is A or B able / Disable to visit each other, trusted switch forces the data from A to B block or release.

5. The Analysis of Safety and Efficiency

5.1. *Safety analysis*

FTNCB-SCD follows the specified protocol in GB in identity authentication, trusted platform authentication and platform status assessment process. Certification and the safety of assessment is not reduced.

Sometimes the judging time of controlling flow is longer than the time of data flow transmission, but as long as the controlling flow completes judgment can we update the control policy of trusted switch or communication parties, enabling subsequent control of illegal traffic.

5.2. *Efficiency*

Compared FTNCB-SCD with common TNCA architecture, the efficiency gains are reflected in two aspects:

1)Improve the legitimate business data efficiency

According to the FTNCB-SCD processes, legitimate business data reach the receiver in real-time, thus it can avoid the influence of the business data in real time due to trusted connection architecture certification and assessment.

2)Improve the trusted state assessment efficiency within the expected time

The trusted network connection architecture in GB each trusted network connection process requires network visitors, network controllers to collect trusted state in real-time, and this process is consuming system resources, because each device`s inconsistent speed acquisition decrease the efficiency of state assessment.

In FTNCB-SCD, each device previously submits trusted state acquisition to trusted network controller with a certain period, a time when we need to access a certain communication parties, trusted network controller can quickly access based on the maintenance assessment table, which can enhance efficiency of the trusted state assessment; only when the status of the communication parties do not meet an updated cycle or do not exist, can it ask communication parties to report the real-time trusted state.

6. Conclusion

The paper puts forward a trusted network connection frame based on the separation of controlling flow and data flow, although there may be that the state is not real-time or latest in special circumstances, compared to high real-time to industrial control systems, military and other fields, FTNCB- SCD is able to ensure the real-time business data transmission, improve communication participants efficiency in trusted state assessment. The next step, we will realize a prototype system as soon as possible to verify FTNCB-SCD functional rationality and determine a reasonable acquisition cycle of the trusted state, to ensure the maximum safety and efficiency.

References

1. Chang-xiang Shen, Network space security strategy thinking and Revelation [J], financial electronic, 2014(6):1-3.(In Chinese)
2. Chang-xiang Shen, Huan-guo Zhang, Huai-min Wang, research and development of trusted computing [J]. China Information Science (Chinese edition), 2010, 40 (2): 139-166. (In Chinese)
3. GB / T 29828-2013 Information security technology trusted computing specifications trusted connection architecture [M], Beijing: China Standard Press, 2013.(In Chinese)

Application of Partial Least Squares Algorithm Based on Kullback–Leibler Divergence in Intrusion Detection

Xian-ping YU, Shan-xiong* CHEN and Xi-hua PENG
College of Computer and Information Science , Southwest University
Chongqing, 400715, China

Mao-ling PENG
Chongqing City Management College,Chongqing, 400715, China
Email:yuxianp@126.com,
**Email: csxpml123@126.com,*
huangai1234@126.com

With the increasing widespread of network applications, the role of network security is becoming more and more important in computer networks. The analysis and discrimination of network data stream and then the discrimination of intrusion behaviors is an important direction of network security research. In network intrusion detection, this paper introduces a nonlinear regression method -- partial least squares to predict the network behaviors. At the same time, in the calculation of partial least squares residuals, the paper adopts the Kullback Leibler - divergence as an iterative calculation standard so as to improve the detection speed and accuracy.

Keyword: Intrusion detection; Partial least squares; Kullback–Leibler divergence; Network security.

1. Introduction

Through collecting information of operating system, application program, network packet, and so on, the intrusion detection system detects the behaviors which violate security policies or endanger the safety of the system. A successful intrusion detection system can not only enable the system administrator to understand any changes in the entire network system, but also provide support for the development of network security policy. The strategy and scale of intrusion detection system should change based on the change in the network threat, system structure and security needs.

At present, there are many techniques for intrusion detection, and from the perspective of detection target, which can be divided into: the host-based IDS[1,

* Corresponding author.

2], the network-based IDS[3] and the host-network-based detection system [4];from the perspective of detection content, which can be divided into: anomaly behavior-based detection and attack mode-based misuse detection, behavior-attack mode-based detection and the detection of privilege program execution [5], etc. from the perspective of technology adopted, such as statistical methods[6], artificial intelligence method, including naive Bayesian classification[7], data mining, expert system, neural network, artificial immune system, Petri network, Markov chain, hidden Markov model (HMM), autonomous Agent, mobile Agent, machine learning and other technologies. Intrusion detection system has developed new technologies to adapt to the new environment in the face of high speed and large scale network needs. This paper has conducted the intrusion behavior detection by using regression analysis and partial least squares (PLS) in the prediction theory and improved the convergence conditions of partial least squares, the study has used the Kullback - Leibler divergence as the criteria for normal and abnormal behaviors, and thus more accurately and quickly detected network intrusions.

2. Regression Fitting and Limitations of Partial Least Squares

Partial least squares regression analysis adopts the component extraction method, to find the comprehensive variable which can best show the original data information from variable X as the main feature information F. And the basis to extract feature information is the original variable information contained is the largest. That is $Var(F) \rightarrow max$. Partial least squares is used for intrusion detection, the various fields in network protocol packets are taken as independent variables, the detection results are taken as the dependent variables. Due to the high multiple correlation of the field variables network protocol themselves, so the partial least squares are used for regression analysis, and the protocol field variables and regression coefficient of detection results are obtained, in this way the corresponding intrusion detection model can be established. Because the detection results are used to identify the intrusion behavior, the detection model in this study adopts the partial least-squares regression of single variable.

$F_0(F_0 \in R^n)$ is the standard variation of the dependent variable y, $E_0$is the standard matrix of X independent variable set. According to the principle of partial least squares regression, firstly, the components $u_1$is extracted from F_0, $u_1=F_0c_1$,$||c_1|| = 1$; Then, the components $t_1$is extracted from it, $t_1=E_0w_1$,$||w_1|| = 1$. since C_1 is a invariant, so $c_1=1$, $u_1=F0$. For the solution of partial least squares, it is needed to make covariance between U_1 and T_1be the maximum. Namely,

$$Cov(t_1, u_1) = \sqrt{Var(t_1)Var(u_1)}r(t_1, u_1) \rightarrow max. \qquad (1)$$

It can be obtained through the iterative calculation

$$E_i = t_{i+1}p_{i+1}^T + E_{i+1}F_i = t_{i+1}r_{i+1} + F_{i+1}. \quad (2)$$

Wherein, p_1, r_1 are the regression coefficient, and

$$p_{i+1} = \frac{E_i^T t_{i+1}}{\|t_{i+1}\|^2} r_{i+1} = \frac{F_i^T t_{i+1}}{\|t_{i+1}\|^2}. \quad (3)$$

This is noted as residual matrix:

$$E_{i+1} = E_i - t_{i+1}p_{i+1}^T = (E_{11}E_{12}, \dots, E_{1p}). \quad (4)$$

$$F_{i+1} = F_i - t_{i+1}r_{i+1}. \quad (5)$$

Finally, the regression model F_0 of t_h. is obtained,

$$F_0 = \sum_{i=1}^{m} r_i t_i + F_m. \quad (6)$$

Because of t_h is the linear combination of E_0, then the following can be obtained.

$$t_h = E_{h-1}w_h = E_0 \prod_{j=1}^{h-1}\left(I - w_j p_j^T\right) w_h = E_0 w_h$$

$$Wherein, w_h = \prod_{j=1}^{h-1}\left(I - w_j p_j^T\right) w_h. \quad (7)$$

Then,

$$F_0 = \sum_{i=1}^{m} r_i E_{i-1} w_h + F_m. \quad (8)$$

If $x_j = E_{0j}y = F_0$, then, $\alpha_j = \sum_{h=1}^{m} r_h w_{hj}$, wherein, w_{hj} is the jth component of w_h , $finally$,the regression equation is expressed as:

$$\hat{y} = \alpha_1 x_1 + \alpha_2 x_2 + \dots + \alpha_p x_p . \quad (9)$$

The regression coefficient of x_j is $\alpha_j = \sum_{h=1}^{m} r_h w_{hj}$, here, the regression coefficient is the parameters of the model. From the calculation process of partial least squares regression, The greater the contribution of parameter variable X_j in constructing feature component t_h $(thegrreaterthew_{hj})$, the greater the role of t_h in the interpretation of the detection result y (and the greater, the r_h), then x_j has the greater coefficient in the final partial least square regression model, the greater the impact is.

From the solution process of partial least squares regression coefficients, the method has good regression ability, and does not need too many samples, which is especially suitable for those situations with difficult data acquisition, incomplete information. But in the network intrusion detection, the correlation between the protocol fields and the variable sets does not fully obey Markoff Gauss's assumption, and the traditional partial least squares will lead to the a higher deviation of the regression parameters, resulting in the decrease of the detection accuracy. Therefore, the Kullback-Leibler divergence is introduced in this study to represent the residuals, the Kullback-Leibler divergence is adopted to measure the difference between the two matrices, to strengthen the constraints of partial least squares regression analysis, to ensure the accuracy of the regression parameters, and to improve the detection accuracy.

3. Partial Least Squares of Kullback-Leibler Divergence Is Used for Intrusion Detection

The Kullback Leibler divergence is introduced in partial least squares to extract the difference between the independent variable set X and the feature vectors. The iterative calculation gradually reduces the difference between the above two. When the appropriate threshold is reached, the independent variable set is regarded to approximately fit the dependent variable, and the fitting coefficient is the model parameters we need to solve. Here, we define two probability distribution functions *p(x)* and Kullback (x) Q - Leibler divergence as follows:

$$D(p \parallel q) = \sum_{x \in X} p(x) log_2 \frac{p(x)}{q(x)}. \quad (10)$$

Wherein, *X* refers to the set of all possible events, *p(x)* and *q(x)* refer to the probability density functions. Kullback–Leibler divergence does not satisfy triangle inequality conditions, namely,$D(p \parallel q) \neq D(q \parallel p)$, and the value is greater than or equal to 0, when it is equal to 0, the two sets are considered to contain the same information.

In order to demonstrate and analyze the solving process of the Kullback Leibler - divergence for partial least squares regression parameters, the derivation process is further given. It can be known according to Equations (4) (5), residual matrix is the product of independent variable minus the ingredients extracted and the regression coefficient, after the Kullback Leibler divergence is introduced, the residual is represented as:

$$E_{i+1} = D\left(E_i \parallel t_{i+1} p_{i+1}^T\right) = \sum_{x \in X} E_i log_2 \frac{\|E_i\|_F}{\|t_{i+1} p_{i+1}^T\|_F}. \quad (11)$$

$$F_{i+1} = D(F_i \parallel t_{i+1} r_{i+1}) = \sum_{x \in X} F_i log_2 \frac{\|F_i\|_F}{\|t_{i+1} r_{i+1}\|_F}. \quad (12)$$

And the weight of the component w_{i+1} is

$$\frac{E_i^T(t_{i+1}p_{i+1}^T)}{\|E_i^T(t_{i+1}p_{i+1}^T)\|_F} = \frac{1}{\sum_{j=1}^{p} Cov^2(E_{ij,}(t_{i+1}p_{i+1}^T)_i)} \begin{pmatrix} Cov(E_{i1,}(t_{i+1}p_{i+1}^T)_i) \\ Cov(E_{i2,}(t_{i+1}p_{i+1}^T)_i) \\ \vdots \\ Cov(E_{ip,}(t_{i+1}p_{i+1}^T)_i) \end{pmatrix}. \quad (13)$$

Wherein, $t_{i+1} = E_i w_{i+1}$, and the regression coefficient is finally obtained as follows:

$$\alpha_j = \sum_{h=1}^{m} r_h w_{hj}^* = \frac{F_{h-1}^T t_h}{\|t_h\|_F} w_{hj}^* \quad (14)$$

$w_{hj}^*$is the jth weight of w_h^*. In intrusion detection, the greater the regression coefficient of partial least squares means the more obvious the feature vector of the intrusion behavior, and it plays a greater decisive role for anomaly detection.

4. Experiments and Analyses

This experiment used the KDD CUP99, the data set conducted an intrusion detection in MIT Lincoln laboratory to evaluate the project in 1998 America's Defense Advanced Research Project Agency (DARPA).The data set contains TCPdump network connection and system audit data in nine weeks, and simulates various types of users, a variety of network traffic and attack means, making it just be like a real network environment. The raw data acquired by the TCPdump are divided into two parts: training data in 7 weeks, which probably contains more than 5000000 network connection records, and the detection data in the remaining 2 weeks may contain 2000000 network connection records. The data set contains a total of 4 major categories of network attacks: (1)Denial-of-Service (DoS):attempts to illegally interrupt or interfere with the normal operation of the host or network;(2)Remote to Local (R2L) : unauthorized access from remote host; (3)User to Root (U2R): local unauthorized users' unauthorized access to local super users or administrator's privileges; (4)Surveillance or Probe: Illegally scan the host or network, look for loopholes, and search the system configuration or network topology.

Table 1 shows the effect of the partial least square method based on KL divergence and other algorithms in the detection of CUP99 KDD data. We randomly divide seven subsets of data and then respectively detect the training time and the detection time. From the table, it can be seen that the method proposed in this paper is lower than those of other methods in training time and detection time. This is because the partial least squares regression is used, and the construction of the model and the fitting time is fast, so the detection time is short.

Table 2 shows the detection rate and false positive rate of the method used in this study and other methods. It can be seen that the detection rate of the method in this study for probe and DoS is slightly lower than other methods. Other detection results are better than other methods.

Table 1 Training time and detection time

k- nearest neighbor		C.45 Decision tree algorithm		Naive Bayesian classification algorithm		Partial least squares based on KL divergence	
Training time (s)	Detection time (s)	Training time (s)	Detection time(s)	Training time (s)	Detection time (s)	Training time(s)	Detection time(s)
1274	368	3223	589	1094	357	1036	297
783	218	1857	379	627	199	731	127
924	305	1546	352	705	218	911	217
831	289	2051	328	732	226	801	177
902	274	1783	419	828	195	893	163
857	265	2311	425	683	208	847	186
914	257	1903	388	746	233	847	193

Table 2 Detection results of intrusion detection

Detection type		normal	Probe	Dos	U2R	R2L
k- nearest neighbor	Detection rate (%)	98.27	96.31	93.52	87.32	97.73
	False positive rate (%)	0.8	1.05	1.34	2.53	0.92
C.45 Decision tree algorithm	Detection rate (%)	98.59	97.42	98.74	85.51	97.92
	False positive rate (%)	0.95	0.97	1.02	2.43	0.87
Naïve Bayesian classification algorithm	Detection rate (%)	99.03	97.68	95.79	90.58	98.01
	False positive rate (%)	0.84	0.94	1.12	1.23	0.97
Partial least squares based on KL divergence	Detection rate (%)	98.59	96.06	94.51	93.26	98.74
	False positive rate (%)	1.07	1.21	0.93	2.27	0.93

5. Conclusions

In this paper, a partial least square based on KL divergence used in intrusion detection is put forward, and the method introduced the KL divergence in the residue calculation of partial least square, and the divergence is used to represent the difference between the two quantities. This weakens the multiple correlation of the field variable of the network data set, accelerates the convergence rate and improves the efficiency and accuracy of intrusion detection. Because the KL divergence does not satisfy the triangle inequality, and it is not symmetric for the difference measure, so the follow-up study is needed to demonstrate the effect of the asymmetry of the divergence on the detection accuracy.

Acknowledgments

This work was supported by the National Natural Science Foundation of China(61303227),the Fundamental Research Funds for the Central Universities (XDJK2014C039, XDJK2016C045), Post Doctoral Fund of Southwestern University(swu1114033).

Reference

1. Sufatrio, and R. H. C. Yap, "Improving host-based IDS with argument abstraction to prevent mimicry attacks," Recent Advances in Intrusion Detection, vol. 3858, pp. 146-164, 2006.
2. G. Creech, and J. K. Hu, "A Semantic Approach to Host-Based Intrusion Detection Systems Using Contiguous and Discontiguous System Call Patterns," Ieee Transactions on Computers, vol. 63, no. 4, pp. 807-819, Apr, 2014.
3. D. Joo, T. Hong, and I. Han, "The neural network models for IDS based on the asymmetric costs of false negative errors and false positive errors," Expert Systems with Applications, vol. 25, no. 1, pp. 69-75, Jul, 2003.
4. M. Andreolini, M. Colajanni, and M. Marchetti, "A collaborative framework for intrusion detection in mobile networks," Information Sciences, vol. 321, pp. 179-192, Nov 10, 2015.
5. I. Corona, G. Giacinto, and F. Roli, "Adversarial attacks against intrusion detection systems: Taxonomy, solutions and open issues," Information Sciences, vol. 239, pp. 201-225, Aug 1, 2013.

6. S. Ganapathy, K. Kulothungan, S. Muthurajkumar, M. Vijayalakshmi, P. Yogesh, and A. Kannan, "Intelligent feature selection and classification techniques for intrusion detection in networks: a survey," Eurasip Journal on Wireless Communications and Networking, Nov 27, 2013.
7. A. Broumand, M. S. Esfahani, B. J. Yoon, and E. R. Dougherty, "Discrete optimal Bayesian classification with error-conditioned sequential sampling," Pattern Recognition, vol. 48, no. 11, pp. 3766-3782, Nov, 2015.

Research on Security of MD5 Algorithm Application

Xiao-ling ZHENG

Information School, Capital University Of Economics And Business, Beijing, 100070, China
E-mail: zxl@cueb.edu.cn

With rapid development of modern computer network technology and the wide application of electronic business and electronic government services, encryption technology is an essential component of information security and research efforts on encryption algorithm has gained importance. This paper introduces the origins and principle of MD5 algorithm and analyzes the collision issue in MD5 algorithm and the impact of security breaches in the field of information security. Thus the detailed methods to improve MD5 algorithm application security are subsequently proposed.

Keywords: MD5; Encryption algorithm; Collision attack.

1. Introduction

Since Rivest developed MD2 algorithm in 1989, new round research of people to encryption algorithm was started, and then MD3 and MD4 algorithm was pushed out. In order to enhance the security of algorithm and satisfy information security requirement, the fairly mature MD5 algorithm is proposed.

MD5 is the English abbreviation of message digest, and was jointly developed by MIT computer science lab and Rivest of RSA Data Security Inc in the early of 1990s. MD5 is always deemed as a very secure encryption algorithm and is mainly applied to information security field as digital signature and password certification, etc. Nevertheless the research shows that, MD5 algorithm can be attached and broken through via collision, security of MD5 encryption algorithm application is challenged. This paper shall introduce MD5 algorithm process, analyzes the collision issue in MD5 algorithm and the impact of security hole to information security field. On this basis, the details measures and methods to improve MD5 algorithm application security are proposed.

2. Encryption Principle of MD5 Algorithm

MD5 algorithm processes the inputted information via 512-bits grouping, each group is also divided into sixteen 32-bit sub-groups, after a series of processing, output of algorithm is composed of four 32-bit groups, after cascading of these four 32-bit groups, a 128-bit hashed value shall be created.

In MD5 algorithm, the information is at first filled, so that the result of the bit length deriving remainder from 512 is 448. The filling method is to fill a 1 and many 0 after the information, and the filling shall not be stopped until above conditions are satisfied; after this result, the information length before filling (presented by 64 bit binary) shall be enclosed. In MD5, four 32-bit are called integer parameter of linked variable, and they are respectively A=0x01234567, B=0x89abcdef, C=0xfedcba98, D=0x76543210. After these four linked variables are set well, four rounds circulated calculations are started, the frequency of circulation is the quantity of 512 bit information grouping in the information.

Above four linked variables are duplicated to another four variables, A to a, B to b, C to c, D to d. The main circulation has four rounds, with 16 times' operation for each round, at each operation three of a, b, c, d are conducted by nonlinear function operation by one time, then all results acquired are added by the fourth variable, and all results are loop-shifted by a variable number toward right, and added by one of a, b, c, or d, finally the result shall substitute one of a, b, c, or d. The following are four nonlinear functions used for each operation, with one function for each round.

$$F(X,Y,Z) = (X \wedge Y) \vee (\overline{X} \wedge Z)$$

$$G(X,Y,Z) = (X \wedge Z) \vee (Y \wedge \overline{Z})$$

$$H(X,Y,Z) = X \oplus Y \oplus Z$$

$$I(X,Y,Z) = Y \oplus (X \vee \overline{Z})$$

Wherein, $\oplus$ is XOR, $\wedge$ is and, $\vee$ is or, - is opposite sign.

After completing all this, A, B, C, D are respectively added by a, b, c, d. Then the next grouping data are used to continue with operation algorithm, finally the cascading of A, B, C, D is outputted, A is low bit, D is high bit, DCBA constitutes the 128 bit output result.

3. Defect and Impact of MD5 Algorithm

The nature of MD5 algorithm is a Hash function. Hash function compresses the information of any length into fixed length value via hash algorithm, and this is called message digest. At present the attack to Hash function mainly comes from collision attack, i.e., to find to different information digests with same Hash function value. E.g., for Hash(M1)=H, a M2 is found to derive Hash(M2)=H, M1 and M2 are called a pair of collision. The collision issue of MD5 algorithm seriously threats the information system security, and incurs extremely great impact to information security field of electronic business, electronic government affairs, as well as password certification, etc.

3.1. *Impact to security of electronic business*

In order to protect privacy information of customer and avoid network attack in the electronic business system, usually the ID information submitted by user is done by a series of operations as formatting, encryption and digital signature, etc, and MD5 algorithm computing message digest is used to prevent falsifying, and form a digital certificate, and user ID is identified by the digital certificate issued by the user. The user's digital certificate can be imported to client, when the client proposes login request to server, the system automatically derives user ID information from digital certificate, and whether the certificate is falsified is judged by computing information digest. During each trading, the system only needs to verify the digital certificate, usually it does not need to input user name and password. Since many years this method is also deemed secure, if MD5 algorithm is broken through, the digital certificate can be falsified.

3.2. *Impact to security of electronic government affairs*

The electronic government affair is that, the government authority adopts modern computer and network technology to shift the management and service function to the network to complete it, and at the same time realize recombination and optimization to government organization structure and work process, and surpass restriction of time, space and department division, and provide to whole society the overall management and service with top quality, high efficiency, transparent specification. Usually it shall have the main functions as public affair mail, receiving and dispatching document management, state documents approval, department brief report, etc, as well as auxiliary functions as schedule arrangement, individual affair management, archive management, official document signature and stamp, etc. The electronic document of the government presents authority and has the legal and administrative effect, if the document is changed during online transmission process, e.g., if the "not" in the "not approve" in the examined official document is removed, the consequence shall be unthinkable. At present, in order to prevent falsifying in the electronic government affair system, usually MD5 algorithm shall be used to create message digest of these electronic official document when transmitting and saving these electronic official documents, once the electronic official document is falsified spitefully, when the electronic official document is started up, the message digest shall be re-created to check and find the falsified one, and then the falsified official document shall lose the effect. Also, professor Wang Xiao-yun theoretically describes the security hole of this method for ensuring completeness of electronic official document.

3.3. *Impact to password certification security*

MD5 is an irreversible encryption algorithm, thus the data after MD5 algorithm encryption cannot be decrypted, the data cannot be really decrypted until the original information is re-inputted, and is once more processed by MD5 algorithm to derive the same message digest and it is once more identified by the system. Therefore MD5 algorithm shall be used to encrypt system password or user password of Web application, and the message digest acquired is saved in the database to prevent the consequence that the leaked password saved in the database is directly acquired by the attacker. It is obvious that once MD5 algorithm is broken through, the security in case of password certification cannot be guaranteed.

4. The Measures and Methods to Improve MD5 Algorithm Application Security

MD5 algorithm is mainly used for digital signature and password certification, etc. MD5 algorithm is improved to essentially enhance the security of application. Nevertheless for the password saved in the database via MD5 message digest form, the security can also suffer threat of dictionary attack in addition to the possible breakthrough of MD5 algorithm. The attacker shall not only have password dictionary with massive data volume, but also establish many MD5 original text/cipher text comparison database, to quickly find MD5 cipher text of ordinary password, this is the high efficiency approach to decode MD5 cipher text. In order to improve security of MD5 algorithm in the application of password certification, etc, the encryption method can be improved on the basis of MD5 algorithm.

4.1. *MD5 algorithm based improvement to encryption method*

MD5 algorithm processing process can be changed, or intervene information shall be added in the user password, so that cipher text information in MD5 algorithm cipher text database is no longer the simple MD5 message digest value.

4.1.1. *Transformation to MD5 processing process*

(1) The frequency of MD5 processing process is added, the basic thinking is that, a user password in need of MD5 encryption is conducted by two times or many times encryption, i.e., the 128 bit message digest value is once more conducted by MD5 computing.

(2) The message digest value is intercepted. The basic thinking is that, at first the user password is conducted by one time MD5 computing, to derive MD5 message digest value; then some values of them are selected to once more conduct MD5 computing, and derive the final result.

(3) Split message digest value. The basic thinking is, at first the user password is conducted by one time MD5 computing, to derive MD5 message digest value H; then H is divided into two 64-bit groups of left and right, and then it is again respectively conducted by MD5 computing, to derive related message digest value, which is respectively presented by HL and HR; HR and HL is then (front and rear) connected into a character string, to once more conduct MD5 computing to it, and derive the final result.

(4) Enclosed with self defined encryption algorithm. The basic thinking is, at first the self defined encryption algorithm is used to encrypt the user password to derive the cipher text; then the cipher text is conducted by MD5 computing to derive MD5 message digest value. The self defined encryption algorithm is endless, e.g., the data in need of encryption is grouped by taking ten characters

as one group (if it is less than 10, it shall be supplemented by blank); each character shall correspond to single bit cipher key (if the cipher key is more than 10 it shall be intercepted, if it is less than 10 it shall be supplemented by 0); each bit shall be of character interchange subject to corresponding cipher key value and the position of the value (e.g., the first bit cipher key value is 2, the first bit character is interchanged with second bit character), it is thus interchanged until 10 bits are all interchanged as per related cipher key value.

4.1.2. *Transformation to MD5 encryption content*

(1) Enclosed with specific character string. The basic thinking is, the user password is added by specific prefix or postfix, including number, alphabet and specific sign, etc, e.g., a segment specific character string "!m%T#?@)>" is added before the password, or a string of random code (such as verification code), the user password is lengthened up to over 20 bit, and then it is encrypted via MD5 algorithm.

(2) The character string determined by additional content. The basic thinking is, the inputted user name and system time is deemed as additional information, then "user name+ user password+ system time" is conducted by MD5 algorithm processing.

(3) The random character string automatically created by the additional system. The basic thinking is, the system automatically creates a random character string R, when the user inputs the password, the password and random character string R are respectively conducted by MD5 encryption computing, and then two cipher texts acquired are computed as per bit.

4.2. *Improvement to MD5 algorithm*

The above mentioned is the method to improve password security without modifying MD5 algorithm, if the user password data is exposed due to some leaks, the method can greatly increase the difficulty of breaking through the user password, to improve the security of MD5 for password certification application, etc. Nevertheless for security threat to applications as digital signature and password certification, etc, the most effective, reliable and convenient method to prevent the collision attack is to improve MD5 algorithm itself. The characteristic of this improvement method is that, the data before and after encryption are very similar, but it cannot be broken through. The basic thinking is to modify the initial value of MD5 buffer register.

The key of MD5 algorithm is the four buffer registers of A, B, C, D, their initial values are: A=0x01234567, B=0x89abcdef, C=0xfedcba98, D=0x76543210. These four values can be the initial seed, during a series of also, or computing, etc, they play a very critical role. The four values of A, B, C, D are hexadecimal 4*8=32 bit, the probability space of breakthrough is calculated, the possibility of breakthrough shall be smaller provided that there are more changes. In fact, if the initial value is slightly changed, e.g., one bit of them is changed (for example, D=0x76543210 is changed to D=0x76545210), new MD5 has algorithm shall be created without changing other part of algorithm.

5. Conclusion

MD5 algorithm possesses an important position in the information security field application. For MD5 algorithm, at present a pair of collision can be found within fairly short time, provided that effective security measure is taken, e.g., MD5 algorithm is improved, or it is of deformation use, actual application of MD5 algorithm shall not be impacted irrespective of whether MD5 is broken through or MD5 collision is found. Therefore MD5 algorithm also has wide application space in the aspects of digital signature and password protection, etc.

References:

1. Wei Xiaoling, Research and application of MD5 encryption algorithm, Information technology, 2010 In Chinese

2. Gao Hongbo, Su Ping, MD5 algorithm and the improvement during user password encryption application, Logistics technology, 2010 (17)

   In Chinese

3. Yi Jun, QiuMeixian, Design of user password certification scheme on the basis of ACSII code and random number, Computer and digital engineering, 2011 In Chinese

4. Lin Zongchao, C# based MD5 encryption algorithm application, Changchun Polytechnic University Journal (natural science version), 2011, 36(2) In Chinese

5. Luo Heping, Application of MD5 encryption algorithm in the software registration code protection mode, Fujian Computer, 2011, 27(8) In Chinese

6. Zheng Xiaosong, Chu Lili, Zhang Tianle, Improvement and application of MD5 encryption algorithm, Digital technology and application, 2012 (8) In Chinese

7. Sun Yang, System security login research on the basis of MD5 encryption algorithm, Computer CD software and application , 2013 (6) In Chinese

8. Xu Qi, MD5 encryption algorithm research, Fujian Computer, 2014, 30(3) In Chinese

9. Luo Zhengping, Lin Yufeng, Improvement of Tornado code duplication algorithm on the basis of MD5 encryption, Zhejiang Normal university Journal (natural science version), 2015 (1) In Chinese

10. Wang Xiong, Zhu Zhixiang, Xu Huihui, MD5 encryption reverse breakthrough and security improvement, Journal of Xi'an College of Arts and Sciences (natural science version), 2014, 17(1) In Chinese

The Establishment and Evaluation of the Campus Network Security System Quantification and Index System Based on ABC Screening Method

Lei-lei DENG

Institute of information technology, Jilin Agricultural University, Changchun, Jilin Province, China
E-mail: deng_ll@163.com

Bing LIU

School of computer and information technology, Beijing Jiaotong University, Beijing, China
E-mail: 342687048@qq.com

With the rapid development of information technology, the Internet has become an important communications tool for information sharing. However this inevitably brings about a security risk and thus network security has gained significance in current information technology research. Therefore, an evaluation system of network security indicators is now an essential technique. This thesis focuses on the specific issues of network security evaluation using the ABC method and subsequent analysis of each influencing factor of campus network security evaluation according to the effects index is conducted according to the size of weights and networking safety evaluation of the fuzzy comprehensive evaluation method.

Keywords: Network security; ABC algorithm; AHP; Fuzzy comprehensive evaluation.

1. Introduction

With the development of computer networks and widespread popularity of Internet, information has become the core of modern social life. Whether the network security we established is reasonable and scientific concerns its ability on evaluation, which related to whether we can improve network security level by evaluating stability. If we want to establish a sound, reasonable and scientific evaluation, we should follow the guiding principles of science feasibility, comparability and stability.

You can delete our sample text and replace it with the text of your own contribution to the proceedings. However we recommend that you keep an initial version of this file for reference.

2. Selection of Indexes and Determination of Weights

2.1. *The principle of ABC method*

This paper will introduce a large scale AHP decision operation method which is simple and effective called ABC screening method. Using this method we can simplify the evaluation and calculation process of large scale AHP.ABC screening method is based on Pareto chart which is an effective chart method used to find a major factor from a number of factors.

The left vertical axis stands for either weight value or absolute value while the right vertical axis stands for cumulative frequency value expressed by percentage. Abscissa indicates the various factors, sorted by weight and effect in the shape of rectangular from left to right, affecting the problem. The curve we draw according to the numbers on left vertical axis and the cumulative percentage on right vertical axis is called Pareto curve.

2.2. *Principles and procedures of AHP*

Steps of AHP:

(1)Determine the overall target through a deep understanding of the system.

(2)Establish a multilayered hierarchy structure, separate the system into different classes according to target and function.

(3)Compare each pair of elements on the same layer treating an element on the last layer as standard. Determine their relative importance according to the judgment scale then establish pairwise comparison judgment matrix in the following format.

Table 1 Judgment matrix

A_k	B_1	B_2	......	B_n
B_1	b_{11}	b_{12}	......	b_{1n}
B_2	b_{21}	b_{22}	......	b_{2n}
...	...	...		...
B_n	b_{n1}	b_{n2}	......	b_{nn}

Obviously, any judgment matrix should satisfy

$$b_{ii} = 1, b_{ij} = \frac{1}{b_{ji}} (i, j = 1,2,...,n). \quad (1)$$

(4)single hierarchical sorting

The so-called single sorting refers to the order of importance of the various factors on upper layer. It is represented by the eigenvectors of judgment matrix.

2.3. *Application of ABC method*

In this paper, we adopt expert scoring approach to calculate weight value of indicators on the same layer in the form of survey table judged by experts. We get the simplified model of this evaluation system by ignoring factors in B and C classes.

We gain average of weight by applying ABC method on the first layer's evaluating indicator and asking 10 experts to do questionnaire survey. Taking an expert's survey result for example to calculate weight of optimal index.

Table 2. Optimal index of a layer

indicators	B1	B2	B3	B4	B5	B6	W
B1	1	3	7	4	7	5	0.4403
B2	1/3	1	3	1/3	5	1/3	0.1055
B3	1/3	1	1	1/3	3	1/3	0.1410
B4	1/4	3	5	1	5	2	0.2128
B5	1/7	1/5	1	1/5	1	1/5	0.0376
B6	1/5	3	5	1/2	5	1	0.1628

By using the analytic hierarchy method we get: CR=0.0707, W = (0.4403, 0.1055, 0.1410, 0.2128, 0.0376, 0.1628) CR<0.1.It can clearly be seen that it is a effective investigation as the consistency of this expert is good. Do the same analysis on other 9 experts' questionnaire and then we get the average weight of each index: $\overline{W}$ =(0.4419,0.1132,0.1453,0.2346,0.0308,0.1738), we can get ABC chart of index on this layer based on this data.

We can know from the figure that physical security belongs to class C factors, so this index and its sub-index can be ignored. In the meanwhile, do normalization and we get the normalized weight W' =(0.3586,0.1170,0.1015, 0.2425,0.1804).

Apply the same processing method on the second layer's evaluating indicator. Then we screen operational safety indicators, data security indicators, system security strategy indicators, safety technical measure indicators, safety measure indicators and calculate their weights (all take one expert's survey for example),at last we get simplified index system as follows:

Table 3. Simplified m of optimal evaluation index

First index	weight	Second index	weight
Operation security	ω_1 =0.1170	Access control measures	ω_{11}=0.3523
		Audit tracking measures	ω_{12} =0.4828
		Risk analysis	ω_{13} =0.1649
Data information security	ω_2 =0.1015	Information transmission security	ω_{21} =0.4711
		Data Integrity	ω_{22} =0.2587
		Data encryption	ω_{23} =0.2702
System security strategy	ω_3 =0.1804	Operating system database access control measures	ω_{31} =0.3048
		User authentication	ω_{32} =0.3908
		Data backup	ω_{33} =0.3044
Security technology measures	ω_4 =0.3586	Anti-virus measures	ω_{41} =0.3797
		Server backup	ω_{42} =0.2963
		Anti-hacker measures	ω_{43} =0.3240
Security systems and measures	ω_5 =0.2425	Organization	ω_{51} =0.6112
		Incident handling plan	ω_{52} =0.3888

In this paper, we use the weight gained from ABC method as index weight.

According to the theory of fuzzy mathematics, we evaluate the network security in order to determine the network security level.

3. Evaluate Campus Network Security System on the Basis of the Fuzzy Comprehensive Evaluation Method

Fuzzy quantitative evaluation method determine the user's satisfaction degree to the network security. Given the existence of fuzziness in the process of network security evaluation, we use the knowledge of fuzzy comprehensive evaluation and quantitative indicators of network security evaluation to define new weight vector and establish a mathematical model of fuzzy quantitative evaluation via AHP which combine qualitative and quantitative, systematic, hierarchical. We use this fuzzy comprehensive evaluation method to make network security evaluation more fair, rational, scientific.

3.1. *Completing fuzzy comprehensive evaluation of network security level need to go through the following steps:*

(1)Select factor set U and review set V

Factor U={operation security(u1),data information security(u2),system security strategy(u3),security technology measures(u4),security system measure(u5)} evaluation has four grades which means that review set V ={very safe(v1),safe(v2),basic safe(v3),not safe(v4)}

(2)Determine the single factor evaluation vector

Factor U={operation security(u1),data information security(u2),system security strategy(u3),security technology measures(u4),security system measure(u5)} evaluation has four grades which means that review set V ={very safe(v1),safe(v2),basic safe(v3),not safe(v4)}

$$R_1 = \begin{pmatrix} 0.2 & 0.3 & 0.3 & 0.2 \\ 0.2 & 0.3 & 0.3 & 0.2 \\ 0.1 & 0.2 & 0.3 & 0.4 \end{pmatrix} \quad R_2 = \begin{pmatrix} 0.1 & 0.1 & 0.3 & 0.5 \\ 0.1 & 0.3 & 0.5 & 0.1 \\ 0.2 & 0.5 & 0.2 & 0.1 \end{pmatrix} \quad R_3 = \begin{pmatrix} 0.2 & 0.3 & 0.4 & 0.1 \\ 0.3 & 0.2 & 0.4 & 0.1 \\ 0 & 0.1 & 0.1 & 0.8 \end{pmatrix} \quad R_4 = \begin{pmatrix} 0.1 & 0.1 & 0.2 & 0.6 \\ 0.4 & 0.3 & 0.2 & 0.1 \\ 0.0 & 0.1 & 0.2 & 0.7 \end{pmatrix}$$

$$R_5 = \begin{pmatrix} 0.2 & 0.2 & 0.3 & 0.3 \\ 0.2 & 0.2 & 0.3 & 0.3 \end{pmatrix}$$

Then calculate basing on fuzzy comprehensive evaluation, the process is as follows:

$$\begin{pmatrix} 0.2 & 0.3 & 0.3 & 0.2 \\ 0.2 & 0.3 & 0.3 & 0.2 \\ 0.1 & 0.2 & 0.3 & 0.4 \end{pmatrix} = (0.19 \quad 0.28 \quad 0.31 \quad 0.23)$$

$$B_2 = A_2 \circ R_2 = (0.4711 \quad 0.2587 \quad 0.2702) \begin{pmatrix} 0.1 & 0.1 & 0.3 & 0.5 \\ 0.1 & 0.3 & 0.5 & 0.1 \\ 0.2 & 0.5 & 0.2 & 0.1 \end{pmatrix} = (0.13 \quad 0.26 \quad 0.32 \quad 0.29)$$

$$B_3 = A_3 \circ R_3 = (0.3048 \quad 0.3908 \quad 0.3044) \begin{pmatrix} 0.2 & 0.3 & 0.4 & 0.1 \\ 0.3 & 0.2 & 0.4 & 0.1 \\ 0 & 0.1 & 0.1 & 0.8 \end{pmatrix} = (0.18 \quad 0.2 \quad 0.31 \quad 0.31)$$

$$B_4 = A_4 \circ R_4 = (0.3797 \quad 0.2963 \quad 0.3240) \begin{pmatrix} 0.1 & 0.1 & 0.2 & 0.6 \\ 0.4 & 0.3 & 0.2 & 0.1 \\ 0.0 & 0.1 & 0.2 & 0.7 \end{pmatrix} = (0.16 \quad 0.16 \quad 0.2 \quad 0.48)$$

$$B_5 = A_5 \circ R_5 = (0.6112 \quad 0.3888) \begin{pmatrix} 0.2 & 0.2 & 0.3 & 0.3 \\ 0.2 & 0.2 & 0.3 & 0.3 \end{pmatrix} = (0.2 \quad 0.2 \quad 0.3 \quad 0.3)$$

$$B = A \circ R = (0.1170 \quad 0.1015 \quad 0.1804 \quad 0.3586 \quad 0.2425)$$

$$\begin{pmatrix} 0.19 & 0.28 & 0.31 & 0.23 \\ 0.13 & 0.26 & 0.32 & 0.29 \\ 0.18 & 0.2 & 0.31 & 0.31 \\ 0.16 & 0.16 & 0.2 & 0.48 \\ 0.2 & 0.2 & 0.3 & 0.3 \end{pmatrix} = (0.17 \quad 0.20 \quad 0.27 \quad 0.36)$$

4. Relevant Countermeasures of Improving the Network Security

Lists According to the structure characteristics of the JiLin Agricultural University campus network and security risk it faces, combined with quantitative results of network security evaluation system, authors think that the whole school digital campus network security system should include the following parts: Network security connection and isolation, network monitoring, network virus prevention, network security vulnerability scanning, identity authentication system. In the design of school network security system, we use the systemic, overall security strategy. By means of network isolation we effectively reduce the propagation of threats (virus, horses) and improve the security of information. In order to realize partition isolation management of whole campus network, we first use firewall to isolate campus network and external network, then isolate campus entrance network with network segments like teaching area, office area, dormitory area partitively by using routing and firewall.

5. Conclusions

According to the quantitative evaluation results of network security index we design security system of JiLin Agricultural University digital campus network. This system uses firewall, intrusion detection, virtual private network, anti virus technology to achieve the construction of network security system. Although the campus network security system has a higher safety factor, It is far from absolutely safe. Factors that affect campus network's safety are constantly changing and attack mode of hackers and virus are constantly updating. The only way to ensure network safety is considering the real situation. Using the latest technological achievements in security technology, timely adjust security policies and strengthen safety management, then we can improve security of our network.

References

1. NI Xiao-Gang, F Cao, HJ Song. *Research on quality evaluation based on improved AHP algorithm for certain weapon.*(2011)
2. D Karaboga, B Basturk. *On the performance of artificial bee colony (ABC) algorithm.* (2008)
3. XW Wang, RZ Zou, M Huang. *ABC Supporting QoS Unicast Routing Scheme Based on Beehive Algorithm.*(2009)
4. LI Mudong,W Xiong,Q Liang.*Wireless Sensor Networks Node Localization Algorithm Based on Improved ABC Algorithm.*(2013)
5. HK Duan.*The Research of the Management of the Network Security in Higher Vocational School.*(2012)
6. W Stallings.*Network Security Essentials*.(2010).

A Secure and Efficient Certificateless Signature Scheme in the Standard Model

Hong-zhen DU

School of mathematics and Information Science, Baoji University of Arts and Sciences, Baoji, China
E-mail: hongzhendu@163.com

Certificateless public key cryptography is an attractive paradigm which combines advantages of both traditional public key cryptography and identity-based cryptography because it avoids using certificates and does not suffer from key escrow. In this paper, the author proposed a certificateless signature (CLS) scheme built upon bilinear pairings and proved its security in the standard model. The scheme turns out to be more efficient than other proposed CLS schemes in the standard model, and the signing algorithm needs no pairing operation while the reverse operation requires only three pairing computations.

Keywords: Certificateless public key cryptography; Certificateless signature; Standard model; Unforgeability.

1. Introduction

Identity-based public key cryptography (ID-PKC) was introduced by Shamir [1] in 1984. It avoids the certificate management problem in traditional PKC. However, there exists a drawback called private key escrow in an ID-PKC since it involves a Private Key Generator (PKG) who knows a user's private key. In 2003, Riyami and Paterson [2] introduced the notion of certificateless public key cryptography (CL-PKC), which is an intermediate between traditional PKC and ID-PKC. It can eliminate the certificate management problem in a traditional PKC and the private key escrow in ID-PKC.

There are a lot of fruits about CL-PKC, to name some [3-12]. Certificateless signature (CLS) is one of the most important security primitives in CL-PKC. Many CLS schemes [5-8] have been constucted and these schemes are provably secure in the random oracle model. However, it has been shown that when random oracles are instantiated with concrete hash functions, the resulting scheme may not be secure [9]. Recently, efforts have been made to construct CLS schemes in the standard model to overcome this problem. Liu et al. [10] proposed the first CLS scheme in the standard model. However, Xiong et al. [11] point out the scheme is insecure against the Type II adversary's attack. Yu et al. [12] proposed a CLS scheme without random oracles. Unfortunately, Yuan et al. [13] prove that the scheme is universally forgeable by both Type I and Type II adversaries.

This paper proposes an efficient CLS scheme in the standard model. The length of public key of a user in the scheme is only one group point, which is shorter than that of most existing certificateless schemes. It achieves higher efficiency because no pairing operation is needed in the signing algorithm while the reverse operation requires only three pairing computations.

2. Preliminaries

Let G_1 and G_2 be multiplicative cyclic groups of the same prime order p. A bilinear pairing is a map e: $G_1 \times G_2 \rightarrow G_2$ which satisfies the properties:

(1) **Bilinearity:** $e(u^a, v^b) = e(u, v)^{ab}$, for any $u, v \in G_1$ and $a, b \in Z_p^*$.

(2) **Non-degeneracy:** There exists $u, v \in G_1$, such that $e(u, v) \neq 1$.

(3) **Computability:** There is an efficient algorithm to get $e(u, v)$, for all $u, v \in G_1$.

The author will review two computational problems as follows:

–Computational Diffie-Hellman Problem (*CDHP*):

Given g^a, $g^b \in G_1$, for unknown values $a, b \in Z_p^*$, to output g^{ab}.

–Non pairing-based Generalized Bilinear Diffie-Hellman Problem (NGBDHP):

Given g^a, $g^b \in G_1$, for unknown values $a, b \in Z_p^*$, to output a tuple (g^{abc}, g^c), for $c \in Z_p^*$.

3. A Certificateless Signature Scheme in the Standard Model

3.1. *The basic scheme*

In this section, I present an efficient certificateless signature scheme which consists of the following five algorithms:

Setup: The KGC chooses groups G_1 and G_2 of same prime order p such that an admissible pairing e: $G_1 \times G_1 \rightarrow G_2$ can be constructed and picks a random generator $g \in G_1$. Then it picks a random $\alpha \in Z_p^*$ and computes $g_1 = g^{\alpha}$. Let $H_1 : \{0, 1\}^* \rightarrow (0, 1)^n$, H_2: $\{0, 1\}^* \rightarrow Z_p^*$ and H_3: $\{0, 1\}^* \rightarrow (0, 1)^l$ be three collision-resistant cryptographic hash functions (Integers n, l are the output lengths of hash functions H_1 and H_3, respectively). Also, it randomly chooses h, $v' \in G_1$ and a random n-length vector $U = (u_i)$, where $u_i \in G_1$ for $i=1,\ldots,n$ and a random l-length vector $V = (v_i)$, where $v_i \in G_1$, for $i=1,\ldots,l$. The published public parameters are *param*: $\{e, G_1, G_2, g, g_1, H_1, H_2, H_3, h, v', U, V\}$ and the master secret key is α.

Partial-Private-Key-Extract: Given an identity ID, the KGC picks a random value $R \in Z_p^*$ and computes $u = H_1(ID, R)$. Let $u[i]$ denote the ith bit of the bit-string u, and $\mu \subseteq \{1, \cdots, n\}$ be the set of all i for which $u[i] = 1$. Then the KGC computes $psk = (h^{H_2(ID,R)} \prod_{i \in \mu} u_i)^{\alpha}$ and sends psk and R to the user with ID.

UserKeyGen: Pick a random $x \in Z_p^*$ as the secret value and set the public key as $pk_{ID} = g_1^x$.

CL-Sign: Given a message, a signer's identity *ID*, partial private key and secret value pair (psk, x), this algorithm works as follows:

(1) Set $v = H_3(m)$ and let $v[i]$ be the ith of the bit-string v, and define $\upsilon \subseteq (1, \cdots, l)$ be the set of indices i such that $v[i] = 1$.

$$(\sigma_1, \sigma_2) = ((psk)^x (v' \prod_{i \in \upsilon} v_i)^r, g^r)$$

(2) Pick a random $r \in Z_p^*$ and compute.

Output the signature $S = < R \| \sigma_1 \| \sigma_2 >$.

Verify: Given a message-signature pair (m, S), a verifier performs as follows:

(1) Set $u = H_1(ID, R)$, $v = H_3(m)$.

(2) Accept (m, S) if and only if the following equation holds.

$$e(\sigma_1, g) = e((h^{H_2(ID,R)} \prod_{i\in\mu} u_i), pk_{ID}) e(v' \prod_{i\in\upsilon} v_i, \sigma_2).$$

3.2. *Security analysis*

Theorem 1. *The proposed CLS scheme is existentially unforgeable against adaptive chosen-message attack (EUF-CMA2) under the assumptions that the NGBDHP and CDHP are intractable.*

The theorem follows from Lemmas 1 and 2.

Lemma 1. *Assume that a EUF-CMA2 adversary A_1 has an advantage ε against the proposed scheme when running in a time t, making q_e queries to the Partial-Private-Key-Extract oracle, q_{pk} queries to the Public-Key-Extract oracle and q_s queries to the Signing oracle. Then there exists an algorithm C that can solve the NGBDHP with probability $\varepsilon' \geq \varepsilon / (4q_s(l+1))$,*

within a time $t' \leq t + O((nq_e + q_s(n+l))T_{mul} + (q_e + q_{pk} + q_s)T_{\exp})$ *, where T_{mul} and T_{exp} denote the costs of a multiplication and an exponentiation in G_1, respectively.*

Proof. Suppose *C* is given a challenge of a random instance of the *NGBDHP*:

Given g^a, $g^b \in G_1$, where values a, $b \in Z_p^*$ are unknown to *C*. *C*'s goal is to output two elements g^{abx}, $g^x \in G_1$, after interacting with A_1.

–Setup: Let $l_v = 2q_s$. *C* randomly chooses an integer k_v such that $0 \leq k_v \leq l$. Assume that $l_v(l+1) < p$ for given values q_s, k_v and l, then *C* randomly picks the following integers:

Pick a random $x' \in Z_p^*$ and compute $h = g^{x'}$. Choose x_i, $y_i \in Z_p$, for i=1,…,n, and let $X = \{x_i\}$ and $Y = \{y_i\}$. Pick $t' \in Z_{l_v}$, $w' \in Z_p$ and $t_i \in Z_{l_v}$, $w_i \in Z_p$, for i=1,…,l, and let $T=\{t_i\}$ and $W=\{w_i\}$.

For ease of analysis, we let $u = H_1(ID, R)$ for an identity ID and a random value R, and define $\mu \subseteq \{1, 2\ldots, n\}$ be the set of all i for which $u[i] = 1$. For a message m, we let $v = H_3(m)$ and define $\upsilon \subseteq \{1, 2..., l\}$ be the set of indices i such that $v[i] = 1$. Further we define the following functions.

$$F(u)=\sum_{i\in\mu}(-1)^{x_i}\ (\mathrm{mod}\ p)\ ,\ J(u)=\sum_{i\in\mu}y_i\ (\mathrm{mod}\ p)\ ,\ K(v)=t'+\sum_{i\in\upsilon}t_i-l_vk_v\ ,$$

$$L(v)=w'+\sum_{i\in\upsilon}w_i\ .$$

C sets public parameters *param* as follows:

$$h=g^{x'}\ ,\ g_1=g^a,\ u_i=(g^b)^{(-1)^{x_i}}g^{y_i}\ ,\ \text{for } i=1,\ldots,n.$$

$$v'=(g^b)^{t'-l_vk_v}g^{w'}\ ,\ v_i=(g^b)^{t_i}g^{w_i}\ ,\ \text{for } i=1,\ldots,l.$$

Obviously, the following equations hold:

$$\prod_{i\in\mu}u_i=(g^b)^{F(u)}g^{J(u)},\quad v'\prod_{i\in\upsilon}v_i=(g^b)^{K(v)}g^{L(v)}\ .$$

Return the public parameters *param* to A_1.

–Partial-Private-Key-Extract: If this query is on an identity ID, C performs as follows: Select a value $R\in Z_p$ such that $F(u)=0\ (\mathrm{mod}\ p)$ for $u=H_1(ID, R)$, and compute the partial private key as

$$psk=(h^{H_2(ID,R)}\prod_{i\in\mu}u_i)^a=(g^{x'H_2(ID,R)}(g^b)^{F(u)}g^{J(u)})^a=g_1^{x'H_2(ID,R)+J(u)}\ .$$

Then insert the triple (ID, psk, R) in a list psk^{list} and output psk and R.

–Public-Key-Extract: C keeps a list pk^{list} of user public key. If this query is on an identity ID, C returns the previously defined value if it exists. Otherwise, C chooses a random $x\in Z_p^*$ as the secret value, computes $pk_{ID}=g_1^x$, and inserts the tuple (ID, x, pk_{ID}) in the list pk^{list} and outputs pk_{ID}.

–Secret-Value-Extract: Upon receiving a query for a secret value of an identity ID, $\mathcal{C}$ returns the corresponding entry if it exists. Otherwise, $\mathcal{C}$ executes a Public-Key-Extract query itself to generate a tuple (ID, x, pk_{ID}) and adds the tuple to the list pk^{list}, and returns the secret value x.

–Public-Key-Replacement: If this query is on an identity ID, $\mathcal{C}$ checks whether a tuple (ID, x, pk_{ID}) is contained in the list pk^{list}. If it does, $\mathcal{C}$ sets $pk_{ID} = pk'_{ID}$ and adds $(ID, x = \perp, pk_{ID})$ to the pk^{list}. Otherwise, $\mathcal{C}$ executes a Public-Key-Extract query itself to generate (ID, x, pk_{ID}), then sets $pk_{ID} = pk'_{ID}$ and adds $(ID, x = \perp, pk_{ID})$ to the pk^{list}.

–Signing-Oracle: If this query is on an identity ID and a message m, $\mathcal{C}$ first recovers the corresponding tuple (ID, psk, R) from the list psk^{list} and the tuple (ID, x, pk_{ID}) from the pk^{list}, sets $u = H_1(ID, R)$ and $v = H_3(m)$, then chooses a random $r \in Z_p^*$ and computes $(\sigma_1, \sigma_2) = ((pk_{ID})^{x'H_2(ID,R)+J(u)}(v'\prod_{i \in \upsilon} v_i)^r, g^r)$, and returns $S = < R \,||\, \sigma_1 \,||\, \sigma_2 >$.

Forgery: A_1 returns a forged signature $S^* = < R^* || \sigma_1^* || \sigma_2^* >$ for an identity ID* and public key pk_{ID^*} on a message m*. $\mathcal{C}$ computes $u^* = H_1(ID^*, R^*)$ and checks whether the equation $F(u^*) = 0 \pmod p$ holds. $\mathcal{C}$ stops the simulation if it does. Otherwise, $\mathcal{C}$ computes $v^* = H_3(m^*)$ and checks whether the equation $K(v^*) = 0 \pmod p$ holds. If it does not hold, $\mathcal{C}$ aborts. Otherwise, $\mathcal{C}$ can compute and output

$$\left(\frac{\sigma_1^*}{pk_{ID^*}^{x'H_2(ID^*,R^*)+J(u^*)}\sigma_2^{*L(v^*)}}\right)^{F^{-1}(u^*)}$$

$$= \left(\frac{pk_{ID^*}^{x'H_2(ID^*,R^*)+J(u^*)} g^{baxF(u^*)} \sigma_2^{*L(v^*)}}{pk_{ID^*}^{x'H_2(ID^*,R^*)+J(u^*)}\sigma_2^{*L(v^*)}}\right)^{F^{-1}(u^*)}$$

$$= g^{abx}.$$

$\mathcal{C}$ outputs (g^{abx}, g^{x}) as a solution to the *NGBDHP* instance.

Now we assess the probability for the above events: Pr [$\neg$ E$_1$] $\geq$1/2.

Since $(t' + \sum_{i \in \upsilon} t_i) < l_v (l+1)$, $l_v k_v < l_v (l+1)$ and $l_v (l+1) < p$, we have

$$\Pr[\neg E_2] = \Pr[K(v^*) = 0 \ (\bmod p)] = 1/(2q_s(l+1)).$$

So, $\mathcal{C}$'s advantage $\varepsilon' \geq \dfrac{\varepsilon}{4q_s(l+1)}$.

Lemma 2. *Assume that a EUF-CMA*2 *adversary A_2 has an advantage ε against our scheme when running in a time t, making q_{pk} queries to the Public-Key-Extract oracle, q_s queries to the Signing oracle. Then, there exists an algorithm $\mathcal{C}$ that can solve the CDHP with probability $\varepsilon' \geq \varepsilon / (2q_s(l+1)q_{pk})$, in a time $t' \leq t + O(q_s(n+l)T_{mul} + (q_{pk} + q_s)T_{\exp})$,* where *$T_{mul}$ and T_{exp} denote the same quantities as in Lemma* 1.

Lemma 2 can be formally proven in the same way as that of Lemma 1. So, I omit it here.

3.3. *Efficiency analysis*

The author denotes “Pr” a pairing operation, “Sm” a scalar multiplication in G$_1$ and “Exp” an exponentiation in G$_1$, and “P-K-S” size of public key.

Table 1. Efficiency Comparison

Schemes	Signing	Verification	P-K-S
Liu[10]	6Exp	6Pr	2 points
Yu[12]	7Exp	5Pr+1Exp	2points
Yuan[13]	3Exp	6Pr+1Exp	2points
My scheme	3Exp	1Exp +3Pr	1 point

As is shown in Table 1, my scheme is the most efficient scheme in terms of the number of pairing operations required and the length of public key.

4. Conclusions

This paper constructs an efficient CLS scheme which is provably secure in the standard model. It achieves high efficiency and the length of public key is short. In addition, it has a simple and flexible structure and can be easily extended to a CLS scheme with additional properties such as certificateless proxy signatures in the standard model.

Acknowledgments

This work is supported by the National Natural Science Foundation of China (Grant No. 61402015), Scientific Research Project of Shaanxi Provincial Education Department (15JK1022).

References

1. A. Shamir. Identity-based cryptosystems and signature schemes. in Proc. Crypto'84, Santa Barbara, CA, 1984, pp. 47–53.

2. S. Al-Riyami, K.G.Paterson. Certificateless public Key cryptography. In Proceedings of ASIACRYPT 2003, LNCS 2894, Springer-Verlag, 2003, pp. 452-473.

3. B. Libert, J. J. Quisquater. On Constructing Certificateless Cryptosystems from Identity Based Encryption. M. Yung et al. (Eds.): PKC 2006, LNCS 3958, Springer-Verlag, 2006, pp. 474–490.

4. Alexander. W. Dent. A survey of certificateless encryption schemes and security models, International Journal of Information Security, 2008, 7(5), pp. 349-377.

5. Hong-zhen Du, Qiao-yan Wen. Efficient and Provably-secure Certificateless Short Signature Scheme from Bilinear Pairings. Computer Standards and Interfaces, 31(2), (2009), pp. 390-394.

6. K. Y. Choi, J. H. Park, D. H Lee. A New Provably Secure Certicateless Short Signature Scheme. Computers and Mathematics with Applications, (2011), 61(7), pp. 1760-1768.

7. Yeh K. Hui, Tsai K. Yu, F. C. Yen. An efficient certificateless signature scheme without bilinear pairings. Multimed Tools Appl. Doi: 10.1007/s11042-014-2154-4.

8. S. Horng, S. Tzeng, P. Huang, et al. An Efficient Certificateless Aggregate Signature with Conditional Privacy-Preserving for Vehicular Sensor Networks. Information Sciences, 317 (2015), pp. 48-66.

9. M. Bellare, A. Boldyreva, A. Palacio. An uninstantiable random oracle-model scheme for a hybrid-encryption problem. Proc. Eurocrypt 2004, LNCS 3027, pp. 171–188.

10. J. K. Liu, M. H. Au, and W. Susilo. Self-generated-certificate public key cryptography and certificateless signature / encryption scheme in the standard model.

11. In Proceedings of ASIACCS '07, 2007, pp. 273-283.

12. H. Xiong, Z. Qin, F. Li, An improved certificateless signature scheme secure in the standard model, Fundamenta Informaticae, vol. 88, no. 1-2, 2008, pp. 193-206.

13. Y. Yu, Y. Mu, G. Wang, Q. Xia, Improved certificateless signature scheme provably secure in the standard model, IET Information Security, 2012, 6(2):102-110.

14. Y. Yuan, C. Wang. Certificateless signature scheme with security enhanced in the standard model. Information Processing Letters 114 (2014) 492–499.

A Cloud Storage Encryption Scheme in the Limited Bandwidth Environment

Wen-juan CHENG[a] , Miao-miao ZHOU[b] , Bing TONG and Shi-xiang TANG

School of computer and Information, Hefei University of Technology, Hefei, 230000, China

[a]E-mail: cheng@ah.edu.cn,

[b]E-mail: miaomiaozhou@mail.hfut.edu.cn

To tackle the problems of encrypted cloud storage in a limited bandwidth environment, we proposed a scheme that divided encryption block of plaintext according to the content changes. The scheme based on the optimized AES algorithm and exhibits improved efficiency and security of data synchronizing in the limited bandwidth environment.

Keywords: Cloud security; Cloud storage; AES algorithm; Block encryption.

1. Introduction

Cloud storage security issues has caused widespread concern in academia and industry, related research has focused on three domains that's about data security storage, security audit and access control of ciphertext[1]. This paper starts with the secure storage of data. For the traditional cloud storage, users upload plaintext to the cloud, then the cloud server encrypting their data. In this paper, we transferred the encryption part of the plaintext to the client. When a large number of encrypted data between the local and cloud need synchronize, it will increase network load and may easily cause network congestion. In this paper, we presented a blocking encryption algorithm. It improved the efficiency and security in the process of data synchronization under the limited bandwidth environment.

2. Cloud Storage Encryption Scheme in the Limited Bandwidth Environment

2.1. *Solution description*

Xiong[2] proposed CloudSeal scheme to provide data confidentiality protection, but the shortage is that it is shared. D'Angelo[3] proposed CoClo scheme to

[b] Corresponding author.

achieve a lightweight client tool, but when the user expressly minor changes, local plaintext encrypted into ciphertext, the ciphertext should fully synchronized to the cloud server, consuming network resources.

The scheme highlighted proposed blocking encryption algorithm. It firstly optimized the AES algorithm, and improved algorithm according to the principle of Content Defined Chunking (CDC).

2.2. *The definition and composition of cryptography [4]*

A cryptosystem defined as S S = (M, C, K, E, D), which M is the plaintext space (also said the information space), C is the ciphertext space, K is the key space, E is an encryption mapping family, E = {fk: M->C | k ∈K}, D is the decryption mapping family, D = {gk: C-> M | k ∈K}.

We supposed that m represented plaintext and c represented the ciphertext. Encryption transformation E (k, m) denoted as Ek (m).The decryption transformation D (k, c) denoted as Dk (c). If $\forall m \in P$, $D_{Kd} \times E_{Ke}(m) = m$ set up, called the cryptosystem has confidentiality; if $\forall m \in P$, $E_{Ke} \times D_{Kd}(m) = m$ is true and the decryption key can be known by only one Data transfer entities, we can say that cryptosystem has certification.

2.2.1. *Improvements of AES encryption algorithm in low-bandwidth environments*

AES is a kind of grouping iterative encryption algorithm, it can effectively resist linear cryptanalysis, checking points attacks and powerful attacks, it has advantages about key lengths and flexible packet length, high efficiency and high security, etc. The algorithm used to encrypt each round by the four transformation, that is round keys XOR, S-box transformation, row replacement and mixed columns.

In the encryption and decryption process of AES, except for the final round, each round of operations including the above four steps, column confusion need to use multiplication on finite field GF (2^8), it is difficult to program implementation, while vulnerable to timing attacks. Based on the literature [5], using look-up table method to realize algorithm after comprehensive consideration for wheel operation , with the look-up table to achieve, it consumes a certain amount of storage space, but the required storage space is not large, and further improving the safety and operational efficiency .

Suppose the state array element is $a_{i,j}$, round key array element use $k_{i,j}$ to represent, $b_{i,j}$ represent output of byte substitution, then byte substitution process can be expressed as: $b_{i,j} = SBox[a_{i,j}]$.

SB0x represent finding S-box transformation:

$$\begin{bmatrix} e_{0,j} \\ e_{1,j} \\ e_{2,j} \\ e_{3,j} \end{bmatrix} = \begin{bmatrix} 02 & 03 & 01 & 01 \\ 01 & 02 & 03 & 01 \\ 01 & 01 & 02 & 03 \\ 03 & 01 & 01 & 02 \end{bmatrix} \begin{bmatrix} SBox[a_{0,j}] \\ SBox[a_{1,(j+1)\bmod 4}] \\ SBox[a_{2,(j+2)\bmod 4}] \\ SBox[a_{3,(j+3)\bmod 4}] \end{bmatrix} \oplus \begin{bmatrix} k_{0,j} \\ k_{1,j} \\ k_{2,j} \\ k_{3,j} \end{bmatrix}$$

$$= \left(\begin{bmatrix} 02 \\ 01 \\ 01 \\ 03 \end{bmatrix} \bullet SBox[a_{0,j}] \right) \oplus \left(\begin{bmatrix} 03 \\ 02 \\ 01 \\ 01 \end{bmatrix} \bullet SBox[a_{1,(j+1)\bmod 4}] \right) \oplus \tag{1}$$

$$\left(\begin{bmatrix} 01 \\ 03 \\ 02 \\ 01 \end{bmatrix} \bullet SBox[a_{2,(j+2)\bmod 4}] \right) \oplus \left(\begin{bmatrix} 01 \\ 01 \\ 03 \\ 02 \end{bmatrix} \bullet SBox[a_{3,(j+3)\bmod 4}] \right) \oplus \begin{bmatrix} k_{0,j} \\ k_{1,j} \\ k_{2,j} \\ k_{3,j} \end{bmatrix}$$

And then to define 4 T tables:T0[x], T1[x], T2[x], T3[x]

Using the above four tables, each round of four operations in encryption process can be expressed as in Eq. (2).

$$\begin{bmatrix} s'_{0,j} \\ s'_{1,j} \\ s'_{2,j} \\ s'_{3,j} \end{bmatrix} = T_0[s_{0,j}] \oplus T_1[s_{1,(j+1)\bmod 4}] \oplus T_2[s_{2,(j+2)\bmod 4}] \oplus T_3[s_{3,(j+3)\bmod 4}] \oplus \begin{bmatrix} k_{0,j} \\ k_{1,j} \\ k_{2,j} \\ k_{3,j} \end{bmatrix} \tag{2}$$

The above 4 T tables can be calculated in advance by the S-boxes, stored in the array. Each round of operation only query T table and make 4 multiplied by 16 times XOR operation. Relative to multiplication on finite field GF(2^8) repeatedly, the operation of look-up table greatly improve the efficiency and can resist timing attacks and improve security.

2.3. *Divided blocking encryption algorithm according to the contents*

The technique of detecting duplicate data block[8] is divided into fixed blocking detection technology, slider blocking technology, variable block-detection technology.

Original and revised document use CDC principle to block file respectively, the binary difference of blocking result is only distributed in modified attachment. Concrete blocking is determined by fingerprint, fingerprint is a kind of the hash value of the file contents. 1981 Harvard University professor Rabin presented Rabin fingerprint algorithm[9], the algorithm has high computational efficiency, the results of any data showing the uniform characteristics, commonly used to quickly compare and identify duplicate data. By using a polynomial over a finite field to implement fingerprint marks. Given an n-bit message M, as in Eq. (3).

$$M=M1+M2+....+Mn. \quad (3)$$

Use it as a n-1 order polynomial on finite field GF(2)

$$F(x)=M_1+M_2x+....+M_nx^{n-1}. \quad (4)$$

selection of irreducible k order polynomial p (x) On the finite field GF (2), then the fingerprint of message M

$$r(x)=f(x) \bmod p(x). \quad (5)$$

r (x) is the k-1 order polynomial.

Specific implementation: The scheme combines Rabin fingerprint algorithm with sliding window thinking to achieve Variable-length block according to content. Rabin's fingerprint defined two integers D and r firstly. Assuming in the position K, data hash value of fixed window is f. If f mod D = r, then this position is a block boundary, shown in Fig 1. Repeat this process until the entire file is partitioned. File is divided into data blocks of variable length. Data block size within the specified range, so that all of the data block size to achieve the desired distribution.

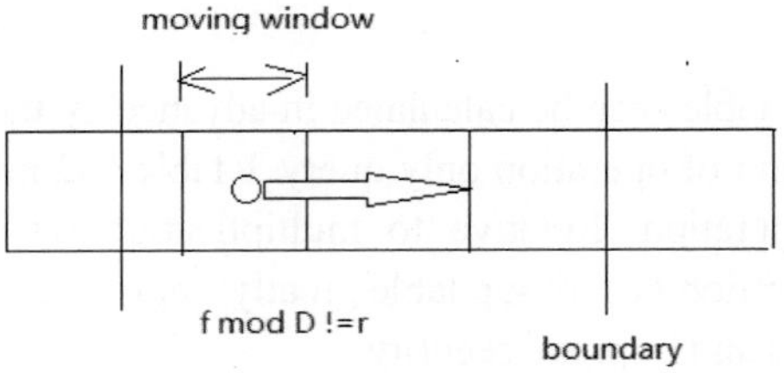

Fig.1. Variable length blocking based on content

3. Experimental Results and Scheme Performance Analysis

The technique of Eucalyptus is used to build small cloud platform, using two Dell servers, two computers, respectively, as a trusted third party, cloud servers, and A, B client. Using Xdelta to calculate the incremental ciphertext. Network bandwidth is 1MB/s. Compare This scheme and the existing programs, to comprehensive consideration of its encryption and decryption performance, communication / storage load and computing performance. As shown in Table 1.

Table 1. Overhead of uploaded to the cloud after native encryption.

Plaintext size (MB)	File encryption time t1 (ms)	Keyencryption time t2 (ms)	Synchronization time t3 (ms)	Encryption proportion of total time T (ms)
1.03	117	93	1102	16%
2.18	247	90	2256	13%
4.85	542	105	5015	11.43%
8.23	904	101	7994	11.17%
10.04	1102	86	9910	10.7%

From Table 1, in the limited bandwidth environment, encryption overhead percentage decreases with the increase of files that stored in the cloud. And decryption process takes up smaller occupancy ratio. For storage system, the overall impact of the performance brings in cloud computing overhead cost is acceptable.

Further testing superiority and efficiency of the scheme compared to AES encryption. Using AES algorithm first, in the host A, file encrypted locally then uploaded to the cloud server. Modify the file locally ,then update the file stored in the cloud server, recording the uplink synchronization time, host B downloaded update files to the local from cloud server , recording the downlink synchronization time; using variable-length blocking encryption algorithm repeat the above steps.

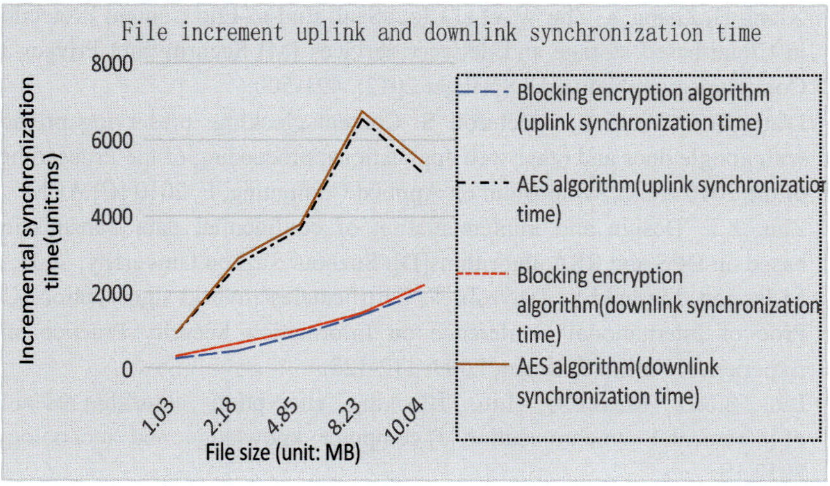

Fig. 2. File increment uplink and downlink synchronization time under two algorithms.

From the Fig.2, we can conclude that compared to AES encryption, the proposed encryption scheme can greatly shorten synchronization time in the limited bandwidth environment.

4. Conclusions

The proposed encryption scheme about cloud storage transferred the encrypt part of the plaintext to the client from cloud server, which ensured the data security. Based on the optimized AES encryption algorithm to introduce, the paper focuses on the introduction of block encryption algorithm. It can efficiently synchronize encrypted data between the local and cloud. The results show that cloud storage efficiency has improved significantly in the limited bandwidth environment, and also improved the security in the stored procedure.

Acknowledgments

In this paper, the research was sponsored by the National Natural Science Foundation of China (Project No. 51274078) and Major Teaching Research Project of Anhui Province (Project No. 2014zdjy015).

References

1. Takabi H, Joshi JBD, Ahn G. Security and privacy challenges in cloud computing environments. IEEE Security & Privacy, 2010,8 (6): 24-31.
2. Xiong H, Zhang X, Zhu W, et al CloudSeal: End-to-End Content Protection in Cloud-based storage and delivery services [M] Security and Privacy in Communication Networks Springer 2012:. 491-500.
3. D'angelo Q Vitali F, Zacchiroli S. Content cloaking: preserving privacy with google docs and other web applications; proceeding of the Proceedings of the 2010 ACM Symposium on Applied Computing, F, 2010 [C] ACM.
4. Zhu, Z.F. Design and implementation of confidential data transmission based on DES and RSA algorithms[D]. Suzhou: Suzhou University, 2005.
5. Li Fa-gen, Masaaki S, Tsuyoshi T. Certificateless hybrid signcryption [C]. Proc of International Conference on Information Security Practice and Experience. Berlin: Springer, 2009: 112-123.
6. Liu, S.&L, Ma.&F.Q, Liu. Blocking encryption algorithm research of incremental synchronization [J].computer knowledge and technology, 2012,10.
7. Rabin Michael O. Fingerprint by random polynomials. 1981, Technical Report TR-15-81, Center for Research in Computing Technology, Harvard University.

Research on IDS Alert Aggregation Based on Improved Quantum-behaved Particle Swarm Optimization

Jing ZHANG†, Bin YU and Jun-quan LI
Zhengzhou Institute of Technology, Zhengzhou,450001,China
†E-mail: zhangjing8673@163.com

In this paper we propose a new approach to reduce excessive duplicate alerts and high false positive rates in IDS. We used an improved quantum-behaved particle swarm optimization (IQPSO) algorithm by introducing multiple segment processing and absorption wall. During Alert aggregation processing, we calculate similarity of alert by fuzzy membership function firstly, then optimize attribute weights and similarity threshold by IQPSO. Experimental results show that the algorithm is effective in alert aggregation and gives better results in reducing false positive rate and duplicate alerts.

Keywords: IDS; Alert aggregation; Fuzzy membership; Absorption wall; IQPSO.

1. Introduction

IDS is short in false positive rate, massive duplicate alerts etc. which make administrators analyze and manage these alerts difficultly[1]. Alert aggregation as well as alert clustering is an effective way to solve this difficulty[2].

Vainikka[4] aggregates large-scale alerts based on temporal series model in specific sequence. Njogu[5]presents the similarity clustering method to reduce the number of alerts based on the alerts significance. Li[6] proposes clustering algorithm based on Particle Swarm Optimization (PSO), that overcomes the shortage of fall into local minimum value easily in traditional K-means algorithm. PSO is relatively simple and easy to understand as it is similar to human decision[8]. Whereas, traditional PSO converges faster and easy to fall in premature and local optimization. QPSO[11] is a new PSO model introduced by Sun form quantum mechanics and well in simpler calculation process and lower complexity. But, there is still a problem of premature convergence in QPSO.

This paper advances the Improved quantum-behaved particle swarm optimization (IQPSO) algorithm by introducing multiple segment processing and absorption wall theory. Firstly, it aggregates alerts based on fuzzy membership function. Then, it optimizes attribute weights and similarity threshold by IQPSO algorithm. Experimental analysis with dataset KDDCUP 99 shows that this approach is effective in alert aggregation and gives better results in reducing false positive rate and duplicate alerts.

The remainder of this paper is organized as follows. Section 1 describes the background and related work; Section 2 provides the alert aggregation model; Section 3 presents the alert aggregation processing; Section 4 presents our experiment and discusses the results obtained; and Section 5 concludes the paper.

2. Alert Aggregation Model

As is shown in Fig.1., alert aggregation model is presented. Firstly, it pre-processes the alert in uniform format; Then it aggregates alerts by the fuzzy membership function; and finally, it optimizes variables by IQPSO.

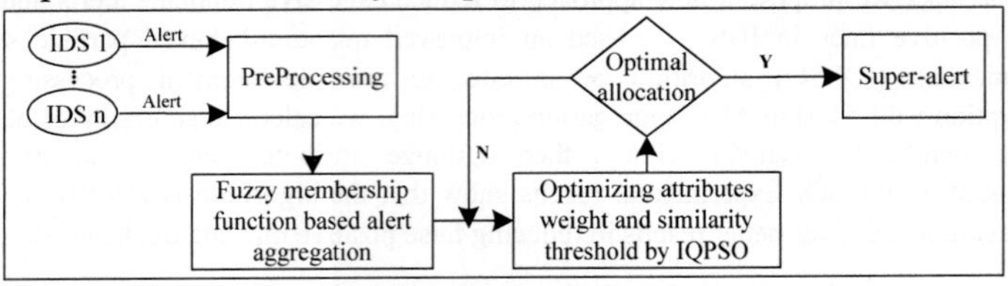

Fig.1. Alert aggregation model

2.1. *Preprocessing*

Alert format may be defined as $Alert = (ID, Type, Priority, Protocol, TimeStamp, SenserID, SrcIP, DstIP, SrcPort, DstPort, Msg)$.Then alert is encapsulated into a packet form based on IDMEF model structure.

2.2. *Alert similarity analysis*

This section is mainly about calculating alert similarity through similarity fuzzy membership function S. The definitions about S are as follows.

(1) Aiming at ID, $Type$, $Priority$, $Protocol$, $SenserID$, $Port$, Msg, $S = 1$ if they are the same between two alerts; otherwise, $S = 0$;

(2) It is shown the calculation of S with IP attribute as Formula 1 expression. In which, $sim(ip_i, ip_j)$ is represented the same number from MSB (Most Significant Bit) between ip_i and ip_j in binary;

$$S(ip_i, ip_j) = sim(ip_i, ip_j). \tag{1}$$

(3) S with $TimeStamp$ is defined as Formula 2. T_{min} and T_{max} respectively represents the minimum and the maximum time interval.

$$S(t_i,t_j)=\begin{cases} 1 & \left|t_i-t_j\right| \le T_{\min} \\ \dfrac{T_{\max}-\left|t_i-t_j\right|}{T_{\max}-T_{\min}} & T_{\min}<\left|t_i-t_j\right|<T_{\max} \\ 0 & otherwise \end{cases}. \tag{2}$$

Due to the different importance of each alert attribute, we calculate the similarity of alerts with respectively attribute weight w. So that the total similarity of two alerts $R(a_i,a_j)$ is shown as Formula 3.

$$R(a_i,a_j)=\sum_{k=1}^{n} w_k \cdot S(x_{ik},x_{jk}),\ \ \sum_{k=1}^{n} w_k = 1. \tag{3}$$

If $R(a_i,a_j) \ge \delta$ (δ : similarity threshold), we aggregate the alerts a_i and a_j. In which, δ and w are obtained by improved quantum-behaved particle swarm optimization algorithm in Section 3.

3. IQPSO Algorithm Optimizing

In this paper, we achieve the alert aggregation by attribute similarity fuzzy membership function. Alerts will be aggregated effectively on the control of attribute weights and similarity threshold by IQPSO algorithm.

3.1. *Alert aggregation*

On the basis of alert aggregation model mentioned above, the procedure of alert aggregation after preprocessing is shown in Fig.2..

Input: alert set in uniform format $A=\{n \in N \mid a_1,a_2,\cdots,a_n\}$, δ and w
Output: Super-Alert

Begin
Obtain δ and w by training sample set with IQPSO algorithm
for i=1 **to** n
  for j=1 **to** n
  if (a_i does not belong to any one clustering)
    Create a new cluster C_i and make $a_i \in C_i$
  else if ($R(a_i,a_j) \ge \delta$)
    if (a_j does not belong to any one clustering)
      Add a_j into C_i
    else Merge the clusters what a_i and a_j belong to
End

Fig.2. Alert aggregation processing

3.2. *Parameter optimization by IQPSO*

According to the iteration number, the search process will be divided into three stages. Each stage begins with the initialization of all the particles positions. In order to guarantee the superiority of particle swarm, the latter stage is beginning with all the particles locally optimal positions and the global best positions in the final of previous stage. However, some particles may run out of effective solutions spatial in the search process. So that, we introduce absorption wall theory, whenever the particles have updated their own positions in the search process, it may determine whether they hit or fly out the boundaries or not. When the particles crash or get past the boundaries of the available space, the particles will stay on the boundary which they meet with.

3.2.1. *Coding and fitness function*

Dimensions are $n+1$, in which the front n dimensions represent attribute weight $w_1, w_2, \cdots, w_n$, the $n+1$ dimension represents the similarity threshold δ. Assumed that, particle i's current position is $x_i = (x_{i1}, x_{i2}, \cdots, x_{i(n+1)})$ and optimal adaptation position is $p_i = (p_{i1}, p_{i2}, \cdots, p_{i(n+1)})$; particle swarm $(i_1, i_2, \cdots, i_{(n+1)})$ optimal adaptation position is $p_g = (p_{g1}, p_{g2}, \cdots, p_{g(n+1)})$.

Fitness function y is defined as Formula 4. In which, TR represents the number of similar alerts actually; TA represents the number of aggregated alerts; FR represents the number of no aggregated alerts and simultaneously dissimilar alerts actually; FA represents the number of no aggregated alerts.

$$y = \frac{TR}{TA} \cdot \frac{FR}{FA} \quad . \tag{4}$$

3.2.2. *Parameter optimization*

The number of particle is M, δ and w are obtained by IQPSO.

Step1: Initializing particle current position and local best position, and searching for the optimal position initially on the basis of fitness function y;

Step2: Determining whether the number of iterations reach the next stage or not, if the answer says yes, then reinitializing all the particle positions;

Step3: Calculating average optimal position: $mbest(C_T) = \frac{1}{M}\sum_{i=1}^{M} p_i$, in which C_T is the number of iterations currently;

Step4: Computing rand-position $p_i = \varepsilon \cdot p_i + (1-\varepsilon) \cdot p_g$, $\varepsilon \in rand[0,1]$, and update present particle position $x_i = p_i + \alpha \cdot (mbest(C_T) - x_i) \cdot \ln(1/\mu)$, $\mu = rand[0,1]$. C_{Max} is the maximum number of iterations, α is defined as contraction-expansion factor and $\alpha = (C_{Max} - C_T)/(2 \cdot C_{Max}) + 0.5$ generally;

Step5: Analyzing whether the particle position is out of bounds or not, if yes indeed, letting the particle position equal to the boundary position;

Step6: Updating the particle local optimum position and the particle swarm global best position based on fitness function y ;

Step7: Determining whether the number of iterations reach the maximum number or not, if yes indeed. end algorithm; otherwise, $C = C + 1$, pass to step2;

Optimal solution $(w_1, w_2, \cdots, w_n, \delta)$ will be obtained with the ending of IQPSO. Meanwhile, in order to improve the accuracy of IQPSO, training set should be updated constantly by LRU to replace the categories in training set.

4. Experiment Work

In order to verify the effectivity of the approach, 10% dataset about 40,000 records are randomly selected from KDDCUP 99. The subset are consist of 94% normal data and 6% anomalous data. About 4/5 dataset are randomly selected as training set subset, while the rest data are accounted for test set. Particle number and dimension are respectively set to 20 and 11.

Defined $Simplify-rate = \dfrac{the\ numble\ of\ reduced\ alerts\ by\ aggregation}{total\ number\ of\ alerts}$, the aggregation results are shown in Table 1. The $Simplify-rate$ is between 86.7% and 93.2% so that it is effective to reduce the number of alerts by applying IQPSO algorithm.

Table.1 Aggregation result

Iteration number	Original alert	Alert aggregation	Simplify rate (%)
10		317	86.7
20		260	89.0
30	2379	201	91.6
50		162	93.2
100		208	91.2

The comparison results are shown in Table.2, in which DR and FPR respectively represent detection rate and false positive rate.

Table.2 Aggregation algorithm comparison result

Iteration number	QPSO [11]		IQPSO	
	DR(%)	FPR(%)	DR(%)	FPR(%)
10	62.9	3.56	74.3	2.82
20	69.4	3.02	83.8	2.19
30	77.2	2.58	89.1	1.67
50	83.8	2.30	93.2	1.06
100	88.6	1.74	96.1	0.81

As Table 2 shown, IQPSO gives better results in DR and FPR than QPSO[11] under the same iteration number. When 100 iterations advanced, the detection rate is 96.1% while the false positive rate is 0.81% only in IQPSO.

In summary, the proposed approach can be effectively applied to alert aggregation process.

5. Conclusions

We present a IDS alert aggregation approach on the basis of improved quantum-particle swarm Optimization in this paper. As a result of experiment with KDDCUP 99 dataset, this approach can aggregate IDS alerts effectively.

Future work: (1) Obtaining more dataset from the actual network to test and validate the approach; (2) After the alert aggregation, it should do more research on alert correlation so as to detect attacks intentions and restore attack scenario.

Acknowledgments

This work is supported by university project-Research on Cyber-Space information security and related key technologies.

Work partially supported by grant 2-4570.5 of the Swiss National Science Foundation.

References

1. Amoroso E, Intrusion detection — An introduction to Internet surveillance, correlation, trace-back, traps, and response. Intrusion Net Books. 1999.
2. H Nguyen, Jia W L. An efficient approach to reduce alerts generated by multiple IDS products [J]. Journal of Network Management. 2014.
3. Chun L, Han S. An SR-ISODATA Algorithm for IDS Alerts Aggregation[J]. IEEE International Conference on Information and Automation. 2014.
4. Vainikka, Debrah. Processing intrusion detection alert aggregates with time series modeling[J]. Information Fusion Journal. 2009, 10(4): 312-324.
5. J Njogu H W, Luo J W. Using alert cluster to reduce IDS alerts[A]. ICCSIT 2010[C]. Chengdu, China, IEEE Press, 2010. 467-471.
6. Li Y Z, Yang G. Anomaly detection for clustering algorithm based on particle swarm optimization[J]. Journal of Jiangsu University of Science and Technology (Natural Science Edition), 2009, 23(1): 51-55.

7. Vaarandi R, Podins K. Network IDS alert classification with frequent itemset mining and data clustering[A]. CNSM 2010[C]. 2010. 451-456.
8. WEN Z W, LI R J. Fuzzy C-means clustering algorithm based on improved PSO[J]. Application Research of Computers, 2010, 27(7): 2520-2522.
9. Mohammad M, Hamed G. Classifying IDS Alerts Automatically for use in Correlation Systems[J]. IEEE. 2014.
10. FEI A, DONGX L. Hierarchically clustering IDS alarms using a GA with vary-lengthed chromosomes[A]. ISIP China: IEEE Press, 2010.172-177.
11. Sun J and Xu W B. A global search strategy of quantum-behaved particle swarm optimization[C]. Proceedings of the IEEE conference on Cybernetics and Intelligent Systems. 2009,111-116.
12. Lin B Q, Bo F Z. Online Mining of Attack Models in IDS Alerts from Network by a Two-Stage Clustering Method[C]. CSS 2013. 2013, 104-116.
13. Taqwa A, Maheyzah M S et al. A Taxonomy on Alert Aggregation Techniques[C]. International Symposium on Security Technologies. 2014.

The Modeling Method of Cryptography Protocols Based on Modified Finite State Machine

Ming-qing ZHANG, Shu-qin DONG[†], Hong-shan KONG, Xiao-hu LIU and Hui GUAN

Zhengzhou Institute of Information Science and Technology, Zhengzhou, 450001, China

[†]*E-mail: dongshuqin377@126.com*

Communicating finite state machines can be used to describe communication protocols; however due to cryptographic operations in cryptography protocols, they undergo state explosion when describing cryptography protocols. In order to overcome this problem, a modeling method of cryptography protocols based on modified finite state machine is proposed in this paper. Firstly, the finite state machine is modified by adding elements into the formal definition of traditional finite state machines to express cryptographic operations and the related communication entity of each operation. In addition, the formal definition of Finite State Machine of Cryptography Protocols (CPFSM) is provided. Secondly, the transition diagram of CPFSM is enriched by changing colors of the nodes in traditional transition diagrams, and adding stripes and flags into the nodes. Thirdly, the general steps to build the CPFSM of a cryptography protocol are described. Lastly, the method is proven to be efficient and valid in describing cryptography protocols and provides increased precision in simulating cryptography protocols.

Keywords: Cryptography Protocol; Modified Finite State Machine; Cryptographic Operation; Transition Diagram.

1. Introduction

Currently, cryptography protocols are widely used in many fields to protect private communication messages against divulging. It's a good way to find leaks of cryptography protocols by formally analyzing them [1-4]. However, the influence of cryptography protocols on the performance of networks can't be judged through formal analysis. Simulation, with the advantages of its economy, security and repeatability, provides an effective means to evaluate the influence of cryptography protocols on communication networks.

Formal models of cryptography protocols should be built before testing them on virtual communication networks. The modeling method, based on Finite State Machine (FSM), has a great advantage in known formal modeling methods, and many communication protocols are designed and implemented based on FSM, such as TCP protocol and RSVP protocol. Moreover, many simulation tools, such as OPNET and OMNeT++, support the simulation mechanism based on FSM. Therefore, FSM models of cryptography protocols can easily convert to simulation models.

However, traditional communicating finite state machines [5-7] can only reveal the law of state transition between different states. Only by adding states can we be able to describe cryptography protocols with them, it means that the state of corresponding communication entities changes once as they do a cryptographic operation. When the cryptography protocol is complex, the number of states will be so huge that will cause a state-explosion problem and seriously affect the performance of the system.

Therefore, with the consideration of the features of cryptography protocols, we propose a modeling method of cryptography protocols based on modified finite state machine in this paper. The validity of the modeling method is proved by taking Internet Key Exchange (IKEv2) protocol as an example.

2. The Modeling Method of Cryptography Protocols

2.1. *The formal definition for the FSM of cryptography protocols*

To solve the problem in describing cryptography protocols with traditional communicating finite state machines, we modified the formal definition of traditional finite state machines by adding two elements to express cryptographic operations and the related communication entity of each cryptographic operation. The modified finite state machine describing cryptography protocols can be defined formally as below:

Definition 2.1. *The Finite State Machine of Cryptography Protocols (CPFSM) can be expressed with a 9-tuples model, as in Eq.* (1).

$$CPFSM = (Q, E, \Lambda, \Omega, \delta, \varphi, \psi, q_0, F). \tag{1}$$

Where, Q is the set of finite states and its elements can be expressed as q_0, q_1, q_2 and so on. E is the set of communication entities and its elements can be expressed as e_1, e_2, e_3 and so on. Λ is the set of finite input events and its elements can be expressed as i_1, i_2, i_3 and so on. Ω is the set of finite output events and its elements can be expressed as o_1, o_2, o_3 and so on. δ is the state transition function, and it is defined as $\delta : Q \times \Lambda \to Q$, for $\forall(q_k, i_l) \in Q \times \Lambda, \delta(q_k, i_l) = q_{k+1}$ means that the state of *CPFSM* will transfer from q_k to q_{k+1} when reading the event of i_l, and $k, l \in N$. φ is the cryptographic operation function, and it is defined as $\varphi : E \times \Lambda \to \Lambda$, for $\forall(e_g, i_l) \in E \times \Lambda, \varphi(e_g, i_l) = i_l'$ means that when the communication entity e_g of

CPFSM reads the input event i_l, it encrypts i_l or signs i_l, then i_l turns to i_l', and $l, g \in N$. ψ is the event output function, and it is defined as $\psi : Q \times \Lambda \times E \rightarrow \Omega$, for $\forall (q_k, i_l, e_g) \in Q \times \Lambda \times E$, $\psi(q_k, i_l, e_g) = o_h$ means that when the communication entity e_g of *CPFSM*, which is at the state of q_k, reads the input event i_l, it outputs event o_h, and $k, l, g, h \in N$. q_0 is the initial state of *CPFSM*, and $q_0 \in Q$. F is the set of final states of *CPFSM*, and $F \subseteq Q$.

2.2. *The transition diagram of CPFSM*

Based on transition diagram of traditional finite state machines, we propose a transition diagram of CPFSM to vividly express the CPFSM. The communication entity of each operation is expressed by adding a flag into the node of the traditional transition diagram. The cryptographic operations are expressed by changing colors of the nodes or adding stripes into the nodes. The symbols in transition diagram of CPFSM are defined in detail, just as shown in Fig.1, in which verifying is the reverse operation of signing, and decryption is the reverse operation of encryption.

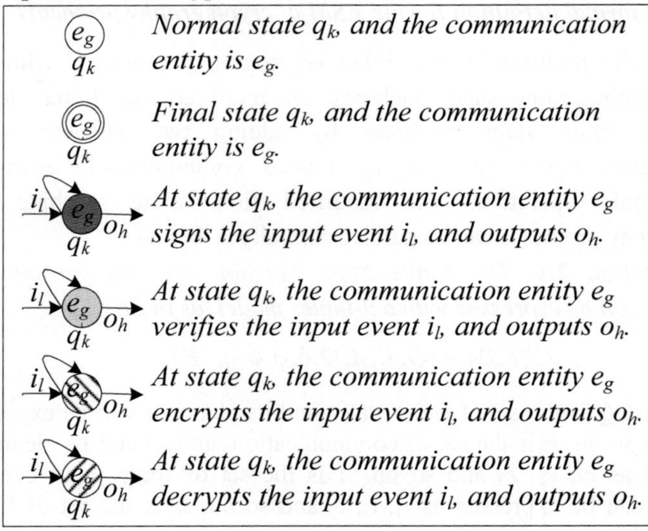

Fig.1. Symbols' definition of the transition diagram

The general transition diagram of CPFSM can be drawn based on the above definitions, and it is shown in Fig.2.

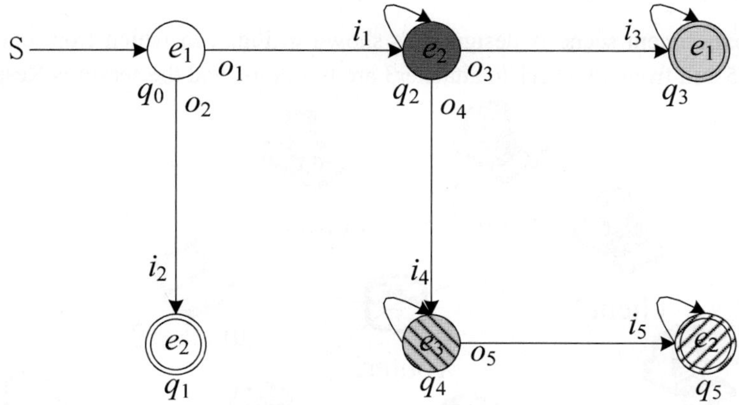

Fig.2. The transition diagram of CPFSM

3. General Steps to Build CPFSM

The general steps to build CPFSM is described as follows:

Firstly, the protocols should be analyzed carefully. The hierarchy of a cryptography protocol should be cleared when analyzing it, its cryptographic operations and cryptography algorithms utilized should be found out according to its operation principle.

Secondly, the events occurred in cryptography protocols should be listed. They are divided into three aspects considering the event source. One part of them may come from external associated components of the protocols. Another part of them may be produced between different processes when the CPFSM is realized by using multiple processes. The third part of them may be internal events that come from the process itself.

Thirdly, the events response table should be established. A state transition condition should be first chosen when determining the state transition, and then the inner cryptographic operations and the actions that need to be performed after the transition should be determined, finally the end state of the state transition should be determined.

Fourthly, the transition diagram of CPFSM should be implemented based on the above analysis.

4. Simulation Experiments in OMNeT++

By taking IKEv2 protocol as an example, we carry out several simulations using OMNeT++ simulator to verify the validity of the modeling method and to evaluate the efficiency of IKEv2 simulation models.

4.1. *Experiment scene and simulation parameters*

The experiment scene is designed as shown in Fig.3, in which from client1 to client5 and from attacker1 to attacker3 are Initiators, and the server is Responder.

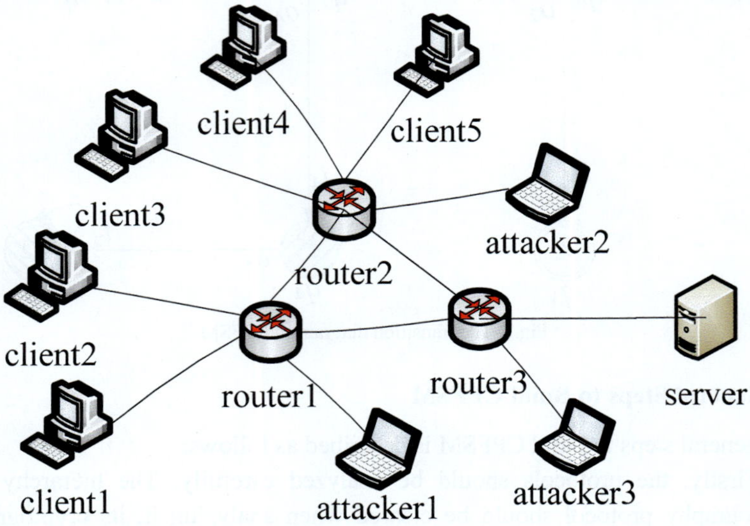

Fig.3. The experiment scene

The simulation parameters are listed as follows: The simulator is OMNeT++, the simulation time is 200ms, the traffic type is UDP, the encryption algorithm is AES-128, and the hash function is SHA-1. For each cryptography algorithm, we use Cryptlib [8] to implement it.

4.2. *Simulation results*

In order to verify the validity of the modeling method, we establish FSM of IKEv2 protocol using communicating FSMs, and establish CPFSM of IKEv2 protocol using the above modeling method. We simulate them in OMNeT++ under a DoS attack conducted by the attackers. The number of response messages sent by the server is counted, and simulation results are shown in Fig.4.

It can be seen from Fig.4, due to the DoS attack, the number of response messages sent by the server increases rapidly after 3ms, and the increment speed of response messages becomes slowly after 30ms when establishing the simulation model of IKEv2 protocol using CPFSM, for the server will only respond to the following encrypted messages when the IKE_SA is established [9]. At last, the number of response messages reaches a steady level at 110ms, it means the IPSec_SA is established. While establishing the simulation model of IKEv2 using FSM, the time cost in establishing IKE_SA extends to 70ms, after

70ms the response messages increase with a ladder shaped growth, and reach a steady level at 170ms, for there are many states to do cryptographic operations that cost much time. The results show that the CPFSM is valid in describing cryptography protocols and more efficient than traditional communicating FSMs.

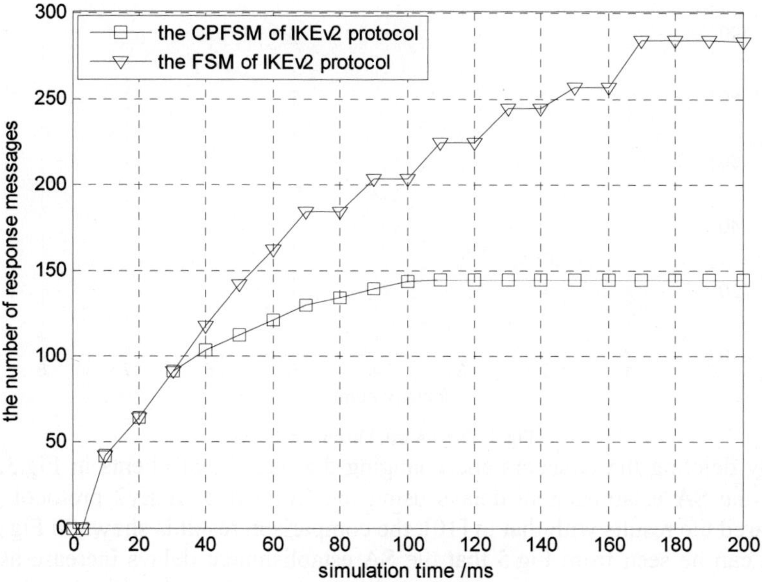

Fig.4. The number of response messages

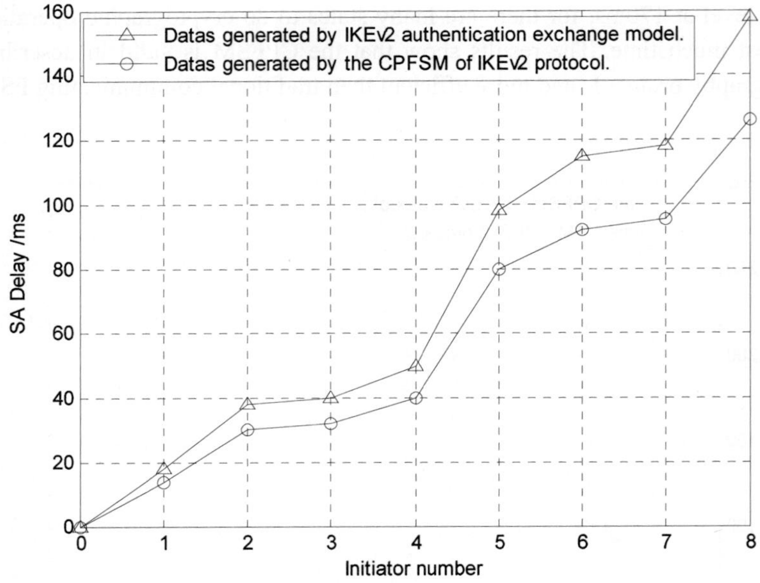

Fig.5. The SA establishment delays

By deleting the attackers and changing the number of clients in Fig.3, we tested the SA establishment delays using the CPFSM of IKEv2 protocol, and compared the results with that in [10], the comparison result is shown in Fig.5.

It can be seen from Fig.5 that the SA establishment delays increase as the number of Initiators increases, and at the same number of Initiators, the SA establishment delay of the simulation model implemented by the CPFSM of IKEv2 protocol reduces by 20 percent. The results show that the simulation model implemented by the CPFSM has higher precision than that in [10].

5. Conclusion

The paper proposes a modeling method of cryptography protocols based on modified finite state machine, which effectively solves the state-explosion problem in describing cryptography protocols with traditional communicating FSMs, and the simulation models of cryptography protocols implemented by the method have higher precision. The modeling method lays a foundation to do simulation analyses of cryptography protocols. The next step, we will further enrich the forms of transition diagram of CPFSM.

References

1. C. Meadows,Formal Analysis of Cryptography Protocols,*Encyclopedia of Cryptography and Security,* 490-492 (2011).
2. A. Pankova and P. Laud,Symbolic analysis of cryptography protocols containing bilinear pairings,in *Proc. IEEE 25th Computer Security Foundations Symposium (CSF)*,(Cambridge MA, USA, 2012).
3. B. Blanchet,Security protocol verification: Symbolic and computational models,in *Proc. the 1st International Conference on Principles of Security and Trust(POST'12)*,(Tallinn, Estonia, 2012).
4. S. Meier and B. Schmidt,The TAMARIN prover for the symbolic analysis of security protocols,in *Proc. the 25th International Conference on Computer Aided Verification(CAV 2013)*, (Saint Petersburg, Russia, 2013).
5. B. Bollig,Communicating Finite-State Machines, *Formal Models of Communicating Systems: Languages, Automata, and Monadic Second-Order Logic*, 117-150 (2006).
6. P.M. Deniélou and N. Yoshida,Multiparty session types meet communicating automata,*Programming Languages and Systems*(Springer, Berlin Heidelberg, 2012).
7. P.M. Deniélou and N. Yoshida,Multiparty compatibility in communicating automata: Characterisation and synthesis of global session types,*Automata, Languages,and Programming* (Springer, Berlin Heidelberg, 2013).
8. P. Gutmann,*Cryptlib security toolkit version 3.4.2*(2015), http://www.cs.auckland.ac.nz/~pgut001/cryptlib.
9. H. Patel and D. Jinwala,Modeling and analysis of internet key exchange protocolv2 and a proposal for its variant,in *Proc. the 6th ACM India Computing Convention*,(New York, USA, 2013).
10. M. Kasraoui, A. Cabani and H. Chafouk,IKEv2 authentication exchange model in NS-2,in *Proc. IS3C2014,* (Taichung, Taiwan, 2014).

A Fast Mura Detection Method Based on Immersion Simulation

Ye-Jian ZHANG and Hyonam JOO

Dept. of Display Engineering, Hoseo University,
Asan, Chungnam, South Korea
[†]E-mail: ldol31627@naver.com
hnjoo@hoseo.edu

Joon-seek KIM

Dept. of Electrical Engineering, Hoseo University,
Asan, Chungnam, South Korea
E-mail: joonskim@hoseo.edu

Numerous defects can occur in the process of manufacturing display panels. In particular, a defect called mura is one of the most difficult defects to detect using conventional image processing algorithms. It usually appears as relatively dark or relatively bright regions with very low contrast against the background when the panel is viewed by an imaging device. We have developed a fast mura defect detection method based on the conventional watershed algorithm. The flooding step of the watershed algorithm is carefully re-designed to detect mura defects that exist both inside and at the boundary of an image. The just noticeable difference (JND) technique is used to quantify the level of the mura defects. Experiments show that the proposed algorithm is efficient and provides rapid detection of low-contrast mura defects.

Keywords: Immersion simulation; Just noticeable difference (JND); Mura; TFT-LCD; Watershed.

1. Introduction

The thin film transistor liquid crystal display (TFT-LCD) is one of the most popular display devices widely used in smart-phones, monitors, televisions and other electronic devices. Many kinds of defects can show up in the TFT-LCD manufacturing process. In particular, a defect called mura is one of the most difficult one to detect using conventional image processing algorithms. The mura defects have no definite shape, no clear contours, non-uniform brightness values and low contrast value against the background. To solve this problem, many automatic mura detection techniques have been developed by researchers.

The mura detection mothed can be roughly divided into two categories, first, the direct mura detection category [1] and, second, the background elimination category [2,3,4]. Cheng [1] uses a Haar wavelet transform to detected mura on the polarizer. Yun [2] uses a principal component analysis (PCA) with k principal components for background reconstruction. It can detect muras without the knowledge of both the shape and location of them. But it is difficult to find the best k value automatically. Lu and Tsai [3] use a singular value decomposition (SVD) method with k largest singular values for background reconstruction. It can easily detect micro-sized defects, but have difficulties detecting big-size low-contrast muras correctly. The discrete cosine transform (DCT) is used in [4] for background reconstruction.

We propose a mura detection method similar to the watershed algorithm in the sense of immersing the 3 dimensional image topography into the water, and by computing the depth of the catchment basins, muras. The concept of Vincent and Soille's [5] watershed algorithm is used to speed up the immersion process.

Section 2 describes a set of basic definitions to use in the algorithm. In section 3, we describe our new mura detection algorithm. Experimental results and performance analysis are given in section 4 followed by a conclusion in section 5.

2. Basic Definitions

Vincent and Soille [5] use the immersion simulation to find the watershed lines. We modify their simulation method to be more suitable for the mura defect detection. The input image is figured as a 3-dimensional topographical island surrounded by an ocean. Before describing our immersion simulation, we will first give a definition of both sea water and fresh water.

The sea water is defined as the water surrounding the ground (input image). While the sea water seeps into the ground, the salt and other impurities in the sea water are filtered by the ground. When it finally fills the catchment basin, it becomes the fresh water. The filtering process is assumed to be fast enough that the water level of both the sea water and the fresh water are always equal while the ground is immersed into the ocean.

Using definitions in [5], let I denote a two dimensional grayscale image, p be a pixel of I, $p \in [0, size)$, where $size$ is the number of pixels in image I, $N(p)$ denote the set of neighbors of a pixel p in four or eight connectivity, $p' \in N(p)$, h denote the gray level of I, h_{min} and h_{max} denote the minimum and the maximum gray level of I. In topography h_{min} and h_{max} means the lowest and highest altitude. Let $Depth(p)$ denote the depth of fresh water at point p, $p \in [0, size)$. Let $Label(p) \in \{FRESH\_WATER, SEA\_WATER, INIT, MASK\}$ be labels to classify pixel $p \in [0, size)$, where $INIT$ is the initial value of $Label(p)$. $MASK$ is defined in flooding step in section 3.3. Let $B_i, 0 \leq i < 8$, denote the set of boundary pixels of image I. There are eight boundaries in an image, two horizontal boundaries, two vertical boundaries, and four corner boundaries. Let $width$ and $height$ denote the width and height of image I. Let N_{B_i} denoted the number of elements in B_i. For a horizontal boundary $N_{B_i} = width$, for a vertical boundary $N_{B_i} = height$, and for a corner boundary $N_{B_i} = \frac{width}{2} + \frac{height}{2}$.

3. Proposed Mura Detection Algorithm

Our algorithm is composed of the following 4 steps: (1) Boundary construction step, (2) Initial sorting step, (3) Flooding step, (4) Mura defect quantification step.

3.1. *The boundary dam construction step*

In order to detect the muras at the boundary of the image, dams should be constructed first at two horizontal boundaries, two vertical boundaries and four corner boundaries of the image. The process of boundary dam construction is a one dimensional one and is decomposed into three steps. The dam construction in forward direction, the dam construction in backward direction, and finally taking the minimum height of the two previously constructed dams. Let $B_i(n)$ be a grayscale value at pixel n in boundary $B_i, 0 \leq n < N_{B_i}$, where N_{B_i} is the number of pixels in boundary B_i. Let $B_{Fi}(n) = B_i(n), B_{Bi}(n) = B_i(N_{B_i} - n - 1)$, $0 \leq$

$i < 8$. The grayscale pixel values at the boundaries are replaced by the dam. Fig.1 shows the constructed boundary dam.

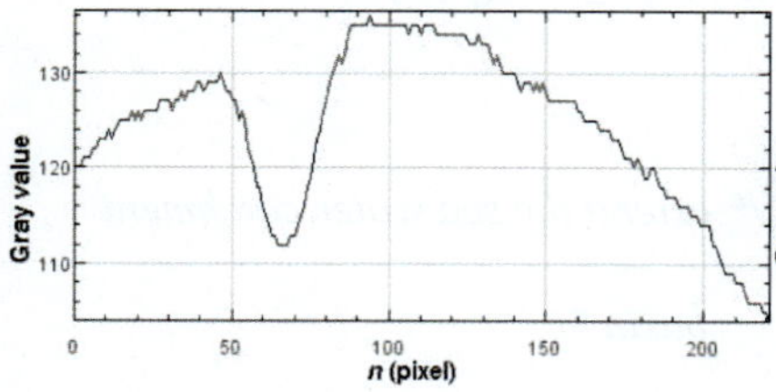

(a) Image boundary

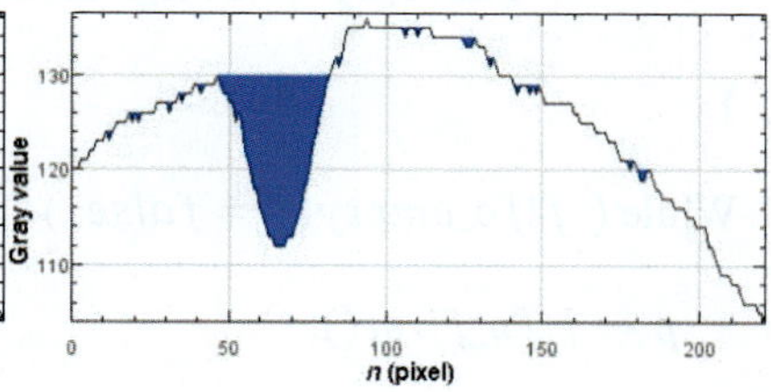

(b) The constructed boundary dam

Fig.1.The boundary dam construction.

3.2. *The initial sorting step*

To speed up the computations, the input grayscale image with the constructed dams is sorted by the gray level as in [5]. Let $I_{in}(p)$ denoted the sorted image.

3.3. *The flooding step*

Let $Depth(p)$ be the depth of the fresh water at pixel p in the fresh water, $p \in [0, size)$ while the image is flooded by the sea water. $Depth(p)$ will be used to quantify the mura in section 3.4. We use a first-in-first-out (fifo) data structure (queue) and a breadth-first searching for fast computation as in [5]. Functions to put and to retrieve a pixel from a queue are defined as $f\_add(p)$ and $fifo_first()$respectively together with$fifo_empty(\,)$. (see [5] for more details).

Algorithm 3.3. The fast $Depth(p)$ calculation algorithm:

$\forall\, p \in [0, size), \{\, Label(p) = \ INIT, D(p) = 0 \,\}$

For ($h \ = \ h_{min};\ h \ \le \ h_{max};\ h{+}{+}$) {

For ($\forall\, p \in [0, size),\ I_{in}(p) = \ h$)

If ($p \in B_i, 0 \le i < 8$) { /* *pixel p at the boundary of the image*

$Label(p) \ \leftarrow \ SEA\_WATER$; } *will be labeled with sea water* */

```
        Else { Label(p) ← MASK;
            If ( ∃ p′ ∈ N(p), Label(p') = SEA_WATER ) {
                Label(p) ← SEA_WATER ; fifo_add(p); } }
    }
    While ( fifo_empty() = false ) { /* extend the sea water catchment
        p ← fifo_first();                           basin */
        For( ∀ p′ ∈ N(p) ) {
            If (Label(p') = FRESH_WATER or Label(p') = MASK ) {
                Label(p') ← SEA_WATER; fifo_add(p'); } }
    }
    For ( ∀ p ∈ [0, size), I_in(p) = h ) {
    /* newfound pixel p not belong to sea water that will belong to fresh water */
        If ( Label(p) = MASK ) Label(p) ← FRESH_WATER;
    }
    For ( ∀ p ∈ [0, size), h_min ≤ I_in(p) ≤ h ) {
        /* all fresh water level up */
        If ( Label(p) = FRESH_WATER ) Depth(p) ← Depth(p) + 1;
    }
} /* all process end */
```

3.4. *Mura defect quantification step*

$Depth(p)$ can be considered as the difference between the gray value at p within the mura region and the gray value of the background surrounding the mura.

When $Depth(p)$ exceeds a certain threshold, the pixel is classified as a mura pixel. We use the formula of just noticeable difference (JND) to determine the threshold to classify the mura pixels. The JND is used in many literatures [4] for mura quantification and is defined by the Semiconductor Equipment and Materials International (SEMI) [6]. The formula of JND is as follow:

$$SEMU = \frac{|C_X|}{\frac{1.97}{S^{0.33}+0.72}}, \ |C_X| = \frac{G_M}{G_B}.$$

SEMU is an approximation of human eye's sensitivity regarding mura size and contrast. Cx is the contrast between background and mura region. G_M is the average of the difference between background and mura region, that equal to the average of $Depth(p)$ where p belongs to the mura region. G_B is the average intensity of background region. S is the area of mura region.

4. Experimental Results

4.1. *Performance about detecting low-contrast area mura*

To evaluate the performance about detecting low contrast mura, we randomly-select four acquired image of TFT panel without mura. Ten different relative gray levels (1 to 10) of artificial rectangular-shaped mura defects are added in each image. The result of proposed mura detection method is compared to three other mura detection methods. Lu and Tsai's SVD based method [3], Yun's PCA based mothed [2], Chen and Kuo's DCT based method [4]. Figure 2 shows the result of our experiments.

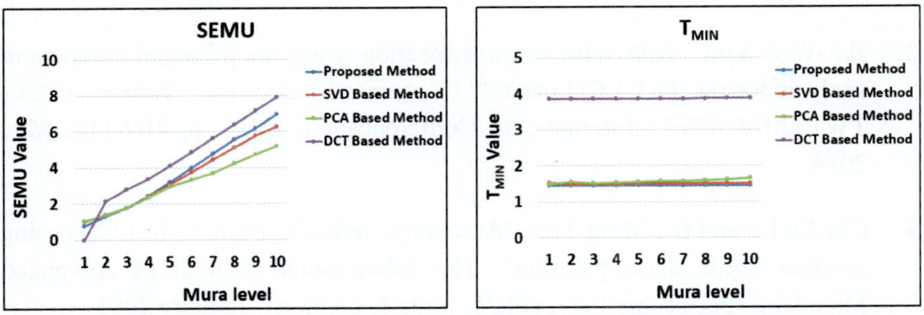

(a) (b)

Fig.2. The experimental result of the minimum detectable mura level. (a) SEMU. (b) T_{MIN} .

In Fig. 2(a), the sensitivity of algorithm to mura defect is measured as SEMU, where the larger the SEMU is the more sensitive the algorithm is to the mura. It shows that our algorithm is more sensitive than PCA and SVD based method, but less sensitive than DCT based one. In Fig. 2(b), the minimum threshold value (T_{MIN}) that can separate mura from non-mura is measured, which also measures the goodness the background fitting. The T_{MIN} value calculate from the proposed method is much smaller than DCT. The total processing time of the proposed algorithm is much faster (1180ms) compared to the others, SVD(3723ms), DCT(4439ms), and PCA(5399ms).

5. Conclusions

We develop a fast mura defect detection algorithm based on immersion simulation. The experimental results show that the proposed mura detection algorithm has a great capability of detecting low-contrast mura. However, the proposed algorithm also still makes some errors in complex imaging situations. The problems and the solution to them will be studied further and will be presented in our next paper.

Acknowledgement

This work is supported by the BK21 project.

References

1. Chi-Cheng Cheng, "Application of the Haar wavelet to mura detection for polarizer", Industrial Technology (ICIT), 2013 IEEE International Conference on, IEEE, pp.1080-1085, February 2013.

2. Jim-Woo Yun, "Automatic mura inspection using the principal component analysis for the TFT-LCD panel ", Consumer Electronics – Taiwan (ICCE-TW), 2014, IEEE, International Conference on, IEEE, pp.109-110, May 2014.

3. Chi-Jie Lu and Du-Ming Tsai, "Automatic defect inspection for LCDs using singular value decomposition", The International Journal of Advanced Manufacturing Technology, vol.25, Issue 1, pp.53-61, January 2005.

4. Liang-Chia Chen and Chia-Cheng Kuo, "Automatic TFT-LCD mura defect inspection using discrete cosine transform based background filtering and

'just noticeable difference' qualification strategies," Measurement Science and Technology, vol. 19, Issue 1, pp. 1–10, January 2008.

5. Luc Vincent and Pierre Soille "Watersheds in digital spaces: an efficient algorithm based on immersion simulations" IEEE Transactions on Pattern Analysis & Machine Intelligence, vol.13, Issue 6, pp.583 - 598, June 1991.

6. SEMI 2006 Definition of measurement index (SEMU) for luminance mura in FPD image quality inspection (SEMI D31–1102, Semiconductor Equipment and Materials International).

An Empirical Analysis of Cryptographic Misuse on Different Platforms

Tian-lu ZHANG, Yuan-yuan ZHANG, Hui WANG and Hui LIU

Dept. of Computer Science and Engineering, Shanghai Jiao Tong University
Shanghai, China
E-mail: zhangtianlu@sjtu.edu.cn

Cryptographic misuse is an increasingly common issue in real-world systems. In this paper, we collected and summarized 224 cryptography vulnerabilities in the CVE database over the previous five years and analyzed the implementation of cryptography systems in 131 common Android application packages (APKs), to understand why certain cryptographic misuses are more likely to appear in certain scenarios. We present a systematic analysis about the pertinence between certain cryptographic misuses and the different characteristics of three actual platforms (mobile, embedded and server). Thereafter, we propose several lightweight countermeasures to alleviate cryptographic misuse.

Keywords: Cryptographic misuse; Software security.

1. Introduction

Implementing cryptography correctly could provide strong security guarantees, but the reality is that turning the complicated cryptographic algorithms and protocols into real working systems correctly is a difficult and error-prone task. Moreover, due to a lack of basic cryptographic knowledge by average programmers, the misuse of cryptography is becoming one of the most common issues in real-word.

Cryptographic misuse is widely concerned by researchers. Das *et al.* investigate the bad design of the cryptography libraries [1], Lenstra *et al.* reveal the misuse of public-key cryptosystem in real working system [2], and Cairns *et al.* focus on the software developers to discuss why cryptography system fails [3]. However, without a comprehensive perspective, these proposed researches only present some specific aspects of the cryptographic system, such as certain cryptographic protocol or application. Furthermore, they do not consider a practical application scenario in which cryptosystem works to draw broader conclusions about the kinds of cryptographic misuse that occurs in practice.

In this paper, we collect and summarize 224 vulnerabilities which are related to cryptographic misuse in the CVE database [7]from 2010 to 2015, and analyze the implementation of cryptography systems of 131 common Android APKs. The results show that the causes of cryptographic misuses are closely related with the different characters of various practical application scenarios. Finally, some lightweight mitigations are recommended to avoid common pitfalls in cryptographic implementation.

2. Cryptographic Misuses and Platform Characteristics

In this paper, we focus on the different characteristics of the mobile, embedded and server platform, and discuss the pertinence between certain cryptography vulnerabilities and the different characteristics of these platforms.

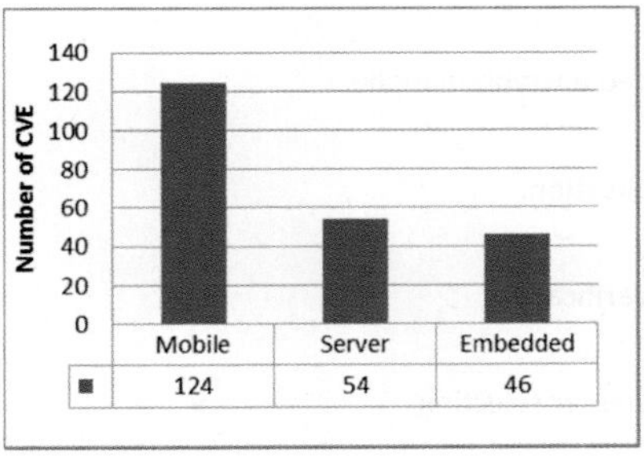

Figure 1: Categories of the CVEs grouped by different platforms.

We collect 224 cryptography vulnerabilities in the CVE database from 2010 to 2015, and analyze cryptography system implementation of 131 common Android APKs. Figure 1 shows the category of 224 CVEs according to the three different platforms.

Table 1 Categories of cryptographic vulnerabilities at the primitive, protocol, or application layer on mobile, server and embedded platform.

Vulnerabilities type	Mobile platform	Embedded platform	Server platform
Cryptographic primitive:			
Hard-coded encryption key	√		
Plaintext storage keys and authenticators		√	
Weak cryptographic components			√
Low PRNG seed entropy		√	
Cryptographic protocol:			
Certificate misconfiguration			√
Wrong authenticated encryption mode			√
Cryptographic application:			
Invalid certificate verification	√		
unreasonable parameter selection	√		

Based on the analysis and classification of the vulnerabilities, we draw a conclusion that specific cryptography misuse is more prone to arise in certain platform. Table 1 shows eight kinds of cryptographic vulnerabilities on three platforms, these vulnerabilities are grouped by cryptographic primitive, protocol, or application layer. As mentioned in the following sections, the specific misuses appear on certain platforms result from different features of each platform.

2.1. *Mobile platform*

With the booming of the mobile industry, a lot of security and cryptographic issues emerge. These problems are closely related with the new mobile structure design, quickly application development iteration speed and the lack of specialized cryptographic knowledge by the mobile developers.

2.1.1. *Customizing SSL/TLS usage by developers causes invalid certificate verification and insecure error handling process.*

Android allows developers to customize SSL/TLS usage, unfortunately, it is complex to implement it correctly with various cryptographic libraries, this often results in invalid certificate verification problems and insecure certificate error handling process.

Invalid SSL/TLS certificate verification. Generally, Android verify SSL/TLS certificates by the system itself, but developers usually misuse non-default self-designed *Trust manager* interface, or extend *SSL Socket Factory* class to accept all certificates. In addition, all hostnames will be allowed if *Allow All Host name Verifier* class is invoking. Moreover, some logic mistakes will bypass all certificates checks for SSL/TLS connections, such as the Apple's 'goto' bug which is produced by unwary developers by adding one redundant goto statement (CVE-2014-1266). In our investigation, 115 CVEs are associated with invalid certificate validation, some of which are about trusting all certificates or hostnames and others are using expired or self-signed certificates.

Insecure certificate error handling process. Android *Webview* UI is used by many mobile web applications to present web pages and communicate with web servers. When an app opens a HTTPS web page, the HTTPS URL is passed to Android for verifying the certificate. With a valid certificate, the *Webview* will show the page, otherwise, *Webview* passes the error handling process to the app and waits for the result. Generally, *Webview* will shield the page directly by default. But if the error handling process is rewritten by developers and ignores the certificate error, the result will be returned to *Webview* and go on visiting the page even though the certificate is illegal. However, programmers often rewrite the error handling process.

2.1.2. *Lack of visual security indicators when implementing SSL/TLS*

Non-browser software whose URLs are usually underlying is widely deployed on mobile platform. When a non-browser app transmits data or accesses Internet, there is often none visual feedback provided by the Android system or app to the users whether or not the connection is secure. In this case, most of the time users do not realize whether the SSL/TLS protocol is correctly used and the certificate is valid or not, the security assurances are totally dependent on the application implementation. Worse still, some wrong warning information will be displayed to users by apps. Even the warning message is meaningful, users may ignore it due to the lack of secure awareness.

2.1.3. *Insecure key management*

Key management includes key generation, exchange, usage, storage, and destruction. A mistake in any of these steps can subvert the entire security of the cryptography system. However, common mobile developers who lack cryptography knowledge will pay more attention to the function of the apps instead of cryptography implementation. Thereby, encryption key generation and storage are usually broken even in some security-critical applications.

Hard-code encryption key. We analyze the key generation methods of 131 Android apps, 23 of which use hard-code encryption keys include some financial related software. Attackers can read the keys directly from the source codes or even closed-source apps by reverse-engineering. Nine CVEs reflect this problem. For example, before IOS version 8.1, some vulnerable apps rely on the hardware UID for its encryption key(CVE-2014-4448).

Plaintext storage cryptographic key or login credential in SD card. As we know, SD cards in mobile devices are publicly readable to the apps which are granted the *READ_EXTERNAL_STORAGE* permission. However, in our investigation, some backup apps will store the authenticators or credentials like passwords and session IDs in plain text into the SD cards without any protection. The attacker is able to obtain the authenticators and take complete control of the authenticated sessions.

2.2. *Embedded platform*

Embedded devices such as home routers, printers, video surveillance systems, and medical implants are widely used. With the widespread usage and the specific characteristics, the cryptography misuse problem on embedded platform is becoming an increasingly important issue.

2.2.1. *Low PRNG seed entropy due to hardware limitation*

Pseudo-random number generator (PRNG) is used to generate random numbers which is seeded by entropy. In general, entropy is gathered from physical sources such as mouse and keyboard activities, disk I/O operations, and specific interrupts on server PC. However, embedded devices do not include a mouse, keyboard and hard disk, only interrupt events can be used as an entropy sources. Some weak random numbers may be generated on embedded platform which will influence a great many cryptographic primitives.

For example, the RSA modulus N_1 and $N_2$of two different devices will have a common factor, if anyone of the random prime number P and Q is generated by PRNG with limited entropy. An adversary can decompose N_1 and N_2 by extracting common factor, and then calculate the RSA private key.

2.2.2. *Plaintext storage in the easily acquired firmware images*

Firmware images of embedded devices can be downloaded from Internet. Therefore, secrets in the firmware can be easier to obtain by attackers. Some negligent development vendors may include RSA or SSH private keys, web-login admin credentials, and weak password hashes inside their firmware images. There are 34 CVEs related to this problem, and Costin *et al.* extract 109 RSA private keys from 428 firmware images in 2014 [4].

2.3. *Server platform*

Web server plays a unique role in encryption communication, encrypted storage and identity authentication. However, a lot of cryptographic misuses arise due to unreasonable parameter selection and wrong encryption mode usage by ignorant developers. More seriously, a simple cryptography vulnerability can affect many users' information security because of the multi-user feature of the servers.

2.3.1. *Certificate misconfiguration in Public Key Infrastructure (PKI)*

A security-critical X.509 certificate is used for the authentication of a server during SSL/TLS protocol implementation. Some properties are needed by a valid certificate: **1)** digitally signed by a trusted CA; **2)** within the validity period; **3)** issued for the correct hostname. However, a remarkable amount of webmasters employ invalid certificates either do so intentionally or lack expert knowledge. For example, they may deploy self-signed and expired certificates, certificates with mismatched hostnames, or certificates signed by an unknown CA. In case X.509 certificate validation fails, SSL/TLS warning messages are present to users. Generally, it is hard for the common users to decide whether the messages imply a Man-In-The-Middle attack or not. Fahl *et al.* collect 1887 certificates from the internet, of which 21 are expired, 45 are signed with unknown CA, and 112 are issued for the wrong hostnames [5].

2.3.2. *Unreasonable authenticated encryption mode*

Strong encryption algorithm together with strong authentication algorithm does not means strong authenticated encryption. In general, encryption-then-MAC authenticated encryption mode is deemed to be secure. However, ASP.net framework uses the Mac-then-Encrypt mode which is vulnerable to chosen-ciphertext attacks. The active adversary could implement Padding Oracle Attack (POA) and Timing Attack to brute-force ciphertext based on the oracles returned by the vulnerable servers. A recent example is the POODLE attack, which reveals that a MITM attacker can exploit padding oracle to recover the cookies on the vulnerable authenticated encryption mode (CVE-2014-8730).

2.3.3. *Weak cryptography components*

The RSA cryptosystem usually fails catastrophically when weak, factorable keys or low exponents by ignorant webmasters. 768-bit RSA modulus can be factored easily nowadays, and low public exponents like *3*without Optimal Asymmetric Encryption Padding (OAEP) suffer from broadcast attack or related message attack [6]. In real-world systems, there are still a lot of weak keys. 14 CVEs present the weak key usage problem. Freak attack which is announced as a serious SSL/TLS vulnerability allows attackers to force servers to use 512-bit RSA key that can be factored easily (CVE-2015-0204).

3. Mitigation

We now suggest a set of countermeasures at primitive, protocol, or application layer that would likely help average developers to reduce the corresponding cryptographic misuse problems.

Cryptographic primitive:

(1) Do not use a constant key for encryption,

(2) Do not store sensitive information in plaintext anywhere,

(3) Save the PRNG output at shutdown and reload it into the entropy when embedded devices reboot.

(4) Use a strong encryption key. That is, symmetric encryption key is not less than 128-bit and asymmetric encryption key is not less than 1024-bit [8].

Cryptographic protocol:

(1) Use key-pinning strategy to pin public key in the local, which can avoid MITM attacks effectively,

(2) Use AES-GCM which is proved to be secure as the authenticated encryption mode.

Cryptographic application:

(1) Use standard libraries for SSL/TLS implementation, and use black-box fuzzing to detect the behavior when an app receives an invalid certificate,

(2) Do not depend on the cryptographic library's defaults.

4. Conclusion

In this paper, we investigate the mistakes that arise when implementing cryptography in real-world systems, and firstly analyze the pertinence between certain cryptographic misuses and the different characteristics of three actual platforms (mobile, embedded and server) systematically. The findings of our investigation suggest that some certain cryptography vulnerabilities widely appear in the specific platform. Finally, some countermeasures are proposed for the common developers that could help to alleviate the cryptographic misuse problems.

References

1. Das, Somak, *et al.* "*IV= 0 Security Cryptographic Misuse of Libraries.*" (2014).

2. Lenstra, Arjen, *et al. Ron was wrong, Whit is right.* No. EPFL-REPORT-174943. IACR, 2012.

3. Cairns, Kelsey, and Graham Steel. "*Developer-Resistant Cryptography.*"

4. Costin, Andrei, *et al.* "*A large-scale analysis of the security of embedded firmwares.*" USENIX Security Symposium. 2014.

5. Fahl, Sascha, *et al.* "*Why Eve and Mallory love Android: An analysis of Android SSL (in) security.*" Proceedings of the 2012 ACM conference on Computer and communications security. ACM, 2012.

6. Boneh, Dan. "*Twenty years of attacks on the RSA cryptosystem.*" Notices of the AMS 46.2 (1999): 203-213.

7. The MITRE Corporation. Common vulnerabilities and exposures (CVE). `http://cve.mitre.org/`.

8. Cryptographic key length proposal. `http://www.keylength.com/`

A Study on Fusion System of Network Security Incident Management Based on Machine Learning Technology

Ling-xing YANG

College of Physics and Electric Engineering, Qujing Normal University,
Qujing, Yunnan 655011, China
E-mail: 84759653@qq.com

Zheng-tao YU

Faculty of Information engineering and Automation, Kunming University of Science and Technology
Kunming, Yunnan 650500, China
E-mail:ztyu@hotmail.com

Due to the rise in popularity of Internet applications, security problems are becoming increasingly significant. The various types of network security problems include the complicated structure of computer viruses and attack information that are well concealed from the network security system, requiring the deployment of a large number of heterogeneous security devices search for every possible threat in order to maintain security protection. However, these isolated systems lack effective linkage and the large amount of information they produce is difficult to be organize and utilize, hampering the administrative staff's ability to monitor real status of network and to make timely response to attacks. This paper proposes the fusion system of network security incident management based on machine learning technology to extract these underlying security incidents. The improved expectation maximization algorithm was introduced to make preprocessing and correlation analysis for the original security data and to generate hierarchical standardized data step by step to identify the source of threats, and provide convenience for administrative staff to make effective responses.

Keywords: Data mining; Risk assessment; Information fusion; Expectation maximization algorithm; Machine learning.

1. Introduction

The network security is needed everywhere in the information society. It is released on the weekly newspaper of the CNCERT/CC on November 6, 2015 that network security problems may occur at any time. The security incidents show a trend of diversification, network viruses producing new variants, and virus source sites from overseas account for 51.2%. Moreover, with network intrusion, the number of tampered domestic government website increased by 48.9% over the previous week and the types of security vulnerability are also increasing. All of these network security problems mainly concentrate on financial field such as bank, so we are in a very insecure network environment [1]. The network security situation is still severe, and the national development strategy of "Internet +" concerns the national economy and people's livelihood. The safety problems are inevitable, while viruses, Trojan virus, data theft, tampering of web pages, network invasion, hackers attacking, unauthorized access and other network events exert constant threat to the user's network security.

Due to the complexity of network security, we need deploy a large number of heterogeneous security devices to build a security system, such as intrusion detection system, antivirus system, firewall, vulnerability scanning system, security authentication system, and so on, which can solve corresponding network security problems respectively. However, these independent and dispersed security devices have no effective linkage with many problems: the huge amounts of security incidents are hard to be organized and managed in a unified manner; the security devices work independently, and the information they produce is disorderly and unsystematic so it can hardly capture the complete attack process of intruders; the security dynamic state cannot be controlled in an all-round way and management of security incidents lags behind as a result of the independence from each other and risk assessment not in time. Therefore, it is an urgent need to integrate these security devices to improve the effectiveness of network security, and researchers at home and abroad have made a lot of work in this area. Valdes & Skinner [2-3] suggested using the generality similarity and minimal matching rules of the attributes of early warning to construct the correlation analysis system of security incident. Benjamin Morin proposed the scene recognition technology [4] based on time sequence pattern recognition, and Steven Cheung put forward the attack scene recognition technology [5] based on expert system. Xinzhou Qin proposed the incident correlation method [6-7] based on statistics causal analysis. In recent years, the research in this field achieved new progress, for instance, MM Siraj suggested the predictable real-time multi-sensing intrusion alarm correlation analysis framework [8]. Based on these research results and adopting the expectation maximization algorithm of machine learning technology, this thesis puts forwards a new fusion method of network security incident which will be discussed in details in the following sections.

2. The General Methods of Security Incident Fusion

The processes of security incident fusion generally are: collection of security incident, pretreatment and standardization, filtering of security incident, clustering and merger of security incident, correlation analysis of security incident, risk assessment, etc. Finally theses links integrate to form attack positioning and security warning, so as to effectively achieve security protection.

Collection, pretreatment and standardization of security incident: the fusion system should collect comprehensive information about security incidents as much as possible, including all security information produced by security devices of all types on different operation systems such as log information, security early warning information and so on, so as to obtain valuable data via pretreatment methods such as correlation analysis. It will involve data transmission in display of the collected data on local terminal, storage on local terminal or uploading to other hosts or integration of the display, storage and uploading. Usually, the syslog protocol or simple network management protocol is adopted for communication so as to ensure the security of data transmission. Finally, make standardized processing of all collected data so that the fusion system can make unified processing of different data. The format of data can follow the intrusion detection message exchange format (IDMEF) put forward by the Defense Advanced Research Projects Agency (DARPA) and the Internet Engineering Task Force (IETF) and Intrusion Detection Working Group (IDWG) [9].

Filtering of security incident: we must filter the data, as the amount of information produced by the security devices is very huge yet the valuable data is quite few. This work is quite complicated, and researchers have achieved many research results in this aspect, so we can make a little modification and use them in the system for reference.

Clustering and merger of security incident: through data preprocessing, it shields low-level details of the operating system and security device types, and after standardizing all security data types, build a model by correlation analysis to classify the security incidents according to the existing knowledge and safety rules. After the information of new security incidents is captured, the model will automatically identify the known security category it belongs to so as to decide whether the alarm information is valuable or not. For the security information not belonging to the known category, the model can further judge whether it is safe, if so, a new security category will be established. The model can make adaptive adjustment according to the safety data, removing useless information, and obtain valuable information through the expectation maximization algorithm.

Correlation analysis of security incident: any security incident is not isolated, but has a foundation. We can discover its inner link through correlation analysis to find its attacking intent. The early warning information of a continuous period can form an alarm sequence by aggregation and correlation analysis, and multiple alarm sequence can constitute an attack scene [10]. The key of correlation analysis is to model safe behaviors, and the modeling methods generally used include attack-tree modeling and causal correlation technology modeling, which have good effect of application and can be integrated into the system.

Risk assessment: risk assessment is to estimate and evaluate the potential risks of the system. Objectively, the actual network is not safe and has certain risks, so how to estimate the risk of network is also one of the key technologies of the system. Researchers have had comprehensive consideration on the research of network risk assessment, which can be directly applied to the system, as long as taking into consideration the dynamic and real-time nature of risk assessment.

3. Fusion System Design of Multi-source Security Incidents

3.1. *Introduction of functions of fusion system*

The security incident fusion system can provide analysis engine for online security incidents fusion and analyze and process all kinds of security information, aiming to discovering the attack incidents and attack host affecting the network security. It acquires precise alarm information from massive security data, increasing the authenticity of system risk assessment, providing reliable evidences for the security administrator, eliminating security hidden danger in time, and removes the influence of security incidents on network. The fusion system can analyze the security information produced by the mainstream security devices in the current market, such as all kinds of log information, information of network intrusion detection system, firewall information, anti-virus information, hardware information, etc.. The fusion system interacts with the unified security management platform, to provide management and control functions, achieve implementation of various kinds of security policies, control commands and rules upgrade interfaces for the unified security management platform dispatching. Its control center can monitor and manage multiple websites, and realize the functions, such as display of the comprehensive alarm data, controlling the allocation of security policies, the alarm data process and asset information management, for each monitored website.

3.2. *Structure of fusion system*

The function modules of fusion system mainly include: data collection module, pretreatment and standardization module, fusion analysis module, and response and output module. The fusion analysis module is the key part of the system, which can realize filtering, alarm validation, clustering, correlation, risk assessment, etc.. The response and output module mainly achieves interaction with the alarm information of control center, corresponding response to the alarm information, and processing of local alarm information. Its structure is shown in Figure 1, and the key technologies to realize each module are introduced in the fourth section.

4. Analysis of Key Technologies

4.1. *Log filtering technology*

Log information contains a large amount of data but most of the data is redundancy, so it is necessary to filter the log information. The common web server log files and database log files will produce a large number of users' access failure incidents, which is normal in general. The thesis analyzes the log filtering technology by analyzing log samples which are taken from the Modern Education Technology Center of Qujing Normal University.

Log sample 1:

[Sun Nov 10 01:22:36 2015] [error] [client ***.***.***.***] File does not exist: http://tswh.qjnu.edu.cn/TeachView.asp?id=14

[Sun Nov 10 01:22:36 2015] [error] [client ***.***.***.***] File does not exist: http://tswh.qjnu.edu.cn/TeachView.asp?id=18

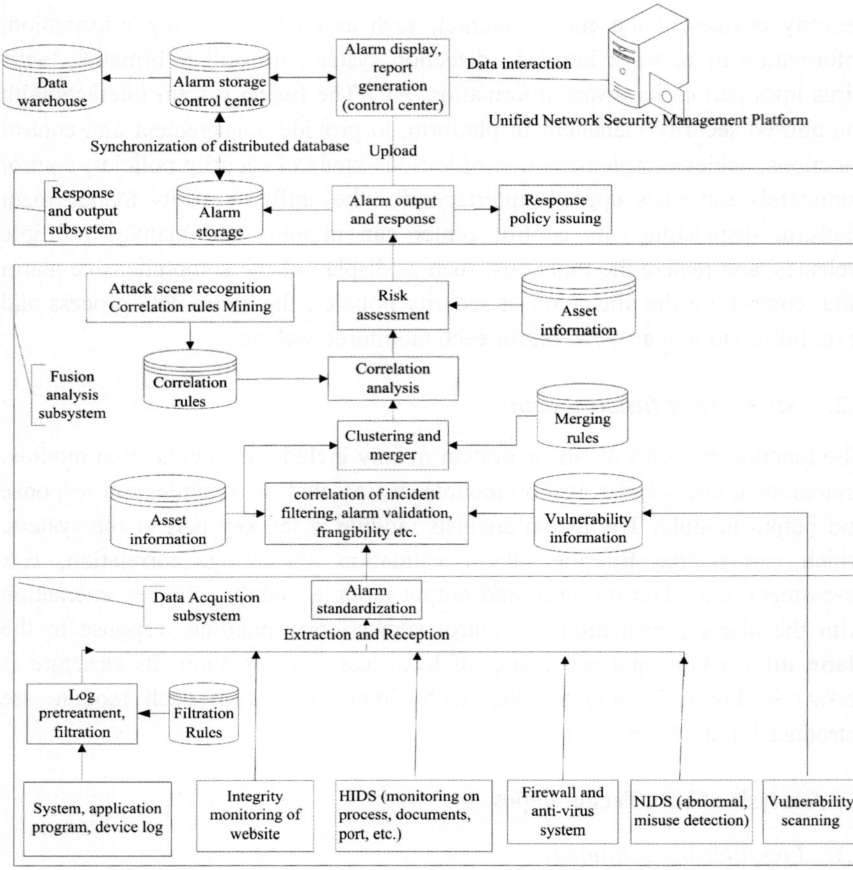

Figure 1 Structure diagram of fusion system

This may be caused by inexistence of resources or modified page or attack. If it is attack, there must be a lot of access records of the same IP, and it can be identified whether it is abnormal through the statistical number of access.

Log sample 2:

[30/Oct/2015:15:04:49 -0400] "GET /scripts/..%c1%1c../winnt/system32/

/cmd.exe?/c+dir+c: HTTP/1.0" 404 315

[30/Oct/2015:15:04:55 -0400] "GET /scripts/..%c0%af../winnt/system32/

/cmd.exe?/c+dir+c: HTTP/1.0" 404 315

This type of log contains cmd.exe,root.exe,_mem_bin,msadc,/winnt/c+dir and other character string. If it can match the log format of Nimda worms, it can be basically determined to be Nimda worms. This type of log can be filtered by rules to determine whether to match the known specific pattern string. An excellent product of log analysis is ossec – hids and can be applied to the fusion system for reference according to the actual situation.

4.2. *Pretreatment, standardization and decoding of security incidents*

The data type and format produced by each security device is obviously different from others. In order to use the unified analysis methods and the association rules, the data must be normalized to shield the differences of various kinds of data type. Therefore, a suitable data model should be chosen to include all security information and design algorithm to achieve the mapping of all kinds of security information to standardized format. This system takes the IDMEF data model for reference to select a proper data structure based on actual situation to model the data standardization, and shield the difference of security incidents by making a mapping table with number ID as a condition of mapping. In order to make the system easy to expand, the system reserves a security incident, and they have a unified internal number, name of behavior, grouping and classification, such as ID, Name, Type Name, and Group Name. Therefore, the standardization processing can be completed by acquiring the external ID of security incident by decoding, inquiring the corresponding internal ID by mapping table and finally getting the internal classification information in security knowledge base according to the internal ID. The model of standardization is [11]:

```
TypeDef Struct Standard_Alert_Type      // security alert data format
{   DateTime      EventBeginTime;    // security event start time
    String        IDS_Name;    // IDS generating the alert
    String        MapTableName;    // map table name
    String        NetProtocol;    // network protocol
String       ServiceNames;    // services
    SOURCE        SourceName;   // source message triggering the event
```

```
TARGET        TargeName;      // target message attacked
CLASSIFICATION    ClassName;       //action name,group,hierarchical
ASSESSMENT     AssessmentName;       //assessment name
CORRELATION_DATA Correlation_Data;   // correlation information
ADDITION_DATA   Additional_Data; //additional data
}Standard_Alert_Type;
```

The Standard_Alert_Type defined above can be used to describe all information of heterogeneous security events, which shields categorical differences between different event systems and contains categorical information after service identification and alert ID mapping for the convenience of subsequent correlation analysis.

The system adopts regular expression to analyze alert data and obtain specific fields on the basis of predefinition regulation. For example, the log information of the network intrusion detection system Snort is: 3/26-00:04:17.670821 [**] [1:1419:9] SNMP trap udp [**] [Classification: Attempted Information Leak] [Priority: 2] {UDP} 202.203.131.179:162 -> 202.203.208.78:162. And its analysis regulation is[4]:

```
<ids>  <!--1:2323:33 type alert-->
<ids>  <!—alert of type 1:2323:33--><name>snort</name>
  <method>net_socket</method>
<regex>^(\d+/\d+-\d+:\d+:\d+).\d+\s+[**]  [\d:(\d+):\d+]  \.+[Classification: (\.+)]  [Priority:  (\d)]  {(\.+)}  (\d+.\d+.\d+.\d+)\p*(\d*)  -> (\d+.\d+.\d+.\d+)\p*(\d*)
</regex>
<order>time,id,classtype,priority,protocol,srcip,srcport,dstip,dstport</order>
<mapping>snort_classtype,snort_id</mapping></ids>
```

Timestamp, ID number, classification name, priority, protocol type, source IR, source port, target IP, and target port field can be extracted. After every and each field is extracted, standardization mapping shall be completed with regular expression specified by the mapping element.

4.3. *Clustering and merger of security incidents*

There are many methods for clustering of security incidents. This thesis takes the expectation maximization algorithm based on statistical ideas to realize it, and the principle of the expectation maximization algorithm can be seen in [12]. The initial clustering can adopt the clustering algorithm based on rules, and the idea of which is: if the security devices produce similar alarm information in a short period, they are likely to be attacked, and when the times of appearance of statistical specified factors such as ID, source, target, and service in a certain period reach a certain requirement, the alarms at the same conditions occurring in the following certain period can be merged. This method works effectively for merging scanning attack and alarm caused by wrong configuration [11].

Actual situation, however, is more complex, and often it cannot be simply determined safe or not and cannot be identified as which type of security incident. What's more, rules can be only formulated from data. Hence, the expectation maximization algorithm based on some measurement rules to realize cluster can reflect the real situation more. First, it defines the model data "m" of known security incident which is dynamic and updating, unknown security incident "s", and the standard to measure the similarity of the two "r" which is uncertain sometimes. Based on the idea of statistics, when there is an unknown incident, it calculates the probability value of "s" belonging to "m" through the expectation maximization training of known and unknown data, and when the algorithm convergence occurs, the result is the value of similarity degree of some attribute of "s" and "m". Accordingly, it automatically affiliates "s" to some "m". According to the Bayesian formula, the regular calculation is:

$$p(r|m,s) = p\,(m,r|s)/p\,(m \vee s). \tag{1}$$

According to Philipp Koenh's statistical machine translation method [13], we can directly get the calculation formula of the generality that a similar new security incident belongs to the known module data:

$$t(m|s) = \frac{\Sigma(m,s)c(m|s;M,S)}{\Sigma m\,\Sigma_{(m,s)}\,c(m \vee s;M,S)}\,. \tag{2}$$

Where, M is the collection of module data, and s is the data collection of security incident that has been determined. Figure 2 is the pseudo-code of expectation maximization algorithm:

```
Input:set of SecurityEvent Data and Templet Data(S,M)
output:Membership Degree Probability t(m|s)
Setting ct(m|s)=0;t_tal(s)=0;t(m|s)=StatisticalValue;
Repeat
  foreach (s,m) in (S,M)
    foreach s in S
      st(s)=0
      foreach m in M
        st(s)+=t(m|s)
      end
    end
    foreach s in S
      foreach m in M
        ct(m|s)+=t(m|s)/st(s)
          t_tal(s)+=t(m|s)/st(s)
      end
    end
  end
  foreach s in S
    foreah m in M
      t(m|s)+=ct(m|s)/t_tal(s)
    end
  end
```

Figure2 Algorithm of EM in Security Incident Cluster

5. Conclusions

On the basis of analysis of the existing research results, this thesis designs and realizes the fusion system of network security incidents based on machine learning technology, and trains the data of security incidents and module by the expectation maximization algorithm to make the clustering less depend on priori knowledge; learn security rules from it, and constantly perfect the clustering of security incidents. This system is applied in Qujing Normal University and achieves good effects, greatly reducing the burden of safety management personnel and improving work efficiency.

References

1. http://www.cert.org.cn/.

2. Valdes A, Skinner K. Probabilistic Alert Correlation[A]. *Proceedings of the 4th International Symposium on Recent Advances in Intrusion Detection.* Springer-Verlag, 2001. 54-68.

3. A.Valdes and K.Skinner, "Adaptive, Model-Based Monitoring for Cyber AttackDetection," presented at RAID 2000 Conf,Oct.2000:80-92.

4. Benjamin M, Herve D.*Correlation of Intrusion Symptoms: An Application of Chronicles,* Proc. of the 6th International Symposium on Recent Advances in Intrusion Detection, Pittsburgh, PA.USA: Springer-Verleg,2003.

5. Steven C, Ulf L, Martin F.*Modeling Multistep Cyber Attacks for Scenario Recognition,* Proc of Third DARPA Information Survivability Conference and Exposition.Washington,2003.

6. Xinzhou Qin and Wenke Lee. Statistical Causality of INFOSEC Alert Data. *In proceedings of Recent Advances in Intrusion Detection* 2003, LNCS 2820, p.73-94; Springer-Verlag.

7. Qin Xinzhou. A Probabilistic-based Framework for INFOSEC Alert Correlation, Master's thesi, Georgia Institute of Technology, 2005.

8. MM Siraj, HHT Albasheer, MM Din. Towards Predictive Real-time Multi-sensors Intrusion Alert Correlation Framework, *Indian Journal of Science and Technology*, Vol 8(12), 70658, June 2015.

9. http://www.ietf.org/rfc/rfc4765.txt

10. Andrew P.Moore, Robert J.EllisonRichard C. Linger. *Attack Modeling for Information Security and Survivability,* CMU/SEI Technical Note,2001.

11. Zhang Zhi-jun , A Study and Implementation on Fusion System of Network Security Incidents. Master's thesis, Yunnan University(2009).

12. http://www.cnblogs.com/biyeymyhjob/archive/2012/07/21/2603020.html

13. Philipp Koehn. *Statistical Machine Translation.* Cambridge University Press.(2010).

Sybil Attack Detection Method Based on Geographic Information in ZigBee

Mei-gen HUANG†, Bin YU, Zhi-yin KONG and Wei-wei ZHOU
Zhengzhou Institute of Information Science and Technology
Zhengzhou, 450004, China
†*E-mail: huang_meigen@163.com*

Currently, the damage potential of Sybil attack is serious in ZigBee. In this paper, our proposed Sybil attack detection method allows the cluster head to identify different Sybil nodes by comparing the RSSI value and geographic information to make an accurate detection of Sybil attack. Both the security test and the experimental results demonstrated that the proposed method can detect Sybil attack efficiently at small expenses of communication and calculation.

Keywords: ZigBee; Sybil attack; Geographic information; Cluster head.

1. Introduction

Sybil attack was put forward by Douceur in [1] firstly. The core characteristic of Sybil attack is presented as one node with multiple identities. The node launching attack is called malicious node. Those attached to malicious node are Sybil node. ZigBee technology is a new kind of wireless sensor network technology with the characteristics of large capacity and low cost [2].However, Its nodes are always exposed to complex environment without supervision, which make it easy to be attacked by malicious node.

Newsome et al. proposed the wireless resource detection method in [3]. Specifically, he made use of the random listening strategy with certain possibility to find out Sybil nodes that can't broadcast information at appointed channel. However, this method will not work when the ZigBee nodes have multiple antennas. Gunhee Lee et al. put forward another inspection method for Sybil attack based on node calculation capacity in [4]. He came to get Sybil node through operation time of repeated encryption and decryption process. From this point, the cost of this method is large. P.Raghu Vamsi and Mingxi Li et al. performed another way to detect Sybil attack based on RSSI through collaboration to capture the same RSSI value during communication in [5, 6]. Similarly, the communication cost is large.

According to whether there is cooperation between malicious nodes, Sybil attack can be divided into two categories: (1).Basic Sybil attack, namely, without any cooperation between malicious nodes; (2). Collaborative Sybil attack, in this case, malicious nodes cooperate with each other. For the above reasons, this mode has wider range of attack damage. To overcome above shortages, we propose a method for Sybil attack detection in the ZigBee based on geographic information after deep analysis of Sybil attacks in ZigBee.

2. Network Topology

ZigBee network support three kinds of topology structure, star topology network, the tree topology network and the network topology network, respectively. ZigBee network topologies are mapped to clusters of network logically according to the relationship between parent and child node. The parent node becomes the only cluster head in each of the clusters. All child nodes become a node within the cluster. The cluster network is shown in Fig.1.

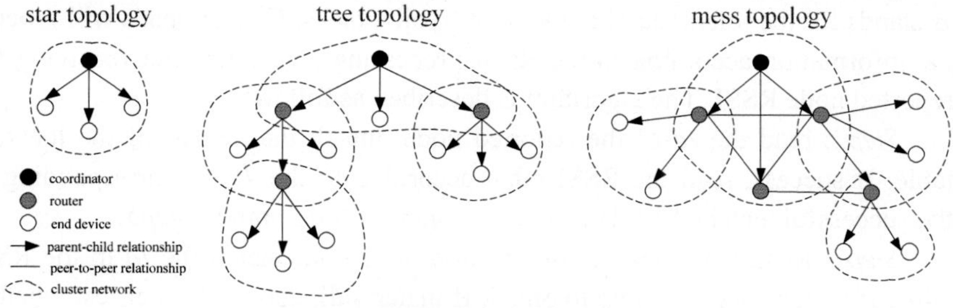

Fig.1. Partition of cluster network

We make the following assumptions based the above analysis.(1)

3. Sybil Attack Detection

3.1. *Establish node position library*

After ZigBee network boot Sybil attack detection process, the parent node to become cluster head, and perform the Sybil node doubt mechanism. All child nodes become a node within the cluster which its father node belongs to. Cluster head start timer countdown τ. Values τ are set by the cluster heads based on cluster nodes, then set up node position library $Command_1 = \{\tau\}$ within the cluster. All cluster nodes report its geographic location after receiving the $Command_1$. Cluster head stop receiving the geographic information from the node within the cluster when is timer τ is out. The cluster head put the received information into the location table and establish the corresponding RSSI table.

(1) Node location table

The node location table has 3 columns, *Id, Position* and *Index*, are represent for the identify, the location information and corresponding RSSI table entry of each node within the cluster. Each node owns an RSSI table.

(2)RSSI table

The RSSI table has 4 columns. Therein, *ID* is represent for node that communicate with the node in the location table. $RSSI_1$, $RSSI_2$ and $RSSI_3$ are represent for the new, the latest and the old RSSI value for the node in itself.

3.2. *Establish node RSSI table*

After the countdown τ, Cluster heads set up a $Command_2 = \{f(\alpha)\}$, which means that the location library is established. The node within cluster will work in the normal communication situation after getting *Command*$_2$. After communication with neighbor, the node will make a decision whether to report to the cluster head according to the probability $f(\alpha) = 1 - \alpha$. Threshold value α stands for the tolerance of network to Sybil attacks. Cluster heads will process the information according to the RSSI processing algorithm after receiving the reported node RSSI. The algorithm is described as follows:

Step1: read the *Id* of the reported node, match the *Id* part of the location table. If success, read the RSSI table according to the *Index* corresponding to the successful matched *Id*. Then jump to *Step2*.If fail, jump to *Step5*.

Step2: Read neighbor communication node's *Id*, match the *Id* in the RSSI table. If match success, jump to *Step3*, If match fail, make a further test whether exist in the location table. If exist, jump to *Step4*. Otherwise, jump to *Step5*.

Step3: read the RSSI value, refresh the corresponding $RSSI_1$ part. The update rules is: copy $RSSI_2$ to $RSSI_3$, copy $RSSI_1$ to $RSSI_2$, replace them $RSSI_1$ with the new RSSI value. Then, jump to *Step6*.

Step4: write the node ID to ID part in the RSSI table, and write the RSSI value into the $RSSI_1$ part. Then jump to *Step6*.

Step5: add the node to the Sybil set named *SybilCollect*. Then jump to *Step6*.

Step6: finish.

3.3. *Sybil nodes identification*

As to one Sybil node with multiple identities, it can report the true geographical location (the same as the malicious nodes), and can also be reported to the false location (unlike the malicious nodes). Cluster heads by traversing location table and RSSI table can find out the two kinds of Sybil node described above.

Considering the influence of environment on the wireless communication, there will be a certain deviation during the node position, so we design a distance deviation called δ .when the distance between two location is less than δ , we consider them to be the same location. The values of δ is associated with network density and communication radius.

(1)Traversing Location table

Location table is the summary within all cluster nodes' location, based on the principles of one node occupy one location. If multiple nodes appear on the same location, we define it as Sybil node. Therefore, Cluster heads traverse the location table to get the nodes whose distance deviation is less than δ , and add them into the $SybilCollect$.

(2)Traversing RSSI table

Cluster heads traverse the entire RSSI table according to the $Index$ order in the geographical location table. For every RSSI entry in the table, the cluster head read the ID field to find the node from the geographical location table and get the $Position$ field. Cluster heads calculate Euclidean distance of the two nodes $D = \sqrt{(x_1 - x_2)^2 + (y_1 - y_2)^2}$. The distance D is called reported distance. The coordinate of reported node is (x_1, y_1) , and the coordinate of neighbor communication is (x_2, y_2) .The distance of d is related to the RSSI value of reported node and neighbor communication nodes calculated by Eq. (1).

$$P_r(d) = P_r(d_0) + 10n\log_{10}(d_0 / d) \quad . \tag{1}$$

$P_r(d)$ is received signal strength, generally taking the RSSI value. In order to eliminate the influence of environment, we take an average value of RSSI by $\frac{1}{3}\sum_{j=1}^{3} RSSI_j$ rather than get the RSSI value directly; $P_r(d_0)$ stand for the path loss corresponding to the distance d_0; n is the signal propagation attenuation factor ranging from 2 to 5. Eq.(1)is converted to the follow Eq. (2).

$$\frac{1}{3}\sum_{j=1}^{3} RSSI_j = P_r(1) + 10n\log_{10}(1/d) \quad . \tag{2}$$

We can calculate d between two nodes. When $|d - D| \geq \delta$, cluster heads will add the reported node and neighbor node into the $SybilCollect$.

4. Experiment and Result Analysis

4.1. *Experimental scheme*

To verify the performance of the method we proposed, we use the ZigBee hardware experimental platform designed by us, and download the Z_Stack [7] protocol stack containing the Sybil attack detection to the CC2530 [8]. We choose the mesh network topology, and are divide it into 5 clusters of network with a total of 30 ZigBee nodes. Among them, there are 4 malicious nodes(1 router and 3 end devices), 10 Sybil nodes(2 routers and 8 end devices).

During the experiment, the ID node take a *IEEE* physical address, and the node's geographical position take 2d location coordinates. ZigBee network communication has 11 channels. The communication radius of node is 50 m. Other parameters set as follows: $\tau = 1s$, $\alpha = 0.8$, $\delta = 3m$, $n = 3$, $P_r(1) = -40dbm$.

4.2. *Security test*

The experimental environment is open and flat space. The geographical location of the reported Sybil node should be to the geographical location of the 30 m range from the malicious node location. The distance between the reported Sybil node and malicious node location should be less than 30 m. Also, the Sybil node can upload no geographical location information. The distance of Sybil node deviate from the malicious node is labeled L. Experiments are conducted independently for 3 times, the number of Sybil nodes with $L < \delta$, $L \geq \delta$, $L = \varnothing$ are (1,9,0), (2,7,1), (1,8,1), respectively. In this experiment, the locations reported have big difference, but the detection rate of Sybil is up to 100%, so the method can improve the security of ZigBee network remarkably.

4.3. *Performance analysis*

The performance analysis is based on the cluster network unit. We make some assumptions before the analysis: The number of nodes within the cluster is m. Each node has an average number of n neighbor nodes. Each node has an average number of p communication times with its neighbor nodes in its lifespan. The number of Sybil node within the cluster is q.

We make some comparisons among our method with [4, 5]. k stands for the times of encrypted. In Table 1, the node's cost of communication and computation is better than those of [4, 5]. The cost of storage and computation of cluster head is little larger than that of [4]. More importantly, our method has advantages in Sybil node detection rate, which provides higher security.

Table1 Cost comparison among different methods

	cluster head in this paper	cluster nodes in this paper	Literature [4]	Literature [5]
cost of storage	$(11n+14)m$ Byte	$8q$ Byte	$7m+6q$ Byte	$14n+8q+p$ Byte
cost of communication	3	$np(1-\alpha)+1$	$O(n)$	$O(n^2)$
cost of computation	$mnp(1-\alpha)+2m+3$ times of AES	$np(1-\alpha)+6$ times of AES	kn times of AES	$O(n^2)$ times of AES

5. Conclusions

In this paper, Sybil attack has been divided into two categories: Basic Sybil attack and Collaborative Sybil attack. On the basis of deep study of ZigBee stack and Sybil attack, a new Sybil attack detection method is proposed, which is based on the matching of geographic information and RSSI to detect the basic Sybil attacks. Both security test and experimental results show that the proposed method has a low cost and high detection rate, which effectively enhances the security of ZigBee in practical application.

References

1. J. Douceur, "The Sybil attack", Peer-to-Peer Systems: First International Workshop (ITPTS 2002), Lecture Notes in Computer Science 2429, Springer-Verlag, March 2002:251-260.
2. Alliance Z B. ZigBee 2007 specification. Online: `http://www. zigbee. org/Specifications/ZigBee/Overview. aspx, 2007, 45: 120.`
3. J. Newsome, E. Shi, D. Song, and A. Perrig, "The Sybil Attack in Sensor Networks: Analysis & Defenses", In Proc. of 3rd IEEE/ACM Information Processing in Sensor Networks (IPSN'04), April 2004: 259-268.
4. Gunhee Lee, J.L.D.K., An Approach to Mitigating Sybil Attack in Wireless Networks using ZigBee. ICACT, 2008: 1005-1009.
5. P. Raghu Vamsi, K.K., A Lightweight Sybil Attack Detection Framework for WSNs. 2014.
6. Mingxi Li, Y.X.X.W., A Regional Statistics Detection Scheme against Sybil Attacks in WSNs. TrustCom, 2013. 12: 285-291.
7. Texas Instruments. Z-Stack Developer's Guide [EB/OL]. (2012).[2013-04-28]. `http://www.ti.com.`
8. Texas Instruments. CC2530_datasheet [EB/OL]. (2011).[2013-04-28]. `http://www.ti.com.`

Research on Quantum Key Network Model

Lei SHI†, Yi-xi GUO and Chen-Hui MA
Zhengzhou Institute of Information Science and Technology, Zhengzhou,450001, China
†E-mail: 409162319@qq.com

A quantum key network that shields equipment and communication networks is proposed to address the issue of complicated key relations of equipment in Quantum Key Distribution (QKD) network. Taking into account the key relations of nodes in quantum key network, a quantum key network model to study the key relations in QKD network is developed using graph theory. The paper firstly provides a detailed introduction to the principle of QKD and its limitations, then studies the topology structure of QKD network and mechanism of the quantum key distributed service, and finally adopts graph theory to construct a key relations based quantum key network model to study key distributing processes in QKD network.

Keywords: Quantum Key Distribution (QKD) Network; Quantum network of secrets; Key relation.

1. Introduction

In order to extend the quantum key distribution distance and realize of quantum key network service requirements, quantum key distribution key relay and the key routing function must be increased on the basis of the original technology of QKD[1-4].

The paper firstly provides a detailed introduction to the principle of QKD and its limitations, then studies the topology structure of QKD network and mechanism of quantum key distributed service, and finally adopts graph theory constructing a key relations based quantum key network model and studies key distributing process in QKD network under the built model.

2. Quantum Key Distribution

2.1. *Principle of quantum key distribution*

Quantum key distribution is a kind of technology that carries quantum information, transmits via the quantum channel, and establishes a shared key through the classical channel among legitimate users[5]. Its characteristics can be summarized as follows:

(1) The security of quantum key distribution is based on fundamental principles of quantum mechanics, which can guarantee unconditional security in theory. However the current classical cryptographic techniques can only be achieved based on the calculated safety.

(2) Secret sharing must be based on sharing quantum media, namely quantum keys are paired. There are essentially different from the classical cryptography which generates key from a single-point sources of noise.

(3) In addition to quantum media, the classic communication media must exist. The classic communication medium can be public, not secure.

2.2. *Quantum key distribution limitations*

Quantum key distribution has incomparable advantages over classical cryptography, and at the same time, there are also some obvious limitations:

(1) limited transmission distance..

(2) t can't meet the demand of multi-user.

In order to extend the quantum key distribution distance and realize of quantum key network service requirements, quantum key distribution key relay and the key routing function must be increased on the basis of the original technology of QKD. The paper defines the following concepts to elucidate the idea:

Quantum Key Generation (QKG), refers to the process in which generating shared security of key by quantum code at both ends of quantum channel.

Quantum Key Service (QKS), refers to the process that on the basis of obtaining the secure key at the Quantum level, realizing quantum key network services to provide key applications for equipment by Quantum Key network services in the classic network layer through the key relay routing realize and key route.

3. QKD Network

3.1. *QKD network topology*

QKD network is composed of two networks, quantum network and classic network Quantum network consists of quantum channel and classic network consists of classical channel[6].

The node in the classic network does not affect the network topology. And the interconnected relationship between the network nodes in quantum layer directly determines the QKD network topology.

QKD networks are generally irregular mesh topology. Mesh topology has the following basic characteristics:

(1) In the network, the nodes are interconnected and does not exist an isolated network node;

(2) Between any two network nodes, there is at least one path;

(3) In the quantum layer, the nodes are not completely interconnected.

3.2. *QKG centralized management mechanism*

Each QKD network node composed of two functional modules, QKG and QKS. The QKS functional module connect several QKG functional module. Depending on the numbers of QKG connected to QKS, QKD network nodes have different functions.

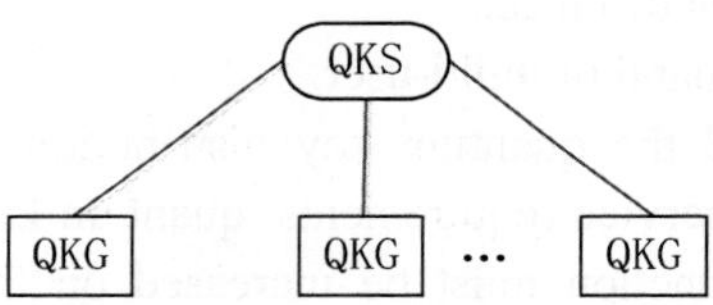

Fig.1.QKG centralized management mechanism

QKS uses a centralized management mechanism to manage its QKGs. The principle of management mechanism is shown in Figure 1. One QKS connects Multiple QKG, each QKG can adopt different quantum codes such as single photon phase coding, a single photon polarization coding, continuous variable coding, free space coding to generate security keys. However, the generated security key is centrally managed by QKS to achieve key relay and key routing function.

3.3. *QKS service mode*

Combining traditional centralized key management, This paper study quantum key distributed service. Traditional centralized key management model shown in Figure 2.

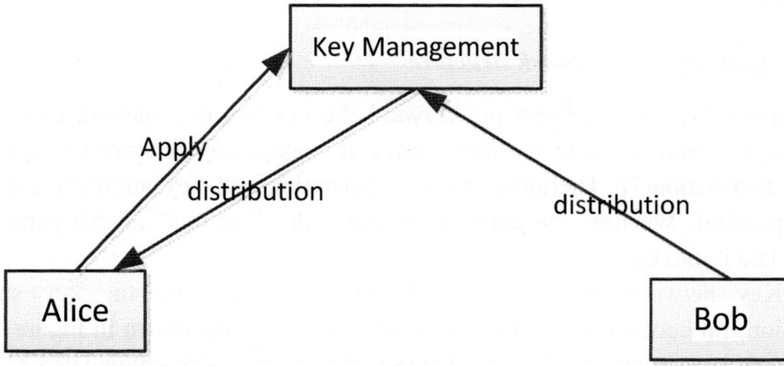

Fig.2.Centralized management mechanism

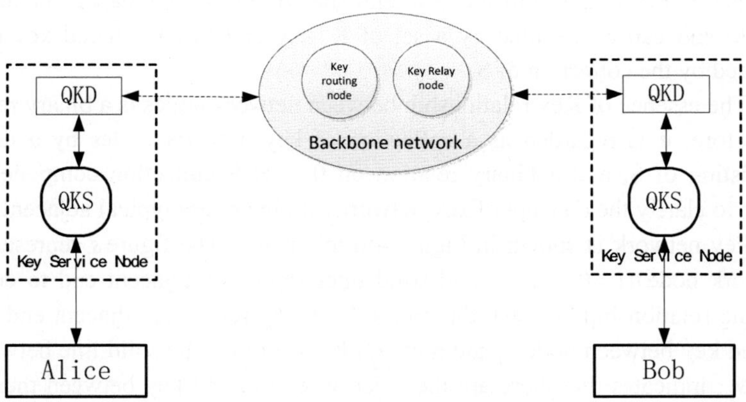

Fig.3.Quantum Key Distributed Services Manner

First, Alice apply from key management for keys to communicate with Bob. Second, key management accepts the applications, generates the key, and distributes the key to users Bob and Alice.

Quantum Key Distributed Services manner shown in Figure 3.Alice apply to local QKS for key, local QKS accepts the applications After key negotiation with multiple QKSs in the network, the QKS corresponding to Alice forms the shared key with the QKS corresponding to Bob. And then Bob acquires the key from its QKS. In the whole key distribution process, there are several QKSs participate in the key distribution. Each QKS has equal status, whose key is obtained by hop consultation, without a centralized management and control of equipment. The mode of this key service in this paper is called quantum key distribution services.

4. Quantum Key Network

4.1. *Quantum key network structure*

European SECOQC project put forward the concept of "network of secrets" whose function is merely to store, push and manage key generated by quantum key distribution[7]. Therefore the key generation and key application can be independent. We uses the concept of "network of secrets" in this paper, and translate it into key network.

Key network, is composed of network nodes and the key sharing relationship between them[8-9]. Network node structure shown in Figure 4.The network node consists of several QKG and one QKS with abbreviated as QKS node. Shared key between network nodes can be divided into the adjacent end to end shared key and arbitrary end to end shared key. In this paper, the adjacent end to end can be denoted by a set of R, any end to end shared key can be denoted by the collection of S.

The essence of Key relationship between network nodes is a binary relation. Therefore, it is regarded as a collection of key network nodes by a network consisting of S, and a binary relation on the set S collection components. In order to clarify the concept of key networks, a nine nodes typical adjacent end to end key network is shown in Figure 4in this paper. The figure s_i represents the network node $i(i=0,1,...,9)$, and solid lines represent adjacent end to end key sharing relationship between the nodes. letters R_{ij} represent adjacent end to end shared key between node s_i and node s_j. For example, the solid line between s_1 and s_2, indicates that there are the adjacent end to end key between them, and the adjacent end to end shared key is called $R_{1,2}$

4.2. *Quantum key network model*

The diagram of key network, is defined as a network diagram , which consists of a collection of network nodes which is called S and its key relationship on the set S. The set of S and R constitute the diagram of adjacent end to end key network, which can be denoted by {S, R}. The set of S and K constitute the diagram of any end to end key network, which can be denoted by {S, K} Combining with the graph theory, we give two definitions of network diagram.

Definition 4.1.the diagram of adjacent end to end key network: end to end adjacent key network diagram is a simple non-fully connected graph which can be represented by the tuple $Q=(S,R)$. Where: $S=\{s_1, s_2, ..., s_n\}$, the set S is a finite non-empty set, which is on behalf of the key network nodes of the network.

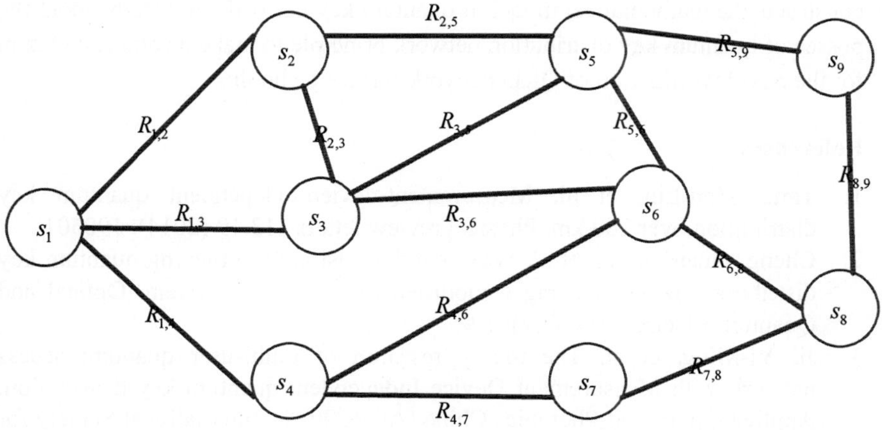

Fig.4.adjacent end to end key network

$R=\{(s_i,s_j)\in S\propto S\mid s_i\neq s_j\}$,the relationship (s_i,s_j) indicates the presence of the adjacent end to end shared key between network nodes s_i and s_j, the adjacent end to end shared key can be denoted by $R_{ij}=(s_i,s_j)$ between network nodes s_i and s_j.

Definition 4.2.the diagram of any end to end key network: Any end to end key network diagram is a simple fully connected graph which can be represented by the tuple $Q=(S,K)$. Where: $S=\{s_1,s_2,\ldots,s_n\}$, is a finite non-empty set, which is on behalf of the key network nodes of the network. $K=S\propto S=\{(s_i,s_j)\mid s_i\neq s_j\}$, (s_i,s_j) indicates that any end to end shared key between network nodes can share key, and an arbitrary end to end shared key can be denoted by $K_{ij}=(s_i,s_j)$ between network nodes s_i and s_j.

Thus, quantum key distribution network key mathematical model can be used in the form of a four-tuple representation.

Definition 4.3.quantum key network key distribution model: quantum key network key distribution model can be a four-tuple (S,R,K,f), where: S is a collection of quantum key network nodes of the network. R is a collection of adjacent end to end shared key in the quantum key network. K is a collection of arbitrary end to end shared key in the quantum key network. f is a mapping function from the collection R to collection K, $f:R\rightarrow K$.

5. Conclusions

On the basis of deep study about QKD network topology and distributed service mode, relying on key relationships, and based on the graph theory, the paper constructs the mathematical model of quantum key network, and study about the posses of quantum key distribution network principle to make a solid foundation for the next investigation of QKD network service technology.

References

1. Tang, Yan-Lin, et al. Measurement-device-independent quantum key distribution over 200 km. Physical review letters 113.19 (2014): 190501..
2. Cheng, Guang-ming, et al. Wavelength division multiplexing quantum key distribution network using a modified plug-and-play system. Optical and Quantum Electronics (2014): 1-9.
3. Ji, Yi-Ming, et al. The theory research of multi-user quantum access network with Measurement Device Independent quantum key distribution. Applied Optics and Photonics China (AOPC2015). International Society for Optics and Photonics, 2015.
4. Wang, Shuang, et al. Field and long-term demonstration of a wide area quantum key distribution network. Optics express 22.18 (2014): 21739-21756.
5. C. Kollmitzer M. Pivk. Applied Quantum Cryptography. Lect. Notes Phys. 797 (Springer, Berlin Heidelberg, 2010).
6. WEN H, HAN Z F, HONG P, et al. Quantum key distribution networks layer model. Proceedings of SPIE.(Bellingham:SPIE,2007).
7. R. Alleaume. Secoqc white paper on quantum key distribution and cryptography. (Secoqc-WP-v5, 2007).
8. TAO Z. Fundamental of quantum key distribution network. (He Fei, University of Science and Technology of China, 2008).
9. HAN W .Protocols and mechanisms in the quantum key distribution networks. (He Fei, University of Science and Technology of China, 2008).

Research of Data Security Strategy MC-R Based on Cloud Computing

LI Ling, MEI Shengmin, ZHANG Hairong, TANG Haiyan
College of Communication Engineering ,Jilin University
Changchun 130012, Jilin, China
liling2002@jlu.edu.cn , 1131772142@qq.com

Cloud computing provides convenient, economic and highly efficient services. However, with its rapid development in recent years, cloud computing's security issues are of increasing importance and data storage security has emerged as the most pressing issue currently. In this paper, we studied cloud computing and data storage security issues and proposed the MC-R strategy to tackle customer data privacy problems. MC prevents data leakage during data download and upload through masking and concealing data in the client while R enciphers data with the computing prowess of cloud computing. Lastly, we tested the strategy and through data analysis, the result of the tests demonstrates that it can successfully mask and conceal data and protect data privacy.

Keywords: Cloud computing security, Data storage security, MC-R strategy, Mask and conceal data.

1. Introduction

Cloud computing, distributing its tasks in a huge Resource Pool, enables users to gain computing power, storage space, tailored information services and opportunities of saving energy and cost, has become a focus in IT domain since October 2007, when IBM and Google declared cooperation. In recent years, emerged as a revolutionary paradigm for dealing with the development needs of computing resources and distributed applications , combined with its dominant power in IT industry, cloud computing has been taken into account by more governments in their IT policies and strategies[1].

Currently, most enterprises still take a wait-and-see attitude towards cloud computing despite its superiorities such as convenience, financial economy, high scalability and paying on demand, because a series of existing security issues including privacy data leakage , tampering or unauthorized access and storing users' data in the cloud instead of their own databases has made them lose faith in service providers. In this paper, the MC-R strategy is proposed, which would decrease the risk of data leakage due to its unique value of guaranteeing data security during transmission and storage.

2. Present Situation of Cloud Computing and Data Storage Security

2.1. *Present situation of cloud computing security*

Cloud computing is a synthesis of existing technologies like grid computing , SOA , Web 2.0 and virtualization , which features dynamic service computing and flexible service contracts, has led to a major change in the IT field where users are exposed to more security crisis. Apparently, applications corresponded with cloud computing are not the sole sufferers as hostile attacks can also do harm to cloud computing performance.

2.2. *Present situation of data storage security*

In cloud computing , data storage and manipulation are both provided in the form of services , so it possesses solid characteristics in terms of data security . Furthermore, storing data in the servers in the Internet causes more security problems in the process of transmission. Besides, cloud computing is based on existing distributed networks, where each computer on the network can be regarded as a node, and each of which would access to the others theoretically through a certain means without reliable security protection.

Considering the above-mentioned problems, issues of data storage security are discussed in this paper.

A privileged strategy aiming at deficiecy and the encryption of novel information called 'MC encryption' is put forward, which confirms the safety when transferring data to the cloud, thus alleviates the crisis of confidence caused by data storage in the third party .

In recent years, researches motivated by diversified standpoints bounding up with cloud computing storage security are all launched limited to respects of the cloud itself rather than more unique points. In [13] and [14] , data integrity and validity is explained, and in [15] , it mainly describes user access .In this paper, considering from the respect of users, basing on the data itself and carrying on sectional encryption on privacy data both at the client and the cloud ,an innovation point is introduced to achieve a high degree of data privacy as well as guarantee the security during upload and download.

3. Design of MC-R Strategy

As is shown in figure 1, MC-R strategy is divided into two parts: one is the MC encryption/decryption part operating on the client side ; the other one is the asymmetric RSA encryption/decryption part operating on the cloud.

In general, users directly upload or download data after logging in the cloud, and the data have a chance of being intercepted during transmission and storage. The MC-R strategy, in which the cloud storing part performs in blocks at the user side and data has been encrypted before upload to the cloud , can prevent information leakage. After being transmitted, data are RSA encrypted via the powerful computational ability of cloud computing, and then they are stored in the cloud sever. Procedures mentioned above availably ensure data safety.

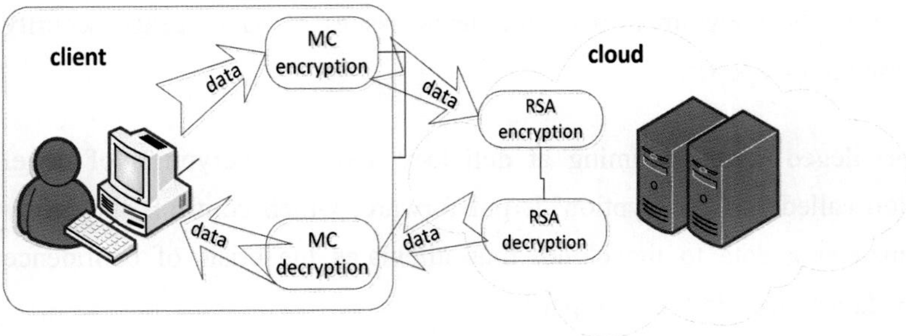

Figure 1. General Structure of MC-R Strategy

3.1. *MC encryption strategies at user side*

The designed MC Encryption Strategy is a coordination of three parts: the Digital Camouflage module, the Data hiding module and the Labeled data module. Among them, the Digital Camouflage module makes up the core digital data in a document by making only superficial changes ,so as to provide a high degree of guarantee that data can not be let out ; The Data hiding module hides data among the false information to further ensure the security ; The Labeled data module aims at recovering the truthful data that are hidden among the large amount of false one.

3.1.1. *Digital camouflage module*

To enterprises , companies and individuals , digital data in documents are always crucial. To prevent the leakage of sensitive digital information, a bran-new Digital steganography algorithm called 'Digital makeup algorithm' is proposed.

The core idea of the algorithm is as follows: Make up each series of digital in files which is called 'NUM' through Digital makeup algorithm and assign its numerical value as 'Mask'. Formulas of the digital makeup and digital remover are listed:

$$MASK = NUM - K_1 \bmod K_2 + K_2 \tag{1}$$

$$NUM = MASK + K_1 \bmod K_2 - K_2 \tag{2}$$

Where K_1 is a 64 bit plastic random value, $K_1 = random\ (1, 2^{64})$, and it is a constant to current files. K_2 is a plastic random value associated with S . Assume S as the current file size and $K_2 = random(1, S)$. The secret key K_1 and K_2 are both private key ,and they are only known by the users themselves.

As it reports in 'Special listing Corporation 2010 annual financial report analysis': In 2010 the listing Corporation asset impairment losses amounts to 235.747 billions yuan , which increased 39.496 billions than that of 2009 ,an increase of 20.13%; In 2010, the impairment loss proportion in net profits is 14.31% , which decreased 19.05% than that of 2009 ,an decrease of 57.10%.

After processed by Digital steganography algorithm , statistics are as follows : In 2041, listing Corporation asset impairment losses amounts to 3.338878 billions yuan , which increased 42.5127 billions than that of 2040 ,an increase of 51.44% ; In 2041, the impairment loss proportion in net profits is 45.62% , which decreased 50.36% than that of 2009 ,an decrease of 88.41%.

It can be seen that Digital makeup algorithm perfectly completes digital makeup , all figures have been made only superficial changes in paragraphs and they are fully staged their own . Meanwhile , as the MOD function does not exist inverse function , the original data can't be obtained by derivation of inverse function method to decipher MASK value. So, the MOD encryption can only be deciphered through brute force manner.

3.1.2. *Data hiding module*

As can be seen from table 2 , current databases are not using this method because it would increase storage consumption. In this paper , considering the privilege of cloud computing that it can weaken the drawbacks of data hiding and its capability of aiming directly at the hiding of a small amount of private data , the Digital makeup algorithm is implemented as a part of data encryption, and the practicability of improving data security performance at the price of additional memory consumption is discussed.

As figure 2 shows, the Data hiding module selects a certain amount of false data randomly from the false database and adds the false data to the real data to achieve data hiding by mixing up false data and real data. The Data hiding module mainly achieves its function by controlling three parameters : m, α, β

The process of data hiding is as follows : There may be inserted n bytes false data with a possibility of α in every m bytes of real data , and how much data to be inserted depends on two parameters : α, β ,where α represents the possibility of inserted n false data in every m bytes , and its value ranges from 0 to1 , where β is the upper limit value of n ,which represents the data size inserted each time, and n ranges from 0 to β. The data will be hidden better and the consumption of resources is larger when α and β are at bigger values while m is at a smaller value.

3.1.3. *Labeled data module*

To extract real data when decrypting the data, real data and false data need to be marked up respectively in the process of data hiding.

The real data extraction section is designed referred to traditional digital watermarking technology which marks up the data basing on data themselves, which exists two drawbacks:

1. There may be difficulties in identifying whether the data belong to users if the data is insufficient.

2.The dependent relationship between watermarks and data makes it difficult to divide them while data extracting.

In consideration of the problems above, a more concise and self-adapting key string marking method is constructed according to the characteristics of data themselves.

The newly-generated L bit key string (This key string is saved by the users) is connected with real data and false data in series respectively and when they are connected with false data , a certain bit in the key string is tampered. Then, combine a tag block with a set of data as a vector each of which can be judged whether it is real data according to the tag blocks. The independence of the blocks and the data effectively avoids the phenomenon that watermarks are hard to be removed ,so this advantage ensures the raw data to be clear and readable.

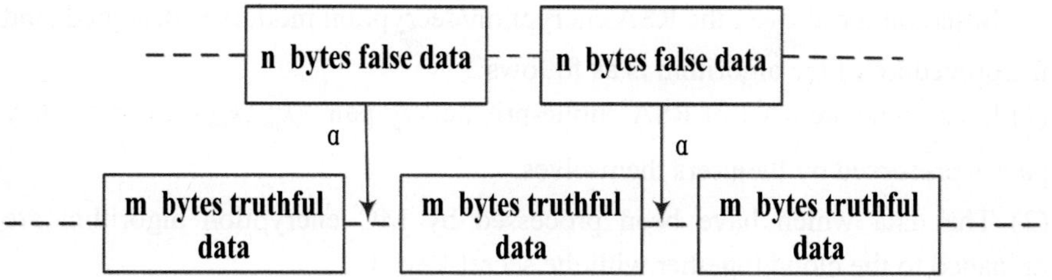

Figure 2. Insertion of false data

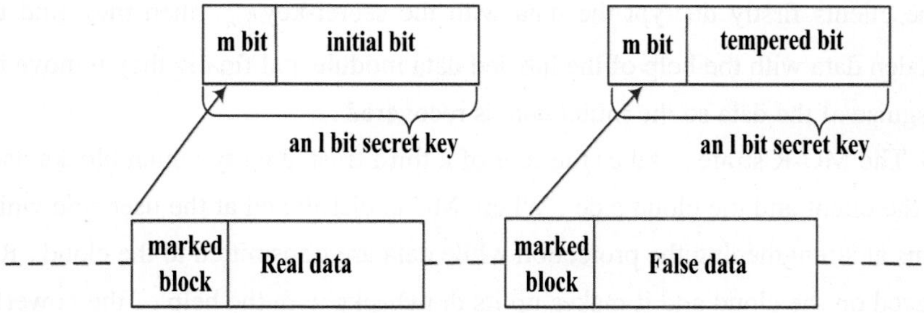

Figure 3. Process of data marker

3.2. *RSA module in the cloud*

Symmetric encryption algorithm and Non symmetric encryption algorithm are two kinds of relatively mature encryption ones. For Symmetric encryption algorithm, despite of its applicability of large amount of data encryption, adopting a same secret key results in deficiency of security. Moreover, it doesn't apply to distributed network for its inherently problems such as the difficulty of key management and the cost .Similarly, although Non symmetric encryption algorithm supports a high security, it does not apply to encryption and decryption for big data because of the low speed of encryption and decryption and the demand of amount of computation. With the powerful computing capability of cloud computing which efficiently makes up for the large amount of cost of RSA, the intractable problems caused by massive data is avoided as the encryption is deployed aiming at the core privacy data rather than all the data .

Based on the above , the RSA encryption/decryption module is designed ,and the procedure of the algorithm is as follows:

(1) Users generate a set of RSA public-private key pair (k_{pub}, k_{pri}) ,then the key pair is preserved by the users themselves.

(2) The data which have been processed by MC encryption algorithm are uploaded to the cloud together with the secret-key k_{pub}.

(3) The re-encryption process is completed by the secret-key k_{pub} on the cloud , hence the process of data encryption is completed .

(4) Users send download requests and download the encrypted file to the client . The clients firstly decrypt the data with the secret-key k_{pri} ,then they find the hidden data with the help of the labeled data module and finally they remove the disguise of the data so the initial data is recovered .

The MC-R strategy takes the role of a third trusted party which blocks itself to the client and the cloud side . Where MC is distributed at the user side which aims at strengthening the protection while data are transmitted to the cloud , R is placed on the cloud and it makes up its drawbacks with the help of the powerful computing cap- acity of the cloud thus it protects data privacy in a more credible way .

4. Simulation and Performance Analysis of MC-R Strategy

The programming process involves 6 modules : the Digital Camouflage module , the Data hiding module ,the labeled data module, the Cloud RSA module, the Real data extraction module and the Digital cleansing module .

4.1. *Digital steganography algorithm performance analysis*

For the sake of testing how digital percentage has influenced on the performance of the algorithm, the document size is fixed to 1020 bit and the digital proportion is transformed（5%，10%，20%，30%，40%，50%，60%）.Test the Digital makeup and the Digital remover time respectively and show the results in figure 4 where the full line represents documents digital makeup time ,the dotted line represents documents digital remover time, the horizontal ordinate represents digital percent and the longitudinal coordinate represents Digital makeup/remover time. All of the above are counted in milliseconds.

It is clearly to see:

1. The Digital makeup/remover time markedly increases when the digital percentage is 5%-20% while it gradual declines when the percentage is 20%-30% ,and it gradual increases a second time when it counts 30%-60%. In the figure , noting that the pit is at 30% ,that is, the algorithm demonstrates more excellent performances when digital percentage is approximately 30% without consideration of situations when Digital proportion is very low .

2. The document encryption time and decryption time are appro- ximately the same if the digital percentage is at about 5% or at 20%-30%. However, document decryption time is evidently lower than the encryption time. The complexity of the encrypt- tion formula and the decryption formula are exactly the same, but the results show significant differences that have not been expected .

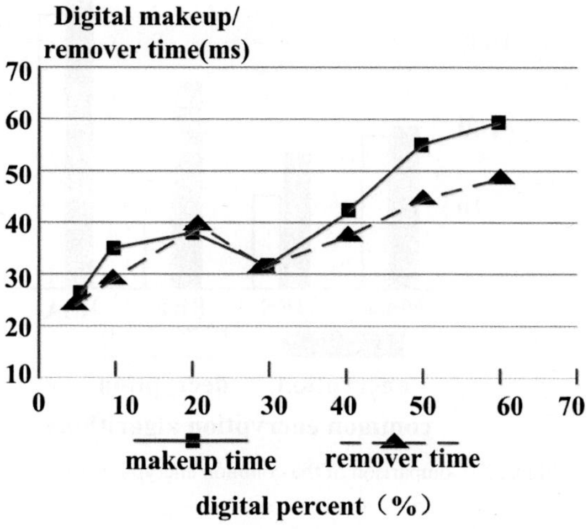

Figure 4. Effects of changes in the digital proportional

To observe the performance of the algorithm visually, compare the algorithm with traditional encryption algorithms(DES, PBE,RSA) and show the results in figure 5, where the longitudinal coordinates represents the logarithm of time consuming, counting in milliseconds.

In figure 5, the encryption process is described as the solid cylinder and the decryption process as the transparent one. It can be concluded that the time that Digital steganography algorithm consumes is close to the symmetric encryption algorithm DES, and the consumption of Digital makeup and Digital remover are both not more than 100ms . That is to say , Digital steganography algorithm is a fast encryption algorithm attributed to its fast processing ability of document encryption and decryption ,thus it can be applied to documents that belong to individuals or enterprises which require high privacy.

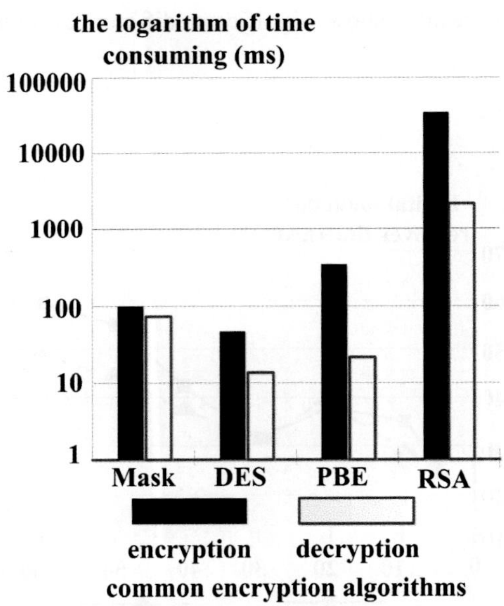

Figure 5. Comparison of the common encryption algorithms

4.2. *Data hiding performance analysis*

Figure 6 shows tests on the time consumption of data hiding and the original data recovery where the active line denotes data hiding , the dotted line denotes data reduction ,and the longitudinal coordinates denotes the time that false data addition and initial data consumes, and the data are measured in millisecond . In this section, the scheme is evaluated by altering the document size, and the parameter size is set to $m = 4, \alpha = 0.6, \beta = 4$.The coming tests tell that the extreme point of data hiding and time reduction consumption is when $\alpha = 0.6$.

It's obviously to find that data addition time and initial data recovery time gradually increase linearly as document size increases, and the time that data recovery consumes is evidently more than that of false data addition.

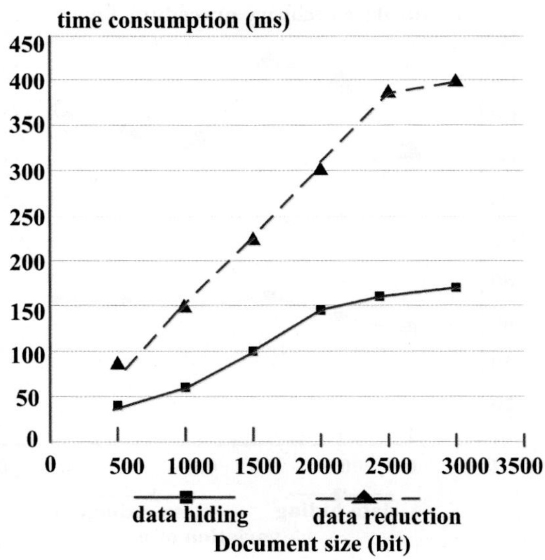

Figure 6. Influences of document size changes on data hiding

As is shown in figure 7, the horizontal ordinate stands for the variation of parameter α, while the longitudinal coordinates stands for the completion time of data hiding process or the data recovery procedure. The document size is 1000 bit and the parameter is set to $m = 4, \beta = 4$. Then alter the value of α and test the completion time of data hiding and data reduction recovery . After that , set $\alpha = 0.6, \beta = 4$ and alter m, then repeat the operation above. Figure 8 shows the testing result , what is different from figure 7 is that the horizontal ordinate represents the variation of parameter m . Finally, set $m = 4, \alpha = 0.6$ and alter β,and then repeat the operation above again .Test results are shown in figure 9 and what differs from figure 7 is that the horizontal ordinate signifies the variation of β.

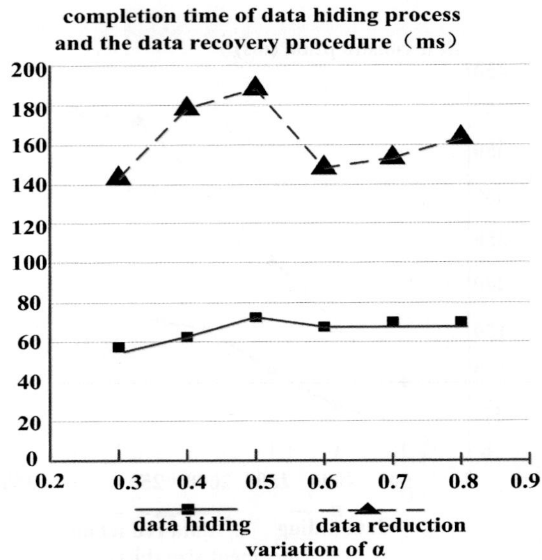

Figure 7. Effects of parameter α on data hiding

It can be seen obviously from figure 7 that the completion time of data hiding and initial data recovery both reach their maxima when $\alpha = 0.5$. When $\alpha < 0.5$, the two completion time mentioned above increase as α rises. Moreover , the two completion time drop sharply in pace with the increase of α when $0.5 < \alpha < 0.6$. Besides, when $\alpha > 0.6$, the completion time gradually increases with the increase of α .

From figure 8, it can be seen that with m increasing ,the completion time of data hiding and data recovery both gradually drop and the reduction speed slows down by degrees.

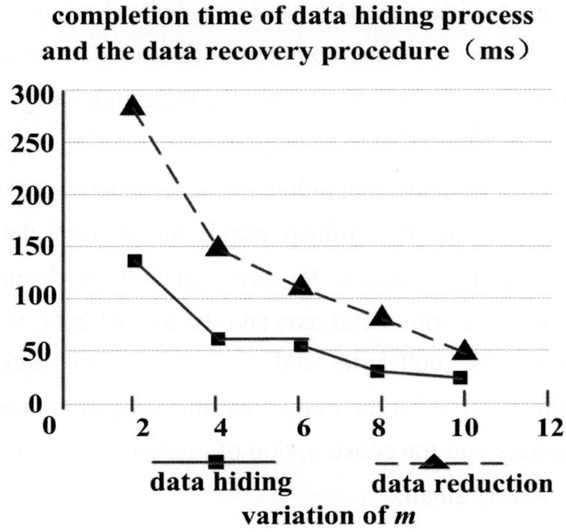

Figure 8. Effects of parameter m on data hiding

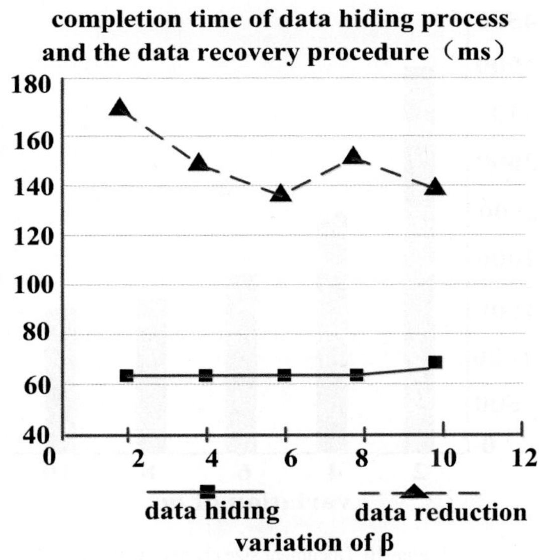

Figure 9. Effects of parameter β on data hiding

Through the observation of figure 9, it can be easily concluded that varied value of n makes no difference to data hiding ,instead it has a great influence on data recovery. When $n < 6$, the completion time of data recovery gradually decreases ,and when $n = 6$, the time reaches the minimum value.

Alter the value of m, α, β successively and test the size of documents after data hiding in order to test how data hiding influences memory consumption.

In figure 10, the horizontal ordinate stands for m (real data interval) and the longitudinal coordinate stands for the variation of document size, the measurement of both the unit lateral axis and the axis of bank are in bytes. The initial document size is 1000 bytes and set $\alpha = 0.6, \beta = 4$ and then alter the value of m. In figure 10, it can be drawn that the sizes of documents gradually drop as m increases and the consumption of memory is extremely large when the value of m is very small.

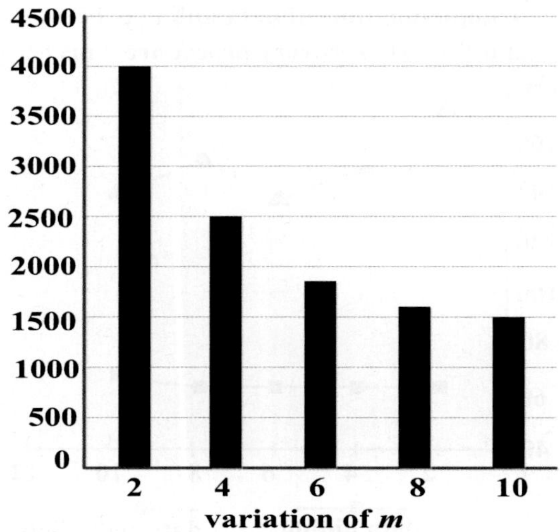

Figure 10. Document size changes with m

In figure 11, set $m = 4, \beta = 4$ and alter the value of α. Obviously, when the horizontal ordinate represents α (addition probability of false data) and the horizontal ordinate represents the variation of document size, the size of documents gradually becomes larger in pace with the increase of α.

In addition to the above , as it in figure 12 where the horizontal ordinate denotes β (data quantity that the false data has added) and the longitudinal coordinates denotes variation of document size, conclusions can be drawn that the size of documents shows an upward tendency as β become larger .

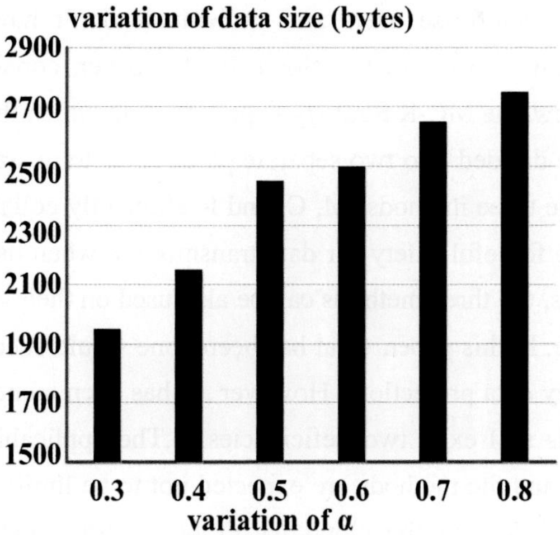

Figure 11. Document size changes with α

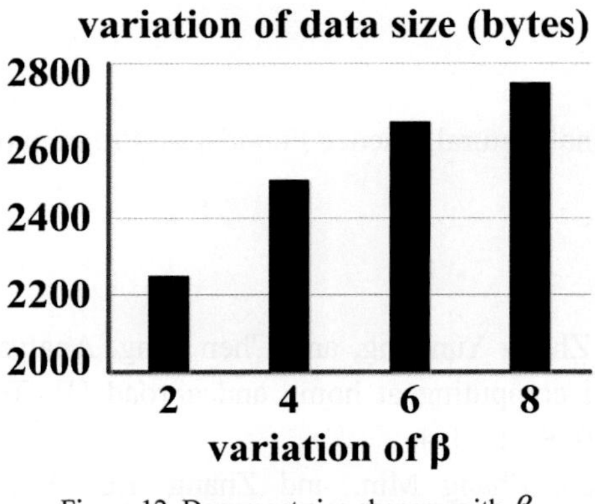

Figure 12. Document size changes with β

From the experimental results above, noting that the data hiding method costs a great quantity of extra consumption, and the better data be hidden, the more the extra consumption is. That is to say, data hiding method does not apply to massive data, instead, it can be appropriately applied to a small amount of private data and it efficiently ensures the security of private data.

5. Conclusion

Nowadays, many enterprise users and individuals don't have faith in their private data security storing in the cloud. In this paper, considering from the users' point of view, the MC-R Strategy is proposed, in which the client side and the cloud side are divided into two separate parts, so as to guarantee the privacy of users' data. The three methods: M, C, and R efficiently collaborate with each other and provide forceful safety for data transmission when users interact with the cloud. Besides, the three methods can be also used on their own or applied to common database. In this paper, what has been done would successfully achieve the goal of privacy data protection . However ,as has been mentioned above, the proposed methods still exist two deficiencies: 1.The applicability needs to be further improved and the methods are expected not to be limited to textual data. 2.The integrity of data in the cloud hasn't been tested and verified before decryption. In the light of the above two reasons, there is still need for further improve in these two points.

Acknowledgement

Sponsored by National Natural Science Foundation Program (61371092).

References

1. Fang Bingyi, Zhang Yunyong, and Chen Ying. Analysis of the development of cloud computing at home and abroad [J]. Telecommunications Sci- ence, 2010, 8(1)： 1-4.
2. Feng Dengguo, Zhang Min, and Zhang Yan. Researches on Cloud Computing Security [J]. Software Journal 2011， 22(1)： 71-83.
3. Chen Y P， Paxson V and Katz R H. What's New About Cloud Computing Security? [J/OL]. Technical Report No. UCB/EECS.2010(1):1-8.
4. Batard F, Boudaoud K, Kamel M. Web 2.0 Security: State of the Art[C]. In Proceedings of the 5th Conference On Security in Network Architecture and Information Systems (SARSSI), 2010:649-653.

5. Hogben G. Privacy, Security and Identity in the Cloud[C]. ENISA. OASIS/EEMA Identity conference, 2010:24-31.
6. ENISA. Benefits, risks and recommendations for information security[R]. European Network and Information Security Agency, 2009.
7. Cloud Security Alliance. Security Guidance for Critical Areas of Focus in Cloud Computing V2.1. Technical report[R]. Cloud Security Alliance, 2009.
8. Archer J, Boehme A, Cullinane D. Top Threats to Cloud Computing V1.0[R]. Technical Report. Cloud Security Alliance, 2010:1-14.
9. Hu Guangyong. Research on data security storage strategy based on Cloud Computing [J]. Computer measurement and control, 2011.19(10)：2539-2541.
10. Delettre C，Boudaoud K.and Riveill M. Cloud Computing, Security and Data Concealment[C]. International Conference on Information Science and Cloud Computing, 2011:424-431.
11. Yang J S and Choi H K. IP Based Security Architecture of Virtual Network in Cloud Computing System[C]. Wireless Communications and Mobile Computing Conference, 2012: 709-715.
12. Almorsy M，Grundy J and Ibrahim A S. Collaboration -Based Cloud Computing Security Management Frame- work[C]. 2011 IEEE 4th International Conference on Cloud Computing, 2011:364-371.
13. Kumar P S, Subramanian R and Selvam D T. Ensuring data storage security in cloud computing using sobol sequence[C]. 2010 1st International Conference on Parallel, Distributed and Grid Computing, 2010:217-222.
14. Tribhuwan M R，Bhuyar V A and Pirzade S.Ensuring data storage Security in cloud Computing through two-way handshake based on token management[C]. Advances in Recent Technologies in Communication and Computing, 2010:386-389.
15. Kumar A, Lee BG and Lee HJ. Secure Storage and Access of Data in Cloud Computing[C]. 2012 International Conference on ICT Convergence, 2012: 336-339.
16. Ge T, Zdonik S. Fast. Secure Encryption for Indexing in a Column-Oriented DBMS[C]. Data Engineering, 2007. ICDE 2007. IEEE 23rd International Conference on，2007:676-685.

Security Mechanism Analysis and Research of Hadoop Cloud Computing Cluster

Hong-ye XUE
Xi'an University of Science and Technology
Xi'an, China
E-mail: xuehy60@163.com

Rui-tao ZHAI
Xi'an University of Science and Technology
Xi'an, China
E-mail: zrt2152@163.com

In this paper, we studied and proposed solutions to the hidden dangers in the security mechanism of Hadoop cloud computing cluster. By analyzing the security mechanism of Hadoop cluster, the paper identifies several security vulnerabilities as such user authentication and certification, and proposes the several solutions to improve the security mechanism of the Hadoop cloud computing. Regarding the data leak that users experience during download or upload, we present a digital envelope technology to encrypt the data transmitted. Additionally, a cryptographic algorithm is adopted to encrypt the virtual disk in cloud disk to prevent data lost. The improvement to the dispatcher in the cluster can enhance the stability of the host node and avoid the system dysfunction. Experimental results demonstrate the effectiveness of the proposed strategy.

Keywords: Hadoop; Cloud computing frame; Cluster; Security mechanism.

1. Introduction

Cloud computing is the further development of Distributed Computing (DC) and Grid Computing (GC). It makes the resources of storage and computing to be resource pooling, to provide corresponding services to users dynamically and on-demand through virtual technology, its features are dynamic contractions, high reliability and low cost, etc.

Hadoop is a kind of basal cloud computing of distributed framework, due to it based on the open source platform in Java which has a extraordinary position in the enterprise cluster building, both of industry and academia adopt Hadoop as a standard second-round development and study platform of cloud computing. However, in the face of the mass data processing in cluster and the guarantee of data security, its security mechanism has some significant hidden danger; it is very hard to ensure the security of cloud computing through the traditional data security technology.

2. Hadoop System

2.1. *Hadoop framework*

Hadoop is an open source distributed computing platform which belongs to Apache software foundation. The Hadoop which based on Hadoop Distributed File System (HDFS) and Google MapReduce[1] provides users with the low-level details transparent distributed infrastructure system. It is shown in the Fig.1:

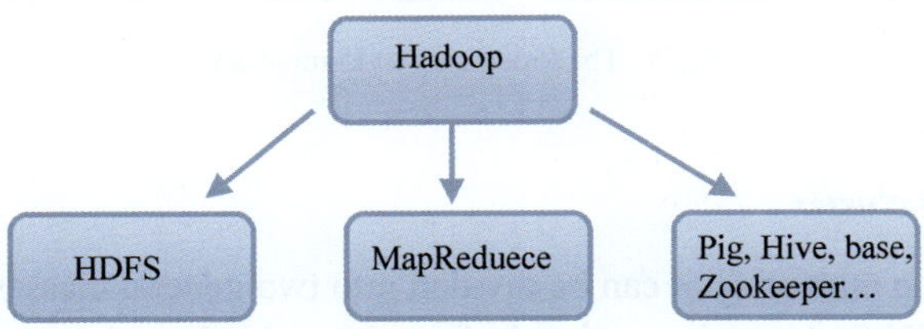

Fig. 1. Distributed Infrastructure System of Hadoop

HDFS is a distributed file system with a distributed storage and parallel computing architecture, in the construction of the cluster, HDFS has a name node (NameNode) and multiple datanode (DataNode), and each node is a computer. In its low-level, files were cut into multiple block, these blocks dispersed on different data nodes, each Block can also copies several data on different data node, in order to achieve the purpose of fault tolerance, name node is the core of the HDFS, it not only records the file blocks, where these blocks come from, but also records the state of each data node, and other important information [2].MapReduce is a kind of parallel computing architecture; its core concept is dividing and conquering the data. The principle of parallel processing is shown in Fig. 2:

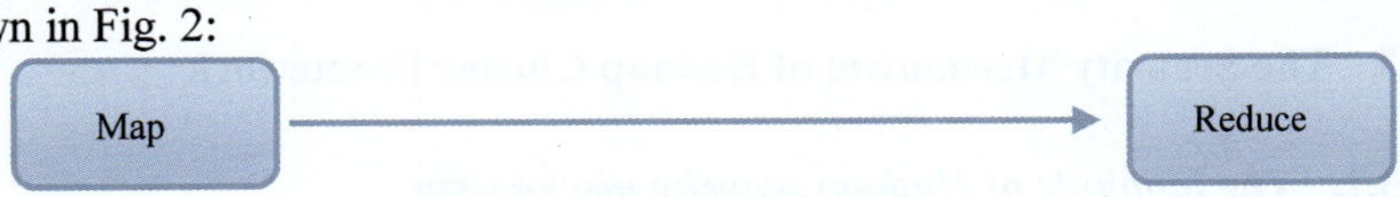

Fig. 2. The Processing of MapReduce

One of the functions Map does the work like this: firstly scans and records the processed elements and data. Then, processes the interested data and acquire the intermediate data. The other function Reduce acts as collecting and collating intermediate data and output the final result. That clearly shows sorting and finishing the intermediate results for subsequent processing in the Fig. 2.

In MR, there is one JobTracker works as the master control and several TaskTrackers, the former is responsible for scheduling and management of the latter. The JobTracker could distribute task to idle TaskTracker, let it run in parallel, and is responsible for the supervision, if one of a node down, JobTracker will hand over the task to another TaskTracker, in order to execute no-break[3]. Its processing framework is shown in Fig.3:

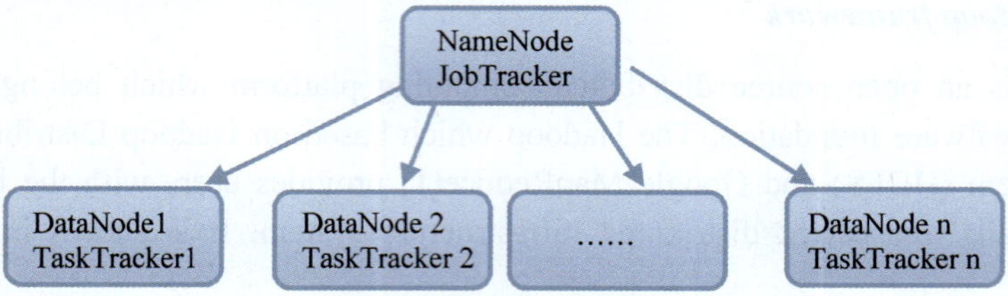

Fig. 3. The Processing of Framework

2.2. *Hadoop cluster*

For the Hadoop cluster[4], it can be divided into two general classes: Master and Slave. One HDFS cluster is consisted of one NameNode and several DataNode, the NameNode works as main server, be responsible for management of the name space of the file system and the access operation of the file system by client; the DataNode of the cluster manage the storage data. MapReduce framework is consisting of one JobTracker which runs separately on the main node and each TaskTrackers which run on each nodes of the cluster. The main node take charge of dispatching the every task which be consist of a job, all of these task distributed on the different nodes. The executive condition will be monitored by main node. When one job has be submitted, JobTracker will receive the submitted job and configuration information, then dispatch the configuration information to the slave nodes, dispatch task and monitor the execution of TaskTrackerat the same time[5]..

3. The Security Mechanism of Hadoop Cluster Framework

3.1. *The loophole of Hadoop security mechanism*

Hadoop is always short of security mechanism at present, its main performance is shown at two parts: the authentication between users and the security authentication between servers.

Neither the NameNode nor JobTracker is lack of security authentication in user services, The client user name and the user group name must assigned by user-self. For example, if the user can control the computer which be used to submit the job, If the user uses the following code in Table 1 in the program, the controller can submit job by any identity, and then steal the resources belongs to others[6].

Table 1. The Codes for user's submitting job by any identity

```
conf.set ("user.name", root);
conf.set ("group.name" root);
```

3.2. *The current situation of Hadoop cluster security mechanism*

Hadoop provides two security mechanisms: Simple and Kerberos. Simple mechanism (default) adopts SAAS protocol. Based on the Kerberos mechanism, Hadoop basis realize these security mechanism below: (1) RPC security mechanism; (2) HDFS security mechanism; (3) MapReduce security mechanism.

3.3. *Hadoop cluster adopt Kerberos mechanism for authentication*

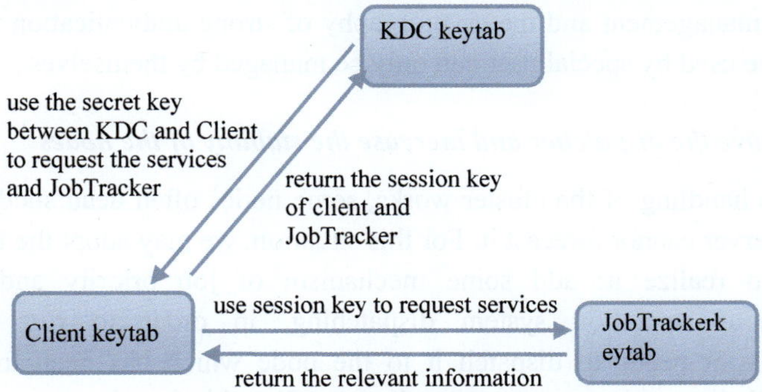

Fig. 4. The Processing of Kerberos authentication

As shown in Fig.4 ,we can see:

- The KDC forward the Ticket to Client. Because this Ticket is requested to send to Service, cannot be known by Client, so the KDC use the secret key which between KDC and Service when before the start of the protocol to encrypt the Ticket and sent it to Client. Meanwhile, in order to share the secret key between the Client and the Service, KDC encrypt the Session Key by the secret key between KDC and Client and return it to the Client,
- In order to implement the delivery of the Ticket, Client forwards the received Ticket to Service. Because the Client doesn't know the secret key between KDC and Service, it can't modify the information of ticket. Meanwhile, the Client decode the received Session Key, and pack the user name, user address (IP) to be Authenticator and encrypt it by Session Key, sent it to Service,

- After the Service receive his Ticket, it will decode the Ticket by the secret key between Service and KDC, thereby acquiring the Session Key and user name, user address (IP), service name, and validity[7]. Then it decode the Authentication by Session Key to acquire the user name, user address (IP), to compare these information with the user name, user address (IP) which decoded from the Ticket to authenticate the identity information of Client.If there is any result returned from service, return it to the Client.

4. Conclusions

4.1. *Data encryption of the cloud computing platform*

Aim at the problems of data leak, we could adopt cryptographic algorithm to protect the data in the data center of the cloud port, in the scenario of cloud computing, the function of virtual disk encryption with the administration of the secret key can disable the administrator to check the sensitive data through hook the tenement's virtual disk[8], ensure the business data cannot be lost or leaked out even when the equipment of data center has been stolen, with the algorithm parameter management and the cryptography of strong authentication to ensure the resource used by special user can only be managed by themselves.

4.2. *Improve the dispatcher and increase the stability of the nodes*

During the handling of the cluster works, some nodes often dead suddenly, but the main server cannot forecast it, For this situation, we may adopt the following methods to realize it: add some mechanism of job priority and support heterogeneous operation system dispatching, in order to run the task successfully, it needs to dispatch it to the node which has been installed a corresponding operation system. In order to realize this function, it needs every TaskTracker to report its operation system type to the JobTracker at the beginning of starting it, so as to dispatch.

4.3. *"Escort" of handling transmit data*

In Hadoop, MapReduce is parallel processing framework, during processing data, uploading to the cloud, sometimes it will be threatened from the outside of the cloud, sometimes the interception will occur when the user access to the files, We should adopt the technology base on the digital envelope to encrypt the transmitting data, during this process the public and private key codon-pair and session key are involved, adopt the session key to encrypt the transmitting data symmetrically, ensure the speed of the encryption and decryption, reduce the system consumption.

Acknowledgments

This research is supported by the National Natural Science Foundation of China (Granted No. U1261114) and the Xi'an University of Science and Technology Cultivation Foundation Project (2014032). All of the authors declare that there is no conflict of interests regarding the publication of this article and would like to thank the anonymous referees for their valuable comments and suggestions.

References

1. BEDRA A. Getting started with Google App engine and conjure [J]. IEEE Internet Computing, 2010, 14(4):85-88.
2. Shin-gyu Kim, Hyuck Han, Hyeonsang Eorn, Heon Y. Yeorn. Toward a Cost-effective Cloud Storage Service, The 12th International Conference on Advanced Communication technique (ICACT),2010:99-102.
3. Z. Cheng et al., "An Elastic Replication Management System for HDFS," Workshop on Interfaces and Abstractions for Scientific Data Storage, IEEE Cluster 2012, 2012.
4. IBM. IBM introduces ready-to-use cloud computing[EB/OL]. http://www03.ibm.com/press/us/en/pressrelease/22613.wss, 2012-12-05.
5. WANG L, VON LASZEWSKI G, YOUNGE A, etal. Cloud computing: a perspective study[J]. New Generation Computing, 2010, 28(2): 137-146.
6. ALMULLA S A, YEUN CY. Cloud computing security management[C]. 2010 2nd International Conference on Engineering System Management and Applications, ICESMA 2010, 2010: 1-7.
7. SCHWARZKOPF R, SCHMIDT M, STACK C, etal. Checking running and dormant virtual machines for the necessity of security updates in cloud environments[C]. Proceedings - 2011 3rd IEEE International Conference on Cloud Computing Technology and Science, Cloud Com 2011, 2011:239-246.
8. ZISSIS D, LEKKAS D. Addressing cloud computing security issues[J]. Future Generation Computer Systems, 2012, 28(3): 583-592.
9. SONEHARA N, ECHIZEN I, WOHLGEMUTH S. Isolation in cloud computing and Privacy-Enhancing technologies[J]. Business & Information Systems Engineering, 2011, 3(3), 155-162.

Security Vulnerability Analysis Assessment Method of Power Information Network

Yong-bin ZHAO

State Grid Liaoning Electric Power Supply Co., Ltd.,
Shenyang, 110006, China
E-mail: zhaoyb@ln.sgcc.com.cn

Tao ZHANG

State Grid Smart Grid Research Institute,
Nanjing, 210003, China
E-mail: zhangtao@sgri.sgcc.com.cn

Bo ZHANG and Jun HOU †

Nanjing University of Science and Technology,
Nanjing, 210094, China
†E-mail: 274365054@qq.com

A power information network risk assessment method of power information network information based on vulnerability analysis graph mode is proposed. The results of several vulnerability scanning tools are the data source of this method. The accuracy rate of one single scanning tool is considered as the reliability and the set of scanning results is considered as a reliability vector. By analyzing every reliability vector, the vulnerability reliability in a single vulnerability analysis graph can be calculated. A risk assessment is given in a small-sized power information network using the introduced method under three attack circumstances with varying periods of time. The experimental results demonstrate that the assessment of power information network risks is viable for this assessment.

Keywords: Power information network; Risk assessment; Vulnerability analysis.

1. Introduction

many researchers have carried out some researches on network risk assessment. The main methods usually use some rules to make an assessment [1,5], such as TCSEC, ITSEC, CC, IOS/IEC 17799, BS 7799 and ISO 13335. Because of the

†Corresponding author.

lack of effectiveness, it can only estimate power information network risk level in the long run and can't detect the real-time attack that the power information network is undergoing. Grid enterprise information construction has reached a very high level, so information security issues become increasingly prominent. Therefore, dynamic risk assessment method becomes a hot topic in this field.

P.A.Porras proposed an M-Correlator alarm processing model[1], this model uses tree-structured Bayes spread method, which associates alarm, the relevance between alarm and target and the importance of recourses together. It can also get the related threats by dealing with the secure issues, making an assessment on its level, that is, high, medium or low. Because all the objects related in this method are all isolate alarms, this model can't make a complete assessment on the whole attack. Stephen Boyer[2] and others proposed a Stellar assessment model. This model is made up of rebuild module and security risk assessment module in the attack process. Between them, attack process security risk assessment is finished by a series rules compiled in advance by experts. The disadvantages lie in that these rules are compiled completely by experts' experience. Besides, it takes a lot of time and energy and it's quite subjective.

This paper focuses on the problems of power information network security risk assessment. Based on the vulnerability analysis graph model. This model discomposes the whole power information network risk into the weighted sum of each node's in the power information network.

2. Security Vulnerability Analysis Assessment

Threat, is the system anomaly traffic or invader's attack action on the system, which will probably do harm to the security of power information network or asset. It's the component of the risk. Vulnerability, is the weakness which can be threatened to be used in the asset or asset group. It's also called loophole. It mainly includes the weak points, which can cause threats on the power information network and system, such as, privilege escalation, denial of service, buffer cache overflow and so on. The existence of vulnerability makes a system much easier to be used by threat to attack and do damage to the asset.

Power information network security risk assessment is a process to analyze and confirm risk. The principle is showed in Fig.1. The procedure of power information network security risk assessment in this paper mainly includes the following steps:(1)Preparations for risk assessment mainly mean to know the system situation, determine assessment objects and provide assessment data objects for the data analysis process.(2)Find out the system and use vulnerability scanning to find out the potential vulnerability in all power information network nodes (3)Find out the threat program confronted. According to power information network nodes' attainable own vulnerability, attack the utilization rule of vulnerability and produce state vulnerability analysis graph and then find the existed behavior in the system.(4)According to the reliability of the occurrence of vulnerability and the complexity of being used, calculated the occurrence possibility of the success attack.(5)Computer security loss. According to the potential harm on asset by vulnerability and the harm on asset when attack happens, calculate the loss of power information network asset.

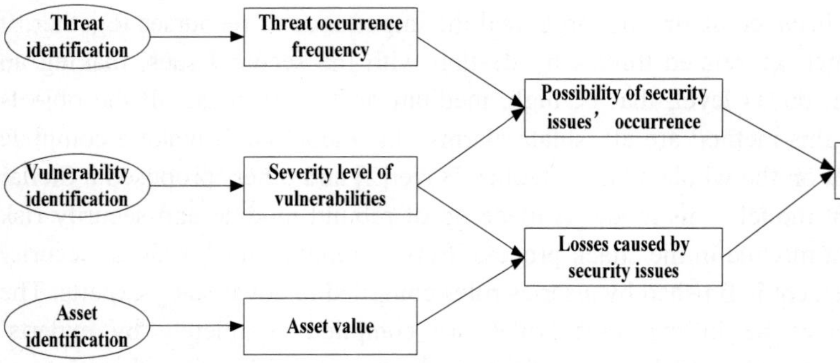

Fig. 1. The illustrative diagram of power information network security risk assessment.

This paper, according to the vulnerability analysis graph's hierarchical framework and vulnerability's logical relationship, designed a power information network security risk quantification assessment framework as Fig.2 shows.

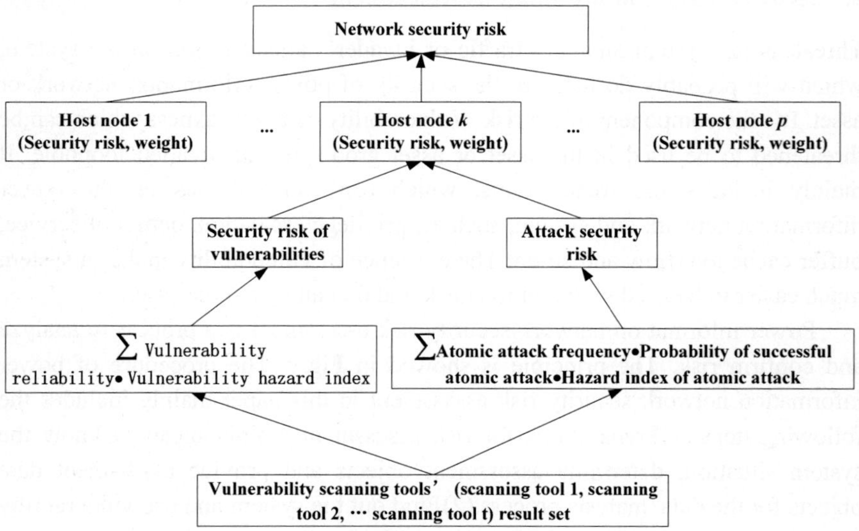

Fig.2. Quantified assessment structure of power information network security risk.

This bottom-up framework, firstly based on vulnerability analysis graph, use various kinds of vulnerability scanning tools to detect existed vulnerability group in all nodes. It further calculates the vulnerability reliability and possibility of successful atomic attack. Combined with each vulnerability hazard index, atomic attack frequency and its hazard index, the vulnerability security risk and attack risk of the node can be calculated, then security risk of the single node can be assessed. Finally, combined with the weight of each node in the power information network, the security risk of the whole power information network can be quantified

Because of the uncertainty of vulnerability analysis graph itself, this paper imports an idea of vulnerability analysis vulnerability graph to represent support degree or credibility existed in the single vulnerability of nodes, written as f. written as e vulnerability hazard index is a direct evidence of this vulnerability gravity degree, so the vulnerability gravity degree can be used to measure its hazard index. National Vulnerability Database is one of the most authoritative vulnerability information databases at present. This database from several aspects like vulnerability usage method, usage complexity, number of target identification and influence of information's privacy, integrity and usability gives the vulnerability gravity measurement, whose value ranges from 0 to 10. Combined with the sign of Common Vulnerabilities and Exposures (CVE), to look up the corresponding gravity from National Vulnerability Database and it becomes the vulnerability hazard index

The product of vulnerability reliability and hazard index of vulnerability analysis graph can represent the risk of single existed vulnerability in nodes.

$$R_v = f \times e. \quad (1)$$

Among them, f is the reliability of single existed node. *e* is the hazard index of single vulnerability in the node.

Now, attacks aimed at power information network are mostly several-step-combined attack, that is, attack by several atoms altogether. What is called atom attack is that attacker uses single vulnerability of the node to carry out attack. Therefore, an attack is made up of series attack by atoms.

Definition(2.1):atom attack frequency. During a period, the number of attack by single atom in the node is written as c. It can be got by attacking log data to be input to statistical analysis.

Definition(2.2):the probability of success in atom attack is written as p. Analyzing the whole power information network system, it can be found that the success attack by atoms is at random and is influenced by the scanning result of the vulnerability and complexity of vulnerability usage. In the formal research, the probability of successful atom attack is usually marked by experts, which make it quite subjective. In order to avoid the weakness, this paper according to the reliability of vulnerability used by vulnerability analysis graph in the atom successful attack, combined with Common Vulnerability Scoring System(CVSS), quantify the attribute set of single vulnerability, define the successful atom attack probability(p)as the product of vulnerability reliability of vulnerability analysis graph(f) and the usage complexity of this vulnerability(exp)[3]. That is,

$$p = f \times exp. \tag{2}$$

Among them, f represents the vulnerability reliability of vulnerability analysis graph. The detailed computing method will be given as follows. exp represents the usage complexity of this vulnerability. In order to satisfy the computing probability less than 1, modify the computational formula of the usage complexity of this vulnerability in CVSS as:

$$\exp = 2 \times \text{AccessVector} \times \text{AccessComplexity} \times \text{Authentication}. \tag{3}$$

Definition(2.3): The hazard index of atom attack: the hazard index of the successful attack by the single atom in the node, written as r. This paper uses the damage of power information network system security nature by the vulnerability in the vulnerability analysis graph to describe the hazard index of atom attack. Referring to the concept of information security property calculability in reference[3], the security property of vulnerability can be divided as *ConfImpact, IntegImpact*and*AvailImpact[6].* According to the method of calculating vulnerability damages in CVSS, define the hazard index of successful atom attack

$$r = p \times [10.41 \times (1 - (1 - ConfImpact) \times (1 - IntegImpact) \times (1 - AvailImpact))]. \tag{4}$$

Definition(2.4): The security risk of atom attack R_a: the risk of successful occurrence of vulnerability by outer attack in the power information network. Because one -time high hazard index attack maybe more serious than over one-time low hazard index attack, when calculating the security risk of atom attack, use atom attack frequency and the product of 10's power of atom attack hazard index to represent the security risk of the atom attack.

$$Ra = c \times 10r. \tag{5}$$

Among them, c is the attack frequency of the single atom, r is the hazard index after the successful attack by the single atom.

Definition(2.5): Security risk of the node R_h. Security risk of one single nod is made of two parts, that is, security risk and security risk of atom attack:

$$R_h = \sum_{i=1}^{m} R_{v_i} + \sum_{j=1}^{n} R_{a_j} . \tag{6}$$

Among them, m is the sum of vulnerability in each node h, n is the sum of successful atomic attacks in a single node h, R_{v_i} is the security risk of single vulnerability calculated with formula (1), R_{a_j} is the security risk of single attack by the atom calculated with formula (5).

Definition(2.6): power information network security risk R_{N} , the influence on each node made by outer attack to power information network can be represented by the sum of all nodes' security risk.

$$R_{\mathrm{N}} = \sum_{k=1}^{p} \omega_k R_{h_k} . \tag{7}$$

Among them, p is the sum of all nodes in the power information network, ω_k is the weight of single node h_k. This can be generated by system administrators according to the importance degree of the service in the nodes, topological structure of the node, the number of access service and some other aspects. System administrators will give the status I_k of each node in the power information network, which can be referred to in chart 1 and also be generated from normalization. In the practical process, different modification can be made to fit different system. R_{h_k} is the single security risk calculated by formula (6).

According to Fig.2, the power information network security risk quantified assessment framework, it is clear that in order to assess the security risk of the whole power information network system, firstly, it's necessary to calculate all vulnerability's security risk and atom-attack security risk of single node. Yet, before calculating vulnerability's security risk Rv and atom-attack security risk of single node R_a, it's necessary to calculate each vulnerability's reliability, vulnerability hazard index e, probability of success atomic attack p and atom attack hazard index r. Among them, the calculation of vulnerability reliability of vulnerability analysis graph f plays a key role.

3. Experimental Verification and Analysis

The power information network below is designed to verify the practicability and effectiveness of the risk assessment model and the power information network risk assessment method based on the vulnerability analysis graph. The topological structure of the power information network is shown as Fig.3. This power information network system has three servers, that is, a web server, an FTP server which is used for important files and data's back up and an Oracle database server which helps provide database service for the Web server. Attackers can visit these three servers in the power information network system directly. The access authority is User authority. These three servers can also visit each other by User authority.

Use three vulnerability scanning tools, Nessus, X-Scan and ISS, to scanning vulnerability in three servers. The scanning results are shown in chart 3. The accuracy rates are respectively 0.98, 0.90 and 0.94.

Three kinds of scanning tools have all detected vulnerability CVE-2011-1871, so its reliability is the highest. Similarly, vulnerability CVE-2010-4562 is detected by two scanning tools, so its reliability is the second highest. Vulnerability CVE-2007-0066 is only detected by Nessus. Although the accuracy rate of Nessus is the highest among three scanning tools, the reliability is the lowest because of the lack of sufficiency which results from the least number of evidences. The calculating results are corresponding to the actual situation.

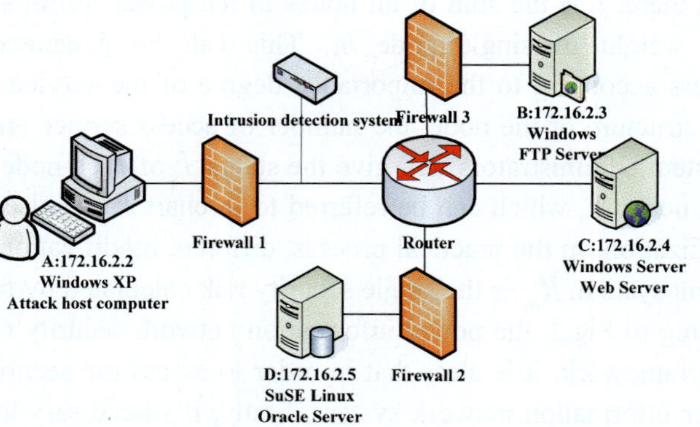

Fig. 3. The Simulation of Power information network topological graph.

Table1. Scanning results

Scanning tools	Node		
	Web server	FTP server	Oracle server
Nessus	CVE-2010-4562 CVE-2011-1871 CVE-2007-0066	CVE-2004-2111 CVE-2011-4800	CVE-2002-0060 CVE-2000-0800
X-Scan	CVE-2011-1871	CVE-2004-2111	CVE-2002-0060 CVE-2000-0800
ISS	CVE-2010-4562 CVE-2011-1871	CVE-2009-1439 CVE-2012-0450	CVE-2002-0060 CVE-2000-0800

Similarly, the vulnerability reliabilities of CVE-2004-2111,CVE-2011-4800, CVE-2009-1439 and CVE-2012-0450 on FTP server's nodes can be calculated, that is, 0.441,0.192,0.1835and 0.1835. And those of CVE-2002-0060,CVE-2000-0800 on Oracle database server's nodes are 0.5 and 0.5.

Table2.Security risks of vulnerability

Server node	Code of vulnerability	Vulnerability reliability in vulnerability analysis graph	One single vulnerability risk value	Total value of vulnerabilities
FTP server	CVE-2004-2111 (8.5)	0.441	3.7485	7.29315
	CVE-2011-4800 (9.0)	0.192	1.728	
	CVE-2009-1439 (7.8)	0.1835	1.4313	
	CVE-2012-0450 (2.1)	0.1835	0.38535	
Web server	CVE-2010-4562 (4.3)	0.313	1.3459	6.6037
	CVE-2011-1871 (7.8)	0.543	4.2354	
	CVE-2007-0066 (7.1)	0.144	1.0224	
Oracle server	CVE-2002-0060 (7.5)	0.5	3.75	8.75
	CVE-2000-0800 (10.0)	0.5	5	

4. Conclusion

The vulnerability analysis graph is model-based power information network vulnerability analysis techniques. Based on the situation of electric power information network, using bottom-up analysis method, a hierarchical power information network security risk assessment framework is proposed. The assessment process is as follows: firstly using vulnerability scanning tool to detect the vulnerability information in the power information network nodes, as well as associating the vulnerability information which attacks relying on with vulnerability information of the node itself to build the state vulnerability analysis graph, further calculating the vulnerability reliability vector and attack reliability vector of the node, combined with the each vulnerability's hazard index and the attack hazard index to calculate the vulnerability security risk and the attack security risk of the node, then assessing the security risk value of a single node; Secondly, combined with the weight of each node in the power information network itself, and eventually to quantify the security risk from the single node to the whole power information network.

Acknowledgments

This work is supported by the Basic and Prospective Project of SGCC SGRIXTKJ[2015]614.

References

1. P.A.Porras, M.W.Fong and A.Valdes. *A Mission-Impact-Based Approach to INFOSEC Alarm Correlation.* Recent Advances in Intrusion Detection, Springer Berlin Heidelberg, (2012),pp. 95-114.
2. S.Boyer, O.Dain and R.Cunningham. *Stellar: A fusion system for scenario construction and security risk assessment.* Proceedings of 13th IEEE International Workshop on Information Assurance, IEEE, (2015),pp.105-116.
3. P.Mell, K.Scarforne. *A Complete Guide to the Common Vulnerability Scoring System (CVSS) Version 2.0.* `http://www.first.org/cvss/cvss-guide.`
4. S.Hariri, G.Qu, T.Dharmagadda, et al. *Impact analysis of faults and attacks in large-scale power information networks.* IEEE Security & Privacy, Vol.11,no.5,(2013),pp.49-54.
5. Li QM, Li J . *Rough Outlier Detection Based Security Risk Analysis Methodology.* China Commucations, Vol.9,no.7,(2012), pp.14-21.

Design on Security Linkage Strategy of Power Information Network Terminal

Zhi-peng SHAO, Wei-wei LI and Qian-mu LI†
State Grid Smart Grid Research Institute,
Nanjing, 21003, China
†*E-mail: liqianmu@126.com*

This paper proposes a security linkage strategy algorithm to accomplish the performance evaluation of network safety, which effectively decreases the amount of computation and improves efficiency. Moreover, different security applications have their own requirements for safety, so that this paper thoroughly considers the security service types of various applications. The methods to compute network safety scores based on fuzzy logic are designed for four different kinds of services, fulfilling security applications' requirements. In addition, this paper gives full considers the situation that current network conditions are not representative of future situations, but current network status changes usually show certain trends which can predict the future conditions, thus providing more comprehensive network information to security linkage strategy.

Keywords: Smart grid; Security linkage strategy; Power information network terminal.

1. Introduction

Grid enterprise information construction has reached a very high level, so information security issues become increasingly prominent.. Traditional security strategy based on utility functions usually takes RSS value and other parameters into consideration. Xia R et al. [1] use the most optimized utility functions to achieve the balance between users' satisfaction and efficiency of network security. Li QM et al. [2] proposed a user-centric security strategy Linkage algorithm, which emphasizes users' satisfaction and only applies to non-real-time security applications. Li QM, Zhang H et al. [3] proposed a Linkage algorithm based on Game Theory. The algorithm bases on the Bayesian Nash equilibrium, for which reduces the delay of Linkage and make users always connect to the safest network using the highest utilization of network and the most appropriate security cost. Despite scholars have proposed lots of algorithms for security Linkage judgment, contradiction between cost and performance exists, and application requirements cannot be satisfied. Moreover,

†Corresponding author.

according to research status domestic and overseas [4], there is few research on framework that support security strategy Linkage, while efficient Linkage framework can improve the performance of the entire security Linkage decision effectively. Therefore, security Linkage technology is still a research emphasis and hotspot. This paper proposes a security Linkage decision algorithm on account of terminal control and network assistance

2. Security Linkage Strategy of Power Information Network Terminal (SLSPIT)

2.1. *Pre-process*

This paper puts forward two tasks during pre-process. The first task is the pre-decision for Linkage. Make network Linkage decision in advance through current network RSS and estimated dwell time. The second one is the selection of candidate network. Networks that don't meet requirements will be left out by considering terminal movement speed and dwell time, so that the number of candidates can be decreased and the complexity of the entire algorithm is lowered.

A Linkage will be forced to operate quickly when terminal feels the RSS value of current service network is lower than the threshold RSSth, in order to avoid interrupting service. For this reason, the target network should have a comparably high rank among available networks. Terminal movement speed selection. A network supports its own maximum moving speed. For example, Wi-Fi can only support walking speed 5km/h, while UTMS and WiMax (802.16e) can both support moving speed more than 120km/h, which satisfies urban transport. Therefore, we can remove Wi-Fi from the candidate list.

Selection of expected dwell time. Dwell time presents the time of terminal staying in a candidate network. Too short dwell time will cause frequent Linkage and result in decrease of service quality and customers' satisfaction. For this reason, we will make a pre-selection among candidates based on terminal expected dwell time and remove networks whose expected dwell time is shorter than 1 min. The procedure of pre-selection among candidate network is shown in Fig.1.

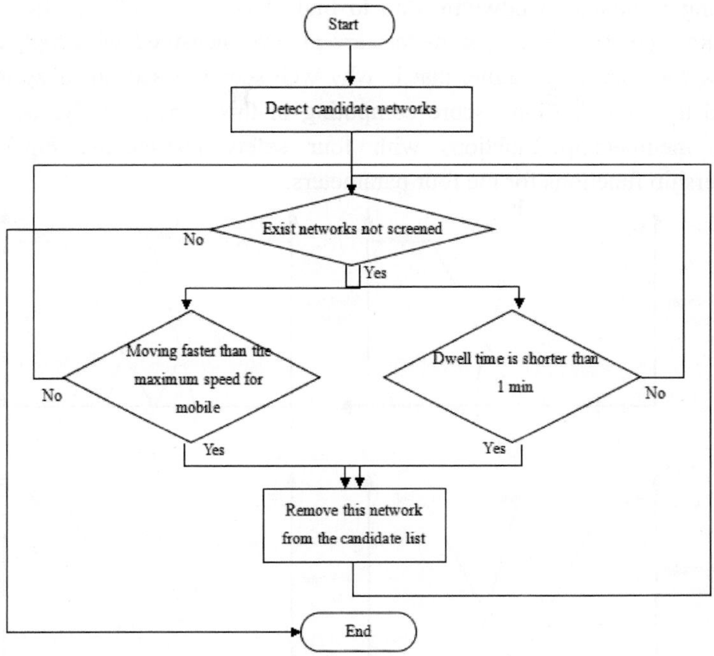

Fig. 1. Flowchart of network pre-selection.

2.2. *Computing network safety score through fuzzy logic*

It is known that safety is an important indicator to evaluate a network. Previous algorithms calculate safety in the terminal and scores depend on safety parameters of networks. Networks need to be calculated respectively, so that the computing complexity increases along with the number of available networks, which is an enormous waste of terminal computing power. Therefore, based on the Linkage framework, this paper adopts the method that the network is responsible for safety score computing. It makes the most of computing abilities of networks, greatly reduces the amount of terminal computing and increases the practicability of the algorithm. In addition, safety parameter requirements varies due to different kinds of application security services. This is considered thoroughly to design four fuzzy logic systems aimed at different kinds of security services to accomplish computing of network safety scores. Next, we will expand details from two aspects, design for membership functions and fuzzy logic rules.

Through pretreatments above, we can get candidates that meets terminal characteristic demands. In the section, we consider network safety parameters including Available Bandwidth, End to End Delay (E2EDelay), Jitter, and Bit Error Rate (BER). These parameters are always measured with high and low because they are very vague, that is why web scores based on fuzzy logic are applied to network safety score computing in this paper. Firstly, we need to design membership functions with four safety parameters. Fig.2 shows membership functions for the four parameters.

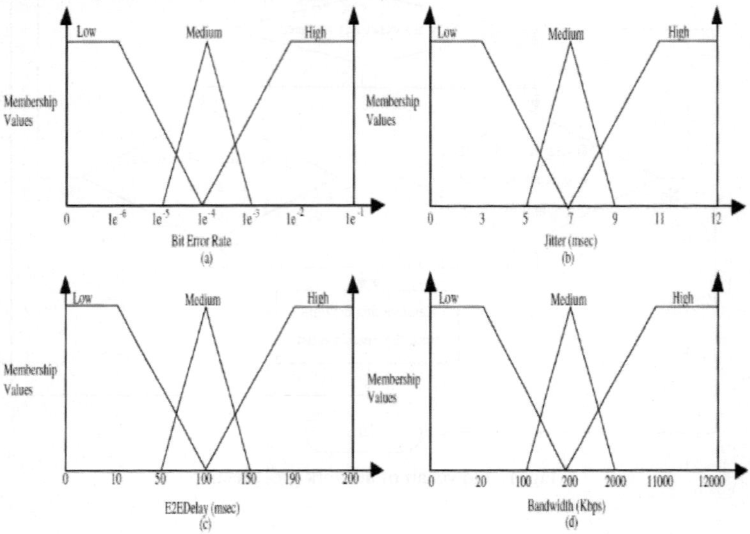

Fig. 2. Membership functions for input parameters.

From the introduction above, different kinds application security services have various safety requirements. Therefore, this paper thoroughly considers the effect on security Linkage decision from current kind of application security service on account of security Linkage decision algorithm based on fuzzy logic. Four different fuzzy logic rules are respectively designed for call security services, streaming security services, interactive security services and background security services. Table1 describes safety requirements for different kinds of security services.

Table 1. safety requirements for different security services.

Security services	BER	E2EDelay	Jitter	Available Bandwidth
Call security services	Unnecessarily Low	Low	Low	Unnecessarily High
Streaming security services	Unnecessarily Low	Low or Medium	Low	High
Interactive security services	Low	Medium	Unnecessarily Low	Unnecessarily High
Background security services	Low	Unnecessarily Low	Unnecessarily Low	Medium at least

For this paper, each kind of security services has 81 (3*3*3*3 = 81) rules. There are 4 * 81 =324 rules for four kinds of security services. Due to space limitation, this paper just gives several sample rules for each security services, which is shown in Table 2.

Table 2.fuzzy sample rules for different kinds of security services.

Rule Number	BER	E2E Delay	Jitter	Band width	Linkage Score
		Call security services			
1	Low	Low	Low	Low	High
25	Low	High	High	Low	Low
50	Medium	High	Medium	Medium	Low
81	High	High	High	High	Low
		Streaming security services			
1	Low	Low	Low	Low	Low
25	Low	High	High	Low	Low
50	Medium	High	Medium	Medium	High
81	High	High	High	High	Medium
		Interaction security services			
1	Low	Low	Low	Low	Medium
25	Low	High	High	Low	Low
50	Medium	High	Medium	Medium	Low
81	High	High	High	High	Low
		Background security services			
1	Low	Low	Low	Low	High
25	Low	High	High	Low	Medium
50	Medium	High	Medium	Medium	Medium
81	High	High	High	High	High

As can be seen from Table 2, each fuzzy rule is strictly designed by safety requirements of different kinds of security services. Other rules can be designed in this way.

2.3. *Network safety score prediction based on GM (1, 1) model*

safety scores will be stored in network terminal information database. These scores change with network conditions. Current web conditions cannot present future web conditions. But recent trends of the network can predict the future conditions, so that this paper designs a safety score prediction model on account of an one-step and single-variable grey forecast model GM(1, 1). Detailed procedure is shown as follows.

Suppose that the real safety score at time t is , the prediction safety score is , the number of samples is n, and the interval time between samples is a unit of time.

$$PScore_{t+1} = GM(RScore_t, RScore_{t-1}, \ldots\ldots, RScore_{t-n+1}) . \quad (1)$$

is the predicted safety score for the next time. GM is the prediction method of grey prediction model which was mentioned in the first paragraph. Parameters are sample values of network safety made of history ones.

Next we will take an example to explain. Assuming that the execution cycle of the algorithm is 1 second, sample size n=3, and current time is t, then .At the first three time points there was no enough dates to accomplish prediction, so that predicted value occurs from time T+3. The predicted value comes from real safety scores at T, T+1, T+2. Similarly, predicted value comes from real safety value at T+1, T+2, T+3. We call the model as metabolism GM (1, 1) model.

So far we have two network ranking lists: a web-based ranking list of the current network safety calculated values and a ranking list based on future network safety predicted values. Suppose that the rank result is shown as Table 3:

Table 3.real score and hypothetical values of prediction score.

Network	Real score (RSocre)	Real rank	Prediction score (PScore)	Prediction rank
WLAN	85	1	80	2
UMTS	80	2	85	1
...	...	...	...	...
WiMAX	50	n	70	N

As shown in the table above, WLAN is in the first place among candidates by current web safety computing results, while its score drops to 80 and is in the second place by network prediction result. The prediction value of UMTS rises to 85 and is in the first place. We can find that safety of UMTS has an upward trend and WLAN shows a downward trend. In the future the score of UTMS will exceed that of WLAN. We should make a security Linkage to UTMS to reduce the amount of Linkagees, avoid unnecessary network Linkagees and reduce the "ping-pong effect".

2.4. *Network selection*

As the last step if security Linkage judgment, network selection is decisive. Security Linkage decision algorithm proposed in this paper considers parameters including real network safety values, predicted network safety values and energy cost.

Firstly, we need to analyze effects that the real and predicted values of network safety have on network selection. The real values of network safety reflect real conditions of current network and the predicted values present prediction conditions of future networks. A main criterion for Linkageing selection is proposed here: if the prediction value of candidates is greater than the prediction of current network service, and the prediction is greater than the acceptable threshold, Linkage network, otherwise stay on the current network.

On this basis, a network filtering rule is put forward: if the real value of a candidate is lower than acceptable network safety threshold, remove this candidate network. This filtering rule is raised to exclude radical network Linkage. A radical network Linkage is an unreliable network Linkage whose prediction value is in the first place but is greater than threshold on the condition that the real values of candidates are lower than the threshold.

Define as the real network safety score of candidate network N running type security service. Define as prediction safety score. Service network C runs security service 'type' and the real network safety score of isPS_{type_C}, prediction safety score is PS_{type_N}. Current acceptable network safety threshold is S_{th}. Then candidate network N can be used as the Linkage target network in following condition.

$$\begin{cases} PS_{type\_N} > PS_{type\_C} \\ PS_{type\_N} > S_{th} \\ S_{type\_N} > S_{th} \end{cases}$$

3. Conclusion

This paper proposed SLSPIT Algorithm. On the basis of analyzing differences between this algorithm and the others, this paper expounds the main idea of this algorithm and in detail describes key steps: pre-process, network safety score computing based on fuzzy logic, network safety prediction and security network selection based on GM (1, 1) prediction model.

Acknowledgments

This work is supported by the Basic and Prospective Project of SGCC SGRIXTKJ[2015]216.

References

1. Xia R, Xu F, Zong CQ, Li QM, Qi Y, Li T, *Dual Sentiment Analysis: Considering Two Sides of One Review.* IEEE Transactions on Knowledge and Data Engineering. 2015, 27(8): 2120-2133..
2. Li QM. *Multiple safety Constraints Finding Paths Algorithm in TMN.* INFORMATION. 2011, 14(3): 731-737.

3. Li QM, Zhang H. *Information Security Risk Assessment Technology of Cyberspace: a Review.* INFORMATION. 2012, 15(11): 677-683.
4. Yang F, Li X, Li QM, Li T. *Exploring the Diversity in Cluster Ensemble Generation: Random Sampling and Random Projection.* EXPERT SYSTEMS WITH APPLICATIONS. 2014, 41(10): 4844-4866.

State Grid Network Attack-defense Graph Generation Method

Cheng ZHOU[†] and Jia-xuan FEI

State Grid Smart Grid Research Institute
Nanjing, 210003, China
[†]*E-mail: zhoucheng@sgri.sgcc.com.cn*

The attack-defense graph is a model-based network vulnerability analysis technique. Utilizing the characteristics of State Grid, this paper extends the attack-defense graph model and proposes a state attack-defense graph model. The state attack-defense graph use rules to model the attacker, and display all threat propagation paths which are generated by the attacker exploiting the dependence relations among vulnerabilities in the target network. In conjunction with prevention and control measures for vulnerability, the corresponding protection solution is proposed. In order to automatically generate the state attack-defense graph according to the network's topology information, reachable relationship of nodes and vulnerability information, a generating algorithm of the state attack-defense graph is proposed.

Keywords: State Grid network; Security strategy; Attack-defense graph.

1. Introduction

With continuing expansion of the size of State Grid network, a variety of network threats is also increasing. Designing an efficient electric power state attack-defense graph model has become one of the main tasks of the national grid information security in recent years. The main method of the area is modeling the entire network abstractly and obtaining the behaviors and the states the network system may have through the model, and then simulate an attack on the overall network system security objectives for analysis [1, 2]. Since the establishment of the model is simple than the extract of regular models and this technique can find the relationship between the unknown attack patterns and vulnerabilities, vulnerabilities and network components.

In recent years in the field, literature [3] proposed the use of Privilege Graphs to describe the intruder privilege escalation process. The node of the Privilege Graphs represents the permissions set that users and groups have, the connection between the nodes represent the privilege transfer caused by the use of vulnerability. It reflects the users owning starting node permissions can acquire permission which target node represents by using the vulnerability exists. Different ways to the attacking goal represent the different attacking process the Intruders conducted. Privilege Graphs describe the change of the attacker's right during the attack. The attack tree model is proposed by literature [4], using and – or tree structure to analyze the vulnerabilities of the network. A bottom-up structure to represent the process of the target attacks is provided on the system. It can be used to model complex network environment and attacking scene, determine the feasibility of an attack and attack path and then to determine which attack is most feasible or most likely to occur. The main problem existing is that the ability of the tree structure to represent the relationship of the complex vulnerability is limited. In literature [5], defense graph model is proposed and the main method is using directed graph to represent the using process. The node of the directed graph represents the security state of the system and use the attack templates to describe the attacking behavior and then generate offensive diagram of a system from the target state reversely through the existing attack templates. If succeed, it indicates that the system has vulnerabilities.

What the State Grid Network attack-defense graph mainly study is that attackers use the vulnerabilities of network nodes to permeate, reflecting the change of the attackers' action and the change of the system state. This paper expands the State Grid Network attack-defense graph and proposes the modeling method of the State Grid Network attack-defense graph. This method establish the model of the attackers' behavior based on the rules, showing all the routes which are threated and spread by the attackers using the dependencies between the vulnerability in the target network and giving the corresponding protect proposal which combined the prevention and control measures of the vulnerability.

2. The Definition of Attack-defense Graph

Definition 2.1*The State Grid Network attack-defense graph is a state transition system graph of an State Grid network SADG=(S, T, s_0, S_G). S is the collection of the security state node, representing the network security state; T is the collection of the edges in the graph, representing the change relations of the network security state and each edge represent an atomic attack which leads to the security state of the State Grid network changing from one state to another.*

$s_0 \in S$ is the initial security state of the network and $SG \subseteq S$ is the target state collection of the attackers.

Definition 2.2*Node of the security state. In the State Grid Network attack-defense graph, the node of the security state is represented by a two-div tuple (hostid, privilege). hostid is the name of the node whose security elements has changed in the network security state. These nodes can be divided by functions as follows: defense, isolation devices, routers, switches, servers, firewalls, smart grid terminals etc. Privilege is the rights which the attackers obtained in the hosted node when the network getting the security state. These rights are Root, User and None. Root has the highest right which indicates that attackers can conduct any program in the node; User is the second which indicates that attackers can only conduct some specific behaviors which have been authorized; None is the lowest that the attackers nearly have no rights to conduct any program.*

Definition 2.3*Change of the security state. In the State Grid Network attack-defense graph, the change of the security state is represent by a 5-div tuple (τid, vid, r, p, d). τid is the serial number of the security state, vid is the serial number of the vulnerability which is used by the atomic attack, r is the damage after a successful atomic attack, p is the probability of a successful atomic attack and d is the defensive measure when the atomic attack occurs. For example, there is a change (τid, vid, r, p, d) from a security node ($host_m$, privilege) to another ($host_n$, privilege), which indicates that node $host_m$ used the vulnerability in node $host_n$ to attack node $host_n$, the attack risk index is r, the probability of a successful attack is p, the network node d can take measure d to defense the atomic attack.*

Definition 2.4*Attack route. The attack path is represented by a 3-div tuple (src_host, dst_host, sequence). src_host is the node identifier to attack, dst_host is the node identifier which has been attacked and sequence is the attack sequence of the attack sequence=$\perp \to \tau 1 \to \tau 2 \to \ldots \to \tau l \to \Diamond$. "$\perp$" is the beginning identifier of the sequence, "$\Diamond$" is the end identifier of the sequence, $\Diamond \in S_G$, $\tau_i \in T(1 \leq i \leq l)$ is the atomic attack, τ_i is the direct precursor of $\tau_{i+1}$and τ_{i+1} is the direct successor of τ_i.*

A continuous attack process caused by the vulnerability and the up relationship among the nodes is showed in the State Grid Network attack-defense graph, so attack-defense graph is an important prediction to generate an State Grid Network attack-defense graph. This article define the up relationship as a 4-div tuple (src_host, dst_host, protocol, port). The structure is as follows:

Table 1. Node up relational structure.

Src_host	Dst_host	Protocol	Port
192.168.1.1	192.168.2.2	TCP	2380

Among them, src_host represents the source node, protocol represents the connection protocal between nodes and port represent the port connecting two nodes. src_host and dst_host can be represented by IP address. For example in table 2, the node up relation entry (192. 168. 1. 2, 192. 168. 2. 2, TCP, 2380) represents that the node whose IP address in the network is 192. 168. 1. 2 can use the TCP protocol through port 2380 to connect the node whose IP number is 192. 168. 2. 2. That traverse all nodes in the network based on the Firewall Rules, Routing Rules and some the network configuration information such as NAT can generate the up relation table of all the nodes in the network and the table represents the up relation of all the nodes.

3. Attack-defense Graph Modeling

Vulnerability using rule is a description of the attack behavior from an attacker's perspective using vulnerabilities to attack and is an important basis to analyze the attack path a specific attacker may take. Finish an atomic attacks need to meet certain preconditions. An attacker's access to the target node will be promoted after attacking successful. Therefore, we write Vulnerability using rule into a map from the premise and the structure is shown in Table 2.

Table 2. Vulnerability using rule

Atomic attack	Pre-Condition				Post-Condition
	192.168.2.2	Dst_priv	Vul_id	TCP	
GoodTech Telnet Server Buffer Overflow	Root	None	CVE-2005-0768	See Figure 2	Root

Among them, atomic attack is the name of Atomic Attack, the attack premise is represented by Pre-Condition, the attack consequence that the right the attacker gets in the target host computer after a successful attack is represented by Post-Condition. The attack premise can be represented as (src_priv, dst_priv, vul_id, connection). Among them, the least right the attacker has in the attack node is represented by src_priv, the least right the attacker has in the target host computer is represented by dst_priv, vul_id is the vulnerability identify the atomic attack used and connection represent the up relation between two target nodes and the structure is shown in Table 1. For example the Vulnerability using rule entry in table 2represents that GoodTech Telnet Server has buffer overflow vulnerabilities(serial number is CVE-2005-0768) which leads to the result that a remote attacker sends malformed and very long data to the server, which result in the buffer overflow, covering the instruction pointer to obtain Root privileges of the target node and remote execution of arbitrary code. The premise of the rule is that the target node has CVE-2005-0768 vulnerability and the attack consequence is obtaining the Root right of the target node. The using rule can be describes as (GoodTech Telnet Server Buffer Overflow, (Root, None, CVE-2005-0768, (192. 168. 1. 2, 192. 168. 2. 2, TCP, 2380)), Root).

An attacker firstly attacks the nodes in the network which haves vulnerabilities and connects with the node which the attacker is in from the attacker's node. If attack successfully, the attacker obtains elevated privileges in the node been attacked. The attack will attack from the node which has been attacked under capacities permit conditions, so again until capture the target node and achieve the stated objectives. However, protective measures are made to prevent attacks to the vulnerabilities from vulnerabilities that exist on the node. In the modeling of the State Grid Network attack-defense graph, we base on the assumption of unity and think that the right the attacker gets in a node has no effect in attacking more times again and the attackers will not launch repeated attacks.

Input:

(1) RT - Up to relational tables for all nodes in the network topology

(2) VS - The set of vulnerabilities for each node

(3) IB –Vulnerability repository been constructed and use rules table

(4) s0 - The initial state of the network nodes

Output:

The State Grid Network attack-defense graph modeling method uses the Depth-first traversal to add initial security state nodes into a security state queue and traversals every security state node in the security state queue, acquiring the collection of the vulnerability nodes which can be get to any element in the collection. To each vulnerability in the collection of vulnerabilities, if satisfies the requirements of the use rule and the network security state is not in the queue, a new security state and a change of the security state from the current security state to a new one are generated and add the new security state node into the security state queue at the same time; if satisfy the Vulnerability using rules but the network security state have been in the state queue after using it, that is, we only generate a change from the current security state node to a new one. If not satisfied, ignore the vulnerability and continue the cycle above until traversal all the nodes in the security state nodes in the security queue. Lastly, construct a completed State Grid Network attack-defense graph based on the relation of the change of security state.

Let the network's security state number is N, the number of the nodes each security can get is H, the number of the vulnerabilities of every nodes is M and the complexity of the algorithm is $O(N \times H \times M)$.

Theorem 3.1*The complexity of the State Grid Network attack-defense graph method is $O(N \times H \times M)$.*

Proof. *The first step of the algorithm is to set up a security state queue state_queue and set it empty. The second step is to add s_0-the initial security state of the State Grid network to the state queue and mark it as non traversal. In step three, start traverse the whole security state queue and get the security state nodes that are not been traversed. The node that the initial security state node s_0 corresponds to ish_0.Get the set of the other nodes that are reachable to s_0 by searching through the reachable relationship among nodes, namely reachable_hostids. The number of elements in the set reachable_hostids is H. In the fifth and sixth steps, traverse through the nodes in reachable_hostids. If hi belongs to the set reachable_hostids, then get the set of vulnerability points of the node from hi, namely vuls. The number of the elements invulsis M. From the seventh step to the twenty-second, traverse through the set vuls. If v_j belongs to vuls, obtain a new network security state node by matching the using rules of the vulnerable point, namely s. If s doesn't belong to the state_queue, add it to the state_queue and mark it as non traversal .Otherwise, don't add it to the state_queue. Repeat the above process until the elements in the state_queueare all traversed. Then the algorithm ends. At the end of the algorithm, the number of elements in the state_queue is N. The whole algorithm includes three cycles, so the time complexity of the State Grid network state attack-defense graph is $O(N \times H \times M)$as can be seen from the third, fifth and seventh steps of the algorithm..*

4. Simulation Experiment and Analysis

MulVAl-a logical inference that designed and implemented by CyberSecurity Lab of the University of Kansas (http://www.arguslab.org/mulval.html)is used in the paper to analyze the vulnerabilities of a segment from State Grid network. The main idea is to use Datalog language to describe the configuration of network and the attackers' attack behavior and system information. MulVAL records the inference rules when the security strategy can't be satisfied. As the

MulVAL model shows in Figure 1, it's input mainly has four parts: Network configuration information, host configuration information, Datalog description file of security strategy and the interaction rules of the attackers' attack behavior that are described with Datalog. Finally attack path is combined into a logical attack graph by using the model of attack-defense graph.

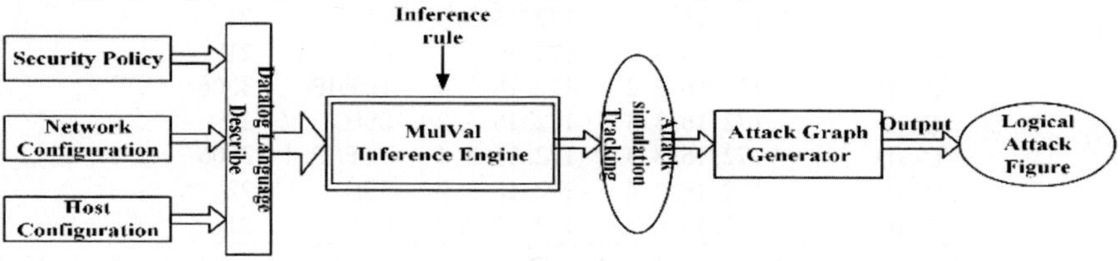

Figure1. System structure diagram of MulVAL

In figure 5, the node where the attacker is in is A. There are network server B, FTP server C and MySQL database server D in the target network. Meanwhile, each node in the network is running Linux operating system. By using the Nessus vulnerability scanner and Nmap scanning tool, the node information of server B, C and D are shown in Table 3.

Table 3. Node Information of server

ID(or IP)	Server	Protocol	Open port	Vulnerable point's ID
B(172. 16. 3. 2)	ssh	SSH	22	CVE-2012-5975
C(172. 16. 3. 3)	ftp	FTP	21	CVE-2009-4006
D(172. 16. 3. 4)	mysql	TCP/IP	3306	CVE-2012-5613

The external firewall is to restrict access to the internal and external network. The attack nodes of the external network can only access the Network server B and FTP server C through the external firewall. While behavior of other direct accesses to the internal network's other hosts from external network is prohibited. The servers between the internal networks can access each other with User right, which is not restricted by external firewall. The reachable relationship between nodes is shown in Table 4.

Table 4. The reachable relationship between nodes

ID(or IP)	A(172. 16. 2. 1)	B(172. 16. 3. 2)	C(172. 16. 3. 3)	D(172. 16. 3. 4)
A(172. 16. 2. 1)	0	1	1	∅
B(172. 16. 3. 2)	∅	0	1	1
C(172. 16. 3. 3)	∅	1	0	1

Reachable relationship entry between nodes is shown in Table 5.

Table 5. The reachable relationship entry between nodes

Reachable relationship	Sourse node	Target node	Protocal	Open port
A→B	172. 16. 2. 1	172. 16. 3. 2	SSH	22
A→C	172. 16. 2. 1	172. 16. 3. 3	FTP	21
B→C	172. 16. 3. 2	172. 16. 3. 3	FTP	21
B→D	172. 16. 3. 2	172. 16. 3. 4	TCP/IP	3306
C→B	172. 16. 3. 3	172. 16. 3. 2	SSH	22
C→D	172. 16. 3. 3	172. 16. 3. 4	TCP/IP	3306
D→B	172. 16. 3. 4	172. 16. 3. 2	SSH	22
D→C	172. 16. 3. 4	172. 16. 3. 3	FTP	21

In the initial state, the attacker has Root permissions on the attack node A and common User permission on the internal server node B and C, but the server D has no permissions, namely None. Now the target of the attacker is to obtain the MySQL's root of server node D. Although the attacker cannot access the MySQL server D from the host A, because of the dependence of vulnerability, the attacker can according to the exploitation rules of vulnerability point that are shown in Table 6 to implement the attack to achieve the target.

Table 6. Exploitation rules of vulnerability point

Atomic attack	Pre-Condition				Post-Condition
	src_priv	Dst_priv	Vul_id	connection	
SSH Server Root Authority Promoting	Root	User	CVE-2012-5975	A→B	Root

Through the analysis of the vulnerability and attack behavior of each node in the network and the modeling method of State Grid network state attack-defense graph, the State Grid network state attack-defense graph in the experimental network environment is shown in Figure 2.

As can be seen from the generated State Grid network state attack-defense graph, there are two attack paths from the attack node A to the target node D, namely A→B→D and A→C→D. The probability, harm and prevention measures of each atomic attack on the attack paths are clearly shown in State Grid network state attack-defense graph. According to the analysis of State Grid network state attack-defense graph that the model reflect the real attack-defense situation of the network system and it can help the manager identify the vulnerabilities of the network system, the potential security threats defense measures faced in order to avoid the occurrence of attack. designed and its formal definition is given. The method of modeling the State Grid network state attack-defense graph is given. In the search process, the method dismisses the vulnerabilities that have no relation with attack target, which reduce the solution space of the problems. Prove that the complexity of the algorithm is O (N×H×M) through our analysis. In the end, by experimenting in a network attack scene, the State Grid network state attack-defense graph model and the feasibility of its generating algorithm are verified.

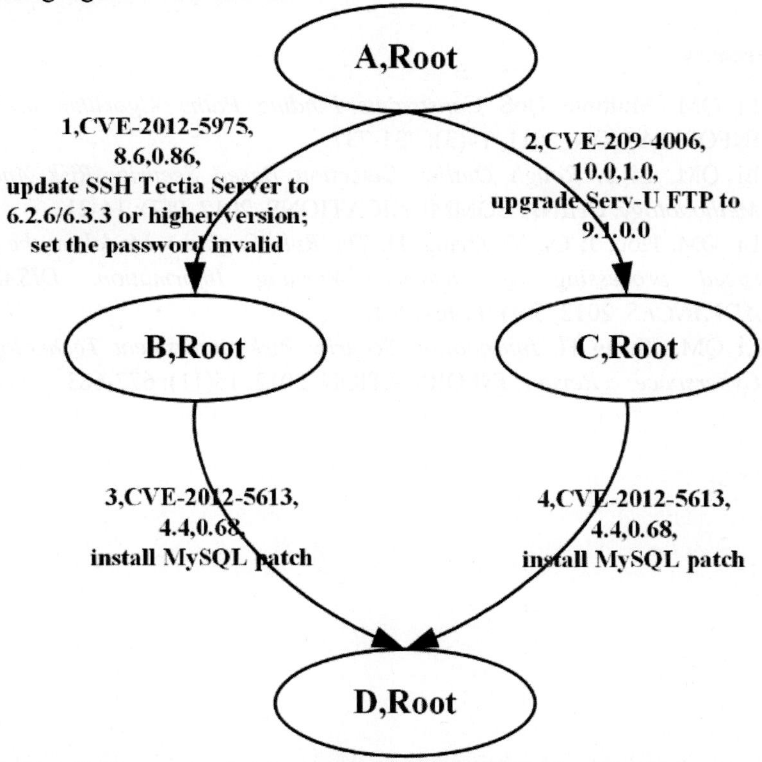

Figure 2. The state attack-defense graph generated from experimental environment

5. Conclusion

In this paper, attack-defense graph model is extended, the model of State Grid network is designed and its formal definition is given. The method of modeling the State Grid network state attack-defense graph is given. In the search process, the method dismisses the vulnerabilities that have no relation with attack target, which reduce the solution space of the problems. Prove that the complexity of the algorithm is O (N×H×M) through our analysis. In the end, by experimenting in a network attack scene, the State Grid network state attack-defense graph model and the feasibility of its generating algorithm are verified.

Acknowledgments

This work is supported by the Basic and Prospective Project of SGCC SGRIXTKJ[2015]614.

References

1. Li QM. Multiple QoS *Constraints Finding Paths Algorithm in TMN.* INFORMATION. 2011, 14(3): 731-737.
2. Li QM, Li J. *Rough Outlier Detection Based Security Risk Analysis Methodology*. CHINA COMMUNICATIONS. 2012, 9(7): 14-21.
3. Li, QM; Hou, J; Qi, Y; Zhang, H. *The Rule Engineer Model on the high-speed processing of Disaster Warning Information. DISASTER ADVANCES.* 2012, 5(4): 1196-1201.
4. Li QM, Zhang H. *Information Security Risk Assessment Technology of Cyberspace: a Review.* INFORMATION. 2012, 15(11): 677-683.

Under the Cloud-Based ECC Dynamic Password Authentication Scheme Design

Hong GAN and Dan PAN

Guangzhou City Construction College
GuangDong; Guangzhou; China
ganhongvip@163.com

The password-based authentication scheme requires users to use low-entropy passwords for identity authentication, thus the authentication process does not require public key infrastructure and users to store long symmetric key security hardware; providing high user convenience. Existing low cloud authentication security technology is not able to efficiently resolve highly complex problems, therefore the proposed password-based authentication method provides a simple solution to maximize the advantages of a password-based authentication scheme. We proposed several improvements in the scheme and analyzed its security capabilities to verify its feasibility for public cloud or private cloud environment.

Keywords: Cloud environments; EEC; Dynamic password Certification

1. Introduction

Dynamic Password (OTP: One-Time Password, also known as one-time Password) technology is the earliest scientists in the United States. Lamppost put forward in 1981.The technology is based on a mathematical algorithm to produce the password sequence, calculated from the previous password value under a password value. Users in every time they log in to use a different password, the password is generated on the client, and only the user knows. After the server receives the password by using their user identity by means of the relevant certification.

Thereafter, the researchers to password-based authentication way to do a lot of research. In 2000, Hwang and Li was proposed based on Mega mall public password system of the remote user authentication scheme, this scheme is a combination of smart card technology, through the timestamp mechanism can resist replay attack, do not have to be stored on the server user name and password. Then Juan, teal.[8] proposed a password authentication key agreement scheme based on smart card, upon completion of the remote system and the user's two-way authentication generated is used for communication between the two sides on the basis of the session. In 2002, Chine et al.[9] in this paper, a remote user authentication protocol based on passwords, this scheme only USES hash algorithm, and implements the bidirectional authentication, the user password with independent options at the same time, the server does not need to store all kinds of information are used to verify the identity of the users. Then many scholars put forward improvement to the agreement. In 2011, Chen et al.[4] proposed a new remote user authentication scheme based on smart card, although successfully implement two-way authentication, but there is still a replay attack and personating attack. Literature [5] proposed a strong two-factor authentication scheme based on password and smart card, through the use of smart CARDS and Chan Xian Ha function reduces the computational burden, can resist various attacks, it will be a one-time password (OTP) sent to the registered mobile phone number, but the SMS (Short Message System) system can't guarantee real-time transmission, data may still be intercepted.

In 1987, N.K blitz and Miller has proposed a more secure remote user authentication mechanism based on ECC. Use of elliptic curve cryptography system can improve the efficiency of plan implementation, saves storage space, reduce the consumption of the network resources. Recently, remote authentication scheme based on ECC was applied in cloud computing environment. Literature[12]proposed a two-way authentication and dynamic password authentication scheme based on ECC, will transfer to encrypt plaintext information protection, make plan in such aspects as safety, operation speed, storage performance has improved. In 2009, Yang and Change in this paper, a dynamic ID based on ECC remote bidirectional authentication and key agreement scheme, the scheme was proved to exist still counterfeit attack and insider attack. Literature of this scheme is improved, and is suitable for the cloud computing environment. Can be seen from the above literature, the existing identity authentication scheme based on password there are still many defects. Based on the above reasons, this chapter put forward a based on cloud users and cloud service providers on both sides of the password authentication of identity authentication scheme, make it suitable for public cloud or private cloud environment.

2. Authentication Scheme Design

In this paper, a dynamic password authentication scheme based on ECC. The program consists of system initialization, user registration, login and the password change phase and certification.

2.1. *Symbol table wrong solutions of symbols are described below*

U_A: Cloud users.
PW_A: Cloud user password.
CS: Cloud server.
E: Definition of elliptic curve on finite field Fq, among them, q is a big prime number.
P: A point on the E, n is the order a big prime number.
Ek()/Dk() : Encryption/decryption algorithms, among them, the symmetric key k said.
H (): Hash Function.
UR, US: Cloud Users Responded to Public and plate Keys.
SR, SS: Cloud Server CS of Public and Private Steel.

2.2. *Scenario is divided into four stages*

Initialization Phase: the server and the user on the elliptic curve cryptography parameters agree, server to choose their own private key to SS, and generate a public key SR = SS x P. By the same token, the user choose his private key to US, the public key UR = US x P. Users and cloud server open your public key to each other and keep their own private key, and the elliptic curve public parameters. Here the safety of the elliptic curve for multiple users to use.

User Registration Stage: when the user wants to access the cloud resource must first be registered to the cloud server. The registration process description as shown in figure 1.

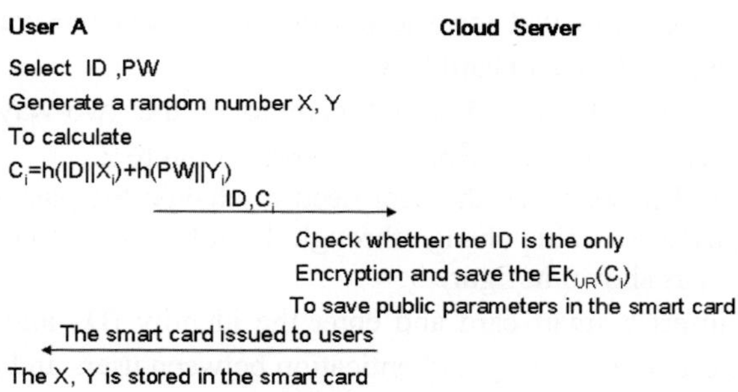

Fig.1 User Registration Phase

Stepl. U→CS: ID, C_i. Registered users of cloud to cloud server request, the identity of the users to select their first lazed and password PW, and generate two random Numbers X_i, Y_i, calculate the $C_i = h(ID||X_i) \oplus h(PW||Y_i)$, the ID, the Ci sent to the cloud server. **Step2.**CS→U: Smart Card. Cloud server after receiving the message, query the database ID exists, if there is asking the user to enter the new ID for registration, in order to make sure the ID is the only one. Will get Ek_{UR} (C_i) with the user's public key to encrypt (C_i), and the user ID of the one-to-one correspondence after stored in the database. Then public parameters stored in the smart card, and sent to the user through the security channel. **Step3.**After receiving the smart card users will 2 randomized parameters X_i, Y_i, and stored in a smart card.

Login And Authentication Stage: when a user UA wish to use the cloud services, through normal channels login cloud server and two-way authentication. Its execution process is as follows.

Stepl. U_A→CS:Ek_{UR})(C_i), a.Users first insert the smart card to the card reader, and password to enter the user identity IDA PW_A, calculation, $C_i = h(ID||X_i) \oplus h(PW||Y_i)$, $a = Ek_{SR}(ID_A||X_i||Y_i)$, log messages sent M_1=< $Ek_{uR}(C_i)$, a> to the cloud server. **Step2.**CS →UA: Challenge. Cloud server CS after receiving the message the M_1, and using the server private key to decrypt the Dkss(a) get IDA, X_i, Y_i, and will be saved as a X_i, Y_i. In the database query whether there is any IDA, if the user exists, the verification $Ek_{uR}(C_i)$? = $Ek_{uR}(C_i)$, or terminate the agreement. Produce two random X_{i+1}, Y_{i+1}, cloud users public key is used to calculate *challenge*=$Ek_{uR}(ID_A||X_i||Y_i||X_{i+1}||$

$Y_{i+1})$, cloud server message M_2=<challenge> send to cloud users U_A, and temporary (X_{i+1}, Y_{i+1}). **Step3.**UA→CS: $Ek_{UR}(C_{i+1})$, b. Cloud users to use their own private key decryption $Dk_{US}(challenge)$ get ID_A, X_i, Y_i, X_{i+1}, Y_{i+1}, $X_i?=X_{i+1}$, $Y_i?=Y_{i+1}$, if equal, cloud users of cloud server certification successfully. Then, calculate the $C_{i+1}=h(ID_A||X_{i+1})\oplus h(PW_A||Y_{i+1})$, $b=Ek_{SR}(X_{i+1}||Y_{i+1})$, and the<$M_3$= Ek_{UR})(C_{i+1}), b> CS sent to the cloud server. **Step4.**CS→UA: ACK. Cloud server after receiving the message decrypted Dkss(b), get X_{i+1}, Y_{i+1}, validation $X_i?=X_{i+1}$, $Y_i?=Y_{i+1}$, if equal cloud server for user authentication is successful, UA and certification success message sent to users, or terminate the agreement. At the same time will be in the database $Ek_{UR}(C_i)$ updated to $Ek_{UR}(C_{i+1})$, so that the next visit, otherwise declined to visit. **Step5.**After the news that the success of cloud users receive certification to random number update of a smart card to X_{i+1}, Y_{i+1}.

At this point, the cloud and cloud completed the two-way authentication between the user. The process description is shown in figure 2.

Password Change Phase: when the user need to change the password for various reasons, can be password value change through the following process. Its execution process description as shown in figure 3.

Stepl. User insert a smart card and enter the identity ID_A and PW_A password first need to complete the two-way authentication between users and cloud servers, if not through the authentication, refused to change password and feedback to the user to change password information. **Step2.**Smart card and twice prompt the user input new password value PW^*_A, this is done to ensure the correctness of the new password value. Then, choose 2 new smart card random number X^*_i, Y^*_i, calculate $C^*_i=h(ID_A||X^*_i)\oplus h(PW^*_A||Y^*_i)$, and C^*_iencryption for $Ek_{UR}(C^*_i)$ sent to the cloud with IDA. **Steps.**ID_A in cloud server, query the database, the corresponding $Ek_{UR}(C_i)$ updated to $Ek_{UR}(C^*_i)$, and reply to the user password change information of success. **Step4.**User after receiving the news of the cloud server, the smart card in the X_i, Y_i, updated to X^*_i,Y^*_i.

3. Safety analysis

Safety analysis has been made to the below for the above.

Proposition 1: The Scheme Can Resist Replay Attack. **Proof:** Assume that the attacker attempts to replay the hacking to login request message M_1=<$Ek_{UR}(C'_i)$, a>, a> to achieve the purpose of through CS authentication, users must know the U_A random number X_i, Y_i, due to the random number of one-time makes the attacker can replay the message.

Proposition 2: The scheme can resist counterfeit attack and denial of service attacks. **Proof:** First of all, the attacker can impersonate server cheat users, because he doesn't have cloud server private key SS, and so cannot be of a, b to decrypt, unable to calculate the random number, can't judge authentication was successful.

Second, the attacker to defraud the server can't fake a legitimate user trust, because a login request message M_l to know password values, and the attacker does not know.

In our scheme, the cloud data saved in the database of the certification C_i contains a random number of X_i, Y_i, and X_i, Y_i change will inevitably lead to change, once passed the certification, the database will store the next authentication password C_{i+1}, that is to say, the authentication data when C_i authenticate users a unique identifier, through authentication of cloud users to log on to the cloud computing platform, to resist the fake attack and denial of service attacks.

Proposition 3: the scheme can resist the middle attack. **Proof:** In this scenario plaintext only on the client side, certification for use in a random number, the information such as user ID and password PW in encrypted form transmission, even if the attacker access, based on the intractability of discrete logarithm characteristics is difficult to obtain effective information. In addition, two random X_i, the use of Y_i is not easy to make the attacker more speculation and forge the authentication data, thus able to resist the middle attack.

Proposition 4: The scheme can resist privileged insiders attack. **Proof:** Because of the cloud save password is to use the user's public key to encrypt, if no user public key, an attacker is unable to get the user's password, even if the cloud server manager is not available. So can effectively prevent the attack from inside the cloud server for user password.

Proposition 5: The scheme can provide two-way authentication. **Proof:** In order to realize the two-way authentication, the user must prove his identity to the cloud server, and the cloud server must also prove his own identity to the user. In the scenario, the user and the cloud server by verifying the value of the random number to determine the identity of each other, because the random number X_i, Y_i can be used only once, even if an attacker to obtain the value of the random number that he attacked when the value is invalid.

Therefore, the scheme can provide two-way authentication.

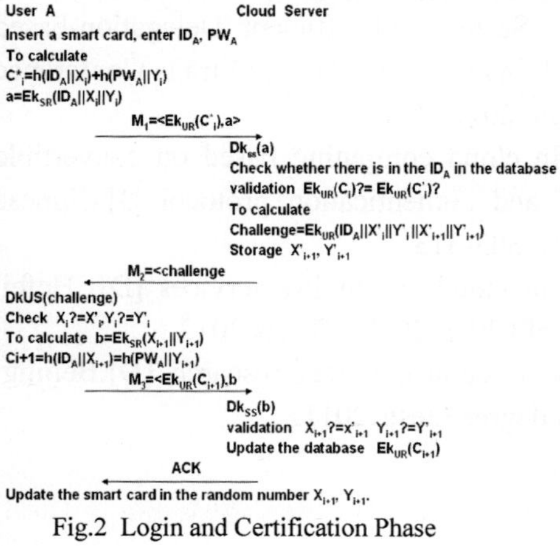

Fig.2 Login and Certification Phase

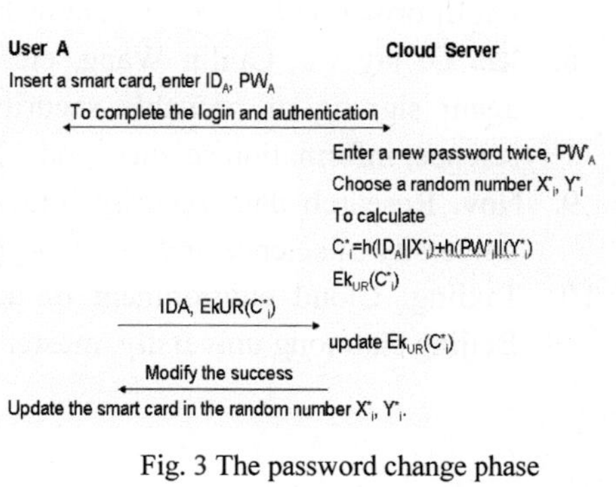

Fig. 3 The password change phase

4. Conclusion

This paper proposes a dynamic password authentication scheme based on ECC. The scheme is based on the cloud users and cloud service providers both sides to implement two-way authentication, the elliptic curve discrete logarithm of difficult Xenia strengthened the protection of users' information, and can according to user requirements for secure password change. The scheme in this paper, the scheme design, through the study of the safety analysis of the scheme, the scheme can resist most of the attacks, such as replay attacks, man-in-the-middle attack, fake attack, denial of service attack, privileged insiders attack, etc., improve the security of the scheme. This scheme is applicable to public clouds or private cloud environment.

References:

1. Liu Lin dong, wu Lin. USB key identity authentication based on cloud computing technology research [J].Journal of gang dong the second normal college,2011,31 (5) : 78-84.
2. Xu Kai,A landing on cloud computing problem of authentication technology[J].Science, technology and engineering,2011,1(6) : 1275-1377.
3. Li jian. PKI application in the cloud computing research [J]. Information network security, 2011, 8:44-47.
4. Jian-xun zhang peoples koshi Zheng Chao. Cloud computing research progress review [J].Computer application research, 2010127 (2) : 429-434.
5. Deng-goo Deng; Zhang min, Zhang Yan etc. Cloud computing security research[J].Journal of software,2011,22 (1) : 71-83
6. TH Chen. An Advanced ECC Dynamic ID-Based Remote utual Authentication Scheme for Cloud Computing[A].In:2011 Fifth FTRA International Conference on Multimedia and Ubiquitous Engineering[C].2011,155-159.
7. WS Juan, JY Chiu, HY Chang. A Secure and Efficient Delegation-based uthentication Scheme in Public Clouds[A].In: The 1st Cross-Straits Conference On Information Security[C].Hangzhou: 2011,96-102.
8. Xin Qi jay wu, Guilin Wang, etc. In cloud computing based on convertible agent signing of provable security and authentication protocol [J].Chinese science, information science, and 2012:303-313.
9. Nov. Research data security issues in cloud computing services [D]. Hefei: university of science and technology of China, Ph.D. Thesis,2012.
10. Taxiing. Cloud environment of access control model research [D].Beijing: Beijing Jiao tong university, master's degree thesis,2011.

11. Security Guidance for Critical Areas of Focus in Cloud Computing V3.0[DB/OL].http://www.cloudsecurit lliance.Org/guidance /csaguide.v3.0.pdf.
12. John Ratting house, James Ran. Cloud Computing: Implementation, Management, and Security[M],2009.

Image Encryption Algorithm Based on Unified Chaotic System and Lifting Wavelet Transformation

Kun ZHANG

School of Mathematics and Statistics, Chuxiong normal university
Chuxiong Yunnan 675000, China
zhangkun@ cxtc.edu.cn

In order to tackle the security problem of image transmission across public networks, a new image encryption algorithm based on unified chaotic system and lifting wavelet transform is proposed in this article. Firstly, the image is decomposed horizontally and vertically by lifting wavelet transform to obtain sub band images. Secondly, utilizing the sort permutation and the binary XOR operation from the unified chaotic series, the algorithm can achieve the encryption of the sub band images. Thus, the recipient of the images can correctly restore the sub band images and reconstruct the original images by a decryption algorithm. Finally, the analysis of algorithm security is conducted with theory analysis and computer simulation. The experiment results demonstrate that the new chaotic encryption algorithm based on unified chaotic system and lifting wavelet transform is feasible and provides higher security.

Keywords: Lifting wavelet transform; Unified chaotic system; Encryption algorithm; Lyapunov exponent.

1. Introduction

With the rapid development of multimedia and network technologies, image encryptions become more and more important, and image encryption schemes have been increasingly studied to meet the demand for secure image transmission over the Internet. Traditional image encryption algorithm such as data encryption standard (DES), has the weakness of low-level efficiency when the image is large [1].

In mathematics, a wavelet series is a representation of a square-integrable function by a certain orthonormal series generated by a wavelet. Because of the good time-frequency localization characteristics, scale variation characteristics and direction characteristics, wavelet has been widely used in many fields, especially in image coding [2]. Sweldens used a new wavelet construction algorithm that does not rely on Fourier transformation, but on lifting scheme to construct wavelet in time domain, then he established the second generation wavelet transform theory [3].In recent years, lifting has been chosen in the JPEG2000 standard [4].

Since the chaos theory was used in applications to cryptology from the 1980s, the chaotic encryptions have gained more and more attentions. It seems that chaotic maps may be useful both in traditional cryptology and in secure line signal generation which hides data effectively [5].Chaotic systems are characterized by the sensitive dependence on initial conditions and system parameters, pseudorandom property, no periodicity and topological transitivity. Therefore, the use of chaos in cryptography is of great interest in many areas, including databases, Internet banking, software, and security of communication channels, in order to preserve confidential data from indiscretion attacks of enemies, spies, opponent, cryptanalysts, etc.

In 2002, Lü and Chen found a new chaotic system bearing the name of the Lu system, thereby bridging the gap between the Lorenz and Chen attractors [6]. In the same year, Lü et al. unified above the three chaotic systems into one chaotic system which is called unified chaotic system [7]. The unified system is a discrete chaotic system with the steady complexity, and the pseudo-random sequences generated by the unified system are suitable for use in information encryption.

The rest of the paper is organized as follows. In section 2, we give a brief overview of the lifting scheme. In section 3, the mapping equation of unified chaotic system is introduced. In section 4, a new image encryption algorithm based on unified chaotic system and lifting wavelet transform is proposed. In section 5, we analyze the security of the proposed image encryption algorithm and evaluate its performance through various tests such as statistical analysis, differential analysis, etc and compare the results. Finally, some conclusions are given in section 6.

2. Lifting Wavelet Transform

The lifting wavelet transform could be divided into the following three stages: split, prediction, and update [8].

(1)Split: First, the input signal $s_j = \{s_{j,k}\}$ was divided into two smaller subsets $e_{j-1}$and o_{j-1}.where $o_{j-1}$was also known as wavelet subset. The simplest split was that s_j was divided into two groups according to parity, then e_{j-1}wasknown as the even sequence ando_{j-1}known as the odd sequence. This split wavelet was expressed as:

$$Split(s_j) = (e_{j-1}, \quad o_{j-1}) . \tag{1}$$

(2) Prediction: Based on the correlation of raw data, the predicted $P(e_{j-1})$ of the even sequence e_{j-1} was used to predict the odd sequence o_{j-1} .The prediction stages was expressed as:

$$d_{j-1} = o_{j-1} - P(e_{j-1}) . \tag{2}$$

where d_{j-1} are detail coefficients or wavelet coefficients.

(3) Update: The idea of update was to find a better subsets e_{j-1} ,which maintained some scalar features of the original signal. The computed wavelet subset d_{j-1} could be used to update e_{j-1}, which made the latter maintain the same scalar features. An operator U could be constructed to update e_{j-1}, which was defined as follows:

$$s_{j-1} = e_{j-1} + U(d_{j-1}) . \tag{3}$$

After successive inverse update and prediction steps, we can interleave these data sets to obtain the original set of samples.

3. The Unified Chaotic System

In 2002, Lü et al. produced a unified chaotic system which contains the Lorenz and Chen systems as two extremes and the Lü system as a special case. The unified chaotic system is described by [9].

$$\begin{cases} \dot{x} = (25\alpha + 10)(y - x) \\ \dot{y} = (28 - 35\alpha)x - xz + (29\alpha - 1)y \\ \dot{z} = xy - \dfrac{\alpha + 8}{3} z \end{cases} . \tag{4}$$

where the constant parameter $\alpha \in [0,1]$. The unified chaotic system can be reformulated in the following canonical form [10]:

$$\begin{bmatrix} \dot{x} \\ \dot{y} \\ \dot{z} \end{bmatrix} = \begin{bmatrix} a_{11} & a_{12} & 0 \\ a_{21} & a_{22} & 0 \\ 0 & 0 & a_{33} \end{bmatrix} \begin{bmatrix} x \\ y \\ z \end{bmatrix} + x \begin{bmatrix} 0 & 0 & 0 \\ 0 & 0 & -1 \\ 0 & 1 & 0 \end{bmatrix} \begin{bmatrix} x \\ y \\ z \end{bmatrix} . \tag{5}$$

According to this critical value, the whole family of (4) or (5) chaotic systems can be classified as follow: when $\alpha \in [0, 0.8)$ in (4), systems (4) belong to the generalized Lorenz system, since with these values of α in (4) has $a_{12}a_{21}>0$ in (5); when $\alpha \in [0, 0.8)$ in (4),it belongs to Lü system, since in this case$a_{12}a_{21}=0$ in (5); when $\alpha \in (0.8, 1]$ in (4),it belongs to the generalized Chen system, for which $a_{12}a_{21}<0$ in (5).Examples of the corresponding attractors with α=0.4, α=0.8 and α=1 are shown inFigure.1(a),(b) and(c), respectively.

4. Encryption Algorithm

Image data has strong correlations among adjacent pixels. In order to disturb the high correlation among pixels, an image total shuffling matrix is used to shuffle the position of the plain-image. Let us assume that the image system is space-invariant and that the channels of the source image H are jointly stationary, i.e.,

$$H = \{h_{ij} | 1 \le i \le m, 1 \le j \le n\} . \tag{6}$$

where h_{ij} denotes pixel (*i*, *j*) of $m \times n$ image. The steps involved in the implementation of our encryption algorithm based on unified chaotic system and lifting wavelet transform can be summarized as shown below.

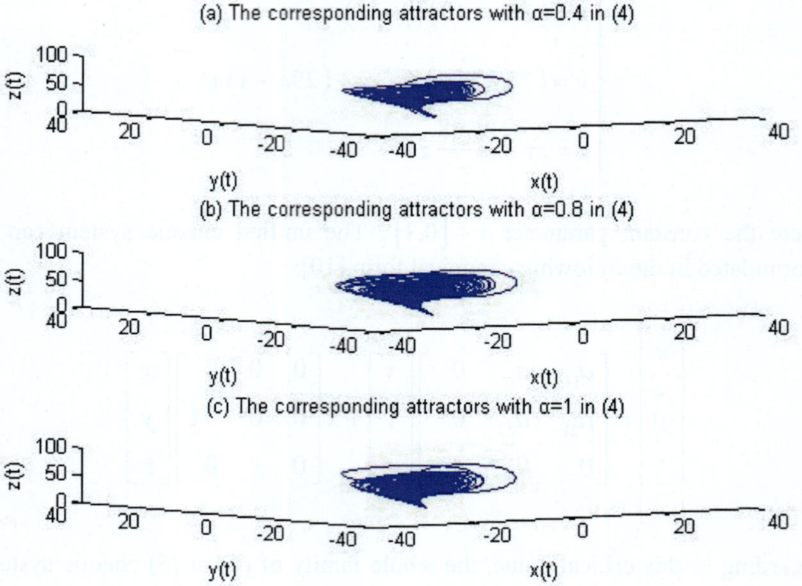

Fig. 1. The corresponding attractors with α=0.4, α=0.8 and α=1 in (4).

Step 1:Set unified chaotic system parameter α, the system initial value $x(0)$,$y(0)$,$z(0)$ in (4),and generate unified chaotic system chaotic sequence x_n,y_n,z_n.

Step 2: In lifting wavelet transform, original image decomposition produces four bands of data, such as approximation coefficients matrix (*LL*) and detail coefficients matrices *HL*, *LH*, *HH*.

Step 3: Calculate the size of the four coefficients matrices, and the four coefficients matrices is respectively changed to four dimensional vector in the order of rank ll_k, hl_k, lh_k and hh_k,.

Step 4: Let the chaos sequence x_k sort descending or ascending, it achieves a new sequence, and use the new sequence location index to produce the replacement encryption of digital image vector ll_k',hl_k',lh_k' and hh_k'.

Step 5: Generate a new chaotic sequence x_n':

$$x'_n = \frac{x_n - \min}{\max - \min}. \quad (7)$$

where x'_n binary form are $x'_n = \left(0.b_{k1}b_{k2}\cdots b_{kp}\right)$, $b_{ij} = \{0,1\}$. use x'_n sequence to produce X_k.

$$X_k = b_{k1}b_{k2}\cdots b_{kp}. \quad (8)$$

Step 6: Calculate encrypted image vector C_k:

$$\begin{aligned} CLL_k &= X_k \oplus ll'_k \\ CHL_k &= X_k \oplus hl'_k \\ CLH_k &= X_k \oplus lh'_k \\ CHH_k &= X_k \oplus hh'_k \end{aligned}. \quad (9)$$

where the $\oplus$ is XOR operation. The encryption process is finished.

The decryption algorithm is similar to the encryption algorithm. That is, for the encrypted image, firstly, decrypt approximation coefficients matrix of encrypted image using unified chaotic system with the same parameters and initial values as that used in encryption, and then anti-shuffle the resulting image, we will get the approximation coefficients matrix of original image.

5. Experiment Analysis

Experimental analysis of the proposed image encryption algorithm in this paper has been done. The experiment is using the platform of Matlab 2009a. The image is decomposed by Haar wavelet lifting scheme and the unified chaotic system parameter is,$x(0)=0$,$y(0)=0$,$z(0)=1$. The top Lyapunov exponent of this system was 0.5241 by Wolf's algorithm is used to identify the dynamic behavior of chaotic system, and the results show that the system is a chaotic system[11]. The plain-image with the size 150×240 is shown in Fig. 2(a). The encrypted image is shown in Fig. 2(b),and is rough-and-tumble and unrecognizable. As Fig. 2(c) shows the decrypted image using the same encryption key is an exact version of the original image. Fig. 2 (d) shows the error between the original image and decrypted image, which is zero.

Fig. 2. The results of color image encryption algorithm .

5.1. *Key space analysis*

For a secure image cipher, the key space should be large enough to make the brute force attack infeasible. In this algorithm, the initial conditions and parameters can be used as keys, and the confusion sequence $x(n)$ is also dependent of both the encryption parameter and the iterative time $x(0),y(0),z(0)$. Since the unified chaotic system parameters are floating-point numbers, key space of the algorithm is very large..

5.2. *Histograms analysis*

The image histogram is important statistical characteristics of digital image, it can illustrate how pixels in an image are distributed by graphing the number of pixels at each color intensity level [12]. The histogram of the encrypted image is fairly uniform and is significantly different from that of the original image that is the encrypted image is unrecognizable as shown in Fig 3. It is clear that the histogram of the encrypted image is fairly uniform and significantly different from the respective histograms of the original image and hence does not provide any clue to employ any statistical attack on the proposed image encryption procedure.

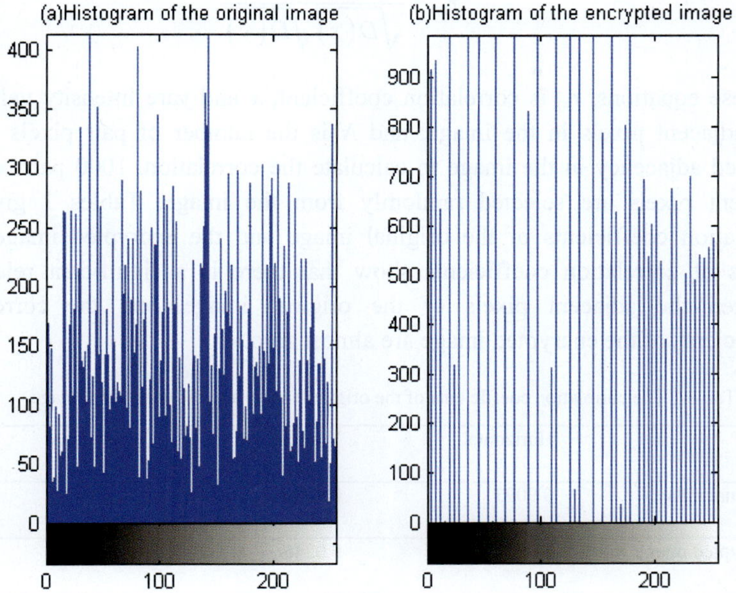

Fig. 3. The histogram of the original and encrypted image

5.3. *Correlation coefficient analysis*

To test the correlation between two vertically adjacent pixels, two horizontally adjacent pixels, and two diagonally adjacent pixels in a cipher image, respectively, the procedure is as follows: First, A thousand pairs of two adjacent pixels are selected randomly in vertical, horizontal, and diagonal direction from the original and encrypted images. Then, calculate their correlation coefficient using the following two formulas[13]:

$$E(x)=\frac{1}{N}\sum_{i=1}^{N}x \ . \tag{10}$$

$$D(x)=\frac{1}{N}\sum_{i=1}^{N}[x-E(x)]^2 \ . \tag{11}$$

$$COV(x,y) = \frac{1}{M \times N} \sum_{i=1}^{M} \sum_{j=1}^{N} [x - E(x)][y - E(y)]. \tag{12}$$

$$r_{xy} = \frac{COV(x,y)}{\sqrt{D(x)}\sqrt{D(y)}}. \tag{13}$$

In these equations, r_{xy} is correlation coefficient, x and $y$are intensity values of two adjacent pixels in the image, and N is the number of pair pixels of the selected adjacency in the image to calculate the correlation. 1000 pairs of two adjacent pixels are selected randomly from the image. Tables 1 give the correlation coefficients of the original image and the encrypted image. The values of correlation coefficients show that there is a significant relevance between the adjacent pixels of the original image, and the correlation coefficients of the encrypted image are almost zero.

Table 1 The correlation coefficients of the original image and the encrypted image

	Horizontal	Vertical	Diagonal
Original image	0.9093	0.9006	0.8469
Encrypted image	0.0030	0.0246	0.0426

6. Conclusion

The unified chaotic system is a highly complex nonlinear dynamic system and is a highly complex nonlinear dynamic system. In this paper, an image encryption scheme based on unified chaotic system and lifting wavelet transform is presented. All parts of the proposed encryption algorithm were simulated using computer code. Theoretical and experimental results indicate that the encryption image histogram distribution of the proposed scheme is so even that the entropy measured is almost equal to the ideal value. Differential analysis showed that a swiftly change in the original image will result in a negligible change in the image. Consequently, the proposed scheme has a high security which is due to characteristics of unified chaotic system.

Acknowledgments

This research was partially supported by the National Natural Science Foundation of China (No. 11261001).

References

1. K.Sakthidasan, Sankaran, B.V.Santhosh Krishna. A new chaotic algorithm for image encryption and decryption of digital color images, *International Journal of Information and Education Technology*, Vol. 1, No. 2, June 2011,pp137-141

2. Zhang Yanyan, Huang Qitao, Han Junwei. Lifting Wavelet-Based Progressive Compression and Real-Time Rendering to Large Terrain. *Journal of Computer-Aided Design & Computer Graphics*, 2010,22(8):1352—1359.

3. Wim Sweldens. The Lifting Scheme: A Custom-Design Construction of Biorthogonal Wavelets. *Applied and Computational Harmonic Analysis*. 3(2), 1996:186–200.

4. WANG Jing-zhong, LI Dan. Watermarking algorithm for infrared image based on chaotic sequence and JND. *LASER & INFRARED*, 2009,39(5):562-565.

5. Mieczysław Jessa, DATA ENCRYPTION ALGHORITHMS USING ONE-DIMENSIONAL CHAOTIC MAPS. *IEEE International Symposium on Circuits and Systems*, May 28-31, 2000:711-714.

6. JINHU LU, GUANRONG CHEN. A NEW CHAOTIC ATTRACTOR COINED. *International Journal of Bifurcation and Chaos*, Vol. 12, No. 3 (2002) 659-661.

7. JINHU LU, GUANRONG CHEN, DAIZHAN CHENG, SERGEJ CELIKOVSKY. BRIDGE THE GAP BETWEEN THE LORENZ SYSTEM AND THE CHEN SYSTEM. *International Journal of Bifurcation and Chaos*, Vol. 12, No. 12 (2002) 2917-2926.

8. Zhong Ji, Lan Zhu, Xing Yang , Lipeng Jiang. Single wave extraction in continuous intracranial pressure signal with lifting wavelet transformation and discrimination rules. *EURASIP Journal on Advances in Signal Processing* ,2011, 2011:43

9. Junan Lu, Xiaoqun Wu, Jinhu Lü. Synchronization of a unified chaotic system and the application in secure communication. *Physics Letters A*. 305,2002: 365–370

10. G. R. Faulhaber. Design of service systems with priority reservation. 1995 *IEEE Int. Conf. Communications*, pp. 3–8.

11. Alan WOLF, Jack B. SWIFT, Harry L.SWINNEY and John A. VASTANO. DETERMINING LYAPUNOV EXPONENTS FROM A TIME SERIES. *Physica D* ,1985,16:285-317

12. Xiaojun Tong, Minggen Cui. Image encryption with compound chaotic sequence cipher shifting dynamically. *Image and Vision Computing*, 26 (2008):843–850.

13. Saeed Bahrami, Majid Naderi. Image Encryption Using a Lightweight Stream Encryption Algorithm. *Advances in Multimedia*, Volume 2012, Article ID 767364,8 page

Research on the Security of Massive Network Data Based on Hadoop

Feng ZONG

Shandong Yingcai University,
Jinan, Shandong, 250104, China
E-mail: nfxzf@163.com

To tackle the security issues of massive network data, this paper utilizes the fuzzy K-algorithm and Naive Bayesian classification to develop a joint classification algorithm, and Mahout technology to develop a classification algorithm for feature extraction based on the MapReduce framework of parallel computing. The establishment of the corresponding model and training allows the joint classifier to determine the abnormal traffic, so as to develop a comprehensive network anomaly traffic detection system, to improve the security of the massive network data processing platform.

Keywords: Hadoop; Big data; Network traffic; Network security; Parallel computing.

1. Introduction

Security problem is an important problem which restricts the development and popularization of cloud computing technology. Although researchers have carried out a lot of research work for cloud security issues, but after the introduction of the mobile Internet massive network data processing business, the existing cloud computing platform based on Hadoop still need to strengthen the security of data flow detection.

The traditional intrusion detection technology has great limitations in the cloud computing platform[1]. Because of the application of virtualization technology and distributed computing technology, the traditional network based intrusion detection technology can not effectively detect the virtual host, and the host based intrusion detection technology can not detect the hacker's network attack. At the same time, the traditional intrusion detection technique in detection of high speed mass of network data flow, the detection efficiency is often not ideal and accurate. And now, more and more network attacks using the information hiding in network message, many trojan virus needs to flow through the test to identify.

The massive network data processing platform based on Hadoop is in the network environment, it needs to receive the massive data stream collected in real time, and at the same time, it needs to provide a large amount of data access interface for all kinds of data users. The network security of the platform has the requirement of rapid detection and detection of abnormal traffic, and the traditional network security technologies, such as data encryption and security authentication, can not solve the security problem of the massive network data processing platform. Therefore, in view of the massive network data processing platform architecture, in addition to the traditional network security equipment, including firewall, network, intrusion detection and other equipment, but also the need for massive data flow detection technology used in massive network data processing platform for research, mainly including improve the detection accuracy and processing speed of two aspects to consider, to carry out related research work.

2. Analysis of Cloud Computing Security

2.1. *Research on network attack technology for Cloud Computing*

Cloud computing uses a network based service model, and according to user needs to provide users with all kinds of hardware and software resources and data information [2]. On behalf of the products have EC2 IBM, BlueCkmd Amazon, Google's Engine App and other [3]. Massive network data processing platform based on Hadoop also has the network interface for platform management and data stream receiving and storage, which is similar to most of the existing cloud services, and it needs to provide services to users in the Internet. At the same time, in recent years, in view of the network cloud computing cluster attack [4] has been increased sharply. At present, the attacks against the cloud mainly include illegal access, cloud platform vulnerability attacks, abuse of authority attacks, cloud computing environment based on the host or network attacks, process hijacking and other conditions.

2.2. *Analysis of abnormal traffic detection technology in cloud computing environment*

For the security problem of cloud computing, researchers have carried out a lot of research work, many cloud security technology has been effectively applied to a variety of cloud computing applications, including the design and deployment of cloud network firewall, intrusion detection system. However, the traditional intrusion detection technology is mainly aimed at the physical network defense, and generally only to a single network or object detection and cloud computing environment is extremely complex and diverse, it has cross region, summarization, virtualization and other features, the use of traditional intrusion detection technology has been unable to meet the information security needs of cloud computing. Therefore, researchers have proposed many intrusion detection technologies which are suitable for cloud security, and have used the research results to show that there is an urgent need for the network intrusion detection method based on the characteristics of the characteristics of the detection system and the two advantages of abnormal behavior detection system.

On the basis of previous studies, this paper proposes a distributed anomaly traffic detection technology based on MapReduce, which is designed to be more efficient and fast response to the special nature of cloud computing environment, and proposes a distributed anomaly traffic detection technology based on classifier combination. Its function is to carry on the fast detection to the cloud platform network export flow, and locate the abnormal flow. The technology of network traffic data using flow statistical characteristics of the flow detection, and the use of historical data on the training of real flow classifier modeling, and then the new data acquisition and model matching analysis, based on a variety of classification algorithm combined detection method, determine the detection of data flow is normal, to achieve efficient and practical purposes.

3. Distributed Anomaly Traffic Detection Based on Classifier Combination

3.1. *Frame description*

Based on Mahout technology, distributed anomaly traffic detection technology, based on the fuzzy K- mean and Naive Bayesian classification algorithm, using the detection probe in the mass network data processing platform network exit location of traffic data to detect and analyze [5], can realize the large cloud computing platform of the network traffic near real-time anomaly detection.

Different from the traditional research of intrusion detection technology, this paper presents the abnormal flow detection and calculation, in order to flow records in the form of HDFS in the Mahout storage traffic characteristics, and based on the MapReduce technology in the framework of its rapid analysis and processing, to achieve the storage and efficient traffic record of abnormal traffic detection. The data flow detection method is more efficient than the data packet analysis, and does not involve user privacy. The anomaly traffic detection technique proposed in this paper is a complete solution for the practical cloud computing environment. At the same time, with the network hardware monitoring equipment, the system can be applied to the large data center of the anomaly traffic near real-time detection. Combined with the related technologies of cloud storage, the storage and re analysis of network traffic can be realized.

3.2. *Classification algorithm selection and Implementation*

Distributed anomaly traffic detection technology based on classifier, as a module of massive network data processing platform, is used to realize the detection of cloud platform network traffic and the determination of abnormal traffic. In the design of the algorithm, it is fully considered the practicability and high efficiency, and it has been run on the center server of the test network. The basic idea of the algorithm is to construct a training model based on historical data, to match the new measurement data and the model, and to determine whether the new measurement data is abnormal data by using the series. The model is constructed based on the historical data, and then the model is performed to determine the flow records. In this paper, fuzzy K- mean and Naive Bayesian classification algorithm to determine the flow of the method to determine the flow data, and based on Mahout Technology to achieve classification algorithms on the MapReduce framework of large data classification calculation.

Mahout is a run on Hadoop for machine learning and data analysis of distributed software framework. It uses MapReduce realizes a series of scalable data mining algorithms, including logistic regression algorithm, Bayesian classifier, hidden Markov model, K-means clustering algorithm and min hash clustering algorithm and singular value decomposition algorithm and so on. At the same time, mahout as the Apache foundation of open source projects, currently there are many researchers on the was expanded and improved, the support of the algorithm is also more and more, such as neural network, vector similarity, principal component analysis, and so on.

3.3. *Combined classifier decision algorithm*

The traffic characteristics of different network applications have a big difference, this paper based on the traffic statistical characteristic index to detect the traffic flow of massive network data processing platform, and based on the Mahout technology for rapid classification of traffic records, detect the abnormal traffic, improve the safety of massive network data processing platform. First, the traffic flow statistics feature index selection technique is used to find a set of the highest recognition degree in the above feature index, and then use the classifier to learn the training. In the selection of the statistical characteristics of the flow, if an index can reflect the attributes of the classification, the index is a valuable indicator. In the actual feature selection, the data characteristic index often has a lot of redundancy, even the value of the index. Therefore, this paper needs to choose the index which has a large correlation with the data classification, and the index of the selected feature is not related to each other.

Joint decision algorithm is used to calculate the current traffic statistical samples and historical data sample approach to analysis, the fuzzy K- mean and Naive Bayesian classification model, the specific includes two parts, the historical data of offline learning and the flow of data in line classification. At the same time, in order to verify the accuracy of the classification algorithm, we can use the sample flow data collected in the following experiments to analyze the data. The calculation is as follows: read the statistical information of a data stream, after data preprocessing, get the data flow characteristic index value, according to the flow rate and normal determine the classification number, and initialize the cluster center point, calculate the Euclidean distance and membership value of the cluster center points of each type of samples, repeat operation until the membership value of each sample data is stable, then determine whether the sample data is abnormal flow. Then use the training of Naive Bayesian classifier, to determine the abnormal. Finally, using the fuzzy K- mean algorithm and Naive Bayesian classifier algorithm, the data is finally abnormal decision. Fuzzy K- means algorithm is unsupervised classification algorithm, Naive Bayesian classifier is supervisee's classification algorithm, combined with supervised and unsupervised classification algorithm, and you can avoid the defects of a single algorithm, more comprehensive network traffic anomaly detection.

4. Conclusion

This paper proposes an anomaly traffic detection technology based on MapReduce technology, the data processing can be achieved by using distributed parallel computing mode, the efficiency of massive data flow detection, the technology introduces the feature selection technology, extracting valuable traffic classification data from traffic data, the technology based on classifier combination detection technology, fuzzy K- mean value algorithm is unsupervised classification algorithm, through the combination of supervised and unsupervised classification algorithm, can improve the security of massive network data processing platform.

However, cloud platform security involves systems, servers, networks, users and other aspects of the content, so the cloud platform for security work, in addition to the deployment of traditional security defense equipment, but also the need for a comprehensive consideration, and for different cloud platform application scenarios, build a perfect network security system, based on the need for further research and deepening of the main issues.

Acknowledgments

This work is supported by Project of National Natural Science Foundation of China(61501284), The 2015 Research on the development of soft science in the national economy and social information of Shandong Province(2015EI063), The 2015 Key project of statistical research of Shandong Province(KT15090), The 2015 experiment research project of Shandong Yingcai University(ycsy201512), The 2015 Research on the development of soft science in the national economy and social information of Shandong Province(2015EI060), The 2015 Business management research project of Shandong Province(J201547), The 2015 National Statistical Science Research Project(2015LY74).

References

1. Lin Wen-hui. Research on Key Technologies of Massive Network Data Processing Platform Based on Hadoop [D].Beijing: Beijing University of Posts and Telecommunications, 2014.4 (in Chinese).

2. AnnbrustM, Fox A, Griffith Ret al., A View of Cloud Computing, Commun Acm,53 □ 2010 50-58.

3. BhardwajS, Jain L, Jain S, Cloud Computing: A Study of Infrastructure as a Service (IAAS),International Journal of engineering and information Technology,2 (1)2010 60-63.

4. ZissisD, Lekkas Ds Addressing Cloud Computing Security Issues, Future Gener Comp Sy, 28 (3) 2012 583-592.

5. AgarwalD, Gonzdlez J M, Jin Get al., An Infrastructure for Passive Network Monitoring of Application Data Streams, 2003.

An Improved Real-time Dendritic Cell Algorithm for Intrusion Detection

Shu-yang WANG[†], Xiao-dong MU,Peng ZHAO and Dian ZHAO
Department of information engineering, Xi'an High-tech Institution,
Xi'an Shannxi, 710025, China
[†]*E-mail: 749547759@qq.com*

With the increasing need of computer network intrusion detection for efficient, lightweight and real-time analysis, a real-time dendritic cell algorithm for intrusion detection is proposed to solve non real-time problems of classical system. The antigens are randomly presented by dendritic cells in time series. Once all antigen cells have migrated, the antigens will be immediately assessed and the output will be generated, the characteristic of real-time analysis. The pseudo code of real-time analysis dendritic cell algorithm is also presented, and it is tested in the KDD CUP99 dataset. The results of the experiments demonstrate that the real-time DCA has high detection accuracy and excellent real time performance.

Keywords: Dendritic cell algorithm; Danger theory; Intrusion detection; Real-time analysis.

1. Introduction

In 2005, based on the danger theory, a Dendritic Cell algorithm (DCA) was proposed by Julie Greensmith according to the function and behavior of dendritic cells[1]. DCA is a promising algorithm with a number of advantages: it does not need a data training process and it is a lightweight intrusion detection algorithm. In addition, the DCA is able to perform temporal correlation in a monitoring system, where multiple data sources (signals and antigens) are fused according to some causal relationships [4].

The DCA has been successfully used in SYN port detection, botnet detection and so on, showing its excellent detection efficiency with high detection rate and low false positive rate. However, the traditional DCA is an off-line analysis algorithm for intrusion detection, which is difficult to achieve an instant response. Thus, in recent years, many research focus on proposing a real-time DCA for on-line intrusion detection. In the work of [2], Gu uses "segmentation" to divide the original piece of data into multiple pieces in order to achieve real-time or near real-time detection. Based on the traditional off-line

DCA, this paper designed a real-time DCA, which analyzes every antigen timely, and the algorithm is tested in the KDD CUP’99 data set.

2. The Dendritic Cell Algorithm

A dendritic cell is a type of antigen-presenting cell (APC), which can catch, process, and reveal antigens efficiently. In immunology, there are four main types of signals, namely pathogen associated molecular patterns (PAMPs), safe signals (SSs), danger signals (DSs) and inflammatory cytokines (CKs). As shown in Figure 1, DCs can divide into 3 different maturity levels in different immune signaling differentiate, “immature”, “semi-mature” and “mature”.

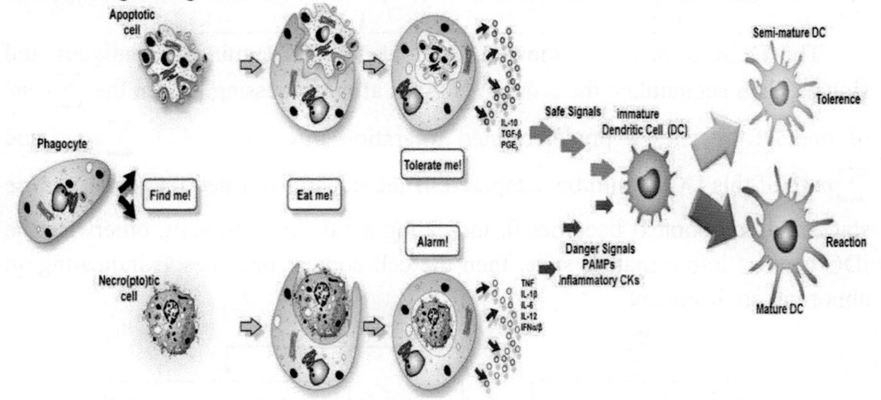

Fig.1.DC transformation

DCA simulates the process of immune system, that is, it can get antigens presenting through dendritic cells, perceive the danger level of environment and react to it. Firstly, immature DCs (iDCs) are produced to collect and sense the antigen signals around. While these signals are safe signals that promote the apoptosis of normal cells, the iDCs will transform to ‘semi-mature’, it indicates that the environment is normal. While the iDCs get dangerous signals of antigen or abnormal cell death, they transform to ‘mature’, and it indicates an anomalous environment.

The input data of DCA are antigens and signals from the environment (PAMPs, DSs, SSs, CKs). Each cell has the capacity to catch antigens, collect signals and fuse them to calculate the output signals (csm, semi, mat). Since the conversion process in the biological immune system is complex, the DCA simplify the processing according to biological experiments, using the weighted sum equation to express for signal integration process.

$$C_i = \frac{((W_{PAMP_i} * \sum PAMP) + ((W_{SS_i} * \sum SS) + (W_{DS_i} * \sum DS))}{W_{PAMP_i} + W_{SS_i} + W_{DS_i}} * \frac{1+I}{2}. \quad (1)$$

Where C_i represents the output signals, C_1, C_2 and C_3 represent the costimulatory molecule signal value (csm), the semi-mature signal value ($semi$) and the mature signal value (mat). I represents the inflammation signal. W_{PAMP_i}, W_{SS_i} and W_{DS_i} represent the weights used for PAMP, SS and DS, respectively. Common weights used for signal processing shown in table1.

Table 1 Weightsfor signal processing

W	*PAMP*	*DS*	*SS*
csm	2	1	2
semi	0	0	1
mat	2	1	-1.5

The DCA principle is showed in Figure 2. iDCacquire the antigens and signals, then accumulate the 3 output signals after processing. When the $\sum csm$ of one DC reaches a predetermined migration threshold (MT), $\sum semi$ and $\sum mat$ of this DC should be compared. If the iDCtransformed into semi-mature state, and cell context becomes 0, indicating a safe environment; otherwise the iDC convert into a mature state, then the cell context becomes 1, indicating an abnormal environment.

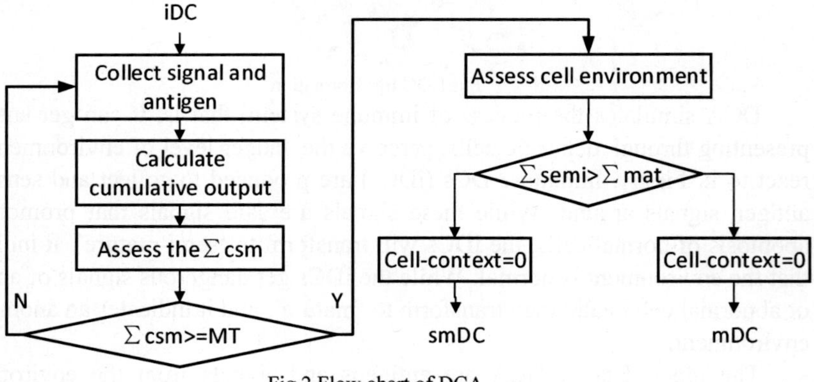

Fig.2.Flow chart of DCA.

After all these antigens are processed, the calculated value for the cell context is used to derive the nature of the response by measuring the number of DCs that are fully mature, is presented as mature context antigen value (MCAV). The closer the MCAV is to 1, the more likely that the environment is abnormal. Therefore a threshold value should be set, while MCAV is greater than this value, the environment should be judged as abnormal.

3. Real-time DCA Detecting Algorithm

DCA algorithm can be divided into 4 phases: pre-processing and initialization phase, detection phase, context assessment phase and classification phase. The main task of the pre-processing and the initialization phase is feature reduction and signal categorization, then extracting PAMP, DS, SS signals. Detection phase process the input signals with weight fusion, to obtain output signals, and then accumulate the output signals until it reaches the migration threshold. By comparing the $\sum semi$ and $\sum mat$, context assessment phase determine the iDC converted to smDC or mDC. Finally, the classification phase will calculate MACV, to determine whether there is an exception exists. It is obvious that DCA algorithm is offline, unable to analyze data in real time, it is difficult to meet the needs of online intrusion detection.

To solve this problem, in work of reference[2], Gu proposed a real-time DCA algorithm based on segmentation, when the number of antigen samples achieve a certain amount or the sampling time reaches a predetermined time, then the classification stage is entered beforehand to calculate the MCAV. It is equivalent to the original data is fragmented. Apparently, the smaller the fragmentation is, the batter real-time performance is possible, but the detection accuracy decreases; while the greater the fragmentation, the worse real-time performance, when fragment number is 1, the algorithm degenerates into original offline DCA algorithm.

This paper presents a real-time DCA algorithms, the basic idea is as follows: Create a pool of 100 DC, and randomly set a migration threshold within a certain range for each DC. When one data enters, the data number is the antigen number, the antigen were randomly presented to 10 DC cells. DC continuous acquire antigens, accumulate and update antigens signals, when there is a DC satisfy the migration conditions, the DC convert to smDC or mDC depending on the size of $\sum semi$ and $\sum mat$ .Then labeled all the antigens presented by this DC. Mark all antigens 0 while DC convert to smDC, indicating normal, or mark antigens 1 while mDC, indicating abnormal. Record the number an antigen is labeled and the times of label 1, when the former is equal to the number of being presented, output the MCAV immediately. If MCAV is greater than abnormal threshold value, the antigen is determined abnormal, otherwise normal. Details as algorithm 1.

```
Algorithm 1 real-time DCA algorithm
Input: antigens and signals (SS, PAMP and DS)
Output: mature context antigen value (MCAV)
Initialization;
Creat a DC pool including 100 DCs;
Foreach itemdo
Select 10 DC from DC poor;
      ForeachDCdo
        add prensent antigen to DC antigen sampling list;/* Preprocessing & Initialization phase */
        get signal from tiem;
        calculate signal value;/* Detection phase */
        calculatecsm,semi and mat, update csm,semi and mat;
        ifcsm>MT
           output the iDC from DC pool;
           create a new iDC intoDC pool;
        end if
     end for
   ifsmDC > mDC then /*Context Assessment phase */
        cell-context = 0;
   else
        cell-context = 1;
   end if
   foreach antigen of this DCdo /* Classification phase */
        antigen++;
        if cell-context == 1
              Ag-mature ++;
        end if
        if Ag-antigen==10
           MCAV = Ag-mature / Ag-antigen ;
        end if
  end for
End For
```

4. Experimental Results and Analysis

This paper selects a 10% subset of KDD CUP99, which is applied to intrusion detection authoritative and standard data sets, for the test, and each piece of data is an antigen. Signal selection is the same with the reference [3], select 10 items feature from 41 dimension attributes of the data set as 3 kind signals of DCA algorithm: PAMP signals: serror rate, srvserror rate, same srv rate, dst host serror, dsthost rerror rate; DS signals: count and srv count; SS signals: logged in, srv different host rate and ds host count

Convert all signals to interval [0,100] according to linear function normalized method, then select the average value of each kind of signals under a normal network as a reference value, and the size of each data signal is related to its distance from the reference value.

Set DC pool size 100 in the test, and migration threshold is a random number from 100 to 200.Select different types of attack form the data set to do the following test: Test 1: Select 500 normal data and 500 smurf attack data. Therefore the test experiences a conversion form normal to abnormal and experiences a wave of attacks; Test 2: Select 300 normal data + 400 smurf data + 300 normal data. Therefore the test experiences 2 environmental conversions; Test 3: Select 250 normal data + 250 smurf data + 250 normal data + 250 nepture data, therefore the test experiences 3 environmental conversions. The results are shown in Fig 3 and Table 2.

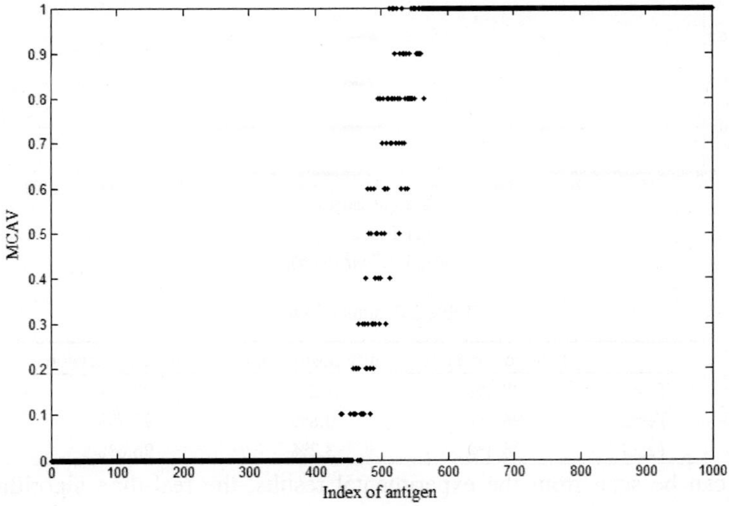

(a) Test1

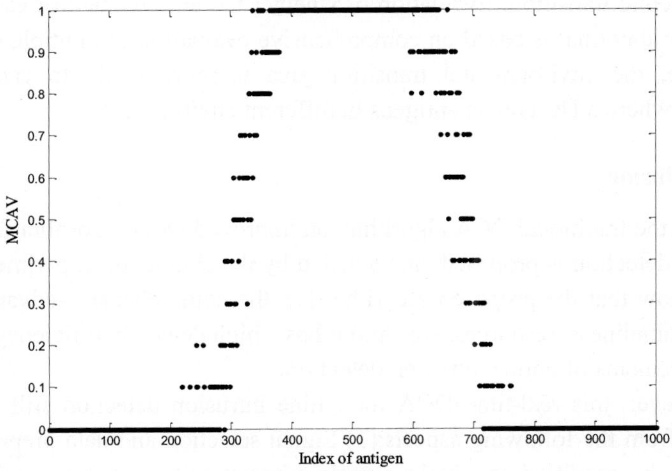

(b) Test 2

Fig.3. Result of Test .

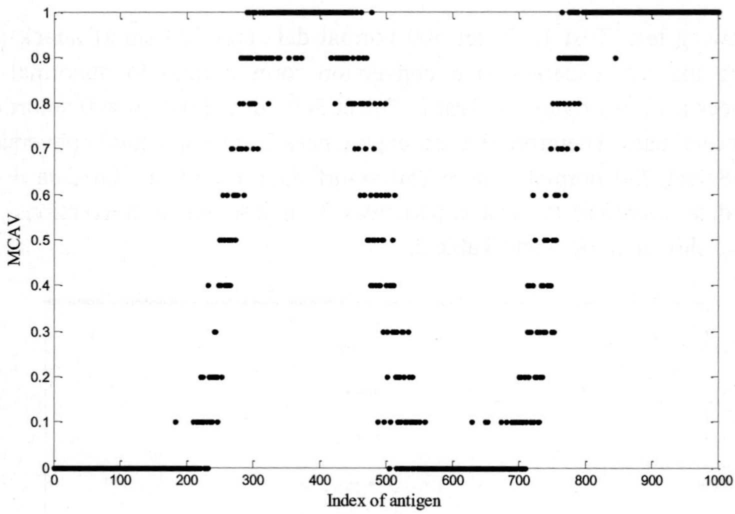

(c) Test 3

Fig.3. (*Continued*).

Table 2 Results of 3 tests

	True positive rate	False positive rate	Detecion precision
Test1	99.2%	1.2%	99.0%
Test2	96.7%	0.8%	97.7%
Test3	96.4%	3.2%	96.6%

It can be seen from the experimental results, the real-time algorithm has high detection rate and low false alarm rate, and the detect errors mainly in the environmental transition. Evaluation of whether the environment of each DC is normal or abnormal is based on comprehensive evaluation of multiple antigens. Therefore, the environmental transition area is more likely to cause false positives where a DC collect antigens in different environments.

5. Conclusion

Based on the traditional DCA algorithm, an improved DCA algorithm for online intrusion detection is proposed, and verified by the simulation experiments. The results show that the proposed algorithm has the comprehensive advantages in terms of timeliness, resources, etc. And it has a high detection efficiency to meet the requirements of online intrusion detection.

However, this real-time DCA for online intrusion detection still needs to improve from the following aspects:(1) Signal selection and data preprocessing stage can be modified to obtain signals automatically and more suitable.(2) Dividing normal and abnormal method is too simple. The threshold setting can be combined with fuzzy theory and other methods to improve the effect.(3) The detection precision is not good in conversion zone. It can speed up or slow down the speed of output DCs, reducing the impact of the following antigens to the current antigen.

References

1. Greensmith J, Aickelin U andCayzer S. Introducing dendritic cells as a novel immune-inspired algorithm for anomaly detection,In:*Proc. of the 4th International Conference on Artificial Immune Systems*(Banff, Canada,2005)
2. Gu FandAickelin U. Integrating real-time analysis with the dendritic cell algorithm through segmentation.In: *Proc. of the 11th Annual Conference on Genetic and Evolutionary Computation*(Montreal, Canada, 2009).
3. Gu F, Greensmith J andAickelin U. *Further exploration of the dendritic cell algorithm: antigen multiplier and moving windows*, ICAIS, Phuket, Thailand: Springer,(2008).
4. Chelly Z andElouedi Z. *A survey of the dendritic cell algorithm*. Knowledge and Information Systems, (2015).

N out of *N* Extended Color Visual Cryptography Scheme

Bin YU, Xian-huan ZHANG* and Zheng-xin FU

Zhengzhou Institute of Technology, Zhengzhou, 450001, China
*E-mail: *zhangxianhuan1989@163.com*

This paper firstly provides a formal definition of the n out of n extended color visual cryptography scheme (ECVCS) based on the XOR cipher, where a color secret image and k color cover images are encoded into n shares in such a way that the n shares present cover images individually and any n shares and above will recover the secret image while any less than n shares, will not reveal any information about the secret image. The proposed scheme in the paper has no extra expansion and it can easily trade the visual quality of the recovery image with the visual quality of shares by changing the value of a certain parameter in the scheme. The validity of the proposed scheme is verified by formal proofs, and its feasibility is demonstrated by computer simulations.

Keywords: Color visual cryptography; CVCS; ECVCS; Pixel expansion; Secret sharing.

1. Introduction

A *k* out of *n* visual cryptography scheme ((*k*, *n*)-VCS), first formally defined by Naor and Shamir [1], is a special kind of secret sharing, which encodes a secret image into *n* shares in such a way that the stacking of any *k* shares can recover the secret image, while any less than *k* shares provide no information about the secret image. Verheul et al. [2] first proposed color visual cryptography scheme (CVCS) which can encode color images. Color image presenting color closing to the real nature, includes more information and is more beautiful compared with binary image. For the widespread of digital camera, computer, mobile phone and so on, the collection and transmission of color image reaches to unprecedented depth and breadth. So the requirement for protecting color image is more urgent.

The scheme proposed by Verheul *et al.* is called Same Color (SC) model. The SC model does not allow the superposition of pixels with different colors, with the exception of the identity ($\circ$) and the annihilator ($\bullet$) colors. Hence, the shares have to be constructed in such a way that each column in the distribution matrices have elements taken from the set $\{i,\circ,\bullet\}$, for some color i . Thus, when we superpose several transparencies, we never have a pixel of color i superposed with a pixel of color j. Blundo et al. [3] mainly research the maximum contrast issue of SC model and redefine contrast $\alpha = (h-l)/(h+l)$ by analyzing weak contrast condition. Koga et al. [4] and Yang et al. [5] improved the pixel expansion in the scheme of [2] and [3]. In the General model [6], there are no restrictions about the superposition of pixels and the superposition operation satisfied the real properties of color superposition. In [7] Hou proposed a method that first splits the secret image into the cyan, magenta, and yellow components and then uses ad-hoc (2, 2)-threshold schemes to share those components. Chen et al. [8] based on $(k,k)-VCS$ by random grids (RG) proposed $(k,n)-CVCS$ by RG through adding extra $n-k$ bits in the process of encoding a color image. Wang et al. [9] based on XOR proposed a full-recovery $(n,n)-CVCS$ without pixel expansion.

Despite many wonderful results on CVCS, each share image generated by CVCS is noise-like and may cause suspicion. Moreover, if some party takes part in several CVCSs, and have several noise-like share images, it will be inconvenient for him to manage those shares. The extended color visual cryptography scheme (ECVCS) does not have the above-mentioned short-comings. In an ECVCS, each share has some content in it. Moreover, different shares generated by the same ECVCS can have different contents. In recent years, many studies (referring to[10-12]) have been dedicated to implement ECVCS. Kamath et al. [10] proposed an ECVCS making using of Jarvis error filter, a key table and specialized tables for coding. Christy et al. [11] proposed a method that uses Back Propagation Network (BPN) for extended color visual cryptography. BPN is used to produce the two shares. The size of the image produced is same as that of the original image. Guo et al. [12] proposed a (k,k) RG-based ECVCS that needs neither extra pixel expansion nor any basis matrices, which are inevitable in conventional solutions of EVCS. In addition, the proposed scheme can easily trade visual quality of the recovery image with the visual quality of shares by setting a certain parameter in the scheme from small to large. In order to improve the visual quality of the recovery image, the paper proposes a $(n,n)-ECVCS$ without pixel expansion.

This paper is organized as follows. In section 2, we give the formal definition of ECVCS. In section 3, we propose a $(n,n)-ECVCS$ based on probability. In section 4, we formally prove the correctness of the proposed scheme. In section 5, we give some experimental results to demonstrate the feasibility of the proposed scheme. The paper is concluded in section 6.

2. Basic Notions

In order to describe easily, the symbols and their meanings used in the paper are shown in Table 1 and the paper considers only the most commonly used 24-bit RGB model.

Table 1. The symbols and their meanings

Symbols	Meanings	Symbols	Meanings
$\varphi=\{1,2,\cdots,n\}$	Participant set	$\oplus$	XOR
SI	Color secret image	m	Pixel expansion
$SI(i,j)$	The color of pixel in *SI* with coordinate $[i,j]$	$S_1,S_2,\cdots,S_n$	*n* shares
$S_t(i,j)$	The color of pixel in S_t with coordinate $[i,j]$	$P(A)$	Event A occurrence probability
P_c	The probability that equals to c, $c\in C$	RI	Recovery image
ρ,ρ'	Probability constant, $0<\rho,\rho'<1$	B	Share matrix
$RI(i,j)$	The color of pixel in *RI* with coordinate $[i,j]$	$\bullet$	Black color
$XOR(M)$	The result XOR all columns in M		

Definition 1 A set $C=(c_1,c_2,\cdots,c_{2^{24}})$ includes all colors in 24-bit RGB model.

Definition 2XOR color pixels refers to bitwise XOR the colors of each pixel. The formula is as follows:

$$c_u \oplus c_v = a_0a_1\cdots a_{24} \oplus b_0b_1\cdots b_{24} = (a_0\oplus b_0)(a_1\oplus b_1)\cdots(a_{24}\oplus b_{24}) = z_0z_1\cdots z_{24} = c_w$$

Where $c_u,c_v,c_w \in C, a_0,\cdots,a_{24},b_0,\cdots,b_{24},z_0,\cdots,z_{24}$ belongs to $\{0,1\}$.

Definition 3 XOR shares refer to XOR the colors of each pixel with same coordinates in the shares one by one.

$$S_u \oplus S_v = S_u(i,j) \oplus S_v(i,j)$$

In the process of encoding a color pixel $SI(i,j)$ in the color image, $\overline{SI(i,j)}$ constitutes the non-secret pixel color set $\overline{C}$ ($\overline{C} \subseteq C$), thus $\overline{SI(i,j)} \neq SI(i,j)$, $P_{\overline{SI(i,j)}} > 0$, $\{SI(i,j)\} \cap \overline{C} = \varnothing$.

Definition 4 In the n out of n extended color visual cryptography scheme, when encoding a color $SI(i,j)$ in the secret image, there exists a matrix B with size $n \times 1$, which decides the color of pixel in n shares with same coordinates. Satisfy the following four conditions.

(1) XOR n colors in B equals to r which satisfies $P_{SI(i,j)} = P(r = SI(i,j)) > P_{\overline{SI(i,j)}} = P(r = \overline{SI(i,j)})$;

(2) For any subset $\{i_1, i_2, \cdots, i_v\} \subseteq \{1, 2, \cdots, n\}$ ($v < k$), XOR v colors in B equals to r which satisfies $P_c = P(r = c) = \rho$ ($\forall c \in C$);

(3) $\forall c \in C$ and $c \neq Cov_t(i,j)$, satisfy $P(B(t,1) = Cov_t(i,j)) > P(B(t,1) = c)$ ($t = 1, 2, \cdots, n$);

(4) XOR n colors in B equals to r, $\forall \overline{SI(i,j)} \in \overline{C}$ ($\overline{C} \cup SI(i,j) = C$), which satisfies $P_{\overline{SI(i,j)}} = P(r = \overline{SI(i,j)}) = \rho'$.

Condition 1 is weak contrast condition, which presents recovery probability of secret color is larger than non-secret color in recovery image. The larger $P_{SI(i,j)}$ is, the better visual quality the recovery image has.

Condition 2 is security condition, which present one can't obtain any information about secret image from any less than n shares. For participate subset $\{i_1, i_2, \cdots, i_v\}$, XOR v colors in B equals to r. All values of r can be any color in set C with same probability, constructing a noise-like image.

Condition 3 can guarantee that the share appear the information in the cover image. Similar to weak contrast condition, the appearing probability of a color in the cover image is larger than any other color for any line in matrix B.

Condition 4 is crosstalk preventing condition which guarantees that in the recovery image non-secret color will not appear in a special image. All non-secret color appearing in recovery image with same probability constructs a noise-like image which will not affect the recovery of secret information.

3. The Proposed (*n*, *n*)-ECVCS

This section gives the secret sharing algorithm of $(n,n)-ECVCS$. The algorithm encodes a color secret image S and n cover images $Cov_1, Cov_2, \cdots, Cov_n$ into n meaningful shares. Through setting the value of β, we can easily trade the visual quality of the recovery image with shares.

3.1. *The secret sharing algorithm*

Input: A color secret image S and n cover images $Cov_1, Cov_2, \cdots, Cov_n$ with size of $a \times b$

Output: n shares $S_1, S_2, \cdots, S_n$ with size of $a \times b$

Step 1. Let $i = 1$, presenting row counter;

Step 2. Let $j = 1$, presenting column counter;

Step 3. Random generate a bit *b*, which is 0 with probability β and 1 with probability $1-\beta$;

Step 4. If *b* is equal to 0, skip to step 5 else to step 7;

Step 5. Random generate $n-1$ colors $c_1, c_2, \cdots, c_{n-1}$ and compute $c_n = S(i,j) \oplus c_1 \oplus c_2 \oplus \cdots \oplus c_{n-1}$;

Step 6. The result of random permuting $c_1, c_2, \cdots, c_n$ is $d_1, d_2, \cdots, d_n$. Let $E = [d_1\ d_2\ \cdots\ d_n]^T$, Skip to step 10;

Step 7. Let $d_1 = Cov_1(i,j), d_2 = Cov_2(i,j), \cdots, d_n = Cov_n(i,j)$;

Step 8. Random generate a color c_{n+1} and integer $e\,(1 \le e \le n)$;

Step 9. Let $d_e = c_{n+1}$, so matrix $Q = [d_1\ d_2\ \cdots\ d_n]^T$;

Step 10. Let matrix B equal to matrix E or Q. Assign the element of B to shares $S_1, S_2, \cdots, S_n$ at the location $[i, j]$;

Step 11. Let $j = j+1$. If $j \le b$, return to step 3 else to step 12;

Step 12. Let $i = i+1$. If $i \le a$, return to step 2 else end the flow.

3.2. *The secret recovery algorithm*

XOR n shares can recover the secret image.

$$RI = S_1 \oplus S_2 \oplus \cdots \oplus S_n$$

4. Validity Analysis

In the section we analyze the validity of the scheme in the paper and prove that the scheme can recover the secret information and satisfies the security condition. Shares can present the information in cover images and non-secret color in recovery image won't have crosstalk with secret color.

Lemma 1. If $c_1, c_2, \cdots, c_t$ is t deterministic colors ($t \ge 0$) and c is a random color, the result of $c_1 \oplus c_2 \oplus \cdots \oplus c_t \oplus c$ ($c_1, c_2, \cdots, c_t, c \in C$) is a deterministic color.

Proof. Let $c' = c_1 \oplus c_2 \oplus \cdots \oplus c_t$, so c' is a deterministic color. The result of $c' \oplus c$ a deterministic color XOR a random color is random.

Theorem 1. The secret information can be recovered by XOR n shares.

Proof. From the secret sharing algorithm, in the process of encoding $S(i, j)$, the probability of matrix B equal to matrix E is β and equal to matrix Q is $1-\beta$. $XOR(B) = S(i, j)$ is the result of XOR all the columns of matrix E. $XOR(Q) = Cov_1(i, j) \oplus Cov_2(i, j) \oplus \cdots \oplus Cov_n(i, j) \oplus Cov_e(i, j) \oplus c_{n+1}$ is the result of XOR all the columns of matrix Q (due to $Cov_e(i, j) \oplus Cov_e(i, j) = \bullet$ and $Cov_e(i, j) \oplus \bullet = Cov_e(i, j)$, the reason why XOR $Cov_e(i, j)$ is to annihilate $Cov_e(i, j)$ in $Cov_1(i, j) \oplus Cov_2(i, j) \oplus \cdots \oplus Cov_n(i, j)$). From lemma 1, the result of $XOR(Q)$ is random. Thus the recovery probability of secret color is

$P_{S(i,j)} = \beta + (1-\beta)/2^{24}$. $\forall \overline{SI(i,j)} \in \overline{C}$ $(\overline{C} \cup SI(i,j) = C(\overline{C} \cup SI(i,j) = C))$, the recovery probability of non-secret color is $P_{\overline{S(i,j)}} = (1-\beta)/2^{24}$.

In summary, the result is $P_{SI(i,j)} > P_{\overline{SI(i,j)}}$ which guarantees that the secret information can be recovered.

Theorem 2. Secret information can't be obtained by XOR any less than *n* shares.

Proof. For the subset $\{i_1, i_2, \cdots, i_v\} \subseteq \{1, 2, \cdots, n\}$ $(1 \le v < k)$, the element in matrix Q is only concern with *n* cover images $Cov_1, Cov_2, \cdots, Cov_n$, from which the secret information can't be obtained. $c_{i_1}, c_{i_2}, \cdots, c_{i_v}$ is taken from matrix *E* randomly and let $r = c_{i_1} \oplus c_{i_2} \oplus \cdots \oplus c_{i_v}$.

(1) If $c_n \notin \{c_{i_1}, c_{i_2}, \cdots, c_{i_v}\}$, for the reason $c_{i_1}, c_{i_2}, \cdots, c_{i_v}$ is generated from step 5 in secret sharing algorithm, *r* is random.

(2) If $c_n \in \{c_{i_1}, c_{i_2}, \cdots, c_{i_v}\}$, suppose $c_{i_v} = c_n$.

$$\begin{aligned} r &= c_{i_1} \oplus c_{i_2} \oplus \cdots \oplus c_{i_{v-1}} \oplus S(i,j) \oplus c_1 \oplus c_2 \oplus \cdots \oplus c_{n-1} \\ &= S(i,j) \oplus c_{j_1} \oplus c_{j_2} \oplus \cdots \oplus c_{j_u} \end{aligned}$$

Where $c_{j_1}, c_{j_2}, \cdots, c_{j_u}$ is the result of annihilating $c_{i_1}, c_{i_2}, \cdots, c_{i_{v-1}}$ from $c_1, c_2, \cdots, c_{n-1}$. Thus $c_{j_1}, c_{j_2}, \cdots, c_{j_u}$ is generated randomly by step 5 in sharing algorithm, *r* is random.

In summary, $\forall c \in C$, if $b = 0$, $P_c = P(r = c) = 1/2^{24}\beta$, which satisfies the security condition in definition 4. The secret information can't be obtained from any less than n shares.

Theorem 3. The share can present information in the cover image.

Proof. Matrix Q contains information in the cover image, the probability of which is $P(Q(t,1) = Cov_t(i,j)) = (1-\beta)(n-1)/n$ ($P(Q(t,1) = Cov_t(i,j)) = (1-\beta)(n-1)/n$) and $P(Q(t,1) = c_{n+1}) = (1-\beta)/n$. The colors in matrix *E* are all random. $\forall c \in C$ and $c \neq Cov_t(i,j)$, $P(B(t,1) = Cov_t(i,j)) = (1-\beta)(n-1)/n + (1-\beta)/2^{24}n + \beta/2^{24}$,

$P(B(t,1)=c)=(1-\beta)/2^{24}n+\beta/2^{24}$. So $P(B(t,1)=Cov_t(i,j))>P(B(t,1)=c)$ which satisfies the condition 3 in definition 4.

Theorem 4. The image constructed by the non-secret color $\overline{SI(i,j)}$ won't have crosstalk with the secret information in the recovery image which is obtained by XOR n shares.

Proof. From theorem 1, $\forall \overline{SI(i,j)} \in \overline{C}$ ($\overline{C} \cup SI(i,j) = C$), the probability of non-secret color is $P_{\overline{S(i,j)}} = (1-\beta)/2^{24}$. Thus from the condition 4 in definition 4, the recovery of secret information won't be affected.

5. Experimental Results and Analysis.

In order to verify the validity of the secret sharing algorithm, in this section a $(3,3)-ECVCS$ is implemented and we analyze the experimental results.

Fig. 1. The experimental result of $(3,3)-ECVCS$ where $\beta = 0.5$

$RI_1 = S_1 \oplus S_2$ $RI_2 = S_1 \oplus S_3$ $RI_3 = S_2 \oplus S_3$

Fig. 1. (*Continued*)

As is shown in the Fig.1 SI is the secret image lena. Cov_1, Cov_2, Cov_3 are the cover images baboon, airplane, peppers. S_1, S_2, S_3 are shares. RI_1, RI_2, RI_3 are the results of $S_1 \oplus S_2$, $S_1 \oplus S_3$, $S_2 \oplus S_3$. RI is result of $S_1 \oplus S_2 \oplus S_3$. From the figure we know that each share can present the information in the cover image and XOR three shares can recover the secret information. Due to $Q = [Cov_1(i,j)\ Cov_2(i,j)\ Cov_3(i,j)]^T$, in which $d_e = c_4$, XOR any two colors in Q there exists the cases of $Cov_1(i,j) \oplus Cov_2(i,j)$, $Cov_1(i,j) \oplus Cov_3(i,j)$, $Cov_2(i,j) \oplus Cov_3(i,j)$. Thus, XOR any two shares can present the information in the image superimposed by two cover images which won't appear secret information.

6. Conclusions

The paper proposes an $(n,n)-ECVCS$, in which each share have meaningful content. In addition, the proposed scheme can easily trade the visual quality of the recovery image with the visual quality of share images by setting parameter β. Due to sharing the color image straightly without halftone processing, the share and recovery image have better visual quality.

References

1. Naor M, Shamir A. Visual cryptography[C]. Lecture Notes in Computer Science, 1995, 950(1):1-12.

2. E. Verheul and H.V. Tilborg. Constructions and Properties of k out of n Visual Secret Sharing Schemes[J]. Designs Codes and Cryptography, 1997, 11(2): 179-196.

3. C. Blundo, A. De Bonis, and A. De Santis. Improved schemes for visual cryptography. Designs, Codes and Cryptography, 24:255-278, 2001.

4. H. Koga and H. Yamamoto. Proposal of a lattice-based visual secret sharing scheme for color and gray-scale images. IEICE Trans. on Fundamentals of Electronics, Communication and Computer Sciences, 81-A(6):1262-1269, 1998.

5. C.N. Yang and C.A. Laih. New colored visual secret sharing schemes Designs. Codes and Cryptography, 20:325-335, 2000.

6. A. Adhikari and S. Sikdar. A new (2,n)-visual threshold scheme for color images. In Proceedings of the Indocrypt 2003, 2904:148-161. Springer Verlag, LNCS, 2005.

7. Hou Y. Visual cryptography for color images[J]. Pattern Recognit, 2003, 36(7):1619-1629.

8. Chen T, Tsao K. Threshold visual secret sharing by random grids[J]. Journal of System & Software, 2011, 84(7):1197-1208.

9. Daoshun W A, Lei Z A, Ning M A, et al. Two secret sharing schemes based on Boolean operations[J]. Pattern Recognition, 2006, 40(10):2776–2785.

10. Kamath M, Pareb A, Salyankar A, et al. Extended visaul cryptography for color images using coding tables[C]. Communication, Information & Computing Technology (ICCICT), 2012 International Conference on. IEEE, 2012:1-6.

11. Christy J I, Seenivasagam V. Construction of color Extended Visual Cryptographic scheme using Back Propagation Network for color images[C]. Computing, Electronics and Electrical Technologies (ICCEET), 2012 International Conference on. IEEE, 2012:1101-1108.

12. Guo T, Liu F, Wu C K. k out of k extended visual cryptography scheme by random grids[J]. Signal Processing, 2014, 94(1):90-101.

Research on Automatic Identification Technology of the Car Key Tooth Code Based on the Spectral Clustering Method

Chun-xian WANG [1,a], Shang-wen DING [2,b] and Fan ZHANG [1,c]

[1]*School of Mechanical Engineering, Xuancheng Campus, Hefei University of Technology, China, 242000*

[2]*Department of Basic Courses, Xuancheng Campus, Hefei University of Technology, China, 242000*

[a]*cxwang2004@126.com*, [b]*dshou1@126.com*, [c]*879179437@qq.com*

This paper proposes a car key tooth code automatic identification method based on the spectral clustering method to tackle the problem of the current low efficiency and high costs of artificial and mechanical identification methods of the car key tooth code. By using the general auto key fixture, the tooth height of different keys is transformed into to an easily identifiable single detection chip height, which is associated with the contour of the car key image. The car key tooth code is obtained by calculating the vertical coordinate of the extreme points of the contour line in the car key image, which are processed in accordance with the following method. Firstly, the key tooth edge is obtained with the spectral clustering classification method and the extreme points at the edge of the tooth are determined with the minimum and maximum method. Secondly, the relative heights of the extreme points to the key's horizontal edge are determined and the corresponding key tooth code is obtained. Lastly the effectiveness of the method proposed in this paper is verified by a car key image.

Keywords: Car key code; Image segmentation; Spectral clustering; Maximum value.

1. Introduction

Identification of the car key tooth code is the important one of steps of assembly about car key lock, which directly affects the efficiency of steps in the process of assembly about the car lock. So it is of great importance for quick and accurate identification on the car key tooth code [1]. At present, the domestic car key identification methods mainly include artificial identification and mechanical automatic identification, etc. the artificial identification is not only with low identification accuracy and production efficiency, but also high labor intensity. Mechanical identification technology overcomes the shortcomings in this area. Currently it is most widely used due to high production efficiency. However, it has high standards for occasional error codes and single key identification types due to the mechanical manipulation in the identification process, which causes to mechanical loss. With the increase types of car keys and the number of car keys, these above methods have seriously affected the efficiency of car lock assembly [2].

In recent years, with the rapid development of image identification technology, the image identification technology is likely to be used for the identification of key tooth code. In the field of image processing, the research and application of spectral clustering for image segmentation algorithm arouses widespread concern [3-5]. The spectral clustering algorithm based on the sample data is mainly implemented by defining the similarity matrix between data points, then calculating the eigenvectors and corresponding eigenvalues of similarity matrix, finally, obtaining different data points by clustering eigenvectors. The spectral clustering algorithm has the following advantages, such as it is simple and difficult to fall into local optimal solution and it also has the ability to identify the non-convex distribution clustering. So the spectral clustering method for image segmentation can cluster different shapes of key images and effectively segment special shapes of key tooth from the image background. Aiming at the automatic identification technology of the car key tooth code, this paper presents automatic identification method about the cay key code based on the spectral clustering method. Firstly, the car key edges are obtained by using the spectral clustering method for image segmentation and then the extreme values of the edge curve in the car key image is determined, finally, the car key codes are obtained by calculating these extreme values.

2. Composition and Working Principle Of Identification System

Identification system about the car key code are consisted of the universal key fixture, lighting, industrial CCD camera, image acquisition card and computer so on based on digital image processing technology. Its working principle has the following contents. First, different types of car key tooth heights are transformed into single and easily identifiable detection sheet height by the general car key fixture, and then a CCD camera and image acquisition card is used to input image information into the computer for digital image processing the contour of the detection sheet is obtained by image segment technology. Finally the appropriate image processing program is developed to obtain the key tooth code by image processing program calculating the size of the detection sheet contour.

2.1. *Design of the key fixture*

In the visual inspection system, one of steps about the car key code identification is to convert key information into height information of detection sheet, which showed it was very crucial to design a universal key identification fixture. The developed universal key detection schematic diagram is showed in Fig.1. Firstly, the detection sheet is used to imitate the blade, and jack up the detection sheet when the key is inserted into the key hole of the fixture, secondly, the jacking height of the detection sheet is indirectly measured by using the adjusting screw to jack up the detection sheet on the supporting plate when the key is inserted into the key hole to adapt to different car keys. The detection sheet is not jacked up if it blocked the key hole when mistakenly inserting into other key holes. The key is compressed by the detection sheet.

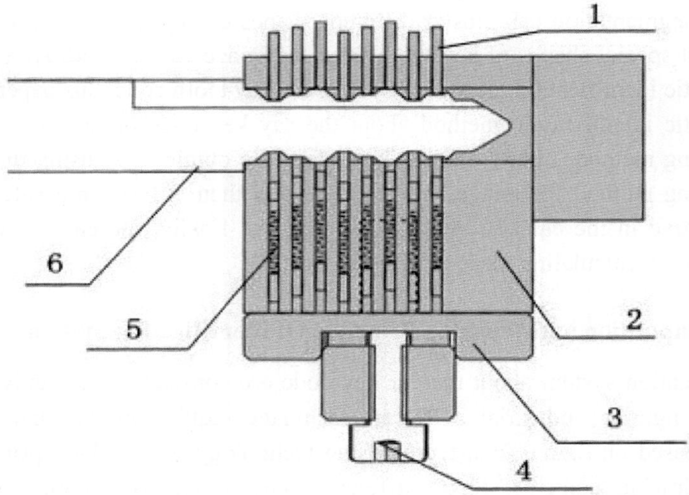

1. Key detection sheet; 2. Key fixture seat; 3. Detection sheet supporting plate; 4. Adjustment screw; 5. Spring; 6. Key to be detected

Fig.1 Schematic diagram of universal key detection fixture

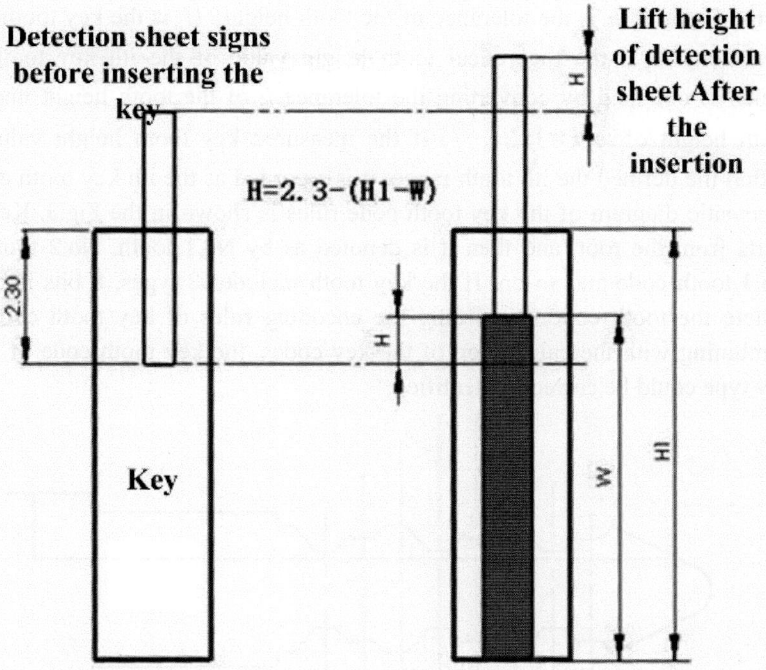

Fig.2 Schematic diagram of detection sheet signs

A calculation relation diagram between the key tooth height and detection sheet height are shown in the Fig.2. As shown in the Fig.2, the height information of the detection sheet could be found by the elevated height of the detection sheet after the key is inserted.

2.2. *Encoding rules of key code*

In the developed prototype system, the height of the detection sheet is adjusted through the screw on the fixture when measuring various car keys. The height of the detection sheet is measured as the key code precise standard by the system by inserting the real key, and the really key tooth height is convert into an image reference value after appropriate conversion, which obtained by the CCD camera. The really key tooth height value is called as the tooth height offset. After obtaining the tooth height offset, the tooth height measured at any position is [1, 2]:

$$H_i = H_0 + h_i. \tag{1}$$

In the formula, h_i is the tolerance of the tooth height; H_0 is the key tooth height deviation; H_i is the theoretical tooth height value of the ith key tooth code which is obtained by converting the tolerance h_i of the tooth height under the tooth height offset $i = 1, 2, 3, \cdots$. If the measured key tooth height value falls within the defined the ith tooth range, it is recorded as the ith key tooth code. A schematic diagram of the key tooth code rules is shown in the Fig.3. Key code starts from the root, and then it is denoted as by No.1 tooth, No.2 tooth, and No.3 tooth code and so on. If the key tooth includes 8 types, 8 bits is used to denote the tooth code. According the encoding rules of key tooth codes and combining with the calculation of the key codes, the key tooth code of certain key type could be correctly identified.

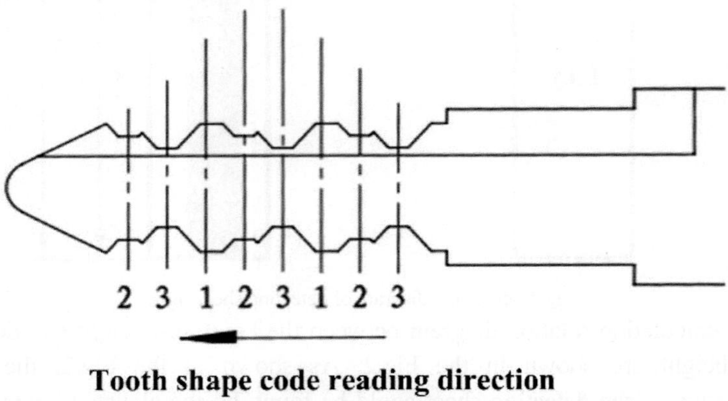

Fig.3: Schematic diagram of the key tooth code number

In the prototype system, the actual height of the detection sheet is compared with the theoretical tooth height value H_i in the standard limited range of each key tooth code so as to determine the key tooth code about the car key image, which is calculated according to Formula (1). The prototype system about the key tooth is automatically detected and identified by the image identification technology.

3. Identification of Key Tooth Codes

The detection sheet of the original image is obtained by the industrial CCD camera, which is converted into the digital image by the image acquisition card and then transfer to the image processing module of the system. Firstly, the original image is pre-processed and noise eliminated, and then the image is segmented, and finally the height information of the key detection sheet is obtained through the image processing algorithm and finally the corresponding tooth code is determined. The basic principle of image segmentation algorithm based on the spectral clustering method is to regard image pixel points as a weighted graph $G(V,E)$. Malik et al. [6] obtained the approximate solution using the above formula by solving the second smallest eigenvalue of the Laplace matrix according to the spectral graph theory. Fowlkes et al. [7] adopted the Nyström extension technology to construct an approximate Laplace matrix by making use of some sampling points of the data set. This method is able to effectively reduce the computational complexity, which method achieves good effect in practice. This paper will adopt the spectral clustering theory and make use of Nyström extension technology to segment key images. Firstly, the edge about the car key tooth image is segmented by using the spectral clustering classification method, and then the extreme points at the tooth edge about car key image are determined by utilizing the extreme value method [8], and then the relative heights between the key horizontal edge and the extreme point are obtained, and finally the corresponding number of the key tooth codes are obtained.

4. Identification Verification of the Key Tooth Codes

To describe the key tooth code identification process in this paper, the car key image is taken as an example. The car key image is shown in Fig.4 (a). Firstly, using the spectral clustering method to divide key images into the background class, the key class and the tooth code class. Secondly, just as segmentation results shown in Fig.4 (b), the tooth code class about the key image clustering result is used to extract the tooth code boundary, And then just as the specific tooth code boundary shape is shown in Fig.4 (c), the unbroken edges are obtained by utilizing the upper and lower symmetry of key tooth edge about the key image to connect the fractured edges, which result is specifically shown in Fig.4. Finally, it is found in the Fig.5,the vertical height of the tooth codes about a car key image is finally obtained by finding local extreme point of edges about the key image.

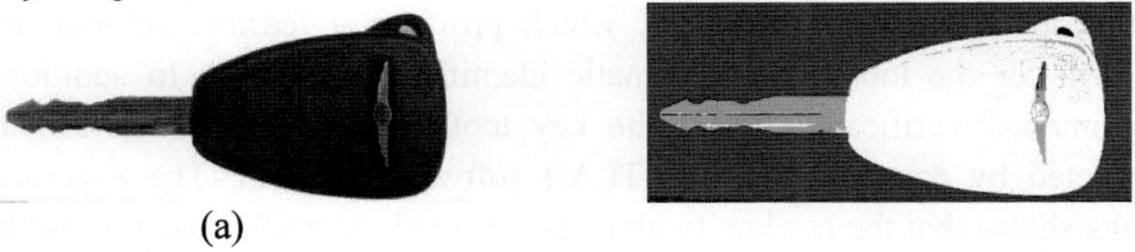

(a) (b)

Fig.4 Segmentation results of spectral clustering image: (a) original car key image (b) spectral clustering segmentation result (c) extracting the tooth code edge (d) supplementing the fractured edge of the image

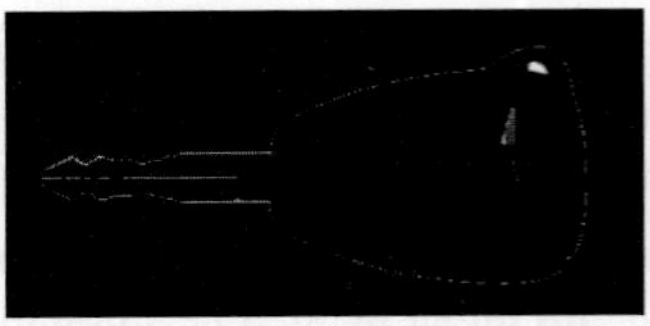

(c)

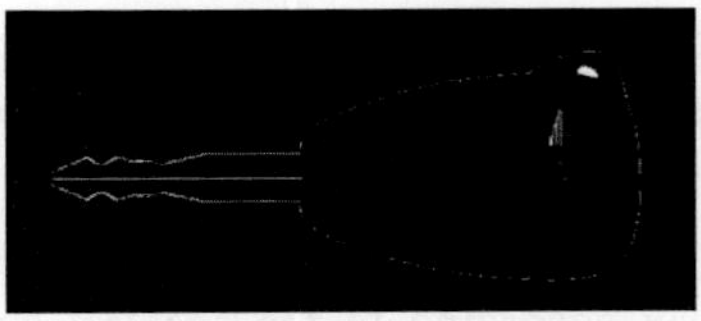

(d)

Fig.4 (*Continued*)

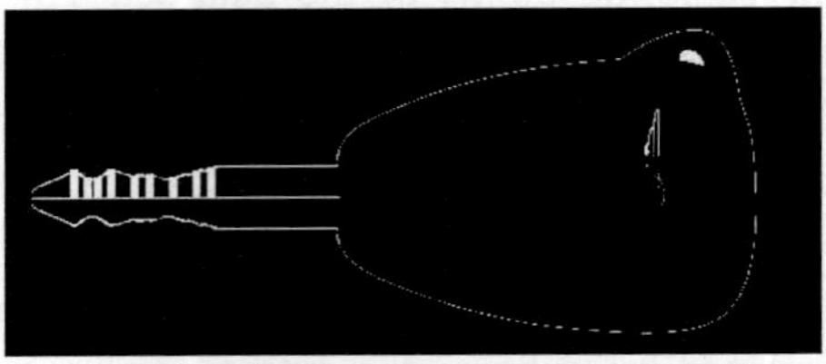

Fig.5 Identification of key tooth code height

It could be observed from Fig.5 that the height of the tooth codes is obtained by calculating extreme points of the tooth code curves. Aiming at solving the problems such as low efficiency and high cost of the current artificial and mechanical identification on car key codes, the proposed tooth code automatic identification method based on the spectral clustering theory is proposed in this paper by measuring the height of the tooth codes about the key image. This method in this paper can effectively identify the tooth codes about a car key, which solves the low efficiency and high cost problems presented in the current artificial and mechanical methods about a car key tooth code identification.

5. Conclusion

The tooth code identification method about a car key based on the spectral clustering theory is presented in this paper. The tooth code boundary image about a car key is obtained by the spectral clustering method and the corresponding tooth code height is obtained by calculating the relative distance of the extreme point relative to the horizontal line on the boundary curve of the tooth code about car key image, which provides a feasible solution to the problem for the tooth code automatic identification method. In addition, the experimental verification about the key tooth code identification scheme is conducted by compiling the MATLAB software program. The experimental results shows that the car key tooth code automatic identification method based on the spectral clustering method could effectively solve the low efficiency and high cost problems presented in the current artificial and mechanical methods about a car key tooth code identification.

References

1. SU Xue-man and WU Yan-ming. Study of Control System for Lock Assembly Machine [J]. CHINESE HYDRAULICS & PNEUMATICS, 11:31-33(2008)
2. NI Zheng. Design and realization of automatic identification system for multiple key shapes [J], MACHINERY DESIGN & MANUFACTURE, 12:51-53(2009).
3. Wang Na and Li Xia. Active semi-supervised spectral clustering based on pairwise constraints. Acta Electronica Sinica, 38(1): 172−176(2010)
4. Ersahin K, et al. Segmentation and classification of polarimetric SAR data using spectral graph partitioning. IEEE Transactions on Geoscience and Remote Sensing, 48(1): 164−167(2010)
5. Alzate C and Suykens J A K. Multiway spectral clustering with out-of-sample extensions through weighted kernel PCA. IEEE Transactions on Pattern Analysis and Machine Intelligence, 32(2): 335−347(2010)
6. Fowlkes C, et al. Spectral grouping using the Nyström method. IEEE Trans. on Pattern Analysis and Machine Intelligence,26:214-225(2004). [doi: 10.1109/TPAMI.2004.1262185]
7. Fowlkes C. et al., "Spectral grouping using the nystrom method[J]. IEEE Trans.pattern Anal.mach.intell, 26(2):214-225(2004).
8. ZHANG Yan-hong, et al. A Watershed Segmentation Algorithm Based on Morphology Reconstruction and Maxima Mark [J]. Computing Technology and Automation, (2):78-81(2015).

Session 4

Databases and Information Systems

High Dimensional Feature Matching and Retrieval Based on Pre-ranking Algorithm

Shuai ZHU, Hong-wei ZHAO and Ping-ping LIU*

College of computer science and technology, Jilin University, Changchun 130012, China

Key Laboratory of Symbolic Computation and Knowledge Engineering of Ministry of Education

Changchun 130012,China

**Email: liupp@jlu.edu.cn*

Image retrieval technology has experienced rapid development in recent years and the image retrieval methods based on gist features and SIFT features are increasingly getting more popular. These image features are high-dimensional features and could potentially be simplified to improve the accuracy of image retrieval. In this paper, we studied the existing methods, moved the calculation of the distance between the image and image database offline and ranked the images offline. During a user search, only a few function values are required to be calculated to find the closest image. Based on the ideology of the algorithm, we have carried out the image retrieval based on gist and SIFT features respectively. The experimental results demonstrate that the speed and accuracy of the image retrieval are improved when the image retrieval is applied to the gist features. The accuracy of the image retrieval is improved by 6.76% when image retrieval is applied to SIFT features. Therefore, the pre-ranking algorithm is an excellent image retrieval algorithm for dealing with high-dimensional features.

Keywords: Computer vision; High-dimensional feature; Image retrieval; Pre-ranking.

1. Introduction

With the development of Internet technology, people's life and production need the support of massive data. Such a large scale of data makes people both excited and worried. People are excited about the rich data of the Internet but also worried about the "Curse of dimensionality"[1]. In the era of big data, how to reduce the feature dimension and accelerate the speed of image retrieval has become a key issue[2].

Image features extracted from the image has a high dimension[3]. The general method of solving the high dimensional feature image retrieval is to

*Corresponding author.

reduce the image dimensionality. We use principal component analysis to reduce the dimensionality and use hash method to encode the features to calculate the Hamming distance between codes .So we can describe the similarity between images[4,5,6].There are some method such as local sensitive hash algorithm, spectral hashing algorithm, iterative quantization algorithm (ITQ),etc. Local sensitive hash algorithm is a popular method of reducing dimension in previous years[7]. It maps the feature in the high dimensional space to the N hash table by some hash functions. All the points in the space are in each hash table. For a query, calculate its N hash function to find out the hash bucket which it falls into. Calculate the distance between the query and all points in the hash bucket, find the nearest point. Local sensitive hash algorithm is efficient and still has a good effect in the case of high dimensional data .Spectral hashing is performed by minimizing the similarity of images. After the problem is relaxed, the eigenvector and eigenvalue of the Laplasse matrix are calculated, and the threshold value is converted to the binarization feature vector[8]. The iterative quantization algorithm is to reduce the data dimension first, and then we can through the iterative calculate the best rotation matrix that make the rotation error smallest, the data after reducing dimension is multiplied by the rotation matrix to get the binary encoding[9].

We studied the existing methods. All of them need to calculate the distance between the image and image in the database when the user search, so we can find the most similar images. It makes the speed very slow. We sorted the image of each dimension off-line. Users can find the most similar image through calculating the value of a few functions. The accuracy of the retrieval is high, is near direct calculation of Euclidean distance.

In the second part, the paper introduces the principle of the algorithm, in the third part it describes the image retrieval algorithm based on gist features, in the fourth part it describes the image retrieval algorithm based on SIFT features, in the fifth part it is the experimental results.

2. Principle of Pre-ranking Algorithm

2.1. *Introduction of pre-ranking algorithm*

We know that when a data set is searched in disorder, a query is required to traverse the data set. When the data set is very large, this method is very complex. If you sort the data set first, it will be much more convenient. When the curve fitting is performed, the location of the query can be found only by calculating the function value according to the key words.

2.2. *Principle of pre-ranking algorithm*

A data set for the X, at first we carry on PCA dimensionality reduction, feature vector length decreased from P to n dimension. The data set XX. is obtained after dimension reduction.

$$XX=\begin{bmatrix} a_{11}a_{12}\cdots a_{1n} \\ a_{21}a_{22}\cdots a_{2n} \\ \vdots \\ a_{m1}a_{m2}\cdots a_{mn} \end{bmatrix}$$

There are m features, feature is the n dimensional vector.

(1)We calculate the length of the m feature.

$D_m=\sqrt{a_{m1}^2+a_{m2}^2+\cdots+a_{mn}^2}$ according to it we sort and then curve fitting. curving use the quintic function. So we get function f_0 ().

The dimension of k (k=1,2,3,...) dimension is based on the m feature. In the same way, we get the function f_k () (k=1,2,3,...).Dependent variable is the line number in a matrix.

(2)According to feature length d of the image to be tested, the f (d) is calculated and the location y is obtained, we search near y and get the set of location L.

The dimension of k (k=1,2,3,...) dimension is based on the M feature. In the same way, we get the set of location L_k

As shown in Figure 1, we calculate the intersection of $L_0, L_1,..., L_k$,and get the result L.As shown in Figure 2,it is the flow chart of pre-ranking algorithm

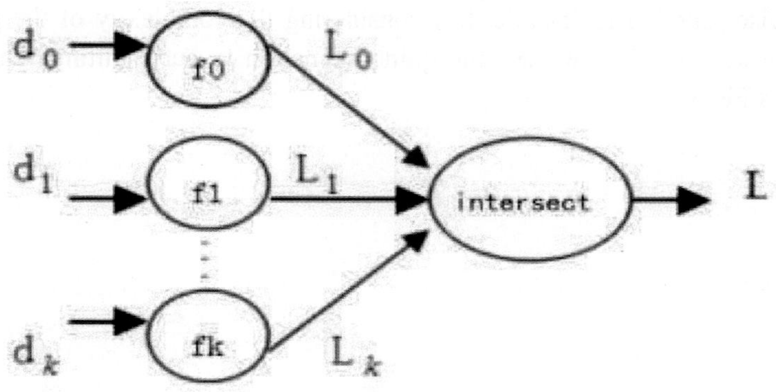

Fig.1 Figure of pre-ranking algorithm

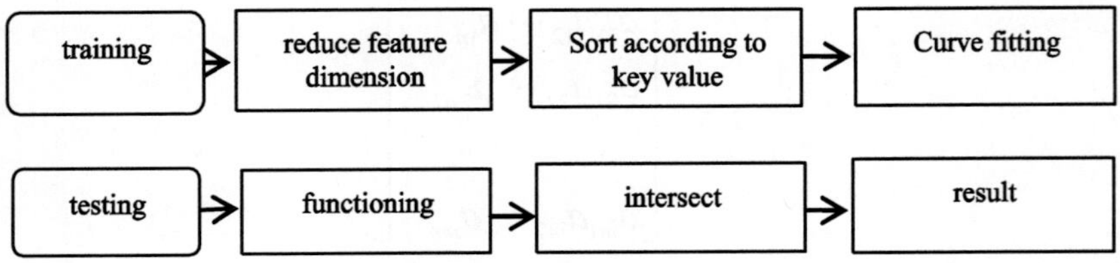

Fig.2 Flow chart of pre-ranking algorithm

3. The Image Retrieval Algorithm

3.1. *Image retrieval based on gist features*

If the image is small, we can't extract enough SIFT features, we turn to extract gist features. Because one feature in each picture can not generate frequency histogram, direct clustering will lead to a large error, so at this time we can not use bow method[10]. Then the commonly used method is PCA+ITQ, it is used to reduce the dimensionality of the feature vector, so we can calculate Hamming distance of image features rather than Euclidean distance.

Our algorithm is a little diferent from traditional algorithm.

(1)extract Gist feature of images[11]

(2)use PCA to reduce dimension

(3)use algorithm in 2.2 (1).

We consider a variety of fitting functions in the curve fitting, and the piecewise function is feasible. But considering the complexity of the program and the actual effect, we use the quintic function to curve fitting. The fitting effect is Fig.3:

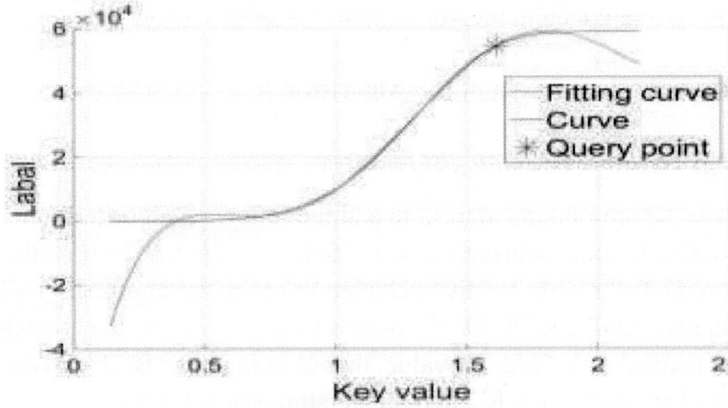

Fig.3 Figure of Curve fitting

When we are testing:

(4) use algorithm in 2.2 (2).

we search near y and get the set of location L. This function is as follows:
Find(s_0 , y_0 ,d-,d+)
y_0 is the approximate location of the input: s_0 is the sorted array: d-, d+ represents the minimum and maximum value of the output position set.

3.2. *Image retrieval based on sift features*

The commonly method is to extract the SIFT features when the image resolution is high. Because of the larger resolution, each image can be extracted from dozens to hundreds of sift features. At this time, the traditional approach is the bow method, clustering to generate the word bag and frequency histogram. Our method is based on bow, which is added to the pre-ranking, it improves the accuracy of image retrieval.

(1)Extract the SIFT features, clustering, do bow, calculate the frequency histogram.

(2)use PCA to reduce dimension

(3)use algorithm in 2.2 (1).

(4)The length d of a vector in the feature vector set M in testing picture.
use algorithm in 2.2 (2).L in the corresponding image similarity plus 1. If M is not empty, return the (4).

(5)the relative similarity = image similarity / number of SIFT feature in the picture.

(6)We sort pictures according to the relative similarity, we get MIX. Image sequences IX obtained by traditional bow method. MIX and IX in front of a certain number of images intersect to get I.

(7)The optional: Geometric verification for a few images in I.

4. Results and Comparison of the Algorithm

4.1. *Image retrieval based on gist features*

We compare the pre-ranking algorithm and the following algorithms:
ITQ: we define hashing scheme H(X) = SGN ($X \widetilde{W}$), $\widetilde{W} = WR$ the optimal rotation matrix R through iterative calculation optimization min||B - VR||2 first random matrix and the SVD decomposition to obtain the corresponding orthogonal matrix as the initial R value, then R is fixed for B, B=sgn (V * d).We carry out SVD to update the R, alternate iterating several times .
LSH: $\widetilde{W}$ is a Gauss random matrix, we rotate the original data[12].
PCA-RR: $\widetilde{W} = WR$, W which is a matrix of the direct PCA dimension reduction, is a randomly generated orthogonal matrix, is also an ITQ initialization form.
SKLSH: this method is based on the random feature map for the approximate translation invariant kernel[13], which is used by the Gauss kernel with the bandwidth setting as the average distance to the nearest distance of fiftieth[14].

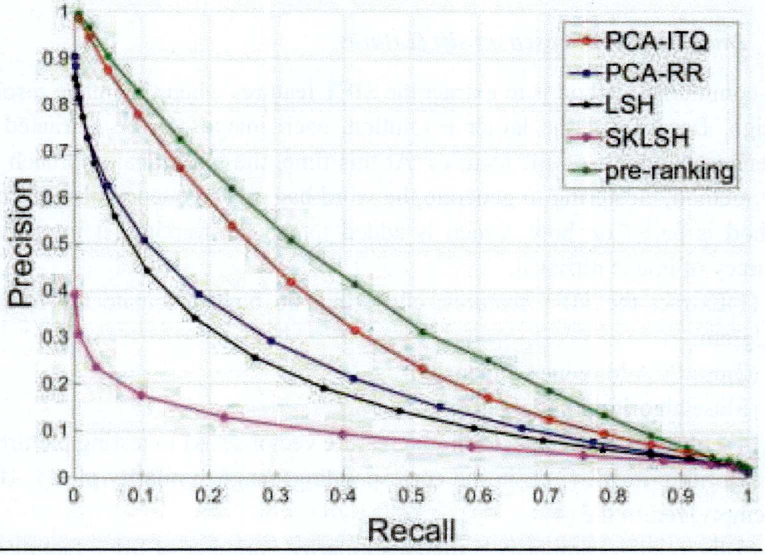

Fig.4 Figure of Algorithm Comparison

From the picture Fig.4, we can see that the accuracy of the algorithm has been improved obviously, and the operating speed of the algorithm is also improved, which reduces the time of image retrieval.

4.2. *Image retrieval based on sift features*

This program retrieve the database, take the first 11 images, and then change the input and output number of image, the average value of the accuracy and recall rate is as follows Table.1:

Table.1 Accuracy comparison of algorithm

algorithm	Bow	Bow+ Geometric verification	Pre-ranking	Pre-ranking+ Geometric verification	Bow+pre -ranking	Bow+pre-ranking+ Geometric verification
Precision	51.00%	81.00%	49.11%	85.27%	67.14%	87.76%
Recall	12.44%	19.76%	11.23%	22.46%	14.27%	23.87%

We can see the pre-ranking algorithm improve the accuracy of the bow algorithm. The actual operating time of the algorithm is not significantly increased. The pre-ranking algorithm alone is not as good as bow, but the combination of geometric verification, the pre-ranking algorithm is better than bow; and combining the two get the best accuracy.

5. Conclusion

This paper proposes a method based on the pre-ranking algorithm where the images are sorted offline and users can find the most similar images through the calculation of the value of a few functions. From the results from the image retrieval based on gist features comparison, it can be demonstrated that the accuracy and operating speed of the algorithm has been improved, which reduces the time of image retrieval. The results from the image retrieval based on SIFT features comparison demonstrated that the pre-ranking algorithm improves the accuracy of the bow algorithm but the actual operating time of the algorithm is not significantly increased. Although the pre-ranking algorithm alone is not as good as bow algorithm, but the combination of geometric verification, the pre-ranking algorithm is better than bow algorithm in terms of accuracy and recall rate.

Acknowledgments

This work is supported by National Natural Science Foundation of China (no.6110115), Natural Science Foundation of Jilin Province, China (no.20140101184JC, 20150520063JH).

References

1. ZH CH Y,ZH H C. Multi-modal robust local feature descriptor[J].Optics And Precision Engineering,2015,Vol. 23(5)(in Chinese)
2. K X W,F H Y. Image retrieval method based on image Hashi[P].Liao Ning Province CN200910220599.9,2010(in Chinese)
3. G J J. Image retrieval based on bilinear map and hash algorithm[D].Zhong Bei University,2014.(in Chinese)
4. Y L P.A relative histogram feature description for face recognition[J]Optics And Precision Engineering,2014,Vol. 22 (1)(in Chinese)
5. L ZH M, ZH J. Semi supervised manifold learning for hyperspectral image classification[J]Optics And Precision Engineering,2015,Vol. 23(5)(in Chinese)
6. S X R,W ZH Y. Unsupervised detection for general purpose of image[J]Optics And Precision Engineering,2014,Vol. 22 (1)(in Chinese)
7. Montréal, Québec, Canada. Similarity estimation techniques from rounding algorithms[J].34th Annual ACM Symposium on Theory of Computing, May 19-21, 2002
8. Y Weiss, A Torralba, R Fergus Spectral Hashing[J].Proc Nips.2008
9. Yunchao Gong and Svetlana Lazebnik. Iterative Quantization: A Procrustean Approach to Learning Binary Codes[J].Department of Computer Science, UNC Chapel Hill, NC, 27599.2011
10. P ZH M,J L,H Y M. Multi focus image super-resolution fusion based on multi scale sparse dictionary[J].Optics And Precision Engineering,2014,Vol. 22 (1)(in Chinese)
11. X T.Image retrieval method based on visual attention model and Gist feature[J]Guangxi Normal University,2014(in Chinese)
12. A. Andoni and P. Indyk. Near-optimal hashing algorithms for ap-proximate nearest neighbor in high dimensions[J]. Communications of the ACM, 2008.
13. A. Rahimi and B. Recht. Random features for large-scale kernelmachines[J]. NIPS, 2007
14. M. Raginsky and S. Lazebnik. Locality sensitive binary codes fromshift-invariant kernels[J]. NIPS, 2009.

An Improved Integration Solution of Heterogeneous Materials Data Based on NoSQL

Min CAO and Pan-pan CHEN*

Institute of engineering and computer science, Shanghai University
Baoshan district, Shanghai, China
E-mail:cpp8238065@163.com

This paper proposes a custom E-R diagram to organize the MongoDB dataset schema to utilize its free model and dynamic expansion characteristics. This allows for NoSQL data source integration of the heterogeneous data and the tackling of problems regarding heterogeneous data integration. Additionally, an algorithm is developed to convert global GSQL to local MongoDB query statement through the metadata of MongoDB.

Keywords: MongoDB; Custom E-R diagram; GSQL.

1. Introduction

Now each enterprise has many applications or websites with different data sources, which are storing in the databases and files independently, and cannot interact directly. In fact, a lot of data have relation with others, but users cannot access to and use these data in a unified way. A reliable way is needed to support the interaction and summary between heterogeneous data sources, which promotes the development of the heterogeneous data integration. The research of heterogeneous data integration has been the focus and hotspot to the academia and companies. Heterogeneous data integration, major research the data integration process in dissimilar network communication environment, heterogeneous data sources, different operating systems and different software development environment.

Materials science is closely connected with engineering technology, which includes physics, chemistry, metallurgy, and so on. In the process of research about material science, a large amount of data is generated, including material properties data, experiment data, results data, and so on. These data are related, however, are kept in isolation by the major research institutions, have no elation with others. Need to provide a unified way to access to various data in materials

* Corresponding author.

research agency. Material data is related to the authors` patent, causing many data sources cannot provide the data directly, only willing to provide query interface. Meanwhile, most of the material database researchers lack the knowledge about information sharing, and even many data sources are simply txt, excel and other documents, which are difficult to provide a mature, standard query interface. At the same time, the data size of material experiment data is huge, has not complex BI logic, data query logic is simple. In order to achieve the efficient management of these data, NoSQL database could be provided for storing.

With the rapid development of web applications, there are more and more data, which do not need complex combination query and high degree of consistency. Meanwhile because of the slow query speed of relational database, large cost, and poor scalability limitations, NoSQL is already more and more important. Experimental data in materials science, data volume is large, query logic is simple, so NoSQL is the best choice. Meanwhile MongoDB is relatively close to the relational database documentation database, not only to solve the dynamic expansion of the database, but also the freedom of custom data model to meet the requirements of NoSQL data features, and to meet the characteristics of relational databases.

To solve the unified way to access material data, this paper proposes a multi-tier architecture data integration framework based on heterogeneous data warehouse and middleware. System implement data warehouse by MongoDB, and implement data integration with MongoDB data warehouse by middleware. This paper will discuss the implementation of query parse process which is key content in the integration of heterogeneous materials data based on MongoDB.

2. Correlational Research

Heterogeneous data integration research includes data warehouse[1], federated database[2],and middleware[3]. Heterogeneous data integration solves the integration for each heterogeneous data source. Previous studies of heterogeneous data integration mainly to achieve integration of relational databases, XML documents[1-3]. Or implement heterogeneous data integration by full-text search using Lucene with relational databases, XML documents, and unstructured data[4]. Because NoSQL has free model and dynamic expansion characteristics, few achieve NoSQL data source integration.

MongoDB is an open source document database which is based on the distributed files, is a dynamic model database, without specific table structure. MongoDB support WEB application well, and is designed to improve the performance and scalability of concurrent storage. Files stored in the collection with BSON format, and the object-oriented features. The data has no imposed-consistency, and has no mandatory referential integrity. It has AutoSharding function, provides backup and recovery mechanisms, supports dynamic query, has good SQL friendliness, and multilingual open-source driver package[5-7].

In order to solve the integration of MongoDB data sources, firstly system must obtain MongoDB data schema information, which is different from the past relational database, it can be read directly. As MongoDB is free model, unable to obtain complete data schema information directly, need to manually define MongoDB data schema. This paper proposes an custom E-R model, to describe the MongoDB data schema, which need to save in XML. Then the metadata information about MongoDB could create base on MongoDB schema information. To solve the transformation of the global query language to the mongo query language. As well as other common problems of heterogeneous data integration need to be resolved, such as the return result merging.

In this paper, the relevant meta-data will be organized based on MongoDB schema. Then the entire query parsing process is achieved about converting global GSQL to the MongoDB query statements.

3. System Overall Framework

This paper presents amulti-tier architecture integrated framework which is combining middleware and data warehouse. To solve the lack of basic data operation and the necessary interface problems which are caused by complex and diverse heterogeneous material data. Meanwhile, ensuring the security and consistency of data, improving data processing performance as possible. Concrete frame structure shown in Figure 1.

Adding data warehouse module and cache module in traditional middleware system framework of heterogeneous data integration. And provide a virtual view database which is logical database to manage global schema information. The core of the framework, including query parsing, result integration and establish metadatabase. The implementation of query parsing process about NoSQL data source MongoDB, and generating MongoDB metadata is researched in this paper.

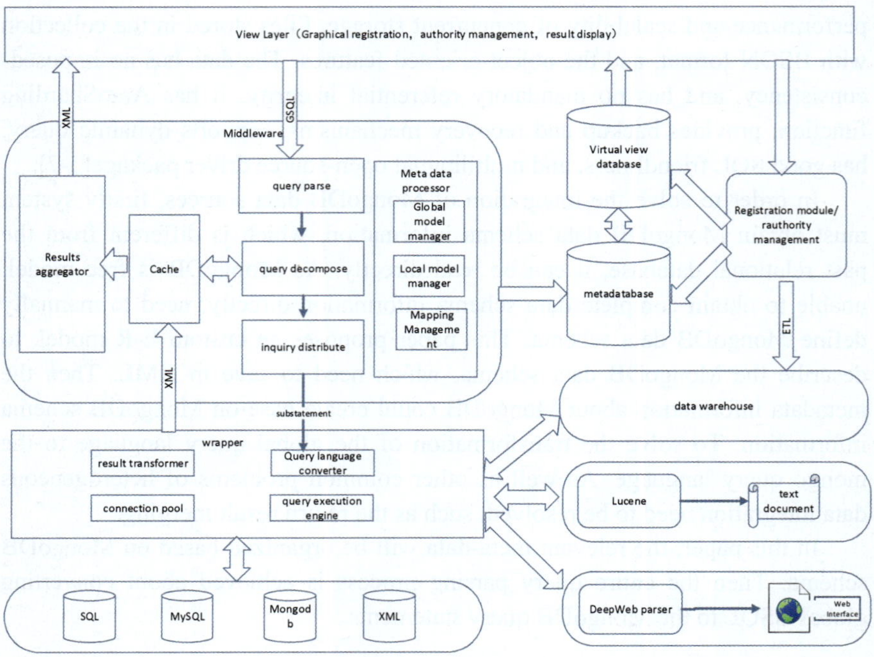

Figure 1.The system overall frame

4. Generate MongoDB Metadata

Metadatabase is the basis of the framework. The metadata includes local data source schema information, which includes the link information of local data sources, user name, password, and table structure information, database field attribute information and so on; global schema information, which is a logical view database customized based on local data schema and specific business. And providing a virtual view of the database, which is a subset of the global schema, to each individual user based on user privileges and specific business. This way providing an unified way to access to various forms of the underlying data source. Meanwhile, including mapping information between global schema and local schema, this is used for achieving converting GSQL to local query statements of each local data source, as well as integrating the return results about the each local data source. No matter what kind of metadata information, schema information of local data sources must be obtained firstly. MongoDB is a free model, and dynamic expansion .It does not provide information for the database schema by itself, in order to generate MongoDB relevant metadata database, must obtain schema information of MongoDB database firstly.

4.1. *MongoDB modeling*

This paper designs a custom E-R diagram based on specific type of data of MongoDB, and the free model characteristic of MongoDB, which is used for describing MongoDB data schema. The custom E-R diagram is shown in figure 2 as follows.

Wherein the dotted line of the "optional field" represent optional fields, two circles of "Array field" represent an array fields, and the extensible filed represent the filed has subfield.

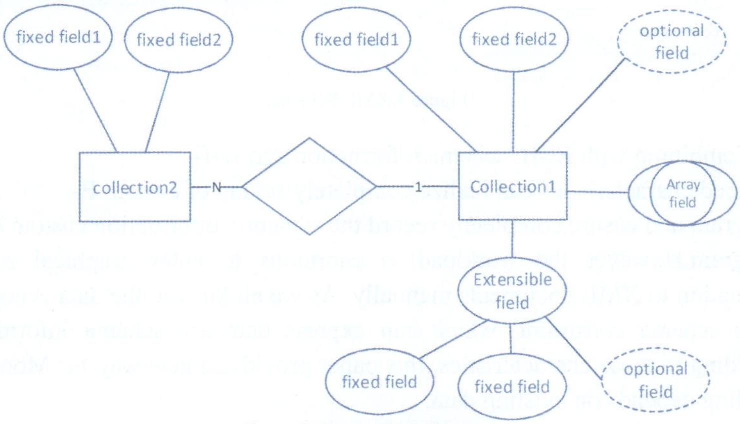

Figure 2.Custom E-R Diagram

This custom E-R diagram expresses MongoDB database schema information vividly. This paper designs optional fields to address the dynamic model feature. MongoDB should be designed for all possible fields which maybe dynamic extended, with detail at the beginning. For solving specific array type data format this paper designs array fields. This model can display MongoDB database schema with detail, is easily to understand to developers. However graphical-based model is difficult as metadata for query parse in data integration and providing support to the integration modules of return results. So a formal describing language must be provided to describe the custom E-R diagram.

4.2. *Storage class E-R diagram model in XML*

The formal describing language commonly used include Z language, LTL, CTL, BNF paradigm which can describe a specific model, such as CTL and LTL are suitable for describing sequential logic system, Z language is good for the system model based on state. These languages are lack of good readability.XML is self-describing, extensible Markup Language, platform-independent, and good readability. It has the structure shown in Figure 3as follows:

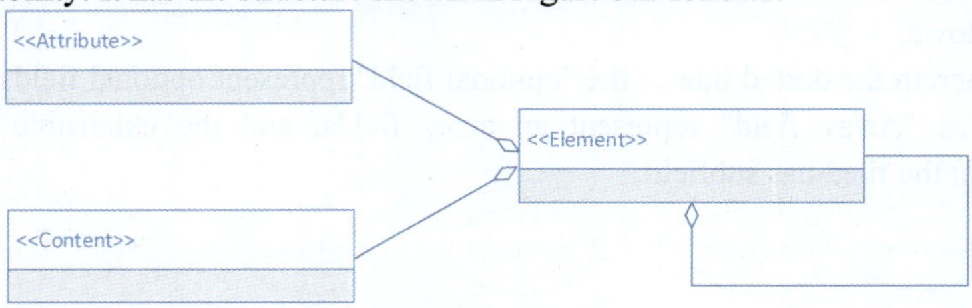

Figure 3.XML Schema

Combining with XML schema information and self-described characteristics can realize completely saving of custom E-R diagram and ensure completely record the semantic information custom E-R diagram.However the workload is enormous to enter graphical schema information to XML documents manually. As we all known, the data is conform to the schema constraint, which can express database schema information. According to these characteristics, this paper provides a new way for MongoDB modeling depends on existing data.

4.3. *Semi-automatic MongoDB modeling*

The Bson of MongoDB data is a kind of data that its schema is same as the XML schema, so all of MongoDB data can be converted into XML. XML schema information can be extracted through the existing API to XSD which is a form of an XML data model. The specific process is in Figure 4 as follows:

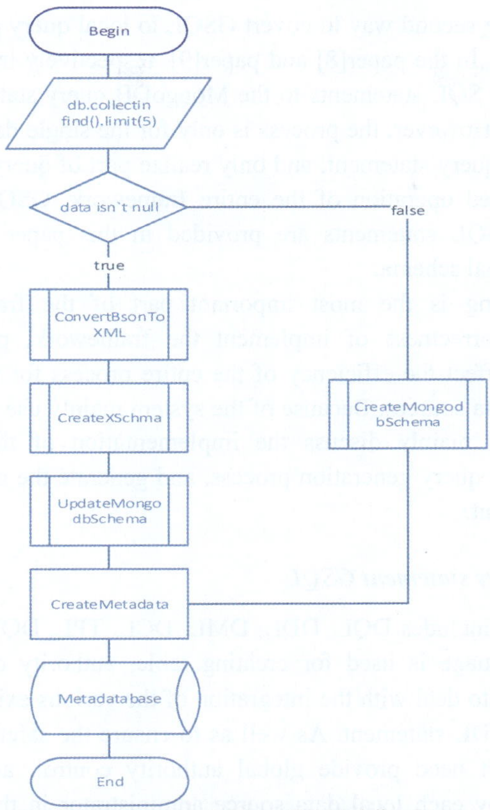

Figure 4.Semi-automaticMongoDB Modeling Process

Because of the dynamic model feature, the data and information which is taken from semi-automatic MongoDB modeling process cannot completely express schema of the entire data collection. So the schema which is automatically generated need to manually combine the custom E-R diagram by the database administrator. Then the local data patterns, the global pattern, as well as other related metadata database information need to be perfect by the final MongoDB schema information.

5. MongoDB Query Parsing

There are two ways of data unified operation in general, one is to provide a unified standard, like the SQL statement is unified standard to relational databases. But there are many database products, which are different in the structure. It would be difficult to provide a unified standard. The other way is to realize different query transformation of the system through third party.[8] This paper will use the second way to covert GSQL to local query statement of each local data source .In the paper[8] and paper[9], respectively introduces the way of converting the SQL statements to the MongoDB query statement and Hbase query statement. However, the process is only for the single data source, cannot parse the global query statement, and only realize part of query paring function. To achieve unified operation of the entire framework, GSQL statements are extended from SQL statements are provided in this paper for virtual view database and global schema.

GSQL parsing is the most important part of the framework, it will determine the correctness of implement the framework, parsing algorithm efficiency, and affect the efficiency of the entire process for the integration of heterogeneous data sources. Because of the system mainly use in the data query, this chapter will mainly discuss the implementation of the transformation process, optimize query generation process, and generate the optimal efficiency subquery statement.

5.1. *Global query statement GSQL*

Traditional SQL includes DQL, DDL, DML, DCL, TPL, DQL, and CCL. The DDL, DCL language is used for creating table, authority control, etc. This system is mainly to deal with the integration of the various existing database do not need parse DDL statement. As well as to ensure the safety of various data sources, does not need provide global authority control, authority assigned would be done by each local data source administrator in the local database. According to the business needs of the system, temporarily achieve global query statement to DQL, DML statement. This section will discuss the specific analysis to achieve more complex DQL statements.

5.2. *GSQL parsing process*

Query parsing process, converting global GSQL statements into local query statements for each data source that can be executed through the metadatabase that provided before. There are two possible solutions to complete a global query to MongoDB query in this paper. One parses GSQL to global MongoDB query statement firstly, and then converts global MongoDB statement to local MongoDB query statement through metadatabase. The other decomposes the GSQL to local GSQL that is only related to each local data source, and then converts local GSQL to MongoDB query statement. As there are many other kinds of data sources, in order to enhance the system extension this paper will choose the second way. So that when a new local data source is added, simply convert local GSQL statements to local data source query statement, and it is uncorrelated with other data sources. Specific query parsing process is as follows:

(1) Write GSQL statement through specific business and virtual view database, such as “select * from T1 where F1 # V1 connector F2 # V2;”(for the administrator can be directly write the query statement through global schema, can omit this step).Including F1 represents field, T1 represents table name, V1 represents a constant, # represents the operator ‘<’, ‘=’, ‘like’,etc, connector represents ‘and’ or ‘or’.
(2) Convert GSQL based on virtual view database to global GSQL based on global schema, such as “select F1, F2, F3[],F4! , F5, F6,F7 Where F1 # V1 connector F2#V2”;
(3) Decomposes the global GSQL to local GSQL that is only related to each local data source, such as
“select F1,F2,F4!,F6 From D1.T1 Where F1 # V1 connector F2#V2”;
“Select F1,F3[],F6,F7 from D2.T3 where F1 # V1”;
(4) Converts local GSQL to MongoDB query statement, such as “db.collection.find({“F1”:V1},{“F2”:1,”F3”:1,”F4”:1,”F5”:1})”.
(5) Get the link information of local data source, user name, password, and server path, and then establish a database connection, execute the query, and returns the result. Each local data source back results are converted into XML format.
(6) The return XML results will be combined by results aggregator through mapping information from metadatabase.
(7) Display the results according to the specific application and self-describing information in XML.

5.3. *Generate query statements*

The main work is to generate each local data source query statement can really execute in query parsing, this section will gradually discuss specific query parse process.

(1.)Generated GSQL based on global schema

Input: Select * from T1 where F1 # V1 connectorF2#V2;

Algorithm:

I.Split GSQL by SQL keyword, such as select, from, where, etc. into the select substatement, the where substatement, and the from substatement.

II.If the select substatement is‘*’,replace ‘*’ to columnFieldIDs[] that in table based on the from substatement in virtual view database.

III.Split the select substatement and the where substatement by character ‘,’ into columnFieldIDs[] and whereFieldIDs[].

IV.Get each related field from columnFieldIDs by virtual view database and global schemamapping information. (getGlobalSelectFieldsByMap (columnFieldIDs, xmlFilePath))

V.optimizeWhereStr(getGlobalWhereStrFieldsBYmap(whereFieldIDs, xmlFilePath));

Output:

select F1,F2, F3[],F4! , F5, F6,F7Where F1 # V1 connector F2#V2;

(2.)Decomposes global GSQL to local GSQL

Input: select F1,F2, F3[],F4! , F5, F6,F7Where F1 # V1 connector F2#V2;

Algorithm:

I.Same as the first step in Generated GSQL based on global schema.

II.Same as the third step in Generated GSQL based on global schema.

III.Get all related local field from columnFieldIDs by global schemaand local schemamapping information. Specific algorithm is as follows:

For each columnFieldIDs

(a)Get all local field which is related with the global field, such as F2 has mapping information as follows:

{"map":[
{"value":"LocalFiledID1.value+LocalFiledID2.value","type":""},
{"value":"LocalFiledID3.value","type":""}
]}

LocalFiledID1, LocalFiledID2, and LocalFiledID3 that the only global ID for field will be got to store in localFieldIDs[];

(b)Sort localFieldIDs to ensure all local field in the same local data source get together;

(c)According to sorted localFieldIDs, split the select substatement into eachlocalFieldIDs[][] that is each local data source related select fields;

IV.Get eachwhereFieldIDs[][] by the same way. If the where substatement include substatement, recursive implementation of this operation.(The all Filter conditions in the where substatement in global GSQL do not need constrainedlyuse for local GSQL)

V.Get the table information by eachlocalFieldIDs and eachwhereFieldIDs, and store in eachFromIDs[][];

VI.If the tables in the same database have reference relations, get foreign key field and update eachwhereFieldIDs.

VII.Join the columnFieldIDs, the eachwhereFieldIDs, and the eachFromIDs to generate multiple local query substatement.

Output:

select F1,F2,F4!,F6 From D1.T1 Where F1 # V1 connector F2#V2;

select F1,F3[],F6,F7 From D2.T3 where F1 # V1;

(3.)Convert local GSQL to MongoDB query statement

Input: Select ** from ** where ***;

Algorithm:

I. Same as the first step in Generated GSQL based on global schema.

II. Decomposes the select substatement and the where substatement into multiple select fields and where fields only related to the collection through the from fields.

III. Same as the third step in Generated GSQL based on global schema.

IV. According to the MongoDB query syntax, creating Json format string based on the select field. e.g.{age:1, name:1,birthday:1,address:1}.

V. According to the SQL operator and the MongoDB operator semantic mapping relations that store in metadatabase, converting the where fields into Json format string like { $or : [{F1: {'$gt': V1}}, {F3:/V3/}]}.

VI. Join together into multiple MongoDB query statement. Meanwhile implement relevant query through DBRef according to the relationship between each collection.

Output:

db.collectin.find({ $or : [{F1: {'$gt': V1}}, {F2:/V2/}]},{"F2":1,"F3":1,"F4":1,"F5":1}).

The first step to generated GSQL statement based on global schema which is combined by a only table, meanwhile complete optimizing the where substatement. The second step to decompose global GSQL to local GSQL based on the mapping information which provide a unique global ID for each field which used for quickly locating. The last step to convert local GSQL to MongoDB query statement based on the syntactic analyzer and lexical analyzer which designs to code the GSQL keyword and MongoDB keyword mapping information. Through the above process complete converting global GSQL statement to MongoDB statement.

5.4. *Implementation*

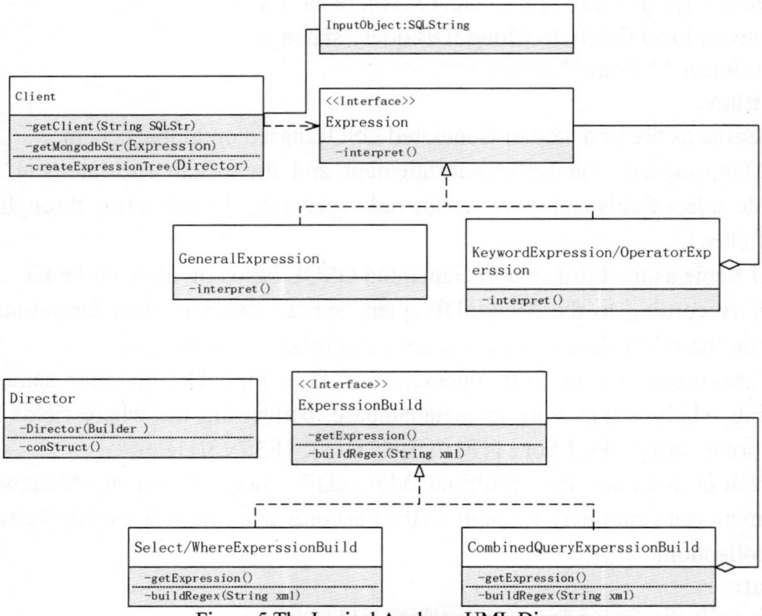

Figure 5.The Lexical Analyzer UML Diagram

This section will discuss the implementation converting GSQL statements into MongoDB statements. Coding based on interface to improve the scalability of the system, to ensure to uniformly implement semantic transformation operation about each keyword and operator. Meanwhile implement the lexical analyzer with regular expression, so that each parse string for keywords and operators can store in configuration files. The syntax tree will be constructed dynamically for specific GSQL statement's keywords and operators through builder pattern. And then generating MongoDB statements though parsing syntax tree. Specific design shown in Figure 5.

Coding lexical parser, through the above way to increase the extensibility of the system, when the new keyword mapping relationship is added or updated, only need to update the corresponding API, and the change is independent and transparent to other keywords. Meanwhile, a composite pattern is used for solving the recursive structure of combination query to ensure structure more clear.

6. Conclusions

This paper is mainly to solve NoSQL data source query parsing problem which is rarely involved with the heterogeneous data integration. To solve the MongoDB free model characteristics, designed a custom E-R diagram to organize the MongoDB schema information, and design a way to automatically generate the formal describing language to store the MongoDB schema through the data which reflect the schema information. Meanwhile, the algorithm is achieved about converting global GSQL statement to local MongoDB query statement through the meta data of MongoDB, and design the query parser`s core lexical analyzer. System has achieved converting global GSQL to the MongoDB query statement, which is satisfied the simple query operation on the material business. Later, in order to improve the framework support for other business, need to implement the complex combination query parsing, transaction operation, stored procedures and other related operation about converting GSQL statements to local query statement.

Acknowledgments

This work is supported by the Shanghai science and technology committee project (14DZ226120).

References

1. Ramamurthy K R, Sen A, Sinha A P. An empirical investigation of the key determinants of data warehouse adoption[J]. Decision support systems, 2008, 44(4): 817-841.
2. Bent G, Dantressangle P, Vyvyan D, et al. A dynamic distributed federated database[C]//Proc. 2nd Ann. Conf. International Technology Alliance. 2008.
3. Xiong Fengguang, Han Xie. Research and implementation of heterogeneous data integration based on XML[J]. Electronic Measurement & Instruments, 2009. 9th International Conference on. 2009:711-715
4. Tianyuan L, Meina S, Xiaoqi Z. Research of massive heterogeneous data integration based on Lucene and XQuery[C]//Web Society, 2010 IEEE 2nd Symposium on. IEEE, 2010: 648-652.
5. Liu Y, Wang Y, Jin Y. Research on the improvement of MongoDB Auto-Sharding in cloud environment[C]//Computer Science & Education (ICCSE), 2012 7th International Conference on. IEEE, 2012: 851-854.

6. Chodorow K. MongoDB: the definitive guide[M]. " O'Reilly Media, Inc.", 2013.
7. Dede E, Govindaraju M, Gunter D, et al. Performance evaluation of a MongoDB and Hadoop platform for scientific data analysis[C]//Proceedings of the 4th ACM workshop on Scientific cloud computing. ACM, 2013: 13-20.
8. LiuGuan,Research On SQL And MongoDB Data Conversion Technology[D].Sichuan ,Sichuan Normal University,2013
9. Tang Tao,Research On SQL conversion engine based on Hbase[D].ChengDu,School of Computer &Engneering,2014

Technical Research on Parameter Extraction of Tibetan Speech Synthesis under the Circumstance of "Digital Silk Road"

Jin-xi ZHANG

Lanzhou University of Finance and Economics
LanZhou GanSu, 730020, China
E-mail: 582361484@qq.com

Based on background knowledge of the "digital silk road" construction, this paper researches the digital speech technology which can support silk road of economic development of western minority regions. With regards to voice information processing, Mel-scale Frequency Cepstral Coefficients(MFCC) is the speech characteristic parameter frequently used. Human auditory sensing characteristics concerning the variation of feelings to different frequencies can be detected by this parameter. Therefore, MFCC is particularly suitable for use in speech synthesis. Based on the theoretical principle of MFCC parameter extraction, this paper conducts an in-depth research on the configuration parameters and HMM modeling and applies it into the parameter extraction of Tibetan speech synthesis. This lays a solid foundation to the realization of HMM Tibetan speech synthesis and provides technical reference for speech recognition and synthesis of minority languages for mobile clients.

Keywords: Digital silk road; Tibetan speech synthesis; Parameter extraction; HMM modeling.

1. Introduction

With the acceleration of economic globalization, social informationization and regional integration, information network technology and its application with its representative of network, cloud computing and big data application has greatly changed economic society running mode all over the world and global competitive landscape. The basis, strategic and leading position of message communication industry has become increasingly prominent in the development of economic society. Nowadays, "digital silk road" carries more missions, which is also an important hand to create economic belt of Silk Road. Its construction will promote the facilitation of cooperation in transportation, trade and business, finance, cultural technology and health care and become a bridge for cooperation and win-win situation.

Under the circumstance of national "Digital Silk Road", this paper researches on digital speech technology which can support the economic development of Silk Road western minority area and provides some technical support for new Silk Road economic zone construction by using the Internet thinking to activate the ancient "Silk Civilization" new engine. According to the research on the mechanism of hearing, it is found that human ear has different auditory sensitivity to different frequency and has great influence on 200Hz and 5KHz speech signal. In this paper, the Mel is a measure of the tone which human ear can perceive.

2. Theoretical Basis of MFCC Parameter Extraction

2.1. *Mel frequency scale*

Mel frequency parameter (MFCC) is the parameter extracted from Mel scale frequency domain. Mel frequency scale is close to frequency resolution by human ear and is more suitable to human's auditory features in the synthesis process. The relation between Mel scale and frequency can be expressed as the following approximation, as in Eq. (1), f is frequency and its unit is Hz.

$$Mel(f) = 2595 * \lg(1 + f / 700). \tag{1}$$

2.2. *MFCC parameter extraction method*

The method to get Mel frequency coefficients is to make the time domain signal to do time / frequency conversion, and the logarithm of the energy spectrum of the triangular filter bank in accordance with the Mel scale distribution, and then the output of the filter bank to do discrete cosine transform (DCT), so that the former N dimensional vector is called MFCC. The process of MFCC is shown in Figure 1.

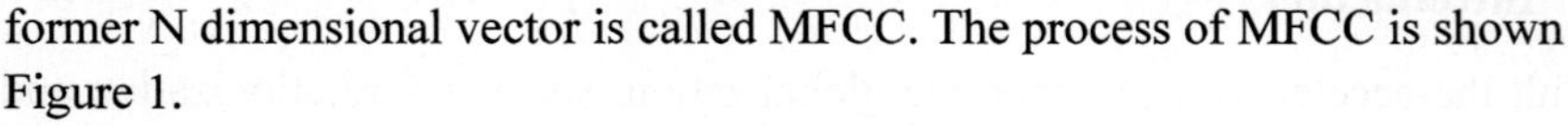

Figure.1.MFCC Parameter Extraction Process.

(i) Separate the speech signal input and then make fast conversion(DFT), as in Eq. (2),Among them $x(n)$ is speech signal, N is the point of changes.

$$X_a(k) = \sum_{n=0}^{N-1} x(n) e^{-j2\pi k/N}, 0 \le k \le N \quad . \tag{2}$$

(ii) The triangle filter output is all signal width and defined signal filter group (including M triangle filters) with center frequency $f(m), m = 1,2,...M$, here it refers to $M=24$.Triangle filter frequency response is defined as in Eq. (3),Among them $\sum_{m=0}^{M-1} H_m(k)=1$.

$$H_m(k)=\begin{cases} 0, k<f(m-1) \\ \dfrac{2(k-f(m-1))}{(f(m+1)-f(m-1))(f(m)-f(m-1))}, f(m-1)\le k\le f(m) \\ \dfrac{2(f(m+1)-k)}{(f(m+1)-f(m-1))(f(m+1)-f(m))}, f(m)\le k\le f(m+1) \\ 0, k\ge f(m+1) \end{cases}. \quad (3)$$

Triangle filter output is all the signal width within the frequency width and its formula is as in Eq. (4),Among them l= 1,2,....,24.

$$Y(l)=\sum_{k=o(l)}^{c(l)} \frac{k-o(l)}{c(l)-o(l)}\left|X_n(k)\right| + \sum_{k=c(l)}^{h(l)} \frac{h(l)-k}{h(l)-c(l)}\left|X_n(k)\right|. \quad (4)$$

(iii) Logarithmic operation for $Y(l)$, as in Eq. (5),Among them l= 1,2,...., 24.

$$\ln(Y(l)). \quad (5)$$

(iv) The discrete cosine transform (DCT) is performed to obtain the Mel frequency parameter (MFCC), as in Eq. (6):

$$C_i=\sum_{i=1}^{24} \ln(Y(l))\cos[i(l-\frac{1}{2})\frac{\pi}{24}]. \quad (6)$$

Among them i= 1,2,..., P,P are the orders of MFCC parameter (P=24).

2.3. *Dynamic differential parameter extraction*

The MFCC parameters described above can only describe the static characteristics of the speech parameters, and the difference of these static characteristics can describe the dynamic characteristics of speech. The combination of static and dynamic characteristics can improve the performance of the system. The calculation formula of difference parameters is as in Eq. (7):

$$d_t=\begin{cases} C_{t+1}-C_t, t<K \\ \dfrac{\sum_{k=1}^{K} k(C_{t+k}-C_{t-k})}{\sqrt{2\sum_{k=1}^{K} k^2}} \\ C_t-C_{t-1}, t\ge Q-K \end{cases}. \quad (7)$$

Among them, d_t represents t difference; C_t represents t frequency of the coefficient; Q represents coefficients frequency stage; t represents differential coefficient, 1or 2 can be removed(This paper selects 2).

3. Related Configuration Parameters

The related configuration parameters discussed in this paper are as follows. ("#" is the explanation)

 # Example of an acoustical analysis configuration file

SOURCEFORMAT = HTK# Give voice file format

TARGETKIND = MFCC_0_D_A # Coefficient of identifiers

 # Unit = 0.1 micro-second:

WINDOWSIZE = 250000.0# = 25 ms =Time span of frame

TARGETRATE = 100000.0 # = 10 ms = Cycle of frame

NUMCEPS = 12 # 12 initial MFCC coefficient (from c1 to c12)

USEHAMMING = T # Use of window

PREEMCOEF = 0.97 # Pre weighting coefficient

NUMCHANS = 24 # Filter channel number

CEPLIFTER = 22 # Coefficient length

 # The End

From the list of parameters, a total of 78 coefficients are extracted from each signal frame by MFCC analysis.

4. Selection of Synthetic Base

In speech synthesis, word, syllable, vowel sound and phoneme can be used as recognition element. This paper uses phoneme (Tibetan Lhasa dialect phonemes have 50 phonemes with moderate phoneme number) as a synthetic element. According to the research findings of Tibetan phonetics, the phoneme collection table of Tibetan Lhasa dialect is finally confirmed and the corresponding Latin is given (See table 1).

Table 1. Tibetan Lhasa dialect phonemes and corresponding Latin table[2]

IP	Writin	IP	Writin	IP	Writin	IP	Writin	IP	Writin	IP	Writin	IP	Writin	IP	Writin	IP	Writin	IP	Writin
c	c	kh	kh	ph	ph	tʂ	q	ɕ	x	tɕh	txh	e:	ew	o	o	yˀ	yb	ɛ	el
ch	ch	l	l	r	r	tʂh	qh	ʂ	ss	ˀ	ab	eˀ	eb	o:	ow	ø	f	ɛ:	elw
h	h	m	m	s	s	w	w	ʦ	ts	a:	aw	I	i	u	u	ø:	fw	ɛˀ	elb
j	j	n	n	t	t	ŋ	ng	ʦh	tsh	a	a	i:	iw	u:	uw	øˀ	fb	ẽ	eu
k	k	p	p	th	th	ɳ	nn	tɕ	tx	e	e	iˀ	ib	y:	yw	ĩ	il	ỹ	yu

5. HMM Modeling

Hidden Markov model is the main technology of acoustic modeling. In the modeling, we use the 7 state continuous HMM model, as is shown in figure 2. The model consists of 7 states {S1, S2, S3, S4, S5, S6, S7}. Among them, S2, S3, S4, S5, S6 are active state while S1 and S6 are non-divergent state(no observation function). The observation function Bi is Gaussian distribution with diagonal matrix and its transformation can be shown by a_{ij}.

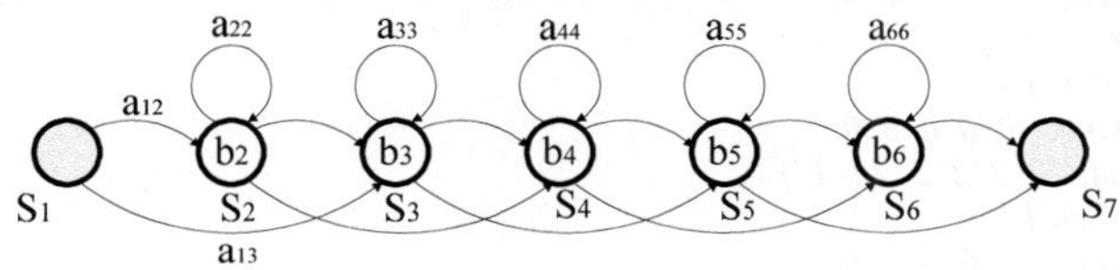

Figure 2 Seven state HMM modeling basic structure[4]

6. MFCC Parameter Extractions

6.1. *Initialization*

Before the model training, we must have first initialized the parameters of the HMM model. HTK tool has two available commands: Hinit and HCompv. In this paper, we use HCompv. HCompv is the smooth initialization for HMM modeling. All States of the HMM model are beginning to have the same mean vector and the change vector. General initialized command forms are as follows, HCompv -A -D –T 1 -S trainlist.txt -M model/hmm0flat \-H model/proto/hmmfile -f 0.01 nameofhmm. And trainlist.txt contains all the.mfcc data. In the process, HCompv also produces variable vFloors file in the initialization model. vFloors file is (../models/qst001/ver1/cmp/vFloors), which includes the overall change vectors of multiplying factor (See List1), a total of four (varFloor2, varFloor3, varFloor1, varFloor4. The initial setting here is VFLOORSCALESTR Vector 4 0.01 0.01 0.01 0.01.

~v varFloor1
<Variance> 75
1.655392e-02 8.970978e-03 2.350296e-03 2.006636e-03(……)4.803030e-05 4.664139e-05
……

List 1. variable base macro file vFloors

6.2. *Training*

HTK tool HRest is used for evaluation, changes and optimization model parameter. The general commands are as follows, HRest -A -D -T 1 -S trainlist.txt -M model/hmmi -H vFloors \-H model/hmmi-1/hmmfile -l label -L label_dirnameofhmm. Among them, trainlist.txt list all the training mfcc file. During this process, the HMM model of the training is repeated for many times.

```
/proto/qst001/ver1/state-5_stream-4_mgc-75_lf0-3.prt . . .
States  :  2  3  4  5  6 (width)
 Mixes  s1:  1  1  1  1  1 ( 75 )
 ( 75 )
 Num Using:  0  0  0  0  0
 Mixes  s2:  2  2  2  2  2 ( 1 )
 ( MSD  <=  1 )
 Num Using:  0  0  0  0  0
 Mixes  s3:  2  2  2  2  2 (  1  )
 ( MSD  <=  1 )
 Num Using:  0  0  0  0  0
 Mixes  s4:  2  2  2  2  2 (  1  )
 ( MSD  <=  1 )
 Num Using:  0  0  0  0  0
 Parm Kind:  USER
 Number of owners = 1
 SegLab   :  aa
 maxIter  :  20
 epsilon  :  0.000100
 minSeg   :  1
 Updating :  Means Variances MixWeights/DProbs TransProbs
```

List2. Training process for the phoneme aa

List 2 is the training process for phoneme aa, evaluation and changes for original modeling proto, optimization modeling parameter, means, variances, mix weights/dprobs and transprobs, ect.

7. Conclusions

MFCC simulates the processing characteristics of the human ear to the speech to some extent and also use the application of the human ear's auditory perception, which has better robustness in the aspect of the channel noise and the spectrum distortion. In speech synthesis, we must first extract the speech parameters (including MFCC parameters) and then use the parameter generation algorithm based on dynamic feature to generate the HMM model. We should calculate the MFCC and logF0 parameter according to the HMM modeling (this process is actually an inversing process). Finally, MFCC parameters and other parameters are input together into the voice synthesizer. Therefore, extraction of MFCC lay the foundation for speech synthesis.

References

1. T. fukada, K. Tokuda, T. Kobayashi, S.Imai. An adaptive algorithm for mel-cepstral analysis of speech[C]. ICASSP, 1992.Vol1, pp 137-140.

2. LI Guanyu, MENG Meng. Research on Acousti Model of Large-vocabulary Continuous Speech Recognition for Lhasa Tibetan [J].Computer Engineering, 2012, 38(5):189-191.
3. Htkbook.http://users.ece.gatech.edu/~antonio/htkbook/htkbook.html[OL].
4. Nicolas Moreau.HTK (v.3.1): Basic Tutorial.2002.
5. Tokuda, Yoshimura, Masuko, Kobayshi, Kitamura, Speech parameter generation algorithms for HMM-based speech synthesis[C], ICASSP.2000. vol.3, PP1315-1318.

The Research on Distributed Classification-based Hybrid Index Mechanism

Qing WU
School of Computer Science and Technology, Hangzhou Dianzi University
City, State ZIP/Zone, Country Hangzhou, 310018,China
E-mail: llcpu@foxmail.com

Liang WU
School of Computer Science and Technology, Hangzhou Dianzi University
City, State ZIP/Zone, Country Hangzhou, 310018,China
E-mail: wuliang901112@163.com

The emerging web text data contain features such as obscure concepts and uncertain word boundaries. Given that the existing traditional index cannot support it efficiently, the paper proposes a distributed classification-based hybrid index model by combining the suffix array's ability to support phrases with uncertain word boundaries and the reverse index's high query efficiency and its ability to support sorting query results. It takes advantage of the Map/Reduce frame's ability to presort web texts and develop a Map/Reduce frame-based distributed hybrid index model on its own classification results set.

Keywords: Reverse index; Hybrid index; Text classification; Distributed; Map/Reduce.

1. Introduction

Based on the advantages of suffix array and reverse index[1], reverse index is a kind of index facing words[2]. Its advantages is supporting presorting query results. Suffix array index[3]are very applicable to the languages with uncertain word boundaries and can support phrase query very well, the paper tries to raise a kind of hybrid index mechanism based on the combination of two indexs. A suffix array index is built for classification text data. The query result from suffix array index is a continuous interval and every value in the interval marks the position of the queried word in document sets, so an inverted list can be prefabricated for the query result interval to support result sets sequence.

Map/Reduce is a distributed computing programming frame based on hadoop platform and a kind of parallel programming pattern used for the parallel calculation of massive data[4]. The implementation process is shown in Fig.1.

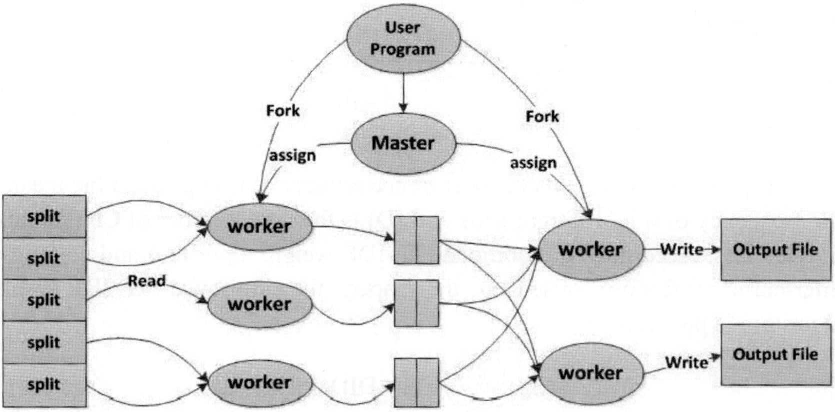

Fig.1. The implementation process of Map/Reduce

According to the parallel processing advantages of Map/Reduce model and aiming at the phenomenon that the construction of traditional index with massive previous data consumes relatively much time, the paper conducted distributed processing based on classification-based hybrid index. The paper uses the improved TF-IDF algorithm to extract the subject terms from web text and regards the data with similar themes as the same class to store. According to the data themes with different classes, distributed classification-based hybrid index is built to improve search and storage efficiency.

2. The Classification Model Based on Prejudgment

Semantics-based KNN classification algorithm divides web text into K classes, namely C = {C1, C2, C3, C4, C5,.....Ck} and applies "ICTCLAS Chinese word segmentation system" to conduct Chinese characteristics segmentation[5]. Term frequency - inverse document frequency (TF-IDF) algorithm represents the importance of words for one text and TF (term frequency) and IDF (inverse Document Frequency) are related to the importance of words[6]. Traditional keywords extraction algorithm only considers the relation between keywords and the number of texts including keywords and ignores the distribution of keywords in one class and misjudgment the weight of rarely used words.

Aiming at the lack of weight functions in traditional TF-IDF and combining the knowledge relating to information theory, the paper adopts inter-class uniformity DIdc to represent the distribution of one word among the words of the same class.

$$DI_{DC}(t_i) = \sqrt{\sum_{j=1}^{|D|}\left(n_{i,j} - \overline{n_{i,j}}\right)^2 / (|D| - 1)} / \overline{n_{i,j}} \cdot \tag{1}$$

In Eq. (1), ni,j represents the occurrence number of ti in j, ns,j is the mean of the frequency of ti in different texts and [D] is the total number of Chinese texts in one class. According to traditional TF-IDF weight algorithm and combining inter-class uniformity raised in the paper, the improved TF-IDF weight algorithm is put forward.

$$(ti,j)= W_{i,j} \times(1 - DIDC(ti)). \tag{2}$$

In Eq.(2), DIDC is the inter-class uniformity obtained from Eq. (1) and ω(ti,j) is the final weight of ti. When the obtained web text data is represented by feature factor, every feature will get a corresponding weight and the feature item of keywords with high weight can well represent relevant theme information of the text. We store the text data with similar themes in one data set.

3. Distributed Hybrid Index Model

The paper first applies prejudgment-based classification model to web text data, then operates web text data on Map/Reduce[7] distributed model, rapidly classifies text data and stores results at different nodes of hadoop.

The paper tries to build suffix array and reverse index-based hybrid index storage mechanism for every class of data by combining the features of suffix array including supporting phrase query, improving the adaptability to the language with uncertain boundaries and providing self-index function, and the feature of reverse index including inverted list beneficial to sorting query results.

Phrase query results of suffix array index are mapped into an interval in suffix array and every value in the interval of the array marks thee positions of queried word in text set, so the reverse index based on queried word can be built on the interval to store the inverted list.

3.1. *Correlating reverse index*

How to obtain the corresponding inverted list of the interval after suffix array-based query and obtaining result interval, is the key problem the paper needs to solve. Generally, the problem is about how to determine a position in one interval to convert interval and inverted list problem into point to point problems. The corresponding inverted list can be obtained after getting the query result interval of suffix array[8], if the determined only position in interval and the pointer of inverted list are correlated. The paper uses the longest common prefix array to solve the mapping relation between interval and inverted list.

Theorem 3.1. Suffix array interval SA and its corresponding LCPA are provided. The least value in LCPA with the first element excluded is the LCPA of all character strings in the suffix array interval.

Hybrid index model raised in the paper stores the corresponding inverted list index of suffix array query results at the corresponding position of the least value except for the first element in the corresponding longest common prefix array interval of the results interval of the suffix array.

Proof. The query result intervals A and B of query words p and q in suffix array are provided and A is the subinterval of B. Assume the longest common prefixes of A and B are P and Q, |P|>|Q|. Therefore, the corresponding least values of intervals A and B in the longest common prefix are different.□

In conclusion, the query result intervals of different prefix arrays won't be mapped into the same position.

3.2. *Map/Reduce hybrid index model*

Another difficult is how to build distributed hybrid index mechanism for every class. Map/Reduce[7] is a kind of programming model related to the achievement of handling and producing massive data sets. Traditional indexing technologies can be improved by taking advantages of hadoop-based Map/Reduce distributed computing performance.

Through the analysis of the flows of every class building distributed hybrid index that we can take advantage of Map/Reduce distributed computing model to improve efficiency at the three core points including suffix array building, query interval determination and query interval correlating reverse index. The first Map/Reduce procedure calculates suffix array SA in the current class based on all suffixes of web texts of every class as input data; the second Map/Reduce procedure calculates which intervals are applicable to correlating reverse index based on the output data of previous Map/Reduce as input data; the third Map/Reduce procedure calculates longest common prefix array and correlates reverse index based on the query interval of the previous output as input. The details about Map/Reduce distributed hybrid index model are shown in Fig.2.

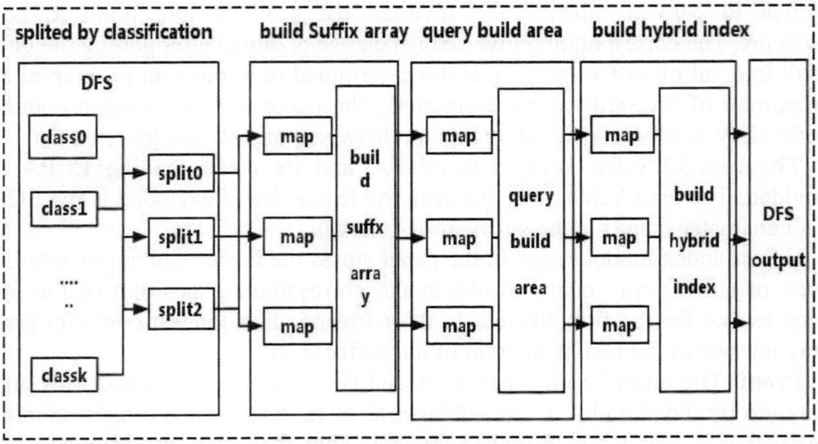

Fig.2. Distributed hybrid index model

4. Experiment and Results Analysis

Experiment environment: The experiment adopts Hadoop-0.22.0 version to build a Hadoop colony experiment platform. The configuration of every Hadoop node is as follows: Inter(R) Pentium(R) D CPU 3.4GHz 4G RAM.100000 text data is obtained through micro blog as the data set TextData of the experiment.

The analysis of classification performance: The experiment will conduct experiment classification comparison to traditional TF-IDF classification algorithm and the improved TF-IDF algorithm in the above text. Three classes of experiment data is chose according to micro blog text and experiment is conducted by taking advantage of the text data obtained after the preprocessing of those data. The effect are shown as Table 1 and Table 2.

Table 1 Classification effects figure of traditional TF-IDF

	Education	Amusement	Health
Number of texts	250	250	250
Classification texts	176	157	208
Classification accuracy	70.4%	62.8%	83.2%
Search accuracy	63.3%	65.4%	81.5%

Table 2 The classification effects figure of the improved TF-IDF algorithm

	Education	Amusement	Health
Number of texts	250	250	250
Classification texts	193	167	208
Classification accuracy	77.2%	69.6%	90.8%
Search accuracy	69.7%	70.4%	83.4%

The above experiment data and results show that the improved TF-IDF algorithm has obvious effects improvement in the accuracy of text classification and also improve search accuracy.

Index performance analysis: Experiment data are divided into six types, namely education, amusement, science and technology, health, gymnastics and tourism. Map/Reduce-based parallel model builds hybrid index for every class. Fig.3 compares the different efficiency of queried words with different lengths based on the benchmark of the number of queried results of 30. It appears from experiment results that the query time is better with the increase of length of queried words. And Fig.4 obtains the query time of Top-k under the precondition of comparing the length of queried words. It can be seen from results that hybrid index is slightly superior to reverse index mechanism when the length of queried words is 5, which indicates that hybrid index supports the query of the languages with uncertain word boundaries and reserves the features of reverse index supporting sorting query results.

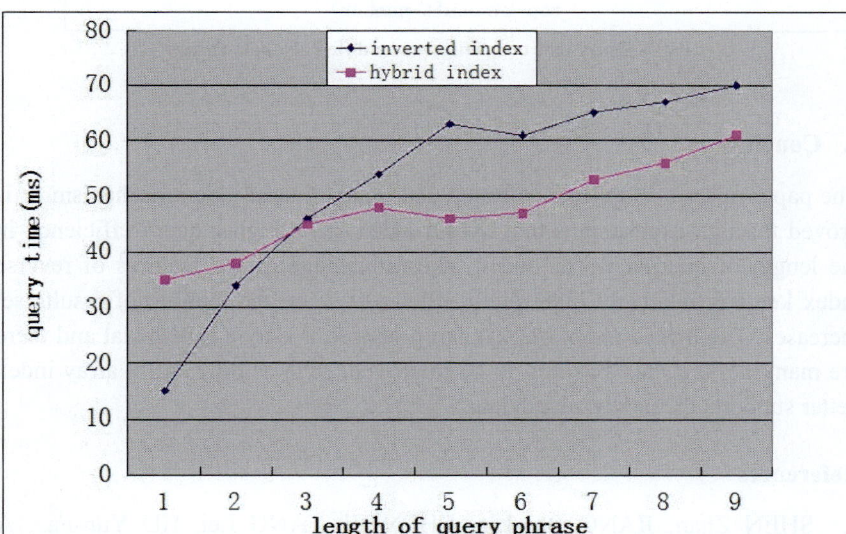

Fig. 3. Query time comparison under different lengths of queried words

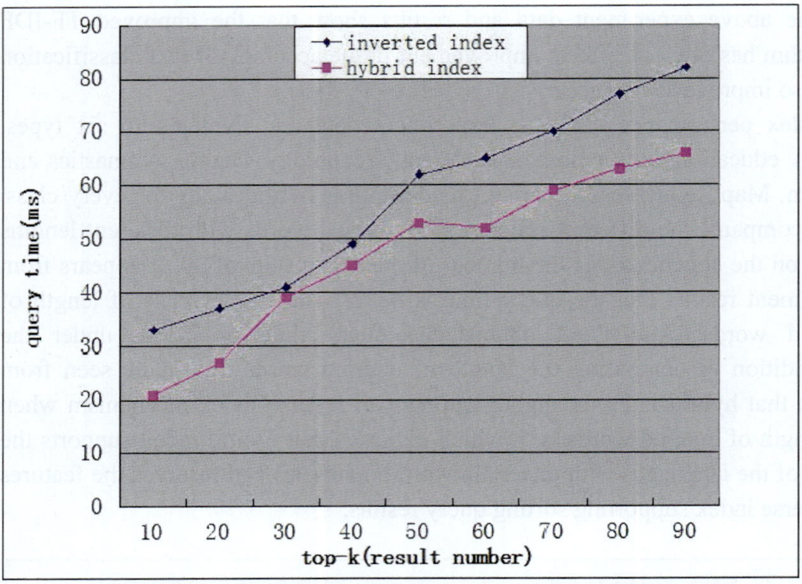

Fig. 4. Query time comparison under different top-k numbers

5. Conclusions

The paper raises a Map/Reduce-based distributed hybrid index mechanism. It is proved through experiments that hybrid index has a higher query efficiency in the length of queried words and it takes advantage of the features of reverse index keeping relatively high query efficiency when the number of results set increases. The hybrid index mechanism proposed is only a initial trial and there are many deficiencies awaiting to be improved, such as how suffix array index better supports the newly added data.

References

1. SHEN Zhan, JIANG Bao-Lin, CHEN Yi, TANG Lei, HU Yun-Fa. A Survey on Full-Text Index Model[J]. Computer Science. 2004(05).
2. Liu Xing Yu. A Research of Full-Text Retrieval Based on Inverted Index[D].Huazhong University of Science and Technology,2004.
3. HE Meng, MUNRO J I,RAO S S.A Categorization Theorem on Suffix Arrays with Applications to Space Efficient Text Inde-xes. SIAM Symposium on Discrete Algorithms (SODA) . 2005.
4. Wikipedia. http://zh.wikipedia.org/wiki/MapReduce.

5. Zhang H P, Yu H K, Xiong D Y. HHMM-based Chinese lexical analyzer ICTCLAS[A]. Proceedings of the second SIGHAN workshop on Chinese language processing Volume 17,2003[C]. Sapporo, Japan: Association for Computational Linguistics, 2003:184-187.
6. Li Hai-rong. Semantic classification model of documents based on concept vector space. Library and information service, 2011, 55(24):106-111.
7. Dean J.Ghemawat S.MapReduce: simplified data processing on large clusters [J].Communication of the ACM ,2008,51(1):107-113.
8. Zhang Xijuan. Approximate String Matching based on suffrix Array[D].Xi'an Electronic and Science University,2012.

Rapid Abnormal Identification in Big Earthquake Data Based on Parallel SURF Algorithm

Zhen-xiang LI, Wei-xin ZHANG and Jing-jing YAN
Tianjin Electric Power Research Institute
Tianjin, 300000, China

Jin-shuo LIU† and Ya-bo XU
†*Email: liujinshuo@whu.edu.cn*
School of computer, Wuhan University,
Wuhan, 430072, China

This paper proposes a method to rapidly identify abnormalities in the big data of the seismic wave signal based on SURF algorithm with Hadoop cluster. The model matches the earthquake precursors waveform data images of earthquake monitor stations with the historical earthquake templates one by one, to rapidly determine whether similar changes in the past exist. The experimental results demonstrated that in comparisons to the conventional seismic data abnormalities detection method of wavelet transform, the improved SURF algorithm is 12% better in scales, and has a 13% improvement in matching results. The SURF feature matching algorithm based on Hadoop clusters meets the requirement of the storage and parallel processing of the massive earthquake data, and improves the abnormal identification efficiency of the big earthquake data.

Keywords: SURF algorithm; Big earthquake data; Abnormal identification.

1. Introduction

With the frequent occurrence of earthquakes, accurate earthquake prediction allows people to take effective preventive measures as well as to reduce the loss of property and life. The occurrence mechanism and forming process of earthquakes are complicated and diversified. Generally, the acquirement of seismic trend judgments and assessments involves the extraction of commonality and precursory abnormal messages from big data. Recently, the combination of seismology and information technology, has greatly promoted the earthquake rapid response and long-term earthquake prediction research. By using Big Data Fast Matching Technology[1] , the earthquake source parameters could be obtained without calculating the synthesis of seismic waveform, thus

† Correspondence author.

providing a new efficient algorithm for the earthquake early forecast and rapid response.

At present, plenty of research for time serial of earthquake are mainly using various pretreatment methods such as Principal Component Analysis (PCA)[2] ,Fourier transform[3], Wavelet transform (WT)[4] to get stable characteristic sequence of seismic data, and using data mining such as Neural Network[5] and Support Vector Machines[6] to predict earthquake. The Time Series Similar Pattern Matching Based on Wavelet Transform[7] is used to obtain main characteristics of data by wavelet transforming for time series, and organize it into multi-dimensional index structure R*Tree, but it doesn't combine the different scales of details into the matching algorithm.

However, so far the methods have the disadvantages that calculate slowly which not satisfy the time request. Our model of seismic data abnormally detection by SURF algorithm based on Hadoop, can quickly process the streaming data [8] collected by earthquake sensor from each observation station, which sampling frequency is every one second. Firstly, preprocess the seismic precursor data, eliminating some noise and error data, and draw the seismic wave image as the input of the algorithm with the digital image processing method. Next, call the SURF algorithm based on Hadoop platform to extract and match the stability of seismic data sequence. Then, judge the matching results according to the similarity measure function.

The first part of this paper introduces the relevant research of seismic precursor anomaly data identification. The method of seismic data abnormally recognition using SURF algorithm is discussed in section 3. Section 4 shows the comparison with the efficiency of the single machine and the cluster of seismic anomaly data, and the comparison of the improved SURF algorithm with the original SURF algorithm and the wavelet transform method. The summary of this paper is given in section 5.

2. Method for Identifying Seismic Data

2.1. *The basic flowchart of the model*

The specific flow of seismic data based on Hadoop cluster is shown in Figure 1.When program starts, master server node in Hadoop call a specific program to read the earthquake waveform image and detecting seismic waveform image from HDFS[12,13] file system, then divides the seismic wave image into several data slices and store the earthquake waveform image in the HDFS global shared cache. After that, all the nodes in the Hadoop cluster can read earthquake waveform image for waveform comparison. The master server node creates a number of Map tasks and assigns them to slave node of the cluster for running according to the number of data slicing.

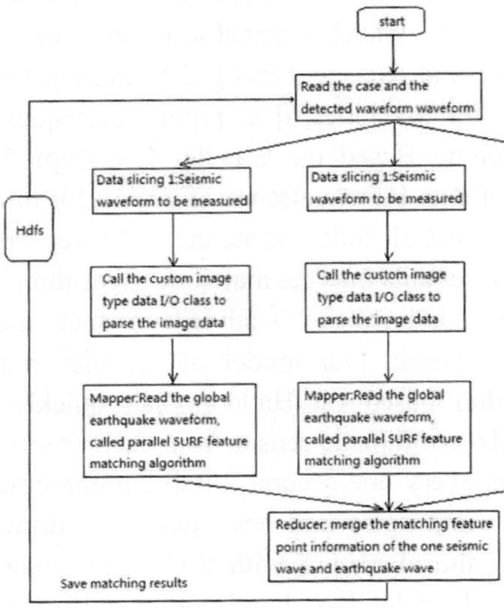

Fig 1 Process of seismic data anomaly recognition based on Clustering

Each slave node first reads data from a data slice, then uses the custom image type data I/O class (Hadoop does not support image data types) to parse seismic data, and transforms the seismic data into key-value pairs< The name of the seismic wave image to be measured, Seismic waveform image >. Then call the Map function defined in advance to process it. The main function of Map is to extract and match the earthquake waveform image and the measured seismic waveform image feature point by executing parallel SURF feature matching algorithm. The final output is the key-value pairs. The function of Reduce is to stipulate the output value of Map function, merge the matching feature point information of the one seismic wave and earthquake wave, and store the result of key-value pairs in the HDFS file system.

2.2. *SURF for abnormal extraction*

Assuming the input time series A, B. SURF is used to extract and match A and B for obtaining feature sequence F1, F2. F1 and F2:

$$F1 = \{f1i, f1j, \ldots f1k, f1l\}$$

$$F2 = \{f2m, f2n, \ldots f2s, f2t\}$$

The f1p (p = i, j, …, k, l) belongs to the feature points of A, and f2p (p = m, n, …, s, t) belongs to the feature points of B. The every two points match in F1 and F2: f1i matches f2m, f1j matches f2n, etc.

Assume that the matching feature points in the F1 are arranged in a sequence of coordinates, and F1' = { f1i, f1j, ... f1k, f1l }. The feature points in the F2 are sorted according to the position of F1, and generate sequence F2' = { f2m, f2n,... f2s, f2t }. In case of i<j<...<k<1 the coordinates of the feature points in F2 should also meet the following relation: m<n<...<s<t. If the coordinates of the feature points are not satisfied with the order, the matching feature points should be deleted. In order to achieve the better removal effect of the screen, it's necessary to dynamically deleted the feature points which is no qualified during comparing the coordinates of the feature points in F2.

3. Experimental Results

The data of earthquake used in experiment 1 is the seismic precursor data collected by each observation stations from 6am. March 21st, 2008 to 2pm. May 13th 2008 in Sichuan province, with generation 100 precursor waveform data per hour. The data to be used is the seismic precursor data collected at Ya'an station with professional metal position shift in Sichuan province from May 15th, 2013 to May 12th, 2008. Test data is divided into the following three groups: 100, 200 and 300 seismic waveform images generated via the precursor data that sampled at one hour intervals during the 30 days before the earthquake. Table 4 lists the experimental data and the various properties of experimental data to be measured: precursor data sampling window, sampling frequency and number of seismic wave series. The precursor data sampling window is the time span of the sampling window to the seismic moment. The number of seismic wave images is the number of the input seismic waveforms, as shown in table fourth 4 lines, the 100 seismic waveforms in the second group is sampled with the frequency of once per hour during the 30 days before earthquake.

Table 1 Comparison of seismic waveform recognition efficiency between single machine SURF algorithm and SURF algorithm

	Single SURF	Cluster SURF	Single SURF	Cluster SURF	Single SURF	Cluster SURF
Experimental data	Group 1 and examples		Group 2 and examples		Group 3 and examples	
Time of feature points matching(h)	27.7	23.1	55.6	39.7	83.3	52.1
speedup	1.2		1.4		1.6	

(1) Efficiency verification

The single serial SURF algorithm and parallel SURF algorithm for Hadoop cluster are used respectively in experiment 1 for feature extraction, and match for the seismic wave image to be measured in the above three groups and the earthquake wave image as well as to dispose experimental data for two methods. Table 1 compares the efficiency of the two methods in the seismic waveform feature matching. TSpeedup respectively shows the run-time proportion of matching the test data in the above three groups and earthquake waveform image with single and cluster of the surf algorithm. In the first three columns, single SURF algorithm compared to the first set of experimental data and earthquake data, which single serial surf algorithm matching time is 27.7 hours while the matching time of cluster parallel SURF algorithm is 23.1 hours. Both the speedup are 1.2.

Table 1 shows the efficiency of the SURF feature matching algorithm in the single node and the cluster with different numbers of seismic waveforms. It can be known from the experimental data that with the increase of the number of seismic waveform images, the amount of data grow increases, both the matching time of single serial SURF algorithm and cluster SURD algorithm become longer. The improvement of operational efficiency between the cluster SURF algorithm and single SUGR algorithm is not obvious when the data is small. It's because cluster needs a certain time to startup, which is accounts for a large proportion of the overall operating time. When the cluster is running, the data transmission between the master node and slave node cost some time. However, because of the proportion of starting time in operating time decreases, the performance of the algorithm is increased with the enlargement of data and algorithm running time increases.

Comparison between SURF algorithm and wavelet transform method

The SURF algorithm and feature extraction method based on Wavelet Transform is used respectively to pairwise match the 10 precursor abnormal waveform sampled with the frequency of once per hour, 30 days before the earthquake in Qingchuan County, Sichuan province. The experimental seismic waveforms are shown in Figure 6. Each waveform image is named according to the sampling time, for instance, the first image named 20070929230000 indicates that it was sampled at 23 of September 29th 2007. Both of those algorithms utilize Euclidean-distance device to measure the similarity of waveform. The matching result of the similar waveform (α = 0.5) is shown in Table 2.

Table 2 results of pairwise matching of the 10 waveform

	Times of waveform matching	Number of waveform matching	Matching rate
Improved SURF algorithm	90	8	8.8%
Wavelet transform	90	6	6.7%

The SURF feature matching algorithm based on Hadoop cluster meets the demand of storing mass seismic data and processing in parallel as well as improving the anomaly recognition efficiency of seismic data benefiting from the powerful function of parallel Hadoop cluster. The improved SURF algorithm solves the problem of original SURG algorithm occurring mismatched feature points in the earthquake waveform matching. It optimizes the processing of scale details and is able to extract the stability of multi scale seismic waveforms, which resolves the lack of scale aspect in wavelet transform algorithm as well as improving the accuracy of seismic data.

4. Conclusion

The anomaly recognition method of seismic data by means of SURF algorithm based on Hadoop platform can not only rapidly extract and match the sass seismic data, but also improve forecasting efficiency. It extracts the multi scale stability of time series by multi scaling property. It is suitable for the matching of different sampling frequency and sampling window size, making applicability more extensive. This algorithm is capable of extracting the time series of stable features and matching quickly with faster speed, and meet the requirements of the big data of earthquake field.

Acknowledgments

This work is supported by National Science Foundation of China 61303214.

References

1. J. Zhang, H. Zhang, E. Chen, et al. Real-time earthquake monitoring using a search engine method.[J]. *Nature Communications*, 2014, 5.
2. L. Chen, C. Y. Zhang. Application of Integrated Comprehensive Evaluation in Earthquake disaster Based on Principal Component Analysis (PCA) and Efficacy Coefficient[J]. *Journal of Kunming College of Metallurgy*, 2012, 28(1): 77-82.

3. Y. Shi, Z. Zhang, J. M. Wang, et al. Investigation on anti-aliasing regularization approach for seismic data[j]. *Progress in geophysics*, 2013, 1: 025.
4. H. L. Li, C. H. Guo. Survey of feature representations and similarity measurements in time series data minig[j].*Application Research of Computers*, 2013, 30(5): 1285-1291.
5. H. G. Ruan, Tan Y H, Lu M M, et al. Particle Swarm Optimization Algorithm of Neural Network and Its Application in Earthquake Prediction[j]. *Computer & Digital Engineering,* 2013, 41(2): 155-157.
6. C. K. Zhang, X. D. Jiang, Z. Y, Zhu et al. Seismic Reservior Discrimination and Attribute selection based on Support Vector Machines. *Oil Geophysical Prospecting*, 2012, 47(002): 282-285.
7. H. Q. Zhang, Q. S. Cai. Time Series Similar Pattern Matching Based on Wavelet Transform[j]. *Chinese Journal of Computers*, 2003, 26(3): 373-377.
8. Z. Hua, L. Wei, J. Q. ianfeng, et a1. An Earthquake Prediction Research Based on Time Series Similarity Matching Algorithm[J]. *Journal of Beijing Electronic Science and Technology Institute,* 2010, 18(2):4 9.
9. C. Yong, D. C. Booth. Prediction efforts prior to the Wenchuan earthquake[M]//*The Wenchuan Earthquake* of 2008. Springer Berlin Heidelberg, 2012: 122-159.
10. H. Bay, T. Tuytelaars, V. L. Gool. SURF: Speeded Up Robust Features: *Proc of European Conference on Computer Vision* , 2006[C]. Austria: Graz , 2006:404-417.
11. H.Bay, A.Ess, V. L.Gool. Speeded Up Robust Features (SURF)[J]. *Computer Vision and Image Understanding*. 2008,110(3):346-359.
12. K. Shvachko, H. Kuang, S. Radia, et al. 2010.The Hadoop distributed file system[J]. IEEE *Symposium on Mass Storage Systems & Technologies*, : 1-10.
13. R. C. Taylor 2010.An overview of the Hadoop/Map/Reduce/HBase framework and its current applications in bioinformatics[J]. *Bmc Bioinformatics*, 11:S1(6): 3395-3407.

tr-HMM: A Recovery Approach of Chinese Abbreviations

Jin-shuo LIU[a], Ya-bo XU[b], Juan DENG[c] and Lina WANG[d]

Computer School, Wuhan University,
Wuhan, 430079, China
E-mail: [a]sureliu@163.com.com, [b]yaboxu@whu.edu.cn,
[c]dengjuan@whu.edu.cn, [d]lnawang@163.com

Chinese abbreviations have been widely used in modern Chinese, and are one of the main sources of unknown words, resulting in the difficulty for correct Chinese character processing. This paper proposes a new approach called tr-HMM (Time Relaxed Hidden Markov Model) to recover Chinese abbreviations to their root words. The tr-HMM is a transformation of HMM, which we have devised as the basic recovery strategy. It firstly considers the abbreviation as the output sequence, and the corresponding root word as the hidden sequence. Subsequently, thetr-HMMrelaxes the time invariant hypothesis in HMM, and extends itself to a non-stationary HMM by making utilizing the time information. Lastly, we utilize the ten folds ten rounds method to prove that the tr-HMM is more eff-ecttive than traditional recovery methods for the Chinese abbreviation recovery problem. The precision of the tr-HMM abbreviation recovery was demonstrated to be 84.3%.

Keywords: tr-HMM, Non-stationary HMM, Chinese Abbreviation Recovery, HMM.

1. Introduction

Chinese abbreviations are commonly used in modern Chinese language, which is even getting more and more highly abbreviated. The abbreviated forms are used almost everywhere in the current Chinese articles, in some of which the proportion of the sentences that contain suspect abbreviated words reaches as high as 20%. The mixed uses of ancient single character words, modern multi-character words, and compound words or other kinds of abbreviations, trouble the correctly Chinese process and comprehension. The recovery of Chinese abbreviations to their root words is very necessary, especially in the field of statistics and information retrieval, since people always tend to prefer abbreviations instead of root words due to their conciseness. For instance, a keyword-based statistical system or information retrieval system may require the two forms, such as 'GuoShiYaoJianJu' (Abbreviation of State food and drug

[b] Corresponding author.

administration) and 'GuoJiaShiPinYaoPinJianDuGuanLiJu' (means State food and drug administration), in order to guarantee the accuracy of the statistical work and not to miss any relevant documents.

Inspired from the pinyin-to-character process of Chinese language, we devise the model tr-HMM. The model proposes the abbreviation recovery problem similar with the pinyin-to-character problem. To convert pinyin to character, firstly note that the most common action for most Chinese that would be taken when encountering a pinyin is to find its candidate character. This problem can be overcome by using an HMM model, since HMM is good at finding the best unseen state sequence. Based on the theory above, experiments have been carried out to verify its correctness [1]. Similarly, it's observed that the recovery of the Chinese abbreviations is very similar with the pinyin-to-character conversion. If the observed abbreviation is regarded as 'observation sequence', and the corresponding unseen root word is regarded as the underlying 'state sequence', then HMM can be used for the Chinese abbreviation recovery problem. Therefore, the Chinese abbreviation recovery problem can be solved by the method based on HMM.

Section 2 will present some related works as well as the three basic HMM problems related with the abbreviation problem. Section 3 will describe the tr-HMM model and show the expansion that is made by tr-HMM aiming at improving the recovery accuracy. Section 4 will show the experiment setup and examine the experiment to predict root words from abbreviations.

2. Related Work

Currently, there are many approaches to the recovery of Chinese abbreviations. However, most of them have numerous limitations. At present, there are two research line for this problem. The first research line is to build an abbreviation dictionary and search through it to find out corresponding original phrases of the abbreviations. In this method, it's important to construct a Chinese abbreviation knowledge database, and restore the abbreviations based on it. Bao [2] uses the ripe relational database to describe the relationship between the abbreviation of new words in modern Chinese and its relevant features. Zhi [3] advances the classification frame of Chinese abbreviations facing to information processing and accomplishes classifying a great quantity of abbreviations. Besides, Wu [4] realizes an automatic identification of modern Chinese abbreviation and automatically produces the abbreviation dictionary using cosine similarity.

The second research line is to predict the original phrase through the analysis of abbreviations according to the constitute laws, such as the abbreviated manners and constituent features, and so on. Chang [5] regards the Chinese abbreviation recovery problem as an error recovery problem, in which he uses some self-defined patterns to help the recovery. Chang [6] also proposed a single character recovery (SCR) model based on the model described above for Chinese abbreviation recovery. Xie [7] applies a heuristic algorithm to extract suspect abbreviation-root pairs, and uses filtering rules concluded from actual observations and Chinese word segmentation techniques to classify the suspect pairs into candidate patterns, and finally restores the abbreviations based on the previous work.

Most of these methods under the traditional research lines have relatively stable precision. However, with the generation of more and more new abbreviations, the dictionary needs to be expanded constantly, and the old laws may be no longer applicable to the new generated abbreviations, making the traditional methods poor in terms of timeliness performance. Moreover, the abbreviations in different fields have different features, so it's better to treat them differently in different fields.

3. Our Model: tr-HMM

The tr-HMM model is a HMM-based model for Chinese abbreviation recovery. Using HMM as the basic recovery strategy, tr-HMM also extends HMM to improve the recovery precision. The framework of tr-HMM is shown as Fig. 1.

The framework of tr-HMM can be divided into three steps: 1) The extraction of abbreviations from training corpus. 2) The preprocess of the abbreviation collection to annotate the time information 3) The training of the model.

Firstly, the collection of observed sequence is needed for the training of the model, therefore a collection of Chinese abbreviation should be extracted from the training corpus. The selected training corpus shouldn't be the corpus just contains formal or official articles and texts, such as People's Daily corpus, for it seems to be difficult to find Chinese abbreviations in this kind of corpus. Moreover, the extraction method should be enabled to extract abbreviations accurately, because the extraction result has a direct impact on the training process. Secondly, as described in step 1), the collected abbreviations will be preprocessed to mark their time information. Program is designed to implement the automatic time information annotation. Thirdly, tr-HMM utilizes HMM model as its basic recovery strategy. tr-HMM relaxes the time invariant hypothesis in HMM, making itself a non-stationary HMM. The training method of tr-HMM is similar with the method of HMM, except that tr-HMM utilizes the time information annotated in step 2) in the training process.

After the three previous steps, tr-HMM can be used to recover the input abbreviations into their root words.

3.1. *Basic recovery model*

In order to describe the recovery model with more details, firstly the recovery process can be regarded as trying to find the best underlying word $\omega_u^m = \omega_1, \omega_2, \ldots, \omega_m$ (which is the root form of the abbreviation), given the surface or observable string of characters $\varepsilon_u^m = \varepsilon_1, \varepsilon_2, \ldots, \varepsilon_m$ (which is the abbreviated form). The recovery process is then equivalent to finding the best word ω_u^*:

$$
\begin{aligned}
\omega_u^* &= \underset{\omega_u^m:\omega_u^m \Rightarrow \varepsilon_u^m}{\arg\max} P(\omega_u^m \mid \varepsilon_u^n) \\
&\cong \underset{\omega_u^m:\omega_u^m \Rightarrow \varepsilon_u^m}{\arg\max} P(\varepsilon_u^n \mid \omega_u^m) \times P(\omega_u^m) \qquad (1) \\
&\cong \underset{\omega_u^m:\omega_u^m \Rightarrow \varepsilon_u^m}{\arg\max} \prod_{i==1\ldots m,\omega_u^m \Rightarrow \varepsilon_u^m} P(\varepsilon_i^* \mid \omega_i^m) \times P(\omega_i \mid \omega_{i-1})
\end{aligned}
$$

In Eq. (1) ε_i^* refers to the surface form, or observable form of ω_i. It always could be the abbreviated form of ω_i. However, it can also refers to the unabbreviated form of the surface form. It's worth noting that this equation is equivalent to the formulation for a HMM to find the best 'state' sequence given the observation symbols. The parameters $P(\varepsilon_i^* \mid \omega_i^m)$ and $P(\omega_i \mid \omega_{i-1})$ represent the output probability and transition probability, respectively. The formulations for $P(\varepsilon_u^n \mid \omega_u^m)$ and $P(\omega_u^m)$ are the respective generation model for the abbreviated word and the language model of the Chinese abbreviations. The analogy provides an approach which uses HMM to solve the abbreviation recovery problem. Besides, the model parameters can be estimated by using an unsupervised training method, which can be directly ported from the Baum-Welch re-estimation formula, such as the generic EM algorithm.

3.2. *Extension on HMM made by tr-HMM*

It's worth noting that most of the abbreviation units of an abbreviation have a clear position feature. For instance, if the abbreviation unit 'Guo' (Abbreviation of National) appears at the head of an abbreviation, such as 'GuoZu' (Abbreviation of National Football Team), 'GuoYu' (Abbreviation of Chinese Language), then it is very likely to be the abbreviated form of the root word 'GuoJia' (means National), instead of 'GuoJi' (means international), 'GuoMin' (means Citizens), or other else. These examples indicate that such position information, namely the time information of the random process, has a big influence on the transition probability and the generation probability. Therefore, time information should not be ignored, but should be used to improve the precision of the model.

Integrating these time information into the transition probability and the generation probability is important and hard. It is unreasonable to simply use the position index to generate a direct impact on the probability, since different abbreviations have different lengths. So this study adopts the ratio of the position index and the length of the abbreviation as the measurement of the position information. Two kinds of position information are calculated in the preprocess of the abbreviation collection. The first is the position information of abbreviation units. The other is the position information of each two hidden states, or root words of the abbreviation units

In the training set, the middling position of s_i and s_j reflects their average position in the Markov process. The closer the value of ω_{ij} gets to its average value in the training set, the more likely that this transition should occur. Otherwise, this transition is more unreasonable. This makes sense in generation probability. Variance is also used in the transition probability. The transition function is redefined as Eq. (2).

$$T(s_i, \varepsilon_i, t_{s_i \varepsilon_i}) = e^{\sqrt{V(\omega_{ij})/\omega_{ij} - E(\omega_{ij})}} \times T^*(s_i, s_j) \qquad (2)$$

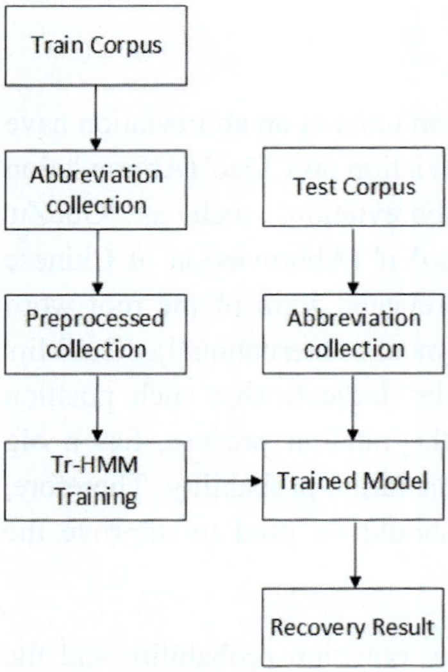

Fig. 1. The framework of tr-HMM

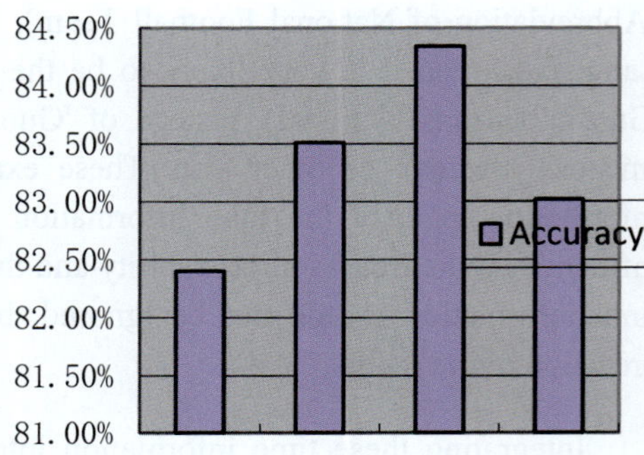

Fig. 2. Comparison among models using different m

4. Experiments and Analysis

In this study, Chinese abbreviations are extracted from the query log and anchor text using Xie's extraction method[7]. Both the query log (1.56GB) and the anchor text (43.1MB) are provided by Sougou laboratory in Beijing, China. Through Xie's extraction method, 8,564 Chinese abbreviations are extracted from the corpus. Among these Chinese abbreviations, 7,364 Chinese abbreviations are randomly selected as the training set and 1200 of them are used as the test set. Moreover, this study selects the 6,873 Chinese characters that are most commonly used as the standard output states table of tr-HMM, and 59,071 Chinese words and characters as the standard hidden states table of tr-HMM. The accuracy is state of the art, which reaches 84.3%.

Since the number of intervals *m* can affect the recovery precision, another experiment is conducted to compare the precision of tr-HMM that using different m. In this study, the value of m is set to 2, 3, 4, and 5 respectively. The experiment result is presented in Fig. 2.

5. Conclusion

Lacking the standardization of the Internet vocabulary, especially the using of Chinese abbreviations, makes supervising the internet public opinion become very difficult. As a special form of unknown words and named entities, Chinese abbreviations are widely used in the modern Chinese texts, resulting difficulties in many aspects of content security. In this preliminary study, the Chinese abbreviation recovery problem is resolved by using the proposed tr-HMM model. tr-HMM is a HMM-based model. Moreover, it relaxes the time invariant hypothesis in HMM, and extends itself to a non-stationary HMM by making enough use of the time information.

With the proposed model, The recovery precision for Chinese abbreviations reaches about 84.3 percent. Although further improvement is expected, the results of this preliminary study are encouraging. It's believed that with a bigger training corpus and model optimization, the result will become better.

Our study of the Chinese abbreviations is just beginning. In the near future, the research of interval mapping for tr-HMM is planned, and a new method to collect Chinese abbreviations will also be explored. These researches should improve the recovery result of tr-HMM. It is expected that more applications will rely on this model for Chinese abbreviation recovery.

Acknowledgments

This work was supported by the National Natural Science Foundation of China (Grant No61303214 and No61303025).

References

1. Xiao Jinghui, & Liu Bingquan. (2005, July). A Non-stationary Hidden Markov Model and its Application on Pinyin-to-character Conversion. Paper presented at the meeting of the 8th Joint Conference on Computational Linguistics, Nanjing, China.

2. Bao Mingling, Kang Shiyong. (2002). *Research on the New Clipped word Based on the Corpus*. Paper presented at the proceeding of SWCL-2002, Beijing, China.

3. Zhi Liu, Zhu Xuefeng, Duan Huiming, & Yu Shiwen. (2006, January). Construction of Chinese Abbreviation Language Knowledge-base. Paper presented at the meeting of the 3rd Seminar on Student Computational Linguistics, Beijing, China.

4. Wu Ziying. (2007). Research methods about automatic identification of modern Chinese abbreviation. Journal of Xinzhou Teachers University.

5. Chang, J. S., & Lai, Y. T. (2004). A preliminary study on probabilistic models for chinese abbreviations. Proceedings of the Third Sighan Workshop on Chinese Language Learning, 9--16.

6. Chang, J. S., & Teng, W. L. (2006). Mining atomic Chinese abbreviations with a probabilistic single character recovery model. Language Resources & Evaluation, 40(3-4), 367-374.

7. Xie Lixing, Sun Maosong, Tong Zijian, & Wang Canhui. (2009). Identification of Chinese Abbreviations using Query Log and Anchor Text. Chinese Computational Linguistics Research Frontiers.

Privacy-Preserving Multi-Keyword Fuzzy Search over Outsourced Encrypted Cloud Data

Xiu-jin SHI† and Ling-zhen YANG

School of Computer Science ,Donghua University ,
Shanghai, 201620, China
†*E-mail:* sxj@dhu.edu.cn

With the rapid development of the e-business, social networking and enterprise information system, the volume of data produced by individuals and enterprises is increasing rapidly, resulting in a rise of cloud storage as an increasing number of enterprises and individuals store their data in the cloud for greater flexibility and economic savings. However the risk of leakage of sensitive user data is still prevalent. Although several keyword search schemes over encrypted data with privacy preserving has been previously proposed, we propose a novel scheme to support the multi-keywords fuzzy search while also supporting Chinese search. We utilize the locality-sensitive hashing technique to solve the fuzzy match and the experiments on real-world data demonstrate that our proposed scheme is accurate, efficient and secure.

Keywords: Cloud computing; Cloud storage; Privacy-preserving; Fuzzy search; Locality-sensitive-hashing

1. Introduction

With the rapid development of the e-business, social networking and enterprise information system, the amount of data produced by individuals and enterprises is increasing heavily. Local storage for individuals and enterprises to use is more and more limited, moreover, once the hardware of local storage doesn't work that may result in the loss of important documents, even lead to the irreparable consequences. As the power of cloud computing became prevalent in the recent years, its easy management, low cost and pay-as-you-use features make the mass of people to outsource their local files into the cloud. Data Security is a matter of public concern and especially when cloud storage service is used . The Infamous data breach incidents occur from time to time, such as the Sony PlayStation privacy leakage. Sony PlayStation data breach was not only a threat to the it's more than 100 million users' personal data, but also made a negative impact on cloud computing, so some enterprises began to rethink cloud computing plans.

Encryption is the most effective way to achieve data confidentiality which also makes effective data utilization a very challenging task. For example, in order to retrieve some relevant documents amongst an encrypted data set stored in the cloud, one may have to download and decrypt all the documents. This is obviously impractical especially when the data volume is very large.
Keyword-based search technique which applied in encrypted scheme has made a lot of significant work in the domestic and overseas. But these works only supported the exactly search of Multi-keywords[1,2] or the fuzzy search of single keyword[3].To date, multi-keyword fuzzy search over encrypted data have acquired some achievements[4,5].In this paper, we propose a novel scheme to efficiently support multi-keyword fuzzy search. Compared to the existing multi-keyword search schemes, we do not need to build predefined keyword dictionary[6]. Since most of the current study adopt the edit distance algorithm to do the fuzzy search which have to build a predefined dictionary. Moreover, the predefined dictionary should be reconstructed when the data owner want to add new documents to the cloud. But in this paper, we propose a novel scheme which based on locality-sensitive hashing (LSH) [7] and Bloom filters . We needn't to build a predefined dictionary with this new scheme. Therefore, our scheme will achieve high efficiency in computing and storage. In addition, the most prominent feature of this paper is that we provide an effective solution which support Chinese Fuzzy search.

2. System Description

2.1. *System model*

Our system include three kind of roles, as shown in Fig.1:the data owner, the data user and the cloud server. In order to protect data privacy, data owner first encrypt the files, then build a secure searchable index for the files, finally outsource both the files and secure index to the cloud server. To search on the encrypted files, the authorized user first obtained trapdoor from the data owner and then submit the trapdoor to the cloud server. After the Cloud server receiving the trapdoor, a search algorithm is executed on the security index, finally , the matched files are returned to the user as a search result. The overall system architecture of our scheme is shown in Fig.1.

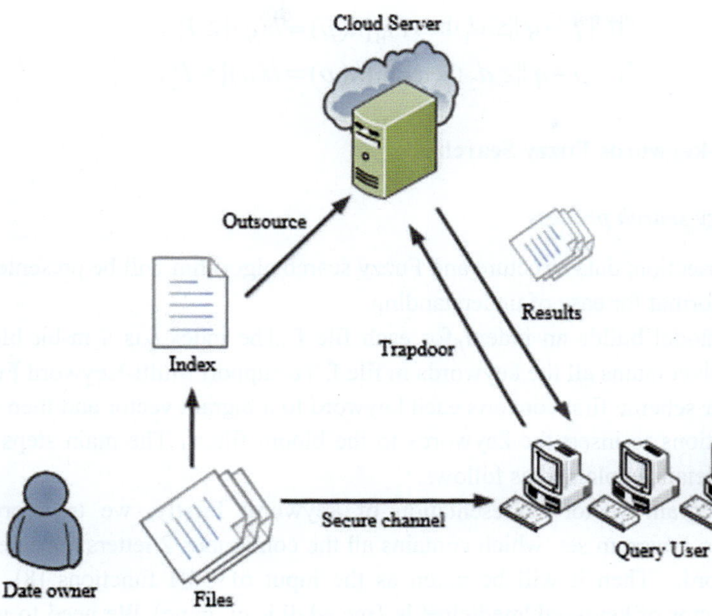

Fig.1:System Model

2.2. *Preliminaries*

There are two important technologies are applied in this paper: Bloom filter and local sensitive hash.

(1) Bloom filter: Bloom filter is a binary vector data structure proposed by Howard Bloom in 1970.It is used to detect whether an element is present in a set. A Bloom filter is an m-bit binary array, initially all set to 0. Then choose k independent hash functions $\mathrm{H}=\{h_i, | 1 \le i \le k\}$,each with range {1,…, m}. Given a set $E=\{e_1, e_2, \ldots e_n\}$, for each element e ∈ E, the bits atpositions $h_1(e), h_2(e), \ldots, h_k(e)$ in the array are set to 1. Given a query for s we check the bits at positions $h_1(s), h_2(s), \ldots, h_k(s)$. If any of them is 0, then certainly s is not in the set E. Otherwise we conjecture that s is in the set although there is a certain probability that we are wrong. This is called a "false positive".

(2)Locality-Sensitive Hashing: LSH is an algorithm for solving the approximate search. Given a distance metric d, such as the Euclidean distance, the LSH function hashes the similar items to the same hash value with high probability. A LSH family $\mathrm{H}=(d_1, d_2, P_1, P_2)$ has the following properties for any p, q ∈ E,as in Eq. (1), (2)

$$\text{if} \parallel p-q \parallel \leq d_1 \text{ then } \Pr_H[h(p)=h(q)] \geq P_1 . \quad (1)$$

$$\text{if} \parallel p-q \parallel \geq d_2 \text{ then } \Pr_H[h(p)=h(q)] \leq P_2 . \quad (2)$$

3. Multi-keywords Fuzzy Search

3.1. *Fuzzy search process*

In this subsection, data structure and Fuzzy search algorithm will be presented in plaintext format for ease of understanding.

Our model builds an index$I_f$for each file f .The index $I_f$is a m-bit bloom filter which contains all the keywords in file f. To support Multi-Keyword Fuzzy search, our scheme first converts each keyword to a bigram vector and then uses LSH functions to insert the keywords to the bloom filterI_f.The main steps and the more details explained as follows.

(1) Bigram vector representation of keyword: Firstly, we transform a keyword to a bigram set, which contains all the contiguous 2 letters appeared in the keyword. Then it will be taken as the input of LSH functions [8]. The bigram vector of keyword 'medicine' is {me,ed,di,ic,ci, in,ne}.We need to use a -bit long vector to represent a bigram set. Each element in the vector represents one of the bigrams. Given a bigram set of one keyword, the element of the vector is set to 1 if the corresponding bigram exists in the bigram set. This bigram set is not sensitive to the position of the misspelled letter. Therefore, a keyword may have many kinds of misspelled shape, but it's vector is still very close to the correct one's.

(2) Bloom filter representation of query/index: As we all known, with the regular hash functions, input two similar keywords even the difference between them is just one letter, but finally they will be mapped to two totally different values. In this paper, we adopt a special kind of hash functions— Locality-Sensitive Hash to build index. LSH function hashes the similar items to the same hash value with high probability. Both the misspelled keyword "medicina" which the data user inputs and the correct one "medicine" will be mapped into the same bucket. Then there will be a success match in the searching process. Hence, the LSH function is the key method to support Fuzzy search.

(3) Inner product of matching algorithm: The finally security index of each file is a bloom filter which contains all the keywords in the file. Firstly, the keyword in the file will be transformed to a bigram set. Then our scheme uses LSH functions to insert the keywords to the bloom filter. Similarly, we can tackle the data user's query in the same way. Our scheme measures the relevance of the query to each file by calculating an inner product between the

index vector and the query vector. If one document contains all the keywords in the user's query, then corresponding bits in the query vector and the index vector will be 1, so the inner product of the match will get a high value.

3.2. *Privacy-Preserving scheme construction*

In this subsection, security and privacy will be introduced in our scheme and symmetric key encryption is used in our scheme [9].

KeyGen(m): Given a parameter m,SK(M_1, M_2, V) will be the security key. Where $M_1, M_2 \in R^{m\times m}$are invertible matrices.

IndexEnc(SK, I):The index I is divided into two vectors$\{I', I''\}$. The process of splitting is as follows:for each $i_k \in I$, if $v_k \in V$ is equal to 1, then set $i'_k = i''_k = i_k$; otherwise, set $i'_k = (1/2)i_k + r$,$i''_k = (1/2)i_k - r$, where r is a random number. Encrypt the index $\{I', I''\}$ into $\{M_1^T \cdot I', M_2^T \cdot I''\}$with$(M_1, M_2)$.Finally,output the security index:$Enc_{SK}(I) = \{M_1^T \cdot I', M_2^T \cdot I''\}$.

QueryEnc(SK, Q): The query is divided into two vectors$\{Q', Q''\}$. The process of splitting is as follows: if $v_k \in V$ is 0, then set $q'_k = q''_k = q_k$;otherwise, set $q'_k = (1/2)q_k + r'$,$q''_k = (1/2)q_k - r'$, where r' is another random number. Encrypt the$\{Q', Q''\}$ into$\{M_1^{-1} \cdot Q', M_2^{-1} \cdot Q''\}$ with (M_1, M_2) . Finally, output the trapdoor:$Enc_{SK}(Q) = \{M_1^{-1} \cdot Q', M_2^{-1} \cdot Q''\}$.

BuildIndex(f, SK, k): Choose k independent LSH functions from p-stable LSH family $H = \{h : \{0,1\}^{26^2} -> \{0,1\}^m\}$. Build a m-bit bloom filter $I_f$as the index for each file . Encrypt the index I_f with the IndexEnc(SK, I):and then output the security index:$Enc_{SK}(I_f)$.

Trapdoor(Q, SK) : Generate a m-bit bloom filter for the queryQ. For each search keyword q_i , insert it into the bloom filter with the same k LSH functions($h_i \in H, 1 \le i \le k$). Use theQueryEnc(SK, Q) to encrypt the query Q , then output the security query$Enc_{SK}(Q)$.

Search($Enc_{SK}(Q), Enc_{SK}(I_f)$) : Output $M_1^T I' \cdot M_1^{-1} Q' + M_2^T I'' \cdot M_2^{-1} Q''$ as the search result of the query Q and the index I_f.

3.3. *Solution of Chinese fuzzy search*

The goal of fuzzy search is trying to return results associated with the user's query. The model described above can successfully complete the English fuzzy search. The homonym and the synonym in Chinese will increase the complexity of fuzzy search. To support the Chinese fuzzy search, the transformation mechanism will be established inside our scheme. When we exact the keywords in a document, the Chinese keyword will be converted to Pinyin with the transformation mechanism, then we can build an index based on the Pinyin. We will discuss the following Scenarios.

(1)The misspelled phonetic: When we enter the phonetic ‘pinguo’ in the Baidu search box, we will get a list of results {Apple’s official website,iphone,iphone6,Apple Mobile Assistant}. For this situation, the fuzzy search is same to the English fuzzy search.

(2)Error Chinese Keywords: If the user enter ‘poor country’ and the like, our system will invert the keywords into the phonetic ‘pinguo’, then matching with the ‘pingguo’ in the index with the LSH functions. Finally, the documents will be returned about the apple.

(3)Synonym processing: There are many synonym in Chinese, such as a synonym of ‘computer’is ‘pc’etc. To tackle the synonym match, we can first turn it into a English keyword. So we should do this work after exacting the keywords of a document and entering the user’s query. Finally, we can successfully complete the synonym match.

For the above three kind of scenarios, our scheme can successfully complete the fuzzy search. However, we may get a low precision rate of fuzzy search when the user’s input is a synonym. To improve the precision rate of synonym match, we can add the number of search keywords in the input. To sum up, our scheme can tackle the Chinese Fuzzy search effectively. If there is a strict requirement on synonym match in the real system, we should take another scheme to tackle this scenario and this work has beyond the scope of this paper.

4. Experiment

We conducted an experiment to evaluate the efficiency of our scheme. Our experiment dataset consists of 2000 English conference papers about computer and science and 2000 Chinese journal articles. We exact 6400 keywords in total. The average number of keywords for each file is 150. The minimum and the maximum are 107 and 180 relatively. We choose $2-stable(\sqrt{3},2,P_1,P_2)-$LSH to build index, $P_1=P(\sqrt{3})=0.558864$, $P_2=P(3/4)=0.285932$,the value of P_1,P_2 are calculated with Eq.(3):

$$-(1-e^{-x^2/2})(\sqrt{2/\pi})/x+Erf[x/\sqrt{2}]\,. \tag{3}$$

Our scheme set k=10,l=32,n=200,m=8000;We complete the experiment on a Lenovo PC with Intel core i5 processor 3.2 GHZ and 8G RAM.

4.1. *Efficiency analysis*

The index generating process mainly consists of two steps: generating Bloom Filter and encrypting index, as shown in Fig.2 and Fig.3 respectively. In Fig.2, we can find that the time consumption of index generation is almost equal to the time cost to generate trapdoor as they have the totally same constructing process. and the time increases linearly with the increasing keywords. Fig.3 shows us that Index encryption time is directly proportional to the number of documents.

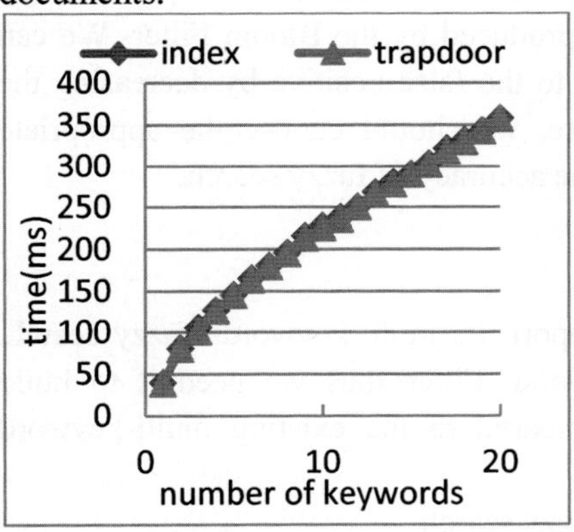

Fig.2:index generation time

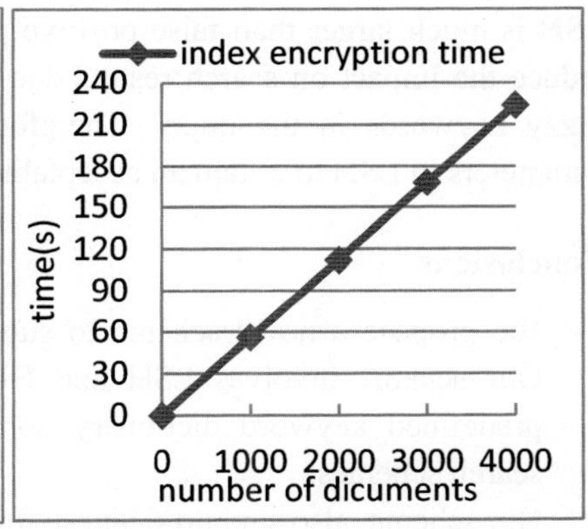

Fig.3: index encryption time

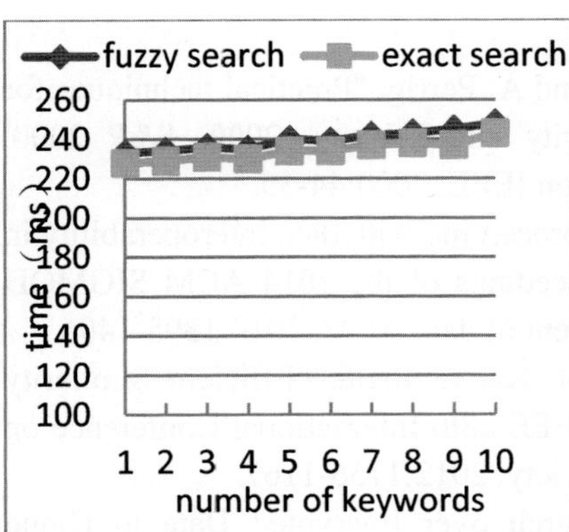

Fig.4: time cost for searching

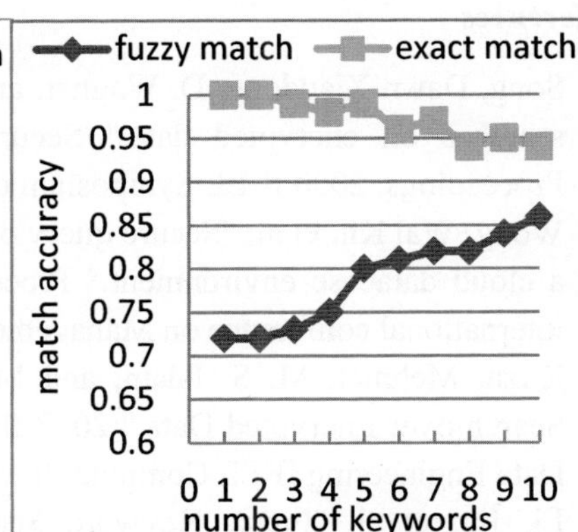

Fig5: match accuracy for searching

The search procedure will be placed in the cloud server in our system model design and thus lessen overhead for data owners and data users .Fig.4 shows that the number of query keywords impact on search time is extremely small due to the Inner product calculation only associated with the length of the index. In addition, the search time of fuzzy search is approximately equal to the search time of exactly search. This reflects the efficiency of our scheme for fuzzy search is extremely high.

4.2. *Accuracy analysis*

Fig.5 shows us that the accuracy of exact search decreasing lightly with the increase of the number of query keywords, from 100% to 94%.But the accuracy of exact search is from 75% to 86%. This due to the false positive produced by LSH is much larger than false positive produced by the Bloom Filter. We can reduce the impact on search results due to the false positive by decreasing the fuzzy keywords in the query. Therefore, we should choose the appropriate parameters in LSH to obtain an acceptable accuracy of fuzzy search.

Conclusions

- We propose a novel scheme to support the multi-keywords fuzzy search. Our scheme involves LSH and Bloom Filter thus we needn't to build predefined keyword dictionary compared to the existing multi-keyword search schemes.
- Our scheme also support Chinese fuzzy search.

References

1. Song, Dawn Xiaodong, D. Wagner, and A. Perrig. "Practical techniques for searches on encrypted data." Security and Privacy, 2000. S&P 2000. Proceedings. 2000 IEEE Symposium on IEEE, 2000:44-55.
2. Wong, Wai Kit, et al. "Secure query processing with data interoperability in a cloud database environment." Proceedings of the 2014 ACM SIGMOD international conference on Management of data ACM, 2014:1395-1406.
3. Kuzu, Mehmet, M. S. Islam, and M. Kantarcioglu. "Efficient Similarity Search over Encrypted Data." 2012 IEEE 28th International Conference on Data Engineering IEEE Computer Society, 2012:1156-1167.
4. Li, Jin, et al. "Fuzzy Keyword Search over Encrypted Data in Cloud Computing." Infocom 2009.9(2010):1 - 5.
5. Chuah, M., and W. Hu. "Privacy-Aware BedTree Based Solution for Fuzzy Multi-keyword Search over Encrypted Data." Distributed Computing Systems Workshops (ICDCSW), 2011 31st International Conference on IEEE, 2011:273-281..
6. Khan, Neelam S., C. R. Krishna, and A. Khurana. "Secure ranked fuzzy multi-keyword search over outsourced encrypted cloud data." Computer and

Communication Technology (ICCCT), 2014 International Conference on IEEE, 2014:241-249.
7. Datar, Mayur, et al. "Locality-sensitive hashing scheme based on p-stable distributions." Proceedings of the twentieth annual symposium on Computational geometry ACM, 2004:253-262.
8. He, Tuo, and W. Ma. "An Effective Fuzzy Keyword Search Scheme in Cloud Computing." International Conference on Intelligent Networking & Collaborative Systems IEEE, 2013:786-789.
9. Curtmola, Reza, et al. "Searchable symmetric encryption: improved definitions and efficient constructions." Proceedings of the 13th ACM conference on Computer and communications security ACM, 2006:79-88.

A Hierarchical Storage Strategy for Hybrid Clusters on a P2P Based Distributed System

Chao-fan TU[1], Qi-fei ZHANG[1,†], Ying-zhuang CHEN[1], Yu-chang ZHANG[1], Wei-dong ZHANG[2], Fan BAI[3], Yin-Chao XUE[1] and Er-teng LIU[1]

[1]*School of Software Technology, Zhejiang University*
Ningbo, 315048, China
[2]*School of Electronics Engineering & Computer Science,Peking University*
Beijing, 100871, China
[3]*Department of Electrical Engineering & Computer Science, Northwestern University*
Evanston, 60201, USA
†*E-mail: zhangqf@cst.zju.edu.cn*

As the energy consumption of storage systems is grows at a staggering rate, hybrid clusters have gained increasing importance as a potential approach to tackle this challenge. By introducing low-power nodes, data-driven companies like Facebook and Baidu have reduced the energy consumption effectively in their Master/Slave based storage systems. However, the Master/Slave based systems have several typical disadvantages such as low scalabilities and single points of failure. The P2P based systems with high scalabilities utilizes file location algorithms instead of table lookup mechanisms, thus resulting in a problem of how to utilize the different storage nodes discriminatively. In this paper, a hierarchical storage strategy called vnode hierarchical remapping (VHR) is proposed based on a P2P distributed system called ZDFS. The strategy guarantees the high scalability and viability of ZDFS, and takes advantage of different storage nodes. Several test cases running on X86 and ARM hybrid clusters are carried out, and the test results demonstrate that the VHR works well, it achieves a good I/O performance and low data access response time while reducing the energy consumption by 44.8%.

Keywords: Storage system; P2P; Hybrid cluster; Hierarchical; Energy-saving.

1. Introduction

It is predicted that the data created will reach for 44 ZB by 2020 from 4.4 ZB in 2013, so the increasing requirement of storage has to be surely accompanied with the explosive growth of data. Some large-scale storage systems were designed and have been deployed, such as GFS [1], Dynamo [2], the open source project – HDFS [3], etc. The challenge of energy consumption has become more and more prominent, the energy consumption of some storage systems are occupied by more than one-third of the whole data centers [4].

Hardware techniques use low-power devices to save energy. Szalay A S, et al applied high-performed SSD by increasing sequential read I/O throughput by an order of magnitude and keeping power consumption constant [5]. Hamilton J, et al constructed a kind of rack which is suitable for low-power Athlon processors [6]. By using lower-power embedded chips and flash devices, Vasudevan V, et al constructed a cluster which has 7 times energy efficiency than by using main-stream devices[7]. With the rapid development of ARM in recent years, ARM based storage devices have been largely applied in practice. 4-core ARM processors are used in the Open Vault project to drive 15 hard disks by Facebook, which are reduced the energy consumption in many aspects [8]. Baidu developed a cloud storage system which consisted by both X86 and ARM nodes, which was claimed that it has improved the storage density by 70% and reduced TCO by 25% [9].

Mixing low-power nodes into storage clusters is an effective approach to construct low-power storage systems. Researches on such hybrid clusters, however, which mostly focus on Master/Slave based systems, the Master/Slave based systems are having some typical disadvantages such as low scalabilities, single points of failure, while the P2P based systems such as Dynamo and Ceph [10]with high scalabilities are now getting more and more attention. Those P2P based systems always use file location algorithms instead of table lookup mechanisms, thus bringing the problem of how to use different storage nodes discriminatively based on P2P.To address this issue, we proposed the hierarchical storage strategy for ZDFS [11], which is an existingP2Pbased distributed storage system.

2. ZDFS

ZDFS introduced the consistent hashing (CH) algorithm to locate a file. Consistent hashing is a special kind of hashing such that when a hash table is resized and consistent hashing is used, only a small portion of keys need to be remapped on average. The CH will build a virtual cycle by the objects' hash value in order, when a file gets its hash value (also called as 'ID'), then it is curtained that which area it may be rejected. So the distributed system like ZDFS did not maintain the file index table. ZDFS has three components, as it is shown in Figure 1: (1)DataNodes, which are the residing host of user data; (2)

Client nodes(s), which acts as spokesman to response the user accessing request, it delegates the I/O transactions with Data Nodes for the end users; (3) Monitor node, a super cute node which maintains global information of storage nodes,

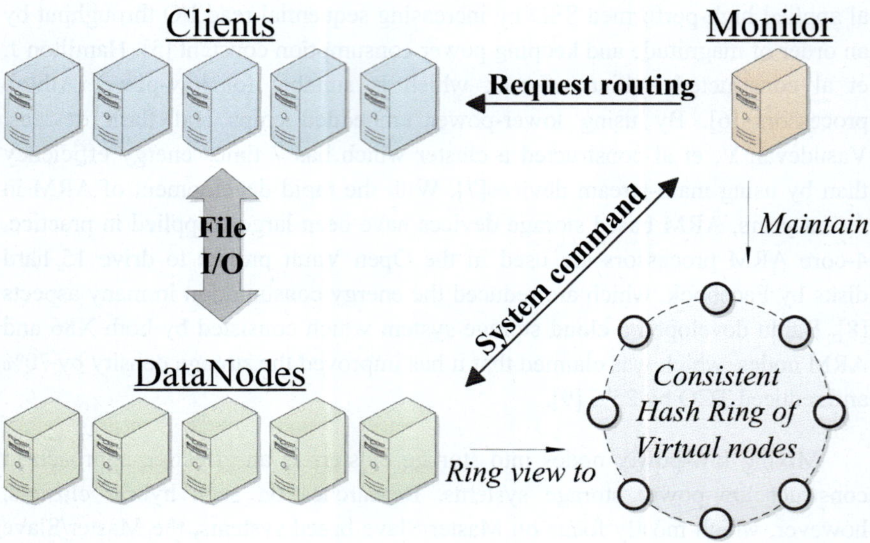

such as the CH chain and the extra coordination of data migration.

Figure 1: System structure

3. Vnode Hierarchical Remapping

There are two kinds of storage nodes in ZDFS. We use the hierarchical strategy to use different kinds of nodes discriminatively, as it is shown as Table 2.

Table2. Nodes' tasks

Strategy	Non-hierarchical	Hierarchical
HighNode	Store primary data and secondary replicas; Perform I/O transactions with Client Node directly	Store primary data ;Perform I/O transactions with Client Node directly
LowNode	The same as HighNode	Store secondary replicas

By using file location algorithms instead of table lookup mechanisms, ZDFS has a good scalability for its P2P structure, thus bringing the problem of how to use different storage nodes discriminatively. In this paper, a hierarchical storage strategy called vnode hierarchical remapping (VHR) is proposed to address this issue and it do not reduce the high scalability. We divide the vnodes set into 2 types called the odd and the even; the odd are mapped to LowNode, while the even are mapped to HighNode, as it is shown in Figure 3.

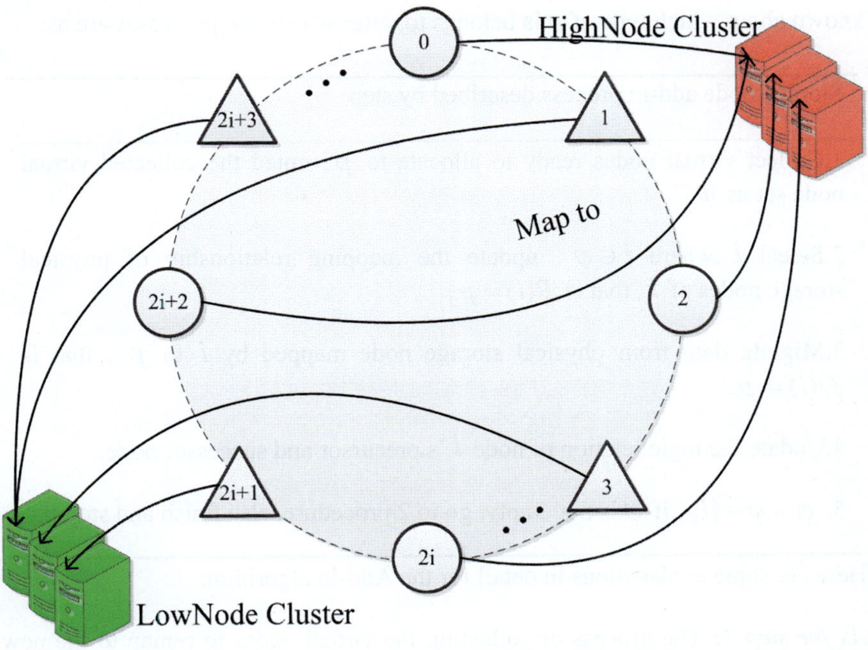

Figure 3: Vnode hierarchy remapping

The descendant node rules are described as bellow:

$$\{vnode(2i)\_next = vnode(2i+1)\ (0 \le i < N/2\ );\ vnode(2i+1)\_next=vnode(2i+3)\}$$

The expression vnode(*)_next is noted as the descendant node of vnode(*), and N represents the total amount of vnodes.The rules are guaranteed that all primary data are stored to HighNode mapped by the even vnodes and all secondary replicas are stored to LowNode mapped by the odd.

We describe the strategy by the Add-in and the Offline processes in a mathematical way, which for the scenarios of nodes add-in to and offline from the storage cluster respectively. Here we describe the strategy in details as the followings.

3.1. *Add-in process*

Let p as the nodes, as the first step, p join to the cluster, the Monitor gets known about which type of p is belongs to, after which, the processes are as:

Storage node add-in process described by step
1.Collect virtual nodes ready to allocate to p, noted the collected virtual node set as φ,
2.Select i ,where $i \in \varphi$, update the mapping relationship of physical storage nodes of i, that is $R(i) = p$,
3.Migrate data from physical storage node mapped by i to p , that is $D(i) = p$,
4.Update the logic relation of node i 's precursor and successor node;
5. $\varphi = \varphi - \{i\}$, if φ is not empty, go to 2 procedure, else finish and stop it.

Here are some explanations in detail for the Add-in algorithm:

As for step 1: The process of collecting the virtual nodes to remap to the new added node of p ; the holding baseline is that the collecting number is even by the number of the type of storage node, for the matter allocating balancing of virtual nodes ;

As for step 2: The function $R(i) = p$ means that virtual node$i$ is mapped to physical storage node of p , at this step, the Monitor updates the mapping relationship, and coordinates p to establish the storage directory related to current virtual node;

As for step 3: The function $D(i) = p$ means that data mapped to virtual node i are stored in physical node of p . The Monitor coordinates that the mapped physical storage node to migrate the data objects to p , and stored in the new storage directory created before;

As for step 4: Let each physical node knows that the precursor and successor node has updated and shall update the mapping table, also including the removal process.

3.2. *Offline process*

Let p as the offline nodes. As the first step, the Monitor automatically detects that p has been offline, it knows the details of p, such as the node's hierarchical type, the virtual nodes set which mapped to p. By following, the offline process is as:

Storage node offline process described by step
1.Note virtual nodes allocated to p as set ϕ,
2.Select x ,where $x \in \phi$, update the mapping relationship of physical storage nodes of x to q,
3.Migrate data from the physical nodes which mapped by x 's first and the second precursor to q respectively , write the first and the second backup area to q 's directory of x ,
4.Update the logic relation of node x 's precursor and successor node;
5. $\varphi = \varphi - \{x\}$, if φ is not empty, go to 2 procedure, else finish and stop it.

As for the realization of offline process, step 2 is essential for remapping the virtual node to other same type physical nodes that is online, like the add-in process, the logic 2 adjacent virtual nodes cannot be mapped to the same physical storage node. Step 3 shall recover the available replica data to the new substituted storage node which stored in the offline node before.

This paper presents a hierarchical virtual node remapping policy by letting different virtual nodes map to different types of hierarchical storage nodes, realized hierarchical storage in a P2P structure, it has the following main running characteristics:

(1) Automatic hybrid cluster management. When the storage node is added or offline, the system automatically uses the mechanisms of assigning or collect-and-reassigning to the corresponding virtual nodes according to the node's type. Meanwhile, the mechanisms are ensure that replica data are

stored in low-power storage nodes where they are mutually different in physical nodes, and both by adapting balancing algorithm, the data system are with high availability.

(2) Not reducing the high scalability. Monitor type nodes are having low load characteristics. In the data migration process, the Monitor's workload is ultra-light , it only responsible to send the appropriate commands to the storage nodes the corresponding virtual nodes mapped to, the data migration are operated independently just between storage nodes.

4. Experiments

We carried out our experiments in a real environment, and its topological structure is shown in Figure 4. HighNodes, LowNodes, one Monitor and one Client are deployed in our test environment; the wire is a scale of 1Gib Ethernet LAN. Multiple power detectors are used to measure energy consumption.

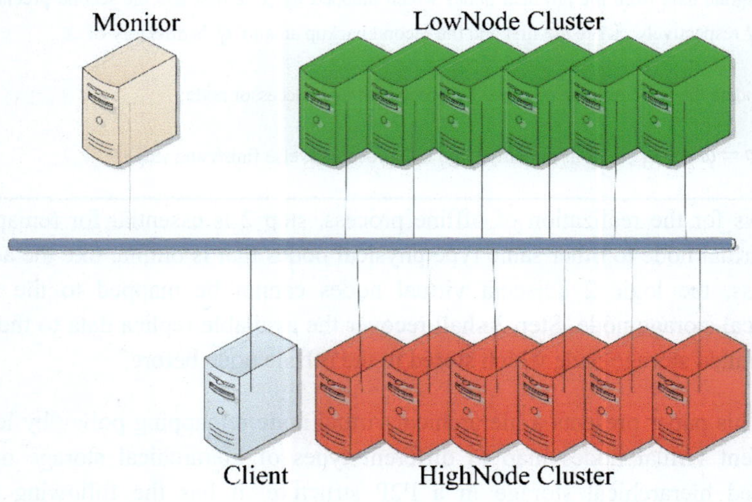

Figure 4: Topological structure

ZDFS is running on Linux boards. Table 3 shows the hardware

configuration of DataNodes, as we can see, HighNode is X86 based, while LowNode is ARM based.

Table3. Hardware configurations

Node	HighNode	LowNode
Processor	3.1GHz Intel i5 2400	600MHz ARM CortexA8
Storage	HDD 500G	Flash 64G
Memory	DDR3 4GB	DDR2 256MB
NIC	10/100/1000 Mbps	10/100 Mbps

4.1. *Energy consumption*

We organized four test cases noted as group, as in Table 4, the configuration for each group is different from each other, the overall energy consumption of each group is also given in Table 4.

Table4. Energy consumption of each test group

Group	Mixing Strategy	Amount		Power (W)
		HighNode	LowNode	
1	--	12	0	708.4
2	--	0	12	69.6
3	Non-hierarchical	6	6	389.5
4	VHR	6	6	390.7

4.2. *Throughput*

We deploy test cases for the performance of throughput with the file size in 500K, 1M, 5M respectively. File scale of each test case is 100G. The test results are as shown in Table 5. Note that we measure the maximum throughput is by the Ethernet port I/O of the Client node.

Table5. Throughput (MB/s) of each test group

Groups	File size		
	500K	1M	5M
1	88.8	89.5	90.9
2	43.1	44.3	50.4
3	87.8	88.0	89.3
4	70.6	87.7	89.6

Group 3 has a slightly high I/O throughput that that of group 4 since the rest of the low-power storage nodes of group 4 are invisible for Client node, however, as we can see from the table, as the file size gets increased, the throughput among the testing groups are becoming nearly same. It is natural that the system bandwidth is becoming a main factor restricting the maximum throughput.

4.3. *Download time*

We download files with a sum scale of 10G for each test group, and the downloaded file is the same for both groups. We pick the average value of download time, and Table 6 shows the testing data:

Table 6. Download time of each test group

Group	Mixing Strategy	File size		
		500K	1M	5M
1	--	120s	118s	117s
2	--	248s	238s	210s
3	Non-hierarchical	244s	236s	170s
4	VHR	149s	120s	118s

In group 3, the user data are stored in HighNode and LowNode with a same mapping method, an object downloaded may come from HighNode or LowNode. We can see that the download time in group 4 is shorter than those of group 3, and it is obviously that data stored in HighNode are getting better response time. The VHR strategy running well for downloading response, with the good using of the hardware resources, and the energy consumption has decreased by 44.8%.

5. Conclusions

With the rapid growth of storage requirements, the energy challenge becomes more and more prominent; mixing low-power nodes into original clusters is a significant method to tackle this problem. P2P based systems with high scalabilities now have been received increasing attention such as Dynamo and Ceph, they use file location algorithms instead of table lookup mechanisms, thus bringing some problems such as how to use different storage nodes discriminatively. To address this issue, a strategy called vnode hierarchical remapping (VHR) is introduced to ZDFS which is a P2P based distribute storage system, and the strategy also guarantees the high scalability and availability of ZDFS. In the final of the paper, some test cases which purposes are to measure the energy consumption and performance running on X86 and ARM hybrid clusters are carried out, the test results indicate that the group using VHR performs well, and also as a consequence, the VHR strategy makes a good use of hardware resources and the energy consumption is reduced by 44.8%. Our future works involve the optimizing of the system, the mechanism of supporting multi-heterogeneous nodes, etc.

Acknowledgments

This work is supported by the National Key Technology Support Program (No.2014BAH23F03), the National Environmental Charity Project(No.20134 67065), the Ningbo Natural Science Foundation (No.2013A610064) and the Ningbo Wisdom Interactive Multimedia Remote Education System (No.2013B10036).

References

1. Ghemawat S, Gobioff H, Leung S T. *The Google file system.ACM SIGOPS operating systems review*. ACM, 2003, 37(5): 29-43

2. Hastorun D. et al. D*ynamo: Amazon's Highly Available Key-Value Store*. SOSP, 2007, 41(6):205--220.

3. Shvachko K, Kuang H, Radia S, et al. The hadoop distributed file system[A]. Mass Storage Systems and Technologies (MSST), 2010 IEEE 26th Symposium, 2010: 1-10

4. Battles B, Belleville C, Grabau S, et al. *Reducing data center power consumption through efficient storage.*(Network Appliance, Inc., 2007) /www.storageconsorcing-datacenter-powensumptn.pdf

5. Szalay A S, Bell G C, Huang H H, et al. *Low-power amdahl-balanced blades for data intensive computing.* ACM SIGOPS Operating Systems Review, 2010, 44(1): 71-75

6. Hamilton J. Cooperative expendable micro-slice servers (CEMS): low cost, low power servers for internet-scale services. Conference on Innovative Data Systems Research. Online Proceedings, 2009

7. Vasudevan V, Franklin J, Andersen D G, et al. F*AWNdamentally Power-efficient Clusters.* HOTOS, USENIX, 2009, 9: 22-22

8. Amber Graner, et al, *Open Compute Project ARM Server Specification,* (Facebook, Inc., 2013) http://www.opencompute.org/wp/wp-content/uploads/2013/01/Open_Compute_Project_ARM_Server_Specification_v0.3.pdf

9. Anna Wang. Chinese Internet Giant Baidu Rolls Out World's First Commercial Deployment of Marvell's ARM Processor-based Server.(Baidu, Inc., 2013.)http://developer.baidu.com/en/events.html

10. Weil S A, Brandt S A, Miller E L, et al. Ceph: A scalable, high-performance distributed file system//Proceedings of the 7th symposium on Operating systems design and implementation. USENIX Association, 2006: 307-320.

11. Qifei Zhang, Weidong Zhang, Linjuan Li, et al. *Cloud Storage System Facing to Small files Based on P2P.* Journal of Zhejiang University (EngineerScience), 2013, 49(1): 8-14

An Improved LSM-Tree Index for NoSQL Data-Store

Lin DAI[†], Jia FU and Chong FENG
Department of Computer Science and Technology, Beijing Institute of Technology, Beijing, 100081, China
[†]*E-mail: dailiu@bit.edu.cn*

The index is one of the most important component in NoSQL database and the B-tree is the currently most widely used index structure. In order to improve the writing performance of B-tree, Log-Structured Merge-Tree (LSM-tree) has been developed. LSM-tree improves writing throughput, but its reading performance is hampered, especially for range queries. In this paper, we propose an indexed LSM-tree (iLSM-tree) to improve the reading performance of the LSM-tree by adding an extra index. To evaluate its performance, we implement iLSM-tree on HBase and perform a series of experiments to compare the iLSM-tree with original HBase which uses LSM-tree. The results demonstrate that the iLSM-tree has improved efficiency.

Keywords: LSM-tree; NoSQL; Index; Reading performance.

1. Introduction

With the increasing amount of data, the world goes into the big data era. Applications need a more efficient data structure to organize data, while traditional relational databases cannot address this problem effectively. Several NoSQL[1-3] data-storesoffer different solutions for large-scale data storage. Since we need to store a large amount of data efficiently, how to index data is an important issue for NoSQL data stores.

B-tree[4] is one of the most frequently used data structure for database index. But B-tree doesn't work well for writing because of the random I/O. LSM-tree[5] is proposed to improve writing performance of B-tree by turning random I/O into sequential I/O. However, reading from LSM-tree is slow because getting a specific data requires iterating all the disk files. Many works[6-8] have been done to improve the reading performance of LSM-tree.

bLSM-tree [6] uses bloom filters to improve reading performance. It reduces query time when the element doesn't exist in some disk stores. The

[†]Corresponding author.

limitation of bLSM-tree is the time of the merge process bound with the timing insertions. pLSM-tree [7] uses Cache Oblivious Look-ahead Array (COLA) [9] to improve reading performance. It stores logical contiguous elements in the same block instead of scattered blocks. But pLSM-tree may consume too much disk space because of the COLA component.

In this paper, we present an improvement base on LSM-tree aims to improve LSM-tree's reading performance. The basic idea is to create an extra index, we note it as INDEX. When searching a data, we firstly search from INDEX to find which subtrees the data locates in. Then we search from the trees on disk to get the wanted data.

The rest of this paper is organized as follows. Section 2 is about the idea of the proposed iLSM-tree. Section 3 evaluates iLSM-tree against LSM-tree. Section 4 concludes this paper.

2. Indexed Log Structured Merge Tree

2.1. *Data structure*

In order to promote the reading performance of LSM-tree, we add an extra index structure to it. Figure 1 is the basic data structure of iLSM-tree. Each entry in the INDEX represents a certain range and it can index several B-tree files. Different from LSM-tree, each B-tree is in the range of the INDEX entry which point to it.

iLSM-tree consists of three parts, i.e., the memory component, the buffer component and the disk component. These three components share a same INDEX.

2.2. *Operations*

2.2.1. *Insert and flush*

When a new data needs to be inserted, it should be written into memory first. With the increase of the size of in-memory component, it will be flushed to disk after certain threshold is reached. To ensure data flushed on disk can be indexed by the INDEX, each in-memory subtree must be flushed to disk separately according to INDEX entry. However, the flush will incur writing small B-tree files to disk. To avoid this condition, we put the in-memory subtrees into a buffer before they are flushed onto disk. We merge the new subtrees into the B-trees in the buffer according to the index range. And then we flush the biggest B-tree in buffer onto disk. An example of flush process is shown in figure 2.

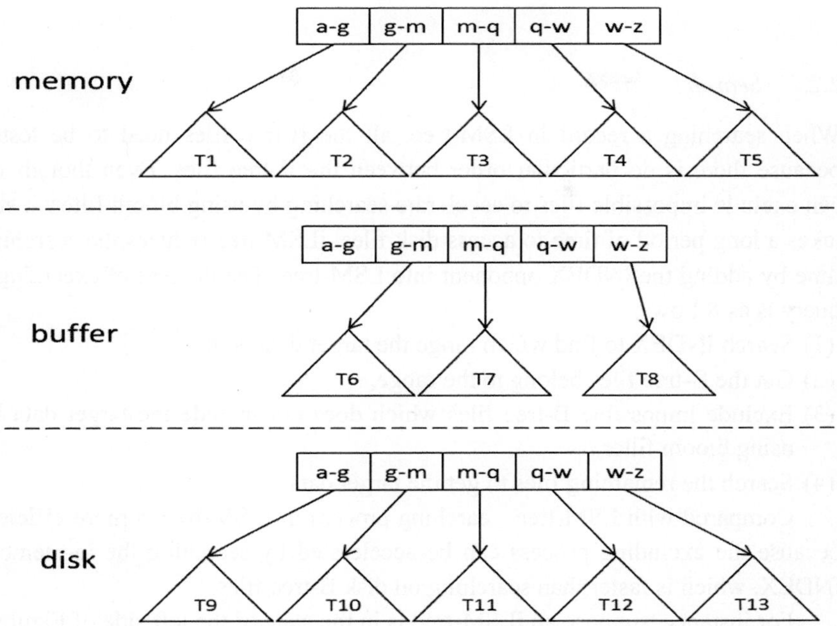

Fig. 1. Three components of iLSM-tree

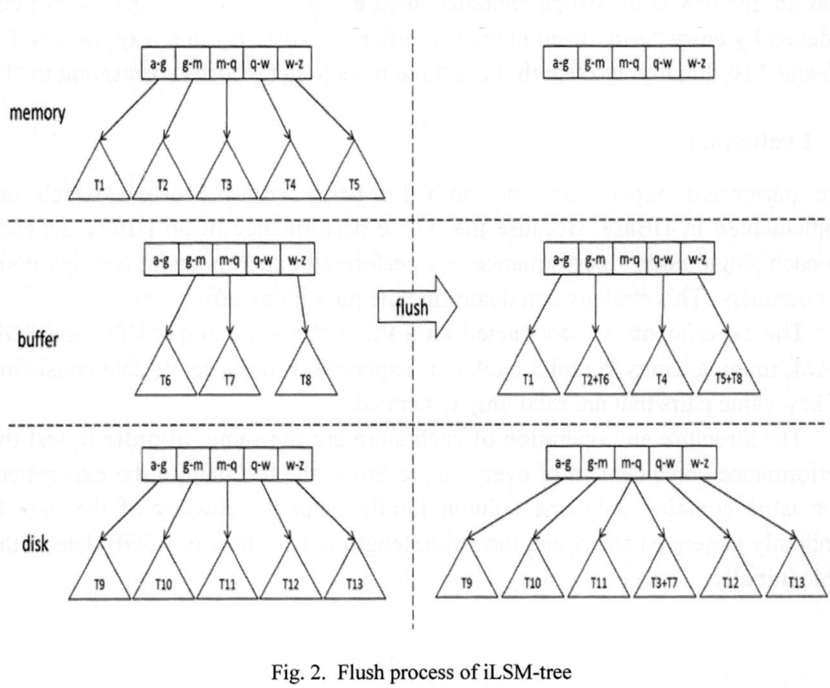

Fig. 2. Flush process of iLSM-tree

2.2.2. *Search*

When searching a record in LSM-tree, all the B-tree files need to be tested because there is no particular order between the B-tree files. Even though we can exclude impossible files to accelerate searching by using bloom filter, it still takes a long period of time to access disk files. iLSM-tree reduces the searching time by adding the INDEX opponent into LSM-tree. The process of executing a query is as follows:

(1) Search INDEX to find which range the target data is in,
(2) Get the B-tree files belong to the range,
(3) Exclude impossible B-tree files which does not include the target data by using bloom filter,
(4) Search the remaining files to get the target data.

Compared with LSM-tree, searching process in iLSM-tree is more efficient because the excluding process can be accelerated by searching the in-memory INDEX, which is faster than searching on disk B-tree files.

For instance, suppose an iLSM-tree is in the state of the left side of Figure 2. When we want to get the value corresponds to "h". Firstly, we search INDEX to find the INDEX entry which contains "h", i.e., "g-m". Then we get the B-trees indexed by entry "g-m" from memory, buffer and disk. By this way, we get T2, T6 and T10. Finally, we search these three trees to get records correspond to "h".

3. Evaluation

We performed experiments on both LSM-tree and iLSM-tree which are implemented in HBase. Because the whole performance of an HBase depends on each single node's performance, we performed experiments in a single node environment. This strategy can determine the pure index efficiency.

The experiments are conducted on a PC with Intel 3.3GHz CPU and 8GB RAM, running Linux kernel 3.13.9. Our experiments use a set of data consisting of key-value pairs that are randomly generated.

The structure and operation of each store are the same. In order to test the performance enhancement of every single Store, the test data in the experiment is a table contains only one column family. And the rowkey of the data is randomly generated string and the string length is 15. There is 1.3GB data in the table initially.

3.1. *Point query performance*

Results of random point query of the two different structures are shown in Figure 3. The X-axis represents the query number and the Y-axis represents the searching time corresponds to the query. As can be observed from the graph, the total point query time of both LSM and iLSM increase linearly as the number of query increases. iLSM-tree outperforms LSM-tree evidently because its INDEX reduces the number of searching on storefiles. In general, the query time of iLSM-tree is about half of that of LSM-tree.

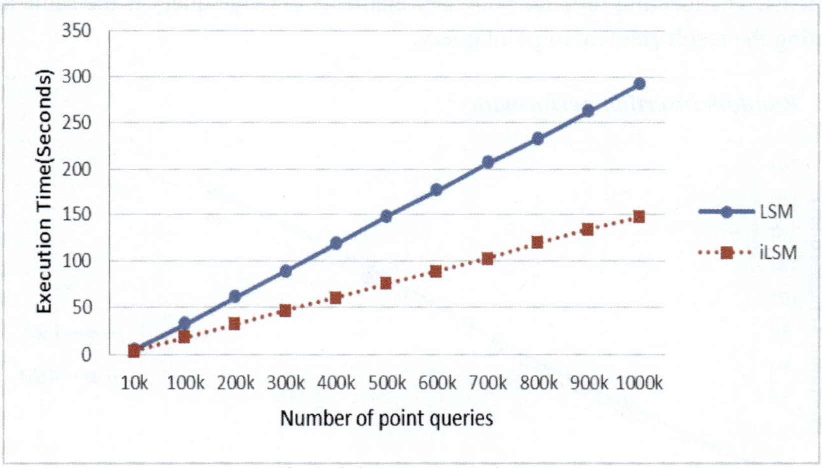

Fig. 3. Point query comparison

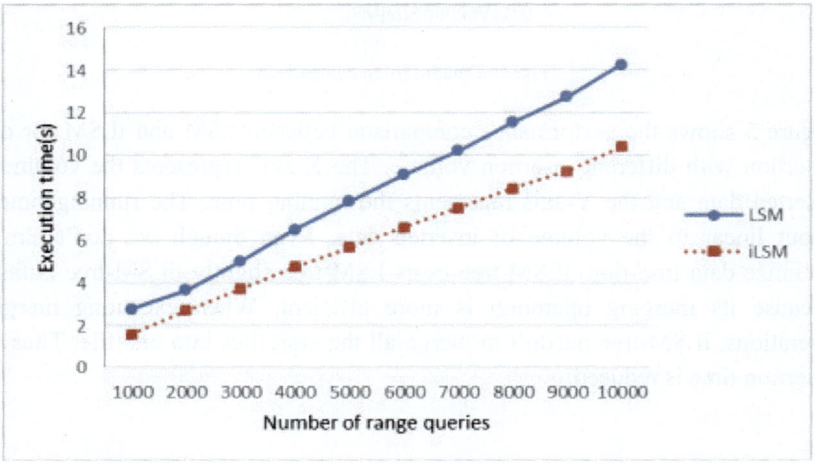

Fig. 4. Range query comparisonRange query performance

We also run experiments on range query task. Figure 4 shows the performance of LSM and iLSM with varying operation number from 1000 to 10000. We randomly choose the ranges and each of them contains 1000 items. From the figure, we can see that in both LSM-tree and iLSM-tree, the running time increase linearly to the number of the queries. LSM-tree consumes about extra 38% time than iLSM-tree does when executing range query. iLSM-tree doesn't outperform LSM-tree on range query as good as on point query. There are two reasons: 1) Range query can't explore bloom filter to exclude impossible trees. 2) The time of range query consists of both locating time and reading time of elements. The locating time for boundary elements in range query is the same as locating the result element of point query.

3.2. *Random insertion performance*

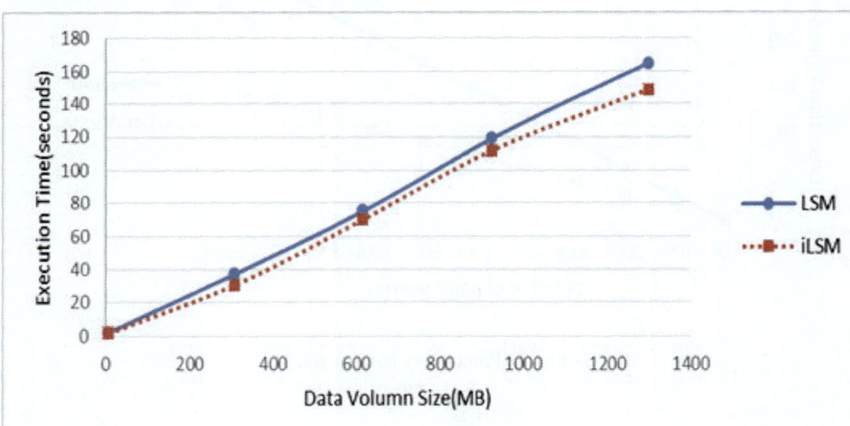

Fig. 5. Data insertion comparison

Figure 5 shows the performance comparison between LSM and iLSM for data insertion with different insertion volume. The X-axis represents the volume of inserted data and the Y-axis represents the running time. The running time is about linear to the volume of inserted data. Even though we don't aim to optimize data insertion, iLSM-tree beats LSM-tree slightly. iLSM-tree is faster because its merging operation is more efficient. When executing merging operations, iLSM-tree needn't to merge all the storefiles into one file. Thus the insertion time is reduced.

4. Conclusion

LSM-tree improves writing performance but sacrifices reading performance of B-tree. To promote reading performance of LSM-tree, we proposed iLSM-tree. iLSM-treereduces the time for selecting the right files in the disk when executing a query. We conducted a set of experiments to evaluate iLSM-tree against LSM-Tree in HBase context. Compared with LSM-tree, iLSM-tree achieves nearly 2 times speed up for the point query and about 1.38 times speed up for the range query. Even though iLSM-tree needs a little more memory space than LSM-tree, it gains promising improvement.

In the future, we will conduct our experiment in distributed environment to examine the performance difference between iLSM-tree and LSM-tree in a distributed environment. Moreover, since split a large amount of data costs much more than split a small amount of data, we will optimize the split strategy to make INDEX split when the data volume is small.

Acknowledgments

This work is supported by NSFC, 61201351, 60803050.

References

1. R. Cattell, *Scalable SQL and NoSQL Data Stores*, ACM SIGMOD Record, Vol. 39 (2010), pp. 12-29.
2. M. Adam, The NoSQL Ecosystem(2011), `http://www.aosabook.o-rg/en/nosql.html`.
3. S. Sherif et al., *A survey of large scale data management approaches in cloud environments*, IEEE Communications Surveys and Tutorials, Vol. 13(2011), pp. 311-336.
4. G. Graefe, B-tree indexes for high update rates, SIGMOD Record, Vol. 35 (2006), pp. 39-44.
5. P. O'Neil et al., The log-structured merge-tree, ActaInformatica, Vol. 33 (1996), pp. 351-385.
6. R. Sears et al., *bLSM: A General Purpose Log Structured Merge Tree*, In: Proceedings ofthe ACM SIGMOD International Conference on Management of Data(2012), pp. 217-228.
7. J. Wang et al., *pLSM: A Highly Efficient LSM-Tree Index Supporting Real-Time Big Data Analysis*, In: Proceedings of International Computer Software and Applications Conference, (2013), pp. 240-245.

8. Z. Zigang, et al., *Pipelined compaction for the LSM-tree*, In: Proceedings of International Parallel and Distributed Processing Symposium Conference, (2014), pp. 777-786.
9. M.Bender et al., *Cache-oblivious streaming B-trees*, Annual ACM Symposium on Parallelism in Algorithms and Architectures(2007), pp. 81-92.

Feature Word Vector Based on Short Text Clustering

Xin LIU[1,†], Bo WANG[1], Yao-yi XI[2], Er-song MAO[1], Sheng-cai KE[1] and Yong-wang TANG[1]

[1]*School of Information and Systems Engineering, PLA Information Engineering University, Zheng Zhou, High-Tech Zone, China;*

[2]*PLA University of Foreign Language, Luo Yang, Jianxi Zone, China*

[†]*E-mail:syliuxinlyl@163.com*

A feature word vector based on short text clustering algorithm is proposed in this paper to solve the poor clustering of short text caused by sparse feature and quick updates of short text. Firstly, the formula for feature word extraction based on word part-of-speech (POS) weighting is defined and used to extract a feature word as short text. Secondly, the word vector that represents the semantics of the feature word was obtained through training in large-scale corpus with the Continuous Skip-gram Model. Finally, Word Mover's Distance (WMD) was used to calculate similarity of short texts for short text clustering in the hierarchical clustering algorithm. The evaluation of four testing datasets revealed that the proposed algorithm is significantly superior to traditional clustering algorithms, with a mean F value of 55.43% on average higher than the second best method.

Keywords: Short text; Feature words; Word vectors; Similarity Calculation; Clustering.

1. Introduction

According to the Analysis Report on User Behaviors of Social APPs in China in 2014, the coverage rates instant messaging (IM), social networking services (SNS) and MicroBlog in the whole netizen population are 89.3%, 61.7% and 43.6%, respectively. Netizen interconnect and delivery speeches freely through these Apps, which generate massive short texts. How to mine and analyze information resources in these short texts through computer technology is of important significance. Text clustering, an unsupervised machine learning method in Natural Language Processing, can organize and classify texts automatically and effectively, thus enabling to get an overall understanding on these disordered text information.

Most of existing clustering methods[1,2] apply the traditional vector space model (VSM) for text expression. This has some shortages: (1) it evaluates text similarity based on morphological similarity, but neglects contribution of synonyms in the text to the sentence similarity. Therefore, it couldn't calculate the deeper semantic similarity between sentences accurately. For example, although “like” and “love” are two synonyms, they are omitted when calculating similarity between two sentences. This won’t increase sentence similarity and thereby influences text clustering performance. (2) Due to the short length of short text, text expression with the traditional VSM will cause serious sparse feature problem. To address this, researchers put forward text clustering methods based on knowledge base[3,4] and text clustering methods based on topic model[5,6].

Text clustering methods based on knowledge base excavate relationship between words to improve clustering effect by making use of rich text features of knowledge bases like HowNet, WordNet and Wikipedia. Chen[3] and Bai Qiuchan[4] expanded key characteristic words of text topic through concept attribute of HowNet, which overcame the sparse feature of short text and improved short text clustering effect to a certain extent. Bouras[7] explored relationship between words in news articles by WordNet and put forward a WordNet-based news document clustering technique. Based on rich short text features of Wikipedia, Banerjee[8] improved accuracy of short text clustering. However, network language is often characteristic of singularity and dynamics. The singularity refers to that existing words are vested with new meanings. Dynamics refers to the quick changes of network language. New words will be created every year. However, many new words are failed to be recorded timely due to the slow update of knowledge bases. As a result, processing network short texts based on knowledge bases will surely influence the short text clustering effect.

The basic idea of text clustering methods based on topic model is to convert texts from high-dimensional feature space into low-dimensional semantic topic space through text modeling by the topic model. This could overcome high-dimensional feature vector in traditional clustering methods. Shi Jianhong[5] and Tang Qiulian[6] made text modeling with LDA (Latent Dirichlet Allocation) model and BTM (Biterm Topic Model) model respectively, and acquired topic distributions of texts. Combining with the K-means clustering algorithm, they realized text clustering. Wang Shaopeng[9] and Yin[10] improved the LDA model independently and improved clustering effect. Although text clustering methods based on topic model overcome shortcomings of previous two types of clustering methods to a certain extent, Mikolov[11] discovered in abundant experiments that topic models like LDA and PLSA (Probabilististic Latent Semantic Analysis) are inapplicable to large-scale data training and processing. Moreover, LDA and other topic models all assume that data conform to exponential distribution. They emphasize on semantic induction from high-frequency data, but neglects existence of low-frequency words. Data on Internet obey long tail distribution[12], which affects application performances of topic models in Internet short text data.

Word vector, a distributed low-dimensional real-valued vector, is generated by large-scale corpus training by neural network linguistic model and is to make related or similar words closer in distance[13]. For example, when calculating similarity between two of “China”, “artificial”, “Beijing” and “intelligence”, “China” and “Beijing” as well as “artificial” and “intelligence” show higher similarity than rest combinations. Mikolov[11] stated that word expression in word vector is more accurate than traditional expressions.

Since word vector is acquired after large-scale corpus training by neural network linguistic model, text expression in Word Vector is not limited by sparse feature of short text and update speed of knowledge base. To increase accuracy of word vectors in calculating text similarity, considering characteristics of word vectors, Kusner[14] used the minimum Euclidean distance sum of word vectors of different texts as semantic similarity of texts. This is called WMD (Word Mover’s Distance).

In view of advantages of word vectors, this paper proposed a feature words vector based short text clustering algorithm. Firstly, every short text was regarded as a cluster and feature words of every cluster were extracted to represent it. This could reduce feature dimension effectively. Secondly, word vectors with semantic information of feature words were acquired by large-scale dataset training with Skip-gram model[13]. This is vectorization of clusters. Finally, semantic similarity between clusters was calculated by WMD and then used in hierarchical clustering algorithm to accomplish short text clustering. Experimental results proved that the proposed algorithm is feasible and has significantly better clustering effect than traditional clustering methods based on vector space model and topic model.

2. Feature Word Vector Based Short Text Clustering Algorithm

This part firstly introduces the basic procedure of feature word vector based short text clustering algorithm and then elaborates key technologies involved one by one.

2.1. *Basic procedure*

Basic procedure of the proposed algorithm is shown in Fig.1. It mainly consists cluster vectorization, short text similarity calculation based on feature word vector and hierarchical clustering algorithm.

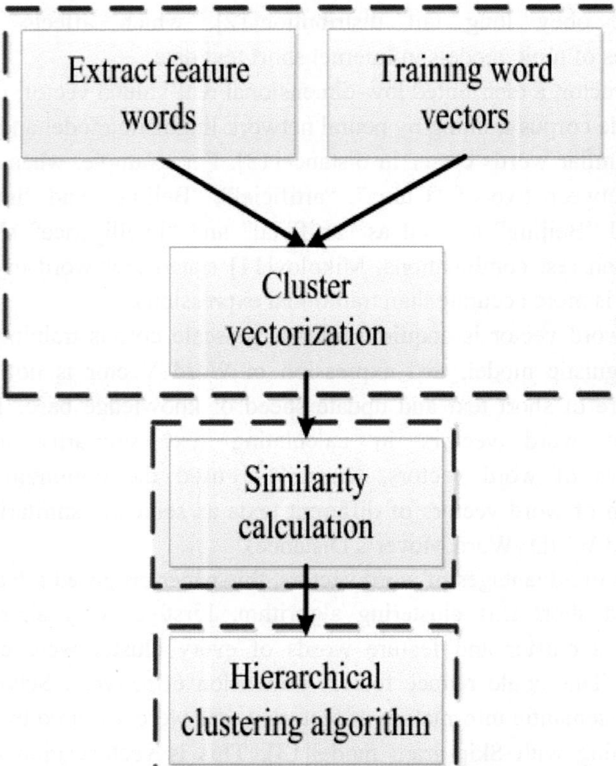

Fig.1. Flowchart of feature word vector based short text clustering algorithm

(1) Cluster vectorization: feature words of clusters are gained through weighted calculation of word POS. Then, vectors of feature words are acquired by training the Skip-gram model. In this way, clusters are vectorized.
(2) Short text similarity calculation based on feature word vector: calculate semantic similarity between vectorized clusters by WMD.
(3) Hierarchical clustering algorithm: use the calculated short text similarity into hierarchical clustering algorithm.

2.2. *Cluster vectorization*

Cluster vectorization includes extraction of cluster feature words and training of word vectors. The following text makes a detail introduction to them.

2.2.1. *Extraction of feature words*

Hierarchical agglomerative clustering algorithm was used for short text clustering. Words in text set will increase continuously when two clusters are combined into a new one. Curse of dimensionality will occur if all words are used to calculate similarity between two clusters, which will influence clustering performance. Hence, feature words were extracted to represent clusters. Generally, nouns and verbs are more important than others. Therefore, a formula to calculate weights of feature words based on word POS was defined in this paper:

$$Weight(w_{id}) = \frac{tf(w_i, \mathrm{d}) \times \log(N / n_{w_i} + 0.01) \times pos_{w_i}}{\sqrt{\sum_{w \in d} [tf(w, \mathrm{d}) \times \log(N / n_w + 0.01) \times pos_{w_i}]^2}} . \tag{1}$$

where $Weight(w_{id})$ is weight of word w_i in text d; $tf(w_i, \mathrm{d})$ is frequency of feature w_i in text d; N is total texts in the text set; n_{w_i} is text amount with the ith word in the text set; pos_{w_i} is weighted value of POS tagging:

$$pos_{w_i} = \begin{cases} 1.5, & w_i \ is \ 'v' \ or \ 'n' \\ 1, & else \end{cases} . \tag{2}$$

When w_i is a noun or verb, pos_{w_i} =1.5; otherwise, pos_{w_i} =1.

During cluster integration, a lot of short texts will concentrate in few clusters if feature words of two clusters are combined simply. Therefore, this paper defined formulas to update weights of feature words:

$$c_{new} = \{\{v(w_i)\} \mid \max_K (Weight(w_i)), w_i \in (c_l + c_k)\} . \tag{3}$$

$$Weight(w_{inew}) = \frac{M \cdot Weight(w_{ik}) + N \cdot Weight(w_{il})}{M + N} . \tag{4}$$

where c_{new} is the new cluster formed by combining c_l and c_k, $v(w_i)$ is feature words vector of the new cluster; $Weight(w_{inew})$ is weight of w_i in c_{new}; M and N are text numbers of c_k and c_l. Through Equation(4), weights of common feature words of two cluster could be increased, while weight of feature words that exist in only one cluster could be decreased. When there are more than K feature words in the new cluster, K feature words with higher weights will be used to represent the cluster.

2.2.2. *Training word vector*

Word vectors were trained by Mikolov's Skip-gram model. The Skip-gram model could be achieved through Hierarchical Softmax and Negative Sampling. In this paper, Skip-gram model based on Hierarchical Softmax was used. Its structure is shown in Fig.2.

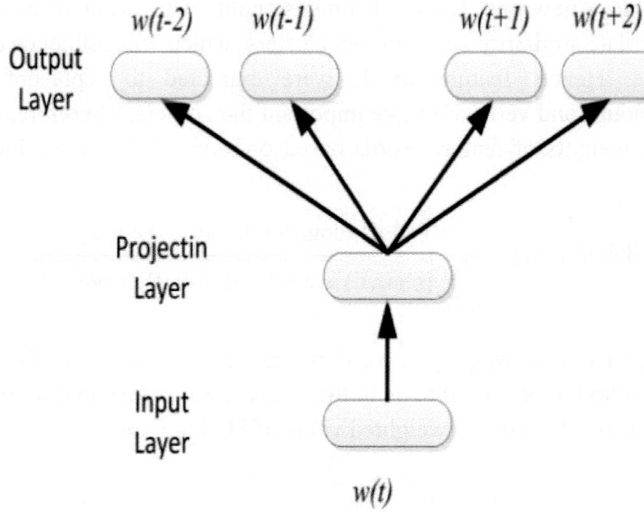

Fig.2. Skip-gram model

It can be seen in Fig.2 that Skip-gram model includes three layers: input layer, projection layer and output layer. It predicts context under the premise of knowing current word $w(t)$. The objective function of Skip-gram model (L) is:

$$L = \sum_{w \in V} \log p(Context(w) \mid w) \,. \tag{5}$$

$$p(Context(w) \mid w) = \prod_{u \in Context(w)} p(u \mid w) \,. \tag{6}$$

Where V is dictionary corresponding to dataset; $Context(w)$ is the context whose distance to w is shorter than C (C generally varies between 5~10). Word vectors with rich semantic information can be gained after Skip-gram model training. More details are available in Reference[11].

2.3. *Short text similarity calculation based on feature word vector*

In this paper, semantic similarity between clusters was calculated by WMD. WMD defines the semantic similarity between two clusters as the minimum sum of distance for all feature word vectors of one cluster "travel" to feature word vectors of the other (Fig.3).

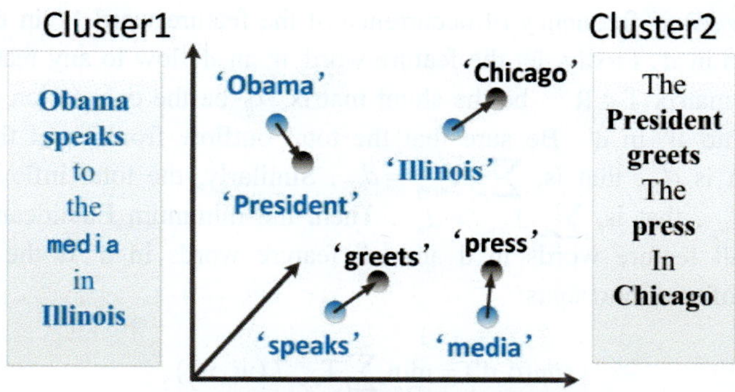

Fig.3. Cluster similarity calculation of WMD

In Fig.3, all non-stop words in two texts shall be mapped onto the same vector space, so that their semantic similarity can be calculated. In other words, the distance sum of all word vectors reaches the shortest only when "Obama" flows to "President", "Illinois" to "Chicago", "speeks" to "greets" and "media" to "press". This distance sum will be taken as the semantic similarity between these two short texts.

2.3.1. *Calculation of semantic similarity between feature words*

When using WMD to calculate semantic similarity between clusters, it has to calculate semantic similarity between feature words firstly. Given a word vector matrix of d feature words $X \in \mathbb{R}^{d \times n}$, if $x_i \in R^d$ is word vector of the feature word w_i in the d-dimensional space, the semantic similarity between feature words can be measured by Euclidean distance:

$$L(w_i, w_j) = \| x_i - x_j \|_2 . \tag{7}$$

where $L(w_i, w_j)$ is semantic similarity between w_i and w_j; x_i and x_j are word vectors of w_i and w_j, respectively. The smaller the $L(w_i, w_j)$, the higher the semantic similarity.

2.3.2. *Calculation of semantic similarity between short texts*

After similarity between feature words was gained through word vector, WMD will calculate the minimum distance sum between all feature words in the short text d to all feature words in the short text d' to measure similarity between these two texts. The total outflow of w_i in d is expressed as:

$$d_{w_i} = \frac{tf(w_i, d)}{\sum_{j=1}^{n} tf(w_j, d)} . \tag{8}$$

where $tf(w_i, \mathrm{d})$ is frequency of occurrence of the feature word w_i in d and n is total words in d. Firstly, let the feature word w_i in d flow to any feature word in d', the matrix $\mathrm{T} \in \mathrm{R}^{n \times n}$ be the shunt matrix, T_{ij} be the conversion degree of w_i in d into w_j in d'. Be sure that the total outflow from w_i at the end of conversion is d_{w_i}, that is, $\sum_{w_j} \mathrm{T}_{w_i w_j} = d_{w_i}$. Similarly, the total inflow into w_j shall be d_{w_j}, that is, $\sum_{w_i} \mathrm{T}_{w_i w_j} = d_{w_j}$. Then, the minimum Euclidean distance between all feature words in d and all feature words in d' is the semantic similarity of two short texts:

$$sim(\mathrm{d}, \mathrm{d}') = \min_{\mathrm{T} \ge 0} \sum_{i,j=1}^{n} \mathrm{T}_{w_i w_j} L(w_i, w_j). \tag{9}$$

Solving details of Equation(9) are introduced in Reference [14].

2.4. *Flowchart of hierarchical clustering algorithm*

The flowchart of proposed feature word vector based hierarchical clustering algorithm is as follows.

Algorithm: Feature word vector based hierarchical clustering algorithm

---

Input: *Cluster set* $C = \{c_1, c_2, ...c_i, ..., c_n\}$ *and* $c_i = \{v(w_m) : Weight(w_m), w_m \in d_i\}$.

Set cluster number as P.

Output: P cluster sets

initialization:

$j := N + 1$

while $|C| > K$:

for $(c_k, c_l) \in C \times C$:

$$sim(c_k, c_l) = \min_{\mathrm{T} \ge 0} \sum_{i,j=1}^{n} \mathrm{T}_{w_i w_j} L(w_i, w_j)$$

$$(c_{n1}, c_{n2}) := \max_{(c_k, c_l) \in C \times C} \{sim(c_k, c_l)\}$$

$$c_j := c_{n1} \cup c_{n2}$$

$$Weight(w_{ij}) = \frac{M \cdot Weight(w_{ik}) + N \cdot Weight(t_{il})}{M + N}$$

$$c_j = \{\{v(w_i)\} \mid \max_K (Weight(w_i)), w_i \in (c_l + c_k)\}$$

$$C := C \setminus \{c_{n1}, c_{n2}\} \cup \{c_j\}$$

$$j : j + 1$$

---

3. Experiments and Results

3.1. *Experimental data*

The proposed algorithm was tested on three English datasets and one Chinese dataset: 20newsgroup_subjects, CLing-2002 dataset, KnCr dataset and Weibo_topic dataset. According to data construction method of Bora[15], this paper chose 5 categories of topic contents in 20 categories of the English text classification general data set 20newsgroup[23] as the experimental dataset, recorded as 20newsgroup_subjects .The topics are "talk.politics.mideast", "comp.windows.x","rec.sport.baseball","sci.med" and "soc. religion. christian" and each sentence has 6.69 words on average.

CLing-2002 dataset: it is composed of 48 article abstracts involving four computer science categories of CICLing2002 Conference, which are collected by Makagonov[16]. These 48 abstracts include 11 of Linguistics, 15 of Ambiguity, 11 of Lexicon and 11 of Text Processing. The CLing-2002 dataset contains a total of 3382 words, averaging at 70.45 words for each abstract. Please see Reference 17 for more details.

KnCr dataset: it consists 900 article abstracts of 16 medical categories collected by D. Pinto[18]. This paper chose five categories, namely, blood, colon, genetic studies, skin and stomach, as experimental data. More details are in Reference 18.

Weibo_topic dataset: data of five events in NLP&&CC2012[24] for studying Chinese MicroBlog Emotion Tendency were chosen as the experimental data .It consists "Philippine army malicious hit Chinese fishing boats", "Officials of the public property", "Han han fight with Fang zhou zi", "Leather shoes jelly" and "Chinese teachers' wages ranked near the bottom of the world" and each sentence has an average of 23.86 words.

3.2. *Evaluation standard*

This paper used the mean F value as the evaluation index of experimental results. F value, the comprehensive evaluation of precision (P) and recall (R), is a common evaluation index of text clustering.

$$P(i,j) = \frac{the\ \ number\ \ of\ \ category\ \ i\ \ in\ \ cluster\ j}{the\ \ total\ \ text\ number\ \ in\ \ cluster\ j}. \tag{10}$$

$$R(i,j)=\frac{the\ \ number\ \ of\ \ category\ \ i\ \ in\ \ cluster\ j}{the\ \ total\ \ text\ \ numbuer\ \ of\ \ category\ \ i}. \tag{11}$$

$$F(i,j)=\frac{2P(i,j)R(i,j)}{P(i,j)+R(i,j)}. \tag{12}$$

where $P(i,j)$, $R(i,j)$ and $F(i,j)$ are precision, recall and F value of category i in the cluster j. The category i with the highest $F(i)$ in the cluster j was taken as the final F value. The overall clustering effect is evaluated by the mean F:

$$F=\sum_i \frac{|i|\times F(i)}{\sum_i |i|}. \tag{13}$$

3.3. *Experimental settings and result analysis*

To verify feasibility and validity of the proposed algorithm, VSM[19], LDA[20]and BTM[21] were used for text expression. Semantic similarity between short texts was calculated by cosine similarity. The mainstream hierarchical clustering algorithm was used as the control group. Evaluation results were recorded as VSM, LDA and BTM. After feature word vectors of clusters were extracted, similarity between short texts were calculated by using cosine similarity and WMD[25], respectively. Clustering was accomplished with hierarchical clustering algorithm. According to number of categories of datasets, number of clusters was set *P*. Evaluation results were recorded FWV-COS and FWV-WMD. Parameters in LDA model and BTM model were set according to Reference 6. Number of topics S was set 12; hyper-parameters α and β were determined empirical values: α=50 / S and $\beta = 0.01$; and iteration time was set 2000. In this paper, English word vectors chose word vectors[26] published by Mikolov, while Chinese word vectors were acquired by Skip-gram model training of "Full Web News Data of Sogou Labs" [27] and "MicroBlog Data of Huawei Labs" [22].

Five clustering method were used to four experimental datasets. The mean F value was used as the evaluation index of clustering effect. Results are shown in Table 1.

Table 1 Clustering assessment of four experimental datasets

	20newsgroup_subjects	Cling-2002	KnCr	weibo_topics
VSM	0.164	0.263	0.150	0.332
LDA	0.215	0.328	0.325	0.333
BTM	0.323	0.355	0.362	0.412
FWV-COS	**0.598**	**0.514**	**0.461**	**0.589**
FWV-WMD	**0.610**	**0.526**	**0.493**	**0.612**

According clustering assessment in Table 1, clustering method based on topic model is superior to clustering method based on VSM model. This indicates that when there are few data features, VSM-based clustering which neglects relationship between synonyms and extracts features by calculating TF-IDF will be greatly influenced by sparse data of short text. The clustering method based on BTM model is better than that based on LDA model. This is because LDA makes document modeling directly and has to make statistics on probability distribution of documents-topics, which is impossible when there are few feature words of short text. But BTM model establishes models to any common word pairs in the text, which makes for shortcomings of the LDA model. The proposed algorithm is far superior to all contrast methods. With respect to four experimental datasets, the mean F value of the proposed algorithm isaveragely55.43% higher than the second best method that is based on BTM model. Among four experimental datasets, 20newsgroup_subjects has the least average words in every text, showing the most serious data sparsity. However, the mean F value of FWV-WMD is 88.85% higher than that of BTM. This demonstrates that word vectors gained from large-scale data training carry with rich semantic information and won't be influenced by data sparsity of text. According to FWV-COS and FWV-WMD, WMD is better than traditional cosine similarity calculation in exploring semantic similarity between word vectors, thus achieving better clustering effect.

4. Conclusion

A feature word vector based short text clustering algorithm is proposed in this paper. Through weighted word POS, it could extract feature words of clusters more accurately. Moreover, it overcomes problem caused by data sparsity of short text by taking advantages of properties of word vector and achieve higher similarity calculation accuracy between short texts by improving WMD. Experimental results prove that the proposed algorithm could improve clustering effectively. The proposed algorithm is used in hierarchical clustering algorithm in this paper and will be used in other mainstream clustering algorithms (e.g. K-means and FCM), aiming to search for the optimum clustering effect.

Acknowledgments

This work is supported by National Natural Science Foundation (（14BXW028）).

References

1. Hong-guang Suo, Yu-wei Wang. An improved means algorithm for document clustering[J].Journal of Shandong University(Natural Science),2008,43(1):61-64. "In Chinese"
2. Xia Zhang, Su-zhen Wang, Yi-xin Yin. Research of text clustering based on fuzzy granular computing[J]. Computer Science, 2010, 37(2):209-211."In Chinese"
3. Chen X, Zhang Y, Cao L, et al. An Improved Feature Selection Method for Chinese Short Texts Clustering Based on HowNet[M]//Computer Engineering and Networking. Springer International Publishing, 2014: 635-642.
4. Qiu-chan Bai, Chun-xia Jin. Short text clustering based on concept feature expansion[J]. Journal of Changchun Normal University(Natural Science) , 2011, 30(5): 29-33."In Chinese"
5. Jian-hong Shi, Xing-shu Chen. Discovering topic from Chinese microblog based on hidden topics analysis[J]. Application Research of Computers. 2014,31(3):700-704."In Chinese"
6. Qiu-lian Tang. Short text clustering method based on BTM[D]. Anhui University,2014."In Chinese"
7. Bouras C, Tsogkas V. A clustering technique for news articles using WordNet[J]. Knowledge-Based Systems, 2012, 36: 115-128.
8. Banerjee S, Ramanathan K, Gupta A. Clustering short texts using wikipedia[C]//Proceedings of the 30th annual international ACM SIGIR conference on Research and development in information retrieval. ACM, 2007: 787-788.
9. Shao-peng Wang, Peng Yan. Research of the clustering based on LDA using in network public opinion analysis[J]. Journal of Shandong University(Natural Science), 2014, 49(09): 129-134.
10. Yin J, Wang J. A dirichlet multinomial mixture model-based approach for short text clustering[C]//Proceedings of the 20th ACM SIGKDD international conference on Knowledge discovery and data mining. ACM, 2014: 233-242.
11. MIKOLOV T, CHEN K, CORRADO G, et al. Efficient estimation of word representations in vector space[J]. arXiv preprint arXiv, 2013:1301.3781.

12. Murphy K P. Machine learning: a probabilistic perspective[M]. MIT press, 2012.
13. Mikolov T, Sutskever I, Chen K, et al. Distributed representations of words and phrases and their compositionality[C]//Advances in neural information processing systems. 2013: 3111-3119.
14. Kusner M J, Sun E D U Y, Kolkin E D U N I, et al. From Word Embeddings To Document Distances[J].
15. Bora N N, Mishra B S P, Dehuri S. Heuristic Frequent Term-Based Clustering of News Headlines[J]. Procedia Technology, 2012, 6: 436-443.
16. Makagonov P, Alexandrov M, Gelbukh A. Clustering abstracts instead of full texts[C]//Text, Speech and Dialogue. Springer Berlin Heidelberg, 2004: 129-135.
17. Shrestha P, Jacquin C, Daille B. Clustering short text and its evaluation[M]//Computational Linguistics and Intelligent Text Processing. Springer Berlin Heidelberg, 2012: 169-180.
18. Pinto D, Rosso P. KnCr: A short-text narrow-domain sub-corpus of medline[J]. Proceedings of TLH-ENC06, 2006: 266-269.
19. Qimin C, Qiao G, Yongliang W, et al. Text clustering using VSM with feature clusters[J]. Neural Computing and Applications, 2015, 26(4): 995-1003.
20. Guo L, Chun-Jie Z, Zhi-Yuan Z. A text clustering method based on weighted LDA model[J]. Journal of Chemical & Pharmaceutical Research, 2015, 7(3).
21. Yan X, Guo J, Lan Y, et al. A biterm topic model for short texts[C]//Proceedings of the 22nd international conference on World Wide Web. International World Wide Web Conferences Steering Committee, 2013: 1445-1456.
22. Wang H, Lu Z, Li H, et al. A Dataset for Research on Short-Text Conversations[C]//EMNLP. 2013: 935-945.
23. http://www.ai.mit.edu/people/jrennie/20Newsgroups/
24. http://tcci.ccf.org.cn/conference/2012/
25. http://matthewkusner.com
26. http://code.google.com/p/word2vec
27. http://www.sogou.com/labs/dl/ca.html

Research of Components Identification and Extraction Based on Software Design Documentation

You-qun SHI and Xiao-yan GUO

School of Computer Science and Technology
Donghua University, Shanghai Songjiang, China
Email:yqshi@dhu.edu.cn,774881584@qq.com

Hong-yun XU

School of Information Science and Technology
Donghua University, Shanghai Songjiang, China
Email: xjyc2000@163.com

Currently, there are no components identification and extraction methods are that further specify the components retrieval targets from the software design document. Therefore, this paper proposes a method for components identification and extraction based on XML document by using a multi-agent system to learn keywords and semantics from the XML document transferred from UML-based software design document. Thereafter OWL, a descriptive language, is used to verify the correctness and completeness of the derived results. The experiment verifies the effectiveness of the proposed method, thus providing a reliable foundation for future works on component retrieval.

Keywords: XML document; Component; Multi-agent system; OWL.

1. Introduction

In recent years, in the field of identification and extraction about components [1] from software design software, researchers have proposed their own methods from different business models or goals or strategies and so on, including Create-Read-Update-Delete (CRUD), domain analysis and cluster analysis. However, these methods are lack of the unified semantic and business supporting models, and the reuse ratio and flexibility of components nearly be neglected. In view of this, this paper proposes a method of components identification and extraction, of which the main idea is using XML technology to re-encoding the software design document and extracting the components from the XML document through a multi-agent system [2] and forming the structure of target system with the context constraints analysis method [7].

2. Components in software design document

The description of component in UML [4] is illustrated in Fig.1. The figure depicts a component which is named UserManage.Fig.1 (a) is an abstract representation of the component; it hides the structural details of UserManage and only marks the interface of component's implementation. What's more, we can see from Fig.1 (b) that the component contains two implementation classes which are named Login and Register, these classes implement the interface offered by UserManage.

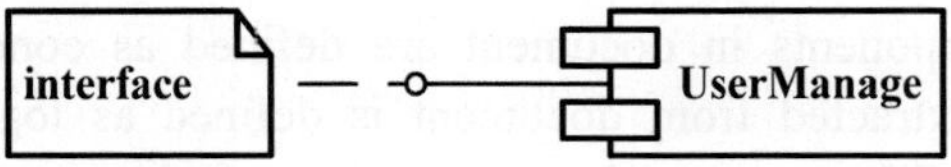

(a) Interface and Component: hide the detail

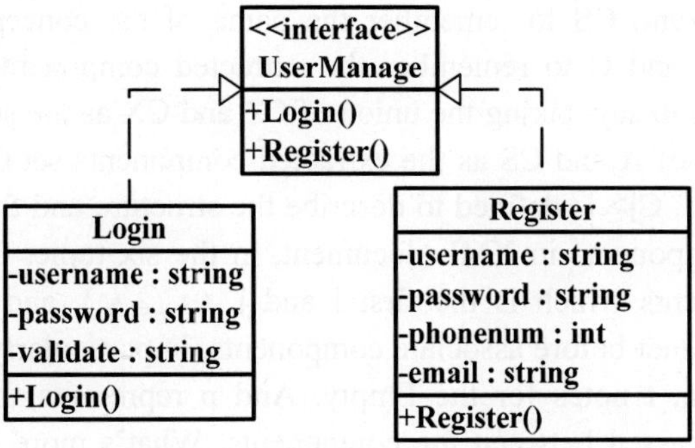

(b) Interface and Component: show the detail

Fig.1 Components concept in UML

In UML-based software design documentation, specifications about components include function that it provides and depends on, and the I/O parameters, and component's type and interface. For example, an e-commerce logical service component which is descripted by the system specifications is shown in Table 1.

Table 1 Example of component description

Name	ShopcartManage
Type	logical service
Input Parma	Id, num, price, weight
Function	generate orders, add goods, delete goods
Depending Functions	Shopcart, NumUpdate, OrderManage, GoodsManage
Interfaces	public void AddtoShopcart(String id), public void DeletefromShopcart(String id), public int CreateOrder(Int num, Double price, Double weight)

3. Components identification and extraction

To be distinguishable, the components in document are defined as concept components, the components extracted from document is defined as logical components. We also define CZ to remember the name of the concept components in component diagram, CX to remember the name of the concept components in sequence diagram, CS to remember the name of the concept components in class diagram, and C to remember the extracted components. And C=(CZ∪ CX)∩CS. That is to say, taking the union of CZ and CX as the set A, then taking the intersection of A and CS as the extracted components set C. besides, a six tuple<Ci, t, p, r, f, Cj> is defined to describe the structure and the mutual relationship of the components in XML document, in the six tuple, Ci and Cj represent the components which is the first i and j. ($i, j \in N$), and t represents the conditions to be met before associate components, in particularly, if there isn't needed condition, t notes for the Empty. And p represents the collection of parameters that passed between the components. What's more, r represents the relationship between the components, including incoming labels, etc. and f represents the state of the connection between components. If the current component own subsequent associated components, f marks next, on the other hand, f marks end. The identification and extraction is completed by a multi-agent system, and the workflow of MAS is shown in Fig.2.

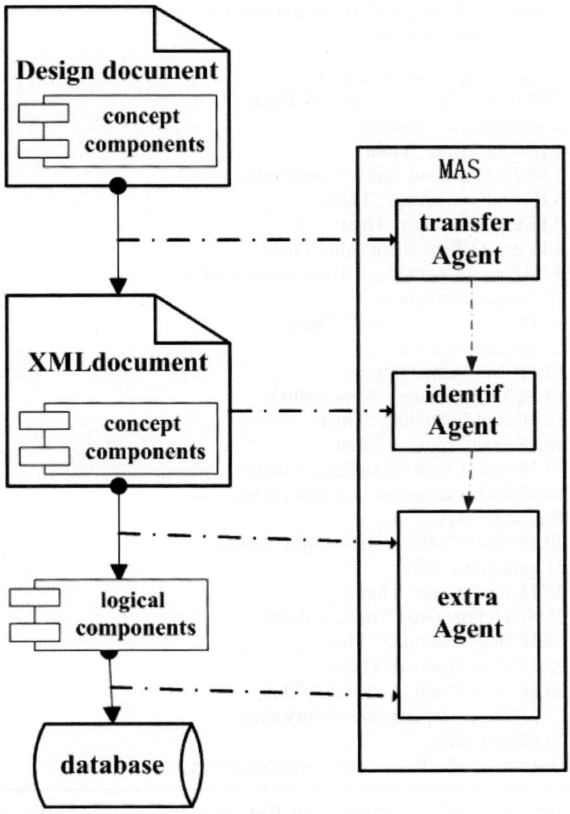

Fig.2 Workflow of MAS

Algorithm1 is the identification process of identifAgent which identify the concept components in XML document.

Algorithm1.*ComponentIdentification (D)*
Input: XML document D.

1.Travers XML document D;
2.**IF** find "UML: Component" **Then**:
3.generate a component;
4.**IF** find "name" **Then**:
5.SET(component.name = nameValue);
6.**IF** find "incoming", **Then:**
7.**IF** exsit Producer **Then**:
8.**IF** exsit Client clientValue **Then:**
9.SET(component dependency clientValue);
10.Output component;
11.**IF** find "UML: Class" **Then**:
12.generate a class;
13.**IF** find "name" **Then:**
14.SET(class.name = nameValue);
15.**IF** find "incoming" **Then**:
16.**IF** exsit Producer **Then**:
17.**IF** exsit Client clientValue **Then:**
18.SET(classdependency clientValue);
19.Output class;
20.**IF** find "UML: Collaboration" **Then:**
21.generate a class;
22.**IF** find "name" **Then**:
23.SET(class.name = nameValue);
24.**IF** find "incoming" **Then**:
25.**IF** exsit Producer **Then:**
26.**IF** exsit Client clientValue **Then:**
27.SET(classdependency clientValue);
28.Output class;
Output: Collection of concept components.

Based on the recognition process of the concept components, Algorithm2 is the extraction process of extraAgent which extract the concept components as logical components from the XML document. when received the collection of concept components offered by identifAgent, extra Agent begin to extract the components with algorithm2: The component name whether is a member of collection of logical components which is described as C= （CZ∪CX）∩CS, as showed by line 2-4 in the algorithm 2.If yes, to obtain the related components and the related parameters according to the dependency property values of the component. As showed in line 5-7.And to gather the logical components into the database and return them, as shown in line 8-9.

Algorithm2.*ComponentExtraction()*
Input: Collection of concept components.
1.generate a logic components collection;
2.Travers the concept components collection;
3.**IF** Ci in CZ || Ci in CX **Then**:
4.**IF** Ci in CS **Then**:
5.**IF** Find(Ci. incoming = Cj) **Then**:
6.**SET**(Ci. Specification=Find(Specification between Ci and Cj));
7.add Ci into logic component set;
8.SAVE(logic component collection);
9.RETURN(logic component collection);
Output: Collection of logical components C.

4. Topological structure of target system

The context constraint analysis method is proposed to connect these logic components into the topology of the target system. The workflow of context constraint analysis method is descripted as follows:

(1) Define the collection G to remember the topological sequence, G Initial is empty.
(2) Traverse the Collection of logical components C, if there is a relationship between Ci and Cj, we create the tuple<Ci,Cj> and put it into the collection G. continue the process until there is no new tuple is created.
(3) Traverse the collection G, for each item in G, such as<Ci,Cj>,we create the edge Eij between the vertexes Ci and Cj. Continue until there is no new edge created.
(4) The topological structure of target system is obtained.

5. Description of the example

In this paper, we take a shopping cart management module of a commercial system for an example. We investigate the component model in the design documentation of the commercial system, including component diagram, class diagram and sequence diagram. As it is shown in Fig.3, we build a multi-agent system based on JADE [3] platform.

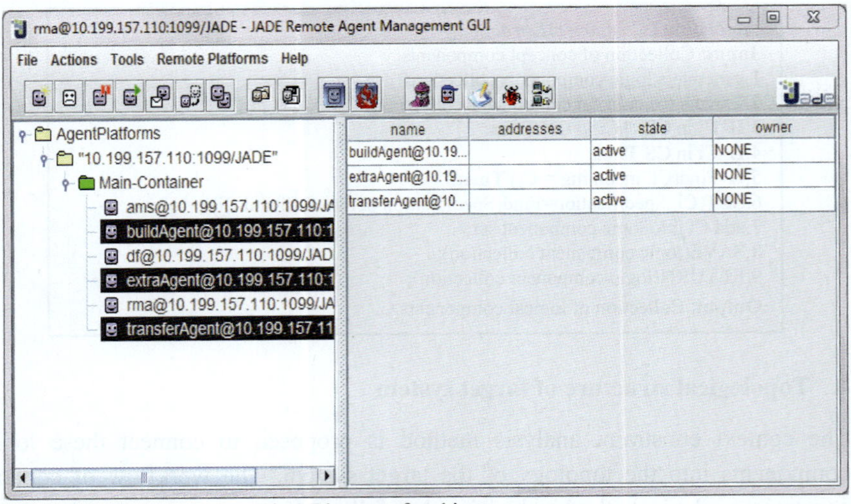

Fig.3 Diagram of multi-agent system

transferAgent which learn the keywords and semantics [6] and re-encoding the software design document into XML document and send the result to extraAgent with the ACL [5] message, extraAgent which identify and extract the components from the XML document begin to work when received the document and its status turned into active from idle, shown in Fig.4. The process of extraAgent depends on Algorithm1 and extraction method proposed in this paper.

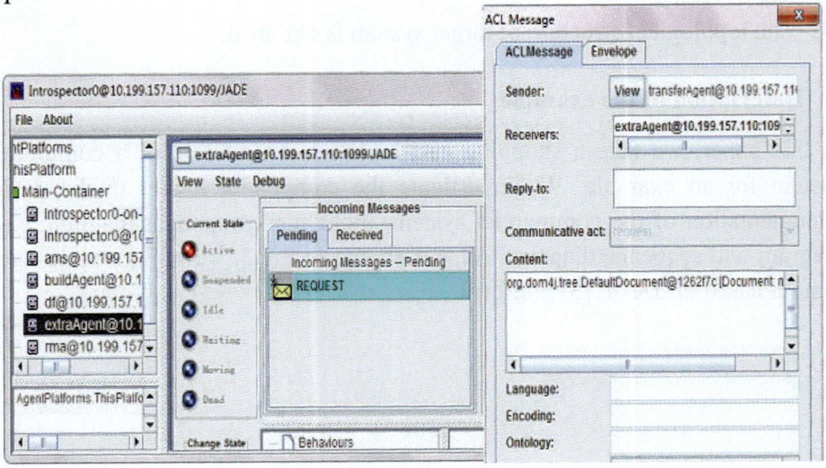

Fig.4 Messages received by an extraAgent

According the component model in document:

CZ={ShopcartManage,OrderManage,FavoriteManage,FavoriteInfo,UserIte mInfo,UserManageInfo,Login,ErrorHandle}.CX={ShopcartManage,AddtoShopcart,ShowShopcart,DeleteFromShopcart,CreateOrder,NumUpdate}.CS={ShopcartManage,AddtoShopcart,DeletefromShopcart,CreateOrder}.the collection of extracted components C={ShopcartManage, AddtoShopcart, DeletefromShopcart, CreateOrder }.After the extraction, each concept component can be described with component description specifications before sent as the ACL message to buildAgent by transferAgent, including component's name, the input parameters, the output parameters, return values, interface and dependencies. Once received the message, the status of buildAgent change into active from idle too, and the received message is parsed, which is to form the topology of the target system with the context constraint analysis method proposed in this paper. The result of buildAgent is shown in Fig.5:

```
My local name is:buildAgent
My globally unique name is:buildAgent@10.199.157.110:1099/JADE
I am running in a location called:Main-Container
Which is identified uniquely as:Main-Container@10.199.157.110
And is contactable at:10.199.157.110
Using the protocol:jicp
<AddtoShopcart,empty,(customerid,goodsid,goodsname,buynum),incoming,next,CreateOrder>
<CreateOrder,empty,(customerid,goodsid,goodsname,buynum),incoming,end,ShopcartManage>
<DeleteFromShopcart,empty,(customerid,goodsid),incoming,end,ShopcartManage>
```

Fig.5 Construction result about system architecture

As a result, the topology structure of the shoppingcart management module obtained. The result is shown in Fig.6.

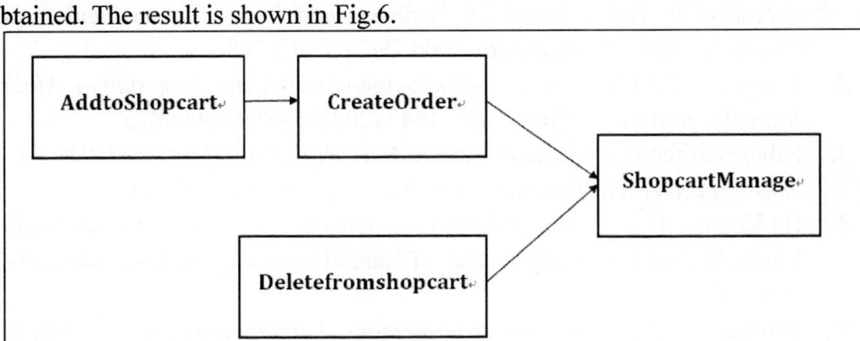

Fig.6 Shoppingcart management module architecture diagram

To verify the result, using automated tool ArgoUML to map the contents of the XML document into a document described by OWL [8], the following conclusions can be drawn:

(1) (CreateOrder, rdfs: subClassOf, ShopcartManage);

(2) (DeleteFromShopcart, rdfs: subClassOf, ShopcartManage);

(3) (AddtoShopcart, rdfs:subClassOf, CreateOrder);

(4) domain(incoming)= CreateOrder, Range(incoming)= ShopcartManage;
(5) domain(incoming)=DeleteFromShopcart, Range(incoming)= ShopcartManage;
(6) domain(incoming)= AddtoShopcart, Range(incoming)= CreateOrder;

In combination with the semantic[9] described by OWL, we can take the architecture of the module of shoppingcart management (Fig.5) for comparison, the relationship between the components and the components described in the architecture is basically consistent with the components described in the document OWL, that is to say, the result obtained is of accuracy and efficiency.

6. Conclusion

This paper presents a method for components recognition and extraction based on software design document. Multi-Agent is applied to identify and extract components, and build the target system architecture. The next priority is to get a logical component of ontology description, and take scientific and reasonable steps to judge logic components and inosculation between the physical artifacts for reliable component retrieval and query.

References

1. Wan G Zhongjie, Xu Xiaofei, Zhan Dechen. *Componentgranularity optimization design based on business model sta-bility evaluation [J].* Chinese Journal of Computers, 2006,29(2) :239 2 248.
2. Wang, L.-C., Chen, S.-F.: *AMulti-AgentMulti-Issue Negotiation Model.* Journalof Software 13(08), 1637–1643 (2002) ISSN: 10009825.
3. Fabio Bellifemine, Giovanni Caire, *JADE PROGRAMMER'SGUIDE. http://Sharon.cselt.it/projects/jade/doc/programmersguide.pdf*
4. He Keqing, Jiang Hong, and HeFei .*Extended UML with role modeling[J].* China, Wuhan University Journal of Natural Science(WUJNS), 2001,6(1-2) :175-182.
5. Shoham, Y.: *Agent oriented programming. Artificial Intelligence* 60(1), 51–92 (1993).
6. Axel Korthaus, Michael Schwind, Stefan Seedorf. *Leveraging Semantic Web technologies for business component specification Web Semantics Web Semantics*. Science, Services and Agents on the World Wide Web 5, 2007:130~141.

7. Ren,Z., Anumba, C.J., Ugwu, O.O.: *The development of a multi-agent system for construction claims negotiation.* Advances in Engineering Software 34(11-12), 683–696(2003)
8. Bohring H., Auer S. *Mapping XML to OWL Ontologies[J].* Lecture Notes in Informatics (LNI). 2005,V72:147-156
9. Gruber T. R. A Translation Approach to Portable Ontology Specifications[J]. Knowledge Acquisition. 1993, 5:199-220

Missing Data Processing Model Based on E-M Algorithm and Its Application in Fault Diagnosis

Yan-an SHEN and Yan-qing QI

Management Engineering Section, Army Officer Academy,
Hefei, China
E-mail: 756534439@163.com

Liang CHEN

Graduate Management Unit, Army Officer Academy,
Hefei, China
E-mail: 499364237@qq.com

Low quantities, structural complexity, prone to variable degradation and numerous failures, are some of the characteristics of an aero-engine and thus it is a great challenge to apply the fault diagnosis and preventive maintenance. In order to overcome such problems, we put propose the missing data processing model based on the expectation maximization algorithm. We estimate the parameters' point estimates of Weibull proportional hazard model using this algorithm and calculate the maintenance interval based on aero-engine' availability constraints.

Keywords: Fault monitoring; Missing data; Maintenance decision.

1. Introduction

In data acquisition field when observer is recording failure data some parts of aero-engine is still in normal work condition due to the different components of investment time. Moreover with the improvement of engine reliability it is harder and harder to get failure data. This forms the characteristics of the failure data random truncation or missing.

Marking the data set of variables as Y, the observed data as Y_{obs}, and the missing data as Y_{mis}. (1)If the conditional probability $P(Y_{mis}|Y)=P(Y_{mis})$ is set up, it is called missing completely at random (MCAR). (2)If the conditional probability $P(Y_{mis}|Y)=P(Y_{mis}|\ Y_{obs})$ is set up, it is called missing at random (MAR). In this condition missing data depends on other observed variables Y_{obs}, but does not depends on the variables' missing parts Y_{mis}. (3)If there is a dependency among the missing data, missing parts Y_{mis} and observed variables

Y_{obs}, it is called missing not at random (MNAR). The mechanism of relationship between 3 types of missing data is shown in Fig. 1.

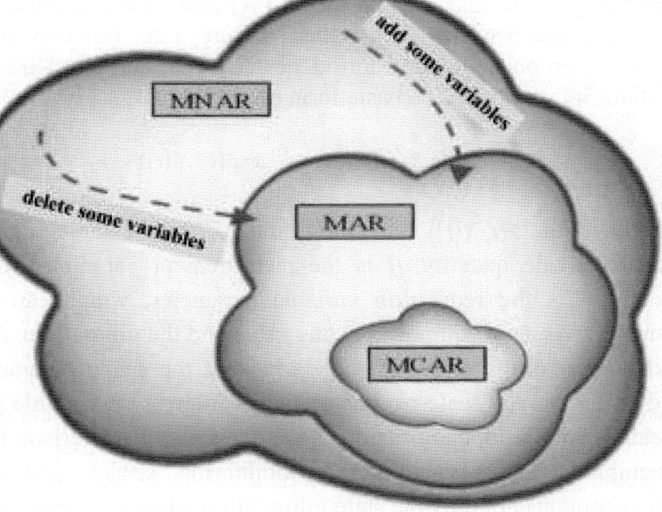

Fig. 1. Three missing data mechanisms and their mutual relations.

In view of the aero-engine' running status, we use the vibration value of monitoring methods to detect fault values. There exists missing phenomenon in fault monitoring process and the type of missing data is called for MAR.

2. The Missing Data Processing Model Based on E-M Algorithm

2.1. *Maximum likelihood estimation*

On the basis of the existing missing data samples, maximum likelihood estimation (MLE) takes the occurrence probability of the observed values to be biggest as the estimate criterion $\hat{\theta}_y$, the maximum likelihood estimator of the parameter θ,makes it the most possible to obtain the sample data in the process of observation, and the corresponding θ should also be the most closed to the real parameters. Take the incomplete variable Y_k of the observation data as unknown variable θ, and construct likelihood function and likelihood equation which can contain the information of parameter θ.

$$l(\theta|Y_{obs}) = \ln L(\theta|Y_{obs}) \ . \tag{1}$$

$$\frac{\partial}{\partial\theta} l(\theta|Y_{obs}) = 0 \ . \tag{2}$$

The maximum likelihood estimator $\hat{\theta}_y$ can be obtained. In this article, the mathematical model used to deal with the random missing fault monitoring data is the Weibull proportional hazards model (WPHM). This model assumes that covariates are independent each other, failure rate function of different individuals are proportional, and introduces covariate to reflect the equipment running status information. The basic form of WPHM is:

$$\lambda(t, X(t)) = \frac{\alpha}{\beta}\left(\frac{t}{\beta}\right)^{\alpha-1} \exp(\gamma \cdot X(t)) . \tag{3}$$

In the equation, $\lambda(t, X(t))$ is the failure rate; *X(t)*is the value that keeps track of the characteristic quantity, β is the measurement parameter of the basic failure rate,; γ is the regression variable parameter, which can reflect the relationship between the equipment status value and the failure rate. A variety of sample data in reality can be fitted by adjusting the shape parameters of the weibull distribution, the scale parameter and the regression variable parameters. When dealing with equipment maintenance decision, characteristic information of the equipment can be obtained by monitoring, sensors and so on. The information contains not only the state information when the equipment operates normally, but also contains the sample information when the equipment is in fault state. After obtaining a set of condition information that reflecting the integrated degree of the equipment, the specific parameters of the weibull proportional hazards model can be determined.

According to the formula (3), the equipment reliability function at the moment t and the state *X(t)* can be obtained:

$$R(t, X(t)) = \exp\left[-\int_0^t \exp(\gamma \cdot X(t)) d\left(\frac{t}{\beta}\right)^{\alpha}\right] . \tag{4}$$

The failure density function is:

$$f(t, X(t)) = \lambda(t, X(t)) \cdot R(t, X(t)). \tag{5}$$

2.2. *Missing data processing model*

Applying the expectation maximization (EM) algorithm to find the maximum likelihood estimator is credit to Dempster, Laird and Rubin. The algorithm is just designed for looking for MLE. Every iteration mainly includes 2 steps:

E step is numerical integration, $Y_{mis}^{(t)}$is predicted based on complete data Y_{obs} and known parameter estimate value. Namely acquire the expectation (condition expectation) towards likelihood function about missing data. M step is derivative operation. A new estimate value $\theta^{(t+1)}$is given based on Y_{obs} and

Y_{mis}, the expectation fetch maximum value at point $\theta^{(t+1)}$. It forms a iteration $\theta^{(t)} \to \theta^{(t+1)}$ the new estimate value $\theta^{(t+1)}$ leads to the maximum value. Making use of EM algorithm to solve WPHM model is as follows.

The E step: Unite formula(1)~formula(5), the consociation probability density likelihood function of equipments is as follows.

$$L(\alpha,\beta,\gamma)=\prod_{i=1}^{k}\lambda(t_i,X(t_i))\prod_{j=1}^{N}R(t_j,X(t_j)) . \tag{6}$$

In the formula, N means the sample total amount of data, r means that there is r breakdown data in the N, rest N-r piece is censored data, who work normally without breaking down to the monitoring points.

The logarithm likelihood function can be got when formula (6) is derivative

$$\ln L = k\ln\frac{\alpha}{\beta}+\sum_{i=1}^{k}\left[(\alpha-1)\ln\left(\frac{t_i}{\beta}\right)+\gamma\cdot X(t_i)\right]-\sum_{j=1}^{N}\left\{\left(\frac{t_j}{\beta}\right)^{\alpha}\exp[\gamma\cdot X(t_j)]\right\} . \tag{7}$$

The M step: when the partial derivative of ln$L$ towards parameter α、β、γ is work out, and each formula is equaled to 0, nonlinear equations are got.

$$\begin{cases}\dfrac{\partial \ln L}{\partial\alpha}=\dfrac{k}{\alpha}+\displaystyle\sum_{i=1}^{k}\ln\left(\frac{t_i}{\beta}\right)-\sum_{j=1}^{N}\left\{\left(\frac{t_j}{\beta}\right)^{\alpha}\ln\left(\frac{t_j}{\beta}\right)\exp\left[\gamma\cdot X(t_j)\right]\right\}=0\\ \dfrac{\partial \ln L}{\partial\beta}=-\dfrac{k\alpha}{\beta}+\displaystyle\sum_{j=1}^{N}\left\{\frac{\alpha}{\beta}\left(\frac{t_j}{\beta}\right)^{\alpha}\exp\left[\gamma\cdot X(t_j)\right]\right\}=0\\ \dfrac{\partial \ln L}{\partial\gamma}=\displaystyle\sum_{i=1}^{k}X(t_i)-\sum_{j=1}^{N}\left\{X(t_j)\left(\frac{t_j}{\beta}\right)^{\alpha}\exp\left[\gamma\cdot X(t_j)\right]\right\}=0\end{cases} . \tag{8}$$

According to the iterative algorithm, the value of parameter α、β、γ can be got. The estimate processes of parameters is shown in Fig. 2.

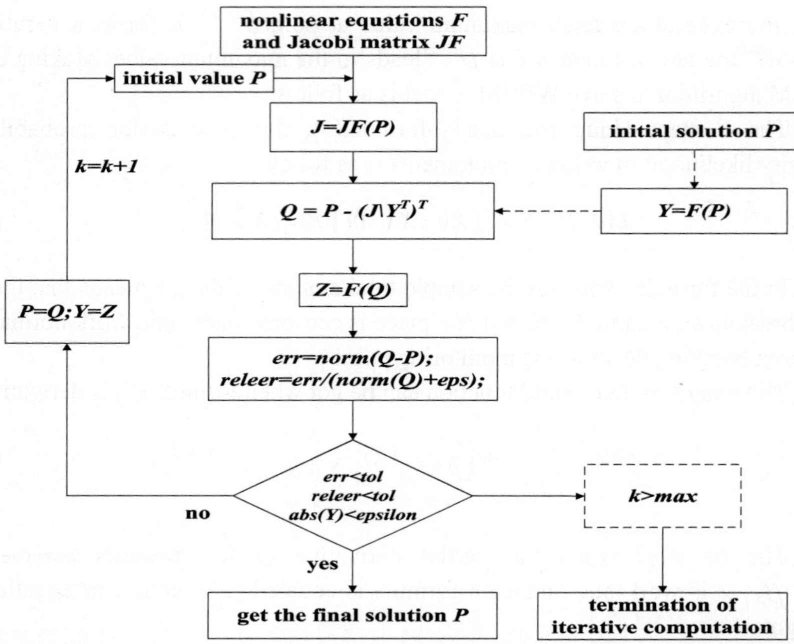

Fig. 2. Using missing data processing model to solve the estimating value in nonlinear equations.

The input parameter *F* is nonlinear equations system to be solved. The *JF* is Jacobi matrix of equation set. The *P* is the initial value; the *tol* is convergence tolerance of *X*, the *epsilon* is convergence tolerance of *F*, the *max* is the max iteration number of times. After a suitable *P* is inputted, through a certain number of times operation, one of the best approximate solution of the equation set(8) can be work out, that are estimate values of parameter α、β、γ of the WPHM.

3. Dynamic Reliability Assessment

3.1. *Data collection*

The monitoring data of engine bearing is collected by investigation. This is a typical indirect monitoring situation. The true state of the bearing is not observed, but it is not related to the measurement of the vibration monitoring data. Table 1 lists the state monitoring data during the period of the bearing. At the early stage of the bearing, the vibration intensity of the vibration intensity is relatively stable. However, with the occurrence and development of the defects, the monitoring value of the vibration intensity is increasing.

Tab.1. Engine bearing condition monitoring data.

data serial no.	total flight time(h)	vibration intensity(mm/s)	data serial no.	total flight time(h)	vibration intensity(mm/s)
point 1	8	1.0376	···		missing data
···		missing data	point 17	126	5.7891
point 3	18	1.1523	point 18	152	7.5246
point 4	24	1.2331	point 19	158	7.5334
···		missing data	point 20	224	8.2517
point 8	40	1.2753	point 21	232	8.7435
point 9	60	1.3265	point 22	246	9.1052
point 10	76	3.0421	point 23	268	14.1021
point 11	90	4.5772	point 24	290	20.2355
point 12	108	5.2130			

According to the method in Section 2, the application of MATLAB programming calculates the parameters: α =5.3422; β =820.6502 and γ =0.3470. So as to get the bearing of the WPHM:

$$\lambda(t,X(t))=\frac{5.3422}{820.6502}\left(\frac{t}{820.6502}\right)^{4.3422}\exp(0.3470\cdot X(t))\ . \tag{9}$$

3.2. *Dynamic maintenance decision*

A decision model of maintenance timing based on state maintenance is established from the perspective of availability.

$$A_w(T)=\frac{\int_0^{t_i} R(t,X(T_i))dt}{\int_0^{t_i} R(t,X(T_i))dt+R(t,X(T_i))\cdot T_p+[1-R(t,X(T_i))]\cdot T_c}\ . \tag{10}$$

Type: T_P for the average preventive maintenance time; $T_C$for the average repair time. The type (10) is performed to obtain the maximum time of$A_W(T)$. In this paper, the most close to the time monitoring data T_m is (158, 7.5334), and the failure rate of λ is 0.000069502.Set a judge function

$$g(t)=\gamma X(t)\geq\ln\frac{\beta^{\alpha}\cdot\lambda_m}{\alpha}-(\alpha-1)\ln t\ . \tag{11}$$

Assuming that t' for monitoring cycle, monitoring points. When the closest data of T_m+t' is substituted into formula (1), the failure rate threshold $\lambda_{m+t'}$ of state monitoring strengthen zone can be obtained. Now we can make a dynamic maintenance decision graph *g(t)* about time *t* as shown in Fig. 3.

As can be seen from Fig. 3, when the engine working time is less than 150h, the operation of its bearing parts is good. When the engine working time is reach to 150h, the bearing will appear failure symptom. At this time we should improve condition frequency. When the engine working time is reach to 220h, the bearing' failure symptom is very obvious. More and more failure state will appear such as burns, friction marks, damage, gap, serious wear and tear, which will affect the normal flight of the aircraft.

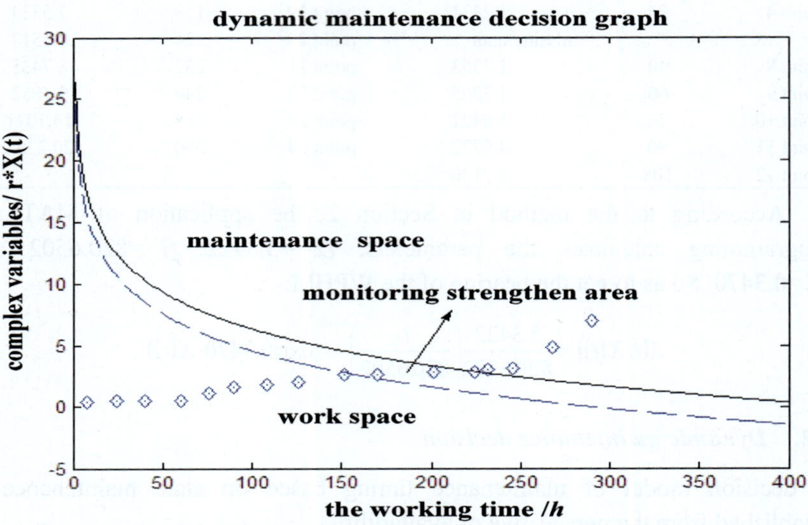

Fig. 3. Engine bearing dynamic maintenance decision graph.

4. Conclusion

In this paper we study on the missing data processing model based on E-M algorithm. Through the algorithm model we also estimate the parameters' point estimates of WPHM. Finally the maintenance interval of the aero-engine is calculated by the equipment availability constraints. The missing data processing model is verified feasibility during the test in the process of engine maintenance decision-making.

References

1. Gao Ping, WU Su, Jia Xi-sheng. Reliability Model of Complex System and its Parameters Estimation Method [J]. Journal of System Simulation, 2009, 21(13):4140-4142.In Chinese.
2. Samrout M, Chatelet E, Kouta R. optimization of maintenance policy using proportional hazard model [J]. Reliability Engineering and System Safety, 2009, 94(1):44-52.

3. Liu Zhi-yong, Wang Li-xin, Cheng Zhong-hua. Preventive maintenance decision optimication of simple system considering task [J]. Manufacturing Automation, 2013, 35(8):64-67.In Chinese.
4. Mohammed Sbihi, Christophe Varnier. Single-machine Scheduling With Periodic and Flexible Periodic Maintenance to Minimize Maximum Tardiness [J]. Computers & Industrial Engineering, 2008, 55(4): 830-840.
5. Chinyao Low, Chou-Jung Hsu, Chwen-Tzeng Su. Minimizing the make-span with an availability constraint on a single machine under simple linear deterioration [J].Computers & Mathematics with Applications, 2008, 56(1): 257-265.

Keyword Parallel Search over RDF Data Based on Semantic Association

Shuang CHEN and Jing-bin WANG
College of Mathematics and Computer Science, Fuzhou University, Fuzhou,350108, China
shuangchen_fzu@163.com, wjbcc@263.net

Existing RDF keyword search studies focus on constructing smallest trees or subgraphs which contain all query keywords, but neglect the semantic association between RDF data. Thus, this paper proposes the keyword parallel search over RDF data based on semantic association (KPSRSA)) algorithm which utilizes a score function to measure semantic association by combining OWL ontology and the probability model. It uses a distributed database Hbase as a storage medium and Mapreduce to perform parallel query, which queries sub-clusters with semantic association in Map phase and constructs a series of associated clusters as query results in Reduce phase. The experimental results demonstrate that the KPSRSA algorithm improves the precision and relevance of search results and keywords. In addition, distributed storage and parallel computing inquiry has improved scalability.

Keywords: Semantic association; OWL; Keyword search; Mapreduce.

1. Introduction

With the rapid development of Semantic Web, RDF has been widely used in many fields with its advantages of flexibility and efficiency. The resource description framework (RDF) is the standard for data representation on the web[1].While common users lack expertise of the structured query language and underlying data patterns, it is difficult to use RDF data. Thus, an efficient keyword search is important tool for exploring and searching large data corpuses whose structure is either unknown, or constantly changing.

Existing RDF keyword search studies mainly can be divided into two categories. The first one was to construct structured query by using query keywords. Elbassuoni S et al. [2] translated keywords into the conjunctive query and then got SPARQL query. While its real-time response was not ideal because the process of extracting structural information needed lots of time overhead.

The another methods[3,4,5] searched results of keywords on the graph data loaded to memory directly ,and matched keyword to each node on the graph. Because these answer models based on the search smallest tree or sub-graph, which suffered from incompleteness of information and redundancy among answers. Gao [6] proposed an approach that searched keyword within a radius r nodes and perform the intersection to form a series of connected subgraph as query results. But these methods above are not applicable to handle large graph data and easily lost the semantic relationships between RDF data.

Combining the advantages of existing RDF keyword query solutions and deficiencies existing, we proposes a KPSRSA algorithm in this paper. Finally, experiments show that our techniques are scalable and help to improve the relevance of search results content and keywords and precision.

2. KPSRSA Algorithm

Firstly, it uses OWL ontology and information theory of probability model to measure semantics association between keyword and query result. Secondly, we uses distributed database Hbase as a storage medium and Mapreduce[7] to perform parallel query. When executing a query, it executes parallel expansion to get semantic association α-i clusters closely around keyword q_i in map phase; it makes join to construct a series of connected graphs as query result in reduce phase. Existing keyword query studies against an RDF graph mostly matched keywords only on literal nodes, while URI nodes involve more information that users want to know. Therefore, our work matches keywords both on literal and URI nodes. A node can fully or partly contains one keyword. KPSRSA algorithm applies a completely different relevancy-connected cluster answer model[6] to provide rich structural information concerning the relevance of results and keywords to improving query precision.

The KPSRSA algorithm consists of following steps, outlined below:

Step_1: Create hbase tables which include ontology semantic tables, instance triples tables and index tables;

Step_2: Establish type-based distributed model to store RDF data by category;

Step_3: Enter a keyword query Q, and calculate threshold α;

Step_4: Execute parallel query in Map phase, and get semantic association α-i clusters closely around keyword q_i of Q;

Step_5:Severalα-i clusters make join in Reduce phase and return a series of clusters contain all keywords as a result; The algorithm ends.

Our framework of KPSRSA algorithm consists of two parts: data distributed storage and Mapreduce query, as shown in Figure 1.

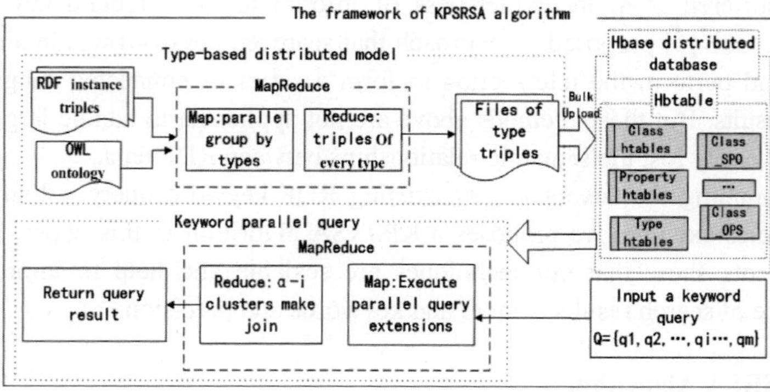

Fig. 1. Overall framework of KPSRSA algorithm

Most existing programs defined smallest subgraph or tree as query result, but there were two major drawbacks: first, the lack of integrity of the information the users want to query, the second is costly computational cost to calculate the minimal query path. In actual query, legitimate query results can be arbitrary-shaped rather than smallest subgraph or tree with the limitation of the path length leading to the semantic information of query results is missing or incomplete. Our work adopts a relevancy-connected cluster answer model, and give the definition of keyword query results as follows.

Definition 1: Query result Given a keyword query Q={ $q_1, q_2,\ldots, q_i,\ldots, q_m$}, the URI or literal node containing the query keyword is called keyword node. Query result is represented as connected clusters (denoted as triples set) which contains all keyword nodes ,where any two triples can be connected by its subject or object, or other triples to form connected graph clusters. If elements in two triples sets are not identical, they are considered as different query results.

Definition 2: α-i cluster A node connected to keyword node is called candidate node on RDF graph. Sort semantic scores between candidate nodes and keyword node; take candidate node whose score is greater than threshold α to construct semantic association α-i cluster (denoted as triples set) closely around i-th the keyword q_i.The threshold α is for evaluating the degree of semantic association, which is larger, more tightly semantic associated between candidate node and keyword node, otherwise vice versa. The value of α is determined by statistical information of instance triples and OWL ontology information. See specific formula for α as in Eq. (2) in 2.2 section.

2.1. *Building type-based distributed model*

Given our observation that nodes with the same type often share similar type-neighborhoods[5], we induce a distinct set of partitions for RDF Graph based on the types in RDF Graph. Our solution builds a type-based distributed storage model that handles realistic RDF data sets with tens of millions of triples. Given a keyword query, we use the type-based partition model to prune the search space, leading to much better efficiency. We group underlying RDF graph into different groups based on its types and store different groups in hbase tables of different types. Besides, we analysis and store OWL information to provide the basis for the calculation of semantic score and query reasoning. Specific design of Hbase tables and storage contents are described in Table 1.

Table 1. Hbase tables and description of storage

TableName	The description of storage
OWL_Table	Store owl information, the definition of classes and properties in ontology
Index_S_Table	Stores instances triples with subject S as key, and the number of triples containing subject S
Index_O_Table	Stores instances triples with object O or literal as key, and the number of triples containing object or literal
ClassName_SPO	Stores instances triples (S,P,O) which belong to the type ClassName
ClassName_OPS	Stores instances triples(O,P,S) which belong to the type ClassName

2.2. *Calculating semantic association estimation*

There are main factors which measure sematic association, such as node weight, edge weight, number of edge and so on. Lin et al.[8] proposed an information theory to estimate sematic similarity, which achieve good performance of the application in studies [2]et al. Motivated by these observations, we present a comprehensive study to address the keyword search problem over big RDF data combining information theory of the probabilistic model and OWL ontology. We define the evaluation function (SAE, Semantic Association Estimation) as in Eq. (1) and Eq. (2) for dynamically calculating query thresholds α depending on the enter keyword query .

Assume that t represents a RDF triple composed by subject, predicate and object. Enter a keyword query Q={ $q_1, q_2, \dots, q_i, \dots, q_m$}; i-th query keyword q_i, whose the j-th candidate object is expressed aso_{ij} ;the connection predicate between q_i and $o_{ij}$is expressed as p_{ij}. RDF graph consists of n classes, which are expressed as C={ $c_1, c_2, \dots, c_k \dots, c_n$}. Eq. (1)for evaluating semantic association is defined as follows

$$\mathrm{SAE}(q_i, o_{ij}) = \frac{\sum_{k=1}^{n} C_{ijk}}{\frac{Sum[t(p_{ij})]}{Sum}} \cdot Sum[t(q_i, o_{ij})] \; . \tag{1}$$

$$\text{wherein } C_{ijk} = \begin{cases} 0 & \text{if } c_k \text{ doesn't define } p_{ij} \\ 1 & \text{if } c_k \text{ defines } p_{ij} \end{cases} \quad i=1,2,3,..m;k=1,2,3\ldots n.$$

In Eq. (1),$\sum C_{ijk}$ indicates the number of classes with defined property p_{ij}, which can be obtained from the table OWL_Table. Sum represents the total number of RDF triples. $Sum[t(q_i, o_{ij})]$indicates the number of triples, of which subject or object contains the keyword q_i triples and object or subject is o_{ij}.$Sum[t(p_{ij})]$indicates the number of triple which has predicate p_{ij}.

When the value of $\mathrm{SAE}(q_i, o_{ij})$ is greater thanα, add o_{ij} to α-i cluster and construct a new α-i cluster for q_i. Eq. (2)for calculating threshold α is defined as follows.

$$\alpha = \mathrm{Average}\left(\sum_{i=1}^{m} \mathrm{SAE}(q_i, o_{ij})\right) \; . \tag{2}$$

2.3. *Mapreduce building search strategy*

A keyword query $Q=\{q_1, q_2,..., q_i,..., q_m\}$ composed of m keywords, which can be matched any nodes on RDF graph, subject ,object or literal. According keyword node may appear in different situations on RDF graph, the process is divided into four kinds, as shown in Figure 2. The black directed edge indicates extended edge, and the grey directed edge indicates under-extended edge. Here we group nodes on RDF graph into four categories. (i)URI(S),node described by URI, only in the subject;(ii)URI(O),node described by URI, only in the object;(iii)URI(S/O),node described by URI, both in subject and object;(iv)Literal, node described by literal, only in the object.

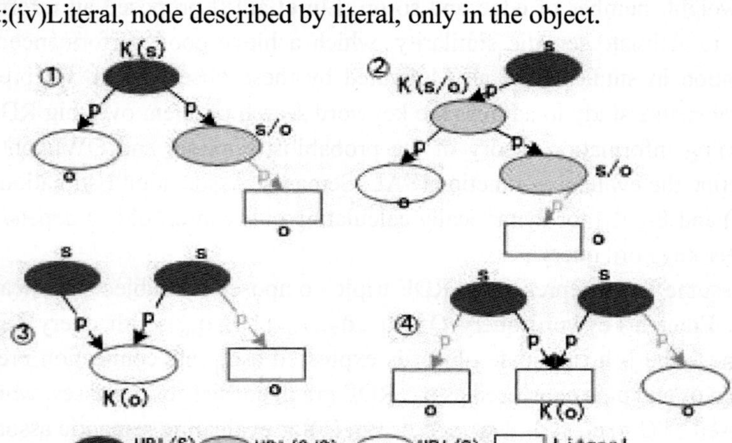

Fig. 2.Four query expansions

KPSRSA algorithm executes the following strategies over RDF graph in different cases.

(1) Query-expanl: When URI(S) contains q_i, obtain triples whose SAE is greater than α from ClassName_SPO table, and then construct a new α-i cluster.

(2) Query-expan2: When URI(O) contains q_i, obtain triples whose SAE is greater than α from ClassName_OPS table, and then construct a new α-i cluster.

(3) Query-expan3: When URI(S/O) contains q_i, obtain triples whose SAE is greater than α from ClassName_SPO and ClassName_OPS tables, and then construct a new α-i cluster.

(4) Query-expan4: When literal contains q_i, obtain triples of which SAE is greater than α from ClassName_OPS table, and then construct a new α-i cluster.

Next, we introduce the process of KPSRSA algorithm in detail from the pretreatment, Map strategy and Reduce strategy three aspects. Firstly, calculate each SAE(q_i, o_{ij}) value for each $q_i$of Q and the threshold α during the pre-processing stage. Second, execute four expansion strategies as described above to get semantic clusters closely around keywords in Map phase, using α and SAE to prune search space, leading to much better efficiency and higher precision of result. Finally, all semantic clusters from Map phase make join to each other in Reduce phase, and return query result as described in Definition 1. The procedure of Mapreduce strategy is shown in Figure 3.

Map phase

```
Input: Q={ q1 , q2,..., qi,..., qm }
Output: <key,value>
Initialize α , <qi , [ SAE(qi, oi1) ···. SAE(qi, oij)]>
if    qi ∈ URI(S) [ // i ∈[ 1, 2···.m]
        execute Query-expan1;
        output(<i, <qi,(qi, p,o)>>);
]else if qi ∈ URI(O) [
        execute Query-expan2;
        output(<i, <qi,(s, p, qi)>>);
]else if qi ∈URI(S/O) [
        execute Query-expan3;
        output(<i, <qi, qi, p,o)>>)
      or output(<i, <qi,(s, p, qi)>>);
]else if qi ∈ Literal [
        execute Query-expan4;
        output(<i, <qi,(s, p, qi)>>);
]
```

Reduce phase

```
Reduce:[(k1,values1)]->(k2,values2)
   identical  k1 make join
   obtain α -i clusters for each qi //i ∈{1, 2...,m}
 for each (value in values1){
    List1<1,< q1,( q1, p,o)>> = α -1 cluster;
    List2<2,< q2,( q2, p,o)>> =  α -2 cluster;
           ......
    Listi<i,< qi,( qi, p,o)>> = α -i cluster;
           ......
   Listm<m< qi,( qi, p,o)>> = α -m cluster;
}
  α -i clusters of different  qi  make join
   Join(List1, List2)
 output(k2, values2);
```

Fig. 3. Mapreduce processing strategy

3. Experiment and Analysis

In the experiment, the hardware environment includes Intel (R) Core(TM) i5-3470,CPU3.40GHz and 8GB memory. The software is as follows: Ubuntu Linux 14.10, java programming language. There are 4 nodes to run experiment.

We conducted the experiment using two real RDF datasets: dblp [9] and DBpedia [10]to further test our algorithm. The basic parameters of datasets are shown in Table 2. We pick representative queries composed of 1 to 5 keywords,Q1 ~ Q5queries test dblp dataset, and Q6 ~ Q10queries test DBpedia dataset. The queries are shown in Table 3.

Table 2. The configuration of datasets

Dataset	Trinples(M)	Input File	Properties	Classes
dblp_2007	11.02	951MB	43	18
dblp_2008	12	1.03 GB	43	18
DB3.7	14.33	1.90GB	1662	336
DB3.8	16.96	2.30GB	1794	376
DB3.9	21.88	3.00GB	2352	570

Table 3.Sample query workload.

Query	Keywords	Dataset	Query	Keywords	Dataset
Q1	algorithm	dblp	Q6	Annevelink,1995	DBpedia
Q2	Michael, database	dblp	Q7	Franklin, Caching, Doctoral ,Dissertation	DBpedia
Q3	Kevin , statistical	dblp	Q8	Peter,Haase	DBpedia
Q4	Abiteboul, adaptive , algorithm	dblp	Q9	Annevelink,Databases	DBpedia
Q5	Kazutsugu,Johanna,software, performance	dblp	Q10	SIGMOD, Data Mining, Database	DBpedia

We assessed query performance from the precision and query response. The precision refers to correct_num /num, wherein the correct_num is the number of correct triples in query results and the num is the total number of triples query returned. Query response time is the average of 10 times. The precision of experimental results on both dblp and DBpedia datasets is shown inFigure4 and Figure 5 respectively. Figure 6 and Figure 7 show the response time for queries in Table 3.

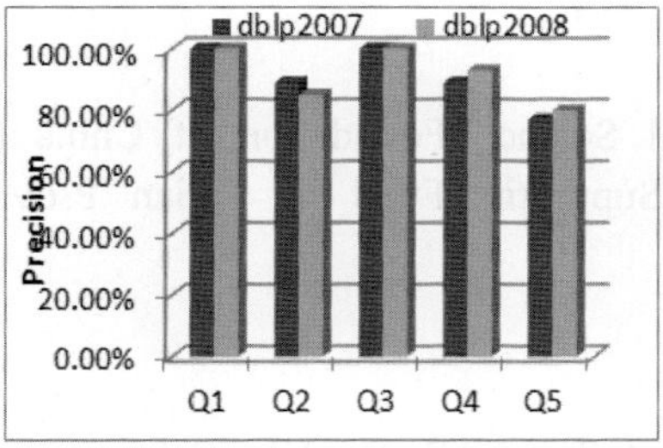

Fig. 4.Query Precision of dblp dataset

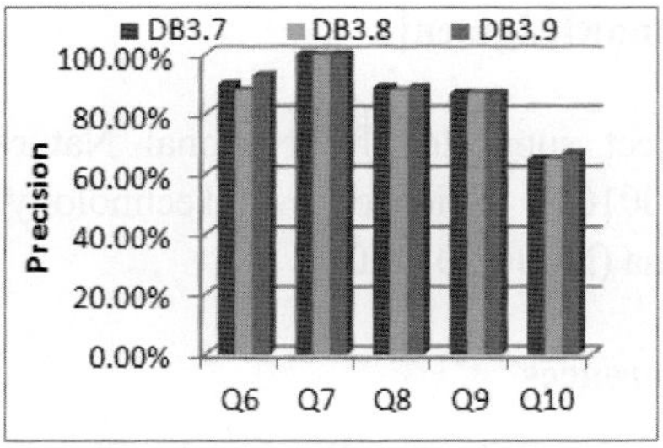

Fig. 5. Query Precision of Dbpedia dataset

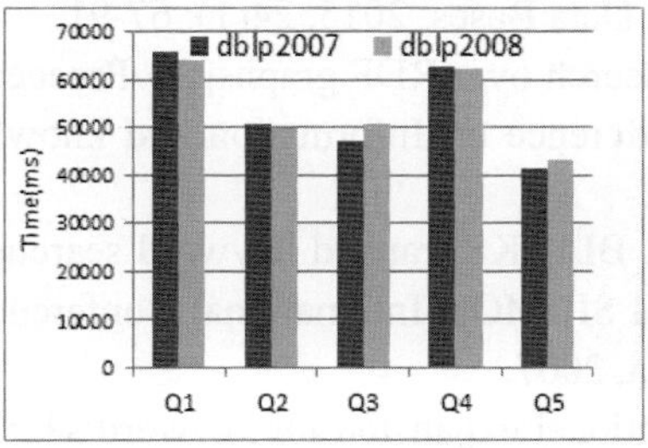

Fig. 6.Query response of dblp dataset

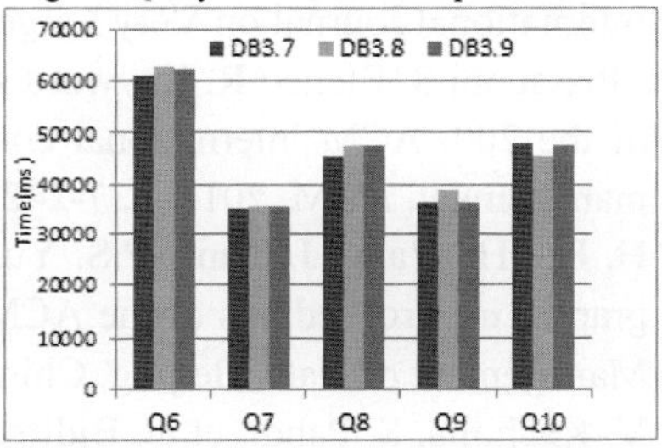

Fig. 7.Query response of Dbpedia dataset

From Figure4 and Figure5, it can be seen queries Q1, Q3 and Q7 with high precision close to 100%. Because query keywords of Q3 and Q7 have higher sematic correlation than others, which gain higher precision and faster query response. Average precision of Q1~Q10 query results is between 90% -100%, indicating that the KPSRSA algorithm helps to ensure the relevance of search results and keyword content, leading to improve the precision of answer.

4. Conclusion

We studied the problem of keyword search on big RDF data and proposed semantic association-based parallel solution: (i)we construct a distributed storage model at the type level from RDF data; (ii) during query evaluation, we leverage semantic association estimation to prune away a significant portion of RDF data from the search space, and use Mapreduce to proceed parallel query for efficiently accessing data. Experiments on two real datasets showed that our solution is efficient and scalable over large RDF graph data. However, our work didn't consider optimal query path, so an interesting future direction is to optimize query path for optimizing query on large RDF dataset.

Acknowledgments

Project supported by National Natural Science Foundation of China (No. 61300104), Science and Technology Supporting Fund of Fujian Province, China (No.JG2014001)

References

1. Kaoudi Z, et al. RDF in the Clouds: A Survey[J]. The VLDB Journal—The International Journal on Very Large Data Bases, 2015, 24(1): 67-91.
2. Elbassuoni S, Blanco R. Keyword search over RDF graphs[C]//Proceedings of the 20th ACM international conference on Information and knowledge management. ACM, 2011: 237-242.
3. H. He, H. Wang, J. Yang, P.S. Yu, BLINKS: ranked keyword searches on graphs, in: Proceedings of the ACM SIGMOD International Conference on Management of Data, Beijing, China, 2007.
4. V. Kacholia, S. Pandi, et al. Bidirectional expansion for keyword search on graph databases. In VLDB, 2005.
5. Le W, Li F, et al. Scalable keyword search on large rdf data[J]. Knowledge and Data Engineering, IEEE Transactions on, 2014, 26(11): 2774-2788.
6. Gao B J. Information-complete and redundancy-free keyword search over large data graphs[C]//Proceedings of the 21st ACM international conference on Information and knowledge management. ACM, 2012: 2639-2642.
7. Dean J, Ghemawat S. MapReduce: simplified data processing on large clusters[J]. Communications of the ACM, 2008, 51(1): 107-113.
8. Lin D. An information-theoretic definition of similarity[C]//ICML. 1998, 98: 296-304.
9. http://lsdis.cs.uga.edu/projects/semdis/swetodblp
10. Auer S, BizerC et al. Dbpedia: A nucleus for a web of open data[M]. Springer Berlin Heidelberg, 2007:722-735.

Tamper Detection of Batch Websites Based on Text Comparison

Shi-yang CHEN
School of Electronics Engineering and Computer Science, Peking University
Beijing 100871, China
Email: chenshiyang@pku.edu.cn

Hao MA
Computer Center, Peking University,
Beijing 100871, China
Email: mah@pku.edu.cn

Qing-jie CHEN
School of Electronics Engineering and Computer Science, Peking University
Beijing 100871, China
Email: tjchern@pku.edu.cn

Currently, information search on websites is an indispensable part of daily life. It is an important platform to obtain resources, such as regular notifications or current affairs about relevant companies, schools or other organizations. However, websites are prone to tampering by malicious attacks and thus tamper detection for websites is an important countermeasure to maintain the credibility and integrity of information found on websites. In this paper, we propose a highly feasible batch website tamper detection method based on text comparison. Different algorithms for text comparison have been proposed to analyze various websites with with varying degrees tamper detection using three factors: time efficiency, accuracy of detection and memory consumption. The experiments demonstrated that different algorithms have varying performances in terms of website tamper detection but nevertheless the string comparison method has more advantages under normal circumstances.

Keywords: Tamper detection; Text comparison; String comparison; Hash.

1. Introduction

The 36th statistical report on Internet development in China, published by China Internet Network Information Center (CNNIC), puts that until June 2015, the scale of Internet users of China has reached to 668 million, which means the rate of Internet population is up to 48.8% in China[1]. As the Internet becomes a lifestyle, more people are eager to obtain information from Internet. Therefore, it's important to find an efficient website tampered detection method with good universal and high efficiency, which can contribute to improve the safety level of the website.

Researchers have proposed many different solutions for tampering detection of websites. In[2] a website security monitoring system based on users perspective is designed and implemented. An integrated anti-tamper system in[3] is also established to actively detect attacks and dynamically defend tamper attack for Websites. In[4], Madhuri proposed the reversible watermarking scheme in medical image for tamper detection and recovery. Ali Kadhim has proposed a different approach where a text document is signed by shifting individual words slightly left or right from their original positions to make the center of gravity for each line fall in with the middle point of intended line[5].Data hiding technique[6] can also applied in websites tamper detection.

In this paper, feasible methods are proposed for websites tamper detection, especially batch pages tamper detection, contributing to different tamper characteristics.

The rest of this paper is organized as follows. Section 2 proposed a core information detection method. Section 3 shows our system design for experiments and experimental results. Finally, we conclude this paper in section 4.

2. Core Information Detection

Our study focus on the unique characteristics of bulk websites. We propose the core information detection. What really matters a website is the homepage and corresponding JS, CSS and image file. Hence we only concern these four information in core information detection. The detection process shows in Fig. 1.

(1) Getting the source code of the website through URL;

(2) Extracting the core information. Get the corresponding JS, CSS and images;

(3) Filtering interference information. Random number and frequent changed information should be removed, so that the detection results with a high reliability.

(4) Compare the homepage and corresponding JS, CSS and image file with the historical data of last detection time respectively.

(5) If they are the same, then determine the website is normal. Or prompt website administrator the content and location of changing website.

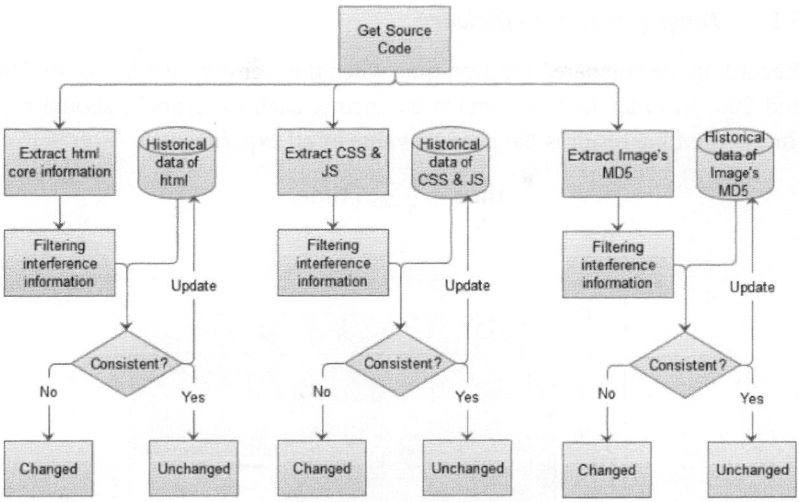

Fig. 1. Process of core information detection

3. Experimental Design and Result Analysis

Table 1. The analysis of 200 websites detection time consumption (time: s)

Item \ Test	Test 1	Test 2	Test 3	Test 4	Test 5	Average
Download (s)	320.9708	292.5495	312.5443	295.4727	299.9382	304.2951
Contrast(MD5) (s)	62.3271	58.8778	54.8941	54.0427	57.4229	57.1717
Total(s)	383.2979	351.4273	367.4384	349.5154	357.3611	361.8080

From Table 1.we can see that the average detection time of 200 websites using core information detection method with MD5 comparison algorithm is 361.8080s. An important step of core information detection is text comparison[8-10]. There are text comparison algorithms based on string comparison, hash and text compression. Each algorithm has its own characteristic.

Next, we will analyze the efficiency, accuracy and memory consumption of those 4 different comparison algorithms – string comparison, hash based text comparison (MD5, SHA-1) and compression based text comparison. The comparison algorithm is applied on fourth step of core information detection which is also the most important part of this method.

3.1. *Tamper detection efficiency*

Recording the compare detection time when the websites number is 50, 100, 150 and 200. In order to avoid inevitable errors, each experiment should be run 5 times. The final result is the average value of all experiments.

$$\text{time} = \frac{1}{5}\sum_{i=1}^{5} \text{time}_i \quad . \tag{1}$$

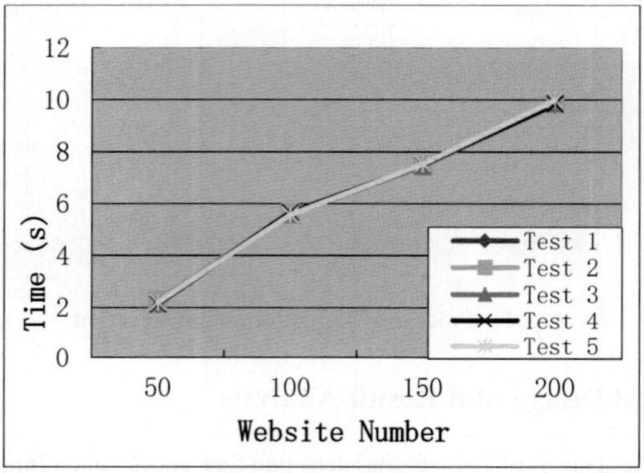

Fig. 2. String comparison algorithm

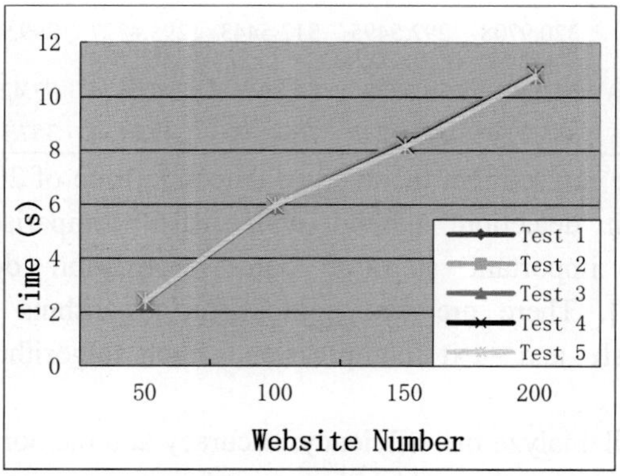

Fig. 3. Detection time of MD5 algorithm

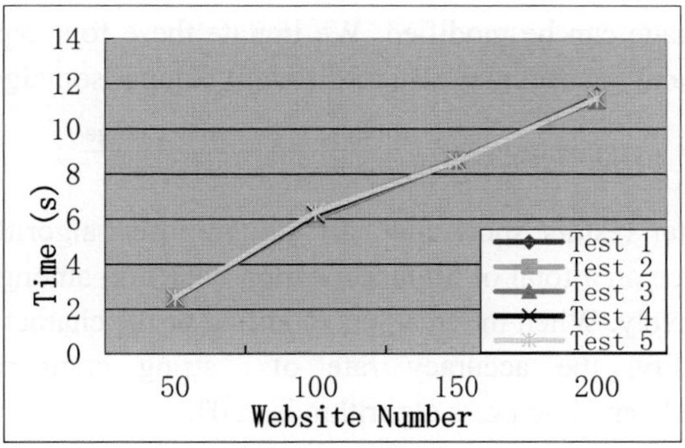

Fig.4. SHA1 algorithm

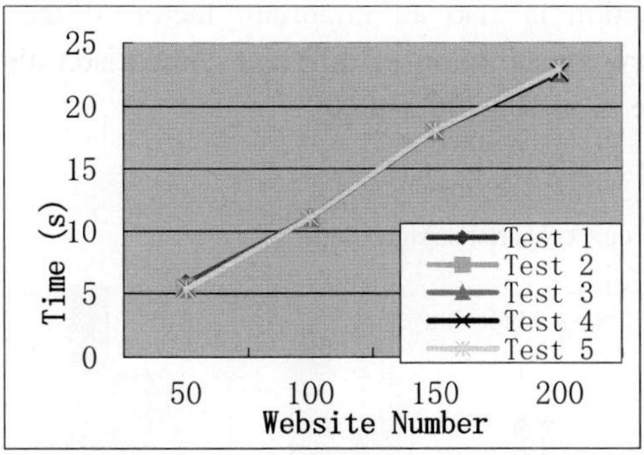

Fig. 5. Compress Algorithm

From Fig. 3.-Fig. 5. we can see when the number of websites is increasing, tamper detection time increased along. Compress algorithm consumes the longest time when the website number is 50, 100, 150 or 200. When the website number is 200, it is nearly two times longer for compress algorithm to the other algorithms. String comparison algorithm is always performs the best. And its advantage even grows with the increase of website number. The MD5's performance is relatively better than SHA-1.

3.2. *Accuracy rate of tamper detection*

The essence of web tamper is malicious modification of website's source code or images. The key to core information detection is to identify whether the website's source code or pictures is changed. The file of source code can be seen as text. And the text tamper can be classified to three categories: add, delete and modify. The image can be modified. We imitate these four types of tamper in the experiment and get accuracy rate of different comparison algorithms.

$$\text{Accuracy rate}=\frac{\text{Number of detective change}}{\text{Number of actual change}} \quad . \tag{2}$$

Experimental results show that, all the proposed algorithms have great positive influence on a total of 50 modification detection among a large number of files, respectively. When the image is modified or the character of text is add, delete or modify, the accuracy rate of string comparison algorithm, hash(MD5,SHA1) and compress algorithm is 100%.

3.3. *Memory consumption of tamper detection*

Memory consumption is also an important factor of the tamper detection. Recording memory consumption of different comparison algorithms when the number of website is 50,100,150 and 200.

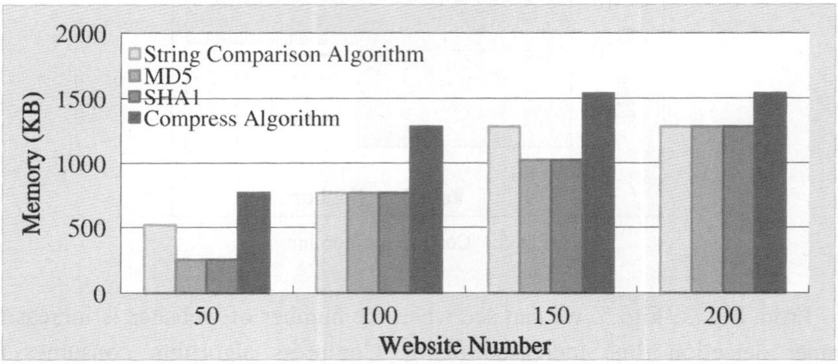

Fig.6. Memory consumption of the four algorithms

The results shows in Fig. 6. The MD5 and SHA1's performance on memory consumption is always the same when testing different website batches. Compress algorithm is always consumes the most memory. Compared with hash algorithm, string comparison algorithm consumes another 256K memory when the website number is 50 or 150. When the website number is 100 or 200 string comparison algorithm's performance is as good as hash algorithm.

4. Conclusion

In this paper, serious of methods of websites tamper detection, which especially focus on batch pages tamper detection have been proposed. All these tamper detect methods are based on text contrast and have been realized in different ways. Experimental results show, string comparison algorithm has the best performance in terms of time efficiency. Each algorithm has a good performance on accuracy rate of tamper detection. Moreover, MD5 and SHA1 can obtain the best performance of memory consumption. Therefore, different algorithms of core information detection can feasibly be chosen under various situations.

References

1. The 36th"Statistical Report on Internet Development in China" published by China Internet Network Information Center (CNNIC)
2. Yaping Chu, Wenping Liu, Xiaoying Wang. Design and Implementation of a Website Security Monitoring System from Users'Perspective.2010 IEEE.978-1-4244- 7618-3 /10
3. Jiuyuan Huo, Hong Qu, Liqun Liu. Design and Implementation of Automatic Defensive Websites Tamper-Resistant System. JOURNAL OF SOFTWARE, (VOL.7, NO. 10, OCTOBER 2012)
4. Madhuri B. Kulkarni, Ramesh T. Patil. Tamper Detection & Recovery in Medical Image with secure data hiding using Reversible watermarking. International Journal of Emerging Technology and Advanced Engineering. Website: www.ijetae.com (ISSN 2250-2459, Volume 2, Issue 3, March 2012)
5. Ali Kadhim Mousa. Tamper Detection in Text Document .Um-Salama Science Journal Vol.5(2)2008
6. Sandipan Dey, Hameed Al-Qaheri, SugataSanyal, Embedding Secret Data in Html Web Page, arXiv.org(2010)
7. SHA Hong-Zhou, LIU Qing-Yu, LIU Ting-Wen, ZHOUZhou, GUOLi, FANGBin-Xin, Survey on Malicious Webpage Detection Research(2015)
8. Alstrup S, Brodal GS, Rauhe T. Pattern matching in dynamic texts. Proc 11th Annual Symposium on Discrete Algorithms 2000; 819–828
9. Cormode G, Paterson M, Sahinalp SC, Vishkin U. Communication complexity of document exchange. Proc 11th Annual Symposium on Discrete Algorithms 2000; 197–206
10. Muthukrishnan S, Sahinalp SC. Approximate nearest neighbors and sequence comparison with block operations. Proc 32nd Symposium on Theory of Computing 2000; 416–424

Research on Text Clustering Based on Hybrid Simulated-Genetic Algorithm

Xiao-qin WU
Key Laboratory of Network and Intelligent Information Processing, Hefei University, Hefei, Anhui 230601, China
E-mail: w2361@163com

The genetic algorithm has strong capabilities in global optimization but it has a high likelihood of falling into local optimums. In contrast, the simulated annealing algorithm has strong capabilities in local optimization but lack capabilities in global optimization. By combining the advantages of simulated annealing algorithm and genetic algorithm this paper proposes a hybrid simulated-genetic algorithm (HSGA) to perform text clustering. We use HSGA specifically to optimize the initialization of the cluster centers for every iteration in the K-means clustering algorithm that is used to cluster text data. In addition, we also utilize the adaptive genetic algorithm to extract the eigenvalues of the text data, which performs dimensionality reduction and further improve the performance of the clustering. Experimental results demonstrate that the Hybrid simulated-genetic algorithm for text clustering not only improves the accuracy and recall rate of the text clustering, but also exhibits high efficiency.

Keywords: Genetic algorithm; Text clustering; TF-IDF method; Vector space model.

1. Introduction

Text clustering is one of the main methods in text mining and information retrieval, which defines the similarity and category of texts through unsupervised learning that searches the similar ones among the text sets [1]. Among multiple typical algorithms of text clustering, K-means text clustering is widely used because of its simplicity and effectivity. Researchers improve the K-means clustering algorithm [2] for its sensitivity to the selection of the initial clustering center. K-means text clustering algorithm [3] based on semantic deals with the dimension and sparseness of the text data set, and is more complicated. Since Standard-Genetic-Algorithm-based algorithm searches larger space, clustering center method based on genetic algorithm initializing K-means algorithm is likely to fall into local optimal solution, thus reduces the accuracy of clustering algorithm. Simulate Anneal Arithmetic is applied to clustering algorithm [4]. But there are more parameters in Simulate Anneal Arithmetic, and is likely to be partially optimized, reducing the efficiency. Text clustering algorithm based on agglomerative hierarchical clustering techniques [5] is often faced with the difficulty of selecting the merge points or split points. The text clustering method based on genetic algorithm and self-organizing feature map network [6] optimizes the clustering center selection, while the initial weights of the network is hard to define. Aiming at the problems of the k-means clustering algorithm, a kind of text clustering method with Hybrid simulating-genetic algorithm is put forward, and satisfactory clustering outcome was obtained through experiments. The accuracy and precision of the text clustering is improved by this method, the high efficiency of the algorithm is also verified.

2. Text Clustering Process

2.1. *Text preprocessing*

Text preprocessing before text clustering transforms the unorganized text described with human natural language into the structured form that can be identified and processed by computer. Text preprocessing transforms the text to string only composed of entries by deleting punctuation marks, stop words and rare words. Then the words should be divided for there is no space between the words in the Chinese text, which should be accomplished by word segmentation. Last, feature items, i.e. Character, word, phrase, etc., that can represent the text features should be extracted to combine the synonyms and near-synonyms to one semantic unit. For the simplicity and high-efficiency of Vector Space Model(VSM), the depiction of the text uses VSM mainly. In VSM, a document is composed of a certain number of feature words. If D is a set of documents with m documents, then $D(d_1, d_2 \cdots\cdots d_m)$, d_i is the feature vector of the i th document, then $D(t_1, t_2 \cdots\cdots t_n)$, t_i $(i = 1 \cdots\cdots n)$ is the i th feature items. Giving each feature item t_i a weight w_i ,document D can be described as $D(w_{i1}, w_{i2} \cdots\cdots w_{in})$, w_{ij} $(i = 1 \cdots\cdots m; j = 1 \cdots\cdots n)$ is the weight of the j th feature item of document d_i. The paper uses improved $TF - IDF$ method[7] to compute the weights of feature items, the particular computing formula , as in Eq. (1).

$$w_{ij} = \frac{m_{ij}/n_j \times \log\left(\frac{M}{n_j+1}\right)}{\sqrt{\sum_{k=1}^{n}[m_{ik}/n_k \times \log\left(\frac{M}{n_k+1}\right)]^2}}. \quad (1)$$

In the formula, m_{ij} is the number that the feature item t_j appears in the document d_i, M is the sum of all the documents, n_j is the number of the documents with the feature item t_j.

2.2. *The measure of text similarity*

Cosine similarity function method and distance function method are often used to measure the text similarity. The paper applies the method of cosine similarity between vectors. The particular formula for computing the similarity between documents d_1 and d_2, as in Eq. (2).

$$Sim(d_1, d_2) = \frac{\sum_{k=1}^{n} w_{1k} w_{2k}}{\sqrt{\sum_{k=1}^{n} w_{1k}^2}\sqrt{\sum_{k=1}^{n} w_{2k}^2}}.. \quad (2)$$

In the formula, w_{1k}, w_{2k} are weights of the k th characteristic value in documents d_1, d_2.

3. K-means Based on Hybrid Genetic Algorithm

3.1. *Encoding*

The paper improves the clustering center in k-means algorithm with Hybrid genetic algorithm, and then accomplishes k-means algorithm with improved clustering center, thus gets rather ideal clustering outcome. Integer encoding scheme can be applied. Chromosome is composed of clustering centers, while the number of clustering center is changeable, so the length of the chromosome is changeable too. The particular encoding form is as follows: $\{a_1, a_2, \cdots\cdots a_n\}$, among which a_i is the i th clustering center($1 \le a_i \le M$, n is the number of clustering center, M is the sum of documents).

3.2. *Fitness function*

The definition of fitness function affluences the efficiency of the whole algorithm. The clustering outcome will be better when the class distance is greater and the within class distance is smaller. The paper sets the fitness function according to the class distance and the within class distance, as in Eq. (3).

$$f(x) = \frac{\min(\sqrt{\sum_{i=1}^{k}\sum_{j=1}^{k}(c_i - c_j)^2}}{\frac{1}{k(n_i - 1)}\sum_{i=1}^{k}\sqrt{\sum_{j=1}^{n_i}(x_j - c_i)^2}}. \tag{3}$$

In the formula, c_i is the i th center, n_i is the document number of the i th class center, k is the number of the clustering centers.

3.3. *The crossover operator*

The paper combines the methods of single point insertion and single point cross. The main procedure of single point insertion is as follows: determining the cross point according to crossover probability, cutting a length of gene of long chromosome, the specific length of which can be a random integer among $[k/3, k/2]$, k is the length of the chromosome, then inserting the gene into the crossing point of another shorter chromosome. Single-point cross method is used for two individuals with same or similar length of chromosome, mutating the latter part to cross.

3.4. *The mutation operator*

The article uses the even mutation operator, and the particular process is as follows:1) An random integer is produced within $[1, len]$ with the mutation probability p_m as mutation point, len is the length of chromosome;
2)A random number r is produced within $(0,1)$, N is the sum of documents, computing X_i and rounding with formula (12). If the outcome is duplicate with other genes of the chromosome, computing should be done again.

3.5. *The procedure of the clustering algorithm based on hybrid genetic algorithm*

Genetic algorithm has rather strong capability of global optimizing and is likely to fall into the most improved solution partly, while simulated annealing algorithm has rather strong capability of seeking improvement partly but is lack of capability of overall optimizing. Combining the characteristics of simulated annealing algorithm and genetic algorithm, Hybrid simulated-genetic algorithm (SGA) is used in text clustering. The particular procedure is as follows:

(i) Initializing parameters, such as population size M, crossover probability pc, mutation probability pm, max iteration MGEN, temperature cooling coefficient C_i, annealing initial temperature T_i, etc.

(ii) Producing M number of initial population at random, evolving generation counts as $t_1 = 0, t_2 = 0$;

(iii) Assessing the fitness value $f(x_i)$ of population individuals $p(t)$;

(iv) Implementing the selection operation $p(t) \rightarrow p(t)'$: the mutation operation: $p(t)' \rightarrow p(t)''$;

(v) Implementing simulated annealing state function to produce new individual x_i'

(vi) If $f'(x_i) - f(x_i) \leq 0$,then individual x_i' is accepted, or else individual x_i' is accepted according to the probability $\min\{1, \exp(-(f'(x_i) - f(x_i))) / T_i\} > \varepsilon$ ($0 \leq \varepsilon \leq 1$ random number)

(vii) Calling simulated annealing algorithm $p(t)''' \rightarrow$ *SimulateAnnealing* $[p(t)'']$;

(viii) Picking out the most optimized individual $p(t)''''$ from $p(t)$ and $p(t)'''$ with optimizing selection model

(ix) If the termination condition is meet, outputting the optimized individual, or else $k+1 \rightarrow k$ back to (3);

(x) Taking the optimized individual k as clustering center $c_1 \ldots\ldots c_m$;

(xi) Computing $\|x_i - c_j\|$ and $\|x_i - c_n\|$, if $\|x_i - c_j\| < \|x_i - c_n\|$,then x_i is classified to the set with c_j as the center, $i, j, n = 1 \ldots\ldots m$;

(xii) Computing the mean value of coordinates of all points in each clustering as the new clustering center;

(xiii) Repeating (2)(3) till the change of c_j is less than the given threshold;

(xiv) Outputting the text clustering outcome.

4. The Analysis of Experimental Results

4.1.1. *Evaluation criterion*

F-Measure is employed as evaluation criterion of clustering algorithm, which is defined as in Eq. (4).

$$F - Measure = \frac{\sum_j (n_j \times F(j))}{\sum_j n_j} . \tag{4}$$

$F(j)$ is the measured value of subset j , $F - Measure$ is the total measured value.

4.1.2. *Experimental analysis*

The document sets was composed of 200 documents that downloaded from the modern Chinese corpus in the national language commission website http://www.cncorpus.org/ccindex.aspx, there are 40 documents respectively for each set of law, economy, computer, history and energy. Dimensionality reduction with genetic algorithm and text clustering with hybrid genetic algorithm are implemented by Java. MyEclipse7.0 is used as Development platform in the experiments, and SQL2000 for database. The parameters in experiment one are as follows: population size M=100, Maximum number of iterations MGEN=200, probability of crossing pc=0.9, mutation probability=0.01. The parameters in experiment two are as follows: population size M=80, Maximum number of iterations MGEN=300.

To testify the performance of feature reduction with genetic algorithm, first getting original feature words set after pre-processing and words- segment of the texts of the five classes of documents, then feature extracting to original feature words set with genetic algorithm. The experiment outcome is as Fig.1.

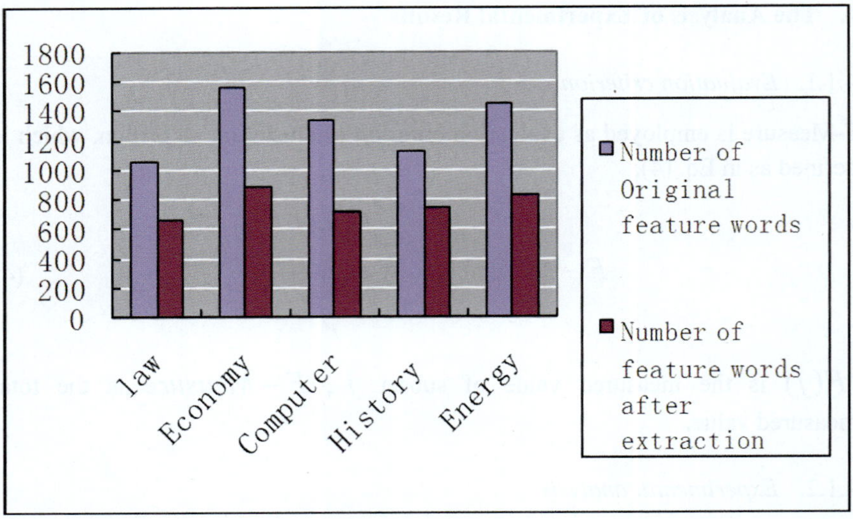

Fig.1: Text feature extraction results

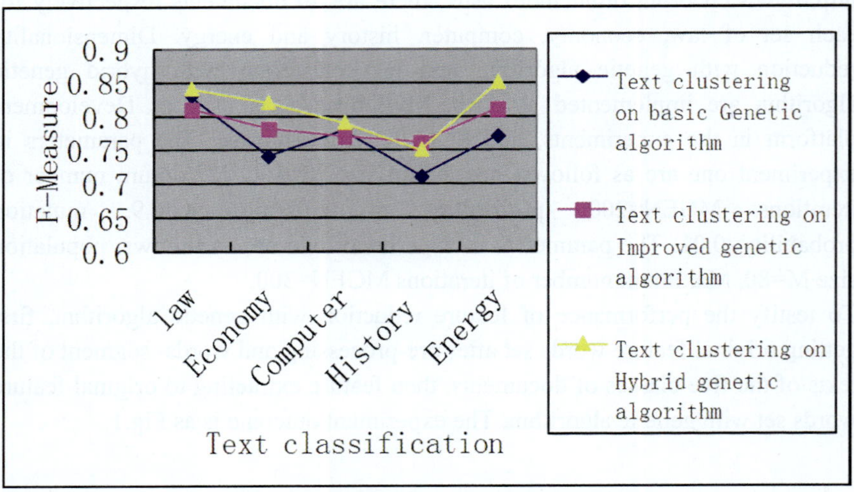

Fig.2: The comparison of clustering algorithms

Hybrid genetic algorithm clustering algorithm improves a lot both in clustering quality and algorithm performance, the performance comparison with basic Genetic clustering algorithm Improved genetic clustering algorithm and Hybrid genetic clustering algorithm is as Fig.2.

5. Conclusions

The paper combines the characteristics of simulated annealing algorithm and genetic algorithm, used Hybrid simulated- algorithm(HSGA) in text clustering, so as to optimize the original clustering center of K-means clustering algorithm, then do text clustering with optimized K-means clustering algorithm, and extract the feature value of the text with self-adaption genetic algorithm, thus get the end of dimension reduction. The method improves greatly the operating efficiency and text clustering accuracy of K-means clustering algorithm, but the shortcoming exists too. The clustering outcome is frequently random in part as the amount of documents increases, and converges slowly. The algorithm should be improved further hereafter so as to improve the convergence speed.

Acknowledgments

This work is supported by Natural Science key Foundation of Anhui Province (Grant No. KJ2013A226) and key Constructive Discipline of Hefei University (Grant No. 2016xk05).

References

1. A. Ahmad and L. *Dey, A k-mean clustering algorithm for Hybrid numeric and categorical data,* Data and Knowledge Engineering Elsevier Publication, 2007 (63). pp:503-527.
2. Min-yin Wang Siqing.*Improved K-means clustering based on genetic algorithm Computer Application and System Modeling(*ICCASM*),*2010 International Conference *on* (Volume:6).pp: 636-639 .
3. Yan-wei Hu, Zheng Qin, Zhong-zhi Zhang, *Intrusion detection algorithm based on simulated annealing and K—mean clustering,* Computer Science.2010.6(6)pp:122-124.
4. Xiao-qin Chang, An Yuan, *Text clustering method based on genetic algorithm and SOM network.* Journal of Computer Applications,3(2008). pp:21-22.
5. Xin-wu LI. *Research on Text Clustering Algorithm Based* on *Agglomerative Hierarchical Clustering,* Journal of Computational Information Systems 5:3(2009).pp:1081-1087.
6. Aggrawal C C, Yu P S. *Finding generalized projected clusters in high dimensional spaces* [A]. Proc of SIGMOD, Dallas,USA,2000, pp:70-81.

7. F Beil, M Ester , X Xu, *Frequent Term - Based Text Clustering,*. In Pro, 2002ACM SIGKDD Int . Conf. Knowledge Discoveryin Databases (KDD'02) . Edmonton , Canada : ACM Press , 2002 :436 - 442
8. Han J, Kamber M. *Data Mining* : *Concepts and Techniques* , San Francisco : Morgan Kaufmann Publishers , 2007 :398 - 45.
9. A Hotho, G Stumme. *Conceptual Clustering of Text Clusters,* In Proceedings of FGML Workshop [C] . Special Interest Group of German Informatics Society ,2002 :37
10. Jolion J M, Meer P, Bataouche S. *Robust Clustering with Applications in Computer Vision,* IEEE Transactions on Pattern Analysis and Machine Intelligence, 1991, 13(8): 791-802.

Study on the Regional Atmospheric Lidar Data Storage Model Based on Ontology

Zhi-rong ZHOU and Deng-xin HUA

School of Mechanical & Instrumental Engineering, Xi'an University of Technology, Xi'an, 710048, China

Hao CHEN† and Yi-kun ZHANG

School of Computer Science & Engineering, Xi'an University of Technology, Xi'an, 710048, China
†E-mail: haozi2638@163.com

Zhi-rong ZHOU

Zhonghang Electronic Measuring Instruments Co., Ltd, Xi'an, 710118China

Ontology is an effective method to solve the problem of heterogeneous atmospheric lidar data. The traditional method of ontology storage cannot be directly applied to atmospheric lidar data and thus this paper proposes an ontology storage model which establishes a mapping mechanism from the ontology of lidar data to the object-oriented data model (OODM). The atmospheric lidar data storage model is developed by analyzing the characteristics of atmospheric lidar data and the ontology syntax of OWL DL. The experimental results demonstrated that this storage model has high query efficiency and is viable for application in the sharing and usage of atmospheric lidar data.

Keywords: Lidar data; Storage model; Ontology; Object-oriented data model.

1. Introduction

Regional air pollution problems have been considered as a serious threat to public health and environmental safety. The regional air pollution problems are very intractable, and require monitoring the regional air with efforts of regional cooperation. In recent years, a number of regional atmospheric monitoring networks have been built using lidar[1-2]. However, the lidar data suffer the issue of varying degree of heterogeneity in structure and semantic etc., which severely delay the progress of lidar data sharing and usage.

With the abilities of expressing and reasoning in semantic, ontology can describe the inner relationships between various atmospheric parameters concepts or terms, and reveal the hidden relationships between them by logical reasoning.

Lidar data contains many atmospheric parameters and generate large amount of data[3]. The data are strongly correlated and the ontology structure is complex. In addition, it requires huge amount of storage resource. The existing storage methods have not been applied to atmospheric lidar data storage. In this paper, we study the relationship between the lidar data and ontology structure. Based on the object-orient data model, we propose a mechanism for mapping lidar data ontology to object-oriented storage model, and develop and object-oriented storage model.

2. Lidar Data Ontology

To build the atmospheric lidar data storage model, the definition of the lidar data ontology and object-oriented data model is given as follows.

Definition 1A lidar data ontology O consists of five elements {C, R, A, I, X}, where C is a set of lidar data's concepts; Ris a set of relationships; A is a collection of attribute sets for each concept and relationship; I is a set of lidar data's instances and X is a set of axioms[4].

For each concept ci, where ci∈C, represents a set of objects of same kind, and can be described by the same set of attributes denoted by AC(ci). Each relationship ri(cp,cq), then ri ∈ R, represents a binary association between concepts cp and cq, and the instances of such a relationship are pairs of (cp, cq) concepts objects. The attributes of ri denoted by AR(ri). Each axiom in X is a constraint on the concept's and relationship's attribute values or a constraint on the relationships between concepts objects. Each constraint can be expressed as a prolog like rule.

Definition 2 An object-oriented data model (OODM) of lidar data is a finite set of class declarations. OODM is a tuple S= {Cs, As, Ds}, where Cs is a finite set of class names; As is a finite set of attribute names; Ds is a finite set of class declarations. Ds contain exactly one declaration. The declaration of definition is defined as follows:

Class C is-a $C_1,\ldots,C_k$ *type-is T*,

In which T denotes a type expression built according to the following syntax[5]:

$T \rightarrow C|$

Union $T_1,\ldots,T_k$ *End* |

Set of T|

Record $A_1{:}D_1,\ldots,A_k{:}\ D_k$ *End*

where the is-a part of a class declaration allows one to specify inclusion between the sets of instances of the involved classes, the Type-is a part of specifies through a type expression the structure assigned to the objects that are instances of the class.

3. The Mapping Method and Storage Mode Based on the OODM

The ontology is constituted of structure and instance, and an object-oriented database is constituted of OODM and database instance.

We develop the mapping rule from ontology to OODM of lidar data based on the syntax of OWL DL.

Let S= {Cs, As, Ds} is the corresponding OODM of lidar data's ontology OS, φj is the mapping rule of structure transformation, so, S= φ (Os)={Cs, As, Ds}.The mapping algorithm is described in class identifier (Table 1) and instance (Table 2).

The mapping rule from OODM to a relational database is defined as follows: for the class of OODM, to create class identifier, name, type and is stored in table Class; class variables is stored in table Property, and property identifier is created. The property and character of the class variables correspond with the Type and Character in Table Property. The table PropertyOf stores the identifier of class and property. The table SubSupClass stores the identifier of parent and child classes which expressed the inheritance relationship in the two classes. The table InstanceValue stores the property and value of object corresponds with the object of OODM. The identifier of Property corresponds with the identifier of table InstanceValue and the property value are stored in table Value. The table InstanceOf stores the identifier of class and the identifier

Table 1 Identifier mapping algorithm

Syntax of ontology O_S	Mapping Method
$c_i \in C$, $r_i \in R$,	add $\varphi(c_i)$ to Cs ,add $\varphi(r_i)$ to Cs
$c_i \in C$, $A^C(c_i) \in A$	add $\varphi(A^C(c_i))$ to As
$r_i \in R$, $A^R(r_i) \in A$	add $\varphi(A^R(r_i))$ to As
$C \subseteq C_1 \cup C_2 ... \cup C_k$	create(Class C *type-is Union* $T_1,...,T_k$) add to Ds
$C \subseteq C_1 \cap C_2 ... \cap C_k$	create(Class C *is-a* $C_1,...,C_k$) add to Ds
type(C)	create(Class C *type-is* T) add to Ds
$U \subseteq C$, $U \subseteq U_i$ or $\geq 1 U \subseteq C_i$ or $T \subseteq \forall UD_i$ or $T \subseteq \leq 1 U$	create(Class C type-is *Record* $A_1{:}D_1,...,A_k{:}D_k$ End) add to Ds
$R \subseteq C$, $R \subseteq U_i$ or $\geq 1 R \subseteq C_i$ or $T \subseteq \forall RC_i$ or $R=(R_0)$	create(Class C *type-is Record* A: *Set of* T) add to Ds

Table 2 Instance mapping algorithm

Syntax of ontology O_S	Mapping Method
$o{:}C_1$	create $o{:}type(C)$
$(o,o_i){:}R_i$ or $(o,v_i){:}U_i$, $R_i, U_i \in C$, $o_i \in O_S$	create $o=<a_1{:}v_1, a_2{:}v_2,..., a_k{:}v_k>$, $a_i \in A$, $v_i \in V$
$o_i \in O_S$, $o_1=o_2=...=o_k$, $o_i \neq o_j$	create o add instance(S)

of object. The property value and the special constraint conditions are stored in the table Restriction, and correlated with each other in the identifier of class and object.

4. Application Example and Experimental

We show the atmospheric lidar data ontology storage model using the lidar data of Laser Radar Center of Remote Sensing of Atmosphere of Xi'an University of Technology. According to **Definition 1**wecan get a lidar data ontology $O_{lidar}=\{C_{lidar}, R_{lidar}, A_{lidar}, X_{lidar}\}$, where $A_{lidar}=A^C{}_{lidar} \cup A^R{}_{lidar}$.. We construct the data storage structure of lidar data ontology O_{lidar}. It will compare with the storage model of OODM with Native XML or XML have easy to extend and the vertical mode of RMDB in different ontology's instance scale.

Experimental setup computer CPU name Intel(R) Core(TM) 2 Duo E7500 2.93GHz, and the operator system is windows server 2003 SP2, and SQL server 2005. We investigated has three types of query: querying all the instances of a class named A; searching all instances of the parent of a class named B; querying all the instances named C. Taking the limitation of computer memory in experiment setup into consideration, the four different sizes of atmospheric lidar data ontology instances will be used, such as 1×103, 2×103, 1×104, 2×104.

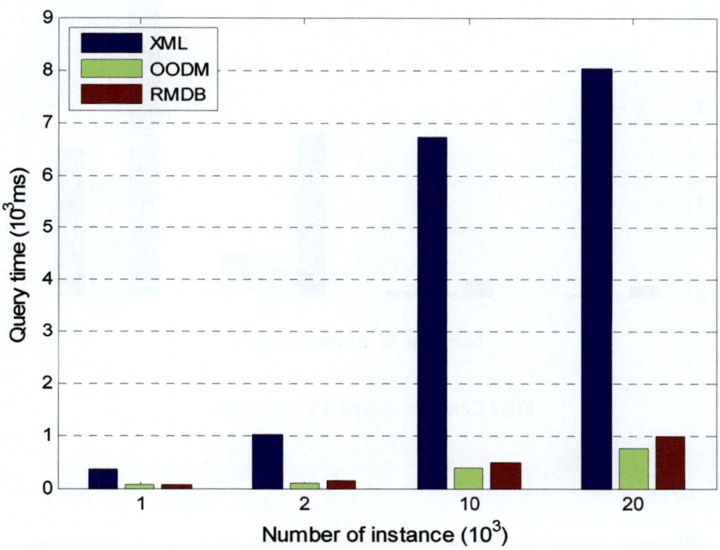

Fig.1 Compare of type A's query time

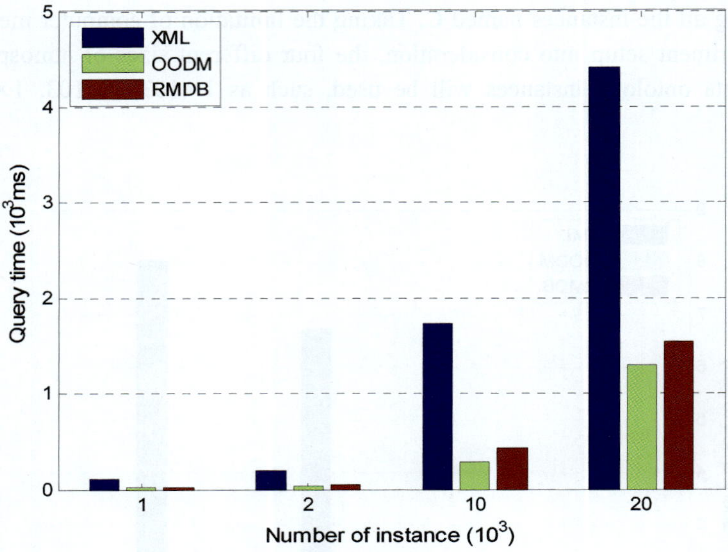

Fig.2 Compare of type B's query time

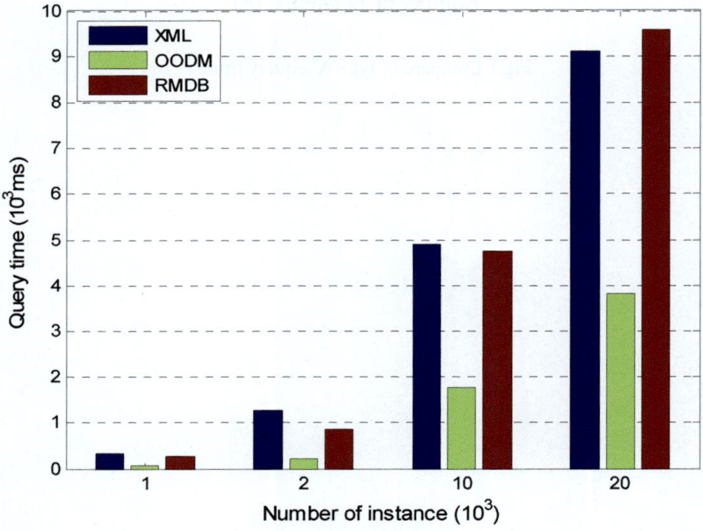

Fig.3 Compare of type C's query time

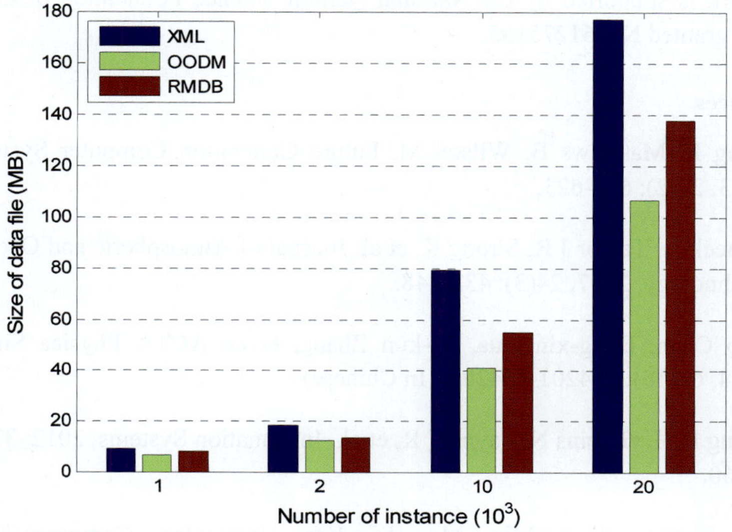

Fig.4 Compare of data file sizes

Fig. 1, Fig. 2 and Fig. 3, show that the XML have the longest query time. The Fig.4 shows that increasing in the number of instances will results in bigger data file size and requires longer query times. Thus, it reveals that with the increase of atmospheric lidar data instances of ontology, XML storage model will consume more time and occupy more storage and memory space compared to other methods. OODM and RMDB storage method is superior to the Native XML method in query times and data file sizes. Fig.1, Fig.2 and Fig.3, show that the consuming time of the RMDB method is greater than the OODM in all three types of queries.

5. Conclusion

In this paper, we investigate the atmospheric lidar data ontology, the representation method and mapping mechanism of its OODM based on the characteristics of atmospheric lidar data, and proposes a data ontology storage model based on object-oriented model. This storage model is strongly extensible with high query efficiency. It is mainly developed for the atmospheric lidar data.

Acknowledgments

This work is supported by the National Natural Science Foundation of China (NSFC) granted No. 61275185.

References

1. Yang E, Matthews B, Wilson M. Future Generation Computer Systems, 2013, 29(2): 612-623.

2. Wiacek A, Taylor J R, Strong K, et al. Journal of Atmospheric and Oceanic Technology, 2007, 24(3): 432-448.

3. Hao Chen, Deng-xin Hua, Yi-kun Zhang, et al. ACTA Physica Sinica, 2014, 63(15): 154201-154204. (In Chinese)

4. Wang H H, Gibbins N, Payne T R, et al.. Information Systems, 2012, 37(7): 33-60.

5. Fu Zhang, Zhong-Min Ma, Li Yan. Integrated Computer-Aided Engineering, 2011, 18(4): 327-347.

The Research of User Profile Model in Personalize Search

Yi SONG
Computer Department, Harbin Hude University
Harbin, Heilongjiang, China.
E-mail:songyiyouxiang@163.com

This paper researches on the application of a user interest model in personalized search. For a given user, we view his query history and documents of interest so as to mine user interest data from him or her. According to the vector space model, we represent the user profile as a vector, which is formed through classification of a select group of user query words. The new approach used in this paper is that the vector of user interest is constructed from the user profile. Experimental results demonstrate that this approach exhibit good description performance with regards to user interest and it lays a reliable foundation for future research on personalized search.

Keywords: Personalized search; User Interest; User profile; Query expansion.

1. Introduction

The traditional retrieval system can meet the needs of users, but it did not meet the needs of different purposes, different times, different backgrounds of the user's search needs. so user search did not effectively meet the needs of the individual, it is difficult to accurately obtain the information from the mass of information. For example, users enter "user interest" queries, For our study of personalized search, we need to get research information, and for ordinary users, may need sports or entertainment interest, personalized search engine is based on the above problems, also is the inevitable result of information growth, personalized search engine to facilitate user needs, and then find the user's interest, personalized service through the collection and analysis of user information to achieve the purpose of active recommendation. Personalized service to achieve information to find people, on-demand services, reduce the burden on users, personalized recommendation is the first need to establish a user's description, only when the user's interest, preference and access patterns and other user information can be well understood by the system, it is possible to achieve the ideal personalized service. According to user search history, user interest mining, which is the core and key technology of personalized service, is to be used to search the user's interest, which is based on the user's interest. This is to establish an effective user interest model to describe user search history and user interest. The paper has carried out the research on the user interest model in personalized search.

2. User Interest Model

2.1. *User Interest model representation*

The model is a mathematical tool for the abstract description of the real world or some kind of motion. The output of the model can be used to approximate the real world, such as the weather forecast model. Information retrieval model is given the representation of documents, the representation of query, and the matching process of query and document. User interest mining can be based on user interest mining and implicit user interest mining, implicit user interest mining: Based on Web content mining and Web Log Mining Based on, this paper studies the user's interest by content mining. Users usually submit query information to search engine, search results, if not satisfied, then continue to find relevant documents, or modify the query information, search again, until the satisfaction of the information so far, we have to build user interest model, we need to obtain the user's interest in history. That is, the relationship between the user's search history and the user's interest is represented by constructing the user interest model. Fan of the query classification, put forward to a category of personalized search by mapping the query, but for concurrent query of interest recognition is not obvious. By adding a query expansion improved the user interest model can not only identification of user interests preference categories, and effectively identify the category of query. The user interest model is the feature space to describe user's interest preference. M=[Q, C, R (Qi, Cj, T, D].

2.2. *System structure*

The user to enter a query to the search engine, through the search engine returns the relevant documents, we through the segmentation module user query word processing, the same will document segmentation, after feature selection feature list and will word query and user document DQ matrix composition, through common TF * IDF method computing query in a document the number of occurrences. By text classification method, the user clicks the document classification, which constitutes the document and category feature matrix. Using the DC algorithm to synthesize the user interest feature matrix DQ, then learn the user interest, and finally the experimental results, we find that the class query has an effect on the user's interest.

Input: query string and related documentation;
Output: the degree of preference for the category of interest;

(1) the user input query and the related documents are represented as vector form Q= (Q1, Q2,... Qn)D= (D1, D2,.... .Dn);
(2) through the traditional tf*idf computing query query in the document feature weight W, forming the query document feature matrix MQD;
(3) the documents are classified by SVM classifier, and the feature matrix of document classification is formed by MDC;
(4) the batch Rcchio algorithm MQD and MDC synthesis of MQC user model;
(5) by the user model M the user's preferences for the type of D;
(6) for query expansion and query appear, to (1).

2.2.1. *Document and query feature matrix* M_{DQ}

User search history we use vector space representation, the use of TF-IDF to find out the weight of each word. The purpose of this step is to generate a matrix of all the articles, all the words. This matrix with the characteristics of these text, the user query with vector Q= (Q1, Q3, q2,......... ..Qn), D= (D2, D3, D1, D) is represented by the search engine query returned by the document vector space.............. D_m), such as m, DQ, W, query, m*n, and N, the weight of the corresponding document is calculated by the improved tf*idf, Finally form the document and query feature matrix of M_{DQ}, where each row represents a document, representing a query.

2.2.2. *Document and class feature matrix* M_{DC}

Classification method based on the classes to represent resources, document resources classification is conducive to recommend to users interested in this kind of document. In theory, the error rate of classification of Bias is the smallest, the experimental results show that Naive Bayesian is very difficult to resist the noise, support vector machine (SVM) by constructing a non-linear function and low dimension of input space data is mapped to high dimensional points in attribute space, and then find a meet the classification requirements of the optimal separating hyper plane, and make it in order to ensure the classification accuracy and maximize super plane two layers of blank area. This method is globally optimal and there isn't a learning problem, fundamentally speaking, it is used to solve binary classification problem for a category, find out a classification, making the category of positive and negative examples fall in the classification of surfaces on both sides, and meet the classification: to a distance equal to the recent positive and negative examples, and all classified plane and positive examples or counterexamples distance of a classification. SVM method has the advantage of using a small training set, the computation is small, the classification accuracy is high, so we use the SVM classifier for text classification, The experimental data using the data from famous site automotive, financial, IT, health, sports, tourism, education, recruitment, culture, military, ten text, a total of 80000 text, we used: sports, military, education, automotive, tourism, IT six kinds of users interested in the text of the experiment. 30000 of them were used for training and 12000 for testing. The classification results and performance evaluation are shown in Table 1 , Performance Evaluation is about 0.9.

Table 1 Feature Matrix MDC

Sports	Military	Education	Tourism	IT
0.92	0.01	0.16	0.03	0.12
0.86	0.27	0.13	0.24	0.15
0.45	0.89	0.07	0.17	0.32
0.28	0.19	0.92	0.24	0.67

2.2.3. *Query and class feature matrix M_{QC}*

We can get the document and query feature matrix DQ of the user's search history, and the document and class feature matrix DC, which can be found in these two matrices through the document has the relevant contact, and then learn to the user query and the class relationship matrix. Specific learning algorithm is as follows:

(1) feature matrix dimension reduction

Because the vector space (VSM) is too large, the computation speed is slow, we use singular value decomposition (SVD) method, the M_{DQ} method will be decomposed into U*R*VT, U and V is orthogonal matrix, R is the diagonal matrix, so that the feature matrix can be reduced:

$$M'_{DQ} = U * R^{+} * V^{T} \quad . \tag{1}$$

R+——R inverted;

(2) Query and class feature matrix M_{QC}

Self-learning's core idea is to update and improve the characteristics of the current user model space. The better strategies include LR and Rocchio, We use a simple adaptive Rocchio algorithm in text classification, which has a decomposition of the document query matrix:

$$D^t = M_{QC} = \frac{N_i^{t-1}}{N_i}\sum_{k=1}^{m} D^{t-1} + \frac{1}{N_i}\sum_{k=1}^{m} M^T{}_{DC(k,i)}\ M'{}_{QD(k,j)}\ . \qquad (2)$$

Dt——User interest in t;

Nit-1 - the number of documents that are accumulated to the T-1 and the I from the 0 moment;Dt-1 - interest in t-1;Ni - the number of relevant documents in the category I. After the algorithm, the feature matrix and the feature matrix MDC are synthesized, and the query and the feature matrix MQC are obtained, which can be seen in Table 2, where each row represents a class and each column represents a query.

Table 2 Feature Matrix MQC

Document interest		Yao Ming	laptop	football	Rocket
Sport	0.86	0.97	0.18	0.98	0.78
Military	0.57	0.01	0.12	0.15	0.69
Education	0.62	0.07	0.13	0.06	0.16
IT	0.43	0.15	0.96	0.13	0.09

(3) User interest model

Query and class feature matrix M_{QC} represents a class of users interested in sports, military, education, automotive, tourism, IT six categories, each column is the user input query, D, C, Q:, M=[Q, R, D], T, C, R, D, query, By sorting the weights of the D of interest, you can dig out the user's preference, and then the model user's information is recommended. For example, the user in the first day of input query for Yao Ming, return the relevant documents, through the R (Qi, CJ) to draw the corresponding category of interest value of 0.97, said the user is relatively high interest in sports.

3. Experiment

Through the above algorithm, we carry on the experiment, the experiment results are shown in Figure 1, the graph is a user's interest in the 30 day of the sports, the military, the education, the automobile, the traveling, the IT class under the condition of change.

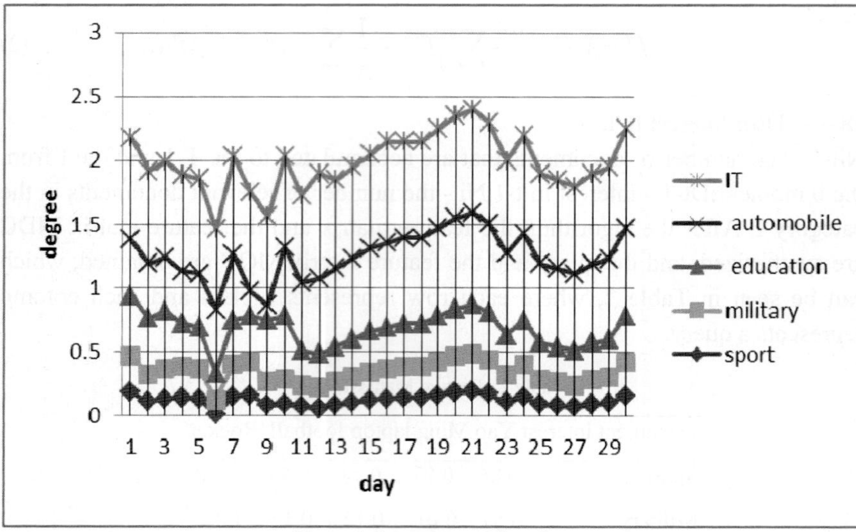

Figure 1 Interest trend line chart

Sort the category according to interest, the higher the weight of the user's preference for a large degree, the degree of interest will be recommended to the user. At the same time, from the picture, we can see that the user has long-term interest and short-term interest, the user's long-term interest can be seen from the stable trend, the user preferences for sports and education two categories, and for military categories, occasionally a few days, the military class is relatively high interest, speculation is short-term interest, the car's interest is not high, it can be inferred that the user's interest in car. Corresponding to the tourism, IT, the change curve of interest is not regular, and the high and low, it can be inferred that the user and the category of low interest correlation.

4. Conclusion

we can get the user interest categories, such as: Q, query D, in the experiment, we can get user interest categories, such as: C Data mining and other related technologies, the user interest category of preference mining, in User interest model is characterized by: the user interest model is automatically constructed through the search history. The model can effectively identify the user interest; it is a adaptive learning algorithm and good performance. Our approach has shortcomings, because users are not interested in long-term interest, users are interested in short-term interest accumulated to a certain extent may evolve into a growing interest, which requires us to learn and update the user interest model. It can be found that users are interested in the application of personalized user product recommendation, social network mining, personalized search and sorting, and so on.

Acknowledgments

This work is supported by the Natural Science Foundation of Heilongjiang Province of China (No. F2015046）, the National Science Foundation of China (No. 61173074) .

References

1. Kumar, M Vikram. Disclosure of User's Profile in Personalized Search for Enhanced Privacy. International Journal of Applied Engineering R, 2015, 10:36358-36363
2. Nicolaas Matthijs · Filip Radlinski. Personalizing Web Search using Long Term Browsing History - Microsoft Research [J]. Web Search and Data Minin, 2011. 36-45
3. Anirban Majumder · Nisheeth Shrivastava. Know Your Personalization: Learning Topic level Personalization in Online Services - arXiv.org e-Print archive, International World Wide Web Conferences [J],2013: 30-40
4. Nicolaas Matthijs and Filip Radlinski .Personalizing Web Search using Long Term Browsing History, ACM International Conference on Web Search and Data Mining (WSDM),2011.1021-1028

The Research on the Application of Photometric Redshifts Based on Spark Platform's Data Mining Technologies

Wei-yang QIAN*, Hong-bing QIU, Jun-yi WANG and Jie-lin FU

Key Laboratory of Cognitive Radio &Information Processing,
Ministry of Education , Guilin University of Electronic Technology,
Guilin 541004, China
**E-mail: 398157889@qq.com*

The quantity of astronomical data has been growing at an exponential rate, creating unprecedented challenges in astronomical data mining. The rapid development of distributed cluster technologies and cloud computing platform provide new research ideas and methods for massive data processing and analysis. The distributed cluster technology Spark is experiencing a meteoric rise, and shows comparative advantages in terms of iterative machine learning and interactive data mining applications. In this paper, we use the latest release of Sloan Digital Sky Survey photometric data set to explore the suitability and application problems of the data mining technologies based on Spark in the massive astronomical survey data, providing a new methodology for large-scale astronomical data mining.

Keywords: Data mining; Machine learning; Photometric redshifts; Spark platform.

1. Introduction

In recent years, sky surveys projects ongoing or already completed such as: SDSS surveys [1], VLT / VIRMOS Survey [2], VST surveys [3] provides a rich array of data resources for the study of the origin and evolution of the universe. Faced with massive data, we will be up against many unprecedented challenges. Using data mining techniques to solve astronomy "data avalanche" issue effectively is crucial for the development of astronomy. In the last few years, photometric redshifts (photo-z) for large samples of normal or active galaxies have become crucial for a variety of cosmological applications[4]. In order to estimate photometric redshifts more effectively and accurately, we need to develop a number of effective automated analysis tools. At the same time, the emergence and development of distributed clusters and cloud computing platforms is making data storage and processing become more efficient and convenient, the combination of distributed computing technology and astronomical data mining will become a necessity. Spark is one of the rapid development of the current open source distributed computing cluster platform based on memory, it has many characteristics, such as rapid, general and simple, the iterative machine learning algorithms and interactive data mining application has a very high efficiency. However, in spite of the obvious advantages of Spark in data mining applications, it hasn't yet be applied in instances of massive astronomical data. Our experiment explored the adaptability and application in photometric redshift valuation on Spark platform by data mining technology according to the latest data set of the Sloan digital sky survey SDSS-DR12.The following sections mainly includes: 1. The preprocessing of the SDSS photometric data set, make it can be read and processed on Spark platform efficiently; 2. Parameters' optimization of the data mining algorithm implemented on Spark platform, in order to increase the accuracy of the photometric redshift estimation;3. The influence on the time of photometric redshift's estimation due to the change of the number of cluster nodes.

2. Photometric Redshifts

The technique of photometric redshifts has experienced a relatively long history. The first application of photometric redshift estimation may date back to the 1950s(Baum[5]). Baum [6] proposes using photometric data to evaluate redshifts and has developed a photometric redshift estimation algorithm in 1962. In Puschell's article(1982)[7], he had used broadband photometry data to estimate the redshift of dark radio galaxies. Lo and Spillar (1986) [8] used the word "photometric redshift" in the title of the article (Photometric Redshifts of Galaxies) for the first time. Today, neural networks, random forest method, Bayesian and a lot of other data mining algorithms have been successfully applied to the photometric redshifts evaluation ([9]- [11]). Although many researchers already have an in-depth exploration and research on data mining methods to estimate photometric redshifts , they only focused on improving the accuracy of photometric redshift estimation, while ignoring the massive time of training photometric redshift evaluation model due to the outdated technology. Especially with the development of large-scale sky survey project, the photometric data grew rapidly, it is meaningful for us to think about how to improve the accuracy of photometric redshifts valuation under conditions of large data sets, while reducing time for training estimation models significantly, This paper first proposed to use the data mining technology based on the Spark platform to reduce the annoying time of training photometric data models which are massive and complex.

3. The Experiment Workflow and Algorithm

3.1. *Data mining technology on the Spark*

The experiment in our paper was based on Spark, which is an open source code frame for very large data process application. Data mining algorithms running on it are transformed from traditional data mining algorithms , making it possible to distribute massive data for processing. MLib is a data mining algorithms library implemented on Spark platform, it has integrated a lot of algorithms such as: decision trees, logistic regression, support vector machines and Naive Bayes et al. [12]. In this paper, we focused on the Multi-Layer Perceptron with Quasi Newton Algorithm (MLPQNA) method and its implementation on MLib.

3.2. *The MLPQNA regression model*

Quasi-Newton Algorithms (QNA) are variable metric methods for finding local maxima and minima of functions . The model based on this learning rule and on the MLP network topology is then called MLPQNA[13].Feed-forward neural networks provide a general framework for representing nonlinear functional mappings between a set of input variables and a set of output variables .One can achieve this goal by representing the nonlinear function of many variables by a composition of nonlinear activation functions of one variable, which formally describes the mathematical representation of a feed-forward neural network with two computational layers (Eq. (1)):

$$y_k = \sum_{j=0}^{M} w_{kj}^{(2)} g\left(\sum_{i=0}^{d} w_{ji}^{(1)} x_i\right) \tag{1}$$

A multi-layer perceptron may be also represented by a graph, as shown in Fig. 1: the input layer (x_i) is made of a number of perceptron equal to the number of input variables (d); the output layer, on the other hand, will have as many neurons as the output variables (K). The network may have an arbitrary number of hidden layers (in most cases one). In a fully connected feed-forward network, each node of a layer is connected to all the nodes in the adjacent layers. Each connection is represented by an adaptive weight, which represents the strength of the synaptic connection between neurons $w_{kj}^{(l)}$. The response of each perceptron to the inputs is represented by a nonlinear function, referred to as the activation function. The above equation assumes a linear activation function for neurons in the output layer. The MLP is a network model propagate submitted data from the input to the output layer. Each neuron of a hidden layer is represented by a nonlinear activation function of the sum of inputs from all previous layer neurons, multiplied by weights . After propagating the input data, at the output layer, the learning error is evaluated (in our case by means of the mean square error), and then the backward phase is started, in which a learning rule is applied, by adapting the neuron connection weights in such a way that the error function is minimized. Then the input data are submitted again and a new cycle of learning is achieved. The algorithm stops after a chosen number of iterations or if the error becomes less than a chosen threshold.

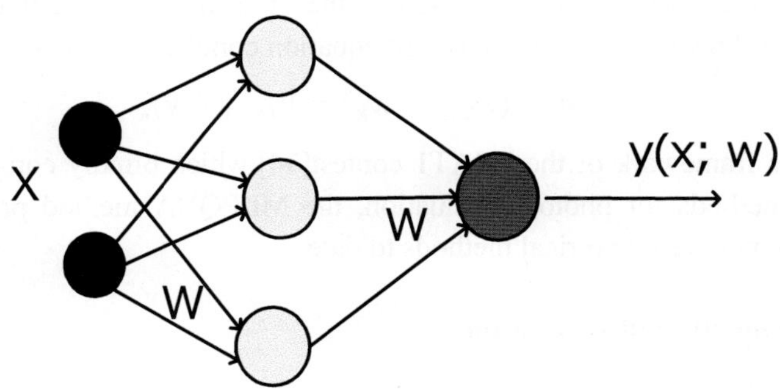

Fig. 1. Topology of MLP

The learning rule of our MLP is the QNA, which differs from the Newton algorithm in terms of the calculation of the Hessian of the error function. The traditional Newton method uses the Hessian of a function to find the stationary point of a quadratic form. The Hessian of a function is not always available and in many cases it is far too complex to be computed. More often we can only calculate the function gradient, which can be used to derive the Hessian via N consequent gradient calculations. The gradient in every point w is in fact given by Eq. (2):

$$\nabla E = H \times (w - w^*) \tag{2}$$

Where w corresponds to the minimum of the error function, which satisfies the condition(Eq. (3)):

$$w^* = w - H^{-1} \times \nabla E \tag{3}$$

The vector is $H^{-1} \times \nabla E$ known as Newton direction and it is the traditional base for a variety of optimization strategies. In practice, QNA is an optimization of learning rule based on a statistical approximation of the Hessian by cyclic gradient calculation. Instead of calculating the H matrix and then its inverse, the QNA uses a series of intermediate steps of lower computational cost to generate a sequence of matrices that are more and more accurate approximations of H^{-1}. More rigorously, given w_k a partial solution to the optimization problem at the iteration k(we want to converge to the optimal solution w^*), when w_k and w_{k+1} lie near the optimal solution w^*, within which $H\ (w)$ is positive definite, we can write as in Eq. (4).

$$H_k(w_{k+1} - w_k) = \nabla^2 f_k(w_{k+1} - w_k) \sim \nabla f_{k+1} - \nabla f_k. \tag{4}$$

The Quasi-Newton method chooses the Hessian approximation A_{k+1}, we require to follow the well-known secant equation condition(Eq. (5)):

$$A_{k+1}(w_{k+1} - w_k) = \nabla f_{k+1} - \nabla f_k. \tag{5}$$

In the framework of the PHAT1 contest[14],which blindly compared most existing methods for photo-z evaluation, the MLPQNA method proved to be among the two best empirical methods to date.

4. Experiments and Discussion

4.1. *The data*

The Sloan Digital Sky Survey is the forerunner of modern wide-field surveys. It combines multiband photometry and fiber-based spectroscopy, thus providing both photometric data for a very large number of objects and spectroscopic information for a smaller, but still significant, subsample of the same population. Photometric redshifts methods have been tested on the various data releases of the SDSS which, over the years, has become a sort of benchmark data set against which to test old and new methods. Currently, the latest SDSS-DR12, its data capacity breaks through more than 100TB, contains nearly 500 million stars' and galaxies' accurate photometric data, and includes more than 300 million celestial objects' spectral data. In this experiment, we selected 12 parameters on five bands (u, g, r, i, z) from SDSS DR12 CasJobs as input features for photometric redshifts' estimation, the value of the spectroscopic redshifts serve as expectations to evaluate data mining algorithms on Spark, The selected input parameters are as shown in Table 1.In the process of extract data from CasJobs, we only chose the data with spectral characteristics and photometric parameters at the same time, in addition we gave up some records which have physical values (for example - 9999). In the end, we obtained 2619593 data records, a total of 1.8 GB of data volume.

Table 1. Photometric redshifts characteristic parametersdescription

meters	ıcteristic
psflMag_u	ıitudeof point spread function, u band
psfMag_g	ıitudeof point spread function, g band
psfMag_r	ıitudeof point spread function, r band
psfMag_i	ıitudeof point spread function, i band
psfMag_z	ıitudeof point spread function, z band
petroR50_[ugriz]	of Petrosian radius
petroR90_[ugriz]	of Petrosian radius
lnLStar_[ugriz]	ikelihood for PSF profile
lnLExp_[ugriz]	ikelihood for exponential profile
lnLDeV_[ugriz]	ikelihood for Vaucouleurs profile
Class	galaxy
Spectroscopic redshift	ı known

4.2. *Parameter optimization and photometric redshifts' estimation*

For supervised methods it is common praxis to split the KB into at least three disjoint subsets: one (training set) to be used for training purposes, i.e. to teach the method how to perform the regression; the second one (validation set) to check against loss of generalization capabilities (also known as over fitting); and the third one (test set) to evaluate the performances of the model. We have chosen the k-fold cross validation in particular, In order to evaluate MLPQNA algorithm implemented under the spark, we use the same training set and testing set to test how it was affected on the results by each internal parameter. Then we choose the optimal internal parameters for estimating photometric redshifts. The process in practice to obtain the optimal setting of each parameter value is adjusting the value of the test parameter with other parameters constant, until the model performance is best. Based on this method, it is concluded that the optimal internal parameters as shown in Table 2.

Table 2. Exploration of the parametric space for MLPQNA

Parameters	Range	optimal value
res	10,20,30	30
dec	0.05,0.1,0.15,0.2	0.1
MxIt	1000,2000,3000	3000

According to the optimal internal parameter values obtained for MLPQNA as shown in Table 2,The results as shown in table 3 includes the time needed for valuation, the scatter, and the fraction of outliers. In Figure 2, we contrast photometric redshift with its spectroscopic redshift. The data in Table 3 shows that MLPQNA algorithm can be well applied in problems of photometric redshifts estimation based on the Spark cluster.

Individual experiments, as well as their comparison with results provided by others, were evaluated in a consistent and objective manner using a homogeneous and standard set of statistical indicators:

– the bias, defined as the mean value of the residuals$\Delta z = z_{spec} - z_{phot}$;

– the scatter, the standard deviation (σ) of the residuals;

–fraction of outliers: where outliers are defined by the condition:
$|\Delta z| > 0.15$

Table 3. The results of spectroscopic redshift estimation under Spark cluster

MLPQNA	Bias	Scatter	Outliers%	Time(s)
$\|\Delta z\| \leq 0.15$	0.0006	0.0056	16.3	130.875
$\|\Delta z\| \leq 0.15$, R≤24	0.0002	0.053	11.7	120.603
$\|\Delta z\| \leq 0.5$	0.0028	0.114	3.8	133.612
$\|\Delta z\| \leq 0.5$, R≤24	-0.0039	0.101	1.7	111.535

Although the data quantity is as high as 1.8G that includes 2,619,593 data records recording 12 input characteristics, it only takes a few minutes to process the data with only 5 compute nodes, which is a Spark cluster whose memory is 1G. By contrast, when estimating the photometric redshift, it will take 2 hours to process the same number of data by using the Perceptron algorithm with Weka. So a conclusion can be easily made that the Data Mining algorithm is better to deal with the estimating task with large data sets than the Perceptron algorithm with Weka.

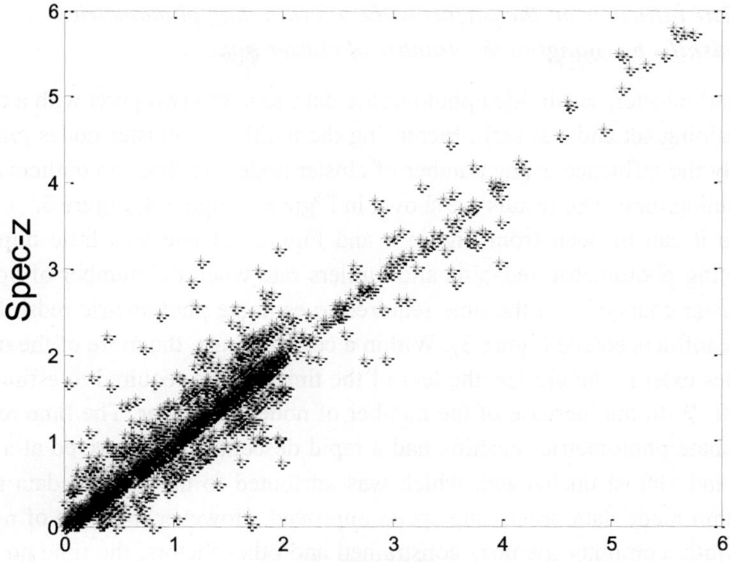

Fig. 2. Spectroscopic redshift-photometric redshift(left)

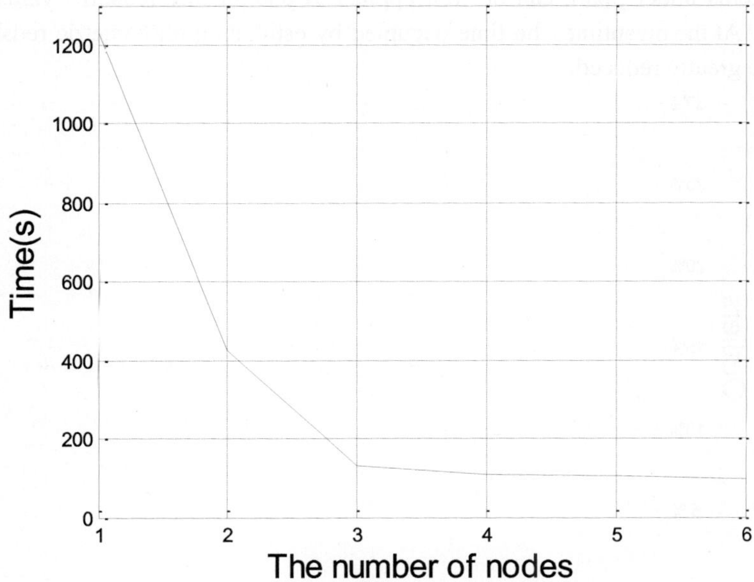

Fig. 3. The relationship between the processing time and the number of nodes in the cluster(right)

4.3. *The influence on the performance of evaluating photometric redshifts by changing the number of cluster nodes*

On Spark cluster, we divided photometric data sets into two parts with a ratio of 3:7 (training set and test set) , Increasing the number of cluster nodes gradually to study the influence of the number of cluster nodes on Bias; on outliers and on the training time. The results are shown in Figure 3, Figure 4, Figure 5.

As it can be seen from Figure 4 and Figure 5,There was little impact on estimating photometric redshifts and outliers rate when the number of nodes in the cluster changed, but the time required to estimate photometric redshifts was greatly influenced(see Figure 3). Within a certain range, the more of the number of nodes exist in the cluster, the less of the time will be required to estimate the redshift. With the increase of the number of nodes in cluster. The time required to estimate photometric redshifts had a rapid descent, finally arrived at a valley value and almost unchanged, which was attributed to the parallel data mining algorithm made data processing speed improved, However, because of network bandwidth, computer memory-constrained and other factors, the time no longer decline. But in general, when the number of nodes in the Sparkc luster is large enough and under the condition of memory space is enough, the data mining algorithms under Spark can be well applied to photometric redshifts valuation issues. At the meantime, the time occupied by estimating photometric redshifts will be greatly reduced.

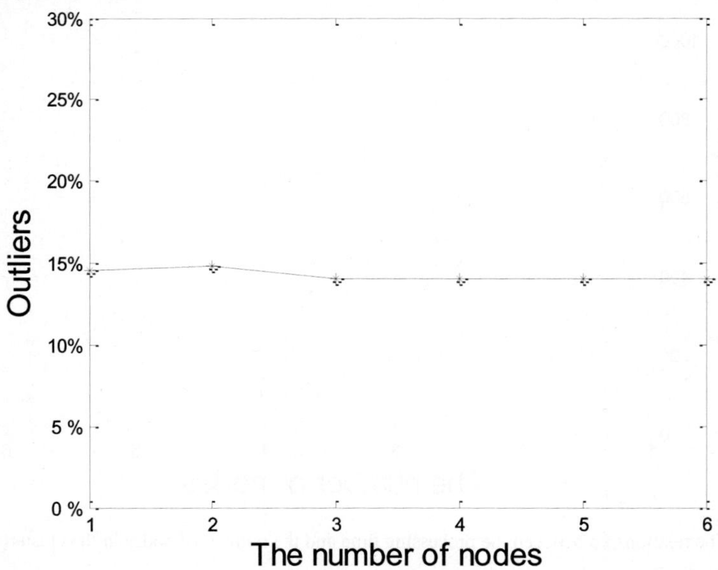

Fig. 4. The relationship between the fraction of outliers and the number of nodes in the cluster

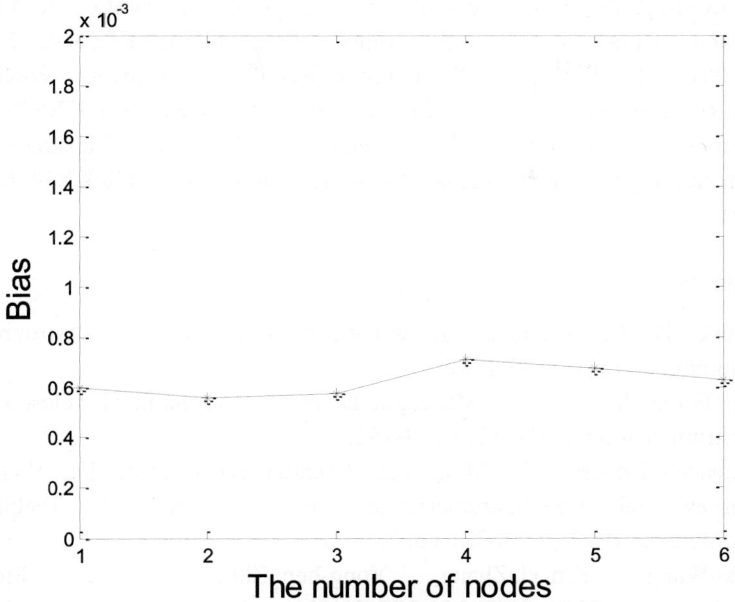

Fig. 5. The relationship between the Bias and the number of nodes in the cluster

5. Conclusion

Spark distributed platforms provides a new and effective tool for data mining techniques in observational astronomy application . In this paper we focus on the application of the photometric redshift estimation by MLPQNA regression model based on the latest data Sloan Survey photometric and spectroscopic data set. We performed an experiment showing that data mining algorithms based on Spark can evaluate massive photometric redshifts quite well. And, through the exploration of the parameter space and code rewriting we implement MLPQNA on Spark successfully. When other conditions remain unchanged, with an increase in the number of computing nodes in the Spark cluster, the speed of model training and the evaluating of redshift was greatly improved, which will make the studies of observational astronomy more efficient. With the development and application of various toolkits for data processing in astronomy, the functions of the Virtual Observatory will be more perfect.

Acknowledgments

This work is supported by the National Natural Science Foundation of China (No.61362006 and No. 61261017), Guangxi Natural Science Foundation

(2013GXNSFAA019334), Foundation of Guangxi Key Laboratory of Wireless Wideband Communication & Signal Processing(GXKL0614202 and GXKL0614101), Key Lab of Cognitive Radio & information Processing (2013ZR08), Innovation Project of GUET Graduate Education(YJCXS201517), Foundation of Science & Technology on Information Transmission & Dissemination in Communication Networks Lab(ITD-U14008/KX142600015 (2014)).

References

1. York D G, Adelman J, Anderson J E, et al. .Astrophysical Journal,2000,120:1579-1587.
2. Le Fevre, Vettolani G, Maccagni D, et al. Astronomical Telescopes & Instrumentation, 2003, 4834:173-182.
3. CapaccioliM,Arnaboldi M,Mancin D,Scaramella R, et al. The VST-VLT survey telescope//Instrumentation and Measurement Technology Conference.1999, 2:776-781 vol.2.
4. DanWang, Yan-xiaZhang, Yong-hengZhao, et al. Progress in Astronomy.2008, 26(3):266-277.(In Chinese)
5. PuschellJ , Owen F N, Laing R A. Astrophysical Journal, 1982, 257: 57.
6. Loh E D, Spillar E J. Astrophysical Journal, 1986, 303:154.
7. D'Abrusco R, Staiano A, Longo G, et al. Astrophysical Journal, 2007, 663: 752.
8. Baum W A. Photoelectric Magnitudes and Red-Shifts//Proceedings from IAU Symposium no.15.New York,USA:Macmillan Press, 1962: 390.
9. Adrian A. Collister, OferLagav. Astrophysics.2004,116:345-351.
10. Samuel Carliles, Tam´asBudav´ ari, S´ebastienHeini,et al.Astrophysical Journal. 2010, 712(1):511-515.
11. Christian Wolf.MNRAS.2009,397, 520–533.
12. Ming-huiZhang, Qing-xinWang.Kunming: Kunming University of Science and Technology, 2012.(In Chinese)
13. Massimo Brescia1, Stefano Cavuoti, et al. MNRAS.2012, 421(2):1155-1165.
14. HildebrandtH, Arnouts S, Capak P, et al.A&A. 2010,523, A31.

Research on Cross Language Information Retrieval of Tibetan Chinese Based on Dynamic Dictionary

Ai-lin LI[1], Hong-zhi YU and Tao JIANG

National Languages Information Technology
Northwest University for Nationalities
Gansu, Lanzhou 730030, China
[1]*Email:lalwxy@163.com*

Cross language information retrieval(CLIR) is a research topic in the field of information retrieval, solve the problem of cross barrier of language is CLIR's core problem. This paper proposes a method with cross language information retrieval of Tibetan Chinese based on dynamic dictionary for query translation and translation ambiguity in cross language retrieval. The Tibetan Chinese electronic dictionary as based knowledge sources, combined with comparable corpus of Tibetan Chinese, extraction of Tibetan Chinese bilingual theme word pair, thus real-time updating knowledge source to solve the problem of the limit of entry number in knowledge dictionary source. According to the characteristics of cross language information retrieval of Tibetan Chinese, using translation expansion techniques and Translation Balanced method, which reduces the number of ambiguity translation, improves the accuracy of translation.

Keywords: CLIR; Information retrieval; Dynamic dictionary; Bilingual theme word pair.

1. Introduction

The characteristic of cross language information retrieval(abbreviation: CLIR) is that the language of query keywords are used by user is different from the language used by the target document. Cross language information retrieval is a research topic in the field of information retrieval, and it has solved the problem of how to cross the boundary of language. So to solve the problem of information retrieval in different languages, we need to establish the corresponding relationship of translation between the language of query keywords are used by the user and the target language. In order to solve this problem that it is the translation of query keywords, there are the following methods: (1) Machine translation technology; (2) Parallel corpus technology; (3)Bilingual dictionary technology. The above two methods need more basic resources to support, moreover, as the limitations of the field, the quality of parallel corpora has a great influence on the translation of the query. With the rapid development of machine readable bilingual dictionary technology, the method of translation based on dictionary translation has become a practical and effective. The phenomenon about the word has a wide range of meanings is very common in various languages, each word in English has 1.678 meanings, each word in the Chinese has an average of 1.397 meanings, there is also the problem of Tibetan. In addition, the query term is short and lack of context support. Based on the above reasons, there are the following main problems in the translation method of query based-dictionary:1)query keywords haven't translation; 2)phrase recognition and translation; 3)semantic ambiguity problem.

This paper analyzes the cross language information retrieval technology based on the dictionary of the latest domestic and foreign, on the basis of this, we proposed a method of cross-language information retrieval of Tibetan Chinese based on dynamic dictionary. Research on cross language information retrieval technology of Tibetan Chinese can not only promote the development of cross language information processing technology of Tibetan Chinese, can also enhance the degree of information technology application in minority areas.

2. Related Research

Research on cross language information retrieval technology of Tibetan Chinese based on dictionary mainly involves three aspects, including query translation, query expansion and translation disambiguation. G.-A. Levow, et al., a bilingual dictionary is used to study the translation of multiple languages [1].Zhang Yuejie, etc., combined with English Chinese Dictionary and machine translation to achieve cross-language information retrieval [2].Wu Dan, et al. proposed a method of cross language query expansion of pseudo relevance feedback and prove the method of query expansion based on query after translation is relative superiority [3].Lisa Ballesteros, et al. in 1998, firstly published a method to solve the problem of translation ambiguity based on co-occurrence technology at SIGIR ACM [4]. Gao J. et al. use the attenuation of the symbiotic model and the syntactic dependency relation to solve the query translation ambiguity [5].

Although the above method in the field of English Chinese, Chinese Japanese or other cross language information retrieval achieved good results, as the Tibetan information processing technology and Tibetan search engine technology is relatively backward, and engaged in the research of cross language information retrieval technology of Tibetan Chinese is relatively small. Therefore, according to the characteristics of text structure and syntactic structure of Tibetan, this paper research on the cross language information retrieval of Tibetan Chinese based on dynamic dictionary.

3. Construction of Knowledge Base Resources

This paper uses Tibet Chinese Dictionary, G Si Zuza Tibetan dictionary, etc. to construct a bilingual dictionary of electronic. Every entry in the bilingual electronic dictionary is set up as table 1:

Table 1. Experimental result of extract bilingual theme word pair

Entry	Speech	Hyponym	Entry Code	Collocation	Semantic Classification Code	Translation Of Words
བར་གསོག་ཁུལ།	noun	བར་གསོག་ཁུལ་མི་འདང་བ།	Dic		Mor-01	Buffer

As the entry of current electronic dictionary of Tibetan Chinese is relatively old, lack of new words, it can't meet the practical application. Therefore, this paper extract bilingual theme word pairs with comparable corpus of Tibetan Chinese, so as to update bilingual dictionary with real time.

4. Build Comparable Corpus of Tibetan Chinese

Bilingual comparable corpus is composed of bilingual texts with similar properties, for example, different website the same day, the same theme of Chinese and Tibetan news, which Chinese and Tibetan are original. The two text are written by different language in the bilingual comparable corpus is completely different writers or reporters with the mother tongue of the event description. Therefore, there is a great hope to extract the corresponding bilingual subject words from the comparable corpus.

The basic ideas of constructing bilingual comparable corpus of Tibetan Chinese is: firstly, collect Tibetan news corpus from the Tibetan website of internet and then cluster the Tibetan news corpus; secondly, find out the words of category theme, and translate words of category theme into Chinese; finally, according to the Chinese theme words, and collect Chinese news corpus, so as to construct bilingual comparable corpus.

5. Text Preprocessing

Segmentation is the foundation work of information retrieval of Chinese and Tibetan, and it is a prerequisite for document retrieval and the establishment of the inverted file. The thesis will achieve word segmentation and labeling with the Hidden Markov Model and B-Gram model–based Tibetan segmentation software which is subject to Kunyu Qi, a professor in Northwest University for Nationalities. Also achieving Chinese word segmentation and labeling with ICTCLAS which is researched and development by Computing Technology, Chinese Academy of Sciences. Then establishing the stop list of Chinese and Tibetan, such as “ད”, “ང”, “ཁ”, “ཨ”. etc.

6. Bilingual Theme Word Pair

This paper uses singular value decomposition to get the theme words in Tibetan and Chinese documents, and gains the maximum possible similarity bilingual theme word pair by computing the similarity between context vectors which is in the words window of the bilingual theme words. The basic idea is: assuming the context of subject words have similarity in the comparable corpus of Tibetan Chinese, and to represent the context of a theme word by means of a vector, the value of vector generally indicate in corpus correlation between the word and words of its context. The main steps of extracting the similar theme word pairs are: (1)respectively do word segmentation and speech tagging of Tibetan corpus and Chinese corpus;(2)select calculation ranges(words window) of context of theme word, and establish the context vector for each topic word by traversing Tibetan corpus and Chinese corpus; (3)calculate the similarity of the corresponding vector of theme words; (4) set a threshold and extract word pair which its weight is greater than threshold, these word pairs are regarded as similar theme word pair. The data of extracting theme word pair is shown in the following table 2.

Table 2. Experimental result of extract bilingual theme word pair

Chinese	Weight	Tibetan	Weight	Chinese	Weight	Tibetan	Weight
China	.1180	ཀྲུང་གོ།	.1096	American	.0738	ཨ་རི།	.0717
bank	.1056	དངུལ་ཁང་།	.0861	Global	.0730	འཛམ་གླིང་ཡོངས།	.0699
Market	.0970	ཚོང་ར།	.0844	Investor	.0712	ཉོ་ཚོང་།	.0659
Company	.0958	ཀུང་སི།	.0808	Finance	.0700	འབྱོར་ལྡན།	.0635
Economic	.0881	དཔལ་འབྱོར།	.0806	Chinese	.0697	རིན་གོང་།	.0633
Investment	.0879	མ་དངུལ་གཏོང་བ།	.0803	Country	.0696	རྒྱལ་ཁབ།	.0629
Billion	.0769	དུང་ཕྱུར།	.0755	Transaction	.0688	ནོར་སྲིད།	.0624

Among, the computation method of the context similarity mainly has the method of Euclidean distance, Cos, Dice, Jaccard and so on. Cosine similarity is used as the measurement method in this paper:

$$\cos(a,b) = \frac{\sum_1^n (a_i \times b_i)}{\sqrt{\sum_1^n a_i^2} \times \sqrt{\sum_1^n b_i^2}}$$

Which, a and b are respectively represented as the context vector of two language text.

7. Inquiry Processing

7.1. *Extracting keywords of pretranslation*

Extracting keywords from user's query is not only a linguistic problem, but also using a lot of technical means. Keep in mind that extract keyword from the query is to translate into the target language, not for keywords matching.

We need to pay attention to the problem of ambiguity for Cross Language Information Retrieval based on dictionary. Each keyword may have more than one meaning which causes the source language to be translated into multiple target languages. In this paper, we focus on the search for reducing ambiguities of the matching of the dictionary, when the extraction of the matching keywords not available, we use backtracking method to improve the coverage of the translation.

7.2. *Pretranslation expansion*

Query expansion in single language information retrieval has been very mature, and short keywords (2~3 keyword) often appear in the search engine, query expansion is complementing the information required for this kind of incomplete query. Keywords are too short may cause ambiguity problem and this paper uses pseudo relevance feedback method to solve this problem.

Query expansion method is as follows: first, the user original input need to be processed in a normal way. Then use the relevance feedback process to get the key words of the extended meaning, the key words are extracted from the training documents of the first 10 of the search frequency, and the training documents are the news corpus of Chinese Tibet net.

After the experiment, the number of the expanded documents is 3, 5, 10, the effect is the best. Put the keywords with query expansion and the original query terms together, take it as original query keywords collection, the collection is the basis of translation.

8. Experiment and Analysis

8.1. *Experimental corpus*

According the basic idea of constructing comparable corpus, this paper uses the web crawler technology to collect experimental corpus. February 2015 to October 2015, we have collected 2496 pair of bilingual documents of Tibetan Chinese and the artificial proofreading. Among, the 1800 pair of documents are used as training documents, the remaining as test document, each document length greater than 400 characters. We obtain78107lemmas after removing repeated lemma in electronic dictionary of Tibetan Chinese.

8.2. *Experimental result*

This paper uses the precision and recall to evaluate the results of cross language information retrieval of Tibetan Chinese based on Dynamic Dictionary. Experimental results are shown in Fig. 1.

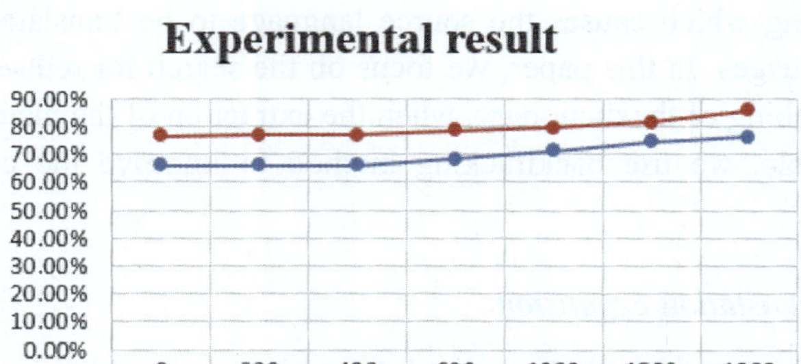

	0	200	400	600	1200	1500	1800
Accuracy	65.96%	66.04%	66.18%	68.27%	71.39%	74.54%	76.08%
Recall	76.65%	76.89%	77.01%	78.62%	79.49%	81.45%	85.69%

The number of Tibetan-Chinese Comparable corpus

Fig. 1. The effect of comparable corpus of Tibetan Chinese on cross language information retrieval of Tibetan Chinese based on dynamic dictionary

9. Conclusion

According to the actual situation of Tibetan information processing, the paper proposes a method for cross language information retrieval of Tibetan Chinese. In view of the shortcomings of the traditional cross language retrieval based on dictionaries, we extract bilingual theme word pair with Comparable Corpus of Tibetan Chinese, so as to real-time Update bilingual dictionary. In translation of keywords, this paper uses the translation extension technology to make the target language more close to the user's meaning, and also can improve the accuracy of translation. Experiments show that this method with cross language information retrieval of Tibetan Chinese based on Dynamic Dictionary has achieved good results in the cross-language information retrieval of Tibetan Chinese, the accuracy reached 86%.

Acknowledgments

This research is supported by Key Laboratory of National language intelligent processing, Gansu Province (Northwest University for Nationalities) and supported by National Natural Fund Project(61262054).

References

1. G.-A. Levow, D. W. Oard, P. Resnik. Dictionary-based techniques for cross-language information retrieval[J]. Information Processing & Management, 2005, 41(3): 523-547.

2. Yuejie Zhang, Yikun Guo, Li Lian, Lide Wu. Implementing Cross-Language Information Retrieval Based on English-Chinese Machine Translation[J].mini-micro systems.2004, 25(7): 1135-1140.In Chinese.

3. Dan Wu, Daqing He, Huilin Wang. Cross-language query expansion using pseudo relevance feedback[J]. journal of the china society for scientific and technical information.2010, 29(2):232-239.In Chinese.

4. L. Ballesteros, W. B. Croft. Resolving ambiguity for cross-language retrieval [C].Proceedings of the 21st annual international ACM SIGIR conference on Research and development in information retrieval (Sigir'98), Melbourne, Australia, August 24-28, 1998:64-71

5. J. Gao, J.-Y. Nie. A study of statistical models for query translation: Finding a good unit of translation [C]. Proceedings of the 29th annual international ACM SIGIR conference on Research and development in information retrieval (Sigir'06), Seattle, Washington, USA, August 6–11, 2006: 194-201.

Optimizing Checkpoint with Record and Replay

Wen-zhe ZHANG, Kai LU and Xiao-ping WANG

Science and Technology on Parallel and Distributed Processing Laboratory, Collaborative Innovation Center of High Performance Computing, State Key Laboratory of High-end Server & Storage Technology, College of Computer, National University of Defense Technology,

ChangSha, 410072, China

E-mail: zhangwenzhe@nudt.edu.cn, kailu@nudt.edu.cn, xiaopingwang@nudt.edu.cn

Checkpoint is a classic method for fault tolerance but its efficiency is hampered by a large overhead due to the dumping of large quantity of data. This paper propose a new checkpoint method which allows for the monitoring and recording of all functions that modifies the data instead of directly copying the data. By replaying the corresponding functions, we can restore the data to the latest state. We demonstrate that this record and replay mechanism is perfectly suitable for the kernel data of a process. Experimental results have shown that our proposed method can effectively reduce the amount of checkpoint data and improve performance.*Keywords*: Checkpoint; Record and replay; Performance; Kernel data.

1. Introduction

Checkpoint [1] is a classic method to achieve fault tolerance. Taking process-level checkpoint as an example, at checkpoint time, all the states of a process will be dumped to non-volatile media (e.g. disk). Thus when failures happen (e.g. power out, system crash), we can restore the process's state using the latest checkpoint. Here the data copying overhead is becoming the bottleneck. Research [2] has shown that for large scale systems whose MTTF (Mean Time To Failure) is continuing decreasing, checkpoint is not acceptable because most of the resources will be dedicated to making checkpoint and thus using checkpoint will lead to the overall system utility to be zero [8-9].

The problem of current checkpoint is its efficiency. It always copies so much data and introduce unacceptable overhead [3]. In order to accelerate the checkpoint process, we propose a new method to reduce the checkpoint data. We are inspired by the record and replay systems [4] which are usually used for debugging. The key idea is, instead of copying the final state of a program, we can monitor the certain functions in the program that change the state. By recording and replaying the certain functions, we can restore the state of the program without directly copying the state. The state of a process could be divided into two parts: (1) the user part and (2) the kernel part. We found that the kernel part (process controlling block, virtual address management, etc) of a process is perfectly suitable for record and replay because the only way a process could modify this part is through system calls thus we can record all the system calls instead of copying all the kernel part of a process at checkpoint time. In this way we can effectively reduce the checkpoint data. We will also show that restoring the kernel data by replaying the corresponding system calls introduces little overhead.

The rest of this paper is organized as follows: we give a brief background of checkpoint in section 2. Section 3 gives the design and implementation of our record and replay mechanism for checkpoint. We show the experiment results in Section 4 and conclude in section 5.

2. Background

Process-level checkpoint dumps all process's state into non-volatile media at checkpoint time. BLCR (Berkeley Lab Checkpoint/Restart) [5] is a representative tool of this kind of checkpoint. It divides the process's state into two parts: (1) the user part and (2) the kernel part. The user part mainly contains all the process's state which could be accessed at user level such as heap, stack, code and data region, etc. The kernel part mainly contains the process's controlling state which could only be accessed through kernel code such as the process's controlling block, opening files, signal stack, etc. At checkpoint time, BLCR would scan and dump these two parts of data. As we will show in our experiment, the amount of the kernel part data accounts for a considerable proportion and it takes time to dump this part. Reducing the amount of this part could help achieve better performance.

3. Design and Implementation

3.1. *Record and replay of system calls*

Instead of dumping the process's data at checkpoint time, we can record the functions that modify the data during execution. Then by replaying the corresponding functions we can restore the data. For the kernel part of a process, it is perfectly suitable for the mechanism of record and replay. Usually it could only be modified through system calls. Moreover, we will show in the experiments that replaying them to restore the kernel data is very fast.

As there are many system calls that may change the kernel data (also some other kernel code will make modifications), our record and replay method is mainly in a case-by-case way:

Virtual memory management. The data structures (e.g. vma structure in Linux) that are used in the kernel to manage a process's virtual memory is an important part. For this part, we mainly monitor the kernel function such as mmap, munmap, mprotect, etc. After system crash we can replay this functions to restore the process's virtual memory. However, two problems remains: (1) current Linux kernel adopts a address randomizing mechanism for security. Our solution for this problem is just turning off this mechanism. (2) The process's stack would be expanded automatically by normal read/write instructions. For this situation, we just record this stack expansion as a special function call. During recovery we will just replay this special function call using mmap to expand the stack.

File and device operation. For opening files or changing the state or the access pointer of files, we mainly record the corresponding system calls and parameters. For file write, we just record the file accessing offset changed by the file write. We do not record file read because the read data must have been stored in the process space and covered by our write protection mechanism. However, as files and other devices are not privately owned by one process, there are some non-deterministic situations we cannot handle. If another process shares the same file or device with the current process, we are not able to guarantee that the state of the file or device can be fully recovered to a consistent point. The same situation happens when a process is communicating with other processes through shared memories or network. Above all, in this case we can just monitor and recover the opened files and the states and file accessing offsets. This is also the limitation of current process-level checkpoint.

Signal Operations. A process may ask kernel to set up some signal handler, or change some signal blocking bits. We just record all the related system calls made by the process. Specially, there may be some signals sent from other processes which are blocked, we will check this special situation at checkpoint time and record it as a special system call. During recovery the signal will be delivered again.

Other Operations. Normally applications seldom make unpopular system calls. We choose to tackle them in a case-by-case way. Getting system information is the mostly used kernel service besides file operations and signal operations. Fortunately there is no need to handle them because the operation will have no side-effects on the process. Socket and network related system calls are currently not supported in this paper. This paper mainly focuses on introducing a new record and replay method for checkpointing process's kernel data. Supporting network and MPI computing would be our future work.

3.2. *Multithreading*

In multithreaded programs, two threads may do system calls at the same time. For simplicity, we tune them to execute system calls in a serial way. This is achieved by introducing a global lock. Thus we can record all the system calls in a serial log and replay them easily. Thread's creation is also recorded as normal system calls.

3.3. *Recovery*

Our recovery process contains two steps: (1) firstly we start a new process and use the replay mechanism to restore all the kernel data of the process. (2) secondly we copy all the backed user data from non-volatile media to main memory.

4. Experiments

This paper introduces a record and replay mechanism to reduce the checkpoint data. In the experiment we mainly show its benefit on reducing the checkpoint data and improving performance. Also to demonstrate the feasibility of this mechanism, we will show the recovering overhead. We implement our system based on BLCR [5] and we compare it with BLCR (BLCR is a state-of-the-art checkpoint tool).

We choose some applications from STAMP [6] and SPLASH-2 [7] benchmark suit which are multithreaded applications with large memory footprint. The applications are also for different application domain and their information are shown in Table 1. In the experiment the checkpoint interval is set to be 10s.

Table 1. Benchmarks (other unmentioned input is by default).

Benchmark Suit	Benchmarks	Problem Scale
SPLASH-2	LU-c	-n7500
	LU-n	-n6500
	Baynes	-r65536
	Intruder	-n6000000
STAMP	Vacation	-t8388608
	Genome	-g80000
	kmeans	Random-n1048576-d64-c16

Our experimental platform is an AMD server with 2.2GHz 12-core CPU and 16GB of physical memory running Linux 3.11.

4.1. *Results*

Firstly, Figure 1 shows the recording overhead we introduce to a program. For all the benchmarks we run them with 1, 2,4 threads, respectively. The baseline in this experiment is native running. For the execution with our recording, there are two main overhead we introduce: (1) we will keep a record of all system calls executed by a process. Thus the more system calls the process executes, the more overhead we will introduce. The numbers above each bar in Figure 1 show the number of system calls recorded. However, recording a system call is pretty simple thus we introduce ignorable overhead. (2) As we serialize the threads' making system calls, the more threads we are running, the more possibility they will conflict on making system calls. This is way the 4-threads version incurs more overhead than 2-threads version and single thread version. Overall, our recording mechanism incurs less than 10% overhead.

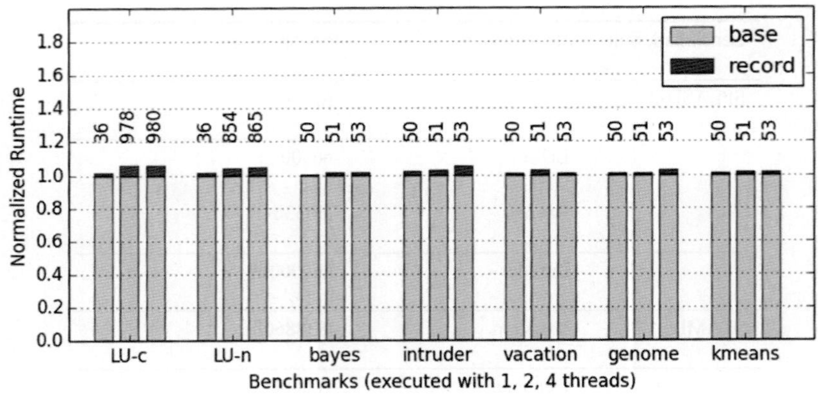

Fig. 1. Recording Overhead.

Figure 2 shows the total copied data in our record mechanism compared with BLCR. The numbers above the bars are the memory footprint (in MB) of the certain benchmarks. As we only try to reduce copying kernel data, the larger the memory footprint is, the less proportion we can achieve the reduction. Thus in Figure 2 we can see for the benchmark vacation our record and replay method could achieve great improvement because of its small memory footprint. Overall, for most applications, our method could reduce the checkpoint data by more than 10%.

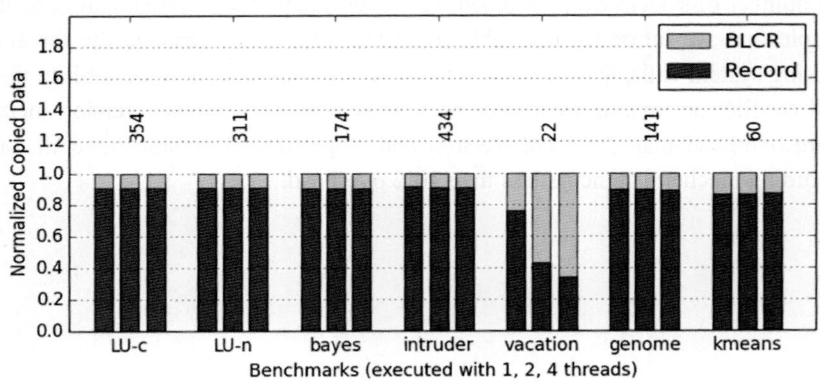

Fig. 2. Reduced Copied Data.

Figure 3 shows the performance improvement due to the reduction of copied data in our mechanism compared with BLCR. Similar to Figure 2, the more data we reduce to copy, the more performance benefit we can get. For the benchmark vacation, we can achieve more than 50% of performance improvement. For other benchmarks, we can achieve around 8% improvement.

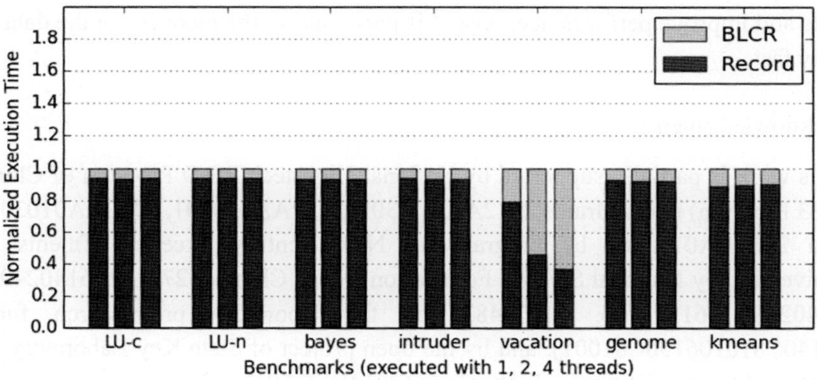

Fig. 3. Performance Improvement.

Finally, Figure 4 shows the recovering overhead of replaying all the system calls to restore the kernel data. Generally, the replaying is very fast. The main overhead comes from the serial execution of threads. The fast replaying shows our work is feasible.

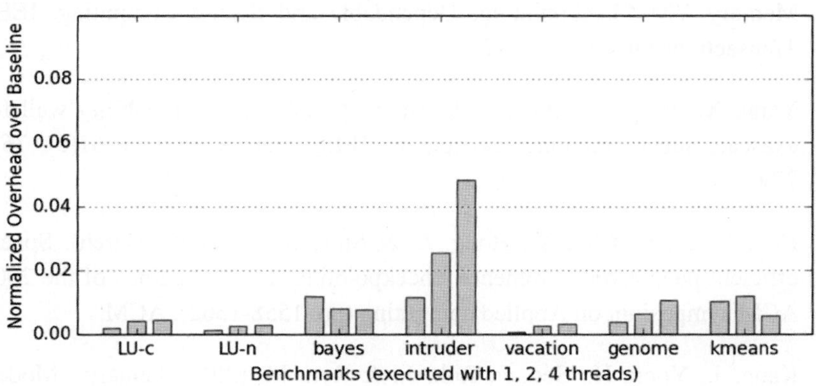

Fig. 4. Replying Overhead.

5. Conclusion

This paper introduces a new record and replay method for checkpointing the kernel data of a process. Compared with traditional checkpoint method that directly copies the kernel data, our work could reduce the amount of checkpoint data and improve performance. Also this paper shows the recovery of the data is very fast.

Acknowledgments

This work is partially supported by National High-tech R&D Program of China (863 Program) under Grants 2012AA01A301, 2012AA010901, 2012AA010303, and 2015AA01A301, by program for New Century Excellent Talents in University, by National Science Foundation (NSF) China 61272142, 61402492, 61402486, 61379146, 61272483, by the laboratory pre-research fund (9140C810106150C81001), and by the open project of State Key Laboratory of High-end Server & Storage Technology (2014HSSA01).

The authors will gratefully acknowledge the helpful suggestions of the reviewers, which have improved the presentation.

References

1. Wang, L., Kalbarczyk, Z., Iyer, R. K., & Iyengar, A. (2015). VM-μCheckpoint: Design, Modeling, and Assessment of Lightweight In-Memory VM Checkpointing. Dependable and Secure Computing, IEEE Transactions on, 12(2), 243-255.

2. Yang, X., Wang, Z., Xue, J., & Zhou, Y. (2012). The reliability wall for exascale supercomputing. Computers, IEEE Transactions on, 61(6), 767-779.

3. Heo, J., Yi, S., Cho, Y., Hong, J., & Shin, S. Y. (2005, March). Space-efficient page-level incremental checkpointing. In Proceedings of the 2005 ACM symposium on Applied computing (pp. 1558-1562). ACM.

4. Kang, J., Yoon, H., Seo, J., Roh, J., & Ryu, M. (2014, January). Model-based Automated Testing using a Record-Replay Mechanism. In Proceedings of the International Conference on Foundations of Computer Science (FCS) (p. 1). The Steering Committee of The World Congress in

Computer Science, Computer Engineering and Applied Computing (WorldComp).

5. Hargrove, P. H., & Duell, J. C. (2006, September). Berkeley lab checkpoint/restart (blcr) for linux clusters. In Journal of Physics: Conference Series (Vol. 46, No. 1, p. 494). IOP Publishing.

6. Minh, C. C., Chung, J., Kozyrakis, C., & Olukotun, K. (2008, September). STAMP: Stanford transactional applications for multi-processing. In Workload Characterization, 2008. IISWC 2008. IEEE International Symposium on (pp. 35-46). IEEE.

7. Bienia, C., Kumar, S., & Li, K. (2008, September). PARSEC vs. SPLASH-2: A quantitative comparison of two multithreaded benchmark suites on chip-multiprocessors. In Workload Characterization, 2008. IISWC 2008. IEEE International Symposium on (pp. 47-56). IEEE.

8. Wang, Feng, et al. "Optimizing LINPACK benchmark on GPU-accelerated petascale supercomputer." Journal of Computer Science and Technology 26.5 (2011): 854-865.

9. Xu, L. I., et al. "Understanding the Impact of BPRAM on Incremental Checkpoint." IEICE TRANSACTIONS on Information and Systems 96.3 (2013): 663-672.

Healthy Diet Personalized Recommendation Algorithm Based on Dietary Records

Yue LI and Han CAO[†]

School of Computer Science, Shaanxi Normal University,
Xi'an, 710119, China
[†]*E-mail: caohan@snnu.edu.cn*

Maintaining a healthy diet is influenced more by the types of food you eat rather than the quantity of food that you eat. In this paper, a multi-objective healthy diet recommended algorithm is proposed according to individuals' dietary records and health conditions. Based on the multi-objective genetic algorithm (MOGA) and taking into consideration the recommended dietary standards and individuals' health conditions, the algorithm evaluates the cumulative and long-term effect of an individual's diet in order to generate a personalized healthy diet recommendation. Experimental results demonstrated that the proposed algorithm is more suitable for application in a personalized recommendation service than the algorithm based on random weighting algorithm.

Keywords: MOGA; Diet recommendation; Nutrition; Dietary records.

1. Introduction

With the improvement of people's living standards, people are not satisfied with the fullness. They begin to pursue delicious and healthy diet. Due to age, gender, physical activity and physiological status, their nutritional needs for food are different4. Facing many types of food, it is still difficult to make a selection of food that meets all their nutrient requirements. Based on healthy eating principles of nutrition, national dietary standards and user information, personalized recommendation service on healthy diet is to provide users with targeted personalized healthy eating plan.

Food service is a very complex task. Scholars began to study how to use a computer to deal with such issues from the 1960's. In 1964, 1 used a linear method to design menus which satisfied user requirements for nutrition and cost. Subsequently, 2 proposed a random approach: random selection menu, and then assessment whether their cost, color, energy, variety and acceptability can meet the demand of users. With the recovery of artificial intelligence, evolutionary computation is used to solve this problem3. At present, there are three main kinds of methods—case-based, rule-based and based on GAs—with nutrition model to balance intake of several key nutrients.

With the rapid economic development, cost is no longer the main factors affecting food choices. Users accumulated intake of nutrients in the past period of time should be added to the recommended strategy. The proposed personalized recommended algorithm on healthy diet, its core is MOGA based on dietary records. Based on national dietary standards and the principle of nutrition, the algorithm considers not only the current user personalized physiological needs, but also the long-term and cumulative effect of diet on the user. Through the analysis of user's dietary records and assessment of user's accumulated intake of nutrients in the past period of time, it adjusts multi-objectives weights.

2. Optimization Model

We treat the problem of recommending and balancing healthy diet as a multi-objectives optimization problem which is to find an optimal composition of foods. Intake of various nutrients is its objective function. There are mutual restraint among the various objectives, that usually one objective optimization may cause reduced performance of other targets.

The multi-objective problem of healthy diet based on nutrition model generally described as in Eq. (1).

$$\min\left|f_i(Y)\right| = \left|\sum_{x_m \in V} x_{mi} \times y_m - s_i\right|. \tag{1}$$

$$Y = (x_1, x_2, \cdots, x_m, \cdots, y_1, y_2, \cdots, y_m, \cdots)$$

There are q objectives(nutrients). Each objective has some parameters:

(i) S_i, recommended intake of nutrients;

(ii) $f_i(Y)$, intake error of nutrients.

Where, V denotes food set, Y is dietary recommendation, food $x_m \in V$, y_m denotes the recommended intake of x_m, x_{mi} denotes nutrient content of x_m.

The end result of healthy diet recommendation is expected to get the minimum $|f_i(Y)|$.

3. MOGA Based on Dietary Records

We decide to solve that multi-objective problem in a heuristic way by using a genetic algorithm (GA) based on dietary records. It is different from traditional GA based on random weighting5 as it adjusts multi-objective weights by analyzing user's dietary records and assessing user's accumulated intakes of nutrients in the past period of time.

GAs are different from traditional optimization techniques as they simulate nature at a very abstract level to get solutions for a variety of demanding problems.

The evolutionary process of biological organisms in nature is simulated by taking an initial population of individuals and applying genetic operators to the selected (normally highly-fit) individuals. Each individual in the population is encoded into a string (chromosome) that represents a possible (candidate) solution to a given problem. The fitness of an individual is evaluated with respect to a given objective function. Highly-fit individuals are reproduced by exchanging genetic information with other highly-fit individuals. This produces new offspring solutions that replace either less-fit individuals or the whole population. This procedure is repeated until finding a satisfactory solution or reaching a pre-set number of iterations.

3.1. *Encoding*

The first step in designing a GA is to encode the candidate solutions to the problem. We apply a real-valued coding of candidate solutions to the problem.

In 7, experts present pagoda graphical representation, which visually tells residents food classification concept and the rational range of intake of all kinds of food every day. We decide to choose 1100 common food items from 6 and then separate those items into 7 groups according to the standard in 7. Creating a composite meal, we select one item from each group. Hence, in our representation, a chromosome contains 7 pairs(x_c, y_c), $c = 1,2,\cdots,7$,as in Table1.

Table 1. Chromosome definition
(a)Food items

Gene	x_1	x_2	x_3	x_4	x_5	x_6	x_7
Food category	Grain	Beans	Milk	Animal food	Vegetables	Fruit	Oil
The number of items	195	97	35	360	207	185	21
Value range	1-195	196-292	293-327	328-687	688-894	895-1079	1080-1100

(b)Recommended intakes

Gene	y_1	y_2	y_3	y_4	y_5	y_6	y_7
Food category	Grain	Beans	Milk	Animal food	Vegetables	Fruit	Oil
Recommended intake	300-500g	50g	100g	125-200g	400-500g	100-200g	25g
Value range	300-500	0-100	50-150	125-200	400-500	100-200	0-25

According to the particularity of the target user, we can also modify the chromosome definition. For example, when we recommend for vegetarians, we can delete gene x_4, y_4 or define the value of gene y_4 is 0.

The GA starts with a random population of candidate solutions. The population size is a few tens and remains constant over all populations.

3.2. *Fitness evaluation*

Each solution of the candidate population is evaluated using the following fitness (objective) function, as in Eq. (2).

$$H = \sum_{i=1}^{q} w_i \left| f_i(Y) \right| = \sum_{i=1}^{q} w_i \left| \sum_{x_m \in V} x_{mi} \times y_m - s_i \right| . \quad (2)$$

$$Y = (x_1, x_2, \cdots, x_m, \cdots, y_1, y_2, \cdots, y_m, \cdots)$$

Where, w_i denotes the weight of each target nutrients. The smaller value of H means better dietary recommendation. The aim of the GA is to minimize this fitness function.

In GA based on dietary records, w_i is not random. It is calculated by analyzing user's dietary records and assessing user's accumulated intakes of nutrients in the past period of time. Detailed calculation steps are as follows:

(i) Calculate cumulative error rate E_i in time t:

$$E_i = \sum_t e_i \ . \quad (3)$$

Where e_i denotes error rate , as in Eq. (4).

$$e_i = \frac{f_i(X)}{s_i} = \frac{\sum_{c \in V} x_{ci} \times y_c - s_i}{s_i} \ . \quad (4)$$

$$X = (x_1, x_2, \cdots, x_c, \cdots, y_1, y_2, \cdots, y_c, \cdots)$$

Where X denotes one item from dietary records within the time t .

(ii) Calculate w_i :

$$w_i = \frac{a^{E_i}}{\sum_{i=1}^{q} a^{E_i}}, (0 < a < 1) \ . \quad (5)$$

where a is Weighting factor.

4. Experiments and Results

In order to evaluate the performance of the proposed GA based on dietary records, we carried out a contrast test with GA based on random weighting.

In this experiment of recommendation algorithm, we aim at an 18-year-old male weighing 63kg under medium labor intensity. Choose three nutrients indicators as recommended objectives: energy, protein and calcium. In Table 2 , recommended daily intakes of nutrients are presented according to the DRIs8.

Table 2. Recommended intakes of nutrients

Nutrients	Energy	Protein	Calcium
RNI/AI	2700kcal	80g	800mg

After several runs of the program, the most advantageous settings for the GA were defined in Table 3.

Table 3. Settings for the GA parameters

Parameter	*Value*
Population size	50
Crossover probability	0.8
Mutation rate	0.085
Iterations	200
The time of error accumulation	10
Weighting factor (^{a})	0.5

For cold start problem, we take random weighting method to produce recommendations t imes for new users. And then record the t times recommendations as dietary records for the next recommendations using GA based on dietary records. Figure 1 shows the changing curve of cumulative error rate of these two algorithms. In Figure 1(a) ,using traditional GA based on random weighting, it changes irregularly. In Figure 1(b) ,we can see that cumulative error rate of the proposed algorithm gradually tends to zero, finally swing around zero.

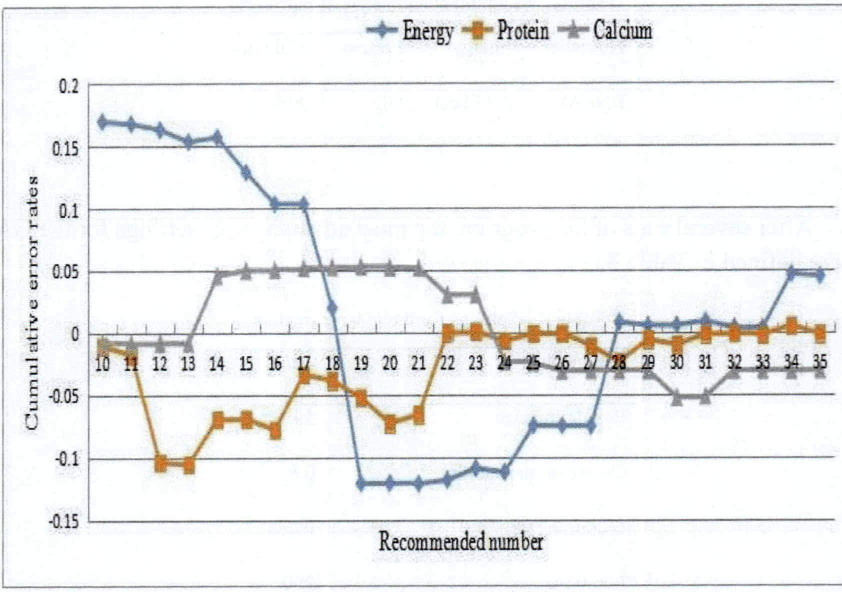

(a)GA based on random weighting

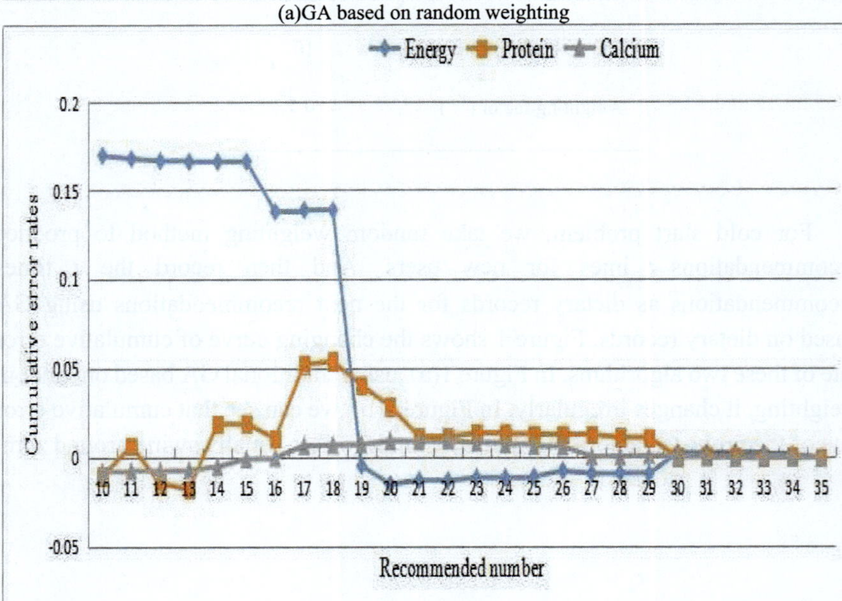

(b)GA based on dietary records

Fig.1. Changing curve of cumulative error rates

Randomly list three items of recommended daily intakes of food for the target users using method based on dietary records in Table 4.

Table 4. Recommended daily intakes of food

Food category	Grain	Beans	Milk	Animal food	Vegetables	Fruit	Oil
1	Black sesame cake 479g	Soybean milk 37g	Yoghourt 107g	Grass carp 157g	Calabash 475g	Apple 139g	Lard 8g
2	Rice flour 311g	High-protein soybean flour 16g	Milk 135g	Salangid 157g	Dry gourd 456g	Mandarin orange 175g	Corn oil 22g
3	Bread 490g	Vegetarian chicken roll 49g	Cream 92g	Ham sausage 151g	Chinese yam 445g	Laiyan pears 138g	Oil mixture 9g

5. Conclusion

The proposed personalized recommended algorithm on healthy diet, its core is MOGA based on dietary records. Through the analysis of user's dietary records and assessment of user's accumulated intake of nutrients in the past period of time, it adjusts multi-objectives weights. Conducting experiments on real food composition data, multi-objective GA based on the dietary records compared with multi-objective GA based on the random weighting. Cumulative error rate of the former gradually tends to zero, finally swing around zero. From the perspective of health considerations, MOGA based on dietary record is more suitable for the personalized recommendation service on healthy diet.

Acknowledgments

Work partially supported by grant 41271387 of the National Natural Science Foundation of China and 999521 of Academician innovation project of Shaanxi Normal University.

References

1. Balintfy J L. Communications of the ACM, 1964, 7(4): 255-259.

2. Eckstein E F. Journal of the American Dietetic Association, 1967, 51(6): 529.

3. Seljak B K. Informatica, 2004, 28: 359-364.

4. K, Gedrich, A, Hensel, I, Binder, et al. European Journal of Clinical Nutrition, 1999, 53(4):309-318.

5. Murata T, Ishibuchi H, Tanaka H. Computers & Industrial Engineering, 1996, 30(4):957–968.

6. Yue-xin Yang. Chinese Food Composition [M]. Beijing: Peking University Medical Press, 2002. (In Chinese).

7. Acta Nutrimenta Sinica,1998,04:5-15. (In Chinese).

8. Acta Nutrimenta Sinica,2001,03:193-196. (In Chinese)

Efficient Approach to Store Big Proteomic Data Based on NoSQL Database

Lin ZHANG
College of Computer Science and Technology, Chongqing University of Posts and Telecommunications, Chongqing ,400065, China
E-mail:601462459@qq.com, bmze@qq.com

Zhe SANG, Xue-Ying YE, Yuan-Hai SHEN, Jun TAN and Ming-Ze BAI
College of Bioinformation, Chongqing University of Posts and Telecommunications, Chongqing 400065, China
E-mail:bmze@qq.com

To solve the inefficient bottleneck problems of the traditional relational databases in big data storage and access, this paper proposes an efficient approach to store big proteomic data based on NoSQL (Not only SQL) database. MongoDB, a typical software of NoSQL, is compared with MySQL in data storage and query performance. The experiment results demonstrate that the query and read speed of NoSQL database has been improved significantly as compared to the traditional relational database, especially for mass unstructured and semi-structured data.

Keywords: Big data; Proteomics; Non-relational database; MongoDB database.

1. Introduction

In recent years, the "Big Data" has penetrated into many industries and business areas, which shown that Big Data not only contains the great scientific value, but also plays an important role in the economic development. For this reason, big data has drawn the great attention of the governments, which has upgraded to the height of national strategy. In September 2008, the Nature magazine first published the "Big data issue" consisting of papers written by House and others, which indicates the influence of big data has been involved in academic and industry fields[1]. In March 2012, the U. S. government invested $200 million to start the "Big Data Research and Development Initiative", which turns out that the influence level of Big Data from academic and commercial behavior to the will of the state[2].

Roughly speaking, big data refers to a collection of data that can't be transmitted ,stored, analyzed and utilized by using existing information technology include the software and hardware tools in a tolerable time[3]. Big data research is of great significance in data intensive disciplines –proteomics. The big proteomic data panoramically reveals human and other organisms' proteins and regulation rules, which can help us unscramble the human and other genomes. The studies on the proteomics data are one of the most important part in the understanding of the health and medical questions.

At present, a data revolution has broken out in the field of life science. After the completion of the human genome project, proteomic data will undoubtedly be one of the biggest, the most important and kernel of the scientific data. Similar to other research fields, the efficiency, quick and mass storage have encountered a bottleneck in their further utilization. Even though the traditional storage solutions can provide reliability and securities, it is difficult to deal with a variety of different demands with the huge amounts of proteomics data[4]. This study proposed an efficient storage method for big proteomics data, by using the non-relational (NoSQL) database from the perspective of the actual production, in the hope of improving the development of the biological science[5].

2. Brief Introduction of NoSQL Database

The so-called NoSQL does not mean there is no SQL, but means "not only SQL"[6]. It is an untraditional relational database whose main features include non-relational, level extensible, distributed and open source. Besides, it also has other characteristics like free and eventual consistency, etc. Because of this kind of the different characteristics from the relational databases, NoSQL databases can adapt to the current status of huge amounts of data. The common storage models of NoSQL include key-value storage, document storage, column storage, graphics storage, XML storage, etc. MongoDB is a typical representative of the document databases[7].

MongoDB is a scalable, high-performance, open source document-oriented database, which is implemented by C++ [8]. MongoDB mainly solves the efficient access of the huge amounts of data. According to the official documents, the data access speed of MongoDB is ten times more than that of MySQL when the data volume is more than 50GB[9].

3. Design and Implementation of Storage Approach for Proteomics Data

3.1. *Storage approach*

Proteomics big data typically include experimental information, protein identification, protein annotation, peptide identification, mass spectra data and so on. Proteomics data have complex relationships among the data mentioned above, with the huge volume of these data, makes that the traditional database increasingly fail to meet the needs of users on the storage of the big proteomics data, with the high maintenance costs, and the complicated code processing. Therefore, a new storage approach has been proposed. Without using the table structure based storage format in traditional data store methods, document storage structure from MongoDB, for storing and managing data. In view of the advantages of MongoDB database, as well as the features of large data and fragmentation of big proteomics data, we use MongoDB to override the performance problems of existing raw file storage and relational database storage.

3.2. *Implementation of the storage approach*

In performance testing, test categories are specifically divided into general data storage and file data storage to compare efficient storage, access and management of proteomics big data.

3.2.1. *General data storage*

General data typically include experimental information, statistics, identification results and other data, They are all in basic types such as numerical, text and others. These data can also be stored by using relational databases, but when the number of experiments increases faster and faster, the bottleneck problems in the management of increasing proteomics database will appear. MongoDB uses the horizontal expansion, document-oriented data model to make data segmentation across multiple servers easily [10]. MongoDB also can automatically process data and load balance across inside the cluster as well as automatically reassign documents, so that the user requests are dynamically assigned to the different machine without the expansion problem. If a cluster requires a larger capacity, we only need to add a new cluster server. MongoDB will automatically transfer existing data to the new cluster server. Compared to MongoDB, a relational database cannot run efficiently in this kind of cluster.

3.2.2. *Mass spectrometry file storage*

Mass spectrometry (MS) is the core technology in the proteomics research, it can measure the molecular weight of the biological macromolecules quickly and accurately. The storage of mass spectra leads to a solid foundation for facilitates in proteomics data. The mass spectra data have the characteristics of high complexity, high flux, large scale and high difficulty of analysis. It is mainly used to identify the peptide and proteins in the samples. Mass spectrometry files are considered as isolated from each other. Each file corresponds to an experiment run, which means a proteomics experiment can contain a lot of mass spectra files. The total number of file types is large, here we choose one of the typical type MGF as an example. The data stored in MS files are shown in figure 1, the main reason choose MGF type is ProteomicsView projects we involved in is using this type[11]. Besides, the PRIDE Cluster and other project are using the MGF type, which is very similar to this type[12]. ProteomicsView is a proteomics database, on which we can analysis, management and display spectra and identifications. PRIDE Cluster is used to calculate the quality of protein identifications from a variety of proteomic mass spectrometry experiments; it is mainly used to assess the peptides identified in the PRIDE database.

Due to the big data characteristics of proteomic mass spectrometry data, when using a relational database, it is easy to make the amount of table reach millions or tens of millions. While the relational database can add an index to query optimizing, whatever a large table-space to optimize, it hardly meets the need for data crush, even database sharding, the cost will be very high. So we can try to pase the proteomics data all at once, then store them into mass spectrum collection of MongoDB. Since the data structure of mass spectrum data is very simple, big data storage performance of MongoDB can be fully reflected. Even if the amount of data reaches tens or hundreds of millions, MongoDB can easily manage without database sharding.

4. Performance Text

4.1. *Construction of experimental test platform*

To compare the storage and read performance of MySQL and MongoDB, this paper runs the instances of MongoDB and MySQL on the same configuration server. The hardware test environment is as follow: 64 bit operating system of Red Hat Enterprise 6.3; memory capacity of 3*1G; the CPU is Intel Xeon E5-2620 2.0GHz; the database version of MySQL is 2.6.7, MongoDB is 2.6.7; the software testing environment using JAVA as the development script. The platform has realized the basic functions of storage, query and so on, and record the testing data, write the test log to provide the basis for further comparison and evaluation.

4.2. *Performance comparison of general data storage*

Test the storage performance for general data of them, add the stopwatch in the key code, and record the execution time of command line. The data volume are 100, 500, 1000, 2000, 5000, 10000, 100000, 500000 respectively. Write the time into the log after each insert. Test three times continuously, and take an average value. As shown in Figure 1, when the number of single inserting data continues to increase, the inserting time of MySQL increases sharply, while the time consuming of MongoDB almost no change, its storage performance has obvious advantages.

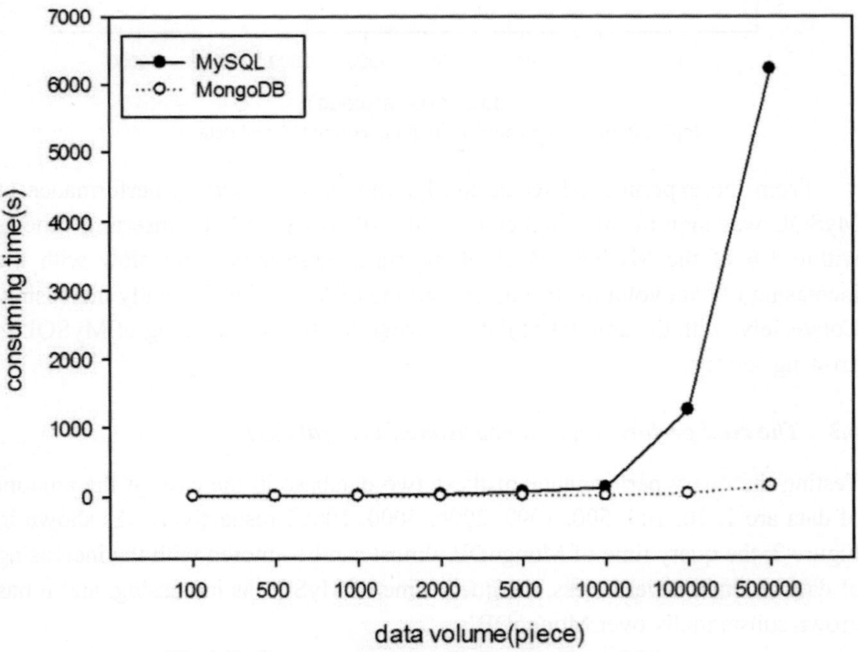

Fig. 1. Performance comparison for inserting General data

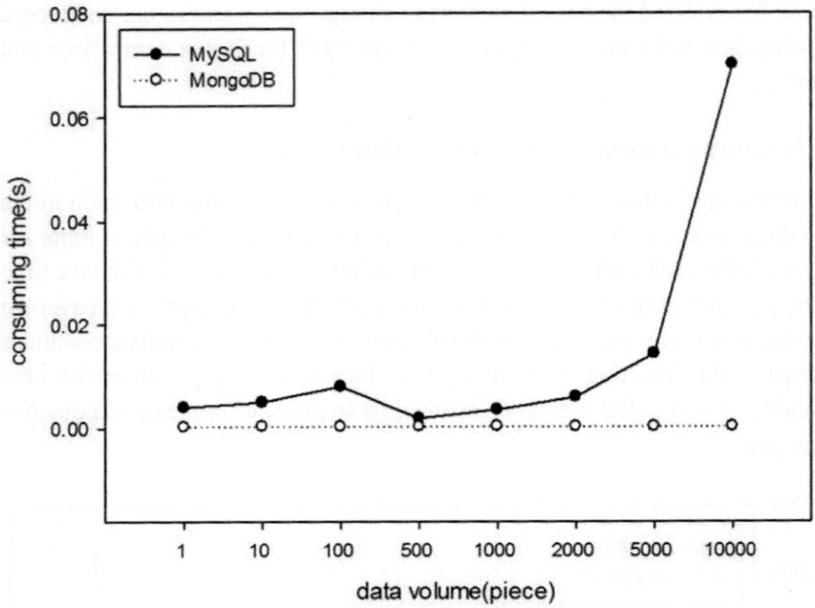

Fig. 2. Performance comparison for querying General data

From the experimental result can be known, the inserting performance of MySQL was significantly higher than that of MongoDB, its inserting time is within 1/6 of the MySQL. Both of inserting performance are slow with the increasing of data volume. The inserting time of MongoDB is gently increasing. Conversely, with the amount of data growing, the time-consuming of MySQL is growing serious.

4.3. *The read performance comparison of general data*

Testing the query performance of these two database in the case of the amount of data are 1, 10, 100, 500, 1000, 2000, 5000, 10000 respectively, As shown in Figure 2, the query time of MongoDB almost can be ignored with the increasing of data volume, nevertheless, the query time of MySQL is increasing, and it has grown substantially over MongoDB's.

4.4. *The read performance comparison of file and MongoDB*

Using the ApacheBench tool to test processing performance of the file and MongoDB respectively, firstly, simulating 10 concurrent users on two systems of processing page for requests simulation in 10, 100,1000,5000, 10000, 20000 times separately, and collect the throughput, test results are shown in Figure 3.

And then simulate 100 users requests for simulation in10000, 20000, 30000, 40000, 50000, 60000 times separately, test results are shown in Figure 4. Each set of data tests five times, removing the highest and lowest of the two sets of data, take the average of the remaining three sets of data. Since once access to a page, then need to read data. With the increment of visit traffic to the page from users, the data read will become very difficult, and even the server will crash. According to the test results, when the amount of data access is not large, MongoDB has no advantage, otherwise, but when the surge in pageviews, the advantage is very obvious.

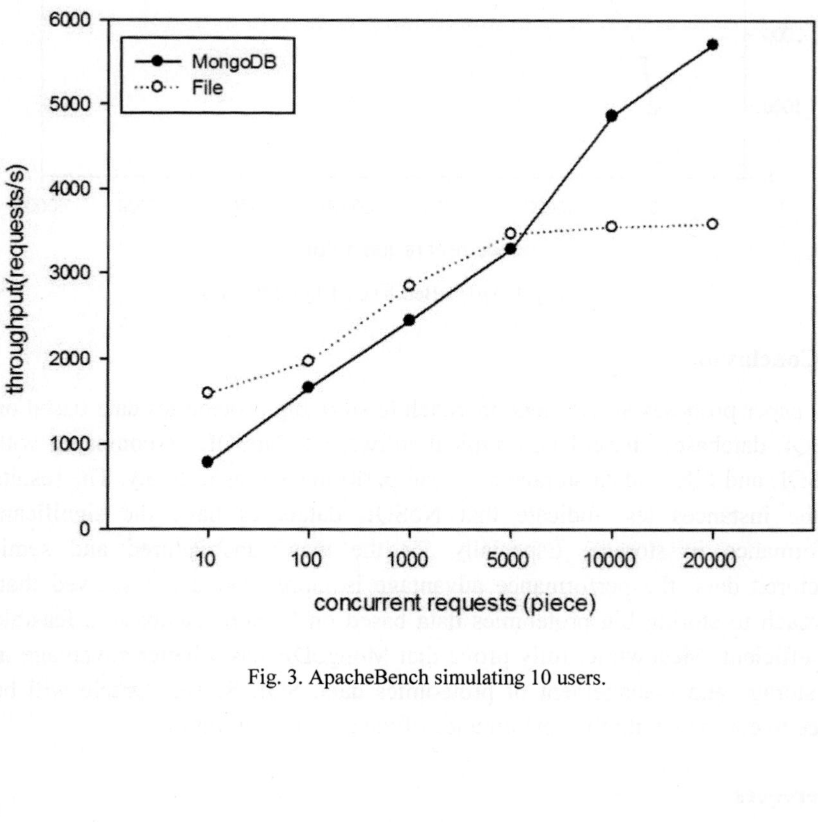

Fig. 3. ApacheBench simulating 10 users.

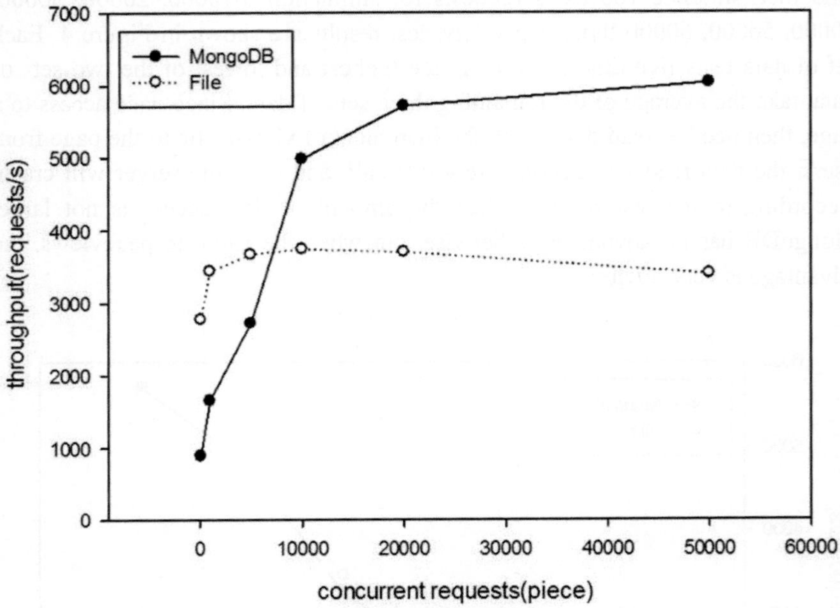

Fig. 4. ApacheBench simulating 100 users

5. Conclusion

This paper proposes an efficient approach to store big proteomics data based on NoSQL database; MongoDB, a typical software of NoSQL, is compared with MySQL and File in data storage and read performance respectively. The results of the instances test indicate that NoSQL databases have the significant performance in storage. Especially for the mass unstructured and semi-structured data, the performance advantage is more obvious. It showed that, approach to storing big proteomics data based on NoSQL database is feasible and efficient. Meanwhile, fully prove that MongoDB has a better advantage in the storage and management of proteomics data. SQL Server, Oracle will be added to compare with the performance of the approach in future.

References

1. Howe D, Costanzo M, Fey P, et al. "Big data: The future of biocuration," Nature, Vol.455, No.7209, pp.47-50, 2008.
2. G.J.Li, X.Q.Cheng, "Study on Big Data: the Major Strategic Fields of Science and Technology and the Development of the Social Economy in the

Future -- Research Status and Scientific Thinking of Big Data," Bulletin of the Chinese Academy of Sciences, Vol.27,No.6, pp.647-657, 2012.

3. Manyika J, Chui M, Brown B, et al. "Big data: The Next Frontier for Innovation, Competition, and Productivity," Technical Report, McKinsey Global Institute,2011.
4. ROBBIN, "A Discussion of NoSQL Database—Why Should Non-Relational Database," http://robbin.javaeye.com/blog/524977.
5. K..Fan, "NoSQL Database Review," Programmer, Vol.2010,No.6,pp.76-78, 2010.
6. Y.Sun, F.Lin, B.J.Wang, "Study on the Key-Value Distributed Storage System for Cloud Computing," Electronica Sinica, Vol. 41, No.7, pp.1406-1411, 2013.B.W. Bestbury, *R*-matrices and the magic square,*J. Phys. A*36, 1947 (2003).
7. G.L.Wang, "MongoDB Database of Applied Research and Program Optimization,"China Science and Technology Information, Vol.20, No.8, pp.93-96, 2011.
8. D.H.Lu, X.B.He, "The Analysis of NoSQL Database," Science And Technology of West China, Vol. 2, No.15, pp.14-16, 2011.
9. MongoDB, http: //mongodb. org/.
10. "Proteomeview: build the view of your proteomes," http: //proteomeview. hupo. org. cn/.
11. Griss J, Foster J M, Hermjakob H, et al. "PRIDE Cluster: building a consensus of proteomics data," Nature Methods, Vol.10, No.2, pp. 95-96, 2013.L.F. Richardson, *Arms and Insecurity* (Boxwood, Pittsburg, 1960).
12. MongoDB Auto-sharding, http: //www. mongodb. org / display / DOCS/ Sharding+Introduction.

Advancing Water Data Retrieval Through a Novel Water Environment Ontology System

Mu-tao HUANG, Xue-ke DONG, Shu-qing LIANG, Na LI and Shuo HE

College of Hydropower & Information Engineering, Huazhong University of Science and Technology, Wuhan 430074, China
E-mail:hmt1973@sina.com

Yong TIAN

South University of Science and Technology of China, Shenzhen, 518055, China
E-mail: 95297626@qq.com

Currently, rapidly locating relevant data sources and assembling the most appropriate data on the Internet is a tremendously difficult task for researchers. To address these issues, this paper proposes the development of a high availability ontology-based water environmental data retrieval and visualization system (OntoWE). The OntoWE prototypes have two significant features. Firstly, it establishes a water environment domain ontology to offer facilities to alleviate semantic heterogeneity and associate semantic information with the data retrieval process. Secondly, it embraces the capability of Service Oriented Architectures (SOA) and Silverlight to leverage the latest protocols of several open web service standards with the Managed Extensibility Framework (MEF). This system provides a centralized and easy-to-use interactive system which enables users to do a one-stop search, access and visualize different types of water data in a single environment. The feasibility and effectiveness of OntoWE system was demonstrated through several investigations about water quality data discovery and retrieval at basin scale in China.

Keywords: Domain ontology; Data retrieval; Semantic web; Service oriented architectures; Water environment.

1. Introduction

Due to the advances in computer sciences and digital earth technologies, large amounts of dispersed water environmental information has been collected by many scientists and organizations in government and academia for different purposes[1].The capabilities to discovery, access to, and integration of information from heterogeneous data repositories through a single tool will be great benefits for hydrologist and environmentalist who try to collect interested data for a particular water environment study. A system named OntoWE was developed to meet these needs.

In this paper we present the system framework and methodologies that are facilitating the development of OntoWE. The resultant prototype provides scientists and common users with a wealth tool that simplify data access, management and publication tasks. The applicability of the system was demonstrated through several investigations about water quality data discovery and retrieval at basin scale in China.

2. OntoWE System Framework Design

The ontoWE system was designed using an architecture that separates the web application interface layer from the service layer, exposing as much of the functionality as possible through an application programmers interface to enable direct client access and interoperability with other systems. Figure1 illustrates the service-oriented, multi-layer architecture proposed for the system. Components and services in each layer perform similar tasks with accordance to the goal of the layer in which they are placed. For example components belonging to the geoportal layer are concerned mainly with two tasks, dealing with the user interface, user interaction, and data visualization and application integration also called business logic or business integration as well as instantiation and invocation of service instances at the service layer.

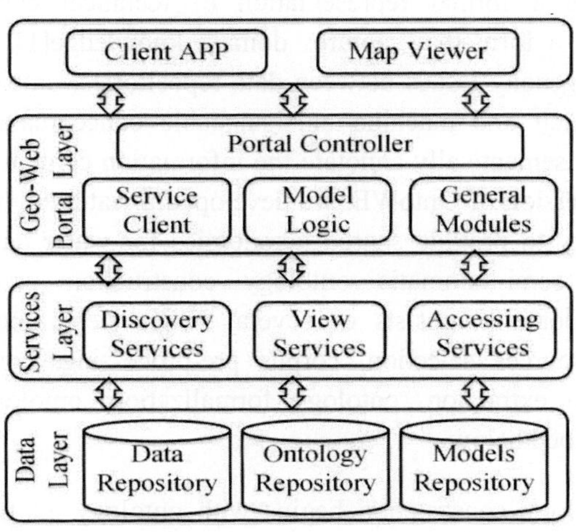

Fig. 1. Data analysis and modeling use case

The service layer comprises a variety of distributed service instances logically clustered according to service types (discovery, view, accessing, etc.). This layer is the most important part of the whole architecture as it provides the interface between the Internet and the web server. The service layer must provide web services by which the client can query the existing datasets and retrieve the data by specifying a few required parameters. Data discovery service provides the functionality for ontology-aided service discovery and semantics-based query. Accessing service contains a variety of service wrappers used to retrieve data from remote data sources by dynamically invoking online web services. View service supports visualization of various data in an integrated hierarchical view.

The main purpose of data layer is to store the metadata of the data files and to provide a mapping between ontology concepts and the datasets being served. To simplify the incorporation of different data formats we assume that the metadata values for different file format will be provided as key value pairs. When a dataset of a specific data format is requested by the user, the particular software routine which is processing the user request will be provided with all the key value pairs corresponding to that specific format.

3. Methodology

3.1. *Water ontology construction*

An ontology is a formal representation of technical concepts and their interrelations in a form that captures domain knowledge[1]. To alleviate the semantic heterogeneity issues between data repositories, ontology is employed to provide explicit and machine-understandable conceptualizations of water information and semantically annotate the information content of web services. In the present version of OntoWE, we developed a water environment domain-specific ontology to provide shared taxonomies for water data discovery and retrieval. Our semi-automatic ontology construction process for water environmental domain consists of several major steps, including ontology learning data sources selection, corpus pre-processing, concept extraction, concept relation extraction, ontology formalization, ontology visualization, which are described below.

Step1 Ontology construction begins with ontology learning data sources selection. Domain corpus was gathered through advices from experts, web pages, documentation, etc. We utilized these corpuses as the information source to facilitate the ontology building process for water environment domain[3].

Step2 A set of natural language processing(NLP)tools including sentence splitter, tokenizer, part-of-speech(POS) taggers, syntactic parsers, stop word filter have been employed to segment texts into grammatically meaningful syntagmatic units and organize them into non-recursive phrasal chunks. For this work, Pan Gu Segment tool 2.3.1.0 software components have been used.

Step 3 A concepts extractor was developed to capture the highly frequent domain terms and phrases (n-grams) and their properties that can correctly represent the key concepts of a corpus of documents in a domain of water environment from the segmented chunks by coupling the TF-IDF (Term Frequency–Inverse Document Frequency) method with seed concepts method to assess the significance of a word within a document in a corpus and complete statistics and regulations.

Step 4 A relation extractor clusters candidate concepts to extract relations and then maps them into meaning representation to facilitate constructing ontology. To this matter, we have implemented several statistical and data mining approaches including conceptual similarity calculation methods, genetic algorithm, K-means cluster analysis, Naive Bayes Network classifier to identify several types of relations(subclass-of relations, mereological relations, instance-of relations, equivalence) between extracted concepts.

Step 5 The aim of this stage is the detection of the classes, subclasses and properties of the ontology and establish the ontology by organizing these concepts and properties in a hierarchy structure. The web ontology language (OWL) has been used to model all kinds of water environment ontologies.

Step 6 An ontology visualization tool was used to manage the versioning of the domain ontology, and modify/improve it.

All these phase executes in semi-automated mode. This set of tools provides ontology engineers with an integrated workbench for corpus management, ontology learning and modelling ontology. Ontology construction tool was developed using C#.Net with embedded version of NLP toolkit. Figure2 shows the GUI for ontology construction and illustrates a part of the water quality ontology obtained from the water environment related corpus.

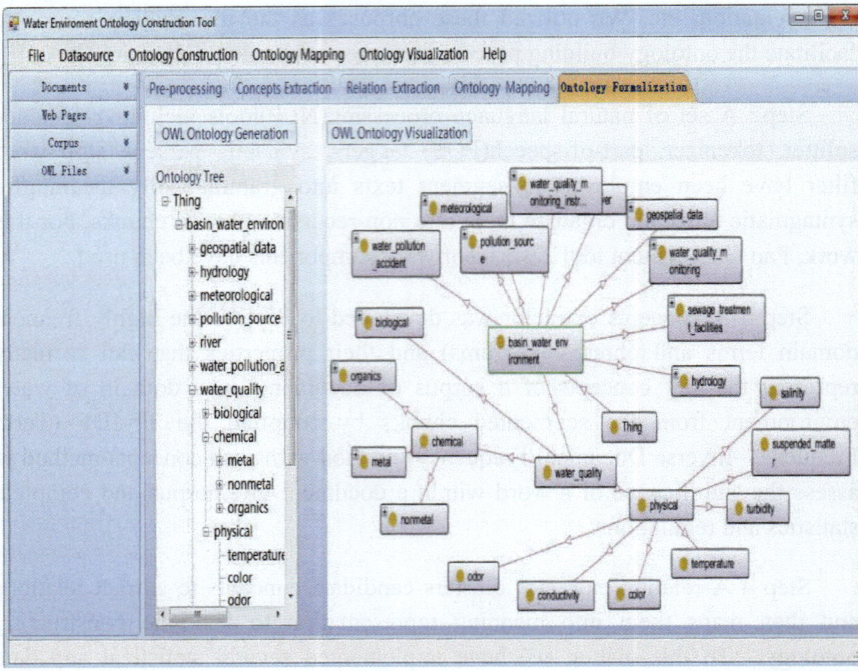

Fig. 2. Water environment construction tool

3.2. *Ontology-based water data retrieval*

The objective of data discovery and retrieval is to help users locate the observation sites of interest, and then directly access and retrieve interested data. In the process of data discovery and retrieval, water environment ontology was employed to establish mappings between the heterogeneous data repositories' controlled vocabularies and specific ontological concepts[2]. The user specifies the query criteria (keyword, time range and geographic area) on the user interface of the web portal. According to the keyword submitted by user, the inference engine derives an answer from the water environment ontology which is a concept hierarchy organizing in a tree structure. OntoWE uses the aforementioned discovery services for this purpose. The discovery services interact with the ontology reasoner through the description logic reasoner interface. Next, the dataSearch module traversals the ontology concept hierarchy and find out available stations satisfying the query criteria for each concept[3].The discovered stations list or series catalog is returned to the map viewer, consequently, a point feature layer used for representing stations is created and added to the map viewer. The user locates a specific station on the map viewer and selects a variable measured at the station, then the data request is sent to the dataMediator. The dataMediator starts invoking and interacting with the access services to retrieve data from remote source, and finally the retrieved data is reformatted and displayed on the user interface.

3.3. *Web portal development*

The web portal of the OntoWE was developed using the C# language based on Microsoft .NET Framework (Version 4.5). The latest .NET Framework provides several unique components which greatly facilitate the development, including Managed Extensibility Framework (MEF), Silverlight, and Language Integrated Query (LINQ). Silverlight is Microsoft's latest solution to delivering rich and interactive experiences for desktop applications. LINQ is a technique for querying data[4]. It is fully integrated into .NET languages like C#, which makes it much easier to query and update data of different source types in developing data-extensive applications like OntoWE.

The main GUI of OntoWE (Figure3) consists of key interactive elements including pull down menus, tree lists, toolbars, floating windows and so on. Additional elements (e.g., scale bar, compass, legend bar, etc.) can be turned on/off as needed. Once the system is started, a world map is lunched. Users can select different aerial imagery as their base map.

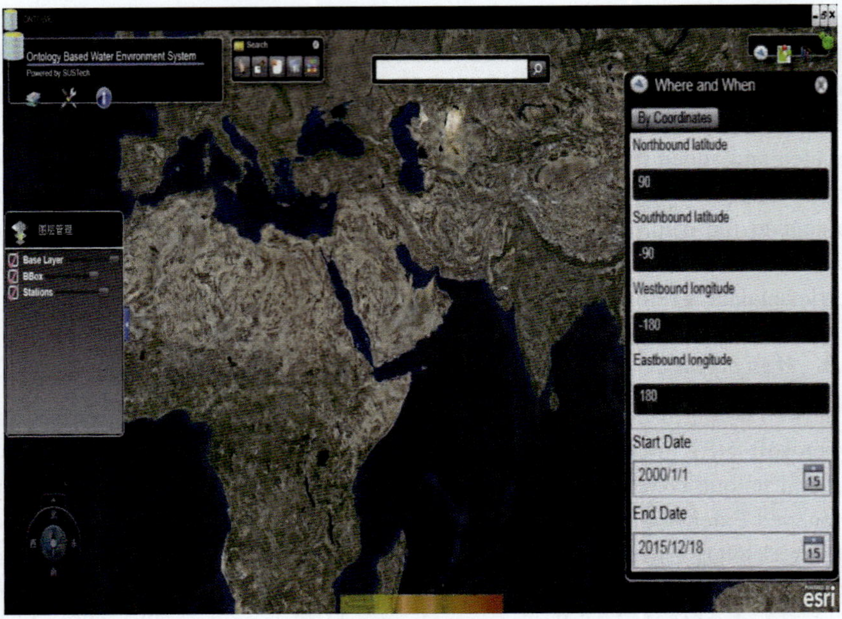

Fig. 3. Main graphic user interface of OntoWE

The system displays elevation data and satellite images at varying levels of detail. Users can manipulate the map, view data in a global view and then seamlessly zoom in to visualize detailed and localized data. Basic view manipulations such as Zoom In/ Out, Pan and Refresh are supported. The GUI provides the user with an integrated environment that provides functionalities to query based on the semantics across the thematic information repositories. For example, the user can first select a geographical extent he/she is interested in and then by selecting a domain of interest (e.g. land cover), the concepts from the shared ontology belonging to land cover domain are automatically retrieved.

4. Case Study

In order to demonstrate the feasibility of the OntoWE prototype, several investigations were made with the goals of discovering and retrieving heterogeneous data to support water quality assessment at basin scale. Figure 4 depicts the results of retrieving data about the PH variable. There are total 962 national water quality stations are discovered. The stations cover the entire China. When selecting a station, all the variables measured at the station will be retrieved and displayed.The first investigation was made aiming at querying PH data from Yangsigang station located in the Yangtze River Basin.A time series panel floating on the map viewer is shown in figure 5. The time series of PH values in 2012 measured at the Yangsigang station are displayed in the panel. The second investigation was made aimed to collect the time series of PH values in 2012 measured at the Heiliuzi stationlocated in the Yellow River basin.As shown in Fig.6, the overall of time series data is plotted in a line graph.

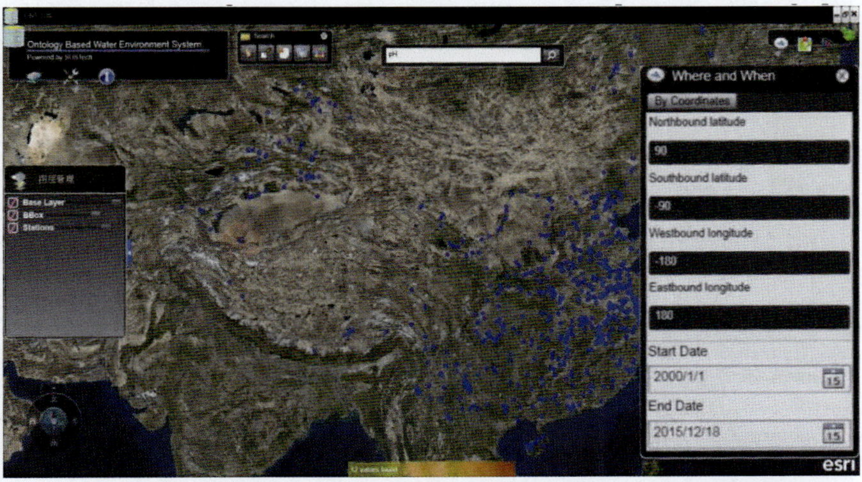

Fig. 4. Example of retrieval of all national water quality stations containing PH data

Fig. 5. Example of retrieval of PH data at the Yangsigang station

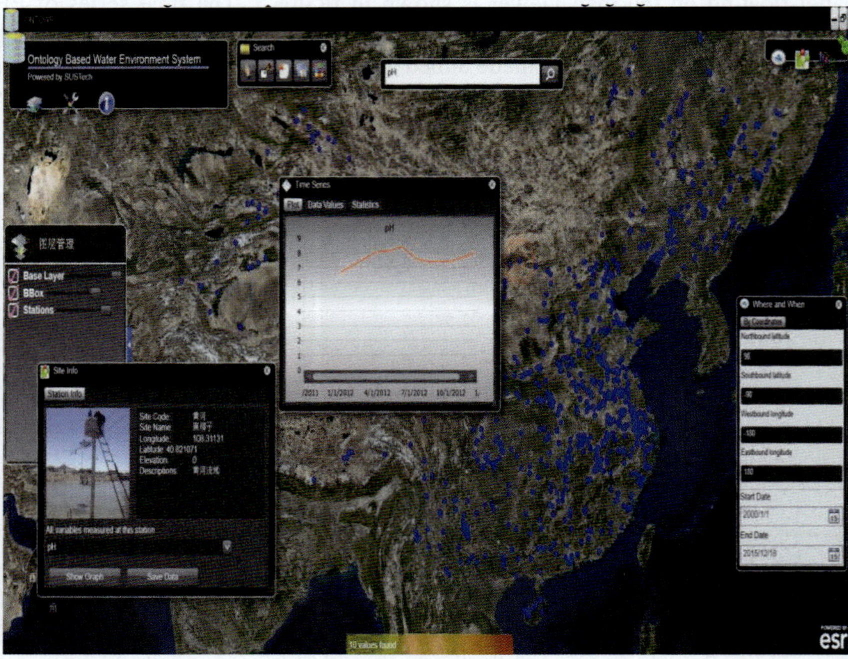

Fig. 6. Example of retrieval of PH data at the Heiliuzi station

5. Conclusion

Academic researchers often involve in collecting multi-source, multi-scale and multi-discipline data within experimental watersheds, observatories, and research sites. Our work makes two major contributions. Firstly, we propose a semi-automatic approach to build a wide-coverage water environment domain-specific ontology from different candidate corpus which provides a cyclical process that involves the successive and flexible application of various NLP techniques and data mining algorithms for ontology learning and ontology modelling. More importantly, this approach is that has been designed to work with Chinese documents. As we know, the vast amount of current ontology learning systems have been developed to work with documents written in English and Ontology-based studies on water environment domain are rather limited. Secondly, OntoWE prototype was developed to provide scientists and common users with a wealth tool that simplify data access, management and publication tasks. In the process of data discovery and retrieval, water environment ontology was employed to establish mappings between the heterogeneous data repositories' controlled vocabularies and specific ontological concepts. The applicability of the OntoWE prototype for discovering and retrieving observations data has been investigated.

Acknowledgements

This research was financially supported by the National Science Foundation of China (NSFC) (No. 51579108 and No. 51209098) and the Fundamental Research Funds for the Central Universities (No. 0118271045 and No. 2014TS153).

References

1. WEI Yuan-yuan, WANG Ru-jing, HU Yi-min and WANG Xue. From Web Resources to Agricultural Ontology: a Method for Semi-Automatic Construction. Journal of Integrative Agriculture, 2012 ,11 (5): 775-783.
2. Huang Mutao, Maidment D R, Tian Yong. Using SOA and RIAs for water data discovery and retrieval. Environmental Modelling & Software, 2011, 26(11):1309-1324.
3. Tian Yong, Huang Mutao. Enhance discovery and retrieval of geospatial data using SOA and Semantic Web technologies. Expert Systems with Applications, 2012, 39(16):12522-12535.
4. Liang Jianming, Gong Jianhua, Li Wenhang, et al. Visualizing 3D atmospheric data with spherical volume texture on virtual globes. Computers & Geosciences, 2014, 68:81–91.

Low Dose Projection Data Reconstruction with a New Regularization

Jun-feng ZHANG[1,*], Yang CHEN[1] and Li-min LUO[1,2]

[1]*Laboratory of Image Science and Technology, School of Computer Science and Engineering, Southeast University, Nanjing 210096, China*

[2]*Centre de Rechercheen Information Médicale Sino-français (CRIBs)*

[*]*E-mail: zhangjf20008@163.com*

Low dose X-ray CT reconstruction is currently a significant research topic in medical imaging. Thanks to the development of compressed sensing, iterative reconstruction with sparse regularization can obtain more satisfactory results than the filtered back projection. As classical total variation cannot reconstruct with noise polluted projection views, we propose a Gamma regulation in tomographic reconstruction, and the experimental results demonstrate better compatibility either in objective evaluation or visual sense than total variation.

Keywords: Computer tomography; Total variation; Gamma regularization.

1. Introduction

Computer tomography (CT) has played an important role in medical imaging and industry seamless test since its introduction in 1970s. However, unlike the industrial applications, the common used X-ray CT in hospitals is harmful for diagnosis, which can induce cancer and other diseases [1]. According to the principles of the CT, the quality of imaging of CT is positive correlation to the radiation dose. Low dose CT, therefore, has become the focus of research, because it can reduce radiation, while improving image quality as soon as possible.

At present, iterative reconstruction with low dose projection data is research hotspot in CT field. Compressed sensing (CS) theory was proposed by Donoho D et al., and was successfully used in Magnetic Resonance Imaging [2]. As is described by CS, TV norm of image is similar to *l1* norm of one dimensional signal. Siddy et al. used the TV norm for three-dimensional divergent beam CT reconstruction with a few number of projection angles [3].Chen et al. suggested a nonlocal method to reconstruct Poisson noised sonogram [4]. Subsequently, low dose CT reconstruction also gained conspicuous result compared with traditional filtered back projection (FBP) algorithm [5, 6].

Although TV norm can obtain considerable result compared with FBP, TV norm is still not l0 norm according to CS. Recently there are many methods to approaches the l0. Hu et al. came forward the l0 norm constrained sparse reconstruction [7]. These methods all obtained better results than TV. However, to my knowledge, Genam et al. suggested l0 norm regularization for image recovery in 1992, which is so-called half-quadratic regularization or concave constraint [8].

To generalize the half-quadratic regularization and reconstruction with noise polluted projected data, we propose a new Gamma regularization in tomographic reconstruction, the result by which is superior to TV. In section 2, we firstly simply review TV norm regularization and half-quadratic regularization. In section 3, the Gamma regularization is defined and analyzed. The performance of the proposed model is verified by experiment in section 4. And we conclude with some remarks in section 5.

2. Preliminaries

2.1. *CT reconstruction with TV model*

The popular TV mode of CT reconstruction can be formulated in discrete form

$$\min \frac{1}{2}\|Gf - y\|_2^2 + \lambda\varphi(f). \tag{1}$$

where the G is imaging system matrix, which can be simply calculated by Siddon's fast ray tracing algorithm [9], f is the vector composed by the discrete attenuation coefficients of the patient' slice with lexicographic order, and y is the vector consisted of project data acquired by projecting patient along an anticlockwise/clockwise rotation. The λ is a balance parameter between fidelity term and constraint term. The common used TV is ROF model [10], which is given below.

$$\varphi_R(f) = \sum_{i=1}^{m}\sum_{j=1}^{n}\sqrt{\left(\nabla f_{i,j}^1\right)^2 + \left(\nabla f_{i,j}^2\right)^2}. \tag{2}$$

Consequently, the problem of CT reconstruction become finding the attenuation coefficients when the projection data is known. Because G is invertible, the problem of (1) is an ill problem.

2.2. *CT reconstruction with half-quadratic model*

The half-quadratic norm regularization is different from the formula (3), which can be given by

$$\varphi_h = \sum_{i=1}^{m} \sum_{i=1}^{n} \left(\varphi\left(\left| \nabla f_{i,j}^1 \right| \right) + \varphi\left(\left| \nabla f_{i,j}^2 \right| \right) \right). \tag{3}$$

where $\varphi(x)$ is a potential function. The common potential functions can be found [11].

3. Gamma Regularization

3.1. *Gamma regularization model*

From the formula (4), with a slightly change, (4) can be rewritten in an obvious definite integration form

$$\varphi_h(f) = \sum_{i=1}^{m} \sum_{i=1}^{n} \left(\int_0^{\left|\nabla f_{i,j}^1\right|} \phi(t) dt + \int_0^{\left|\nabla f_{i,j}^2\right|} \phi(t) dt \right). \tag{4}$$

where ϕ is integral kernel function. Differing from the conventional TV model whose integral kernel is constant function, i.e., $\phi(t) = 1$, we propose a following generalized reconstruction model

$$\min \| Gf - y \| + \lambda \varphi_g(\nabla f). \tag{5}$$

with a new kernel function taking the form of Gamma distribution probability density function

$$\phi(t) = \frac{t^{\alpha-1} \beta^{\alpha} e^{-\beta t}}{\Gamma(\alpha)}. \tag{6}$$

where α is the shape parameter and β is a scale parameter , respectively. The supports of α and β are both [0, ∞], and the curve of corresponding curve changes with different α and β . Apparently, the new potential function takes the form

$$\varphi_g(f) = \sum_{i=1}^{m} \sum_{j=1}^{n} \int_0^{\left|\nabla f_{i,j}^1\right|} \frac{t^{\alpha-1} \beta^{\alpha} e^{-\beta t}}{\Gamma(\alpha)} dt + \sum_{i=1}^{m} \sum_{j=1}^{n} \int_0^{\left|\nabla f_{i,j}^2\right|} \frac{t^{\alpha-1} \beta^{\alpha} e^{-\beta t}}{\Gamma(\alpha)} dt. \tag{7}$$

3.2. *Iterative optimization*

Many methods have been proposed to solve the problem (1). The fixed-point algorithm, conjugate gradient method (CG), is used in this study. Iteration step τ is selected by backtracking line search with auxiliary parameter ρ . On account of the formula of (8), which is a composite function with the inner function $\phi(t)$ and outer integration function $|\nabla f|$, the corresponding derivative can be conveniently obtained by

$$\left(\varphi_g\left(|\nabla f|\right)\right)' = \sum_{i=1}^{m}\sum_{j=1}^{n}\frac{|\nabla f|^{\alpha-1}\beta^{\alpha}e^{-\beta|\nabla f|}}{\Gamma(\alpha)}\operatorname{sign}(\nabla f). \tag{8}$$

By introducing a sufficiently small constant ε to overcome the zero denominator in (8) (when $\alpha < 1$), the Gamma regularization function Eq. (6) can be approximated by Eq. (9):

$$\varphi_g(f) \approx \sum_{i=1}^{m}\sum_{j=1}^{n}\int_0^{\left(\left(f_{i+1,j}-f_{i,j}\right)^2+\varepsilon\right)^{\frac{1}{2}}}\frac{t^{\alpha-1}\beta^{\alpha}e^{-\beta t}}{\Gamma(\alpha)}dt$$

$$+\sum_{i=1}^{m}\sum_{j=1}^{n}\int_0^{\left(\left(f_{i,j+1}-f_{i,j}\right)^2+\varepsilon\right)^{\frac{1}{2}}}\frac{t^{\alpha-1}\beta^{\alpha}e^{-\beta t}}{\Gamma(\alpha)}dt. \tag{9}$$

The corresponding partial derivative of the regularization function Eq. (9) with respect to pixel $f_{i,j}$ is given as

$$\frac{\partial}{\partial f_{i,j}}\left(\Psi_{\Gamma}(f)\right) =$$

$$-\frac{\left(\left(f_{i+1,j}-f_{i,j}\right)^2+\varepsilon\right)^{\frac{\alpha-1}{2}}\beta^{\alpha}e^{-\beta\left(\left(f_{i+1,j}-f_{i,j}\right)^2+\varepsilon\right)^{\frac{1}{2}}}}{\Gamma(\alpha)}\times\left(\left(f_{i+1,j}-f_{i,j}\right)^2+\varepsilon\right)^{-\frac{1}{2}}\times\left(f_{i+1,j}-f_{i,j}\right)$$

$$-\frac{\left(\left(f_{i,j+1}-f_{i,j}\right)^2+\varepsilon\right)^{\frac{\alpha-1}{2}}\beta^{\alpha}e^{-\beta\left(\left(f_{i,j+1}-f_{i,j}\right)^2+\varepsilon\right)^{\frac{1}{2}}}}{\Gamma(\alpha)}\times\left(\left(f_{i,j+1}-f_{i,j}\right)^2+\varepsilon\right)^{-\frac{1}{2}}\times\left(f_{i,j+1}-f_{i,j}\right)$$

$$+\frac{\left(\left(f_{i-1,j}-f_{i,j}\right)^2+\varepsilon\right)^{\frac{\alpha-1}{2}}\beta^{\alpha}e^{-\beta\left(\left(f_{i-1,j}-f_{i,j}\right)^2+\varepsilon\right)^{\frac{1}{2}}}}{\Gamma(\alpha)}\times\left(\left(f_{i,j}-f_{i-1,j}\right)^2+\varepsilon\right)^{-\frac{1}{2}}\times\left(f_{i,j}-f_{i-1,j}\right)$$

$$+\frac{\left(\left(f_{i,j-1}-f_{i,j}\right)^2+\varepsilon\right)^{\frac{\alpha-1}{2}}\beta^\alpha e^{-\beta\left(\left(f_{i,j-1}-f_{i,j}\right)^2+\varepsilon\right)^{\frac{1}{2}}}}{\Gamma(\alpha)}\times\left(\left(f_{i,j}-f_{i,j-1}\right)^2+\varepsilon\right)^{-\frac{1}{2}}\times\left(f_{i,j}-f_{i,j-1}\right)$$

$$=-\frac{\left(\left(f_{i+1,j}-f_{i,j}\right)^2+\varepsilon\right)^{\left(\frac{\alpha}{2}-1\right)}\beta^\alpha e^{-\beta\left(\left(f_{i+1,j}-f_{i,j}\right)^2+\varepsilon\right)^{\frac{1}{2}}}}{\Gamma(\alpha)}\times\left(f_{i+1,j}-f_{i,j}\right)$$

$$-\frac{\left(\left(f_{i,j+1}-f_{i,j}\right)^2+\varepsilon\right)^{\left(\frac{\alpha}{2}-1\right)}\beta^\alpha e^{-\beta\left(\left(f_{i,j+1}-f_{i,j}\right)^2+\varepsilon\right)^{\frac{1}{2}}}}{\Gamma(\alpha)}\times\left(f_{i,j+1}-f_{i,j}\right)$$

$$+\frac{\left(\left(f_{i,j-1}-f_{i,j}\right)^2+\varepsilon\right)^{\left(\frac{\alpha}{2}-1\right)}\beta^\alpha e^{-\beta\left(\left(f_{i,j-1}-f_{i,j}\right)^2+\varepsilon\right)^{\frac{1}{2}}}}{\Gamma(\alpha)}\times\left(f_{i,j}-f_{i,j-1}\right)$$

$$+\frac{\left(\left(f_{i,j-1}-f_{i,j}\right)^2+\varepsilon\right)^{\left(\frac{\alpha}{2}-1\right)}\beta^\alpha e^{-\beta\left(\left(f_{i,j-1}-f_{i,j}\right)^2+\varepsilon\right)^{\frac{1}{2}}}}{\Gamma(\alpha)}\times\left(f_{i,j}-f_{i,j-1}\right). \tag{10}$$

Algorithm 1: Reconstruction Gamma Regularization

Input : projected data y

Output: reconstructed image f

1. **Set** λ, α, β, ρ, τ, N, $k=1$
2. **Initialize** f_0, g_0, γ_0
3. **while** $\|g_k\|>\varepsilon$ or $k<N$
4. **while** $R(f+\tau\gamma)>R(f)+\alpha\tau R(f)^T\gamma$
5. $\tau=\rho\tau$
6. **end**
7. $f_{k+1}=f_k+\tau\gamma_k$
8. $g_{k+1}=\Delta R\left(f_{k+1}\right)$
9. $\vartheta=\dfrac{\|g_{k+1}\|_2^2}{\|g_k\|_2^2}$
10. $\gamma_{k+1}=-g_{k+1}+\vartheta g_k$
11. $k=k+1$
12. **end**

Let $R(f) \equiv \|Gf - y\| + \lambda\varphi_g(\nabla f)$, combining (10), the gradient g of $R(f)$, can be easily obtained. To calculate the conjugate gradient γ, Fletcher-Reeves (FR) formulate is used with the help of an auxiliary parameter θ. The stop criterion is the minimum norm ε of the gradient or maximum iterative number N. The algorithm outline is given in the algorithm 1.

4. Simulation Data Results

We present numerical result for 2-D CT reconstruction from simulated NCAT phantom [11] and Modified Shepp-Logan (MSL) phantom data, which are both composed by 256×256 pixels and the size of each pixel is 1mm×1mm. The projection data are composed with 367 radial bins per view. We reconstructed the all 180 views projected data and corresponding noise polluted projected data, respectively. The singram of the phantoms are shown in the Fig 1. To simulate the noise contaminated projection data, we add Gauss noise to the projection data. The standard deviation used in this experiment is 1.

To demonstrate the proposed algorithm' preponderance, we compare the reconstruction results with the regularization TV norm regularization. For TV and Gamma regularization, we perform quantitative evaluation (PSNR). The PSNR is defined via (11)

$$PSNR(R,I) = 10\log 10\left(\frac{(\max(I))^2}{\frac{1}{mn}\sum_{i=1}^{m}\sum_{j=1}^{n}\left(I_{i,j} - R_{i,j}\right)^2}\right). \tag{11}$$

where $I_{i,j}$ is the original phantom and $R_{i,j}$ is the reconstructed one.

The parameters in different methods were adjusted manually to provide the best reconstruction results. In the experiments, we found the scale parameters and shape parameters in the Gamma regularization for a specific phantom is relative stable. The reconstruction results are illustrated in the Table 1 and the Fig. 2. In Fig. 2, we can see the proposed reconstruction algorithm with Gamma regularization can perform the TV regularization and the results either the all noise-free or noised polluted projection data. The Gamma regularization was robust to noise, however, the TV regularization reconstruction with noised always bring in artifacts. From the Table 1, we can see the PSNR of Gamma regularization is higher than TV either the projection data was added the noise or not.

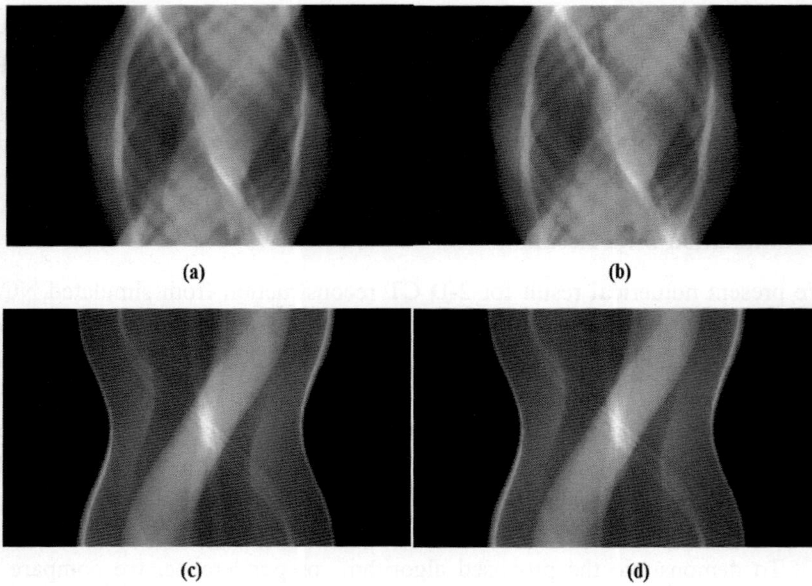

Fig.1:Simulation singram with the NCAT phantom and MSL phantom: (a): noise-free projection data of NACT phantom.(b): noisy projection data of NACT phantom. (c): noise-free projection data of MSL phantom data, (D): noisy projection data of NACT phantom MSL.

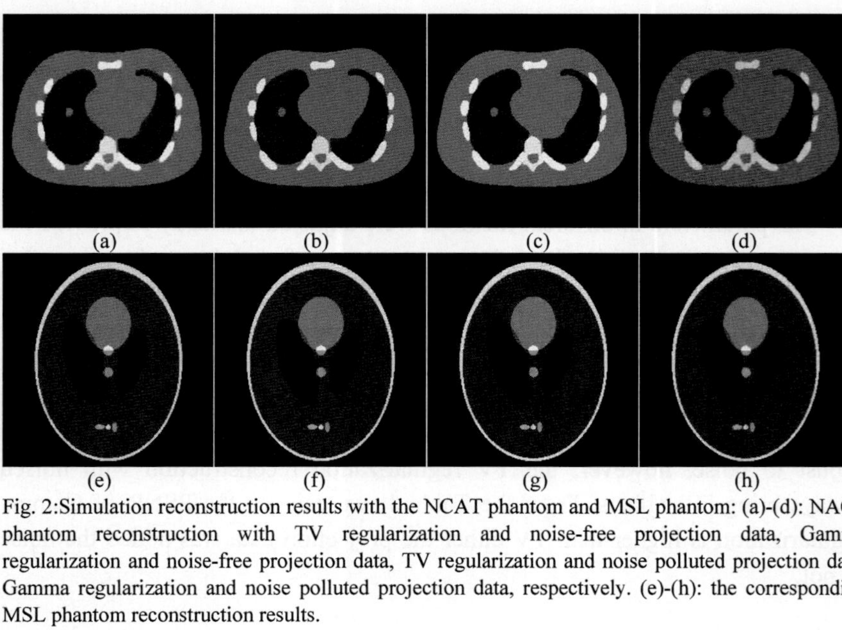

Fig. 2:Simulation reconstruction results with the NCAT phantom and MSL phantom: (a)-(d): NACT phantom reconstruction with TV regularization and noise-free projection data, Gamma regularization and noise-free projection data, TV regularization and noise polluted projection data, Gamma regularization and noise polluted projection data, respectively. (e)-(h): the corresponding MSL phantom reconstruction results.

Table 1: The PSNR of different algorithms.

phantom	method	noise-free	noise(σ=1)
NCAT	TV	43.1845	29.7253
	Gamma	61.4031	30.8660
MSL	TV	42.4411	34.9261
	Gamma	57.1798	40.5955

5. Conclusion

A new low dose iterative reconstruction model with gamma regularization was proposed in this paper. Through the numerical experiments, the proposed Gamma penalty manifested the same performance as half-quadratic penalty. The reconstruction results significantly outperformed that of TV. However, the parameters of the model are more than TV model, so how to choose the proper parameters is still a problem in the future work.

References

1. Brenner, D. J., Elliston, C. D. , Hall, E. J. and Berdon, W. E., Estimated risks of radiation-induced fatal cancer from pediatric CT. American Journal of Roentgenology, 176, pp. 289-296, 2001.
2. Donoho, D., For most large underdetermined systems of linear equations the minimal linear equations the minimal l1 norm solution is also the sparsest solution. Communications on Pure and Applied Mathematics. 59, pp. 797–829, 2006.
3. Sidky, E. Y. , Kao , C. M., and Pan, X., Accurate image reconstruction from few-views and limited-angle data in divergent-beam CT. Journal of X-Ray Science and Technology, 14, pp, 119-139, 2006.
4. Chen, Y., Feng, Q., Luo, L. M., Shi, P. and Chen, W., Nonlocal prior Bayesion tomographic reconstruction. Journal of Mathematical Imaging and Vision, 30, pp. 133-146, 2008.
5. Yu, H. Y. and Wang, G., Compressed sensing based interior tomography. Physics in Medicine & Biology, 54, pp. 2791–2805, 2009.
6. Pan, X., Sidky, E. Y. and Vannier, M. , Why do commercial CT scanners still employ traditional, filtered back-projection for image reconstruction?. Inverse Problem, 25(12), 2009.
7. Hu, Y., Xie, L. , L. Luo, L., J. C. Nunes and C. Toumoulin, L0 constrained sparse reconstruction for multi-slice helical CT reconstruction. Physics in Medicine & Biology, 56(4), pp. 1173-1189, 2011.

8. Geman, D. and Reynolds, G. Constrained restoration and recovery of discontinuities. IEEE Transactions on Pattern Analysis and Machine Intelligence. 14, pp. 367–383, 1992.
9. Siddon, R., Fast calculation of the exact radiological path of a three-dimensional CT array. Medical Physics, 12, pp. 252–255, 1985.
10. Rudin, L. I.S., Osher and Fatemi, E. Nonlinear total variation based noise removal algorithms. Physica D. 60(1), pp. 259-268, 1992.
11. Segars, W. P. and Tsui, B. M. W., Study of the efficacy of respiratory gating in myocardial SPECT using the new 4-D NCAT phantom. IEEE Transactions on Nuclear Science, 49(3), pp. 675-679. 2002.

Session 5

Artificial Intelligence and Multimedia

HMMs Based Faults Diagnosis for Rotor-Gear-Bearing Transmission System

Chang-jian FENG

Department of Mechanical Engineering, Dalian Nationalities University, Dalian, Liaoning, China

E-mail: jdfcj@dlnu.edu.cn

This paper proposes a new fault diagnosis scheme based on continuous density Hidden Markov Model (HMM) for vibration signals. Features extracted from vibration signals of rotor-gear-bearing transmission system are used to train HMMs to represent various running conditions. The feature vectors based on the node energies of wavelet packet decomposition are extracted from the vibration signals. Faults can be identified by selecting the HMM with the highest probability. The proposed method was tested by measuring the data of rotor-gear-bearing transmission system and has been demonstrated to be accurate and feasible.

Keywords: HMM; Faults diagnosis; Vibration signal; Wavelet packet decomposition.

1. Introduction

Gears and bearings are the most universally used machine elements. With higher requirements in operating speed, applied load, and lighter weight, there is a general increase in premature failures in bearing and gear components due to excessive wear and material fatigue. Such premature failures often result in substantial losses, and sometimes may even lead to catastrophic consequences.

Due to the measuring data from faulty rotor-gear-bearing transmission system is time-varying. In fact the fault diagnosis problem is a problem of dynamic pattern recognition [1]. A dynamic pattern is a multidimensional pattern that evolves as a function of time. The pattern is not only contains spatial information but also temporal information. Therefore, it is reasonable to adopt a double stochastic approach for classification of the patterns. Hidden Markov Models can enable modeling, not only spatial phenomena, but also time-scale distances. The HMM can be used to solve classification problems associated with time-series input data such speech signals or vibration signals [1-9], and can provided a suitable solution by means of its modeling and learning capability even though it does note have enough exact knowledge[2]. This paper proposes a new fault diagnosis scheme based on continuous density Hidden Markov Model (HMM) for vibration signals.

2. Probability Theory for Faults Diagnosis

Faults diagnosis problem of rotor machine is defined the classification of type of faults, ω_j, given sequential input pattern $\boldsymbol{X}_t$ at time *t*. Input pattern $\boldsymbol{X}_t$ is mathematically defined as an object described by a sequence of features at time *t*[2].

$$\boldsymbol{X}_t = (x_1, x_2, \ldots, x_d). \tag{1}$$

The space of input pattern $\boldsymbol{X}_t$ consists of the set of all possible pattern: $\boldsymbol{X}_t \subset R^d$, R^d is a *d*-dimensional real vector space.

The *k* observed vectors up to time *t* are defined as,

$$\boldsymbol{\Phi}_{t-k} = \{\boldsymbol{X}_{t-k+1}, \ldots, \boldsymbol{X}_{t-1}, \boldsymbol{X}_t\}. \tag{2}$$

The set of possible fault types ω_j forms the space of classes $\boldsymbol{\Omega}$:

$$\boldsymbol{\Omega}(t) = \{\omega_1, \omega_2, \ldots, \omega_c\}. \tag{3}$$

where *c* is the number of classes.

The faults diagnosis task can be considered to be the finding of function *f*, which maps the space of input patterns $\boldsymbol{\Phi}_{t-k}$ to the space of classes $\boldsymbol{\Omega}$.

The probability of specific signal is already known, and is called prior probability. When identifying a specific fault, a decision can be made only by selecting the type of signal ω with the highest a prior probability $P(\omega)$. The decision is probably unreasonable. It is more reasonable to determine the type of time series after observing the trend of vibration signals of major variables, namely, to get the conditional probability $P(\omega \mid \boldsymbol{\Phi}_{t-k})$.This conditional probability is called a posterior probability. Decision-making based on the posterior probability is more reliable, because it employs a prior knowledge together with the observed fault features. Classification of an unknown pattern X_t corresponds to finding the optimal model $\hat{\omega}$ that maximizes the conditional probability $P(\omega \mid \boldsymbol{\Phi}_{t-k})$ over the whole time series of the type ω. One can apply Bayes rule to calculate the a posterior probability,

$$P(\hat{\omega} \mid \boldsymbol{\Phi}_{t-k}) = \max_{\omega} \frac{P(\boldsymbol{\Phi}_{t-k} \mid \omega) P(\omega)}{P(\boldsymbol{\Phi}_{t-k})}. \tag{4}$$

The conditional probability $P(\omega \mid \boldsymbol{\Phi}_{t-k})$ comes from comparing the shapes of fault models with the input observations, while the prior probability $P(\omega)$ comes from the fault probability. Since $P(\boldsymbol{\Phi}_{t-k})$ is independent of $\hat{\omega}$, thus,

$$P(\hat{\omega} / \boldsymbol{\Phi}_{t-k}) \propto \max_{\omega}\{P(\boldsymbol{\Phi}_{t-k} \mid \omega) P(\omega)\}. \tag{5}$$

In fact it is difficult to calculate an a priori probability $P(\omega)$, which satisfy the following equation.

$$\sum_{j=1}^{c} \omega_j = 1. \tag{6}$$

The HMM can successfully treat an identification of faults of dynamic pattern under a probabilistic or statistically framework. In the faults diagnosis problem, the HMM is used to estimate the conditional probability $P(\omega \mid \boldsymbol{\Phi}_{t-k})$.

3. Application of HMM

3.1. *The structure of HMM*

The following parameters are needed to define a mixed-gaussian density continuous HMM [3,4,7]:

(1) The number of states of the model, *N*.

(2) The number of observation symbols in the alphabet, ***M***. If the observations are continuous then *M* is infinite.

(3) A set of state transition probabilities $\boldsymbol{A} = \{a_{ij}\}$.

$$a_{ij} = P(q_{t+1} = j \mid q_t = i), 1 \le i, j \le N. \tag{7}$$

where q_t denotes the current state.

Transition probabilities should satisfy the normal stochastic constraints,

$$a_{ij} \ge 0, 1 \le i, j \le N. \tag{8}$$

and,

$$\sum_{j=1}^{N} a_{ij} = 1, \quad 1 \le i \le N. \tag{9}$$

(4) A probability distribution in each of the states, $\boldsymbol{B} = \{b_j\{k\}\}$.

$$b_j(k) = p\{\boldsymbol{o}_t = v_k \mid q_t =_j\}, \quad 1 \le j \le N, 1 \le k \le M \quad (10)$$

where v_k denotes the k-th observation vector, and $\boldsymbol{o}_t$ the current parameter vector.

Following stochastic constraints must be satisfied,

$$b_j(k) \ge 0, 1 \le j \le N, 1 \le k \le M. \quad (11)$$

Usually the probability density is approximated by a weighted sum of M Gaussian distributions G,

$$b_j(\boldsymbol{o}_t) = \sum_{m=1}^{M} c_{jm} G(\boldsymbol{\mu}_{jm}, \boldsymbol{\Sigma}_{jm}, \boldsymbol{o}_t). \quad (12)$$

Where, c_{jm} =weighting coefficients; $\boldsymbol{\mu}_{im}$ =mean vectors; $\boldsymbol{\Sigma}_{jm}$ =covariance matrix. The initial state distribution, $\boldsymbol{\pi} = \{\pi_i\}$.

Where,

$$\pi_i = p(q_1 = i), \; 1 \le i \le N. \quad (13)$$

Thus HMM with mixture probability distributions is denoted as following,

$$\lambda = (\boldsymbol{A}, c_{jm}, \boldsymbol{\mu}_{jm}, \boldsymbol{\Sigma}_{jm}, \boldsymbol{\pi}). \quad (14)$$

3.2. *Training of HMM*

According to the above definition of an HMM, there are three problems of interest [4]. The Evaluation Problem can be solved by Forward Algorithm and Backward Algorithm. The problem also can be solved by Viterbi Algorithm. The Decoding Problem can be solved by Viterbi Algorithm. The Training Problem can be solved by Baum-Welch Algorithm [4,7].

The full steps for training of an HMM is as following:

(1) Input the numbers of hidden states, initial probability distribution $\boldsymbol{\pi}$, initial state transition probabilities, the error e of iteration, the maximization number of iteration L and observations $\boldsymbol{O}$.

(2) Initial Gauss function parameters, $\overline{c}_{jm}$, $\boldsymbol{\mu}_{jm}$ and $\boldsymbol{\Sigma}_{jm}$ are estimated by k-means algorithm. Then the initial HMM λ_0 is gained.

(3) According to the Baum-Welch Algorithm, the each parameters $\boldsymbol{A}$, c_{jm}, $\boldsymbol{\mu}_{jm}$ and $\boldsymbol{\Sigma}_{jm}$ of HMM are re-estimated. In this step, Multi-observation (from

various load conditions) can be considered. Therefore the HMM $\overline{\lambda}_i$ re-estimated by i-th iteration.

(4) According to the Viterbi Algorithm, the output probability $P(\boldsymbol{O} \mid \overline{\lambda}_i)$ of re-estimated HMM $\overline{\lambda}_i$ with the observations $\boldsymbol{O}$ is calculated. Then increasing error of output probability between the twice iterations. If the error is satisfied the given error e in the first step, the re-estimated HMM is taken as the final HMM. But if the error is not satisfied given the condition error e, then calculation flows to the step (3).

(5) If the number of iterations exceeds maximization number L, then the training exits.

3.3. *Choice and initialization of HMM*

A six-state HMM (initialized) is illustrated in Fig. 1. In this model, transitions among the states occur only from left to right. This kind of HMM is referred to a left-right HMM. A detailed explanation of HMMs is provided in [4].

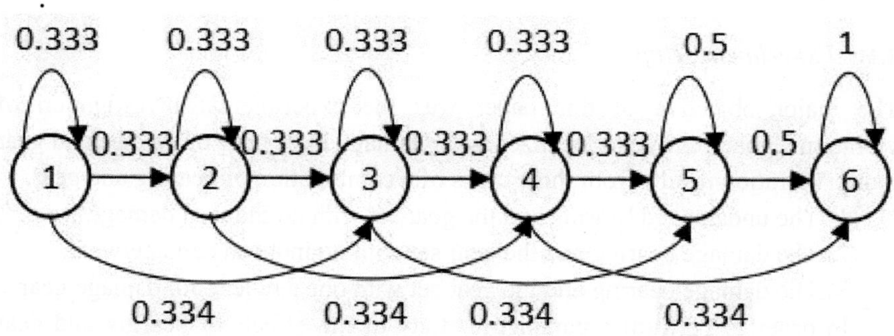

Fig. 1. Initialized six-state left-right HMM.

3.4. *Fault diagnosis based on HMMs*

The various HMMs that represent several distinct faults (norm condition is contained) are trained by the collect data. A single running state (Norm or a fault) of rotor-gear-bearing transmission system is identified by the following steps shown in Fig. 2.

The c types of faults are considered, the probabilities of the observation sequences given all the HMMs in the previously modeled by history database. The HMM which the probability is maximum, determines the type of the fault.

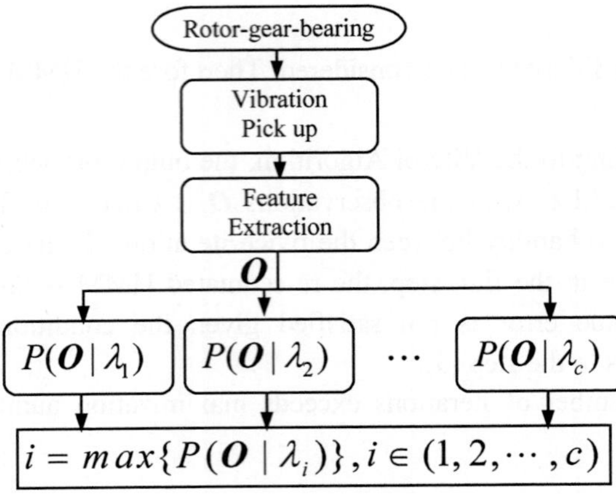

Fig. 2. Fault diagnosis based on HMMs.

4. Experiment and Results

4.1. *Experiment setup*

The major objective of this paper was the experimental investigation of vibration signatures due to localized wear/damage in bearing outer race and gear tooth. Vibration results from three cases of a combination of bearing and gear.

(1) The undamaged bearing and the gear set with no induced damage/wear.

(2) The damage bearing and the gear set with no induced damage/wear.

(3) The damage bearing and the gear set with one single tooth damage gear.

In order to perform a parametric study of the effects of bearing and gear damage on the vibration signatures of the system, vibration study for three different cases above were carried out using the test rig shown in Fig. 3.

The test rig consists of two identical spur gears on two shafts with one attached to the electric motor driver while the other is attached to a water-braking system to provide loading onto the gears, each shaft is supported by two bearings. The driver of the gear test rig consists of a 75Hp motor connected through a belt-pulley driving system that can 6 provide a maximum speed of up to 8000 rpm.

Fig. 3. Rotor-gear-bearing test rig.

Fig. 4 shows the test gear with single tooth damage. Fig. 5 shows the test bearing with the damage of outer race.

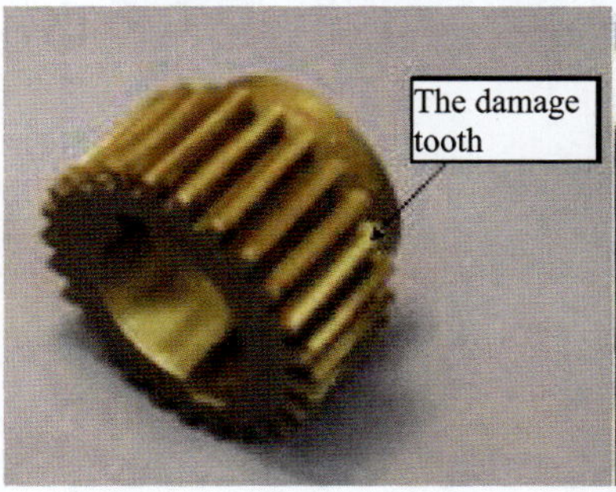

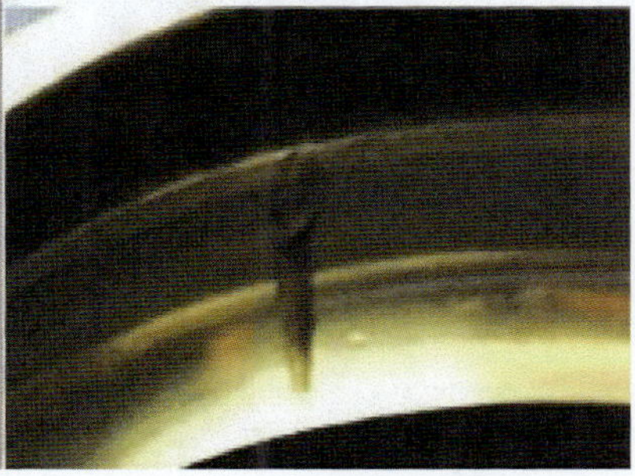

Fig. 4. Gear with single tooth damage. Fig. 5. Bearing with outer race damage.

In the time Signal figures, only 1600 points are chosen within 32768 total points. Time signals with undamaged the gear and undamaged bearing of y-direction are shown in Fig. 6. Time signals with undamaged gear and damaged bearing of y-direction are shown in Fig. 7. Time signals with damage gear and damage bearing of y-direction are shown in Fig. 8. Only y-direction vibration signals are considered.

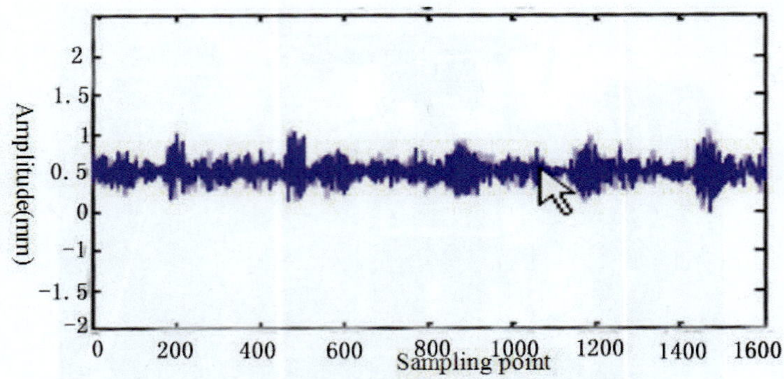

Fig. 6. Time signals for undamaged gear & undamaged bearing.

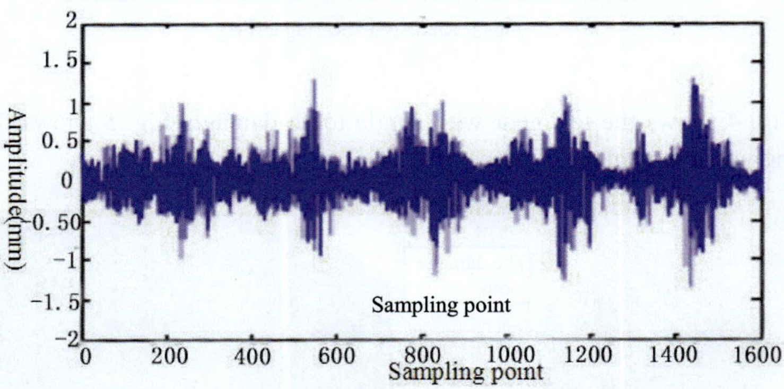

Fig. 7. Time signals for undamaged gear & damaged bearing.

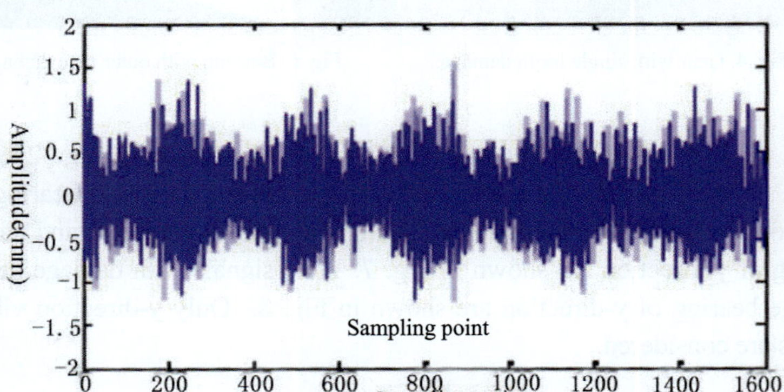

Fig. 8. Time signals for damaged gear & damaged bearing.

4.2. *Features extraction with wavelet packet decomposition*

The features used for a specific fault must only be correlated with this specific fault and uncorrelated (or unnoticeable corrected) with all the other faults. To illustrate this, if the energy of a certain frequency band is used as one of the features for type-one fault, then the energy of this band must only be affected by the presence of type-one fault and be unchanged (or minimally affected) by the presence of other faults. Thus a new feature extraction method is considered. The signal is divided into several small window segments of equal length. Wavelet packet decomposition (WPD) is applied to the segments of the signal in each window. A detailed review of WPD can be found in [10]. The feature vector for each window consists of selected node energies of the WPD. This process of WPD is illustrated in Fig. 9.

Fig. 9 shows the three wavelet packet decomposition. *(i,j)* represents the i-th layer and j-th node. For example, (3, 0) represents the third layer and 0 th node of WPD. We obtain the coefficients of all the nodes. The time signals S_{ij} are reconstructed from the coefficients. All the nodes in third layer are considered. Then the whole signal is obtained as following,

$$S = S_{30} + S_{31} + \cdots + S_{37} \quad . \tag{15}$$

Thus the energy of node is as following,

$$E_{3j} = \int \left| S_{3j} \right|^2 dt = \sum_{k=1}^{n} \left| x_{jk} \right|^2 \quad . \tag{16}$$

Where x_{jk} represent amplitude of reconstructed discrete signal. Therefore the observation feature vector is constructed as following.

$$\boldsymbol{o}_t = [E_{30}, E_{31}, \cdots, E_{37}] \tag{17}$$

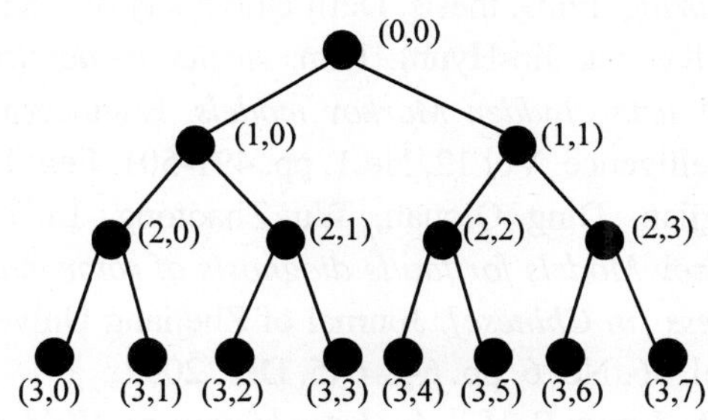

Fig. 9. WPD of vibration signal.

4.3. *Experiment results*

Initial HMM is as Fig. 1. The number of components of gauss mixture is 5. The result of 15 times test of fault diagnosis is illustrated in Table 1.

Table 1. The result of diagnosis.

Test (15times)	Normal	Fault-1	Fault-2
Normal	15	0	0
Fault-1	1	14	0
Fault-2	1	1	13

Normal, Fault-1 and Fault-2 represent the three cases described in section 4.1 separately.

5. Conclusion

HMMs with gauss mixture densities are introduced into faults diagnosis of rotor-gear-bearing transmission system based on vibration signal. In this method, HMM models were trained to represent various fault conditions. The method were test with experimental data collected from rotor-gear-bearing test rig. It was shown that this method is executable and effective.

Acknowledgment

This work is supported by the Fundamental Research Funds for the Central Universities (No. DC 120101013).

References

1. Alexander Ypma, *Learning methods for machine vibration analysis and health monitoring,* Ph.D. thesis, Delft University of Technology, 2001.
2. Kee-Choon Kwona, Jin-Hyung Kim. *Accident identification in nuclear power plants using hidden Markov models*, Engineering Applications of Artificial Intelligence, Vol 12, No.1, pp. 491-501, Feb. 1999.
3. Feng Changjian, Ding Qiquan, Wu Zhaotong, Li Zhinong, *Study on Hidden Markov Models for faults diagnosis of rotor machine in the whole run-up process [in Chinese],* Journal of Zhejiang University (Engineering Science), Vol. 36, No. 6, pp. 642-645, Dec. 2002.
4. Rabiner L R, Juang B H, *An Introduction to Hidden Markov Models, IEEE ASSP Magazine*, Vol.3, No.2, pp. 4-6, January, 1986.

5. Hasan Ocak, Kenneth A. Loparo, *HMM-Based Fault detection and Diagnosis Scheme for Rolling Element Bearingcs*, Journal of Vibration and Acoustics, vol. 127, pp. 299-306, No. 8, Aug. 2005.
6. Feng Chang-jian, Kang-jing, Wu-bin, Hu Hong-ying, *Application in Fault Diagnosis of Rotary Machine Based on Theory Of DHMM Dynamic Pattern Recognition [in Chinese],* Journal of Dalian Nationalities University, No. 3, pp. 12-15,May,2005.
7. Heqiang, Heying, *Extended programming using matlab* (in Chinese), Tsingthua University press, Beijing, 2002.
8. Juang B H, Rabiner L R, The Segmental k-Means Algorithm for Estimating Parameters of Hidden Markov Models. IEEE Trans. ASSP, Vol.38, No. 9, pp. 1639-1641, 1990.
9. Lito Wang, Mostafa G. Mehrabi, Elijah Kannatey-Asibu, Jr., *Hidden Markov Model-based Tool Wear Monitoring in Turning*, Journal of Manufacturing Science and Engineering, Vol. 124, August, 2002.
10. Chui, C. K., *An Introduction to Wavelets (Wavelet Analysis and Its Applications)*, Academic Press, 1992.

Transformer Fault Diagnosis Using Restricted Boltzmann Machines

Jing XU* and Cheng LIU
Department of Computer Science, North China Electric Power University, Baoding, Hebei, China
**E-mail: ncepuxujing@163.com*

In this paper, we developed a RBM classification model and tested its performance. The RBM transformer fault diagnosis classification method increases the training of pre-training sets and provides an improved average rate of correctly classified faults. This method is applicable to a large number of training samples and has high scalability. Comparisons to the BPNN and SVM methods demonstrate that RBM achieves on average a higher accuracy rate of fault diagnosis, which is suitable for engineering needs.

Keywords: Power transformer; Fault diagnosis; Deep learning; RBM.

1. Introduction

In transmission and distribution of power systems, power transformers are key components, its health is directly related to the safe and stable operation of the entire power system in case of failure which will lead to a partial blackout even a large area, it is bound to cause huge economic losses. Therefore, transformers must be routinely examined to find incipient faults and to catch any potentially extended deterioration as early as possible[1]. Application of dissolved gas-in-oil analysis (DGA) in the diagnosis of faults in electrical insulation of transformers is a common practice.

Many applications for Restricted Boltzmann Machines (RBMs) have been developed for variety of machine learning techniques. RBMs are usually used as feature extractors for another learning algorithm or to provide a good initialization for deep feed-forward neural network classifiers[2] and train data.

In this paper, we will introduce a generative model RBMs, which includes its mathematical representation and related learning algorithm. We also demonstrate that RBMs can be successfully adapt to predict the classes when given DGA data. We first use IRIS data set testing RBMs classification performance test, and then use it in the transformer fault diagnosis, the test results show that the performance of the proposed approach prevails better than that of back propagation neural network (BPNN) and support vector machine (SVM) methods.

2. Restricted Boltzmann Machines

2.1. *Deep learning*

In 2006, Hinton et al. at University of Toronto introduced Deep Belief Networks (DBNs)[3], with a learning algorithm that greedily trains one layer at a time, and exploiting an unsupervised learning algorithm for each layer, a Restricted Boltzmann Machine (RBM)[4]. Inspired by the architectural depth of the brain, neural network researchers have wanted for decades to train deep multi-layer neural networks. We apply deep learning by building a machine learning model with multiple hidden layers training samples layer by layer feature transformation, the samples in the feature space representation of the original conversion the new features in another space, so as to achieve the desired results of the experiment. Since 2006, deep networks have been applied with success not only in classification tasks[5], however also in regression, information retrieval, dimensionality reduction, modeling motion, modeling textures, object segmentation, robotics, natural language processing, and collaborative fltering[6,7].

2.2. *RBMs*

A RBM contains two layers of units(m visible units V=(V1,...Vm) and n hidden units H=(H1,...Hn), The RBM is a probabilistic model that uses a layer of hidden binary variables to model the distribution of a visible layer of variables. An RBM is a model associated with a graph shown in Fig. 1.

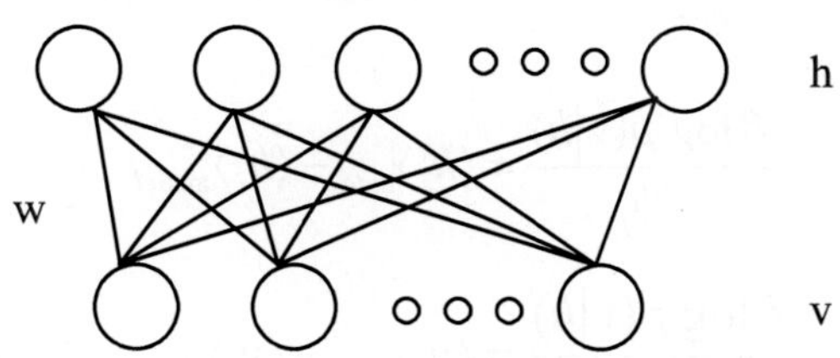

Fig. 1. A graph of RBM with hidden and visible varibles.

Visible units to represent the observed data and the hidden units to capture relation the two observed variables. All the units are binary variables, and this means that all the values from $(v,h) \in \{0,1\}^{m+n}$. RBMs as a system with energy function is defined as

$$E(v,h|\theta)=\sum_{\mathrm{i}=1}^{n}\mathrm{a}_{\mathrm{i}}\mathrm{v}_{\mathrm{i}}-\sum_{j=1}^{m}b_{j}h_{j}-\sum_{i=1}^{n}\sum_{j=1}^{m}v_{i}w_{ij}h_{j}\,. \tag{1}$$

With parameters in the Eq. (1), the θ ={w, a, b}, a={a_i, i=1,…,n}, b={b_j, j=1,…,m} are biases term associated to visible and hidden units respectively.

$$P(\mathrm{v},\mathrm{h}|\theta)=\frac{\exp(-E(v,h|\theta))}{Z(\theta)},Z(\theta)=\sum_{v,h}\exp(-E(v,h|\theta))\,. \tag{2}$$

Where $Z(\theta)$ is a partition function. The likelihood function is presented as follows

$$P(v|\theta)=\frac{\sum_{h}\exp(-E(v,h|\theta))}{Z(\theta)}\,. \tag{3}$$

As we have noticed in the Eq. (2) and Eq. (3), we need to compute parameter that's why we train the RBM model. The derivatives of the log-likelihood function is

$$\frac{\partial\log P(v|\theta)}{\partial\,\theta}=\sum_{t=1}^{T}\langle\frac{\partial(-E(v^{(\mathrm{t})},h|\theta))}{\partial\,\theta}\rangle_{p(h|v^{(t)},\theta)}-\sum_{t=1}^{T}\langle\frac{\partial(-E(v,h|\theta))}{\partial\,\theta}\rangle_{p(v,h|\theta)}\,. \tag{4}$$

In this Eq. (4), <*>p is the P mathematical distribution

$$\frac{\partial\log p(v|h)}{\partial w_{ij}}=\langle v_i h_j\rangle_{data}-\langle v_i h_j\rangle_{model}\,. \tag{5}$$

$$\frac{\partial\log p(v|h)}{\partial b_{j}}=\langle h_j\rangle_{data}-\langle h_j\rangle_{model}\,. \tag{6}$$

$$\frac{\partial\log p(v|h)}{\partial a_{i}}=\langle v_i\rangle_{data}-\langle v_i\rangle_{model}\,. \tag{7}$$

2.3. *Contrastive Divergence (CD) algorithm*

CD was proposed by Hinton[8,9,10], which is different from Gibbs, Hinton proposed when using the training data initialize v0, we need only the operation of K-step Gibbs that will get well likehood.

Base on CD fast learning algorithm RBM primary procedure is :

- Inout : training sample x_0, The number of hidden layer units are m, learning rate is ε , Maximum training cycle is T,
- output: weight w, the bias of visible is a, the bias of hidden is b,
- training period: Initialization the parameters, make the visible layer initial units V_1=X; w,a,b Randomly selected minimum,
- For t=1,2,…,T,
- For j=1,2,…,m(for all hidden units),
- Computing $P(h_{1j} = 1|v_1)$, $P(h_{1j} = 1|v_1) = \sigma(b_j + \sum_i v_{1i} w_{ij})$,

From the condition of the distribution $P(h_{1j}|v_1)$ siphon $h_{1j} \in \{0,1\}$,

- End for,
- For i=1,2,…n(for all visible nuits),
- Computing $P(v_{2i} = 1|h_1)$, $P(v_{2i} = 1|h_1) = \sigma(a_i + \sum_j w_{ij} h_{1j})$,

From the condition of the distribution $P(v_{2i}|h_1)$ siphon $v_{2i} \in \{0,1\}$,

- End for,
- For j=1,2,…,m(for all hidden units),
- Computing $P(h_{2j} = 1|v_2)$, $P(h_{2j} = 1|v_2) = \sigma(b_j + \sum_i v_{2i} w_{ij})$,

$$- w \leftarrow w + \varepsilon(P(h_1 = 1|v_1)v_1^T - P(h_2 = 1|v_2)v_2^T)$$

$$- a \leftarrow a + \varepsilon(v_1 - v_2)$$

$$- b \leftarrow b + \varepsilon(P(h_1 = 1|v_1) - P(h_2 = 1|v_2))$$

2.4. *Classification RBMs model*

In the paper, we first built RBMs classifier, the bottom layer of the model is stacked by a number of layers of RBMs, and the top of the layer is added to the final layer of the desired output variable, which is the classification layer, as shown in Fig. 2. As to top level units we use softmax classifier outputs, a corresponding sample which belongs to different states of probability, the maximum probability of the state is classified.

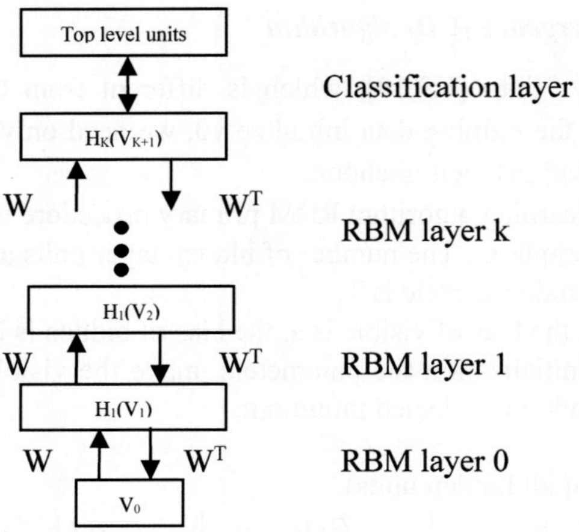

Fig. 2. Classification RBMs model.

3. Experiment

3.1. *Transformer fault diagnosis*

(1) Data selection

(a) Sample selection. We selected multiple project site records transformer oil chromatography-line monitoring data occurred failures before and after a short period of time, this data are unlabeled, it can be used as a pretraining samples. For sample fine-tuning stage use a small amount of sample labels, though collecting fault transformer test experimental data obtained.

(b) Characteristics of selected variables. We choose H_2, CH_4, C_2H_6, C_2H_2, CO, CO_2 which feature gas content as model input. Since the DGA data differs, in order to reduce the differences between the input data, calculation errors decrease, using Eq. (8) for each gas to standardize and improve diagnostic accuracy. X_{new} is the gas that normalized, X is original gas, X_{mean} is training set or test set representing gas content, X_{std} is the standard deviation X

$$X_{\text{new}} = \frac{X - X_{mean}}{X_{std}}. \tag{8}$$

(c) Transformer status codes. Six types transformer fault diagnosis is a multi-classification task, the diagnosis can be divided into normal, low temperature heat, high temperature overheating, partial discharge, low energy discharge and high energy discharge, of which in turn encoded as shown in Tab.1.

Table 1. Transformer status codes.

Schedule	Capacity
normal	(0,0,0,0,0,1)
low temperature heat	(0,0,0,0,1,0)
high temperature overheating	(0,0,0,1,0,0)
partial discharge	(0,0,1,0,0,0)
low energy discharge	(0,1,0,0,0,0)
high energy discharge	(1,0,0,0,0,0)

(2) Transformer Fault Diagnosis implementation process. We select the sample and characteristic variables, Then we build classification model based on RBM training, using the training set of unlabeled samples to RBM training through CD algorithm, the final sample by using a label for the entire network Back-Propagation algorithm fine-tuning , save the results, and test.

(3) The comparison results are presented in Tab. 2. The result of Tab. 3 experiment shows that RBM is a very promising method to classify and it gains better than other methods.

Table 2. Transformer fault classification case on the different pre-training sets.

Pre-training	Turning sets	Test sets	Correct rate
100	300	80	78.37%
500	300	80	84.62%
1000	300	80	87.43%
1500	300	80	89.96%

Table 3. Transformer fault classification case base on BPNN and SVM on the different training sets.

Methods	Parameter	Pre-training	Test sets	Correct rate
BPNN	Epochs[a]=1500 Ir[b]=0.01	80	80	53.46%
		160	80	62.78%
		180	80	73.98%
		300	80	79.69%
SVM	C[c]=2048 R[d]=0.03	80	80	60.62%
		160	80	73.84%
		180	80	82.43%
		300	80	85.96%

Note: Table notes.

[a,b] Sample footnote BPNN maximum number of iterations and learning rate.

[c,d] Sample footnote SVM rules coefficients and kernel parameters.

4. Conclusion

In the contest, we build the RBM classification model and test it's performance, we find base on the RBM transformer fault diagonsis classification method can becoming well and it will train the increase of the pre-training sets increasing, Fault average correct classification rate increasing, the method is applicable to a large number of training samples, scalability, and compared to BPNN, SVM method we conclude RBM get higher average accuracy rate of fault diagnosis, it can better meet the engineering needs.

References

1. Z. Zhang, Y. L. Zhu, *Transformers*, Vol. 47, pp. 59-62, March 2010. (in Chinese)
2. R. Salakhutdinov, A. Mnih, and G. Hinton, Restricted boltzmann machines for collaborative filtering, in *Pro. of the 24th international conference on Machine learning (ACM'07).*
3. H. Mobahi and R. Collobert (eds.), Deep learning from temporal coherence in video, in: *International Conference on Machine Learning (ACM'09),*(Canada, 2009).
4. H. Larochelle and Y. Bengio (eds.), Classification using discriminative restricted boltzmann machines, *in Pro. of the25th international conference on M-achine learning (ACM'08),* (Helsinki, Finland, 2008).
5. H. Larochelle and M. I. Mandel (eds.), *Learning algorithms for the classification restricted boltzmann machine,* Journal of Machine Learning Research,Vol. 13, pp. 643–669, 2012.
6. Y. Bengio, *Foundations and Trends in Machine Learning*, Vol. 2, pp. 1–127, 2009.
7. Hinton G, *Momentum*, Vol. 9, pp. 926, 2010.
8. Hinton and Y.W. The (eds.) , *Neural computation*, Vol. 18, pp. 1527–1554, 2006.
9. A. Patel and S. Sundararajan (eds.), Semi-supervised classification using sparse Gaussian process regression, in: *International Joint Conferences on Artificial Intelligence*, (2009), pp. 1193–1198.
10. J. Weston and F. Ratle (eds.), Deep learning via semi-supervised embedding, in: *International Conference on Machine Learning (ACM,'08)*, (Helsinki, Finland, 2008).

An Improved Particle Swarm Optimization

Li-kun WU* and Jian ZHOU

College of Telecommunications and Information Engineering, Nanjing University of Posts and Telecommunications,
Nanjing, Jiangsu, China
**E-mail: 1196683627@qq.com*

To tackle the premature convergence problem of the Particle Swarm Optimization, we proposed an improved algorithm was proposed. Chaotic sequence is utilized to pretreat the positions of particles to introduce randomness, and then the reverse learning ability of the worst individual particle is introduced into the velocity update iteration of the particle. The simulation results demonstrate that the improved algorithm significantly decreases the premature convergence of particle swarm optimization.

Keywords: Premature problem; Particle swarm optimization; Reverse learning ability.

1. Introduction

In 1995, Kennedy and Eberhart proposed a swarm intelligence algorithm---PSO[1](Particle Swarm Optimization, PSO). Although the algorithm exits the problem of low convergence precision and premature convergence, PSO is also widely used in power systems[2], computer field[3] and so on, because of its simplicity, fast convergence speed and advantages of less adjustable parameters. Scholars have also proposed a series of improved algorithm. Shi[4] and Eberhart proposed an improved algorithm, in which the inertia weight linearly decreases with the number of iteration increase. In the early period of algorithm, the inertia weight is larger, which contributes to searching the range of optimal solution. With the increasing of the number of iteration, the inertia weight becomes smaller, which contributes to enhancing the local search ability. However, when dealing with multidimensional and multimodal complex problem, the improved algorithm also persists premature convergence.

In order to overcome the problem of premature convergence, an improved PSO algorithm was proposed. Firstly, chaotic sequence was utilized to pretreat the positions of particles, and then the reverse learning ability of the worst individual particle was introduced into the velocity update iteration of particle to make the particles overcome premature convergence in later iterations. Tests on the multidimensional and multimodal complex functions shows that our algorithm significantly improves the premature convergence of the PSO.

2. Particle Swarm Optimization and CBMPSO

PSO[5] is the simulation of the foraging behavior of birds. In the PSO, each particle can be viewed as a solution to the problem in the feasible space. The state of the particle is described by its position vector and velocity vector. All the particles adjust their state to find the position of global optimum according to their own flight experience and the flying experience of their companion.

Suppose that the swarm composed of n particles and D-dimension search space. Position vector of $i'th$ particle: $x_i = (x_{i1}, x_{i2}, \cdots x_{ij} \cdots x_{iD})$, $1 \le i \le n, 1 \le j \le D$, velocity of $i'th$ particle: $v_i = (v_{i1}, v_{i2}, \cdots v_{ij} \cdots v_{iD})$, $1 \le i \le n,\ 1 \le j \le D$, historical best position of $i'th$ particle: $pbest_i = (pbest_{i1}, pbest_{i2} \cdots pbest_{ij} \cdots, pbest_{iD})$, $1 \le i \le n,\ 1 \le j \le D$, best position of the swarm: $gbest = (gbest_1, gbest_2, \cdots gbest_k \cdots gbest_D)$, $1 \le k \le D$, the swarm's best position is determined by the following formula:

$gbest = \min(f(pbest_1), f(pbest_2), \cdots f(pbest_k) \cdots f(pbest_D))$, $f(x)$ is the fitness function.

At each step, all particles update their position and velocity vector:

$$\begin{aligned} v_{id}(t+1) = w * v_{id}(t) + c_1 * rand() * [pbest_{id}(t) - x_{id}(t)] \\ + c_2 * rand() * [gbest_d(t) - x_{id}(t)]. \end{aligned} \tag{1}$$

$$x_{id}(t+1) = x_{id}(t) + v_{id}(t+1) \tag{2}$$

Where, $1 \le i \le n, 1 \le d \le D$, i is the $i'th$ particle, d is the dimension of search space, t is the number of iterations, c_1, c_2 are acceleration factor, $rand()$ is random number, usually $[0,1]$, the parameter w is the inertia weight. The first section of the expression (1) shows the inertial velocity of particle. The second section is the cognitive part of the particle, which reflects the self-awareness ability of the particle. The third section is the social part of the particle, which reflects the information share and mutual cooperation ability of the particles.

PSO has the problem of low convergence precision and premature convergence, so some scholars proposed many improved algorithms, such as CBMPSO.

In CBMPSO[6] (CBM Particle Swarm Optimization), the reverse learning ability of the worst particle of the population was introduced to help particle escape from the local optimization. The improvement reflected in introducing the reverse particle of the worst particle of the population, which is away from the local optimization. So it can help the particle escape from the local optimization. The following is the improved velocity formula:

$$\begin{aligned} v_i(t+1) = wv_i(t) &+ c_1 rand(pbest_i(t) - x_i(t)) \\ &+ c_2 rand(gbest(t) - x_i(t)) \\ &+ c_3 rand(pp'_g(t) - x_i(t)). \end{aligned} \tag{3}$$

Where, w is the inertia weight, c_1, c_2, c_3 are acceleration factor, $rand$ is random number, usually $[0,1]$. $pp'_g(t)$ is the reverse particle of the worst particle of the population.

$$pp'_g = \begin{cases} a + b - (m_1 pp_g + m_2 pbest_i) & rand < p \\ 0 & rand > p \end{cases}. \tag{4}$$

Where, a and b is the upper and lower limits of the particle's position, pp_g is the worst position of the population, m_1 is random number, usually $[0,1]$. $m_2 = 1 - m_1$. During the solving of the reverse particle, we introduce individual optimization $pbest_i$, which improves the diversity of the population and increases the ability of learning new space. But the worst position of the population is not always useful. So we should make the particle take effect at the probability of p, which riches the learning content and avoid the performance of over learning.

Then the above improved algorithm exits defect when deal with multidimensional and multimodal function. In the later iteration of CBMPSO, when the particle is lost in local optimization, the worst position of the population is hard to help find the global optimization because it is too far away from the global optimization.

3. An Improved PSO

To overcome the premature convergence, we proposed an improved PSO in this paper. Firstly, chaotic sequence was utilized to pretreat the positions of particles to make them have randomness, and then the reverse learning ability of the worst individual particle was introduced into the velocity update iteration of particle group to help the particle escape from the local optimization.

Firstly, we adopt the chaotic system to deal with the position of the particles, which not only doesn't change the randomness in initialization period, but also increase the diversity of population and the ergodicity of particle search.

Although the CBMPSO is useful to help the particle escape from the local optimization at a certain degree through introducing the reverse learning ability of the worst position of population, when deal with the multidimensional and multimodal function, it is hard to help particle escape from the local optimization. So the reverse learning ability of the worst individual particle was introduced in the velocity update iteration of particle.

$$\begin{aligned} v_i(t+1) = wv_i(t) + c_1 rand(pbest_i(t) - x_i(t)) \\ + c_2 rand(gbest(t) - x_i(t)) \\ + c_3 rand(pp'_i(t) - x_i(t)). \end{aligned} \tag{5}$$

$$pp'_i = \begin{cases} a + b - (m_1 pp_i + m_2 pbest_i) & rand < p \\ 0 & rand \geq p \end{cases}. \tag{6}$$

Where, pp'_i is the reverse particle of the worst individual, pp_i is the worst individual particle of the population. pp'_i takes effect at the probability of p. From the improved velocity update formula(5), we can know the velocity of the particle depends on four parts. The first part is the inherit from the last velocity of the particle; the second part is the ability of learning from its own optimization; the third part is the ability of learning from the swarm's optimization; the last part is the reverse learning ability of the worst individual particle. When the particles are lost in local optimization, the first three part is hard to help escape from the local optimization because it is close to local optimization. But the last part can help because it is away from the local optimization.

3.1. *The process of the improved algorithm is following:*

Step 1: Set the initialization parameters of the algorithm.

Step 2: Initialize the position and velocity of the particles. Chaotic system was utilized to pretreat the positions of particles. Suppose the fitness function of the particles is $f(x)$, we can calculate the value of particle's fitness.

Step 3: Calculate the $pbest_i, gbest, pp_i$ according to the value of particle's fitness function, then calculate the pp'_i according to the expression (6).

Step 4: Update the velocity and position of the particles according to the expression (5) and (2).

Step 5: Calculate the value of particle's fitness function $f(x_i)$. If $f(x_i) < f(pbest_i)$, use the current x_i update $pbest_i$. If $f(x_i) < f(gbest)$, use the current x_i update $gbest$.
Step 6: If $f(x_i) > f(pp_i)$, use the current x_i update pp_i. Then calculate pp_i' according to the expression (6).
Step 7: Iteration from step 4 until reaching the final step.

4. Simulation Results

In order to test the performance of the improved PSO, we conduct simulations compare with the CPSO[7] (Chaos Particle Swarm Optimization), GPSO[8] (Grouping Particle Swarm Optimization), LH-DMPSO[9](LH-DM Particle Swarm Optimization) and CBMPSO through the multidimensional and multimodal function Ackley and Rastrigin.

Parameter settings: five algorithms parameter setting are basically the same. Population size m=50; range of the particle's velocity [-30,30]; range of the particle's search space [-100,50]; acceleration factor $c_1 = c_2 = 1.5$, $c_3 = 1$; inertia weight $w = 0.7898$;dimension sizes: 50; number of iterations: 100. In CBMPSO and the improved algorithm $p = 0.1$.

The simulation results are shown in Fig. 1 and Fig. 2. In Fig. 1 and Fig. 2, the dotted line shows the simulation result of improved PSO's single run, the other curve describe the meaning fitness of the five algorithm which run 50 times.

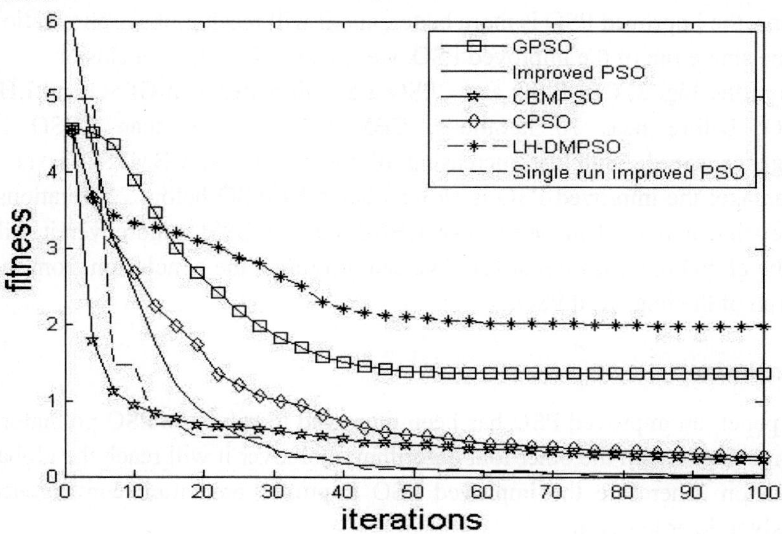

Fig. 1. Ackley function.

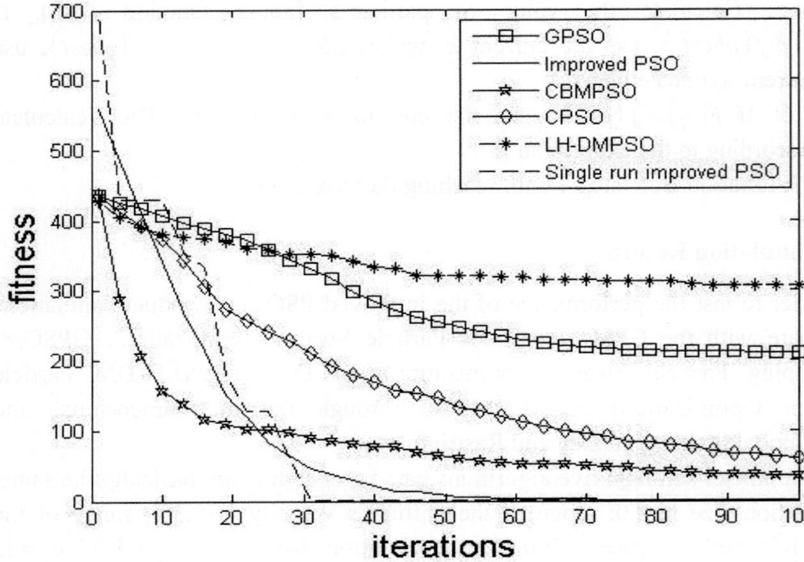

Fig. 2. Rastrigin function.

From the Fig. 1, CBMPSO is superior to GPSO, LH-DMPSO and CPSO in convergence speed and performance; before near 25 iterations, the improved PSO is slow to CBMPSO in convergence speed, but with the increasing of the iterations, the improved PSO is more better, and it will reach global optimization. From the single run of the improved PSO, we can also draw the conclusion.

From the Fig. 2, CBMPSO and CPSO are both better than GPSO and LH-DMPSO; before near 70 iterations, CBMPSO is faster than CPSO in convergence speed, with the increasing of the iterations, CBMPSO is at a disadvantage; the improved PSO is slower than CBMPSO before 25 iterations, but after that it is evident better than CBMPSO and CPSO, moreover it will reach the global optimization at last. We can also draw the conclusion from the single run of the improved PSO.

5. Conclusion

In this paper, an improved PSO has been improved to solve the PSO premature problem is better than the other four algorithm, moreover it will reach the global optimization. Therefore the improved PSO improves premature convergence obviously in later iteration.

Acknowledgments

Work partially supported by grant 2-4570.5 of the Swiss National Science Foundation.

References

1. J. Kennedy, R. Poli, T. Blackwell, Swarm Intelligence, vol. 1, no. 1, pp. 33-57, 2007.
2. Ting-chang Zhang, Guang-fei Geng, Power System Technology, vol. 36, no. 2, pp. 158-162, 2012 In Chinese.
3. A. Salman, I. Ahmad, S. A1-Madani, Microprocessors and Microsystems, vol. 26, no. 8, pp. 363-371, 2002.
4. Y. Shi, R. Eberhart, *A modified particle swarm optimizer*, Proceedings of IEEE International Conference on Evolutionary Computation, Piscataway, NJ, USA, 1998, pp. 68-73.
5. Xiao-feng Xie, Wen-jun Zhang, Zhi-lian Yang, Control and Decision, vol. 18, no. 2, pp. 129-134, 2003 In Chinese.
6. Ya Wen, Guo Li, Chen Xu, Applications and Research of Computer, vol. 30, no. 1, pp. 82-85, 2013 In Chinese.
7. Xian-lun Tang, *Theory and application of chaos particle swarm optimization*, Chongqing: Chongqing University, 2007 In Chinese.
8. Guo-an Liu, *Research of improved PSO and its application in image retrieval*, Harbin: Harbin Engineering University, 2008 In Chinese.
9. Wu Liu, Jian Zhou, *A LH-DM strategy based particle swarm optimization algorithm*, International Conference on Computer Information Systems and Industrial Applications, Atlantis Press, 2015.

Modified MFCC Methods Based on Differential Power Spectrum and Power Law for Robust Speech Recognition

Gao-yun LI
School of Electrical Engineering, Northwest University of Nationalities, Lanzhou, Gansu, China
E-mail: ligaoyun@xbmu.edu.cn

Xiong WANG
College of Education Technology, Northwest Normal University, Lanzhou, Gansu, China
E-mail: wxyf3222@wo.cn

This paper proposes a new feature for robust speech recognition. This method combines the benefits of differential power spectrum and the power law. The extracted features from this combined method are known as mel frequency differential power cepstral coefficients (MFDPCC).The speech recognition performance of MFDPCC features is compared to the conventional mel frequency cepstrum coefficients (MFCC) features using fuzzy radial basis function (FRBF) neural network under different noise level and different vocabulary. The experiment results demonstrate that the proposed MFDPCC feature has higher recognition rate and better robustness than MFCC.

Keywords: Differential power spectrum; Feature extraction; MFCC; Speech recognition.

1. Introduction

Feature extraction is a crucial step of the speech recognition process. The most popular features in the speech recognition system are most likely the MFCC. It can obtain the more accuracy results of speech recognition under a non-noise condition. But, accompany with deterioration of the environmental noisy condition as well as the increase of the speech vocabulary, the MFCC method's speech recognition capabilities decrease dramatically, showing the unsuitability of the usage in the strong noisy conditions and large vocabulary recognitions. In this paper, a new feature extraction method has been proposed to overcome the limitation of MFCC in noise speech. This method attempts to achieve robustness based on differential power spectrum (DPS) and power law. DPS based representation is robust with respect to the noise whose spectrum is flat.

According to Steven's Power Law, logarithmic compression can be replaced with the exponential operation[1]. We refer to this new feature extraction method as mel frequency differential power cepstral coefficients (MFDPCC).

The remainder of this paper is organized as follows: Section 2 provides a brief overview of the differential power spectrum. Stevens' power law is explained in Section 3. In Section 4, we introduced our proposed method, MFDPCC. Section 5 describes the recognition model of fuzzy radial basis function neural network. The recognition experiments and their results are described in Section 6.

2. Differential Power Spectrum

If we assume that the obtained speech signal under noise environment is y(n) and its power spectrum is $Y(\omega)$. $Y(\omega)$ is the fast Fourier transform of y(n). y(n) can be formulated as in Eq. (1).

$$y(n) = x(n) + v(n)(0 \le n < N). \tag{1}$$

where N is the frame length, y(n) represents a given frame of a speech signal that is pre-emphasized and hamming-windowed, x(n) is the noise-free speech signal, and v(n) is the ambient noise signal.

If we assume that the noise and speech signal are mutually uncorrelated, the power spectrum of the obtained speech signal can be formulated as in Eq. (2).

$$Y(\omega) = X(\omega) + V(\omega). \tag{2}$$

where $X(\omega)$ is the power spectrum of the noise-free speech signal x(n) and $V(\omega)$ is the power spectrum of the noise signal v(n).

The DPS in continuous frequency domain is defined as in Eq. (3).

$$D(\omega) = \frac{dY(\omega)}{d\omega} = \frac{dX(\omega)}{d\omega} + \frac{dV(\omega)}{d\omega} = D_X(\omega) + D_V(\omega). \tag{3}$$

where $D_X(\omega)$and $D_V(\omega)$are the differential power spectrum of the given frame of noise-free speech and noise signal. In discrete frequency domain, Eq. (3) can be recast as in Eq. (4).

$$D(k) = \sum_{l=-M}^{P} w_l Y(k+l) = D_X(k) + D_V(k) = Y(k) - Y(k+1). \tag{4}$$

where M and P are the orders of the differential equation, w_l is some real-valued weighting coefficients, and $0 \le k < K$, K is the length of FFT.

By differential operation of power spectrum, each spectral peak is split into two, one negative and one positive. The flat part of the power spectrum is transformed into some values approximating to zero. Because spectral peaks convey the most important information in speech signal, so DPS preserves spectral peaks means that the DPS representation does not lose information contained in the speech signal. On the other hand, noise spectrum is often quite flat. The differentiation operation will cause the flat part of the spectrum to be near zero. Hence we can expect that DPS based representation is robust with respect to the noise whose spectrum is flat[2,3]. This motivates us to investigate DPS for robust speech recognition. The paper proposed DPS operation after FFT in conventional MFCC features extraction algorithm.

3. Steven's Power Law

Stevens' power law[4] describes a relationship between the intensity of a physical stimulus and its perceived magnitude. The general form of the law as in Eq. (5).

$$\psi(P) = kP^{m}. \tag{5}$$

where P is the intensity of the physical stimulus, $\psi(P)$ is the subjective magnitude of the sensation evoked by the stimulus, m is an exponent that depends on the type of stimulation and k is a proportionality constant.

The MFCC procedure uses logarithmic compression for intensity-loudness conversion because human ears perceive loudness in decibel scale. In accordance with Steven's Power Law, the paper proposed replaces logarithmic compression with the exponent.

4. Mel Frequency Differential Power Cepstral Coefficients (MFDPCC) Feature Extraction Method

In this section, mel frequency differential power cepstral coefficients (MFDPCC) feature extraction method and its difference from the conventional MFCC feature extraction method are discussed. Figure 1 illustrates the block diagram of the MFDPCC feature extraction method. And the block diagram of the MFCC feature extraction method is shown in Fig. 2.

There are two difference in these two methods. One is using DPS operation after FFT in MFDPCC features extraction algorithm. The other is replaces logarithmic compression with the exponent.

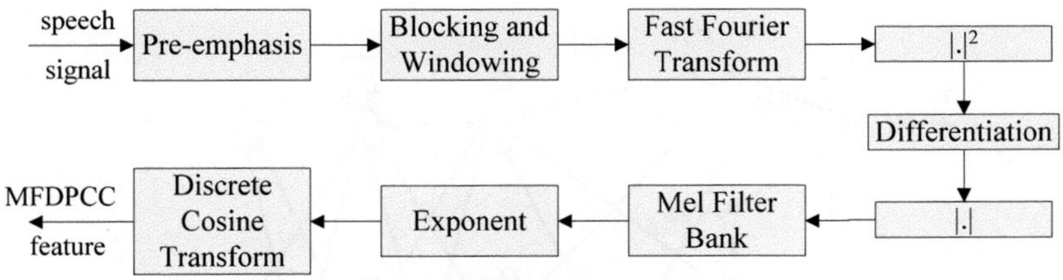

Fig. 1. Block diagram of MFDPCC feature extraction algorithm.

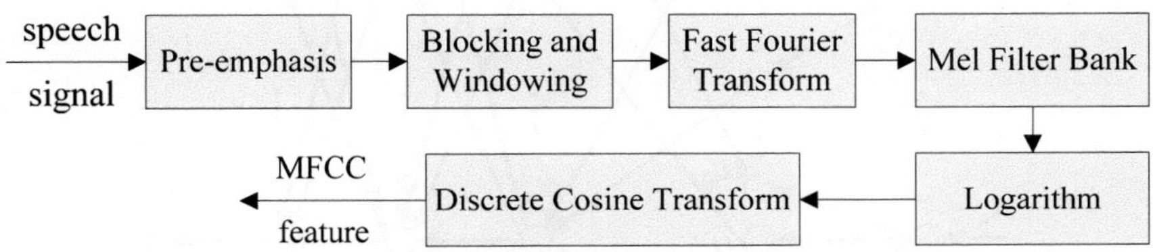

Fig. 2. Block diagram of MFCC feature extraction algorithm.

The calculation process of MFDPCC is as follows: ①The speech signal is pre-emphasized using H(z)=1-0.97Z-1. ②Framing blocking and frame shift are performed with 256 and 128 samples per frame, respectively. ③The hamming window is used on the pre-emphasized signal of a given frame. ④Make the FFT to obtain signal power spectrum. ⑤Compute the differential power spectrum of the signal. ⑥Pass the signal through the Mel frequency coordinate triangle filter groups. ⑦ exponential compression of the signal after the Mel filters with the exponent being 0.33.⑧Make the discrete cosine transform to the signal and obtain the MFDPCC coefficients.

5. Fuzzy Radial Basis Functional Neural Network

The structure of FRBF neural network is shown in Fig. 3[5,6]. It is combination of fuzzy systems and neural networks. It consists of five layers: input layer, fuzzy layer, fuzzy inference layer, normalization layer and output layer.

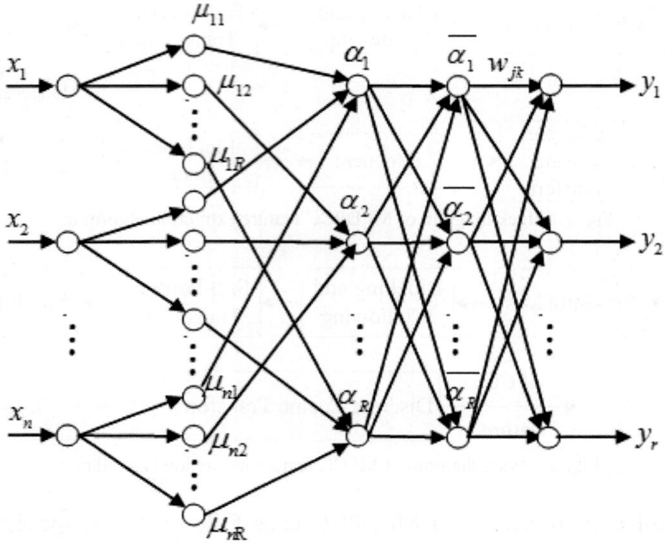

Fig. 3. Structure of FRBF neural network.

The first layer is the input layer. The input layer nodes, which transfer input value to the next layer, are connected directly with the feature vector component x_i (i=1, 2, …, n) of input speech signal, here n is the dimension of the input data.

The second layer is fuzzy layer. Each node in this layer represents a linguistic variable. Its role is calculating membership matrix μ_{ij} of each linguistic variable value's fuzzy set to which each input component belongs. The Gaussian membership function is expressed as in Eq. (6).

$$\mu_{ij} = \exp\left(-\frac{(x_i - c_{ij})^2}{\sigma_{ij}^2}\right), i = 1,2,\cdots,n; j = 1,2,\cdots R. \quad (6)$$

where c_{ij} and σ_{ij} are respectively the center value and the width of the membership function, R is the number of rules.

The third layer is fuzzy inference layer. Its function is calculating the degree of the role by multiplying them as in Eq. (7).

$$\alpha_j = \prod_{i=1}^{n} \mu_{ij}. \quad (7)$$

The fourth layer is normalization layer, which realizes normalized calculation. The output of the jth node in this layer can be expressed in Eq. (8).

$$\overline{\alpha_j} = \alpha_j / (\sum_{j=1}^{R} \alpha_j). \tag{8}$$

The fifth layer is output layer, which realizes clear calculation. The result of the jth node in the output layer is calculated in Eq. (9).

$$y_k = \sum_{j=1}^{R} w_{ik} \overline{\alpha_j}, k = 1,2,\cdots r. \tag{9}$$

where w_{jk} is the weight between the jth node in the normalization layer and the kth node in the output layer.

The parameters needing adjusting in the network are the center values and width of the membership function and the weights between the normalization layer and the output layer. A two stage algorithm for the parameters learning of the network is presented, which first determines the center values and width of the membership function according to the classification information of training samples, and then adjusts the weights between the fourth layer and the fifth layer by the gradient descent method.

6. Experimental Methods

All speech samples in the experiment are isolated words. The sampling rate of speech signal is 11.025 kHz. In the experiment, speech data of 30 words are used pronounced by 16 persons respectively in presence of noise for different SNR values (15, 20, 25 and 30 dB) and in the environment of noiselessness. And each person pronounces each word 3 times. Among them nine persons' speech data are used to train the network, and seven other persons' speech data under relevant SNR condition are used to recognize. Since the speech data file's lengths are different, in order to conveniently processing the case, we make the time normalization process to the extracted coefficients. Each word's single pronunciation will be normalized into 1024 dimensions speech feature vector series, which will be input the following FRBF neural network.

The recognition performance of the MFDPCC feature extraction method is compared with that of the MFCC method. The word recognition rate results are listed in Table 1.

Table 1. Word recognition rate (%) in MFCC and MFDPCC features.

Words	features \ SNR(dB)	15	20	25	30	Clean	Maximum Difference
10	MFCC	95.24	95.71	96.67	96.67	97.14	1.90
	MFDPCC	96.19	96.67	97.14	97.14	97.62	1.43
20	MFCC	94.05	94.52	95.00	95.47	96.19	2.14
	MFDPCC	95.71	96.19	96.67	97.14	97.62	1.91
30	MFCC	92.54	93.17	94.44	95.24	95.87	3.33
	MFDPCC	93.17	94.13	94.92	95.71	96.19	3.02

7. Conclusion

The experimental results showed that the MFDPCC feature presented in the paper has the advantages of high precision and strong robustness. It will provide the research foundation for further study of anti-noise speech recognition.

References

1. JOHN SAHAYA RANI ALEX, NITHYA VENKATESAN, Modified MFCC Methods Based On KL-Transform And Power Law For Robust Speech Recognition, in Journal of Theoretical and Applied Information Technology, Vol. 67, No. 2 (2014), pp. 527–532.
2. Jing-dong Chen, Kuldip K. Paliwal, Satoshi Nakamura, Cepstrum Derived From Differentiated Power Spectrum For Robust Speech Recognition, in Speech Communication, Vol. 41 (2003), pp. 469–484.
3. Yan-ping Zhao, Study on robust speech recognition method of isolated word in small vocabulary, Master's thesis, Jilin University (2006), “In Chinese”.
4. Stevens, S.S., On The Psychophysical Law, in Psychol, Vol. 64 (1957), pp. 153–181.
5. Gao-yun Li, The study of the speech recognition based on the optimized RBF neural network, Master's thesis, Taiyuan University of Technology (2006), “In Chinese”.
6. Qi-hong Wang, Emitter Identification Based on Fuzzy RBF Neural Network, in Marine Electric & Electronic Technology, Vol. 27 (2007), pp. 310-313, “In Chinese”.

A Hybrid PBIL-Based ICA Method

Ai-yi ZHANG* and Hai-yan QUAN†

Faculty of Information Engineering and Automation, Kunming University of Science and Technology,
Kunming, China
*E-mail: *xiaozhangaiyi@163.com; †quanhaiyan@163.com*

Independent Component Analysis (ICA) is the focal point in blind signal processing (BSP). It aims to separate the relatively independent signals from the mixed signal source. FastICA is widely used because of its simplicity and fast convergence rate. However, it is extremely sensitive to the initial values, which affects the separation effect and even inconvergence if the initial values are not chosen appropriately. In order to solve the problem, a new method based on PBIL to combine ICA is proposed. The learning rate and the learning model in PBIL are used to optimize the separation matrix in ICA, before the kurtosis is used to evaluate the effective values. The proposed method effectively avoids the problems in sensitivity of the initial values. Experiment results from the mixed speech signals data shows that the method has obvious advantages over FastICA on both separation effect and algorithm performance analysis.

Keywords: ICA; PBIL; Kurtosis; FastICA.

1. Introduction

Blind signal processing, which the word "Blind" means that there are no training data and no prior knowledge of system of parameters. Independent Component Analysis (ICA) as a parallel method can be used in BSP. This method seeks for a linear coordinate system to produce signals that are mutually statistically independent[1].

The PBIL is a new but emerging stochastic optimization approach [2,3]. Distinct from the common evolutionary computation methods, such as GA and particle swarm optimization (PSO) [4], which relies on a unique probability vector to guide the whole search process. In this paper, we develop and explore a hybridization of the ICA and PBIL: ICA-PBIL.

The rest of the paper is organized as follows. We briefly introduce the background of the ICA and PBIL in Secs. 2 and 3, respectively. In Sec. 4 by embedding the PBIL into the ICA method, we proposed a new hybrid optimization algorithm: ICA-PBIL in details. We demonstrate the performance comparison between the regular ICA method and proposed ICA-PBIL in the optimization of mixed speech signals and the algorithm per-formance. In Sec. 5, we conclude the paper with some remarks and conclusions.

2. Independent Component Analysis

The original driver of ICA research was the Cocktail-Party problem[1], the basic ICA model is a generative model, and it describes how the observed data is generated by a mixing process. Assume n mutually independent random variables $s=(s_1,s_2,\cdots,s_n)^T$, whose linear combination generates n random variables $x=(x_1,x_2,\cdots,x_n)^T$, i.e. $x=\mathbf{A}s=\sum_{i=1}^{n}a_i s_i, i=1,2,\cdots,n$, $\mathbf{A}$ is the mixing matrix. The theme of the ICA is to find a separating matrix $\mathbf{W}$, which can make the output signal are independent to each other, the form is as follows:

$$y(t)=\mathbf{W}x(t)=\mathbf{WA}s(t). \tag{1}$$

The random variable with zero mean value, whose fourth-order cumulant is kurtosis, which is

$$\text{kurt}\,(y)=E\{y^4\}-3\left(E\{y^2\}\right)^2. \tag{2}$$

The non-Gaussian is usually measured by the absolute value of kurtosis. The greater the kurtosis value is, the stronger non-Gaussian is, which can be used to separate the mixed signals. At the same time, the pre-processing signals is also important in ICA. The most useful pre-processing steps are the elimina-tion of mean and whitening. The detailed excuses can be seen in the reference No.5.

3. PBIL (Population-Based Incremental Learning)

In the simplest binary PBIL, a real-valued probability vector $P=(p_1,p_2,\cdots,p_n), 0<p_l<1, i=1,2,\cdots,n$ is used to create new binary individuals $x=(x_1,x_2,\cdots,x_n)$ as follows. With n random numbers r_i between $[0,1]$, we have: if $r_i \geq p_i, x_i=1$, else $x_i=0$ [6]. After all the individuals are generated in this way, their fitness is evaluated, and select K best of them, $\mathbf{x}^{Best}$, is chosen to update the probability vector :

$$\mathbf{P}^{New}=(1-\alpha)\mathbf{P}^{\mathbf{Old}}+\alpha\frac{\mathbf{x}^{Best}}{\mathbf{x}^{Old}}. \tag{3}$$

where $\alpha\in(0,1]$ is a learning rate parameter of the algorithm.

4. Fusion of ICA and PBIL: ICA-PBIL

In this section, the PBIL discussed above is incorporated into the original ICA, namely ICA-PBIL. In the ICA-PBIL, when a random W solution candidate is needed, it is not generated in a "pure" random way like in the regular ICA method. Instead, it is controlled by a random binary matrix of the PBIL, $v=[v_1,v_2,\cdots,v_m]^T, i=1,2,\cdots m$. Here are the steps of the ICA-PBIL:

Input signal: $x(t)$

Output signal: $y(t)$

(1) Get the input signals pre-processed.

(2) Initialization. Setting the initial learning rate α in Eq.4. M is the size of the candidates pool, $v=[v_{1:D},v_{2:D},\cdots,v_{m:D}]^T, i=1,2,\cdots m$, where D is the dimension of the individuals.

(3) Setting the iteration times i=1. Transforming the M binary particles into decimal vectors. $W = (w_{M,1}, w_{M,2}, \cdots, w_{M,D})^T$.

(4) Using Eq.2 $y(t) = W\tilde{x}(t)$, evaluating every particle according to Eq.3. Then rank each particle kurtosis value from greatest to least, the result is named $F = (f_1, f_2, \cdots, f_M)$.

(5) Choosing K best candidates according to priority principle of kurtosis from F, $x^1_{1:M}, \cdots x^1_{i:M}, \cdots, x^1_{K:M}$, and are then used to build up a new candidate pool according to using Eq.4, $p_2(x)$.

(6) Using $p_2(x)$ to select the new binary particles from the initial binary particles to conduct the next round evaluating.

(7) Judging the algorithm convergence by $|w_{n+1}-w_n| \geq \varepsilon, \varepsilon = 0.0001$. If it does not converge, then go to the step (2) to go on evaluating. Otherwise, the optimal particle is the separating matrix W^i.

(8) According to Eq.3, we can get the output signal $y(t)$.

(9) Simulations and Performance Analysis

4.1. *Simulation*

The original ICA was used to solve the Cocktail-Party problem[1], whose aim is to get the everyone's speech signal clearly. The experiment select 3 way speech signal to test the new method. The simulation parameters are used to analysis the performance of FastICA and ICA-PBIL here are the same. A total of 8,000 sampling points of the speech signals have been run. In the experiment, M represents the population size is 100. Because of the input signal is 3, so the $D = 9$. Setting the $K = M/2$. In order to analysis conveniently, the experiment have the amplitude normalized. The same mixing matrix as in the above Eq.1 is,

$$\mathbf{A}=\begin{bmatrix}0.8147 & 0.9134 & 0.2785\\ 0.9058 & 0.6324 & 0.5469\\ 0.1127 & 0.0975 & 0.9575\end{bmatrix}$$

The original input 3 way speech signal, which including man, music, and dragon, which is illustrated in Fig. 1, respectively. Figure 2 shows respectively the mixed signal, which is formed by the original signal and the mixed matrix **A**. The separating effect of ICA-PBIL are illustrated in Fig. 3 respectively. The separating results of FastICA are shown in Fig. 4.

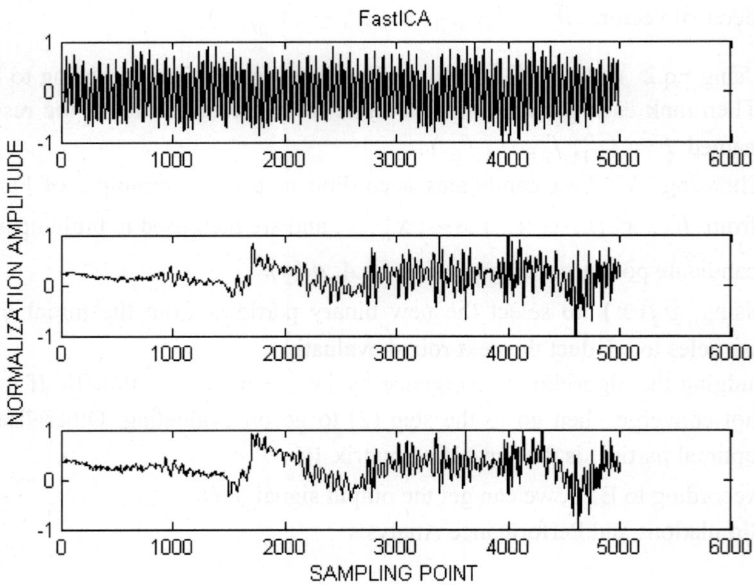

Fig. 1. The original speech signal.

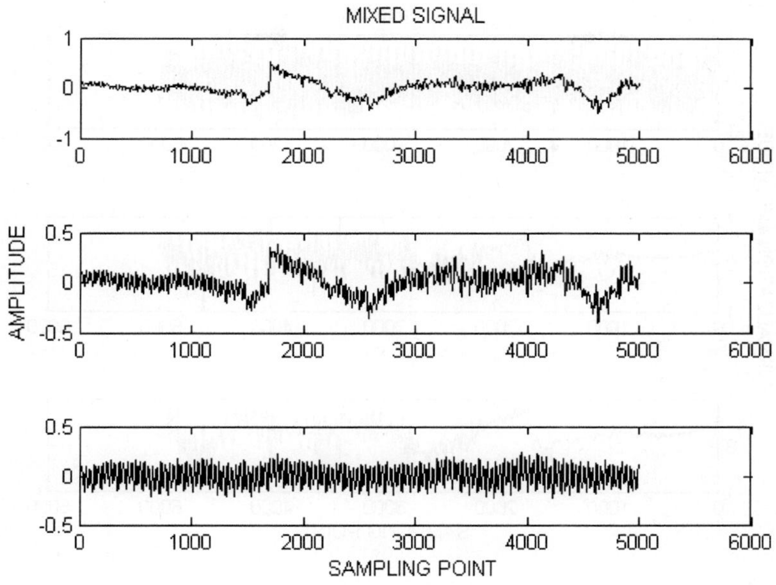

Fig. 2. Mixed speech signals.

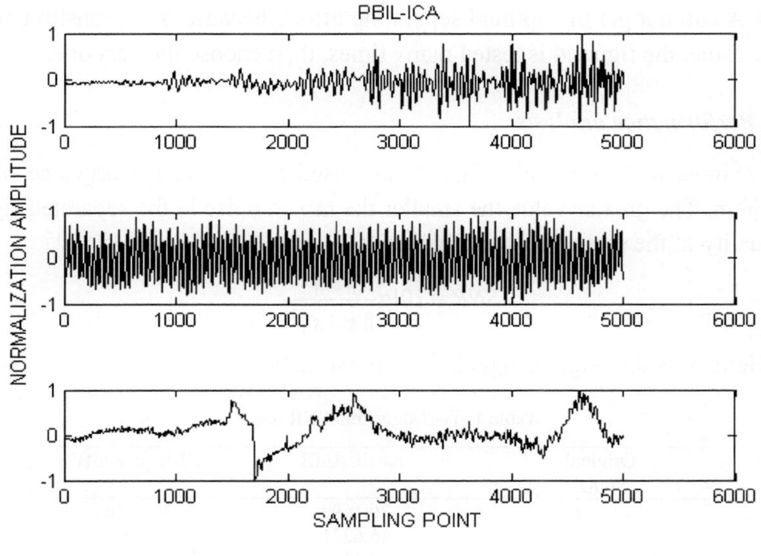

Fig. 3. PBIL-ICA processing result.

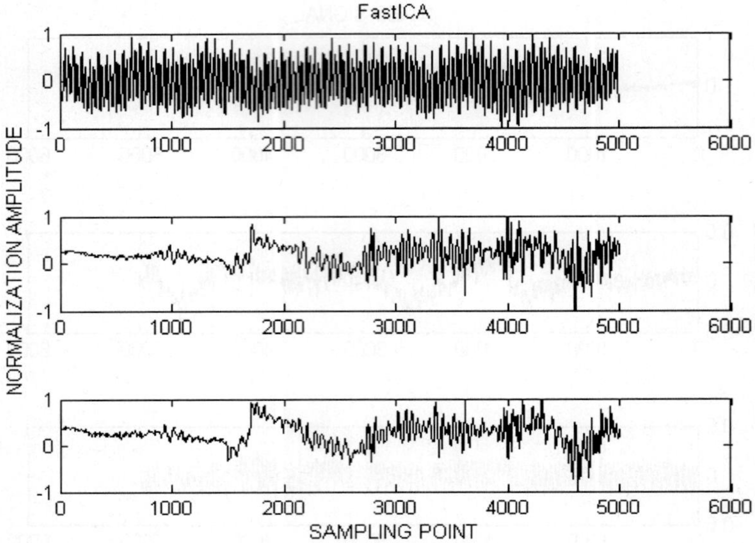

Fig. 4. FastICA separating result.

The simulation results show that the ICA-PBIL has the higher quality of separating effect than the FastICA. However, during the experiment, the FastICA can not get the optimal separating effect, because of its sensitive to the initial value, the figure 4 is tested many times, then choose the best one.

4.2. *Performance analysis*

SNR (Signal to Noise Ratio)[7]is always used to test the performance of the algorithm. The greater value the smaller the mixed noise in the separated signal, the quality of the speech signal is higher.

$$SNR = 10\lg \frac{\| s \|^2}{\| \hat{s} - s \|^2}. \tag{4}$$

Here, s is the original signal, $\hat{s}$ is its estimation signal.

Table 1. Two algorithm SNR result.

Original Signal	FastICA/dB	PBIL-ICA/dB
1	30.1699	30.6556
2	16.6231	16.7910
3	20.6026	21.2317
average	22.4652	22.8928

Table 1 shows that the ICA-PBIL has the higher quality than the FastICA of the separating speech signals. To summarize, it is obvious that the proposed ICA-PBIL is well capable of out performing the FastICA method in term of convergence efficiency when coping with this challenging mixed speech signal optimization problem.

5. Conclusion

In this paper, we develop a hybrid optimization approach, ICA-PBIL, by merging the ICA and PBIL together. It can be observed that the employment of the PBIL in the ICA-PBIL indeed results in an enhanced convergence performance by the experiment. Compared with the original ICA, better optimization results are obtained by using the ICA-PBIL. The ICA-PBIL overcomes the shortcoming of FastICA, which use the learning rate and model to update the distribution of the particles. Unfortunately, the "No Free Lunch" theorem is a fundamental barrier to the exaggerated claims of the power and efficiency of any specific optimization algorithm[8]. The optimal result is obtained by the expense of the computation, because of the binary coding. Therefore, in our future work, we are going to further study how to insure the time of the new method.

Acknowledgments

This work is supported by National Natural Science Foundation of China (No. 41364002), State Science Foundation of Yunnan (No. 2009ZC048M) and Science Grant of Kunming University of Science and Technology (No. KKZ3201103022). The authors are graceful for the support of the grants.

References

1. Xizhi Shi, Blind Signal Processing: Theory and Practice[M], SHANGHAI JIAO TONG UNIVERSITY PRESS, 2011.
2. Baluja S (1995) An empirical comparison of seven iterative and evolutionary function optimization heuristics[J]. Technical report CMU-CS-95-193, Carnegie Mellon University
3. Servet I, Trave-Massuyes L, Stern D (1997) Telephone network traffic overloading diagnosis and evolutionary computation techniques [C], Proceedings of the 3rd European conference on artificial evolution, Nimes, France, October 1997, pp 137–144
4. Engelbrecht AP (2005) Fundamentals of computational swarm intelligence. Wiley, West Sussex

5. LIU F. The research of ICA and ICA's multilayer expansion algorithm[D]. Qingdao: Ocean University of China, 2013:8-12 (In Chinese)
6. Gao Xiaozhi, Wang Xiaolei, A hybrid PBIL-based harmony search method[J], Neural Computing & Applications. Jul 2012, Vol. 21 Issue 5, pp. 1071-1083. 13 p
7. JI Ce, HU Xiang-nan, ZHU Lichun et al. Improved Higher Order Convergent FastICA Algorithm[J], Journal of Northeastern University (Natural Science), 2011, 32(10): 1390-1391 (In Chinese)
8. Wolpert DH, Macready WG (1997) No free lunch theorems for optimization. IEEE Trans Evol Comput 1(1): 67–82
9. Jiang Qun. Optimization Techniques by Building Population-based Probabilistic Models: From Algortithms to Applications[M]. Shanghai Jiao Tong University Press, 2010.
10. Aapo Hyvarinen, Juha Karhunen, Erkki Oja. Independent Component Analysis[M], Publishing House of Electronics Industry, 2007(1)
11. Lu Wei, Rajapakse JC. ICA with Reference[C]//Prose of the 3rd International Conference on ICA and Blind Source Separation. [S. l.]: Springer, 2001

Fuzzy Clustering and Deep Neural Network-Based Image Segmentation Algorithm

Zhi-jie LIN

School of Data and Computer Science, Sun Yat-sen University, Guangzhou, China

Shi-jing ZHANG

Department of Optoelectronic Information Science and Engineering, Huazhong University Of Science and Technology, Wuhan, China

Image segmentation is an essential research topic in the field of image processing, which primarily functions to separate figures into multiple disjoint regions. In most computer imaging scenarios, segmentation serves as the primary procedure for the further image understanding. In this paper, we propose a novel algorithm based on deep neural network and modified fuzzy clustering model. We enhance the clustering model with the incorporation of Markov random field theory to build up the spatial information model. To resolve the challenges influencing the performance of the traditional neural network, we adopt the deep neural structure to enhance the feasibility and robustness of the network. We compare our model with other state-of-the-art algorithms, using numerical and visual simulation to test the effectiveness,. Our experimental results verify that both accuracy and efficiency are promoted simultaneously. We attained a high segmentation accuracy of 93.6% with our proposed method.

Keywords: Image segmentation; Fuzzy theory; Deep learning; Neural network; Natural image; Clustering accuracy.

1. Introduction

Image segmentation is the primary step in the procedure of image processing to image analysis which is the basis for the further image understanding. Image segmentation refers to separating the image into the characteristics of regional extracts interested in technology and the process of target. In the recent years, researchers continue to improving the original method and using some theories and methods of the other subjects for image segmentation, a large volume of novel segmentation methods are proposed [1].

According to the literature reviews, the existing approaches for segmenting images could be categorized as the following types. (1) Threshold value method. Threshold value method is a simple and effective method of image segmentation of target and the background which is particularly useful for images with fierce background differences. The basic idea is to use one or more of the thresholds as the grayscale measure criterion to divide image into several parts, the pixel gray value with same class belongs to the same goal. (2) Boundary tracking method. The basic ideas of boundary tracking method start from the edge of a point in the gradient map to search for and connect adjacent edge points, so as to realize the image boundary detection. (3) Wavelet transform based approach. Wavelet transform is developed on the basis of Fourier analysis which not only holds the good time domain and frequency domain localization features, but also has the characteristics of multi-resolution analysis. Edge detection method based on the wavelet analysis of the advantage is its multi-scale property, every scale wavelet transform image edge information will be provided.

Fuzzy theory is a relatively new mathematical tool with fuzzy uncertainty, it can be implied from large amounts of data mining technology. Neural network has good generalization ability and numerical approximation ability, it can deal with numerical value preserves rate and compared with the basic neural network the fuzzy neural network can generate more detailed result. General training sets tend to have more redundancy, the training of the neural network in this set will often cause a phenomenon and the fuzzy set analysis can filter out the redundant information so as to improve the generalization ability of the neural network. To ascend the performance of the contemporary segmentation algorithms, we adopt the deep neural network theory with the fuzzy clustering technique to form the novel methodology. The reminding of the manuscript is organized as follows. In the section 2, we introduce the basic theory and corresponding modification on fuzzy clustering and neural network. In the section 3, we introduce optimized novel algorithm for natural image segmentation. In the sections 4, we simulate the proposed approach compared with the other algorithms. In the final part, we summarize the research and finalize further modification orientation. The result proves the feasibility of our method compared with other state-of-the-art ways.

2. The Prerequisite and Priori Knowledge

2.1. *The modified fuzzy clustering algorithm*

The development of the theory of fuzzy clustering (FC) promotes the application in the production practice, in turn, the needs of practical application promote the fuzzy clustering theory constantly to get enriched. With the development of the theory, the fuzzy clustering has obtained widespread application in many fields, and have achieved satisfactory effect and significant benefit. In modern scenario we will select fuzzy c-means (FCM) algorithm as the representative of the soft clustering model whose overall performance is satisfactory. However, when the FCM method is applied to image segmentation tasks, the relationship between pixel data in spatial domain is completely ignored, if there is a big noise, image tends to make the split out in many areas of discrete holes or clutter [3].

To overcome the drawbacks, we introduce the spatial information into the traditional model for optimization. In the formula 1~3, we demonstrate the basic steps of the traditional fuzzy c-means algorithm.

$$J(U,V)=\sum_{i=1}^{c}\sum_{k=1}^{n}(u_{ik})^{m}(d_{ik})^{2} \quad k=1,2,\cdots n; i=1,2,\cdots c. \tag{1}$$

$$v_i=\left[\sum_{k=0}^{n}u_{ik}^{m}\cdot x_k\right]/\left[\sum_{k=0}^{n}u_{ik}^{m}\right]. \tag{2}$$

$$u_{ik}=\left[\left(1/d_{ik}^{2}\right)^{1/(m-1)}\right]/\left[\sum_{j=1}^{c}\left(1/d_{ik}^{2}\right)^{1/(m-1)}\right]. \tag{3}$$

Where the $J(U,V)$ represents the objective function, $(d_{ik})^2$ is the Euclidean distance between the classes. To incorporate with spatial information, we need to introduce the MRF model with pseudo likelihood degree of approximation. By statistical theory, wo-dimensional grid field of a certain relationship between lattice can be considered with MRF model. Hameraley-Clifford theorem further pointed out that the joint probability distribution of MRF can be equivalent as the Gibbs distribution expressed in the formula 4.

$$P(z)=W^{-1}\exp\{-U(z)\}. \tag{4}$$

W is the normalized constant and $U(z)$ is energy function. If we consider the second order neighborhood system of interaction between two points, it can be used in statistical physics Potts model and energy function could be expressed as the following form.

$$U(z)=\sum_{i\in S}\sum_{j\in N(i)}V_2(z_i,z_j). \tag{5}$$

MRF theory aims to describe the relationship between adjacent pixel space provides a powerful tool and in order to reach the global optimal segmentation of the image, approaches tend to be under the framework of statistics using such as simulated annealing, Gibbs computation of stochastic optimization methods which could be found in [2]. The final pixel classification for the conditional probability can be expressed as formula 6.

$$P_G\left(z_i \mid z_{N(i)}\right)=\left[\exp\left(\beta\sum_{j\in N(i)}\delta(z_i,z_j)\right)\right]/\left[\sum_{z_i}\exp\left(\beta\sum_{j\in N(i)}\delta(z_i,z_j)\right)\right]. \tag{6}$$

We apply the proposed conditional probability on the distance measurement criterion in traditional FCM for modification as formula 7.

$$d_m^2\left(x_i,v_k\right)=d^2\left(x_i,v_k\right)/P_G\,. \tag{7}$$

The novel standard contains the characteristics of pixel domain information as well as local neighborhood distribution information of pixels.

2.2. *The traditional Neural Network (NN) for image segmentation*

The back propagation neural network is a neural network in the study of one of the most widely used network model using negative gradient descent algorithm, which effectively overcome the single-layer perceptron challenges and contains only a input layer, hidden layer and output layer of three layer back propagation neural networks, many scholars have proved his universal approximation ability. In the figure one, we illustrate the traditional neural network structure.

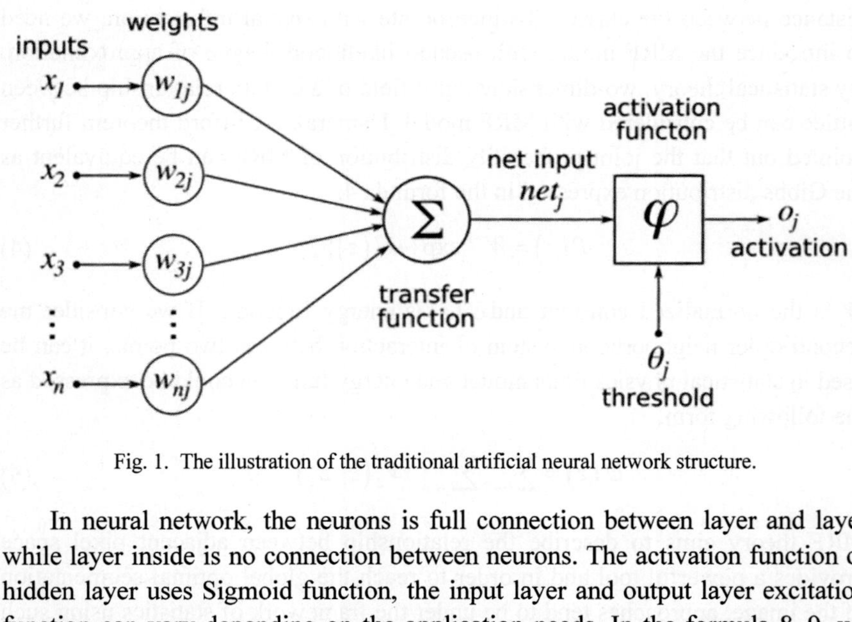

Fig. 1. The illustration of the traditional artificial neural network structure.

In neural network, the neurons is full connection between layer and layer while layer inside is no connection between neurons. The activation function of hidden layer uses Sigmoid function, the input layer and output layer excitation function can vary depending on the application needs. In the formula 8~9, we show the neurons and the network mathematical model, respectively.

$$a=f\left(\sum_{i=1}^{q}w_ix_i+b_i\right). \tag{8}$$

$$a^{m+1}=i^{m+1}\left(w^{m+1}a^m+b^{m+1}\right),\qquad m=1,2,3,\cdots,M-1\,. \tag{9}$$

However, the traditional neural network model is suffering from the following drawbacks. (1) Network topology is difficult to determine. Layer is overmuch or number of neurons in layer can make complex network structure, significantly increase the amount of calculation and to extend training time. (2) Study time is long with slow convergence speed. Due to generation of oscillation phenomenon can lead to network in the process of training increase learning time slows down the rate of convergence. (3) Can't jump out of local minima. There are a number of minimum point in the error surface and in the process of gradient descent are likely to fall into a local minimum and can't jump out.

3. Enhanced Deep Neural Network Model

Convolution of CNN layer have played an important role in the effective local feature extraction. DBN adopted in the matter of characteristics of sample did not feature extraction module which is actually new characterization of original data. If we can improve the structure of matter while not affect the layer under the premise of greedy algorithm to implement effective local feature extraction, DBN effect will be better. Visible layers in the matter of the state of each unit is determined jointly by all the hidden layer units, we improve the structure of the matter. The formula 10 shows the optimization of the objective function [4].

$$J(W,b)=\left[\frac{1}{m}\sum_{i=1}^{m}J\left(W,b;x^{i},y^{\to i}\right)\right]+\frac{\lambda}{2}\sum_{l=1}^{n_l}\sum_{i=1}^{s_l}\sum_{j=1}^{s_{l+1}}\left(W_{ij}^{l}\right)^{2}. \tag{10}$$

The optimized model could be roughly categorized as following four steps. (1) Determine the depth of the neural network based on positive linear activation function layers and each layer contains number of neurons. (2) Linear activation function and the cost function are selected, the use of data without a label for unsupervised automatic coding training model step by step. (3) Use label data on the depth of layer includes classification prediction with linear neural network supervision and training to further adjusting parameters. (4) Model based on the study to the characteristics of data to classify the new sample.

4. Experiment and Simulation

In this section, we conduct experimental simulation visually and numerically. To verify the robustness, we run our algorithm on different data sets. In the figure 2, we demonstrate the individual process experiment on proposed deep structured segmentation algorithm. In the figure 3, we compare our method with the other state-of-the-art algorithms. In the Table 1, we show the numerical comparison result. It could be reflected from the result that in most of cases, our algorithm outperforms. The highest segmentation accuracy has been reached by method proposed by us with the numerical value of 93.6%.

Fig. 2. Individual process experiment on the proposed deep structured segmentation algorithm.

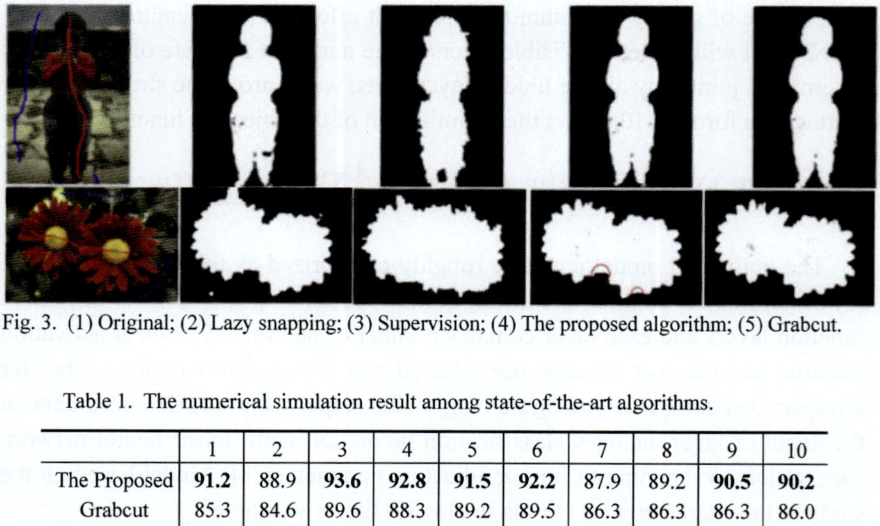

Fig. 3. (1) Original; (2) Lazy snapping; (3) Supervision; (4) The proposed algorithm; (5) Grabcut.

Table 1. The numerical simulation result among state-of-the-art algorithms.

	1	2	3	4	5	6	7	8	9	10
The Proposed	**91.2**	88.9	**93.6**	**92.8**	**91.5**	**92.2**	87.9	89.2	**90.5**	**90.2**
Grabcut	85.3	84.6	89.6	88.3	89.2	89.5	86.3	86.3	86.3	86.0
Lazy snapping	88.2	86.0	92.3	89.1	88.7	87.6	86.9	88.5	87.1	86.5
MOF	83.1	80.5	88.7	87.5	88.4	88.2	87.2	88.2	87.5	87.2
Supervision	90.6	**89.3**	91.5	91.3	89.9	88.9	**88.9**	**90.5**	89.3	88.7

5. Conclusion

This paper proposes the novel fuzzy clustering and deep neural network based image segmentation algorithm. We introduce the fast and efficient algorithm to train the traditional neural network with deep structure for segmenting images. We achieve the state-of-the-art performance on the challenging standard datasets, the effectiveness and feasibility of the algorithm is verified. Our segmentation accuracy has reached 93.6% which holds time transgressive significance.

References

1. Wang, Fan, et al. "Synthetic aperture radar image segmentation using fuzzy label field-based triplet Markov fields model." IET Image Processing 8.12 (2014): 856-865.
2. Zhang, Luming, et al. "Representative discovery of structure cues for weakly-supervised image segmentation." Multimedia, IEEE Transactions on 16.2 (2014): 470-479.
3. Bhatia, Meenu, and SayleeGharge. "Segmentation of brain MR image using fuzzy local Gaussian mixture model." Electrical Insulation Conference (EIC), 2015 IEEE. IEEE, 2015.
4. Bi, Chujian, et al. "SAR image change detection using regularized dictionary learning and fuzzy clustering." Cloud Computing and Intelligence Systems, 2014 IEEE 3rd International Conference on. IEEE.

Color Cast Correction of Color Image Based on Improved Frankle-McCann Retinex

Hui-ling SHI[1], Jian-yong CAI[*1,2,3], Jin-qi CHEN[1], Yu-si CHEN[1] and Fei-yang TONG[1]

[1]*College of Photonic and Electronic Engineering, Fujian Normal University*
[2]*Key Laboratory of Optoelectronic Science and Technology for Medicine Ministry of Education, Fujian Normal University*
[3]*Fujian Provincial Engineering Research Center for Optoelectronic Sensors and Intelligent Information, Fujian Normal University*
Fuzhou, Fujian350007, China
[*]*E-mail: cjy@fjnu.edu.cn*

A color cast correction algorithm based on improved Frankle-McCann Retinex is proposed to correct images which are influenced by illumination. To improve on the original algorithm, the distance-weighting factor with Gauss function is introduced, and a linear stretch with the mean and the standard deviation is carried out. Experimental results demonstrate that the algorithm in this paper has improved correction effect on the color cast image.

Keywords: Color cast image; Color constancy; Frankle-McCann retinex; Distance-weighting with gauss; Mean; Standard deviation; Linear stretch.

1. Retinex Theory

The basis of Retinex theory [1] is about that the color of objects is determined by reflectance of an object. The color of the object is not affected by the nonuniform illumination. Namely the Retinex theory is based on consistency (color constancy) [2]. From the principle of Retinex theory, an image S(x, y) can be defined as in Eq. (1) and Eq. (2):

$$S(x,y) = R(x,y) \bullet L(x,y). \tag{1}$$

$$\log S = \log R + \log L. \tag{2}$$

where *L(x, y)* represents the illumination and *R(x, y)* is reflectance of objects. The purpose of image enhancement based on Retinex is to estimate the illumination L from image S, so we can obtain the reflection image $R(x,y)$. To improve the visual effect of the image just as the human visual system, in processing, the image is usually transferred to the logarithmic domain. But in fact, many algorithms estimated $R(x, y)$ directly [3]. This paper proposes a color cast correction algorithm based on improved Frankle-McCann Retinex to correct images which are influenced by illumination.

2. Frankle-McCann Retinex Algorithm and Its Improvements

2.1. *Classical Frankle-McCann Retinex algorithm*

A critical concept in the Frankle-McCann Retinex [4] algorithm (FMR) is the comparison of a destination pixel value to that of other source pixels. The manner in which comparison pixels are chosen is fundamental to the computational efficiency of the algorithm. The comparison pixels are defined by following a path from a destination pixel to neighboring source pixels in the image. The path is showed in Fig. 1

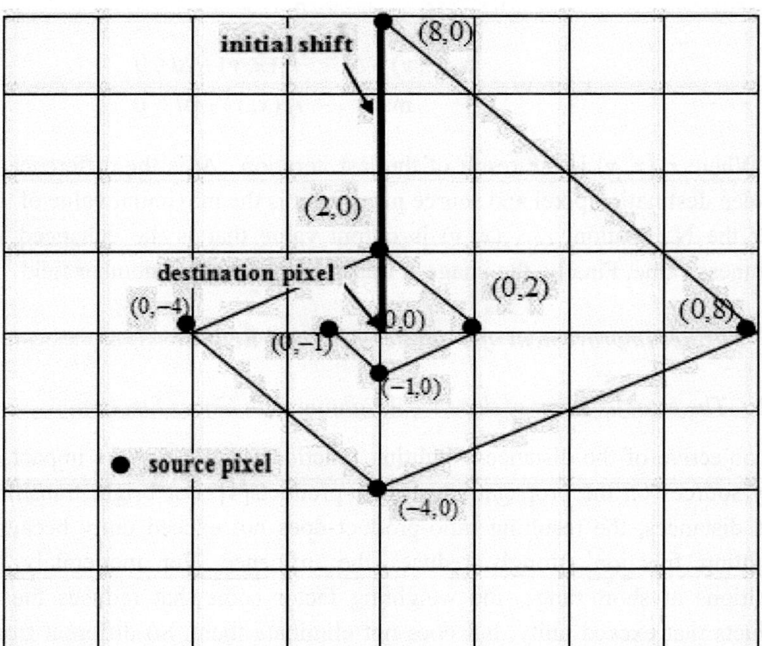

Fig. 1

Long-distance interactions between pixels are computed first and then progressively shorter distance interactions are computed. The direction between pixels also changes at each step, forming an inward spiral. At each step, the comparison is performed by the ratio-product-reset-average operation. When processing an image, the image is first initialized to a constant. In Figure 1, the first point (initial shift, 0) compare with the origin of coordinate system (0, 0) at the beginning of the first iteration, the process continues until the spacing decreases to a separation of 1 pixel. The initial spacing value between comparison pixels is 2^p, where $p = fix\ (\log_2{}^{\min(nrows,\ ncols)-1})$, *nrows* is the image width, *ncols* is the image height, and *fix* indicates rounding to the nearest integer toward zero. For the next step, the spacing is halved, shift =shift/2, and the direction changed. This process continues progressively until the distance shrinks to the nearest neighbor. The comparison processes are in Eq. (3) and Eq. (4):

$$r_{n+1}(x,y) = \frac{r_n(x,y) + r_n'(x,y)}{2}. \tag{3}$$

$$r_n'(x,y) = \begin{cases} r_n(x,y) + \Delta l & r_n(x,y) + \Delta l \le 0 \\ \max & r_n(x,y) + \Delta l > 0 \end{cases}. \tag{4}$$

Where $r_n(x, y)$ is the result of the last iteration, Δl is the difference value between destination pixel and source pixel, max is the maximum value of $s(x, y)$. After the N iteration, $r_{n+1}(x, y)$ is output value that is the enhanced image brightness value. Finally, the image is transferred to the real number field

2.2. *Further improvement of Frankle –McCann Retinex*

2.2.1. *The establishment of distance weighting with Gauss function*

The objective of the distance-weighting function is to lessen the impact of far away sources on the propagation of ratio-products[4]. For bright transitions at large distances, the resulting ratio-product does not exceed unity because the weighting function strongly reduces the influence. For moderately bright transitions at short range, the weighting factor somewhat reduces the ratio-products that exceed unity, but does not eliminate them. So different from the traditional FMR algorithm, we add a distance-weighting factor with Gauss function w in Eq. (4). Expression is shown in Eq. (5). It was to reduce the influence of a bright source as a function of the radial distance from the destination. Distance weighting with Gauss function is given in Eq. (6).

$$r_n'(x,y) = r_n(x,y) + \Delta l \cdot w. \tag{5}$$

$$w = f^{power}. \tag{6}$$

$$f(x,y) = \frac{1}{2\pi\sigma^2} e^{-(x^2+y^2)/2\sigma^2}. \tag{7}$$

$$3\sigma = \text{initial shift} \quad \sigma = \text{initial shift}/3. \tag{8}$$

Where f is the Gauss function. given in Eq. (7). Plane figure of Gauss is shown in Fig. 2. The Gauss distribution is a bell shaped curve, the closer to the center, the greater the value is, the farther away from the center , the smaller the value is. And according to the properties of Gauss function,99. 7% of the values are within the range of 3 standard deviations from the mean value, so we can define 3σ=initial shift, σ=initial shift/3, as in Eq. (8). The destination pixel (0, 0) as the origin of Gauss, and the (x, y) of the Gauss function is (0, shift) and (shift, 0) which are source pixel on the path in Fig. 1. Weight value w depends on position of (x,y) on the Gauss curve. When the power=0.01, the experiment result of image processing is the best.

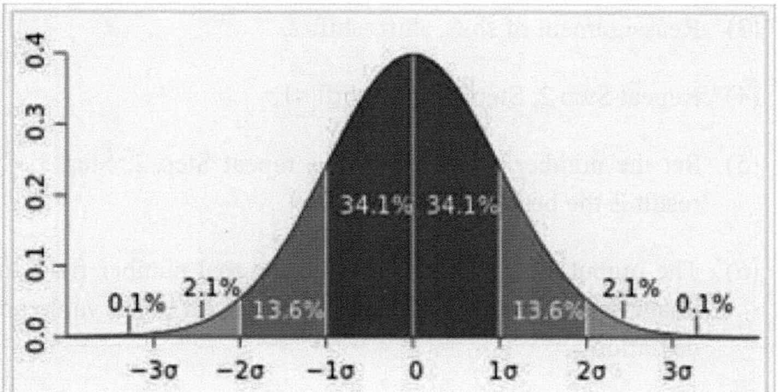

Fig. 2

2.2.2. *Linear stretching with mean and standard deviation*

The processing effect of the traditional FMR algorithm is not very good if it is directly converted to real number field. In order to further enhance the global brightness contrast, the following method is proposed. A linear stretch with mean (*Mean*) and standard deviation (*Var*) is carried out after the image is transformed to a real number field. Firstly, the *Mean* and *Var* of the image is calculated, and the *Min* and *Max* values of each channel are calculated by using the Eq. (9).

$$\begin{aligned} Min &= Mean - 3Var \\ Max &= Mean + 3Var. \end{aligned} \tag{9}$$

Finally, the linear mapping is performed for each pixel, as in Eq. (10):

$$R(x,y) = \frac{Value - Min}{Max - Min} \cdot (255 - 0). \tag{10}$$

An overflow judgment is add, as in Eq. (11):

$$\begin{array}{ll} R(x,y) > 255 & \mathrm{R(x, y) = 255} \\ \mathrm{R(x, y) > 0} & \mathrm{R(x, y) = 0.} \end{array} \tag{11}$$

The processes of the improved algorithm in this paper are:

(1) The input image is transferred to the logarithmic domain, the data type is converted to double type, and initialization,

(2) Determine the initial shift variable, Begin to compare,

(3) Reassignment of shift, shift=shift/2,

(4) Repeat Step 2, Step 3, until |shift|<1,

(5) Set the number of iterations N , repeat Step 2, Step 3, Step 4, The result is the best when N=8,

(6) The output image is converted to the real number field and then the image is processed by a linear stretch with mean value and standard deviation.

3. Experimental Results

The simulation experiment is carried out by using MATLAB. In order to improve the accuracy and practicability of the algorithm, a large number of color cast images were corrected with improved Frankle-McCannRetinex. The experimental results show that algorithm in this paper can produce a good correction result for the color cast images. Correction images under different illuminations and their comparison are shown in Fig. 3-Fig. 5.

(a) (b) (c) (d)

Fig. 3. (a) color cast image, (b) color corrected by FMR, (c) color corrected by improved FMR and (d) original image.

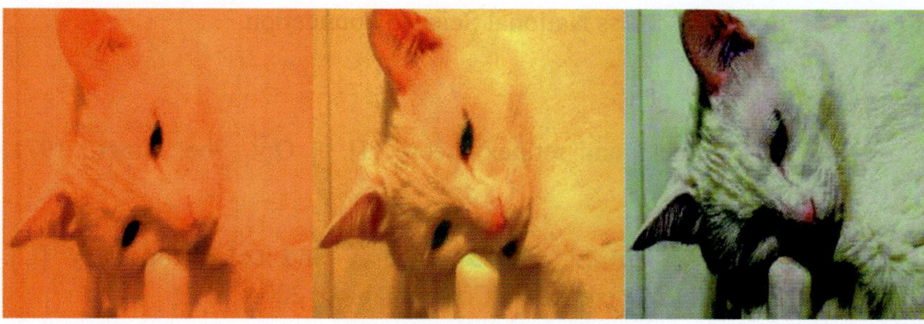

(a) (b) (c)

Fig. 4. (a) color cast image, (b) color corrected by FMR, and (c) color corrected by improved FMR.

(a) (b) (c)

Fig. 5. (a) color cast image, (b) color corrected by FMR, and (c) color corrected by improved FMR.

4. Conclusion

This paper proposes a new color correction method based on improved Frankle-McCannRetinex algorithm. Through MATLAB simulation experiments, the results show that the proposed algorithm has good correction effect under different illuminations. From the experimental results, compared with the classical algorithm, the improved algorithm has better color correction result for the color image.

Acknowledgments

This work is supported by grant 2015H4007 of the Fujian province 2015 strategic emerging industries special committee fund. Work partially supported by grant 2-4570.5 of the Swiss National Science Foundation.

References

1. J. McCann. Lightness and retinex theory [J]. J. Opt. Soc. Amer., 1971, 61(1)1–11.

2. G.D. Finlayson, E. Trezzi. Shades of gray and color constancy [C]. Proceeding of 12th Conference on Color Imaging, 2004.

3. E. H. Land and J. J. McCann, ''Method and system for reproduction based on significant visual boundaries of original subject,'' U.S. Patent No. 3,553,360 1971.

4. ted J. Cooper, Farhan A. Baqai: Analysis and extensions of the Frankle-McCann Retinex algorithm[J].J. Electronic Imaging, 2004,13(1): 85-92.

Simulation of Chinese Ink Animation Based on Navier-Stokes Equations

Wei-wei LI*

Department of Information Engineering, Shandong Youth University of Political Science, Jinan, 250103, China
Key Laboratory of Information Security and Intelligent Control in Universities of Shandong, Jinan 250103, China
**E-mail: lww@sdyu.edu.cn*

The difficulty of simulating Chinese ink animation in computer is a prevalent issue and in this paper, we propose the use of Navier-Stokes equations to control the motion of the Chinese ink to form animations. This method can reflect the intrinsic physical properties of fluid motion, and it can realistically simulate various natural and physical phenomena. The equations were resolved by the semi-Lagrange method in this paper. The calculation of the equations is too complicated for real-time simulation, so GPU (Graphics Processing Unit) is used to accelerate the calculation rates. Experimental results have demonstrated the feasibility and viability of the proposed method and it greatly simplifies the production process of Chinese ink animation.

Keywords: Chinese ink animation; Navier-stokes equations; GPU (Graphics Processing Unit).

1. Introduction

Chinese Ink Animation is evolved by the Chinese traditional painting, and it has formed the national animation industry with Chinese characteristics[1]. But because of the miscellaneous workmanship, Chinese it once abandoned by the animator. Now, the digital technology has injected new vitality for it, animation production efficiency is improved greatly[2].

The existing methods of Chinese Ink Animation computer simulation focus on the ink painting. The simulation of ink painting is comparatively ripe[3-8]. Strassmann proposed a Brush model which has characteristic of Chinese painting[9]. Lee proposed a model which combine ink and paper[10], but his

Diffusing Algorithm is based on pixel, Authenticity diffusion effect is poor. Way simulated the Chinese landscape painting through drawing the texture and strokes[11], but this method is tedious and the effect is lack of Chinese ink and lasting appeal. Shi Yongxin proposed an ink and wash drawing model based on Particle System[12], to some extent this method partially simulated the ink painting, but realization of this algorithm is difficult and simulating effects is lack of reality. Cao Yi[13] proposed a method based on image which can transfer two-dimensional picture to Chinese ink painting, but the brush model has the same mechanism and not agree with the diversification of the line in the actual painting.

The simulation of ink painting is not ideal, the effect of reduce the miscellaneous workmanship is limited. Computer animation based on Navier-Stokes equations is becoming more and more mature. Simulation based on Navier-Stokes equations can reflects intrinsic physical properties of fluid motion and realistically simulate various natural physical phenomena. Liu Youquan[14] have successful simulated realistic smoke animation based on Navier-Stokes equations. Yue Wang [15] simulated real-time cloud based on physical models. Li Weiwei [16] simulated realistic flame animation based on Navier-Stokes equaitons.

We proposed a simulation method based on Navier-Stokes equations to explore new ways to simulate Chinese Ink Animation.

2. Fluid Simulation Based on Navier-Strokes Equations

Fluid simulation based on Navier-Strokes equations can exactly describe the variation of fluid motion; the calculation result of these equations can meet the physical nature and motion characteristics of the real phenomenon.

The Navier-Stokes equations for incompressible flow[17]:

$$\frac{\partial u}{\partial t} = -(u \cdot \nabla) - \frac{1}{\rho}\nabla p + v\nabla^2 u + F \,. \tag{1}$$

$$\nabla \cdot u = 0 \,. \tag{2}$$

Where t is time, F is external forces, u represents velocity field, v is the kinematic viscosity, ρ is the fluid density, p is pressure field.

The first term on the right-hand side of Equation 1.1 is advection term. Imagine squirting ink into fluid. The ink is advected along the fluid's velocity field. The second term is pressure term. Because the molecules of a fluid can move around each other, when force is applied to a fluid, the molecules close to the force push on those farther away, and pressure builds up. The third term is the diffusion term. Viscosity is a measure of how resistive a fluid is to flow. The third term is External Forces. This term encapsulates acceleration due to external forces applied to the fluid[18].

First, we use Helmholtz-Hodge decomposition theorem to simplify the equations.

Helmholtz-Hodge Decomposition Theorem[19]:

A vector field w on D can be uniquely decomposed in the form: $w = u + \nabla p$,

Where u has zero divergence and is parallel to ∂D; that is, $u \cdot n = 0$ on ∂D.

We can use the Helmholtz-Hodge Decomposition Theorem to define a projection operator, P, that projects a vector field w onto its divergence-free component, u. If we apply P to Equation1, we get:

$$P\frac{\partial u}{\partial t} = P(-(u \cdot \nabla)u - \frac{1}{\rho}\nabla p + v\nabla^2 u + F)). \quad (3)$$

Because u is divergence-free, so is the derivative on the left-hand side, so $P(\partial u/\partial t) = \partial u/\partial t$. Also, $P(\nabla p) = 0$, so the pressure term drops out. We're left with the following equation:

$$\frac{\partial u}{\partial t} = P(-(u \cdot \nabla)u + v\nabla^2 u + F). \quad (4)$$

We first compute what's inside the parentheses on the right-hand side. From left to right, we compute the advection, diffusion, and force terms. Application of these three steps results in a divergent velocity field, w, to which we apply our projection operator to get a new divergence-free field, u.

Step by step to solve the equations is as follows[19]:

$$\mathbf{u}_0(\mathbf{x}) \xrightarrow{advect} \mathbf{u}_1(\mathbf{x}) \xrightarrow{diffuse} \mathbf{u}_2(\mathbf{x}) \xrightarrow{force} \mathbf{u}_3(\mathbf{x}) \xrightarrow{project} \mathbf{u}_4(\mathbf{x})$$

Advection: $\mathbf{u}_1(\mathbf{x}) = \mathbf{u}_0(\mathbf{x} - \delta t \mathbf{u}_0(\mathbf{x}))$

Viscous Diffusion: $\mathbf{u}_2(\mathbf{x}) = \mathbf{u}_1(\mathbf{x}) - \delta t v \nabla^2 \mathbf{u}_1(\mathbf{x})$

Applied External Forces: $\mathbf{u}_3(\mathbf{x}) = \mathbf{u}_2(\mathbf{x}) + \delta t \mathbf{F}(\mathbf{x})$

Projection:
$$\nabla^2 p(x) = \nabla \cdot u_3(x)$$
$$u_4(x) = u_3(x) - \nabla p(x)$$

3. Acceleration by GPU

Simulation based on Navier-Stokes equations can accurate computing the motion of fluid, so we simulate the Chinese Ink Animation through this method, but calculation of this method is complicated, so it is hard to meet the real-time demand of the Computer Graphics.

Using GPU to solving the equations has unique advantages [20]: parallelism, high intensive operation, reduce the CPU and GPU data communication. The new hardware features greatly accelerates the computation speed. We use GPU to accelerate the solvation of the Navier-Stokes, so we can conquer the trouble of the complicated computing in order to real-time simulation.

Solving the Navier-Stokes equations using GPU as follows, each frame following this operation process, the result of this operation is as enter of the next operation:

(1) Advect density field by calling advect() fragment program.

(2) Advect velocity field by calling advect() fragment program.

(3) Set source for the fluid by calling splat() fragment program to add velocity to velocity field and density to density field.

(4) Vorticity Confinement.

(5) Solving the diffusion term by calling divergence() fragment program.

(6) To control the fluid by exert External Force.

(7) Convert divergence velocity field to zero divergence velocity using pressure field.

advect()fragment program as follows:

```
void advect(float2      coords : WPOS,
out   float4      x New   : COLOR,
uniform float     timestep,
uniform float      dissipation,.
uniform float      rdx,
```

*divergence()*fragment program as follows:

```
void divergence(half2      coords  : WPOS,
out  half4      div    : COLOR,
uniform half       halfrdx,
uniform sampler RECT w)
{  float2pos = coords - timestep * rdx * f2texRECT(u, coords);
x New = dissipation * f4texRECTbilerp(x, pos);  }
```

4. Add Ink

This system exerts ink and external force to fluid through clicks and drag mouse, here we call it pulses. Click the speed texture, and draw a spot, the red channel storage x axis velocity component, and the green channel storage y axis velocity component. We use splat() fragment program which proposed in the Section 2. Check the distance between each fragment and the spot which mouse click to calculate the color value which should add to the texture. Using the formula as follows:

$$c = F\delta t \exp\left\{\frac{(x-x_p)^2+(y-y_p)^2}{r}\right\}. \quad (5)$$

Where (x,y) is the position of fragment, (x_p,y_p) is the position of the pulse, r is the radius of the pulse, F is the external force which is exerted by mouse.

5. Experiment Results

The process of Chinese Ink Animation simulation on computer is shown in Fig. 1:

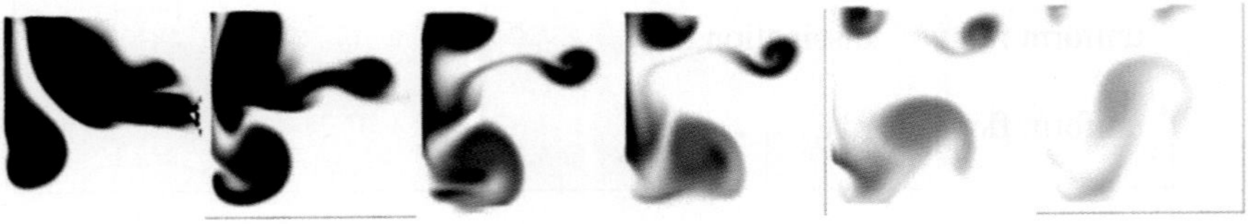

Fig. 1. The process of Chinese ink animation.

The computation based on Navier-Stokes equations is high complexity compared to the before simulation method, but this method can accurate solving the motion of fluid, and can accurate describe the changes of the flowing ink. The effective of the simulation is ink and lasting appeal and the animation production process is greatly simplified.

6. Conclusions

In this paper, we use the method based on Navier-Stokes to explore Chinese Ink Animation. The Governing Equations of Fluid Mechanics is Navier-Stokes equations and the solving method is semi-Lagrangian. We accelerate the realization speed by calculating on GPU. We use splat() fragment program to add ink and external force to fluid. As shown in figure 1 is the effect of simulation of Chinese Ink Animation on computer. The production speed is fast and the ink colour is dye-in-the-wood.

Acknowledgments

This work is supported by the 12th Five-year Education Science Key Plan of Shandong Province (No. 2013GZ042), the scientific research project of Shandong Youth University of Political Science (No.2015QN10) and the Teaching Reform Project of Shandong Youth University of Political Science (No. 201417).

References

1. Dan Luo, Development and application of digital ink animation [D]: Hunan University of Technology, Zhuzhou, 2013, In Chinese

2. Xiao-yu Xie, Mergence of science and art: Research on Ink-Wash Animation [D]: Shanghai University, Shanghai, 2011, In Chinese

3. Da-jin Li, Cheng-jie Bai. An efficient rendering method of wash-ink strokes and its applica-tion[J]. Journal of Computer-Aided Design & Computer Graphics. 2014, 26(3): 356-363, In Chinese

4. Xiu-jin Wang. Research on the simulation of Chinese paiting [D]. Tianjin University, Tianjin. 2008, In Chinese

5. Yan Luo, Jiang-mei Luo, Zhongfu Wu, Qing Li. Graphical simulation algorithm for chinese traditional ink painting based on Perlin noise [J]. Journal of Chongqing University. 2014, 37(7):131-135, In Chinese

6. Jia-chuan Sheng. Computerized learning and classification of traditional Chinese IWP(Ink and Wash Paintings). Tianjin University, Tianjin. 2013

7. Bin Yu. Chinese Ink-Wash Painting Styled Rendering of 3D Models [D]. Tianjin University, Tianjin. 2006, In Chinese

8. Ya-feng Qi, Ji-zhou Sun, Yi Shang. Basic Art Characters and Graphical Simulation for Chinese Ink Wash Drawing [J]. Journal of Image and Graphics. 2003, 8(5):562-566

9. Strassmann S. Hairy brushes[C]. Computer Graphics Proceeding. Dallas: ACM SIGGRAPH, 1986:225-232

10. Lee J. Diffusion rendering of black ink paintings using new paper and ink models [J]. Computers and Graphics, 2001, 25(2):295-308

11. Way D L, Shih Z C. The synthesis of rock textures in Chinese landscape painting [C]. Manchester: Proceedings of Eurographics, 2001:123-131

12. Shi Yongxin. Graphical simulation algorithm for Chinese ink-wash drawing by particle system [J]. Journal of computer-aided design & computer graphics.2003, 15(6):667-672

13. Yi Cao. Research on Image Based Rendering of Chinese Ink Painting [D]: Jilin University, Changchun, 2012

14. You-quan Liu. Study on Acceleration Techniques of Physically Based Computer Animation [D]. Chinese Academy of Sciences, Beijing, 2005, In Chinese

15. Wang Yue. Real-Time Cloud Simulation Based on Physical Models [D]. Jilin University, Changchun, 2008, In Chinese

16. Wei-wei Li. New idea of flame simulation in real-time [J]. 2008, 26(6):571-575, In Chinese

17. A. J. Chorin and J. E. Marsden. A Mathematical Introduction to Fluid Mechanics [M]. New York: Springer-Verlag, 1990.

18. Scott Jacobs. Game Programming Gems 7 [M]. Charles River Media, 2008

19. Jos Stam. Stable Fluids [J]. In Proceeding of SIGGRAPH. 1999, 6, P121-128

20. Wolfgang Engel. Gpu Pro 3: Advanced Rendering Techniques [M]. A K Peters, 2012

A Retinal Image Segmentation Algorithm Based on Threshold Segmentation

Hong-qiang ZHANG

College of electrical engineering, Northwest University For Nationalities, Lanzhou, 730030, China

E-mail:954914142@qq.com

Shu-wen WANG*

College of electrical engineering, Northwest University For Nationalities, Lanzhou, 730030, China

E-mail: shuwenwang@163.com

Cong MA

College of electrical engineering, Northwest University For Nationalities, Lanzhou, 730030, China

E-mail:1216881372@qq.com

Bing-kun PI

College of electrical engineering, Northwest University For Nationalities, Lanzhou, 730030, China

E-mail:294171424@qq.com

There are two major limitations with the existing retinal blood vessels segmentation method: high computational complexity and poor real-time capability. In order to overcome these limitations, this paper proposes a simple retinal image segmentation algorithm based on threshold segmentation. Firstly we select a point in the gray image and compares this point and other points for differences in gray value. Through this method, we can determine whether this point is on the blood vessels image. Secondly,, we set the threshold to eliminate noise, according to the connectivity of blood vessels. Finally, we obtain the retinal image segmentation results, which demonstrate that this algorithm can effectively extract the retinal blood vessels distribution, which has a good reference value.

Keywords: Retinal vascular images; Blood vessels image segmentation; Threshold segmentation.

*Corresponding author.

1. Introduction

Retinal blood vessel is the only deep microvascular in the human body what can be directly observed without any trauma, its physiological status check is very important for the diagnosis and treatment of some disease, just like high blood pressure, diabetes, atherosclerosis and other cardiovascular diseases. More importantly, the shape and structure of the retina cannot be obtained by naked eye, it have very strong concealment, at the same time the possibility of forgery is very low. Compared with face, iris and fingerprint identification system, the retina identification system is more difficult to be cheated; it is a more secure recognition system. it will have better application prospect in such aspects as identification and security.

At present, many scholars have done a thorough research about the fundus retinal vascular distribution at home and abroad. According to whether there need the characteristics of the data rules provided by standard image, the existing retinal blood vessels segmentation method divided into two categories: unsupervised method and monitoring method [1]. Unsupervised methods mainly include local filtering method, the locally adaptive threshold method [2] and blood vessel tracking method [3], etc. Supervised methods include blood vessels segmentation method based on ridge let[4] and pixel classification based on neural network[5]. However, through the analysis of the existent retinal blood vessel extraction method we can find that, most of the retinal blood vessel extraction algorithm of segmentation accuracy is not high, and they need very high computational complexity and their real-time performance are not strong. So it is difficult to have high request for real-time used in clinical widely.

To the two major defects in the existing retinal blood vessels segmentation method, the high computational complexity and real time capability is not strong, this paper proposes a simple retinal image segmentation algorithm based on threshold segmentation. First select a point in the gray image, comparing this point and other points of the difference of gray value. In this way we can find out whether this point is on the blood vessels image. The second step, according to the connectivity of blood vessels, by setting the threshold to eliminate noise. Finally we will obtain retinal image segmentation results. This algorithm can effectively extract retinal blood vessels distribution, and the computational complexity of it is not high, the real time capability of it is strong. It will have a good reference value.

2. The Retinal Image Segmentation Algorithm Based on Threshold Segmentation

The implementation process of the retinal image segmentation algorithm based on threshold segmentation: First, convert color images to gray image, and then to get the image pixel inversion and using adaptive image enhancement to enhance the image. Second, determine whether there is a blood vessel image by comparing the grey value of the point with the grey value of the surrounding matrix in size, and then set the threshold to determine whether this point is that points on the image for blood vessels. Last, get the target image by setting the length of blood vessels to be the threshold for filtering.

2.1. *The preprocessing of retinal image*

From Figure 1 and Figure 2 we can find that: the original image is color image, and the blood vessels are deep red mesh lines; the target image is black and white image, and the blood vessels are white mesh lines. If we want to vascular images, extracted from the original, we need to preprocess the original image at first.

The first step, convert color images to grayscale. As shown in Figure 3, after converted to grayscale the color of blood vessels became to gray, and they are not very obvious, compared with the original the image resolution was decreased.

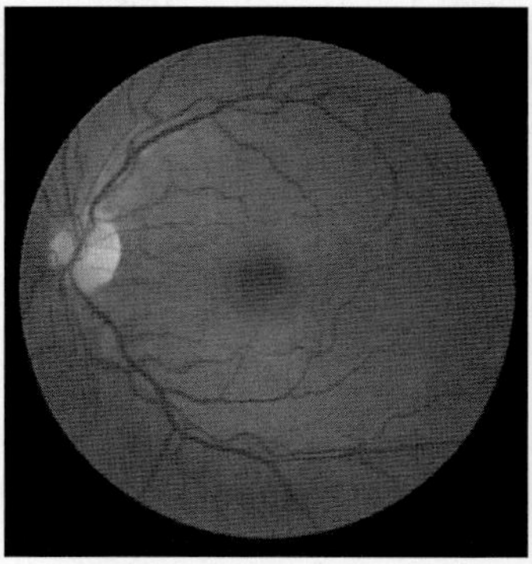

Fig.1. The original image.

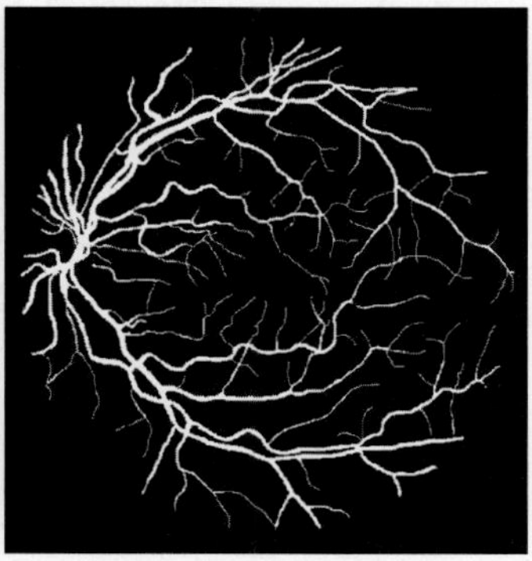

Fig. 2. Result of manual segmentation.

The second step, as shown in Figure 4: get the inversion image of gray image in pixels, and highlights the blood vessel image. The result is not very clear.

So the Figure 4 needs to be enhanced. We can enhance the image contrast to get the enhanced images.

Specific method of contrast enhancement: set the threshold of contrast ratio, the threshold contrast within the scope of expanding into the global; put the scope of the threshold into the global.

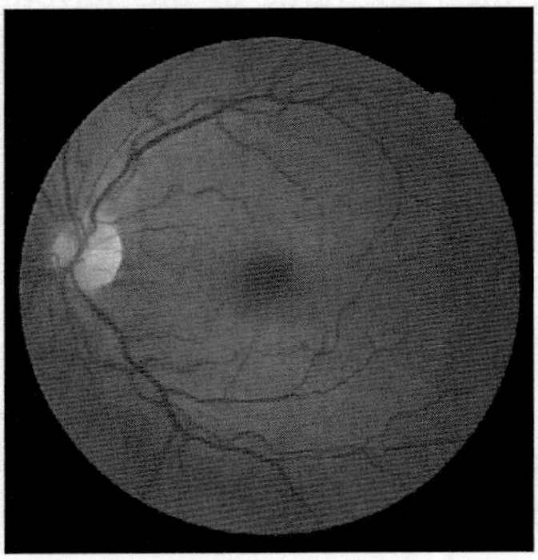

Fig. 3. Grayscale.

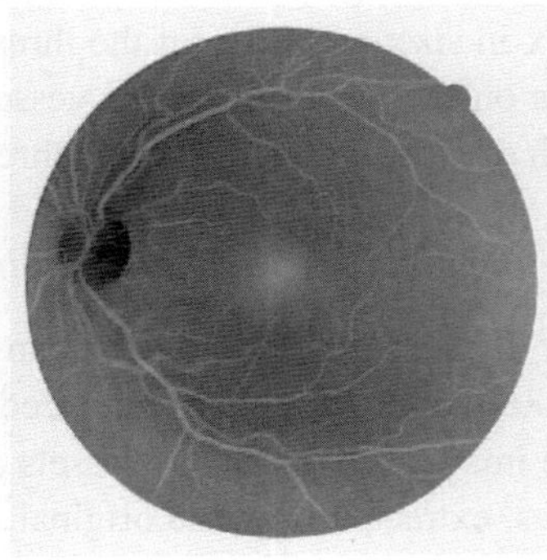

Fig. 4. The result of pixel inversion.

Given an image, the pixels in the image are divided into two categories, C1 and C2, according to the threshold t. The C1 class contains all the pixels whose gray value is in the range of $[0,\dots,t]$. The C2 class contains all the pixels whose gray value is in the range of $[t+1,\dots,255]$. The probability distribution of the two kinds of grey value is:

$$w_1 = \Pr(C_1) = \sum_{i=0}^{t} p_i = w(t)\,. \tag{1}$$

$$\mathrm{w}_2 = \Pr(\mathrm{C}_2) = \sum_{\mathrm{i}=0}^{\mathrm{t}} \mathrm{p}_\mathrm{i} = 1 - \mathrm{w}(\mathrm{t})\,. \tag{2}$$

As the contrast range of Figure 4 is not big, it delimits the scope of the threshold. So the enhancement effect will not obvious if we just enhance contrast only once. Multiple contrast enhancements can obtain more effect. From Figure 5 and Figure 6 we can find that: after 4 times enhancements, the distribution of the retina has been obviously.

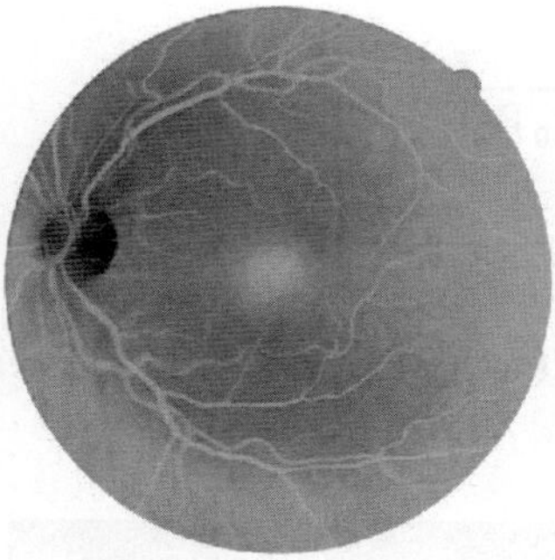

Fig. 5. Enhance contrast once.

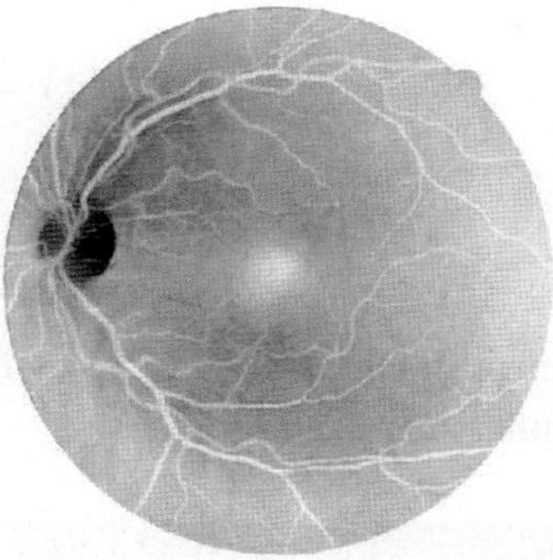

Fig. 6. Enhance contrast 4 times.

2.2. *Setting threshold to get retinal blood vessels*

Through the analysis of retinal blood vessels it is not hard to find that: the brightness of the retinal blood vessels and other parts has obvious difference, and the retinal blood vessels have obvious connectivity. According to these two characteristics, this article decide to determine whether there is a blood vessel image by comparing the difference of the grey values between the point and the surrounding points within the matrix .The specific process: one by one to compare the grey value of the point and the point within the surrounding 11×11 matrix. And record the number of which pixels have the greater grey value. If the number is between 1 and 55 the point will be judged to be one of the blood vessels, and make its grey value to be 1 (binary image).Because the pixel gray value and neighborhood spatial relationships are involved, so this paper use two-dimensional maximum entropy method to determine the threshold. The two kinds of entropy are defined as follows:

$$H_0(s,t) = -\sum_{i=0}^{s}\sum_{j=0}^{t} P0_{ij}(s,t)\log P0_{ij}(s,t). \tag{3}$$

$$\mathrm{H_1(s,t)} = -\sum_{\mathrm{i=s+1}}^{\mathrm{L-1}}\sum_{\mathrm{j=t+1}}^{\mathrm{L-1}} \mathrm{P1_{ij}(s,t)\log P1_{ij}(s,t)}. \tag{4}$$

Among the two formulas $P0_{ij}$ and $P1_{ij}$ are:

$$P0_{ij}(s,t) = \frac{P_{ij}}{\sum_{K=0}^{s}\sum_{J=0}^{t} P_{KJ}} \quad . \tag{5}$$

$$P1_{ij}(s,t) = \frac{P_{ij}}{\sum_{K=s+1}^{L-1}\sum_{I=t+1}^{L-1} P_{KI}} \quad . \tag{6}$$

Select the threshold vector (s,t) makes $H(s,t) = H_0(s,t) + H_1(s,t)$ reaches maximum value.

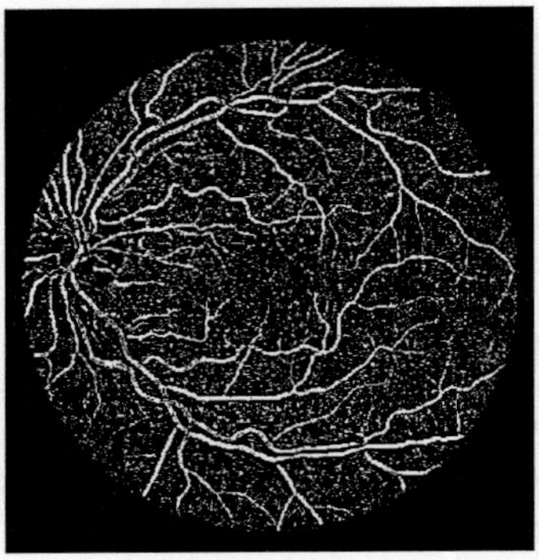

Fig. 7. The extraction result of Figure 5.

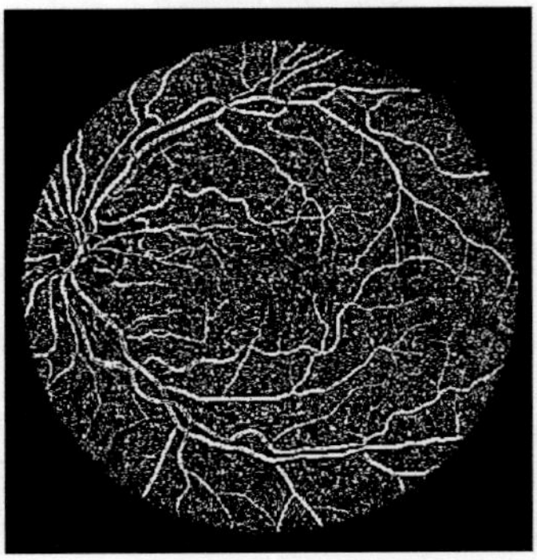

Fig. 8. The extraction result of Figure 6.

After the preliminary judgment, vascular image has obvious emerged. The processing results of Figure 5 and Figure 6 are Figure 7 and Figure 8 respectively. The details in the results of Figure 7 and Figure 8 are clear, but there are more noise in Figure 8.

2.3. *Set a threshold to remove noise*

Through the Figure 7 and Figure 8 we can clearly distinguish the retinal blood vessels, but there still have very much noise, especially in Figure 8, which will cause many problems for clinical application in the future. So we need to remove the noise. There are many ways to remove the noise and we use the threshold denoising method. Because the entire blood vessel image is continuous, if we selecting appropriate length threshold for the part of the continuous, we will remove noise.

Target and background are assumed to be two kind of different probability distribution:

$$\frac{p_0}{P_T}, \frac{p_1}{P_T}, \dots, \frac{p_t}{P_T} . \tag{7}$$

And

$$\frac{p_{t+1}}{1-P_T}, \frac{p_{t+2}}{1-P_T}, \dots, \frac{p_{L-1}}{1-P_T} . \tag{8}$$

Definition:

$$H_B(t) = -\sum_{i=0}^{t} \frac{p_i}{P_T} \log_2 \frac{p_i}{P_T} . \tag{9}$$

$$H_W(t) = -\sum_{i=t+1}^{L-1} \frac{p_i}{1-P_T} \log_2 \frac{p_i}{1-P_T} . \tag{10}$$

The best threshold is t which can make $H_B(t) + H_W(t)$ to be the maximum entropy:

$$t = \text{Arg}\{\text{Max}\{H_B(t) + H_W(t)\}\} . \tag{11}$$

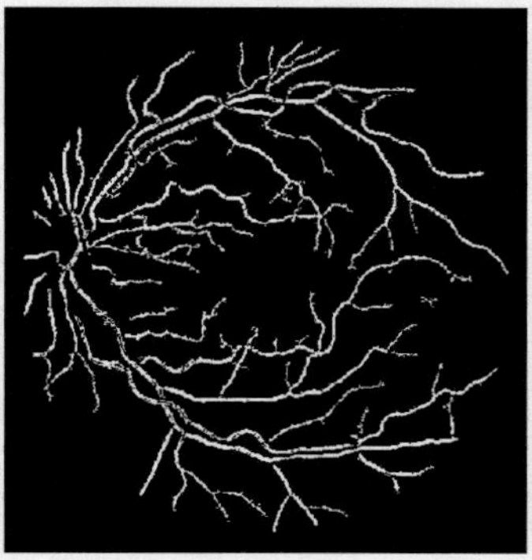

Fig. 9. Figure 7 after denoising.

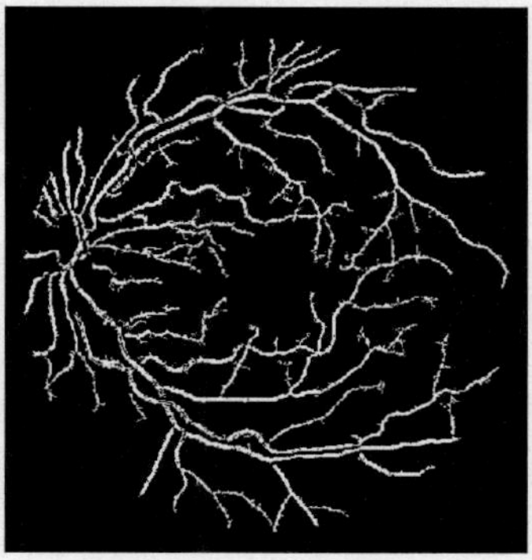

Fig. 10. Figure 8 after denoising.

Selecting different threshold for Figure 7 and Figure 8, the denoising results is Figures 9 and 10.

3. Analysis of Experimental Results

Varying degrees of image enhancement will get different segmentation results. However, the image enhancement will cause image distortion when it is too strong. So this paper has carried on the two experiments, splitting two images which have been enhanced once and twice separately, comparing the results with the manual segmentation result. The experimental results are as follows:

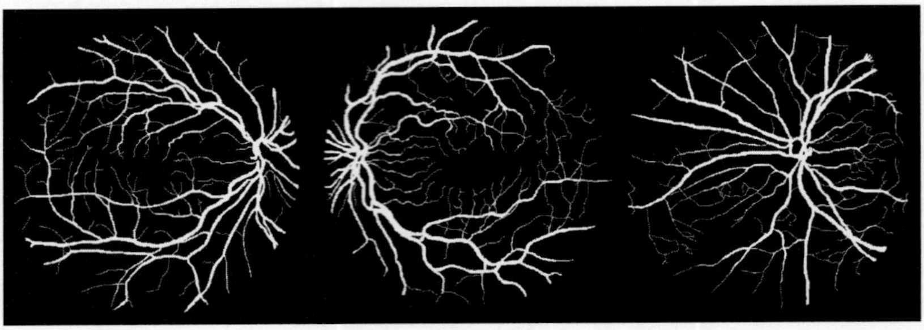

Fig. 11. Manual segmentation results.

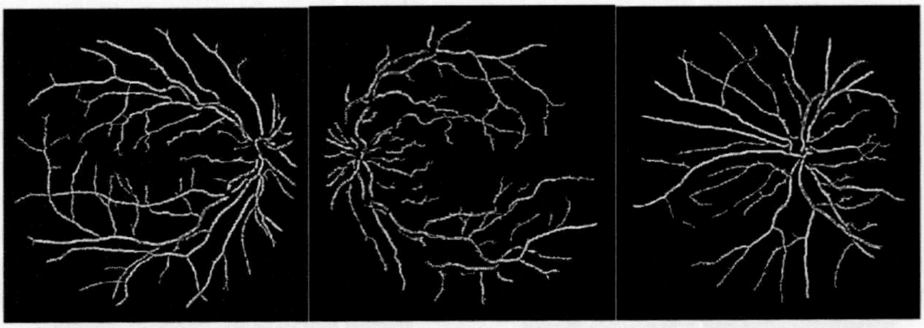

Fig. 12. The segmentation results with the algorithm of this paper (image is enhanced once).

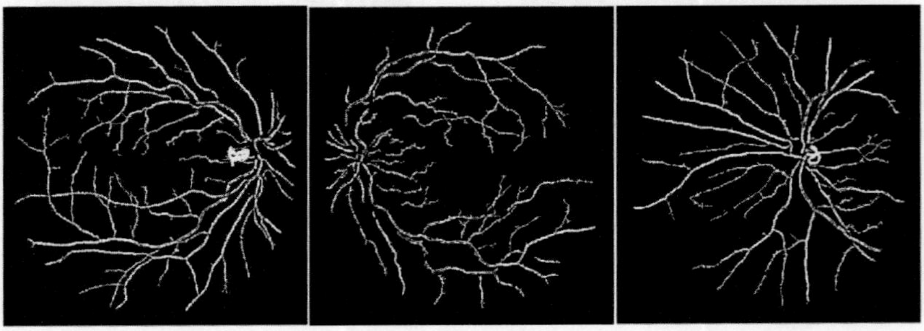

Fig. 13. The segmentation results with the algorithm of this paper (image is enhanced twice).

First of all, take the accuracy as the key. Through the comparison of Figure 11 and Figure 12 and Figure 13 we can find that: the algorithm of this paper has high accuracy and it can find out the basic framework and main branches of the retinal image accurately. Although the result of the images which was enhanced twice compared with the result of the images which was enhanced once is much better in the details, but there is not a big difference between them.

On the other hand, take the running time as the key. Comparing the running time of two experiments there was so little difference between them, as shown in Table 1. In this paper, the running time of this algorithm consists of three parts: the preprocessing of retinal image, determine whether there is a blood vessel image, remove the noise. Algorithm in this paper takes about 33 seconds to get the target image on average, has a good real-time performance.

Table 1. The running time of two experiments.

Sequence number	Enhanced once	Enhanced twice
1	29.406	34.687
2	33.984	39.27
3	32.688	31.781
4	33.531	33.266
5	32.672	34.203

4. Conclusion

The existing methods of retinal blood vessels segmentation have two problems, the high computational complexity and the weak real-time performance. For the two problems, this paper puts forward a simple retinal image segmentation algorithm based on threshold segmentation. First, convert color images to gray image, and then to get the image pixel inversion and using adaptive image enhancement to enhance the image. Second , determine whether there is a blood vessel image by comparing the grey value of the point with the grey value of the surrounding matrix in size, and then set the threshold to determine whether this point is that points on the image for blood vessels. At last, get the target image by setting the length of blood vessels to be the threshold for filtering. The experiments prove that, the algorithm of this paper can segment the fundus images of blood vessels effectively, and it has high accuracy and strong instantaneity. Because this algorithm still have some shortage in the blood vessels image segmentation and image denoising, so in this paper, the segmentation results have some problems like details missing and partial distortion. How to avoid these deficiencies, further improve the accuracy of segmentation, will be the future research direction.

Acknowledgments

This work is supported by the National Natural Science Foundation of China (No.61261042) and the scientific research innovation team about the key technologies of Internet of Things of Northwest University For Nationalities.

References

1. Fraz M M, Remagnino P, Hoppe A, et al. Blood vessel segmentation methodologiesin retinal images-a survey[J]. Computer Methods and Programs in Biomedicine, 2012, 108(1): 407-X33.
2. AI-Rawi M, Qutaishat M, Arrar M. An improved matched filter for blood vessel detection of digital retinal images[J]. Computers in Biology and Medicine, 2007, 37(2): 262-267.
3. Saleh M D, Eswaran C. An efficient algorithm for retinal blood vessel segmentation using h-maxima transform and multilevel thresholding[J]. Computer Methods in Biome-chanics and Biomedical Engineering, 2012, 15(5): 517-525.
4. Yin Y, Adel M, Bourenname S. Retinal vessel segmentation using a probabilistic tracking method[J]. Pattern Recognition, 2012, 45(4): 1235-1244.
5. Wu C H, Derwent J J K, Stanchev P. Retinal vessel radius estimation and a vessel center line segmentation method based on ridge descriptors[J]. Journal of Signal Processing Systems for Signal Image and Video Technology, 2009, 55(1-3): 91-102.

A Rapid Object Detection Algorithm Based on Deformable Part Models

Chun-wei LI*, Hong-tao YU, Shao-mei LI and You-jun BU
National Digital Switching System Engineering & Technological R&D Center, Zhengzhou, 450002, China
**E-mail: lichunwei15@126.com*

To solve the speed bottleneck of deformable part models in the detection process, this paper proposes a cascade deformable part model with rapid computation of feature pyramids. As the speed of the detection is largely determined by feature computation and object location, we propose a two-stage acceleration method. Sparsely-sampled feature pyramids on the scale are firstly utilized to approximate finely-sampled feature pyramids and then combined with the cascade algorithm in the location process. The resultant sequence model is utilized to evaluate parts sequentially so as to rapidly remove most object hypotheses of small possibilities. The experimental results on Pascal VOC 2007 dataset and INRIA dataset demonstrate that the proposed method accelerates the speed of detection with minor loss in detection precision.

Keywords: Deformable part model; Feature computation; Cascade detection.

1. Introduction

Object detection is one of the key technologies and research hotspots in computer vision. As one of the most popular object detection algorithms currently, Deformable Part Model (DPM) [1] has achieved excellent results in the famous PASCAL VOC challenge in the field of object detection and has been extended to pedestrian detection, face detection and many other fields. But the extraction of Histogram of Oriented Gradient (HOG) [2] pyramids and object location of DPM require high computing cost and can't satisfy actual application requirements. For this reason, researchers have carried out a series of researches on the acceleration of DPM in recent years. The existing DPM accelerating researches mainly focus on the following two aspects:

Acceleration of single-category DPM [3,4] pruned unpromising object hypotheses to reduce computing cost. The former required a special recognition dataset. The latter utilized the hierarchical part model with multiple resolutions to judge object hypotheses. [7] optimized the order of the filter evaluation through an active part selection which is similar to [3]. [5] searched for global optimal classification results in all possible image regions but its effectiveness greatly depends on the robustness of the boundary. [6] utilized GPU in parallel but it required higher requirements for computer hardware.

Acceleration of multi-category DPM [8, 9] utilized linear combination of a number of parts to compress the number of effective parts used in the model. These approaches obtained detection results of category hierarchies by learning a set of shared parts. [10] utilized locality sensitive hashing algorithm to approximate convolution computation.

In summary, the main focus of current researches is to speed up the object location, however pays less attention to accelerate feature computation. So as to further accelerate the speed of DPM, the acceleration problem of feature computation should be considered. Therefore we propose a two-stage accelerating algorithm for DPM: firstly utilizing sparsely-sampled feature pyramids on the scale to accelerate the process of feature computation; and then utilizing cascade algorithm to accelerate the process of object location. For ease of narration, we call the proposed approach as Cascade Deformable Part Model with Fast Feature Pyramid (FCDPM).

2. Fast Feature Pyramids Based on Power Law

In the sliding window model based on multiscale feature pyramids to solve the problem that the model size is not the same as the object size, it needs to extract image feature under every scale and position to generate fine feature pyramids. The feature obtained has high accuracy but with high computation cost. Some researchers have found the features between scales satisfy the power law [11,12]. Therefore we propose to utilize the power law and have a choice to compute features of some reference scales and then the features of reference scales are utilized to approximate that of nearby scales.

2.1. *HOG feature approximate computation between scales*

This section gives a brief introduction about the power law of the statistics of multiscale images. Let I denote the target image and let I_s denote I at scale s. The size $h_s \times g_s$ of I_s is s times the size $h \times g$ of I. Let Ω be HOG feature mapping function and computes the corresponding HOG features: $C = \Omega(I)$. We define $f_\Omega(I_s)$ as:

$$f_\Omega(I_s) \equiv \frac{1}{h_s g_s s} \sum_{ijs} C_s(i,j,s) \text{where } C_s = \Omega(I_s)\,. \tag{1}$$

Thus $f_\Omega(I_s)$ denotes the global mean of C_s computed over locations (i, j) and scale s of the image$I$.

Let $\Phi(I)$ denote the statistic of I and $E[\cdot]$ denote the mathematical expectation over an ensemble of images. According to [20], the ratio of $E[\Phi(I_{s1})]/E[\Phi(I_{s2})]$ computed over at scales $s1$ and $s2$ depends only on the ratio of $s1/s2$. Thus obtained the power law followed by $E[\Phi(I_s)]$:

$$E[\Phi(I_{s1})]/E[\Phi(I_{s2})] = (s1/s2)^{-\lambda_\Phi}. \tag{2}$$

If decomposing an image I into K smaller images $I^1 \dots I^K$, thus we can obtain $I = [I^1 \dots I^K]$. Because HOG is shift invariant and ignoring boundaries, $\Omega(I) = \Omega([I^1 \dots I^K]) \approx [\Omega(I^1) \dots \Omega(I^K)]$. According to this conclusion we obtain:

$$f_\Omega(I) \approx \sum f_\Omega(I^k)/K\,. \tag{3}$$

That means $f_\Omega(I) \approx E[f_\Omega(I^k)]$. Substituting into Eq. (1) yields:

$$f_\Omega(I_{s1})/f_\Omega(I_{s2}) \approx (s1/s2)^{-\lambda_\Omega}\,. \tag{4}$$

Using the above power law, let $s1 = s, s2 = 1$ of Eq. (4), thus we obtain$f_\Omega(I_s) \approx f_\Omega(I)s^{-\lambda_\Omega}$. This conclusion applies not only to the original image, but also to sampling window ω of I and ω_s of I_s. Expanding yields:

$$\frac{1}{|\omega_s|}\sum_{i,j\in\omega_s} C_s(i,j) \approx \frac{1}{|\omega|}\sum_{i,j\in\omega} C(i,j)\, s^{-\lambda_\Omega}\,. \tag{5}$$

Because $\sum_{\omega_s} C'/|\omega_s| \approx \sum_\omega C/|\omega|$, then $C' \approx \mathrm{R}(C, s)$, we can obtain:

$$C_s \approx \mathrm{R}(C, s) \cdot s^{-\lambda_\Omega}\,. \tag{6}$$

Therefore we utilize the information contained in $C = \Omega(I)$ to approximate C_s.

2.2. *HOG feature pyramid approximate computation*

Standard feature pyramid computation of DPM is to compute $C_s = \Omega(\mathrm{R}(I, s))$ at every scale s. There are 10 scales per octave in DPM, C_s needs to repeat the computation of 10 times to extract multiscale features. The above approximate computation of HOG features is extended to the approximate computation of HOG feature pyramid. Firstly we begin to compute $C_{s'} = \Omega(\mathrm{R}(I, s'))$ by choosing several reference scales based on the average interval (for instance choosing one reference scale per octave, that means $s' \in \{1, 1/2, 1/4, \dots\}$). The rest intermediate scales are to compute $C_s \approx R(C_{s'}, s/s')(s/s')^{-\lambda_\Omega}$ based on the nearest reference scale. The diagram of the computation process is shown in Figure 1.

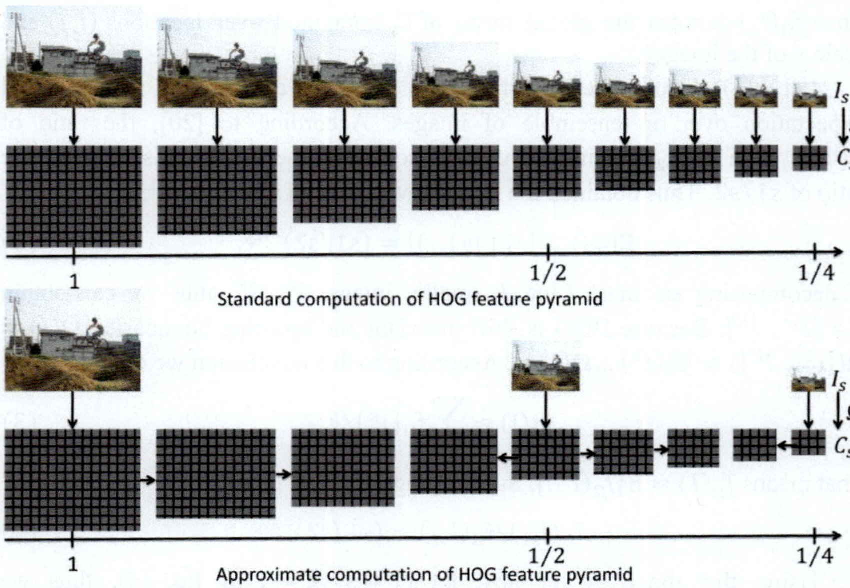

Fig. 1. Approximate computation of HOG feature pyramid (Top: standard computation of HOG feature pyramid; Bottom: approximate computation of HOG feature pyramid).

3. Object Location of DPM with Cascade Algorithm

3.1. *Object location process of DPM*

This section begins with a brief introduction about object location of DPM. DPM is a two-layer model, in which the root filter w_0 is to describe the overall contour of target objects and n parts allow for a certain displacement relative to the root filter to describe details of target objects and deformation features. The i-th part is composed by filter w_i and deformation model $d_i (i = 1, \dots, n)$. An object hypothesis is defined by $\{p_0, p_1, \dots, p_n\}$, among them p_0 indicates the position of w_0 and p_t indicates the position of the t-th part.In order to detect the position of the target object, we compute the overall score of the object hypothesis according to the most likely part configuration:

$$\mathrm{score}(p_0) = \max_{p_1, \dots, p_n} \mathrm{score}(p_0, \dots, p_n) \,. \tag{7}$$

where

$$\mathrm{score}(p_0, \dots, p_n) = w_0^T \phi_\alpha(p_0, H) + \sum_{i=1}^{n} w_i^T \phi_\alpha(p_i, H) - d_i^T \phi_d(p_i, p_0) + b. \tag{8}$$

and H indicates the previously computed HOG feature pyramid of I, ϕ_α indicates the HOG feature of the corresponding position and ϕ_d indicates the deformation feature. b is to distinguish different components.

For an object hypothesis $\{p_0, p_1, \dots, p_n\}$, we only know the root position p_0 and then the part position p_t is computed by maximizing the part appearance score minus the deformation cost caused by the displacement relative to the root:

$$p_i = \underset{p}{\operatorname{argmax}}\, w_i^T \phi_\alpha(p, H) - d_i^T \phi_d(p, p_0)\,. \tag{9}$$

where p indicates the possible location of parts.

3.2. *Rapid object location with cascade algorithm*

In DPM, the overall score is required to computed at every window position of every scale which includes performance scores and deformation costs of all parts. However objects are usually found in a limited set of positions, thus we propose to combine cascade algorithm in the process of object location. In DPM with $n+1$ parts (including the root filter), a global threshold T and a sequence of $2n(t_1, t'_1, t_2, t'_2 \dots, t_n, t'_n)$ intermediate thresholds are utilized to construct a sequence model. At every root position $p_0 \in H$, the score is evaluated by carrying out n stages (needs to evaluate n parts). In every stage of the evaluation, there are two chances for pruning.

If the score at the position p_0 with the first $l(l = 1, \dots, n)$ parts, that means $w_0^T \phi_\alpha(p_0, H) + \sum_{i=1}^{l-1} w_i^T \phi_\alpha(p_i, H) - d_i^T \phi_d(p_i, p_0) < t_l$, the object hypothesis at position p_0 is pruned directly without evaluating the scores of $w_l \sim w_n$ parts.When computing the score of part w_l, we need to search over $\delta \in p$ relative to root position p_0. If the score of first l parts minus $\phi_d(\delta, p_0)$ is below the intermediate threshold t'_l, that means $w_0^T \phi_\alpha(p_0, H) + \left(\sum_{i=1}^{l-1} w_i^T \phi_\alpha(p_i, H) - d_i^T \phi_d(p_i, p_0)\right) - d_l^T \phi_d(\delta, p_0) < t'_l$, δ is skipped.

4. Cascade Deformable Part Model with Fast Feature Pyramid

For proposed algorithm of FCDPM, sparsely-sampled feature pyramids on the scale and the cascade algorithm are utilized to speed up the process of object detection. The corresponding algorithm is shown below:

Input: detected image I;

filter$\{w_0, w_1, \dots, w_n\}$;deformation model$\{d_1, \dots, d_n\}$;

global thresholdT;intermediate threshold$(t_1, t'_1, t_2, t'_2 \dots, t_n, t'_n)$;

Output: position collection of target objects$D$;

FOR $s = s_i (i = 1, \dots, m)$
$C_{s_i} = \Omega(\mathrm{R}(I, s_i))$
    FOR $s = s_{ik} (k = 1, \dots, r)$
$C_{s_{ik}} \approx \mathrm{R}(C_{s_i}, s_{ik}) \cdot {s_{ik}}^{-\lambda_\Omega}$
    END FOR
END FOR
$H \leftarrow \{(C_{s_1}, C_{s_{11}}, \dots, C_{s_{1r}}), \dots, (C_{s_m}, C_{s_{m1}}, \dots, C_{s_{mr}})\}$
$D \leftarrow \emptyset$
FOR $p_0 \in H$
$s = w_0^T \phi_a(p_0, H)$
  FOR $i = \{1, \dots, n\}$
  IF $s < t_i$ THEN PRUNE p_0
    FOR $\delta \in p$
      IF $s - d_i^T \phi_d(\delta, p_0) < t'_i$ THEN PRUNE δ
$q = \max_p w_i^T \phi_a(p, H) - d_i^T \phi_d(p, p_0)$
    END FOR
$s = s + q$
  END FOR
  IF $s \geq \mathrm{T}$ THEN $D \leftarrow D \cup \{p_0\}$
END FOR
RETURN D

5. Experimental Results

5.1. *Experiment preparation*

In order to evaluate the performance of the proposed algorithm, the average precision (AP) is used as the evaluation index. Experiments are conducted on PASCAL VOC 2007 dataset and INRIA dataset compared with original DPM and some other acceleration algorithms. AP is defined as follows:

$$\mathrm{AP} = \int \mathrm{Precision(Recall)\,dRecall}\ . \tag{10}$$

The bigger the value of AP $\in [0,1]$, the better the performance of the algorithm.

5.2. *Experimental Results of Pascal VOC 2007*

Pascal VOC 2007 is a generic object detection dataset which includes 20 categories of object images. Through above description, let nApp denote the number of scales approximated by one nearest reference scale. When nApp = 0, that is the finely-sampled multiscale feature pyramid. We first discuss the effect on AP and detection speed relative to DPM of different values of nApp. The corresponding results are shown in Figure 2.

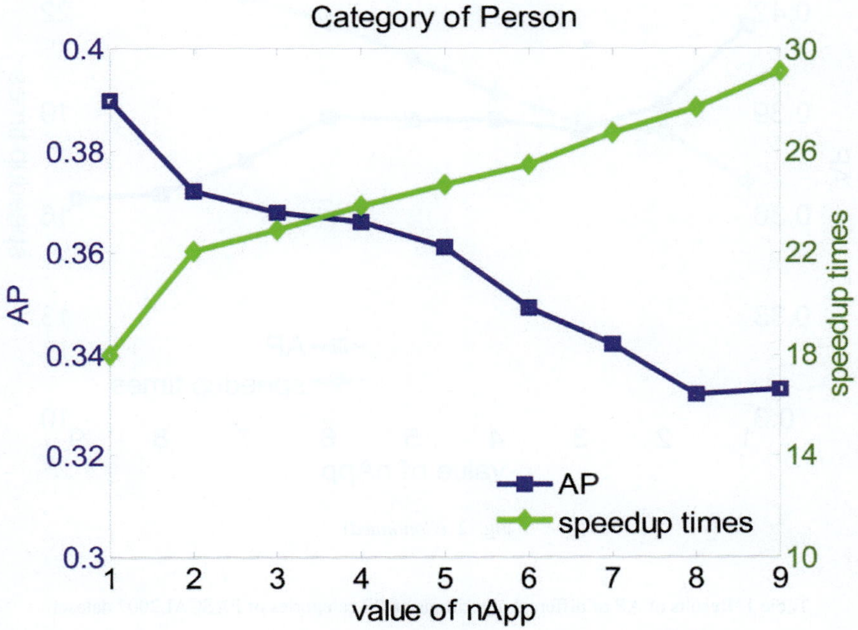

Fig. 2. Effects of different values of nApp on the detection speed and precision.

We can find that the overall trend of AP is to continue to decline with the increase of nApp and the overall trend of speedup times relative to DPM is to continue to rise. This shows that the bigger the value of nApp the faster the detection speed and the smaller the value of AP. Therefore the proposed algorithm can achieve a balance between detection accuracy and precision through adjusting the value of nApp.

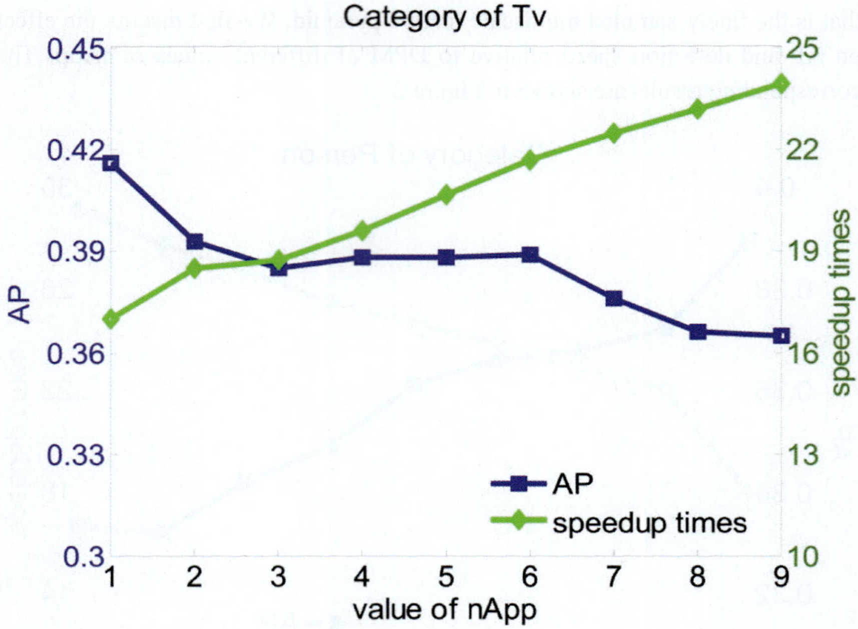

Fig. 2. (*Continued*)

Table 1. Results of AP of different algorithms on 20 categories of PASCAL2007 dataset.

	Aero	Bicycle	Bird	Boat	Bottle	Bus	Car	Cat	Chair	Cow
DPM	32.1%	59.9%	10.6%	13.5%	24.9%	47.7%	48.9%	27.5%	17.4%	27.0%
CSC	33.6%	58.5%	10.2%	13.4%	25.0%	44.7%	49.2%	28.0%	17.1%	27.2%
CF	27.6%	58.6%	10.5%	10.6%	16.5%	52.7%	42.1%	27.6%	12.9%	29.1%
BB	30.6%	53.9%	8.7%	10.4%	22.5%	43.2%	38.9%	17.5%	13.5%	22.6%
$FCDPM_9$	35.9%	57.6%	8.4%	11.8%	26.9%	44.3%	48.1%	18.0%	14.7%	22.8%
$FCDPM_5$	35.5%	58.6%	10.2%	11.6%	27.4%	46.5%	50.6%	19.4%	16.4%	23.4%
$FCDPM_1$	37.0%	59.6%	10.3%	11.2%	27.4%	44.3%	50.8%	20.6%	17.9%	23.0%

Dog	Horse	Mbike	Person	Plant	Sheep	Sofa	Table	Train	Tv	Mean
14.4%	57.4%	50.0%	38.4%	13.3%	21.0%	36.8%	31.1%	47.5%	42.3%	33.0%
13.5%	57.7%	50.0%	38.5%	14.1%	21.6%	36.8%	28.6%	47.4%	42.0%	32.8%
15.3%	55.2%	44.6%	26.3%	12.4%	22.7%	38.6%	32.8%	44.8%	32.2%	30.6%
9.0%	55.7%	47.2%	27.4%	11.1%	17.1%	28.3%	23.3%	44.5%	38.4%	28.2%
8.7%	55.3%	46.0%	33.3%	13.3%	19.2%	29.5%	25.9%	44.5%	36.5%	30.0%
9.9%	53.2%	47.0%	36.6%	15.0%	22.8%	32.4%	26.8%	43.1%	38.8%	31.3%
11.6%	57.9%	50.8%	39.0%	15.2%	23.5%	34.4%	26.0%	47.0%	41.6%	32.4%

In Tab. 1, we compare proposed FCDPM with original DPM and several other speedup algorithms, including CSC[3], CF[4] and BB[5] in Pascal VOC 2007 dataset. The subscript of FCDPM indicates the value of nApp.

Table 2. Average running time (measured by second) on PASCAL2007 dataset.

	Feature Computation	Location	Sum	Speedup times
DPM	0.376	9.197	9.573	1.00
CSC	0.376	0.439	0.815	11.74
CF	0.548	0.438	0.986	9.71
BB	0.376	1.287	1.663	5.53
$FCDPM_9$	0.090	0.251	0.341	28.10
$FCDPM_5$	0.110	0.275	0.385	24.87
$FCDPM_1$	0.193	0.318	0.511	18.73

The average feature computation time, location time, full time and speedup times relative to DPM of the 20 categories are reported in Tab. 2. According to Tab. 2, CSC, CF and BB have achieved a speedup of about 10 times compared with original DPM and the proposed method runs almost 30 times faster than original DPM. When nApp = 9, FCDPM achieves the fastest speedup times but the drop of AP is also the most. Taken a comprehensive consideration of detection precision and speed, the method in the paper has great advantages over CF and BB. When nApp = 1, the mean AP is 32.4% which is similar to CSC and the detection speed is 1.6 times of CSC.

5.3. *Experimental results of INRIA*

INRIA is a common pedestrian detection dataset. The results of AP of above algorithms on INRIA dataset is shown in Figure 3. The running time is reported in Tab. 3. It can be found that FCDPM obtains similar detection results in the field of pedestrian detection.

Table 3. Average running time (measured by second) on INRIA dataset.

	Feature Computation	Location	Sum	Speedup times
DPM	0.766	14.425	15.191	1.00
CSC	0.766	0.670	1.441	10.54
CF	1.242	0.445	1.687	9.00
BB	0.766	1.477	2.243	6.77
$FCDPM_9$	0.157	0.323	0.480	31.65
$FCDPM_5$	0.212	0.354	0.566	26.84
$FCDPM_1$	0.326	0.443	0.769	19.75

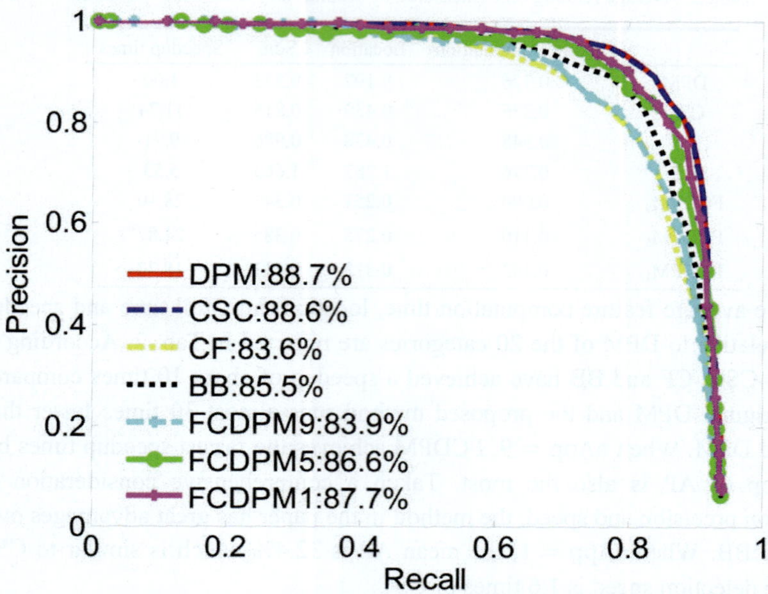

Fig. 3. Recall-Precision curves of different algorithms on INRIA dataset.

6. Conclusion

For the detection process of DPM, in the paper we propose a two-stage acceleration method to speed up the detection process: firstly sparsely-sampled feature pyramids on the scale are utilized to speed up the process of feature computation; then cascade algorithm is utilized to speed up the process of object location thereby significantly improving the detection speed of the model. The experimental results on Pascal VOC 2007 dataset and INRIA dataset show that the algorithm in the paper apparently accelerates the speed of detection with minor loss in detection precision. The next step is to speed up the convolution computation in the process of detection which is complementary to previous work [8]. It is expected to obtain a significant effect of acceleration when combined with each other; and it also can be combined with current popular object proposals [13] to further accelerate the detection speed.

Acknowledgments

This work is supported by 2014BAH30B01 of the Chinese National Key Technology Support Program and 61521003,61572519 of the Chinese National Natural Science Foundation.

References

1. Felzenszwalb P, Girshick R, McAllester D, et al. Object detection with discriminatively trained part based models [J]. IEEE Transactions on Pattern Analysis and Machine Intelligence, 2010, 32 (9): 1627-1645.
2. Dalal N and Triggs B. Histograms of oriented gradients for human detection [C], Proceedings of the IEEE Computer Society Conference on Computer Vision and Pattern Recognition, 2005: 886-893.
3. Felzenszwalb P, Girshick R, McAllester D. Cascade Object Detection with Deformable Part Models[C]. Proceedings of IEEE Computer Society Conference on Computer Vision and Pattern Recognition, 2010:2241-2248.
4. Pedersoli M, Vedaldi A, Gonzàlez J, et al. A coarse-to-fine approach for fast deformable object detection[J]. Pattern Recognition, 2015, 48(7):1844-1853.
5. Kokkinos I. Bounding Part Scores for Rapid Detection with Deformable Part Models[C]. Proceedings of the 12th European Conference on Computer Vision, 2012: 41-50.
6. Gadeski E, Fard H O, Borgne H L. GPU deformable part model for object recognition[J]. Journal of Real-Time Image Processing, 2014: 1-13.
7. Zhu M, Atanasov N, Pappas G J, et al. Active Deformable Part Models Inference[C]. Proceedings of the 13th European Conference on Computer Vision, 2014:281-296.
8. Song H O, Girshick R, Zickler S, et al. Generalized Sparselet Models for Real-Time Multiclass Object Recognition[J]. IEEE Transactions on Pattern Analysis & Machine Intelligence, 2015, 37(5):1001-1012.
9. Pirsiavash H. Steerable part models[C]. Proceedings of the 2012 IEEE Computer Society Conference on Computer Vision and Pattern Recognition, 2012:3226-3233.
10. Dean T, Ruzon M, Segal M, et al. Fast, Accurate Detection of 100,000 Object Classes on a Single Machine[C]. Proceedings of the 14th International Conference on Computer Vision, 2013:1814-1821.

11. Ruderm D L. The statistics of natural images[J]. Network Computation in Neural Systems, 2009, 5(4):517-548.
12. Dollar P, Appel R, Belongie S, et al. Fast Feature Pyramids for Object Detection[J]. IEEE Transactions on Pattern Analysis & Machine Intelligence, 2014, 36(8):1-14.
13. Hosang J, Benenson R, Dollar P, et al. What makes for effective detection proposals?[J]. IEEE Transactions on Pattern Analysis & Machine Intelligence, 2015:1-12.

Simulation Study on Ground Operation Efficiency of Beijing New Airport Airfield Area

Hao-ning WU
Planning and Design Institute, China Airport Construction Group Corporation of CAAC, Beijing, 100101, China
E-mail: wuhaoning@vip.sina.com

Yan-chi GUO
Beijing New Airport Construction Headquarters, Capital Airports Holding Company, Beijing, 102600, China
E-mail: gyc10000@sina.com

Tong MU and Xiong LI†
Planning and Design Institute, China Airport Construction Group Corporation of CAAC, Beijing, 100101, China
†E-mail: lixiong_cacc@163.com

An effective and feasible analysis on airport ground operation efficiency and capacity is of great significance for the overall planning of an airport construction project. Utilizing the Beijing New Airport as the test location and applying the simulation software Simmod, the ground operation efficiency and the flight delay time in southward and northward operation directions of the airport is studied in this paper. Based on simulations and taking into account the configuration of terminal building, three apron taxiway operation patterns were proposed, analyzed, and compared through simulation. The simulation results indicate that under the current construction scheme, the Beijing New Airport is expected to run with an average ground delay time of 2.72 minutes for departure flights and 58 seconds for arrival flights in target year, which is of high operation efficiency. Over half of ground delays of departure flights is attributed to take-off waiting time, another 1/5 happens in the angle area between main buildings. When the three apron taxiways within the angle area operate in two-out and one-in pattern, ground delay time is minimized.

Keywords: Civil aviation; Airport capacity; Simulation; Beijing New Airport; Simmod.

1. Introduction

China has been witnessing rapid development of her aviation industry, which is now the second largest aviation system in the world, in these years. Needless to say, the soaring aviation market leaves the airport systems not many choices except enlarging the airport system scale to tackle the booming demand of capacity. Under such a context, as an alternative to relieve operation pressure of the Beijing Capital International Airport and to better the experience of air travelers in Beijing-Tianjin-Hebei region, construction of Beijing New Airport (Hereinafter referred to as BNA) is imperative. With the current plan of 4 runways (3 vertical and 1 horizontal), BNA is the first one who applies non-parallel runway configuration in China. Given the complicated runway configuration and characteristic design of terminal building in BNA, and to better direct the planning, design and operation of the new airport, it is necessary to conduct in-depth exploration into ground operation efficiency of its airfield area via computer simulation.

In general, there are three approaches to evaluate airport capacity and operation efficiency: data statistics, mathematical theory and computer simulation. (1) Method of data statistics is used to estimate airport capacity through drawing a capacity envelope graph based on existing statistical information of airport flow. As a frequently-used approach for capacity analysis in early stage, it accompanies disadvantages that it only evaluates established operation pattern of existing runway system in busy airport, which lacks prospectiveness [1,2]. (2) Approach of mathematical theory could be harnessed to calculate runway capacity through proposing proper assumption, establishing mathematical equations of airport ground operation parameters. It is mainly used for macroscopic capacity evaluation, lacking consideration on operation details and commonality [3,7]. (3) Approach of computer simulation is at present the most popular solution to evaluate airport capacity and efficiency. Via establishing operating environment and control rule models through simulation software, it reflects airport operation status with reality, and reaches to airport capacity based on analysis on simulated operation data [8,11]. Simmod and TAAM are the mainstream simulation modeling software for airport capacity evaluation [12].

Employing the BNA as research object and applying Simmod for computer simulation and modeling, in this paper a comprehensive analysis on airport ground operation efficiency under different conditions is performed, and recommended schemes are put forward. Conclusions in this paper might be a reference and instruction for planning, construction and operation pattern selecting of multi-runway systems in Chinese large airports.

2. Airfield Layout and Operation Rules of BNA

In current phase of the BNA construction project it is to build 4 runways for a yearly passenger throughput of 72 million. The layout of its airfield is shown in Fig. 1. The planned terminal building, targeting at a yearly passenger throughput of 45 million, applies a centralized combinational configuration, with the 5 concourses distributed in "centrally radial" shape. Taking the main landing direction as example, the runway operation pattern employed is: West 1 Runway (W1) and North 1 Runway (N1) only used for take-off; West 2 Runway (W2) and East 1 Runway (E1) mainly used for landing, and E1 could be used for assisted take-off in morning departure peak. Runways operate independently.

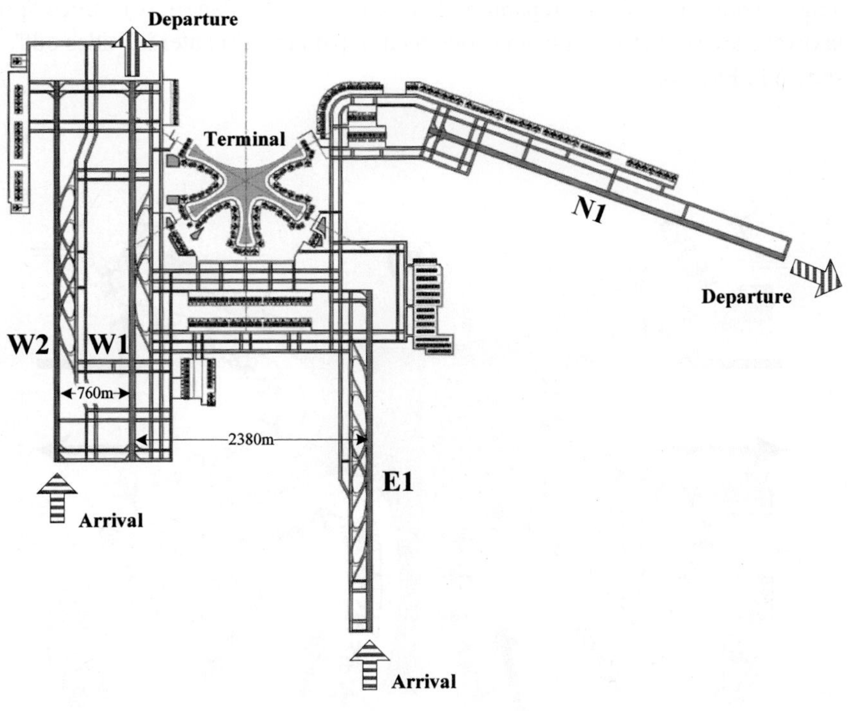

Fig. 1. Airfield layout and runway operation pattern of BNA.

Taxiing routes should be reasonably and appropriately setup, based on airport operation, by the principle that main taxiways such as parallel taxiways, western and eastern contact taxiways etc. should be operated in monodirectional fashion. Taxiway system of airfield could be divided into four areas based on the average taxiing speed (from 5km/h to 46km/h): push-out taxiway, apron taxiway, main taxiway and high speed taxiway.

Based on the terminal configuration of BNA, four "Harbours" (i.e. the angle area between concourses) are formed in the airside. In light of this and combing with the layout setting of apron taxiways, three apron operation patterns are considered in this paper: Pattern (a) - unidirectionally operated double apron taxiways are planned in angle area, as shown in Fig. 2(a). Pattern (b) - unidirectionally operated double apron taxiways are planned in angle area. In addition, a push-out waiting position is set in the meantime based on space in the area, satisfying push-out waiting of one E type plane and two C type planes, or two E type planes, as shown in Fig. 2(b). All departure flights must push to adjacent waiting slot for preparation before taxiing out. Pattern (c) - three apron taxiways are set in the angle area, operated in pattern of "center in, sides out", as shown in Fig. 2(c).

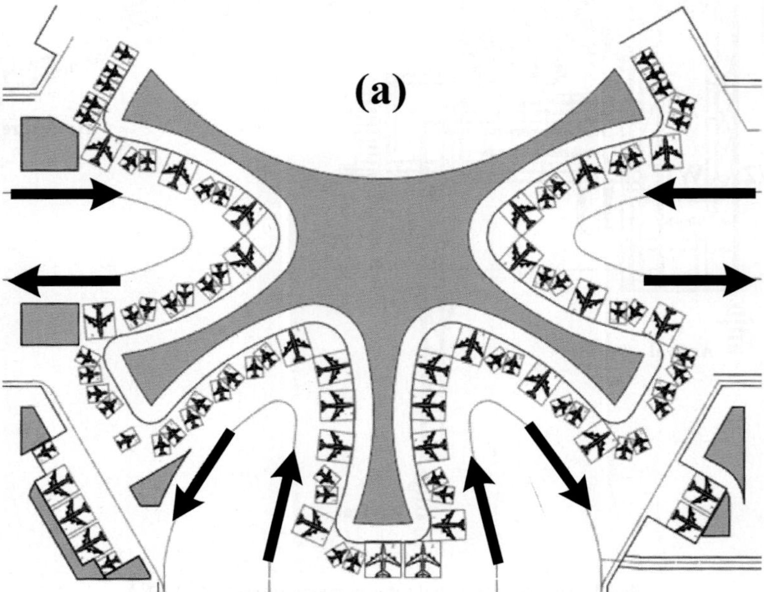

Fig. 2. Apron taxiway operation patterns in BNA.

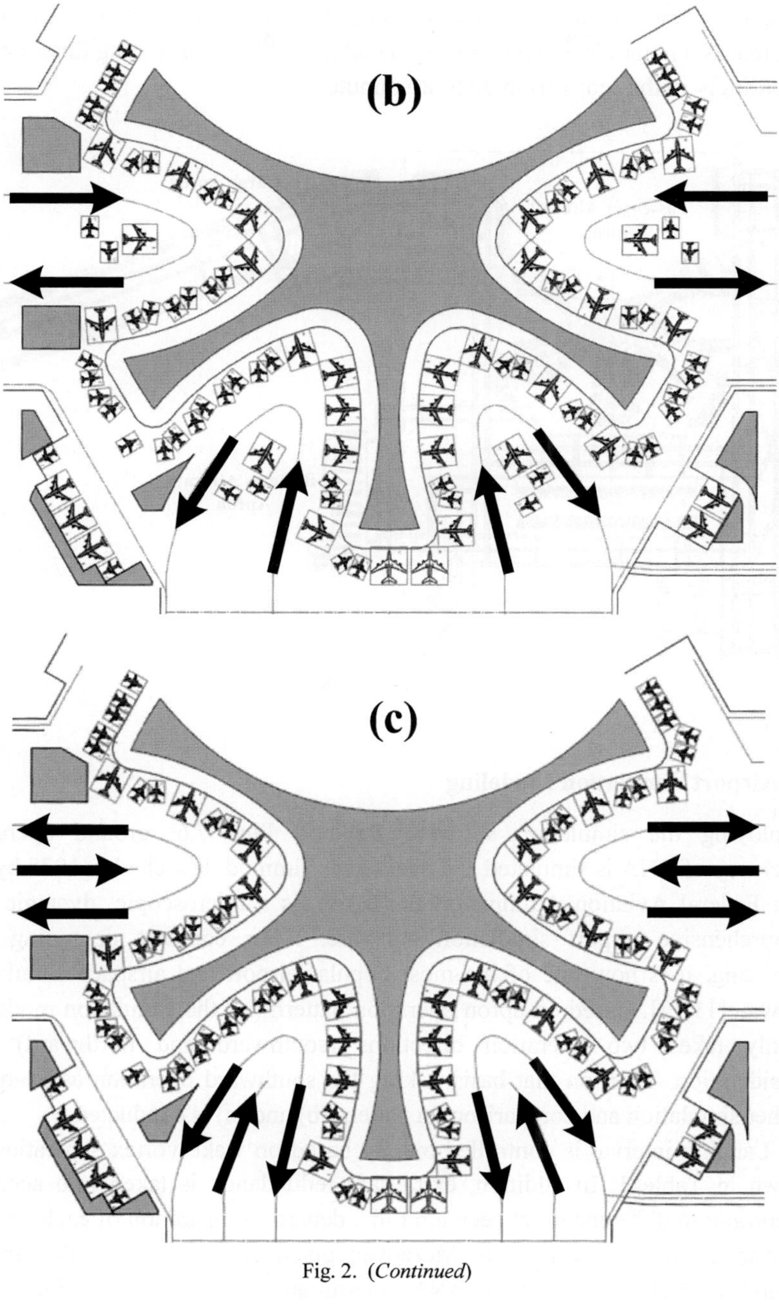

Fig. 2. (*Continued*)

As shown in Fig. 3, there are 322 gates in airfield, among which 197 for passenger plane, 40 for cargo aircraft, and 85 for corporate aircrafts. Based on differences among plane types corresponded boarding and alighting times are set accordingly in the scope from 30 to 80 minutes.

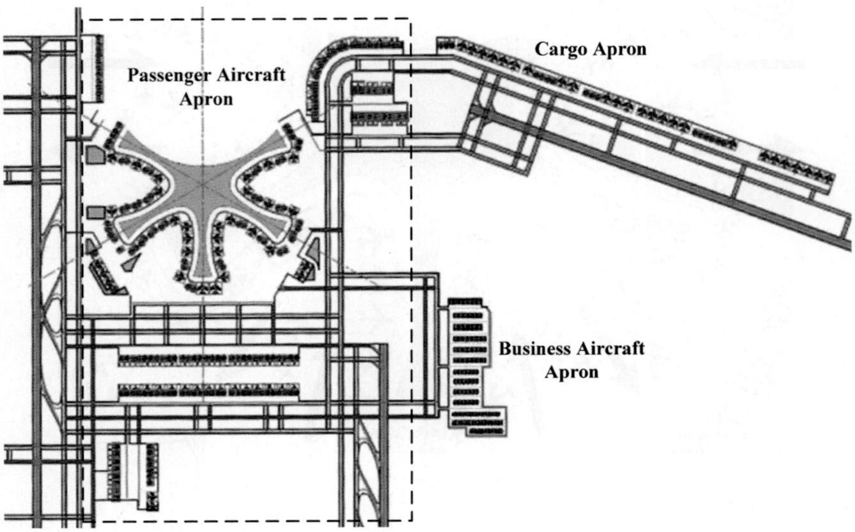

Fig. 3. Apron distribution.

3. Airport Simulation Modeling

Employing the simulation software Simmod Plus 7.6, ground operation efficiency of BNA is simulated and evaluated. Simmod, launched in 1978 by the U.S. Federal Aviation Administration (FAA), is a microscopic, dynamic and comprehensive airport simulation software. After constant upgrading and perfecting, it is now one of the most popular airport and airspace simulation software[11,12]. Based on apron operation pattern (a), the simulation modeling mainly takes two operation directions (southward and northward) into consideration. Then on that basis, taking the southward operation as example, further simulation and comparison on pattern (b) and (c) is conducted.

Landing interval is controlled mainly based on wake vortex separation, as shown in Table 1. In addition, extra safe redundancy is taken into account. According to differences between aircrafts, departure separation of each runway is arranged at 80~140 seconds. Moreover, given the influence of the Beijing Capital International Airport on BNA in terminal airspace, departure interval of

3 minutes is considered for western runways in morning time of 7:30-8:30, and a same departure interval is considered for eastern runways in morning time of 8:30-9:30. When one single runway is in alternate operation and distance from landing flight to runway is less than 8km, departure flights are forbidden to taxi out from waiting point.

Table 1. Wake vortex separation of landing flights.

Latter aircraft	Former aircraft		
	A380	Heavy	Medium
A380	8km	6km	6km
Heavy	12km	8km	6km
Medium	13km	10km	6km

Based on predicted flight volume of BNA and requirement of targeted yearly transportation volume of the terminal building, three typical daily flight schedules are planned in simulation, as shown in Table 2.

Table 2. Typical daily take-off and landing flights.

Yearly passenger throughput (person-time)	Typical daily aircraft movements	Aircraft movements in peak hour
3000	808	80
4500	1210	95
6000	1600	115

Taking the pattern (a), under northward operation, as example, the simulated operation demonstration is shown in Fig. 4.

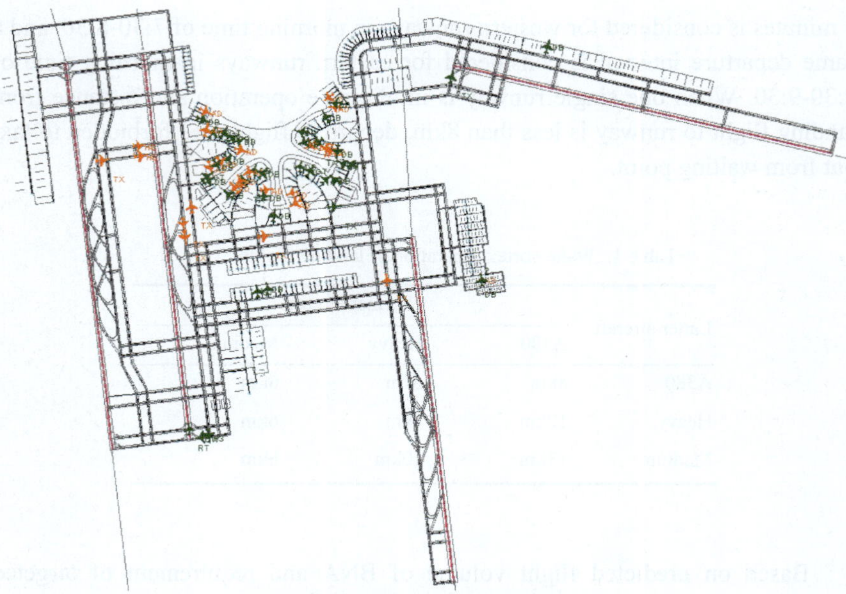

Fig. 4. Simulated operation demonstration.

4. Operation Results and Analysis

Table 3 gives out the average ground delay times under different daily flight volumes when the airport is running in northward and southward directions. In calculation of comprehensive delay time, the proportion of operation in Northern and Southern directions is temporarily considered as 9:1. When the passenger throughput is 45 million person-times, average ground delay time of departure and arrival flights is 2.72 minutes and 58 seconds respectively, which stands for a high operation efficiency. When the passenger throughput reaches 60 million person-times, average ground delay time of departure flights is 4.41 minutes, which is still a sound efficiency of ground operation.

Table 3. Average ground delay time.

Yearly passenger throughput (person-time)	Typical daily aircraft movements	Departure flight average ground delay			Arrival flight average ground delay		
		Northward	Southward	Mean value	Northward	Southward	Mean value
30 million	808	1.32’	1.33’	1.32’	0.57’	0.49’	0.56’
45 million	1210	2.73’	2.63’	2.72’	0.97’	0.83’	0.96’
60 million	1600	4.43’	4.21’	4.41’	1.42’	1.15’	1.39’

For departure flights using boarding gates, the total delay time consists of three parts: (1) take-off waiting, including waiting for take-off at runway entrance and delay of push-out; (2) delay in angle area of main terminal buildings, including waiting in apron taxiway and waiting caused by interference due to push-out of other flights; and (3) taxiing delay occurs in other areas. Table 4 presents details and proportion of each part. With increase of flight volume, take-off waiting and taxiing delay in other areas grows obviously; while delay in angle areas grows slowly, with merely slight change of delay time. When passenger throughput exceeds 45 million person-times, proportion of delay time in angle area is relatively low, accounting for 1/5 or 1/6 of total delay time, indicating that it is not the bottleneck of airport ground operation.

Table 4. Constitution of ground delay of departure flights using boarding gates.

Yearly passenger throughput (person-time)	Airport operation direction	Total ground delay of departure flight	Take-off waiting	Delay in angle area	Taxiing delay in other areas
30 million	Northward	1.61	0.83	0.68	0.1
	Southward	1.51	0.82	0.6	0.09
	Mean value	1.6	0.83	0.67	0.1
		Proportion	51.8%	42.0%	6.2%
45 million	Northward	3.41	1.83	0.75	0.83
	Southward	3.36	1.88	0.72	0.76
	Mean value	3.41	1.84	0.75	0.82
		Proportion	53.9%	21.9%	24.2%
60 million	Northward	5.47	3.05	0.85	1.57
	Southward	5.25	3.02	0.91	1.32
	Mean value	5.45	3.05	0.86	1.55
		Proportion	55.9%	15.7%	28.4%

Fig. 5 gives the aircraft movement in daily time frame under a passenger throughput of 45 million person-times. The total movement is 1210 flights, among which 90 flights in each peak hour.

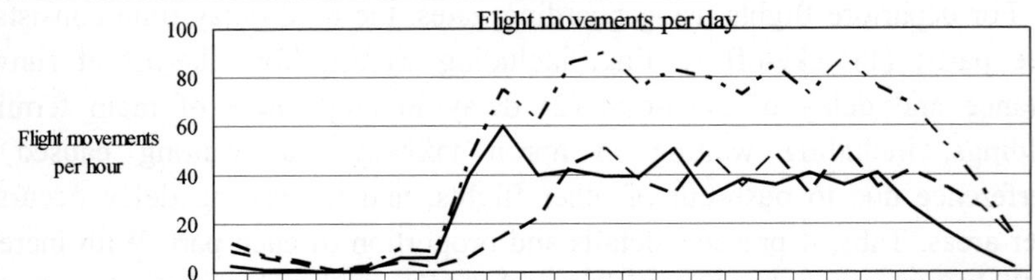

	1	2	3	4	5	6	7	8	9	10	11	12	13	14	15	16	17	18	19	20	21	22	23	24
Arrival	9	6	4	1	2	4	3	6	15	22	44	51	37	32	49	35	49	32	52	35	42	35	27	13
Departure	3	1	1	0	1	6	6	40	60	40	42	39	39	51	31	38	36	41	36	41	27	17	9	2
Total	12	7	5	1	3	10	9	46	75	62	86	90	76	83	80	73	85	73	88	76	69	52	36	15

Fig. 5. Distribution of aircraft movements in daily time frame.

Table 5 presents the average ground delay time of departure and arrival flights, under different daily flight volumes, in the three apron taxiway operation patterns. Overall analysis indicates that the lowest ground delay time and highest operation efficiency shows in pattern (c). Which is because, separation of taxiing routes of departure and arrival flights leads to less interference.

Table 5. Average ground delay time of pattern (a-c).

Apron taxiway operation pattern \ Yearly passenger throughput	30 million person-times		45 million person-times		60 million person-times	
	Departure	Arrival	Departure	Arrival	Departure	Arrival
Pattern (a)	1.33	0.49	2.63	0.83	4.21	1.15
Pattern (b)	1.53	0.33	2.71	0.7	4.13	1.03
Pattern (c)	1.11	0.35	2.40	0.60	3.96	0.84

5. Conclusion

In this paper, a systematic analysis on ground operation efficiency of airfield of BNA was conducted. Based on layout of the new airport, three apron taxiway operation patterns were planned. Harnessing the simulation software Simmod, simulation study on ground operation efficiency, delay time and its constitution under the three patterns was performed. Results of all endeavors above mentioned are as follows:

(1) When the yearly passenger throughput is 45 million person-times, as to the construction scheme in current stage of BNA, the average ground delay time of departure flights is about 2.72 minutes, and that of arrival flights is about 58 seconds, indicating that the airport is running in high efficiency, and the target yearly transportation volume could be reached.

(2) As to flights using boarding gates, over half of ground delay of departure flights is caused by take-off waiting, only 1/5 happens in angle area between main buildings. Furthermore, this part accounts a smaller proportion when flight volume grows, proving that it is not the bottleneck of airport operation.

(3) When the three apron taxiways in angle area operate in "two-out and one-in" pattern, compared with other two patterns, the ground delay time of both departure and arrival flights minimizes. The reason, also the merit is that the separation of taxiing routes of departure and arrival flights leads to fewer interference.

It should be noted, however, that the simulation study in this paper only works for the capacity and delay time of the airport under normal operation. What's more, flight delay in simulation is normally less than that in actual cases, since influencing factors such as air traffic flow control, bad weather, airlines, military actions and aviation events, etc. are excluded in the study.

Acknowledgments
This work is supported by the National Key Technologies R&D Program (2014BAJ04B02).

References

1. E. P. Gilbo, Airport capacity: representation, estimation, optimization, *IEEE Transactions on Control Systems Technology*, 1(3), pp. 144-154, (1993).
2. Ming-hua Hu, Song Liu, Lan-gen Su, Research of airport capacity estimation model based on statistic analysis, *Journal of Data Acquisition & Processing*, 15(1), pp. 74-77, (2000). In Chinese
3. R. D. Neufville, A. R. Odoni, *Airport systems planning, designs, and management* (McGraw-Hill, New York, 2002).
4. Jing Yu, Yun Pu, Runway capacity probability model and capacity curve, *Journal of Traffic and Transportation Engineering*, 2(4), pp. 99~102, (2002). In Chinese
5. Yong Chen, Yi-hua Cao, Yong Zhou, Estimation of Beijing international airport capacity, *Flight Dynamics*, 23(4), pp. 86-89, (2005). In Chinese
6. Hai-qi Guo, Jin-fu Zhu, Calculation models of capacity and delay for closely spaced parallel runway, *Journal of Traffic and Transportation Engineering*, 8(4), pp. 68-72, (2008). In Chinese

7. Xin Chen, Research on capacity evaluation and optimization methods at airport airside, PhD thesis, Nanjing University of Aeronautics & Astronautics (2007). In Chinese
8. C. Wang, X. Y. Zhang, X. H. Xu. Simulation study on airfield system capacity analysis using SIMMOD, in *Proc. 2008 International Symposium on Computational Intelligence and Design*, (Wuhan, China, 2008).
9. W. Gao, S. Y. Jiang. Simulation study on closely spaced parallel runway analysis using SIMMOD plus, in *Proc. 2010 International Conference on Intelligent Computation Technology and Automation*, (Los Alamitos, CA, USA, 2010).
10. Wei Gao, Chao-wei Huang, Research on capacity evaluation for Chongqing TMA, *Journal of Civil Aviation Univ. of China*, 28(5), pp. 1-4, (2010). In Chinese
11. Hai-yang Yu, Hua-qing Hu, Jin-jin Yao, Computer emulation methods for aviation capacity evaluation of airports, *Air Traffic Management*, (2), pp. 21-25, (2009). In Chinese
12. A. S. Huang, D Schleicher, G. Hunter, Future flight demand generation tool, in *Proc. AIAA 4th Aviation Technology, Integration and Operations (ATIO) Forum*, (Chicago, IL, USA, 2004).

Designs of Interface on the Local Mobile Communication Data Marts

Shi-hong ZHANG
Department of Information technology,
Hainan Vocational College of Political Science and Law,
Haikou, China
E-mail: qinhao3806@163.com

To accommodate the needs of local mobile communications, the interface of data marts are designed using the data warehouse and ETL2. The interface of the data warehouse is composed by the user interface, the interface traffic, the billing interface, etc. ETL2 is designed by processes involving extracting, FTP, clearing and loading. The results demonstrate that the designs can reduce the impact and stress of the data warehouse, and are important supplements to the extension of the data warehouse.

Keywords: Data warehouse; Data mart; User interface; ETL2.

1. Introduction

In the construction of the municipality mobile communication data mart, the interface design of data mart includes data warehouse interface design and ETL2 design. Interface of the data warehouse is made up of user interface, business interface, billing interface, new business interface, major client interface and competition interface, including the implementation of related table design. In the design of ETL data mart, there are two ideas: one is the direct transmission between libraries, which is not pass through files, directly from the table of data warehouse, putting the corresponding record inserted into the table of the corresponding municipality data mart. The other way is that each local files, generated from the data warehouse, is inserted into the corresponding local data mart tables. The first way can be finished by the data warehouse; while the second way is achieved through the ETL process, which includes generating various cities files[1], the FTP entering into the server of the data mart and then loading. This paper mainly analyses the second design way and address it ETL2

2. Data Warehouse Interface

2.1. *User interface design*

2.1.1. *Monthly balance design*

DMD PRODUCT EXTFAMILYNO YYYYMM: this table shows user's familiarity numbers of GSM voice service, allowing users to define a maximum of 5 family- numbers, for the current effective GSM users; DMD PRODUCT EXPIP YYYYMM: affiliated property sheet binding IP express users and fixed telephone users; DMD PRODUCT EXTFUNC YYYYMM: providing product's information for clients, including the user's home service; DMD PRODUCT EXTFUNCNEXT MS: user programmable function of DWD layer product information effective cycle under the table;

2.1.2. *Calendar design*

DMD PRODUCT YYYYMMDD: it is a daily table for the user's full information, which only store all on-line users until this day and the daily amount of extraction the on-line user data. DM PRODUCT YYYYMMDD: it is a daily wide table for the user, including all on-line users until this day and the off-line users from beginning of this month to the date. DWD PRODUCT EXTFUNC YYYYMMDD: it is a programmable function information table for the user, saving the data of a day, daily total quantity extraction.

2.2. *Business interface design*

Detail record table: It mainly includes calling detail records, roaming detail records and the corresponding later detail records. Calling detail records, in accordance with the principle of "day + cities" distribution, is stored in the data warehouse and open to the data mart; Later detail records, in which daily later voice detail records are stored; while the roaming detail records have the details of other provinces' users roaming into the target province; Related data table of business volume: it mainly includes two kinds of data tables, one is detail list of business, mainly recording data of users' business, such as detailed data of long-distance roaming users, which is day information table to store multiple records, including daily calling bills TAB and month calling bills. Another is calling transfer list, mainly recording data details, separated and call related detail data information, including user calling transfer schedule and users call return table;

Related tables of the user-level business: it mainly records the user's business volume, one record for one user, including the detail and contain the user daily and cumulative tableand user monthly record table.

2.3. *Accounting interface design*

2.3.1. *Level 3 bills*

Current month bill: It refers to the bill formed from the account during the month and the offset pre-existing, which allows users pay the bill in the next cycle payment, so post-paid users are not in the list of arrearage users. At the same time, due to the different significance between this bill and the historical bill, they will be separately to store so as to make the data processing and query easy. Statement of account of the current month including the monthly bill, the users monthly billand the users monthly bill item.

2.3.2. *Accounting payment table*

Accounting payment table mainly includes payment information table, bank payment information table and customer capital balance record table. Payment information table consists of two pieces of main tables, one is the payment record table, recording the payment information of users, a capture to a record; The other is the payment detail table, recording specific strike a balance. For example, if a client pay three-months overdue bills for three phones, nine records will be recorded in this table, including users payment record table and user payment detail table; Bank Payment Information Table has corresponding records in the payment record table; Customer Capital Balance Record Table records the changes of every account funds, including every payment and every charger pin.

2.3.3. *Accounting information table*

Accounting information table includes information table of all accounts and individual accounts. It refers to: Accounting information table, It records all accounts, including information table of personal and public account; Non-public fund information table, It records all fund information of individual account, including pre-paid and post-paid personal prestored information; The individual account precipitation fund table, It records the account fund information at the condition of users off-grid or other abnormal off-grid.

2.4. *Competition interface design*

Rival data table: it mainly records information about customers and large customers of competitors, including its customers' monthly table and large customers' monthly table, to hold monthly large customer's information of competitors. Rival data table exchange between networks: it mainly includes the communication monthly table and competitors daily business table.

3. ETL2 Design

Through extraction, FTP, deletion and loading, ETL2 extracts DMD detailed data and DM integrated query data from the data warehouse, generates municipality data files and FTP is put into a designated server, and then loaded into the data warehouse. For detail files, they should be loaded into the data mart[2].

3.1. *Extraction (extract)*

3.1.1. *Function Description*

Reading the name of the table and municipality code configuration file; Transferring table name and municipality code parameters , extracting data according to the designated table name by parameters and municipality code to; Batch extraction, according to a configuration file, respectively to extract multiple tables and municipality data ; Background database supporting oracle and db2; Supporting table name automatic matching , such as configuration files or parameters. For example, if the name of the table is attached with yyyymmdd or yyyymm, the program will do automatic replace according to the incoming billing cycle; if the municipality parameter value is 999 or is null, extract full table data of the target table.

3.1.2. *Programming*

Extract the oracle to do database design[3].Transform the existing e_extract procedures and it is packaged as extract_mart. Tcl. At the moment of extracting the oracle data, transferring e_extract program. At present, e_extract extraction procedure has not been able to do municipality extraction, the previous program should be transformed and packaged to gain the municipality extraction mechanism and generate municipality target files according to the demand of different cities.

Invocation style is as follows:

e_extract -e /data -t 2012-01-10 -c cityid -p yyyymmdd001 –d user/pwd@linkdb -o config_file. Among them, -c cityid parameter is incoming municipality code information, -o config_file parameter is the configuration information file in extraction table, in which sql statement used for extracting data. Transferring e_extract command named files extracted and generated table_name. Cityid. Yyyymmdd. MMDDHH, consistent with - c parameters which add the cityid information and procedures.

At the moment of extracting the db2 data, there are two ways to support [4]. One is a direct transfer db2 extraction tools export, the generated data file is named as table_name. Cityid. Yyyymmdd. MMDDHH.The other is transferring the extract ing process of the version db2 and extracting generated multiple municipality files at the same time. Its design idea and transfer method are similar to oracle.

3.1.3. *Extraction method*

Configuration environmental variables: MART_DATADIR is deposit directory of generated data files, while MART_TRACEDIR is the log file directory configuration parameter file, the default is data_mart. File formats: The set table_nocitylist "user_right user_user"; The set city_list "999"; Among them: city_list needs to extract data of municipality code list. Table_list needs to extract the data list, if the table is in accordance with the accounting cycle, such as dw_call_detail_201201, configured it dw call detail YYYYMM in the configuration file.

Table nocitylist: there is no table of city_id field

The caller program extract_mart. tcl to extract data

Extract_mart. TCL - d [conn string] [op_time] - p - t [timestamp] - [file_name] f -u (DDH) -v (RWH)

If the -f [file_name] parameter is not designated, read data_mart. CFG directly.

3.2. *FTP and removal*

3.2.1. *Function description*

It can be used for file transfer between two servers, passing extracted files directly to the target server[5]. Transfer all files of source directory of FTP to the target path of assigned machine. Before FTP, Check the integrity of data files in accord with the configuration files, and record the error log for the missing or incomplete files. After FTP, record success and error log of FTP. Based on the successful cases of FTP, delete the files of the source directory.

3.2.2. *Process design*

Do file transmission between assigned original path and target path; Check the number and size of the files before transmission. If the file size equals zero, there will be no transmission but recording log; Delete success files of FTP.

3.2.3. *Loading (e_load)*

After datas are extracted from data warehouse to the target server, they need to be loaded into the data mart relatively. The loading of data mart uses and develops a ETL product called "e_load_ctl", which supports Oracle 8i, Oracle 9i, DB2 7.2 EEE, DB28 and so on. Under the UNIX operational system, it can be compatible with IBM AIX, SUN Solaris, HP - UX system, etc. After completing ETL2 process, a data warehouse of data mart is built and the next step is to do data mining, data analysis process in data warehouse.

4. Conclusion

The interface design of mobile communications data mart, in prefecture-level cities, is a complex process. This design, including the interface design of the data warehouse and ETL2 design, initially completes the interface design of data mart. Its advantages are: First, do special treatments in loading detail record of municipality data mart. After the cleaned-up detail record files are separated in line with municipality, they will be directly put into the warehouse, which can reduce the e pressure on data warehouse; Second, data layer generated in the data warehouse, which support data mart to do integrated query, is performed by the data warehouse and as an important supplement of the expansion of data warehouse. Certainly, as the increasing volumes of data, the in-depth information of data marts needs further data mining and analysis. As a result, the interface design of data mart needs to be constantly improved so as to meet consumers' changing requirements.

References

1. China Mobile Communications Corporation, On China Mobile Provincial Level Management and System Specification (Version 1.5) [S].
2. Kenneth C. Laudon, Jane P. Laudon, "Management Information Systems," Beijing: Higher Education Press Pearson Education, 2003, pp. 102-103.
3. Microsoft Corporation, "SQL Server2000 Architecture and XML/Internet Support," Washington: Microsoft Press, 2001, pp. 89-90.

4. D. A. Keim, C. Panse, M. Sips, "Visual Data Mining in Large Geospatial Point Sets," IEEE Computer Graphics and Applications, vol. 24, 2004, pp. 36-44.
5. Tim Chenoweth, Karen Corral, Haluk Demirkan, "Seven Key Interventions for Data Warehouse Success," Communications of the ACM, Oct. 2006, pp. 38-39.

DOA Estimation Algorithm of Coherent Weak Targets in Strong Interference Environment

Yan-jie CHENG, Zheng-tang LIU, Wen YANG, Hui MA and Hui-min GAO

LuoYang Electronic Equipment Test Center, 471000, Luoyang, Henan, China

In order to estimate the spatial orientation of weak signal accurately, DOA estimation algorithm for coherent weak target signal in strong interference environment was proposed. Firstly, this algorithm carried out the decorrelation of the coherent weak signal via modified Toeplitz matrix. Then, the strong interference signal corresponding to the feature vector was removed from the subspace. Finally, DOA estimation of the weak signal was accomplished by making use of MUSIC algorithm. Simulation results indicate that the algorithm can eliminate the influence of strong interference signal effectively.

Keywords: DOA estimation; Strong interference; Coherent signal sources.

1. Introduction

The conventional DOA estimation methods, such as ESPRIT and so on, are very difficult to detect the weak signal accurately, which leads to a great influence on the accuracy of DOA estimation. Therefore, it is necessary to suppress the strong interference signal in order to achieve the DOA estimation of the target signal[1]. Firstly, the decorrelation of received signal has been finished by constructing Toeplitz matrix amended, and then the feature vector corresponding to the strong interference signal is removed from the signal subspace. Finally, MUSIC algorithm is used to estimate the weak signal DOA. The algorithm does not need to predict the direction of the strong interference signal, and it has good suppression performance on the non-stationary noise. Compared with the interference blocking algorithm, its computation is smaller.

2. Signal Model

Assuming that the receiving antenna array is M-element linear array of the array element spacing $d = \lambda/2$. In the observation period, a total of M narrow-band signal is received. We assume that the number of target source is $N-J$, the number of Strong interference source is J. For the convenience of narrative, we tagged the former A signals are strong interference. The incident power and the incident angle are respectively: σ_i^2, θ_i. The received signal of M element among the array at t time is expressed as accordingly:

$$x_m(t) = \sum_{i=1}^{N} s_i(t) \exp\{j(m-1)\pi \sin(\theta_i)\} + n_m(t) \tag{1}$$

Wherein, $s_i(t)$ is the complex envelope of the i information source; $n_m(t)$ is AWGN of M array element at t time, not related in space time. Its power is σ_n^2. Then the data covariance matrix of array signal is:

$$\boldsymbol{R}=E\left\{\boldsymbol{X}\boldsymbol{X}^{\mathrm{H}}\right\}=\boldsymbol{A}(\boldsymbol{\theta})\boldsymbol{R}_s\boldsymbol{A}(\boldsymbol{\theta})^{\mathrm{H}}+\sigma_n^2\boldsymbol{I} \tag{2}$$

Where $\boldsymbol{R}_s=E\left\{\boldsymbol{S}(t)\boldsymbol{S}(t)^{\mathrm{H}}\right\}$.

3. DOA Estimation Algorithm for Coherent Weak Signal

Since the N narrow-band signals may be associated or even coherent. For convenience of analysis, here we consider the worst case, namely the N narrow-band signal are all coherent. Now, rank($\boldsymbol{R}$)=1, making an eigenvalue decomposition for covariance matrix $\boldsymbol{R}$, the number of large eigenvalues is 1. The dimension of the corresponding signal subspace feature vector is also 1. Therefore, in order for rank($\boldsymbol{R}$)=N, it is necessary for the source covariance matrix to decorrelate [2]. For the coherent sources on the same initial phase, the available signal power of source covariance matrix can be expressed as $\boldsymbol{R}_s$. Substituting $\boldsymbol{R}_s$ into (2) formula, we obtain the first row elements of the data covariance matrix: $\boldsymbol{R}_{1,1}...\boldsymbol{R}_{1,M}$.

$$\boldsymbol{R}_s=\begin{bmatrix}\sigma_1^2 & \sigma_1\sigma_2 & \cdots & \sigma_1\sigma_J & \cdots & \sigma_1\sigma_N\\ \sigma_2\sigma_1 & \sigma_2^2 & \cdots & \sigma_2\sigma_J & \cdots & \sigma_2\sigma_N\\ \vdots & \vdots & \ddots & \vdots & \ddots & \vdots\\ \sigma_J\sigma_1 & \sigma_J\sigma_2 & \cdots & \sigma_J^2 & \cdots & \sigma_J\sigma_N\\ \vdots & \vdots & \ddots & \vdots & \ddots & \vdots\\ \sigma_N\sigma_1 & \sigma_N\sigma_2 & \cdots & \sigma_N\sigma_J & \cdots & \sigma_N^2\end{bmatrix}\quad \begin{cases}\boldsymbol{R}_{1,1}=\sigma_1\alpha+\cdots+\sigma_J\alpha+\cdots+\sigma_N\alpha+\sigma_n^2\\ \boldsymbol{R}_{1,2}=\sigma_1\alpha e^{j\beta_1}+\cdots+\sigma_J\alpha e^{j\beta_J}+\cdots+\sigma_N\alpha e^{j\beta_N}\\ \vdots\\ \boldsymbol{R}_{1,M}=\sigma_1\alpha e^{j(M-1)\beta_1}+\cdots+\sigma_J\alpha e^{j(M-1)\beta_J}+\cdots+\\ \quad\sigma_N\alpha e^{j(M-1)\beta_N}\end{cases} \tag{3}$$

Wherein, $\boldsymbol{R}_{1,i}(i=1,...,M)$ represents the i th elements in the first row of $\boldsymbol{R}$. $\alpha=(\sigma_1+\cdots+\sigma_J+\cdots+\sigma_N)$, $\beta=\dfrac{2\pi d\sin(\theta)}{\lambda}$. Taking the conjugate of $\boldsymbol{R}_{1,i}(i=1,...,M)$, and writing in vector form, we can derive

$$\boldsymbol{V}=\begin{bmatrix}1 & \cdots & 1 & \cdots & 1\\ \mathrm{e}^{-j\beta_1} & \cdots & \mathrm{e}^{-j\beta_J} & \cdots & \mathrm{e}^{-j\beta_N}\\ \vdots & \ddots & \vdots & \ddots & \vdots\\ \mathrm{e}^{-j(M-1)\beta_1} & \cdots & \mathrm{e}^{-j(M-1)\beta_J} & \cdots & \mathrm{e}^{-j(M-1)\beta_N}\end{bmatrix}\bullet\begin{bmatrix}\sigma_1\alpha\\ \vdots\\ \sigma_J\alpha\\ \vdots\\ \sigma_N\alpha\end{bmatrix}+\begin{bmatrix}\sigma_n^2\\ 0\\ \vdots\\ 0\end{bmatrix}=\boldsymbol{AS}+\sigma_n^2\boldsymbol{W} \tag{4}$$

Wherein, $\boldsymbol{s}=\begin{bmatrix}\sigma_1\alpha & \cdots & \sigma_J\alpha & \cdots & \sigma_N\alpha\end{bmatrix}^{\mathrm{T}}$; $\boldsymbol{W}$ is the $M\times1$ dimension vector in which the first element is one,others are zero. Reconstructing of a new Toeplitz matrix $\boldsymbol{R}'$ with V:

$$\boldsymbol{R}' = \text{Toeplitz}(\boldsymbol{V}) = \begin{bmatrix} \boldsymbol{R}_{1,1}^{*} & \boldsymbol{R}_{1,2}^{*} & \cdots & \boldsymbol{R}_{1,M}^{*} \\ \boldsymbol{R}_{1,2} & \boldsymbol{R}_{1,1}^{*} & \cdots & \boldsymbol{R}_{1,M-1}^{*} \\ \vdots & \vdots & \ddots & \vdots \\ \boldsymbol{R}_{1,M} & \boldsymbol{R}_{1,M-1} & \cdots & \boldsymbol{R}_{1,1}^{*} \end{bmatrix} = \boldsymbol{A}\boldsymbol{R}_s'\boldsymbol{A}^{\mathrm{H}} + \sigma_n^2\boldsymbol{I} \tag{5}$$

Wherein, Toeplitz($\boldsymbol{V}$) is represented by the Toeplitz matrix formed by vector V; $\boldsymbol{R}_s' = \text{diag}(\boldsymbol{s})$, $\text{diag}(\boldsymbol{s})$ is represented by the diagonal matrix formed by vector S;I is the unit matrix of $M \times M$. By type (5), the Toeplitz matrix reconstructed is full rank, namely rank($\boldsymbol{R}'$)=N ,the decorrelation of coherent source is realized.

We consider the situation firstly when the number of strong interference source is equal to 1. Assuming the N source is a strong interference signal, the other is the target signal. Define a $(M-1) \times M$ dimensional matrix is P:

$$\boldsymbol{P}^{\mathrm{H}}(\theta) = \begin{bmatrix} 1 & -\mathrm{e}^{j\beta} & 0 & \cdots & 0 \\ 0 & 1 & -\mathrm{e}^{j\beta} & \cdots & 0 \\ \vdots & \vdots & \ddots & \ddots & \ddots \\ 0 & 0 & \cdots & 1 & -\mathrm{e}^{j\beta} \end{bmatrix} \tag{6}$$

Well, obviously

$$\boldsymbol{P}^{\mathrm{H}}(\theta)\boldsymbol{A}(\theta) = \boldsymbol{P}[\boldsymbol{a}(\theta_1), \boldsymbol{a}(\theta_2), ..., \boldsymbol{a}(\theta_N)] = [\boldsymbol{b}(\theta_1), \boldsymbol{b}(\theta_2), ..., \boldsymbol{b}(\theta_N)] \tag{7}$$

when $\theta = \theta_N$, $\beta = \beta_N$,the last column is 0. The formula can be simplified as:

$$\boldsymbol{B}(\theta) = [\boldsymbol{b}(\theta_1), \boldsymbol{b}(\theta_2), ..., \boldsymbol{b}(\theta_{N-1})] \tag{8}$$

The process fully shows that the eigenvector of strong interference signal has been removed by using the matrix T. That is to say, as long as the incident azimuth θ of the strong interference source is obtained, matrix P can be used to transform the array manifold matrix, to eliminate the impact of strong interference. n the same way, when there are many strong interference sources in the space, the matrix needs to be amended as $\boldsymbol{P}^{\mathrm{H}} = \prod_{j=1}^{J} \boldsymbol{P}_j$. The dimension of matrix $\boldsymbol{P}_j$ is $(M-j) \times (M-j+1)$. The form of matrix is the same as the formula (6), but the value of β_i is different.

At this point, the modified data covariance matrix $\boldsymbol{R}_Y$ is

$$\boldsymbol{R}_Y = \boldsymbol{P}^{\mathrm{H}}\boldsymbol{R}'\boldsymbol{P} = \boldsymbol{P}^{\mathrm{H}}\boldsymbol{R}_s'\boldsymbol{P} + \sigma_n^2\boldsymbol{P}^{\mathrm{H}}\boldsymbol{P} \tag{9}$$

In the formula, the noise term becomes $\sigma_n^2\boldsymbol{P}^{\mathrm{H}}\boldsymbol{P}$. Diagonal loading of data matrix $\boldsymbol{R}_Y$ becomes $\boldsymbol{R}_d = \boldsymbol{R}_Y/\gamma + \boldsymbol{I}$ .The eigenvalue decomposition of the matrix $\boldsymbol{R}_d$ has been done,then

$$\boldsymbol{R}_d = \sum_{i=1}^{N} \hat{\lambda}_i \boldsymbol{u}_i\boldsymbol{u}_i^{\mathrm{H}} + \sigma_n^2 \sum_{i=N+1}^{M-1} \boldsymbol{u}_i\boldsymbol{u}_i^{\mathrm{H}} = [\boldsymbol{U}_s \quad \boldsymbol{U}_n] \begin{bmatrix} \boldsymbol{\Sigma}_s & \\ & \boldsymbol{\Sigma}_n \end{bmatrix} \begin{bmatrix} \boldsymbol{U}_s^{\mathrm{H}} \\ \boldsymbol{U}_n^{\mathrm{H}} \end{bmatrix} \tag{10}$$

In the formula, $U_s = [u_1, u_2, ..., u_N]$ is the signal subspace, and $U_n = [u_{N+1}, u_{N+2}, ..., u_{M-J}]$ is the noise subspace.

DOA estimation formula for the weak target can be obtained by music algorithm:

$$\hat{\theta} = \arg\min_{\theta} \left\{ a^{\mathrm{H}}(\theta) U_n U_n^{\mathrm{H}} a(\theta) \right\} \tag{11}$$

4. Simulation Results

In this section, we present several simulation examples to illustrate the performance of the proposed algorithm as compared to some of the existing methods. We assumed that the array is uniform linear array with 8 sensors and the antenna spacing is half wavelength. The additive noise is uniform white noise, and the weak target signal and the strong interference signal are coherent signals[3]. *SNR* is defined as the ratio of the power of the source signal to that of the additive noise at each sensor, i.e., $SNR = 10\log_{10}(\sigma_s^2/\sigma_n^2)$; *JSR* is defined as the ratio of the power of the interference signal to that of the source signal at each sensor, i.e., $JSR = 10\log_{10}(\sigma_j^2/\sigma_s^2)$; *JSR* is defined as the ratio of the power of the interference signal to that of the additive noise at each sensor, i.e., $JNR = 10\log_{10}(\sigma_j^2/\sigma_n^2)$ .Where, σ_s^2 is the power of the source signal , σ_j^2 is the power of the interference signal, σ_n^2 is the power of the additive noise.

Example 1. Spectral resolution of the algorithm with strong interference.

In this examples, we assumed that two strong interference signals of equal power with angles $\theta_1 = -20^{\circ}$ and $\theta_2 = 10^{\circ}$ and $JSR = 120\text{dB}$, one weak source signals with angles $\theta_3 = 20^{\circ}$ and $SNR = 5\text{dB}$. Fig. 1 plots the normalized spatial spectrum curve using ordinary MUSIC algorithm, and Fig. 2 plots the normalized spatial spectrum curve using proposed algorithm.

It can be concluded from Fig. 1 that convectional MUSIC algorithm can estimate the spatial position of the strong interference signals, while neglect the target signal which to be estimated. It can be seen clearly from Fig. 2 that after strong interference rejection, the proposed algorithm effectively removes the influence of strong interference.

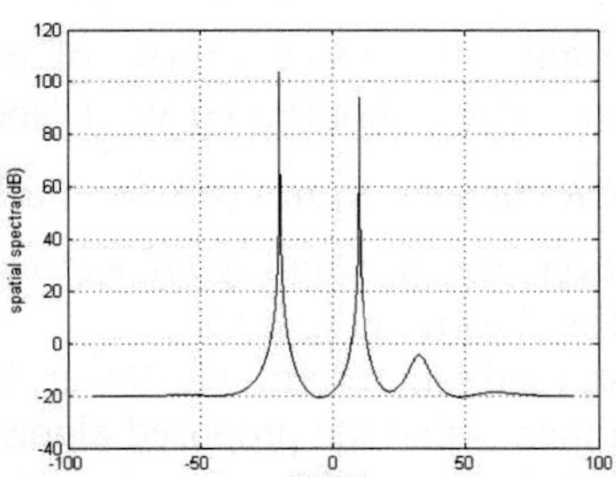

Fig. 1. Spectral curve of MUSIC algorithm.

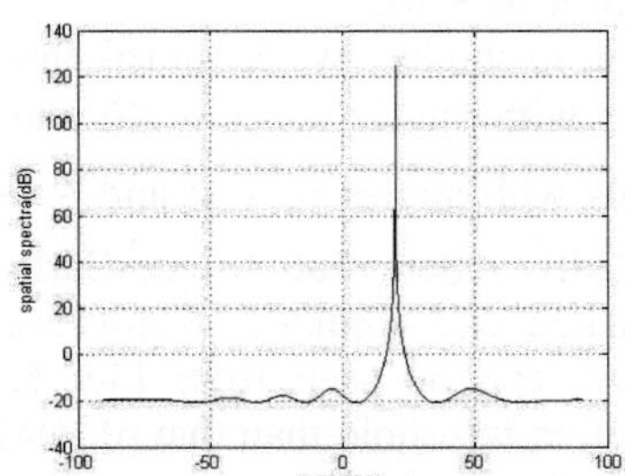

Fig. 2. Spatial curve of proposed algorithm.

Example 2. Performance comparison of spatial spectrum estimation of the proposed algorithm and JJM.

In this examples, we assumed that two strong interference signals of equal power with angles $\theta_1 = -30^\circ$ and $\theta_2 = -50^\circ$. When there is only one target signal, the incident angle is 10 degrees and when there are two target signals, the incident angle is -30 degrees and 20 degrees respectively. $JSR = 100\text{dB}$ and $SNR = 5\text{dB}$. Fig. 3 gives a comparison of the spatial spectrum estimation performance of the proposed algorithm and the JJM algorithm when there is only one weak target signal. It can be seen from Fig. 3 that when the number of weak target signal is 1, the proposed algorithm and JJM can all effectively overcome the influence of strong interference and accurately estimate the spatial orientation of the weak target signal. However, the accuracy of proposed algorithm is slightly higher than that of JJM. Fig. 4 gives another comparison of the spatial spectrum estimation performance of the proposed algorithm and JJM when there are two weak target signals. It can be seen clearly from Fig. 4 that when the number of target signal is 2, JJM algorithm completely failed to work, only the two false peaks are estimated, however, proposed algorithm can effectively estimate the spatial position of weak target signal, which shows that the proposed algorithm has better estimation performance for weak target signals.

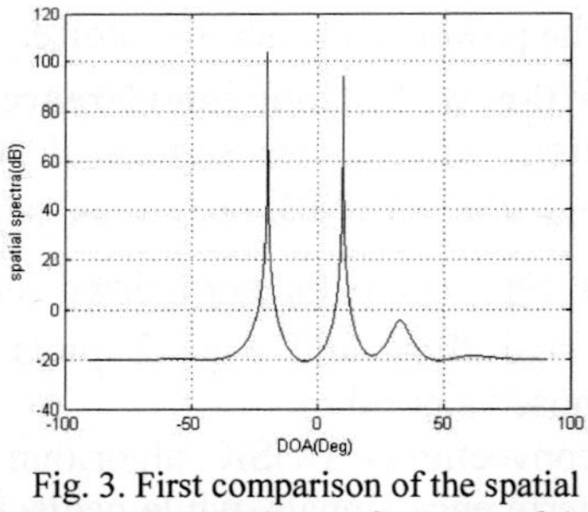

Fig. 3. First comparison of the spatial spectrum estimation performance of the proposed algorithm and JJM.

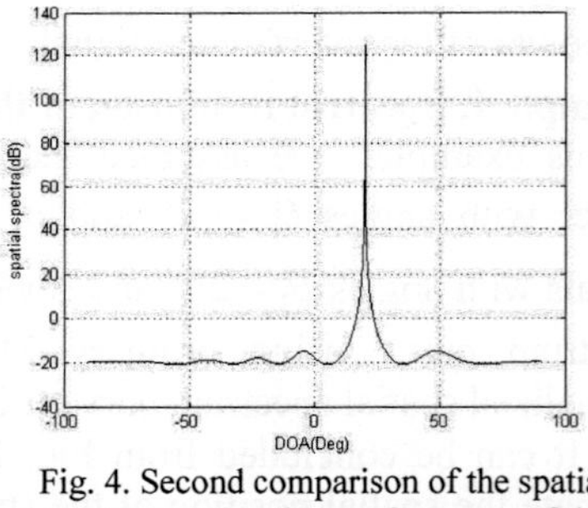

Fig. 4. Second comparison of the spatial spectrum estimation performance of the proposed algorithm and JJM.

Example 3. Performance comparison of proposed algorithm and JJM for Variable of SNR.

In this examples, we assumed that two strong interference signals of equal power with angles are $\theta_1 = -30^\circ$ and $\theta_2 = -60^\circ$, $JSR = 100\text{dB}$,two weak source signals with angles $\theta_3 = 10^\circ$ and $\theta_4 = 20^\circ$. SNR changes from -2dB to 20dB by step 2dB. After 1000 Monte-Carlo simulation ,the probability of success is calculated, and simulation results is achieved as shown in Figure 5.

As can be seen from Fig. 5, the proposed algorithm has lower SNR resolution threshold than that of JJM, which means that the proposed algorithm have better performance in suppressing strong interference signals.

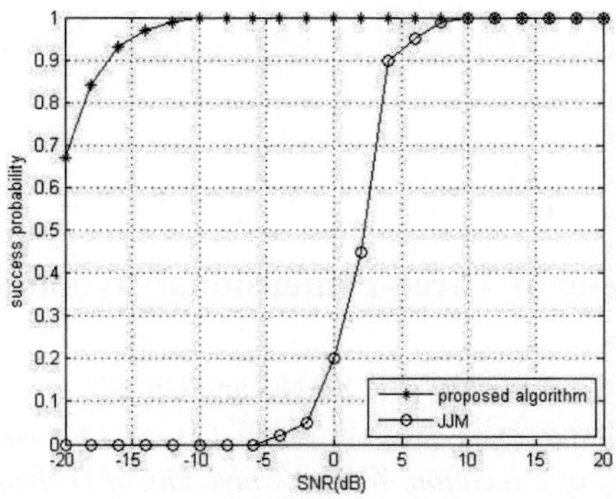

Fig. 5. Comparison of the success probability of the proposed algorithm and JJM with different SNR.

5. Conclusion

In this paper, we have proposed a very efficient DOA estimation method for weak coherent signals with strong interference environment. Firstly, via the modified Toeplitz matrix, the decorrelation of the coherent weak signals is carried out in this algorithm. Then, the feature vector of the strong interference is removed from the signal subspace. Finally, the DOA of the weak signal is estimated with the MUSIC algorithm. A number of simulations demonstrate that our proposed method provides a better DOA estimation performance than traditional method, especially for correlated signals.

References

1. Li Hongbing, Guo Yi, Gong Jian et al. *DOA estimation method of coherent weak signal source under strong interference background 'In Chinese'[J].* modern radar, 2012, 9 (34): 45-49.
2. Cheng-xiao Su. *An interference inhibition of DOA estimation algorithm based on uniform circular dipole array'In Chinese' [J].* Signal processing, 2010, 26(9): 1355-1360.
3. Sao J.T., Steinberg B,*Reduction of Sidelobe and Speckle Artifacts in Microwave Imaging: the CLEAN Technique[J].*IEEE Trans on Antennas and Propagation ,1988, 36(4): 543-556.
4. Grough P.T.,*A Fast Spectral Estimation Algorithm Based on the FFT[J].*IEEE Trans on SignalProcessing, 1994, 42(6): 1317-1322.

Research on Model of Three-Dimensional Dynamic Ship Domain

Ting XU*, Jie YANG and Qin SU

Key Laboratory of Fiber Optic Sensing Technology and Information Processing, Ministry of Education, Wuhan University of Technology,

WuHan, HuBei 430070, China

**E-mail: 1508186160@qq.com*

To ensure the safe navigation of ships, this paper proposes a three-dimensional model for dynamic ship domain by integrating ship wave and turbulent region theories, taking the impact of water and wind into consideration by utilizing quantitative analysis to update the equations of lateral boundary and longitudinal boundary in accordance. Furthermore, data about the experiences of ship pilots is applied to adjust the model with a coefficient correction method. The experimental results demonstrate that the established model has higher scalability compared with existing models. In addition, the model's performance in the experiments also demonstrates that our model is a better model to simulate actual shipping conditions.

Keywords: Ship domain; 3D model; Quantitative analysis; Coefficient correction.

1. Introduction

Ship domain was firstly introduced in Fujii model by Fujii in the 1960s, which defines the distance between ships to avoid stepping into surrounding domain of the other. After that, many improved models are proposed by foreign scholars, such as Goodwin model[1,2] and P.A. Davis model[3]. Based on the research of foreign experts, Professor Bi Xiuying[4] established dynamic ship model by taking the theory of ship collision risk into consideration. Then Professor Sun Licheng[5] presented a novel definition of ship domain by concentrating on the investigations of avoidance behavior of ship pilots[6]. However, due to the complexity of inland waterways, shallow water effect and quay phenomenon will occur frequently, leading to the limitation and ineffectiveness of these 2D models. Thus based on water features of China, Professor Xu Zhouhua[7] initially proposeda three-dimensional ship domain model.

Ship domain is affected by multiple factors, such as the surrounding environmental and human factors, etc. However, since most scholars are limited to the study of ship and rarely consider the environment factors, leading to the no availability of conventional modeling methods and low ineffectiveness of dynamic ship domain. Based on the quantitative study of the impacts of multiple factors, a three-dimensional model of dynamic ship domain is established.

2. Ship Domain Modeling

There has been no unified definition of the ship domain, synthesizing domestic and foreign documents[8], we defined ship domain as a space that kept to avoid collision, and the majority following ships should avoid entering this space to ensure safe driving. The 3D model of ship dynamic security fields should be cut in an "ovate[7]" which located in rectangular. As shown in Figure 1(a), the length and width of cuboid are respectively the length and width of ship domain. As shown in Figure 1(b), the three dimensional ship domain remains as the "ovate", the ship is not in the center of the oval, but to some extent skew.

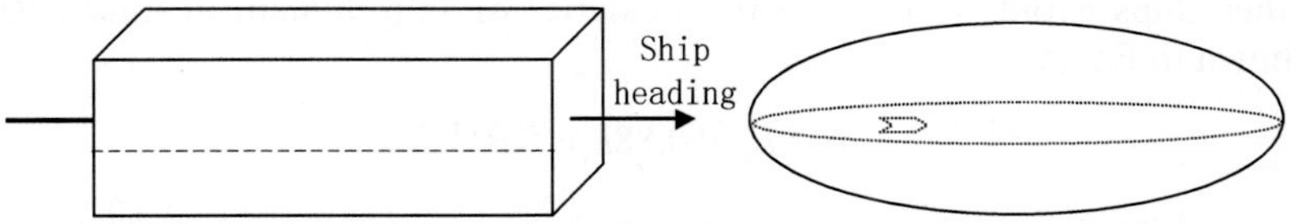

(a) Size of 3D module in ship domain(b) Conception of 3D model in ship domain

Fig. 1. Three-dimensional model of the ship domain.

The length c above the horizontal surface is mainly considering bridge traffic environment, it's the height of ship add a fixed safe distance. The length d below the horizontal surface is the maximum draught of ship plus a fixed safe distance. In this paper, due to the factors to consider is limited, so only calculate the length of two short axis simply: the safe distance above water and under water are 0.1 times the height of the ship ,as shown in Eq. (1) and (2):

$$c = H - D + 0.1H. \tag{1}$$

$$d = D + 0.1H. \tag{2}$$

Where, H represent the height of ship, D on behalf of the draft of ship.

2.1. *Ship dynamic domain parameters*

2.1.1. *Lateral boundary of the ship domain*

The influence of pier turbulence zone to lateral boundary of the ship domain is large, experts from the Yangtze River waterway Design Institute[9,10] given the formula of the width of the bridge Pier turbulence[11] by researching, as shown in Eq. (3):

$$E = K_c K_s f(v,b,h) = 0.88 K_s V^{0.75} b^{0.56} h^{0.44}. \tag{3}$$

Where, E is total width of pier turbulence; K_c is a dimensionless coefficient; K_s is associated with the pier; V the flow velocity; b is pier width; h is the depth of water. Similar to Eq. (3), the interference region of ship wave E_s is shown in Eq. (4):

$$E_s = f(v_0, B, D) = 0.88 k_s v_0^{k_1} B^{k_2} D^{k_3}. \tag{4}$$

Where, k_s is associated with ship shape; v_0 is the speed of ship; B is the breadth of ship. By querying relevant references[11], the values of k_1 , k_2 , k_3 is set as 1. 23,0. 40,0. 60. While interference region of ship wave is the area which other ships avoid, so the lateral boundaries of ship domain in Inland River is shown in Eq. (5):

$$b = E_s = 0.88 k_s v_0^{1.23} B^{0.40} D^{0.60}. \tag{5}$$

2.1.2. *Longitudinal boundary of ship domain*

When the ship is in reverse, it is actually a uniform deceleration motion, this theory is proved to be feasible in practice[12,13]. So the reverse stopping distance can be estimated by following empirical estimation formula, is shown in Eq. (6):

$$S_s = C \cdot V_k T_s. \tag{6}$$

Where, S_s is reverse stopping distance; C is distance coefficient; V_k is reversing speed; T_s is reverse time. In order to deal with emergency situations, the execution time $t_{execution}$ is consisted with three parts: reaction time of driver is $0.5{:}1.5s$, cabin operation time is $0.7{:}1.0s$, and host execution time is $4{:}6s$, therefore the safe distance S_T is at least, as shown in Eq.(7):

$$S_T = v_0 t_{execution} + S_s. \tag{7}$$

In conclusion, the longitudinal boundaries of ship domain should be, as shown in Eq. (8):

$$a = S_T + L = v_0 t_{execution} + C v_0 T_s + L. \tag{8}$$

Where, L is the length of ship.

2.2. *Impact factors analysis of dynamic ship domain*

2.2.1. *The effect of water flow in the dynamic ship domain*

The direction of flow effect the dynamic ship domain, this paper focus on the condition of ship under uniform oblique flow. Under oblique flow, if still using the previous method, the model is as shown in the dashed oval of Fig. 2. When the ship comes in the areas of A and C, this ship is not located within the dashed oval, but in the vessel's navigation routes, there is no doubt it will affect vessel's safe navigation. In the areas of B and D, the vessel will never arrive. Therefore, the existing model of ship domain needs to be reconsidered.

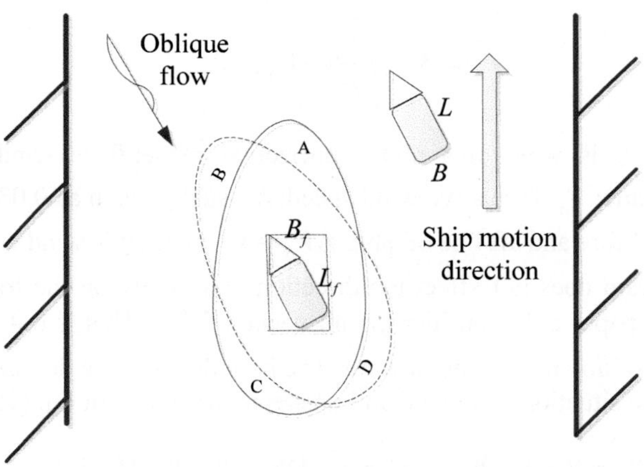

Fig. 2. The field of the ship under the condition of oblique flow.

In this paper, using the yaw cause by oblique flow as the breakthrough point. The length and width of the ship is defined as B_e and L_e . It can be regarded that a change in ship domain is the change of equivalent size of vessel. So we can get Eq. (9) and Eq. (10):

$$L_e = L\cos\omega + B\sin\omega. \tag{9}$$

$$B_e = L\sin\omega + B\cos\omega. \tag{10}$$

ω is the ship's yaw angle, L_e is effective length of ship under oblique flow; B_e is effective width of ship under oblique flow. So the ship domain boundary is shown in Eq. (11) and Eq. (12):

$$a = v_0 t_{execution} \cos\omega + C v_0 T_s \cos\omega + L_e. \tag{11}$$

$$b = 0.88 k_s (v_0 \cos\omega)^{1.23} B_e^{0.40} D^{0.60}. \tag{12}$$

2.2.2. *The effect of wind in the dynamic ship domain*

This paper assumes the force of the wind is constant in a relatively short time. According to the theory of ship maneuvering, can get the drift velocity of the ship as Eq. (13)when the wind effect on the ship.

$$V_f = e^{-0.14 V_s} \cdot V_b. \tag{13}$$

V_f is the drift velocity by the effect of wind; V_b is drift velocity of stopping ship; V_s is the velocity of the ship in wind. V_b is as shown in Eq. (14),

$$V_b = K \cdot \sqrt{\frac{B_a}{B_w}} \cdot V_a. \tag{14}$$

Where, B_a is wind area above horizontal plane; B_w is wind area under horizontal plane; V_a is relative wind speed; K usually taken as 0.038~0.041; the component of fore and aft line of ship is $V_{fx} = V_f \cdot \cos\varsigma$; ς is wind chord angle.

Wind beam does not affect the direction of velocity on the fore and aft of ship. So this paper only consider the influence of V_{fx} . That is only considering the situation of downwind and upwind. The boundary of ship domainis:

When the situation is upwind and upstream, as shown in Eq. (15):

$$\begin{cases} a = (v_0 - u - v_{fx}) t_{execution} + C \cdot (v_0 - u - v_{fx}) T_s + L \\ b = 0.88 k_s (v_0 + u - v_{fx})^{1.23} B^{0.40} D^{0.60} \end{cases}. \tag{15}$$

When the situation is upwind and downstream, as shown in Eq.(16):

$$\begin{cases} a = (v_0 + u - v_{fx}) t_{execution} + C \cdot (v_0 + u - v_{fx}) T_s + L \\ b = 0.88 k_s (v_0 - u - v_{fx})^{1.23} B^{0.40} D^{0.60} \end{cases}. \tag{16}$$

When the situation is downwind and upstream, as shown in Eq. (17):

$$\begin{cases} a = (v_0 - u + v_{fx})t_{execution} + C\cdot(v_0 - u + v_{fx})T_s + L \\ b = 0.88k_s(v_0 + u + v_{fx})^{1.23}B^{0.40}D^{0.60} \end{cases} . \quad (17)$$

When the situation is downwind and downstream, as shown in Eq. (18):

$$\begin{cases} a = (v_0 + u + v_{fx})t_{execution} + C\cdot(v_0 + u + v_{fx})T_s + L \\ b = 0.88k_s(v_0 - u + v_{fx})^{1.23}B^{0.40}D^{0.60} \end{cases} . \quad (18)$$

2.3. *Validation of the model calculation*

Choose main kind of vessel in Yangtze river to verify the established dynamic domain[11]. The information of the selected ship is shown in Table 1.

Table 1. Scale size of general cargo ship.

Length(L/m)	Width(B/m)	Draft(D/m)	Height(H/m)
280	42.6	6.8	17.5

Speed v_0 is set to 13 kn, wind speed v_f is $3.0m/s$, velocity takes $1.5m/s$, set astern at about $120s$, take $7s$ as driver's reaction time. According to the established model, the parameters of ship domain are shown in Table 2.

Table 2. Ship domain of general cargo ship.

The state of water flow	The state of the wind	The lateral axis/ship (times)	The longitudinal axis/ship (times)
downstream	downwind	0.85	9.55
	upwind	0.82	9.46
upstream	downwind	1.46	7.21
	upwind	1.43	7.11

As shown in Table 2, the size of lateral and longitudinal axis is affected by wind and flow. According to the experience of pilots, the horizontal axis of ship domain in general cargo vessel is three times the length of ship, the longitudinal axis is about $7 \sim 10$ times. Comparing with above results, lateral axis of the calculated model is shorter than the empirical data of pilots, but the longitudinal axis is similar to the experience data.

2.4. *Correction of the model*

Here choose correction coefficient X to modify the size of the lateral boundary b, as shown in Eq. (19):

$$b = 0.88\, Xk_s (v_0 \pm u)^{1.23} B^{0.40} D^{0.60} . \tag{19}$$

The correction coefficient is influenced by flow. X takes $6 \sim 7$ when ship sailing downstream, X takes $3 \sim 4$ when ship sailing upstream. After revise the model, calculate the parameters under the conditions of four types, the result is as shown in Table 3.

Table 3. Ship domain of general cargo ship (after the model verified).

The state of water flow	The state of the wind	The lateral axis/ship (times)	The longitudinal axis/ship (times)
downstream	downwind	4.23	9.77
	upwind	4.12	9.67
upstream	downwind	4.38	7.34
	upwind	4.30	7.25

The revised lateral boundary is in accordance with the empirical data. According to the data, the proportion that $500 \sim 3000$ tons of ship accounted for total ship is the largest in Yin Gong Zhou segment. Therefore, this article chooses the ship of 2000 ton represented the general ship in Inland River, the ship parameters are shown in Table 4:

Table 4. Scale size of general ship in Inland River.

Length(L/m)	Width(B/m)	Draft(D/m)	Height(H/m)
210	34	5.5	15.4

Using the revised ship dynamic domain model calculate the parameters of ship domain in Yin Gong Zhou segment, the results are shown in Table 5.

Table 5. Ship domain of general ship in Inland River (after the model verified).

The state of water flow	The state of the wind	The lateral axis/ship (times)	The longitudinal axis/ship (times)
downstream	downwind	4.55	9.77
	upwind	4.42	9.67
upstream	downwind	4.71	7.35
	upwind	4.62	7.25

According to the experience data, lateral axis of ship domain is $4 \sim 5$ times the length of ship, longitudinal axis is about $7 \sim 10$ times, the average boundary of the calculated ship domain is consistent with empirical data. Therefore, the revised coefficient of ship dynamic model is thought to be reasonable.

3. Quantitative Analysis of Model Impact Factors

3.1. *The analysis of water effect*

In the actual voyage, there are likely to encounter the oblique flows. So we discuss the influence of the uniform oblique flow. The ship information is set as Table 1, take the ship speed v_0 to $13kn$, the wind speed v_f in average wind speed $3.0m/s$. Under downwind situation, astern takes about $120s$, $t_{execution}$ set to $7s$ and the low velocity takes $1.5m/s$, then analysis ship domain when the angle of the oblique flow is change between $0°$ to $60°$, the result is shown in Fig. 3.

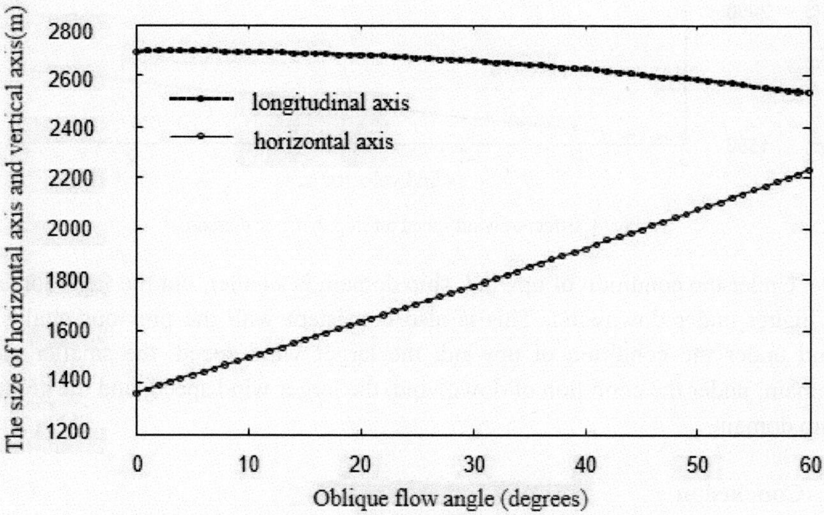

Fig. 3. The change of ship dynamic domain under uniform oblique flow.

As shown in the Fig.3, oblique flow's influence on the horizontal axis of the ship domain is larger. With the increase of the angle of oblique flow ,the horizontal axis shows the tendency of gradually become bigger. This is because as the angle of oblique flow getting larger, cause a large transverse velocity of the ship, so it makes the horizontal axis larger. The oblique flow also has a certain influence in the longitudinal axis of ship domain. Due to the oblique flow, the actual speed that a ship in the water become smaller, so that the longitudinal axis decrease with the increase of the angle of oblique flow.

3.2. *The analysis of wind effect*

The setting of other parameters are the same as section 3.1 except the wind speed, set the wind speed change between $-3{\sim}3m/s$, the result is shown in Fig. 4.

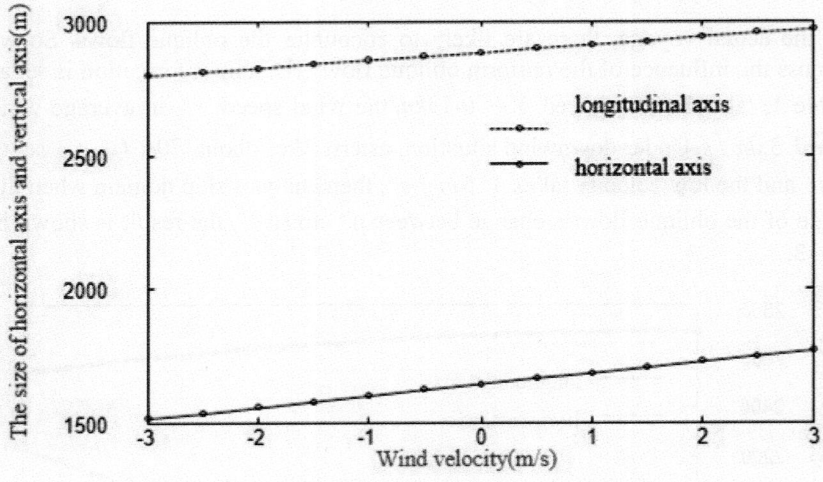

Fig. 4. Effect of wind speed on ship dynamic domain.

Under the condition of upwind, ship domain is smaller, but the field domain is bigger under downwind. This is also consistent with the previous analysis. And under the condition of upwind, the larger wind speed, the smaller ship domain, under the condition of downwind, the larger wind speed, and the greater ship domain.

4. Conclusion

This paper analyzes the ship domain from the perspective of space. In combination with the ship it factors and external environment factors, a dynamic three-dimensional model of the ship domain is established, which simulates the dynamic security domain of a normal sailing ship. This model is verified by using empirical data in the main channel of Yangtze River and then relative parameters are adjusted to be more suitable in reality. The experimental results show that the model is closer to the actual condition after the adjustment. What's more, a quantitative analysis of multiple factors affecting the ship domain is performed, revealing the inner links among ship domain, flow and wind, which is beneficial for deeply understanding the size changing of ship domain.

Acknowledgments

This work was supported by National Science Foundation of China (NSFC 51479159).

References

1. E.M.Goodwin. Determination of Ship Domain Size. Proceedings of International Conference on Mathematical Aspects of Marine Traffic, pi 03-127. London, Academic Press, 1977.
2. E.M.Goodwin. A statistical study of ship domain. The Journal of Navigation, 1975, vol. 28, no. 3, pp. 328-344.
3. P.V.Davis, M.J.Dove, C.T.Stockel. A computer simuation of marine traffic using domains and arenas. The Journal of Navigation, 1980, vol. 33, no. 2, pp. 215-222.
4. Xiu-yin Bi. Research of ship's collision risk and collision avoidance decision-making model[D]. Dalian: Dalian maritime university, 2000.
5. Li-cheng Sun. Research of mathematical model on ship collision avoidance decision-making[D]. Dalian: Dalian maritime university, 2006.
6. QiLe. Ship domain modeling in sight of one another based on AIS data. Journal of Dalian maritime university, 2011.2.
7. Zhou-hua Xu. Research of 3D model of ship domain in inland waters[J]. Journal of wuhan university of technology, 2004 (3), 380-383.
8. TianXin. Research of inland ship domain in specific waters[D].Dalian: Dalian maritime university, 2009.
9. ZhuangYuan. Research of key techniques of bridge navigation conditions [D]. Wuhan: Wuhan university of technology. 2008.
10. Shwu-Jingchang, Deng-Teng Hsiao and Wei-Chih wang. AIS-based Delineation and Interpretation of Ship Domain Models[C]. Department of Communication, Navigation and Control Engineering National Taiwan Ocean University, 2014.10.
11. Huang Yin. Research and application of model of ship domain under the action of wind in inland[D]. University of electronic science and technology, 2012.

12. TAM C K, BUCKNALL R, GREIG A. Review of collision avoidance and path planning methods for ships in close range encounters[J]. Journal of Navigation, 2009.
13. S.J. Chang, G.Y. Hsu, J.A. Yang, et al. Vessel traffic analysis for maritime Intelligent Transportation System. Proc[J]. IEEE 71st Vehicular Technology Conference, VTC 2010 Spring, Taipei, R.O.C., 16-19 May 2010.

Forearm Gesture Interface for Gaming via an Ordinary Camera

Cheng-bin ZENG† and Ji-qian LIU
School of Information Science and Technology, Guizhou Institute of Technology, Guiyang, Guizhou, China
†E-mail: cbzeng@qq.com, Liujiqian@git.edu.cn

Natural human-computer interaction is an active research topic in the field of computer vision with widespread applications and one important application is in computer game. In this paper, we propose a novel method using forearm gesture as the input of the Tetris game via an ordinary camera. We use the particle filter to track the movement of the forearm and thus obtain directional information. Thereafter, the directional information is mapped into the input of the Tetris game. In comparison with existing human-computer interaction (HCI) systems which require expensive equipment such as stereo cameras, our system only requires an ordinary camera. Experimental results demonstrate that our method effectively tracks the movement of a human forearm, and implement real-time control for the Tetris game.

Keywords: Human-computer interaction; Tracking; Particle filter; Tetris game.

1. Introduction

Natural human-computer interaction based on computer vision is an active research area and has widespread applications, especially in computer games. It is an exciting experience for users to play games using their limb actions while not using the keyboard and mouse. Nowadays, many famous game manufacture-rs, such as Sony and Microsoft, are researching on integrating the natural human computer interface into their products. It is reported that the basis of the next version of Xbox 360 will be Project Natal, which will enable the players to control and interact with the Xbox 360 through a natural human-computer interface [1].

The difficulties of designing a natural human computer interface lie in how to understand the human's gesture properly and how to interact with the players in real time. There are some research works on natural human computer interact-

Fig. 1. The proposed system. The forearm gesture as the system input . The player uses his forearm to control the movement of the block in the Tetris game via an ordinary camera. The red rectangle indicates the original position of the forearm. The green rectangle denotes the current position of the forearm.

ion for games. Wang *et al* [2] applied the recognition of the human body gesture to the box game. Yin et al [3] integrated a gesture interface to a commercial online dance game through tracking the movement of the player's face and hands. But both of these researches focus on recovering the human body poses using depth images, which require expensive stereo cameras to obtain.

In this paper, we design a natural human computer interface for the Tetris game via an ordinary camera. As illustrated in Fig. 1, an ordinary camera captures the movements of the player's forearm. Through tracking the movements of the forearm, we get the directional information (left, right, up, and down). According to the directional information, we can control the behavior of the blocks in the game. That is, the leftward or rightward information means moving the blocks left or right. The upward information means rotating the blocks. And the downward information means dropping the blocks faster.

We use particle filter [4] to track the movement of the forearm. Particle filter has been applied to many fields, such as 3D human tracking [5] and head pose tracking[6]. All of these applications show that particle filtering is very effective in estimating the state of the object with nonlinear and non-Gaussian movement. We obtain the directional information through comparing the position of the forearm in the current frame and the former frame. Thus the player can control the movement and the rotation of the blocks in the Tetris game.

Compared to the other human-computer interaction systems which use expensive equipments such as stereo cam-eras, our system only needs an ordinary camera. This is the main novelty of our approach and will be beneficial to the widespread use of human-computer interaction.

2. Forearm Gesture Control System

We treat the forearm motion tracking as Bayesian filtering problem. Given a sequence of image z1: t= {zi, i=1... t}, we seek filtered estimation of state st of the forearm position at time t. Particle filter is used to represent the probability distribution by a set of random samples with associate weights.

As for the forearm motion tracking, one particle represents one state of the forearm. The main steps of particle filter used to forearm motion tracking are: 1) Initialization, i.e., computing p(s0); 2) Computing the likelihood; 3) Resampling, i.e., reduce the effects of particle degeneracy.

2.1. *Initialization*

In order to get the position of the forearm, we only need to know the coordinate of the central pixel of the detection window in the current frame. Then, the position of the forearm in the current frame is easy to compute according to the geometrical relation between the centroid and the size (64×128 pixels) of the detection window. Note that we track only the location of the forearm, not including the other motion information such as scale and rotation.

Thus, the state s_t of the forearm is represented as the coordinate (x_t, y_t) of the centroid of the detection window. As mentioned above, one particle represents one state of the forearm. We then use a 2-dimensional normal distribution $N_2(\mu, \Sigma)$ as the proposal distribution to generate the initial particle set. The expected value μ is the state vector s_0, and the covariance matrix Σ is a 2×2 identity matrix.

2.2. *Computing the likelihood*

Through the step of initialization, we have generated sample windows, i.e. the particles. For each particle, we need to estimate how well the particle fits the current frame, i.e. the likelihood This is the most important step of particle filter. The likelihood of each particle is calculated according to its HOG[7] feature. We first record the decision value of the HOG feature of the detection window in the former frame (See Fig. 2 (e)). Because we use radial basis function SVM, the decision value is calculated by

$$K(v',v) = \exp(-r\|v'-v\|^2) \ . \quad (1)$$

where r is kernel parameter, v is the support vector, and v' is the HOG feature vector.

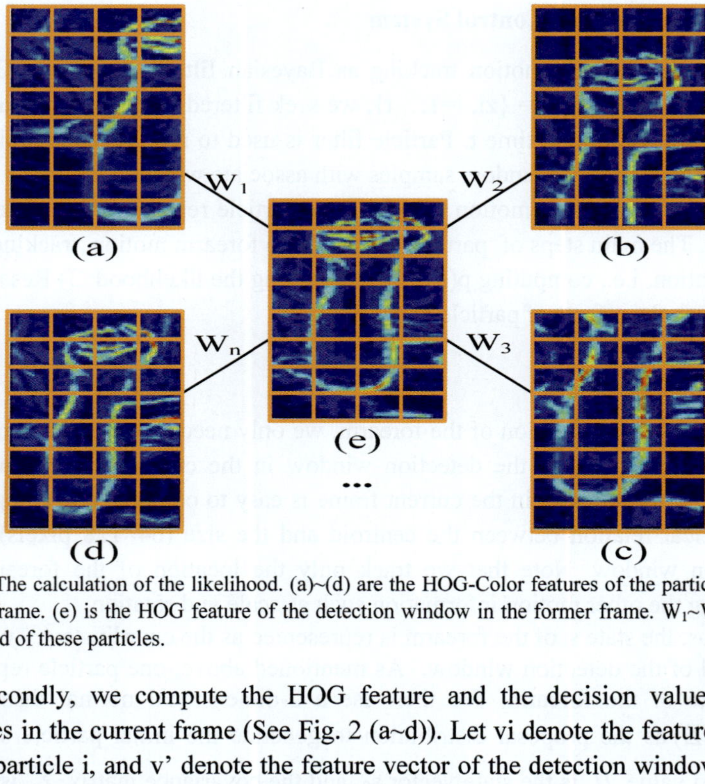

Fig. 2. The calculation of the likelihood. (a)~(d) are the HOG-Color features of the particles in the current frame. (e) is the HOG feature of the detection window in the former frame. W_1~W_n are the likelihood of these particles.

Secondly, we compute the HOG feature and the decision value of the particles in the current frame (See Fig. 2 (a~d)). Let vi denote the feature vector of the particle i, and v' denote the feature vector of the detection window in the former frame. Then the likelihood of the particle i is given by

$$W_i = \frac{1}{\sqrt{2\pi}} \exp\left(\frac{-((K(v_i,v) - K(v',v))^2}{2}\right). \quad (2)$$

2.3. *Resampling*

Given the state st-1 of the forearm at the former frame, we can use the normal distribution to generate the particle set at the current frame, and get the state st. This is the basic form of particle filter. But this process will generate the particle degeneracy phenomenon, which implies that a large computational effort is devoted to updating particles whose contribution to the prediction is almost zero [4]. To reduce to effects of degeneracy, we use the resampling method described in [9], which eliminates particles that have small weights and concentrates on particles with large weights.

3. Experimental Results

3.1. *Tracking*

We use 50 particles obeyed the normal distribution for particle filter tracking. As illustrated in Fig. 3, each green rectangle represents a particle. The likelihood of each particle is based on its HOG feature. We also compare our approach with the mean shift tracking [8]. As illustrated in Figure 3(a), the mean shift will

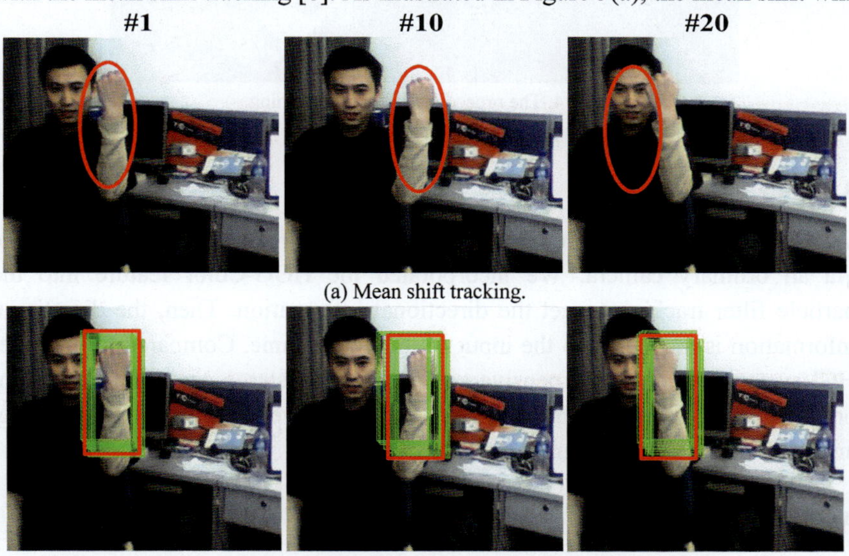

(a) Mean shift tracking.

(b) Our approach (each green rectangle represents a particle).

Fig. 3.Tracking the movement of the forearm in a video.

track the object lost sometimes. However, our proposed method can track the movement of the forearm robustly under real time.

3.2. *Gaming*

The directional information is obtained by comparing the location of the forearm in the current frame and the former frame. Then, the blocks in the game can move and rotate with the movement of the forearm of the player through the interface of Windows API. Figure 4 illustrates the procedure of our HCI gaming.

Fig. 4. The procedure of our HCI gaming.

4. Conclusion

We proposed a novel approach using forearm gesture as the input of the game via an ordinary camera. We incorporated the HOG-Color feature into the particle filter tracking to get the directional information. Then, the directional information is mapped into the input of the Tetris game. Compared to the other HCI systems which use expensive equipments like stereo cameras, our system only needs an ordinary camera. About 10 users have played our HCI gaming, and most of them showed great interest in it.

Acknowledgments

Work partially supported by the Innovation Team of Guizhou Provincial Education Department under Grant No [2014] 34.

References

1. Xbox, "Introducing Controller-Free Gaming & Entertainment," `http://www.xbox.com/en-US/live/projectnatal/`.
2. Y. Wang, T. Yu, L. Shi, and Z. Li, "Using Human Body Gestures As Inputs For Gaming Via Depth Analysis," Proc. of IEEE Int'l Conference on Multimedia & Expo (ICME), 2008.
3. T.K.Yin, C.M.Manders, F.Farbiz, and etc, "Integrating a Gesture Interface to A Commercial Online Dance Game," Proc. of IEEE Int'l Conference on Multimedia & Expo (ICME), 2009.

4. M. S. Arulampalam, S. Maskell, N. Gordon, T. Clapp, "A tutorial on particle filters for online nonlinear/non-gaussian bayesian tracking," IEEE Transactions on Signal Processing, 50(2):174–188, 2002.
5. E. Ricci and J.M Odobez, "Learning Large Margin Likelihood for Realtime Head Pose Tracking," in IEEE Int. Conference on Image Processing (ICIP), Cairo, Nov. 2009.
6. Balan,A., Sigal, L., Black, M., A quantitative evaluation of video-based 3D person tracking. IEEE Workshop on VS-PETS, 349-356, 2005.
7. N. Dalal and B. Triggs, "Histograms of oriented gradients for human detection," IEEE Conference on Computer Vision and Pattern Recognition (CVPR),2005.
8. D. Comaniciu and P. Meer, "Mean Shift: A Robust Approach Toward Feature Space Analysis," IEEE Trans. Pattern Analysis and Machine Intelligence (PAMI), vol. 24, no. 5, pp. 603-619, May 2002.
9. Isard, M, Blake, A.," Condensation-Conditional density propagation for visual tracking," Int.J. Computer Vision (IJCV), 29(1):5–28, 1998.

Distributed Parallel Stochastic Dynamic Programming Algorithm Based on MPI and Multithread for Long-Term Optimal Operation of Cascaded Hydropower Stations

Dong-qing ZHOU*, Shi-yu PENG and Kang-li SUN
School of Computer Science and Technology, Dalian University of Technology,
Dalian, Liaoning, China
**E-mail: zhoudq@dlut.edu.cn*

Xiu-feng LI
Yunnan Power Dispatching Center
Kunming, Yunnan, China
E-mail: 26240067@qq.com

Chun-tian CHENG
Institute of Hydropower and Hydroinformatics, Dalian University of Technology,
Dalian, Liaoning, China
E-mail: ctcheng@dlut.edu.cn

Stochastic dynamic programming (SDP) is widely adopted in a long-term optimal operation of large-scale hydropower systems. In this paper we propose a distributed parallel stochastic dynamic programming algorithm based on Message Passing Interface (MPI) and a peer-to-peer parallel paradigm (DPSDPoM). To deal with the disadvantages of redundancy in communications and memory-consumption during calculation in the peer-to-peer parallel paradigm, we propose a DPSDPoM with multithread algorithm (DPSDPoM-MT) which reduces costs between processes in each machine. The two algorithms are compared through the optimization scheduling of three reservoirs on Lancang Jiang Dam Cascade using time-elapse and memory consumption. Experimental results demonstrate that the improved algorithm can reduce computing time and alleviate memory consumption effectively.

Keywords: Stochastic dynamic programming; Distributed parallel computation; MPI; Multithread.

1. Introduction

The long-term optimal operation for cascaded hydropower stations is of great significance[1]. Because of the large-scale and high dimensionality of the optimization problem it is necessary to adopt effective optimization method.

Stochastic Dynamic Programming (SDP) method has been widely applied to long-term optimal operation of cascaded hydropower stations[2]. As the number of reservoirs and discrete variables increases, the problem of "curse of dimensionality" will occur[3], and at the same time the computational cost increases dramatically. In order to reduce the time-consuming and improve efficiency, Wang et al[4]. proposed the multi-core Parallel Stochastic Dynamic Programming (PSDP) method that splits the computation task into many subtasks, implements parallel computing by the multi-core parallel framework Fork/Join, which greatly shortens the calculation time elapse. PSDP, however, is still a stand-alone parallel algorithm which performance is limited and could not easily extend.

With the development of the High Performance Computing (HPC) technology, distributed parallel computing based on MPI (Message passing Interface) has been widely studied. Jin et al[5]. proposed multi-core parallel system based on MPI and OpenMP. Li et al[6]. proposed a peer-to-peer parallel dynamic programming algorithm based on MPI protocol for multi-reservoir system optimization. These algorithms take full advantages of cluster and dispatch the discrete water level combinations to different nodes, which effectively alleviates the "curse of dimensionality" and reduces each node's memory consumption. In this paper we analyze the peer to peer parallel model's advantages and drawbacks and propose a improved algorithm which based on MPI and multithread, and compare them from the aspects of time-consuming and memory consumption. Experimental results show that these improvements can effectively reduce the computation time and alleviate the memory consumption.

2. Distributed Parallel Stochastic Dynamic Programming

2.1. *Mathematical model*

Generally the problem of long-term optimal operation of cascaded hydropower stations uses several months or years as one period of optimization, one month or ten days as one stage in one period, and finally gets the maximum total output of all hydropower stations, the maximum guaranteed output or other goals with constrains of reservoirs and others. In the Solution of SDP, the state variable and decision variable should be discretized first. In this paper, we only consider the correlation of inflow between each hydropower station, and assume that the inflow between each stage is independent. In the procedure of computing global maximum benefit, We get each month's remained benefit expectation according last month's remained benefit and the this month's outputs of reservoirs. Finally we can obtain the global maximum benefit of the whole period and each month's best initial water levels and outputs by back-tracing.

Let M be the number of hydropower stations, T be the period number of scheduling cycle, the remaining value of the benefit is a recurrence equation as in Eq. (1).

$$E_{t+1}(Z_{t+1}) = \max\left\{\sum_{u=1}^{U} P(Q_t^u)[B(Z_t, Q_t, Z_{t+1}) + E_t(Z_t)]\right\}. \quad (1)$$

Where Z_t is initial water level vector of stage t; $E_t(Z_t)$ is the remaining benefit expectation of stage t; U is the number of inflow vectors in each stage; Q_t^u is the u th inflow vector in stage t; $P(Q_t^u)$ is the probability of u the inflow vector occur; and $B(Z_t, Q_t, Z_{t+1})$ is the total output at stage t. The calculation process and results' back-tracing are shown in Figure 1.

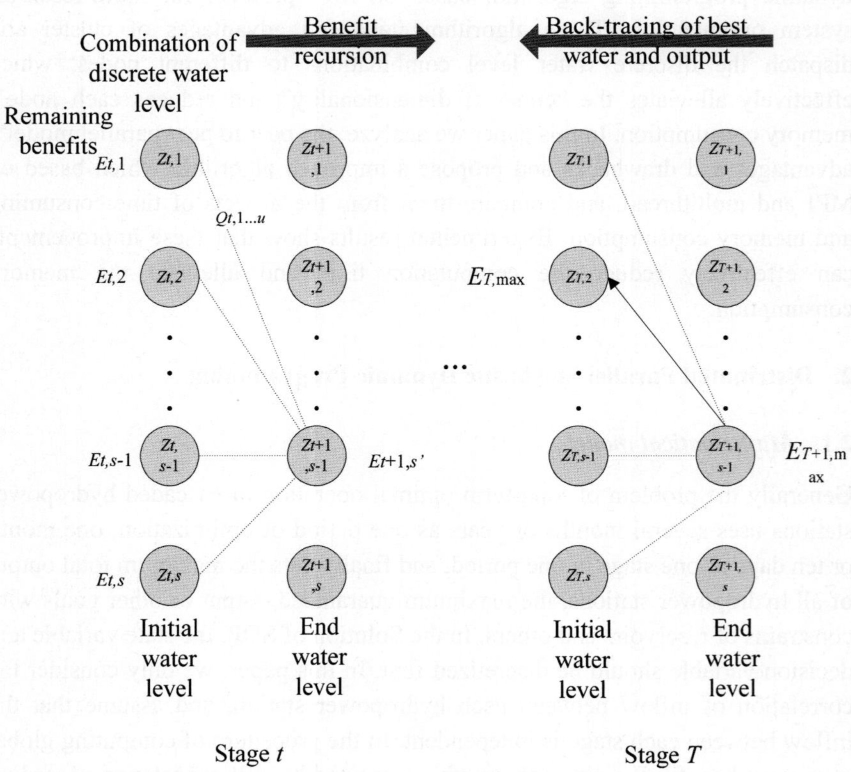

Fig. 1. Remaining benefit recursion and back-tracing.

Hydropower stations have to meet the following constraints:

$$V_m^{t+1} = V_m^t + Q_m^t - R_m^t; \tag{2}$$

$$V_{m,\min}^t \le V_m^t \le V_{m,\max}^t; \tag{3}$$

$$R_{m,\min}^t \le R_m^t \le R_{m,\max}^t; \tag{4}$$

$$N_{m,\min}^t \le N_m^t \le N_{m,\max}^t. \tag{5}$$

Where m denotes the number of stations, V_m^t is the initial capacity of station m at stage t, which has the explicit relationship with water level Z_t and can also be used as state variable in SDP; Q_m^t is the inflow of station m at stage t; R_m^t is the outflow of station m at stage t, containing power flow and spillages; N_m^t is the output of station m at stage t, which can be calculated by end water levels, inflows and stations' output curves.

In addition, the initial water levels at first stage are constrained by given values, and all variables are nonnegative.

2.2. *DPSDPoM and DPSDPoM-MT*

Referring to the peer-to-peer parallel paradigm which proposed in [6], we propose and implement a distributed parallel stochastic dynamic programming on MPI (DPSDPoM) algorithm, which takes the randomicity of inflow into consideration. DPSDPoM divides the computing process into two types: peer process and transfer process. The discrete water level combination variables are stored in different peer processes. Peer processes are responsible for calculating the benefits of the combinations which are stored in them, sending their data to the transfer process and receiving data from transfer process which is forward from another peer process. There is only one transfer process, which is responsible for data transmission and synchronization. The computing progress is paralleled through spread combinations to different peers.

During the DPSDPoM's iterative stage, the peer processes first initialize vector Z, vector E and matrix C. Z is the water level combinations which stored on current process; E is used to store the best remaining benefits of current process's water level combinations at each stage, its initial value is 0; C is used to store the last stage's water level combinations which maximize current stage's remaining benefits. Peer processes send Z and E to transfer process and wait for Z' and E' from other peer processes through transfer process. Z' is considered as the initial water level combination and Z as the end water level combination, and we can calculate the best remaining benefits. Then E and C will be updated and E is considered to be the parameter in the next stage's calculation. After all stage's calculations finished, the transfer process back-traces the result, sending the optimal combination to all peer processes, and receiving the last stage's optimal combination and sending it again until getting all optimal combinations at each stage.

The implementation of parallelism and reduce of memory of DPSDPoM is at the expense of massive communications. This algorithm works well, but still has some deficiencies:

- There are many redundant communications since every process receives its own data;
- During the back-tracing, transfer process needs to query the water level combinations from all peers for the best last stage's water level combination but just gets one peer's data, which leads to extra data transmission;
- The data between two processes which are on the same machine need to be sent to each other through transfer process. This transmission will cost much time and could be avoid.

In order to solve these problems, DPSDPoM with multi-thread (DPSDPoM-MT) algorithm is proposed:

- Each process calculates its own data first during every stage's calculation, and then transmits its data to transfer process. Transfer process excludes this process when sending data to all peers;
- At each stage matrix C just stores the process number and its index of last stage's best water level combination instead of the combination values, which avoid the query progress in back-tracing;
- Keep only one peer process in every machine, use multi-thread to parallel the calculation on each machine, which greatly alleviate the communications between peers.

The flow chat of DPSDPoM-MT' s iteration and back-tracing is shown in Figure 2 and Figure 3.

3. Experiment and Analysis

The proposed method is tested on LanCang Jiang Cascade. Partial characteristic parameters of involved reservoirs are shown in Table 1. Figure 4 shows the spatial distribution of these reservoirs.

Table 1. Parameters of reservoirs.

Reservoirs	Dead level(m)	Normal level(m)	Capacity(MV)	Max inflow(m3/s)
Xiaowan	1166.00	1240.00	4200	2340
Dachaoshan	882.00	899.00	1350	1800
Nuozhadu	765.00	812.00	5850	3528

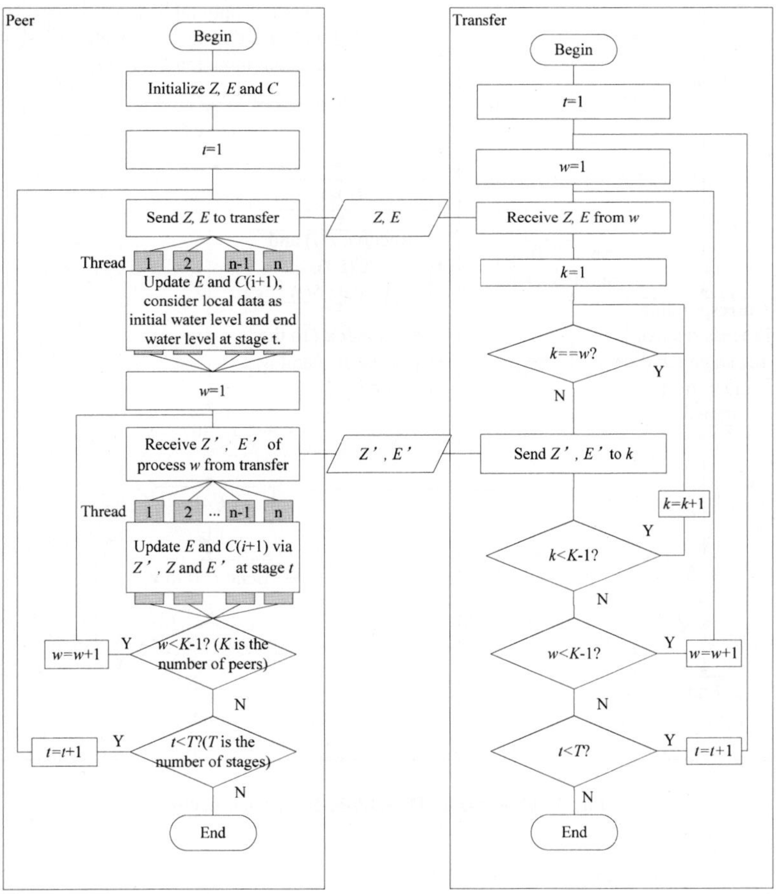

Fig. 2. Flow chat of DPSDPoM-MT's iteration.

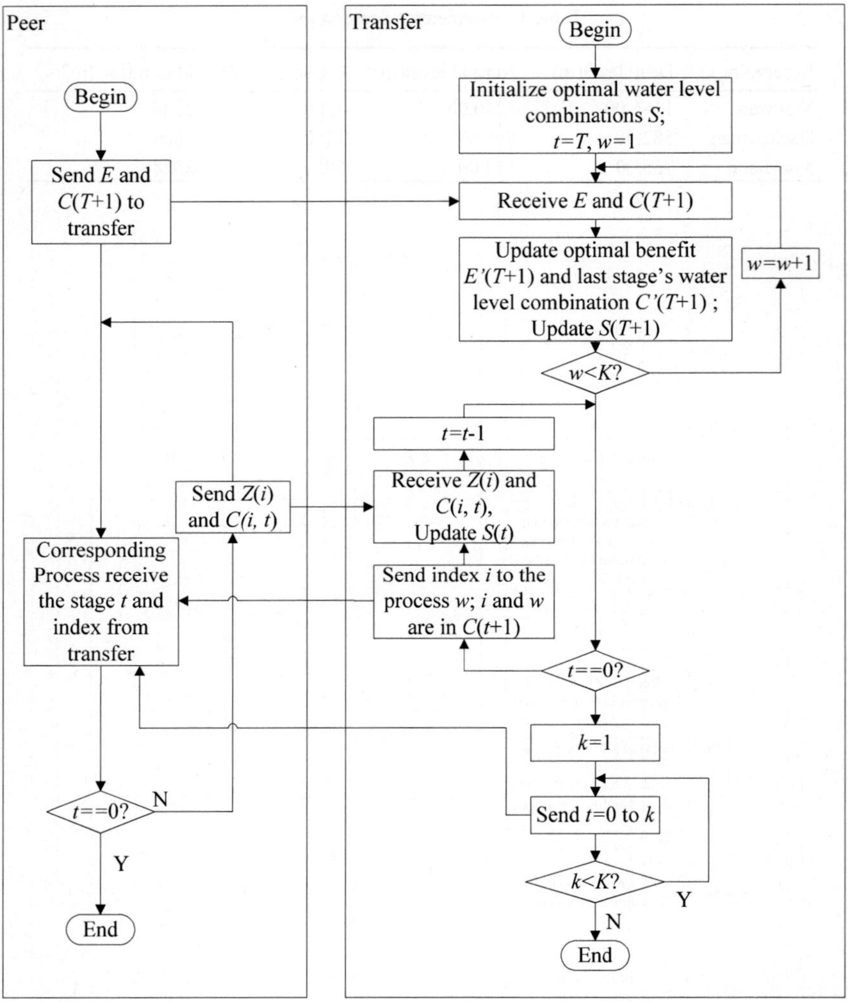

Fig. 3. Flow chat of DPSDPoM-MT's back-tracing.

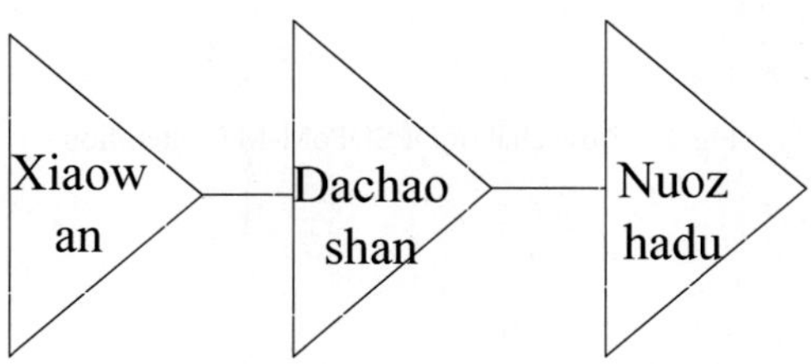

Fig. 4. position relation of cascade hydropower stations.

3.1. *Experimental environment and design*

Considering for load balancing, we assigned roughly the same number of water level combinations for each peer. Combination m_k which stored on peer k is calculated according to Eq. (6):

$$\begin{cases} m_k = \alpha + 1 & k \le \beta \\ m_k = \alpha & \beta < k \le K \end{cases}. \tag{6}$$

Where

$$\alpha = floor(N / K); \tag{7}$$

$$\beta = N \bmod K. \tag{8}$$

N is the total number of water level combinations; K is the number of peers; the function $floor()$ gets the max Integer which smaller than or equal to the given float number; "mod" means complementation.

3.2. *Speed-up ratio and efficiency*

Speed-up ratio is the proportion of time-elapsed in serial and parallel computation; Efficiency is the proportion of speed-up radio and core's number, which reflects the utilization of multi-cores. The formulation of Speed-up ratio and efficiency are shown in Eq. (9) and Eq. (10).

$$S_p = T_1 / T_p; \tag{9}$$

$$E_p = S_p / p. \tag{10}$$

Where T_1 is the time-elapsing of serial computation; T_p is the time-elapsing of computation with p parallel units. The Experimental result is shown in Figure 5 and Figure 6. DPSDPoM-MT reduces the overhead of the multiple processes and inter-process communications in each node, so it is more efficient than DPSDPoM.

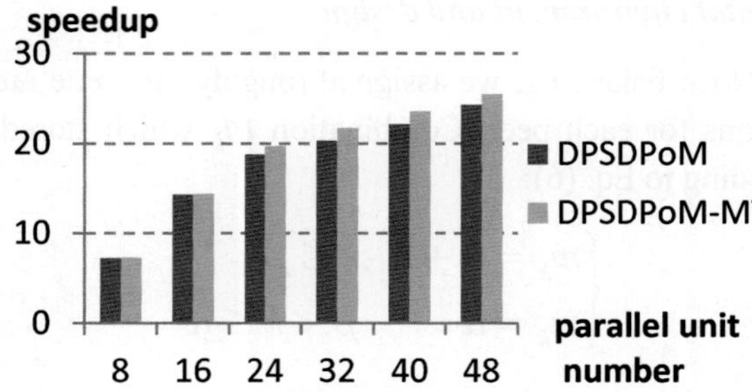

Fig. 5. Comparison of speed-up.

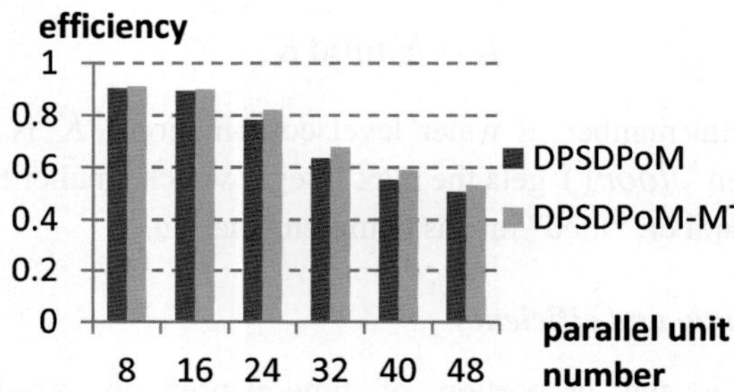

Fig. 6. Comparison of efficiency.

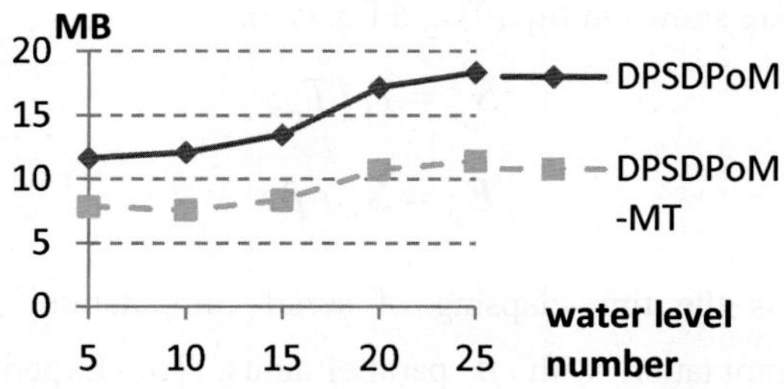

Fig. 7. Memory consumption over water level discrete number.

3.3. *Memory consumption*

When computing scale comes to particularly huge, nodes' memories are likely insufficient, which would cause memory overflow problem. In order to compare memory consumptions in the calculation progress, we monitor the memory changes of each node during the calculation and compare the largest memory usage of these algorithms. The average of memory usages of nodes in different discrete number of water levels are shown in Figure 7.

DPSDPoM-MT costs fewer memories during calculation for it avoids the consumption of multi-processes and inter-process communications in one node. With the increase of computation scale rise, this advantage would be more obvious.

4. Conclusion

Stochastic dynamic programming algorithm is widely adopted in the long-term optimal operation of cascaded hydro stations. Traditional SDP and PSDP which based on the Fork/Join are limited by the computational resources of stand-alone. Traditional high performance computation which represented by MPI is applied widely. In this paper, 1) the peer-to-peer computing model based on MPI (DPSDPoM) is implemented; 2) DPSDPoM-MT algorithm which improved from DPSDPoM is proposed; 3) the two algorithms are compared in many aspects. Experimental results show that these algorithms can effectively alleviate the problem of “curse of dimensionality” and DPSDPoM-MT performances better than DPSDPoM in computation efficiency and memory usage.

Acknowledgments

This work is supported by the Major International Joint Research Project from the National Nature Science Foundation of China (51210014).

References

1. Cheng C T, Shen J J, Wu X Y, et al. Practical solution strategies and methods of large-scale complex hydropower system operations (in Chinese). Journal of Hydraulic Engineering, 2012, 43: 785-795.
2. Cerisola S, Latorre J M, Ramos A. Stochastic dual dynamic programming applied to nonconvex hydrothermal models[J]. European Journal of Operational Research, 2012, 218(3): 687-697.
3. GUO S L, CHEN J H, LIU P, et al. State-of-the-art review of joint operation for multi-reservoir systems(in Chinese)[J]. Advances in Water Science, 2010 (4).
4. Wang S, Cheng C T, Wu X Y, et al. Parallel stochastic dynamic programming for long-term generation operation of cascaded hydropower stations (in Chinese). Sci China Tech Sci (Chin Ver), 2014, 44: 209–218, doi: 10.1360/092013-800.

5. Jin H, Jespersen D, Mehrotra P, et al. High performance computing using MPI and OpenMP on multi-core parallel systems[J].
6. Li X, Wei J, Li T, et al. A parallel dynamic programming algorithm for multi-reservoir system optimization[J]. Advances in Water Resources, 2014, 67: 1-15.

BFSDPOP: DPOP Based on Breadth First Search Pseudo-Tree for Distributed Constraint Optimization

Zhen HE
College of Computer Science, Chongqing University, Chongqing, China
E-mail: hezhen127287@163.com

Zi-yu CHEN
College of Computer Science, Chongqing University, Chongqing, China
E-mail: chenziyu@cqu.edu.cn

DPOP is an efficient algorithm based on the Depth First Search (DFS) Pseudo-tree for distributed constraint optimization problems in multiagent systems (MAS). DFS Pseudo-tree is able to help achieve parallelism due to the relative independence of nodes lying in different branches. However, we often get a chain-like pseudo-tree with few branches in our experiments, which greatly impairs the algorithm performance. Therefore we propose a new DPOP algorithm called BFSDPOP which uses Breadth First Search (BFS) Pseudo-tree as the communication structure. The two advantages are that BFS Pseudo-tree can help the algorithm achieve more parallelism as it has more branches; and BFS Pseudo-tree shortens the communication path and requires less communication time because the height of a BFS Pseudo-tree is often much lower than that of a DFS Pseudo-tree from the same constraint graph. To overcome the cross edge constraints in BFS Pseudo-tree which can easily result in large utility message size, a method of Cluster Removing is proposed. In the experiment, we compare BFSDPOP with the original DPOP and the result shows that BFSDPOP outperforms the original DPOP in most cases, which demonstrate the excellent attributes that BFS Pseudo-tree has over DFS Pseudo-tree.

Keywords: Multiagent system; Distributed constraint optimization; Breadth first search pseudo-tree; DPOP.

1. Introduction

Presently, multiagent systems (MAS) are widely deployed in real life to accomplish distributed satisfaction and optimization tasks. As a basic and practical framework for MAS problems, Distributed Constraint Optimization Problem (DCOP) has become a research hotspot in artificial intelligence area. To solve DCOPs, Petcu and Faltings proposed an inference-based algorithm—

DPOP [1] which uses the principle of Dynamic-Programming. It just requires a linear number of messages and is able to deal with large DCOPs of low induced-width. Afterwards, Petcu and Faltings presented two other improved algorithms: ODPOP[2] and MBDPOP[3] to deal with memory-bounded problems. In addition, James and Keith[4] tried to construct a non-traditional pseudo-tree structure using distributed best-first search traversal but had to deal with backedges and crossedges simultaneously.Function filtering is used in [5] to exploit utility bounds for smaller runtimes and Branch consistency is used in [6] to deal with hard constraints and large message size.

In our study, we caught the idea from another point--the pseudo-tree structure. The height of a BFS Pseudo-tree is often much lower than that of a DFS Pseudo-tree from the same constraint graph, which means the communication path is shorter and the communication time expense is lower. BFS Pseudo-tree is also better than DFS Pseudo-tree on parallelism as the former has more branches and more agents can compute concurrently.

The rest of the paper is structured as follows: Section 2 presents DCOP definitions and notations; Section 3 illustrates the details of BFSDPOP and the theoretical analysis of its advantages and disadvantages; Section 4 is the experiment part, where we compare BFSDPOP with the original DPOP. Finally, we conclude in Section 5.

2. Definitions and Notations

2.1. *Distributed constraint optimization*

A DCOP (Distributed Constraint Optimization Problem) is defined as a tuple $< X, D, R >$, where$X$={X_1,...,X_n} is a set of variables,$D = \{D_1, ..., D_n\}$ is a set of finite variable domains and$R = \{r_1, ..., r_m\}$ is a set of relations.A relation r_i is any function with the scope $(X_{i_1}, ..., X_{i_k})$, $r_i: D_{i_1} \times ... \times D_{i_k} \rightarrow \mathbb{R}^+$ which denotes how much utility is assigned to each possible combination of values of the involved variables.Without loss of generality, a solution to DCOP is an assignment to all variables that maximizes the total utilities, which is the sum of all relations shown by Eq. (1).

$$X^* = argmax_{x \in D} \sum_i r_i \tag{1}$$

As unary and higher arity relations can be easily expressed by binary relations with little modifications, we only deal with binary relations in this paper. We also assume each agent is assigned a single variable since multiple local variable cases can be transformed to single variable ones.

2.2. *DFS and BFS pseudo-tree*

To enable parallel computation, the original constraint graph is often prioritized to DFS or BFS pseudo-tree.A DFS and BFS pseudo-tree example from the same constraint graph is given in Fig. 1. To describe a pseudo-tree, the definitions are given as follows:

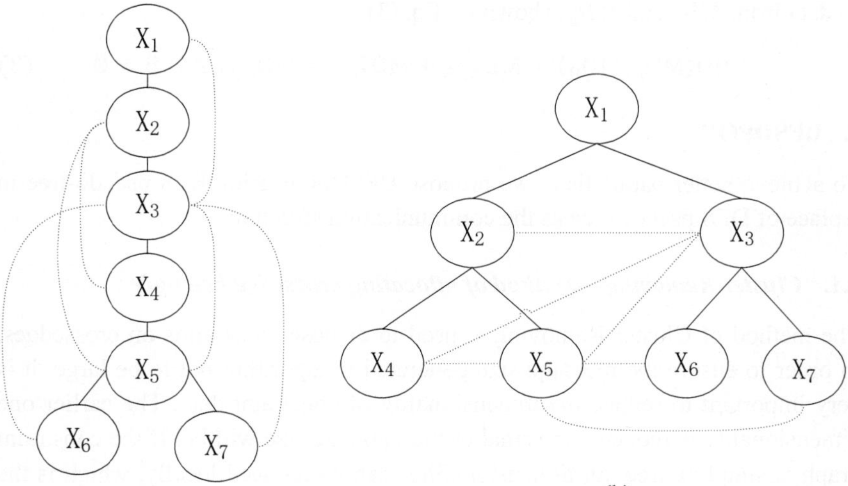

(a) (b)

Fig. 1. An example of DFS pseudo-tree (a) and BFS pseudo-tree (b) from the same constraint graph.

- P_i-the parent of nodeX_i(e.g. $P_2 = X_1$ in Fig. 1(a) and (b)).
- C_i-theset of children of node X_i (e.g. $C_1 = \{X_2, X_3\}$ in Fig. 1(a) and (b)).
- N_i- neighbors of node X_i(e.g. $N_2 = \{X_1, X_3, X_4, X_5\}$ in Fig. 1(a) and (b)).
- PN_i-theset of pseudo neighbors of node X_i, $PN_i \subseteq N_i$.
- $E(X_i, X_j)$-the edge connecting node $X_i$and X_j.
- $BE(X_i, X_j)$- back edge, a non-tree edge in DFS Pseudo-tree.
- $CE(X_i, X_j)$- cross edge, a non-tree edge in BFS Pseudo-tree.
- $CT(X_i, X_j)$-the constraint on edge $E(X_i, X_j)$.
- CEC_i-cross edge cluster: aset of cross edges that connect the mutual node X_i(e.g.$CEC_3 \subseteq \{E(X_2, X_3), E(X_3, X_4), E(X_3, X_5)\}$ in Fig.1(b)).
- $DIM = \{dim_1, \ldots, dim_n\}$ – the set of dimensionalities and dim_i is the dimensionality corresponding to node X_i with the size of $|D_i|$.
- $MD_S, S \subseteq DIM$ - the multi-dimensional data that involves the dimensionalities in set S;$CT(X_i, X_j) = MD_{\{dim_i, dim_j\}}$.

- $RD_{dim_i}(MD_S)$ - the operation of reducing the dimensionality dim_i, shown by Eq. (2).

$$\mathrm{RD_{dim_i}(MD_S) = min_{v \in D_i}(MD_S) = MD_{S\backslash\{dim_i\}}, dim_i \in S} \tag{2}$$

- $UD(MD_A, MD_B)$ - the operation of uniting two multi-dimensional data MD_A and MD_B, where $MD^A_{A \cup B}$ and $MD^B_{A \cup B}$ denote the extended multi-dimensional data from MD_A and MD_B, shown by Eq. (3).

$$\mathrm{UD(MD_A, MD_B) = MD^A_{A \cup B} + MD^B_{A \cup B} = MD_{A \cup B}, A \cap B \neq \emptyset} \tag{3}$$

3. BFSDPOP

To achieve better parallelism, we propose BFSDPOP using BFS pseudo-tree in replace of DFS pseudo-tree as the communication structure.

3.1. *Cluster Removing—Method of allocating crossedge belonger*

The method of Cluster Removing is used to dispose constraints on crossedges. In order to ensure the message size generated in algorithm not to be large, it is very important to reduce the dimensionality of constraint data. The earlier one dimensionality is reduced, the smaller the message size will be. If the constraint graph is simply a tree, all dimensionalities can be reduced locally, which is the best case. So, it is very important to carefully determine which one of the two nodes on a cross edge computes the constraint because each constraint should be considered only once. We call the process as Allocating Crossedge Belonger and the constraint on a crossedge should be computed by the belonger node.

We propose the method of Cluster Removing to allocate crossedge belonger. The procedure is as follows:

(1) For each node X_i, compute the max size crossedge cluster CEC_i;

(2) Select out the largest size crossedge cluster CEC_k;

(3) If CEC_k is empty, terminate;

(4) For each $CE(X_j, X_k) \in CEC_k$, set $CE(X_j, X_k)$ belongedto X_j. That is, $CT(X_j, X_k)$ should be computed by X_j. Then remove $CE(X_j, X_k)$ from all *CECs* if it exists;

(5) Loop.

The cross edges in BFS Pseudo-tree can result in larger utility message size than that in original DPOP with DFS Pseudo-tree but Cluster Removing helps BFSDPOP overcome this problem. With the help of Cluster Removing, we can easily exploit the excellent attributes of BFS Pseudo-tree on parallelism and communication time without causing too large utility message.

3.2. *The BFSDPOP Algorithm*

The detailed procedures of BFSDPOP are shown by Algorithm 1.

Algorithm 1: *BFSDPOP for Distributed Constraint Optimization Problem*

$BFSDPOP(X, D, R)$: each agent X_i executes:

Procedure Preprocessing

01: Generate BFS Pseudo-tree by Algorithm 1

//now X_i knows N_i, P_i, C_i, PN_i, CEC_i

02: Allocate crossedge belongers by Cluster Removing

Procedure Initialize

03: Unite the local constraints to MD_{S_i}

04: **if** X_i is a leaf agent **then**

05: **if** dim_i of MD_{S_i} is reducible **then**

//dim_i of MD_{S_i} is reducible when all constraints involved

// with dim_i are gathered together in MD_{S_i}

06: Reduce the dimensionality dim_i, that is $MD_{S_i} = RD_{dim_i}(MD_{S_i})$

07: Send MD_{S_i} to P_i by utility message $UTIL_i$

When received $UTIL_j$ from X_j

08: Unite MD_{S_i} and MD_{S_j}, that is, $MD_{S_i} = UD\left(MD_{S_i}, MD_{S_j}\right)$

//MD_{S_j} is the multi-dimensional data wrapped in $UTIL_j$

09: **if** all utility messages from children have been received **then**

10: **foreach** $dim_k \in S_i$ in MD_{S_i} **do**

11: **if** dim_k is reducible **then**

12: Reduce the dimensionality dim_k, that is, $MD_{S_i} = RD_{dim_k}(MD_{S_i})$

13: **end**

14: **if** X_i is the root **then**

15: Compute V, $V_k \in V$ if X_k is reduced here //V_k is the optimal value of X_k

16: **for each** X_k in C_i **do**

17: Send V to X_k by value message $VALUE_i$

18: Terminate execution

19: **end**

20: else

21: Send MD_{S_i} to P_i by utility message $UTIL_i$

When received $VALUE_j$ **from** X_j

22: Compute V, $V_k \in V$ if X_k is reduced here

23: Set $V = V \cup V' \backslash V_{P_i}$ //V' is the optimal value set wrapped in $VALUE_j$;

//V_{P_i} is the optimal value of P_i

24: **if** X_i is not a leaf agent **then**

25: **for each** X_k in C_i **do**

Send V to X_k by value message $VALUE_i$

end

Terminate execution

The $UTIL_i$ and $VALUE_i$ in the algorithm represent two types of messages transmitted by agents--the utility message and value message. The former contains the multi-dimensional utility data and the latter contains a set of optimal agent values.

4. Experimental Evaluation

As can be seen in Fig. 2(a), with the increase of agent number, the runtime increases and BFSDPOP expends less time. The positive result of BFSDPOP comes from the fact that the communication path of BFS Pseudo-tree is shorter than that of DFS Pseudo-tree.

There are more branches in a BFS Pseudo-tree while a DFS Pseudo-tree maybe chain-like. So BFS Pseudo-tree also exceeds DFS Pseudo-tree on parallelism, which is another influencing factor on algorithm runtime. The attributes of BFS Pseudo-tree are thus proved more excellent. It can be inferred that BFSDPOP is more appropriate for cases where communication time cannot be neglected, which is often the exact situation in real scenarios.

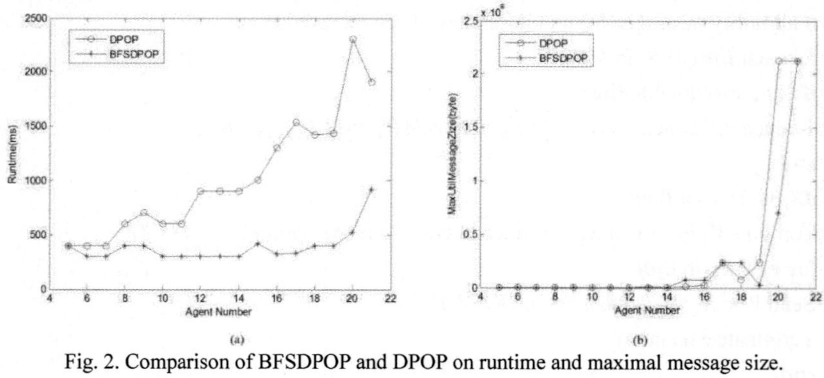

Fig. 2. Comparison of BFSDPOP and DPOP on runtime and maximal message size.

Same with DPOP, the complexity of BFSDPOP also lies in the size of utility message, which can be seen from Fig. 2(b). Compared on maximal message size, BFSDPOP is prior to DPOP in most cases.

We also see abnormal points in the figures like the maximal message size when agent number is 21 in Fig. 2(b). The reason is that the complexity of DCOP cannot be completely described by agent number. Though agent number cannot totally describe the problem complexity and may result in abnormal points, the curves still generally exhibit regular trends, which isconvictive on showing the algorithm performance.

5. Conclusion

In this paper we presented a new complete algorithm for solving DCOPs by replacing the communication network structure of DFS Pseudo-tree with BFS Pseudo-tree, considering that BFS Pseudo-tree is more excellent than DFS Pseudo-tree on both communication time and parallelism. The crossedges in BFS Pseudo-tree may result in very large utility message size but the Cluster Removing method perfectly solves this problem. By experimental evaluation, BFSDPOP proves to be much better than original DPOP on runtime and also slightlyprior on utility message size.

Acknowledgments

This work is funded by Chongqing University Postgraduates' Innovation Project (Project No. CYS14018).

References

1. Adrian Petcu and BoiFaltings,*DPOP:A scalable method for multiagent constraint optimization,*in Proceedings of the 19th International Joint Conference on Artificial Intelligence, IJCAI-05 (Edinburgh, Scotland, August 2005), pp. 266-271.
2. Petcu, A. &Faltings, B.,*ODPOP: An Algorithm for Open/Distributed Constraint Optimization,* AAAI, AAAI Press (2006), pp. 703-708.
3. Petcu, A. &Faltings, B.,*MB-DPOP: A New Memory-Bounded Algorithm for Distributed Optimization,*in Proceedings of the 20th International Joint Conference on Artificial Intelligence, IJCAI-07 (Hyderabad, India, January 2007), pp. 1452-1457.
4. James Atlas andKeith Decker, *A Complete Distributed Constraint Optimization Method For Non-Traditional Pseudotree Arrangements,* in Proceedings of the Sixth Intl. Joint Conf. on Autonomous Agents and Multiagent Systems, IFAAMAS (2007), pp. 741-748.
5. Brito, I. and Meseguer, P., *Improving DPOP with function filtering,* in Proc. of AAMAS (2010), pp. 141–158.

6. Ferdinando Fioretto, Tiep Le, William Yeoh, Enrico Pontelli and Tran Cao Son, *Improving DPOP with Branch Consistency for Solving Distributed Constraint Optimization Problems,* Principles and Practice of Constraint Programming, Vol. 8656 of the series Lecture Notes in Computer Science (2014), pp. 307-323.

An Integrated Interframe Video Coding Scheme Based on Adaptive Directional Motion Search and Improved Mode Decision

Zhi-gang YANG*, Hong-bin WANG† and Tao CHEN‡

College of Information and Communication Engineering, Harbin Engineering University,
Harbin, 150001, China
E-mail: *zgyang@hrbeu.edu.cn, †wanghongbin@hrbeu.edu.cn, ‡chentao@hrbeu.edu.cn*

In this paper, an improved interframe coding scheme consisting of both the adaptive directional motion search and improved mode selection is proposed to reduce the computational complexity of video coding. The motion direction is divided into four regions, and different multi-hexagon templates are designed for each region to enhance directional search, which can improve the search accuracy. Subsequently, the improved mode decision that integrates the detection of all zero blocks is proposed for further computation reduction. Experimental results demonstrate that the proposed scheme can reduce encoding time by an average of 60% while maintaining almost the same coding efficiency as existing fast interframe coding schemes.

Keywords: Motion search; Mode decision; Adaptive search templates; Video coding.

1. Introduction

Video coding has greatly progressed due to the increasing interests in broadcast, communication, internet and other multimedia applications. Removing interframe redundancy in continuous video sequence is the key to obtain high compression efficiency. Therefore, motion estimation and compensation with variable block size, sub pixel and multiple reference frames [1] are adopted in the second generation video coding standards like H.264 [2], which can approximately save 50% bitrate than prior standards. At the same time, these interframe coding modules also contribute the heaviest computational burden to the whole video encoding.

Many fast search algorithms which can reduce the complexity of motion estimation have been proposed in recent years, such as three-step search algorithm (TSS), diamond search algorithm (DS), unsymmetrical-cross multi-hexagon-grid search (UMHexagonS) [3]. Among these algorithms, UMHexagonS has better prediction accuracy and coding performance, but its computation complexity is still high. Some algorithms have been proposed to solve the problem [4]. As for fast mode decision, the information of adjacent macroblocks (MBs) can be used for predicting the possible encoding mode to reduce the computation [5].

In this paper, a fast interframe coding scheme including both adaptive directional motion search and improved mode selection is proposed to reduce the computational complexity of video coding. The rest parts of this paper are organized as follows. In Section 2, adaptive directional motion search are presented. In Section 3, all zero block detection and mode decision are used together for further computation reduction. In Section 4, experimental results are shown to demonstrate the effectiveness of the proposed method. Finally, the paper is concluded in Section 5.

2. Adaptive Directional Motion Search

The multi-hexagon template adopted by the UMHexagonS algorithm has been proved to be efficient when the movements in a video are mainly in the horizontal direction. As for vertical or other directional motion pictures, it will spend more search steps to find the best matched block, or sometime the second best matched block.

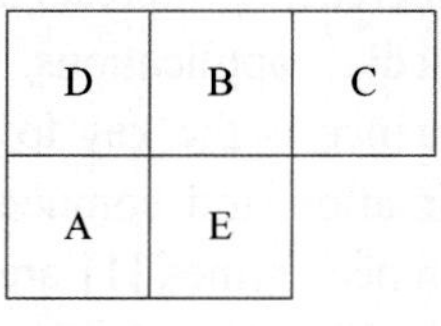

Fig. 1. Adjacent blocks of current block.

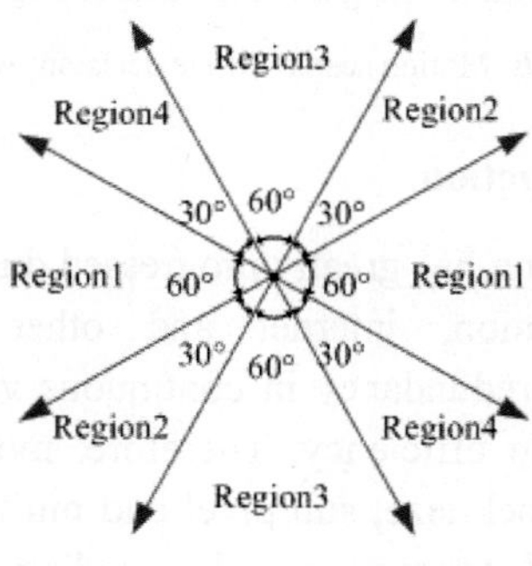

Fig. 2. Region division of motion vector.

Adaptive multi-hexagon search templates are proposed to improve the search accuracy and speed. Firstly, motion vectors (MVs) of adjacent blocks are taken into consideration. As shown in Fig. 1, block A, B, C and D are the adjacent blocks of current block E. And the motion vectors of these adjacent blocks are mv_a, mv_b, mv_c and mv_d respectively. All the motion vectors can be located in one of the four regions as shown in Fig. 2. If two or three adjacent motion vectors among mv_a, mv_b and mv_c (replaced by mv_d if unavailable) are in the same region, the corresponding template (as shown in Fig. 3(a-d)) will be adopted in motion search. If all the three vectors are in different regions, the original template shown in Fig. 3(a) will be used. The detailed adaptive search steps can be found in our previous work [6].

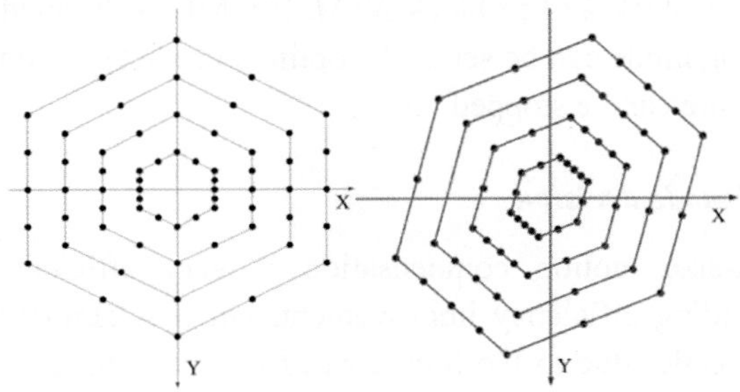

(a) Template of Region 1 (b) Template of Region 2

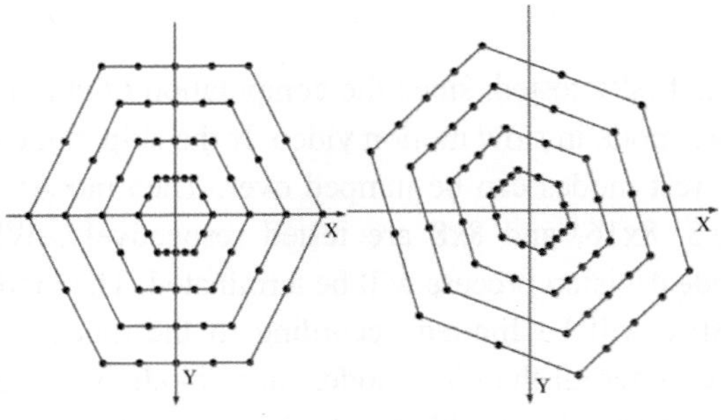

(c) Template of Region 3 (d) Template of Region 4

Fig. 3. Adaptive multi-hexagon search templates.

3. Mode Decision

3.1. *All Zero Block (AZB)*

In interframe coding, the coefficients of some residual blocks are relatively small and usually all zeros after transform and quantization. Such kind of block is called all zero block. If ABZs can be detected before transformation and quantization, the processes of transformation, quantization, inverse transformation and inverse quantization can be omitted to reduce the computational complexity of encoding. Let T_{ZERO} (usually $T_{ZERO} = 0.707STEP_{QP}$ [7]) denotes the all zero block threshold of block 4×4, then the AZB detection condition for block $N \times M$ is as follows.

$$SAD_{N\times M} < N_{BLOCK} \times T_{ZERO}. \tag{1}$$

Where $SAD_{N\times M}$ is the sum of absolute difference of block $N \times M$, and N_{BLOCK} is the numbers of block 4×4 in block $N \times M$. If a MB is detected to be an AZB, the corresponding mode can be set as the optimal prediction mode and the mode selection procedure can be stopped.

3.2. *Improved mode decision*

Variable block-size motion compensation is very efficient for prediction accuracy and coding efficiency improvement, but it is almost the most costly part in video encoder due to the high cost of motion estimation. An improved mode decision scheme integrated with AZB detection is proposed to reduce the computational complexity in this paper. The specific mode decision process is shown in Fig. 4.

Skip mode is firstly tested, since the computation of skip mode is not high and it is the major mode in slow motion video. If the skip mode is detected to be an AZB, all the rest modes can be jumped over. Then modes of macro block-size 16x16, 16x8, 8x16, and 8x8 are tested respectively. When an AZB is detected, the mode decision process will be terminated. The modes of sub block-size 8x4, 4x8, 4x4 will be limited according to the mode decision result of macro block-size. After all the inter modes, intra mode is tested only if at least one of the MBs among adjacent blocks A, B, C, and D (as shown in Fig. 1) is intra-coded or unavailable, or at least one MV during the inter motion search exceeds search range.

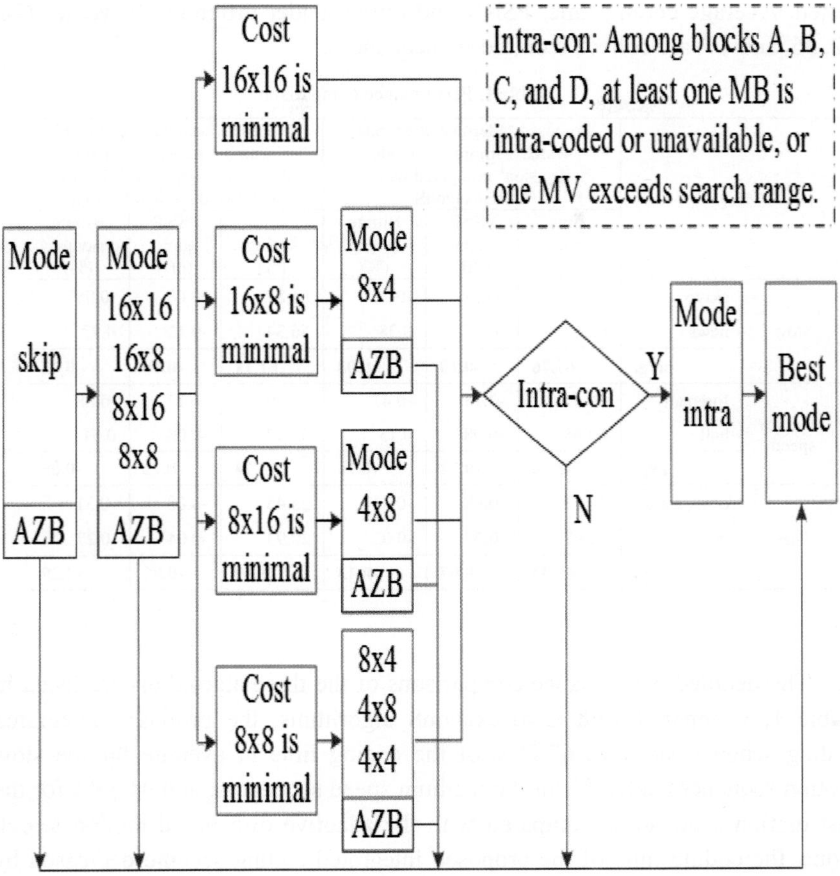

Fig. 4. Improved mode decision.

4. Experimental Results

The proposed interframe video coding scheme integrated with adaptive directional motion search and improved mode decision is tested with the H.264 reference software JM10.1 on a PC platform (Intel Core i5, 2.3GHz, 2G RAM). The main coding conditions are as follows: reference frame number 5, search range 32, UVLC, RDO off, IPPP, 100 frames to be coded, frame rate 30Hz, and the other parameters use the default settings. Six sequences are selected, including two slow motion sequences "akiyo" and "news", two medium speed motion sequences "foreman" and "hall", and two fast motion sequences "bus" and "coastguard". Besides the proposed integrated scheme, the adaptive directional search algorithm alone and the UMHexagonS algorithm are also tested. Average coding time, PSNR and bitrate under different QP values (28, 32, 36, and 40) are collected on the six sequences.

Table 1. Performance comparison.

Seq.		Proposed "adaptive directional search + improved mode decision" compared with UMHexagonS			Proposed "adaptive directional search + improved mode decision" compared with only "adaptive directional search"		
		Time saving (%)	PSNR gain (dB)	Bitrate saving (%)	Time saving (%)	PSNR gain (dB)	Bitrate saving (%)
Slow	akiyo	71.88	-0.08	-0.32	65.87	-0.08	-0.90
	news	63.64	-0.12	0.38	56.34	-0.11	0.93
	avg.	**67.76**	**-0.10**	**0.03**	**61.11**	**-0.10**	**0.02**
Medium speed	foreman	61.65	-0.15	-0.47	54.10	-0.17	-0.68
	hall	62.68	-0.08	0.15	53.37	-0.06	0.51
	avg.	**62.16**	**-0.11**	**-0.16**	**53.74**	**-0.12**	**-0.08**
Fast	coastguard	48.71	-0.08	-0.24	35.45	-0.08	-0.51
	bus	41.95	-0.07	-0.02	20.93	-0.04	-0.27
	avg.	**45.33**	**-0.07**	**-0.13**	**28.19**	**-0.06**	**-0.39**

The detailed performance comparisons of the three algorithms are listed in Table 1. Compared with UMHexagonS algorithms, the proposed integrated coding scheme can save 67.76% of the coding time in average for the slow motion sequences, 62.16% for the medium speed sequences, and 45.33% for the fast motion sequences. Compared with the adaptive directional motion search alone, the coding time of the proposed integrated coding scheme decreased by 61.11% for slow motion sequences, 53.74% for medium speed sequences, and 28.19% for fast motion sequences. Since some sub block-size modes are skipped during the fast mode decision, the PSNR dropped about 0.1 dB. Thus, the proposed integrated coding scheme can provide a good tradeoff between coding speed and performance.

5. Conclusion

In this paper, an interframe video coding scheme integrated with adaptive directional motion search and improved mode decision is proposed to reduce the computational complexity of video coding. Adaptive directional search are adopted to improve the search accuracy, and fast mode decision are applied for great computation reduction. Experimental results show that the proposed integrated scheme provides a good tradeoff between coding speed and coding performance.

Acknowledgments

This work was supported in part by the National Natural Science Foundation of China (61201238 and 61571146), and the Fundamental Research Funds for the Central Universities (HEUCF140812).

References

1. T. Wiegand, H. Schwarz, A. Joch, F. Kossentini and G. J. Sullivan. Rate-Constrained Coder Control and Comparison of Video Coding Standards. *IEEE Trans. Circuits and Systems for Video Technology*, Vol.13, No. 7, pp. 688-703, 2003.

2. Draft ITU-T recommendation and final draft international standard of joint video specification (ITU-T Rec.H.264/ISO/IEC 14496-10 AVC), JVT of MPEG and VCEG, JVT-G050r1, May, 2003.

3. Z. Chen, J. Xu, Y. He, and J. Zheng. Fast Integer-pel and Fractional-pel Motion Estimation for H.264/AVC. *Journal of Visual Communication and Image Representation*, Vol. 17, No. 2, pp. 264-290, 2006.

4. W. Zhao, S. Xu. Research and optimization of UMHexagons algorithm based on H.264. *Int. Conf. Multimedia Information Networking and Security*, pp.600-603, 2012.

5. Wang H, Yang Y. Fast mode selection based on texture segmentation and view prediction in JMVC. *Int. Conf. Communication Technology*, pp.192-196, 2012.

6. Z. Yang, H. Wang. An Adaptive Directional Motion Search Algorithm of Video Coding. *Int. Conf. Artificial Intelligence, Software Engineering and Industrial Application*, 2015.

7. Y. Zhao, Y. Yuan. All-zero block detecting algorithm based on look-up threshold tables in H.264. *Int. Conf. Digital Content, Multimedia Technology and its Applications*, pp.183-187, 2010.

Fast Mode Decision Based on Motion Coherence for P-Frame Video Coding

Zhi-gang YANG[*], Ling-yong XU[†] and Tao CHEN[‡]

College of Information and Communication Engineering, Harbin Engineering University,
Harbin, 150001, China
E-mail: [*]zgyang@hrbeu.edu.cn, [†]xulingyong@hrbeu.edu.cn, [‡]chentao@hrbeu.edu.cn

In this paper, fast mode decision strategies based on motion coherence for P-frame coding are proposed to accelerate the video encoding procedure. Firstly, mode prejudgment strategy based on neighborhood macroblocks (MBs) is introduced. According to the coherence of adjacent movement, the left and up MBs in current frame and the current-position and right MBs in previous frame are used to predict the mode of current MB. Secondly, mode combination strategy based on motion coherence is implemented to combine blocks in sub-type with similar motion vectors (MVs) into a block in macro-type. Lastly, the overall fast mode decision scheme is proposed and the performance of the proposed scheme is verified through comparative experimental results using JM reference software.

Keywords: Fast mode decision; Motion coherence; Video coding.

1. Introduction

The transform and motion compensation hybrid coding framework is commonly adopted in the second generation video coding standards like H.264/AVC [1]. The variable block-size motion compensation is a key technique in this coding scheme. Full inter modes including SKIP, 16×16, 16×8, 8×16, 8×8, 8×4, 4×8, and 4×4 blocks, followed by intra mode are usually used in P-frame coding to obtain a high compression efficiency[2]. These structures cause the computational complexity of full-mode motion estimation/compensation is much higher than other video coding modules.

Many kinds of fast inter-mode decision schemes have been reported to reduce the computation of interframe coding [3-6]. For instance, a MB tracking-based fast mode decision algorithm is proposed in [3]. The information of adjacent MBs is used for predicting the possible encoding modes to reduce the computation [4]. Early termination and adaptive threshold techniques are adopted in the mode decision procedure [5].

In this paper, fast mode decision strategies for P-frame coding are proposed to reduce the computational complexity of video coding. The rest parts of this paper are organized as follows. In Section 2, different strategies including mode prejudgment based on neighborhood MBs and mode combination are introduced, and then the overall fast mode decision scheme is presented. In Section 3, experimental results are shown to demonstrate the effectiveness of the proposed method. Finally, the paper is concluded in Section 4.

2. Fast Mode Decision

2.1. *Mode prejudgment based on neighborhood MBs*

If the possible mode of current MB can be early predicted, the motion estimation procedure of the rest modes can be reduced. In general, skip and 16×16 modes account for the largest proportion of the final mode statistic. Therefore, a mode prejudgment strategy for skip and 16×16 modes is proposed.

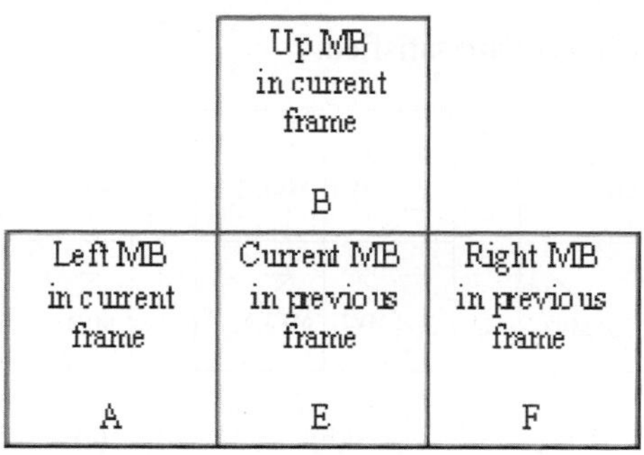

Fig. 1. Neighborhood MBs for mode prejudgment, two in current frame and two in previous frame.

Table 1. Prediction values of the neighborhood MBs.

Mode	Skip	16×16	16×8, 8×16	8×8	8×4, 4×8, 4×4	Intra	Unavailable
Pred Val	0	1	2	4	7	9	10

As shown in Fig. 1, there are total four neighborhood MBs used in mode prejudgment. From the aspect of spatial movement coherence, the left MB A and up MB B in current frame are selected. From the aspect of temporal correlation, the current-position MB E and right MB F in previous frame are chosen. According to the mode of the neighborhood MBs, the prediction values of the neighborhood MBs are listed in Table 1. Then $PVAL_{ADD}$ is calculated as follows.

$$PVAL_{ADD} = PVAL_A + PVAL_B + PVAL_E + PVAL_F. \quad (1)$$

If $PVAL_{ADD} < 5$, the current MB are prejudged to be SKIP or 16×16 modes.

2.2. *Mode combination*

Adjacent blocks in sub-type with similar MVs can be combined into a block in macro-type. Assume that MV0, MV1, MV2, and MV3 are the MVs of four 8×8 blocks as shown in Fig. 2 and they are all from the same reference frame, then the mode combination rules are as follows.

(a) 16×8: if the difference between MV0 and MV1, and the difference between MV2 and MV3 are both less than one integer pixel.

(b) 8×16: if the difference between MV0 and MV2, and the difference between MV1 and MV3 are both less than one integer pixel.

(c) 16×16: both (a) and (b) are satisfied.

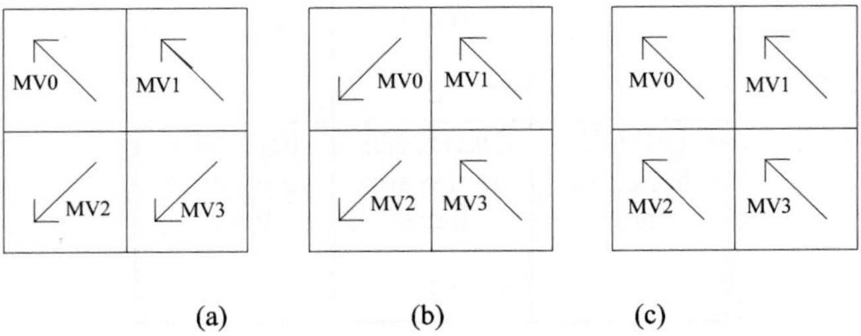

Fig. 2. Illustration of MVs used in mode combination.

2.3. *Overall scheme of the proposed fast mode decision*

The overall scheme of the proposed fast mode decision is shown in Fig. 3, including mode prejudgment based on neighborhood MBs and mode combination.

Mode prejudgment is firstly applied. If $PVAL_{ADD} < 5$, a simple mode decision procedure will be chosen. Motion estimation is only performed on 16×16 and 8×8 modes, then followed by 8×8 mode combination. The final mode is selected among SKIP, 16×16 and 8×8 modes. If $PVAL_{ADD}$ >= 5, a multiple-comparison mode decision procedure will be chosen. 16×16, 16×8, and 8×16 modes are firstly tested. If the best mode of MB E (shown in Fig. 1) is SKIP mode, then directly jump to the temporal-spatial correlation analysis, otherwise the rest modes of sub block-size 8×8, 8×4, 4×8, 4×4 will be limited according to the mode decision result of macro block-size.

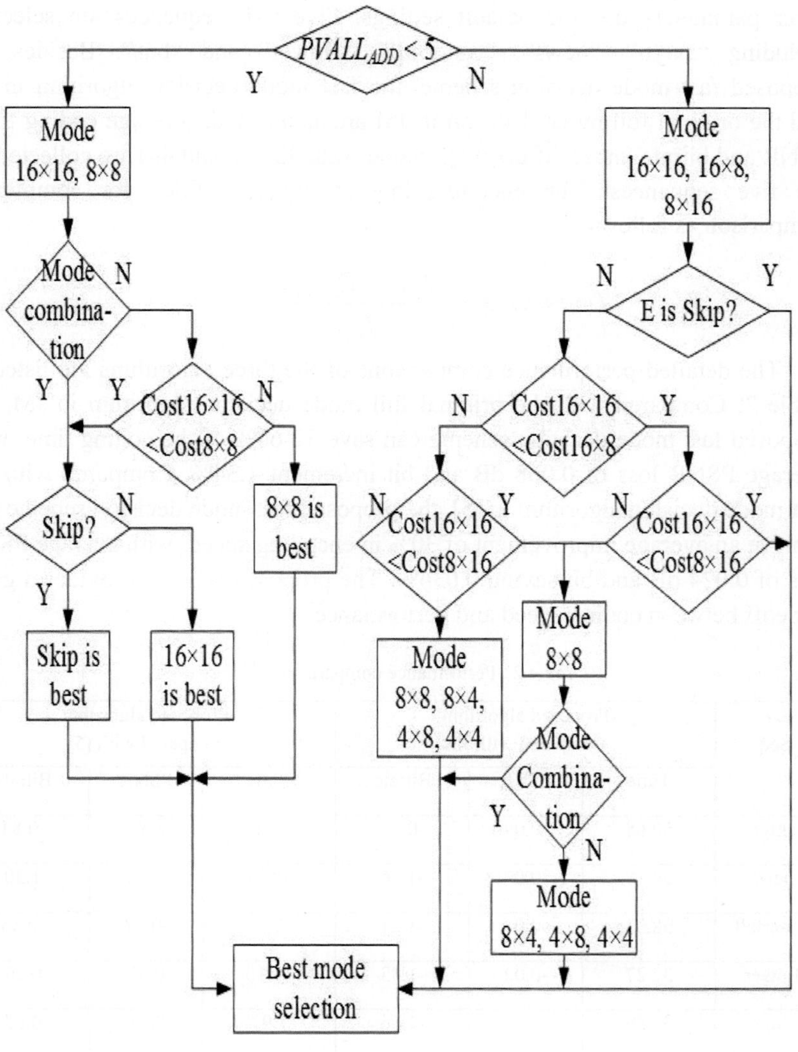

Fig. 3. Proposed fast mode decision.

3. Experimental Results

The proposed fast mode decision scheme is tested with the H.264 reference software JM10.1 on a PC platform (Intel Core i3, 2.53GHz, 2G RAM). The main coding conditions are as follows: reference frame number 4, search range 32, UVLC, RDO off, IPPP, 100 frames to be coded, frame rate 30Hz, and the other parameters use the default settings. Five CIF sequences are selected, including “akiyo”, “news”, “waterfall”, “flower” and “bus”. Besides the proposed fast mode decision scheme, the fast mode decision algorithm in [5] and the original full mode decision in JM are also tested. Average coding time, PSNR and bitrate under different QP values (28, 32, 36, and 40) are collected on the five sequences. The encoding-time saving is defined for complexity comparison as follows.

$$Timesaving = \frac{T_{ref} - T_{proposed}}{T_{ref}} \times 100\% . \quad (2)$$

The detailed performance comparisons of the three algorithms are listed in Table 2. Compared with the original full mode decision algorithm in JM, the proposed fast mode decision scheme can save 32-60% of the coding time, with average PSNR loss of 0.068 dB and bit increment 1.34%. Compared with the fast mode decision algorithm in [5], the proposed fast mode decision scheme can achieve an average improvement of 30% in encoding speed, with average PSNR loss of 0.024 dB and bit saving 0.036%. The proposed scheme provides a good tradeoff between coding speed and performance.

Table 2. Performance comparison.

Seq.	Proposed algorithm compared with JM			Proposed algorithm compared with [5]		
	Time	PSNR	Bitrate	Time	PSNR	Bitrate
akiyo	60.68	-0.09	-0.83	47.25	-0.05	-0.84
news	54.18	-0.09	-1.56	38.12	-0.01	1.30
waterfall	58.02	-0.07	-1.21	47.94	-0.07	-0.55
flower	32.27	-0.02	-1.43	11.10	0.00	0.20
bus	32.89	-0.07	-1.66	7.97	0.01	0.07

4. Conclusion

In this paper, fast mode decision strategies for P-frame coding, including mode prejudgment based on neighborhood MBs and mode combination are proposed to reduce the computational complexity of video coding. Experimental results show that the proposed fast mode decision scheme can achieve a speed-up factor of 32-60% with no obvious coding performance loss.

Acknowledgments

This work was supported in part by the National Natural Science Foundation of China (61201238 and 61571146), and the Fundamental Research Funds for the Central Universities (HEUCF140812).

References

1. Draft ITU-T recommendation and final draft international standard of joint video specification (ITU-T Rec.H.264/ISO/IEC 14496-10 AVC), JVT of MPEG and VCEG, JVT-G050r1, May, 2003.

2. T. Wiegand, H. Schwarz, A. Joch, F. Kossentini and G. J. Sullivan. Rate-Constrained Coder Control and Comparison of Video Coding Standards. *IEEE Trans. Circuits and Systems for Video Technology*, Vol.13, No. 7, pp. 688-703, 2003.

3. B. G. Kim, C. S. Cho. A Fast Inter-Mode Decision Algorithm Based on Macro-Block Tracking for P Slices in the H.264/AVC Video Standard. *IEEE Int. Conf. Image Processing*, pp. v301-v304, 2007.

4. H. Wang, Y. Yang. Fast mode selection based on texture segmentation and view prediction in JMVC. *Int. Conf. Communication Technology*, pp.192-196, 2012.

5. X.X. Wang, Z.C. Lu. Optimization algorithm of fast mode decision for H.264/AVC inter-prediction. *Journal of Computer Applications*, Vol. 30, No. 6, pp. 188-194, 2010.

6. C. Crecos and M. Y. Yang, Fast Inter Mode Prediction for P Slices in the H264 Video Coding Standard, *IEEE Trans. Broadcasting*, vol. 51, no. 2, pp. 256-263, 2005.

A Spatial Analysis of Urban Taxi Drivers' Working Pattern

Xiang-yu LI[1], Wen-jun WANG[1], Lin PAN[1], Ning YUAN[1,2*] and Shan GAO[3]
[1]*School of Computer Science and Technology, Tianjin University,*
[2]*Department of Basic Courses, Academy of Military Transportation, PLA,*
[3]*Information Engineering Institute, Tianjin University of Commerce,*
Tianjin, China
[*]*E-mail: ningyuan@tju.edu.cn*

Taxis equipped with GPS can record their trajectory and generate huge amounts of data. We can analyze the behavior of taxi drivers and search for similarities and common characteristics in their working patterns. In this paper, we utilize taxi GPS data collected form Tianjin city to analyze taxi drivers' working pattern. Firstly, we determined taxis' parking place by detecting stopping points and measured the operating range. Secondly, we studied the taxis' working pattern by comparing the relationship between three representative locations in taxis' behavior: parking place, working center and city center. Thirdly, we analyzed the spatial pattern from two perspectives of direction and distance. Lastly, we studied the income efficiency of different taxis from different parking places and working centers. The research results demonstrated that the taxis' individual mobility behavior has clear similarities: The taxi drivers' operating pattern has a characteristic of moving toward the city center and most of the working centers distribute in positions between parking places and the city center. The discoveries are significant for urban public infrastructure construction, government's management of the taxis and taxi drivers' strategy selections.

Keywords: Taxi GPS; Spatial data mining; Working pattern; Radius of gyration.

1. Introduction

As an important part of urban transportation, taxi carries a considerable part of urban travel. Taxis equipped with GPS can be regarded as a sensor of taxi drivers' and residents' behavior and urban traffic flow. Recently, lots of related works are about human behavior researching[1-5], hotspots discovering[6], urban planning[7-12], and transportation planning[13-16].

Jiang et al.[1] researched on human movement patterns through over 72,000 passengers' trajectories. Chen et al. [2] used taxi trajectories to discover frequent trajectories between a given source and destination. Liu et al. [3] used taxi trajectories and smart card data form metro and bus to quantify and visualize urban transport pattern. Liang et al.[4] proposed the distribution of passenger travel distance is more general fits the exponential distribution rather than power law distribution. Tang et al.[5] revealed the law of urban human mobility through the taxi GPS data collected from Harbin. Wang et al. [6] analyzed frequent travel pattern by passenger pickup and drop-off location in different hotspots. Zheng et al. [7] discovered inefficient connectivity between two regions by looking at actual versus expected distance required to travel between these two regions. Liu et al. [8,9] mined the mobility of urban human and the land use variations based on taxi trajectories. Pan et al. [10] put forward a new method by using taxi trajectory data to classify the urban land use features. Yuan et al. [11]combined a hierarchical road network decomposition, general human mobility and points of interest of each region to uncover the functionality of different regions. Zhang et al. [12] analyzed the urban taxi drivers' refuel behavior based on GPS data, and built a system that can monitor the energy consumption of the city. Wu et al. [13] introduced a novel method to explore urban human mobility based on social media check-in data. Castro et al. [14] proposed a summary of using taxi GPS data to analyze people's mobility and activities, which includes social dynamics, traffic dynamics and operational dynamics.

Human dynamics can be researched through a variety of data, such as mobile phone data [15], GPS trajectory data[16-19], social network check-in data [20],wireless network trajectories [21], etc.

Gonzalez et al.[15] used mobile call records for statistical research, they found that human trajectories show a high degree of temporal and spatial regularity. Zheng et al. [16] proposed an approach based on supervised learning to infer people's motion modes from their GPS logs. Liu et al. [17] analyzed trajectory data from 3000 taxi drivers in Shenzhen, summarized operating differences between top drivers and ordinary drivers. Yuan et al. [18] analyzed mobility patterns of taxi drivers and passengers, and built a recommending system for both taxi drivers and passengers. Zhang et al. [19] found that there are significant patterns under the OD flows constructed from taxis' random motion. Cho et al. [20] used cell phone location data and records from two online location-based social networks, they found that humans experience a combination of periodic movement that is geographically limited and seemingly random jumps correlated with their social networks.

Current research on taxi working patterns are mostly from the perspective of the city, such as origin and destination locations, hotspots and landmarks in the city. These researches were based on the mixture of taxi trajectories but ignored taxi individuals' characteristics and individual operating patterns. In this paper, we analyze the spatial working pattern of urban taxi drivers in Tianjin city based on over 3000 taxis' trajectories in a month.

Our contributions list in the followings:

(1) We proposed a method for identifying taxi parking places. We identified most of the parking places by the method and found parking places and residential area has a similar spatial distribution;

(2) Taxi individuals' spatial mobility activities are random, but they have the characteristic of moving toward the city center;

(3) Taxi drivers will neither work around their homes(parking places) nor the city center but work around between homes and the city center;

(4) The relationship between income efficiency and working center.

2. Dataset

The taxi GPS trajectory data we used in this study are collected from 3500 drivers in Tianjin city. The dataset was continuously collected in Oct. 2012, a total of 31 days. Each GPS record consists of several significant attributes. Table1 provides a description of taxi trajectory data.

Table 1. Data sections of taxi GPS data in Tianjin city.

Taxi ID	Timestamp	Longitude	Latitude	Occupied
E00864	2012-10-01 17:50:19	117.17947	39.092183	0
E00864	2012-10-01 17:51:13	117.17973	39.09015	0
E00864	2012-10-01 17:52:46	117.1798	39.089867	1
E00864	2012-10-01 17:53:46	117.18165	39.0893	1

Since the raw data contains noise, we processed the data at first. (1) We excluded trajectory data located in Binhai New Area(Another district away from Tianjin City); (2) Trajectories beyond the downtown area were excluded. If over half of the trajectory was outside the downtown area, data will be discarded for the day; (3) Discarded inactive data. If a taxi parked in the same location for a whole day, data of that day would be discarded; (4)After the previous steps in the process, taxis with a sum of active days over 25 could be remained as our research data. Finally, we got 2435 taxis' trajectory as the research data.

3. Results

3.1. *Parking place and working center detection*

First, we detected taxi parking places. We found that most of taxis didn't lead a continuous work for 24 hours so that we can detect parking places from longest and most frequency staying locations. Taxi ownership in Tianjin is private, so we can conclude that most of the parking places are not far from taxi drivers' homes.

We determined the longest staying locations for each taxi. Simultaneously, we divided the Tianjin map into grids by warps and wefts at the precision of 0.001, so that we could make each longest staying point drop into a certain grid. The area of each grid is about 98m*98m. We selected the most frequent drop-in grid of each taxi. If over 60% days of the longest staying locations located in a same gird of the valid days, the average coordinate in the most frequency grid would be regarded as the parking place. The method got notable results in the experiment. Compared with the map of Tianjin city, we found that parking places and residential areas lead almost the same distribution. We could find that fewer parking places are located in the city center area and suburbs(Fig. 1a).

Radius of gyration is an important indicator to describe the range of human spatial mobility in human dynamics. We use it to describe the mobility pattern of taxis in this paper. The radius of gyration of object ***a*** at time ***t*** is defined as follows:

$$r_g^a(t) = \sqrt{\frac{1}{n_c^a(t)} \sum_{i=1} (r_i^a - r_{cm}^a)^2}. \quad (1)$$

In the formula, r_{cm} indicates the average of all location coordinates in the statistical period, it stands for the centroid of a trajectory; r_i indicates all trajectory points, in our dataset, it was coordinate data from GPS trajectory; $n_{c(t)}$ is the amount of points on the trajectory through the time period. We regard the centroid of trajectory as the working center of a taxi driver in the day. In addition, we defined the average location of the working centers as the working center of the taxi.

After our calculation and statistics, we got a spatial distribution of taxis' trajectories centroids (Fig. 1b) and probability density distribution of gyration radius (Fig. 1c). We regard the centroids as working centers of taxi drivers. From Fig.1b we discovered that working centers are more concentrated in city centers. We define the mean of all working centers as city center because the mean coordinates locate in the center area of Tianjin city. Gyration radius in line fitted a normal distribution with a mean of 5.049. Compared with real data and fit line, we could see there was a certain amount of drivers tended to work in a large area.

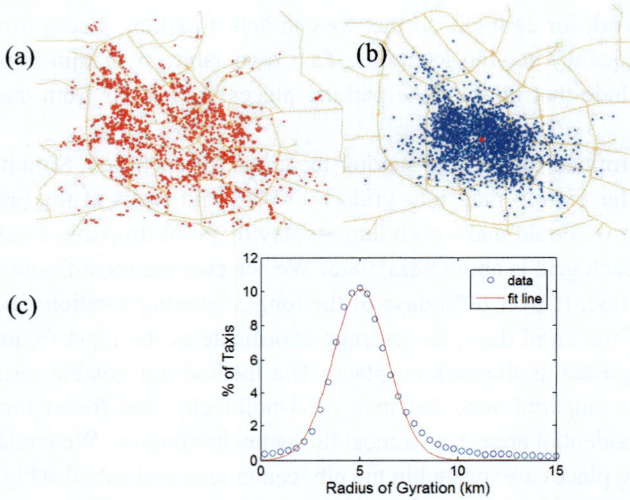

Fig. 1. (a) Spatial distribution of parking places. (b) Spatial distribution of working centers. Red triangle in the map center indicates the mean of all working centers (city center). (c) Probability density distribution of gyration radius.

We visualized each taxis' gyration radius in different parking places to explore the relationship between gyration radius and parking place (Fig. 2a). First, we divided the range of gyration radius into four intervals. Then we chose the city center as the center of circles, and define circles with a radius from 0km to 15km by an increment of 3km. In each of the five annular areas, the proportions of parking places with different gyration radius were computed (Fig. 2b). From the city center to downtown areas, the value of gyration radius with the increase of distance from city center to different parking places also had a tendency to increase. That was, the farther away from the city center to parking place, the taxi driver was more inclined to work in a larger area. This phenomenon was most likely due to a taxi drivers' potential operating pattern.

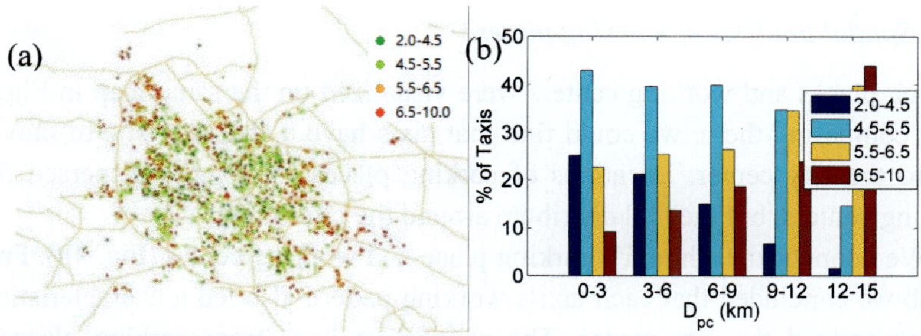

Fig. 2. Relationship between spatial distribution of parking places and gyration radius. (a) Distribution of gyration radius of different taxi drivers with different parking places. (b) With the increasing distance from parking place to city center, the proportion of gyration radius.

We defined D_{pw}^{a}as the distance from parking place to working center of taxi a, and R^{a} as the gyration radius of taxi a. Then we definedC^{a}:

$$C^{a}=\frac{R^{a}}{D_{pw}^{a}}. \tag{2}$$

C^{a} was used to evaluate the possibility of whether a taxi driver prone to work around its parking place. A greater C^{a} indicated the more possibility of a driver to work around its parking place.It is shown in Fig. 3 that parking places near city center have a larger C^{a}. With the increase of the distance from parking place to city center, C^{a} led a decreasing trend. So we could conclude that taxis whose parking places near city center would operate around parking place, but others with a lower C^{a} usually operate further. According to experience, people believe that taxis usually operate around the city center. Then we led a deep research on such empirical operating pattern.

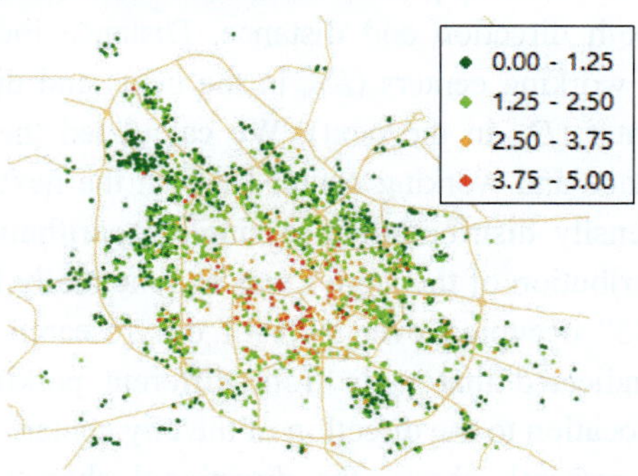

Fig. 3. Spatial distribution of C^{a}.

3.2. *Spatial analysis of working pattern*

Parking places and working centers were visualized on the same map in Fig.4a. After comparing them, we could find that taxis have a characteristic of moving toward the city center. Locations of parking places were more dispersed than working centers, but they all distribute around the city center.

We connected each taxi's parking place and working center (Fig. 4b). From Fig.4b we concluded that each taxi's working pattern also led a characteristic of moving toward the city center. The connecting lines from parking places to working centers were presented as a radiation pattern. There was also a phenomenon that location points and connecting lines were still aparse in the city center. It means that taxis from different parking places may choose a downtown area not far from their parking places as working centers.

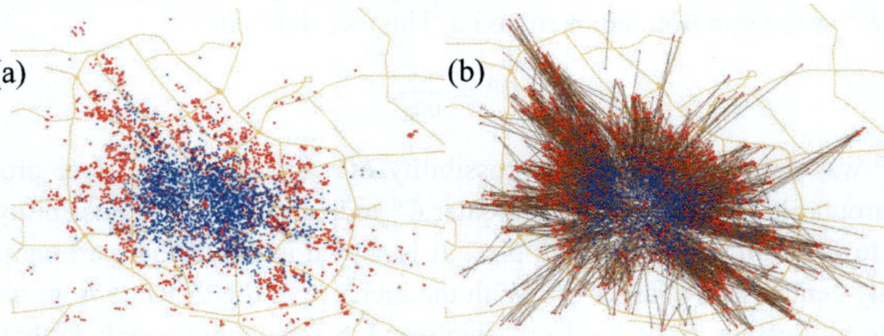

Fig. 4. (a) Spatial distribution contrast of parking places and working centers. (b) Connecting lines between parking places and working centers.

We verified the working pattern observed and experience based from two perspectives of both direction and distance. Distance includes distance from parking places to working centers (D_{pw} in the next) and distance from parking places to city center (D_{pc} in the next). We calculated the angle between city center, parking place and working center (A_{cpw} in the next) of each taxi, made the probability density distribution in a single logarithmic coordinate system (Fig. 5a). The distribution of the angles was exponentially fitted. Taxis with the angle less than 45° occupied over 91% of our research data (Fig. 5b). The research above indicated that taxis from different parking places tended to operate around a location to the direction of the city center.

Through the research above, the directional characteristics of operating pattern was discovered. Next we uncovered the spatial operating pattern in the distance perspective. We analyzed probability density distribution of D_{pc} and

D_{pw} (Fig. 6a), as well as the ratio of the two distances (Fig. 6b).The two kinds of distances are all normal distributed with their means of 3.709 and 7.087. D_{pc} is often bigger than D_{pw}. The difference of two distances' distribution indicated that taxi drivers didn't tend to work around the same center (the city center), though we have proved taxis have a characteristic of moving toward the city center. The ratio of D_{pw} and D_{pc} also normal distributed with a mean of 0.543. As for most of the taxis, they would neither operate around parking place nor city center, their working center often located between the two meaningful locations.

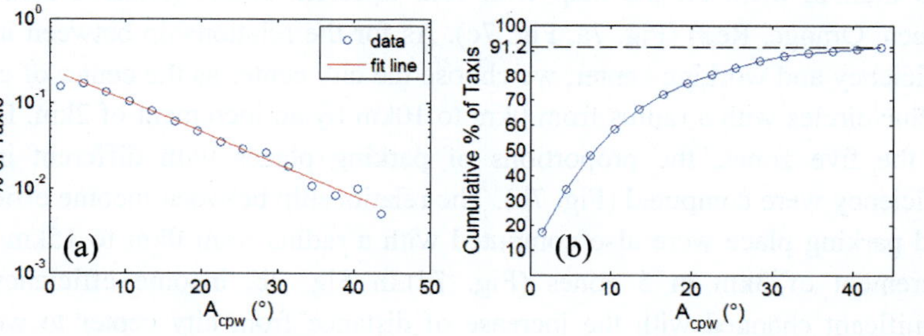

Fig. 5. (a) A_{cpw} Probability density distribution. (b) A_{cpw} Cumulative probability density distribution.

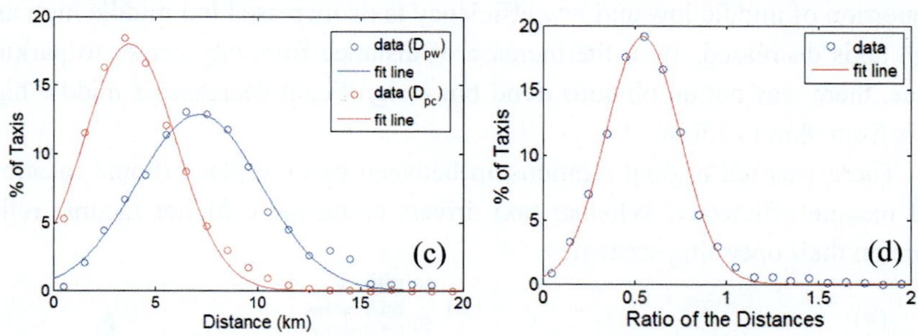

Fig. 6. (a) Probability density distribution of D_{pw} (red) and D_{pc} (blue) (b) Probability density distribution of the ratio of D_{pw} and D_{pc}.

This phenomenon maybe caused by taxi drivers are more familiar with the surroundings around their parking places (home locations), hunting for passengers far away may result in higher costs; Another suppose was that drivers must go back to the parking places regularly but operate around city center can carry more passengers. Overall, the city center and parking places both impacted on the working centers.

3.3. *Spatial analysis of working efficiency*

Income efficiency is concerned by taxi drivers and it is one of the important evaluation criterions about top drivers. Income amount and efficiency could be calculated from GPS data. In this section, we searched the relationship between income efficiency and two important positions: working center and parking place.

According to the income efficiency distribution from low to high, we divided the taxis into four categories (Low, Middle Low, Middle High, High) and marked them on the map with four different colors (Dark Green, Light Green, Orange, Red) (Fig. 7a, Fig. 7c). As for the relationship between income efficiency and working center, we choose the city center as the center of circles, define circles with a radius from 0km to 10km by an increment of 2km. In each of the five zones, the proportions of parking places with different income efficiency were computed (Fig. 7b). The relationship between income efficiency and parking place were also computed with a radius from 0km to 15km by an increment of 3km in 5 zones (Fig. 7d).In Fig. 7b, income efficiency was significant changed with the increase of distance from city center to working center. With the increase of distance from city center to working center, the proportion of middle low and low efficiency taxis increased but middle high and high taxis decreased. With the increase of distance from city center to parking place, there was not an obvious trend but a significant decrease of middle high taxis from 9km to 15km.

There was not a great relationship between parking place (home location) and income efficiency. Whether taxi drivers could get a higher income relies more on their operating strategies.

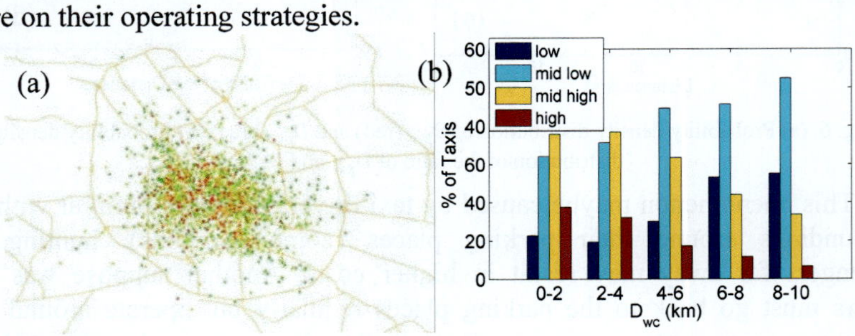

Fig. 7. Relationship between income efficiency and two locations: working center and parking place. (a) Spatial distribution of taxis' income efficiency with different working centers. (b) Tendency of four kinds of income efficiency with the increase of the distance form city center to working center. (c) Spatial distribution of taxis' income efficiency with different parking places. (d)Tendency of four kinds of income efficiency with the increase of the distance form city center to parking place.

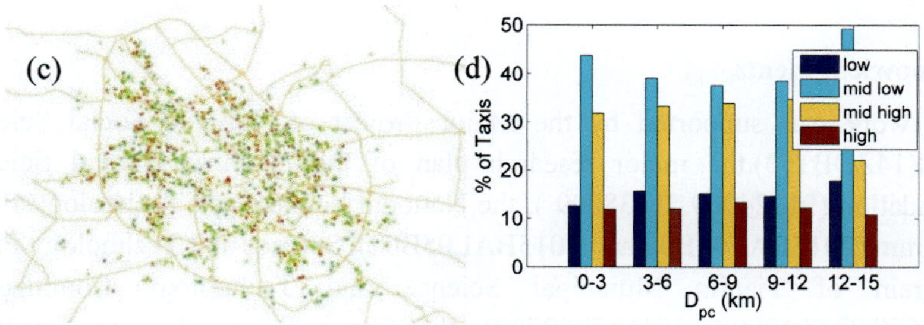

Fig. 7. (*Continued*)

4. Conclusion

In this paper, we first proposed a method to identify taxis' parking places. In this way we got the spatial distribution of parking places and found the spatial distribution consistency of parking places and residential areas. Gyration radius from human dynamics was used to measure taxi working ranges and uncovered the range of operating pattern from randomness trajectories. Three meaningful locations, parking place, working center and city center were defined and analyzed their spatial distributions and relationships. Through the analysis of direction, we discovered the characteristic of operating towards city center. From further research, we concluded that most of the taxi drivers would neither operate around their parking places (home locations) nor the city center, they were more likely to choose the location between parking places and city center as their working centers. In addition, we carried out a research about income efficiency. The research found that there was not a great relationship between parking place (home location) and income efficiency. Whether a taxi driver could get a higher income more relies on the driver's operating strategies, of course, not only limited to working centers.

Taxi is an important part of urban transportation. The research uncovered urban taxis' spatial working pattern from taxi GPS trajectories. This pattern may be generated due to taxi drivers' strategy or the ownership of taxis. Taxis in Tianjin city are privately held but not taxi companies held. Research results are significant in urban planning, the management of taxis and other aspects of urban transportation. The results can also explain the phenomena of some drivers refuse to carry passengers in some locations or routes. With the widely using of GPS on a variety of carriers, other trajectory data collection and the construction of smart cities, our methods and search results can be applied to urban human mobility, urban structure changing and some other related areas.

Acknowledgments

This work was supported by the Major Project of National Social Science Fund(14ZDB153),the major research plan of the National Natural Science Foundation (91224009,51438009), the National Science and Technology Pillar Program (2015BAL05B00 and 2015BAL05B02), Science and Technology Pillar Program of Tianjin Municipal Science and Technology Commission (13ZCZDGX01099,13ZCDZSF02700), the Ocean Public Welfare Scientific Research Project under Grant No. 201305033,National Science and Technology Program for Public Well-being(2012GS120302), Tianjin Municipality innovation fund project for small and medium-sized technology-based firms(14ZXCXGX00542)

References

1. Jiang B, Yin J, Zhao S. Characterizing the human mobility pattern in a large street network[J]. Physical Review E, 2009, 80(2): 021136.
2. Chen G, Chen B, Yu Y. Mining frequent patterns from GPS tracks[C]//Computational Intelligence and Software Engineering (CiSE), 2010 International Conference on. IEEE, 2010: 1-6.
3. Liu L, Biderman A, Ratti C. Urban mobility landscape: Real time monitoring of urban mobility patterns[C]//Proceedings of the 11th International Conference on Computers in Urban Planning and Urban Management. 2009: 1-16.
4. Liang X, Zheng X, Lv W, et al. The scaling of human mobility by taxis is exponential[J]. Physica A: Statistical Mechanics and its Applications, 2012, 391(5): 2135-2144.
5. Tang J, Liu F, Wang Y, et al. Uncovering urban human mobility from large scale taxi GPS data[J]. Physica A: Statistical Mechanics and its Applications, 2015.
6. Yuan J, Zheng Y, Xie X. Discovering regions of different functions in a city using human mobility and POIs[C]//Proceedings of the 18th ACM SIGKDD international conference on Knowledge discovery and data mining. ACM, 2012: 186-194.
7. Zheng Y, Liu Y, Yuan J, et al. Urban computing with taxicabs[C]//Proceedings of the 13th international conference on Ubiquitous computing. ACM, 2011: 89-98.

8. Liu Y, Kang C, Gao S, et al. Understanding intra-urban trip patterns from taxi trajectory data[J]. Journal of geographical systems, 2012, 14(4): 463-483.
9. Liu Y, Wang F, Xiao Y, et al. Urban land uses and traffic 'source-sink areas': Evidence from GPS-enabled taxi data in Shanghai[J]. Landscape and Urban Planning, 2012, 106(1): 73-87.
10. Pan G, Qi G, Wu Z, et al. Land-use classification using taxi GPS traces[J]. Intelligent Transportation Systems, IEEE Transactions on, 2013, 14(1): 113-123.
11. Wang H, Zou H, Yue Y, et al. Visualizing hot spot analysis result based on mashup[C]//Proceedings of the 2009 International Workshop on Location Based Social Networks. ACM, 2009: 45-48.
12. Zhang F, Wilkie D, Zheng Y, et al. Sensing the pulse of urban refueling behavior[C]//Proceedings of the 2013 ACM international joint conference on Pervasive and ubiquitous computing. ACM, 2013: 13-22.
13. Wu L, Zhi Y, Sui Z, et al. Intra-urban human mobility and activity transition: evidence from social media check-in data[J]. 2014.
14. Castro P S, Zhang D, Chen C, et al. From taxi GPS traces to social and community dynamics: A survey[J]. ACM Computing Surveys (CSUR), 2013, 46(2): 17.
15. Gonzalez M C, Hidalgo C A, Barabasi A L. Understanding individual human mobility patterns[J]. Nature, 2008, 453(7196): 779-782.
16. Zheng Y, Li Q, Chen Y, et al. Understanding mobility based on GPS data[C]//Proceedings of the 10th international conference on Ubiquitous computing. ACM, 2008: 312-321.
17. Liu L, Andris C, Ratti C. Uncovering cabdrivers' behavior patterns from their digital traces[J]. Computers, Environment and Urban Systems, 2010, 34(6): 541-548.
18. Yuan N J, Zheng Y, Zhang L, et al. T-Finder: A recommender system for finding passengers and vacant taxis[J]. Knowledge and Data Engineering, IEEE Transactions on, 2013, 25(10): 2390-2403.
19. Zhang W, Li S, Pan G. Mining the semantics of origin-destination flows using taxi traces[C]//UbiComp. 2012: 943-949.

20. Cho E, Myers S A, Leskovec J. Friendship and mobility: user movement in location-based social networks[C]//Proceedings of the 17th ACM SIGKDD international conference on Knowledge discovery and data mining. ACM, 2011: 1082-1090.
21. Kim M, Kotz D, Kim S. Extracting a Mobility Model from Real User Traces[C]//INFOCOM. 2006, 6: 1-13.

Research on the Intelligent Blind Cane System Based on Multi-Dimensional Environment Perception

He ZHAO[1], Jun-Yi WANG[2], Kai KANG and Peng LIN

College of Software, Jilin University,
Changchun, Jilin, China
[1]1461756559@qq.com, [2]wangjunyi0825@gmail.com

He ZHAO

College of Software, Jilin University,
Changchun, Jilin, China
1461756559@qq.com

This paper designed an intelligent blind cane system based on multi- dimension environment perception to provide improved protection and safety for the blind. This system utilizes the Arduino platform as the core to connect the hardware, and uses the edge detection algorithm, calibration algorithm (temperature calibration and mean filter), Kalman filtering algorithm to achieve obstacle detection, GPS positioning, traffic light recognition and other functions..

Keywords: Ultrasonic; Kalman filter; OPENCV; Hough transform.

1. Introduction

World Health Organization expresses that the number of the blind all over the world is nearly 45 million currently and that the safety of the blind's travel has become a serious problem to be solved in today's society. In the domestic, the protective measures for the safety of the blind's travel are not in place. Many typhlosoles are designed unreasonable and unscientific and can't provide safety protection for the blind. So they are still at the post-rescue phase at present. Besides, although there are many products like intelligent cane on the market now, the function of some of these products is single and they are of little practical value. Therefore, we designed an intelligent blind cane system which is easy to use and fully functional.

The system includes ultrasonic obstacle detection module, fall detection and alarm module and traffic lights recognition module. The ultrasonic obstacle detection module is necessary for the blind, which uses ultrasonic sensors and voice module to measure the distance between the obstacle and the blind and achieve voice prompts. In traffic lights recognition module, camera is used to capture video containing traffic lights. Then the video is changed into image sequences with the use of OPENCV functions. And the program processes the image and detects the data to recognize the color of the traffic lights in the image. Lastly, in the fall detection module, the system adopts fall detection and Kalman filter algorithm to detect the blind's posture so that the blind can be helped in time.

2. Ultrasonic Testing Barrier Module and Calibration Algorithm

Obstacle measurement is one of the basic functions of intelligent cane, which can be greatly convenient to the blind when they are out. This work system uses ultrasonic sensors to detect obstacles within 5 meters. The ultrasonic echo sounder method, means that ultrasonic transmitting transducer continuously transmit sound pulses, and then receiving transducer receive the ultrasonic wave when the wave meets obstacle, finally the transducer calculates the distance to obstacles according to the speed of sound and time discrepancy.

But this solution is not rigorous. It needs careful process, which is temperature correction and average filtering. Under normal temperature, the propagation speed of ultrasonic wave is 340 meters per second, which is susceptible to the influences of air temperature, humidity, pressure and other factors, especially to the influence of air temperature. Usually for every 1°C rise in temperature, the speed of sound rises 0.6 meters per second. This shows the impact of temperature for ultrasonic testing barrier system cannot be ignored. In order to get a more accurate result, the temperature compensation of the wave velocity must be compensated. The empirical model of velocity and temperature can be obtained by experiment: $V=331.5+0.607T$, and T is the field temperature and V is the actual wave velocity. From the formula, we can see that to get the accurate velocity, the field temperature T must be obtained. DS18B20 (digital temperature sensor) is used to detect the temperature of the field, and to realize the calibration of the actual wave velocity. This is the temperature calibration. The mean filter is a method The ultrasonic ranging process is roughly as shown in Figure 1.

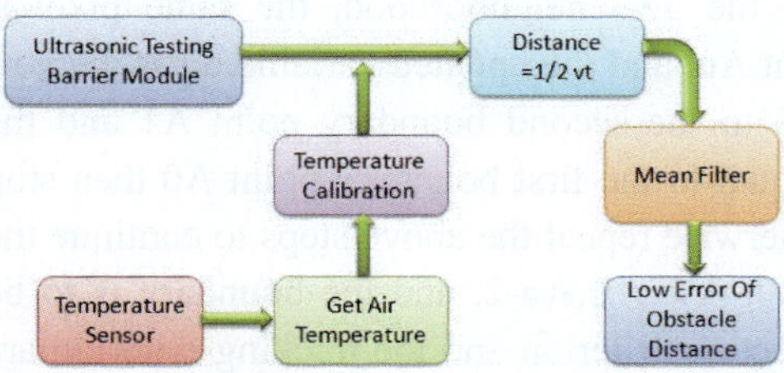

Fig. 1.

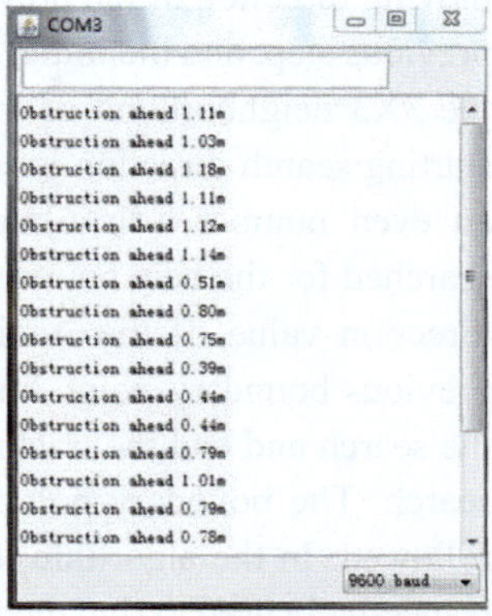

Fig. 2.

Mega Arduino 2560 development board and ultrasonic sensor are connected. When ultrasonic sensor has detected the obstacle information in front of the sensor, the sensor information is converted into distance information. Then the temperature calibration and mean filtering are processed, and the data is accurate to 0.01cm.The result of Arduino serial monitor while ultrasonic sensor ranging is as shown in Figure 2. When the ultrasonic sensor measures that the distance is between 0.5 meters to 2 meters, the voice module starts.

3. Traffic Lights Detection Module

To begin with, the red area in the image should be found. First capture image from the camera, convert the RGB space to HSV space, and the HSV three channels are taken apart into an array of length 3. Then the pixel value of the place where H<15 or H>245 is set to 1, which means the red area, the pixel value of the other places is set to 0, which means non red area. Lastly the program only need to process the places whose pixel value is 1.

Then the program uses the contour tracing algorithm to detect and draw the contour of the red region. First, according to the order of from top to bottom and from left to right, scan image, find the first starting point A with no boundary marker tracking end symbol, which is a boundary point minimum and column value. Then scan direction variable dir is defined, which is used to record the moving direction of the previous boundary point to the boundary point along the previous step, and the initial value of the eight connected region is 7. Then search the 3X3 neighborhood of the current pixel in an anti clockwise direction. The starting search direction is set to: if dir is an odd number, (dir+7)mod8; if dir is an even number, (dir+6)mod8. In the 3X3 neighborhood, the same pixel is searched for the new boundary point An, and the updated variable dir is the new direction value .If the An is equal to the second boundary point A1 and the previous boundary point An-1 is equal to the first boundary point A0 then stop the search and end the tracking, otherwise repeat the above steps to continue the search. The boundary points are A0, A1,……An-2, and the boundary is to be followed. In the algorithm, the detection criterion and the tracking criterion are respectively used to find the first boundary points and find all the boundary points.

Finally, the contour of the red region obtained by the above steps is detected by a circle. Here the program uses the Hough transform (Hof transform), which is based on the statistical regularity of parameter space to estimate parameters. In particular, the (x,y) is transformed into the parameter space (K1,..., Kn), and the possible parameter vector is calculated for each pixel in the Cartesian coordinate system. When the program has dealt with all the pixels, coordinates of the most frequent (one or a few) parameter vector are used as parameters of Cartesian coordinate equation, namely the detected circular.

The identification process of the traffic lights: extract the image from the video file and write the program to identify the red circle area. The original picture is shown in Figure 3, and the recognition results are shown in Figure 4. If the program detects the red circular area successfully, it locates the red area in the image, as shown in Figure 5.

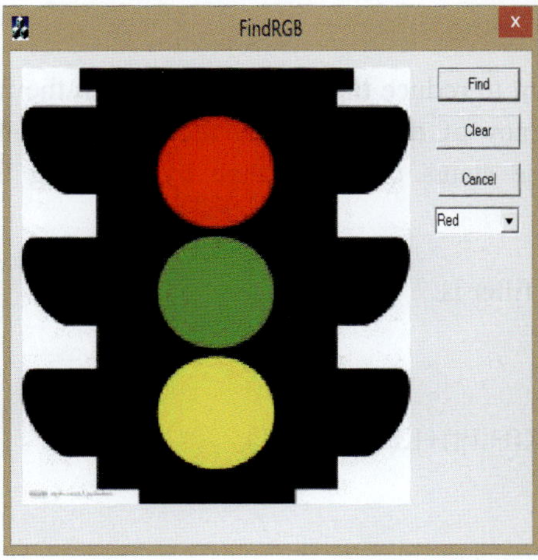

Fig. 3.

Fig. 4.

Fig. 5.

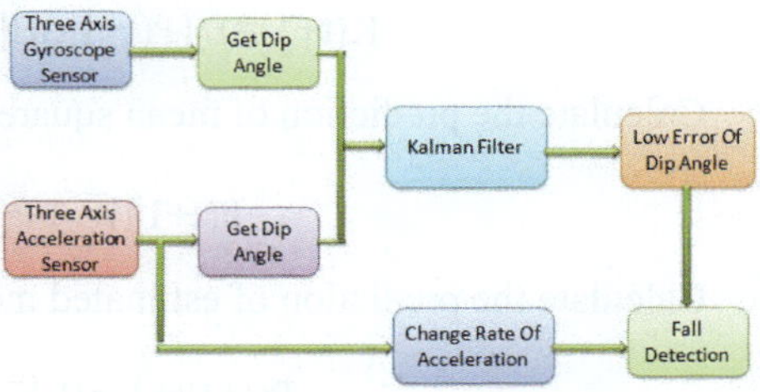

Fig. 6.

4. Fall detection Module and Kalman Algorithm

The module uses the six axis IMU module (including the three axis acceleration and three axis gyroscope) to measure the angle between the stick and the ground, and then the measured data are fused, and the angle with lower error is obtained by using the Kalman filtering algorithm to detect the position of the crutches and determine whether the user falls down. The process is shown in Figure 6.

4.1. *Kalman filtering algorithm*

The system uses the Kalman algorithm to reduce the error of the data in the fall detection, which improves the accuracy of detection. The model reflects the characteristics of the system and the status of the change by selecting the appropriate state variables.

The specific process of Kalman filter is:

Calculate state estimate:

$$X(t+1|t+1)=X(t+1|t)+K(t+1)\varepsilon\,(t+1). \tag{1}$$

Calculate state prediction:

$$X(t+1|t)=\Phi\, X(t|t). \tag{2}$$

Calculate innovation:

$$e(t+1)=Y(t+1)-HX(t+1|t). \tag{3}$$

Calculate the gain of Kalman filter:

$$K(t+1)=1/\{P(t+1|t)H[HP(t+1|t)H+R]\}. \tag{4}$$

Calculate the prediction of mean square error:

$$P(t+1|t)=\Phi P(t|t)\Phi+\Gamma Q\Gamma. \tag{5}$$

Calculate the prediction of estimated mean square error:

$$P(t+1|t+1)=[I-K(t+1)H]P(t+1|t). \tag{6}$$

4.2. *Fall detection algorithm*

In the vertical axis of Z axis, the X axis corresponding to the front and rear of the crutches, Y axis corresponding to the left lateral horizontal axis, and the Y, Z and X axes are orthogonal to each other, and the changes of vector in the spatial direction can be decomposed into three components of X, Z and Y. The prototype of the fall detection algorithm is to determine whether fall or not by a threshold in a Cartesian coordinate system. In the present algorithm, the act of falling is required to include three conditions:

Condition 1: stick changes from upright state to the horizontal state.

Condition 2: stick is close to the horizontal state for a long time.

Condition 3: The change of acceleration is fast.

Most studies show that the duration of the fall action process is not more than 6 seconds. Therefore, when the Z axis acceleration is higher than the threshold and the X axis and Y axis are changed obviously, it is considered to satisfy the condition 1 of falling down. When the acceleration of the Z axis is lower than the threshold, the delay of 10 seconds is needed. And when the state is stable, the acceleration value of the Z axis is still under the threshold, which is considered to satisfy the condition 2 of falling down. According to the shape the walking stick when it falls, the change of the barycenter of the walking stick will be faster than the general situation. Therefore, after meeting the condition 1 and 2, the acceleration is detected again. And when the acceleration is lower than the threshold, the accelerations between 6 seconds before and after needs a differential operation. If the result during this time is higher than the threshold, it is considered to satisfy the condition 3 of falling down. Then trigger alarm processing.

The six axis IMU module is installed in the central position of the staff, and the direction of the 3 measurement is the same as the 3 axes of the coordinate system. The acceleration is obtained, and the inclination angle of the walking stick and the horizontal plane is calculated. If the calculated angle is less than 30 degrees, it can be considered that the information of the fall and the fall of the stick will be sent out as a warning. On the other hand, it is considered to be miscarriage of justice.

Under the static condition, the acceleration vector is $1 \pm 0.15g$. When the walking stick falls, the acceleration vector in each direction will change. At this point, the Kalman filter algorithm is used to deal with the relevant data to reduce the error of the data to improve the accuracy of fall detection.

5. Conclusion

In this paper, a kind of intelligent system for the blind is studied. It is simple and easy to use. It can be used to make a real time data acquisition and processing of the obstacles, whether there is a fall and whether the traffic lights ahead. It also broadcasts in a timely manner, so that protect the blind to a large extent from the disaster, and can also make a sudden emergency call for help, etc. For this product, the system is more practical and applicable. In the future, it will be able to expand and realize the function of more human nature.

References

1. ZeJun Cai, *Survey report on the status quo of the blind.* (2010.10.20). In Chinese.

2. Song Guo. Yu Ying Zhang and Shao Hua Han, *Design and Research on blind travel aid.* (2014.6). In Chinese.

3. China Daily, Japan develops new smart walking stick --- can be for the elderly navigation positioning. 2013.3.22. In Chinese.

4. Li Li Xia, *Application of single chip microcomputer in ultrasonic distance measurement.* (Electronic technique[J]. 2002.6). In Chinese.

5. Zhao Xiao Qiang and Zhao LianYu, *Temperature compensation in ultrasonic distance measurement system, combined machine tools and automatic processing technology*. (2008.Twelfth stage). In Chinese.

6. DouDing network, *The contour detection based on OPENCV.* In Chinese.

7. Wang Fu Sheng and Qi Guo Qing, *Boundary tracking algorithm for object contour in two valued image*. (Journal of Dalian Maritime University.2006.2). In Chinese.

8. Wang Qiang, Hu Jian Ping, Hu Kai, Lu Zhi Min and Hu Wei Ping, *Fast HOUGH algorithm for element detection*. (2000.9). In Chinese.

9. Wang Rong, Zhang Yun and Chen Jian Xin, *Design and implementation of fall detection system using tri-axis accelerometer*. (Nanjing University of Posts and Telecommunications). In Chinese.

Configuration Optimization Design for Satellite Constellation Using Multi-Island Genetic Algorithm

Jun-hua XIANG*, Si-hui HU, Tai-bo LI and Xue-yang ZHANG

College of Aerospace Science and Engineering, NUDT,
Changsha, 410073, P.R.China
E-mail: xiangjunhua@nudt.edu.cn

Utilizing the advantage of increased revisit performance of the low inclination regression orbit; this paper developed the optimization design model considering the constellation configuration, the orbit and the performance, and designed the constellation configuration optimization design process. Based on Multi-Island Genetic Algorithm (MIGA), the multi-objective optimization design of a satellite constellation with rapid revisit in equal time interval is completed. Performance analysis results for satellite constellation optimized indicated that the mission requirements and design constraints are satisfied, and the rapid revisit to the target in equal time interval is achieved.

Keywords: Satellite constellation; Configuration optimization design; Rapid revisit; Equal time interval; Multi-island genetic algorithm.

1. Introduction

The main mission of satellite constellation is realizing continuous and multi-layer coverage to the target, including communication, navigation, observation, and so on [1]. The coverage area is a function of altitude, and the LEO satellite can cover a small area on earth. And the satellite constellation is used to realize continuous and multi-layer or equal time interval coverage to the target area or the latitude bandwidth on earth [2].

LEO satellite can cover the target less than 10 minutes, and satellite has relative motion to the earth. In order to achieve continuous coverage to the target, the number of satellite constellation is too huge to accept from the fees including satellite manufacturing, launch and operation [3]. The Iridium constellation [4], which provides global coverage at all times, has 66 satellites in near circular orbits with the altitude of 780 kilometers and inclination of 86.4 degree. There are six orbit planes spaced 30 degrees apart with 11 satellites in each plane.

The main object of constellation optimization design is to optimize the constellation configuration parameters, including total number of satellites, number of orbit planes, phase-angle, and altitude et al. The optimization process is converting the satellite constellation design criterion to one of the objective functions or one of constraint condition, and building the optimization design model about constellation configuration and constellation performance, then choosing the appropriate optimization algorithm to complete the optimization design according to optimization objectives of the design mission [5, 6].

In paper the design objective is the rapid revisit to the target in equal time interval, and the restrictions include constellation configuration, orbit and performance, then uses Multi-Island Genetic Algorithm to complete the optimization design of satellite constellation with rapid revisit to the target in equal time interval. The performance analysis results for satellite constellation indicated that the mission requirements and the design constraints are satisfied.

2. Optimization Design Model

2.1. *Satellite constellation configuration*

Based on the Walker constellation configuration, the configuration model of earth observation satellite constellation is built, which N satellites are equally divided among P orbit planes with same altitude, eccentricity, inclination and argument of perigee. Each orbit plane has S satellites, namely $N=PS$. The difference between different satellites includes difference of RAAN of different orbit planes $\Delta\Omega$, and the mean anomaly difference of the first satellite in different orbit planes ΔM.

The orbital elements of the first satellite in the first orbit plane are denoted by $(a_0, e_0, i_0, \Omega_0, \omega_0, M_0)$. For a circular orbit, $e_0 = 0$, $\omega_0 = 0$.

Then the orbital elements of the kth satellite in the jth orbit plane can be obtained, as in Eq. (1).

$$\begin{cases} a_{jk} = h_0 + R_e \\ e_{jk} = e_0 \\ i_{jk} = i_0 \\ \Omega_{jk} = \Omega_0 + (j-1)\Delta\Omega \\ \omega_{jk} = \omega_0 \\ M_{jk} = M_0 + (j-1)\Delta M + (k-1)2\pi/S \end{cases} . \tag{1}$$

where $j = [1, 2, \cdots, P]$, $k=[1, 2, \cdots, S]$, and R_e is the earth radius.

2.2. *Regressive orbit model*

The regressive orbit satellite satisfies the regressive equation [7], as in Eq. (2).

$$\frac{2\pi}{\left(\omega_e - \dot{\Omega}\right)T_\Omega} = \frac{N^*}{D^*}. \tag{2}$$

where N^* is the regressive cycles, D^* is the regressive period, ω_e is the angular velocity of earth rotation, $\dot{\Omega}$ is the secular variation rate of RAAN, and T_Ω is the orbital node period.

2.3. *Performance optimization index*

The performance indexes of LEO optical satellite include satellite cost, launch cost, energy consumption of orbital injection, coverage performance for the target, and working performance of payloads, and so on.

(1) Satellite cost

The main factor of satellite cost is the number of satellite, N.

(2) Launch cost

Because satellites in different orbit planes are not fit to launch into orbit with the same rocket, launch cost is influenced by the orbit planes, P and the altitude, h.

(3) Energy consumption of orbital injection

The energy consumption of orbital injection is influenced by the orbit altitude, h. The orbit is lower, and the energy consumption is less.

(4) Target coverage performance

Observation performances of satellite constellation mainly include the following indexes:

- Observations times for the target in everyday, C_{times}
- Average observation time, T_{mean}
- Maximum observation time interval, $T_{\max gap}$
- Minimum observation time interval, $T_{\min gap}$
- Average observation time interval, T_{avegap}
- Mean square deviation of observation time interval, $\Delta T_{\max gap}$ and $\Delta T_{\min gap}$

(5) Payload imaging performance

Payload imaging performances include spatial resolution L, swath width E and field of view θ, where L and E are affected by orbital altitude and satellite payload, and θ is affected by the design of lens and not fit as optimization objective.

3. Optimization Design Process

The design of optical imaging satellite constellation observing assigned target is a typical optimization problem with multi-constraint and multi-objective. The design optimization process is as follows:

a. For the regressive orbit with low inclination, the computer program design is finished firstly, which considering energy consumption of orbital injection, coverage performance, and imaging performance, and can calculate constellation performance according to the setting parameters and the variable parameters of satellite constellation.

b. Starting on the optimization software ISIGHT, and building the integration dialog framework, completing the definition of executive program, input file and output file, and settings of adjustment and output parameters.

c. Finishing the parameter settings of input and output file through the parameter setting dialog framework. The parameter setting dialog framework shows the parse variable of input and output file, which can be set to optimization objectives at the same time. Optimization objectives include the maximum and minimum two ways. The weight and scale factor of the optimization objective parameters in the total optimization function can be set, and also as the type and upper and lower bounds of the parameters.

d. Opening the optimization plan dialog frame, and finish the optimization method selection and parameter settings. The optimization design of satellite constellation with rapid revisit in equal time interval is an optimization problem with multi-constraints and multi-objectives, therefore choose Multi-Island Genetic Algorithm and finish the setting to the sub-population size, the number of islands and the number of generations.

4. Optimization Design Example

4.1. *Optimization design of constellation configuration*

According to the mission characteristics of LEO imaging satellite, and considering that the payload of satellite constellation is video cameras, then to realize rapid revisit of the target in equal time interval with satellite constellation. The latitude and longitude of the target is (30°, 135°). The minimum elevation angle for earth observation is 5°. The main mission constraint is that the observation interval is less than 30 minutes and the average time of observation are more than 5 minutes. Constellation configuration optimization design parameters and video camera parameters for LEO optical imaging satellite are shown in Table 1.

Table 1. Optimization design parameters.

Parameters	Value	Parameters	Value
latitude of target point /deg	30	CMOS pixel size	6μm
longitude of target point /deg	135	focal length	2000mm
simulation steps per day	86400	resolution	4096×3072
simulation time/day	Regressive days, D	diagonal length of area array	30mm
whether or not regressive orbit	Yes		
lower bound of orbit altitude/km	250		
upper bound of orbit altitude /km	1200		

Then Multi-Island Genetic Algorithm (MIGA) is chose to complete the optimization design for satellite constellation configuration. The optimization parameters of MIGA include the sub-population size, the number of islands and the number of generations, which are set as 5, 5 and 200 respectively. So the total optimization steps are 5×5×200=5000. Input constraints are shown in Table 2. Output constraints are shown in Table 3.

Table 2. Input constraints.

Variable	Type	Lower bound	Current value	Upper bound
Number of orbit planes	INTEGER	1	3	3
Satellite number in each plane	INTEGER	1	4	8
Regressive circles	INTEGER	14	15	50
Regressive period / d	INTEGER	1	1	3
Orbit inclination / deg	REAL	20	30.5	60
RAAN / deg	REAL	0.0	0	360
Mean anomaly / deg	REAL	0.0	0	360.0
Difference of RAAN/deg	REAL	0	50	120
Difference of mean anomaly /deg	REAL	0	0	60

Table 3. Output constraints.

Variable	Type	Lower bound	Current value	Upper bound
Orbit altitude/km	REAL	250	0	1200
Satellite number	INTEGER	/	0	14
Observation times per day	REAL	36	0	/
Average observation time/s	REAL	300.0	0	/
Average observation interval/s	REAL	/	0	1800
Spatial resolution/m	REAL	/	0	2.5
Swath width in length/km	REAL	4.0	0	/
Swath width in short/km	REAL	3.0	0	/
Observation interval deviation/s	REAL	/	0	300

The objective function combinations for constellation configuration optimization design are shown in Table 4.

Table 4. Objective definition for optimization design.

Objective parameters	Weighting	Scale factor	Type	Direction	Value
Orbit inclination/deg	1	1	REAL	minimize	0
Orbit altitude/km	1	1	REAL	minimize	0
Satellite number	1	1	INTEGER	maximize	0
Observation times per day	20	1	INTEGER	maximize	0
Average observation time/s	1	1	REAL	minimize	0
Maximum observation interval/s	0.01	1	REAL	minimize	0
Minimum observation interval/s	1	1	REAL	maximize	0
Average observation interval/s	1.0	1	REAL	minimize	0
Maximum observation interval deviation /s	0.01	1	REAL	minimize	0
Minimum observation interval deviation/s	0.01	1	REAL	minimize	0
Satellite-earth distance/km	1	1	REAL	minimize	0
Energy consumption/km/s	1	1	REAL	minimize	0
Spatial resolution/m	1	1	REAL	minimize	0
Swath width in length/km	1	1	REAL	maximize	0
Swath width in short/km	1	1	REAL	maximize	0
Time difference of maximum and minimum observation interval/s	20	1	REAL	minimize	0

After setting up, and starting up the optimization design program to optimize the design for satellite constellation. Design results of satellite constellation configuration which can realize the rapid revisit to the target in equal time interval are shown in Table 5.

Table 5. Constellation optimization design results.

Parameters	Value
Number of orbit planes	3
Satellite number in each plane	4
Regressive circles	15
Regressive period/d	1
Orbit altitude/km	491.4
Eccentricity	0
Orbit inclination/deg	44.19
Right ascension of ascending node/deg	22.95
Argument of perigee/deg	0
Mean anomaly/deg	163.2
Difference of RAAN /deg	96.97
Difference of mean anomaly /deg	7.575

4.2. *Constellation performance analysis*

The orbit characterization and coverage performance of satellite constellation optimized are analyzed. The sub-satellite track is repeated in every one sidereal day, and all the satellites of constellation are evenly distributed in the three sub-satellite tracks. The minimum elevation angle is 5 degrees, and the observation performance to the target point by satellite constellation in each regressive period is shown in Fig. 1. Fig. 1 shows that satellite constellation designed can realize the rapid revisit to the target point in equal time interval. In each regressive period, the satellite constellation can observe 82 times to the target point, and the average time per observation is 463.6s, the minimum observation time is 35.7s, the maximum observation time is 576s.

Coverage percent probabilities to the target point by satellite constellation from sending ask to realizing observation is shown in Fig. 2. Fig 2 shows that the maximum time interval from sending observing ask to completing observation mission with satellite constellation is less than 1200s, namely that the satellite constellation can observe the target at time intervals which not more than 20 minutes.

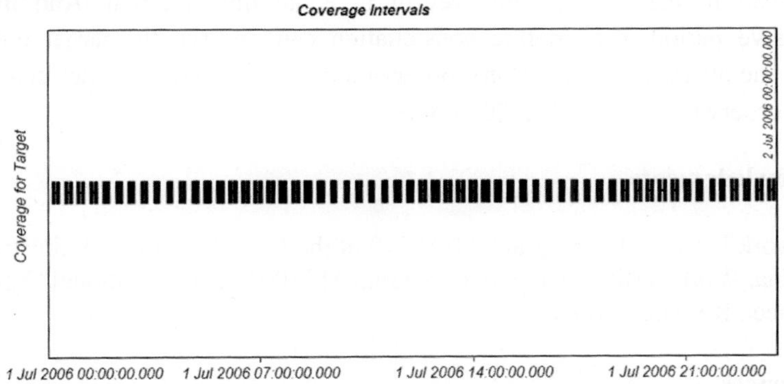

Fig. 1. Observation time distribution map.

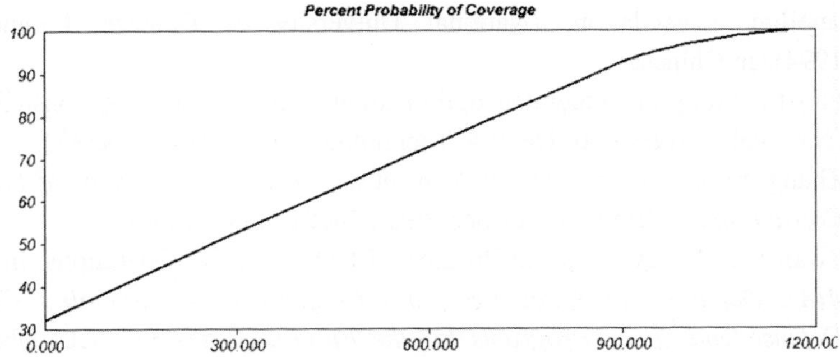

Fig. 2. Coverage percent probability of satellite constellation.

5. Conclusion

For the mission requirements that LEO satellite constellation realizes the rapid revisit to the target point in equal time interval, the paper finished the constellation configuration optimization design considering the constraints including constellation configuration, orbit and performance optimization design and so on, and using the MIGA. The satellite constellation realized the rapid revisit to the target point which latitude and longitude is (30°, 135°) in equal time interval. The constellation has 12 satellites in 44.2 degree inclination near circular orbits with orbital altitude 491.4 kilometers. There are 3 orbit planes spaced 96.97 degrees evenly with 4 satellites in each plane. The mean anomaly difference of the first satellite in different orbit planes is 7.8 degrees. Regressive period is one day and regressive circles are 15. The coverage performance analysis results of satellite constellation to the target point show that the satellite constellation realized the rapid revisit in equal time interval. And in each regressive period, the satellite constellation can observe the target point 82 times, the average time for every observation is 463.573s, the time interval for every observation is less than 20 minutes.

Acknowledgments

This work is supported by grant 20150219 of the Civil Aviation Administration of China. Work partially supported by grant 51320010201 of National Defense Advanced Research Project.

References

1. Bai Hefeng, Research on optimization design and control method of satellite constellation, (National University of Defense Technology, 1994).(In Chinese)
2. Fan Li, Study on integrated optimization design of satellite constellation, (National University of Defense Technology, 2006). (In Chinese)
3. Zhang Yulin, Fan Li, Zhang Yan, et al, *Theory and Design of Satellite Constellations*, (Beijing: Science Press, 2008). (In Chinese)
4. Swan PA. A Revolution in Progress: IRIDIUM LEO Operations, in *Proc. AIAA Defense and Space Programs Conference and Exhibit - Critical Defense and Space Programs for the Future*, (Huntsville, AL. UNITED STATES, 1997).
5. Williams EA, Crossley WA, Lang TJ. Average and Maximum Revisit Time Trade Studies for Satellite Constellations Using a Multiobjective Genetic Algorithm, J*ournal of Astronautical Sciences*, 49(3):385-400(2001).

6. Brochet C, Enjalbert JM, Garcia JM. A Multiobjective Optimization Approach for the Design of Walker Constellation, in *Proc. 50th International Astronautical Congress*, (Amsterdam, Netherlands, 1999).
7. Yang Jiachi. *Spacecraft orbital dynamics and control*, (Beijing: China Astronautic Publishing House, 1995). (In Chinese)

Research on the Topic Evolution of Microblog Based on BTM-LPA

Peng ZHANG[1,†] , Bi-cheng LI[1] and Rui-peng YANG[1,2]

[1]*School of Information and Systems Engineering, PLA Information EngineeringUniversity, Zheng Zhou, High-Tech Zone, China;*

[2]*PLA Academy of Air Defense Forces Command, Zheng Zhou, Erqi Zone, China*

[†]*E-mail: peng001zhang @163.com*

When topic evolution is analyzed by the traditional topic model on the micro blog data, the problem of sparse features arises. In this paper, we propose a new topic evolution method of combined BTM model with community discovery technology, which called BTM-LPA method. Firstly, this method uses the BTM model to select feature words and model in different time windows, and construct the co-word network by using the co-occurrence relationship of feature words in each time window; Secondly, through the community discovery technology, we use the LPA algorithm to find communities in co-word network, where a community represents a subtopic and the similarity measure of subtopics is transformed into the similarity measure of communities; Lastly, the five evolution types of subtopics, which include birth, extinct, merge, split and development, are defined for correlation analysis, the correlations of the subtopics are then set up according to the semantic similarity and temporal relations and the topic evolution is described through content change of subtopics. The experiment results demonstrate that the proposed method in this paper can effectively reflect the evolution process of the micro blog topic.

Keywords: Topic evolution; BTM model; Label propagation algorithm LPA; Community discovery.

1. Introduction

With the rapid development of the Internet, microblog users are growing day by day. Microblog has become a news, opinion published a center, users can freely publish comments on the microblog platform, the comments released by a large group of microblog users has been reflected its strong influence in the public opinion guidance and communication. Some topics can be quickly spread on the microblog, some topics have great influence over a very short period of time. Sometimes micro blog appear some radical comments, once these statements are manipulated or exploited, if not timely and actively respond to, small negative emotions will quickly be amplified, trigger public opinion crisis.

Therefore, it is very important to study the discussion on public events of the micro blog users and the development of the tracking events.

The primary task of the topic evolution is the topic detection, the research on topic detection have many for short text data such as microblog, such as literature[1-4],but the research on the topic evolution of the microblog data is less. At present, many methods of the research of topic evolution is mainly aimed at the data of news or science and technology literature, these methods are not suitable for short text data such as micro blog. Therefore, this paper proposes a new method of micro-blog topic evolution based on BTM-LPA, which combine BTM(Biterm Topic Model) model with community discovery technology .

2. Related Work

Measurement of topic evolution is the dynamic, developmental and differential of the same topic over time[5]. Topic detection and tracking(called " TDT " for short)define a topic as a seed event or activity, and all related events or activities[6],but TDT does not make full use of the time information in the corpus, with the wide application and development of the topic model[7-9], scholars use the topic model, through the introduction of time information in the corpus to carry out the research on the evolution of micro blog topic, has become a hotspot in machine learning, text mining and other fields.

At present, most of the research on the evolution of the topic is based on LDA(Latent Dirichlet Allocation)or its improved model. Literature[7] summarized three kinds of methods based on LDA topic model: (1) integrating the time information in the LDA model, the method is the time information of the text as an observable variable, combined with the LDA topic model to train the distribution of the topic in the text collection, such as Topic Over Time (TOT) model [10]. (2) post-discretized analysis method, this approach is to use LDA or some based on LDA improved model to obtain the topic, and then use the time information of the text to examine the distribution of the topic in the discrete time to study the topic evolution. (3) pre-discretized method, such as Griffiths[11] in 2004 and Hall[12] in 2008 proposed method respectively. This method is to discretize the text into the time window corresponding to time series according to the time information, and then, in order to deal with the text set in each time window, the evolution of the topic with time is finally formed, such as Dynamic Topic Model[13], Continuous Time Dynamic Topic Model[14], Dynamic Mixture Model[15], Multiscale Topic Tomograph Model[16], Incremental Latent Dirichlet Allocation Model[17]. At present, many of the research on topic evolution use the above models or their improved models, such as, in 2012, Hu[18] use the OLDA model to get the subtopics of each time window, five stages of the subtopic evolution, which are generation, extinction, inheritance, split and merge, are defined, then carry on the related analysis to the subtopic. Iwata, T[19] use the topic model to analyze the topic evolution by dividing time into multi-scale. In 2014, Cao[20] proposed a two-channel online theme evolution model based on LDA. Zhao[21] proposed a feature computation model for the evolution of the topic through the in-depth analysis of the characteristics of the dynamic evolution of the topic characteristics with time. There are some research on the evolution of science and technology literature data. For example, Qiao[22] used OLDA model, proposed a kind of scientific and technological literature evolution model based on seed documents. Wang[23] proposed a new approach and a framework to discover the evolution of topics based on dynamic co-word networks and communities within them. Of course, there are some research on the topic of the short text data such as micro blog. For example, Jain. Mona[24] proposed a method for studying user behavior and topic evolution based on time line for twitter data. Cai[25] proposed MLDA model to carry out the topic detection and topic evolution. Zhu[26] designed a coherent topic hierarchy to complete the analysis of the evolution of the micro blog topic.

There are some research on the topic evolution of short text data such as micro blog, but it is relatively less, due to the short text feature of micro blog, lead to feature sparse, so some topics evolution method for the news data is not appropriate for micro blog data. In addition, there will be the generation of new topics and the demise of the old, the number of subtopics is dynamic at each time period, but when the topic model is used, it is often necessary to set the number of subtopics in advance, and the number of subtopics is fixed, which is not consistent with the fact in a certain extent. Based on this, this paper proposes a topic evolution method, which is based on the BTM topic model and community discovery technology, that is the BTM-LPA method, the main purpose of this method is to obtain the feature words in each time window by using the BTM topic model. Therefore, an advantage of this method is that it can not set the number of subtopics in advance, at the same time, the BTM model is a model of the co-words, which overcomes the sparse problem of micro blog data.

2.1. *Basic frame*

Microblog has different characteristics with the traditional long text, that is, the content is short, the format is complex and so on, these make the research methods of topic evolution of the news data apply to the short text data, such as micro blog, the effect is not ideal. In this paper, we try to propose a new method of topic evolution based on the combination of BTM model and community discovery technology. The method first of all is to pre-process the micro blog data, which include the Chinese word segmentation, part of speech tagging and stop word filtering, etc., then, the micro blog data are dispersed to each time window according to the time information of the micro blog. The statistics of the co-words is done at each time window with the micro blog data, under the condition of non fixed number of topics, the BTM is used to model the co-words to obtain the topic feature words of each time window. Then we use the co-occurrence relationship to characterize the semantic relations among the feature words and construct the co-word network. We use the community discovery technology to find communities of each time window, because community reflects the theme of the corresponding documents and the different aspects of the topic, so a community should be a subtopic, community discovery process is a subtopic discovery process, we choose a label propagation algorithm with linear time complexity to find the community at each time window. Then the correlation of subtopics is analyzed, the correlation of subtopics is established according to the semantic similarity of subtopics and temporal relations, the topic is composed of the subtopics with the temporal relations and the content related, topic evolution is described by the change of the content and intensity of sub topics. Because a subtopic is a community, so the similarity measure of the subtopic with different time window is transformed into the similarity measure of community structure, community structure similarity measure is use the algorithm based on the maximum common subgraph. Our method is called BTM-LPA micro blog topic evolution analysis method. The basic framework is shown in Fig 1 with the analysis of the topic evolution of micro blog based on BTM-LPA.

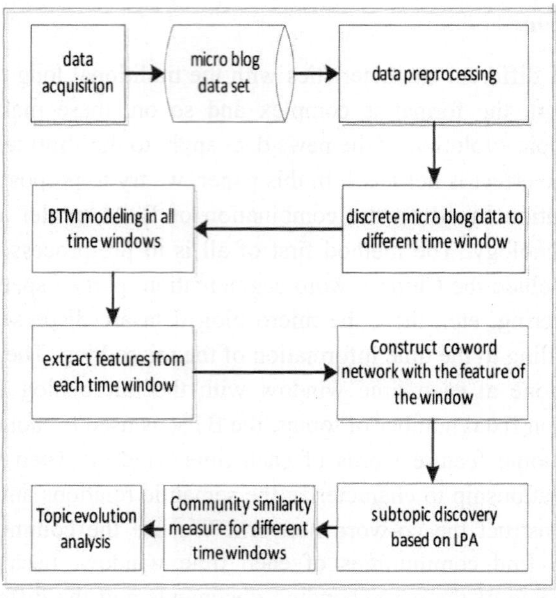

Fig. 1. topic evolution analysis flow chart based on BTM-LPA.

2.2. *Key technical description*

2.2.1. *BTM model*

Micro blog has the characteristics of short text, the feature is sparse, which lead to effect is not ideal for the traditional topic model. So Yan[27] proposed the BTM model, the main idea of the model is that the statistics of the co-words pairs is done in corpus, then modeling is based on the co-words pairs. BTM model overcome a series of problems caused by sparse corpus, the BTM model is shown in Fig 2.

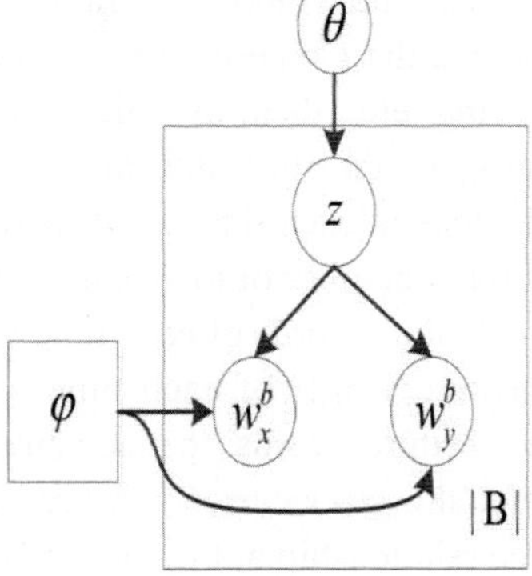

Fig. 2. BTM model.

The BTM model considers that the whole corpus is composed of many subjects, each subject use a certain probability to choose a co-word, the probability of each subject choosing a co-words is equal to the joint probability of the subject choosing respectively the two words in co-words, assuming α and β is Dirichlet priori value, the BTM model is described as follows:

First, for each subject T, the probability distribution $\phi_T : Dir(\beta)$ of the words is generated.

Then, the subject probability distribution $\Theta : Dir(\alpha)$ of the whole corpus is generated.

In the end, we find a subject $T : Multi(\Theta)$ of the co-words b, And then find the two words $w_x^b, w_y^b : Multi(\phi_T)$ in b, the joint probability of the co-word pairs $b = (w_x^b, w_y^b)$ is:

$$P(b) = \sum_T P(T)P(w_x^b \mid T)P(w_y^b \mid T) = \sum_T \theta_T \phi_{w_x^b|T} \phi_{w_y^b|T} . \tag{1}$$

where θ_T represents the probability of the subject in the corpus, $\phi_{w_x^b|T}$ and $\phi_{w_y^b|T}$ represent the emergence probability of the words w_x^b and w_y^b in the subject T .

Compared with the traditional topic model, the BTM model can effectively solve the problem of sparse data, and it is suitable for the analysis of the short text data.

2.2.2. *Feature word extraction and construction of common word network*

The topic evolve over time, which is expressed by the change of feature words for different time periods. In this paper, the BTM model is used to extract feature words from different time windows, where we define feature words as nouns, adjectives, verbs, etc., which contain more semantic information. In order to get the feature words in each time window, we first of all is to pre-process the micro blog data, which include the Chinese word segmentation, part of speech tagging and stop word filtering, etc., then, the micro blog data are dispersed to each time window according to the time information of the micro blog, the statistics of the co-words is done at each time window with the micro blog data, under the condition of non fixed number of topics, the BTM is used to model the co-words to obtain the topic feature words of each time window.

After obtaining the feature words of each time window, we use the co-occurrence relationship to feature words the semantic relations among the feature words and construct the co-occurrence word relationship network by feature words co-occurrence relationship at the same time window. The network of co-words relationship is undirected weighted graph, which express as $G = (G, E)$, G is node set, nodes express feature words in the co-words network, E edge set, the edge of co-word network express the co-occurrence relations of feature words in the same time window, edge weight is the joint probability of co-words, it can be calculated by the formula (1). Through the establishment of the co-word network, the semantic information of the feature words is preserved and the inner link between the words is also loaded, which express more abundant information.

2.2.3. *Subtopic discovery based on community discovery*

The same topic often contains some same or similar core words. In the co-words network, the feature words of the same subtopic is closely related, presenting nodes convergence phenomenon, so as to forming some communities, so we can mining these communities by community discovery technology, thus find feature word set to express a subtopic. community reflects the theme of the corresponding documents and the different aspects of a topic, so a community can be regarded as a subtopic of a topic.

The big number of microblog may lead to the network size of the co-words is relatively large, Therefore, we use label propagation algorithm with linear time complexity for community detection in all time windows, so as to get the subtopics of all time windows. LPA is a kind of semi-supervised learning method based on graph, which is proposed by Zhu[28] in 2001, the basic idea is to predict the label information of unlabeled nodes according to the label information of the labeled nodes. Raghavan[29] first used LPA algorithm for community detection in 2007, and achieved good results. The steps of LPA application in community discovery: (1)initialize for all nodes in the network, and assign a unique label for each node in turn.(2)set the number of iterations to

$t=1$;(3) randomly arrange nodes in the network to generate a sequence X; (4)we follow the order of sequence X, and use the update the formula $L_x(t)=f\left(L_{x_{i1}}(t),\cdots,L_{x_{im}}(t),L_{x_{i(m+1)}}(t-1),\cdots,L_{xk}(t-1)\right)$ to update each node in X. $x_{i1},\cdots,x_{ik}$ is the neighbor node set of x ,where $x_{i1},\cdots,x_{im}$ are these nodes that label have been updated in this iteration, $x_{i(m+1)},\cdots,x_{ik}$ are these nodes that label have not been updated, $L_x(t)$ represents the label of node x at the time t, the label of the node x in the first t iteration according to labels of these nodes which labels have been updated in the first t iteration and these nodes which labels have been updated in the first $t-1$ iteration but have not been updated in the first t iteration to determine; (5) if all the labels of nodes are not changed, then the algorithm stops, otherwise $t=t+1$, go to step (3).

A measure index of the quality of community division is modularity, its calculation formula is:

$$Q=\frac{1}{2m}\sum_{ij}\left(A_{ij}-P_{ij}\right)\delta\left(C_i,C_j\right). \tag{2}$$

where A is the adjacency matrix of the network, M is the number of edges, P_{ij} represents the expected values of the edge with node i and j in the null model, if node i and j belongs to the same community, $\delta\left(C_i,C_j\right)=1$, otherwise it is 0.

2.2.4. *The similarity measure of subtopics*

These communities of all the time window are obtained by label propagation algorithm, these communities represent subtopic, the similarity measure of subtopic of different time window is transformed into the similarity measure of community structure. We use the maximum common subgraph algorithm to carry out community similarity measure, and consider the influence of edge and weight on the similarity measure of community, if the more the same nodes and edges of two communities , the more similarity.

We calculate the similarity of two communities as follows:

$$S(C_m^{t_l},C_n^{t_k})=\alpha\frac{\left|C_m^{t_l}\cap C_n^{t_k}\right|}{\left|C_m^{t_l}\cup C_n^{t_k}\right|}+\beta\frac{\sum S_e\left(\frac{\min\left(w_{ij},w_{i'j'}\right)}{\max\left(w_{ij},w_{i'j'}\right)}\right)}{\max E\left(C_m^{t_l},C_n^{t_k}\right)}. \tag{3}$$

where $C_m^{t_l}$ represents the m-th community in the time window t_l, $C_n^{t_k}$ represent the n-th community in the time window t_k, the first half of the formula is the similarity measure of nodes with the two communities, $\left|C_m^{t_l}\cap C_n^{t_k}\right|$ represents the number of public nodes in two communities, $\left|C_m^{t_l} \cup C_n^{t_k}\right|$ represents the number of union nodes in two communities, the more similar nodes are, the more similarities the two communities are. The second part is the similarity measure of edges with the two communities, $\max E\left(C_m^{t_l}, C_n^{t_k}\right)$ represents the larger number of edges in the two communities, S_e represents the same side of the two communities, w_{ij} and $w_{i'j'}$ represent the weights of the same edges for community $C_m^{t_l}$ and $C_n^{t_k}$,weight values can be obtained by the formula (1), $C_m^{t_l}$ and $C_n^{t_k}$ the weight of the same edges is more similar, the value of $\min\left(w_{ij}, w_{i'j'}\right) / \max\left(w_{ij}, w_{i'j'}\right)$ is close to 1, the sum of the same edges weights approximate represents the same edges number, thus, the edges number of the maximum common sub-graph is obtained, if the more the same edges of maximum common subgraph is, the greater $C_m^{t_l}$ and $C_n^{t_k}$ similarity is. The similarity of the two communities is represented by a linear combination of these two parts, the similarity of these two parts impact on the similarity of two communities by adjusting parameters α and β , $\alpha + \beta = 1$.

2.2.5. *Correlation analysis*

In this paper, the evolution of subtopics is represented by the changes of the community structure, and the community of the time window represents a subtopic.

Let $C_m^{t_i}$ denote the m-th subtopic in the time window t_i , $t_1, t_2, \cdots, t_n$ indicates the order of the time window, and ε represents the threshold value of the evolution relationship.

Definition 1(pre-order related subtopic):the similarity of subtopic $C_m^{t_i}$ and $C_n^{t_j}$ $(t_j \in t_1, t_2, \cdots, t_{i-1})$ is the largest, and it exists $sim(C_m^{t_i}, C_n^{t_j}) \geq \varepsilon$, then $C_n^{t_j}$ is called the preorder related subtopic of $C_m^{t_i}$, recorded as $prior(C_m^{t_i})$.

Definition 2(post-order related subtopic):the similarity of subtopic $C_m^{t_i}$ and $C_h^{t_k}$ $(t_k \in t_{i+1}, t_{i+2}, \cdots, t_n)$ is the largest, and it exists $sim(C_m^{t_i}, C_h^{t_k}) \geq \varepsilon$, then $C_h^{t_k}$ is called the post order related subtopic of $C_m^{t_i}$, recorded as $post(C_m^{t_i})$.

According to the definition of the pre-order and post-order related subtopics, we define the evolution of subtopics as five stages, which contains birth, extinct, merge, split and development, they are defined as follows:

Definition3 (the birth of subtopics): for the subtopic $C_m^{t_i}$, if it not exists $C_n^{t_j} = prior(C_m^{t_i})$, then $C_m^{t_i}$ is called a new subtopic generated in the time window t_i.

Definition 4 (the extinction of subtopics): for the subtopic $C_m^{t_i}$, if it not exists $C_h^{t_k} = post(C_m^{t_i})$, then $C_m^{t_i}$ is called a extinct subtopic in the time window t_i.

Definition 5 (the merge of subtopics): for the subtopic $C_m^{t_i}$, if it exists $C_h^{t_k} = post(C_m^{t_i})$, but have $C_m^{t_i} \neq post(C_n^{t_j})$, and exists $C_f^{t_r} = prior(C_h^{t_k})$, then $C_h^{t_k}$ is obtained by the merge of $C_m^{t_i}$ and $C_f^{t_r}$.

Definition 6 (the split of subtopics): for the subtopic $C_m^{t_i}$, if it exists $C_n^{t_j} = prior(C_m^{t_i})$, but have $C_m^{t_i} \neq post(C_n^{t_j})$, and exists $C_f^{t_r} = post(C_n^{t_j})$, then $C_m^{t_i}$ and $C_f^{t_r}$ is obtained by the split of $C_n^{t_j}$.

Definition 7 (the development of subtopics): for the subtopic $C_m^{t_i}$, if it exists $C_h^{t_k} = post(C_m^{t_i})$ and $C_m^{t_i} = post(C_n^{t_j})$, then $C_h^{t_k}$ develop as $C_m^{t_i}$.

The flow of the algorithm is shown as below:

step1: for all $C_m^{t_i}, t_i \in t_2, t_3, \cdots, t_n$, find $C_h^{t_k} = post(C_m^{t_i})$;

if $post(C_m^{t_i}) = \text{NULL}$;

$C_m^{t_i}$ extinct;

step2: for all $C_m^{t_i}, t_i \in t_1, t_2, \cdots, t_{n-1}$, find $C_n^{t_j} = prior(C_m^{t_i})$;

if $prior(C_m^{t_i}) = \text{NULL}$;

$C_m^{t_i}$ birth;

if $C_m^{t_i} \neq prior(post(C_m^{t_i}))$;

$C_f^{t_r} = prior(post(C_m^{t_i}))$;

$C_m^{t_i}$ and $C_f^{t_r}$ merge into $C_h^{t_k}$;

if $C_m^{t_i} \neq post(prior(C_m^{t_i}))$

$C_f^{t_r} = post(prior(C_m^{t_i}))$

$C_n^{t_j}$ split into $C_m^{t_i}$ and $C_f^{t_r}$;

if $C_m^{t_i} = prior(post(C_m^{t_i}))$

$prior(C_m^{t_i})$ develop into $C_m^{t_i}$;

3. Experiments and Results

3.1. *Experimental data*

Experimental data is micro blog data that is from March 2014 to October about the event of Kunming violent terrorist attacks. According to the release time of the micro blog, micro blog data are discrete distributed to eight time windows. For eight time windows, we select the first 1000 feature words in each time window as the co-word network nodes. The co-word network basic information for eight time windows is shown in the following table:

Table 1. Common word network basic information of each time window.

Time Window	Network Identification	The Number Of Micro Blog	The Number Of Nodes	The Number Of Edges
March	G1	42,118	1,000	241,079
April	G2	8,672	1,000	54,216
May	G3	7,861	1,000	48,634
June	G4	4,797	1,000	22,365
July	G5	4,353	1,000	19,685
August	G6	3,594	1,000	14,685
September	G7	9,426	1,000	65,257
October	G8	5,860	1,000	39,822

3.2. *Experimental result analysis*

3.2.1. *Subtopic discovery results*

In this paper, community discovery for co-word network is conducted based on LPA algorithm in eight time windows, a community represents a subtopic, the following table shows the results of community discovery.

Table 2. Community discovery results in eight time window.

Co-word Network	Community Number	Maximum Community Node Number	Minimum Community Node Number
G1	9	596	18
G2	16	265	9
G3	17	257	7
G4	15	248	7
G5	14	251	5
G6	15	239	6
G7	13	394	6
G8	12	227	8

As can be seen from table 2, the incident immediately made a high degree of attention after it occurred, the number of communities in the first time window is 9, significantly less than that of other time windows, and the maximum number of nodes in the community is significantly more than the other time window, note micro blog discussion focused on a few subtopics in the first time window. To the time window 2, the number of communities increased significantly, which indicate the discussion began to split into more subtopics. Time window 2 to 6, the number of communities and the maximum number of community nodes is not much change, which shows topic is relatively stable in time window 2 to 6. To the time window 7 appear to change, which shows incident has changed significantly and caused public concern.

3.2.2. *Topic evolution analysis*

A community represent a subtopic, topic evolution is explained by the change of the feature words in the community. As shown in Fig 3.

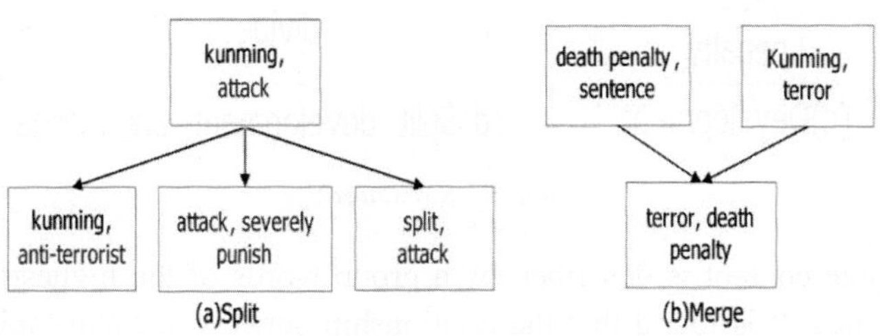

Fig. 3. Correlation analysis of sub-topic.

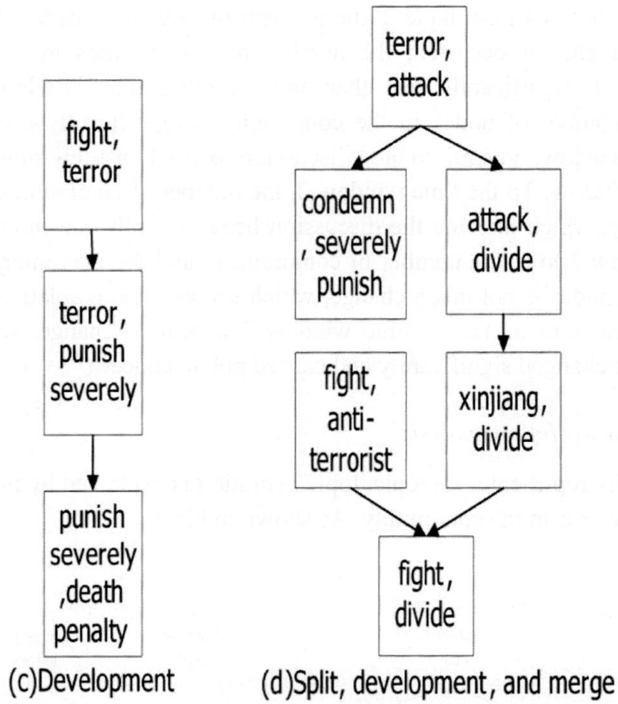

Fig. 3. (*Continued*)

Subtopic content is described by a group words of the highest probability for occurrence. It is found that the relationship between the sub-topics, such as split, merger and succession, and the evolution of these relationships is found. For example, the subtopic of "Kunming, attack" in time window 1split into the three subtopics of "Kunming, anti-terrorist ", "attack, severely punish " and" attack, divide "in time window 2 (see Fig 3 (a)); the subtopics of "death penalty, sentence" and "Kunming, terror" in time window 7mergeas a subtopic of "terror, death penalty" in time window 8 (see Fig 3 (b)); the subtopic of "fight, terror "in time window 5 develop as the subtopics of " terror, punish severely "in time window 6 and " punish severely ,death penalty" in time window 7 (see Fig 3 (c)); the subtopic of " terror, attack" in time window 1 first split into the subtopic of "condemn, severely punish " and "attack, divide "in time window2, the subtopic of "condemn, severely punished" in time window 3 is extinct, the subtopic of "attack, divide " develop into "Xinjiang, divide " in time window 3,and the subtopic of "Xinjiang, divide "merge into " fight, divide " in the time window 4 with the new birth of subtopic of "fight, anti-terrorist "in time window 3 (see Fig 3 (d)).

4. Conclusion

We present a topic evolution method based on BTM-LPA, modeling is based on the co-words pairs of micro blog at each time window by using BTM, and get feature words with each time window; then use the co-occurrence relationship of feature words to construct co-word network in each time window, find the subtopics of all time window by using community discovery technology based on LPA algorithm, therefore, the similarity calculation of subtopics is transformed into the similarity calculation of community structure; In this paper, we define the four kinds of evolution models, which contains birth, extinct, merge, split, the related analysis of the subtopic is carried out according to the semantic similarity and temporal relationship of subtopics. We analyse the content evolution of topic based on microblog data, experiments show that the method proposed in this paper is effective. On the basis of this, the next step will be to study how to use more abundant index to evaluate the performance of the topic evolution model.

Acknowledgments

This work is supported by National Natural Science Fundation(14BXW028).

References

1. Sakaki T, Okazaki M, Matsuo Y. Earthquake Shake Twitter Users: Real-time Event Detectionby Social Sensors. In Proceedings of the19th International World Wide Web Conference, 2010.
2. Popescu A, Pennacchiotti M. Extracting events and event descriptions from Twitter. In Proceedings of the 20th International World Wide Web Conference (Companion Volume). 2011, pp.105-106.
3. Guo J, Zhang P, Tan J, Guo L. Mining Hot Topics from Twitter Streams. In Proceedings of Proceedings of International Conference on Computational Science, 2012, pp.2008-2011.
4. Guo X, Xiang Y, Chen Q, Huang Z and Hao Y. LDA-based online topic detection using tensor factorization. Journal of Information Science, vol. 39, 4: pp. 459-469, 2013.

5. Bin Dan, Fang Li. Review of research methods of topic evolution based on LDA [J]. Journal of Chinese Information Processing, 2010, 24 (6): 43-49. In Chinese.
6. Yu Hong, Yu Zhang, Ting Liu, et al. Evaluation and review on the research of topic detection and tracking[J]. Journal of Chinese Information Processing, 2007, 21 (6): 71-87. In Chinese.
7. HofmannT, editor Probabilistic latent semantic indexing[C]. Proceedings of the 22nd annual international ACM SIGIR conference on Research and development in information retrieval, 1999: 50-57.
8. Griffiths T, Steyvers M. A probabilistic approach to semantic representation [C]. Proceedings of the 24th annual conference of the cognitive science society, 2002: 381-386.
9. BleiDM, Ng AY, Jordan MI. Latent Dirichlet Allocation[J]. the Journal of machine Learning, research, 2003(3):993-1022.
10. Wang X, McCallum A, editors. Topics over time: a non-Markov continuous-time model of topical trends[C]. Proceedings of the 12th ACM SIGKDD international conference on Knowledge discovery and data mining, 2006: 424-433.
11. GriffithsTL, Steyvers M.Finding scientific topics[J]. Proceedings of the National Academy of Sciences, 2004, 101(suppl1): 5228-5235.
12. Hall D, Jurafsky D, Manning CD. Studying the history of ideas using topic models[C]. Proceedings of the conference on empirical methods in natural language processing, 2008: 363-371.
13. Blei DM, Laffeny JD.Dynamic topic models[C]. Proceedings of the 23rd international conference on Machine learning, 2006: 113-120.
14. Wang C, Blei D, Heckerman D. Continuous time dynamic topic models[J]. arXiv preprintarXiv:12063298.2012.
15. Wei X,Sun J, Wang X. Artificial Dynamic Mixture Models for Multiple Time-Series[C]. Proceedings of the International Joint Conference on Artificial Intelligence (IJCAI), 2007:2909-2914.
16. Nallapati RM, Ditmore S,Laffeny JD, etal. Multiscale topic tomography [C].Proceedings of the 13th ACM SIGKDD international conference on Knowledge discovery and data mining, 2007: 520-529.
17. SonyX, Lin C-Y, Tseng BL, etal. Modeling, and predicting, personal information dissemination behavior[C].Proceeding of the eleventh ACM SIGKDD international conference on Knowledge discovery in data mining 2005: 479-488.

18. Yan-Li Hu, Liang Bai, Wei-Ming Zhang. A method for modeling and analyzing topic evolution. ActaAutomaticaSinica, 2012, 38(10):1690-1697. In Chinese.
19. IwataT, YamadaT, SakuraiY, Ueda N. 2011. Sequential modeling of topic dynamics with multiple timescales. ACM Trans. Knowl. Discov. Data 5, 4, Article 19 (February 2012), 27 pages.
20. Jian-ping Cao, You-qing Xia, Feng-cai Qiao, Hui Tu, Xin Zhang. The evolution model of double channel online theme based on LDA. Acta Automatica Sinica, 2014, 40 (12): 2877- 2886. In Chinese.
21. Xu-jian Zhao, Chun-ming Yang, Bo Li, et al. A new method for the evolution of news topic evolution based on feature evolution. Journal of Computers, 2014, 37 (4): 819-831. In Chinese.
22. Shan-zeng Qiao, Ai-li Han. A Way to Construct Evolution Model of Scientific Papers Based on the Seed Document and OLDA Models[C]. International Conference on Mechatronic Sciences, Electric Engineering and Computer (MEC), 2013:900-903.
23. Xiao-guang Wang, Qi-kai Cheng, Wei Lu. Analyzing evolution of research topics with NEViewer: a new method based on dynamic co-word networks [C]. Scientometrics. 2014:1253–1271.
24. Mona Jain, S.Rajyalakshmi, Rudra M. Tripathy. et al. Temporal Analysis of User Behavior and Topic Evolution on Twitter[C]. BDA 2013, LNCS 8302, pp. 22–36, 2013.
25. Guo-yong Cai, Li-bin Peng, and Yong Wang. Topic Detection and Evolution Analysison Microblog[C]. International Federation for Information Processing, 2014:67-77.
26. Jia-hui Zhu, Xu-hui Li, Min Peng, et al. Coherent Topic Hierarchy: A Strategy for Topic Evolutionary Analysis on Microblog Feeds .In: WAIM 2015, LNCS 9098, pp. 70–82, 2015.
27. YanX, Guo J, Lan Y, et al. A biterm topic model for short texts[C]. Proceedings of the 22nd international conference on World Wide Web. International World Wide Web Conferences Steering Committee, 2013:1445-1456.
28. Zhu X, Ghahramani Z. Learning from labeled and unlabeled data with label propagation[R]. Technical Report CMU-CALD-02-107, Carnegie Mellon University, 2002.
29. Raghavan UN, Albert R, Kumara S. Near linear time algorithm to detect community structures in large-scale networks[J]. Physical Review E. 2007, 76(3): 036106.

User Influence Analysis Based on Blogs

Xiang LIU*, Yan JIA, Rong JIANG and Yong QUAN
Dept. of Computer, National University of Defense Technology, Changsha, 410073, China
E-mail: xiang_liu2013@163.com

Social networks play an important and indispensable role in the internet, especially for governments and organizations. Social networks are information diffusion networks with users as the node and the relationships between users functioning as the vehicle. In this paper we propose three different types of algorithms to compute the user influence based on users' behavior of forwarding micro blogs and the symbol of @ in the micro blogs. We evaluate the effectiveness of the algorithm by comparing the results of our algorithms and the trained data in the dataset and the results demonstrate promising performance.

Keywords: Social network; Information diffusion; Forwarding micro blog; User influence.

1. Introduction

With the continuous development of network technology, network shows more and more superiority in people's lives. Social networks are increasingly becoming an important part of people's daily lives. Through micro blog, we can get to know what our good friends was doing, are doing and what they will do. We can see some of the current hot information through the net, such as a star's willing to come to your homeland to host a concert, a movie's being released before long and so on. Micro blog has indeed become indispensable in our lives. In addition, micro blog also plays another important role: product promotion, viral marketing. We know that with the continuous development of network technology, the advertising industry has been transferred from newspapers, radio, television and other traditional media to the internet. Even some of the big events are closely related to the micro blog network. Such as the U.S. presidential election in 2008, MySpace and Facebook, especially Facebook play a very important role. The president has established a good personal image through communication and interaction with supporters on the Internet. Of course there are some negative examples, for example, some criminals use social networks to spread false information, spread rumors. This requires our government to strengthen public opinion monitoring to better ensure the healthy development of the internet. Strengthen the Internet user behavior monitoring, we can accurately grasp the development trend of social networks.

There is too much user information in the Social network that this paper only take forwarding micro blog and @ relationship information in the social network for user influence analysis. When we browsing other people's blogs, we found that some of the micro blog is useful to us or is interesting to us, thus we will forward his blog; likewise when our blog is useful to other users, they will forward our blogs too. For some well-known big V, there will be a lot of micro blog users who forward their micro blog; relatively speaking, we common users will have much less people forward our blogs. In these cases, we believe that the number of users who have more blogs forwarded are more influential than the users who have less users forwarding their blogs. For @ information, to a certain extent, it is more similar with the forwarding behavior; we will carry out a detailed account in this text. In this paper, the third kind of social network user influence calculation method is based on the forwarding level. That is to say, for the case that when the user B forwards a blog of user A, user C forwards the blog of user B, it forms a forwarding chain structure. with social network structure more and more complex, it will form a complex forwarding structure named forwarding tree. In this paper, we will figure out user influence by the forwarding tree. Overall this paper works on the relationship between the forwarding behavior and the content of blogs information to calculate the user influence. Our result show that our algorithm performs rather good.

The rest of this paper organized as follows: the second chapter introduces the previous related work; the third chapter introduces the data sets we use; the fourth chapter introduces our three algorithms: forwarding, @ and forwarding hierarchy; the fifth chapter presents our experimental results; the sixth chapter is the evaluation of the effectiveness of the algorithm; the seventh chapter is the conclusion.

2. Related Work

In recent years, with the study of user behavior in social network deeper and deeper, various methods of research about user influence studying from different all kinds of perspectives emerge in an endless stream. We carried out the analysis of user influence from different angles, and launched it in the view of their own points. This plays a great role in guiding us to understand the user behavior in social network.

Daniel[1] et al. proposes IP algorithm, based on research about influence and passivity. They have got analytical factors by analyzing the behavior of users to click on the URL of others, which will be helpful to future analysis. Adrien[4] et al. through the complex calculation of the way of information transmition, have had put forward a practical model which can be used to guide the present network media to spread information much better and faster. This study can help us understand the present work better, and propose the improvement measures to the present work. What is more, there are some topic-themed anslysis of the user influence. For example, Tang[5] et al. has put forward a topical affinity propagation to simulate the topic level user behavior to analyze the user's influence. TAP model works on the MapReduce model proposed a series of efficient distributed algorithm and show its advantages by the analysis of the effectiveness. Zhang[6] et al. thinks the user behavior is mainly affected by the most intimate friends in his ego network. Based on this understanding, their social influence positioning technology can be a good predictor of user forwarding behavior. From a dynamic point of view, Valerio[3] et al. has analyzed the changes of the user's behavior in social network , and think it better to use OSN model to analyze the change rules of user's behavior. It also can make them to understand the network actions better in the past by OSN model, and also it is better to predict the dynamic changes of the user's behavior in the future.

3. Dataset

We have used the crawler technology to crawl information of users from Sina micro blog continuously, including the data from 2014 March to May. This dataset is used as a prediction dataset. First of all, we need to clean up the data, and remove the accounts which doesn't conform to our analysis. Considering that crawling too much data will lead to cost too much time, and also make analysis quite too slow, so we have selected 200 thousand user's information, each user has blog of on average of 200 articles, a total of 40 million of articles in the blog. Dataset's format is shown as in Table 1:

Table 1. Data format.

Field No.	0	1	2	3	4	5	6
Field Name	Did	Uid	Username	Timestamp	Uid	Did	content

Among them: Uid refers to the user ID ;Did refers to the document ID, and it is the id of the user's blog; Username refers to the user's nickname; Timestamp refers to the time when post his blog; Content refers to the blog content. When we do the data analysis, we will need some information of the blog, such as the information of @ . Therefore, the Content section is an important part of our data set.

Besides, in order to carry out data analysis, we also have chosen some users of Sina micro blogging celebrity to collect data, and probably get 50 users' information. This data format is same as the user data format is same as table 1. This data set regarded as training dataset carries on to forecast the predicting dataset.

4. Methods

Analyzing the influence among the users, blog plays an important role. There are a lot of papers on the study of blog. This article measures the influence between users only from the blog forwarding and the @ information.

4.1. *Forward*

Every blogger may have many posts, each blog is likely to be forwarded by the blogger's friends and such formats of a forwarding behavior.

Based on past experience, we are likely to boil the user's forwarding other people's blog down to two main reasons:

i)This blog has attracted the user who forwarding the blog by the content of the blog; that is to say, the blogger have a certain influence on the user who forwarding the blog.

ii)That is online water army. There are quite a lot of research on exposure of online water army now, and it already has so much mature technology that We don't make a detailed explanation here; and the data set has been cleared about the online water army.

From the above information, I believe that you will have a general understanding of this article about the forwarding blogs; and the following will be described in detail about the forwarding algorithm.

We define V as the user space, including all users in the dataset of this text, define the user i as Vi. Define D as all the blog space, and the j_{th} blog of user I names D_{ij}. The blog posts of user i as D_{vi}.

We have analyzed that the user's forwarding other people's blog just because the user is affected by others, which can reflect the user's influence of the user on other users who has a direct relationship. However, if we just take the number of forwarding behavior to calculate the influence is obviously not enough, we also need to consider the total number of blogs of the user. This is because, although there may be a certain number of users forwarding his blogs, if the number of blogs of the user is quite too small, it will seriously harm the blogger's influence and his fans will decline. This also shows that the blogger does not pay much attention to its fans. Therefore, when we calculate the user's influence on the forwarding relationship, it also need to be reflected in the total number of the users' blogs.

By the above statement, we get the formula for calculating the user's influence by the amount of his blogs which are forwarded and the total number of blogs:

$$I(v_i)=\frac{F(vi)}{D(vi)}. \quad (1)$$

Through this formula, we can figure out the user influence if we have the number of the number of a user's blogs forwarded and the total number of the user's blogs.

4.2. *Symbol of @*

For users who are often or less frequently (but occasionally) used micro blog, there is a sign that everyone is very familiar with which is @. When we are posting a blog, adding a @ symbol in the micro blog, we can make the users who was @ to see our blogs. Of course, this is also divided into several cases:

i) who was @ is the famous big V. And they are people who we seldom communicate with in our daily lives. We @ them just because we have question to consult them or we want to make them see some of our views.

ii) who ware @ are our good friends. They may have minimal influence in the social network, but who we are good friends! We @ each other just to share a thing, or a news, or funny story. Only this and no more just!

Of course, the @ relationship is more complex than the forwarding relationship.

For each micro blog, it is likely consist @ relationship, and for the bloggers, he or she will have many @ relationship, analysis of the number of these @ relationship in coarse granularity, we can draw the following conclusions:

i) The user who @ many people and also many people will @ him. These people are usually more active, and we think that they are welcome.

ii) The user who seldom @ others but there are many people who will @ him. Such people in the social network is not too much. They are often some organizations or medias or individuals which Have high reputation and popularity, such as China Daily, CCTV, Ma Yun, etc..

iii) The user often @ other people, but there is few people will @ him. This situation is not very common. In the social network, some users are very active, but the blog of such users may be too shallow, it is difficult to resonate around other people, so these posts are lack of other people's attention.

iv) Still there are people who seldom @ other people and there are few people will @ him. This person may be online water army, may be some interference users or probably these people are really less active in the micro blog. We may have heard about some of these people that who seldom post blogs, but often read other people's blogs.

See from above, in fact, there may be some people still feel forward and @ relationships are the same, in fact, these two points are different. The difference is in that each blogs, users can @ a number of users, which led to the number of users bigger than the number of users forwarding blogs. We know that when the user A @ other people B, B will has a greater chance to read the blog which consist of the symbol @. As long as he read the blog there will be a certain degree of probability of being influenced. So, in a sense, the @ relationship has more power than the forwarding relationship.

Therefore, through the above elaboration, to calculate the influence of the user, intuitive, we may draw the following formula:

$$I(v_i) = a \times I(i) + b \times I(ii) + c \times I(iii) + d \times I(iv). \quad (2)$$

Among them, I(i), I(ii), I(iii), I(iv) are the influence of the above four kinds of users, a, b, c, d corresponding to the influence coefficients. But after careful analysis, we found a problem: for the user vi, those users who @ vi is equivalent of vi's fans. @ behavior can be understood as that the user has already be influenced by vi (they @vi just because that they are concerned about vi, and this can be understood as having been affected by vi); and to those users who vi @ (of course, some of these users have @ VI already, here we should remove this part of the users), means that vi will be applied to the impact or trying to influence the users (however, whether he really be affected, there is a lot of uncertainty). This is the idea of the @ relationship to calculate the user's influence.

From the above analysis, we come to the conclusion that the influence should be included into two parts: the users that will be affected and the users who have already been affected:

$$I(v_i) = Ied(v_i) + c \times Iing(v_i). \quad (3)$$

Here, Ied represents the number of people influenced which is already confirmed.

Iing represents the number of people is to be influence. The parameter c represent influence coefficient. This parameter is used to deduce Iing from Ied.

Through the analysis of the data, we know that the user data which has been affected in the data set is easy to get. The problem we have to discuss is the acquisition of user data that is about to be affected.

After data analysis, we separate the dataset to four kinds of data:

i)The dataset of the users who @ user vi, named R(vi) . We regard these users as the user vi has already influence.

ii)The dataset user vi @, this dataset names S(vi) .

iii)The dataset is the users who already has @ interaction relationship with user vi, this dataset names T(vi), it's the intersection of dataset R(vi) and S(vi) .

iv) Remove the dataset of T(vi) from the dataset of the users vi @ ,and we name the left dataset Q(vi) . That's to say Q(vi) = S(vi) − T(vi) .

For further analysis, we found that i and ii can deduce iii, in other words i and ii are the past iii.

For iii, the possibility the user vi affect other users around him in the social networks is:

$$P(\text{iii}) = \frac{T(vi)}{S(vi)} = c \tag{4}$$

Then, we rank user influence of the @ behavior by the number the user influence, the formula of the number a user influence is:

$$I(vi) = R(vi) + c \times Q(vi) \tag{5}$$

4.3. *Forwarding hierarchy*

Searching in micro blog, we are very easy to find another problem, that for every blog post, it may be forwarded more than once, it may be forwarded by more than one person. What's more important is that when the user B's blog was forwarded by a user A, it is likely that there will be another user C forwarding B blog, there is still probability that a user D forwarding user C blog, and this forms a forwarding chain.

So for this kind of situation, if we just simply regard the forwarding behavior of user B forwarding user A's blog as the influence factor, obviously it weakened its influence. Therefore, here we have to talk about the problem lies in the forwarding chain composed by the forwarding relationship. And how shall we calculate the user's influence?

We know that not long ago Google has published an article of web page authority algorithm on the field of information retrieval named PageRank. They set score to the web pages about the importance based on PageRank algorithm; and finally based on this score they establish a certain rules to better meet user's search request of information. The forwarding chain of blogs here is similar to the web pages described in PageRank algorithm. So to get the score of the blogger we should add up all the score of each posts in the forwarding chain. There is a need to note that there are a number of blog posts, and there may be a number of blog posts in these posts which are forwarded more than once. Taking this into account, we should differentiate every score of the post and then add them to get the user influence of the specific blogger.

But we found that there are essential differences between the users of social networks and the web pages in PageRank. For example, in PageRank algorithm, for each page, the several links has the same weight. But for each common bloggers, every degree is a post. But the blog is very different, because bloggers even some of the big V, many of the blogs also are not forwarded by others. Although there are so many difference, the thought of the score of each page given by the previous page is still so us much favor. For each user B forwarding blogs of user A and then user C also forwarded the blog from the user B, but no matter whether user C forward blog from user A, the source of the blog is from A. So we believe that A's score is incline by one owing to C's forwarding blog. While for user B, C did not contribute to incline the score of B. (We insist that the size of a blogger's influence is determined by the number of times it is forwarded, but not as the fact that high quality website contributes high score in PageRank)

The dataset can be divided into two parts, one part is the list of blogs without being forwarded. For this part, the contribution of the blogs to the blogger is 0. That's to say these posts can't incline the score of the user. For the other part, it's consist of a list of blogs which is forwarded by others. For this part, every blog make the score of the blogger incline by one.

We can separate several forwarding trees from the source dataset. And these forwarding trees consist of the forwarding forest.

We name the forwarding tree (FT) as Ft(vi) and the forwarding tree is shown in Fig.1; and the forwarding forest (FF) include Ft(0), Ft(1), Ft(2), Ft(3)… and the forwarding forest is shown in Fig. 2.

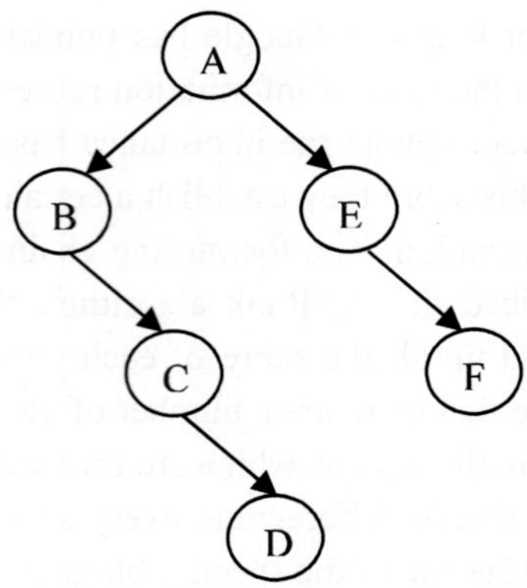

Fig. 1. Forwarding Tree (FT).

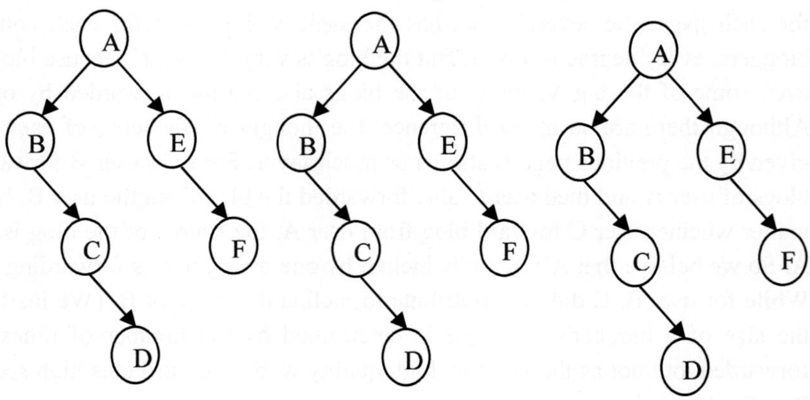

Fig. 2. Forwarding Forest (FF).

Traversal tree structure of all the sub nodes we can get

$$\mathrm{Fscore}(i) = n \ \text{(n is the number of all the sub nodes)}\,. \tag{6}$$

For the forwarding forest:

$$\mathrm{FScore}(vi) = \textstyle\sum_{vi \in V} \mathrm{Fscore}(vi)\,. \tag{7}$$

FScore(vi) is the sum of the contribution value of each node to the root node, and that is the score of each node vi. Obviously the sum of contribution of all other non forwarding relationships is

$$\textstyle\sum_{\mathrm{Fscore}(vi)} 0 = 0\ . \tag{8}$$

At this point, for all the nodes sorted by value, it is ranking of user influence.

5. Results

5.1. *Results of the three algorithms*

According to the analysis of the chapter 4, we design the corresponding algorithm, and finally get the results which is shown is Table 2:

Table 2. Rank of user influence by forwarding behavior and @ behavior.

Forward	@
1708942053	1708942053
2090591961	2482557597
2547916923	2090591961
2482557597	1866402485
1866402485	1649155730
1649155730	2547916923
3249656920	1742703365
1652707015	1725876907

Notes: the number is Uid.

We can see the results of the two algorithms as shown above, and for the result of Forwarding Hierarchy is shown in Table 3:

Table 3. Rank of user influence by forwarding hierarchy.

Forwarding Hierarchy
1708942053
2482557597
1866402485
1649155730
2547916923
2090591961
1725876907
1652707015

Notes: the number is Uid.

5.2. *Evaluation*

For the data obtained in the last section, we compare the results obtained in the last section with the train data and find that forwarding hierarchy performs better and the other two perform alike. The three results consist of three vectors, which need to be standardized and then can be used for the calculation. The standard formula is as follows:

$$I(vi) = \frac{Rx(vi)}{\sum_{vj \in V} Rx(vj)}. \quad (9)$$

Ry and Rz is similar to Rx.

Then we have to carry out the similarity comparison of the three results, the method used here is cosine similarity, the formula is as follows:

$$\mathrm{Sim}(A,B) = \cos\theta = \frac{A \times B}{|A| \times |B|}. \tag{10}$$

Through the above formula, first the standardization, and then calculate the similarity.

The cosine similarity calculation results is shown in table 4:

Table 4. Cosine similarity of three algorithms.

Algorithm	Cosine Similarity
Forward & @	0.719
@ & Forwarding Hierarchy	0.522
Forwarding Hierarchy & Forward	0.499

By calculating the cosine similarity of the three algorithms, we can see that the overall results of the three algorithms are not bad, of which the result of forward and @ relationship based algorithms is close, but it is not too fit with the actual situation. The algorithm based on the forwarding layer fit more with the actual data.

We can see that, it's not good enough to get the user influence just according to the forwarding behavior and the @ relationship. Because it just concerned about the user's information and the user's close friends; but we are more likely to get the user's actual influence from a more comprehensive network structure that is based on the forwarding hierarchy. Therefore, we can strengthen the detection of these more influential people ranked by forwarding level based algorithm. Only do like this can we better grasp the network development trends. And also we can be better to promote our products through these users.

6. Conclusion

Through this article, we can understand the great significance of the user influence in the social network to our society in many aspects. So the research on the user's influence is still in constant. Many experts and scholars have contributed a lot of excellent algorithms in this area, and make a great contribution to our government and enterprises. In this paper, we attempt to come up with a new algorithm on user influence based on the forwarding and the @ symbol in the microblog. We know that the PageRank algorithm is a web ranking algorithm, although there indeed is certain similarities between PageRank and social network users influence calculation, the social network has more of its own characteristics, we also proposed an influence algorithm based on the forwarding hierarchy.

In the next step, we will further calculate the user influence on a fine grain. Previous methods focus more attention on computing users' personal influence, the next step we will pay more attention to explore the influence between the users and bring corresponding algorithm. In order to grasp of the development of social networks more sensitively. And it will be better for the information dissemination related tasks.

Acknowledgments

This work is supported by national key fundamental research and development program (973 program) No. 2013CB329600, 2013CB329604 and National Natural Science Foundation of China No. 61372191.

References

1. Daniel M. Romero and Wojciech Galuba and Sitaram Asur and Bernardo A. Huberman, Influence and Passivity in Social Media. the 20th International Conference Companion on World Wide Web, India, March 2011.
2. Ding Zhao-yun and Jia Yan and Zhou Bin and Tang Fu, Survey of Influence Analysis for Social Networks,Computer Science,2014.
3. Valerio Arnaboldi and Marco Conti and Andrea Passarella,Dynamics of Personal Social Relationships in Online Social Networks : a Study on Twitter, Conference on Online Social Networks, 2013.
4. Adrien Guille and Hakim Hacid and Cecile Favre, Information Diffusion in Online Social Networks: A Survey, ACM, 2013.
5. Jie Tang and Jimeng Sun and Chi Wang and Zi Yang, Social Influence Analysis in Large-scale Networks, ACM SIGKDD, 2009.
6. Jing Zhang and Biao Liu and Jie Tang and Ting Chen and Juanzi Li, Social Influence Locality for Modeling Retweeting Behaviors, Cognitive Computation, 2013.
7. Sai Teja Peddinti and Keith w. Ross and Justin Cappos, "On the Internet, Nobody Knows You're a Dog":A Twitter Case Study of Anonymity in Social Networks, ACM Conference on Online Social Networks, 2009.
8. A. Anagnostopoulos and R. Kumar and M. Mahdian, Influence and correlation in social networks, In KDD '08, 2008.

9. M. D. Choudhury and Y.-R. Lin and H. Sundaram and K. S. Candan and L. Xie and A.Kelliher, How does the data sampling strategy impact the discovery of information diffusion in social media, In ICWSM '10, 2010.
10. Aggarwal C C, Social Network Data Analytics, Springer, 2012.
11. Goyal A and Bonchi F and Lakshmanan L V S, Learning influence probabilities in social networks, SIGKDD, 2009.
12. Ding Z Y and Jia Y and Zhou B, An influence strength measurement via time-aware probabilistic generative model for microblogs, Asia-Pacific Web Conference, 2013.
13. Aral S and Walker D, Identifying influential and susceptible members of social networks, Science, 2012.
14. D. kempe, Maximizing the spread of influence through a social network, KDD, 2003.
15. M. Kitsak and L. Gallos and S. Havlin and F. Liljeros and L. Muchnik and H. Stanley and H. Makse, Identification of influential spreaders in complex networks, Nature Physics, 2010.

A BPNN-Based Model for Predicting Essential Genes and Its Application

Xiao LIU*, Luo XU and Bao-jin WANG

College of Communication Engineering, Chongqing University, Chongqing, 400044, China
**E-mail: liuxiao@cqu.edu.cn*

Hong-ling TANG

Chongqing City Management College, Chongqing, 401331, China

The identification of essential genes is important for understanding cellular mechanisms and determining potential drug targets. Neural Network methods have been widely used in biological fields and in this paper, we construct a Back Propagation Neural Network (BPNN) model to predict essential genes. Three evaluation methods were designed to assess the predicting effect: (1) Self-test on a single organism (Escherichia coli). (2) A BPNN model trained by a single organism (E. coli) is used to predict the essential genes of other 30 organisms. (3) A BPNN model trained by 30 organisms is used to predict the essential genes of another organism (E. coli). In this model, 57 sequence-based features were used to screen the key feature(s) related to gene essentiality and we proposed a method based on Principal Component Analysis, which reduced the quantity of features from 57 to 35 and the prediction performance remained stable. These screened features could be used as key features in computational analysis and biological experiments.

Keywords: Neural network; Essential genes; Principal component analysis; Feature selection.

1. Introduction

Essential genes are the genes indispensable for the survival of an organism[1]. Investigation of essential genes has important practical implications, such as studying the minimal requests for the survival of an organism, revealing the mechanism of cellular life, and development of antimicrobial drug[2]. The experimental methods of identification of essential genes include gene deletions, RNA interference, antisense RNA and transposon mutagenesis. However, experimental methods are time-consuming and expensive, and different experimental methods may yield different results [3]. Therefore, computational prediction methods provide a valuable alternative.

As an important method of machine learning, Artificial Neural Network (ANN) has been applied in bioinformatics research widely[4-6], and was employed to predict essential genes/proteins. Krishnaveni and Sumitra used a Leave-One-Genome-Out and 10-fold cross-validation method to predict the essential genes of 14 prokaryotic organisms, based on Back Propagation Neural Networks (BPNN)[7]. Jiancheng *et al.* proposed a gene expression programming-based method to predict essential protein of *Saccharomyces cerevisiae* by combining some biological features and topological features[8].

In this paper, we constructed a BPNN model to predict *Escherichia coli*'s essential genes, applying 5-fold cross-validation. To evaluate the performance effectively, three evaluation methods were designed to assess the predicting effect: (1) A self-test on a single organism (*E. coli*). (2) A BPNN model trained by a single organism (*E. coli*) was used to predict the essential genes of another 30 organisms. (3) A BPNN model trained by 30 organisms was used to predict the essential genes of another organism (*E. coli*) (see Table 1). Since feature is the major factor for classification, 57 commonly used and sequence-based features were collected and used for the prediction, firstly. And then, we proposed a method based on Principal Component Analysis to screen the key features related to gene essentiality. The features were reduced from 57 to 35, and the prediction performance kept stable (see Table 3). We proposed that the screened features could be used as key features in computational analysis and biological experiments.

2. Materials and Methods

2.1. *Data sources*

The data of the *E. coli* and the other 30prokaryotes (see Table 1) were downloaded from NCBI (http://www.ncbi.nlm.nih.gov/), and category properties of gene essentiality were downloaded from Database of Essential Genes (DEG, http://www.essentialgene.org/) [9].

Table 1. List of the 31 prokaryotic objects.

Object	Object
Bacillus subtilis 168	*Caulobacter crescentus*
Mycoplasma genitalium G37	*Campylobacter jejuni subsp. jejuni* NCTC 11168 = ATCC 700819
Mycoplasma pulmonis UAB CTIP	*Escherichia coli* MG1655
Mycobacterium tuberculosis H37Rv	*Francisella novicida* U112
Staphylococcus aureus NCTC 8325	*Haemophilus influenzae* Rd KW20
Staphylococcus aureus N315	*Helicobacter pylori* 26695
Streptococcus pyogenes MGAS5448	*Pseudomonas aeruginosa* PAO1
Streptococcus pneumoniae	*Pseudomonas aeruginosa* UCBPP-PA14
Streptococcus pyogenes NZ131	*Porphyromonas gingivalis* ATCC 33277
Streptococcus sanguinis	*Salmonella enterica subsp. enterica serovar Typhimurium str.* 14028S
Acinetobacter baylyi ADP1	*Salmonella typhimurium* LT2
Bacteroides fragilis 638R	*Shewanella oneidensis* MR-1
Burkholderia pseudomallei K96243	*Salmonella enterica serovar Typhimurium* SL1344
Bacteroides thetaiotaomicron VPI-5482	*Salmonella enterica serovar* Typhi
Burkholderia thailandensis E264	*Sphingomonas wittichii* RW1
	Vibrio cholerae N16961

2.2. *Analysis model based on ANN*

ANN, which was inspired by the brain synapses, is a mathematical model widely used for classification[10]. In this paper, we employed the popular neural network, *i.e.*, BPNN, for prediction. The training process of BPNN contains two stages: forward propagation of signals and backward propagation of errors, as shown in Fig. 1. If the output is different from the expected output, the error will be backward propagated in the form of gradient descent, which adjusts the weights and threshold values to make the adjusted output approach the expected one, through the continuing recycles. In this paper, we constituted a BPNN model with function *feedforwardnet* in MATLAB R2014a.

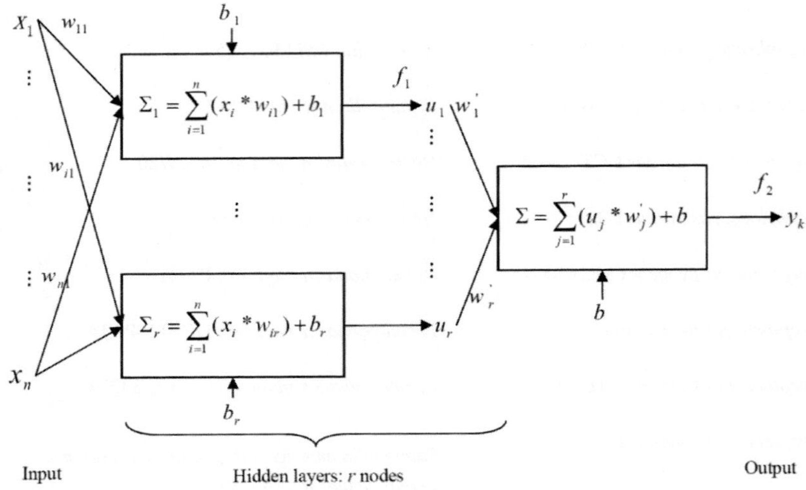

Fig. 1. The structure of a 3-layer BPNN. Input: *x*, *m*: sample size, *n*: dimensions of feature, *w and w'*: weights in the first/second hidden layer, *b*:threshold value, *r*: the number of nodes, *f*:transfer function, *u*:the output of hidden layers, output: *y*, *k*: dimensions of output.

2.3. *Processing of features*

As the genome sequence information is the most basic information, we concentrated on sequence-based features in this study. The commonly used 57 sequence-based features were collected, as shown in Table 2.

Considering the redundancy of the used features, we proposed a method based on Principal Component Analysis (BPCA) to search key features related to gene essentiality. Firstly, the principal component analysis was carried on and the coefficient matrices: *COEFF* were obtained. There were *n* rows corresponding to *n* features and *n* columns corresponding to the *n* principal components, in a *COEFF*. The variable *importance* corresponding to weighted proportion represents the importance proportion of a component. So, the summation of the weighted *importance* of each feature represents the importance level. The importance level of the ith feature (f_i) is defined as Eq. (1).

$$f_i = \sum_{j=1}^{n} |\mathrm{COEF}(i,j) * \mathrm{impotance}(j)|. \tag{1}$$

The relative importance level of the ith feature (F_i) are calculated as Eq. (2):

$$F_i = f_i / f_{max}. \tag{2}$$

where f_{max} is the maximum of f_i.

Finally, BPCA was used to analyze the other 30 organisms and screened 35 features whose F were greater than 82%(see Table 2).

Table 2. Initial and selected features.

Feature	Feature
Length of genes	Molecular weight
Negative or positive strand	Isoelectric Point
Length of amino acids	Silent base compositions about T
Number of mole of the amino acids (A+C+G+S+T)*	Number of mole of the amino acids (A+B+C+D+G+N+P+S+T+V)*
Silent base compositions about C*	Silent base compositions about A*
Silent base compositions about G*	The number of transmembrane amino acids
Number of mole of the amino acids (A+I+L+V)*	Number of mole of the amino acids (F+H+W+Y)*
Number of mole of the amino acids (A+C+F+G+I+L+M+P+V+W+Y)	Number of mole of the amino acids (D+E+H+K+N+Q+R+S+T+Z)
Codon Adaptation Index*	Codon Bias Index
G+C content 3rd position of synonymous codons	Number of mole of the amino acids (B+D+E+H+K+R+Z)*

Table 2. (*Continued*)

Frequency of Optimal codons*	Number of mole of the amino acids (H+K+R)*
The number of transmembrane amino acids in first 60	Number of mole of the amino acids (B+D+E+Z)*
G+C content of the gene	The effective number of codons*
Length of system amino acids	The final prediction of transmembrane helices
Hydropathicity of protein	Cytoplasmic Score *
The frequency of aromatic amino acids*	Cytoplasmic Membrane Score *
Amino acid: A,R,N,D,C,Q,G,H,I,L,K,M,F,P,S,T,W,Y,V	Amino acid: A,R,N,D,Q,E,G,H,I,L,K,F,S,W,Y,V*
The frequencies of rare amino acids	Final Score*
Extracellular Score*	The Hurst exponent
The number of codons that one third-base mutation is removed from a stop codon*	

Note: [a] Key features selected by BPCA are marked by an asterisk:*.

2.4. *Procedure of analysis*

The analysis steps are shown as following:

(1) Data was downloaded from DEG and NCBI.

(2) The commonly used 57 sequence-based features were collected. For comparison, 35 key features were selected by BPCA.

(3) A BPNN model was constructed, trained and used to predict the test data set, with 5-fold cross validation. This process was repeated 50 times to optimize the model based on the maximum of average AUC scores. As non-essential genes is far more than essential genes, an under-sampling strategy was also used to deal with the data imbalance.

(4) Three evaluation methods were designed to assess the predicting effect:

(a) Self-test on *E. coli*. 2/3 of *E. coli* genes were selected randomly as training set, while the rest were used for test.

(b)The BPNN model trained by *E. coli* was used to predict the essential genes of other 30 organisms. All the genes of *E. coli* were used as training set and the other 30 organisms' genes were used as test set.

(c)The BPNN model trained by the other 30 organisms was used to predict the essential genes of *E. coli*. All the genes of other 30 organisms were used as training set and *E. coli* genes were used as test set.

3. Results

Results (see Table 3) show that the AUC score of self-test of *E. coli* was 0.7362, decreased to 0.6071 for prediction of other 30 organisms based on the BPNN model trained by *E. coli*, and rose to 0.7858 for prediction of *E. coli* based on the BPNN model trained by other 30 organisms. Results show the similar decreasing for prediction based on the reduced 35 features.

The features were decreased from 57 to 35 via the BPCA screening. The AUC kept stable after feature screening, 0.7362 vs. 0.7420, 0.6071 vs. 0.6056, and 0.7858 vs. 0.7844. This indicated the validity of the feature screening.

Table 3. AUC of prediction.

Evaluation method	Prediction based on 57 features	Prediction based on 35 features screened by BPCA
Self-test of *E. coli*	0.7362	0.7420
Prediction of other 30 organisms based on the BPNN model trained by *E. coli*	0.6071	0.6056
Prediction of *E.coli* based on the BPNN model trained by other 30 organisms	0.7858	0.7844

4. Conclusion

Effective computational methods for essential genes prediction is of great value. In this paper, a BPNN model was constructed to predict essential genes, and a BPCA method was proposed to screen key features.

The AUC score of self-test was 0.7362. This value dropped to 0.6071 when predicted another 30 organisms based on the model trained by *E. coli*, because the samples provided limited information. On the contrary, the AUC score rose to 0.7858 when predicted *E. coli* based on the model trained by another 30 organisms, because the more samples provided the richer information. Moreover, the AUCs kept stable after feature screening, which indicated the validity of the feature screening. We proposed that the screened features could be used as key features in computational analysis and biological experiments.

Future work includes: (1) More objects with gene essentiality information are needed to train our model. (2) The performance of predicting needs to be promoted further. (3) The features collected and used in this paper may not describe the intrinsic relations of gene essentiality sufficiently, so more effective features are needed.

Acknowledgments

This work was supported by the China Postdoctoral Science Foundation funded project (Grant No. 2012M521673), and the Fundamental Research Funds for the Central Universities (Project No. 106112014CDJZR165503, CDJRC10160011, CDJZR12160007) .

References

1. F.M. Commichau, N. Pietack and J. Stulke, Essential genes in Bacillus subtilis a re-evaluation after ten years. *Mol. BioSyst***9**, 1068 (2013).

2. S.Y. Gerdes, M.D. Scholle and M.D. Souza, From Genetic Footprinting to Antimicrobial Drug Targets: Examples in Cofactor Biosynthetic Pathways. *J. Bacteriol***184**, 16(2002).

3. L. Yang, L. Wang and H. Wang, et al., Analysis and identification of essential genes in humans using topological properties and biological information. *Gene***551**,2(2014).

4. L. Matulewicz, J.F.A. Jansen and B. Matulewicz, et al., Anatomic segmentation improves prostate cancer detection with artificial neural networks analysis of ^{1}H magnetic resonance spectroscopic imaging. *J. Magn. Reson. Imaging***40**,6(2014).

5. Y.C. Chen, Y.C. Chang and W.C. Ke, et al., Cancer adjuvant chemotherapy strategic classification by artificial neural network with gene expression data: An example for non-small cell lung cancer. *J. Biomed. Inform.***56** (2015).

6. T. Waller, R. Nowak and M. Tkacz, et al., Familial or Sporadic Idiopathic Scoliosis - classification based on artificial neural network and GAPDH and ACTB transcription profile. *Biomed. Central.***12**(2013).

7. K. Palaniappan and S. Mukherjee, Predicting " essential " genes across microbial genomes: a machine learning approach. in *Proc.10th Int. Conference on Machine Learning and Applications* (Honolulu, USA, 2011).

8. J. Zhong, J. Wang and W. Peng, et al., Prediction of essential proteins based on gene expression programming. *BMC Genomics*, **14**(Suppl 4):S7 (2013).

9. H. Luo, Y. Lin and F. Gao, et al., DEG 10, an update of the database of essential genes that includes both protein-coding genes and noncoding genomic elements. *Nucleic Acids Res.***42**(2013).

10. 10.I.A. Basheer and M. Hajmeer, Artificial neural networks: fundamentals, computing, design, and application. *J. Micicrobiol Meth.***43**,1(2000).

A Novel Speaker Segmentation Method Fused with Acoustic Event Information

Ze-ping XIAO[1,*], Gang TANG[1], Tong LI[1], Xiang XIE[1,2], Shi-lei HUANG[2] and Hao-bo CHENG[1,2]

[1]*Information and Electronics School, Beijing Institute of Technology,*
[2]*Shenzhen Research Institute, Beijing Institute of Technology,*
Beijing, 100081/Haidian District , China
[*]*E-mail: xiaozeping@bit.edu.cn*

To overcome speaker segmentation in the walkie-talkie radio system's speech, we propose a novel method of recognizing the acoustic presence of push-to-talk clicks. Firstly, a typical speaker segmentation system is realized by GMM with BIC criteria. By moving the time window with different scales, speaker-change points can be determined and the best performance value of F is 65.47%. Secondly, a detector is used in acoustic analysis to locate the acoustic event of push-to-talk click. Lastly, a fusion scheme is designed to take advantage of the both results. The F value of the proposed method can be boosted up to 77.18% with a relative increment of 17.88%. In addition, the recall rate and accuracy rate are improved by 20.01% and 16.07% respectively.

Keywords: Speaker segmentation; Acoustic event detection; Bayes information criteria.

1. Introduction

The information fusion was extensively used in military fields[3] as well as civilian fields and currently it has become a complete discipline. Information fusion technology is widely used in audio processing such as electric motor diagnosis[1], speaker segmentation and clustering with the help of gender information[2].

This paper presents a novel method for unsupervised conversational speaker segmentation. Based on acoustic feature processing, the speaker segmentation is to segment an audio stream into segments of different speakers[9] respectively, which is a pre-processing for speaker clustering, speaker recognition and speaker tracking and has an significant impact on the post-processing performance. The difficulty of the unsupervised speaker segmentation is the audio of walkie-talkie radio which has multiple speakers, channel change and large noises. Traditionally the key point in unsupervised speaker segmentation is to find appropriate metrics to split the audio, the widely applied metrics include

Bayes Information Criteria (BIC), Generalized Likelihood Ratio (GLR), Symmetric Kullback Leibler Distance (KL2)[4], Cross Likelihood Ratio (CLR).

The performance of distance-based speaker segmentation is often limited in practice, as they tend to discriminate different speakers only from the feature of audio itself. Based on our observations and analyses of the radio walkie-talkie audio, push-to-talk click is generated when talks are finished between land commander and pilots. Base on the push-to-talk clicks are a sign of the speaker change point, speaker segmentation technique infused with acoustic event information is proposed in this paper.

The remainder of this paper is organized as follows. The speaker segmentation algorithm is introduced in section 2. In section 3 we describe two methods for the acoustic event detection and choose the feature analysis for the detection of the push-to-talk click. The data we used in the experiments is briefly described in section 4. In section 5 we come up with a fusion scheme which take advantage of the results of speaker segmentation and the acoustic event detection, results are also given in this section. Conclusions follow in section 6.

2. Speaker Segmentation Algorithm

The metrics widely used in unsupervised conversational speaker segmentation include BIC, GLR, KL2, CLR and so on. Due to the BIC distance has a better performance than others on the conversational audio, we use BIC distance in the experiments.

For two audio segments of feature vectors $a=\{y_1...y_t\}$ and $b=\{y_{t+1}...y_T\}$,we assume that they follow Gaussian distribution. The BIC distance is defined as :

$$\Delta BIC(t) = -R(t) + \frac{\lambda}{2}(p + \frac{p(p+1)}{2})\log(T) \cdot \quad (1)$$

$$R(t) = \frac{T}{2}\log|\sum_{ab}| - \frac{T_a}{2}\log|\sum_a| - \frac{T_b}{2}\log|\sum_b| \cdot \quad (2)$$

In the expression, p is the dimension of the vector, λ is the penalty factor, T_a and T_b are the number of audio frames in audio segments a and b, $\sum_a$ and $\sum_b$ are covariance matrices for audio segments a and b, T_{ab} and $\sum_{ab}$ are the number of frames and covariance matrix after the combination of the audio segment a and b . Audioseg[10] is used for speaker segmentation in the experiments.

3. Acoustic Event Detection Algorithm

Acoustic event detection can be classified into two categories. One is feature analysis. In time domain short time energy and zero-crossing rate are always used, while in frequency domain Mel Frequency Cepstral Coefficients (MFCC) and Linear Prediction Cepstral Coefficients (LPCC) are always chosen. For example, when a solitary senior falls down, the accident can be automatically recognized based on the collection and analysis of the frequency features[6]. The other common method is pattern recognition. Commonly-used pattern recognition mechanisms include Support Vector Machine (SVM), Hidden Markov Model (HMM)[7], Gaussian Mixture Model (GMM).

Considering duration of the push-to-talk click is very short and the audio of channel is changing all the time, a robust model for push-to-talk click is very difficult to get training, so in the experiments we use the feature analysis for the acoustic event detection.

4. Experimental Data

Experimental data are collected from the real in-flight aircraft radio communication between land commander and pilots, of which the signal sampling rate is 16 KHz and its amplitude is 16-bit precision. The data sequence is 15 hours long in total including all states from the plane start to stop. The experimental data contain about 120 show-up people, 8000 speaker-change points and 9000 push-to-talk clicks with duration between 10ms to 30ms. In the experiments, frame length is set as 20ms, frame shifting step 10ms, the pre-weighting coefficient 0.97, and 12 MFCCs together with energy plus their 1st and 2nd-derivatives are extracted from each audio frame, leading to 39-dimention acoustic vectors.

5. Algorithm Evaluation and Experimental Results

5.1. *Evaluation algorithms*

The evaluation criterion for the algorithm in experiments is based on parameters include recall (RCL), precision (PRC) and F-value[8]. If the integrated index of F value in the algorithm is bigger, the performance is better and the splitting result is more accurate.

5.2. *Speaker segmentation experiments*

The length of the large window is 600 samples and the window shifting step is 120 samples, while the small window is 300 samples and the moving step is 60 samples. The optimal results are classified in table 3 by the methods of BIC without event detection.

Based on the experimental results, for the airplane audio, the best performance of the BIC criterion can reach 65.47%.

5.3. *Acoustic event detection experiments*

In the experiments, audio data and speaker segmentation data are the same which is introduced in chapter 4. In the experiment we uses time domain feature analysis to detect the location of the push-to-talk click, which is a unsupervised method, all the push-to-talk clicks as a test set.

Time domain features mainly select short time energy (STE) and zero-crossing rate(ZCR). We use window length of 10ms and window step of 10ms to calculate each frame's STE and ZCR.

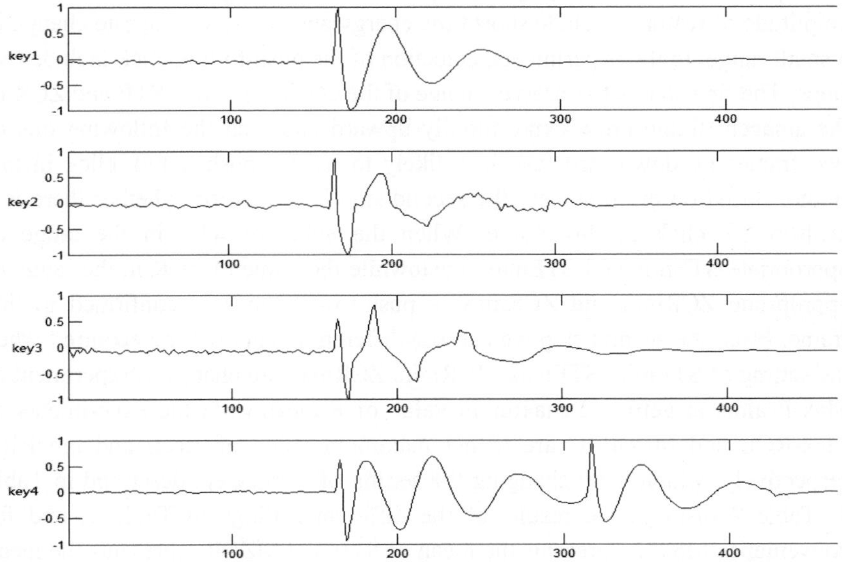

Fig. 1. Different waveforms of push-to-talk click samples.

Figure 1 shows waveforms of four different push-to-talk click samples. It is clear that the amplitude and envelopes of the push-to-talk click change sharply, depending on the airplane type, flying status, background noises and operator's habits, etc., which are the hardship and challenges in robustness acoustic event detection.

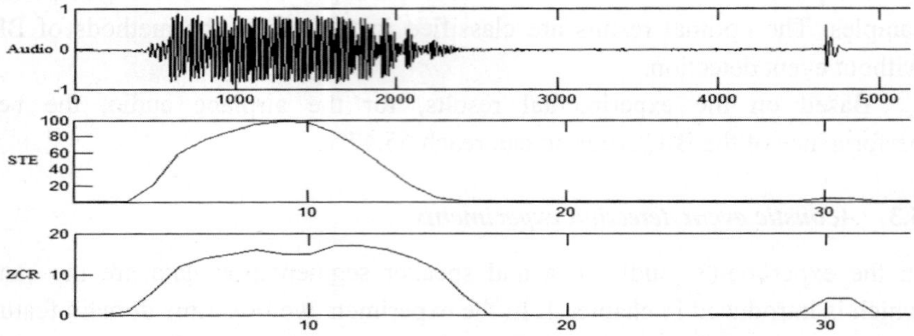

Fig. 2. Waveform of push-to-talk click audio, STE & ZCR.

Figure 2 gives the waveform of audio, short time energy and zero-crossing rate for the first push-to-talk click in figure 1. Different from the silence period and the envelope characteristics at audio position, the features of push-to-talk click position are abruptly going up and then falling down fast, and the amplitude of features include short time energy and zero-crossing rate change in a small range. In the experiments, detection of the push-to-talk click include two steps. The first step is to observe change of the envelope, when STE and ZCR of the adjacent frame grow exponentially upward and then the following one or two frames go downward fast, it is likely to have a push-to-talk click in this frame. Based on the first step, the second step is to confirm whether there is a push-to-talk click in this frame. When the value of STE in the range of appropriate STEmin and STEmax meanwhile the value of ZCR in the range of appropriate ZCRmin and ZCRmax, a push-to-talk click is confirmed in this frame. From the second step we can see different results will be acquired when the setting of STEmin, STEmax, ZCRmin, ZCRmax are changed. Experiment of Max-F aims at getting a maximum value of F meanwhile the experiments of Max-RCL and Max-PRC are to get maximum value of recall and precision respectively, which is by changing the setting of parameters described in Table 1. Table 2 displays the results of the different settings in Table 1, and for convenience MSTE represents the mean of STE and MZCR represents the mean of ZCR.

Table 1. Setting of different experiments.

	STE		ZCR	
	Min	Max	Min	Max
Max-F	$M_{STE}/4$	$M_{STE}*2$	$M_{ZCR}/2$	$M_{ZCR}*2$
Max-RCL	$M_{STE}/8$	$M_{STE}*8$	$M_{ZCR}/8$	$M_{ZCR}*8$
Max-PRC	$M_{STE}/2$	$M_{STE}*3/2$	$M_{ZCR}/2$	$M_{ZCR}*3/2$

Table 2. Different time domain characteristics result (%).

	RCL	PRC	F
Max-F	71.21	69.32	70.25
Max-RCL	95.23	43.06	59.29
Max-PRC	39.13	95.16	55.45

5.4. *Speaker segmentation experiments assisted by event detection method*

Based on our observations there are mainly two kinds of deficiencies in the speaker segmentation results.

(1) Due to the talk gap between land commander and pilots is small and existence of noises, the algorithms do not separate the two speakers in the segments,

(2) Because there are pauses (or breathing) during the talk of the land commander or pilots, the algorithms split the same speaker's audio stream into two segments.

The two deficiencies above can be partly corrected by using the position of push-to-talk click. For deficiency (1), if the push-to-talk click detection accuracy is larger than 95% (Max-PRC experimental results), the scenario is to check whether there is a push-to-talk click within the segment from the speaker segmentation result, and if there exists a push-to-talk click in the audio segment, it will be split into two segments by the position of the push-to-talk click. For deficiency (2), on the basis that the recall ratio of the push-to-talk click is larger than 95% (Max-RCL experimental results), the scenario is to merge the adjacent audio segments if there appears no push-to-talk click within the audio segment in the speaker segmentation result and the gap between the adjacent audio segments is relatively small (in our experiments, the threshold is set as 0.5s).

With the assistance of the acoustic event detection, the experimental results of BIC metric are summarized in Table 3. It is indicated that the performance of speaker segmentation is improved substantially after the addition of the push-to-talk click information. The increase comes from the use of BIC criterion for speaker segmentation with an increase of 17.88%.

Table 3. Experimental results with and without event detection (%).

	RCL	PRC	F
BIC(without event detection)	70.38	61.21	65.47
BIC(with event detection)	84.46	71.05	77.18
Relative Increment	20.01	16.07	17.88

6. Conclusion

This paper firstly fulfills speaker segmentation of the airplane audio record by BIC splitting criteria, and then based on the audio features of walkie-talkie,the speaker segmentation results are corrected by the information of push-to-talk clicks. The speaker segmentation performance can be boosted up to 77.18% with a relative incremental of 17.88% compared with the optimal BIC splitting algorithm. Through the effective use of the acoustic event information in the audio recording, the speaker segmentation performance has been greatly improved. Our future work will focus on refined analysis on audio streams and deeper exploration of acoustic information features to get better speaker segmentation results.

Acknowledgment

The work is supported by the National Natural Science Foundation of China (NSFC): Grant No. 61473041, 61571044, 11161140319, 11590772.

References

1. XiaoTang. Audio fault diagnosis of motor based on information fusion [J]. Computer knowledge and technolog –y ,2013,26:5960-5962.

2. Ore B M, Slyh R E, Hansen E G. Speaker Segmentation and Clustering using Gender Information [C]// Speaker and Language Recognition Workshop, 2006. IEEE Odyssey 2006: The. IEEE, 2006:1-8.
3. Greenway A P. SKIDS data fusion project[C]// Robotics - DL tentative. International Society for Optics and Photonics, 1992.
4. Madikeri S, Bourlard H. KL-HMM Based Speaker Diarization System For Meetings[C]// IEEE International Conference on Acoustics, Speech & Signal Processing. Idiap, 2015.
5. Naresh J, Holambe R S, Basu T K. Unsupervised Speaker Segmentation and Clustering Using TESBCC and Pitch Based Features[C]// Computational Intelligence and Communication Networks (CICN), 2013 5th International Conference on. IEEE, 2013:215-219.
6. ZIGEL Y, LITVAK D, GANNOT I. A method for automatic fall detection of elderly People using floor vibrations and sound proof of concept on human mimicking doll falls[J]. IEEE Transactions on Biomedical Engineering, 2009, 56(12) : 2858-2867.
7. Lojka M, Pleva M, Kiktová E, et al. Efficient acoustic detector of gunshots and glass breaking[J]. Multimedia Tools & Applications, 2015:1-29.
8. Zokaei N, Heyes S B, Gorgoraptis N, et al. Working memory recall precision is a more sensitive index than span[J]. Journal of Neuropsychology, 2014, 9(2):319–329.
9. Yong Ma,Changchun Bao. Research progress of speaker segmentation clustering [J]. signal processing, 2013,09:1190-1199.
10. Gravier G, Betser M, Ben M. audioseg: Audio segmentation toolkit, release 1.2[J]. IRISA, january, 2010

Concept Mining to Chinese News Similarity Measure

Xun ZHOU and Chun-Yao WANG
Industrial Ph.D. Program of Internet of Things,
Feng Chia University, Taichung, Taiwan, R.O.C.

Ying-Chih LIN* and Yu-Min ZHANG
Department of Applied Mathematics,
Feng Chia University, Taichung, Taiwan, R.O.C.
**E-mail: yichlin@fcu.edu.tw*

To determine the similarity measure of news articles, this paper proposes a hybrid approach based on the dictionary and research done by previous studies. We identify representative nouns from news articles, and combine the word similarity metric into the text metric, which helps the news provider to filter out similar articles to the subscriber. The experiments are conducted to examine a set of press releases and news articles, while the results demonstrate that our proposed method outperforms the TF-IDF-based approach.

Keywords: News similarity; Concept term; Cosine similarity; TF-IDF.

1. Introduction

The measure of article similarity is a fundamental step to many studies and applications in *natural language processing* (NLP). Since the sentence can be constructed by different lexicons and syntax as well as the inherent attribute of Chinese, it is challenging to determine the similarity between Chinese articles. On account of the growth of Internet media and micro-blogging services, more and more Chinese articles are proposed on Internet. Sending similar news articles again and again to a news subscriber makes the users impatient. Therefore, we measure the news articles similarity by computing the text metric derived from the conceptual feature of words, so that the highly similar articles can be identified to reduce the reading load of subscribers. The experiments are conducted to compare our method with the well-known TF-IDF approach, and its results demonstrate the accuracy of our method.

---

* Corresponding author.

2. Related Work

The similarity between words can be extended to articles, while some works rely on the *part-of-speech* (POS) of words. Lin et al. adopt different weights to the noun, verb and other POSs to compute the similarity between short Chinese texts [1]. Yu and Wang consider that the important components to a sentence are the noun and verb, and they should have higher weights in the semantic analysis of sentences [2]. Moreover, Luo et al. examine the POS significance from the three kernel SVM functions, and propose that the *F-score* performance of the classification to exclude the noun is worse than the words with other POSs [3]. These works agree that the noun is the important element to a sentence and even an article. As a result, we extend the consistent result to measure the article similarity by combining the word similarity metric into the text metric.

3. Material and Method

The work to measure the news similarity consists of three steps: Chinese segmentation, feature construction and cosine similarity. The details are as follows.

3.1. *Chinese segmentation*

To tackle the article content, a basic step is the Chinese segmentation, while the greedy algorithm of *backward maximum matching* based on a dictionary of enough size achieves over 90% accuracy. We implement this algorithm as the segmentation method. Moreover, our dictionary consists of several reference sources. At first, we translate the dictionary with the Simplified Chinese used by Jieba into the Traditional Chinese, which has about one hundred thousand words. The dictionary contains the POS labels with the ICTCLAS rule, so that we can extract the terms of specific POS labels handily. Based on the Jieba dictionary, some common words are integrated into the dictionary, including the dictionary of Chinese idioms, toponym, academic terms, Taiwan celebrities, hundred family surnames, etc. The number of words in our dictionary achieves 188,033.

3.2. *Feature construction*

There are many models to represent the features of an article, while the *vector space model*(VSM) is one of the widely used [5]. VSM is an algebraic model for representing objects as vectors of identifiers, which is also called the *feature vector*. The process to construct the feature vectors usually requires the evaluation function for computing the weight in each dimension, where the weight is to evaluate the importance of a specific term. The advantage of VSM is to represent unstructured and semi-structured articles as vectors, and hence, many mathematical models can be applied. According to the previous works, we employ the so-called *concept terms* to form the feature vector for each article, and one of the best known metric, TF-IDF, is used as the comparison.

3.2.1. *TF-IDF*

TF-IDF is a statistic metric to evaluate the degree of importance of a word to a document. Its idea is that a word could be a representative of an article if it appears many times in the article and few articles contain it. Suppose that $n_{i,j}$ is the frequency of the j-th word $w_{i,j}$ in the article d_i, and D is the set of all articles. Then, the TF-IDF formula of the word $w_{i,j}$ is as follows:

$$\text{TF-IDF}_{i,j}=\frac{n_{i,j}}{\sum_k n_{i,k}}\times\log\frac{|D|}{|\{i \mid w_{i,j}\in d_i\}|}. \qquad (1)$$

3.2.2. *Concept term*

Though a few methods for the document classification used the POS information, some works have pointed out the good performance of the developed methods based on the POS analysis [1,2,3]. These works also conclude that the noun is the crucial role in a sentence. Based on the conclusion, we extract the nouns and their frequency from a news article to form its feature set, and the feature vector of each article can be derived from the union of all feature sets UFS. Let w_i be the i-th word in UFS. Then, the feature vector $<n_1, n_2, \ldots, n_i, \ldots>$ of an article is constructed as follows: n_i equal to 0 if w_i is not in the article; otherwise, n_i is the number of occurrences of w_i in the article.

In addition, a news article reports a factual account of events, activities, or persons. Since a news of events is in a short and easy to digest form, it should describe five basic factors in a clear way, where these factors are the person, event, time, place and thing, i.e., the so-called *Five Ws*. We call the nouns related to these factors except the thing as the *concept term*. The reason why we exclude the nouns for the thing is that the number of corresponding nouns is large and most of them have no representative. Since our dictionary has the POS tags, all concept terms in an article can be obtained after the word segmentation. Furthermore, when the concept term is in the feature set of the news article, its weight is double in order to highlight the information of the article.

3.3. *Cosine similarity*

With the steps in Section 3.2, each news article can be represented as a feature vector derived from the TF-IDF and the concept term. Therefore, the similarity measure of news articles is transformed into computing the similarity of vectors, where the best known approach is the *cosine similarity*. Given that two vectors A and B are the feature vectors of two articles, the formula of their cosine similarity cos-Sim(A, B) is as follows:

$$\text{cos-Sim}(A, B) = \frac{A \cdot B}{\|A\| \times \|B\|} = \frac{\sum_{i=1}^{n} A_i \times B_i}{\sqrt{\sum_{i=1}^{n} (A_i)^2} \times \sqrt{\sum_{i=1}^{n} (B_i)^2}}. \quad (2)$$

The cosine similarity ranges from 0 to 1, while the value of cos-Sim(A, B) approaching to 1 means that two news are every much alike; on the contrary, they are probably different if cos-Sim(A, B) is close to 0. Once the cos-Sim(A, B) is greater than or equal to the pre-defined threshold, we think that two news articles report similar account.

4. Experimental Evaluation and Discussion

We obtain the test data from the GEO Informatics Inc. The data set contains 24 press releases published by the Taichung Branch, Soil and Water Conservation Bureau Council of Agriculture, Executive Yuan, as well as 2,070 news articles coming from the Internet media. These news accounts may describe the same event but they have great variances in the length, phraseology, focal points, etc. We want to determine whether any news article is similar to a press release. Since every article has the time tag, the experiment accesses each article according their time order, and determines whether the news article is similar to a press release existed.

The feature vector is individually constructed for each news article by using TF-IDF and concept term, followed by applying the cosine similarity with the empirical threshold of 0.8.We evaluate the considered methods using three different criteria as the equation (3). Table 1 shows the experimental evaluation for the four considered methods. TF-IDF method establishes the feature vector by using all nouns in a news article, whereas TF-IDF+ uses the concept terms only; CM also adopts all nouns but gives double weight to the concept term specially, and CM+ considers the concept terms only. The experimental results demonstrate that the CM approach outperforms other considered methods.

$$Precision = \frac{TP}{TP+FP}, \; Recall = \frac{TP}{TP+FN}, \; F\text{-}score = \frac{2 \times Precision \times Recall}{Precision + Recall}. \quad (3)$$

Table 1. Experimental evaluation.

Method	*Precision*	*Recall*	*F-score*
TF-IDF	1	0.6000	0.7500
TF-IDF+	0.8846	0.7667	0.8214
CM	1	1	1
CM+	0.4615	0.6000	0.5217

The precision value of TF-IDF is good but its poor recall rate means that many news articles match no press release. TF-IDF+ slightly improves the recall rate but reduces the precision value, and it usually occurs when two similar articles have different lengths, e.g., a new article reports excerpts from the press release. Take Fig. 1for an example, the article with greater length is the press release, whereas the other comes from the website of chinatimes.com released later. In this example, the TF-IDF method returns the similarity of 0.6520, demonstrated that the similarity measure based on the TF-IDF metric may fail to determine the similar articles with different lengths. Furthermore, the TF-IDF+ method based on the concept term gives the similarity value 0.8730 for the example in Fig. 1, which is higher than the threshold. Furthermore, the CM method gives double weight to the frequency of concept term when computing the cosine similarity, and obtains the similarity value of 0.8229, whereas CM+ outputs the value 0.8906.

全球首創「土石流擴增實境」App搶鮮上市 供稿日期：2015-04-14 14:22

為推廣土石流防災知識，水土保持局推出全球首創「土石流擴增實境」App，軟體結合擴充實境技術，將AR運用在土石流防災宣導，並於4月14、15兩日科技部於臺灣科技大學所舉辦的「行政院災害防救應用科技方案總成果發表會」展出。

結合新技術 宣導新利器

此次「行政院災害防救應用科技方案總成果發表會」中，水土保持局的一大亮點就是「土石流擴增實境」App，水土保持局局長李鎮洋也親至現場解說，早期水土保持局在進行土石流防災宣導時，常會藉由立體模型來輔助說明，雖然能吸引民眾的目光，但模型較笨重，且體積大攜帶不便，僅能侷限固定在室內使用。現今科技發達，水土保持局應用擴增實境（AR, Augmented Reality）技術虛實合一的特性，建置一個虛擬的集水區模型，讓民眾有身歷其境的感受。首度亮相的「土石流擴增實境」App，係利用擴增實境技術，在虛擬的模型上，模擬一段土石流發生的動畫，目前已在Google play開放免費下載，提供民眾進行多視角、可互動的教學體驗，透過動畫瞭解土石流發生的三個發生條件（雨量、土石、坡度），與土石流發生的前兆（眼、鼻、耳），以及土石流災害可能的影響範圍。期以推廣土石流防災教育，達到土石流防災觀念向下扎根的目的，進而省思人與環境互依互存的關係。

運用新科技 展現防災軟實力

發表會現場設有六大主題館，分別為大規模崩塌災害、洪水災害、地震災害防治、氣候變遷之災害衝擊與調適、旱象與水資源與災害資訊管理等六個方面，水保局位於大規模崩塌災害展區，除了「土石流擴增實境」外，另於現場展出無人空拍載具UAV，藉由無人飛機搭載攝影器材，能於災後立即執行空拍任務，由於UAV較不受天候影響，所需人力及經費亦較傳統航拍低廉，近年來於防災工作上已廣為各單位所使用，除上述UAV外，水保局也於會場展示簡易式觀測站，此簡易式觀測站可由人力攜帶至車輛無法抵達之更上游集水區，對於土石流防災監測資訊蒐集，將可更加完備，歡迎有興趣民眾共同蒞臨參與。

土石流擴增實境App 讓你身歷其境 2015年04月14日 21:45 莊舒仲

為推廣土石流防災知識，農委會水土保持局推出「土石流擴增實境」App，軟體結合擴增實境技術AR，運用在宣導土石流防災，4月14、15兩日，科技部在臺灣科技大學發表展出，水保局局長李鎮洋還親臨現場解說。

這套App建置了虛擬的集水區模型，利用擴增實境技術，在虛擬的模型上，模擬一段土石流發生的動畫，讓民眾感覺有如身歷其境，目前已在Google play開放免費下載，期這項技術整合，可達到扎根防災觀念，省思人與環境相互依存關係。

Fig. 1. News with similar topic but different lengths.

The CM+ approach appears good to the example in Fig. 1. In fact, it is easy to have an error output for using the concept terms only, where Table 1 shows the poor precision and recall values of CM+. However, the CM method takes all nouns into account, and hence, reduces the error rate to measure different articles with similar concept terms. In the experiment, though there are variances in the length, phraseology and content among the press releases and news articles, the CM approach can precisely determine the press release which each news article is similar to.

5. Conclusion

Measuring the article similarity is a basic step for many NLP applications. For the news subscriber, it is irritating to receive similar news articles over and over again. However, it is challenging to identify the news reports of describing the same event, because these articles have great variances in the length, phraseology, focal points, etc. This work proposes a hybrid approach based on the dictionary and knowledge of previous studies and ours to combine the word similarity metric into the text metric. The experiments are conducted to examine a set of press releases and news articles, while its results show that our method outperforms the TF-IDF-based approach.

Acknowledgments

We thank the GEO Informatics Inc. and the Taichung Branch, Soil and Water Conservation Bureau Council of Agriculture, Executive Yuan to provide the experimental data. This work is partially supported by the Ministry of Science and Technology under contract number MOST 104-2633-S-035-001.

References

1. P. Lin, Z. Lin, B. Kuang and P. Huang, A short Chinese text incremental clustering algorithm based on weighted semantics and Naive Bayes, *Journal of Computational Information Systems*, **8(10)**, pp. 4257–4268, 2012.
2. Y. Yu and L. Wang, A novel similarity calculation method based on Chinese sentence keyword weight, *Journal of Software*, **9(5)**, pp. 1151–1156, 2014.
3. X. Luo, W. Ohyama, T. Wakabayashi and F. Kimura, A study on automatic Chinese text classification, *International Conference on Document Analysis and Recognition (ICDAR)*, pp. 920–924, Beijing, 2011.

4. S.Q. Long, Z.W. Zhao and H. Tang, Overview of Chinese word segmentation algorithms, *Computer Knowledge and Technology*, **5(10)**, pp. 2605-2607, 2009.
5. G. Salton, A. Wong and C.S. Yang, A vector space model for automatic indexing, *Communications of the ACM*, **18(11)**, p.613-620, 1975.

The Algorithm of Micro Moving Target Detection in the Video Images

Shi-quan AN, Qian-yun WEN* and Qi MENG

College of Computer Science and Technology, Chongqing University of Posts and Telecommunications, Chongqing 400065China

**E-mail: 284966027@qq.com*

In order to effectively replace the background of micro moving targets in the video sequences, it is important to solve the problem of micro moving targets extraction. We propose a new algorithm of micro moving target detection in video images. Firstly, Adaboost was used to train skin samples to obtain the skin color data and determine the threshold range of skin color. Secondly, in order to obtain the rough binary images, we fused the binary images of skin detection with the binary images of micro targets by the Otsu. Thirdly, morphological processing and the holes filling processing were used to overcome the rough binary images, in order to obtain the complete binary templates. Lastly, the algorithm successfully accomplished the background replacement of the video sequences. The experiments demonstrate that the proposed algorithm in this paper is effective, which can segment micro moving targets accurately and complete background replacement.

Keywords: Otsu; Adaboost classifier; Threshold of skin; Morphological; Background replacement.

1. Introduction

With the popularity of the 4 Generation mobile communication technology, it is inevitable that more and more customer services provide a more humane and reliable service to customers. Compared with the original video, this paper can make a better visual effect and protect the privacy of the staffs after the background replacement. This method can realize the effective utilization of video image background, which can increase the credibility of customer services. In the video, there is a larger foreground than the background. And the foreground has not obvious change. So the key problem of replacing the video background is accurately to segment the micro moving target from the background in real time. After the image segmentation [1], morphological processing, background replacement, the original video images can finish the micro moving target segmentation and background replacement of the video images.

On the basis of the binary image of micro moving target by using Otsu to obtain the segmentation threshold, this paper proposed a new way to solve the problem that the foreground color is similar to the background. First, this paper combined skin color detection [2-3]trained by the Adaboost algorithm in the HSV space to get a strong classifier, and obtained the binary images of skin color detection. Then, the two binary images were fused to get the binary images of micro moving target. After that, this paper used the morphological processing to remove noise and fill holes [4]for a complete binary image of micro moving target. Finally, the original video background was replaced by the desired video images to obtain the synthesized video.

2. The Threshold Selection

The micro moving targets have not changed much in the video images, the figure1(a),(b),(c) shows three kinds of micro moving targets. Because the micro moving targets are almost fixed, the traditional methods, for example, the Background Subtraction, the Frames Subtraction, the Codebook, the Mixed Guassian[5]etc, all of that cannot segment from the video images. Because of the similar color between the foreground and the background, illumination, noise, shadow and so on, it is too hard to segment the micro moving target accurately.

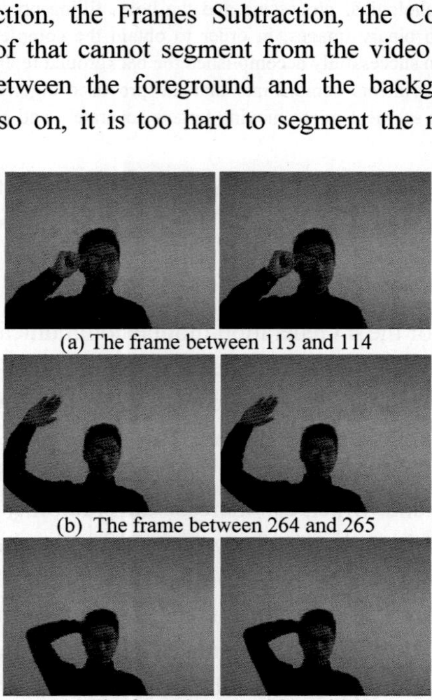

(a) The frame between 113 and 114

(b) The frame between 264 and 265

(c) The frame between 364 and 365

Fig. 1. The micro moving target.

2.1. *The algorithm of Otsu threshold selection*

In 1979, a Japanese scholar named Otsu proposed Otsu that was an algorithm widely used as threshold value[6], but this algorithm was only considered gray level information of the pixel. For a image $f(x,y)$, the segmentation threshold of Otsu was denoted by T. If the image met $f(x,y)<T$, it was judged either the foreground or the background.

2.2. *The algorithm of two-dimensional Otsu threshold selection*

The algorithm of two-dimensional Otsu used the original images and its neighborhood smoothing images to construct a two-dimensional histogram. The image $f(x,y)(1\le x\le M,\ 1\le y\le N)$ was assumed an image which gray level was L .Hence, the two-dimensional histogram increased the complexity of the calculation and limited the useful of two-dimensional Otsu at the same time.

2.3. *Skin color detection threshold selection*

In 1995, Adaboost was proposed by Freund and Schapireis. It is an iterative algorithm[7]that focuses on key data sets. Adaboost selected weak classifiers to train, then the weak classifiers were made up a strong classifier.

Skin color is one of the features of micro moving target, at the same time, HSV space[8] has a characteristic of separating luminance components , which can avoid the effects of brightness. So this paper used Adaboost to train the data sets of skin color in HSV space [9]. The skin color detection is shown in figure 2.

Fig. 2. Skin color detection.

2.4. *K-means combined with skin color detection*

QuZhong, Ma Qingwei et al. proposed a micro moving target detection and segmentation algorithm[10]based on the combination of K-means and skin color detection. First, that paper used K-means to classify pixels, which got the foreground and background respectively. Then, that paper filled the background region with black pixels and filled the foreground region with white pixels.

Finally, that paper got the micro moving target binary images. Because the K-means algorithm is an iterative clustering algorithm, the segmentation processing running time was relatively long.

3. Micro Moving Target Segmentation

When Otsu was applied in to extract the micro moving target, the color of the skin of the micro moving target and the background are so closed that it causes wrong segmentation. As is shown in figure 3, the face and the hand have been deemed to the background. In order to solve the problem, a one-dimensional histogram of Otsu was raised to a two-dimensional histogram. But the running time of the video images processing was also doubled and redoubled. Besides, most of the sequence images after dealing with the morphology and hole filling still could not get the complete binary image template, as shown in figure 4.The micro moving target can be extracted completely by K-means combined with skin color detection, but the real-time performance of the system was sacrificed. The paper fused the binary images obtained by the Otsu and the binary images obtained by the skin color detection, and it was not only solved the problem that the similar color between the micro moving target and the background, but also got the complete binary images. The real-time performance of the algorithm in this paper was better than the previous two kinds of micro moving target extraction algorithm.

Fig. 3. Binary images by Otsu.

Fig.4. Binary images by two-dimensional Otsu.

The algorithm in this paper was mainly divided into three parts: the micro moving target pre-segmentation, the micro-target coarse segmentation and the background replacement.

Specific algorithm steps are as follows:

(1) Enter the original video images.

(2) Use the Otsuto compute the largest valueasa threshold value between the foreground and the background, named T .If the image met $f(x,y)<T$, then the image was labeled as foreground, otherwise was labeled as background. The binary images of micro moving target in video images were obtained at last.

(3) Establish the color sample data sets, split the color manually, and convert the color and non-color data from RGB to HSV. Then the paper extracted and classified the characteristic of skinbyAdaboost to determine the skin color threshold range. At last, the binary images of micro moving target by skin color detection were acquired.

(4) Combine the step (2) with step (3), if $f_e(x,y)$ was white pixels or $f_f(x,y)$ was white pixels, then $f_n(x,y)$ was labeled as white pixels. According to the equation (1) ,it could obtain the coarse segmentation of the binary images.

$$f_n(x,y)=\begin{cases}255, & \begin{array}{l} if\ f_e(x,y)=255 \\ or\ f_f(x,y)=255 \end{array} \\ 0, & otherwise\end{cases}. \tag{1}$$

Where, $f_e(x,y)$ is binary image by the Otsu, $f_f(x,y)$ is binary image by color threshold detection, $f_n(x,y)$ is synthesic coarse binary image of micro moving target.

(5) The Binary images of micro moving target coarse segmentation were obtained by step (4). In order to get a complete micro moving target, the binary images were determined by morphological processing, filling holes pretreatment and so on.

(6) Use the black and white pixels of binary images to obtain relevant information about the background video images and the original video images. Then the paper based on the equation (2) to finish the background replacement,

$$f_t(x,y)=\begin{cases}f(x,y), & if\ f_n(x,y)=255 \\ f_b(x,y), & otherwise\end{cases} \tag{2}$$

Where, $f(x,y)$ is the original video images, $f_b(x,y)$ is the video images of the background, $f_t(x,y)$ is the synthesis of new video images after the background replacement.

3.1. *The pre-segmentation of micro moving target*

This paper respectively pre-segmented and obtained the binary image of micro moving target by Otsu and the binary image of skin by skin color detection as shown in figure 5(a) and 5(b).

(a) Binary image of micro moving target (b) Binary image of skin color

Fig. 5. Pre-segmentation of micro moving target.

3.2. *Coarse segmentation of micro moving target*

The binary image of micro moving target by pre-segmentation based on the equation (1) was got, as shown in figure 6. Because there were some noises and holes in the binary images named coarse binary images. Coarse binary images still influence the integrity of micro moving target, hence, morphology processing and holes filling were needed to complete the binary image of micro moving target.

Fig. 6. Coarsebinary image.

The main procedure of the hole filling algorithm is as follows:

(1) Preprocess the binary images of the micro moving target by morphology.
(2) Find out all holes on the binary image by traversing and get the sequence or array of the contour boundary.

(3) Get the starting point of the interested contour in which found by step (2), then define the closed area as Area, which is structured by the contour and the starting point.
(4) If Area<Area-T, use the white pixels to fill it.
(5) If Area ≥ Area-T, calculate the next contour area and return to the step (3).
Where, Area-T is the max area of hole based on the contour in some video images.
To perform the hole filling algorithm and get the complete binary images of micro moving target, as shown in figure 7.

Fig. 7. Complete binary images.

(6) The process is terminated.

3.3. *The background replacement*

The white pixels and black pixels stand for the foreground and the background. So the paper combined the foreground of the original video images and background of the background video images to finish the background replacement. As is shown in the figure 8.

Fig. 8. Background replacement.

4. Experimental Results and Analysis

The test video was recorded naturally. Figure 9 shows the micro moving target segmentation processing time of three algorithms. Vertical axis stands for the time of micro moving motion segmentation processing, and the transverse is the number that the frames selected randomly based on the video images (220,240, ..., 540). The first algorithm is two-dimensional Otsu, the second algorithm is K-means combined with skin color detection, and the third algorithm is proposed by this paper. As is shown in figure 9, the processing time of the algorithm proposed in this paper is the fastest, moreover, the algorithm is ten times faster than two-dimensional Otsu.

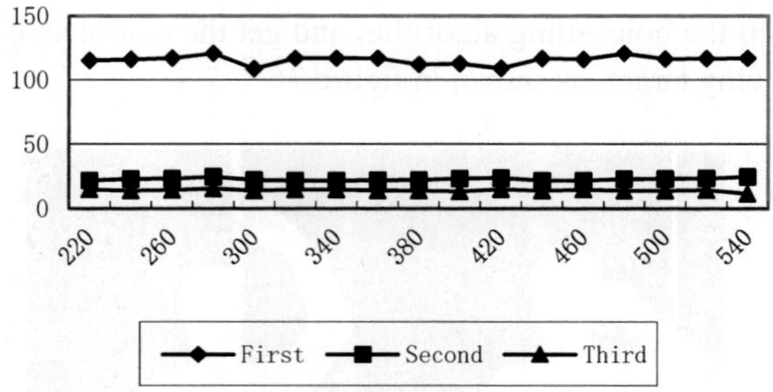

Fig. 9. Segmentation processing time of three algorithms.

Table 1 shows the number of the binary micro moving target images of white pixels by the two-dimensional Otsu, the K-means combined with the skin color detection, the algorithm proposed in this paper and the professional by hand respectively.

According to the number of pixels counted in the Table 1, the accuracy of micro moving target extraction about three algorithms are seen in Figure 10. The P representes the accuracy of two-dimensional Otsu, the Q representes the accuracyof K-means combined with skin color detection and R representes the accuracyof this paper respectively to quantify evaluation. The P , Q , R can be defined respectively as:

$$P = N_e / N_t \,,\; Q = N_k / N_t \,,\; R = N_r / N_t \,. \tag{3}$$

where N_e is the number of white pixels by two-dimensional Otsu, N_k is the number of white pixels by the K-means combined with skin color detection, N_r is the number of white pixels by the algorithm in this paper, N_t is the number of white pixels by the professional. This paper selected 17 frames randomly (frame number Num:220, 240, ... , 540) for calculation, the results are shown in Table 1.

According to the quantitative analysis of three kinds of micro moving target extraction integrity in Table 1, the paper showed that the number of pixels extracted by three kinds of algorithms are13592, 13875, 13994respectively, the number of white pixels by the professional is 14128.

Table 1. The micro moving target extraction integrity of quantitative analysis.

Num	N_e	N_k	N_r	N_t
220	6818	7081	7156	7221
240	7702	7966	8052	8176
260	26568	27961	28186	28475
280	24677	24733	24869	24943
300	25361	25651	25742	26723
320	23801	24466	24581	24605
340	21604	22024	22864	23458
360	16317	16523	16699	16734
380	15227	15478	15537	15625
400	15508	15728	15809	15879
420	15652	15757	15790	16376
440	8434	8567	8866	8962
460	3813	4318	4433	4588
480	4348	4736	4799	4903
500	4328	4627	4812	4899
520	4487	4807	4880	4928
540	4424	4750	4823	4889
AVE	13592	13875	13994	14128

The figure 10 is based on equation (3) to calculate the integrity by two-dimensional Otsu, K-means combined with skin color detection and the algorithm proposed in this paper. The vertical axis is the value of P, Q, R. It is obvious to see that the accuracy of the algorithm proposed in this paper is the highest. The experimental result shows that this algorithm has the highest accuracy in real-time extraction of micro moving target.

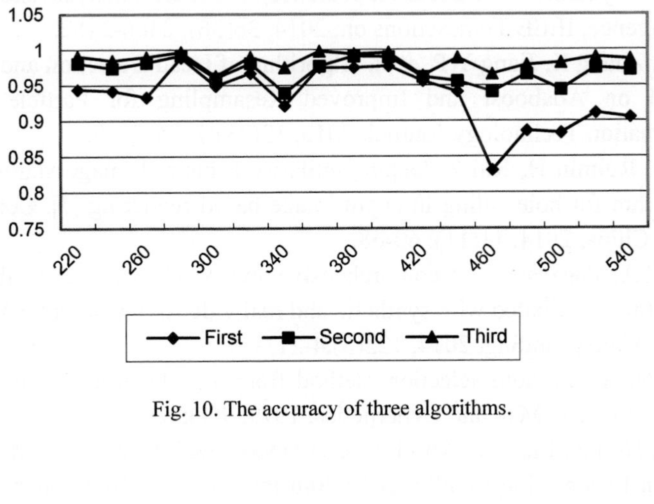

Fig. 10. The accuracy of three algorithms.

5. Conclusion

This paper used the Otsu algorithm combined with skin color detection to solve the problem that the skin color is similar to the background. According to the experimental verification, the algorithm in this paper not only effectively obtains the binary image of micro moving target, but also can extract accurately the micro moving target. In the end, it can replace the micro moving target background with a better effect. The next step of the study is LBP in the YCbCr color space, and using Otsu to segment the Y, detecting, marking and removing the shadow.

Acknowledgments

This work is supported by Outstanding Achievements Transformation Projects of University in Chongqing under Grant No. KJZH14219 and Chongqing Science and Technology Research Project of Chongqing Municipal Education Commission under Grant No. KJ1402002.

References

1. Liu S, Gao D, Yin F. Infrared image segmentation method based on 2D histogram shape modification and optimal objective function[J]. Journal of Systems Engineering and Electronics, 2013, 24(3):528-536.
2. Luo G, Yang S, Tian G, et al. Learning Human Actions by Combining Global Dynamics and Local Appearance[J]. Pattern Analysis and Machine Intelligence, IEEE Transactions on, 2014, 36(36): 2466-2482.
3. Qu Z, Zhang K, Jiang Y P, et al. Algorithm of Head Detection and Tracking Based on Adaboost and Improved Resampling for Particle Filter[J]. Information Technology Journal, 2013, 12(23):7124-7130.
4. Lin S, Ruimin H, Rui Z. Depth similarity enhanced image summarization algorithm for hole-filling in depth image-based rendering [J]. Communications, China, 2014, 11(11): 60-68.
5. Sobral A, Vacavant A. A comprehensive review of background subtraction algorithms evaluated with synthetic and real videos[J]. Computer Vision & Image Understanding, 2014, 122(5):4-21.
6. Otsu N. A threshold selection method from gray-level histogram[J]. IEEE Trans. System. Man and Cyhernetics, 1979, 9(1): 62-66.
7. Jin X, Hou X, Liu C L. Multi-class Adaboost with Hypothesis Margin.[C]// Pattern Recognition (ICPR), 2010 20th International Conference on. IEEE, 2010:65-68.

8. Yogarajah P, Condell J, Curran K, et al. A dynamic threshold approach for skin segmentation in color images[J]. International Journal of Biometrics, 2012, 4(5):38-55.
9. Chatrath J, Gupta P, Ahuja P, et al. Real time human face detection and tracking[C]. //International Conference on Signal Processing and Integrated Networks. IEEE, 2014:705-710.
10. Qu Z, Ma Q W. An Algorithm of Slight Moving Object Extraction in Real-Time Video[J]. Advanced Research on Mechanical Engineering Industry & Manufacturing Engineering, 2011(63-64): 603-606.

The Improved Codebook Algorithm Combined Updating Background and Changing Brightness Range

Zhong QU[1,2,*], Ning XIN[1], Chun-mei LIAO[1] and Chang-zhi CHEN[1,2]

[1]*College of Computer Science and Technology, Chongqing University of Posts and Telecommunications, Chongqing, China*

[2]*Chongqing Engineering Research Center of Software Quality Assurance, Testing and Assessment, Chongqing 400065, China*

[*]*E-mail: quzhong@cqupt.edu.cn*

The establishment of a Codebook background model in RGB color space results in high computational complexity, low segmentation quality and poor immunity power. We proposed the improved brightness range Codebook algorithm under YUV space to overcome the problem of irrational brightness range definition of the algorithm, as well as the background updating method which combined a two-layer Codebook model with a short-sliding window. Firstly, the Codebook background model was built under YUV color space based on the characteristics of luminance and chrominance separation. Secondly, the brightness range was redefined using the average of the Y component of the codeword to tackle the problem of the irrational brightness range definition of the background model. Lastly, a two-layer Codebook model and a short-sliding window were combined to update the background in the process of moving object detection in order to improve the anti-jamming capability. The experiments demonstrated that the improved brightness range can be updated gradually with background changes. Comparing with the original algorithm, this method can update the background effectively, and improve the detection accuracy.

Keywords: Codebook model; YUV color space; Background updates; Brightness.

1. Introduction

Moving object detection is to detect and separate moving object in video sequences through image processing method. It is one of the key technology in intelligent video surveillance and a research focus in the field of computer vision.

Currently, the method of moving target detection can be divided into three categories according to the basic principle of the algorithm: optical flow, inter-frame difference and background subtraction[1]. The optical flow method[2] can achieve a better effect but it has high computation complexity and weak real-time performance. And it is vulnerable to background disturbance and illumination changes; The inter-frame difference method[3] is easy to realize by computer and has light computational load. But the result of this method is not complete and the speed of moving object has great influence on the result; The advantage of background subtraction division is simple, easy realized, and it can adapt to the dynamic background changes. Now it has become a research hotspot in the field of moving objects detection[4]. The background is often dynamic and complicated in the process of actual moving target detection, so how to build and update background model accurately is the key to the research of background subtraction division. The algorithms which were commonly used to build background model mainly include: Kernel Density Estimation method, Gaussian Mixture background model and the Codebook background model. Kernel Density Estimation method[5] is characterized by large memory space, large computation and poor real-time performance. The computational cost of the Gaussian Mixture background model[6] is high, and it is difficult to adjust parameter; The Codebook background model algorithm put forward by Kyungnam Kim[7] is to describe pixels under RGB color space and build background with brightness range and color distortion model standard[8]. The algorithm has high computational complexity, and the luminance and chrominance information of the RGB color space cannot be distinguished so they influence each other to reduce the accuracy of the algorithm.

In this paper, the Codebook background model under YUV color space was built, and we improved the definition of the brightness range in the algorithm, combined a two-layer Codebook model with a short-sliding window method to update background in the process of detection, improved the accuracy and robustness of the algorithm.

2. The Codebook Background Model under YUV Color Space

The RGB color space can be transformed directly to YUV color space by the linear operation. The characteristics of the YUV color space is that the luminance and chrominance information is separated from each other so that they have no interference with each other[9]. This paper built the Codebook model under the YUV color space.

Codebook background model under YUV color space include: background model establishment, the calculation of brightness range and color distortion degree, the calculation of the maximum negative run length and foreground detection. The brightness range under YUV color space:

$$YL = \alpha \hat{Y}_i. \tag{1}$$

$$YH = \min(\beta \hat{Y}_i, \check{Y}_i / \alpha). \tag{2}$$

brightness range:

$$\text{brightness} = \begin{cases} \text{TRUE}, & \text{if } YL < Y_i < YH \\ \text{FALSE}, & otherwise \end{cases}. \tag{3}$$

color distortion degree:

$$colordist = |U_i - \bar{U}_i| + |V_i - \bar{V}_i|. \tag{4}$$

Where, the $\bar{Y}_i$, $\bar{U}_i$, $\bar{V}_i$ are the mean weight of *Y, U, V* components which belong to a codeword, $\check{Y}_i$, $\hat{Y}_i$ is minimum and maximum of the brightness range of the codword.

Moving object detection using the current frame and background frame "subtraction" approach, that is for each pixel in each frame, if it is matched with the codeword of its codebook established in the background model building process, it will be judged as the pixel belongs to the background, and the corresponding code word will be updated. Otherwise it will be judged as the pixel belongs to the foreground.

3. Improved Brightness Range Definition Method and Background Model Update Algorithm

3.1. *Improved brightness range definition method of the Codebook background model based on YUV color space*

There are many wrong detections in the process of moving object detection in the Codebook background model under YUV color space. Such as in the video sequence, a pixel belongs to background at the first, after a period of time the pixel which did not represent moving object was detected as foreground pixel, as shown in Fig. 1, Fig. 2:

Fig .1. The 215frame of the video camera.

Fig. 2. The 722frame of the video test.

The video camera from PETS2001 video set, video test from PETS2000 video set. This paper selected several pixels in figure 1, 2, found that the *Y* components value of the pixels changed as shown in Fig. 3, 4:

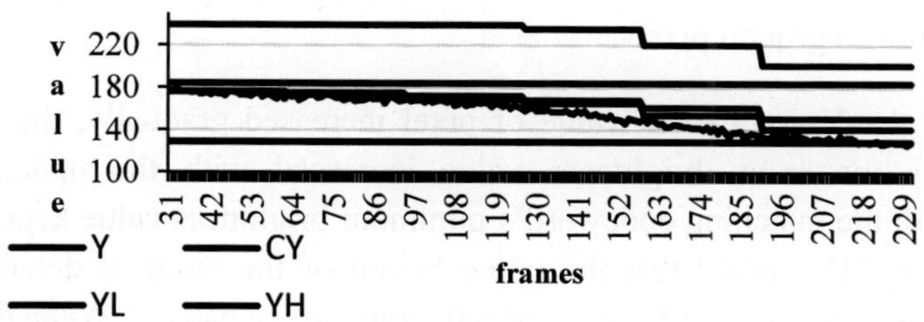

Fig. 3. Pixel (364, 90) in video camera changes from frame 31 to 231.

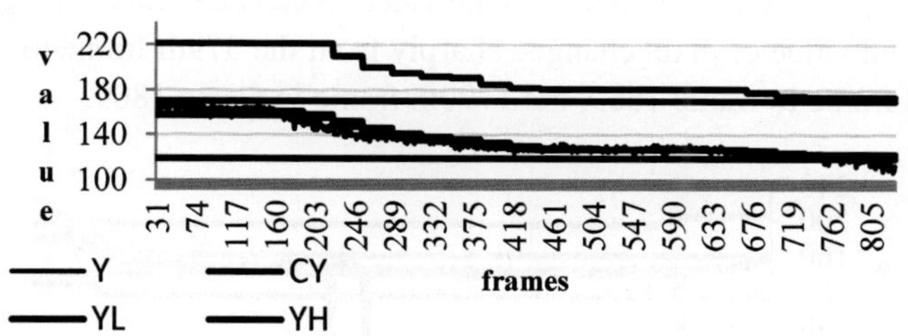

Fig. 4. Pixel (324, 293) in video test changes from frame 31 to 831.

Among Fig. 3, 4,Y is the Y component value of the pixel, CY is the codeword's Y component mean value which corresponding to the pixel, CYL is the codeword's minimum brightness value which corresponding to the pixel (that is $\check{Y}_i$, in the formula (1)), CYH is the codeword's maximum brightness value which corresponding to the pixel (that is $\hat{Y}_i$, in the formula (2)), CYL and CYH change with the update of the background, YL is determined by CYH, YH is determined by CYL and CYH.

From figure 3, 4, we can know that, as the value of the Y component of the pixel gradually fell, the matching codeword's minimum brightness value (the value of the parameter $\check{Y}_i$) decreased with the update of the background, and the maximum brightness value of the matching codewords kept constant, the lower bound of the codeword's brightness range YL is determined by $\hat{Y}_i$ according to the formula (1), so it will remain the same. When the pixel's Y component keeps falling, it will break through the lower bound of the codeword's brightness range become into foreground pixels.

When the Y component value of pixel increased gradually, the matching codeword's maximum brightness value increased with the update of the background, the matching codeword's minimum brightness value kept constant, The formula (2) showed that the upper bound of the range is determined by smaller values of YH and YL, so it basically remains unchanged. When the pixel's Y component continues to rise, it will break through the upper bound of the codeword's brightness and become into foreground pixels.

At the same time, this paper studied the change of the Y component value of pixels that represent moving object in the video. It can be seen from Fig.5 that the Y component value of pixel changed sharply from the 379th frame to frame 395, the 1645th frame to frame 1669, the 1790th frame to frame 1809.

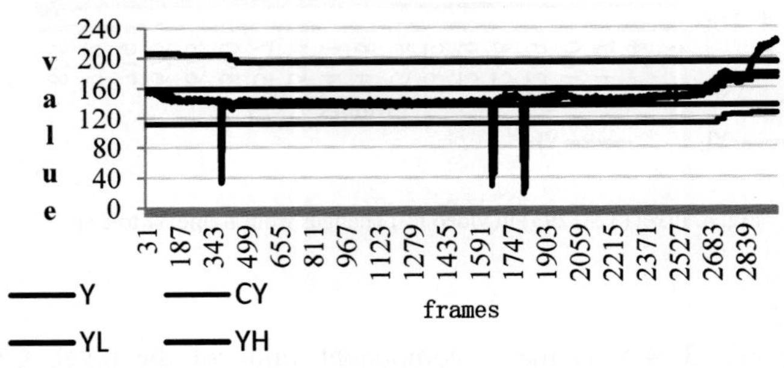

Fig. 5. Y component value of pixel change.

In view of the above analysis and combined with the structure of codeword sunder YUV color space and the background update algorithm, we found that codeword's Y component mean value changed gradually according to the pixel values' change by frame, as it is the average of the pixels for multiple frames, so it update slowly. Therefore, this paper used codeword's $\overline{Y}_i$ define a new brightness range.

$$YL = \overline{Y}_i - T. \tag{5}$$

$$YH = \overline{Y}_i + T. \tag{6}$$

T is a adjustable parameter, generally takes different values between 10 and 40. After redefine, when the Y component value of pixels rise or fall continuously within a certain range, the matching codeword's upper limit and lower limit will be adjusted slowly, namely the brightness range of the codeword can update slowly along with the change of pixel's values, as shown in Figure 6, 7:

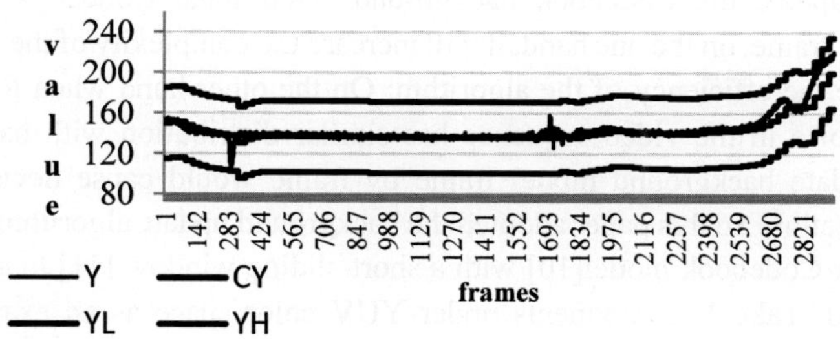

Fig. 6. Pixel (364, 90) in video camera changes.

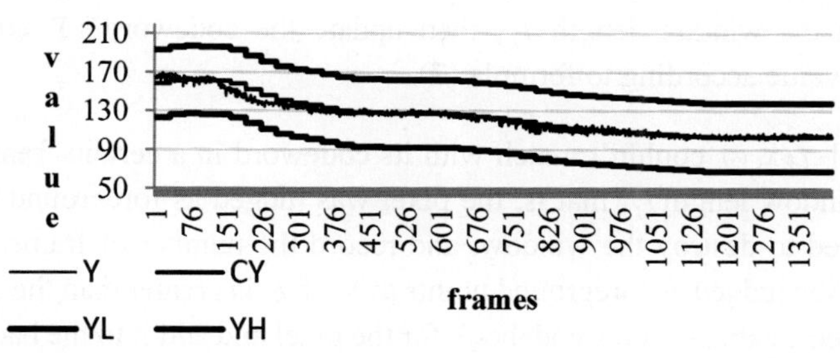

Fig. 7. Pixel (324, 293) in video test changes.

Applying new brightness range defining methods the codewords' parameter changed from $aux_i = \left\langle \check{Y}_i, \hat{Y}_i, f_i, \lambda_i, p_i, q_i \right\rangle$ to $aux_i = \langle f_i, \lambda_i, p_i, q_i \rangle$.

3.2. *The background update algorithm combing a two-layer Codebook model with a short-sliding window*

In the process of moving object detection, new background may appear after the background model training. Common in some moving object stopped and changed into background gradually, such as car stopped in the parking space, and the bag was put on a chair. Besides that, due to factors such as light would cause subtle changes for the background in the process of moving object detection, so we must update the Codebook background. Traditional Codebook model is updated by frame, on the one hand, it will increase the complexity of the algorithm and reduce the efficiency of the algorithm; On the other hand when foreground pixel or noise in the video sequence has similar distribution with background pixels, update background model frame by frame would cause deviation and wrong detection. So this paper adopted the background update algorithm combing a two-layer Codebook model[10] with a short-sliding window [11] to update the background. Take Y components under YUV color space as an example, the specific method is:

(1) If the number of the frames which a pixel $f(x,y)$ was continuously determined as background point is *B*. If *B* is more than T_1, that is, the pixel matched continuously with the same codeword in the background model within the window length T_1, then update the codeword's Y component mean value according to formula (7).

(2) If pixel $f(x,y)$ couldn't match with its codeword in a certain frame within the window length T_1, that is, the pixel was judged as foreground point, so we need to destroy the window, and record the number of frames that the pixel was judged as foreground points as S, if S is greater than the threshold T_2, then establish a new codebook for the pixel and add it to the background model.

(3) If the pixel $f(x,y)$ was judged as foreground pixel again when S is less than T_2 and the pixel have been tested as the background point lasted $2T_1$ frames then update the codeword's Y component mean value according to the nearest T_1 frames' information.

(4) Repeat the above process, until the end of the test.

$$\bar{Y}_i = (\bar{Y}_i + Y_{add}/T)/2\,. \tag{7}$$

Y_{add} is the accumulated value of Y components in the window, T_1, T_2 is the adjustable threshold which comply with the video.

Using the method which combined a two-layer Codebook model with a short-sliding window background update algorithm can update the background timely and reduce the wrong background update.

4. Experimental Results and Analysis

This article selected four groups of typical video file to compare the original Codebook algorithms, Codebook algorithm under YUV color space and the algorithm this paper proposed respectively. We implemented all the experimentsinVisual c++ 2008 and Opencv2.4.3 and ran them on a CPUPencium (R) Dual – Core machine with 2GB RAM. Video camera and the test are from the PETS video sets, video ped and car are from video database of changedetection.net.

(a) (b) (c) (d)

Fig. 8. The results with different algorism of the 296 frame of video camera.

(a) (b) (c) (d)

Fig. 9. The results with different algorism of the 1001 frame of video ped.

(a) (b) (c) (d)

Fig. 10. The results with different algorism of the 772 frame of video test.

(a) (b) (c) (d)

Fig. 11. The results with different algorism of the 726 frame of video car.

In Fig. 8 to 11, (a) is the original video image (b) is the original Codebook algorithm result image, (c) is the Codebook algorithm under in the YUV color space result image, (d) is the algorithm results image which proposed in this paper.

The Fig. 8 shows: the moving object which the original Codebook algorithm detected with large shadow, at the same time there is wrong detection which appeared on the roof at the top right of the image and noise is more; the moving object which the Codebook algorithms under YUV color space detected is complete, reduced the shadow and noise, but there is still wrong detection; the algorithm which proposed in this paper detected the moving object complete and no shadow, reduced the noise and wrong detection mainly.

The Fig. 9 shows: the original Codebook algorithms identified the stationary backpack mistakenly as moving object, and the shadow of moving object is large; the Codebook algorithms under YUV color space failed to detect stationary backpack as the background, but compared with the original algorithm the moving object's shadow is smaller and less noise; This paper's algorithm could update the background and the background is clean, almost no shadow.

The Fig. 10 shows: the original Codebook algorithms identified the stationary car mistakenly as moving object, and in the bottom right picture area appeared wrong detection; the Codebook algorithms under YUV color space failed to detect stationary car as the background, but compared with the original algorithm the car's shadow is smaller and less noise and there is still wrong detection; This paper's algorithm could update the background and the background is clean, almost no noise.

The Fig. 11 shows: the moving object the original Codebook algorithm detected had large shadow, it has a lot noise because the light changed, and there was wrong detection on the place where a car stopped before; the result which Codebook algorithm under YUV color space detected had little shadow and less noise, but there still has wrong detection; This paper's algorithm detected the object accurately and resisted light's change effectively.

Analysis quantitatively the result of the detection using precision rate P and recall rate R, formula is as follows:

$$P = Np / Nt. \tag{8}$$

$$R = Np / Nr. \tag{9}$$

Where Np is the number of pixels being recognized as foreground pixels in one frame; Nr is the number of artificially extracted foreground pixels in one frame; Nt is the number of pixels detected as foreground points in one frame. The formula shows that when the P is higher the ratio of false detection is low (that means the accuracy of detection result is high), when the R is lower the rate of miss detection is higher (that means incomplete foreground detection).The results are shown in Table 1:

Table 1. The compare of precision rate and recall rate between different algorithm.

image	The original Codebook algorithm		Codebook algorithm under YUV color space		the algorithm which proposed in this paper	
	P	R	P	R	P	R
figure 8(a)	22.96%	89.05%	46.99%	92.82%	83.79%	90.02%
figure 9(a)	53.21%	83.63%	67.62%	83.19%	90.41%	82.34%
figure 10(a)	10.77%	97.40%	45.37%	93.30%	86.54%	94.30%
figure 11(a)	56.31%	83.63%	68.26%	82.96%	91.40%	82.63%

The Table 1 showed : Comparing with the original algorithm, the improved algorithm of Codebook model based on updating background and changing brightness range improved the accuracy rate and the recall rate was slightly lower. It demonstrated that the algorithm this paper proposed had lower error detection rate, high accuracy, but a slight leak.

5. Conclusion

In this paper, we established Codebook background model under YUV color space and put forward the improved brightness range Codebook algorithm under YUV space aimed at the problem of the irrational brightness range definition of the algorithm, at the same time this paper put forward the background updating method which combined a two-layer Codebook model with a short-sliding window. Experiments proved that our proposed algorithm gives better precision than the original Codebook algorithm. It is easy to implement and suitable for complex scenarios of moving object detection.

Acknowledgments

This work is supported by Outstanding Achievements Transformation Projects of University in Chongqing under Grant No. KJZH14219 and Chongqing Science and Technology Research Project of Chongqing Municipal Education Commission under Grant No. KJ1402002.

References

1. Gross R, MatthewsI, Baker S. Active Appearance Models with Occlusion[J]. Image and Vision Computing, 2006, 24(6): 593-604.

2. Xiaojing Song, Seneviratne L. D., Althoefer K. A Kalman Filter Integrated Optical Flow Method for Velocity Sensing of MobileRobots[J]. IEEE/ASME Transactions on Mechatronics, 2010, 16(3):551-563.

3. Gao Hongzhi, Green R. A Robust Moving Object Segmentation Algorithm[C]. Proceedings of the 2007 International Conference on Wavelet Analysis and Pattern Recognition, 2007(1): 214-217.

4. Ke-xue D, Guo-hui L, Dan T, et al. Prospects and Current Studies on Background Subtraction Techniques for Moving Objects Detection from Surveillance Video[J]. Journal of Image & Graphics, 2006, 11(7):919-927.

5. Dawei Li, Lihong Xu, Goodman E. A fast foreground object detection algorithm using Kernel Density Estimation[C]. IEEE International Conference on Signal Processing, 2012:703-707.

6. Yan R, Song X, Yan S. Moving object detection based on an improved gaussian mixture background model[C]. International Colloquium on Computing, Communication, Control, & Management. IEEE, 2009:12 - 15.

7. K. Kim, T. H. Chalidabhongse, D. Harwood and L. Davis. Real-time Foreground-Background Segmentation using Codebook Model[J]. Real-time Imaging, 2005, 11(3):167-256.

8. Qu Zhong, Ma Qingwei, Zhang Qingqing. Research on the algorithm of micro-movement target tracking and extraction in video by multi-thread technology[J]. Computer Science, 2012, 39(4):265-268.

9. Lei Fei, Huang Wenlu, Wang Xueli. Underwater moving targets detection based on codebook model under YUV color space[J]. Computers and Applied Chemistry, 2014, 31(4):416-420.

10. Sigari M H, Fathy M. Real-time Background Modeling/Subtraction using Two-Layer Codebook Model[C]. International Multiconference of Engineers & Computer Scientists, 2008: 1-5

11. JIANG Ke, LI Ai-hua, SU Yan-zhao. Moving Targets Detecting Algorithm in Video Based on Improved Codebook Model[J]. Journal of University of Electronic Science and Technology of China, 2012, 41(6):932-936.

SVM-Based Clinical Decision Support Algorithm under Medical Big Data Architecture

Jie HOU
School of Medical English and Health Communication, TianJin Medical University, TianJin, China
E-mail:houj@tmu.edu.cn

Xi-kun ZHANG
School of Science and technology, TianJin Open University, TianJin, China

Yao-gang WANG
School of Public Health, TianJin Medical University, TianJin, China
E-mail: wyg@tmu.edu.cn

Big Data technology has experienced rapid development in recent years and has demonstrated its effectiveness when implemented inclinical diagnostic decision support. Current research of big data focuses largely on data storage architecture, the exploration on big clinical data mining and decision making strategy is relatively less. This paper discusses the parallel big medical data mining method under Spark architecture and proposes the optimized support vector machine (PCSVM) algorithm to provide qualitative data for clinical diagnostic decision support.

Keywords: Big data; Spark; SVM; Clinical decision.

1. Introduction

With the rapid development of informatics of healthcare, standard EHR(electronic health record) and CIS(Clinical Information System) are being widely used. As a result, healthcare industry has accumulated a large number of medical related data, including the patients' medical records, diagnosis results, medical imaging, etc. Medical data show to be an explosive growth trend, which is facing a series of processing problem , such as, big volume, complex dimension relationships, high demand of interactive response. Applying big data technology to medical field, doctors and researchers will fully share more medical information resources , improving their medical decision making level. Through model analysis and data mining, big healthcare data resources can describe the phenomenon of life , predict the occurrence rule of diseases, explore clinical characteristic and therapy of some diseases, thus saving medical cost.

Google successfully predicted the H1N1 flu outbreak by the users' online search record in early 2009. By combining big data processing techniques with traditional monitoring methods, their "Flu Trends system" can forecast the future one week of influenza infection in the United States [1]; American Flatiron Health company, which committed to collecting and analyzing tremendous amounts of clinical data to analysis and predict of cancer treatment, has obtained Google venture sector investment over 100 million US dollars.

Big Data technology can be more effectively applied to clinical decision-making. Compared with the traditional evidence-based medicine, clinical decision support systems based on big data technology has advantages of low rate of misdiagnosis, and realizes remote clinics and real-time monitoring of biology data functions. The research of the US Metropolitan pediatric intensive care shows that, the clinical decision support systems can avoid the 40% of adverse drug events. Many medical institutions around the world (such as the UK's NICE, Germany IQWIG etc.) has begun comparative effectiveness research (CER) project and has achieved initial success.

Clinical decision-making system which is supported by traditional databases and Hadoop framework cannot get rapid, real-time response. Spark as an open source cluster computing system based on memory computing, analyzes data more quickly. Its optimization design based on memory provides distributed computing framework similar to MapReduce, which makes Spark achieve more faster response speed. This paper discuss an optimized SVM algorithm of medical decision support system based on Spark architecture for its advantages of high-performance, high flexibility, and compatible to Hadoop ecosystem.

2. Relevant Work

Cloud computing as a new parallel processing technology incorporates features of grid computing, distributed computing and parallel computing, so it has superior performance in big data computing and network storage [2]. Since 2003, four papers about Google File System [3], structured data table---BigTable [4], parallel data processing computing model---MapReduce[5] and distributed lock service---Chubby[6] respectively laid foundation of cloud computing infrastructure technologies. Thus Apache launched a corresponding open source cloud computing platform---Hadoop[7], which pushed the research of cloud computing into a peak. Since the advent of big data era, the amount of data and the scale of the problem to be addressed appear to be blowout type growth, combining the traditional algorithm with cloud computing technology to expand data processing and throughput become a hot topic. So far most domestic and international researches on cloud computing and parallel algorithm are based on Hadoop platform and MapReduce parallel computing framework. However, MapReduce computing model belongs to intensive I/O type, which is very suitable for large amounts of data offline reading and writing. However, when used for iterative algorithms or high demand of real-time applications, the asynchronous bottleneck between CPU and I/O will be enlarged, MapReduce appears to be more inadequate. Aiming at this problem, the University of California, Berkeley AMP (Algorithms Machines People) laboratory developed the Spark system. Spark is a memory-based computing system, it enhance speed of computing that is applicable to memory scene to a great extend[8].

Collobert et al. first proposed the parallel SVM learning algorithm[9] for a large-scale data. During the training phase, large-scale problems are broken down into a number of random smaller-scale sub-problems, then training support vector machine for each sub-issue at the same time. Support vector machine are combined to get the final classifier. Catanzaron et al., who utilize the robust matrix computing power of GPU to achieve an efficient SVM training. Although SVM algorithm based on graphics processors have greatly improved, it still cannot solve the larger data set computing problems. Bickson et al. implemented SVM parallel processing based on MPI(Message Passing Interface) [10]. Their parallel scheme is based on peer to peer grid environment. In this environment, there is no middleware managing and allocating assignments. However, MPI does not support asynchronous communication mechanism, the process of algorithm has to take synchronous approach, so that it cannot apparently improve the training efficiency. According to MapReduce parallel programming model proposed by Google, Chu Chengtao et al. who applied MapReduce to machine learning firstly, realized many kinds of machine learning algorithms[11], including linear support vector machine algorithm based on MapReduce. Deng Kun et al.'s report[12] also pointed out that the way of dividing the sample set uniformly and randomly into a number of different sizes of data subsets, then training each subset to get the support vector machine which will be merged into classifier finally turned out to be more effective to linear support vector machine. Alham et al.[13] applied the above distributed SVM idea in large-scale image annotation based on Hadoop distributed platform, and achieved good results. But there is a serious problem in this way---the larger number of divided training sets the less time for each one being trained, which leads to the result that the final number of integrated support vectors of Support Vector Machine will be more, then accurate rate will be reduced accordingly.

3. Optimized SVM Algorithm Based on Spark Architecture

3.1. *Parallel cascade algorithm*

According to the implementation mechanism of Hadoop and MapReduce platform, this paper presents a parallel cascade SVM algorithm---PCSVM, the system architecture is as figure 1. The algorithm is a three step process:

Step1: dividing the sample set into several groups uniformly and randomly;

Step 2: training and optimizing each of these small data blocks;

Step 3: merging the supported vectors of each small data block obtained in step2.

Repeating the above three steps.

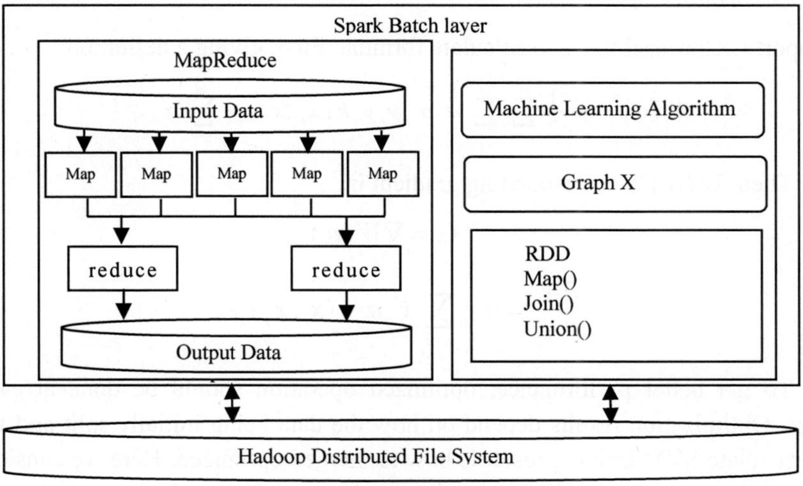

Fig. 1. System architecture.

In order to avoid the potential impact on the performance of the classifier because of large distribution of initial training data set, the algorithm uses feedback method to appropriately adjust the initial classifier in the training process, as a result, each small data set obtained support vector more accurately, so that improving the accuracy of classification.

Taking three-layer parallel support vector machine as an example: in the first layer, the original data set is divided into blocks during Map process; then in the Reduce process, every small data set will be trained in order to output the corresponding support vector; finally, which will be merged finally. In the integration process, we adopt a feedback optimization method, which will be described in detail in the next section. The second layer repeats the operation of the first one. The last layer does not need to block the data set, that means there's no more operations, but to training data D7, obtaining their support vector SV7, and then output the training models.

In specific application process, we can set different subsets according to the actual situation, thus using different cascade layers to be trained, then merging them layer by layer until the last one. In each layer of the merger process, it is important to remove the non-support vector machine as early as possible, in order to speed up the training process. After such an operation, the final model is relatively simple, and each set independently of each other, so it can well realize concurrent execution.

3.2. *Distributed optimization*

Support vector machine is to calculate formula. First, giving a definition,

$$W(\alpha) = -\frac{1}{2}\sum_{i=1}^{n}\sum_{j=1}^{n}\alpha_1\alpha_j y_i y_j k(x_i, x_j) + \sum_{i=1}^{n}\alpha_i \quad . \tag{1}$$

Then $\mathrm{W}(\alpha)$'s corresponding gradient is:

$$\mathrm{G} = \nabla W(\alpha) \quad . \tag{2}$$

$$\mathrm{G}_i = \frac{\partial W}{\partial \alpha_i} = -y_i \sum_{i=1}^{n} y_j \alpha_j k(x_i, x_j) + 1 \quad . \tag{3}$$

To get better performance, optimized operation should be done at each stage. Optimization results depend on how the data being initially split and the intermediate SVM training result is how to merged optimized. Here we consider the gradient ascent algorithm and discuss how to deal with the combination effectively. Gradient ascent algorithms and gradient descent algorithm are of similar principle, the difference between lies in gradient ascent algorithm is to find the maximum value, but the gradient descent algorithm is to find the minimum.

$$W_i = -\frac{1}{2}\alpha_i^T Q_i \alpha_i + e_i^T \alpha_i . \tag{4}$$

$$G_i = -\alpha_i^T Q_i + e_i \ . \tag{5}$$

In formula (4) and (5), Q is a nuclear matrix, e_i is a matrix of all elements are 1. According to the formula (6), gradients of SVM1 and SVM2 are combined, and then being input to SVM3. SVM3 is used to test whether the sub-data blocks 1 and 2 meet the KKT (Karush-Kuhn-Tucker) optimal condition. If not, the data that does not meet the KKT will be combined with the classifier optimized in the last step in the next iteration process.

$$W_3 = -\frac{1}{2}\begin{bmatrix}\alpha_1\\ \alpha_2\end{bmatrix}^T \begin{bmatrix}Q_1 Q_{12}\\ Q_{21} Q_2\end{bmatrix}\begin{bmatrix}\alpha_1\\ \alpha_2\end{bmatrix} + \begin{bmatrix}e_1\\ e_2\end{bmatrix}^T \begin{bmatrix}\alpha_1\\ \alpha_2\end{bmatrix} \ . \tag{6}$$

$$G_3 = -\begin{bmatrix}\alpha_1\\ \alpha_2\end{bmatrix}^T \begin{bmatrix}Q_1 Q_{12}\\ Q_{21} Q_2\end{bmatrix} + \begin{bmatrix}e_1\\ e_2\end{bmatrix}. \tag{7}$$

3.3. *Implementation of the PCSVM*

Suppose to build n-tier support vector machine, the current number of iteration layers (or cascading layers) is i, the total number of cascading layers of cascade is λ .

Then,

$$\lambda = 1 + \lfloor \log_2(MapNum) \rfloor \ . \tag{8}$$

Figure 2 depicts the flow chart of PCSVM algorithm. It's realization process is as follows:

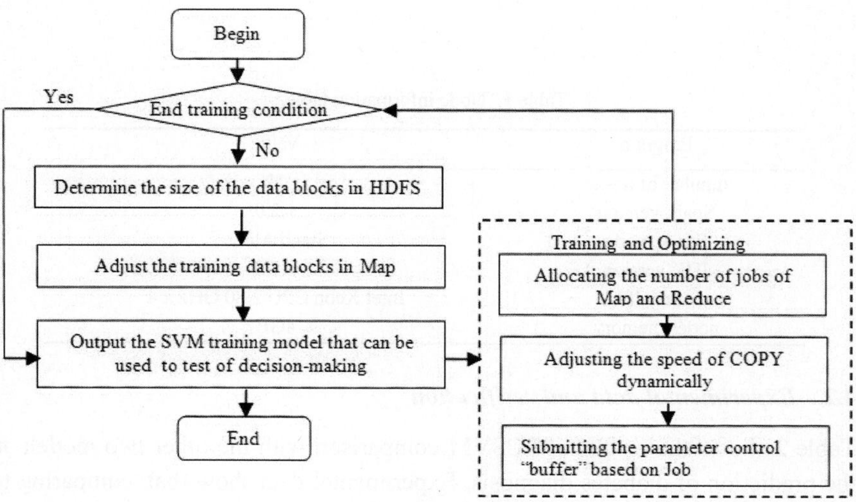

Fig.2. Flow chart of PCSVM algorithm.

(1) Judging the number of the current iteration layers;
(2) If the number of iteration layer is not the smallest, then the data set will be divided into 2^{n-i} small data blocks uniformly and randomly during Map process, each small data block will be trained independently during Reduce process. Feeding back and optimizing the support vector we get, subtracting one iteration layer;
(3) Else, the iteration operation will end, then output the training model.

4. Demonstration and Analysis of Experimental Results

This section evaluates the PCSVM algorithm based on Spark parallel framework, comparing it with SVMWithSGD and LibSVM algorithm. SVMwithSGD is a linear support vector machine training algorithm in SparkMLlib (a package of some common machine learning algorithms implemented by Spark, including classification, regression, clustering, dimensionality reduction, etc.), which uses the parallel gradient descent method to train the support vector.

4.1. *Experimental environment*

Attributes information of nodes in experimental environment are shown in Table 1.

Table 1. Node information table.

Program	Value
number of nodes	12
Spark version	1.2.0
Spark mode	Stand Alone
JDK version	1.7.0
nodes CPU	Intel Xeon CPU 2.80 GHz x 4
nodes memory	4GB

4.2. *Experimental data and verification*

Table 2 shows the results of PCSVM comparison with the other two models in the prediction of diabetes diagnosis. Experimental data show that, comparing to LibSVM and SVMWithSGD, PCSVM algorithm is most effective in Type I and Type II diabetes decision and prediction. After testing the algorithm, the optimal linear kernel parameters C=3.301, σ=0.004. Under optimal conditions, the accuracy of classification linear kernel function will be greatly improved.

Table 2. Results of different SVM models.

Algorithm	Penalty parameter	Kernel parameter	Testing data set					
			TP	FN	TN	FP	Accuracy (%)	Specificity (%)
SVMWithSGD	16	0.109	119	1	108	9	95.78	92.31
LibSVM	3.031	0.004	115	5	106	11	93.25	90.60
PCSVM	0.004	3.301	119	1	105	8	96.20	99.17

4.3. *Analysis of the experimental results*

In this paper, we propose a parallel gradient descent algorithm based on Spark platform and do relevant verification through experiments from accuracy and running time aspects, which compare the PCSVM with SVMWithSGD and the classic serial algorithm LibSVM under different iterations and data size conditions. Experimental results show that accuracy of the proposed algorithm is higher than SVMWithSGD in Spark environment. Furthermore, its speed is much faster than LibSVM especially for very large data sets. Within a certain range, the more the number of iterations, the higher the accuracy of PCSVM, but it is more time consuming for the price. Therefore, we chose the number of iterations N=200 as a compromise choice to ensure the accuracy of BMB> PGD and take a shorter time.

5. Conclusion

PCSVM algorithm breaks the barriers that SVM algorithm can quickly and efficiently handle only small data sets. PCSVM algorithm can do classification and prediction quickly of large-scale data sets, solving the problem of non-linear large-scale data and ensuring a certain degree of accuracy . PCSVM algorithm limits the size of SVM training model, so it has a constant time complexity and space complexity. The algorithm will have widely applicable value in medical diagnosis decision.

Acknowledgments

This work is supported by the National Natural Science Foundation of China (Grant No. 71473175) and the Tianjin Science and Technology Commission (Grant No. 15ZCZDSY00500).

References

1. Ginsberg J, Mohebbi M H, Patel R S, et al. Detecting influenza epidemics using search engine query data[J]. Nature, 2009, 457(7232): 1012-1014.
2. ZHANG J, GU Z, ZHENG C. Survey of research progress on cloud computing[J]. Application Research of Computers, 2014, 27 (2):429 -433.
3. GHEMAWAT S, GOBIOFF H, LEUNG S. The Google file system[J]. Proceedings of the Nineteenth ACM Symposium on Operating Systems Principles. New York: ACM Press, 2003 : 29-43.
4. CHANG F, DEAN J, GHEMAWAT S, et al. Bigtable: a distributed storage system for structured data[J]. ACM Transactions on Computer Systems, 2008, 26(2) : 205- 218.
5. DEAN J, GHEMAWAT S. MapReduce: Simplified data processing on large clusters[J]. Communications of the ACM, 2014, 51(1): 107-113.
6. BURROWS M. The chubby lock service for loosely-coupled distributed systems[C]. Proceedings of the 7th USENIX Symposium on Operating Systems Design and Implementation. Berkeley: USENIX, 2013: 335-350
7. O'Driscoll, A., Daugelaite, J., and Sleator, R. D., Bigdata, Hadoop and cloud computing in genomics. J. Biomed. Inform. 2013, 46(5): 774-781.
8. ZAHARIAM, CHOWDHURYM, DAST, et al. Resilient distributed datasets: a fault-tolerant abstraction for in-memory cluster computing[C]. Proceedings of the 9th USENIX Conference on Networked Systems Design and Implementation. Berkeley: USENIX, 2012: 141 -146.
9. Collobert, R., S. Bengio and Y. Bengio, A parallel mixture of SVMs for very large scale problems. Neural computation, 2012. 14(5): 1105-1114.
10. Bickson, D., E. Yom-Tov and D. Dolev, A Gaussian belief propagation solver for large scale support vector machines. Arxiv preprint arXiv, 2013: 1658
11. Chu, C.T., et al., Map-reduce for machine learning on multicore. Advances in neural information processing systems, 2011. 19: 281.

12. Kun, D., L. Yih and A. Perera, Parallel SMO for Training Support Vector Machines. Proceedings of the 2nd USENIX Conference on Hot Topics in Cloud Computing. Berkeley: USENIX, 2010: 10.
13. Alham, N.K., et al., A distributed SVM for image annotation, in Fuzzy Systems and Knowledge Discovery (FSKD), 2010 Seventh International Conference

High-Quality Reconstruction of 3D Model

Xing-ming LIU, Tie CAI, Rong-zhi GUI, Hui-jing WANG and Jun-yao LIU
Computer Science, Shenzhen institute of Information and Technology, Shenzhen, Guangdong, China
E-mail: xlium@126.com

The scanner of three-dimensional reconstruction has become popular in the common practice of quality measuring, quality control, and cultural heritage et al. In this paper, we presented an algorithm to produce high-quality of photorealistic textured model, which aligned and integrated range images into a common system, reconstructed the geometric shape of object; In the next step, the captured color-images are back-projected onto the reconstructed surface and removed the artifact with a composite weighted strategy. The experimental result shows our presented method can produce high quality photo-realistic results with a low computational cost.

Keywords: 3D model; Range image; Reconstruction; Texture mapping.

1. Introduction

Three-dimensional scanning has been widely used for many years in reverse engineering, three-dimensional measuring, quality control, art-designing, visualization of cultural heritage object [1-5]and medical implementations (e.g. body shape evaluation for medicine purpose). For example, if one used the robotic arm for grasping and manipulating the target objects, it important to estimate the size and orientation of the target object from the capture views as well as reconstruction the three-dimensional of the geometric information, which will help the robotic arm to success grasp the target object and interact with it. Moreover, we also can re-design or modify the reconstruction digital model for purpose of other using, like manufacture or processing.

However, because of the limited field of view (FOV) of capture view, it usually can't acquire all the data from just one view of the target model, especially when the target object with complex geometric shape and topology as well as the geometric size is big. In this case, the range image should be captured around the target objects from the different views or put the objects on a turntable and the system provides a cylindrical scan. And the captured range images must be aligned, or registered into a common coordinate system, and integrated to get a complete 3D model[6].

In order to register all range images into a common coordination, some systems attached the scanner to a coordinate measurement machine that tracks its trail of its movement and orientation. With this help, the range images of different coordination systems can be aligned into a common coordination, and integrated to obtain the geometric model. The most successful method is Iterative Closet Point algorithm (ICP) proposed by Besl and Makay[7], Chen[8], and Zhang[9], which is applied to register range images into a common coordination system.

However, above of all these steps is the reconstruction of its geometric model (size and the shape of object), lack of the visual appearance will limit its application in the area of visual displaying, art-designing, and cultural heritage areas[10, 11]. So it is of paramount important to capture the images of the target object and back-projected the capture views onto the reconstructed 3D model to recover the visual appearance of object, and to remove the visual artifact that caused by variable illuminations, the change directions of capture views, non-perfect reconstruction model, non-lambert surface and other reasons. In this paper, an approach to reconstruct the textured model of an object is proposed(both the geometric and visual appearance of the object). And in our proposed approach, the following tasks should be concerned: (1) the registration of the range images into a common coordination system to construct a single 3D model and (2) the projection between the capture views and the reconstructed model to get a texture mapping, which is a 3D-2D texture mapping. Of course, to texture map for a visual reconstruction, a composite-weight strategy is applied to blend texture in the overlapped region to remove artifact visual of the final reconstructed result, resulting a photorealistic texture model.

2. System Principles

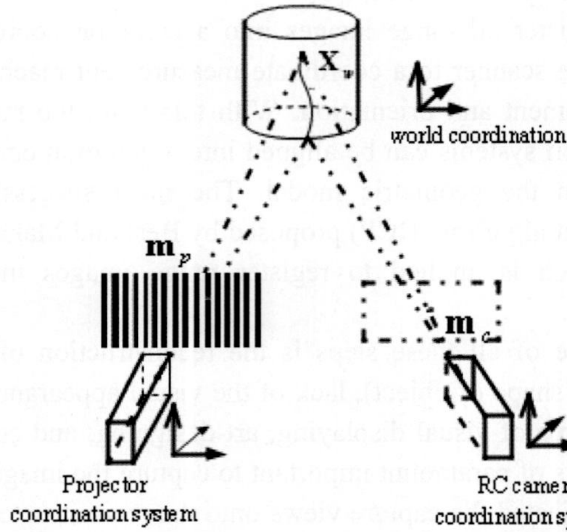

Fig. 1. Principles of the triangulation algorithm. The projector provides structural illuminations and using RC camera to capture the images, with the help of triangulation theory, 3D space points are computed by intersecting of the scan line.

The principle of our prototype for the scanning device is shown in Fig.1, which compose a digital light projector(DLP) that projects man-made stripe to object and with a CCD camera capture the deformation images. And with the help of triangulation algorithm, the depth value of the target object can be deduced. Suppose an object space point is $\mathbf{X}_w$, and its corresponding image in the CCD camera and the projector is $\mathbf{m}_c$ and $\mathbf{m}_p$ respectively, then based on the triangulation algorithm, the process can be expressed as follows:

$$\begin{cases} \mathbf{m}_c = \mathbf{R}_c\mathbf{X}_w + \mathbf{t}_c \\ s_c\tilde{\mathbf{m}}_c = \mathbf{K}_c[\mathbf{I}\,|\,\mathbf{0}]\tilde{\mathbf{X}}_c \\ \mathbf{m}_c = \hat{\mathbf{m}}_c - \boldsymbol{\delta}(\mathbf{m}_c;\boldsymbol{\theta}_c) \\ s_p\tilde{\mathbf{m}}_p = \mathbf{K}_p[\mathbf{R}_s\,|\,\mathbf{t}_s]\tilde{\mathbf{X}}_c \\ \mathbf{m}_p = \hat{\mathbf{m}}_p - \boldsymbol{\delta}(\mathbf{m}_p;\boldsymbol{\theta}_p) \end{cases} \quad . \tag{1}$$

Here, $\mathbf{m}_c$ $\mathbf{m}_p$ subscript means the coordination in CCD or Projector system, $\mathbf{R}$ $\mathbf{t}$,c $\boldsymbol{\delta}(\mathbf{m};\boldsymbol{\theta})$ is the camera parameter that can be known from calibration, $\tilde{\bullet}$

represents homogeneous coordination, $\widehat{\mathbf{m}}_c$ is the ideal non-distortion image point, and $\mathbf{m}_c$ is the measurement image point of $\mathbf{X}_w$. $\mathbf{R}_s$ $\mathbf{t}_s$ is represent as follows:

$$\begin{cases} \mathbf{R}_s = \mathbf{R}_p \mathbf{R}_c^{-1} \\ \mathbf{t}_s = \mathbf{t}_p - \mathbf{R}_p \mathbf{R}_c^{-1} \mathbf{t}_c \end{cases} . \tag{2}$$

$\mathbf{R}_s$ $\mathbf{t}_s$ is the transformation between the CCD camera and projector system. If the camera parameters is known(from camera calibration procedure), then object space points $\mathbf{X}_w$ can be deduced.

2.1. *Registration*

Using the Scanner system to acquire the range image around the target object based on the coordination system of local scanner. Then range images must be aligned, or registered into a common coordination system.

The intrinsic of registration is to find the rotation matrix R and translation vector t that minimized the distance target range images with the help of overlap area. Let $S_i(i=1,\cdots,m)$ and $S'_k(k=1,\cdots,n)$ be the adjacent range images that have common overlap areas, and let $X_{i,j}(j=1,\cdots,N_i)$ and $X'_{i,j}(l=1,\cdots,N_i)$ be the corresponding points on the range images S_i and S'_k, respectively. The problem of registration is to compute R, t with minimization of the following equation:

$$F(R,t)=\sum_{i=1}^{m}\sum_{j=1}^{N_i} d^2(RX_{i,j}+t,X'_{i,j}) \tag{3}$$

Here, $d(X,X')$ denote the distance of the corresponding points in the range images.

The ICP registration algorithm consists two steps: in the first step, it need the corresponding points in the area of the overlap of target images; In the second step, an optimization procedure is applied to compute a fine registration that reduce minimization of distance of the target range images. in our approach, we interactive select the points between the overlap area of range images as the candidate corresponding points to compute initial transformation, and put this initial transformation as the optimization procedure input to get fine transformation, reduce the distance of the Eq.(3). The general ideal is iterated until some convergence criterion is satisfied. However, sometimes the algorithm may converges to a local minimum, depending on the initial transformation, selecting points usually can avoid this situation, and have a good convergence.

Moreover, the aligned multiple range images must be integrated to reconstruct the geometry and topology of the target object from the capture range images, and to build a unified, non-redundant surface 3D model. Which like reduce the data noise, remove the outliers, and repaired the parts of surface that lost sampling area. In our approach, we use Delaunay-based method to achieve it, similar like paper[12].

2.2. *Texture mapping and blending*

In order to reconstruct a photorealistic 3D textured model, the captured color images must be registered with the 3D model (2D-3D registration) and texture map onto the surface of the reconstructed model. The color image acquisition methodology requires only inexpensive hardware: a household digital camera or a high-resolution mobile phone, and with the digital advice to capture details from a set of views that cover the whole surface of the object.

Then, the acquired color images are registered with respect to the reconstructed model M (usually the model is in the form of mesh), of course, there are many methodology to achieve this, either by attach the color-camera on the scanner system and through calibration to accurate be determined, or by interactive selection of corresponding pair points, each methodology have advantages and disadvantages, none is prior. In our approach, the latter case is adopted. We interactive select the space and the image point corresponding: ($X_i \leftrightarrow x_i$), and use the Maximum Likelihood to determine the projection P that minimize the following equation:

$$\sum_i d(x_i, PX_i)^2. \tag{4}$$

$$P = KR\left[I \mid -\widetilde{C}\right]. \tag{5}$$

here, $K, R, \widetilde{C}$ is the camera parameters, and using the Gold standard algorithm[13] to compute the projection P.

Fig. 2. Texture mapping.left: the reconstruction geometric model; Middel and right: texture mapping the corresponding color images onto the reconstruction model, getting the texture patch.

Given this registration, the color images can be back-projected onto the surface of the model (see Fig. 2), and followed with a composited weighted strategy to blending the visual artifacts, resulting a photorealistic 3D model. More details is in the literature[14].

Fig. 3. Results of our experiment. Top left: the point form of the reconstruction object, and its triangular mesh model. Bottom: views of the texture reconstruction of results, which reconstructs both the geometric and its appearance attribute.

3. Experimental Results

We used our scanner to capture the range images, which composed one DLP projector (project pattern man-made stripes onto the measurement object) and a CCD camera(Imaging Source, 1280x960 pixel) to capture views. The scanner system is calibrated with Zhang[15] approach, pose planar pattern in a few different orientations in a volume area. The camera parameters (both internal and external parameters of camera) are determined, and the radial lens distortion is also recovered, then based on Eqs. (1) and (2), the space points of range image can be calculated, and the capture range images in a local coordination system are aligned into a common coordination to establish the 3D model.

Thereafter, a wine-chinaware with a height about 30cm is digitized using our scanner system, which is a type of art in our daily life. 8 views around the target model are captured to recover all the surface, and then registered and integrated into a single 3D model using our proposed approach (see top of Fig. 3), which consist of about 2,500,000 triangles. Furthermore, we interactive select the space and image corresponding point and using the Eqs. (4) and (5) to compute the projector matrix and back-projected onto the surface. And a composited weight strategy is followed to remove the artifacts or seams on the reconstruction surface, producing a photorealistic of the final reconstruction (see Fig. 3). And due to our reconstruction model is a glossy object , there have some flash artifacts in the final experimental results which affect the quality of experimental results, these problems will be resolve in our further research.

4. Conclusion

This paper proposes an algorithm for high-quality reconstruction for 3D models by aligning and integrating range images into a common system and reconstructing the geometric shape of object. The experimental results demonstrate that our proposed method can produce high quality photo-realistic results at low computational cost.

Acknowledgments

Work is support Guangdong National Science Foundation and the Shenzhen Science and technology project under contract numbers 015A030310511, JCY20150417094158019, and the Shenzhen Intelligent color modeling engineering lab is also acknowledgment.

References

1. CRocchini, PCignoni, CMontani and RScopigno, Multiple textures stitching and blending on 3D objects, In Eurographics Rendering Workshop, (1999).
2. FChen, G.MBrown and MSong, Overview of three-dimensional shape measurement using optical methods, Opt Eng **39**, 10(2000).
3. H.PALensch, WHeidrich and H-PSeidel, Automated Texture Registration and Stitching for Real World Models., in Proc of the 8th Pacific Conference on Computer Graphics and Applications: IEEE Computer Society, (2000).
4. FBernardini, H Rushmeier, I.M Martin, J Mittleman and TaubinG, Building a digital model of Michelangelo's Florentine Pieta, IEEE COMPUT GRAPH **22**, 59(2002).
5. F Blais, Review of 20 Years of range sensor development, J Electron Imaging**13**, 231(2004).
6. K Ikeuchi, T Oishi, J Takamatsu, R Sagawa,A Nakazawa, Kurazume R, et al., The Great Buddha Project: Digitally Archiving, Restoring, and Analyzing Cultural Heritage Objects, Int J Comput Vision**75**, 189(2007).
7. P.J.Besl and H.D McKay, A method for registration of 3-D shapes, IEEE T Pattern Anal **14**, 239(1992).
8. Y Chen and G Medioni, Object modeling by registration of multiple range image, in Proc. IEEE International Conference on Robotics and Automation, (1991).
9. Z Zhang, Iterative point matching for registration of free-form curves and surfaces, Int J Comput Vision**13**, 119(1994).
10. M Karaszewski, R Sitnik and E Bunsch, On-line, collision-free positioning of a scanner during fully automated three-dimensional measurement of cultural heritage objects, Robotics and Autonomous Systems **60**, 1205 (2012).
11. J Geng, Structured-light 3D surface imaging: a tutorial, Advances in Optics and Photonics **3**, 128(2011).
12. A Vrubel, ORP Bellon and L Silva, A 3D reconstruction pipeline for digital preservation, in Proc. IEEE Conference on Computer Vision and Pattern Recognition, (2009).
13. L.Y Liu, Y Gene, G Wolberg and Zokai S, Multiview Geometry for Texture Mapping 2D Images Onto 3D Range Data, in Proc. IEEE Computer Society Conference on Computer Vision and Pattern Recognition, (2006).

14. X.M Liu, X Peng, Y Yin, X.L Liu, W Wu, Generation of photorealistic 3D image using optical digitizer, Applied Optics **51**, 1304(2012).
15. Z Zhang, A Flexible New Technique for Camera Calibration, IEEE Trans Pattern Anal Mach Intell **22**, 1330 (2000).

The Parallel Implementation of Deep Neural Decision Tree Based on Spark

Zhi-chang HUANG, Jun-yi WANG†, Lin ZHENG and Jie-lin FU

Key Lab of Cognitive Radio & Information Processing, the Ministry of Education, Guilin University of Electronic Technology,
Guilin, 541004, China
†E-mail: wangjy@guet.edu.cn

We present a deep neural decision tree based on Spark - a novel approach that unifies classification tree with the representation learning functionality known from deep belief network and runs on the Spark to dramatically decrease the training time of the model. Firstly, we introduce a stochastic, differentiable, and therefore back-propagation compatible version of decision tree, guiding the representation learning in lower layers of deep belief networks. Furthermore, we make an parallel implementation for the decision tree back-propagation method based on Spark. We show experimental results on the Sloan Digital Sky Survey Data Release 7(SDSS-DR7) star/galaxy set and find out it scales well with the cluster size and have on-par or superior results in the classification accuracy when compared to state-of-the-art model which are used on the data set.

Keywords: Spark; Deep learning; Decision tree; Parallelization; Classification.

1. Introduction

Decision tree [1,2,3] have a rich and successful history in machine learning in general and the astronomy data mining in particular. Their performance has been empirically demonstrated to outperform most state-of-the-art learners when it comes to astronomy objects classification[4]. They are inherently able to deal with multiclass problems, handle discrete and continuous attribute data at the same time. However, decision tree just operates on the input space which is typically predefined and left unchanged. Moreover, with the development of the new-generation of sky survey and time domain observations, the amount of astronomical data quickly grows by exponential order of magnitude. How to classify and predict these large-scale data rapidly and effectively becomes a serious problem.

One of the consolidated findings of modern, deep learning approaches is that their joint and unified way of learning feature representations together with their classifiers greatly outperforms conventional feature descriptor & classifier pipelines, whenever enough training data and computation capabilities are available. To more exciting, unifying appealing properties from representation learning as known from deep architectures with the divide-and-conquer principle of decision trees[5], can obtain superior or on-par performance with the state-of-the-art in MNIST and ImageNet dataset. And the authors in [5] have discussed how to integrate them in existing deep learning frameworks such as Caffe[10], MatConvNet[11], etc.

Spark[6] is a fast and general environment for large scale data processing especially for iterative algorithms, developed by the University of California, Berkeley AMP Lab(Algorithms, Machines, and People Lab). For iterative situations, Spark can run programs much faster than Hadoop [7] MapReduce because of resilient distributed dataset(RDD)[8]. Using Spark to do large-scale data analytics can greatly improve the efficiency. However , it is not assigned to support the workloads of existing deep learning networks.

Thus, in order to use Spark to classify and predict the massive and complex astronomy data with the state-of-the-art algorithms effectively, in this paper we discuss the parallel implementation of the deep neural decision tree based on Spark. The rest of this paper is organized as follows. We first introduce the theory of neural decision tree in section 2. Section 3 we illustrated the parallel implementation of the neural decision tree based on Spark. Section 4 presents our experiment environment, as well as accuracy and time results of our algorithm. Finally, Section 5 summarizes our work.

2. Deep Neural Decision Tree

Consider a classification problem with input and (finite) output spaces given by X and Y , respectively. A decision tree is a tree-structured classifier consisting of decision (or split) nodes and prediction (or leaf) nodes. Decision nodes indexed by N are internal nodes of the tree, while prediction nodes indexed by L are the terminal nodes of the tree. Each prediction node $l \in L$ holds a probability distribution π_l over Y . Each decision node $n \in N$ is instead assigned a decision function $d_n(\cdot;\Theta): X \to [0,1]$ parametrized by Θ ,which is responsible for routing samples along the tree. When a sample $x \in X$ reaches a decision node *n* it will be sent to the left or right subtree based on the output of $d_n(x,\Theta)$. Once a sample ends in a leaf node l, the related tree prediction is given by the class-label distribution π_l. In the case of stochastic routings, the leaf predictions will be averaged by the probability of reaching the leaf. Accordingly, the final prediction for sample x from tree T with decision nodes parametrized by Θ is given by

$$P_T[y \mid x, \Theta, \pi] = \sum_{l \in L} \pi_{ly} u_l(x \mid \Theta) . \tag{1}$$

Where $\pi = (\pi_l)_{l \in L}$ and π_{ly} denotes the probability of a sample reaching leaf l to take on class y, while $u_l(x \mid \Theta)$ is regarded as the routing function providing the probability that sample x will reach leaf l. Clearly, $\sum_l u_l(x \mid \Theta) = 1$ for all $x \in X$.

In order to provide an explicit form for the routing function we introduce the following binary relations that depend on the tree's structure: $l \swarrow n$,which is true is l belongs to the left subtree of node n, and $n \searrow l$, which is true if l belongs to the right subtree of node n. We can now exploit these relations to express u_l as follows:

$$u_l(x \mid \Theta) = \prod_{n \in N} d_n(x; \Theta)^{1_{l \swarrow n}} \bar{d}_n(x; \Theta)^{1_{n \searrow l}}, \tag{2}$$

where $\bar{d}_n(x;\Theta) = 1 - d_n(x;\Theta)$, and 1_P is an indicator function conditioned on the argument P. Although the product in (2) runs over all nodes, only decision nodes along the path from the root node to the leaf l contribute to u_l, because for all other nodes $1_{l \swarrow n}$ and $1_{n \searrow l}$ will be both 0(assuming $0^0 = 1$).

In the next we consider decision functions delivering a stochastic routing with decisions defined as follows:

$$d_n(x;\Theta) = \sigma(f_n(x;\Theta)) . \tag{3}$$

where $\sigma(x) = (1 + e^{-x})^{-1}$ is the sigmoid function, and $f_n(\cdot;\Theta) : X \to R$ is a real-value function depending on the sample and the parametrization Θ. Here we take the output of deep belief network output as $f_n(\cdot;\Theta)$. Each output unit of deep belief network corresponding a $f(\cdot;\Theta)$.

2.1. *Learning trees by back-propagation*

Learning a decision tree modeled as described above requires estimating both, the decision node paramentrizations Θ and the leaf predictions π. For their estimation we adhere to the minimum empirical risk principle with respect to a given data set $T \subset X \times Y$ under log-loss, i.e. we search for the minimizers of the following risk term:

$$R(\Theta, \pi; T) = \frac{1}{|T|} \sum_{(x,y)} L(\Theta, \pi; x, y) \quad . \tag{4}$$

where $L(\Theta, \pi; x, y)$ is the log-loss term for training sample $(x, y) \in T$, which is given by

$$L(\Theta, \pi; x, y) = -\log(P_T[y \mid x, \Theta, \pi]) \; . \tag{5}$$

and P_T is defined as in (1).

We consider a two-step optimization strategy, described in the rest of this section, where we alternate updates of π in a way to minimize (4).

2.1.1. *Learning decision nodes*

All decision functions depend on a common parameter Θ, which in turn parametrizes each function f_n in (3). So far, we make no assumptions about the type of functions in f_n, therefore nothing prevents the optimization of the risk with respect Θ for a given π from eventually becoming a difficult and large-scale optimization problem. As an example, Θ could absorb all the parameters of a deep neural network having f_n as one of its output units. For this reason, we will employ a Stochastic Gradient Descent(SGD) approach to minimize the risk with respect to Θ, as commonly done in the context of deep neural networks:

$$\begin{aligned} \Theta^{(t+1)} &= \Theta^{(t)} - \eta \frac{\partial R}{\partial \Theta}(\Theta^{(t)}, \pi; B) \\ &= \Theta^{(t)} - \frac{\eta}{|B|} \sum_{(x,y) \in B} \frac{\partial L}{\partial \Theta}(\Theta^{(t)}, \pi; x, y) \end{aligned} \; . \tag{6}$$

Here, $0 < \eta$ is the learning rate and $B \subseteq T$ is a random subset of samples from the training set. Although not shown explicitly, we additionally consider a momentum term to smooth out the variations of the gradients. The gradient of the loss L with respect to Θ can decomposed by the chain rule as follows

$$\frac{\partial L}{\partial \Theta}(\Theta, \pi; x, y) = \sum_{n \in N} \frac{\partial L(\Theta, \pi; x, y)}{\partial f_n(x; \Theta)} \frac{\partial f_n(x; \Theta)}{\partial \Theta} \; . \tag{7}$$

Here, the gradient term that depends on the decision tree is given by

$$\frac{\partial L(\Theta,\pi;x,y)}{\partial f_n(x;\Theta)} = d_n(x;\Theta)A_{n_r} - \bar{d}_n(x;\Theta)A_{n_l} \quad . \tag{8}$$

Where n_l and n_r indicate the left and right child of node n, respectively, and we define A_m for a generic node $m \in N$ as

$$A_m = \frac{\sum_{l \in L_m} \pi_{ly} u_l(x \mid \Theta)}{P_T[y \mid x, \Theta, \pi]}$$

With $L_m \subseteq L$ we denote the set of leaves held by the subtree rooted in node m. Detailed derivations of (8) can be found in the article[5].

2.1.2. *Learning prediction nodes*

Given the updates for the decision function parameters Θ from the previous subsection, we now consider the problem of minimizing (4) with respect to π when Θ is fixed, i.e.

$$\min_{\pi} R(\Theta,\pi;T) \quad . \tag{9}$$

This is a convex optimization problem and a global solution can be easily recovered. If the whole tree is taken into account, and we are jointly estimating all the leaf predictions.

In order to compute a global minimizer of (9) we propose the following iterative scheme:

$$\pi_{ly}^{(t+1)} = \frac{1}{Z_l^{(t)}} \sum_{(x,y')\in T} \frac{1_{y=y'}\, \pi_{ly}^{(t)} u_l(x \mid \Theta)}{P_T[y \mid x, \Theta, \pi^{(t)}]} \quad . \tag{10}$$

for all $l \in L$ and $y \in Y$, where $Z_l^{(t)}$ is a normalizing factor ensuring that $\sum_y \pi_{ly}^{(t+1)} = 1$. The proof of (10) can be found in the article[5]. The starting point $\pi^{(0)}$ can be arbitrary as long as every element is positive. A typical choice is to start from the uniform distribution in all leaves, i.e. $\pi_{ly}^{(0)} = |Y|^{-1}$. It is interesting to note that the update rule in (10) is a step-size free and it guarantees a strict decrease of the risk at each update until a fixed-point is reached.

As opposed to the updated strategy for Θ , which is based on mini-batches, we adopt an offline learning approach to obtain a more reliable estimate of π , because suboptimal predictions in the leaves have a strong impact on the final prediction. Moreover, we interleave the update of π with a whole epoch of stochastic updates of Θ as described in the previous subsection.

3. The Parallelization of Deep Neural Decision Tree

In the last section we have discussed the theory about deep neural decision tree. This section we will focus on the implementation of this model based on Spark. It contains with several phases in processing workflow.

1) *Phase I:* we load training datasets from HDFS into the Spark RDD and make good use of cluster memory.

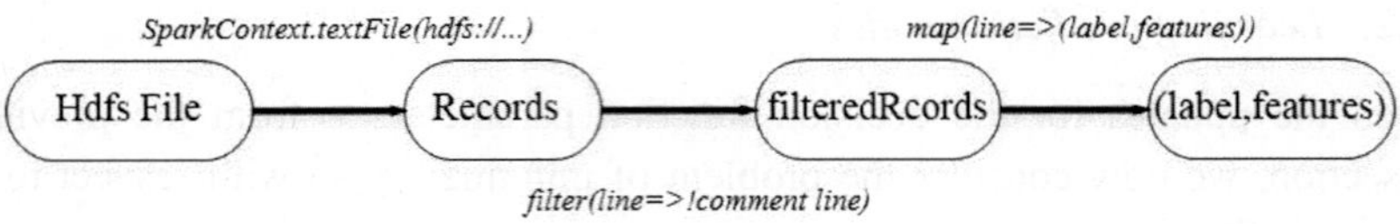

Fig. 1. Transform the dataset into Spark RDD and separate the label and features.

As illustrated in Fig. 1, first, the training dataset will be transformed into Spark RDD format by using a textFile() function. Then a filter() function will be applied on each of records to filter the comment lines . When the filter process is finished, the map() function is applied to transform all records to the (label, features) pairs, which is the input for the deep neural tree to predict the output of X as illustrated in Fig. 2. In Fig. 2 what we should pay an attention to is that BDM means the DenseMatrix in the Breeze library (The same in the following).

2) *Phase II:* in this phase, we initialize the weights of the deep belief network[9] and class-label distriburion for all leafs, the depth of tree, the architecture of network. Then we use map() function to assign all the records to different executors to predict the class-label corresponding to specified x . In all the processing procedure, we also make good use of the breeze library to run the matrix operation in a parallel way, as described in Fig. 2. The getRouting() function returns the routing function matrix for all leafs and get_probabilities_ for() function returns the prediction probability for all labels in Y . Then labelofMax() function is applied to get index of the max prediction probability which is regarded as the final predict class-label corresponding to x .

Algorithm 1 Predict Y For X using Deep Neural Decision Tree Based Spark

```
input: Testset : RDD[(BDM[Double], BDM[Double])]
output: set of label
val q = Testset.map{f =>
        val features = f._1
        val nna = ArrayBuffer[BDM[Double]]()
        val Bm1 = new BDM(features.rows, 1, Array.fill(features.rows * 1)(1.0))
        val features2 = BDM.horzcat(Bm1, features)
        val nna+ = features2
        for (j <- 1 to layer_cnt - 1) {
           val A1 = nna(j - 1)
           val W1 = nn_W(j - 1)
           val aw1 = A1 * W1.t
           val nnai1 = sigmoid(aw1)
           val Bm1 = BDM.ones[Double](nnai1.rows, 1)
           val nnai2 = if(j == layer_cnt - 1) nnai1 else BDM.horzcat(Bm1, nnai1)
           nna += nnai2            }
        val routing = getRouting(nna(layer_cnt - 1), depth_of_tree)
        val predict_prob = get_probabilities_for(leaf_pi, routing)
         labelofMax(predict_prob)
    }
```

Fig. 2. Predict the class-label for the corresponding x using the parallel tree model.

The parallelization of the getRouting() function which is not show explicitly in Fig. 2 can be illustrated in Fig. 3. We start from the root by setting $u_T = 1$, and for each node $n \in N$ that we visit in breadth-first order we set $u_{nl} = d_n(x;\Theta)u_n$ and $u_{nr} = \bar{d}_n(x;\Theta)u_n$. At the end, we can read from the leaves the desired values of the routing function. In the detailed implementation, we separated all the decision nodes at the same level into two parts. The nodes belong to the left subtree of their parent nodes are grouped into a matrix, and the others another matrix. And then multiply them respectively by the last u_T matrix by using the matrix elementwise multiplication. Finally we merged the two matrix as a matrix according to the order of nodes at this level. When we have get the value of the routing function, we use the leaf π matrix with it to get the predict probabilities of class-label by performing matrix multiplication.

Algorithm 2 Calculate the routing function for a record to reache all the leafs of the tree

```
input: nnout : BDM[Double], depth_of_tree : Int
output: routingfunction
var lastoffset = 0
var nextoffset = 1
var leftrout = nnout(::, 0).toDenseMatrix
var rightrout = (leftrout − 1.0) * (−1.0)
val lastTensor = BDM.horzcat(leftrout, rightrout)
for (i < − 1 to depth_of_tree − 2){
    val lastWidth = 1 << i
    lastoffset = nextoffset
    nextoffset+ = lastWidth
    val tensor = nnout(::, lastoffsettonextoffset − 1).toDenseMatrix
    val leftTensor = tensor : * lastTensor
    val rightTensor = ((tensor − 1.0) * (−1.0)) : *lastTensor
    lastTensor = BDM.horzcat(leftTensor(::, 0).toDenseMatrix, rightTensor(::, 0).toDenseMatrix)
    for (j < − 1 to leftTensor.cols − 1){
      val leftcol = leftTensor(::, j).toDenseMatrix.reshape(leftTensor.rows, 1)
      val rightcol = rightTensor(::, j).toDenseMatrix.reshape(rightTensor.rows, 1) }
}
val routingMatrix = lastTensor
routingMatrix
```

Fig. 3. The parallelization of routing function for a record to reaches all the leafs.

3) *Phase III:* in the last phase, we have described the parallelization of computing the values of the routing function $u_l(x;\Theta)$ and the value of the tree prediction $P_T[y|x,\Theta,\pi]$ for each sample (x,y) in the training set. Now we consider the parallelization of updating the leaf distribution π and the parameter Θ by back-propagation. First, we consider the parallelization of π. It can be illustrated as Fig. 4. At the start, a map() function is applied to the RDD training set to get the new π for every sample. And then treeAggregate() function to aggregate the elements of each partition of RDD training set, calculate the sum of π, finally return the averaged and normalized π as the updating value.

Next, we consider the parallelization of updating θ. It is similar to the update of π and can be illustrated as Fig. 5. First, it takes the result of the forward pass (Fig. 2) and the neural network weights as the input, then uses map() function to assign every record in the RDD set to different executors calculate the gradient of the loss L which has been defined in (5), and pass gradient to the last network to train, this part can take reference of [9]. For a local computing node, calculating the gradient of the loss L need the function of getAm( ) and gradOntheta( ).

Algorithm 3 update pi one iter

```
input: train_d : RDD[NDTLabel], last_pi : BDM[Double]
output: next_pi
val train_d1 = train_d.map{f =>
        val label_to_int = f.label.data(0).toInt
        val prob_of_label = f.predict
        val routing = f.routfunc
        val get_pi_on_record = (last_pi(::, label_to_int).toDenseMatrix :* rf.t)/prob_of_label(0, label_to_int)
        last_pi(::, label_to_int) = get_pi_on_record.toDenseVector
        last_pi    }
val init_pi = BDM.zeros[Double](leaf_pi.rows, leaf_pi.cols)
val(pisum, count) = train_d1.treeAggregate((init_pi, 0L))(
        seqOp = (c, v) => {
          val m1 = c._1
          val m2 = m1 + v
          (m2, c._2 + 1)      },
        combOp = (c1, c2) => {
          val m1 = c._1
          val m2 = c._2
          val m3 = m1 + m2
        (m3, c1._2 + c1._2 )      })
val piav = pisum/count.toDouble
val pisum_per_row = Bsum(piav(*, ::))
val next_pi = piav(*, ::) : /pisum_per_row
next_pi            }
```

Fig. 4. The parallelization of updating pi in every iteration.

```
Algorithm 4 Learn tree by back propagation
input: dNDTff : RDD[NDTLabel], nn_W[Array[BDM[Double]]
output: the gradient for all theta
val train_d1 = dNDTff.map{f =>
        val nna = f.nna
        val prob_of_label = f.predict
        val routing = f.routfunc
        val label = f.label.data(0).toInt
        val dn = ArrayBuffer[BDM[Double]]()
        val amatrix = getAm(laef_pi, prob_of_label, routing, depth_of_tree, label)
        val nndn = gradOntheta(nna(layer_cnt − 1), amatrix, depth_of_tree)
        dn+ = nndn
        (f, dn)     }
val train_d2 = train_d1.map{f =>
        val nna = f._1.nna
        val di = f._2
        for(i <− (layer_cnt − 2) to 1 by − 1) {
           val nnd_act = nn_a(i) :* (nn_a(i) * (−1.0) + 1.0)
           val W1|= nn_W(i)
           val nndi1 = if(i + 1 == layer_cnt − 1){
                          val di1 = (di(layer_cnt − 2 − i) * W1) : *nnd_act
                          di1            }
                       else{
                          val di1 = di(layer_cnt − 2 − i)(::, 1 to − 1)
                          val di2 = (di1 * W1) : *nnd_act
                          di2            }
           di += nndi1}
        di += BDM.zeros(1, 1)
        val dw = ArrayBuffer[BDM[Double]]()
        for (i <− 0 to layer_cnt − 1){
           val nndW = if(i + 1 == layer_cnt − 1){
                          (di(layer_cnt − 2 − i).t) * nna(i)
                                                  }
                       else{
                          (di(layer_cnt − 2 − i)(::, 1 to − 1)).t * nna(i)
                          }
           dw+ = nndW              }
        (f._1, di, dw) }
val train_d3 = train_d2.map{f._3 }
use treeAggregate like Algorithm 5 to calculate the sum and average of Gradient.
return the average of gradient for all thetas.}
```

Fig. 5. The parallelization of updating Θ for a mini-batch RDD training set.

They are responding to A_m and the formular (8) respectively as defined in section 2. And the parallelization of the getAm( ) and the gradOntheta( ) function can be illustrated as Fig. 6 and Fig. 7, respectively. They also use the matrix and breadth-first strategy to make use of the cores in a local computing node.

Algorithm 5 Calculate Am For a Generic Node m

input: *leaf_pi : BDM[Double], predict_prob : BDM[Double], routing : BDM[Double]*
output: *The Am matrix for all decision nodes*

```
var leafPredict = leaf_pi(::, *) : *routing.toDenseVector
    leafPredict = leafPredict.t
    leafPredict = leafPredict.toDenseMatrix
for (i <- 1 to depth_of_tree) {
    val leftchild = leafPredict(::, 0 to leafPredict.cols - 1 by 2)
    val rightchild = leafPredict(::, 1 to leafPredict.cols - 1 by 2)
    leafPredict = leftchild + rightchild
    amatrix = BDM.horzcat(leafPredict, amatrix)}
amatrix = amatrix.t
val amatrix1 = amatrix(*, ::) : /predictProb.toDenseVector
val amatrix2 = amatrix1(::, label).toDenseMatrix
amatrix2.t
```

Fig. 6. The parallelization of getAm( ) function.

Algorithm 6 Calculate the gradient of the loss L with respect to theta

input: *nnout : BDM[Double], Amatrix : BDM[Double]*
output: *Thegradientoftheta*

```
var leftchild = leftChildIndex(1) - 1
var rightchild = rightChildIndex(1) - 1
var dw = nnout(0, 0) * Amatrix(rightchild, 0) - (1.0 - nnout(0, 0)) * Amatrix(leftchild, 0)
var dwm = BDM(dw)
val numdeciNodes = (1 << (depth_of_tree - 1)) - 1
for (i <- 2 to numdeciNodes) {
    leftchild = leftChildIndex(i) - 1
    rightchild = rightChildIndex(i) - 1
    dw = nnout(0, i - 1) * Amatrix(rightchild, 0) - (1.0 - nnout(0, i - 1)) * Amatrix(leftchild, 0)
    dwm = BDM.horzcat(dwm, BDM(dw))}
dwm
```

Fig. 7. The parallelization of gradOntheta( ) function.

Algorithm 7 Training decision tree model

input: *training_data : RDD[(BDM[Double], BDM[Double])*
output: *The deep neural decision tree model*

```
Initial weights nn_w
Initial pi of the leafs
for (i < -1 to numepochs){
    broadcast(nn_w)
    perform Algorithm 1 with training_data to get the probability of y, the routing function
    perform Algorithm 3 to update pi
    for(j < -1 to numbatchs){
        get the batch data from training_data
        perform Algorithm 1 with batch data to get the probability of label, the routing function
        perform Algorithm 4 to update weights}
    updating the learning rate for weights
    }
return the deep neural model with the pi and weights
```

Fig. 8. Training decision tree model.

4) *Phase IV:* in the final part. We perform the iteration procedure to update π and Θ, and finally return all the update parameters to the model to predict a record as described in Fig. 2. As Spark is developed for iterative algorithms and interactive data mining, there is no doubts that the iteration in the Spark cluster can run effectively. The iteration can be described as Fig. 8.

4. Experiments

Our experiment illustrate the performance of this deep neural decision tree in star/galaxy classification problem and the speedup for the algorithm running on the Spark cluster.

In order to evaluate our algorithm performance on the star/galaxy classification problem better, we use the same star/galaxy dataset which can be selected from the SDSS Legacy survey by simple Structured Query Language(SQL) queries and calculate the completeness function for the test data set in a magnitude interval as Vasconcellos described in his article [1]. Here, we make a comparison between deep neural decision tree and the functional tree which would be the best classifier for star/galaxy separation explored by Vasconcellos. As illustrated in Table 1, it is obviously the deep neural decision tree can have higher completeness than the functional tree, so we can strongly believe that combining the representation learning method and decision tree together helps to improve completeness of star/galaxy classification.

Moreover, when we used the dataset($20.5 \le r \le 21$, about 3700 records) to execute the experiments on the Spark Cluster on six computers, including 1 master, 5 workers. We changed the number of computing nodes in the cluster

Table 1. The completeness of our neural decision tree on SDSS DR7 Star/Galaxy data set compared with functional tree used by Vasconcellos.

Data Set	Completeness obtained by neural decision tree(%)	Completeness obtained by functional tree(%)
$19 \le r \le 21$[a]	90.68($\pm$2.04)	84.98($\pm$1.08)
$20.5 \le r \le 21$[b]	78.55($\pm$5.32)	74.04($\pm$8.45)

Note:

[a]The SDSS-DR7 star/galaxy records in the magnitude [19.0,21.0], details see [1].

[b]The SDSS-DR7 star/galaxy records in the magnitude [20.5,21.0], details see [1].

and obtained the relationship between the execution time of deep neural decision tree with the number of computing nodes varying as illustrated in Fig. 9. As can be seen from the figure, although the data size is very small, it also can speed up more when training the tree model. As the star/galaxy data set with $19 \leq r \leq 21$ in a single computing node should take a lot of time and may go to wrong as the computer out of memory. So we evaluate the speedup of this algorithm when using star/galaxy data set $19 \leq r \leq 21$ just increase the cores and memory of each node. As time limited, we just took two records on this dataset. When the Spark Cluster with each node a Intel(R) core(TM) 3.40GHz CPU and 1 Gbytes memory, it takes 6932.512 seconds to train and test the tree model. When the Spark Cluster with each node 2 Intel(R) core(TM) 3.40GHz CPU and 12Gbytes memory, it just takes 2004.658 seconds. Thus, we can draw a conclusion that when the data is massive, the neural decision tree runs on spark can dramatically decrease the training time.

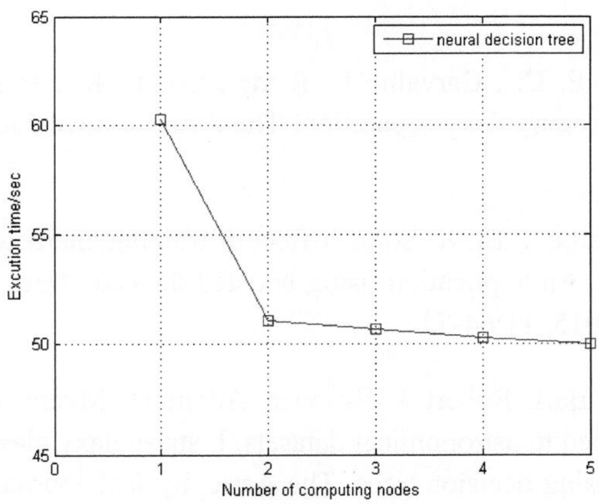

Fig. 9. The execution time of deep neural decision tree with the number of computing nodes varying.

5. Conclusions

In this paper we have shown how to model and train stochastic, differentiable decision tree based on Spark. Prevailing approaches for decision tree training typically operate in a greedy and local manner and single computer, making representation learning and massive data processing impossible. To overcome this problem, we introduced stochastic routing for decision tree, enabling split node parameter learning via back-propagation. By implementing it on Spark, we can dramatically decrease the training time of the model with massive training data. We do some experiments on the SDSS star/galaxy data set, and find it have superior performance than the traditional tree classifiers.

Acknowledgments

This work is supported by the National Natural Science Foundation of China (No. 61362006 and No. 61261017), Guangxi Natural Science Foundation (2013GXNSFAA019334), Foundation of Guangxi Key Laboratory of Wireless Wideband Communication & Signal Processing (GXKL0614202 and GXKL0614101), Key Lab of Cognitive Radio & Information Processing, Ministry of Education (2013ZR08, CRKL150112), Innovation Project of GUET Graduate Education(YJCXS201517), Foundation of Science & Technology on Information Transmission & Dissemination in Communication Networks Lab(ITD-U14008/KX142600015 (2014)).

References

1. Vasconcellos E. C. , Carvalho R. R. de , Gal R. R. , et al. Decision tree classifiers for star/galaxy separation, The Astronomical Journal, 2011, 141: 182-191

2. I. Sevilla-Noarbe, P.Etayo-Sotos. Effect of training characteristics on object classification: An application using boosted decision trees, Astronomy and computing, 2015, 11:64-72

3. Nicholas M. Ball, Robert J. Brunner, Adam D. Myers. Robust machine learning applied to astronomical datasets. I. star-galaxy classification of the SDSS DR3 using decision trees. The Astrophysical Journal, 2006,650:497-509.

4. V.Subhashini, Data mining techniques to classify astronomy objects. NITK Surathkal, 2009.

5. P. Kontschieder, M. Fiterau, A. Crimisi, et al. Deep Neural Decision Forests. In (ICCV), 2015.12

6. Apache spark – lighting-fast cluster computing. URL https://spark.apache.org

7. Hadoop. URL http://hadoop.apache.org

8. M. Zaharia, M. Chowdhury, T. Das, et al. Resilient distributed datasets: a fault-tolerant abstraction for in-memory cluster computing. Technical Report No. UCB/EECS-2011-82. 2011.

9. SparkMLlibDeepLearn. URL https://github.com/sunbow1/SparkMlibDeepLearn.

10. Y.Jia, E. Shelhamer, J. Donahue, et al. Caffe: Convolutional architecture for fast feature embedding. *arXiv preprintarXiv:1408.5093*, 2014. 2

11. A. Vedaldi and K. Lenc. Matconvnet-convolutional neural networks for matlab. CoRR, abs/1412.4564, 2014. 2,6

Session 6

Theory and Software Engineering

Development on Software of Overhead Transmission Line Foundation Design

Qiang CUI

Transmission line engineering department, China Electric Power Research Institute, Beijing, China

E-mail:everjsl@126.com

Sheng-kui LIU

Gan Su Electric Power Design Institute, China, 730050 Lanzhou, Gansu Province, China

E-mail: lanzhoulsk123@163.com

Xian-long LU

Transmission line engineering department, China Electric Power Research Institute, Beijing, China

E-mail:luxianlong@163.com

In order to investigate the actuality and demand of transmission line tower foundation, this paper proposes an engineering design management software which comprises "input of foundation parameters", "design method selection", "design parameters selection", "foundation type selection", "output of design calculation sheets", "output of working drawing" using Visual Basic and Visual C++ developing environment and AutoCAD ObjectARX and VBA Office programming technology. The software can precede foundation parameters calls, inquiry of foundation type selection, foundation optimal design and design result batch output. This software provides a reasonable, precise, fast and economic design tools for the designers, thus to realize the overhead transmission lines tower system, basic engineering design innovation, safety and economic goals.

Keywords: Tower foundation; Engineering design management software; Ground soil and foundation parameters database; Optimization design, Parametric drawing.

1. Introduction

Overhead transmission line project has the industrial characteristics of complicated load conditions, diversified topography and landform and a large number of foundations. Currently, DL/T5219—2014<Technical Regulation for Designing Foundation of Overhead Transmission Line>[1] is the main basis for the engineering design of tower foundation. With the vigorous construction of high-tension projects in China in recent years, the transmission lines gradually develop towards the direction of "large scale, large cross section and large load", and more and more new foundations are applied in the engineering design and construction, while the design methods of many new foundations are not mentioned in the above Regulation, so the supporting calculation methods and software are urgently needed to be provided to the design personnel for purpose of design.

Currently, as the main technical means in the engineering design field, the computer-aided technology replaces the traditional manual design and has the advantages of high efficiency, speediness and convenience and high accuracy. At present, designers compile some design calculation software in accordance with the above Regulation and in combination with the design experience, which solves the engineering problems[2-5]. However, these software adopts the "one-to-one" design thought, namely they face the design, calculation and output of single foundation, so this will easily increase the working strength and error rate of designers. For this reason, an engineering design management software was developed in this paper, which took a transmission line project as object instead of a single foundation in the past.

2. General Framework of Software

2.1. *Software overview*

The software is developed utilizing VB and VC++, regards projects as the design object, uses the cost of foundation body as the target function and integrates the AUTOCAD workstation, Microsoft Office and other software environment and technique as a whole. The software has the functions of "inquiry and calling of foundation database →type selection of foundation → comparison and selection of design methods → determination of design parameters → optimized design of foundation → preparation of design calculations → mapping of working drawings".

2.2. *Composition structure and main functions of software*

Software consists of basis database function zone of foundation, typical foundation optimization and design function zone, optimized design calculation result output function zone and online help function zone, as shown in the figure 1. These 4 parts are not only mutually independent, but also interconnected with each other.

Basis database function zone of foundation. Basis database function zone of foundation integrates the common design parameters of various rocks and soils. Users can edit, call and inquire the geological parameters necessary for design.

Typical foundation optimization and design function zone. Typical foundation optimization and design function zone is the core function zone of software system. Users can implement the optimized calculation of the foundation soil stability, structural reinforcement, etc. and finally propose the most economic and profitable design scheme(For details, see the figure 2).

Optimized design calculation result output function zone. Users can output the calculation sheets and working drawings in batches according to the demands after completing the foundation design, and customize the output contents of the calculation sheet before output.

Online help function zone. Users can call the online help in the software to obtain technical support in case of having operation doubts during the use of software.

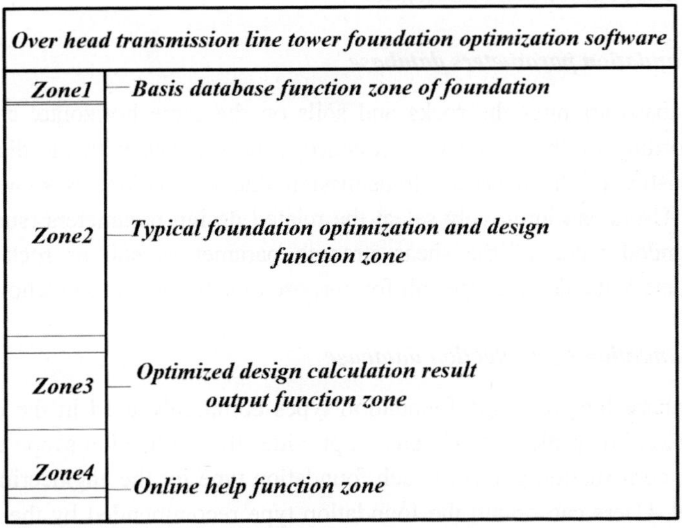

Fig. 1. Basis database function zone of software.

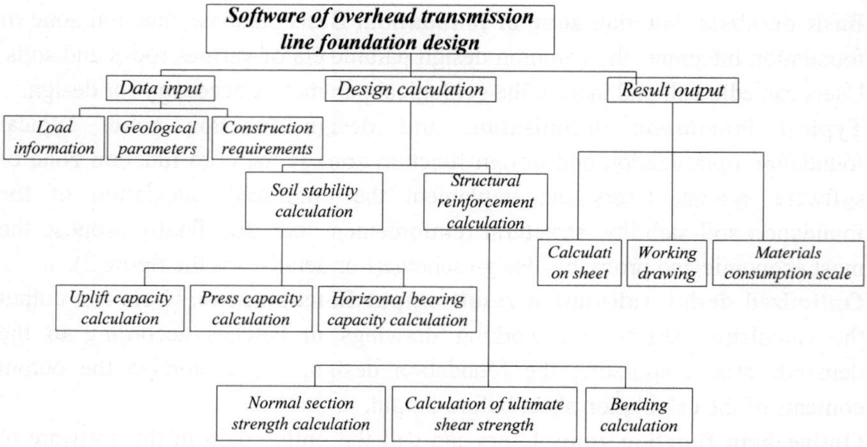

Fig. 2. The calculation content and step of software.

3. General Framework of Software

3.1. *Foundation parameters database*

This database arranges the rocks and soils on the same horizontal coordinate axis according to "hard → soft" sequence in accordance with the distribution characteristics of the overhead transmission line foundation, as shown in the figure 3. Users can intuitively select the related design parameters (such as the recommended value of the shear strength parameters, soil or rock density, porosity, etc.) of a certain type soil for purpose of subsequent foundation design.

3.2. *Foundation type selection database*

This database integrates the foundation types commonly used in the overhead transmission line projects of China and provides the application scope and main design & construction points of each foundation type for the engineering design personnel. Users can obtain the foundation type recommended by the software by importing in the load conditions of tower foundation, geological parameters and environmental conditions.

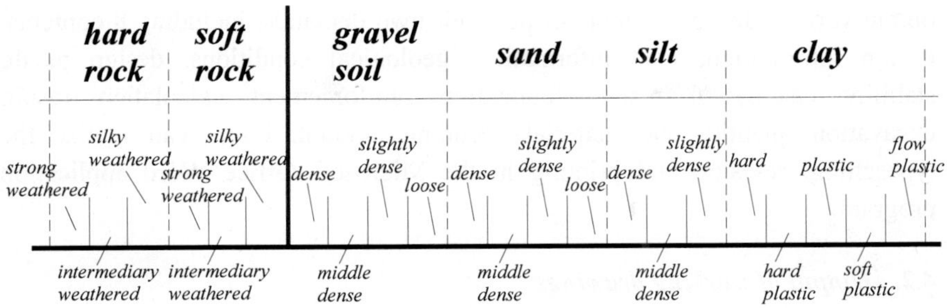

Fig. 3. Foundation parameters database of software system.

In accordance with the evaluation characteristics of different parameters, the software set 4 types of parameter input methods: manual input in text box, selection of table parameters, selection of pull-down list and file import.

Prior to design calculation, the software will implement self-check of the users' input parameters. When certain input parameter has mistaken, the software will mark it at the corresponding location to remind the user of making correction and revision.

4. Output of design results

4.1. *Output of design calculation sheet*

Calculation sheet is the file used by the designers to record the design conditions, calculation result, design scheme and other important information and the most direct reflection of the design result of tower foundation. The software adopts the VBA (Visual Basic for Application) programming technique to implement the secondary development on the Office platform and realize the automatic generation of design calculation sheet for the tower foundation of overhead transmission line.

VBA technology is the built-in programming language in the Microsoft Office integrated office software and a new generation of standard macro language. It is developed on the basis of VB and has a good compatibility with VB. VBA reading of Office Word documents is controlled through the following codes:

Dim doc As Word. Application//define the Office Word object in VBA.
Set doc = Create Object("word. Application")//create new Word program
doc. Documents. Add//create a new blank document

Software provides the functions of automatic customization of the output format and content of calculation sheet for the users. Users can customize and output various design contents as per their own demands, including 8 contents: design information, load information, geological conditions, design result, stability calculation result, foundation reinforcement calculation result, excavation quantity and material spending amount. Users can realize the typesetting, revision and printing in the Microsoft Office Word application program.

4.2. *Output of working drawings*

The software adopts the technology combining the VC++ and ObjectARX and implements the parameter transferring through the external data interface and foundation design module. The whole preparation process of working drawings can be summarized as: preparation of foundation design template→start the AutoCAD→call the ARX file drawing and extraction→implement the parameterized drawing through the manner of component drive and dimension drive on the basis of the template.

5. Conclusion

Main conclusions of this paper are as follows:

(1) Adopt the technique combining VB and ADO to prepare the foundation parameters database. This database arrange the typical foundation soil of China on the same horizontal coordinate axis according to "hard → soft" principle, and users can call and inquire the parameters required for design in accordance with the foundation conditions of the foundation bearing stratum. The typical foundation type database provided by the software to the users integrates the characteristics and application scope of various typical foundations and users can obtain the foundation types recommended by the software through the load condition, geological parameters and environmental conditions.

(2) The software provides a variety of parameter input methods and has the function of verifying the correctness of parameters. The foundation design regards the project as the object, and the design conditions and design information are automatically saved in the project file. Users can call, modify and output all foundation recorded in the project after completing the design.

(3) The software adopts the Visual C++ combined with ObjectARX technique to develop the parameterized drawing module. The parameterized drawing process can be summarized as the completion of adding, editing and deletion of geometric dimension parameter of foundation through the component drive and data drive, so as to finally prepare the project construction drawings.

Acknowledgments

We acknowledge the Science and Technology project of State Grid of China under Grant No.SGSC0000KXKJ1300485.

References

1. Electric Industry Standard of People's Republic of China. Technical regulation for designing foundation of overhead transmission line (DL/T 5219-2014) [S]. Beijing, China Electric Power Press, 2014, in Chinese.
2. Jian-minJia, PengZeng. *Shanxi Electric Power*, 2000, 4(93), pp.32-33, in Chinese.
3. Meng-qiZhang ,Jian-minJia , Qing Guo. *Electric Power Construction*, 2001, 22 (4): pp.44-46, in Chinese.
4. HuiLi, Optimization design CAD system of bore pile foundation of linear tower [D], Chengdu, *Southwest Jiaotong University*, 2006, in Chinese.
5. Pei-quanLiang, Xiao-huaJing. *Electric Power Construction*, 2003, 24 (4): pp. 37-41, in Chinese.

e-CRT: An Embedded Code Reverse Technology

Zhen-xiang LI, Qing LIU and Wei-xin ZHANG*,
University Department, University Name, Tianjin Electric Power Research Institute, Tianjin, 300000 City, China
**E-mail: zhangweixin_cn@126.com*

Jin-shuo LIU† and Ya-bo XU
Computer School, Wuhan University, Wuhan, 430072, China
†Email: liujinshuo@whu.edu.cn

The study of code reverse engineering requires the integration of disassembly and decompiling key technologies. As independent adoption of disassembler and decompiler causes decompiling input restriction, e-CRT is implemented in this paper to overcome this issue. Its sound effects are presented not only through theoretical foundation but also in a specific test case of the smart meter embedded device

Keywords: Code reverse engineering; E-CRT; Smart meter test.

1. Introduction

As an important branch of reverse engineering, code reverse engineering [1]has long been a hot issue in the software engineering field. It targets binary code of ultimate program and takes conversion from machine code to high-level language as a core mission. Furthermore, two kinds of key technologies—disassemble and decompile are involved.

What is noteworthy is that system environment has not been restrained during the study of code reverse technology before. Implementation of embedded Code Reverse Technology (e-CRT) in this paper would not only help to expand application scope of code reverse engineering, but provide new idea for embedded software function test.

Embedded System[2] is a class of special-purpose computer system which focuses on the application and has strict requirements on function, reliability, cost, volume, power consumption, etc. With rather strong independence and rigorous hardware environment, implementation of code reverse technology of this platform is often difficult.

---

† Correspondence author.

The rest of the paper is organized as follows. Related work is discussed in section 2, section 3 talks about our challenge and theoretical analysis, main introduction of e-CRT is illustrated. Disassemble and decompile module is separately elaborated in section 3.1. Finally experimental statistics are presented and direction of future work is proposed in section 4 and 5.

2. Related Works

Disassembly research concentrates on algorithm improvements at home and abroad, such as static disassembly combined with machine learning[3], error detection via control flow [4], mixed disassembly method[5], disassembly based on speculation [6], etc.

Meanwhile, study of decompilation is embodied in: on one hand, melioration of existing decompilers and performance evaluation afterwards, for example, TyDec[7]and Expanded-Desquirr[8]; on the other hand, decompilation of assembly instructions with given restraint, for instance, the nonlinear instruction decompile algorithm[9] and differencing algorithm for decompilation code and source code[10].

Studies above have indeed proved validity and scientificity of disassembly and decompilation. However, as decompilationis actually the follow-up work of disassembly, knowledge module[11], which means some qualifications of the input, should be explicit before decompilation. If disassembly is not associated together with decompilation, free decompilation—decompile with arbitrary conditions, would not complete.

This paper presents an implementation scheme of e-CRT whereby free decompilation on the basis of embedded systems can be fulfilled. Taking smart meters as an example, the experimental results also show superiority of code reverse device designed by the authors.

3. e-CRT

Figure 1 presents main infrastructure of this procedure. The assembly instruction block is generated as the output file and it varies according to the structure of e-CRT. Disassembler takes machine code section as input, and knowledge module contains configuration information about embedded OS and related instruction set.

Decompiler analyzes syntax notations and semantic structure of target block. Code structure analysis technology [11,12] is adopted to generate control flow graph (CFG), data flow graph (DFG) and function call graph (FCG). In conclusion, high-level program segment is organized by comprehensive analysis of the graphs.

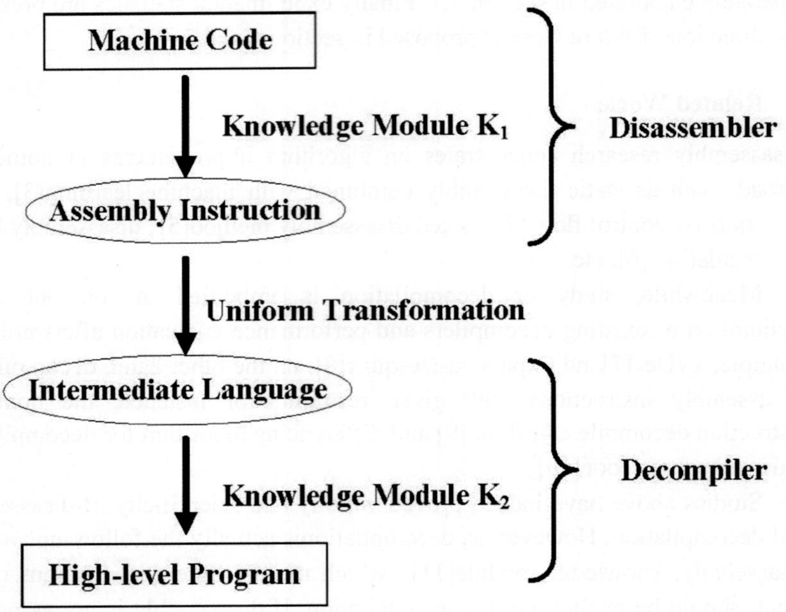

Fig. 1. Structure chart of e-CRT

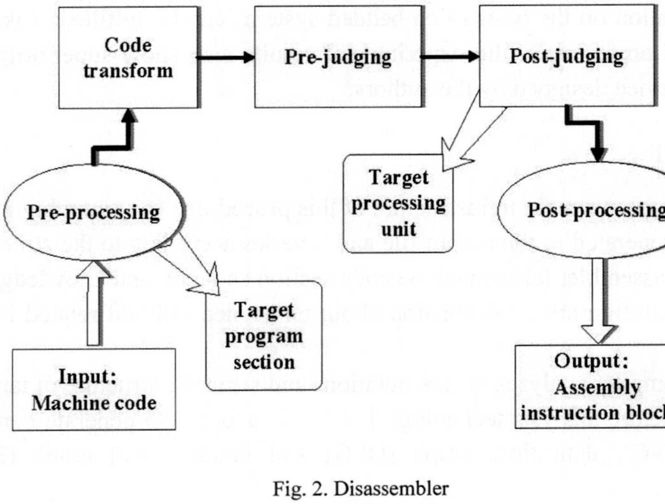

Fig. 2. Disassembler

3.1. *Disassembler*

As shown in figure 2, this disassembler regards machine code section as input, treats

assembly instruction block as output and performs following steps:

Pre-processing of machine code section includes machine code endian adjustment [13], instruction and data blocks separation and target section normalization. Afterwards a target program section which conforms to the next input format is generated.

Code transformation function translates 01 strings into assembly instructions on the basis of knowledge module K1. Owing to embedded memory capacity limit, often it's not possible to complete translation once. Thus, target program section is segmented to proper size and transformed into assembly instruction blocks a couple of times.

Pre-judging of assembly instruction blocks mainly discards syntactically incorrect instructions according to K1. Here define incorrect instructions as instructions which deviate from syntactic rules based on K1.

Post-judging function summarize semantics of instruction block generated in last step to obtain ideal target processing unit that matches best with input machine code section. Alternative targets stem from K1 and TOPSIS decision algorithm[14]is adopted here.

Finally, Post-processing module is implemented to optimize current assembly instruction block.

Compared with previous ones, this disassembler is able to acquire hardware configuration information that accords with machine code as well as output assembly instruction block.*3.2 Decompiler*

The decompiler translates assembly instruction block into uniform intermediate language by substitute regulation shown in Table 1.

Table 1 Substitute rules between assembly and intermediate instruction.

Instruction type	Assembly instruction	Intermediate representation

Assignment	ADD OP1, OP2
	SUB OP3, OP4
	......
		OP1= OP1+OP2
		OP3= OP3-OP4
		......

Unconditional jump	JMP LABEL	GOTO LABEL
Conditional jump	JC, JNC, JE, JZ, JNZ......	Discussed in control flow analysis step.
Procedure call	CALL	Construct a function.
Return	RET, IRET......	RET
Stack	PUSH, POP	PUSH, POP
Other	AAA, DAA......	None

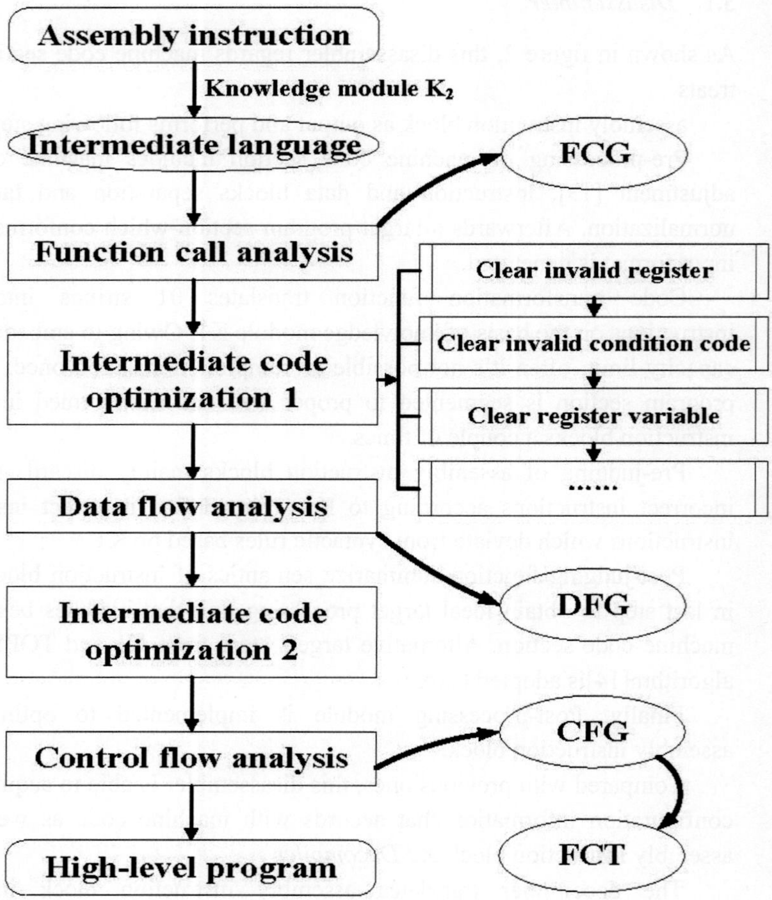

Fig 3. Decompiler.

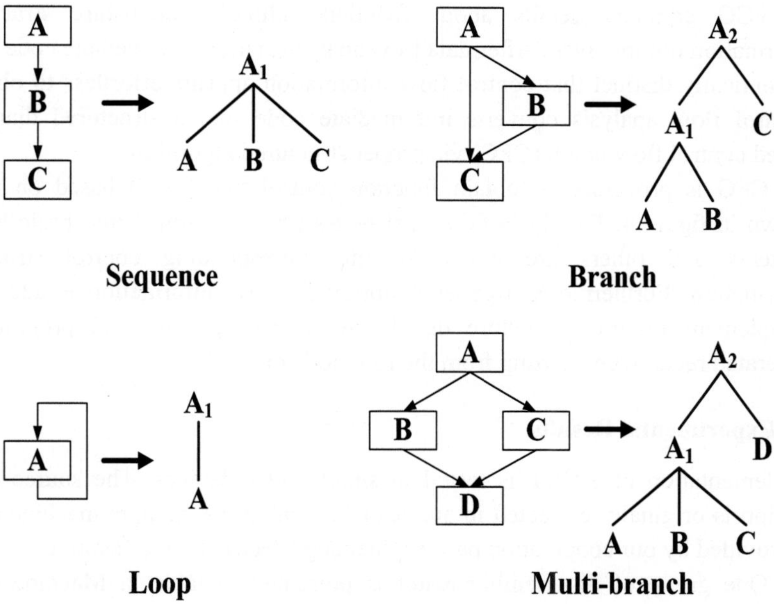

Fig. 4. CFG to FCT templates.

Consequently K2 keeps unchanged during decompiling procedure. The overall process of decompilation is revealed in figure 3. Once intermediate language is formed, target instruction blocks become syntactically unambiguous. For each subroutine, a basic block is built. The entire intermediate representation is transformed into a function call graph (FCG).

A variable is treated as invalid when it has not been used after definition. Often invalid variables are meaningless and can be swept out. Intermediate code optimization 1 is performed to clear invalid register, invalid condition code, register variables, redundant and transition instructions. Expressions with more than two operands are imported to initially shape high-level concept.

To ensure coherence of global data and variable, decompiler collects information about register and condition code throughout target instructions and spread it out across basic blocks. This multi-block information gathering procedure is titled as data flow analysis. A data flow graph (DFG) is formed and it contains information described above. With DFG in hand, global data and variable information are applied into intermediate code, for instance, displacing variable mnemonic, etc. That is exactly the objective of Intermediate code optimization 2.

FCG contains details about function calling relationship, structural information not involved. After data flow analysis, target intermediate code is so semantically distinct that control flow information appears effortless to obtain. Control flow analysis converts intermediate code into a structured diagram called control flow graph (CFG) via proper structured algorithm.

CFG is processed to obtain function control tree (FCT) based on rules shown in figure 4. Finally in FCT, leaf nodes are transformed into basic block contents and others are translated into corresponding control structure information. Furthermore, high-level library function information is added to complement program structure details. As a result, high-level program is generated recursively starting from the root node of FCT.

4. Experimental Results

Implementation of e-CRT is tested in smart meter devices. The source code section is originally extracted in ammeter internal chips. Sample machine code is provided by our cooperation partner Zhejiang Electric Power Institute.

One group of disassembly result is presented in table 2. Machine code section is stored in file sourcecode.mot. File asciicode.txt contains pre-processing result with extended ASCII. After code transformation, file binarycode.txt is generated. Assembly block is stored in file assemblycode.txt and ultimate instructions are included in file optimizedcode.txt.

Table 2. Template code disassembly result.

File	Size(KB)	Time(ms)	Rate(%)
sourcecode.mot	185	-	-
asciicode.txt	225	31	-
binarycode.txt	136	28	60.44
assemblycode.txt	841	7096	-
optimizedcode.txt	537	10258	63.85

Column 2 presents size of input and related intermediate file and column 3 shows time to generate them. Column 4 indicates a reduced size rate after pre-processing and post-judging optimization.

Decompilation is applied in three types of processing unit—Renesas M16C, 78k/0 and Intel 8051. Summary outcome is shown in table 3.

Table 3. Decompiling result.

Type	ω_1(%)	ω_2(%)	Pe(%)
Renesas M16C	13.23	86.77	90.04
Renesas 78k/0	60.64	39.36	90.61
Intel 8051	40.74	59.26	75.86

Column ω1 shows percentage of simple statements in the overall program segment. And similarly, column ω2 shows percentage of compound statements. The "Pe" column presents accurate rate of decompiling results in contrast to actual application program.

5. Conclusion

This paper discusses main idea and frame of e-CRT—embedded Code Reverse Technology. Aiming at decompiling input restriction, a detailed theoretical analysis is carried out and the concept of "free decompile" is proposed. Our implementation of e-CRT coordinates knowledge module with disassembler and decompiler, which ensures veracity of free decompiling and result consistency. Experimental data upon smart meter—a typical embedded device has confirmed the validity of our implementation to meet free decompiling demand.

Future research directions include improvement and integration of algorithms involved in e-CRT and enhancement of result accuracy.

Acknowledgments

This work is supported by National Science Foundation of China 61303214.

References

1. *Related definition of Reverse Engineering, Wikipedia* [EB/OL]. https://en.wikipedia.org/wiki/Reverse_engineering.
2. *The advent of 64GB iNAND embedded flash drives* [EB/OL]. http://www.dzsc. com/data/html/2011-9-3/97488.html 2013-9-4.
3. C.Kruegel, W. K.Robertson, F.Valeur, et al. Static Disassembly of Obfuscated Binaries [C]. *In: USENIX Security Symposium.* 2004, 13: 18-18.
4. N.Krishnamoorthy, S.Debray, K.Fligg. Static detection of disassembly errors [C]. *In: Reverse Engineering, 2009. WCRE'09. 16th Working Conference on.* IEEE, 2009: 259-268.
5. B.Schwarz, S.Debray, G Andrews. Disassembly of executable code revisited [C]. *In: Reverse Engineering, 2002. Proceedings. Ninth Working Conference on.* IEEE, 2002: 45-54.
6. S.Nanda, W Li, L. C.Lam, et al. BIRD: Binary interpretation using runtime disassembly [C]. *In: Proceedings of the International Symposium on Code Generation and Optimization.* IEEE Computer Society, 2006: 358-370.

7. K. Troshina, A.Chernov, Y. C Derevenets, Decompilation: Is It Possible [C]. *In: Proceedings of International Workshop on Program Understanding*, Altai Mountains, Russia, 2009: 18-27.
8. S.Sourjko, R.Krten. Decompiling the ARM Architecture Code [J]. *Electronic Engineering Times*, 2010.
9. M.Shudrak, V.Zolotarev, The New Technique of Decompilation and Its Application in Information Security [C]. *In: Computer Modeling and Simulation (EMS), 2012 Sixth UKSim/AMSS European Symposium on* IEEE, 2012: 115-120.
10. M.CAO, K.CHEN Differencing Algorithm for Decompilation Code and Source Code [J]. *Computer Engineering,* 2009, 4: 015.
11. Z. Liu, F. Chen Research on decompiling technology [J]. *Journal of Computer Science and Technology*, 1994, 9(4): 311-319.
12. L.JIANG, B.ZHOU, et al. Study of Structural Analysis Algorithm for Disassembled Code [J]. *Journal of Chinese Computer Systems,* 2007, 6: 019.
13. J.LIU, X.WANG, et al. A method to process disassembly Endianness for firm-code: China, CN201210489305.4 [P]. 2013-3-13.
14. L.JIANG. Research on Key Techniques for Firm-code Reverse Analysis [D]. *The PLA Information Engineering University*, 2008, 07.

Solving Traveling Salesman Problem Using Artificial Bee Colony Algorithm

Hong-wei JIANG
School of Information Management, Beijing Information Science and Technology University,
Beijing, 100192, China
E-mail: jianghongwei@bistu.edu.cn

The traveling salesman problem (TSP) involves the question: Given a list of cities and the distances between each pair of cities, what is the shortest possible route that visits each city exactly once and returns to the origin city? Additionally, it belongs to the class of NP-complete problems. It has been proved that bionic intelligence algorithms are effective and efficient, with respect to the traditional methods for solving TSP. Artificial Bee Colony (ABC) algorithm is a swarm intelligence optimization algorithm based on the foraging behavior of honey bee swarm. In this paper, we employ the artificial bee colony algorithm to solve TSP, present specific solutions of artificial bee colony algorithm, and conduct a simulation experiment to solve TSP. The results demonstrate that the algorithm can efficiently and rapidly search for optimal or near-optimal solutions.

Keywords: Swarm intelligence; Artificial Bee Colony algorithm; TSP.

1. Introduction

The traveling salesman problem consists of a salesman and a set of cities. The salesman has to visit each one of the cities starting from a certain one (e.g. the hometown) and returning to the same city [1]. The challenge of the problem is that the traveling salesman wants to minimize the total length of the trip. The travelling salesman problem was first formulated in 1930 and is one of the most intensively studied problems in optimization. It is used as a benchmark for many optimization methods [2].

In the theory of computational complexity, TSP belongs to the class of NP-complete problems. Thus, it is possible that the worst-case running time for any algorithm for the TSP increases superpolynomially (perhaps, specifically, exponentially) with the number of cities. In recent years many approaches have been developed to solve TSP that can be divided to exact [3] and approximate approaches [4]. Exact methods can only be used for very small size instances, and for real-world problems, researchers have to apply approximate methods that find near-optimal solutions in a reasonable time rather than an exact method that guarantees to find the optimal solution in an exponential time.

In this paper we solve the travelling salesman problem using ABC algorithm. The rest of paper is organized as follows: In section 2, the ABC algorithm has reviewed and presents the methodology of ABC algorithm. Solution methodology and experimental setup proposed for TSP are given in section 3. The experimental results are shown in section 4, and consequently, a conclusion is described in section 5.

2. Basic Principles of Artificial Bee Colony Algorithm

The Artificial Bee Colonies (ABC) is a novel optimization algorithm that comes under Swarm Intelligence. ABC algorithm is inspired by social behavior of natural bees. The Artificial Bee Colony, introduced by Dervis Karaboga in 2005[5,6,7].The natural bees are very good in searching for some food source. Whenever any bee finds the food, it signals the other bees by its dance. This signals the other bees regarding the quantity and the location of the food source. This helps in directing the other bees towards good sources of food in their search for food. These bees are able to attract a large number of bees and carry forward to search the food area.

In ABC algorithm the bees are divided into three groups: employed bees, onlooker bees and scout bees. Employed bees visited the food source and gather information about food source location and the quality. Employed bees have memory, so they know the places they have visited before and the quality of food there. Employed bees performs the local search and try to exploit the neighboring locations of the food source and search the best places of foods in the surrounding areas of the present value. Onlooker bees are bees that are waiting on the dance area to decide which food source is better. This decision is made on the basis of information provided by employed bees. Onlooker bees perform the global search for discovering the global optimum. Scout bees do a random search for the food. Scout bees discovers the new area which are uncovered by the employed bees, these bees are completely random in nature and their operation of search. Scout bees avoid the search process to get trapped in local minima. In ABC algorithm, first half of the colony consists of employed bees and the second half constitutes by onlooker bees. The number of employed bees is equal to the number of food sources around the hive. The employed bee whose food source is exhausted becomes the scout bees. In ABC algorithm each food source position represents a candidate solution of optimization problem. In optimization problem each solution is associated with the fitness value on the basis of fitness value it is decided that which solution is better. So the nectar amount of a food source corresponds to the fitness value of the associated solution in ABC algorithm. The number of employed bees or the onlooker bees is equal to the number of solutions in the population.

The ABC algorithm generates a random solution or initial population of size N, where N denotes the size of population or total number of food source.

Food source $X_i(i=1,\ldots,N)$ are vectors of D dimension, which corresponding to one employed bee. F(Xi) is the fitness value of the solution Xi or the nectar amount of food source. The iteration times are constrained to "Limit" for each source, and max iteration is constrained to MAX_{pop} for whole population.

Step one: generate N feasible solution randomly.

For i=1 to N

do

$$Xij= Xminj+rand(0,1)(Xmaxj- Xminj). \qquad (1)$$

(j is component of D dimension vector)

Step two: employed bee search good solution in food source neighbor, and calculate the fitness value, if new source fitness is higher than old one, replace it. Search new source formula as follows: For i=1 to N

do

$$V_i^j= X_i^j+\varphi_i^j(X_i^j- X_k^j) . \qquad (2)$$

(new source fitness is $F(V_i)$,if $F(X_i)$lower than $F(V_i)$, make V_i replace $X_{i,}$ otherwise unchanged.)

Step three: for follow bees, according to the probability of positive correlation to employed bee fitness value, choosing one employed bee to neighborhood search. The probability of food source i chosen is:

$$Pi = \frac{F(Xi)}{\sum_{i}^{n} F(Xi)} . \qquad (3)$$

(The ways follow bees search and select the food source is similar to step 2)

Step four: for all food source, if search times reach a certain limit but still do not find better solution around some food source, give up the source and generate new source:

For i=1 to N

do

{limit=0;m=0;

If $F(X_m) = F(X_{m-1})$ then m=m+1;

If m = Limit then

{give up the food source, and generate a new source according to formula(1.1); limit=0;}

}

Step five: Judge whether algorithm meets the end conditions, or get maximum iteration limit MAX_{pop}. If it is, output the optimal solution, otherwise the algorithm into the next iteration.

3. Solution Methodology and Experimental Setup for TSP

TSP can be represented as a graph G = (V, E), where V= {1,2,...,M} is a set of nodes, and $E=\{(i,j) \mid i,j \in V\}$ is the set of all connection edges between them. Each node represents a city, and each edge means the possible path between two related cities. The distance d_{ij} is associated with edge (i, j) and represents the Euclidean distance from city i to city j. The heuristic information is calculated before performing the main algorithm. So, the distances of all edges were calculated and saved. Iteratively, after construction the solutions, the qualities of the gathered solutions are evaluated by the fitness value, which is calculated by sum of the Euclidean distances of the consecutive edges within the tour. To solve TSP using ABC algorithm, at the first step, an initial population (food source positions) is generated via random way considering diversity of population.

For every algorithm there are some control parameters which are used for its efficient working. Hence, there are some control parameters for artificial bee colony algorithm also. We did an extensive literature survey and carried out our own experiments for determining the values of these control parameters. From this we found that the values which we have taken in this experiment are standard values and they are also suitable for this experiment. The first control Parameter is Maximum cycle number: Maximum number of cycles (MCN) equals to the maximum number of generation, we have taken the result for 2500 MCN value. The next parameter in our experiment is maximum number of population and we have taken its value to be 30. Another control parameter is number of runs and we have taken its value in our experiment as 50. It must be noted that each run contains maximum cycle number, which is 2500 in our experiment. The fourth control parameter is Dimension and it depends upon the number of city.

4. Experimental Results

In this section we have tested our approach on the travelling salesman problem with 16 cities. Fig. 1 is the path diagram without being optimized and Fig. 2 is the path diagram with being optimized. Fig. 3 is the convergent iteration curve with ABC algorithm. It can be seen that the application of artificial bee colony algorithm, the path has been significantly optimized. With the completion of the iteration, the path length can quickly converge to the shortest path length. We can also use our proposed algorithm ABC to solve similar optimization problems.

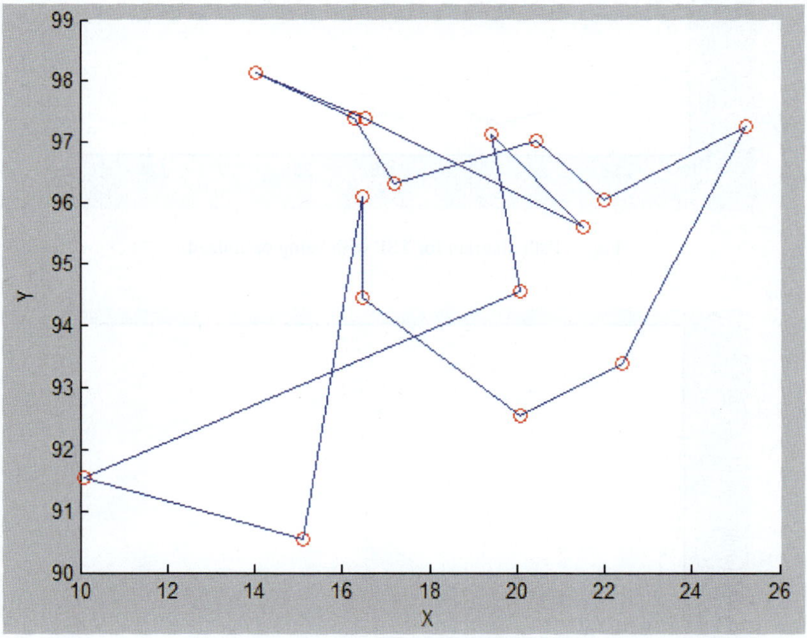

Fig. 1. Path diagram for TSP without being optimized.

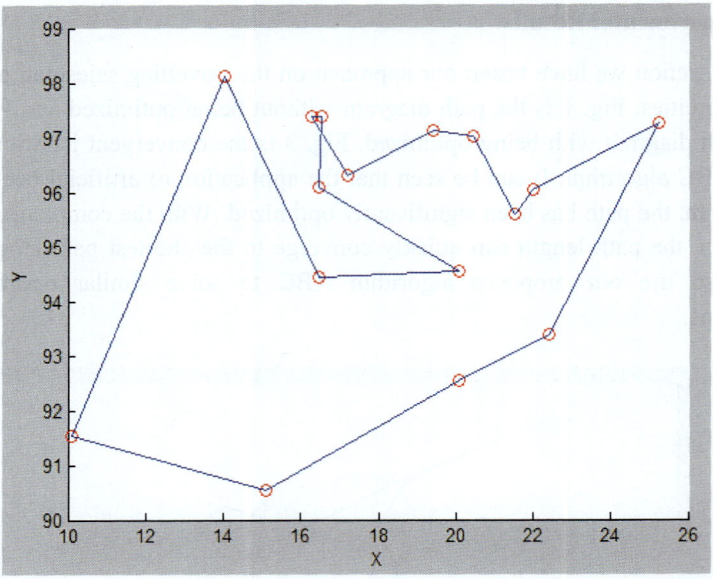

Fig. 2. Path diagram for TSP with being optimized.

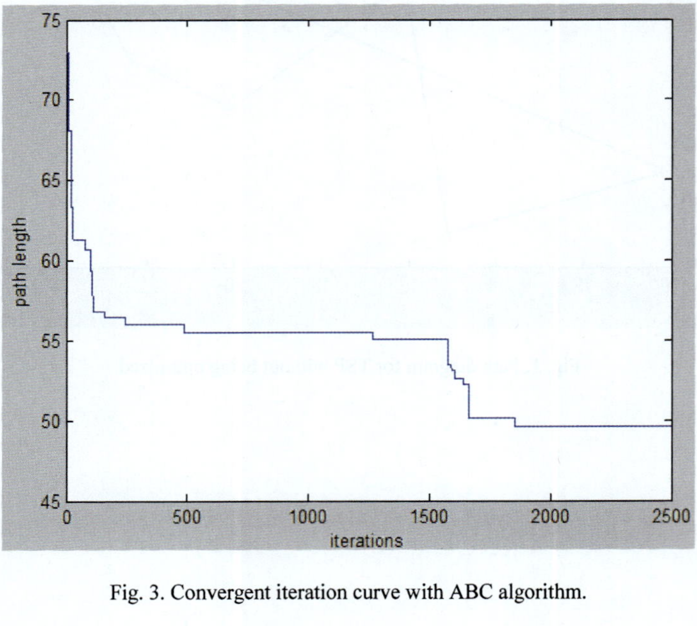

Fig. 3. Convergent iteration curve with ABC algorithm.

5. Conclusion

In this paper, ABC algorithm was introduced for TSP aims to efficiently reduce the complexity of evolutionary algorithms. ABC algorithm has a strong search capability in the graph space and can effectively find an optimal path. Experimental results show that this approach considers both running time and solution quality as well. As a future work, the algorithm will be hybridized with other algorithm to find better results.

Acknowledgments

The research work was supported by Foundation for the Importation and Development of High-Caliber Talents Project of Beijing Municipal Institutions (Grant NO. CIT&TCD201304118).

References

1. G. Reineit, TSPLIB-A traveling salesman problem library, *ORSA Journal on Computing*. 3(4), 376 (1991).
2. Erdogan, G., Cordeau, J.-F., & Laporte, G., The attractive traveling salesman problem, *European Journal of Operational Research*. 203(1), 59 (2010).
3. T. Bektas, The multiple traveling salesman problem: an overview of formulations and solution procedures, *Omega*. 34(3), 209(2006).
4. A. Ugur and D. Aydin, An interactive simulation and analysis software for solving TSP using ant colony optimization algorithm, *Advances in Engineering Software*. 40(2), 341 (2009).
5. D. Karaboga, *An idea based on honey bee swarm for numerical optimization*, Technical Report-TR06, Erciyes University, Engineering Faculty, Computer Engineering Department, Turkey (2005).
6. D. Karaboga, B. Akay, A Survey: Algorithms Simulating Bee Swarm Intelligence, *Artificial Intelligence Review*. 31(1), 68 (2009).
7. Karaboga, D., & Basturk, B, On the performance of artificial bee colony (ABC) algorithm, *Applied Soft Computing*. 8(1), 687 (2008).

Improvement of Gaussian Resampling Algorithm in Particle Filter Algorithm

M.Y. LI* and W.C. XIE

School of Electrical and Electronic Information Engineering, Xihua University, Chengdu, 610039, China

**E-mail: limiaoyi536@126.com*

The improved resampling algorithms commonly in particle filter (PF), increase particles' diversity by making new particles with various methods, and thus improve PF's accuracy. However, they also increase the distance of particle probability distribution before resampling and reduce the actual estimation accuracy. To solve this problem, this paper proposes an improved Gaussian resampling (IGR) algorithm, based on Gaussian Resampling (GR) Algorithm. Under the premise of maintaining the diversity of particles, we enable new particles to contain part of the low-weighted particles' information by conducting proper linear combination with low-weighted particles. Simulation experiments conducted on single variable non-growth model suggest that the improved algorithm reduces the particles' Kullback-Leibler (K-L) distance and improves the final tracking accuracy of PF.

Keywords: Particle filter; Gaussian Resampling; Linear combination; *K-L* distance.

1. Introduction

As a tool that can effectively deal with non-linear and non-Gaussian filter issues, *PF* has been widely applied in areas like tracking of visual targets, image processing and data analysis[1]. The application of resampling algorithm in *PF* solves particles' degeneration and expands *PF*'s application area[2,3]. The basic idea of resampling algorithm is to remove low-weighted particles and copy high-weighted particles, such as cumulative sum weights (*CSW*) algorithm, polynomial resampling (*PR*) algorithm[4]. After many times of calculation iteration, loss of particles' diversity, one factor that restricts PF's accuracy, will emerge[5]. Currently, researchers mainly improve the resampling algorithm by producing new particles after dealing with high-weighted particles in various ways. For example, the paper [6] proposes *GR*. Its main idea is to sample based on the Gaussian distribution with high-weighted particles as the mean, produce new particles and increase particles' diversity. However, with the set of new particles and that of high-weighted particles being highly related and containing no information of low-weighted particles, the *K-L* distance of particle probability distribution is too large, thus affecting room for improvement of the algorithm's performance. The paper [7] adopts Linear Combination Resampling (*LCR*) Algorithm and divides the set of particles before classifying it into different groups. Then it picks proper low-weighted particles by calculating the step length for each to-be-copied high-weighted particles and conducts corresponding linear combination. In this way, the original low-weighted particles' information is reserved to some certain extent but the single high-weighted particle restricts the room for expansion in diversity of the new set of particles.

Based on the two above-mentioned algorithms, this paper proposes an Improved Gaussian Resampling (*IGR*) Algorithm. It produces corresponding Gaussian distribution with high-weighted particles as the mother particle. Then it samples on the distribution and gets initial resampling particle set. Then the final particle set is gained by conducting linear combination between this particle set and low-weighted particles. The improved algorithm improves PF's performance by lessening particles probability distribution disparity before and after resampling and assures the diversity.

2. Particle Filter

The general non-linear motion model can be expressed by formula 1 and formula 2:

$$x_k = f_k(x_{k-1}, \theta_k) . \tag{1}$$

$$z_k = h_k(x_k, \varphi_k) . \tag{2}$$

Where x_k, z_k are respectively the status vector and observational vector at moment *k*; θ_k, φ_k are corresponding transmission noise and observational noise; $f_k(\bullet)$, $h_k(\bullet)$ are non-linear functions.

PF is the *Monte-Carlo* method based on *Bayes* estimation, which tracks and calculates the status and observational data of a group of sample set spreading in the space status [8]. Then it approximates posterior probability density function according to particle x_k^i at moment *k* and weight ω_k^i and gets the best *Bayes* estimation, as shown in formula 3:

$$x_k = E[x_k \mid z_{1:k}] = \int x_k p(x_k \mid z_k) dx_k \approx \sum_{i=1}^{N} \omega_k^i x_k^i \ . \tag{3}$$

PF's steps are as follows:

(i) Initialization of parameters.

$k=0$, initial particle status $x_0^i \sim p(x_0)$ $(i=1,2,\cdots,N)$, initial particle weight, initial particle status variance $\varepsilon^2=1$.

(ii) Calculation of importance weight.

Particles k obey the importance function $q(x_k \mid x_{0:k-1}^i, z_{0:k}) = p(x_k \mid x_{k-1})$

Calculates importance weight after sampling:

$$\omega_k^i = \omega_{k-1}^i p(z_k \mid x_k^i) p(x_k^i \mid x_{k-1}^i) \Big/ q(\bullet) \quad . \tag{4}$$

Normalization of importance weight:

$$\omega_k^i = \omega_k^i \Big/ \sum_{i=1}^{N} \omega_k^i \quad . \tag{5}$$

(iii) Resampling Test and resampling.

Resampling test is conducted according to the weight $\hat{\omega}_k^i$ on the particle set $x_k^i (i=1,2,\cdots,N)$ .When $N_{eff} < N_{thr}$, resampling is ignited to get the particle set $\hat{x}_k^i (i=1,2,\cdots,N)$ and $\hat{\omega}_k^i$ after resampling. N_{thr} is the preset threshold and tested by experiments. N_{eff} is the resampling test value and is obtained by the following formula:

$$N_{eff} = 1 \Big/ \sum_{i=1}^{N} (\omega_k^i)^2 \quad . \tag{6}$$

(iv) Export of estimation.

The export of *PF* consists of export of state estimation and export of particle status variance.

The export of state estimation:

$$\hat{x}_k = \sum_{i=1}^{N} \hat{\omega}_k^i \hat{x}_k^i \quad . \tag{7}$$

The export of particle state estimation:

$$\varepsilon^2 = \sum_{i=1}^{N} \hat{\omega}_k^i (\hat{x}_k - \hat{x}_k^i)^T (\hat{x}_k - \hat{x}_k^i) \quad . \tag{8}$$

(v) $k=k+1$, and recycle to step *ii*.

3. Improved Gaussian Resampling

The main idea of *IGR* is to deal with copying of particles of various weights. There are mainly three kinds of particles: low-weighted particles that do not need copying. They are used as the set of to-be-dealt-with particles to conduct linear combination with high-weighted particles; stable particles that need copying for once only. They are treated as part of the new particle set; high-weighted particles that need copying for many times. With them as the mother particle, the researcher builds corresponding Gaussian Distribution, samples within the high confidence range and gains related middle particles. Then by combining with low-weighted particles, he reduces the correlation with the original high-weighted particles and expands particles' diversity and enables the new particle to contain low-weighted particles' information to achieve the goal of reducing the particle probability distribution disparity before and after resampling.

IGR's main steps are as follows:

(i) Classification of particle set.

Particles are classified into to-be-dealt-with particle set $\{x^i_{\min k}\}$, stable particle set and high-weighted particle set $\{x^i_{\max k}, \omega^i_{\max k}, n^j_{\max}\}$ according to their weight.

(ii) Gaussian Distribution.

IGR builds a Gaussian Distribution with high-weighted particle $x^i_{\max k}$ as the mean, the estimation variance ε^2 of *k-1* step as the variance, namely $\hat{x}^j_k \sim N(x^i_{\max k}, \varepsilon^2)$ .Statistically, sampling conducted in the *95* percent of confidence interval is close to full-range sampling[9,10]. Therefore, the researcher sample on this distribution for $n^j_{\max}$ times and get the initial resampling particle $\{x^i_{firstk}\}$.

(iii) Linear Combination.

IGR conducted linear combination between the resampling particle set $\{x^i_{firstk}, \omega^i_{firstk}\}$ made in the ii step and to-be-dealt-with particle set $\{x^i_{\min k}, \omega^i_{\min k}\}$ and gained the final new particle set. The linear combination was done according to formula 12:

$$\hat{x}^j_k = x^i_{firstk} + KL(x_{\min k} - x^i_{firstk}) \ . \tag{9}$$

Where $\hat{x}^j_k$ is the finally gained new particle; K is the step length coefficient, which is set to regulate the Euclidean distance influence produced by $(x_{\min k} - x^i_{firstk})$, $L$is the proper step length in the $(x_{\min k} - x^i_{firstk})$ direction. For particles that are picked from theto-be-dealt-with particle set, they are supposed to meet the step length's requirement. The step length is gained according to formula 10. The observational weight gained by the finally gained new particle is supposed to be higher than the weight of high-weighted particles or the step length will reduce in half and recalculate new particles.

$$L = \left[1/N\omega^{i}_{\max k} \right]^{1/din} \quad . \tag{10}$$

4. Simulation and Analysis

All the experiments in the paper are conducted in the software condition based on *MATLAB R2014b*, a computer with *Intel CPU dual-core 3.40GHz* and *4GB RAM*. Experiments in this paper adopted *GR* in paper [6] and *LCR* in paper [7]. Models in the experiments are single variable non-growth model, which has been widely applied in econometrics. Models can be described with formula 11 and formula 12:

$$x_k = ax_{k-1} + b\left[x_{k-1} / \left(1 + x^2_{k-1}\right) \right] + c\cos[1.2(k-1)] + \theta_k \quad . \tag{11}$$

$$z_k = \left(x_k^2 / 20 \right) + \varphi_k \quad . \tag{12}$$

Where θ_k , $\varphi_k \sim N(0,1)$; $x_0 = 0.1$; $a = 0.3$; $b = 15$; $c = 3$.

In the experiment, *PF*'s performance are mainly tested in tracking location error and *K-L* distance. The tracking location error is the difference between each step's estimation location and actual location of each algorithm. *K-L*distance, can test the distance between two probability distributions, which is realized by the following formula:

$$D_{KL}\left(x_k^i \parallel \hat{x}_k^i \right) = \sum_i \ln\left(x_k^i / \hat{x}_k^i \right) x_k^i \quad . \tag{13}$$

Where x_k^i is the particles probability distribution before resampling; $\hat{x}_k^i$ is the probability distribution of new particles made in each resampling algorithm. $D_{KL}(\bullet)$ is the *K-L* distance of probability distribution before and after resampling. When it gets smaller, it means the smaller difference between two probability distributions and vice versa.

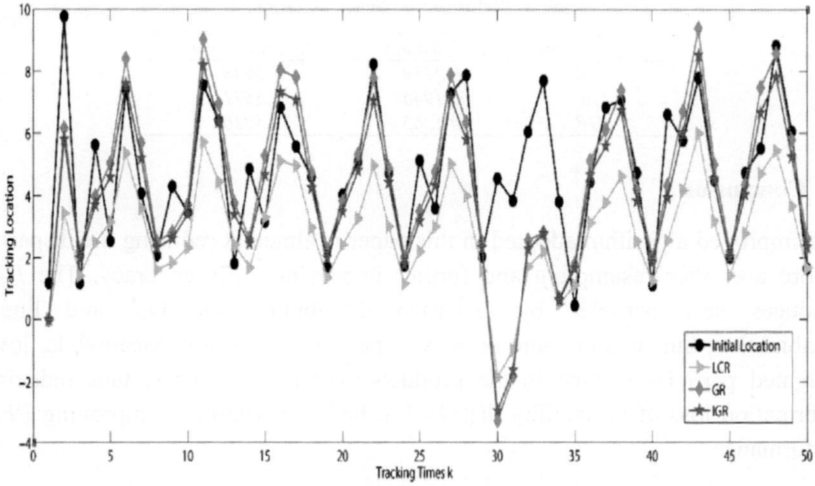

Fig. 1. Tracking location of each algorithm.

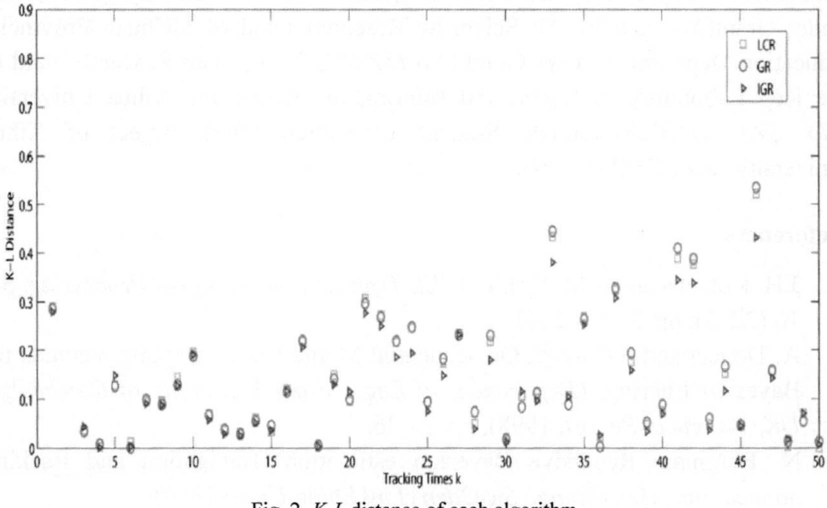

Fig. 2. *K-L* distance of each algorithm.

Figs. 1 and 2 can show that the improved algorithm effectively increases room for improvement of *PF*'s performance after particles' diversity is enhanced by reducing the particle probability distributions before and after resampling. It enhances particles' diversity with *GR*, combines with low-weighted particles, improves information loss of low-weighted particles by resampling and further boosts *PF*'s accuracy. The same result can be shown in Tab. 1 that, the algorithm with shorter *K-L* distance boasts smaller tracking error.

Table 1. Performance of each algorithm.

Performance	*K-L distance*	*Tracking error*
LCR	*0.2154*	*1.5948*
GR	*0.1946*	*1.5571*
IGR	*0.1365*	*1.5026*

5. Conclusion

The improved algorithm adopted in this paper is aimed at reducing the disparity before and after resampling and further improving *PF*'s accuracy. The *IGR* produces new particles by Gaussian distribution sampling and linear combination, thus making sure no loss in particles' diversity. Meanwhile, low-weighted particles engage in the production of new particles, thus reducing information loss of probability distribution before resampling, improving *PF*'s performance.

Acknowledgments

This work is supported by the "Chunhui" plan of Chinese Ministry of Education under Grant(*No. Z2015115*); Scientific Research Fund of SiChuan Provincial Education Department under Grant (*No.15ZA0127*);the Open Research Fund of the Key Laboratory of Signal and Information Processing, Xihua University (*No. SZJJ2015072*);Graduate Student Innovation Fund Project of Xihua University (*No.YCJJ2015204*).

References

1. J.H. Kotecha and P.M. Djuric, *IEEE Transactions on Signal Processing*, **51**, 10 (2003), pp. 2592 - 2601.
2. A. Doucet and S.Godsill, On sequential Monte Carlo sampling methods for Bayesian filtering, (*Department of Engineering University of Cambridge, UK, Technical Report*, 1998), pp. 1 - 36.
3. N. Bergman, Recursive Bayesian estimation: Navigation and tracking applications, (*LinkÊping, Swe2den :LinkÊping Univ* , 1999).
4. E. Belviken and P.J. Acklam, *Auto-matica*, **37**, 1(2001), pp.177 - 183.
5. Y.Yu and Q. Cheng, *IEEE Transactions on Signal Processing*, **86**, 8 (2006), pp.195-203.
6. Z. Rong and T. Jing, *Journal of Coastal Research*, **73**, 1 (2015), pp. 600-605.
7. G.H. Zou, Z.L. Jing and H.T. Hu, *JOURNAL OF SHANGHAI JIAOTONG UNIVERSITY*, **40,** 7 (2006), pp. 1135-1139.

8. M. Sanjeev and S. Maskell, *IEEE Transactions on Signal Processing*, **50**, 2(2002), pp. 174 - 188.
9. M.R. Morelande and S. Challa, *IEEE Transactions on Aerospace Electronic System*, **41**, 15 (2005), pp. 252-270.
10. H.X. Li, T.B. SchonandL. Ljung, *IEEE Transaction on Signal Processing*, **56**,4(2008), pp. 1337-1348.

Fully Discrete Method for the Boundary Integral Equations of Eigenvalue Problems

Xin LUO

College of Applied Mathematics, Chengdu University of Information Technology, Chengdu, 610225, China

E-mail: luoxin919@163.com

In this paper, the fully discrete method is applied for the eigensolutions of the Laplace equation on smooth closed boundaries. The fully discrete method mainly consists of two levels of numerical quadrature: the trapezoidal rule for the integrals including the weakly singularity, and the discrete inner product for the outer integrals. The convergence and error results of the fully discrete method for Steklov eigenvalue problems are provided. Thereafter, the numerical examples demonstrate the efficiency of the fully discrete method.

Keywords: Eigenvalue problems; Fully discrete method; Convergence.

1. Introduction

Consider the Steklov eigenvalue problem: Find u and λ such that

$$\begin{cases} \Delta u = 0, & in \quad \Omega, \\ \dfrac{\partial u}{\partial n} = \lambda u, & on \quad \Gamma, \end{cases} \tag{1}$$

where $\Omega \subset R^2$ is a simply-connected bounded planar domain with smooth closed boundary Γ, u and λ represent the eigenfunction and the associated eigenvalue, respectively. This problem arise from many applications, e.g. the heat flow problems and the free membranes, the study of vibration modes of a structure interaction, and the analysis of stability of mechanical oscillators[3] .

By using the potential theory [5] , the Eq. (1) can be transformed into the following boundary integral equations [5] :

$$c(y)u(y) + \int_\Gamma q^*(y,x)u(x)ds_x = \lambda \int_\Gamma u^*(y,x)q(x)ds_x, \tag{2}$$

where

$$q^*(y,x) = -\frac{1}{2\pi}\frac{\partial \ln|x-y|}{\partial n_x}, \tag{3}$$

and the fundamental solution of Eq. (2) is

$$u^*(y,x) = -\frac{1}{2\pi}\ln|x-y|. \tag{4}$$

Here, $c(y) = \theta(y)/(2\pi)$ is related to the interior angle $\theta(y)$ of Ω at $y \in \Gamma$, especially when y is the smooth boundary points, then $c = 1/2$, and $|x-y|$ denotes the distance between points x and y. Once the eigensolutions λ are obtained by substituting the boundary conditions into Eq. (2), the potential $u(y)(y \in \Omega)$ can be calculated by the following (see [1])

$$u(y) = \frac{1}{2\pi}\left(\int_\Gamma \frac{\partial \ln|x-y|}{\partial n_x}u(x)ds_x - \lambda\int_\Gamma \ln|x-y|\,q(x)ds_x\right). \tag{5}$$

In this paper, the fully discrete method [2] is mainly to deal with the integral smooth and the weakly singular integral which arise in the boundary integral equation of the eigenproblems. The errors of fully discrete method for solving the eigenproblems can obtain the convergence rate $O(h^2)$.

2. Fully Discrete Method

2.1. *Discrete inner product*

Fully discrete method is characterized by special quadrature approximations of the inner-product integral (see [2])

$$(v_1, v_2) = \int_0^1 v_1(x)\overline{v_2}(x)dx. \tag{6}$$

A discrete inner product of (6) can be written as the following form

$$(v_1, v_2)_h = h\sum_{k=0}^{N-1}\sum_{j=1}^{J}\omega_j v_1((k+\xi_j)h)v_2((k+\xi_j)h), \qquad h = 1/N, \qquad \sum_{j=1}^{J}\omega_j = 1. \tag{7}$$

2.2. *Fully discrete method for integral equations*

Assume that the smooth closed boundary Γ of the region Ω can be parameterized by a 1-periodic $C^{2\ell}$ function $\gamma = (\gamma_1(t), \gamma_2(t)) : [0,1] \to \Gamma$, with $|\gamma'(t)|>0$. Under this parameter mapping, Eq. (2) can be converted into the integral equations including definite integrals over $[0,1]$

$$u(t)+\int_0^1 \tilde{q}^*(t,s)\tilde{u}(s)ds=\lambda\int_0^1 \tilde{u}^*(t,s)\tilde{q}(s)ds, \quad t\in[0,1], \tag{8}$$

where

$$u(t)=u(\gamma(t)), \quad \tilde{u}(s)=u(\gamma(s))|\gamma'(s)|$$

and

$$\tilde{u}^*(t,s)=-2\ln|\gamma(t)-\gamma(s)|, \quad \tilde{q}^*(t,s)=-\frac{\partial \tilde{u}^*(t,s)}{\partial n}$$

Defining the following boundary integral operators on $C^{2\ell}$

$$(Ku)(t)=\int_0^1 \tilde{u}^*(t,s)\tilde{q}(s)ds, \quad (Gu)(t)=\int_0^1 \tilde{q}^*(t,s)\tilde{u}(s)ds. \tag{9}$$

Thus, Eq. (8) may be written as the operator form

$$(I+G)u=\lambda Ku. \tag{10}$$

Defining the discrete set

$$\Lambda^h=\{m\in Z:-N/2<m<N/2\}$$

and the trigonometric interpolation space

$$\Gamma^h=span\{e^{i2\pi mx}:m\in\Lambda^h\},$$

and choosing the hat-function

$$v_k(t)=\begin{cases}1-|t-kh|/h, & if\ |t-kh|\le 1\\ 0, & otherwise.\end{cases}$$

Hence the fully discrete method for solving the equation (10) can be stated as: find $u^h\in\Gamma^h$ such that

$$((I^h+G^h-\lambda^h K^h)u^h,\chi)_h=((I+G-\lambda K)u,\chi)_h, \quad \forall\chi\in S_h^r. \tag{11}$$

3. Convergence and Error Analysis

From the logarithmic capacity theory [4] , the eigenvalues of G and G^h are not -1 . Hence, the equation(10) can be rewritten as follows: find $\eta=1/\lambda$ and $u\in C[0,1]$ satisfying

$$\begin{cases}(Mu,\chi)_h=((I+G)^{-1}Ku,\chi)_h=(\eta u,\chi)_h,\\ \|u\|_{0,1}^2=1,\end{cases}\tag{12}$$

and find $\eta^h=1/\lambda^h$ and u^h satisfying

$$\begin{cases}(M^h u^h,\chi)_h=((I+G^h)^{-1}K^h u^h,\chi)_h=(\eta^h u^h,\chi)_h,\\ h\sum_{j=0}^{n-1}(u^h(s_j))^2\,|x'(s_j)|=1.\end{cases}\tag{13}$$

Theorem 3.1. *The approximate operator sequence* $\{M^h\}$ *is the asymptotically compact sequence and convergent to* $\{M\}$ *in* $C[0,1]$, *i.e.,*

$$M^h\xrightarrow{a.c}M,\tag{14}$$

where $\xrightarrow{a.c}$ *denotes the asymptotically compact convergence.*
Proof. From [4], we know that for any bounded sequence $\{y_m\in C^{(m)}[0,1]\}$ there exists a convergent subsequence in $\{K^h y_m\}$. Without loss of generality, we assume $K^h y_m\to z$, as $m\to+\infty$. In addition, G is a smoothing operator and G^h is collectively compact convergent to G. Thus, we have

$$\|M^h y_m-(I+G)^{-1}z\|\le\|(I+G^h)^{-1}\|(\|K^h y_m-z\|+\|(G-G^h)(I+G)^{-1}z\|)\to 0\tag{15}$$

where $\|\cdot\|$ is the norm of the linear bound operator space $L(C^{(m)}[0,1],C^{(m)}[0,1])$. It shows that $\{M^h\}$ is an asymptotically compact operator sequence. Furthermore, for all $y\in C^m[0,1]$ we have

$$\|M^h y-My\|\le\|(I+G^h)^{-1}\|(\|K^h y-Ky\|+\|(G-G^h)(I+G)^{-1}Ky\|)\to 0.\tag{16}$$

Hence, the sequence $\{M^h\}$ is point wisely convergent to M.
Because the sequence $\{M^h\}$ is an asymptotically compact sequence and is point-wisely convergent to M, the proof of the theorem is completed. □

Similar to the main result in the literature [6], we have the following theorem.

Theorem 3.2. *If* $\{\eta_j,u_j\}$ *and* $\{\eta_j^h,u_j^h\}$ *are the eigenvalue and eigenvector of (12) and (13) respectively, then there exist a constant* c_j *and vector functions* $d_j\in C^2[0,1]$ *independent of* h, *such that*

$$\eta_j^h-\eta_j=c_jh^2+O(h^3),\qquad u_j^h-u_j=d_jh^2+O(h^3).\tag{17}$$

4. Numerical Examples

Let $h = 1/N$ be the mesh width and $t_i = ih(i = 0,\cdots,N-1)$ be the nodes. Also let $e(\lambda_i) = |\lambda_i^h - \lambda_i|$ and $r(\lambda_i) = \log_2(e_i^h / e_i^{h/2})$ be the errors and errors ratio respectively by using fully discrete method for solving problem (1).

Example 1. Consider a circular isotropic body with radius R in the plane deformation. The analytic solutions about eigenvalues for this problem is $\lambda_i = i/R, i = 1,2,\cdots$. Assume that the circular deformation problem with radius $R = 1$. The computed eigenvalues and errors of the boundary numerical eigensolutions for Eq. (1) are listed in Table 1.

Table 1. The errors for Example 1.

N	2^4	2^5	2^6	2^7	2^8
$e(\lambda_1)$	1.053E-2	2.654E-3	6.663E-4	1.670E-4	4.179E-5
$r(\lambda_1)$	--	1.989	1.994	1.996	1.998
$e(\lambda_2)$	8.291E-2	2.107E-2	5.309E-3	1.333E-3	3.339E-4
$r(\lambda_2)$	--	1.976	1.989	1.994	1.997
$e(\lambda_3)$	2.726E-1	7.058E-2	1.785E-2	4.489E-3	1.126E-3
$r(\lambda_3)$	--	1.949	1.983	1.991	1.995

Example 2. Consider an elliptical plane body $x^2/a^2 + y^2/b^2 = 1$ with $a = 3$ and $b = 2$ in plane strain deformation. we compute the boundary numerical eigensolutions for Eq. (1) and list the errors in Table 2.

From Table 1 and 2, we can see numerically

$$r(\lambda_i) = \log_2(e^h(\lambda_i)/e^{h/2}(\lambda_i)) \approx 2, i = 1,2,3,$$

which shows that the convergence rate of λ_i is the order of $O(h^2)$.

Table 2. The errors for Example 2.

N	2^4	2^5	2^6	2^7	2^8
$e(\lambda_1)$	1.598E-2	3.947E-3	9.711E-4	2.309E-4	4.615E-5
$r(\lambda_1)$	--	2.018	2.023	2.073	2.323
$e(\lambda_2)$	1.124E-1	3.045E-2	7.634E-3	1.829E-3	3.668E-4
$r(\lambda_2)$	--	1.885	1.996	2.062	2.318
$e(\lambda_3)$	3.055E-2	1.210E-2	3.533E-3	8.880E-4	1.807E-4
$r(\lambda_3)$	--	1.336	1.777	1.992	2.297

5. Conclusion

In this paper, the fully discrete method is applied for the first kind boundary integral equations of eigenvalue problems on smooth domains. The numerical results show that the rate of error convergence for the fully discrete method for solving the problem(1) can achieve $O(h^2)$.

Acknowledgments

This work is supported by Foundation of Chengdu University of Information Technology (NO. KYTZ201505).

References

1. P. Cheng, J. Huang, G. Zeng, Splitting extrapolation algorithms for solving the boundary integral equations of Steklov problems on polygons by mechanical quadrature methods, *Eng. Anal. Bound. Elem.*, 35 (2011), pp. 1136-1141.
2. I. H. Sloan, B. J. Burn, An unconventional quadrature method for logarithmic-kernel integral equations on closed curves, *J. Integral Equations Appl.* 4 (1992), pp. 117-151.
3. P. Cheng, Z. Lin, W. Z. Zhang, Five-order algorithms for solving Laplace's Steklov eigenvalue on polygon by mechanical quadrature methods. *J. Computational Analysis and Applications*, 1(18), (2015).
4. K. Atkinson and I. H. Sloan, The numerical solution of first-kind Logarithmic-kernel integral equation on smooth open arcs, *Math., Comp.*, 56 (1991), pp.119-139.
5. P. Davis, Methods of Numerical Integration, Second edition, Academic Press, New York, (1984).

Properties and Applications of Differential Point of Boolean Function

Jing-wei LI[1,2], Mo-han YANG[1], Dao-guang MU[2] and Xue-jia LAI[1,*]
[1]*Institute of Cryptology and Information Security, Dept of Computer Science and Technology, Shanghai Jiaotong University*
Shanghai,200240, China
[2]*Science and Technology on Communication Security Laboratory*
Chengdu, 610041, China
[*]*E-mail: lai-xj@cs.sjtu.edu.cn*

In this paper, the set of some points, derived at which the degree of a Boolean function can be reduced by at least i, is defined as D_f^i. We show the set of i-DPs (*i*-differential point) is closed to the operation XOR, and the origin i-DP still exists after taking a derivative on the Boolean function at a non-2-DP. In addition, an n-variable non-linear Boolean function of degree d has at most $2^{n-d} - 1$ 2-DPs. We prove that an n-bit cipher whose n component functions have common terms of degree $n - 1$, is not IND-CPA secure. We also show that an n-bit cipher with low degree d can be distinguished with obvious advantage and data complexity $2^d + 1$.

Keywords: Boolean function; Higher order differential; Distinguisher; Fast point; Indistinguishability under chosen-plaintext attack (IND-CPA).

1. Introduction

Higher order derivative[1] was introduced into cryptography in 1994. This paper proposed some basic properties of higher order derivatives on binary functions and the idea of higher order differentials, which is a generalization of original differential cryptanalysis developed by Biham and Shamir[4]. Higher order differential attack uses the differences among associated many texts, instead of considering the differences between two texts in differential attack.

Higher order differentials was first applied to block ciphers by Knudsen[5]. In 1997, Jakobsen and Knudsen showed that the KN cipher, which is proved secure against differential attack and linear attack[5], can be broken by higher order differential attack[6]. Since then, higher order differential attack has extensively been used in cryptanalysis[7-10].

Higher order differential attack is very efficient cryptanalysis method, so the research on properties of higher order derivative of Boolean function is

[*] Corresponding author.

significant. In this paper, our contributions are that we prove that the origin i-DP still exists, after taking a derivative on the Boolean function at a non-2-DP. In addition, an n-variable non-linear Boolean function of degree d has at most $2^{n-d}-1$ 2-DPs.

Furthermore, we show that an n-bit cipher whose n component functions have common terms of degree $n-1$ can be distinguished with significant advantage and data complexity 2^{n-1} and a kind of cipher whose Boolean functions have low degree is not IND-CPA.

The paper is organized as follows. In section 2, we recall the notion of higher order derivatives and define the i-differential point(i-DP). In section 3, we prove some special properties of i-DP of Boolean function.In Section 4, we discuss two kinds of cipher which is not IND-CPA. Section 5 concludes our results.

2. Preliminaries

In this section, we recall some notions of high order derivatives Boolean functions[1] and the definition of fast point[2], you may refer to them to get more details.

Definition 2.1. [1] *Let (S, +) and (T, +) be Abelian groups. For a function: S → T, the derivatives of the f at point a ∈ S is defines as*

$$\Delta_a f(x) = f(x+a) - f(x).$$

The i-th (i> 1) derivative of f at $(a_1, a_2, \dots, a_i)$ *as*

$$\Delta^{(i)}_{a_1,\dots,a_i} f(x) = \Delta_{a_i}(\Delta^{(i-1)}_{(a_1,\dots,a_{i-1})} f(x))$$

where $\Delta^{(i-1)}_{(a_1,\dots,a_{i})-1} f(x)$ *being the (i-1)-th derivative of f at* $(a_1, a_2, \dots, a_{i-1})$. *The 0-th derivative of f(x) is defined to be itself.*

Proposition 2.2. [1] *Let* $deg(f)$ *denote the nonlinear degree of a multi-varible polynomial function* $f(x)$. *Then*

$$\deg(\Delta_a f(x)) \leq \deg(f(x)) - 1.$$

Proposition 2.3. [1] *For any function:* $F_2^n \to F_2^m$, *the n-th derivative of f is a constant. If f:* $F_2^n \to F_2^m$ *is invertible, then* $(n-1)$*-th derivative of f is a constant.*

Proposition 2.4. [1] *Let* $L[a_1, a_2, \dots, a_i]$ *be the list of all* 2^i *possible linear combinations of* $a_1, a_2, \dots, a_i$. *Then*

$$\Delta^{(i)}_{a_1,\dots,a_i} f(x) = \sum_{c \in L[a_1,a_2,\dots,a_i]} f(x \oplus c).$$

Definition 2.5. [2] *For a Boolean function* $f: F_2^n \to F_2$, *if a point* $c \in F_2^n$ *satisfies* $deg(\Delta_c f(x)) \leq deg(f) - 2$, *then c is called a fast point (FP) of f.*

3. Some Properties of i-DP

Let $f(x)$ be a n-variable Boolean function of degree d. By Proposition 2.2, we may know that, in general, the d-th derivative of f is constant. But sometimes, we can adopt a faster way to do this step. By taking a derivative at some specifical points(such as **c**), the degree of $\Delta_c f$ is reduced by more than 1. Here, **c** is so-called fast point in [2][12].

Definition 3.1. *For a Boolean function* $f: F_2^n \to F_2$, *let* $d = deg(f)$. *If a point* $c \in F_2^n$ *satisfies* $deg(\Delta_c f(x)) \leq deg(f) - 2$, *then* **c** *is called a i-DP of f. The set of all i-DPs is called* D_f^i.

Obviously, for a Boolean function, there are 1-DPs, 2-DPs, 3-DPs, etc. It then follows that:

$$D_f^n \subseteq \cdots \subseteq D_f^2 \subseteq D_f^1.$$

Theorem 3.2. *For a Boolean function f, the sum(XOR) of any two i-DPs is still a i-DP of f.*

Proof. Let $f(x)$ be a Boolean function of degree d, point a and b are both *i*-DP of f.According to definition and Corollary, for any *d-i* points$\alpha_1, \alpha_2, \ldots, \alpha_{d-i}$,

$$\sum_{c \in L[a, \alpha_1, \alpha_2, \ldots, \alpha_{d-i}]} f(x \oplus c) = C_1. \quad (1)$$

$$\sum_{c \in L[b, \alpha_1, \alpha_2, \ldots, \alpha_{d-i}]} f(x \oplus c) = C_2. \quad (2)$$

Equation (1) can be written as:

$$\sum_{c \in L[\alpha_1, \alpha_2, \ldots, \alpha_{d-i}]} f(x \oplus c) \oplus \sum_{c \in L[\alpha_1, \alpha_2, \ldots, \alpha_{d-i}]} f(x \oplus c \oplus a) = C_1. \quad (3)$$

In Equation (2), x can be substituted by$x \oplus a$, then

$$\sum_{c \in L[\alpha_1, \alpha_2, \ldots, \alpha_{d-i}]} f(x \oplus a \oplus c) \oplus \sum_{c \in L[\alpha_1, \alpha_2, \ldots, \alpha_{d-i}]} f(x \oplus a \oplus c \oplus b) = C_2. \quad (4)$$

(3) XORs (4), we can get

$$\sum_{c \in L[\alpha_1, \alpha_2, \ldots, \alpha_{d-i}]} f(x \oplus c) \oplus \sum_{c \in L[\alpha_1, \alpha_2, \ldots, \alpha_{d-i}]} f(x \oplus a \oplus c \oplus b) = C_1 \oplus C_2. \quad (5)$$

or

$$\sum_{c \in L[a \oplus b, \alpha_1, \alpha_2, \ldots, \alpha_{d-i}]} f(x \oplus c) = C_1 \oplus C_2. \quad (6)$$

This to say, $a \oplus b$is also i-DP of f. □

Theorem 3.3. *For a Boolean function* $f: F_2^n \to F_2$, if $a \in D_f^i (i > 1)$, $b \in D_f^1 - D_f^2$, then $a \in D_{\Delta_b f}^i$.

Proof. If $a \in D_f^i$, for any d-i points , $\alpha_1, \alpha_2, \dots, \alpha_{d-i}$,

$$\sum_{c \in L[a,\alpha_1,\alpha_2,\dots,\alpha_{d-i}]} f(x \oplus c) = C. \tag{7}$$

α_{d-i} of (7) is substituted by b, then

$$C = \sum_{c \in L[a,\alpha_1,\alpha_2,\dots,\alpha_{d-i}]} f(x \oplus c) = \sum_{c \in L[a,\alpha_1,\alpha_2,\dots,\alpha_{d-i-1},b]} f(x \oplus c) = \sum_{c \in L[a,\alpha_1,\alpha_2,\dots,\alpha_{d-i}]} f(x \oplus c) \oplus f(x \oplus c \oplus b)) = \sum_{c \in L[a,\alpha_1,\alpha_2,\dots,\alpha_{d-i-1}]} \Delta_b f(x \oplus c) = \sum_{c \in L\left[a,\alpha_1,\alpha_2,\dots,\alpha_{d-i-1},\alpha_{\deg(\Delta_b f)-i}\right]} \Delta_b f(x \oplus c). \tag{8}$$

So a is a i-DP of $\Delta_b f$. □

A non-linear Boolean function has many 2-DPs, the upper bound of the number is as follows:

Theorem 3.4. *A n-variables non-linear Boolean function of degree d has at most $2^{n-d} - 1$ 2-DPs.*

Proof. Let f(x) be a n-variable Boolean function of degree d, $a_{l_1,\dots,l_{n-d}}$ denotes the coefficient of the monomial $\prod_{t=1}^{n} x_t / x_{l_1} x_{l_2} \cdots x_{l_{n-d}}$. If point $c = (c_1, \dots, c_n)$ is a 2-DP of f, the coefficients of all monomials of degree d-1 in $\Delta_c f$ are 0. This is to say, there exists the following equations:

$$c_{l_1} a_{l_1,\dots,l_{n-d+1}} \oplus c_{l_2} a_{l_1,l_3,\dots,l_{n-d+1}} \oplus \dots \oplus c_{l_{n-d+1}} a_{l_1,\dots,l_{n-d}} = 0 \ \forall\, 1 \le l_1 < \dots < l_{n-d+1} \le n. \tag{9}$$

For a Boolean function of degree d, there exists a monomial whose coefficient is 1, without loss of generality, we suppose $a_{1,\dots,n-d} = 1$. Considering d equations in (9) for $l_1 = 1, l_2 = 2, \dots, l_{n-d} = 1$ and $l_{n-d+1} \in \{n - d + 1, \dots, n\}$, the coefficient matrix (denoted as A for convenience) of these d equations can be written as

$$\begin{bmatrix} a_{2,\dots,n-d+1} & \cdots & a_{1,\dots,n-d-1,n-d+1} & 1 & 0 & 0 & \dots & 0 & 0 \\ a_{2,\dots,n-d,n-d+2} & \cdots & a_{1,\dots,n-d-1,n-d+2} & 0 & 1 & 0 & \dots & 0 & 0 \\ \vdots & \ddots & \vdots & \vdots & \vdots & \vdots & \ddots & \vdots & \vdots \\ a_{2,\dots,n-d,n-1} & \cdots & a_{1,\dots,n-d-1,n-1} & 0 & 0 & 0 & \dots & 1 & 0 \\ a_{2,\dots,n-d,n} & \cdots & a_{1,\dots,n-d-1,n} & 0 & 0 & 0 & \dots & 0 & 1 \end{bmatrix} (c_1, \dots, c_n)^T = 0. \tag{10}$$

Note that the rank of the above matrix is at least d and also no more than the rank of A, so the rank of A is also at least d, i.e., the number of solutions to (10) is at most $2^{n-d} - 1$. So f has at most $2^{n-d} - 1$ 2-DPs. □

The above theorem established if only if f is a non-linear Boolean functions. And it has totally same form with Theorem 3.1 of [2]. In fact, FP_f is D_f^2.

Obviously, we can have the following propositions[2]:

Proposition 3.5. *A n-variable Boolean function of degree* n *has no non-zero 2-DPs.*

Proposition 3.6. *A n-variable Boolean function f of degree* $n - 1$ *has a unique non-zero 2-DP.*

4. Ciphers which are not IND-CPA Secure

4.1. *Notions of IND-CPA*

The experiment is defined for any private-key encryption scheme $\Pi = (Gen, Enc, Dec)$, any adversary A, and any value n for the security parameter:

The adversarial indistinguishability experiment $PrivK^{eav}_{A,\Pi}(n)$:
1. The adversary A is given input 1^n*, and outputs a pair of messages* m_0, m_1 *of the same length.*
2. A random key k is generated by running $Gen(1^n)$*, and a random bit* $b \leftarrow \{0,1\}$ *is chosen. The ciphertext* $c \leftarrow Enc_k(m_b)$ *is computed and given to A.*
3. A outputs a bit b'*.*
4. The output of the experiment is defined to be 1 if $b' = b$*, and 0*

An n-bit block cipher is a bijection from F_2^n to F_2 which can be viewed as n balanced output component functions from F_2^n to F_2. The degree of a cipher is defined as the maximum degree of the component functions and the optimized degree of a n-bit cipher is $n - 1$ since all component functions are balanced[3].

4.2. *Ciphers whose n component functions have common terms of degree n-1*

Theorem 4.1. *If A n-bit cipher whose n component functions have common terms of degree n-1, the ciphers is not IND-CPA secure.*

Proof. We construct distinguisher D_1,

Distinguisher D_1 is given oracle access to $Enc_k(.)$.
1. D_1 randomly chooses a $(n-1)$-dimensional subspace L of F_2^n such that $m_0 \oplus m_1$ is not in this subspace.
2. D_1 queries all the values of $Enc_k(m_0 \oplus x)$ where $x \in L$ and $x \neq 0^n$.
3. D_1 sums all the ciphertexts and $Enc_k(m_b)$.
4. If the sum equals 0^n or 1^n, output 0; otherwise output 1.

Fig. 1. Higher order differential distinguisher D_1.

The degree of these n Boolean functions is at most $n-1$, so the $(n-1)$-derivative is a linear function of the coefficient of term of degree $n-1$. Due to common terms of degree $n-1$, the higher order differential of these n Boolean functions are same for any $(n-1)$-dimensional subspace.

If the higher order derivatives at the subspace L of the component functions with common terms of degree $n-1$ are 0, then the sum is 0^n when $b = 0$. When $b = 1$, the sum is $Enc_k(m_0) \oplus Enc_k(m_1)$ which is a random sequence of length n. If the higher order derivatives are 1, then the sum is 1^n when $b = 0$and when $b = 1$, the sum is $Enc_k(m_0) \oplus Enc_k(m_1) \oplus 1^n$ which is also a random sequence of length n.

Without loss of generality, we denote p as the probability that the higher order derivatives of the component functions with common terms of degree $n-1$ at L is 0. Then the probability that the derivative is 1 is $1-p$. So the advantage of the distinguisher is

$$p \times \left[\frac{1}{2} + \frac{1}{2} \times \left(1 - \frac{1}{2^n} \times 2\right)\right] + (1-p) \times \left[\frac{1}{2} + \frac{1}{2} \times \left(1 - \frac{1}{2^n} \times 2\right)\right] - \frac{1}{2} = \frac{1}{2} - \frac{1}{2^n}$$

It can be distinguished with advantage $\frac{1}{2} - \frac{1}{2^n}$and data complexity 2^{n-1}. □

It follows that n component functions have common terms of degree $n-1$. Ciphers which meets the strong condition are very few. In fact, this restriction can be relaxed to k Boolean functions, i.e. at least $k(k > \lfloor\frac{n+1}{2}\rfloor)$ component functions have common terms of degree $n-1$. Then if the number of 0s or 1s in the sum is at least k, output 0; otherwise output 1. Similarly, we can compute the advantage is

$$p \times \left[\frac{1}{2} + \frac{1}{2} \times (1 - \frac{\sum_{i=k}^{n} \binom{n}{i}}{2^n}) \times 2\right] + (1-p) \times \left[\frac{1}{2} + \frac{1}{2} \times \left(1 - \frac{\sum_{i=k}^{n} \binom{n}{i}}{2^n}\right) \times 2\right] - \frac{1}{2}$$

$$= \frac{\sum_{i=n-k+1}^{k-1} \binom{n}{i}}{2^{n+1}}$$

Due to $k > \lfloor\frac{n+1}{2}\rfloor$, $\sum_{i=n-k+1}^{k-1} \binom{n}{i}$ includes the middle $\binom{n}{\lfloor\frac{n}{2}\rfloor}$ of binomial coefficient $\binom{n}{k}$. If $2|n$, by using Stirling Approximation we have

$$\binom{n}{\frac{n}{2}} \sim \frac{2^n}{\sqrt{\frac{\pi n}{2}}} \quad n \to \infty$$

$$\frac{\sum_{i=n-k+1}^{k-1} \binom{n}{i}}{2^{n+1}} \geq \frac{\binom{n}{\frac{n}{2}}}{2^{n+1}} \sim \frac{1}{\sqrt{2\pi n}}$$

If $2 \nmid n$, there is similar result. In conclusion, the advantage of distinguisher is not negligible. So this kind of cipher is NOT-CPA secure.

But, similar result cannot be obtained if $k \leq \lfloor \frac{n+1}{2} \rfloor$. The incident that a n-bit sequence has at least k 0s or 1s is true. Then output of the distinguisher is always 0. In other words, there is no advantage.

4.3. *Ciphers whose component functions of low degree*

Theorem 4.2. *If there are all component functions whose degree are most* $d (d < n - 1)$, *the ciphers is not IND-CPA secure.*

Proof. We construct distinguisher D_2,

1.D_2 randomly chooses a d-dimensional subspace L of F_2^n such that $m_0 \oplus m_1$ is not in this subspace.
2.D_2 queries all the values of $Enc_k(m_0 \oplus x)$ where $x \in L$ and $x \neq 0^n$.
3.D_2 sums all the ciphertexts and $Enc_k(m_b)$.
4.D_2 randomly chooses a point c, then $sum = D_c(sum)$.
5.If the sum equals 0^n, output 0; otherwise output 1.

Fig. 2. Higher order differential distinguisher D_2.

The degree of these n Boolean functions is at most d, so the higher oder derivative at d-dimension subspace is constant[11]. The sum is constant when $b = 0$. When $b = 1$, the sum is $Enc_k(m_0) \oplus Enc_k(m_1)$ which is a random sequence of length n. So the advantage of the distinguisher is

$$\frac{1}{2}+\frac{1}{2} \times \left(1 - \frac{1}{2^n}\right) - \frac{1}{2} \times \frac{1}{2^n} = 1 - \frac{1}{2^n}$$

The cipher can be distinguished with advantage $1 - \frac{1}{2^n}$ and data complexity $2^d + 1$. □

As can be seen, the degree of Boolean functions ciphers used must be sufficiently high, otherwise these ciphers are NOT-CPA secure.

In block cipher design, to resist high order differential attack, a cipher should iterate enough rounds to obtain high degree.

5. Conclusion

In this paper, we did some research on higher order derivatives and got some important properties. The set of i-DPs is closed to the operation XOR. And the origin i-DP still exists, after taking a derivative on the Boolean function at a non-2-DP. In addition, an n-variable non-linear Boolean function of degree d has at most $2^{n-d} - 1$ 2-DPs.

Furthermore, we constructed two higher order differential distinguishers and got some results. To resist higher order differential attack, a block cipher should have as many component functions with maximum degree $n-1$ as possible, and as few component functions with common terms of degree $n-1$ as possible.

All the above results are meaningful reference for block cipher design.

Acknowledgments

This work was supported by the National Natural Science Foundation of China (61272440, 61472251, U1536101), China Postdoctoral Science Foundation (2013M531174, 2014T70417) and Science and Technology on Communication Security Laboratory.

References

1. X. Lai, Higher order derivatives and differential cryptanalysis, In Proc."Symposium on Communication, Coding and Cryptography", in honor of James L. Massey on the occasion of his 60'th birthday, Feb. 10-13, 1994, Monte-Verita, Ascona, Switzerland, 1994.
2. M. Duan, X. Lai, M. Yang, X. Sun and B. Zhu, Distinguishing properties of higher order derivatives of Boolean functions, Inf. Sci. 271: 224-235,2014.
3. A. Canteaut, Cryptographic functions and design criteria for block ciphers, Progress in Cryptology-INDOCRYPT 2001, LNCS 2247, pp. 1-16. Springer-Verlag, 2001.
4. E. Biham and A. Shamir, Differential Cryptanalysis of DES-like Cryptosystems, Advances in Cryptology-CRYPTO'90, Proceedings, LNCS 537, pp.2-21, Springer-Verlag, Berlin 1991.
5. K. Nyberg and L. Knudsen, Provable Security Against a Differential Attack, Journal of Cryptology, Volume 8, Number 1, pp. 27-37, Springer Verlag, 1995.
6. T. Jakobsen and L. Knudsen, The interpolation attack on block ciphers, Fast Software Encryption, pp.28-40, Springer Verlag, 1997.
7. S. Moriai, T. Shimoyama and T. Kaneko, Higher order differential attack of a CAST cipher, In Fast Software Encryption, pp. 17-31. Springer, 1998.
8. T. Shimoyama, S. Moriai, and T. Kaneko, Improving the Higher Order Differential Attack and Cryptanalysis of the KN Cipher, Information Security, First International Workshop, ISW'97, LNCS 1396, pp. 32-42, Springer-Verlag, 1998.

9. Y. Tsunoo, T. Saito, M. Shigeri and T. Kawabata, Higher Order Differential Attacks on Reduced-Round MISTY1, In Information Security and Cryptology-ICISC 2008, pp. 415-431. Springer, 2009.
10. Christoph Dobraunig, Maria Eichlseder, and Florian Mendel, Higher-order cryptanalysis of LowMC, IACR Cryptology ePrint Archive 2015: 407, 2015.
11. M. Duan, X. Lai., Higher order differential cryptanalysis framework and its applications, 2011 International Conference on Information Science and Technology (ICIST), 291—297, 2011.
12. Counting and characterising functions with "fast points" for differential attacks, Cryptography and Communications, 2015.

A Study of the Correlation of the Non-Singularity Degree Indexes of the Matrix

Hong-qiang ZHANG

College of electrical engineering, Northwest University For Nationalities, Lanzhou, 730030, China
E-mail:954914142@qq.com

Shu-wen WANG*

College of electrical engineering, Northwest University For Nationalities Lanzhou, 730030, China
E-mail: shuwenwang@163.com

Bing-kun PI

College of electrical engineering, Northwest University For Nationalities, Lanzhou, 730030, China
E-mail:294171424@qq.com

Cong MA

College of electrical engineering, Northwest University For Nationalities, Lanzhou, 730030, China
E-mail:1216881372@qq.com

In this paper, we select 4 indexes that are commonly used to measure the degree of the non-singular of the matrix: the minimum norm of eigenvalue, the minimum norm of singular value, the condition number and the absolute value of the determinant. The Pearson correlation coefficient was calculated for every 2 pairs for the 4 indicators of the random non-singular matrix so as to compare the changes between them and to explore the correlation between these indicators. The experimental results demonstrate that there is a good linear correlation between each pair of the 4 indexes.

Keywords: Non-singular matrix; Non-singularity degree index; Correlation.

1. Introduction

The usual methods of judging the non-singularity of the matrix are calculating the minimum norm of eigenvalue, the minimum norm of singular value, the

* Corresponding author.

condition number and the absolute value of the determinant. If the minimum norm of eigenvalue, the minimum norm of singular value, the absolute value of the determinant is not 0 or the condition number is not infinite, the matrix is non-singular matrix. In practice, we usually use only one method to determine the non-singularity of the matrix. Whether there is a correlation between these 4 indicators? In order to explore the correlation of the 4 indicators, this paper carried out the related experiments.

2. Data Sources and Research Method

2.1. *Research objects and data sources*

Table 1. The values are measured by a matrix whose dimension is 10×10, and the value range is 5.

The minimum norm of eigenvalue	The minimum norm of singular value	The condition number	The absolute value of the determinant
1.8921	0.9735	64.5711	398136
0.2119	0.0576	689.6545	6078
0.6332	0.3257	175.1621	132306
0.8794	0.1236	382.1691	74628
1.2813	0.3664	97.648	161814
1.7218	0.4586	99.0635	231460
0.9687	0.3133	113.6526	53472
0.2581	0.1352	335.343	61336

Table 2. The values are measured by a matrix whose dimension is 5×5, and the value range is 8.

The minimum norm of eigenvalue	The minimum norm of singular value	The condition number	The absolute value of the determinant
2.1177	1.2146	30.2762	956
0.3072	0.0994	228.1818	88
3.5594	2.2642	16.9565	4784
1.9392	0.6099	41.5078	514
2.7346	2.0969	15.8915	2802
0.3546	0.0798	394.3289	152
3	1.901	16.318	2745
1.5071	0.4907	61.2473	558

In this paper, we use MATLAB to obtain two kinds of random matrices. One kind is whose dimension is fixed, and the value range is not fixed. The other kind is whose dimension is not fixed, and the value range is fixed. Use the MATLAB to calculate the 4 indicators of random matrix, the minimum value of the model and the minimum norm of singular value and the condition number and the absolute value of the determinant. As shown in Table 1, the values are measured by a matrix whose dimension is 10×10, and the value range is 5. As shown in Table 2, the values are measured by a matrix whose dimension is 5×5, and the value range is 8.

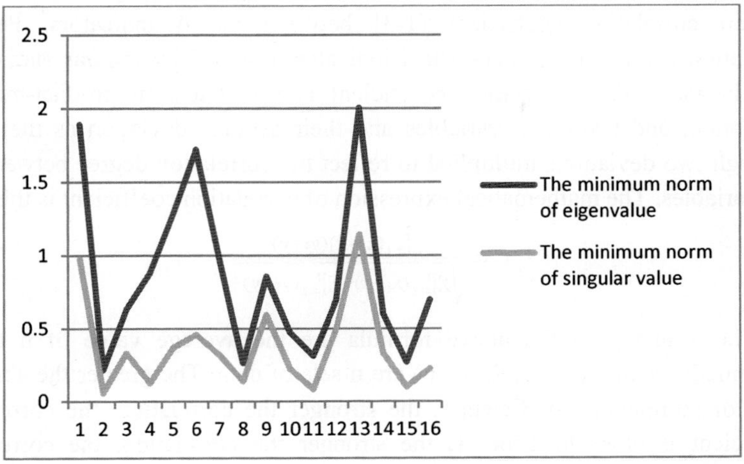

Fig. 1. The changing trend of A and B in Table 1.

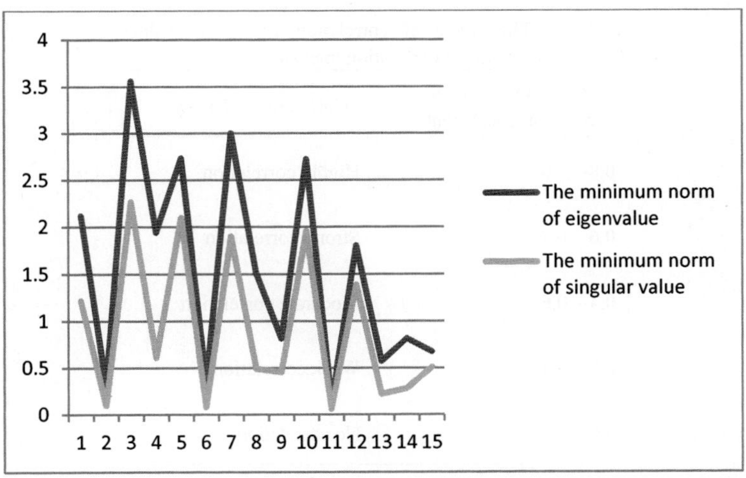

Fig. 2. The changing trend of A and B in Table 2.

From Figure 1 and Figure 2, it can be found that the minimum norm of eigenvalue and the minimum norm of singular value have a good correlation and their changing trend is basically the same. It proves the feasibility of the study. This paper will prove the correlation between the 4 indicators.

2.2. *Research methods*

In this paper, we study the correlation of the 4 indicators by calculating the Pearson correlation coefficient [1-3] between the 4 indicators. Pearson correlation coefficient is a statistical indicator designed by famous statistician Karl Pearson. The correlation coefficient is calculated on product-moment correlation, and takes two variables and their average deviation as the basis. Through two deviations multiplied to reflect the correlation degree between the two variables. The mathematical expression of correlation coefficient is this:

$$r = \frac{\sum_{i=1}^{n}(x_i - x)(y_i - y)}{\sqrt{\sum_{i=1}^{n}(x_i - x)^2 \sum_{i=1}^{n}(y_i - y)^2}}. \tag{1}$$

The x and y in the above formula are the average value of n time's experiments, x_i and y_i (i=1, 2, 3…n) are n sets of data. The greater the absolute value of correlation coefficient r, the stronger the correlation, the correlation coefficient is close to 1 or -1, the stronger the correlation, the correlation coefficient is close to 0, the weaker the correlation. The strength of the variables are related is usually judged by the following values, as shown in Table 3:

Table 3. The range of correlation coefficient values corresponding to the correlation intensity.

The absolute value of correlation coefficient	Correlation intensity
0.8—1.0	Highly correlation
0.6—0.8	Strong correlation
0.4—0.6	Moderate correlation
0.2—0.4	Weak correlation
0.0—0.2	No correlation

3. Data Analysis and Results Discussion

3.1. *Data analysis*

The each other's correlation coefficient of 4 indicators of two cases was obtained by experiments. Matrix dimension is fixed, the values range is not fixed, and such as Table 4, this is one case. Matrix dimension is not fixed, the values range is fixed, and such as Table 5, this is the other case.

A is the Pearson correlation coefficient of the minimum norm of eigenvalue and the minimum norm of singular value, B is the Pearson correlation coefficient of the minimum norm of eigenvalue and the condition number, C is the Pearson correlation coefficient of the minimum norm of eigenvalue and the absolute value of the determinant, D is the Pearson correlation coefficient of the minimum norm of singular value and the condition number, E is the Pearson correlation coefficient of the minimum norm of singular value and the absolute value of the determinant, F is the Pearson correlation coefficient of the absolute value of the determinant and the condition number, in the Table 4 and Table 5.

Table 4. The each other's Pearson correlation coefficient of4 indicators of the matrix whose dimension is fixed.

Matrix dimension is 10 x 10	A	B	C	D	E	F
Values range is 5	0.8436	-0.6623	0.7834	-0.6734	0.8701	-0.6
Values range is 6	0.9407	-0.7104	0.8065	-0.6517	0.8553	-0.5017
Values range is 7	0.8183	-0.6561	0.7175	-0.6744	0.9332	-0.5634
Values range is 8	0.7314	-0.6648	0.7615	-0.7429	0.5643	-0.5741
Values range is 9	0.8661	-0.6437	0.6859	-0.8627	0.8789	-0.6761
Values range is 10	0.7495	-0.6508	0.6304	-0.806	0.707	-0.5726
Values range is 11	0.776	-0.7423	0.5326	-0.8629	0.5235	-0.5252

Table 5. The each other's Pearson correlation coefficient of 4indicators of the matrix whose values range is fixed.

Values range is 8	A	B	C	D	E	F
Matrix dimension is 5 x 5	0.9532	-0.6621	0.8812	-0.6031	0.9445	-0.5112
Matrix dimension is 6 x 6	0.6657	-0.425	0.531	-0.8192	0.6584	-0.4314
Matrix dimension is 7 x 7	0.7998	-0.7446	0.6913	-0.6669	0.8866	-0.4282
Matrix dimension is 8 x 8	0.649	-0.618	0.51	-0.7647	0.6221	-0.4644
Matrix dimension is 9 x 9	0.8643	-0.8243	0.5914	-0.8565	0.8376	-0.7084
Matrix dimension is 10 x 10	0.841	-0.7381	0.6282	-0.772	0.8496	-0.5625
Matrix dimension is 11 x 11	0.5723	-0.5361	0.4905	-0.7448	0.7163	-0.4454

When the matrix dimension is fixed and the values range is not fixed, the relation between correlation coefficient and matrix values range is shown in Figure 3.

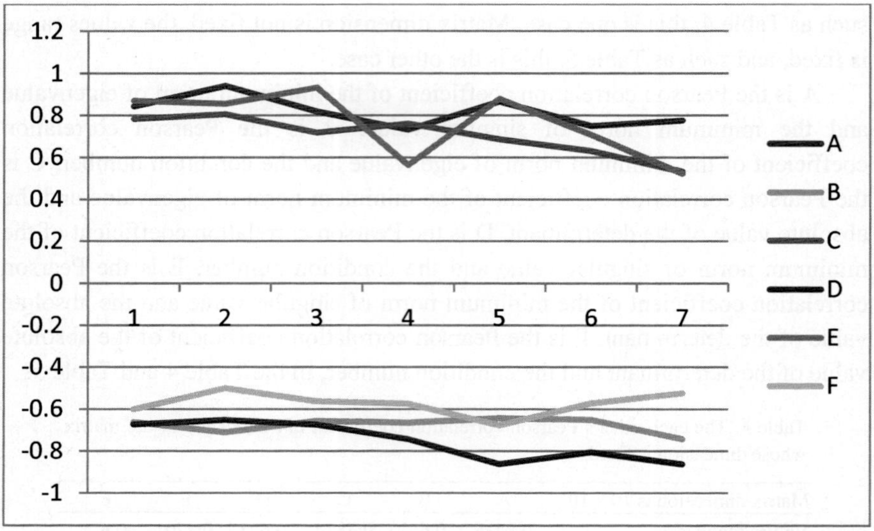

Fig. 3. The relation between correlation coefficient and matrix values range.

When the matrix dimension is not fixed and the values range is fixed, the relation between correlation coefficient and matrix dimension is shown in Figure 4.

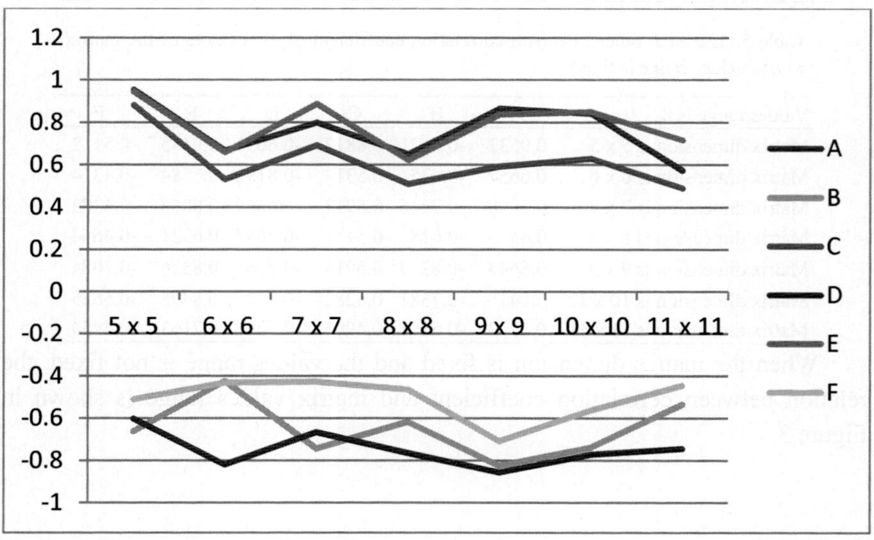

Fig. 4. The relation between correlation coefficient and matrix dimension.

From Table 4 and Figure 3 the following conclusions can be finding:
(1) B and F don't have much change when matrix values range is increase.
(2) A and C and E are getting smaller when matrix values range is increase.
(3) D is getting bigger when matrix values range is increase.
(4) On the whole, take the average of the Pearson correlation coefficient as the correlation decision criteria. The average of A is 0.818, so the minimum norm of eigenvalue and the minimum norm of singular value may be discriminated have highly correlation. The average of B is −0.676, so the minimum norm of eigenvalue and the condition number may be discriminated have strong correlation. The average of C is 0.703, so the minimum norm of eigenvalue and the absolute value of the determinant have strong correlation. The average of D is −0.753, so the minimum norm of singular value and the condition number have strong correlation. The average of E is 0.762, so the minimum norm of singular value and the absolute value of the determinant have strong correlation. The average of F is −0.573, so the condition number and the absolute value of the determinant have moderate correlation.

From Table 4 and Figure 3 the following conclusions can be finding:
(1) A and B and C and E have highly correlation, and the values swing back and forth when matrix dimension is increase.
(2) D and F don't have too much change when matrix dimension is increase.
(3) On the whole, take the average of the Pearson correlation coefficient as the correlation decision criteria. The average of A is 0.764, so the minimum norm of eigenvalue and the minimum norm of singular value may be discriminated have strong correlation. The average of B is −0.649, so the minimum norm of eigenvalue and the condition number may be discriminated have strong correlation. The average of C is 0.618, so the minimum norm of eigenvalue and the absolute value of the determinant have strong correlation. The average of D is −0.747, so the minimum norm of singular value and the condition number have strong correlation. The average of E is 0.788, so the minimum norm of singular value and the absolute value of the determinant have strong correlation. The average of F is −0.507, so the condition number and the absolute value of the determinant have moderate correlation.

3.2. *The results and discussion*

According to the experiment result it can be finding: the minimum norm of eigenvalue and the minimum norm of singular value and the condition number have very good correlation, the correlation of the absolute value of the determinant and the condition number is weaker than the others. But there still have a certain degree of correlation, so to a certain extent, the minimum norm of eigenvalue and the minimum norm of singular value and the condition number and the condition number can reflect each other.

It should be pointed out that, in this paper, the experimental data is limited, the random matrix values range is not big, and so there is a certain degree of error. Such as: when the matrix dimension is fixed and dimension is 10 x 10, the values range is 8, then the Pearson correlation coefficient is:

Values range is 8	0.7314	-0.6648	0.7615	-0.7429	0.5643	-0.5741

When the matrix dimension is 10 x 10, the values range is fixed and it is 8, then the Pearson correlation coefficient is:

Matrix dimension is 10 x 10	0.841	-0.7381	0.6282	-0.772	0.8496	-0.5625

Both the calculation is about the random matrix whose dimension is 10 x 10 and its values range is 8, but the measurement results are different. Because it is the calculation of the random matrix, and the amount of calculation is limited, so there is a certain error. But the experimental data is reliable, so this paper can prove the relationship between the 4 indicators in a certain extent.

4. Conclusion

The minimum norm of eigenvalue and the minimum norm of singular value and the condition number and the absolute value of the determinant are the judgment index of non-singular matrix. In this paper, through calculating the each other's Pearson correlation coefficient of the 4 indicators determines the correlation between the 4 indicators. Although the experimental data is limited, there are some errors, but the experiment of this article proves there is a good linear correlation between each pair of the 4 indicators. How to reduce error and increase the amount of calculation will be the future research direction.

Acknowledgments

This work is supported by the National Natural Science Foundation of China(No.61261042) and the scientific research innovation team about the key technologies of Internet of Things of Northwest University For Nationalities.

References

1. Jun-ping Jia. Statistics In Chinese [M]. Beijing: Tsinghua University press,2004.
2. RODGERS J L,NICEWANDER W A. Thirteen ways to look at the correlation coefficient [J]. The American Statis-tician, 1988, 42(1): 59- 66.
3. Yong-quan DONG, Zhan-min WANG. Some Notes about Correlation Coefficient ρ In Chinese [J]. College Mathematics, 2008, 24(2):182-186.

A Reliability Analysis Method of the Composite Web Services

Yan-jun SHU*, Zhi-bo WU and Yun-ping FENG

School of Computer Science and Technology, Harbin Institute of Technology, Harbin, 150001, China

**E-mail: yjshu@hit.edu.cn*

Service-oriented computing is emerging method to develop extensible computing systems which evolved from component-based software engineering. The complex web services can be composited by simpler, loosely coupled, reusable web services. Reliability is an important factor for choosing, ranking and compositing Web services. However, existing analysis methods of composite web services are rare and majority of them are proposed for component-based software reliability analysis. In this paper, a reliability analysis method for composite Web services is proposed. The architecture of the composite Web service is characterized as a tree which is transformed from its business process execution language (BPEL) description. In addition, several examples are illustrated to demonstrate the effectiveness of the proposed analysis method.

Keywords: Service orientation architecture; Composite web service; Reliability analysis.

1. Introduction

Service-Orientation Architecture (SOA) has played an extremely important role in the evolution of Information Technology in the last decade [1]. It provides the foundations for some of today's most significant advancements, such as Web 2.0, Cloud computing, and the Internet of Things. A complex Web service can be combines simpler, loosely coupled, reusable Web services by using service composition via the Business Process Execution Language (BPEL). Web services composition is an efficient and cost-effective way to develop the modern business applications.

Reliability is a key issue of SOA which has been applied in many critical domains such as military or financial Web services systems. The dynamic nature of internet environment makes the reliability improvement more challengeable. On the other side, the reliability of composite Web services is usually analyzed by the architecture-based software reliability analysis models [2,3]. According to the failure behavior, the architecture-based software reliability analysis models are categorized into the state-based and path-based models. However, both of these two kinds of models are not considering the concurrent circumstance which is a common situation in the operation of composite Web services. Moreover, how to export the architecture of the objective composite Web services is a hard work. The existing reliability analysis models proposed a lot of complex rules to construct the architecture and transition of Web services which is very difficult for users.

In this paper, the architecture of composite Web services is characterized by a construction dependency tree which is named WS-CDT. The WS-CDT can be easily transited form BPEL descriptions. Moreover, the reliability analysis method based on the WS-CDT can be easily applied. Then, some experiments are represented to show the advantages of the method in calculating the reliability of composite Web services.

2. The Constructive Dependency Tree of Composite Web Services

2.1. *Basic compositional structures*

A composite Web Service is composed by integrating existing Web services which can communicate and cooperate with each other to complete missions collectively. The compositional structures can be expressed by a flow chart with transition probability. There are four basic compositional structures.

- ***Sequence*** Structure. The most common structure which represents the sequence Web service preformed at a time. Figure 1 shows the structure's notation.

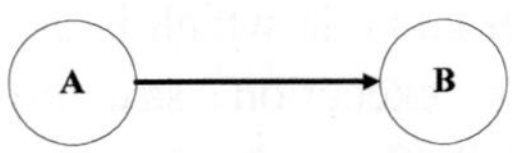

Fig. 1. *Sequence* structure.

- ***If*** Structure. Generally, there are two or more Web services in the if structure. As shown in Figure 2, one of B or C is executed, then the if structure complete.

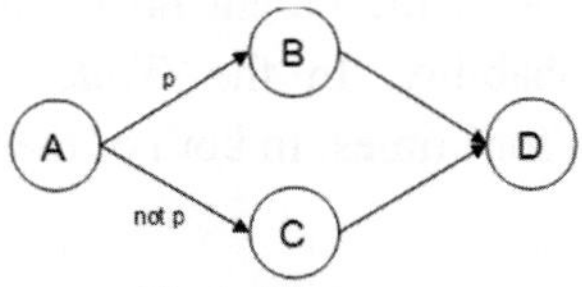

Fig. 2. *If* structure.

- ***Flow*** Structure. One of Web service's important feature. In this structure, B and C services will be executed in parallelism. Moreover, if one of B or C services fails, then the overall task fails. The notation is depicted in Figure 3.

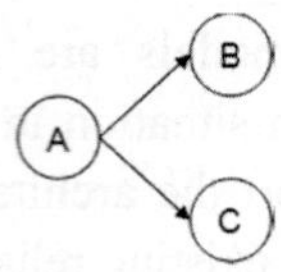

Fig. 3. *Flow* structure.

- ***While*** Structure and ***Repeat*** Structure. In these structures, the condition is judged first. Then, the structure is executed until the condition is false. The notation is shown in Figure 4.

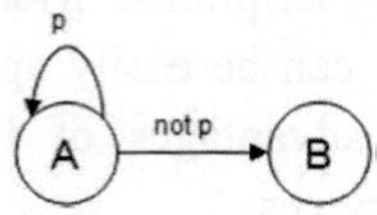

Fig. 4. *While* structure and *Repeat* structure.

2.2. *The definition of the web services composition dependency tree*

The Web Services Composition Dependency Tree (WS-CDT) is a tree. According to the iteration feature of a tree, every *TreeNode* :=<*type*, *parent*, *childList*, *weight*>.

(1) *type*∈{*ServiceNode*, *ControlNode*}. There are two kinds of nodes, the *ServiceNodes*and the *ControlNodes*. The *ServiceNode* is a leaf of WS-CDT which represents the reliability of a component service (a basic service or a composite service). The definition of *ServiceNode* is *ServiceReli*. The *ControlNode* is the internal node which is the father of a leaf. It is used to present the children's execution structure. Thus, a *ControlNode*∈ {*Sequence*, *If*, *Flow*, *While/Repeat*}.

(2) *parent*: WS-CDT *TreeNode*, the father of the tree node.

(3) *childList*:{*child1*, *child2*,…, *childn*: WS-CDT *TreeNode* }.

(4) *weight*: the weight of the tree node, which represents the execution probability $\{p_i\}$ relative to the parent node. In the *If* structure, p_i is the branch execution probability. In the *While/Repeat* structure, p_i is the probability of the loop for i times. In both of these two structure, $\sum_{i=0}^{n} p_i = 1$.

3. Transition from the BPEL to a WS-CDT

The Organization For the Advancement Of Structured Information Standards (OASIS) uses the BPEL as the specification standards of composite service [4]. The architecture of the composite Web service which is characterized by the WS-CDT can be transformed from its BPEL file. There are two steps to implement the transformation: extract the WS-token string from BPEL and mapping WS-token string to WS-CDT.

(1) Extract the WS-token String from BPEL

BPEL has its own syntax rules. The grammatical items include Partner Links, Variables, Correlation Sets, Activity, etc. In BPEL, the structure activity of a composite Web service is a series of basic compositional structures. These structures are nested and iterated. In this paper, the WS-token string is defined to represent the relations between activities and Web services. A WS-token string is a set of tuples. These tuples are nested and iterated. Every tuple is represented as (*basic Web services structure activities, Web services numbers*). There are four kinds of construction activities which are *Sequence, If, Flow and While/Repeat*. The start and the end of activities are denoted by"(" and ")". The *Web services numbers* denote the service of activities. Thus, a WS-token string can be obtained by parsing the BEPL description.

(2) Mapping the WS-token string to a WS-CDT

The WS-CDT is a tree and there are two kinds of node, {(*Service Nodes*), (*Control Nodes*)}. In the above discussion, how the WS-token string is extracted from the BPEL source file has been introduced. As an intermediate representation, the WS-token string can transform BPEL to WS-CDT conveniently and quickly. Scanning the WS-token string in sequence, the characters "(" and ")" mean the start and the end of the *basic Web service structure activities*. The *basic Web services structure activities* of WS-token string are mapped to the *Control Nodes* of WS-CDT. The *Web services numbers* of WS-token string are mapped to the *Service Nodes* of WS-CDT.

4. The Reliability Analysis Method Based on the WS-CDT

The architecture of composite web services is characterized clearly in the WS-CDT. Users can calculate the reliability by integrating the reliability of every service and communication link with WS-CDT. The users need to travel the WS-CDT in Pre-order. If *TreeNode.type* is *ServiceNode*, it means it is a leaf and represents a component Web service. The reliability is *ServiceReli*. The information about reliability can be obtain from services providers, the third party testing, the experts' experience in related fields or the similar web services. However, the determination of the reliability is not the topic in this paper.

Otherwise, *TreeNode.type* is *ControlNode* which means it represents a kind of composition structure. There exist one or several children for a *ControlNode*. Therefore, the subtrees can be partitioned in terms of *TreeNode.childList.* The partition is iterated execution until the *TreeNode.type* is *ServiceNode.* Based on the reliability of subtrees, the reliability for every *ControlNode* can be calculated. The calculation formulas for basic compositional Structure are in Table 1 which have been introduced widely [5]. m is the degree of the *TreeNode* which means there are m children. $R_i$is the reliability of the component web service i. For composition structure, both these two kinds of p_i are recorded in *TreeNode.weight*.

Table 1. Formulas for composition structures.

Composition structures	*Sequence*	*If*	*Flow*	*While/Repeat*
Reliability	$\prod_{i=1}^{n} R_i$	$\prod_{i=1}^{n} p_i R_i$	$\prod_{i=1}^{n} R_i$	$\prod_{i=1}^{n} p_i R_i$

5. Experiments

In this section, a composite Web service of bank transaction is an example for how to apply the proposed method [6]. There are three kinds of web services and they are deposit and withdraw service, invest assessment and three level approval service, loan services. The description and reliability of the component web services are listed in the Table 2.

Table 2. Reliability of the component web services.

No.	1	2	3	4	5	6
Name	Deposit and with draw	loan	Invest assessment	Primary approval	Intermediate approval	advanced approval
R_i	0.782	0.804	0.792	0.791	0.783	0.817

According to 10031 tests of the bank transaction service, *TreeNode.weight* is {0.129, 0.168, 0.703} for the *If* structure and *TreeNode.weight* is {0.262, 0.310, 0.059, 0.005} for the *While/Repeat* structure. As introduced above, the WS-token String can be extracted from the BPEL description of the bank transaction service which is (*If*, (*While/Repeat*, 1)(2)(*Sequence*, 3(*Flow*, 456))). Then, the WS-CDT is derived in Fig.1. By applying the analysis method, WS-CDT is partitioned by three subtrees. The roots of these subtrees are WH, Service 2, SE which represent *While/Repeat,* Service 2, *Sequence* structure in Fig. 5. By further partition, the SE subtree has two subtrees which are Service 3 and FL. FL represents the *Flow* structure. The reliability of WH, Service 2, SE subtrees can be calculated by using the formulas in Table 1 which are 0.684,

0.804 and 0.4. Finally, the reliability of the WS-CDT is 0.527 by calculating the *If* structure formula. Furthermore, users can rank the web services and sensitivities by increasing or decreasing the reliability of component web services.

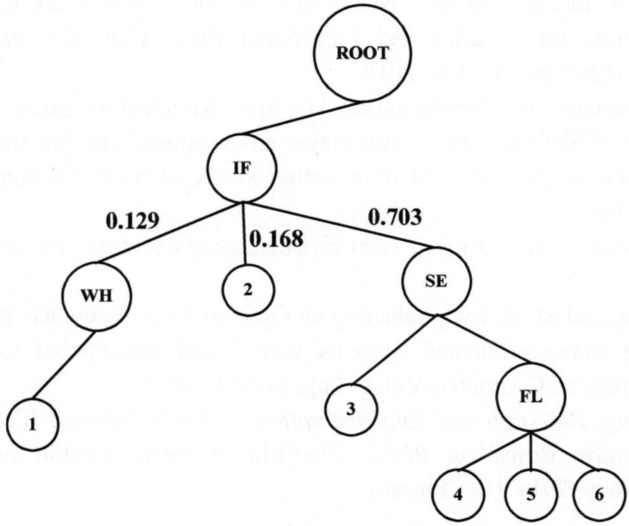

Fig. 5. The WS-CDT of the bank transaction service.

6. Conclusion

This paper proposes a reliability analysis method for composite Web services. The main idea is to transform the BPEL description of the composite web service to a WS-CDT. Then, the reliability is obtained by iterated partition the WS-CDT and calculation the reliability of subtrees. By this way, users can analysis the reliability easily. In future, the reliability functions and execution time will be considered to improve the accuracy of the analysis method.

Acknowledgments

This work was supported in part by the National Natural Science Foundation of China (Grant No.61202091), and the Fundamental Research Funds for Central Universities (Grant No.NSRIF.2016050).

References

1. T. Erl, Diffusion Processes in Advanced Technological Materials, Prentice Hall Publications, 2005.
2. T. Hu, M.Guo, S. Guo, et al: MTTF of composite web services. in *Proc. Int.* Symposium on *Parallel and Distributed Processing with Applications* (*ISPA*), *IEEE*, pp.130-137, 2010.
3. M. Rahmani, A. Azadmanesh, H. Siy: Architecture-based reliability analysis of Web services in multilayer environment. The 3rd International Workshop on Principles of Engineering Service-Oriented Systems. ACM, 2011: 57-60.
4. Information on `http://docs.oasis-open.org/ws-rx/wsrm/200702`
5. Z. Zheng and M. R. Lyu: Selecting an Optimal Fault Tolerance Strategy for Reliable Service-Oriented Systems with Local and Global Constraints. IEEE Trans on Computer, Vol. 64, pp. 219-232,2015.
6. X. Zhang, *Research and Implementation of Fault Tolerant Web Services Composition Based on BPEL*. The Master thesis, Harbin Institute of Technology, 2014. (In Chinese)

Ontology-based Comprehensive Weighted Similarity Algorithm Research

Xian-kun ZHANG, Qian ZHANG* and Xin-ya GAO

College of Computer Science and Information Engineering, Tianjin University of Science and Technology,
Tianjin, China
**E-mail: 381398314@qq.com*

As existing similarity algorithms are hampered by low accuracy and recall rates, a comprehensive ontology-based weighted similarity algorithm was proposed for case retrieval. Taking into account the various attributes of the case, different attribute calculation methods were used and each attribute was weighted in accordance and the similarity of the case was calculated. The similarity algorithm was validated by three psychological counseling cases. By comparing the traditional similarity algorithm based on the nearest distance and the weighted similarity algorithm, this paper demonstrates that the weighted similarity algorithm exhibit higher accuracy.

Keywords: Case-Based Reasoning (CBR); Ontology model; Case retrieval; Similarity algorithm; Psychological counseling.

1. Introduction

Case-based reasoning (CBR) is a set of methods that have a long tradition in the field of artificial intelligence[1], that is depending on previous experience solving the problems through reasoning and machine learning mechanisms[2]. CBR involved the use of some methods to find the same or most similar cases in memory or past cases base and reuse the solution of the original problem in the new issue[3]. As soon as the new issue is solved, it will be addressed to update the original database under the use of learning mechanism[4]. The library of psychological counseling case stores the events that have already occurred. Counselors often recalls his memories of similar events to form a solution for the current event[5]. So, for the psychological consultation cases, CBR is one of the common techniques for psychological counseling case decision.

Case retrieval is the core of CBR, it works with a policy for retrieval from the case library to find a case or cases with the most similar experience to the current problem[6]. Retrieve matching efficiency and quality of the search results is two most important elements of case retrieval. Retrieval process is very important in the implementation of CBR, it is the key factors to influence the efficiency and precision. The most common search methods are the nearest neighbor method, inductive method and knowledge-guided method[7]. There are some disadvantages of the traditional methods on accuracy. This paper uses weighted similarity matching algorithm for case retrieval to improve the efficiency and accuracy.

2. Related Research

Current ontology-based similarity computing methods are mainly divided into four parts which include semantic-distance based, information-content based, propertied based and hybrid-similarity method[8]. Distance based method[9] is the earliest use of ontology similarity calculation method, and ShortestPath method [10] is typical of this kind of algorithm. It is using the concepts in the ontology tree path lengths to quantify the concept of semantic distance between the tree nodes. WeightedLinks method [11] improved the ShortestPath method by using edge weights which allocated to the concept of node. With the continuous improvement of semantic- distance based method, it has developed into the structure of the ontology-based similarity algorithm[12]. Information-based method is using the common parent node information to measure the similarity between two concept nodes. And the node information is measured by p which means the frequency of the concept's occurrence in the ontology. Butthis method does not take into account the information which the child node itself contains. The attribute based method is measured similarity by the number of public properties that the nodes contains.

3. Psychological Counseling Case Retrieval Algorithm

3.1. *Psychological counseling case ontology*

The solution of CBR-based psychological counseling case is formed to find a similar case in the case database based on the supplicants' symptoms, and improved the retrieved case solution according to the actual situation of current cases. So, CBR-based counseling case should at least include two parts which are description and solution. Building counseling case of ontology model which contains information and solutions, solving semantic ambiguity in case ontology construction based on CBR and to quickly and accurately locate callers the cause and symptomatic selected consultation method of psychotherapy, has important significance in preventing further deterioration. This paper build the psychological counseling case ontology model based on the expansion of ABC ontology model.

3.2. *Similarity computation*

Case retrieval is the core part of CBR, which determine the quality of the system to some extent. The common used retrieval methods are nearest neighbor method, templates method, inductive method and knowledge-guided method. This paper uses weighted similarity algorithm to retrieve. The tasks of this part is to select the most similar cases under the current caller's basic information, and then, give the case solutions to the caller as reference. At last make the patient's own advisory programme on the basis of the similar case solution.

The feature attribute of the psychological counseling case can be represented by a feature vector $V = (x_1, x_2 \dots x_n)$. If all the eigenvalues of the two feature vectors are matched, the two case is called the same case. If the partial eigenvalues are not the same, the two case is called similar case. Using Sim to represent the similarity between cases. $Sim \in [0,1]$. The higher the value, the higher the degree of similarity. If Simis equal to 1 ,it means for the same case, otherwise, if it is equal to 0 ,it means for different cases. For two cases A and B, we define two feature vectors $V_A = (a_1, a_2 \dots a_n)$ and $V_B = (b_1, b_2 \dots b_n)$, so the similarity between two eigenvalues of ai and bi is represented by $Sim(a_i, b_i)$.

3.2.1. *Attribute similarity calculation*

(1) Concept name similarity calculation method

Name is the most critical and the most important attribute value of the index. Psychological counseling ontology, to a certain extent, can be unified in the psychological counseling case of the relevant concept name, which provides a convenient for the calculation of the similarity of concept name. If there is a completely same property value between the target case and the source case, then they can be completely matched by the name of the concept. Such as case name, gender and other attributes can be match using this method. Definition 1 gives the method of calculating the similarity between the two psychological cases of the same level node.

Definition 1: Set $Sim_{nam}(a_p, b_p)$ to the attribute of the name matching similarity for case A and case B. Set $N(a_p)$ to the property name of the case A, and the calculation formula is as follows:

$$Sim_{nam}\left(a_p,b_p\right)=\begin{cases}1 & N(a_p)=N(b_p)\\ 0 & N(a_p)\neq N(b_p)\end{cases}. \tag{1}$$

(2) Similarity computation based on time attribute matching

Psychological counseling case has the attributes of time, duration and so on, they can use time attribute matching method. Definition 2 gives a method for calculating the similarity based on time attribute matching.

Definition 2: Set $Sim_{tim}\left(a_p,b_p\right)$ to attribute of the time attribute matching similarity for case A and case B. Set $T\left(a_p\right)$ to the time attribute of the case A. The calculation formula of the time attribute similarity matching is as follows:

$$Sim_{tim}\left(a_p,b_p\right)=1-\frac{\left|T(a_p)-T(b_p)\right|}{Max(T(a_p),T(b_p))}. \tag{2}$$

(3) Similarity calculation based on numerical attribute matching

Numerical value is a kind of common attribute value type. The method can be used to match the attribute of age and degree. The numerical similarity calculation method is based on the absolute value distance formula, which is defined by definition 3.

Definition 3: Set $Sim_{val}\left(a_p,b_p\right)$ to the attribute of the value of the attribute matching similarity for case A and case B. Set $V\left(a_p\right)$ to the numerical value of the case A. The calculation formula of the similarity matching of the numerical value is as follows:

$$Sim_{val}\left(a_p,b_p\right)=1-\frac{\left|NV(a_p)-NV(b_p)\right|}{Max(NV(a_p),NV(b_p),\left|NV(a_p)-NV(b_p)\right|)}. \tag{3}$$

(4) Ontology concept similarity matching based on nearest ancestor

For psychological symptoms, physical symptoms, social functions and other complex attributes, the use of the first three methods can not be used in similarity matching, then you can use the method based on the recent ancestors of the concept of ontology similarity.

If p and q are two nodes in the ontology tree, the distance between them is defined as follows.

Definition 4:

$$dist(p,q)=\begin{cases}0 & p,q \text{ is the same node in the tree}\\ \infty & \text{no common ancestor node between p and q}\\ n & \text{n is the number of edge between p and q}\end{cases}. \tag{4}$$

Then, the concept of the similarity between p and q is calculated as follows.
Definition 5:

$$Sim_{onto} = \begin{cases} 1 & dist(p,q) = 0 \\ 0 & dist(p,q) = \infty \\ \dfrac{\omega * N_3 + 1}{n + \omega * N_3 + 1} & dist(p,q) = n \end{cases} . \quad (5)$$

$dist(p,q)$ presents the distance between p and q, N_3presentsthethe distance between the common parent node to the root node, ω is the adjustment factor, it can be obtained by neural network and other methods. In the field of psychological counseling it is 2. The concept similarity algorithm based on nearest ancestor is described as follows:

Step 1: Find nodes p, q in the ontology;

Step 2: If p and q are the same node, sim=1, the program ends, otherwise go to step3;

Step 3: Find p and q's recent ancestors parent node, if parent node is empty, then sim=0, program ends, otherwise go to step 4;

Step 4: Calculate the distances between parent node and p, q and root, N1, N2, N3 respectively;

Step 5: dist=N_1+N_2, if dist=0, sim=1. If dist=∞, sim=0. Otherwise,

$$Sim = \frac{\omega * N_3 + 1}{dist + \omega * N_3 + 1}$$

3.2.2. *Case similarity calculation*

The similarity between the two cases is the global similarity, which can be defined as the weighted sum of the similarity of each attribute.

Definition 6:

$$Sim(A,B) = \frac{\sum_{p=1}^{n} \theta_p Sim(a_p, b_p)}{\sum_{p=1}^{n} \theta_p} . \quad (6)$$

$Sim(a_p, b_p)$ represents the similarity between two attributes of a_p, b_p, θ_P represents the weight of the attribute p, which is based on the importance of the area in the case. The weights of all attributes are submitted to 1.

3.3. *Case retrieval algorithm*

According to the above analysis, the description of psychological cases similarity algorithm(PCSA) is as follows:

Step 1: Get two feature vectors $V_A = (a_1, a_2 \ldots a_n)$ and $V_B = (b_1, b_2 \ldots b_n)$;

Step 2: For each group of properties, calculate the similarity $Sim(a_p, b_p)$;

Step 3: Calculate the product of the attribute similarity and its corresponding weight, and the sum is case similarity which can presents as CaseSim;

Step 4: The case database in all cases performed Step1- Step3, and get the case similarity set CaseSim[n];

Step 5: Sort CaseSim[n] from big to small, and form a sort queue CaseSim Index[n];

Step 6: If the highest degree of similarity in the queue is greater than the specified threshold, the case is the most similar case, and return this case.

3.4. *Case similarity experiment*

3.4.1. *Comprehensive weighted similarity algorithm experiment*

According to attribute similarity calculation method in 3.2.1 and case similarity calculation method in 3.2.2, respectively compute the similarity between acrophobia and hematophobia, between forced wink behavior and compulsive hand washing behavior, between Obsessive compulsive disorder and depression. The results are shown in figure 1:

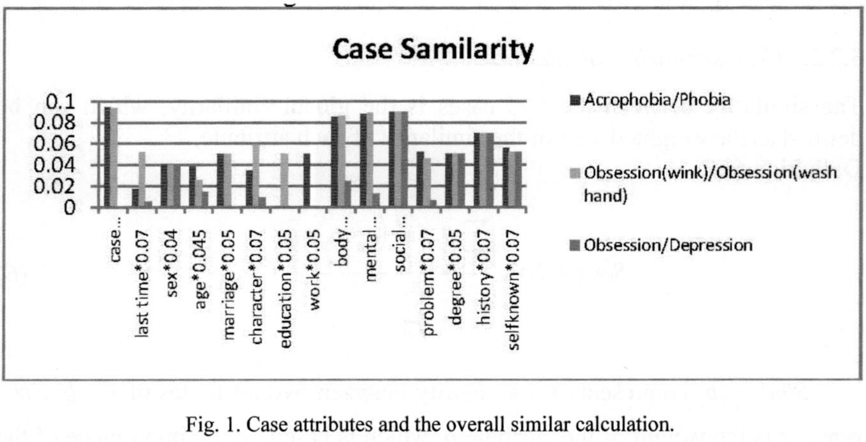

Fig. 1. Case attributes and the overall similar calculation.

As shown in the example above, the attributes of the case are the case name, duration of disease, gender, age, marital status, personality traits, education, work, physical symptoms, psychological symptoms, social functions, problem description, medical history, insight and severity. According to the important degree of diagnosis and the distinction of the case, the corresponding weight is given, and the case similarity is calculated. The similarity between the cases of the disorder is obviously higher than that of the similarity between depression and the case of obsessive compulsive disorder. The experimental results show that the similarity based on the characteristics of the psychological consultation case can reflect the similarity between the case samples, and the validity of the case similarity calculation is verified.

3.4.2. *Comparison of results with the traditional nearest distance similarity algorithm*

Compared with the traditional algorithm based on nearest distance, the similarity of several typical cases of psychological counseling is calculated, and the results are shown in Table 1 and figure 2:

Table 1. Two similarity algorithm results.

No.	Case1	Case2	Nearest distance	Synthetic weighted
1	Obsession(wash)	Obsession(lock)	0.68524	0.85425
2	Test anxiety	Marriage anxiety	0.52869	0.83084
3	Anxiety	phobophobia	0.13001	0.14262
4	Exam fear	Acrophobia	0.62435	0.85984
5	Depression	Depressive neurosis	0.75142	0.89872
6	Mental disorder	Neurosis	0.05328	0.04632
7	Depression	Panic disorder	0.03354	0.0253
8	Anxiety	Panic disorder	0.36752	0.22586
9	Normal problem	Serious problem	0.63287	0.64261
10	ASD	PTSD	0.53245	0.68592

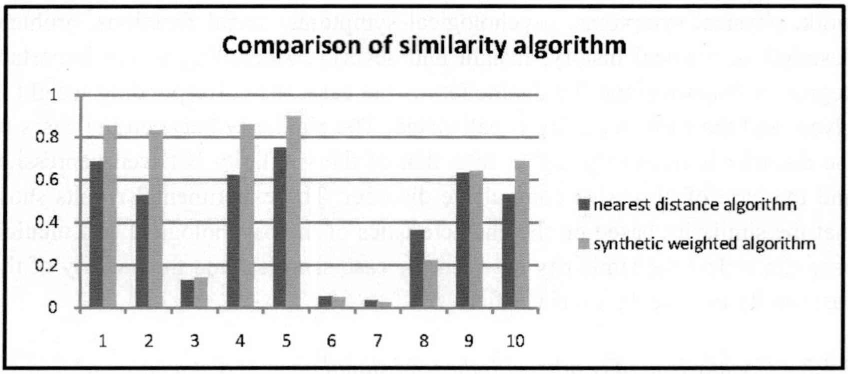

Fig. 2.Two similarity algorithm results.

Compared with the traditional distance based case similarity algorithm,the similarity value obtained by the comprehensive weighted similarity calculation method is more accurate. The main reason is that, for each pair of cases, taking full account of the various attributes of the case, although the amount of calculation increased, the time increased, but there is more comprehensive and more accurately reflect the similarity between cases. Of course, this method also has shortcomings, such as the existence of a large number of weights in the calculation process has a great impact for the system. This can be improved by machine learning or networks technology in the course of the study.

4. Conclusion

Based on the analysis of the case of psychological counseling, this paper constructs a model of psychological counseling case ontology based on the extended ABC ontology model, and designs a case similarity calculation algorithm, which improves the efficiency and accuracy of case retrieval. On the basis of this work, it is also needed to further improve the case base, so that the case can be better realized, and finally to develop a system of psychological consultation and can be reused.

Acknowledgments

This work is supported by Youth National Natural Science Fund (61402331, 61402332), Science and technology innovation fund project of Tianjin(14ZX CXGX00409,14ZXCXGX00531). Address: NO.1038,Dagu South Road, Hexi District, Tianjin, China.

References

1. López, Beatriz. Case-based reasoning: A concise introduction[M]. Spain: Morgan and Claypool Publishers, 2013.
2. Xavior, Anthony M, Anouncia, Margret S. Case-based reasoning (CBR) model for hard machining process[J]. International Journal of Advanced Manufacturing Technology, 2012, 61(9-12):1269-1275.
3. Berkat, Abdellatif. Using Case-Based Reasoning (CBR) for detecting computer virus [J]. International Journal of Computer Science Issues, 2011, 8(4-2):606-610.
4. Guan Hongbo, Yang Baoan. New product introduction management model based on CBR[M]. GuangDong, China: IEEE Computer Society, 2011.
5. Ma Qianguang. From the perspective of psychological counseling case of statistical analysis on students ' mental health[J]. Ideological and theoretical education, 2012, 15(06):64-67.
6. Ye Feng, Zhou Jun. Research and practice of clinical cases of knowledge base based on ontology[J]. Chinese Journal of medical instrumentation, 2012,36(3):188-191.DOI:10.3969/j.issn.1671-7104.2012.03.009.
7. Yuan Guo, JieHu, Yinghong Peng et al. A CBR system for injection mould design based on ontology: A case study[J]. Computer-Aided Design, 2012, 44(6):496-508.
8. Sun Haixia, Qian Qing, Cheng Ying. Summary of the method of semantic similarity computation based on ontology[J]. Library and information technology, 2010, 26(1):51-56.
9. Yang Fangying, Jiang Zhengxiang, Zhang Shanshan. Structure of the ontology-based semantic similarity computing[J]. The development of computer technology, 2013, 23(7):52-56.
10. Zhao Yongjin, Zheng Hongyuan. A study on ontology-based semantic similarity algorithm[J]. Computer applications, 2009, 29(11):3074-3076.
11. Li Wenjie, Zhao Yan. Structure of the ontology-based concept semantic similarity algorithm[J]. Computer engineering, 2010, 36(23):4-6.
12. He Yuanxiang, Shi Baoming, Zhang Yong. Study on ontology-based semantic similarity algorithm[J]. Computer application and software, 2013, 30(11):312-315..

An Expanded Model of Role-Based Access Model Based on Resource Model

Zhi-hong LIANG, Xing-ping SUN* and Qing-yi CHEN

School of Software, Yunnan University
Kunming, Yunnan, 650091, China
**E-mail: sunxp@ynu.edu.cn*

Jun-hua HU and Shu-qiong SUN

Key Laboratory for Software Engineering of Yunnan Province Republic of China
Kunming, Yunnan, 650091, China

In the RBAC model, a resource is represented by an object. As there is close connectivity between objects and operation, the resources accessing control authorization is inconvenient. This paper extends the RBAC object model to the resource model while the resource elements, abstract resources and resource bundles are defined in the resource model. The RBAC operating model is extended and the concept of abstract operations and the operating bundles are proposed. In addition, the relationship between resources and operations are discussed and the grading of the resource and role is proposed.

Keywords: RBAC; Accessing control; Resource model.

1. Introduction

With the development of information technology and the popularization of network, it brings people not only convenience but also a deeper understanding of the Internet. And with the development of the Internet, it also faces another big problem --- the security of the information. To control the security of information we need effective safety management mechanism, and access control is an effective security management mechanism.

International Organization for Standardization (IOS) in its customized security architecture for open systems interconnection reference model (ISO7498-2) gives the definition of a standard security services, these services include authentication, access control, data confidentiality, data integrity, and non-repudiation. Access that controls as one of the five standard security services, it is an important way to guarantee the data security. The Standard for evaluating process of trusted computing system of United States Department of Defense regarded it as an important index for the evaluation of system security. We can see from the above that it is necessary to take access control to improve the system security, and it was already to be the fact without argument.

* Corresponding author.

2. Related Research

Discretionary access control is a kind of access control by treating the subject as a basis , which allows authorize access permission independently of its championed resources to other users or recycle the permissions have been granted from other users. This operation which allows users authorize freely makes it difficult to determine what resources the user has the access permission. So access control will be got stuck on uniformity, and also lack of some relevant safety considerations.

Mandatory access control (MAC) is mainly granting the users and the objects a security level, and the users can not change the level of security which only the manager has the authority. The system will contrast the relative attribute of security level between the access subjects and controlled objects, and then determine whether the access to the main body can access the controlled object.

3. RBAC Model

RBAC is different from DAC and MAC model, because this model introduced the role between the user and the access. First, assignment the roles to users, and then assignment authorities for the roles, finally the user obtain corresponding permissions through the roles.

Although there has been more than one model based on RBAC, RBAC96 has become a widely used authoritative reference because it contains the important aspects of the traditional RBAC models. And it is very close with the RBAC model which raised by the United States national institute of standards and technology. RBAC96 model is a model family, which includes RBAC0, RBAC1, RBAC2 and RBAC3 models. Here will give some introduction about RBAC96 models which is regarded as representative. RBAC0 is also known as the core model, RBAC1 is referred to as the hierarchical model, and RBAC2 is known as constraint model.

RBAC0 model is the foundation model, the other models are developed independently from it. And it mainly contains six basic elements ---the users, roles, conversation, objects, actions, objects and privileges; RBAC1 model is developed from the core model and adds the Hierarchical relationship between the roles which means a role that can be automatically acquired by inheritance of all the relevant rights of an inherited role by one or more roles; The constraint model is built on the basis of the core model and adds the Conception of constraint. And constraints determine whether each component of the core model can be accepted. Constraints can be divided into separation of static and dynamic separation of duties and responsibilities. The former is mainly used in the formulation process of the user and the role and the latter is mainly used in the role of the activation process; the complete RBAC model as mentioned above is mainly includes RBAC0, RBAC1, and RBAC2. The complete RBAC model is shown in the Fig.1[3,4].

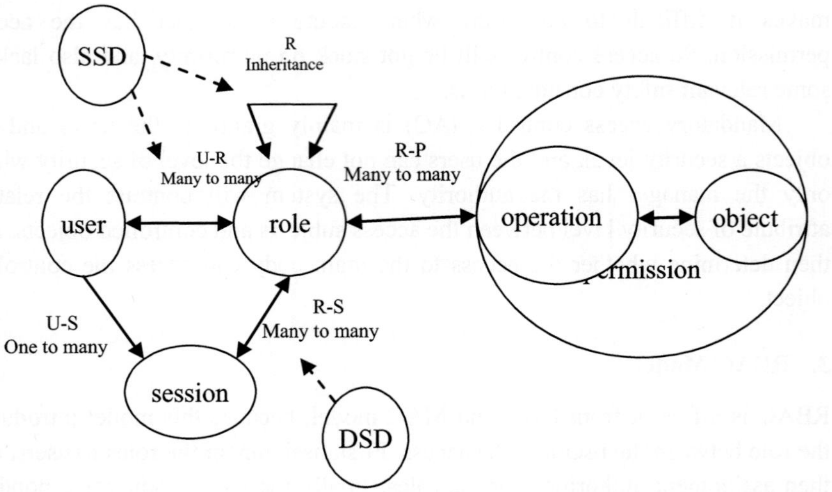

Fig. 1. Complete RBAC model Punctuation marks are used at the end of equations as if they appeared directly in the text.

4. RBAC Resource Model Development

Because of the complexity of the resource itself and the complexity of authorization, the same resource can be put together and set up. And these resources will be accessed only by having a certain degree role. This changes the limit for a single resource setting, and reduces the number of times for the resource setting. In the same way, you can put some of the commonly used operations together; you can also put some common operations of a role together, and this will help reduces the work of setting up a continuous role. According to the ideas shown above, we can expand the resources and operations as well as the resources and roles in the traditional RBAC model.

4.1. *RBAC model of resource development*

In resource development of RBAC model, firstly, the resource model is put forward. Here will introduce the definition of abstract resources and resource constraints as well as the relationship of them. The operation of the original model which is closely with the resource has been unable to meet the current expansion of the model. So the operation should be extended, and then put forward the operation model. In the operation model, it has proposed the definition of abstract operation and operation constraint as well as the relationship between these operations. And then the resource model and operation model are combined to introduce and discuss the relationship between resources and operation of expansion. Finally, the relationship between the resources and the role of the expansion is determined. The role and resources will be set up a strict level and combined by the role hierarchy and resource level, and different levels of roles can access the resources that are lower or the same level, so as to control the access to resources for different levels of roles. The RBAC model of resource development is shown in the Fig. 2.

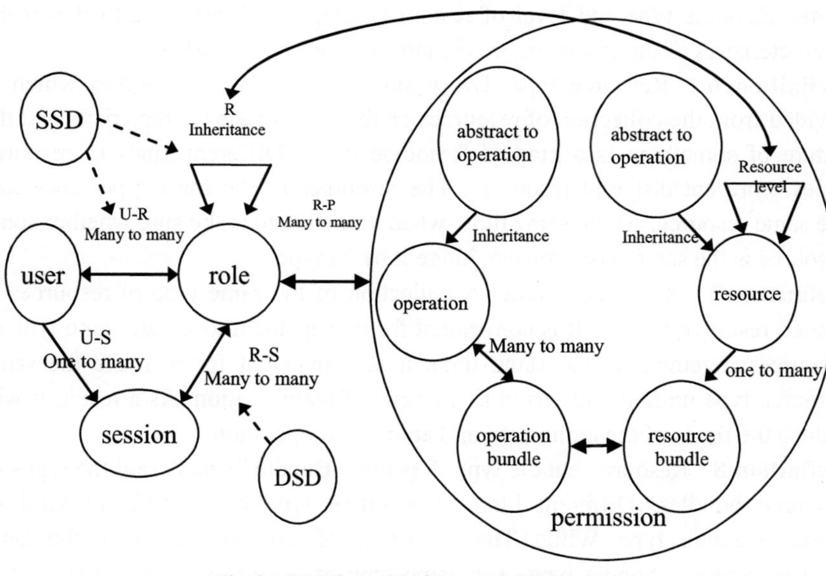

Fig. 2. RBAC model of resource development.

4.2. *Resource model*

Definition 1 Entity: All kinds of equipment, software ,and the data such as physical devices, data files, memory, or process from computer or network and a legitimate users are referred to entity.

Definition 2 Subject: Subject refers to the active entity which can implement operations on other entities and is the sponsor of the operation. Meanwhile ,the

Subject can refer to the user itself as well as the computer terminals and smart phones.

Definition 3 Object: The passive entities which accept other entities operating are the receiving operation and the objects that are in need of protection because of under the effect of the main body. Sometimes it is called the goal. The Information and objects which can be used to be operated can be seen as object. The object can refer to documents, data and records and so on in a computer system environment.

Definition 4 Resource: The collections of objects which can be accessed in the computer system are called resource.

Definition 5 Resource attribute: To be used to describe the characteristics of resources is called resource attribute. For example, describing the resource name, resource type and level of resources, etc., which are used to depict the characteristics of the resources are the attributes of the resources.

Definition 6 Resource type: Every small collection of resources which is divided from the collection of resources on the basis of the characteristic and the nature of something is a kind of Resource types. Different kinds of resource types represent different resources. The resources of the same type represents the same resource. At the same time, when you want to make sure whether some resource is the same type, you can judge it by its type.

Definition 7 Resource bundle: A collection of the same type of resources is named resource bundle. It is convenient for management to tie the same type of resources together. At the same time, it is convenient for to make the same resource type unified authorized at the time of authorization. As a result, it will reduce the times of the authorized and authorized operation.

Definition 8 Resource bundle type: Resource Bundle Type is said the types of resource bundles. Different kind of resource type owns different kind of resource bundle type. While, The same kind of resource type owns the same kind of resource bundle type. The same type of resources are tied together to define a type of resource bundles. In general, the type of resource is regarded as resource bundle type.

Definition 9 Abstract Resource: Abstract resources are the abstraction of resources and a description of resources, which we can form a new base class ,bring out the resources with the same properties and bring the resources of the same properties together.

All the other resources inherit Abstract Resource, who is the father of all the resources. The resource of the same resource bundle have not only the same resource bundle type but also the same resource type and vice versa. But these resources are in need of a resource type to identify itself what kind of resource it belongs to. So the abstract resources represent the upper resources of these resources.

4.3. *Operation model*

In the last section, the operational objects-resources are extended and the definition of Abstract Resource and Resource Bundle have been put forward and the relationship between resources are discussed. In the original model, the operation which is closely related to the model can not meet the extended model ,therefore the operation must also be extended.

Definition 10 Operation: The action which Subject is access to the resources protected by system is defined as Operation. Operation is an action for system access to protected resources .

Definition 11 Operation Attribute: The feature which is used to describe the characteristics of the Operation is defined as Operation Attribute.

For example, the description of the operation's name, a relatively higher operating and what kind of specific operation it is, etc., which are used to characterize features of operations, are the attributes of the operation.

Definition 12 Abstract Operation: Abstract operation is not directly used to operate the protected resource by system. On the contrary, the role of the abstract operation is just a higher level of description to the specific operation, is an abstract description to the specific operation, and is an description to the common property, which is referred to as Abstract Operation.

Definition 13 Abstract Operation: A limited collection of specific operations is referred to as Bundle Operation. These Operation Bundle are usually based on specific circumstances, some Operation Bundle just have only one specific operation ,however, some Operation Bundle have a number of specific operations. These specific Operation are putted together in order to Correspond to the same type of resource. Different levels of user's Operation Bundle on the same type resources is different. Generally speaking, the Operation Bundle corresponding to the high level of the role contains more specific operation than the Operation Bundle corresponding to the low level of the role .

4.4. *The relationship between resources and operations*

According to the definition of Operation in the previous description, we could know that Operation is one or more specific access to resources protected by system, so there is a complex relationship between resources and operations.

As shown in the diagram of the relationship between the operation and the resources. In general, the Operation Bundle and the Resource Bundle is associated, which reduces the number of common operations for the same resource, and also reduces the complexity of adjunction of common operations. The same type of resource can be placed in a same resource bundle, and then the common operation of these resources can be placed in a same Operation Bundle. the resource bundle can be modified, when some resources are unnecessary, the resource can be removed from the resource bundle. And the resource can be added to the corresponding Resource Bundle. The operations mentioned above can also be added to the Operation Bundle. When some specific operations are not required for this Resource Bundle, you can delete them from the Resource Bundle. When the Operation Bundle can not meet the Resource Bundle, some specific operations can be added to the Operation Bundle, in which it can meet the operation of resources.

However, in special cases, some operations can also be directly related to the Resource Bundle and resources. Some special resources can also be directly related to the corresponding Operation Bundle. Some operations of resources are very simple, it is not necessary to create a new Operation Bundle related to the Resource Bundle. These simple operations can be directly related to the resource bundle. Some special resources which the operation is relatively simple, can also be directly associated with the operation. the commonly used individual resources will be operated more times and more complex, so, it is necessary to construct a Resource Bundle to reduce the number of the constructing operation bundle corresponding to the individual resources.

Fig. 3 in the relationship between operation and resources, the solid line between Operation Bundle and Resource Bundle represents the common relationship. The dotted line between the Operation and the Resource, the Resource Bundle represents the uncommon relationship. The dotted line between the Operation Bundle and the Resource also represents uncommon relationship.

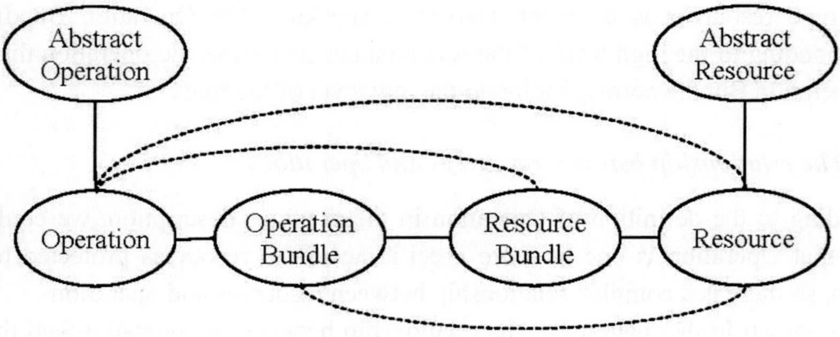

Fig. 3. Relationship between operation and resource.

In the system, the resource type is used to distinguish different resources. So in the system, a resource type table should be created to express different

resources. Because of the variety of resource types, it is impossible to build up all the resources in the system in the beginning. In building up a system, we just need to put the types of common resources in the resource type table. The type of infrequently used resource should not listed in the resource type table. As long as we can modify the resource type table and the required resource types are not present in the resource type table, we can add the type of the resource to the resource type table. some resource type which is no longer used in the system should be deleted from the resource type table.

Similarly, the specific operation is more and different type resources have different operation. In the system, a specific operation table is established, and the operation corresponding to the resource bundle can be obtained from the specific operation table, and then added the operation to the corresponding Operation Bundle. Some specific operations that some resource type need is not exist in the specific operation table, so we can add the specific operation to the specific operation table.

4.5. *Relationship between resources and roles*

In the RBAC model, the role is directly related to authority, and there is no association between roles and resources. In the RBAC model, the role structure is a hierarchical structure in a certain degree. It means that at a high level the role must have the authority owned by low level role. In resource model introduced in the previous chapter, resources are set to a certain level and the relationship between resources and roles can be determined by the level of role and the level of resources in the resource model so that the relationship between roles and resources can be extended. In this section, the relationship between the role and resources is mainly extended, and establish a direct relation between role and resource. So as to make different levels of role access to different levels and other resources. Thereby the role of corresponding level can have access to resources of their own level, and control the access to resources. So as to control the different levels of the role access to different levels of resources.

In the RBAC model, the hierarchy of roles is implemented by the role of the inheritance, and the permissions of the underlying role can be obtained by the senior role. In the resource model, the structure of resources is also a kind of hierarchy structure in a certain degree. Access to resources should be limited by the role level and the resource level. Thus users access to resources can be controlled in the system and resources can be protected.

In RBAC, the relationship of inheritance between roles is an inverted tree. That is to say, the relatively higher roles inherit from the relatively lower roles. This is just a hierarchy of roles, and there is no strict distinction between roles. In order to distinguish the different levels of the role, the role of the strict division level is presented. Every role belongs to a certain level. The level of role can be divided from high to low. For example, the role of the hierarchy can be divided level 1, level 2, level 3, level 4 and level 5. The level 1 is the lowest and is in the lowest level of the role hierarchy. the level 5 is the highest level of role and is in the top of the role hierarchy. Each role must belong to a certain level, in the setting of roles, the hierarchy of role must be determined.

5. Conclusion

In the resource development RBAC model, the same type resources are put together to form a resource bundle, which reduces the number that resource authority are repeatedly set; Similarly, some common operations on resources to put together to form an operation bundle, which reduce the number of settings operation for the resource; In setting permissions for roles, the size of the current permissions to compare and the size of the permissions to be granted are the first. The authority can be granted for the role only if the authority to be granted is greater than the current authority, which reduces the number of granting permissions for roles.

Acknowledgment

This work is funded by Yunnan Provincial Department of Education Fund for Scientific Research of major special projects under Grant No. ZD2014001, and by the Open Foundation of Key Laboratory of Software Engineering of Yunnan Province under Grant No. 2015SE102, 2015SE204.

References

1. Jiang Zenghu, Chert Maohua. Access ControI ModeI Based on Repeated-Role and PRI Task[J], Network Security Technology & Application 2007.
2. BAO lian-cheng, ZHAO jing-bo, A survery on access control teachno-logy [J], Electrical Drive Automation, 2006, 28(4):1-5.
3. ZHANG Rui-qingu, SHU Jian, CAI Ke, LIU Lin-lan, Improved RBAC model based on organization structure[J], Computer Engineering and Design 2009, 30(23).

4. S. Sandhu, E. Coyne, H. Feunstein, Role-Based Access Conrol Model[J] IEEE Computer, 1996, 29(2):38-47.
5. Ravi Sandhu. Rational for the RBAC96 family of access models. Proceedings of the 1th ACM Workshop on Role-based Access Control, ACM1997.

Design and Research of Soft-Parts Based on the JAVA Platform

Meng-xia GU
HuBei University of Technology Engineering and Technology College, WuHan HuBei,
E-mail:787397227@qq.com

This paper discusses the development of soft-parts to achieve software reuse and improve the efficiency of software development. Based on the JAVA platform, we researched the common problems of soft-parts and demonstrated the fundamental steps in constructing applied systems through this system. The tests demonstrate that the application of soft-parts can significantly improve the efficiency of software development.

Keywords: Soft-parts; Software reuse; Software construction.

1. Introduction

A lot of smart plug-in and general parts have been used in electronics or mechanical products, we only need to do a little work to these small parts of a new product. Hardware products always choose existing components, added some non-standard design, It will be high efficiency, good quality and low cost. The software should also be the case[1,2] .

Software is more and more pay attention to the development of its reusability. From the emergence of object-oriented language, until now the concept of "component", all indicate the importance of its reusability. Although there are on the research of the "component", but the meaning too general, and the effect of the size of the particle on reusability is too big.

Small granularity component has the function of independent, encoding level clear, don't need to maintain in general ,and don't have to expand when it is installed. This can improve software quality, but the reusability is small. Component size is larger, the shorter the software development cycle, the higher maintainability, but the waste rate can be very high. In addition, personalized glue code can lead to a potential system defects, and make the system more fragile. Software is not really achieve the purpose of software reuse[3].

Therefore, according to the study in the MIS system, Study a highly plug-and-play system level component, that can be applied to all kinds of management system, realize the desired goals of software reuse [3]. The soft-parts to apply the all kinds of management information system is a big granularity reusable program that is a collection of program code used to accomplish a specific task. It is encapsulated, business-oriented work rather than a system function module with simple single function only[4].

Because of JAVA has excellent cross platform[5], the soft-parts will have more extensive application prospect in the JAVA platform[6]. Therefore, this article mainly introduces the development process and related problems of soft-parts in the JAVA platform.

2. The Main Characteristics of Soft-Parts

(1) The soft-parts is a independent modules of business level. General soft-parts is an encapsulation of application, have an independent function and performance. It puts the software reuse as the target, and contains the applications with multiple independent functions[4] to complete a business work, and each function complement each other to meet the needs of different users in many ways.

(2) Using the top-down model and big reuse granularity. The function and performance of soft-parts have been researched. An abstract and non specific management information system was used as a target, without a specific management information system.

(3) Plug and play. A small amount of standardized soft-parts were designed and convenient to be used to make system more standardized.

3. System Total Design

According to the division system function, the system is divided into the following several parts:

(1) Cover module: Provide the system background of the author, date, etc.

(2) The master control module of application system: Generate menu for the system, and select the corresponding parts for the menu.

(3) The soft-parts module: The programs have been completed, have the corresponding function, to be chosen.

Specific application system structure is shown in figure 1.

Among them, the soft-parts module part is the most important, is chosen to build application by user. Soft-parts collection with all kinds of different function will be developed from soft-parts module 1 to soft-parts module. Each kind of soft-parts contains many parts that is roughly same, but also is different from each other to meet the different needs of different users on the same function. These will be presented in classify in this paper.

(1) The data maintenance class by table: The soft-parts class that are provided to the operator in the form of table to complete all kinds of data maintenance.
(2) The data maintenance class by single data form recording: The soft-parts class that display only one record at a time in the form of form to complete all kinds of data maintenance.
(3) The query class: The soft-parts class that find the needed records in a table or many table according to certain conditions.
(4) The data processing class: The soft-parts that make a corresponding mathematical statistics and various relation operations on the all data or the part of data in the table according to the requirements.
(5) The data communication class: The soft-parts that export the data in current table to another table, or import the data in other table into current table.
(6) The report printing class: The soft-parts that realize all kinds of report printing.

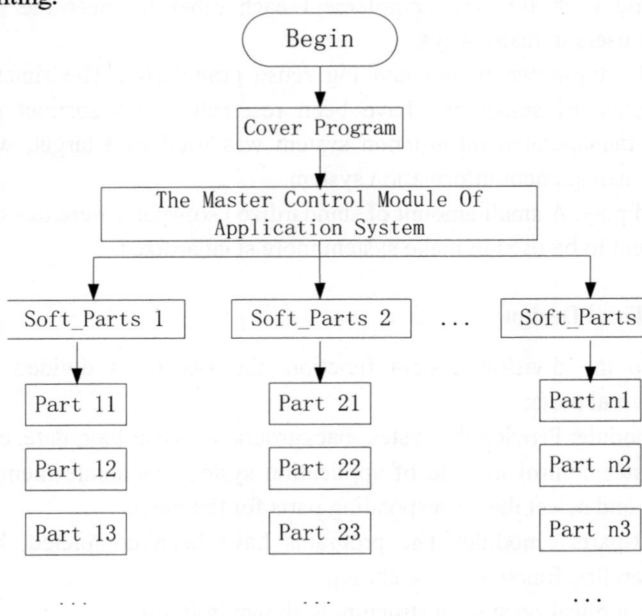

Fig. 1. System structure.

4. The Function Implementation

This section briefly explains the each part of overall design.

4.1. *The cover*

In order to meet the needs of different application system's cover, the user can define the title, author, date, background information in this module. The program can provide users with window size definition, location and other public property by updating it.

4.2. *The control module*

This module is the control center of building the while system, as shown in figure 2.

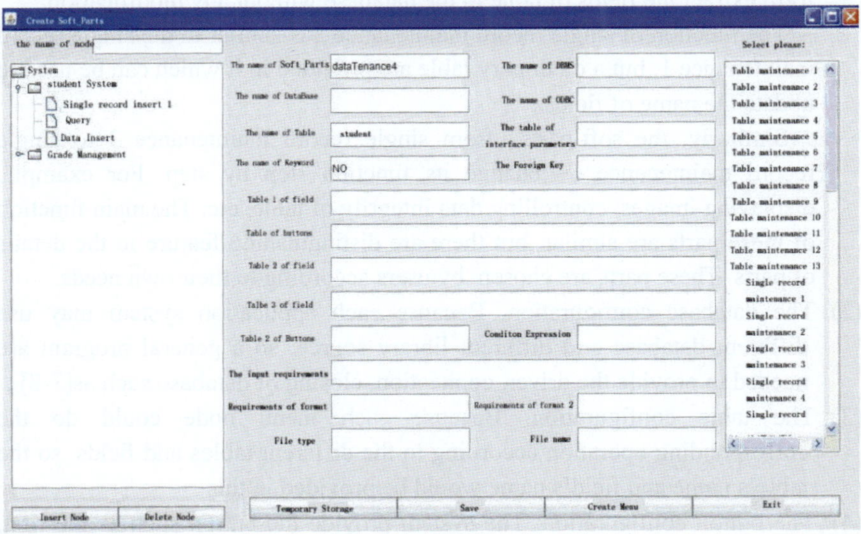

Fig. 2. The control module.

The function provided by the control module as follow.

Setting up the menu node of system. The menu node can be built and shown on the left of figure 2.

Configuration related parameters for the menu node. The specific functions will be achieved by passing the specific parameter to part, as follows.

(1) Choosing the appropriate features. There are many soft-parts with all kinds of function, as shown on the right of figure 2, and users can choose the right parts to build a management system that is consistent with needs. For example, the data maintenance class by table, the data maintenance class by data form recording, the query class, the data processing class, the data communication class, etc.

Taking an example of soft-parts of the data maintenance class by data form recording, it displays only one record at a time in the form of form to complete all kinds of data maintenance, mainly contains data entry, modification, deletion, browsing, etc.

From "single record maintenance 1" to "single recorded maintenance 6", its main function is to provide data maintenance, but there are small differences on the function because of different needs between each other.

For example, in the single record maintenance 1, the single record data maintenance program is built by using text box, button, etc. The program can insert data, update data ,and delete data in the database. The label of the form extract the fields of table in the database without any modification.

The function of single record maintenance 2 is similar to the single record maintenance 1, but a dictionary table are provided in it which can be used to update the name of fields,.

Similarly, the soft-parts from single record maintenance 3 to single record maintenance 6 change its function step by step. For example, displaying images, controlling data integrity of table, etc. The main function of these parts are similar ,but there are distinguishing feature in the details of parts. These parts are chosen by users according to their own needs.

(2) The database configuration. Because each application system may use different database and different library source, so a general program are needed to provide the driver, connection, closing of database such as[7-8] .

(3) The table configuration. Because each menu node could do the corresponding operation according to the different tables and fields, so the table's name and field's name would be provided in this .

(4) The button configuration. The system provide the button such as the first, next, last, previous, query, browse, save, clear, modification, delete, batch, exit, etc. Users may choose these buttons according their needs.

5. Conclusion

For software developers, many module program have similarities, at the same time have a slightly different. So many soft-parts being developed have similar main functions, but there are some local differences in these soft-parts for different users making different choices to increase its generality and save development time.

At present, the layout of the system is defined by the program itself, and can be improved by the users' parameters.

References

1. J. Stanley Warford. Computer Systems[M]. Jones & Bartlett Publishers, 2009:10 .
2. Jonh W. Satzinger. Systems Analysis and Design in a Changing World[M]. Cengage Learning EMEA, 2008:35.
3. Abdellatif, T. and F. Boyer. Anode allocation system for deploying JavaEE systems on Grids[C]. 2009. Hammemet, Tunisia.
4. Xuexian Cheng. Theory and Application of Database. Tsinghua university Press, China. 2014.3: 220-270.
5. Bruce Eckel. Thinking in Java[M]. Upper Saddle River, New Jersey, USA: Prentice Hall, 2006:12.
6. Joshua Bloch. Effective Java[M]. Piscataway, N.J: IEEE Press, 2009 :135.
7. Thomas M. Connolly, Carolyn E. Begg. Database systems: a practical approach to design, implementation, and management[M]. Addison-Wesley, 2009:330.
8. Peter Rob, Carlos Coronel. Database Systems[M]. Cengage Learning EMEA, 2008:256.

An Improved 2-D Coupled Map Lattice Model Based on Radial Basis Function

Shu-wang WANG* and An-ping BAO

School of Electronic Information Engineering, Nanjing College of Information Technology, Nanjing, Jiangsu 210023, China

**E-mail: wangsw@njcit.cn*

An improved 2–D coupled map lattice model based on radial basis function is proposed fit the evolution of an actual spatio-temporal system. A real signal was adopted and by using different coupled map lattice (CML) models, different predicted signals were obtained. The correlation coefficients between the real signal and the predicted signal indicated the fitting capabilities of the models to real system. Simulation results demonstrated that the proposed method can effectively fit the evolution of an actual spatio-temporal system.

Keywords: Coupled Map Lattice (CML); Logistic function; Radial Basis Function (RBF).

1. Introduction

The coupled map lattice (CML) model has high efficiency in the chaos studies, and many known achievements about chaos can be directly used in this model, so the CML model has been an important branch of nonlinear dynamic research.

When the time and space variables of a dynamic system are discretized while its state variable remains continuous, the system becomes a CML system. The CML model has some advantages. First, it has high speed of computing. Second, the calculation can be processed in parallel. Third, we can scan the parameter space then obtain the role of mutual conversion between time and space behavior when the system parameters are changed even the phase diagram of the whole parameter space because of the high computing efficiency. Forth, the results of low-dimensional dynamical systems can be used. So, the CML model will be powerful if it fit the evolvement rule of actual spatio-temporal system[1].

The Logistic function is most commonly used in the CML model. But it lacks universal approximation capability when the dynamical system is reconstructed from the measured time series. Considering the topological structure and interaction among the different parts in the actual physical system, we build an improved 2-D CML model using RBF as the map function to accurately describe the actual system and make the study easy.

2. CML Model

The CML model can be built using different types of local mapping and lattice coupling, so it has many forms. In reality, CML model can be described as

$$x_{n+1}(i)=\sum_{j=-K}^{K}\varepsilon_j f\left(x_n(i+j)\right). \tag{1}$$

or

$$x_{n+1}(i)=f\left(\sum_{j=-K}^{K}\varepsilon_j x_n(i+j)\right). \tag{2}$$

where f is local nonlinear map, t is discrete time step, i is lattice coordinate, K is the lattices number related to current lattice in one direction. ε_i is the spatial coupling parameter and it satisfies

$$\sum_{j=-K}^{K}\varepsilon_j=1. \tag{3}$$

where ε_j is the correlation coefficient between the data of current lattice and related lattice.

In this paper, we use the formula 2, so the two-dimension (2-D) CML model can be described as

$$x_{n+1}(i,j)=f\left(\begin{array}{l}\sum_{m=-K}^{K}\sum_{n=-K}^{K}\varepsilon(i+m,j+n)x_n(i+m,j+n)\\ -\varepsilon(i,j)x_n(i,j)\end{array}\right). \tag{4}$$

$$\sum_{m=-K}^{K}\sum_{n=-K}^{K}\varepsilon(i+m,j+n)-\varepsilon(i,j)=1. \tag{5}$$

$$\varepsilon(i+m,j+n)=\frac{R(i+m,j+n)}{\sum_{j=-K}^{K}\sum_{n=-K}^{K}R(i+m,j+n)}. \tag{6}$$

$$m = -K,\ldots,K\text{, } n = -K,\ldots,K$$

2.1. *CML model based on logistic function*

The most normal local nonlinear map is Logistic function as follow

$$f(x) = \lambda x_n(1 - x_n), \qquad \lambda \in (0,4), \qquad x_n \in [0,1]. \tag{7}$$

The formula 4 can be rewritten as

$$x_{n+1}(i,j) = \mu x_n^{'}(i,j)\left(1 - x_n^{'}(i,j)\right). \tag{8}$$

where $x_n^{'}(i,j) = \sum_{m=-K}^{K} \sum_{n=-K}^{K} \varepsilon(m,n) x_n(i+m, j+n) - \varepsilon(i,j) x_n(i,j)$. K is the lattices number related to current lattice in one direction.

We can get ε using formula 6 and μ can be found by optimizing following formula

$$\min_{\langle \mu,\varepsilon \rangle} \left\| x(i,j) - \hat{x}(i,j) \right\|. \tag{9}$$

where $x(i,j) = (x_1(i,j),\ldots,x_n(i,j))$ is the real signal in lattice (i,j), while $\hat{x}(i,j) = (\hat{x}_1(i,j),\ldots,\hat{x}_n(i,j))$ is the predicted value in the same lattice, and $x_1(i,j) = \hat{x}_1(i,j)$. Consider the 2-D model

$$\hat{x}_n(i,j) = \lambda x_{n-1}^{'}(i,j)\left(1 - x_{n-1}^{'}(i,j)\right). \tag{10}$$

Let $X_n(i,j) = x_{n-1}^{'}(i,j)\left(1 - x_{n-1}^{'}(i,j)\right)$, $n \geq 2$, the optimization is

$$\min_{\mu} \left\| x(i,j) - \mu X(i,j) \right\|. \tag{11}$$

That is

$$\min_{\mu} (x(i,j) - \mu X(i,j))^2. \tag{12}$$

So we can get

$$\mu = \frac{sum(X(i,j))}{sum(x(i,j))}. \tag{13}$$

Then the 2-D Logistic-CML model is obtained[2,3].

2.2. *CML model based on RBF*

Although the CML model based on Logistic map has many advantages, it lacks universal approximation ability. So we use the radial basis function as the local nonlinear map

$$f(x)=\sum_i a(i)\phi(x,t_i). \tag{14}$$

where $a(i)$ is weight matrix, $\{\varphi(x,t_i)\mid i=1,2,\ldots,N\}$ is the base functions, t_i is the center of φ. In reality, Gaussian function is usually used as the base function of RBF

$$\varphi_i(x_i;c_i,\sigma_i)=\exp\left(\frac{-\|x_i-c_i\|^2}{2\sigma_i^2}\right), i=1,2,\ldots m. \tag{15}$$

where x is the n-dimension input vector, c_i is the center of the i th base function and has the same dimension as x. σ_i is an element of sample covariance matrix, and it determine the width of the base function around the center. m is the number of base functions. $\|x_i-c_i\|$ is the norm of vector x_i-c_i, and it shows the distance between x and c_i.

Then we get 2-D CML model based on RBF

$$x_{n+1}(i,j)=\sum_{l=1}^{L} W(l)\exp\left(\frac{-\|x_n'(i,j)-a(l)\|^2}{s}\right). \tag{16}$$

where L is the number of RBF, s indicates the width of the base function, a is the center of the function.

In order to determine the RBF-CML model, the optimization as follow has to be resolved.

$$\min_{\langle W,\varepsilon,a,s,L\rangle}\|x(i,j)-\hat{x}(i,j)\|. \tag{17}$$

ε can be determined by formula 6, s and L are determined from experience. a is the mean value of the measured signal. So the formula 17 can be rewritten as

$$\min_{\langle W\rangle}\|x(i,j)-\hat{x}(i,j)\|. \tag{18}$$

The optimum value of W satisfies

$$y = HW. \tag{19}$$

where $y = x(i,j), H(n,m) = \exp\left(\frac{-\left\|x'(i,j) - a(m)\right\|^2}{s}\right)$, n is the length of $x'(i,j)$.

So

$$W = H^+ y. \tag{20}$$

H^+ is the pseudo-inverse matrix of H defined as

$$H^+ = \left(H^T H\right)^{-1} H^T. \tag{21}$$

Thus the 2-D RFF-CML model is built[4,5].

3. Experiment and Results

We study the degree of resemblance between real measurement signals and predicted signals obtained from model to measure the simulation ability of the model to real system. If the model can commendably track the variation of system, we consider the model can generate the states and their variation of real system. In order to assure the complexity of test data, we adopted EEG (Electroencephalogram) as simulating signal.

We took a sequence with 1000 values. The anterior 800 were used to train parameters and posterior 200 values were used to test the predicted data obtained from the models. The scale of the grid is 5×4, and the terminal condition was supposed periodic, the correlation coefficient was adopted to measure the degree of likelihood between measured data and predicted data. We used those data to respectively test these models, compared the ability to fitness.

Using the different CML model, we can get the fitness results.

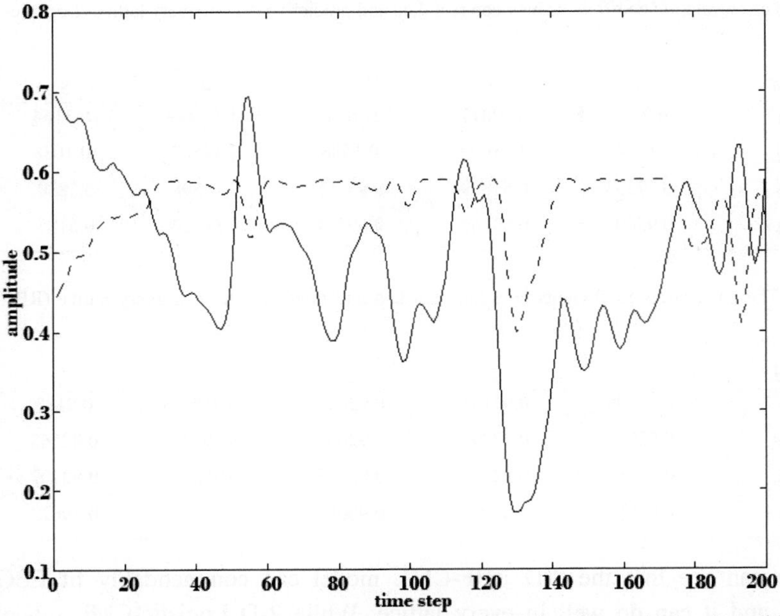

Fig. 1. The fit of Logistic-CML models to real EEG signal in one lattice, the solid lines represent real data, the broken lines represent predictive data.

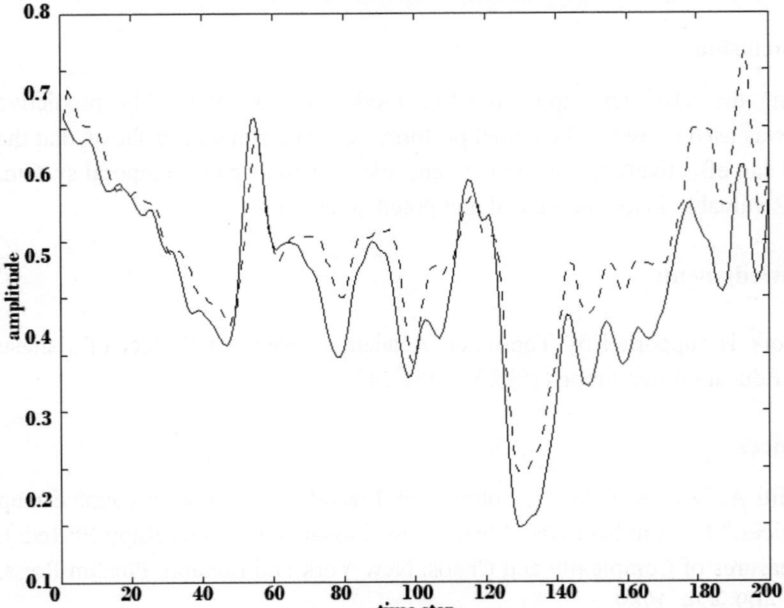

Fig. 2. The fit of RBF-CML models to real EEG signal in one lattice, the solid lines represent real data, the broken lines represent predictive data.

Table 1. The correlation coefficients between real data and predictive data in every lattice (Logistic-CML).

Lattice	1	2	3	4	5
1	-0.01439	0.59017	0.56841	-0.01929	-0.3164
2	0.17949	-0.30515	0.1586	0.34522	-0.1038
3	0.77253	0.81839	0.95953	0.70598	0.5830
4	0.95697	0.82166	0.69524	0.81224	0.6185

Table 2. The correlation coefficients between real data and predictive data in every lattice (RBF-CML).

Lattice	1	2	3	4	5
1	0.91999	0.91101	0.92024	0.91017	0.9183
2	0.82995	0.77299	0.92694	0.89537	0.92568
3	0.93557	0.92312	0.88687	0.90236	0.92292
4	0.95955	0.8744	0.90663	0.93456	0.89622

We can see that the 2-D RBF-CML model can commendably fit EEG signals, and it can do well in every lattice. While 2-D Logistic-CML model cannot do this.

4. Conclusion

By using the RBF, an improved CML model was obtained. The predictive ability was used to assess the model performance. The simulation shows that the method can effectively fit the evolvement rule of actual spatio-temporal system, which is valuable in the theoretical and practical domains.

Acknowledgments

This work is supported by Top-notch Academic Programs Project of Jiangsu Higher Education Institutions (PPZY2015C242).

References

1. Politi A, D'Alessandro G, Torcini, "A Fractal dimensions in coupled map lattices," In: Abraham NB, Albano AM, Passamante A and Rapp PE (eds): Measures of Complexity and Chaos. New York and London. Plenum Press, pp. 409–424, 1989.

2. Diomar Cristina Mistroa, , Luiz Alberto Díaz Rodriguesa, Maria Cristina Varrialeb, “The Role of Spatial Refuges in Coupled Map Lattice Model for Host-Parasitoid Systems”, Bulletin of Mathematical Biology (2009) 71: 1934–1953.
3. Y. Liu, Z-Y. Suna, and L-J. An, “The study of banded spherulite patterns by coupled logistic map lattice model”, Eur. Phys. J. B 62, 481–484 (2008).
4. Henry Leung, Geoffrey Hennessey and Anastasios Drosopoulos: Signal Detection Using the Radial Basis Function Coupled Map Lattice. IEEE TRANSACTIONS ON NEURAL NETWORKS, VOL.11, NO.5, SEPTEMBER 2000.
5. T. Laffargue, P. Sollich, J. Tailleur and F. van Wijland, “Large-scale fluctuations of the largest Lyapunov exponent in diffusive systems”, EPL, 110 (2015) , 10006.

The Key Technology and Algorithm of BDS Software Pseudorange Differential Positioning System

Fei YANG, Jie-lin FU* and Hong-bing QIU

Key Lab of Cognitive Radio & Information Processing, the Ministry of Education, Guilin University of Electronic Technology, Guilin, 541004, China

**E-mail: hmfjl@guet.edu.cn*

In order to solve the problem of a lack of accuracy in absolute single point positioning in certain fields of application, a design scheme of software pseudorange differential positioning system (BDS) is proposed. To tackle the problem of original measurement pseudorange smoothing and denoising, this paper proposes an improved integral Doppler smoothing pseudorange algorithm. An improved weighted least square algorithm is introduced to reduce the influence of measurement noise on the localization to overcome the limitations of the traditional least square algorithm. The experimental results demonstrate that the proposed algorithm can provide a stable planar position accuracy of 2~5m which is three times higher than single point positioning.

Keywords: BDS differential positioning; Implementation; Improved integration; Doppler smoothing pseudorange; BDS differential message; Improved WLS.

1. Introduction

Beidou satellite navigation system (BDS) is the implementation of China's independent research and development of the global satellite navigation system. BDS absolute single point positioning is so affected by troposphere error, ionospheric error, receiver noise that the positioning accuracy is about 10m [1]. It can't satisfy the fields which demand positioning accuracy of submeter for example, ship into port, intelligent transportation and so on. Pseudorange differential technique can eliminate or weaken public error of the single point positioning so as to improve the positioning accuracy to submeter.

[1-6] laid the theoretical foundation of the BDS pseudorange difference. At present, many provinces and cities have done a lot of theoretical researches to promote the construction of BDS pseudo range difference. The [2] compares BDS and GPS pseudorange difference positioning model and describes the BDS pseudorange differential positioning model.[3] proposed a kind of differential message which is used to make up the incomplete BDS constellation by using

GPS. The BDS differential encoding and decoding process is presented by [4,5] proposes a kind of GPS differential message which is used to make up the incomplete BDS constellation. The feasibility of using the GPS-OEM board to realize the GPS pseudorange differential positioning system is verified by the literature[6], but did not do further research and implementation of BDS pseudorange difference. A scheme of BDS pseudorange differential positioning system is presented in this paper, and then it introduces the algorithm and key technology of BDS software differential location system. An improved integral Doppler smoothing pseudorange algorithm is proposed in order to solve the problem of original measurement pseudorange smoothing and denoising. In view of the defects of the traditional least square algorithm, an improved weighted least square algorithm is proposed to reduce the influence of measurement noise on the localization. The experimental results show that the proposed algorithm can provide a stable planar position accuracy of 2~5m.

2. BDS Pseudorange Differential Positioning Principle

The pseudorange differential positioning system includes three parts: the first is reference station, the second is differential data link, the last is user receiver. The reference station is equivalent to a BDS receiver which is fixed to a known exact coordinate, it collect all the satellite ephemeris to calculate satellite instantaneous position (X_s^i, Y_s^i, Z_s^i), the reference station coordinate is (X_o, Y_o, Z_o), the real distance from the satellite to the reference station R_b^i can be calculated by using the satellite and the reference station's coordinates:

$$R_b^i = \sqrt{(X_s^i - X_o)^2 + (Y_s^i - Y_o)^2 + (Y_s^i - Y_o)^2}\ . \tag{1}$$

The pseudorange measured by the reference station is ρ^i, due to the ephemeris error, ionosphere error, troposphere error ρ^i and R_b^i are different. Pseudorange correction is:

$$\Delta\rho^i = R^i - \rho^i . \tag{2}$$

Pseudorange correction change rate is :

$$d\rho^i = \frac{\Delta\rho^i}{\Delta t} . \tag{3}$$

The base station broadcast $\Delta\rho^i$ and $d\rho^i$ to the user. The User receive differential message to correct pseudorange.

$$\rho^i_{carr} = \rho^i_{meas}(t) + \Delta\rho^i + d\rho^i(t - t_0)\,. \tag{4}$$

The coordinates of the user receiver can be calculated by using the modified pseudorange:

$$\rho^j_{carr} = R^j_{user} + C\cdot d\tau + \nu = \sqrt{(X^i_{user} - X)^2 + (Y^i_{user} - Y)^2 + (Z^i_{user} - Z)^2} + C\cdot d\tau + \nu\,. \tag{5}$$

$d\tau$ is receiver clock error, ν is receiver noise. The formula (5) has eliminated the satellite ephemeris error, satellite clock error, ionospheric error, so the differential positioning can improve position accuracy.

3. BDS Pseudo Range Differential Positioning Scheme

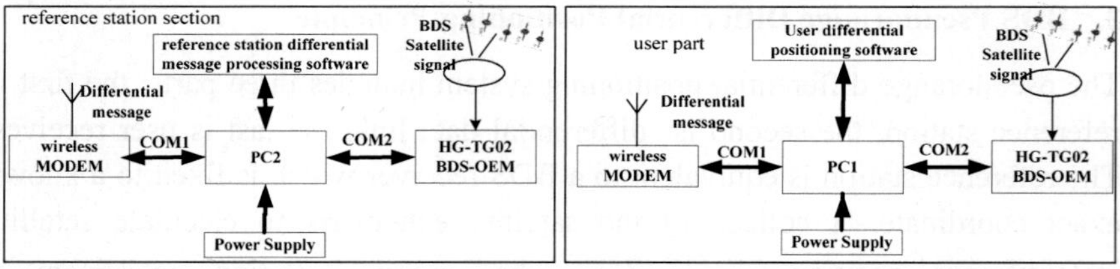

(a) (b)

Fig. 1. BDS pseudorange differential positioning system structure diagram.

BDS pseudorange differential positioning system mainly consists of two parts: the reference section and the user part. Their structures are similar, including the power supply, wireless modem, HG-TG02 original measurement module, PC and software. The difference is the reference section of the BDS-OEM board use the value of original measurement (BDS satellite ephemeris, almanacs, receiver time, epoch count, carrier phase, etc.) to calculate and send differential message. Wireless MODEM broadcasts differential correction message including Z count, pseudorange correction, pseudorange correction change rate[7]. The user receives the differential message by wireless modem and BDS satellite signal by HG-TG02-OEM for pseudorange differential positioning.

The key technology in the design of the system is described as follows:

The first is the decoding of BDS ephemeris. BDS has the different ephemeris from GPSs. It needs respectively decode the D1 code and D2 code format, with reference [8]. The verification mode is BCH(15,11) which can use look-up table method for decoding.

The second is BDS satellite position calculation. The difficulty is that GEO (earth synchronous orbit satellite) needs a coordinate of the inverse transformation, reference [9].

The third is encoding and decoding of BDS differential message. BDS differential message protocol has not been determined. The references [4] proposed a BDS differential message protocol and the method of encoding and decoding.

The fourth is how to guarantee the pseudorange difference position on real-time. We use the two threads in software engineering to parallel process the differential data and the original measurement on real- time.

The fifth is the smoothing and denoising of the original measurements data. The stability and accuracy of the original pseudorange value form the OEM board is insufficient. An improved integral Doppler smoothing pseudorange algorithm is proposed in order to solve the problem of original measurement pseudorange smoothing and denoising. In the view of the defects of the weighted least square algorithm, we optimize weight matrix to reduce the amount of calculation.

The satellite pseudorange calculation formula is

$$\rho = (t_r - t_{sv}) * c \,. \tag{6}$$

Which t_r represents the satellite signal reception time, t_{sv} is the satellite signal launch time, c is light speed.

$$\begin{aligned} t_{sv} = {} & \text{bit*0.02+ms*0.001+codephase/2046000.0+} \\ & \text{codedcophase/2046000.0/1024.0} \end{aligned} \,. \tag{7}$$

bit is 20ms epoch count, *ms* is 1ms epoch count, *codephase* is the integer part of code phase and the *codecophase* is the decimal part. The accuracy of t_{sv} is between *us* and even dozens of *ns*, so the pseudorange accuracy is about 100 meters. The pseudorange accuracy can be greatly improved by using the integral Doppler smoothing pseudorange algorithm. The weighted least square method reduces the influence of measurement noise on the positioning.

3.1. *Pre-processing Doppler smoothing pseudorange algorithm*

Carrier phase smoothing pseudorange algorithm can provide a cm level accuracy of pseudorange, but it is influenced by the loss of carrier-track loop. The price of OEM board which provides carrier phase output is higher than the one provides

Dopler. The pseudorange value of m level can be provided by using Doppler auxiliary pseudorange [10]. Considering most precise position field such as the ship into port, intelligent traffic does not need cm level positioning accuracy, therefore, this paper chooses the lower price BDS-OEM board and uses the Doppler smoothing pseudorange algorithm[11].

$$f_{dopp}^{i} = \int_{0}^{t_k} \hat{f}_{k}^{i} dt = \sum_{k=0}^{K-1} (\hat{f}_{k}^{i} T) \quad . \tag{8}$$

$\hat{f}_{i}^{k}$ it is the value of Doppler frequency shift filter in K time. T is tracking loop filter time. T=100ms.

K is the update number of navigation cycle tracking loop. K =10.

Using Hatch filtering algorithm, integral Doppler smoothing pseudorange:

$$\rho_{s,k}^{i} = \frac{1}{M} \rho_{k}^{i} + \frac{M-1}{M} [\rho_{s,k-1}^{i} - \lambda f_{dopp}^{i}] \quad . \tag{9}$$

$\rho_{s,k}^{i}$ is dopler smoothing pseudorange for K time. ρ_{k}^{i} is the pseudorange for K time. M=100.

Providing a more accurate smoothing pseudorange initial value can achieve rapid high-precision positioning. N=20.

$$\rho_{s,1}^{i} = \frac{1}{N} \sum_{n=1}^{N} \rho_{s,1,n}^{i} \quad . \tag{10}$$

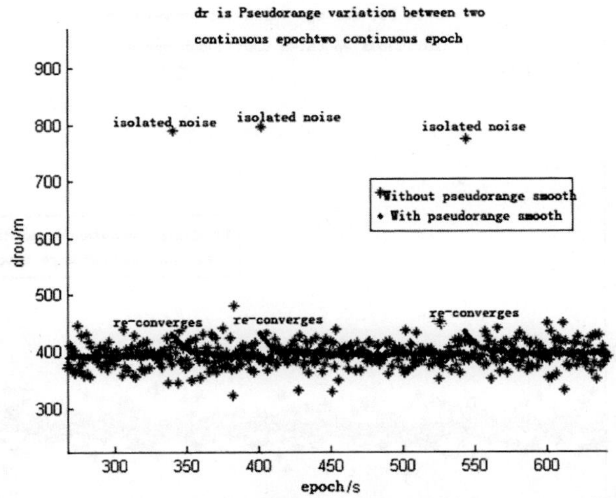

Fig. 2. Integral Doppler smoothing pseudorange without preprocessing.

You can see from Figure 2, due to the impact of isolated noise, the traditional Doppler pseudorange smoothing[11] is discontinuous. As the pseudorange is influenced by receiver noise and multipath effects we may get some error pseudorange. The pseudorange smoothing value re-converges at the error pseudorange. It makes positon results fluctuate. By considering the shortcomings of the Doppler smoothing pseudorange algorithm, an improved algorithm is proposed. A pre-processing Doppler smoothing pseudorange algorithm is proposed.

We find the error pseudorange is isolated point through statistical analysis. We considering the median filter theory, the error isolated point is replaced by an approximate value. Set threshold T is:

$$T = 1.5\frac{1}{100}\sum_{i=1}^{100} d\rho_i . \tag{11}$$

$d\rho_i$ is the change of pseudorange between front pseudorange and later pseudorange .We judge the pseudorange as isolated error pseudorange when the change of pseudorange value exceeds the threshold value. We replace the current pseudorange value by the average value.

$$\rho_k^i = (\rho_{k-1}^i + \rho_{k+1}^i)/2 . \tag{12}$$

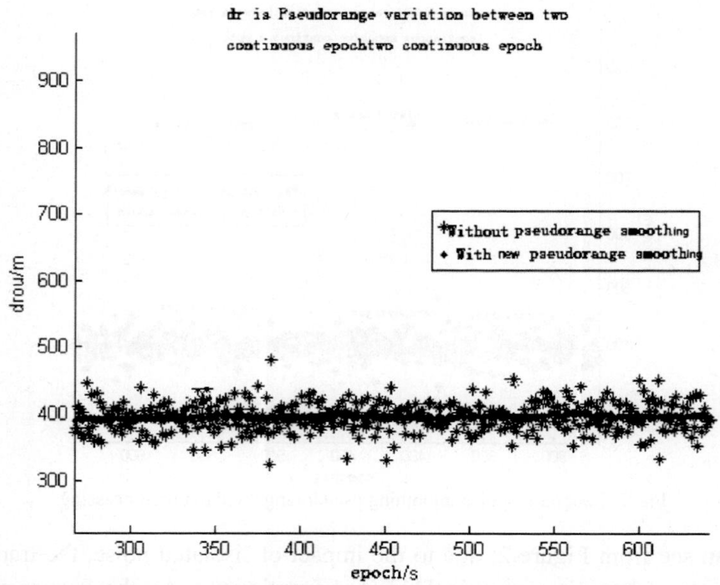

Fig. 3. Integral Doppler smoothing pseudorange with preprocessing.

From Figure 3, we can see after the preprocessing algorithm, we get rid of the isolated error pseudorange and solve the problem of pseudorange re-converges at the error pseudorange. This will let the positioning results become more stable.

3.2. *Carrier-to-noise-ratio-based weighted least squares algorithm*

The traditional least squares method considers the variance of each satellite measurement vector errors are the same. But as the environmental impact, the variance of the satellite measurement vector error is often different. In weighted least squares method, the higher accuracy satellite measurement value get a greater weight and the lower accuracy value get a lower weight. Compared to ordinary least squares solvers, carrier-to-noise-ratio-based weighted least squares algorithm can improve the receiver's positioning accuracy to some extent[12,13].The paper [12] chooses the weight matrix as the reciprocal of the pseudorange variance, this method needs a time delay to generate pseudorange variance. The weight matrix of paper [13] is carrier-to-noise ratio, it can deal with pseudorange on real-time. We take the algorithm of paper [13]. Aiming at the shortage of literature [13],we optimize the weight matrix.

The solution equation of weighted least-squares is

$$Wb = WH * \Delta x . \tag{13}$$

Solution vector is

$$\Delta x = (H^T H)^{-1} H^T b \,. \tag{14}$$

The matrix of H:

$$\begin{bmatrix} \frac{x_1 - \bar{x}_r}{\bar{r}_r} & \frac{y_1 - \bar{y}_r}{\bar{r}_r} & \frac{z_1 - \bar{z}_r}{\bar{r}_r} & 1 \\ \frac{x_2 - \bar{x}_r}{\bar{r}_r} & \frac{y_2 - \bar{y}_r}{\bar{r}_r} & \frac{z_3 - \bar{z}_r}{\bar{r}_r} & 1 \\ \vdots & \vdots & \vdots & 1 \\ \frac{x_n - \bar{x}_r}{\bar{r}_r} & \frac{y_n - \bar{y}_r}{\bar{r}_r} & \frac{z_n - \bar{z}_r}{\bar{r}_r} & 1 \end{bmatrix} . \tag{15}$$

(x_i, y_i, z_i) represents the coordinates of the satellites of number i.

$(\bar{x}_r, \bar{y}_r, \bar{z}_r)$ represents the user's position in the Newton iterative process.

$$\bar{r}_r = \sqrt{(x_i - \bar{x}_r)^2 + (y_i - \bar{y}_r)^2 + (z_i - \bar{z}_r)^2} \,. \tag{16}$$

$b$is pseudorange residual error matrix:

$$b = \bar{r}_r - \rho_i - dRotat - dRtrop - \mathrm{dIonoTime} \tag{17}$$

ρ_i is pseudorange , $dRotat$ error due to the earth rotation, $dRtrop$ is tropospheric propagation delay error, dIonoTime is ionospheric propagation delay error, reference[14] for detail calculation.
W is weight matrix $W = ww^t$, w is :

$$\begin{bmatrix} CN_0 & 0 & 0 \cdots 0 \\ 0 & CN_1 & 0 \cdots 0 \\ \vdots & \vdots & \vdots & \vdots \\ 0 & 0 & 0 & CN_n \end{bmatrix} . \tag{18}$$

CN_i is carrier-to-noise-ratio. The pseudorange measurement error source mainly includes two parts if weight matrix without considering multipath interference. The error source is code phase jitter and dynamic stress error caused by thermal noise, therefore, the carrier-to-noise-ratio is introduced into the calculation of the weighted matrix. Taking full advantage of satellite signal of high carrier-to-noise-ratio can make up for the defects of the traditional least square method.

The accuracy of the weighted least square method is analyzed in the literature [13], but the amount of calculation is not considered. In practical computation, due to the OEM board output value of carrier-to-noise-ratio is through the filter and power amplifier, so the weight coefficient matrix is relatively large, it will increase the number of iterations to compute the user's position. In this paper, the weight matrix of the literature is optimized to reduce the amount of calculation. We normalize the weight matrix as:

$$\begin{bmatrix} 1 & 0 & 0\cdots 0 \\ 0 & \frac{CN_1}{CN_0} & 0\cdots 0 \\ \vdots & \vdots & \vdots \quad \vdots \\ 0 & 0 & 0 \quad \frac{CN_n}{CN_0} \end{bmatrix}. \tag{19}$$

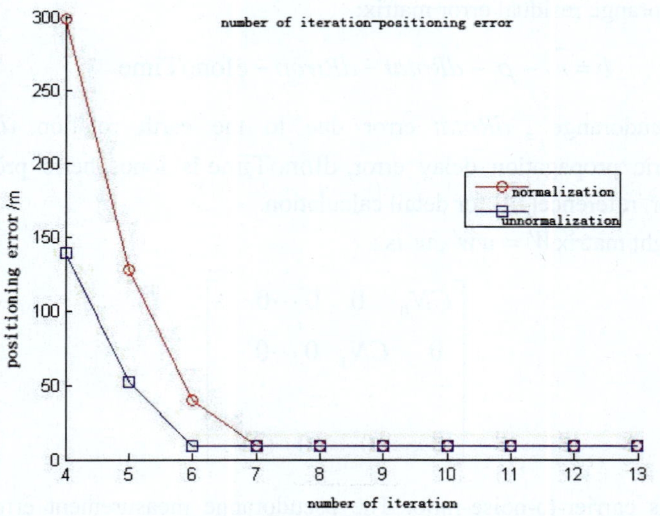

Fig. 4. The number of iterations comparation.

We compare the number of iteration times of normalized and non-normalized weighted least square method and find the weight matrix after normalization can speed up the convergence of the iterative algorithm.

4. BDS Differential Positioning Experiment and Result Analysis

Using the design of BDS pseudorange differential software positioning system, we deal the pseudorange of OEM output with optimized integrated Doppler pseudorange smoothing method. Coordinate system is 2000 national geodetic coordinate system. (x=-2005191.546831, y=5411088.065640, z=2707881.020321) is the accurate coordinates of reference station .The differential message is broadcasted after the differential calculation and differential encoding. The accurate coordinates of user station is (x=2005079.2522, y=5411189.0612, z=2707763.9556).The user receiver gets differential message to modify pseudorange, then conduct the differential positioning by optimized carrier-to-noise-ratio-based weighted least squares algorithm, single point positioning and differential positioning is conducted on software on the same time. We analyse the position results after 2 hours of continuous measurement.

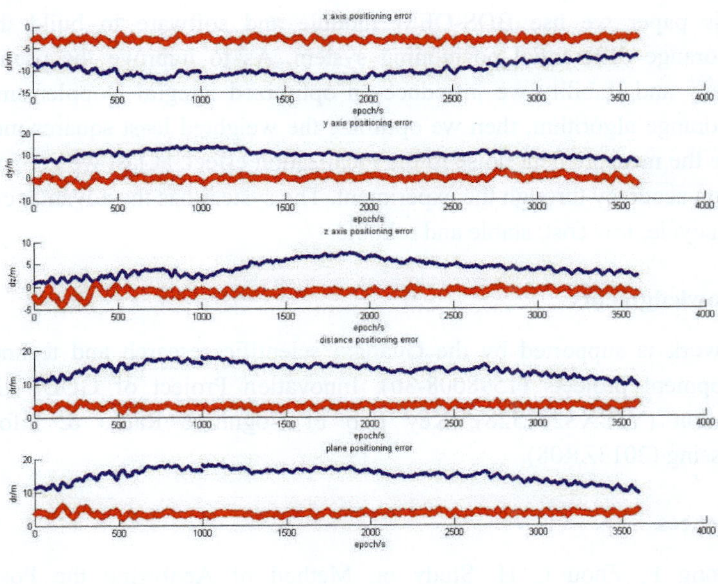

Fig. 5. Positioning error comparison of single point position and differential position.

Table 1. BDS three-dimensional distance position error.

type	max	min	std	mean
single point position	18.178	9.0783	0.0507	14.228
differential position	4.7983	1.6268	0.0041	3.2358

Table 2. BDS two-dimensional planar position error.

type	max	min	std	mean
single point position	18.268	9.3453	0.0608	14.862
differential position	6.1250	2.1512	0.0052	3.5092

From the Figure 4 we can see the single point positioning result changes slowly by the affection of environmental noise, the pseudorange differential weaken this change to a large extent and improve the positioning accuracy. Compared the maximum value, minimum value and mean value of the planar position error from Table 1,we can see the differential positioning accuracy is 2 to 5m increased from 9 to 18m of single point positioning. Positioning accuracy increased about three times.

5. Conclusion

In this paper we use BDS-OEM module and software to build the BDS pseudorange differential positioning system. As to improve the pseudorange accuracy and stability we introduce an optimized integral Doppler smoothing pseudorange algorithm, then we optimize the weighted least squares method to reduce the measurement noise to the localization effect, at last we get 5m planar position accuracy through the experiment. The system has the advantage of short design cycle, low cost, stable and reliable.

Acknowledgments

This work is supported by the Guangxi scientific research and technological development projects (1598008-30), Innovation Project of GUET Graduate Education (YJCXS201528), Key Lab of Cognitive Radio & information Processing (2013ZR08).

References

1. Long F, Zhou C H. Study on Method of Analyzing the Positioning Accuracy of Beidou 2nd Generation Satellite Navigation System[J]. Hydrographic Surveying & Charting, 2009.
2. Wei D, Feng L M.Research on the Technology of BDS Pseudorange Differential Positioning[J]. Global positioning system, 2015.
3. Li Z, Yuan Y, Fan L, et al. Determination of the Differential Code Bias for Current BDS Satellites[J]. IEEE Transactions on Geoscience & Remote Sensing, 2014, 52(7):3968-3979.

4. Ding Yiwei, Pan Shuguo, Wang Denghui, et al. A method of encoding and decoding the Beidou message based on RTCM2.3 format[C]. The sixth China satellite navigation academic conference. 2015.
5. Feng L Y,Lin H J,Yao P.pseudorange single point positioning and differential positioning results precision analysis[J]. Hydrographic Surveying & Charting, 2014.
6. Wen Jichao. Research and implementation of differential GPS positioning system based on OEM board [D]. Central South University, 2011
7. Bo H.RTCM SC - 104 differential GPS (DGPS) data standard format[J]. Telecommunication, 2001(2):11-30.
8. China's satellite navigation system management office. BDS space satellite navigation system signal interface control file public service (version 2.0) [R]. China's satellite navigation system management office, Beijing, 2013.
9. RenGui Ruan, xiao-lin jia, xian-bing wu, etc. About the coordinate rotation method in geostationary orbit navigation satellite broadcast ephemeris fitting study [J]. Journal of surveying and mapping, 2011, 40, 145-150.
10. Yong L, Jing S, Sun G, et al. Doppler-aided rapid positioning method for BDS receivers[J]. Electronics Letters, 2015.
11. Jin Lei, Chen Shuai, Liu Yaling, et al. Research on Navigation Algorithm Based on Integral Doppler Smoothing Pseudorange [J]. aerospace control, 2015, 33 (1).
12. Tian A, Dong D, Ning D, et al. GPS Single Point Positioning Algorithm Based on Least Squares[C]// International Symposium on Computational Intelligence & Design. IEEE Computer Society, 2013:16-19.
13. Chen chen Yu ,Hong lei Qin,Tian ji Jin, et al.Design of weighted least squares positioning algorithm for BD2/GPS based on CNO[J]. The sixth China Satellite Navigation Conference electronic. -S07 BDS/ GNSS user terminal technology, 2015.
14. Xie Gang. Principle and design of GPS [11] receiver. GPS principle and receiver design [M]. Electronic Industry Press, 2009.

A Modified Oblique Projection Beamforming Algorithm with Chebyshev Window Function for Coherent Sources

Xing-hang ZHANG, Yan GUO†, Ning LI, Ai-hong LU and Xiao-yun YUAN
Institute of Communication Engineering PLA University of Science and Technology
Nanjing, Jiangsu Province, China
†E-mail: guoyan_2000@sina.com

Traditional beamforming algorithms have relatively poor performance in conditions of small snapshot numbers, high signal-to-noise-ratio and coherent sources. To address this issue, an oblique projection-based beamforming algorithm is modified in this paper. In this algorithm, the oblique projector is utilized to eliminate the noise of the array input data and enhance the robustness of algorithm. Furthermore, the transformation-based linear constraint matrix may eliminate the interferences, and Chebyshev window function is utilized to suppress the side-lobe level. Simulation results demonstrate that the modified algorithm has good robustness and performance.

Keywords: Oblique projection; Chebyshev window; Low side-lobe; Coherent sources.

1. Introduction

Adaptive beamforming algorithms are widely used in signal processing. The technology changes the array beam-pattern by regulating the weights of amplitude and phase of each element. Existing beamforming algorithms are of variety, many of them have worse performance in the cases of small snapshot numbers, low signal-to-noise-ratio (SNR) and coherent sources. In this paper, the oblique projector is utilized to filter out the noise, and the interferences are filtered by the transformation-based linear constraint matrix T, so the levels of the interferences directions are in the null, which can ensure good performance in the condition of coherent sources. Furthermore, the power from the interference directions may descend to the extremely low level by the matrix T. However, these high side-lobe levels nearby the main-lobe may result in that interferences from these directions make remarkable influence on the output data [1]. So, side-lobe controlling is essential. Chebyshev window function is combined to the oblique projector, which may suppress side-lobe levels according to users' requirement. But, this method cannot solve the problem of coherent sources independently [2,3]. Thus, it is essential to combine these

† Corresponding author.

methods. The computational complexity of the modified algorithm is not higher than the oblique projection algorithm.

2. Signal Model

Consider an N-sensor linear array model for signal-plus-interference and noise illuminated by a desired signal and J uncorrelated interferences. The input data is [4]

$$x(t)=\sum_{i=1}^{J+1} a_i s_i(t)+n(t)=AS_a(t)+GS_g(t)+n(t). \tag{1}$$

where $s_i(t)$ denotes the waveforms of the desired signal and interferences, $n(t)$ is the background noise. It is assumed to be spatially white and uncorrelated with $s(t)$. The linear constraint is $C = [A\ G]$, with $A = a(\theta_1)$, $G = [a(\theta_2),\ldots, a(\theta_{j+1})]$, $S_a(t)=s_1(t)^T$, $S_g(t)=[s_2(t),\cdots,s_{J+1}(t)]^T$, in which A and G denote the phase vectors of the desired signal and interferences, respectively. $S_a(t)$ and $S_g(t)$ represent the desired signal and interferences, respectively. If $S_a(t)$ and $S_g(t)$ are non-coherent, the correlation matrix of the input data is [4]

$$R_x=E\left[x(t)x(t)^H\right]=AR_aA^H+GR_gG^H+R_n. \tag{2}$$

where $R_g=E\left[S_g(t)S_g(t)^H\right]$, $R_a=E\left[S_a(t)S_a(t)^H\right]$, and $R_n=\sigma_n^2 I$. R_a, R_g are the correlation matrix of the desired signal and interferences, respectively. σ_n^2 is the noise power. If $S_a(t)$ and $S_g(t)$ are coherent, the correlation matrix of the array input data $R_x=E\left[x(t)x(t)^H\right]=CR_sC^H+R_n$, where R_s is the covariance matrix of the desired signal and interferences.

3. The TCOP Algorithm

The oblique projection algorithm is widely used in the area of signal processing. The input data is oblique projected into the signal subspace along which oblique direction. The matrix E is defined as the oblique projector [4]. Hence, the array input data can be written as $y(t)=w^H\hat{s}_1(t)=w^H Ex(t)$ [5].

The Chebyshev window or Kaiser window functions is utilized to suppress side-lobes of beam-patterns. This method may avoid the interferences improving the output SINR. The functions are generated by the DSP toolbox of Matlab[2], [6].

The transformation-based linear constraint matrix T is defined as $T^H G = O$, in which O is zero matrix. The matrix T may filter out components in the interference subspace and preserve the components in the signal subspace [7].

The correlation matrix of the data after oblique projected is $R_E = E\left[\hat{s}_1(t)\hat{s}_1(t)^H\right]$, and $\overline{R_E} = T^H R_E T$. Meanwhile, the linear constraint C and the phase vectors of the desired signal $a(\theta_1)$ are transformed into $\overline{C} = T^H C$ and $\overline{a(\theta_1)} = T^H a(\theta_1)$, respectively [7]. So, the weight vector of the transformation-based linear constraint minimum variance (T-LCMV) may be denoted as

$$W_{LCMV} = T \frac{\overline{R_E}^{-1}\overline{C}}{\overline{C}^H \overline{R_E}^{-1}\overline{C}} F. \tag{3}$$

in which $F = [1, 0, \cdots, 0]^H$ is the linear constraint vector.

Now, an adaptive beamforming algorithm is proposed, which is called the oblique projection algorithm with the matrix T and Chebyshev window function (TCOP). The Chebyshev window function or Kaiser window function generates the weight coefficient vector win. So the oblique projector is transformed by [4]

$$E = c(\theta_1)\left(c^H(\theta_1) P_G^{\perp} c(\theta_1)\right)^{-1} c^H(\theta_1) P_G^{\perp}. \tag{4}$$

in which $c(\theta_1) = a(\theta_1)\,\mathrm{e}\, win$, and $P_G^{\perp} = I - G\left(G^H G\right)^{-1} G^H$ [8]. e is the symbol of hadamard product, and win is the Chebyshev window function. Therefore, the transformed steering vector $c(\theta_1)$ is the key to suppress side-lobes of beam-patterns.

In conclusion, the TCOP algorithm is denoted in the chart.

Fig. 1. The chart of the TCOP algorithm.

Consider the N-sensor linear array model, the computational complexity of oblique projection algorithm and T-LCMV algorithm are $O(N^3)$ and $O(N^2)$, respectively [8,9]. Thus, the computational complexity of the TCOP algorithm is $O(N^3)$, not higher than the oblique projection algorithm.

4. Simulation Results

In this section, some simulations are presented to justify the performance of the TCOP algorithm. The linear array of antenna with $N = 16$ is assumed to directional sensors and spaces half of a wavelength apart. The desired source is at 5°. And two interfering sources are at 25° and -27°, respectively. And the interference-to-noise-ratio (INR) is 20dB. All the three signals are sine wave with the same frequency. All simulation results are the average of 100 times.

First, we show the performance of array beam-pattern. Secondly, in the condition of different input SNR or different snapshot numbers, the output SINR and the MSE are compared, respectively.

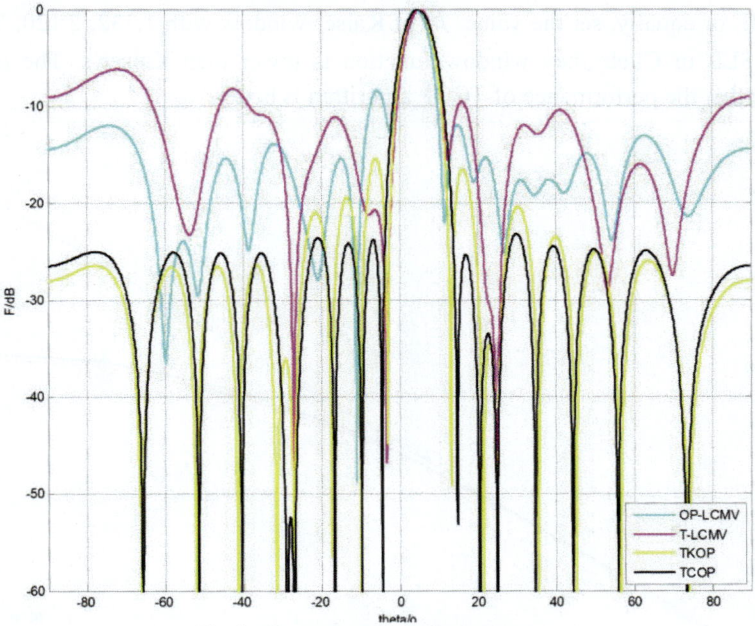

Fig. 2. Comparison of the beam-patterns.

In Fig. 2, in the condition of coherent sources, the side-lobe peaks of the TCOP algorithm are compared with OP-LCMV algorithm, T-LCMV algorithm and the oblique projection algorithm with the matrix T and Kaiser window function (TKOP). In the simulation, the snapshot is 512, and the SNR is 0dB.

The levels of OP-LCMV and T-LCMV algorithms are higher than the other two. The level of OP-LCMV algorithm is not null in the interference directions. In addition, the side-lobes of TKOP algorithm nearby the main-lobe are higher than TCOP algorithm, but the width of main-lobe is comparative with the other three. Furthermore, in the interference directions, the levels of TCOP and TKOP algorithms are extremely low because of the restriction of the matrix T. So, the TCOP algorithm is able to suppress the peaks of side-lobes, realize zero-forcing of the interference directions, but the main-lobe of which is a little wider.

Table 1. Comparison of side-lobe peaks and main-lobe width in different parameters.

Values of SLL(dB)	-25	-30	-40
Chebyshev window(dB)	-23.968	-28.215	-36.774
Kaiser window(dB)	-14.149	-19.513	-27.974

The side-lobe level (SLL) of Chebyshev window is set -25dB, -30dB or -40dB, or equally, set the value β of Kaiser window with 1.332, 2.120, 3.384. The SLL of Chebyshev window function is lower than Kaiser's. The results show that the performance of TCOP algorithm is better.

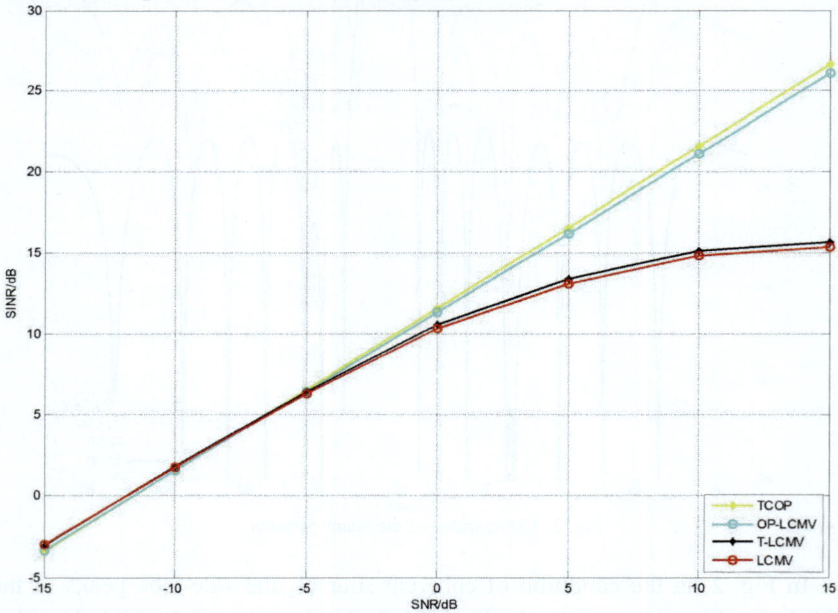

Fig. 3. Comparison of the output SINR in different input SNR.

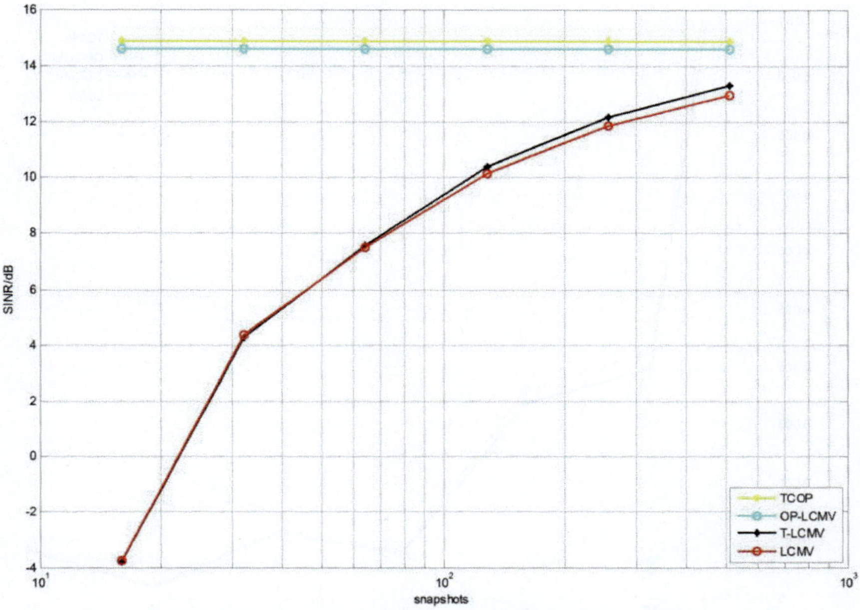

Fig. 4. Comparison of the output SINR in different snapshot numbers.

In Fig. 3, the snapshot number is 512, the SNR is from -15dB to 15dB. The weight vectors are generated by TCOP algorithm. In the low input SNR, the output SINR of the four algorithms are about 11.56dB higher than the input SNR. When the input SNR is higher than -5dB, the output SINR of T-LCMV and LCMV raise different maximum values, while the output SINR of which with the TCOP algorithm and OP-LCMV (LCMV algorithm with oblique projection) algorithm are still increasing. In brief, the TCOP algorithm and OP-LCMV algorithm may improve the output SINR concretely and have better performance, which prove that the two algorithms are robustness.

In Fig. 4, the SNR is 0dB, the snapshot number is from 16 to 512. With the increasing snapshot number, it has almost no effect on the output SINR of the TCOP algorithm and OP-LCMV algorithm. By comparison, when the input SNR is low, the output SINR of T-LCMV and LCMV algorithm are lower than the TCOP algorithm and OP-LCMV algorithm evidently. With the increasing snapshot numbers, the output SINR of T-LCMV and LCMV raise different maximum values, which are still lower than that of TCOP algorithm. The conclusion is that the TCOP algorithm and OP-LCMV algorithm have better performance in different snapshot numbers, which proves that the two algorithms are still robust.

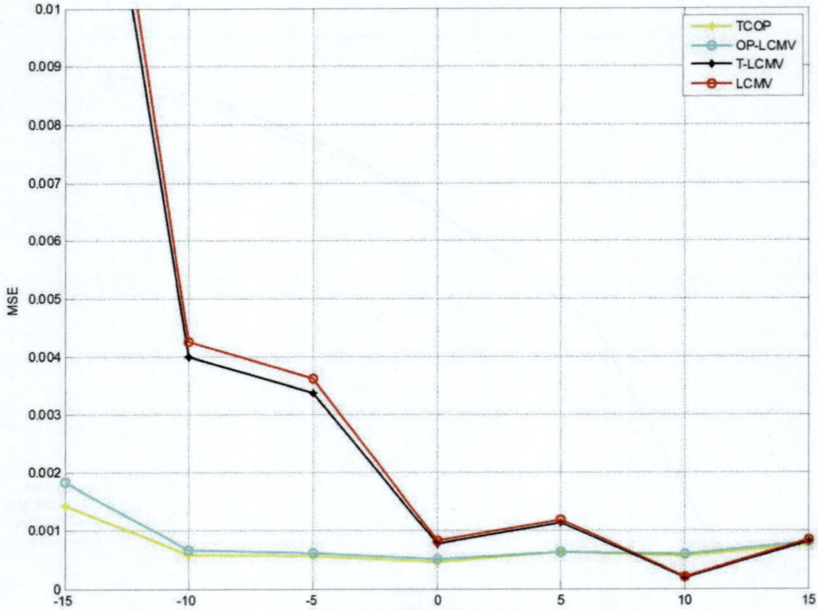

Fig. 5. Comparison of MSE in different input SNR.

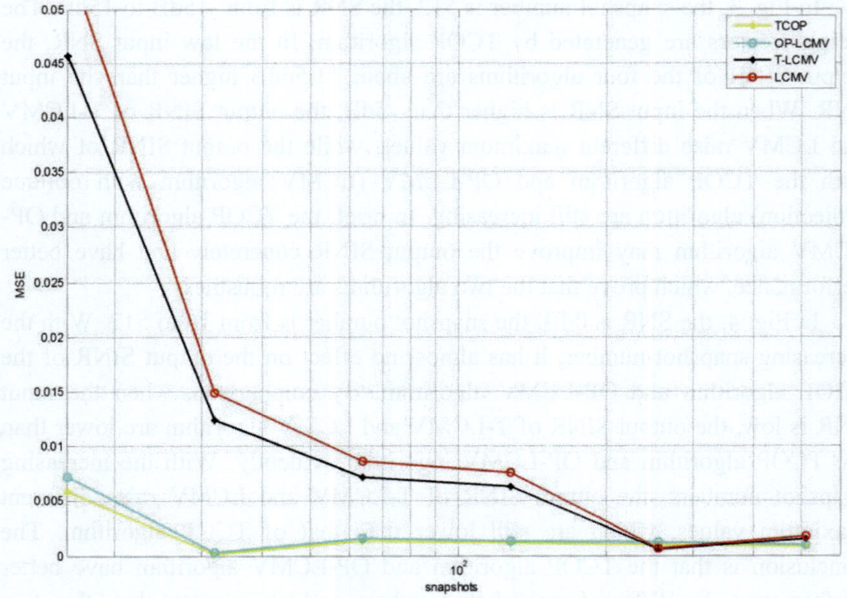

Fig. 6. Comparison of MSE in different snapshot number.

In Fig. 5, the snapshot number is 512, and the SNR is from -15dB to 15dB. When the SNR is low, the MSE of OP-LCMV and TCOP algorithms are small, while the MSE of LCMV and T-LCMV algorithms are high, obviously. With the SNR increasing, the MSE of LCMV and T-LCMV algorithms decrease to the low level, which is close to that of OP-LCMV and TCOP algorithms. Meanwhile, the MSE of OP-LCMV and TCOP algorithms are stable, correspondingly.

In Fig. 6, the SNR is 0dB, and the snapshot number is from 16 to 512. When the snapshot number is small, the MSE of OP-LCMV and TCOP algorithms are small, while the MSE of LCMV and T-LCMV algorithms are high. With the snapshot number increasing, the MSE of LCMV and T-LCMV algorithms decrease to the low level, which is close to that of OP-LCMV and TCOP algorithms. Meanwhile, the MSE of OP-LCMV and TCOP algorithms have little suppressing, correspondingly. The conclusion is that the TCOP and OP-LCMV algorithms have remarkable effect on the MSE suppressing, especially in low SNR or low snapshot numbers. Hence, the two algorithms may descend the error of the original signals.

5. Conclusion

In this paper, the TCOP algorithm modified the performance of beam-pattern, remarkably. In the simulation, the algorithm can descend the peaks of side-lobes. The main-lobe does not become wider apparently, and the interferences are null. In addition, the TCOP algorithm is proposed to assure higher output SINR in the condition of different input SNR or the snapshot numbers. Furthermore, the MSE of the TCOP algorithm is small and stable, which is almost not affected by the input SNR or the snapshot numbers. Finally, compared with the oblique projection algorithm, the computational complexity of the TCOP algorithm is not higher. Generally speaking, in the condition of coherent sources, numerical results reveal that the TCOP algorithm has better performance in different snapshot numbers and SNR, which demonstrates that the algorithm has good robustness and performance.

Acknowledgments

This work is supported by the National Natural Science Foundation of China (61571463, 61371124, 61272487, 61472445 and 61201217).

References

1. X. Xu, Z.F. Ye, Y.F. Zhang, and C.Q. Chang, A deflation approach to direction of arrival estimation for symmetric uniform linear array,IEEE antennas and wireless propagation letters, pp. 486-490 (2006).
2. G.T.F. de Abreu, and R.Kohno, A modified Dolph-Chebyshevapproach for the synthesis of low side-lobe beam-patterns with adjustable beam-width,IEEE Trans on Antennas and Propagation, Vol. 51, No. 10. pp. 3104-3107 (2003).
3. H. Jiang, Z.J. Li, and D. Liu, DOA estimation of ultra wideband signals using multiple constant beam-width beamformers,in *IEEE Int. on Wireless communication and signal processing,*(Nanjing, China, 2009), pp. 1-5.
4. X. Xu, Z. Ye and J. Peng, Method of direction-of-arrival estimation for uncorrelated, partially correlated and coherent sources,IET Microwave antennas propagation, Vol. 1, No. 4. pp. 949 –954 (2007).
5. McCloud M L. and Scharf L A, A new subspace identification algorithm for high-resolution DOA estimation, IEEE Trans on Antennas and Propagation, Vol.50, No.10. pp. 1382- 1389 (2002).
6. M. Luszczyk and D. Mucha, Kaiser-Bessel window weighting function for polyphase pulse compression code, In *Proc. Int. on Microwaves radar and wireless communication,* (Wroclaw, Poland, 2008), pp. 1-4.
7. Q.J. Ding, Y.L. Wang, Y.S. Zhang, and R.F. Li, Transformation-based linearly constrained reduced rank adaptive beamforming, in *IEEE Int. Radar Conference,* (Arlington, USA, 2005), pp. 647-652.
8. N.Suga, and T.Furukawa, Iterative updating of oblique projection matrix,IEEE International Symposium on Intelligent Signal Processing and Communications Systems, pp. 230-234 (2013).
9. L.Wang, R.C. de Lamare, and M.Yukawa, Adaptive Reduced-Rank Constrained Constant Modulus Algorithms Based on Joint Iterative Optimization of Filters for Beamforming,IEEE Trans on Signal Processing, Vol. 58, No. 6. pp. 2983-2997 (2010).

A New Dual-Frequencies Direction Finding Method

Jian-bin ZOU*, Kai GAO, Jun YANG and Er-yang ZHANG
Institute of Electronic Science and Technology, National University of Defense Technology,,
Changsha, 410073, China
**E-mail: zjb_nudt@163.com*

This paper proposes a new direction finding system consisting of a transmitter and two receivers. The phase differences of different frequency signals received by the two receivers are used to resolve interferometer phase ambiguity in this method and the direction is obtained through the phase differences obtained. The simulation results demonstrate the effectiveness of this method.

Keywords: Phase difference, Direction finding, Dual-frequencies.

1. Introduction

Phase interferometer direction finding system has the advantages of high resolution, high sensitivity and good real-time ability, widely applied in angle measurement system in electronic reconnaissance domain. But the contradiction between the maximal range of unambiguous direction measurement and precision of measurement exists in this system [1]. For the problem of the direction finding ambiguity with interferometers, five approaches are commonly used to deal with the ambiguities, including: long-short baseline, stagger baseline, virtual baseline, unambiguous long-baseline interferometer angle measurement method and spatial baseline or arrays [2,3,4]. Though the long-short baseline method could solve the problem of direction finding ambiguity, it can't be realized in wide-band high frequency system because of the short wavelength. Stagger baseline and virtual baseline could solve the problem of physical realization restrict of short wavelength, but the single layout modality in restricted space will affect the measurement precision. Unambiguous long-baseline method needs high signal noise ratio (SNR) to resolve the ambiguity accurately [5]. Most of the paper focus on the direction finding of radiant source, and the signal processing under different circumstance, without considering the non-radiation sources and the frame of the receiver[6,7,8]. For a non-radiation target, most of the method are using multiple sensors or sub-arrays or monopulse technique, which is too complicated to be implemented in practicality [9,10,11].

This paper proposes a new direction finding method, which uses the phase differences of dual-frequencies signals' echo to resolve phase ambiguity, could avoid the length and precision restriction of baseline and suitable for a non-radiation sources.

2. Direction Finding System

This system consists of one transmitter T and two receivers R1 and R2, transmitter and receivers separate from each other. T is settled in the middle of R1 and R2, the space between R1 and R2 is d. T transmits dual-frequencies continuous wave signals against the target in air, R1 and R2 receive the echo signals from the target. The frequencies of transmitted signals are f_1 and f_2 , phase difference between two receivers in frequencies f_1 and f_2 are $\Delta\varphi_1$ and $\Delta\varphi_2$. The direction finding system is as shown in Fig. 1.

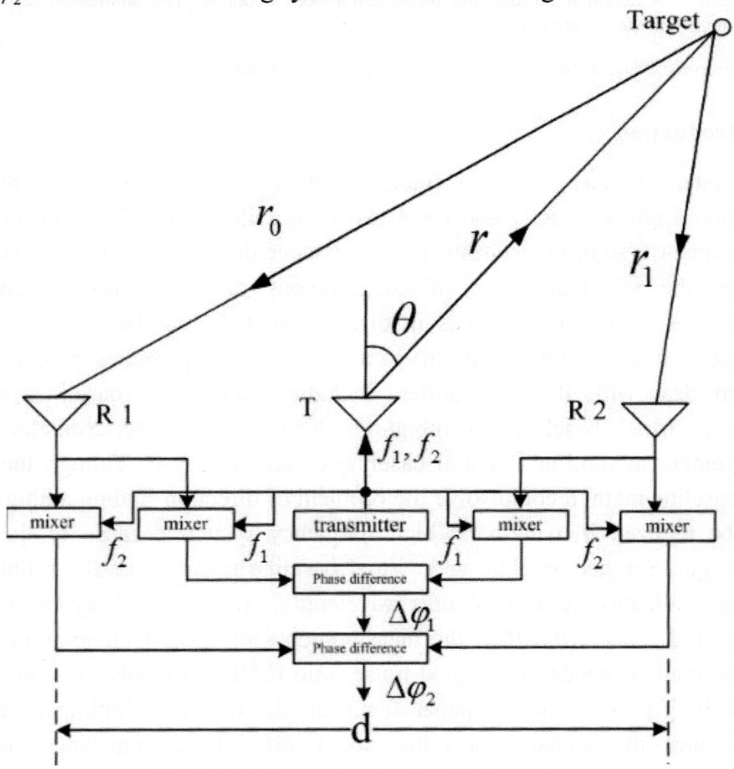

Fig. 1. Dual-frequencies direction finding system.

3. Direction Finding Method

Based on the interferometer direction finding principle, as shown in Fig. 1. Supposed the target is in the direction of θ , $f_1 > f_2$, then we have the phase differences between receivers when frequencies are f_1 and f_2 are:

$$\begin{aligned}\Delta\varphi_1 &= \frac{2\pi d}{\lambda_1}\sin\theta = \frac{2\pi d f_1}{c}\sin\theta = \frac{d}{c}\sin\theta\cdot 2\pi f_1 \\ \Delta\varphi_2 &= \frac{2\pi d}{\lambda_2}\sin\theta = \frac{2\pi d f_2}{c}\sin\theta = \frac{d}{c}\sin\theta\cdot 2\pi f_2\end{aligned} . \tag{1}$$

Where λ_1 and λ_2 are the wavelength of signals when frequencies are f_1 and f_2 , c is the velocity of light. Though R1 and R2 receive different frequency echo signals, the delay time is the same, which is

$$\tau = \frac{d}{c}\sin\theta \ . \tag{2}$$

Phase difference between two different frequency signals of two receivers is

$$\Delta\Phi = \Delta\varphi_1 - \Delta\varphi_2 = 2\pi\tau\left(f_1 - f_2\right) = 2\pi\tau\Delta f \ . \tag{3}$$

If we can get $\Delta\Phi$ accurately, and Δf is known, the only solution of τ is gained, then we can obtain the direction θ .

We can't get $\Delta\varphi_1$ and $\Delta\varphi_2$ directly, can only get the value of them in the range of $[0, 2\pi]$, define them as $\Delta\varphi_{M1}$ and $\Delta\varphi_{M2}$, then $\Delta\varphi_1$ and $\Delta\varphi_2$ can be written as

$$\begin{aligned}\Delta\varphi_1 &= 2\pi k_1 + \Delta\varphi_{M1} \\ \Delta\varphi_2 &= 2\pi k_2 + \Delta\varphi_{M2}\end{aligned} . \tag{4}$$

Where k_1 and k_2 are unknown integers, the problem is how to get them, this is the problem of ambiguity solution.

When $\Delta\Phi = 2\pi\Delta f \frac{d}{c}\sin\theta = 2\pi\tau\Delta f < 2\pi$, that is

$$\Delta f \frac{d}{c}\sin\theta \le \Delta f \frac{d}{c} < 1 \Rightarrow \Delta f < \frac{c}{d} \ . \tag{5}$$

The relationship between $\Delta\Phi$ and τ has no ambiguity, we have

$$\Delta\Phi = \Delta\varphi_1 - \Delta\varphi_2 = 2\pi k_1 + \Delta\varphi_{M1} - \left(2\pi k_2 + \Delta\varphi_{M2}\right) \ . \tag{6}$$

The relationship between $\Delta\varphi = 2\pi fd\sin\theta/c$ $(f = f_1, f_2)$ and τ is as shown in Fig. 2. (1) and (2) are the lines of $\Delta\varphi_1$ and $\Delta\varphi_2$. (3) and (4) are the lines of $\Delta\varphi_{M1}$ and $\Delta\varphi_{M2}$. (1) and (2) are linear growth along with τ , the perpendicular between (1) and (2) means $\Delta\Phi = \Delta\varphi_1 - \Delta\varphi_2$. Because $f_1 > f_2$, from Fig. 2, we can see $\Delta\varphi_1 > \Delta\varphi_2$, and $\tau = d\sin\theta / c$ means different direction θ has different τ . In Fig. 2, supposed θ is in the range of $[0, \pi/2]$, and $\Delta\Phi < 2\pi$.

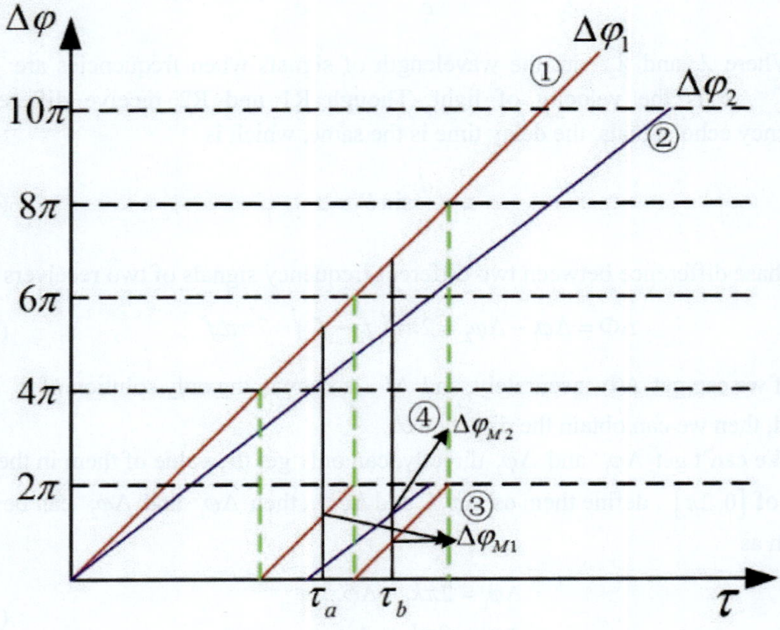

Fig. 2. The relationship between $\Delta\varphi$ and τ.

When the value of $\Delta\varphi_1$ and $\Delta\varphi_2$ exceed 2π , as (1) and (2) shown in Fig. 2. the module of (1) and (2) at 2π become (3) and (4). Based on the relationship between (3) and (4), two situations are discussed. When τ at τ_a , $\Delta\varphi_{M1} > \Delta\varphi_{M2}$, $k_1 = k_2$, we have

$$\Delta\Phi = \Delta\varphi_{M1} - \Delta\varphi_{M2} \ . \tag{7}$$

When τ at τ_b , $\Delta\varphi_{M1} < \Delta\varphi_{M2}$, $k_1 = k_2 + 1$, we have

$$\Delta\Phi = 2\pi + \left(\Delta\varphi_{M1} - \Delta\varphi_{M2}\right) \tag{8}$$

With the $\Delta\Phi$ gained above, we have

$$\tau = \frac{d}{c}\sin\theta = \frac{\Delta\Phi}{2\pi\Delta f} \; . \tag{9}$$

$$\theta = \arcsin\frac{\Delta\Phi \cdot c}{2\pi d\Delta f} \; . \tag{10}$$

Then we can get the direction of the target, and phase ambiguity was solved. For obtaining more high resolution direction, we need high resolution $\Delta\varphi_{M1}$ and $\Delta\varphi_{M2}$, then we can get k_1 and k_2, and high resolution direction θ can be gained by long baseline d, $\Delta\varphi_1$ and $\Delta\varphi_2$.

4. Simulation Results

Supposed that the length of baseline d is 10m, the phase difference measurement error $\delta\Delta\varphi_{M1} = \delta\Delta\varphi_{M2}$, $\Delta f = c/d = 30MHz$ $(\theta < 90^0)$, $f_1 = 5GHz$, $f_2 = 5.03GHz$, sample data length N is 3000, using the DFT method to get phase difference. When SNR=15dB, 20dB, 30dB, and target direction θ changes from 0^0 to 60°, the direction measurement error $\delta\theta$ is as shown in Fig. 3. From Fig. 3 we can see that the measurement error becomes larger along with the θ becomes larger. The measurement error is less than 1×10^{-3} degree when SNR is 20 dB under the simulation parameters.

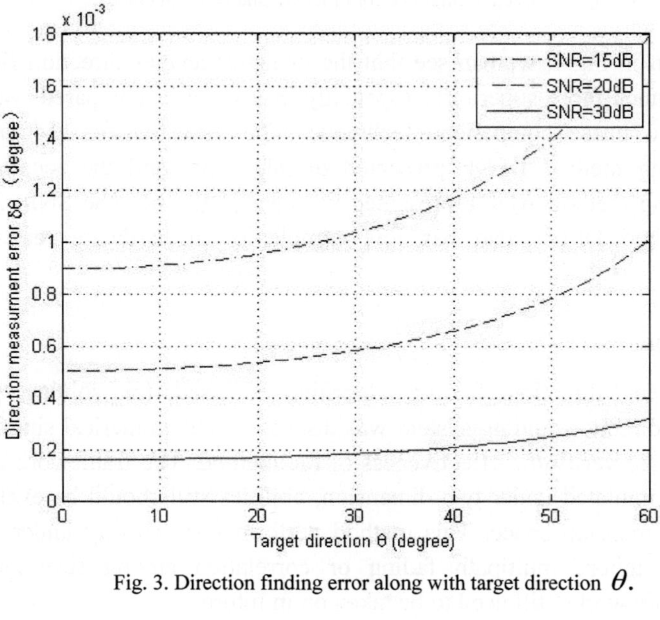

Fig. 3. Direction finding error along with target direction θ.

The direction measurement abilities of the dual-frequencies direction find method (DFDF) and the amplitude and phase comparison techniques (APCT) proposed in paper [10] are analyzed, which shown in Fig.4 below.

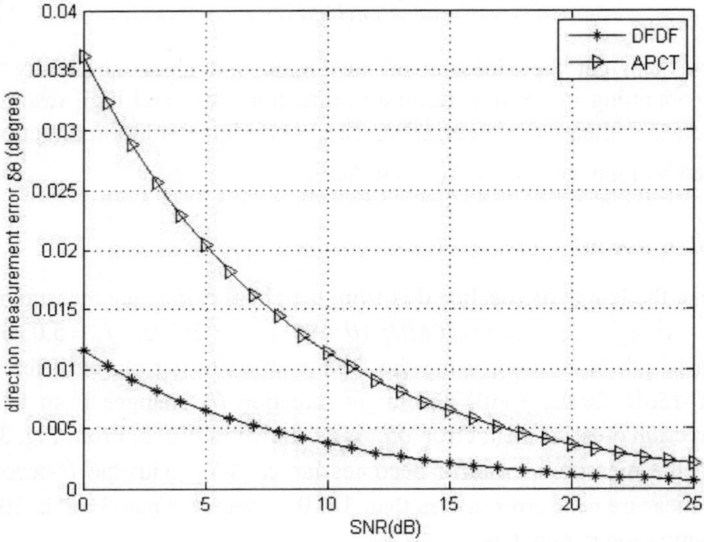

Fig. 4. Direction finding error of DFDF and APCT methods.

As shown in Fig.4, we can see that the dual-frequencies direction finding method has much more superiority especially in low SNR, compared with the amplitude and phase comparison technique. The measurement accuracy is 1.2×10^{-3} using method DFDF presented in this paper and the accuracy is 2.5×10^{-3} using method ADCT presented in paper [10] when the SNR=20dB, and the method DFDF also has low complexity in hardware realization procedure.

5. Conclusion

Dual-frequencies direction finding algorithm is used for solving phase ambiguity in direction finding system was discussed. The numerical simulation results presented verify the effectiveness of the method. The framework of the system only simulated under two-dimension, abilities still should be evaluated under three-dimension space. This method perform satisfactorily under white noise, which ignore multipath fading or correlation among two sources. Therefore, more works still need to be taken on in future.

Acknowledgments

Project supported by the National Nature Science Foundation of China (No.61401476).

References

1. Malloy N J. 'Analysis and synthesis of general planar interferometer arrays'. IEEE ICASSP-83, 1983: 352-355.
2. Bin Liao, Shing-Chow Chan. 'Direction Finding in Partly Calibrated uniform linear arrays with unknown gains and phases'. IEEE Transactions on aerospace and electronic systems, 2015, 51(1): 217-227.
3. Jung-Hoon Lee, Jong-Myung Woo. 'Interferometer direction-finding system with improved DF accuracy using two different array configurations'. IEEE Antennas and wireless propagation letters, 2015, 14:719-722.
4. Jacobs E, Ralston W E. 'Ambiguity resolution in interferometer'. IEEE Trans. On AES, 1981, 17, (2):766-779.
5. Wickersham, D.J. 'Application of the robust symmetrical number system to high resolution direction finding interferometry'. ADA378826, Mar, 2000.
6. Nurbanu Guzey, Hao Xu. 'Localization of near-field sources in spatially colored noise'. IEEE Transactions on instrumentation and measurement, 2015, 64(8):2302-2311.
7. Naresh vankayalapati, Steven Kay, Quan ding. 'TDOA based direction finding maximum likelihood estimator and the Caramer-Rao Bound'. IEEE Transaction on aerospace and electronic systems, 2014, 50(3):1616-1635.
8. Xinyu Zhang, Yang Li, Xiaopeng Yang, etal. 'Sub-array weighing UN-MUSIC: a unified framework and optimal weighting strategy'. IEEE Signal processing letters, 2014, 21(7):871-874.
9. H.T.Hui. 'Improved compensation for the mutual coupling effect in a dipole array for direction finding'. Antennas and Propagation, IEEE Transactions on, 2003, 51(9):2498-2503.
10. Brad R. Jackson, Sreeraman Rajan, Bruce J, etal. 'Direction of arrival estimation using directive antennas in uniform circular arrays'. IEEE Transactions on antennas and propagation, 2015, 63(2): 736-747.
11. Orduyilmaz A, Serin M, Gurbuz A.C, Yildirim A. 'Passive direction finding using amplitude and phase comparison techniques'. Signal processing and Communications Applications Conference, 2014 22nd, pp: 935-938.

Design of an Enhanced DMA with Data Pre-Computing for Digital Image Processing

Peng-yi WU[1,*] and Zhao-lin LI[2,†]
[1]*Institute of Microelectronics, Tsinghua University, Beijing, 100084, China*
[*]*wpy13@mails.tsinghua.edu.cn*

[2]*Research Institute of Information Technology, Tsinghua University, Beijing, 100084, China*
[†]*lzl73@mail.tsinghua.edu.cn*

EDMA (Enhanced Direct memory access) is an important method to transmit data in Digital Signal Processer (DSP) for high speed and real-time processing of digital signal, such as digital image processing, radar signal recognition. However existing DMAs do not use data pre-computation and they are incapable of satisfying the increasing demands of signal processing, target recognition or scientific computing applications. In this paper, we propose a new enhanced DMA design with data pre-computing for digital image processing, which provides more efficient data transfers in modern DSP by integrating several useful arithmetic units for data preprocessing. In comparison to traditional EDMA, the proposed design reduces the DSP's burden of simple calculations and increases the efficiency of data transmission for improved performance..

Keywords: EDMA; Data transfer; DSP; Digital image processing.

1. Introduction

Digital image processing is widely used in radar signal, target recognition and scientific computing applications[1]. Most of digital image processing are completed in DSPs, because DSP is more flexible than Application Specific Integrated Circuits (ASICs). Extracting the relevant calculations, such as matrix addition, matrix weighting which are frequently used is important for the performance evaluation.

CPU is always exhausted when processing those simple calculations. The time is mainly used in data operation and data transference. To transfer data more efficiently, DMA is often used. It is an important data exchange technique used in DSP which could transfer a bulk of data without the intervention of CPU[2].

The traditional DMA, aimed at general application for transferring data, do not have operational units. However, efficient could be largely improved if data have been pre-processed before arriving at the CPU core.

This paper proposes a new methods for digital image processing after analysis an algorithm of infrared processing which has so many repetitive, regular matrix operations.

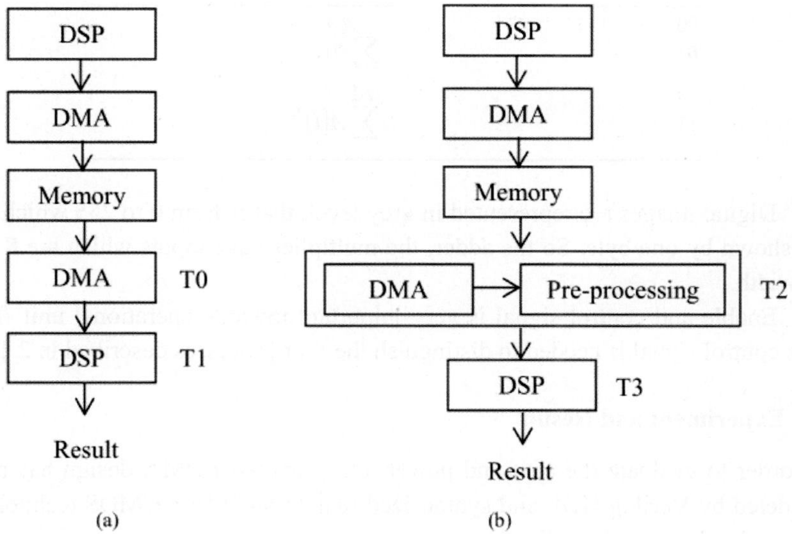

Fig. 1. The comparison of two methods (a) Traditional way (b) New way.

DMA issues write command when there is sufficient data in the data FIFO[3,4,5,6]. There may be a long time since the read controller can process up to four or eight TRs ahead of the write controller. So this time can be made full use of . T2 illustrated in figure.1(b) is a little longer than T0 in (b), but T3 is much smaller than T1.

2. Analysis of Image Processing Algorithm

After reading an code about infrared processing, we extract four repetitive, regular operations used for histogram statistic, correlation images calculation, real-time image averaging, square deviation of real-time figures. The lowercase letter represents a real number while the uppercase ones, a matrix.

$$B = A + a . \tag{1}$$

$$a = \sum A[i]. \quad (2)$$

$$B = aA. \quad (3)$$

$$a = \sum A[i]^2. \quad (4)$$

Table 1. Configuration.

ctr	Operation
00	$A + a$
01	$\sum A[i]$
10	aA
11	$\sum A[i]^2$

Digital images are represented in grey level, that is from 0 to 255 which can be shown by one byte. So the adder, the multiplier have inputs which are 8 bits in width.

Enable and control signal is very important towards operational unit. Two bits control signal is needed to distinguish the four processes described in 2.1.

3. Experiment and Result

In order to evaluate the area and power, the proposed EDMA design has been modeled by Verilog HDL and synthesized in a TSMC 65nm CMOS technology after fully functional verification.

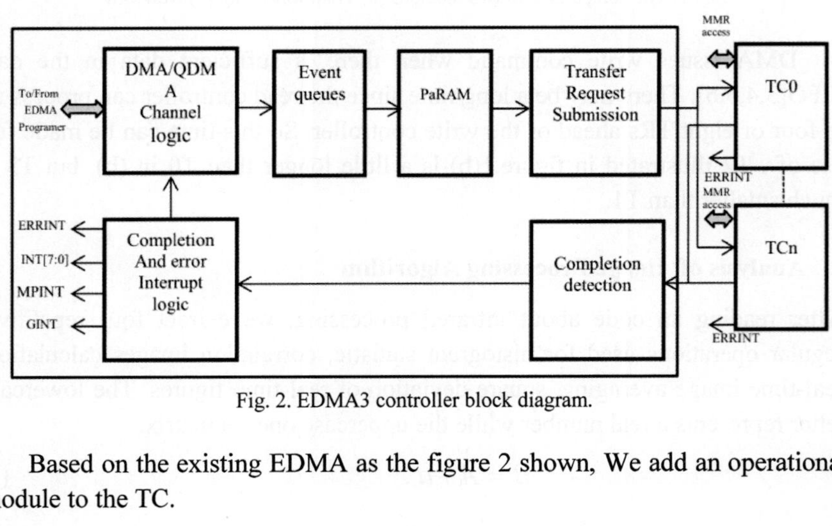

Fig. 2. EDMA3 controller block diagram.

Based on the existing EDMA as the figure 2 shown, We add an operational module to the TC.

As the figure 3 and figure illustrated, the preprocessing of data must go through two steps. The one named 'add or mul', and the other accumulation. There are 16 flowing structures in the design for the Bus width is 128 bit.

The synthesis results are:

Area: 0.42 mm^2

Power: 18.5 mw

Worst delay: 1.16 ns

According to the results, this design can run at 860MHz and the power is relatively low. However, the efficient is improved.

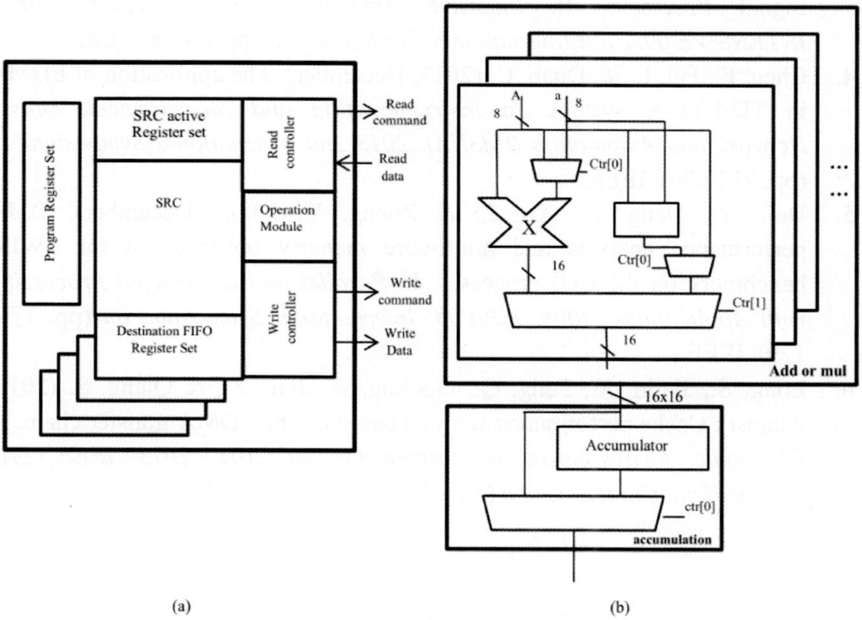

Fig. 3. (a) TC block diagram (b) operation module.

4. Conclusion

This paper presents a new enhanced DMA design with data pre-computing for digital image processing, which provides more efficient data transfers in modern DSP by integrating some useful arithmetic units for data preprocessing. In comparison to traditional EDMA, the proposed design reduces the DSP's burden of simple calculations and increases the efficiency of data transmission for performance improvement. Experiential results show that this design can run at 860MHz, the area and power of the additional arithmetic units for data preprocessing is 0.42 mm^{2}and 18.5 mw, respectively.

References

1. Bier, J. (1997). The evolution of DSP processors. presentation at UC Berkeley.
2. TI, "Enhanced Direct Memory Access (EDMA3) Controller User's Guide" (2015).
3. Lee, M., Jeong, J. H., Kim, J., Shim, Y. S., Lee, H. S., & Kim, S. S. (2009, April). Parallel Data Processing Based on EDMA to Save the Processing Power of a T-DMB Software Baseband Receiver Running on a Digital Signal Processor. In *Intensive Applications and Services, 2009. INTENSIVE'09. First International Conference on* (pp. 34-38). IEEE.
4. Chen, F., Fei, L., & Duan, C. (2013, December). The application of EDMA in TD-LTE-A system. In *Instrumentation and Measurement, Sensor Network and Automation (IMSNA), 2013 2nd International Symposium on* (pp. 972-974). IEEE.
5. Dou, Y., Deng, L., Xu, J., & Zheng, Y. (2008, December). DMA performance analysis and multi-core memory optimization for SWIM benchmark on the Cell processor. In *Parallel and Distributed Processing with Applications, 2008. ISPA'08. International Symposium on* (pp. 170-179). IEEE.
6. Long, S., Jialin, X., Feng, Q., Guoling, B., Jian, Z., & Qiang, S. (2013, August). Cache performance analysis based on the EDMA transfer chain. In *Electronic Measurement & Instruments (ICEMI), 2013 IEEE 11th International Conference on* (Vol. 2, pp. 868-871). IEEE.

A Short Text Similarity Measure Based on Hidden Topics

Hong-chao CHEN[1,2], Xiao-hua GUO[1], Ling-qiang LIU[1] and Xin-hua ZHU[1,2,*]
[1] *College of Computer Science& IT, Guangxi Normal University, Guilin, 541004, China*
[2] *Guangxi Key Lab of Multi-source Information Mining & Security, Guangxi Normal University, Guilin, 541004, China*
[*]*Email: zxh429@263.net*

Similarity measurement plays an important role in the classification of short text. However, traditional text similarity measures fail to achieve a high accuracy because the sparse features in short text. In this paper, we propose a new method based on the different number of hidden topics, which are derived through well-known topic models such as Latent Dirichlet Allocation (LDA). We obtain the related topics, and integrate the topics with the features of short text in order to decrease the sparseness and improve the word co-occurrences. Numerous experiments were conducted on the open data set (Wikipedia dataset) and the results demonstrated that our proposed method improves classification accuracy by 14.03% on the k-nearest neighbors algorithm (KNN). This indicates that our method outperforms other state-of-the-art methods which do not utilize hidden topics and validates that the method is effective.

Keywords: Short text; Similarity measure; Topic model; KNN; Information retrieval.

1. Introduction

The problem of measuring the similarity between two short text become an increasingly challenging task that needs to be solved in natural language processing and related domains, because the different methods of similarity measure generate distinct results, which directly affect the accuracy of these classifiers (such as K-Nearest Neighbor classifier, KNN in short). Examples of such tasks also include web information retrieval[1,2] and text mining[3], in which the computing of similarities between short text has been proved to be an important technique for discovering hidden knowledge from textual corpus. Traditional methods for measuring the similarity of two long texts mainly leverage the word co-occurrences in them, which can achieve good results because of having enough common words to calculate the text similarity. But these methods fail to achieve the desired accuracy on two short text snippets because of providing no enough contexts. For example, "what price is the apple" and "how much is the apple", there is an obvious similarity between the two

[*] Corresponding author.

short texts, but most traditional text similarity measures will get a very low score between these texts.

For above reasons, we are proposing a new short text similarity measures solution along this direction in this paper. With pre-defined number of topics, the popular topic model like LDA[4,5] can generate the different number of latent topics from a related collections and then do topic inference for the short text segment. Let us assume there are two short text segments s1 and s2, we can get different topical proportion of two short text through pre-defined number of latent topics (e.g., 30, 100). If the two short text belong to the same topics, we can incorporate the same topics into the two short text (e.g., s1={s1, 30 topic, 100topic}, s2={s2, 30 topic, 100 topic}). So the two short text share more common words than before, and get a higher similarity score. We validated our method over an open data set[6], on which one text categorization method, K-Nearest Neighbor[7], was used as the classifiers. The performance has been improved 14.03% by our method. This shows the superiority of our method using the combination of the different number of topics over the other methods without hidden topics.

2. Topic Model

Latent Dirichlet Allocation (LDA), first introduced by Blei et al.[4], is a generative process where each document in the text corpus is modeled as a set of topics draw from a mixture distribution over a set of hidden topics. A topic is modeled as a probability distribution over topic words. LDA is a latent semantic analysis (LSA)[8] method, which showed the co-occurrence of terms being used to recover the latent topic structure. In the following, we first introduce LDA generative process and some important parameters.

2.1. *Topic generative process*

Given a collection of M documents D={d1, d2, … , dM}, and the vector wd as the bag of words representation of document d. The generative graphical model is illustrated in Figure 1. It can be used to model and discover the hidden topic structures in the text collections. The generative process mainly has three steps: 1) the document is first associated with a K-dimensional topic mixing vector $\vec{\theta}_d$ which is drawn from a Dirichlet distribution, $\theta_d \sim Dir(\alpha)$; 2) each word wdn in the document is then assigned to a single topic z_{dn} drawn from the multinomial variable, Zdn~Multi($\vec{\theta}_d$); 3) finally, the w_{dn} is drawn from a V-dimensional multinomial variable, wdn ~ Multi($\phi_{z_{dn}}$), where V is the size of the vocabulary.

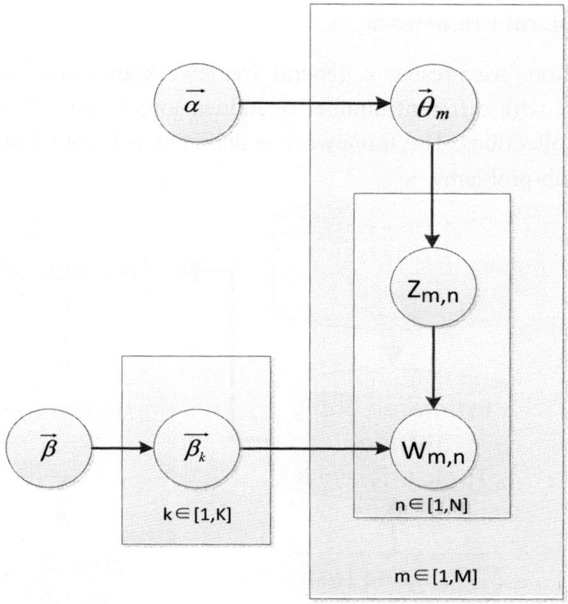

Fig. 1. LDA: a generative graphical model.

2.2. *Important parameters*

There are three important input parameters and one output parameter, which will be used in the following sections, in the above LDA theory: α, β, the number of topics K and document mixing topic vector, the optimal parameters of α and β depend on the topic number and the size of vocabulary in the document collection, and they are typically set as α=50/K and β=0.01[10]. The number of topics is a very important setting parameter, which can affect the interpretability of the extracted topics and accordingly influence the performance of calculating the similarity between two short text snippets. How to decide the number of topics will be discussed in Section 5. There is still an important parameter, document mixing topic vector. This parameter is the mostly related to our work. Through doing topic inference, we obtain each document mixing topic vector, and two similarity short text has the very similarity document mixing topic vector. In this paper, we fix the hyper parameters of α and β as α=50/K and β=0.01. The number of topics K and document mixing topic vector is discussed in the following sections.

3. The General Framework

In this section, we present a general framework that aims at integrating the original text with different number of hidden topics from the related universal document collections. The framework is depicted in Figure 2 and consists of the following sub-problems.

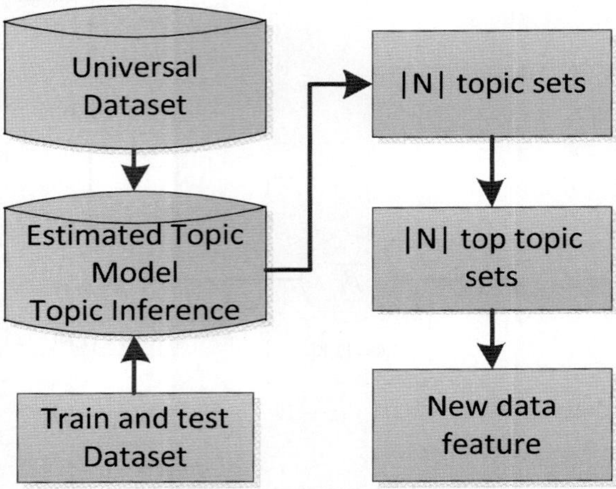

Fig. 2. Our framework to gain the new short text feature.

(i) Use the well-known topic model (LDA) to analysis the hidden topics of the universal dataset to generate estimated topic model.

(ii) Given a set denoted by N, which the size is |N|; we do topic inference over train and test dataset to generate the topic proportion according to each item in N. As a result, we gain |N| different sets of topics mixing vector.

(iii) For each theme in the topic sets, we rank it by the probability in order to get a |N| top topic sets.

(iv) Combine the top topic feature and the original short text segments to form new text feature.

3.1. *Generate |N| topic sets*

In our framework, the first step is that we run LDA over the universal dataset to estimate topic model. Choosing an appropriate universal dataset is a huge challenge, because the quality of universal dataset directly affects the topic mixing vector of the train and test dataset. So the universal dataset should be gained by humans to determine whether or not the estimated topic model from this dataset can help to inference a good document topic mixing vector. After estimating topic model, there still is an important problem that how to generate the topic sets. In this paper, we use a direct way to get topic sets N. Intuitively the pre-defined number of topics is a good way to be used to produce topic sets (e.g. {10,20,…,200,..}). There, we gain |N| different sets of topics as:

$$T=\{T1,T2, \dots , T|N|\} . \tag{1}$$

where each Ti is a topic mixing vector in the form of:

$$T_i = \left\{\vec{\theta}_d\right\}_{m=1}^{M} . \tag{2}$$

where M is the number of short text and $\vec{\theta}_d$ is a topic mixing vector. We do topic inference over the train and test dataset to obtain the |N| topic sets T.

3.2. *Establishing top topic sets*

Table 1 depicts some samples of new short text feature. Given a short text d and the top topic vector, according to each item in N, we will integrate the top topic vector and the original short text, in order that the new short text vector is suitable for the following experiment classifier.

Table 1. Some samples of new short text feature.

snippet1: manufacture manufacturer directory china products manufacturers directory china products manufacturer exporter directory supplier directory suppliers business 50topic3750topic3750topic37 50topic27 50topic27 50topic44 50topic42 50topic13 100topic82 100topic82100topic82 100topic17 100topic17 100topic92 100topic81 100topic71
snippet2: electronics manufacturing procurement homepage electronics manufacturing procurement magazine power products production essentials data management business 50topic27 50topic2750topic27 50topic26 50topic26 50topic19 50topic19 50topic16 50topic48 100topic82 100topic82100topic82 100topic37 100topic37 100topic18 100topic100 100topic86
snippet3: paper true cost overseas manufacture product design costs manufacturing products china manufacturing redesigned product china save business 50topic27 50topic2750topic2750topic42 50topic42 50topic29 50topic36 50topic24 100topic82 100topic82100topic82 100topic92 100topic92 100topic100 100topic87 100topic68
snippet4: machining metal stamping gaskets fasteners searchable database information products services cad drawings business 50topic35 50topic3550topic35 50topic50 50topic50 50topic45 50topic38 50topic31 100topic86 100topic86100topic86 100topic79 100topic79 100topic16 100topic12 100topic88

4. Experiments

In this section we describe the experimental comparison between our methods and alternative state-of-the-art baseline over web-snippet dataset. We validate our method effective through the KNN classifier, on which the similarity measure between two short texts is a key step.

4.1. *Data sets*

We choose the open data set, collected by Phan[11]. This data set consists of two parts, namely corpus and short text snippets. Corpus: Phan prepared various seed crawling keywords coming from distinct domains, ran JWikiDocs to download the corresponding WiKipedia and crawl the relevant pages by following outgoing hyperlinks. After dealing with the crawling data, the final corpus was presented in Table 2. The short text snippets were selected from the results of web search transaction by the predefined phrases of different domains. For each query term put into Google search engine, the top 20 or 30 ranked web search snippets were collected.

Table 2. Some basic statistics of the corpus.

Raw Data: 3.5GB; |Docs| = 461177
Preprocess: removing duplicate documents, HTML tags, navigation links, stop and rare (thresold = 30) words
Final Data: 240MB; |Docs| = 71986;|Vocabulary| = 60649

4.2. *Experiment results*

In order to compare our method with the method without hidden topic, we did an important experiment by training many KNN classifiers on the different single number of topics and measures the accuracy on the test set. The performance of KNN is showed in Figure 3. This figure mainly highlights two points. First, our similarity measure method can achieve an impressive improvement of accuracy. From the Figure 3, we can see that our method with single topic increase the classification accuracy from an accuracy of 73.45% without topical feature to 82.67%. Second, our proposed method always outperforms the method without hidden topic. This also shows the robustness of our similarity measures method.

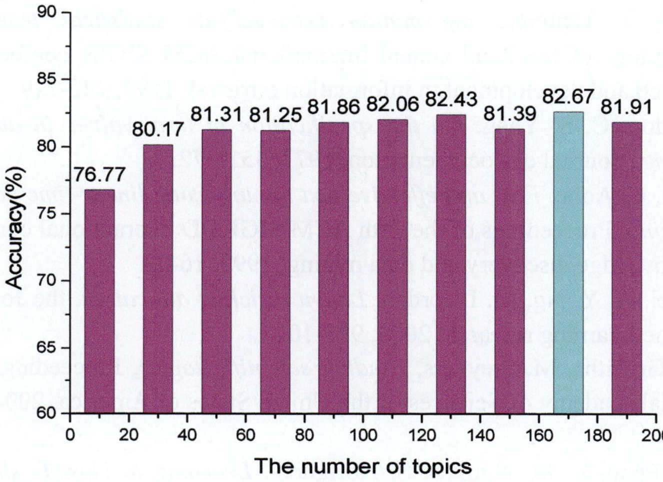

Fig. 3. Classification performance with different single number topic.

5. Conclusion

In this paper, we put forward a method for short text similarity measure. In order to do with the sparseness of short text, various ways have been tried to enhance the representation of short text, including using web-based or topic-based method. These methods solve the problem to certain degree, but still leave much space for improvement. In our method, we integrate the different numbers of topics and the original to form new short text feature. We compare our proposed method against the methods without topics through KNN classifier over one open data set. The experimental results show that our method can increment the classification accuracy by 14.03%. Though we see the advantage of our proposed method clearly in this paper, we can further improve it by exploiting advanced approaches, such as generating more related topics, or exploiting the internal relation of short text to measure their similarity.

Acknowledgments

This work was supported by the National Natural Science Foundation of China under the contract numbers 61462010 and 61363036, Guangxi Collaborative Innovation Center of Multi-source Information Integration and Intelligent Processing.

References

1. Berger, J. Lafferty, *Information retrieval as statistical translation,* Proceedings of the 22nd annual international ACM SIGIR conference on Research and development in information retrieval, 1999, 222-229.
2. G. Salton, C. S. Yang, *On the specification of term values in automatic indexing ,* Journal of documentation, 1973, 351-372.
3. Larsen, C. Aone, *Fast and effective text mining using linear-time document clustering,* Proceedings of the fifth ACM SIGKDD international conference on Knowledge discovery and data mining, 1999, 16-22.
4. M. Blei, A. Y. Ng, M. I. Jordan, *Latent dirichlet allocation*, the Journal of machine Learning research, 2003, 993-1022.
5. T. L. Griffiths, M. Steyvers, *Finding scientific topics*, Proceedings of the National academy of Sciences of the United States of America, 2004, 5228-5235.
6. X. H. Phan, L. M. Nguyen, S. Horiguchi, *Learning to classify short and sparse text & web with hidden topics from large-scale data collections*, Proceedings of the 17th international conference on World Wide Web, 2008, 91-100.
7. J. M. Keller, M. R. Gray, J. A. Givens, *A fuzzy k-nearest neighbor algorithm*, Systems, Man and Cybernetics, IEEE Transactions on, 1985, 580-585.
8. T. K. Landauer, P. W. Foltz, D. Laham, *An introduction to latent semantic analysis*, Discourse processes, 1998, 259-284.

Session 7

Computer Applications

Analysis of the Effective Connectivity of Brain Network Based on Transfer Entropy

Guo-jin ZHANG*, Yan-jiang WANG† and Bai LI

College of Information and Control Engineering, China University of Petroleum (East China),

Qing Dao, 266580, P.R. China

*E-mail: *gjzhang2015@163.com*

†yjwang@upc.edu.cn

Identifying the effective connectivity of human brain is much crucial for understanding the cognition and brain diseases. Transfer Entropy (TE) offers a model-free approach to detect directed information flow between nodes in brain network and is inherently non-linear. In this paper we apply TE to the detection of the effective connectivity of brain network with 998 ROIs (Regions of interest, or nodes). With the resting state functional MRI (rs-fMRI) BOLD time series we obtain the strength of directed effective connection and analyze its relationship with the structural connections.

Keywords: Transfer entropy; Effective connectivity; Blood oxygenation level dependent(BOLD); Functional magnetic resonance imaging (fMRI).

1. Introduction

At present, the research of complex brain network has become a hot spot in the field of neuroscience. Blood oxygenation level dependent functional magnetic resonance imaging (BOLD fMRI) technology provides a new method to explore the brain neural information. The flow of brain information can be traced according to the change of blood oxygen levels. Therefore, the information flow in the brain network, namely the functional connectivity of the brain can be used to explore the interaction between different regions of the brain. It has been widely applied in the field of mental or neurological disorders diagnosis and brain cognitive studies.

The functional connectivity describes the statistical correlations between spatially separated neural units or brain regions, which is undirected, while the effective connectivity reflects directional connection [1]. The brain effective connectivity network describes the influence that one neuron or region exerts over another, which is dynamic and depends on models of interactions [1]. Traditional methods for measuring causal relationship between two brain regions such as Granger Causality (GC) and Dynamic Causal Modeling (DCM) are usually appropriate to linear system or require knowledge about the input to the system and cannot model networks with large numbers of nodes. However, in a complex system--such as the brain-nonlinear interactions between neurons have to be expected and usually uneasy to construct a suitable model of interaction [2]. While Transfer Entropy (TE) is an information theoretic measure, which does not need a model of the interaction and also non-linear. TE offers a stable and accurate approach for identifying directed information flow between nodes in brain network. It was first formulated by Schreiber [3], and then applied to neurophysiological data, such as MEG/EEG or fMRI data.

2. Transfer Entropy

Transfer Entropy is a quantitative measure of information flow between two random processes *X* and *Y*. Mutual Information is usually used to describe correlation between the two systems, which lacks the dynamics and direction. However, TE can overcome this shortcoming, because of its asymmetry, i.e. $TE(X\rightarrow Y)\neq TE(Y\rightarrow X)$. This difference shows the direction of information flow and the causation between *X* and *Y*.

Assume two random variables *I* and *J*, the Mutual Information can be defined as [4]:

$$M_{IJ} = \sum p(i,j)\, log \frac{p(i,j)}{p(i)p(j)} \ . \tag{1}$$

As indicated by Eq.(1), M_{IJ} is symmetric and does not contain any directional information. The direction information can be obtained by adding a time delay *u*, that is:

$$M_{IJ}(u) = \sum p(i_n, j_{n-u})\, log \frac{p(i_n, j_{n-u})}{p(i)p(j)} \ . \tag{2}$$

The direction of the information flow can be seen in terms of the Eq. (2). Then we consider a dynamic system by using the transition probabilities, instead of static probabilities.

Assuming two observable time series $X = \{x_t\}$ and $Y = \{y_t\}$ that can be approximated by Markov processes. Schreiber combined the Kullback-Leibler divergence with Eq. (2), and proposed the basic definition of the transfer entropy from *X* to *Y*, that is:

$$TE(X \rightarrow Y) = \sum_{y_t, y_{t-1}^n, x_t^m} p(y_t, y_{t-1}^n, x_t^m)\, log\left(\frac{p(y_t|y_{t-1}^n, x_t^m)}{p(y_t|y_{t-1}^n)}\right) \ . \tag{3}$$

For general interactions, there may exist longer time delay. So the definition of Transfer Entropy in Eq.(3) for the time series with time delay u can be modified as:

$$TE(X \rightarrow Y) \sum_{y_t, y_{t-1}^n, x_{t-u}^m} p(y_t, y_{t-1}^n, x_{t-u}^m) \log\left(\frac{p(y_t|y_{t-1}^n, x_{t-u}^m)}{p(y_t|y_{t-1}^n)}\right). \quad (4)$$

3. Algorithm

3.1. *Reconstruct the state space*

For time series applications, supposing that there are two observed time series X_t and Y_t . In order to estimate the probability density for obtaining the Transfer Entropy, it is proposed to estimate transition probabilities in high dimensional space. So we need to reconstruct the state space, and use the method of Takens' delay embedding[2] to map the input states into high dimensional space,

$$x_t^{d_x} = \left(x_t, x_{t-\tau}, x_{t-2\tau}, \dots, x_{t-(d_x-1)\tau}\right). \quad (5)$$

Where d_x is the dimension of the high dimensional space, and τ is the embedding delay. Obviously, the process is mainly determined by two important parameters. We can use the approximate Ragwitz' criteria method[2] to optimize parameters d_x and τ .

3.2. *Parameters optimization*

Under the rule of Ragwitz' criteria method, embedding parameters d_x and τ are optimized to minimize the errors in the local prediction of future states.

In the local constant prediction method, unobserved future x_{t+u} is obtained from the mean of the future $x_{t'+u}$ of its neighbors after embedding:

$$\hat{x}_{t+u} = \frac{1}{|U_{t'}|} \sum_{U_{t'}} x_{t'+u} . \quad (6)$$

$U_{t'}$ is the set of $x_{t'}^{dx}$, which is defined as:

$$U_{t'} = \left\{ \mathrm{x}_{t'}^{\mathrm{dx}} : \left\| \mathrm{x}_{t'}^{\mathrm{dx}} - \mathrm{x}_{t}^{\mathrm{dx}} \right\| \leq \varepsilon \right\} . \quad (7)$$

Then we obtain the minimum values of the mean squared prediction error:

$$e^2 = \sum_t (x_{t+u} - \hat{x}_{t+u})^2 . \quad (8)$$

3.3. *Estimating TE*

After the state space of both time series reconstructed, TE is defined by introducing prediction time u:

$$TE(X \to Y) = \sum_{y_{t+u}, y_t^{d_y}, x_t^{d_x}} p(y_{t+u}, y_t^{d_y}, x_t^{d_x}) \log\left(\frac{p(y_{t+u}|y_t^{d_y}, x_t^{d_x})}{p(y_{t+u}|y_t^{d_y})}\right). \quad (9)$$

Then we need to rewrite the estimator according to the concept of Shannon Entropies:

$$TE(X \to Y) = S(y_t^{dy}, x_t^{dx}) - S(y_{t+u}, y_t^{dy}, x_t^{dx}) + S(y_{t+u}, y_t^{dy}) - S(y_t^{dy}). \quad (10)$$

3.4. *Significance analysis*

For data sets with finite length or size, almost any estimator that based on information theory shows bias and statistical errors. In order to estimate accurately, we use an appropriate statistical test of the null hypothesis of independence to evaluate the statistical significance of the TE estimator. Because the distribution of the test statistic is unknown, we use non-parametrical statistical significance test, e.g. permutation test, for detecting the absence of causality. If the p-value is below 0.05, then we consider it as significant at alpha level.

4. Results and Discussions

Experimental data was obtained by functional neuroimaging. We conducted independent resting state fMRI imaging that runs for each of the five participants. The BOLD responses are recorded with a TR of 2000 ms and a TE of 30 ms [6]. The sample rate is 0.5 Hz and the participants were scanned for 20 min. The participants were asked to keep alert and close their eyes. The high-resolution datasets includes 998 ROIs (regions of interest), which has been confirmed to be with higher accuracy. The rsFC and SC matrix of the high-resolution datasets with 998 ROIs are shown in Fig.1. The rsFC and SC matrix are both symmetric, so that functional and structural connections are undirected.

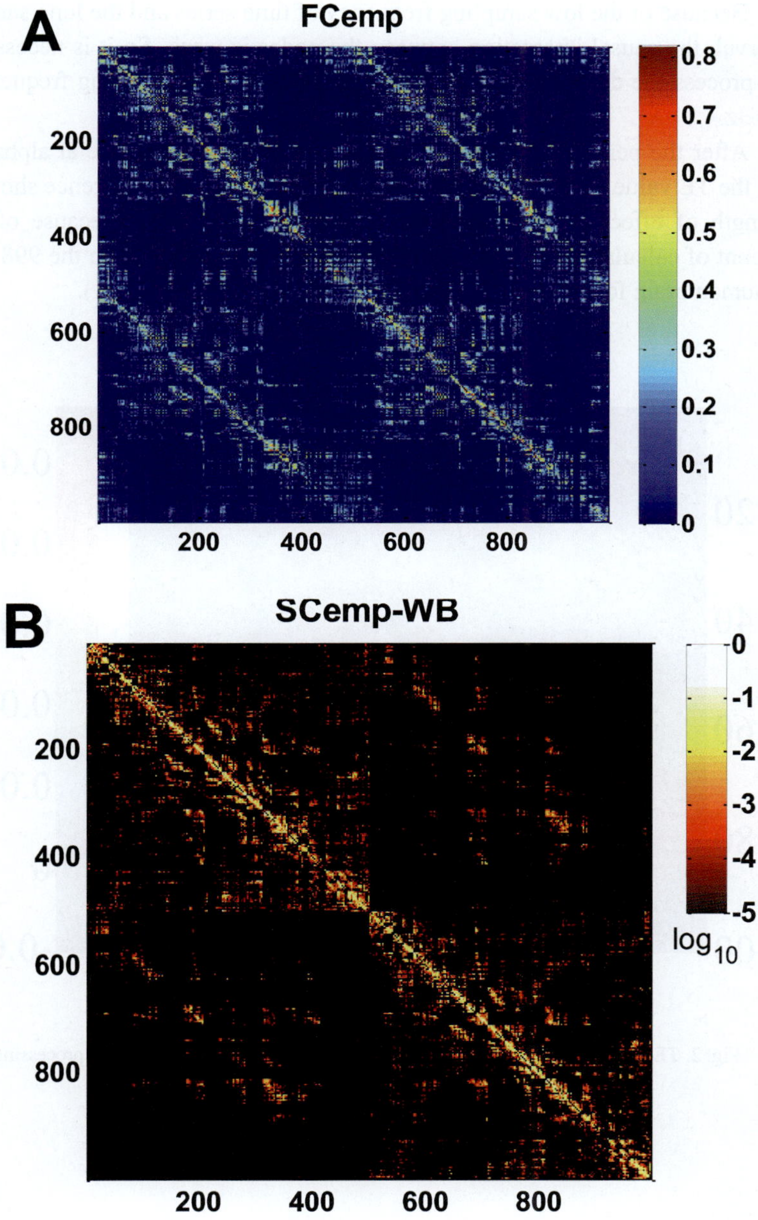

Fig. 1. Empirical datasets:(A)The rsFC matrix of the high-resolution datasets with 998 ROIs; (B) SC matrix (transformed into logarithmic form) of the 998-ROI dataset.

Because of the low sampling frequency of time series and the long sampling interval, the causal interaction between the nodes is weak. So it is necessary to pre-process the data firstly by re-sampling the data with sampling frequency of 100Hz.

After the permutation test, we can get p-values, significance at alpha level and the TE value between two regions. The values of mean difference shows the strength of effective connection between two region pairs. Because of large amount of calculation, we just select 100 BOLD time series from the 998 nodes of human brain for experiment. The TE results shows in Fig. 2 (A).

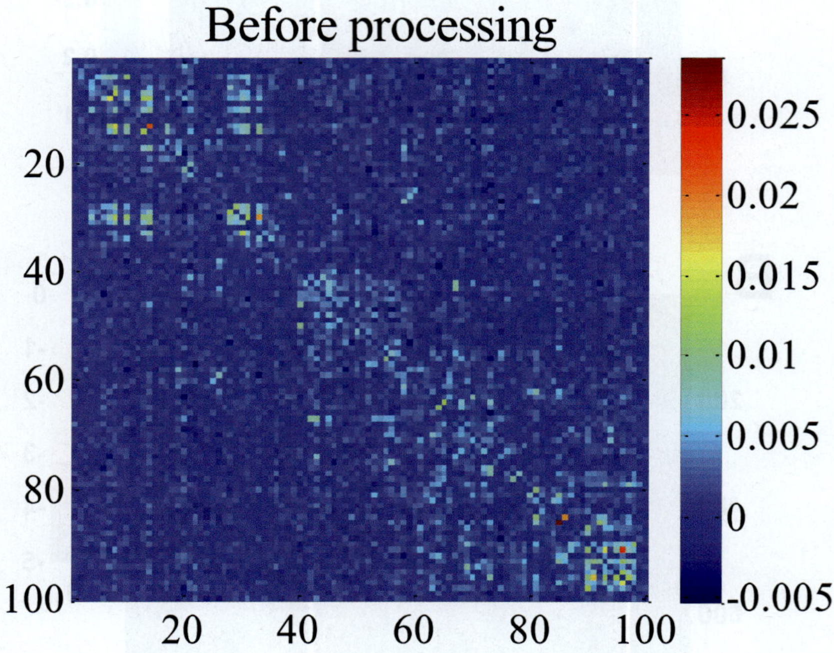

Fig. 2. TE matrix of 100*100 brain regions: (A) before processing; (B) after processing.

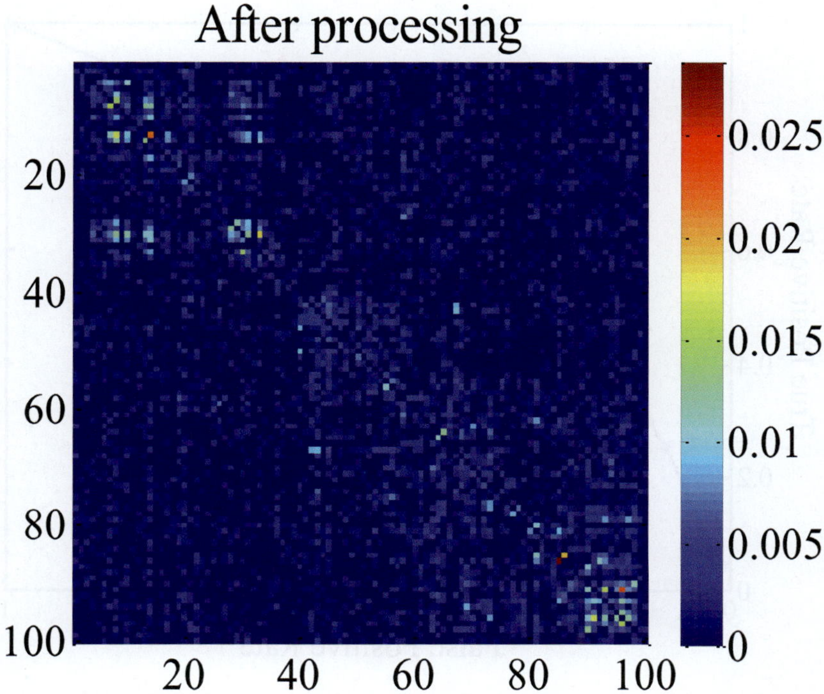

Fig. 2. (*Continued*)

Because weak and non-significant values may be spurious connections, so we remove all the connections whose strength is smaller than 0.001. In addition, all self-connections, the diagonal elements in the TE matrix and negative connections are also excluded. We can see from Fig. 2. that the TE matrix is asymmetric, so we can draw the conclusion that the interaction between the brain regions is directional.

Receiver operating characteristic (ROC) provides an objective and non-parametric method to quantify the performance of the algorithm. TE values are thresholded to make the total number of connections in EC network match with the number of connections in structural connections. TPR of detection is plotted against the FPR. The ROC curve is shown in Fig. 3. When we select the best threshold, the true positive rate is 0.7384, and the false positive is 0.5329, indicating that the TE network is strongly correlated with the structural network.

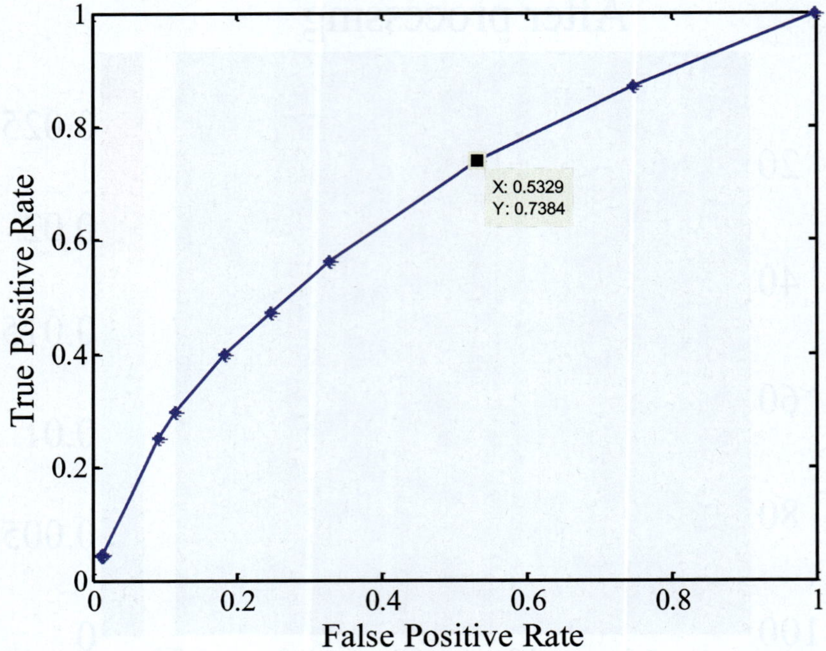

Fig. 3. Comparison of different threshold values of ROC curves.

5. Conclusion

The results presented here constitute a proof of principle that the information theoretic Transfer Entropy measure can be applied on fMRI BOLD time series to identify effective connections between nodes in brain network. And the obtained effective connection has been found closely related to the structural connection.

Acknowledgment

We would like to thank Olaf Sporns for sharing the 998-ROI SC and fMRI datasets. This paper is supported by the China Scholarship Council (201306455001) and the National Natural Science Foundation of P.R. China (Grant No. 61271407).

References

1. Friston, Karl, Rosalyn Moran, and Anil K. Seth. "Analysing connectivity with Granger causality and dynamic causal modelling." Current opinion in neurobiology 23.2 (2013): 172-178.
2. Lindner, Michael, et al. "TRENTOOL: A Matlab open source toolbox to analyse information flow in time series data with transfer entropy." BMC neuroscience 12.1 (2011): 119.
3. Ito, Shinya, et al. "Extending transfer entropy improves identification of effective connectivity in a spiking cortical network model." PloS one 6.11 (2011): e27431.
4. Schreiber, Thomas. "Measuring information transfer." Physical review letters 85.2 (2000): 461.
5. Vicente, Raul, et al. "Transfer entropy—a model-free measure of effective connectivity for the neurosciences." Journal of computational neuroscience 30.1 (2011): 45-67.
6. Hagmann, Patric, et al. "Mapping the structural core of human cerebral cortex." PLoSBiol 6.7 (2008): e159.
7. Ashby, F. Gregory. "An Introduction to fMRI." An Introduction to Model-Based Cognitive Neuroscience. Springer New York, 2015. 91-112.
8. Stephan, Klaas Enno, and AlardRoebroeck. "A short history of causal modeling of fMRI data." Neuroimage 62.2 (2012): 856-863.
9. Friston, Karl J. "Functional and effective connectivity: a review." Brain connectivity 1.1 (2011): 13-36.

Design of a DDS Signal Processing Unit Based on the DSP BUILER Technology

Tao JIA
The First Aviation Academy of Chinese Air Force, XinYang 464000, China

This paper proposes the design process of a DDS signal processing unit based on the SOPC technology. The main hardware is implemented by the NiosII soft core and the corresponding interface module on FPGA chip. The chip EP2C35 is used to control and deal with the signal which comes from the DDS module. Implementation of custom instruction hardware in SOPC Builder introduces the RS coding function. Comparison of software operation results demonstrated that our designed system has faster development and a high performance to price ratio, thus it can be widely applied in many fields of engineering and technology.

Keywords: DDS signal processing unit; SOPC; RS coding; Custom instruction.

1. Introduction

Direct Digital Synthesizer (DDS) is the third generation of frequency synthesis technology, compared with the direct frequency synthesis technology and the phase locked loop frequency synthesis technology, DDS uses the full digital structure, which has the advantages of fast speed, high frequency resolution, low phase noise and high signal purity [1]. Therefore, DDS is widely used in the frequency source design of modern electronic devices such as signal device, radio, radar and so on. There are a variety of DDS chips, such as AD7008, AD9852 and AD9954. The technique of DDS chip is mature; its information is elaborate and it is prone to be used. But the fixed control mode is the advantages and also the disadvantage. The current operating mode, frequency control and other parameters can not meet all the requirements of the actual system.

Since DDS is a kind of digital signal processing concept, it might be designed by FPGA chips to meet the needs of the user system. Usually, DDS might involve complex mathematical models, it is very difficult to realize by using VHDL and other hardware description language. DSP Builder is a system level (or algorithm level) design tool, which is based on a number of software tools. Both system level and RTL level, two design areas of design tools, could be connected to maximize the advantages of both tools. The Simulink module in Matlab software is called and relayed by DSP builder, which is in the form of

Blockset Simulink. A complex algorithm is designed and simulated graphically in Simulink, and then a generation file is converted into a hardware description language (VHDL) file by SignalCompiler and the TCL script that is used to control the synthesis and compilation in QuartusII[2], which greatly improves the efficiency of FPGA development DDS.

In this article, the modularization design method is applied. Take the AM modulation circuit of a signal processing unit for example, applying Cyclone EP2C35 and DSP Builder of Altera company, design a DDS signal source, which has high frequency resolution and stability, adjustable modulation ratio and duty cycle, and fast switching frequency and phase. In the FPGA design of DDS, the Matlab simulation and FPGA design are combined, which makes the waveform simulation of FPGA more intuitionistic, greatly shorten the DDS design and debugging time.

2. System Design

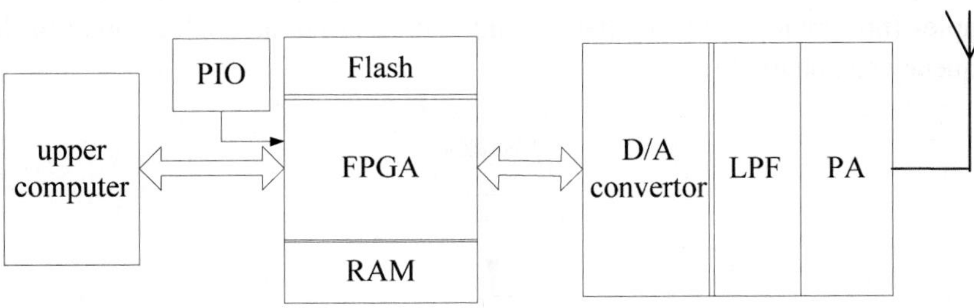

Fig. 1. DDS signal processing unit system overall block diagram.

The overall system block diagram is shown on figure 1. Among them, the upper computer software is written by Lab/Windows CVI software, which is used to control the signal. A FPGA is used as the core control device by the lower computer uses, which is mainly used to receive the control commands and signal parameters, and to generate the corresponding waveforms. The lower computer system is mainly divided into FPGA control unit, waveform storage unit, and wave generating unit. The waveform storage unit mainly includes a Flash and a SRAM. The Flash is used to store all kinds of waveform data. When waveform generate, FPGA will generate the waveform data from Flash into SRAM. Then, the waveform data is read from SRAM according to the cumulative value of the phase accumulator. The waveform generating unit is mainly designed to generate waveform data. Firstly, the waveform amplitude data that is read from SRAM is stored into the D / A converter to produce a the step sequence wave, and then through a low pass filter and power amplifier, the final signal is output.

This design is composed of hardware design and software design. A high cost effective chip EP2C35 of ALTERA Company is chosen as a core chip. The algorithms, such as build phase accumulator, in a FPGA chip are mainly designed by DSP Builder to realize the logic control and coding algorithm. In this way, it has the advantages of fast speed, flexibility, high integration and easy adjustment [3].

3. Operating Principle

3.1. *DDS operating principle*

DDS working principle block diagram is shown in figure 2. Where K and M are positive integers, according to the sampling theorem requirements, the maximum of K should be less than half of M.

In summary, if the sampling frequency is fixed, the frequency of the resulting discrete sequence should be controlled by the phase increment between samples (not greater than π), after holding and filtering, an analog signal of the frequency can be produced.

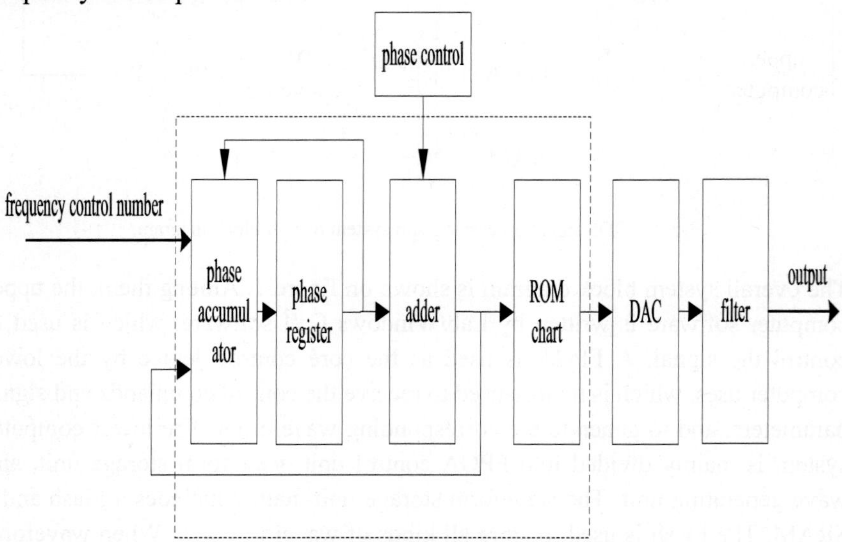

Fig. 2. DDS block diagram.

Its essence is a phase is sampled according to reference frequency source (system clock). From figure 2, A DDS consists of a numerically controlled oscillator (NCO) that includes a phase accumulator and waveform memory (ROM lookup table), a DAC and a low pass filter (LPF). In every clock cycle, the current value of the N-bit phase accumulator and the feedback value are accumulated. The high L-bit of the result is considered as an address of the ROM table, and then the amplitude value is read from the chart and sent it to the DAC. Next, it is converted into a ladder simulation waveform. Finally, an analog signal wave is produced after filtering by the LPF with interpolation effect. Therefore, the output frequency can be changed by changing the frequency control word K.

3.2. *AM modulation principle and DSP Builder*

The design can be processed from top to down by using DSP Builder, which is more suitable for the characteristics of human thinking. The block diagram is as shown in Figure 3. The whole development process includes system modeling, system simulation, converting MDL file to VHDL code conversion, functional simulation, real-time simulation, FPGA target device configuration and so on. The whole design process combines the system described and Hardware implementation organically. The designers can focus on complex algorithms design and greatly improving design efficiency with the help of DSP Builder.

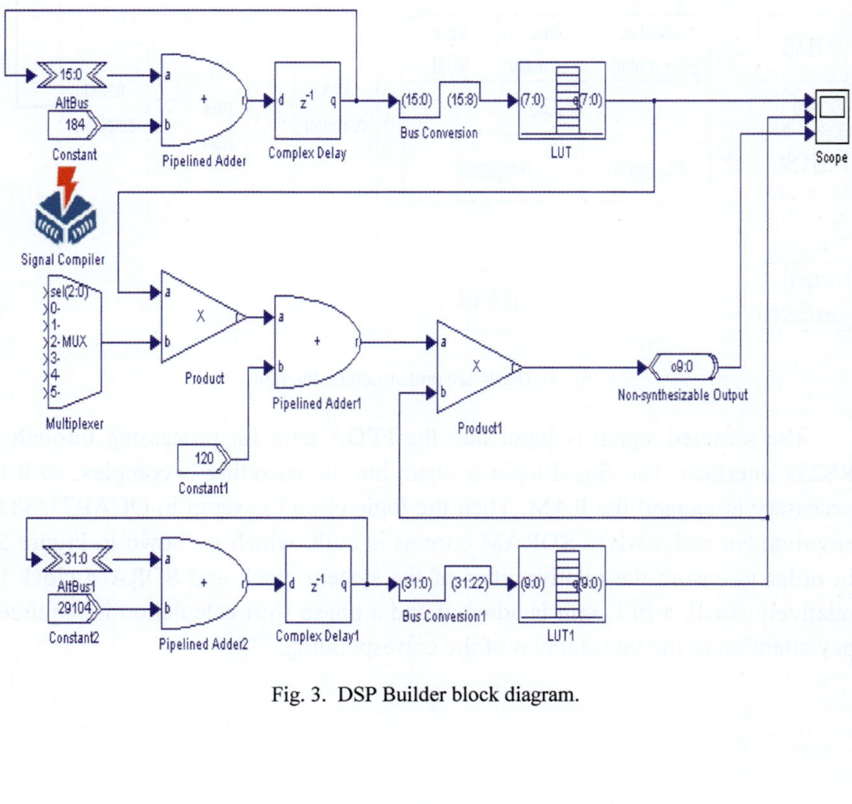

Fig. 3. DSP Builder block diagram.

4. Hardware Design

The signal processing unit is composed of FPGA core chip, DDS module, JTAG, SDRAM and other peripheral circuits, which is shown in Figure 4. The module JIUPITER manufactured by American ROCKWELL company is adopted, which can automatically detect the status of the antenna, quickly capture the satellite signal, short first time (TTFF), no static drift and wonderful dynamic performance. It also can output the carrier phase, can achieve a variety of data by setting. Compared to other products, it has strong anti-blocking ability, easy operation and development. It is very suitable for all kinds of navigation and positioning equipment [2].

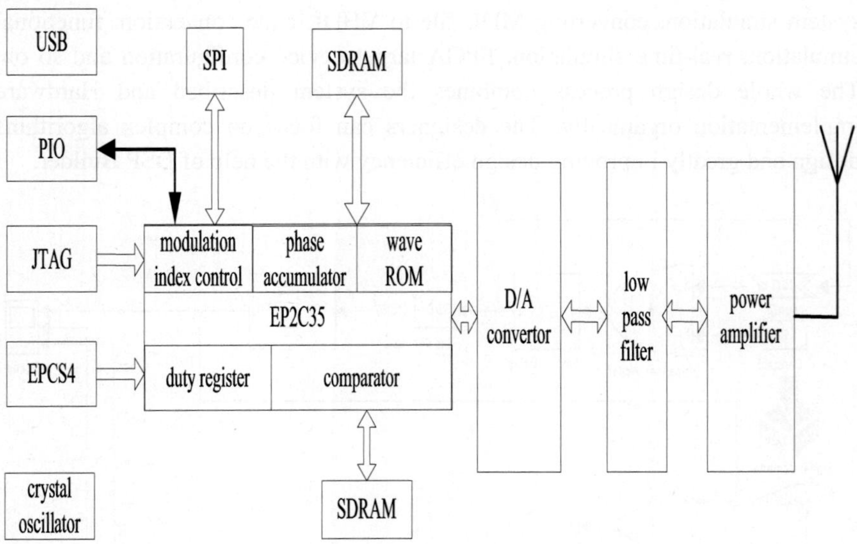

Fig. 4. Hardware unit structure diagram.

The sampled signal is input into the FPGA chip for processing through a RS232 interface. The signal logic is clear, but the encoding is complex, so it is necessary to expand the RAM. Then the logic circuit is setup in QUARTUS8.0 environment and a NIOS SDRAM core as is built, which is shown in Figure 5. In order to ensure the relative jitter of the system clock and SDRAM clock is relatively small, a PLL unit is adopted and a phase shift calculation is required. pay attention to the introduction of the corresponding.

5. Software Design

Extract latitude and longitude, speed, time and other data from the signal processing unit JIUPITER messages whose ID address is 1000. The default output frequency is 1Hz, the corresponding PPS trigger signal frequency is also set to 1Hz. The signal coding, logic control and other work are accomplished in the NIOSII8.0 environment. The APIs in the HAL library are used and the UART input signals and PPS signals are processed in interruption mode [3]. The software workflow is shown in Figure 5.

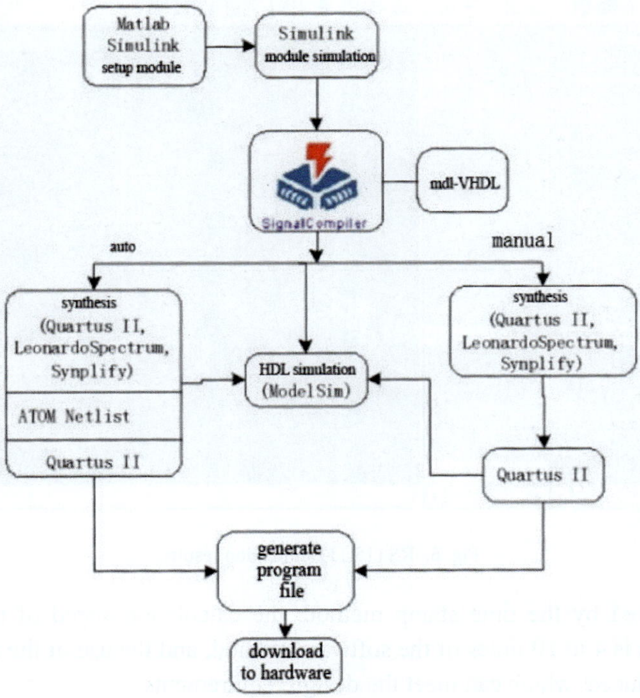

Fig. 5. Software flowchart.

The RS algorithm and CRC algorithm are required by this design. If they are implemented by programming in NIOS, the efficiency is not high; since there are only a few clocks are needed in hardware, the design is more complexity. Therefore, adding custom instructions is applied to resolve this contradiction. By a custom instruction, a sequence of instructions that contain more than one instruction can be reduced to one instruction realized by hardware. The custom instruction logic is directly connected to the NIOSII arithmetic logic unit (ALU), and the NIOSII can be configured as many as 256 custom instructions, which greatly increases the application of FPGA.

Taking RS code for example, as we can see in the system header file, NIOSII is produced by every definition instruction the RS_CI_MACRO and CRC_CI_MACRO macros, which can be directly invoked by the NIOSII code.

Assume the data 08 06 03 01 00 00 03 01 00 00 08 is input into the FPGA encoding using the RS (15, 11), the simulation results are shown in Figure 6, the encoded data is 08 06 03 01 00 00 03 01 00 00 08 07 0b 0a 02.

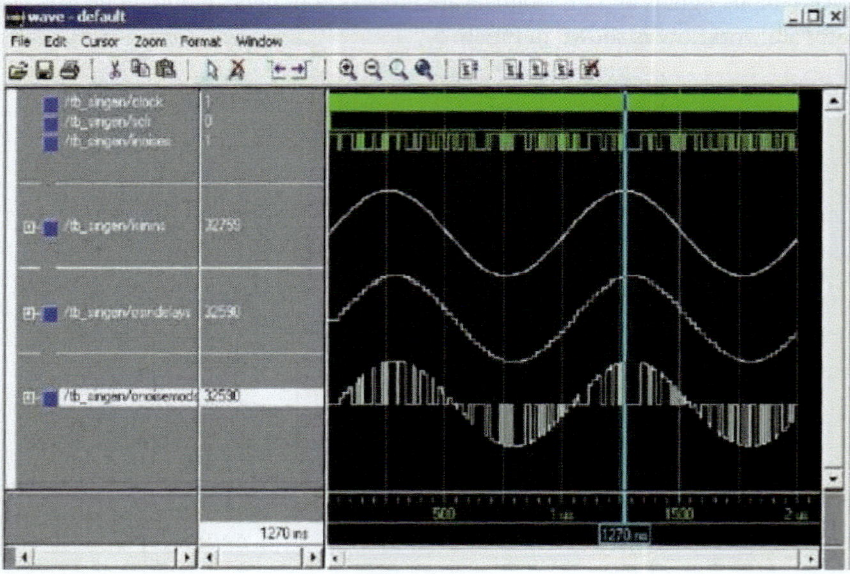

Fig. 6. RS (15,11) simulation results.

Checked by the time stamp method, the calculation speed of the custom instruction is 4 to 10 times of the software method, and the use of the resource is greatly reduced, which can meet the design requirements.

6. Conclusion

Through the actual test, the signal processing unit can accomplish logic control, algorithm realization and different interface transmission efficient and reliable. The design method based on SOPC for system control and man-machine interface is convenient for adjusting and altering, which has the characteristics of short development cycle and high cost efficiency.

References

1. TSUI J B Y. Fundamentals of global positioning system receivers: a software approach[M]. New York: John Wi-ley & Sons lnc., 2000: 133—190.
2. PING L. Improving tracking performance of PLL in high dynamic application[D]. Canada: UCGE reports 20208, the University of Calgary, 2004: 35-55.
3. IANMK. Study on important issues in design higIl dynamic GPS receiver[D]. Beijing: Beijing University of Aeronautics & Astronautics, 2002:48-57.
4. Joel A Seely. The application of FPGA in Soft Defined Radio[J]. Electronic Products China, 2005. 5: 61-62.
5. Li Zhi-Jun. Digital Down Converter in radio monitoring receivers[C]. Transaction of Beijing Institute of Technology, 2008, 28(10): 906-909.

A Performance-Driven DSP Fault Tolerance Approach Based on Loop Optimization

Ze-ming SHAO*, Qing-ping TAN, Jian-jun XU and Jing-fei JIANG
School of Computer, National University of Defense Technology
Changsha, China
**E-mail:szmlonely@163.com*

This paper proposes a DSP fault tolerant approach based on loop optimization known as DSP Loop Optimization Approach (DLOA). DLOA reduces the performance overhead incurred by traditional fault tolerance techniques while maintaining their fault tolerance capabilities. DLOA delays the fault tolerance latency between errors detecting and errors handling to scheduling the software pipeline, increasing performance significantly. The performance experiments and the ion irradiation experiments in the Heavy Ion Research Facility in Lanzhou (HIRFL) demonstrated that DLOA used in SWIFT achieved a 6.2 times average speedup and with its fault tolerance ability unaffected. *Keywords*: DSP; Transient fault; Fault tolerance; Loop optimization.

1. Introduction

During the recent a few decades, processor designers employ the techniques of increasing clock rates, lowing voltage levels, and shrinking feature sizes. However, these techniques make processers more and more susceptible to transient faults which can jeopardize the correct software execution. These transient faults are incurred by the hitting of high energy particles, and they are also known as soft errors[1]. To deal with these issues, hardware-level techniques and software-level techniques have been conducted.

Hardware-level techniques primarily employ architectural redundancy to detect and correct the soft errors. These techniques can achieve significant reliabilities. However, they also introduce significant hardware costs in terms of area and power overhead, which is typically prohibitive for embedded systems.

To mitigate the hardware costs, also to complement with the hardware-level techniques, some software-level fault tolerance techniques have been proposed. Stanford proposed a software redundancy approach known as EDDI [2] wherein all instructions are duplicated and checking instructions are inserted before the "store" and "branches". To protect the control flow, [3] developed a signature-based control flow checking method (CFCSS) wherein a run-time signature is updated and checked in every block. Coalescing [2] and [3], Princeton proposed an efficient method called SIWFT [4]. SWIFT protects both data flow and control flow by applying redundancy to instructions and employing signature-based checking method.

The goal of this paper is to accelerate the traditional software fault tolerance techniques in DSP without reducing reliability. We validate the ability of DLOA by the performance experiments and the ion irradiation experiments in HIRFL, respectively. These experiments shown that DLOA achieved a 6.2 times average speedup, while remaining the reliability, compared to SWIFT.

The remainder of this paper is organized as follows. Section 2 describes the DLOA technique. Section 3 presents and analyses the result of ion irradiation experiments and performance experiments. Section 4 concludes the paper.

2. The Approach Details

2.1. *The DSP fault tolerance issue*

The high-performance digital signal processor (DSP) has a powerful digital signal processing capability, and has been widely used in electronic systems of the spacecraft. Therefore, effective hardening techniques should be applied to DSP software. However, DSP's software pipeline is susceptible to the "branches instructions", which are indispensable for almost every software-level hardening technique. These traditional fault tolerance algorithms incur significant performance overhead in DSP, which is sometimes unacceptable in the real-time systems. To overcome these issues, this paper presents the DLOA approach.

2.2. *Fault tolerance latency delay technique*

To the best of scheduling the software pipeline, DLOA eliminates the branches instructions inserted by the algorithms. To do this, we apply fault tolerance latency delay technique to traditional fault tolerance methods to reduce their performance overhead. DLOA prefers handling errors detected in the loop after the loop finish to handling them immediately to interrupt the loop execution.

Fig. 1 shows the brief idea of DLOA. To mark the errors in the loops, a loop error signature can be used. This signature is assigned to a designated logical register named ERR. DLOA do not eliminate the checkpoints in the loops, and it still detects errors at every checkpoint. DLOA stores the information of errors detected in the loops in ERR, rather than handle them at these moments. When the loop is finish, DLOA checks ERR and decides whether calling error-handling function according to its information. DLOA accelerates the performance at the cost of delaying to handle the errors.

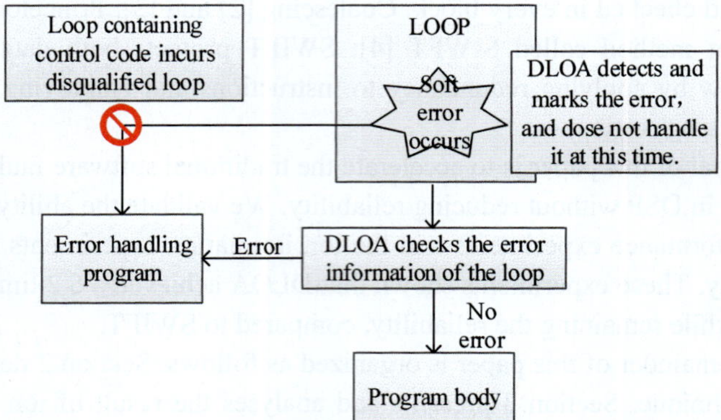

Fig. 1. The idea of DLOA.

There is a defect of DLOA that errors occurring in the loop may propagate to the memory which is typically prohibitive for many fault tolerance methods. If DLOA detects an error and does not call the error handling function instantly, it may store the wrong data to the memory or store a data to the wrong memory. To avoid this, we use this observation to restrict store instructions executing only without errors. Executing store instructions only without errors lets the "store instructions" execute according to the ERR's value. If errors occur, it skips these "store instructions". Or it executes them. This optimization obviously increases reliability and hardly decreases performance.

3. Experiments

In this section, we evaluate the technique detailed in Section 2 in order to determine its performance and to verify the capability to detect faults.

SWIFT is a representative software fault tolerance method, and it detects both control flow errors and data errors. We use our technique in SWIFT for the compared experiments of performance and reliability. This section uses DLOA to abbreviate SWIFT with DLOA, conveniently.

3.1. *Performance evaluation*

We evaluated the performance of those techniques based on CCS5.5 compiler circumstance and C6678 DSP platform. A version was created for each of the SWIFT and DLOA techniques, respectively.

These techniques inserted the fault detection code into the linear assembly programs. The experiments were performed on the following four well-known benchmarks, Matrix Multiplication(MM), Bubble Sort (BS) Fibonacci (FIB), and PI program (PI). These benchmarks were programed in linear assembly, and the original code was unprotected by any fault tolerance technique.

Results were obtained executing each version on a 1Ghz C6678 DSP core with 512Kegabytes of RAM and running under CCS5.5 with Blackhawk XDS560v2-USB System Trace Emulator. Each version was compiled on optimization level 3, and each of them was paralleled efficiently.

The results are shown in Fig. 2. For the DLOA version, the execution time was 2.60. As SWIFT duplicated almost every instruction and introduced control flow detecting code, more than twice instructions were executed on DLOA and SWIFT version compared to the original one. And due to the fault tolerance latency delay technique, the software pipeline had been scheduled successfully on DLOA version, which contributed to the 6.2 times speedup compared to SWIFT.

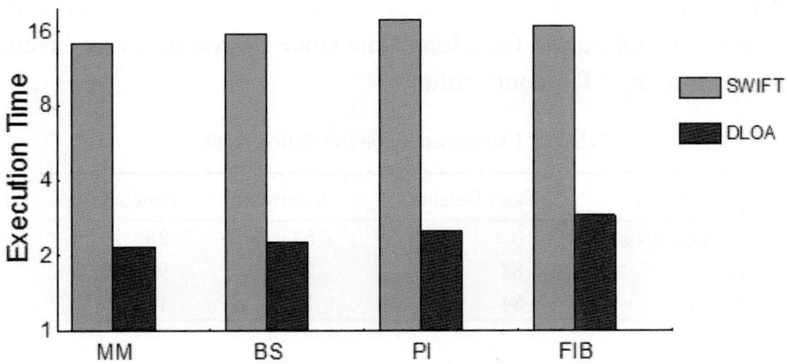

Fig. 2. SWIFT and DLOA performance normalized to original code.

3.2. *Fault detection capability evaluation*

The techniques' capability to detect faults were evaluated by the ion irradiation experiments in HIRFL in Institute of Modern Physics, Chinese Academy of Sciences. To get the ions pass through the chip's substrate and incur the transient fault, the C6678 chip was unsealed and its substrate was polished to around 50 microns.

The experiments were conducted with heavy ion microbeam constructed in the SFC+SSC Cyclotrons Accelerator in HIRFL. The ion irradiation experiments were performed using 86Kr26+. The ions crossing through 30mm air, possess the LET value around 20.52 MeV*cm2/mg approximately with the penetration range of 273.8μm in silicon. The microbeam targeted at the C6678 DSP chip accurately.

Each version from performance evaluation was performed in the irradiation experiments. For the reason that the Sphere of Replication (SoR) of the SWIFT is not including memory and cache, we put data and code in the DDR3 external memory outside the chip which was not irradiated by the microbeam. We did not use either data cache or program cache in these experiments. Therefore, registers became the most susceptible units of the DSP platform, which was in the SoR of the SWIFT.

The execution output was also recorded and compared against known good outputs. The experimental results are shown in Table 1. The incident dose of these experiments was about 18000 ions/cm2s. Each version was injected 107 Kr ions/cm2 totally. The results of each technique were the sum of the four benchmarks respectively. If the execution fails due to a fault being detected, the run is entered into the "Fault Detected" column. If the execution output is not match to the known good one, the run is entered into the "Incorrect" column. If the serial port has not output for a long time since the version was executed, the run is entered into the "Timeout" column.

Table 1. Experimental ion irradiation results.

Benchmarks	Fault Detected	Incorrect	Timeout
Original Code	0	64	28
SWIFT	88	2	9
DLOA	84	1	11

The total run times of each version were numerous at level of millions even ten million. Mostly, the run resulted correct, even the original code builds. Because register files only a small part of the entire chip, from the area's perspective. Therefore, most Kr ions did not hit the register files, in other words, they did not affect the correct software execution.

The Table 1 shows that the SWIFT and DLOA techniques detect most of the faults which yield incorrect outputs. It should be underlined that the SEU model is not suitable for these experiments. It may occur several soft errors at one execution for the experiments, so that the hardening techniques could not correct all of them sometimes. Furthermore, the number of timeout were reduced from 28 in original code to 9 and 11 in these two techniques, respectively. This is because some faults which would have resulted in timeout in the original code are detected in these two techniques builds before the timeout can actually occur.

The ion irradiation experiments were uncontrolled and random, even the same experiment would result different outputs at every time, mostly. It is considered that two techniques share the same order of ability to detect faults if their failure numbers are closed. The failure comprises incorrect and timeout. The failure numbers of SWIFT and DLOA were 11, 12, respectively. This confirms our earlier claims that they are at the same order of magnitude, from the reliability perspective.

4. Conclusion

To mitigate the DSP performance overhead incurred by the traditional software hardening techniques, this paper proposes DLOA. By delaying the fault tolerance latency, DLOA devotes to accelerating the traditional software fault tolerance methods, while maintaining their fault tolerance capability. When compared to the well-known software approach SWIFT, DLOA achieves 6.2 times speedup, while remaining the ability to detect faults.

Acknowledgments

We appreciate our entire laboratory as well as the referees for their valuable comments. This work has been supported by the grants of the National Natural Science Foundation of China (NSFC No. 61202116and No. 61303070) and Ph.D. Programs Foundation of Ministry of Education of China grants 20124307120037.

References

1. R.C.Baumann. Radiation-induced soft errors in advanced semiconductor technologies. IEEE Transaction on Device and Materials Reliability. 2005, 5(3):305-316.
2. N. Oh, P. P. Shirvani, E. J. McCluskey. Error detection by duplicated instructions in super-scalar processors. IEEE Transactions on Reliability, March 2002, 51(1):63–75.
3. N. Oh, P. P. Shirvani, E. J. McCluskey. Control-flow checking by software signatures. IEEE Transactions on Reliability. 2002, 51(1): 111–122.
4. G. A. Reis, J. Chang, N. Vachharajani, R. Rangan, D. I. August. SWIFT: Software implemented fault tolerance. Proc. of International Symposium on Code Generation and Optimization. 2005, 243–254.
5. SONG RuiQiang, CHEN ShuMing, HE YiBai and DU YanKang. Flip-flops Soft Error Rate Evaluation Approach Considering Internal Single-event Transient. SCIENCE CHINA, June, 2015. Vol. 58: 1-12.

The Design and Implementation of Teaching Aids Information Publishing System Based on Glossy Display

Xiang-yu JI[1] and Xiao-dan ZHANG[2]
Huishang Vocational College[1], Qinghai University[2]
Email1: jxyonline@163.com
Email2: zhangxd@ipp.ac.cn

Xiao-dan ZHANG
Xining, Qinghai, China, Qinghai University Ningda Road 251number
E-mail: zhangxd@ipp.ac.cn

An assisted Teaching Information Publishing System (TIPS) based on glossy screen is designed and developed in this paper for displaying teaching information dynamically. This system is composed of one information publishing server and more than one information display client terminals. With C/S program mode and computer network communication, the teaching information can be published to each display terminal accurately and timely. By integrating human perception sensors installed on the display terminals, the observer's position in front of the glossy mirror is confirmed, then the size of the display contents will be adjusted according to the distance between the mirror and the observer. When there is no human or the relative distance is distant, that's to say, it is beyond the set range, the glossy screen will show nothing and shut off its display function for achieving to save power and improve its life. At this time, this glossy screen as an ordinary mirror will be used for checking the teachers and students' dress whether they are proper or not. As a new way of display, it gives the teachers, students as well as the other audiences new experience, thus makes a large improvement for them to receive published information actively.

Keywords: Glossy display; Information publishing system; TCP; OpenGL.

1. Introduction

The mechanism of publishing the teaching information timely and accurately, as well as improving the acceptance degree for the teachers and students, has a very large significance for the smooth development of the teaching work. The traditional publishing ways of teaching information mainly include paper, notice, blackboard newspaper, periodicals, television and so on[1]. There are not only some inadequacies such as the monotony and no timeliness of information dissemination; more importantly, the audience's acceptance degree actively can't be guaranteed. Thus, by means of modern information display and network technology to explore a new kind of teaching information release platform makes a large improvement to the degree of automation teaching.

As a new mode of display, the glossy display mounts the LCD on the rear end of a specular with high reflectance, by using of the high transmittance characteristic of mirrors in one direction, the screen content with a certain brightness will be displayed on the LCD through the mirror. And it'll be an ordinary mirror when the screen is black. So a new type of teaching information publishing system based on the technology of glossy display and network will be introduced in this paper for more convenient, timely and quickly displaying the distributed teaching information and improving the initiative of receiving information for the teachers and students.

2. Requirements and Functions

With the development of information and network technology, the requirements of publishing teaching information accurately and realizing the information synchronization between multiple campuses or display sites are increasingly high. In order to design and develop a TIPS with high reliability and availability, the following aspects should be fully considered.

(1) Stability

Ensuring that the system can run stably under the premise of achieving its functions.

(2) Scalability

In the design of hardware and software, the capacity and redundancy of the system should be considered for the expanding demands.

(3) Easy to operate and maintain

It's necessary to provide a reasonable and handy man-machine interface for the users. And the system should be easily handled by fault in problems or failure.

The main functions should be achieved are described as follows:

(1) The functions of user security authorization and authority management. The administrator or users with administrator privileges can alter and publish the teaching information.
(2) The types of the information be published include text, picture and video.
(3) Archiving that the teaching information can be released to the display terminals timely and the published information should be been saved to log, so that it can be according to.

(4) By the integrating human perception sensors, sensing the position of the observers in front of the mirror and automatically adjusting the size of the display contents.
(5) Closing the functions of display when there is no activity in the mirror or no need to display information.
(6) Releasing the information with pertinence. Different information should be published to different display terminal according to the actual situations.

3. The Overall Architecture Design of the TIPS

The TIPS is composed of the information publishing server and some display terminals. Because of the dispersion of the server and the terminals in physical position, distributed computer network structure is adopted to realize distributed control[2]. The network communication based on C/S mode is used on this system to realize the communication between the various display terminals and the information publishing server.

The server is established for the legitimate certification of the information processing display terminal and the audit, publishing as well as achieving records before the release of the information. The display terminals located in the remote different sites, on the one hand to receive the text, picture or video information from the server; on the other hand to receive the distance signal between the audiences and the glossy screen from the integrating human perception sensors, and then make the corresponding process to the display contents. The overall topological structure is shown as Fig.1

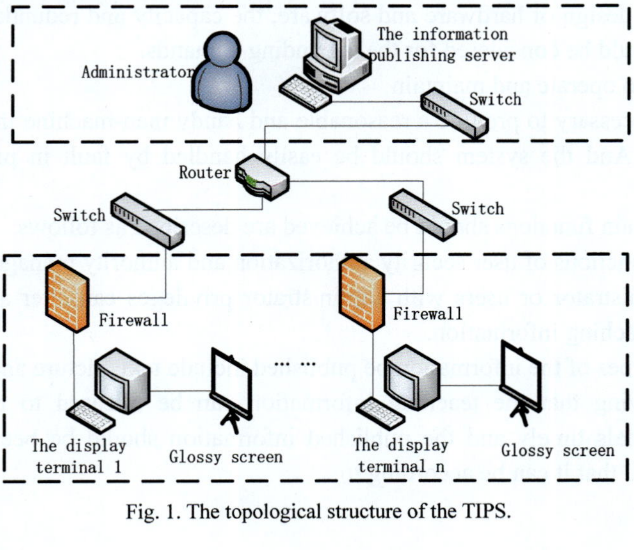

Fig. 1. The topological structure of the TIPS.

4. The Implementation of Hardware

The hardware design of the TIPS mainly includes hardware integration and lower computer sensor circuit and supplemented by the glossy LCD screen[3,4]. The hardware design schematic of TIPS is shown as Fig. 2.

The role of the sensor circuit is to obtain the distance information between the observer and the glossy screen. The core of it is micro-controller. The three perception principles of pyroelectric, ultrasound and camera are adopted to the design of the sensor circuit. By the pyroelectric sensor to get the human dynamic information and the distribution of the observers front of the display is obtained by the camera, then the distance information between the display mirror and the human body will be confirmed through the ultrasonic sensor by measuring the time difference from transmit to receive of the emitted ultrasonic 40KHz. The communication between the sensor circuit and the micro-controller is achieved through the RS232 serial port.

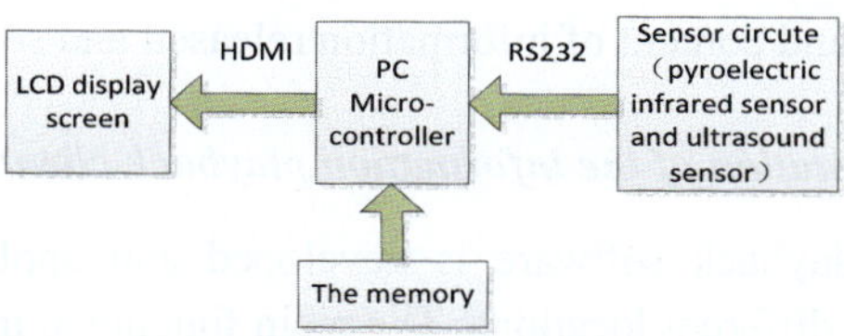

Fig. 2. The implementation of hardware design.

The signals acquired from the pyroelectric infrared sensor are passing to the infrared sensor signal processor chip and are translated into those signals that the micro-controller can identify, thus the body's mobile information can be perceived and then an interrupt signal will be generated and sent to the micro-controller. The ordinary LCD is used as the display device because of its advantages of mature, stable performance, rich interfaces between PC, easy to use and relatively low cost and so on.

5. The Implementation of Software

The software of the TIPS is programmed in C/C++ based on standard TCP protocol[5] under a Windows development environment and it is mainly composed of the information publishing server software and the information playback client software for achieving the functions of user identify, resources configuration, establishment of communication protocol, information reviewing and publishing, information receiving, playback and adjusting.

5.1. *The implementation of the information publishing server software*

The information publishing server software is designed for consisting the information audit module, information transmission module and information dissemination log recording module for publishing the texts, pictures or video information which are passed the safety auditing to each display terminal.

The information should be reviewed by the audit module before it's released. And the audit authority is only owned by the system administrator or the users with administrator privileges. Only the information passed the audit can be published, so that the reliability of the information contents can be guaranteed. The information transmission module[6] based on a reliable TCP protocol connection with the Ethernet as the medium is designed for transmitting the published teaching information from the host server to the each display terminal. The information resource can be from the local file or manual input directly through the interface. The log recording module is for recording the publishing log to make it's evidence-based, which including the user name, date-time, the type and content of information released and so on.

5.2. *The implementation of the information playback client software*

The information playback software is developed and applied to each client terminal located on different locations. The main functional modules include the information receiving module, information playback and adjustment module.

The information receiving module is for receiving the published teaching information including text, picture, video information from the server. In order to ensure the safety of the published information and to release targeted information to the appointed client terminal, the registration service is required to the sever when the each client terminal system starts. Then with the multi-threading processing mechanism, a special listening thread is created for listening and receiving the published information, as well as saving them to local disk.

The information playback and adjustment module is designed and realized on another independent thread to display the received information and it can make the appropriate adjustments about the display size of the contents according to the distance and position signal from the sensor circuit. The OPenGL three-dimensional graphics processing technology is adopted when dealing with the display size of the content on glossy screen along with the distance. The display size is proportional positively to the distance between the observer and the mirror. That's to say, it will be changed to be bigger smoothly when the observer away from the mirror. However, there will be an upper and lower limit in the process of adjustment to ensure that the size of display content won't be unlimited zoom or reduce. When the observer is close enough to the screen, the information size will be a suitable size and keep unchanged which the human eye can comfortably afford. While the body is far away form the mirror and beyond the distance that the sensor can measurement or there is no human activity in front of the glossy mirror for a long time(the timeout can be set at the software interface), the mirror screen will turn off its display screen and as an ordinary mirror.

5.3. *The Determination of a network communication protocol*

TCP with the advantages of providing a connection-oriented and reliable error-free data transmission service is to be the first chose when the based data transfer protocol is confirmed[7]. To ensure the reliability of data transmission as well as the security check of the network information, the unified data structure package shown as Fig. 3 must be complied with between the various devices.

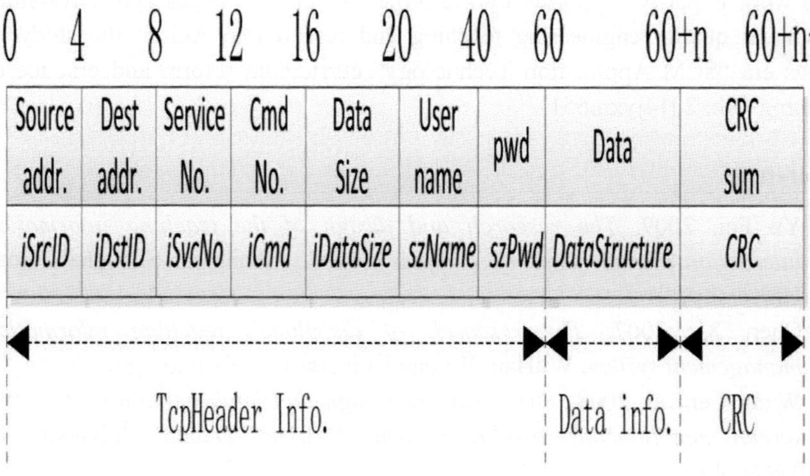

Fig. 3. The unified data structure of network communication.

The common data structure consists of three parts. The first part is 60 Bytes data segment for the TCP header. The second part is the real data packet of network communication with length uncertainty. The third part is the CRC (Cyclical Redundancy Check) sum value for ensure the accuracy of data package. Except that CRC is correct, the data package will be disposed, or the sender will be informed to resend.

6. Conclusion

At present the hardware and software of the TIPS have been completed, and the software simulation results show that it can satisfy the functional requirements of the system very well. Because that the study research of this paper is based on the current actual situation of teaching information on universities. And the glossy LED mirror with the function of adjusting its display size according to the observer's distance as a new way of display is applied to teaching information publishing system for replacing the monotonous way of information dissemination, thus giving the audiences novel experience and improving the initiative to accept the teaching-related information greatly. So the study in this paper and its application will be a very significant value.

Acknowledgments

This work is partly supported by the project of 2014 colleges and universities provincial quality engineering teaching and research in Anhui: the study of things era "SCM Application Technology" curriculum reform and practice of teaching (No. 2014jyxm651).

References

1. Yu Fei. 2009, *The research and design of the teaching information interaction system based on campus network*, Shanghai: Shanghai Fudan University.
2. Chen Xi. 2007, *The research of distributed teaching information management system*, WuHan: Wuhan University of Technology.
3. Wang CenKai. 2008, *The hardware design and implementation of Large-screen simultaneous display system*, DaLian: Dalian University of Technology.
4. Li Zhidong. 2005, *The research and design of LED display control system and dirver*, ChangChun: Jilin University.
5. Sun Xin, Yu Anping. 2008, Detailed in-depth of VC++. Electronics Industry Press, Beijing, China(in Chinese).

6. He Tian. 2004, *The design and implementation of real-time transmission system based on multimedia streaming network*, SiChun: SiChun University.
7. Xiaodan Zhang, Chundong Hu, Peng Sheng, et.al. *Data Server Application Software for Neutral Beam Injection Control System*, Journal of Fusion Energy, 2014 (33):125-129. L. Lamport, *LaTeX, A Document Preparation System*, 2nd edn. (Addison-Wesley, Reading, MA, 1994).

Flow Field Numerical Simulation of Artificial Submerged Cavitating Water Jet Based on Fluent

Chuan-chao LEI[†], Song-sheng DENG, Jin-fa GUAN, Shi-xia ZHANG, Guang-dong GUO, Teng-fei ZHANG and Lian-huan GUO

Department of Petroleum Supply Engineering, Logistics Engineering University, Chongqing, China

[†]*E-mail: 15683416227@163.com*

In order to overcome the shortcoming of small standoff distance of the submerged cavitating water jet, this paper proposes a new artificial submerged cavitating water jet nozzle. Fluent is used to perform the inner flow field simulation of the nozzle and several nozzles' structural parameters are optimized through the total volume integral of vapor. The results demonstrate that the flow accelerates in the convergent section of the inner nozzle and expands in the diffuser. Additionally, cavitation takes place initially in the diffuser and small cylindrical section of the outer nozzle and the nozzles' structural parameters have significant effects on cavitation. The cavitation quality is optimal when the outlet diameter of outer nozzle is 10 mm and the distance from the inner nozzle's outlet to the outer nozzle's convergent is 6 mm.

Keywords: Cavitating water jet; Numerical simulation; Flow field.

1. Introduction

Artificial submerged cavitating water jet is a new form and highly efficient water jet[1]. it can improve the standoff distance of submerged water jet effectively and expands its application[2]. But the relationship between cavitation effect and the nozzle's geometry is not clear, therefore, an accurate research on the nozzle's flow field should be made.

With the rapid development of computer science, fluid mechanics and numerical mathematics, computational fluid dynamics (CFD) have become an important tool to study the law of fluid flow[3], the study shows that this method can lower cost, shorten cycle, and improve efficiency. In this paper, a new type of artificial submerged cavitating water jet nozzle was designed, then, the flow field of cavitating water jet was simulated by Fluent. Obtained the distribution of velocity and volume fraction of vapor, and deepen the understanding of characteristic of flow field and studied the relationship between nozzle's parameters and cavitation.

2. The Structure of Cavitating Water Jet Nozzle

The structure of cavitating water jet nozzle is the coaxial superimposed, a sleeve was used around the high-pressure nozzle for forming an artificial submerged environment. The nozzle consists of three parts, namely the inner nozzle, the foundation support and the outer nozzle (sleeve). The structure and sizes of Artificial submerged water jet nozzle are shown in Figure 1.

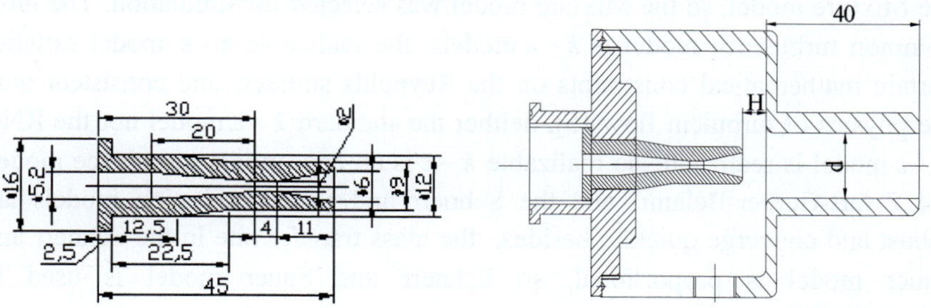

(a)The inner nozzle

(b)The structural sketch map of Artificial submerged water jet nozzle

Fig. 1. Artificial submerged water jet nozzle.

3. Model and Calculation Strategy

3.1. *Meshing*

As seen in Figure 2, the computational domain includes the inner nozzle and the outer nozzle. In order to alleviate computational burden and reduce the computing time, half of the problem geometry is modeled, with an axis boundary at the centerline. GAMBIT was used for meshing , the Quad unit and the Map types was seleted, and the mesh is slightly graded in the plenum to be finer toward the outlet of the inner nozzle .

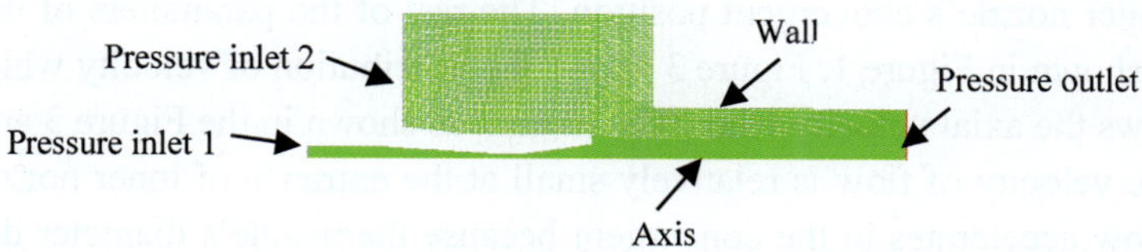

Fig. 2. Meshed domain for flow field semi-section.

3.2. *Models*

High-speed cavitating water jet is a complex flow phenomenon, and an appropriate multiphase model, a turbulence model and a cavitation model should be chosen for simulation. The Mixture and Eulerian models are appropriate for flows in which the phases mix volume fractions exceed 10%[4], and the complexity of the Eulerian model can make it less computationally stable than the Mixture model, so the Mixture model was selected for simulation. The most common turbulence model is $k-\varepsilon$ models, the realizable $k-\varepsilon$ model satisfies certain mathematical constraints on the Reynolds stresses, and consistent with the physics of turbulent flows[5], neither the standard $k-\varepsilon$ model nor the RNG $k-\varepsilon$ model is realizable, so realizable $k-\varepsilon$ is an appropriate turbulence model. the Zwart-Gerber-Belamri and the Schnerr and Sauer cavitation models are robust and converge quickly, besides, the mass transfer rate in the Schnerr and Sauer model is proportional, so Schnerr and Sauer model is used in calculation[6].

3.3. *Boundary conditions*

The boundary conditions of inner nozzle's inlet and outer nozzle's inlet are both pressure inlet, pressure-inlet 1 is 25 MPa, pressure-inlet 2 is 0.2 MPa and pressure-outlet is 0.1MPa. hydraulic diameter and turbulence intensity are selected to describe turbulence and turbulence intensity can be estimated according to the empirical formula[7] .

$$I_{in} = 0.16\,\mathrm{Re}_{in}^{-0.125}$$

4. Computational Results and Discussions

4.1. *Optimization of the d*

In this section, we assume that H is 10 mm, where d denotes the outlet diameter of the outer nozzle, H does the distance between the inner nozzle's outlet and the outer nozzle's convergent position. The rest of the parameters of the nozzle were shown in Figure 1. Figure 3 shows the distribution of velocity while Figure 4 shows the axial velocity when d is 10 mm, as shown in the Figure 3 and Figure 4, the velocity of flow is relatively small at the entrance of inner nozzle, then, the flow accelerates in the convergent because the nozzle's diameter decreases, and the velocity reach a maximum in the cylindrical section and expands in the divergent. After spurt from the inner nozzle's outlet, jet convert the momentum with the surrounding flows continuously and form a strong shearing action. With far away from the inner nozzle's outlet, the surrounding flow coerced by the jet increase, and the velocity of the surrounding flows increase with the axis velocity decrease.

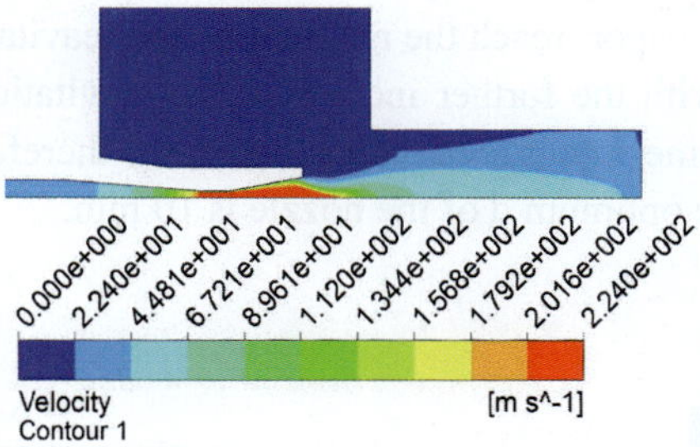

Fig. 3. The coutour maps of velocity.

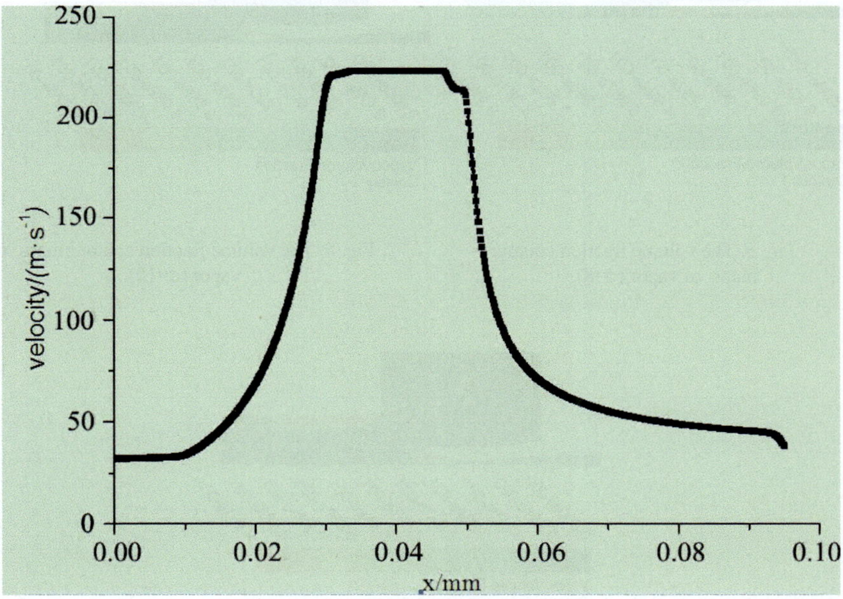

Fig. 4. The curve of axis velocity (d=10).

Figure 5 to Figure 7 shows the volume fraction contour maps of vapor, Figure 8 shows the relationship between d and the volume fraction of vapor. As shown in Figure 5 to Figure 7, cavitation takes place initially in the diffuser and small cylindrical section of the outer nozzle, this suggests that the diffusion angle and submerged environment is conducive to the formation of cavitation. Cavitation is mainly due to the shearing action between jet and surrounding flows. it Can be seen by the Figure 8 that d has a great influence on cavitation, when d is 7 mm, cavitation is weak, then, with the increase of d, cavitation intensity is significantly enhanced, When d is 10 mm, the total volume integral of vapor reach the maximum and cavitation intensity in its strongest, finally, with the further increase of d, cavitation intensity decrease while the total volume integral of vapor decrease, therefore, there is optimal values for d, and the optimum d of the nozzle is 10 mm.

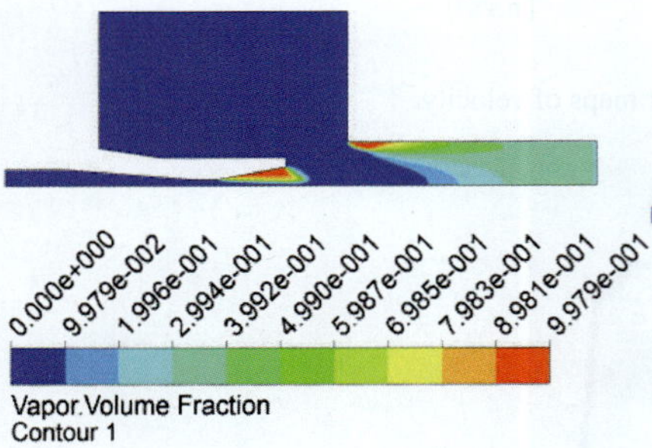

Fig. 5. The volume fraction coutour maps of vapor (d=8).

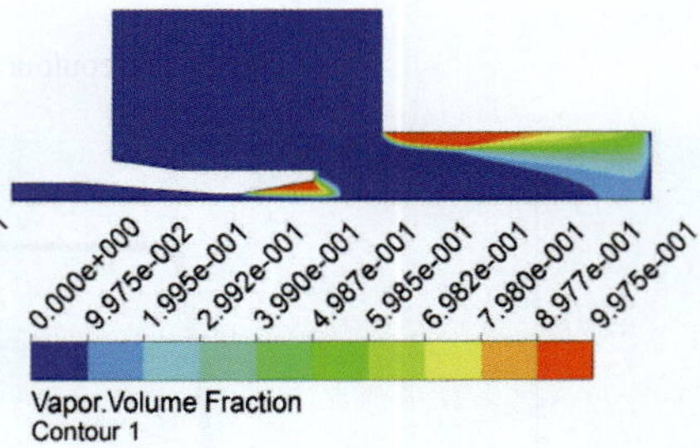

Fig. 6. The volume fraction coutour maps of vapor (d=10).

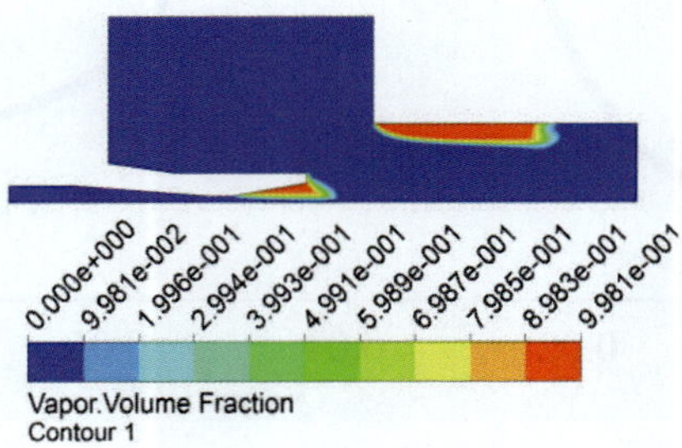

Fig. 7. The volume fraction coutour maps of vapor (d=12).

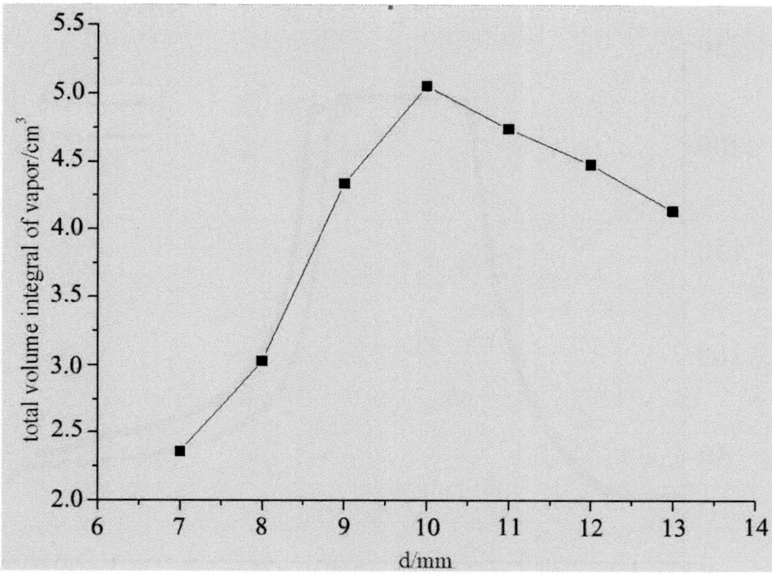

Fig. 8. The relationship between and the total volume integral of vapor.

4.2. *Optimization of the H*

In this section , d was set to 10 mm, the rest of the parameters of the nozzle were shown in Figure 1. Figure 9 shows the axial velocity of different H. it can be seen from Figure 9 that the axis velocity curve is almost coincided before the outlet of the inner nozzle, then to fall both, but the maximum velocity can keep a long distance when H is 6mm. Figure 10 shows the relationship between H and the total volume integral of vapor, we can see that H also has a significant effect on cavitation from Figure 10, when H is 6 mm, the total volume integral of vapor reach the maximum as well as the cavitation intensity, and smaller or larger might hinder the development of cavitation, so the optimum H of the nozzle is 6 mm.

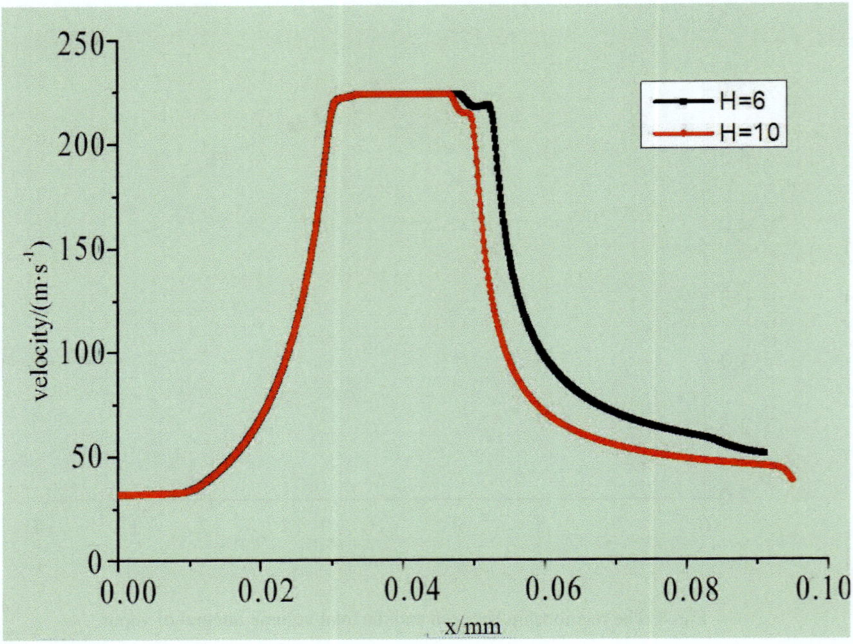

Fig. 9. The axial velocity of different H.

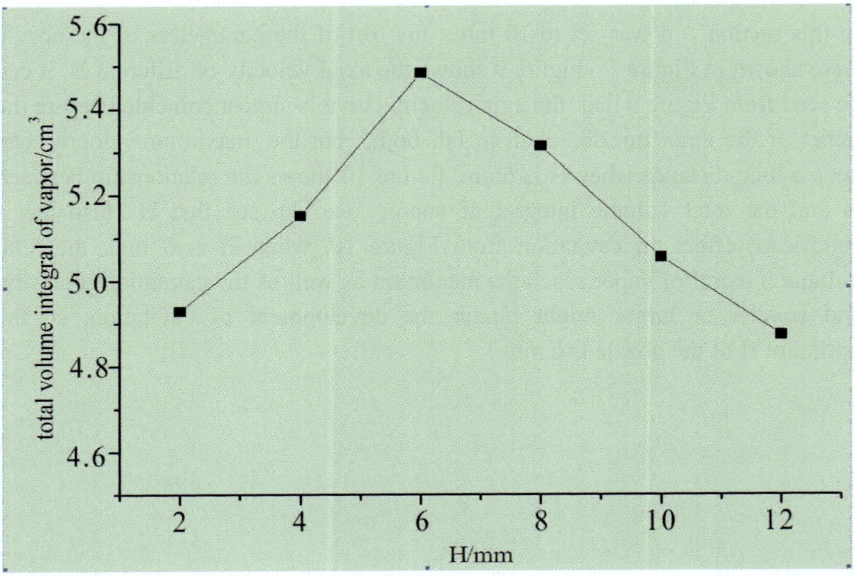

Fig. 10. The relationship between H and the total volume integral of vapor.

5. Conclusion

Based on the CFD software of Fluent, the flow field about cavitating water jet was simulated by the adoption of Mixture model, Schnerr and Sauer cavitation model and Realizable $k-\varepsilon$ turbulent model. The following conclusions are drawn:

(1) cavitation takes place initially in the diffuser and small cylindrical section of the outer nozzle, this suggests that the angular nozzle and submerged environment is conducive to the formation of cavitation.

(2) The axis velocity of flow is relatively small at the entrance of inner nozzle, accelerates in the convergent section and expands in the divergent section, then diminishes gradually in artificial submerged section.

(3) The nozzle's structural parameters have significant effects on cavitation. The quality of cavitation is optimal when the outlet diameter of outer nozzle is 10 mm and the distance from the inner nozzle's outlet to the outer nozzle's convergent is 6 mm.

Acknowledgments

This work is supported by the nature science foundation project in Chongqing(CSTC2009BB7177),Military Supplies and Oil Ministry's project (YX213C208)and youth scientific research funds of Logistics Engineering University(YQ14-420701).

References

1. Xinmin He. The application of high-speed water jet on petrochemical equipment cleaning and derusting [J]. Industrial technology. 2013,104-106. (in Chinese)
2. Meizhou Zhu, Shougen Hu. Study on the Conical Nozzle Configuration and the Performance of Submerged Caviting Water Jets[J]. Chinese Journal of Hydrodynamics, 1998, 13(3):263-268. (in Chinese)
3. Yiyu Lu, Xiaochuan Wang, Yong Kang, et al. Numerical simulation for cavitation water jet flow field through convergent-divergent nozzle [J]. Journal of China University of Petroleum, 2009, 33(6), 57-60. (in Chinese)
4. Xinghua Li, Minge Zhang, Qing Qin, et al. Progress in the numerical simulation for cavitation jet flow field [J]. Chemical Industry and Engineering Progress, 2015, 34(4), 921-929. (in Chinese)

5. Miao Zhang. The Comparision of turbulent and cavitation model and the application of them in convex body cavitation [D]. Xian: Xi'an University of Technology, 2012:17-20. (in Chinese)
6. Fang Tan. Study on Numerical Simulation on Flow Field in Cavitating Cleaning Nozzle [D]. Daqing: Northeast Petroleum University, 2011. (in Chinese)
7. Fujun Wang. Computational Fluid Dynamics-the basic principles and application of CFD [M].Beijing: Tsinghua University Press, 2004:63-108. (in Chinese)

A Cloud Computing-Based Fault Diagnosis Approach for Radar System

Wen SHENG[1a], Zhi-xian ZHANG[2] and Feng JIANG[3]
[1] *Air Force Early Warning Academy, Wuhan, P.R.C*
[2] *Air Force Early Warning Academy, Wuhan, P.R.C*
[3] *Air Force Early Warning Academy, Wuhan, P.R.C*
[a]*sheng_wen@263.net*

This paper proposes a cloud computing based fault diagnosis scheme for radar systems. Based on the gradation diagnosis model and fault separation tree, diagnosis knowledge is represented by an integrated framework; and the direct inference, reverse inference and hybrid inference diagnosis strategies are carried out. Site test results demonstrated that the diagnosis system improves the fault diagnosis accuracy and speed of modern radar fault diagnosis.

Keywords: Cloud computing; Expert system; Fault diagnosis.

1. Introduction

Fault diagnosis when system malfunctions is not only urgent for modern military radars in battlefield, but also for those located in remote regions in peace time. With more and more new technologies introduced, the system structure is becoming more and more complicated, and this leads to the design and application of built in test equipment(BITE) in radar system. However, the BITEs in many cases misleads technicians to an error-free place due to poor diagnosis strategy and knowledge base, thus the research of fault diagnosis approach and expert system realization is becoming a demand in modern radar BITE application.

To solve this problem, this paper presents a cloud computing based fault diagnosis scheme, which can collect and integrate diagnosis knowledge within all the diversified troops located in different regions. A gradation diagnosis model for fault diagnosis in an embedded BITE system and the fault separation tree is employed to guide diagnosis process. To verify its practicability, a visual fault diagnosis expert system is developed, and satisfactory results have been obtained.

2. Cloud Computing Based Fault Diagnosis Scheme

Cloud computing is now a widely used technology in many fields[1]. For fault diagnosis, its advantages not only lies on the fact that people can share the same resource(including knowledge base and diagnosis strategy) at the same time, but also presents an individual platform to process common resource data. In this paper, the cloud can store data concerning with knowledge base and diagnosis strategies, and people in anywhere can retrieve them at anytime according to their requirements. When new fault diagnosis experience is found, people can also upload to the cloud to share it for other users. In this way, all authorized users can access the cloud and share the diagnosis resource, regardless the user is a maintenance engineer of a certain manufacturer, or just a soldier at the radar site. The fault diagnosis cloud block diagram is shown in Fig.1.

3. Gradation Diagnosis Model and Fault Separation Tree

The foundation of gradation diagnosis[2] model is that radar equipment has the speciality of structure and function hierarchy. Usually, the hierarchy structure may be like this: radar system, sub-system such as antenna system and signal processing system, component compartment such as transmitter and receiver, and unit containing every on-site replaceable component, unit is the lowest layer of radar system structure.

According to the structure hierarchy of radar, to guide the diagnosis process, the system is divided into some layers, on every layer the locations and fault causes of errors committed are confirmed one by one, until to the required depth. On every layer, the fault diagnosis is divided into a few steps of examining, hypothesis and verifying. First examining the faults confirmed, then putting forward some assumptions of next fault in the lower lever, and finally verifying which assumptions are true and which assumptions are false among them. These steps can also be considered as nodes of a diagnosis tree, the parent node and children nodes are connected with each other, and the fault sources can be searched from layer to layer. On every later, the fault causality between upper and lower level is analyzed by fault omen, system function and signal feature, etc. and the fault omens are driving conditions for analysis from the upper level toward the lower level.

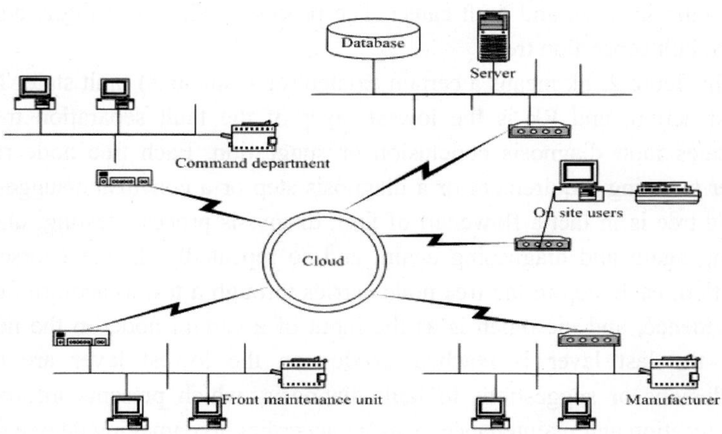

Fig. 1. Fault diagnosis cloud.

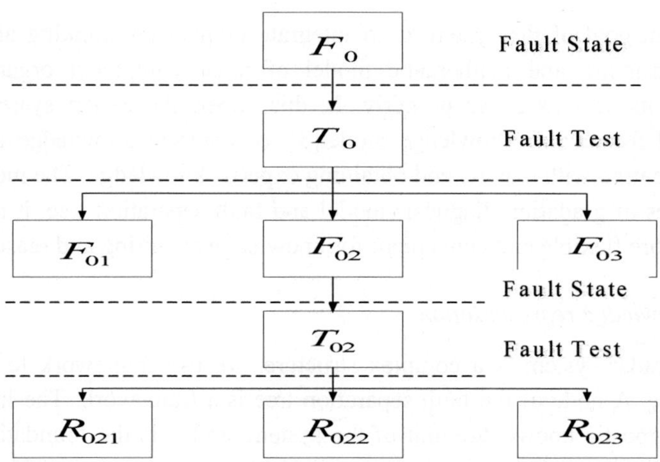

Fig. 2. Sketch of fault separation tree.

Based on the fault tree analysis and gradation diagnosis model, any external omen of a system fault has its internal cause, and any element damage or function degradation will lead to performance changes and function changes of system parts. The process of fault diagnosis is that, from the beginning of system abnormal function that is often represented by the root node of a fault separation tree, the relevant tree nodes are scanned until the node which coincides with the hypothesis is met, and this node is right the fault node indicating location and fault cause. The process is shown in Fig.2, and it is in fact a fault separation tree.

In figure 2, Fk means a certain existent(or suspicious) fault state, Tk means a test action, and Rk is the lowest layer of the fault separation tree which indicates fault diagnosis conclusion or suggestion. Each tree node represents either a testing requirement or a diagnosis step or a conclusion/suggestion, the whole tree is in fact a flowchart of fault diagnosis process: testing, diagnosing, testing again and diagnosing again, and so repeatedly. In the course of fault isolation, each step in the tree node carries through a test to acquire fault omen as evidence, and the omen is as the input of a certain node on the next layer, until the last layer is reached. Nodes on the lowest layer are diagnosis conclusions or suggestions to fault diagnosis, which presents information of fault location and maintenance measure according to damaging degree of system components.

4. Design and Implementation

The design goal of the system is to integrate humanity's thinking ability, the system structure and mathematic model of radar equipment organically to represent its various states properly. In this paper, the expert system adopts integrated framework knowledge model[3] to represent knowledge base after communicating with experts and obtaining experts' knowledge. The model takes advantages of gradation diagnosis model and fault separation tree, it makes the system more flexible and convenient for knowledge acquiring and reasoning.

4.1. *Knowledge representation*

Because radar system is a complex structure, we use framework to represent knowledge. A node of the fault separation tree is a framework. The framework is the diagnostic knowledge unit of the system, and it is the foundation of the diagnostic process that collection omens, detecting an decision-making on any node.

The identical node adopts identical framework, Figure 3 shows the basic framework. A typical framework includes framework name, node identification, node attribute, next layer node identification, testing condition, testing content, standard I/O and diagnosis rule and etc.. The next layer node identification decides the position and property of node in fault separation tree; test condition and content are description to expert action; diagnosis rule is experts' valuable experience. Test condition, contents and diagnosis rule are the mutual slot of middle node framework between root and leaf node. Maintenance measure is a particular slot of leaf node, it is usually a description on how to fix a breakdown.

Framework Name: Node Identification: Node Attribute: (R/M/T): R means root node, M means middle node, T means leaf node: Next Layer Node Identification: Testing Condition: Testing Content: Standard I/O: Diagnosis rule: Maintenance measure: Graphics support:

Fig. 3. Framework of expert system.

4.2. *Inference strategy and diagnosis process*

Based on fault mechanism and expert knowledge, the expert system mainly adopts the direct inference approach, and the reverse inference and mix inferences are also used. The inference process is in fact a fault separation tree search process. There are two types of tree search method: breadth-first search and depth-first search, here the depth-first search method seems to be more feasible and efficient than the breadth-first search method since each node contains several branches as its child nodes and the result is located at the deepest(or lowest)level of the tree[4].

Diagnosis process can be described by the framework knowledge representation: Diagnosis is started by finding obvious errors or abnormal functioning, or carrying out a primary test, fault cause search can be begun from one node of a test layer or from the root node: secondly the framework knowledge of the node which lies in the middle layer of fault separation tree is called repeatedly, and maintaining personnel is reminded to carry on a test action, through diagnosis rule the search depth goes forward, and finally the fault range reduces gradually, till a basic fault source is found.

The run-time separation tree is shown in Fig.4, in which red block represents fault omen, grey block reprensent action and blue block represent the final result.

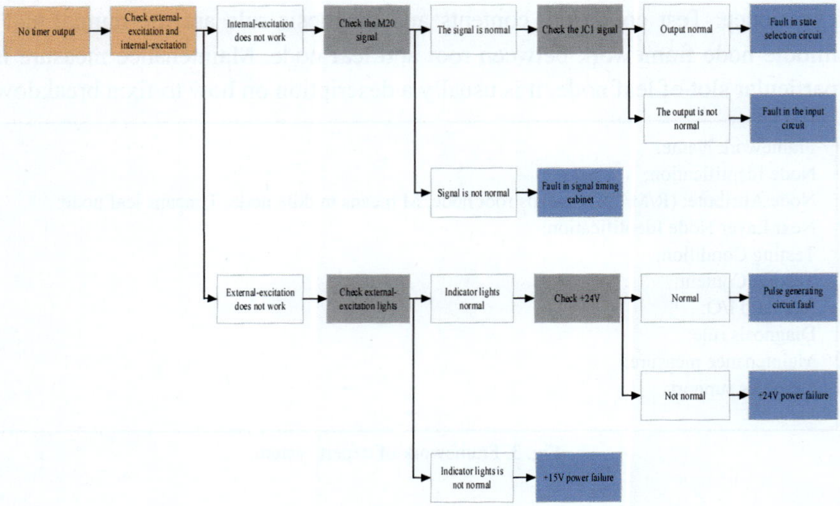

Fig. 4. Run-time screen of diagnosis process.

5. Conclusion

This paper presented a cloud computing based fault diagnosis system scheme, an efficient fault diagnosis expert system for radar based on gradation diagnosis model and fault separation tree model is introduced. Site tests results showed that, cloud has the advantage of sharing diagnosis knowledge for different users at different places. During a diagnosis procedure, the fault search process is more efficient, and a visual diagnosis progress with diagnosis explanation is presented. Under the guidance of the diagnosis system, improvements of fault diagnosis accuracy and speed of BITE for modern radar system have been obtained.

References

1. Xu Fei, “Research on Equipment Fault Diagnosis System Based on Cloud Computing”, Electronics Design Engineering, 10 (2015) 5-7.
2. Liu Bailin, Hao Chongyang, Fan Yuehua, Zhu Meiping,”Design and Realization of Fault Diagnosis Expert System Tools”, Fire Control and Command Control, 5 (2007) 76-77.

3. Fan Yuehua, Xie Zhilong, "Application of Intelligent Fault Diagnosis System in a Weapon System", JOURNAL OF GUN LAUNCH & CONTROL, 4 (2007) 83-85.
4. S.C. Liu and S.Y. Liu, "An Efficient Expert System for Machine Fault Diagnosis", Int. J. Adv. Manuf. Technology, 21 (2003):691-698.

The Application of MES in the Hydraulic Torque Converter Manufacturing Shop

Yue-xin YANG[1,*] and Gong-chang REN[2]

[1]*College of Electrical and Information Engineering, Shaanxi University of Science & Technology,*
[2]*College of Mechanical and Electrical Engineering, Shaanxi University of Science & Technology,*
Xi'an 710021,China
[*]*E-mail: yangyuexin@sust.edu.cn*

In this paper, the actual conditions of the hydraulic torque converter production workshop are analyzed, and the overall architecture, key technology and function module of MES in the production workshop of hydraulic torque converter are present. The use of MES greatly improves the efficiency of the hydraulic torque converter production.

Keywords: Manufacturing shop; Hydraulic torque converter; MES; Web service.

1. Introduction

MES (Manufacturing Execution System) is a production management system for manufacturing enterprise workshop execution layer. MES can provide the following functions: manufacturing data management, planning and scheduling process management, production management, inventory management, quality management, human resource management, work center / equipment management, tools equipment management, procurement management, cost management, production process control, the underlying data integration and analysis, upper data integrated decomposition. Mes could create a solid, reliable, comprehensive and feasible manufacturing collaborative management platform for enterprises.

Therefore, the development of hydraulic torque converter production workshop MES could improve the automatic transmission industry and manufacturing level of automobile manufacturing industry.

2. The Overall Framework of the System

From the three level integrated model of enterprise (Figure 1), it can be seen that MES has built a bridge between the management layer and the control layer. Mes could fill the gap between the management layer and the control layer. It plays an important role in the three tier enterprise architecture. On the one hand, MES can refine and decompose the production management information from the ERP software, which will be transmitted to the control layer. On the other hand, MES can collect the status data of the equipment and instruments.

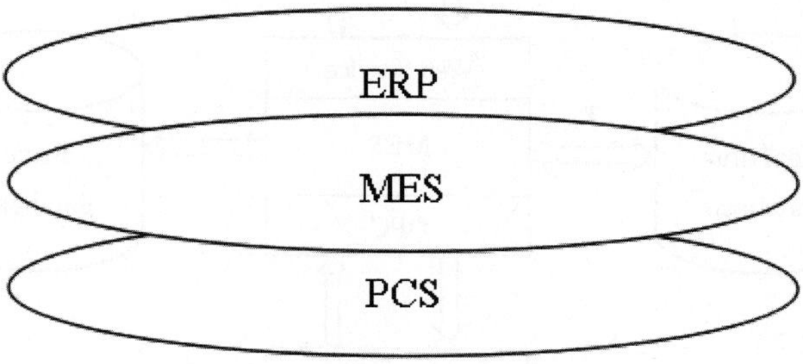

Fig. 1. The three level integrated model of enterprise.

Hydraulic torque converter production line consists of five production areas — production zone of pump wheel, guide wheel production area, production zone of turbine, cover wheel production area and the torque converter assembly production. MES can meet the requirements of production control in the process of assembly and production process of the whole hydraulic converter, and the whole system can meet the requirements of production and assembly.

MES can obtain order information from the ERP, and combine the production workshop equipment, personnel, material conditions for a reasonable arrangement, and the production process of real-time database in the product quality information, equipment status information, testing data, measurement data through the analysis and processing to the form or report form feedback to ERP, to manage the production management decisions.

Combined with the actual situation of the hydraulic torque converter workshop, we present the whole frame design of the hydraulic torque converter workshop MES as shown in Figure 2.

The database of MES in the production workshop of hydraulic torque converter is composed of real-time database and basic database.

Real time database is used to store the following information in real time:

Equipment status information: information of current, voltage, load, speed, etc.;

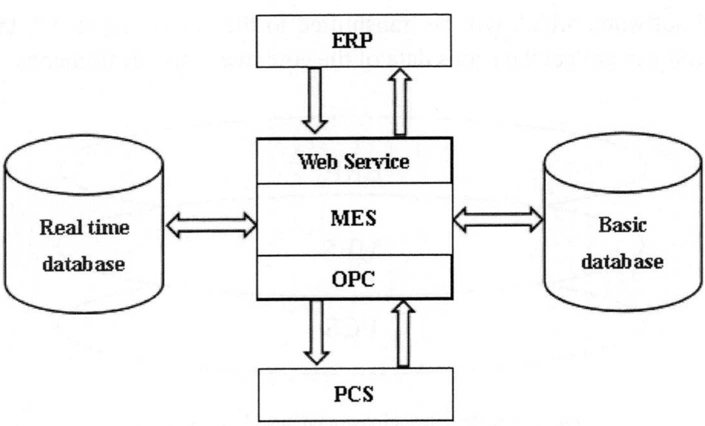

Fig. 2. The whole frame design of the hydraulic torque converter workshop MES.

Product information: encoding, name, composition, etc.;

Quality information: product quality level information;

Measurement information: the main parameters of the product information.

The following information is saved in the underlying database:

The process information of hydraulic torque converter, including the name of each process, the description of the operation process, the time required for the number of workers, the required material information,. The process information support the scheduling and distribution of material;

Inventory information: the classification of materials stored in the warehouse, encoding, name, minimum inventory and other information. The inventory information is mainly used for the issuance of materials and procurement;

Line edge library information: the production line of the edge of the stock information, the information in the production process of real-time changes, so that the timely issuance of material, to ensure the smooth production of the production;

Equipment information: this information is the main storage equipment of the detailed information (such as equipment encoding, equipment name, purchase time, etc.), equipment maintenance information and equipment failure information, the part of the information is used for scheduling;

Personnel Information: this information contains information about the organization structure of the workshop (the team uses a tree structure to describe), the detailed information of the personnel and the association between the organization structure information and the personnel information;

Scheduling information: including production workshop daily scheduling, if there is a good logic of workshop scheduling can generated by code, otherwise you can bulk import in advance (first through fixed excel template editing and database import);

Production process analysis: through the analysis and processing of the information obtained from the real time database, the output statistics, equipment failure causes, quality statistics, etc., this part of the information is submitted to ERP through the interface.

Hydraulic torque converter workshop MES provides two important interfaces for information interaction. It provides methods (such as access to production reports, equipment failure causes and statistical reports, quality statistics, and MES) by using Service Web. The information exchange between MES and PCS uses OPC server to transfer, and the information collected by different manufacturers of different types of OPC protocol is collected and stored in OPC. MES is used to obtain the corresponding information by configuring the tag point name.

3. Key Technology of the System

Web Service is a method of communication between two electronic devices over a network. It is a software function provided at a network address over the Web with the service always on as in the concept of utility computing. It is a standardized way of integrating Web-based applications using the XML, SOAP, WSDL and UDDI open standards over an Internet protocol backbone. XML is used to tag the data, SOAP is used to transfer the data, WSDL is used for describing the services available and UDDI lists what services are available.

OPC Technology(COM/OLE based technology for Process Control). COM/OLE applications are widely used in Industrial Automation and Process Control domains. Since not many programmers are aware of these technologies, I thought to share my experience in OPC and most developers would love to expand their knowledge about COM/OLE application areas.

The purpose of scheduling the production schedule is to generate a detailed short-term production plan for the workshop. Scheduling (Production schedule) indicates the processing time and the end time of each order in the planned range, i.e., the processing procedure of the order of the given resource.

4. Function Modules of the System

Function module of MES in the production workshop of hydraulic torque converter is shown as below:

Resource allocation Module: the functional module manage all kinds of resource, including machines, tools, labor skills, materials, gas equipment, and other items, such as the start of operation must provide the documents. It provides a detailed history of resources, ensures that the correct set of equipment, and provides real-time equipment status.

Scheduling module: the functional module optimizes the production order, such as color sorting, or other features, in order to minimize the adjustment of the equipment in the operation.

Production unit allocation module: The module manages the production logistics. Production scheduling information to form a sequence of presentation and real-time adjustment according to actual production.

Data acquisition module: the module provides an interface link, which is used to obtain the intermediate product and parameter data. These data can be collected from the factory site, and can be collected automatically from the equipment, and ensure the timely update of data.

Quality management module: This module from the production process of collecting real-time measurement information, and the analysis to ensure the strict product quality control, and to identify potential quality problems. The system can prompt the problem to correct the plan, including the related phenomenon, the behavior and the cause of diagnosis.

Production management module: the module of production monitoring and automatically correct or prompted questions existing operators correct production to improve production line in the regulation. These regulation focuses on the monitoring and control of the device, and the successive tracking.

Product tracking module: the module monitoring the use of the products and processing state. State information including processors, raw material suppliers, batch number, serial number, product current status, alarm, rework, and other production related to the unusual circumstances.

The performance analysis module: the module provides real-time production data and results compared with the historical data and expectations. The production performance such as resource utilization, resource utilization, production cycle and plan and standard etc..

5. Conclusion

The application of MES in the production of hydraulic torque converter is greatly improved. The system can timely feedback to the real-time information of the production line to the management personnel. Management personnel through the system can adjust the production in time. Through the application of the system, the combination of ERP and PCS. MES to create a solid, reliable, comprehensive and feasible manufacturing collaborative management platform.

Acknowledgments

This research was supported by Shaanxi province of China science and technology research and development project (No. 2014 GY2-04).

References

1. Liu Ping Ping and Li Long, Design and implementation of the steel enterprise MES based on CICS, Advanced Materials Research, v 779, p1801-1804,2013,Materials, Transportation and Environmental Engineering.
2. Younus Muhammad, Peiyong Cong, Hu Lu and Yuqing Fan, MES development and significant applications in manufacturing -A review, ICETC 2010 - 2010 2nd International Conference on Education Technology and Computer, v 5, p V597-V5101, 2010.
3. Weygandt Steven L, Automatic data collection methods for MES, Instrumentation in the Aerospace Industry : Proceedings of the International Symposium, p 345-354, 1996.
4. Baljet Peter, Manufacturing Execution System: Manufacturing process improvement through plant-wide visibility with MES, National Electronic Packaging and Production Conference-Proceedings of the Technical Program (West and East), v 2, p 1078-1083, 1999.
5. Wang Jin-Ye, Yue Yan-Fang, Wang Jian-Lou, Xin, Zhi-Bo and Yao, Xue-Min, Function model of MES oriented to mechanical blanking workshop, Advanced Materials Research, v 622, p 1479-1483, 2013, Manufacturing Science and Technology III.
6. Long Wen, Research on retrieval of MES components based on ontology, Proceedings - 2009 2nd International Workshop on Knowledge Discovery and Data Mining, WKKD 2009, p 175-178, 2009.
7. Du, Hui, Research and implement of enterprise instant messaging system for MES, International Journal of Advancements in Computing Technology, v 3, n 10, p 240-249, November 2011.
8. Lee SeungWoo, Nam So Jeong and Lee Jai-Kyung, Real-time data acquisition system and HMI for MES, Journal of Mechanical Science and Technology, v 26, n 8, p 2381-2388, August 2012.

K-SVD Dictionary Incremental Learning Algorithm Based on Clustering Theory

Rui-peng LUAN* and Gui-xin SUN

The Chinese People's Liberation Army No:91550,Dalian, 116023, China

**E-mail: lrp_ph@163.com*

To solve the time-consuming problem of K-SVD, a dictionary learning algorithm based on clustering theory is proposed. The proposed algorithm learns incremental dictionary from an incremental training sample set, then leverages clustering theory to combine the initial dictionary and incremental dictionary. Thus it provides a two way optimization for the entire training sample set and significantly increase the efficiency of the K-SVD dictionary learning algorithm for big sample set learning. The image super resolution reconstruction experiment demonstrates that the proposed algorithm exhibits the capability for incremental learning.

Keywords: K-SVD; Clustering theory; Incremental learning.

1. Introduction

Signal sparse representation is one of hot topics in signal processing, which has been applied successfully in several areas of signal processing. For instance, image compression[1], image denoising[2], image inpainting[3], image super-resolution reconstruction [4][5] and achieve positive results. Dictionary learning method is key link of sparse representation. The major dictionary learning method includes Method of Optimal Directions (MOD)[6], Generalized PCA(GPCA)[7], parameter training method[8], and K-SVD[9]. All above dictionary learning algorithm is two way optimization of iterative batch processing, in additional words, in every iteration, all training set will be accessed, and under constraints, minimize cost function, amount of calculation would be huge, not convenient for or barely to handle big sample sets.

Therefore, this paper introduces a K-SVD dictionary incremental learning algorithm based on clustering theory. This algorithm will firstly divide a big sample set into a main training set and several sub training sets, then learn initial dictionary from major training set by K-SVD, later learning incremental dictionary from sub training sets. It will combine dictionaries based on clustering theory, interactively process all sub training sets, to complete learning on big samples sets. This algorithm, compared with whole process, will cost lower internal memory, lower calculation workload as benefits, and meaningful for sparse representation of big sets on program application.

2. K-SVD Algorithm Introduction

K-SVD Algorithm contains 2 key structures, sparse representation coding and dictionary update, K-SVD object function as Eq. (1).

$$\min\{\|X - DW\|\} \text{ s.t. } \|w_i\|_0 \le T_0, \text{for } i \in \{1,...,N\}. \tag{1}$$

$$\|X - DW\|_F^2 = \left\|(X - \sum_{j\neq k} d_j w_j) - d_k w_k\right\| = \|E_k - d_k w_k\|_F^2. \tag{2}$$

$X \in \Re^{n\times N}$ is from all kinds of samples, $X = [x_1,...,x_N]^T$; $D \in \Re^{n\times M}$ is the matrix of dictionary atoms, $D = [d_1,...,d_N]^T$; $W \in \Re^{M\times N}$ is x_i correspond to coefficient matrix of dictionary atom d_j. K-SVD complete sparse coding in order to Orthogonal Matching Pursuit(OMP)[10], update dictionary parameters; during dictionary update, atomic and its related none 0 parameters will be updated by the SVD of E_k, as in Eq. (2).

3. Description of K-SVD Dictionary Incremental Learning Algorithm

The K-SVD dictionary incremental learning algorithm based on clustering theory, firstly divide the big sample set into a major training set and several sub training sets, then learn initial dictionary from major training set, then learn incremental dictionary from one sub training set. After that, initialize original dictionary and incremental dictionary under objective function, adjust atomic weights of dictionary and replace some of atomic weights to establish a new dictionary as an initial dictionary to continue the interaction, until all sub training sets are completed.

Detailed algorithm is demonstrated as below.

Step 1:

Initialize parameter, $t = 1$, the ith column of dictionary D_t is d_i^t, the ith column of parameter matrix W_t is w_i^t, $dis(x, y)$ is the Euclid distance between vector x and y.

Step 2:

For class ω_i, there are N_i samples , which is described as $S = [s_1, s_2,..., s_p]^T$, in the training set, and the mean value vector is $\overline{S}_{\omega_i} = \frac{1}{N_i}\sum_{j=1}^{N_i} S_j$, the discrete extent of the whole set is $T_{\omega_i} = \frac{1}{N_i}\sum_{j=1}^{N_i}\left\|S_j - \overline{S}_{\omega_i}\right\|$. For any two class ω_m and ω_n, the conjunctive entropy is $H(\omega_m,\omega_n) = \ln(\frac{\left\|\overline{S}_{\omega_m} - \overline{S}_{\omega_n}\right\|}{T_{\omega_m} + T_{\omega_n}})$, which is used to describe the easily discrimination level of the two class. And for the classification task, in which the number of the classes is k, the conjunctive entropy between any two classes can form a matrix as Eq. (3). $HM[i,j] = H(\omega_i,\omega_j)$, k is the number of classes, $HM(k)$ is named as class conjunctive entropy matrix, and represents the complicated degree of the whole task.

$$HM(k) = \begin{bmatrix} 0 & H(\omega_2,\omega_1) & H(\omega_3,\omega_1) & \cdots & H(\omega_k,\omega_1) \\ H(\omega_1,\omega_2) & 0 & H(\omega_3,\omega_2) & \cdots & H(\omega_k,\omega_2) \\ H(\omega_1,\omega_3) & H(\omega_2,\omega_3) & 0 & \cdots & H(\omega_k,\omega_3) \\ \vdots & \vdots & \vdots & \ddots & \vdots \\ H(\omega_1,\omega_k) & H(\omega_2,\omega_k) & H(\omega_3,\omega_k) & \cdots & 0 \end{bmatrix}. \quad (3)$$

Divide the big sample set into a main training set Y_1 and some sub training set $Y_2 \cdots Y_p$ by any classing algorithm as the principle that $HM(p) \geq 0$.

Step 3:

Obtain the dictionary D_0 and parameter matrix W_0 from the main training set Y_1 by K-SVD algorithm.

Step 4:

Obtain the dictionary D_t and parameter matrix W_t from the sub training set Y_t by K-SVD algorithm.

Step 5:

Define new object function as Eq. (4). Iteration until conditional convergence, if d_i^0 don't content the conditional convergence, update d_i^0 with d_j^t.

$$\min\{\sum_{j=1}^{M}\sum_{i=1}^{N} u^2_{ij} dis^2(d_j^t - d_i^0) - H(\omega_t,\omega_{t-1})\sum_{j=1}^{M}\sum_{i=1}^{N} u_{ij}\}$$

$$s.t. \sum_{j=1}^{M} u_{ij} = \frac{\left\|w_j^t - w_i^0\right\|^2}{\left\|d_i^0\right\|^2}, for\, i \in \{1,...,N\}. \quad (4)$$

Step 6:

Let $t = t+1$, return Step 4, until $t = p$ (p is the training set number of a big sample set).

4. Experiment and Results

Select the images with different structure and texture, such as Fig. 1. By pre-degradation and extraction of high frequency component, append 1 variance 5×5Gaussian Blur , 1 variance additive noise , 3-desample Bicubic, establish training sample set with 28000 3×3image blocks finally. Divide the sample set into 1 main training set and 2 sub training sets, the conjunctive entropy between any 3 sets can form a matrix as Eq. (5).

Fig. 1. Images of experiment with lenna (left), man (middle), baboon (right).

$$HM(3) = \begin{bmatrix} 0 & 0.823 & 0.772 \\ 0.823 & 0 & 0.516 \\ 0.772 & 0.516 & 0 \end{bmatrix}. \tag{5}$$

The dictionary result of K-SVD, and incremental learning algorithm proposed in this paper, such as Fig. 2. The result of super-resolution reconstruction with the algorithm[4], using above different dictionaries, is shown in Fig. 3. The result of time-consuming comparing above two algorithm, is shown in Table 1.

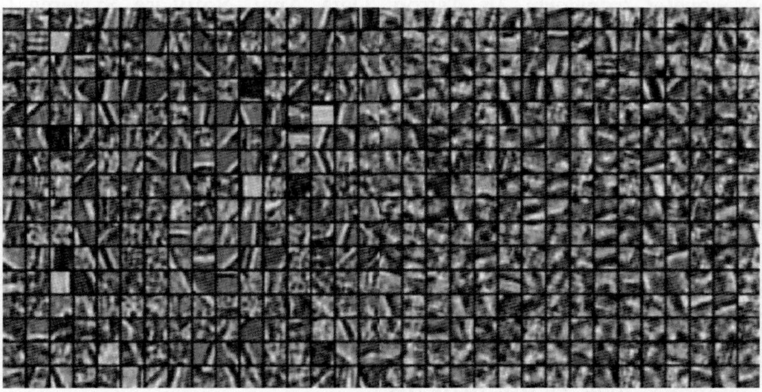

Fig. 2. Dictionary of K-SVD (left) and incremental K-SVD (right).

Fig. 3. Result of SRR with Bicubic (left), K-SVD (middle), incremental learning K-SVD (right).

Table 1. Result of time-consuming.

	K-SVD	Incremental learning K-SVD
Establish Dictionary duration(s)	1674	608

5. Conclusion

Compared with K-SVD, the experiment shows that the K-SVD dictionary incremental learning algorithm based on clustering theory can obtain the capability of incremental learning and better performance with time-consuming. Therefore the algorithm proposed in this paper can cost lower internal memory, lower calculation workload as benefits, and meaningful for sparse representation of big sets on program application

References

1. R.Gastaud, J. L. Starck, *Dynamic range compression: a new method based on wavelet transform*. In Astron. Data Anal. Software Systems Conf., Strasbourg, 2003.
2. M. Elad, M. Aharon, *Image denoising via sparse and redundant representations over learned dictionaries*. Image Processing, IEEE Transactions on, 2006, 15(12):3736-3745.
3. M. Elad, J.L. Starck, P. Querre , *Simultaneous cartoon and texture image inpainting using morphological component analysis (MCA)*. Applied and Computational Harmonic Analysis, 2005, 19(3): 340-358.
4. S. Park, M. Park, M. G. Kang. *Super-resolution image reconstruction: a technical overview*. IEEE Signal Processing Magazine, 2003, 20(3): 21-36.
5. J. D. van Ouwerkerk. *Image super-resolution survey*. Image and Vision Computing, 2006,24(10): 1039-1052.

6. K. Engan, S. O. Aase, J. H. Husoy. *Method of optimal directions for frame design*. Proceedings of IEEE International Conference on Acoustic, Speech, and Signal Processing, Phoenix, AZ, Mar 1999, 2443-2446.
7. R. Vidal, Y. Ma, S. Sastry. *Generalized principal component analysis (GPCA)*. IEEE Transactions on Pattern Analysis and Machine Intelligence, 2005, 27(12): 1945-1959.
8. R. Rubinstein, A. M. Bruckstein, M. Elad. *Dictionaries for sparse representation modeling*. Proceedings of the IEEE, 2010, 98(6): 1045-1057.
9. M. Aharon, M. Elad, A. M. Bruckstein. *The K-SVD: An algorithm for designing of overcomplete dictionaries for sparse representation*. IEEE Transactions on Signal Processing, 2006, 54(11): 4311-4322.
10. Y. C. Pati, R. Rezaiifar, P. S. Krishnaprasad. Orthogonal matching pursuits: Recursive function approximation with applications to wavelet decomposition. Proceedings of the 27th Asilomar Conference in Signals, Systems, and Computers, Pacific Grove, CA, Nov 1993, 40-44.

High Precision Control of the Voltage Stabilizer Based on Neuron PID Control Algorithm

Jun-jie MA

Faculty of Mechanical Engineering & Automation,
Zhejiang Sci-Tech University, Hangzhou, China
E-mail: 449155786@qq.com

This paper discusses the basic principle of the neuron PID controller for the brushless DC motor. Unlike the classical PID controller, the neuron utilizes the deviation, integration and derivative values as inputs and utilizes the proportional, integral and differential gain as the weight of the neuron, thus making the neuron PID controller adaptive. Experimental results demonstrate that the neuron PID controller is a better control method as compared to the classic PID controller.

Keyword: Neuron PID, Smart control, Motor control.

1. Introduction[1]

After decades of development worldwide, there are a lot of researches about control theory. Some of these studies through continuous development and improvement have become mature independent disciplines. And some studies after a period of prosperity, greatly promoted the development of control theory. Although from now on the theory and application of that own is limited. Currently, control theory has penetrated into almost all areas of engineering technology. As a result new issues, themes and subjects branch abundantly appearance.

The most important features of classical control theory are: linear constant objects, single input and output, complete stabilization tasks. Even for these very simple objects, the theories of object description and control tasks are incomplete. Which contribute to the development of modern control theory: the precision mathematization and theorization progress of the classical control theory. This paper discusses the basic principle of the neuron PID controller for the brushless DC motor.

1.1. *The prospect of brushless DC motor [2]*

Currently, energy conservation is the only way of China's sustainable economic and energy development, which will greatly boost the development and application of permanent magnet motors in China. As an important member of the permanent magnet motors, brushless DC motors will also make an important contribution to efficient motor systems architecture and low-carbon industrial production by virtue of the inherent advantage that our country is the world's largest rare earth storage country.

1.2. *Development and research status of brushless DC motors[3-4]*

In recent decades, with the continuous improvement of the performance of permanent magnet materials, further study of microelectronic technology, automatic control technology and power electronics technology, especially the further development of high-power switching devices, coupled with the gradual experience accumulation of brushless DC motor research and development, brushless DC motor technology gradually matured. Which make the brushless DC motor applications and development enter a new stage with the following characteristics:

(1) The range of applications of brushless DC motor began to expand to a high temperature, high vacuum, space constrained and other special occasions.

(2) The trend of development of the brushless DC motor system is to drive the inverter into the inside of the motor, making them together as a miniaturized systems.

(3) The brushless DC motor is moving in miniaturization and ultra-type development direction.

2. Concept and Realization of Neuron PID Control [5]

Artificial neural networks (ANN) is the research hotspot focus on artificial intelligence field since the 1980s. It abstract the brain nerve network from the information processing point of view by establishing some simple model consisting of different ways to connect different networks. The past ten years, the study of artificial neural networks continue to develop and make considerable progress. It has successfully resolved many difficult practical problems in pattern recognition, intelligent robot, automatic control, predictive estimate, biology, medicine, economics and other fields which too difficult for the modern computer. that shows good intelligence.

2.1. *Application of artificial neural network control theory [6]*

The reason why artificial neural network able to be applied in the control area, because it has the following features: (1) with learning systems and characteristics of nonlinear mapping, capable of approximately representing any nonlinear function and the inverse; (2) is highly adaptive and self organized, able to learn and adapt to the dynamic characteristics of severe uncertainty systems; (3) parallel processing of information makes it possible to quickly carry out a lot of computing, information is stored in the distributed neural network element and its connection weights, and therefore has a strong robustness and fault tolerance; (4) the information is converted into the internal network representation, this representation allows both qualitative and quantitative data fuse together.

2.2. *The learning methods of neural network*

The so-called neural network learning, refers to the process that under a set of given information (learning samples), each processing unit status stay the same, but each connection weights continue to be amended so that the network reaches a desired output. Learning algorithm is the main sign which represent the artificial intelligence features of artificial neural network. Without the learning algorithm, artificial neural network lost tempting capacity of self-adaption, self-organization and self-learning ability.

2.3. *Artificial neuron PID controller model [7]*

Artificial neuron model as is shown in Fig. 1, in which, x_i (i = 1,2, ..., n)is the neuron input, w_i (i = 1,2, ..., n) is the connection weight of each input value, θ is the threshold value of neuron threshold, f as a function (also called excitation function). Y is the output of neurons.

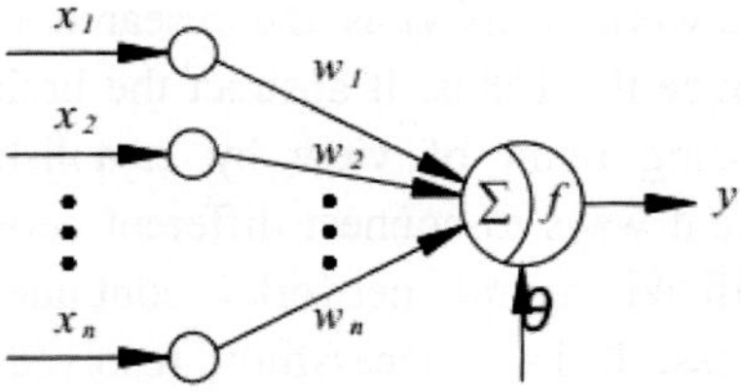

Fig. 1. Neuron model.

f as a function can be linear function, a step function, hyperbolic tangent S type function (symmetric Sigmoid function) and unipolar S function

(Asymmetric Sigmoid function). The relation of Input and output of neurons is as follows:

$$I = \sum_{i=1}^{n} x_i w_i - \theta \qquad f(I). \tag{1}$$

By the formula (1), if we take the deviation value, integration value and derivative value of system as input of neuron, and take proportional gain, integral gain and differential gain as the weights of neuron. Then, the neuron has a PID control function as PID controller. its model is shown in Fig. 2.

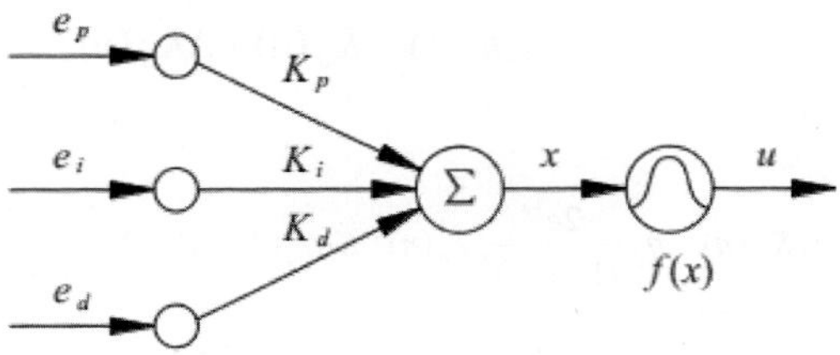

Fig. 2. The model of neuron PID controller.

As is shown in Fig. 2, e_p , e_i and e_d are the three input neuron PID, namely deviation value, integration value and differential value. Take position control as example

$$e_p = \theta_{des} - \theta_{cur} \; e_i = \sum e_p \; e_d = \Delta e_p . \tag{2}$$

In formula above, θ_{dex} is the target angle, θ_{dex} is current angle. In Fig. 2, K_p, K_i and K_d are proportional gain, integral gain and differential gain. At the same time, they also are three link weights of neuron. X an input function f, u is the output of neuron PID. There is:

$$x = K_p e_p + K_i e_i + K_d e_d \qquad u = f(x) . \tag{3}$$

2.4. *Artificial neuron PID learning algorithm*

The difference between Neuron PID Controller and classical PID controller is that the former can be self-learning, self-tuning on K_p, K_i and K_d, improving the output performance of the controller. In this paper, BP learning algorithm do online learning on neural PID.

Take the control of brushless dc motor as example. Because the target is to make $|e_p|$ smallest, therefore, we take neuron PID controller's performance:

$$E=\frac{1}{2}(\theta_{des}-\theta_{cur})^2=\frac{1}{2}e_p^2. \quad (4)$$

Take the hyperbolic tangent S-type function as action function of neuronal:

$$f(x)=\frac{1-e^{-x}}{1+e^{-x}}. \quad (5)$$

The learning algorithm on different gains of neuron PID controller are:

$$K_p(n+1)=K_p(n)+\Delta K_p(n)\ K_i(n+1)=K_i(n)+\Delta K_i(n)$$

$$K_d(n+1)=K_d(n)+\Delta K_d(n). \quad (6)$$

We obtain:

$$K_p(n+1)=K_p(n)+\eta_p\frac{2e^{-x}}{(1+e^{-x})^2}e_p(n)^2\ K_i(n+1)=K_i(n)+\eta_i\frac{2e^{-x}}{(1+e^{-x})^2}e_p(n)e_i(n)$$

$$K_d(n+1)=K_d(n)+\eta_d\frac{2e^{-x}}{(1+e^{-x})^2}e_p(n)e_d(n). \quad (7)$$

The formula above is the iterative learning algorithm of the proportional gain, integral gain and differential gain of neuron PID controller on the control of brushless dc motor.

2.5. *Realization of neuron PID in the angle control of the motor*

In the rotation angle control process of carbon brush drive motor of the voltage regulator, we apply neuron PID control system, the control structure is shown in Fig. 3.

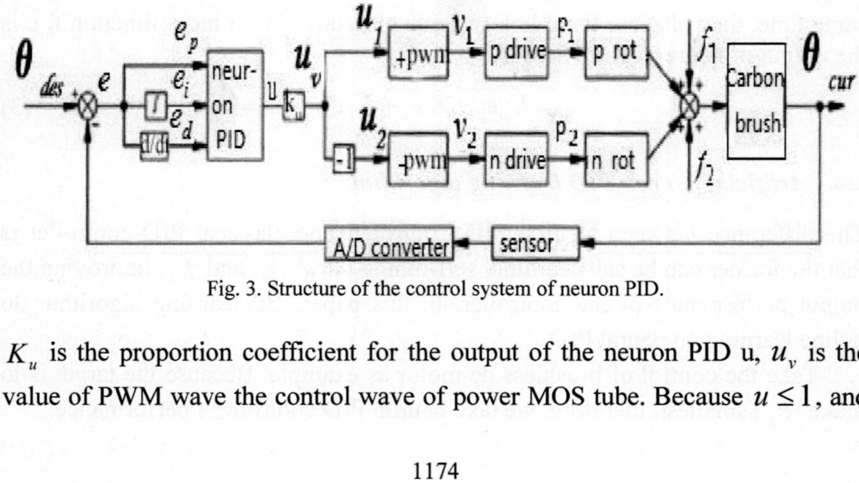

Fig. 3. Structure of the control system of neuron PID.

K_u is the proportion coefficient for the output of the neuron PID u, u_v is the value of PWM wave the control wave of power MOS tube. Because $u \le 1$, and the acceptable range of the driving voltage MOS tube is $0 \sim 5$, so we need multiply K_u to u and get a suitable output voltage value. Which is $u_v = K_u u$

3. Experiment Results and Conclusion

As is shown in Fig. 4, under the step position control process for brushless dc motor, when the parameters of the neuron PID controller differ, the control curves are different. In the parameters above K_u=2, $K_p(0)$=0.01 are the initial value percentage gain, $K_i(0)$=0.00025 is the initial value for integral gain, $K_d(0) = \eta_d = 0$ .As is shown in Fig. 4, we can conclude that the response speed and adjust speed of the neuron PID depends mainly on η_i

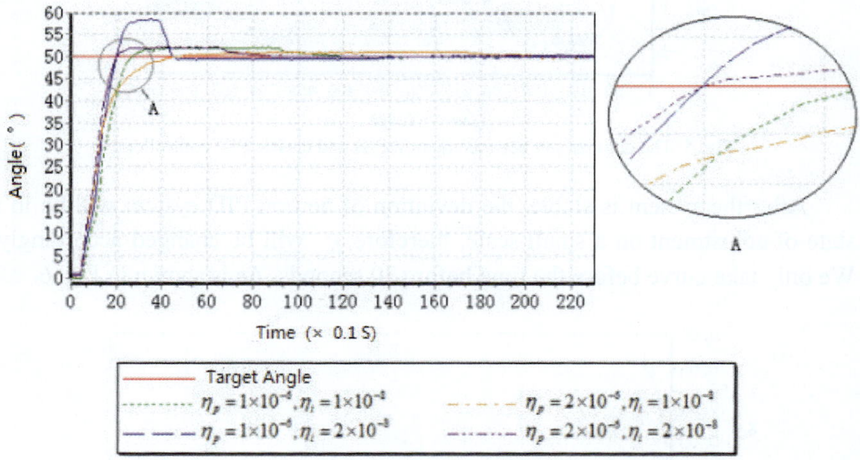

Fig. 4. The control effect of neuron PID when parameter is different.

In Fig. 5, we compare the control effect of the neuron PID and classical PID in the position step control of brushless dc motor. Among them, the parameters of neuron PID are $K_u = 2$, $K_p(0) = 0.01$, $K_i(0) = 0.00025$, $K_d(0) = 0$, $\eta_p = 2\times10^{-6}$, $\eta_d = 0$. The parameters of classical PID control are $K_p = 0.0285$, $K_i = 0.00175$, $K_d = 0$. The initial proportional gain and integral gain of neuron PID are smaller than the corresponding classical PID parameters, but the corresponding speed is faster, adjust time is much less.

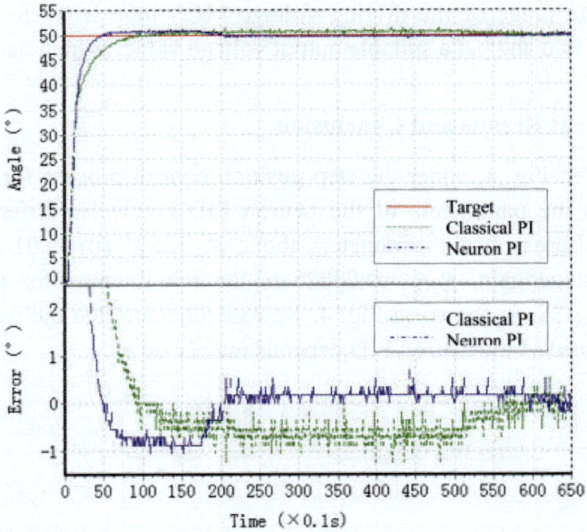

Fig. 5. The comparison between neuron PID and classic PID controllers.

After the system is stable, the deviation of neuron PID system will be in a state of adjustment on a small scale, therefore, K_p will be changed accordingly. We only take curve before the time before 30 seconds. As is shown in Fig. 6.

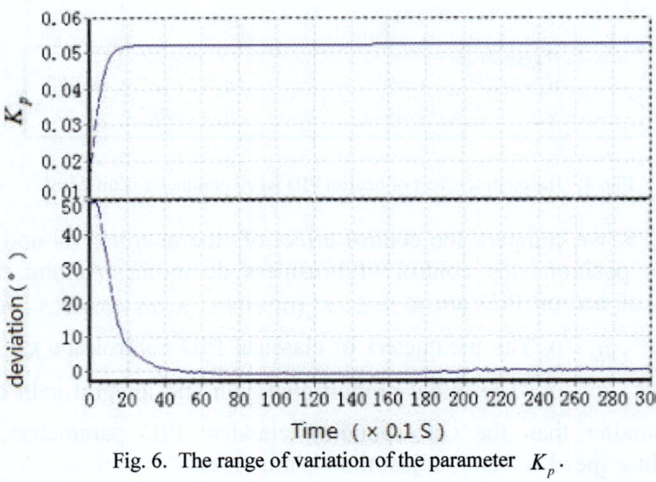

Fig. 6. The range of variation of the parameter K_p.

4. Conclusion

In conclusion, through the neural model, after the adjustment of K_p, K_i, K_d, the control result of neuron PID control is much better than the classic PID control.

Acknowledgments

This work is supported by Science Foundation of Zhejiang Sci-Tech University (ZSTU, Grant No. 13022152-Y) and the Intelligent Multi-Color 3D Printer (ZSTU, Grant No. 14020089-J)

References

1. Weibing Gao, The development and status of control theory--simple remark on complex system and intelligence control. (project report of Science and technology committee State Education Commission on automatic control subject 1994).
2. Changliang Xia, Hongwei Fang, Permanent magnet brushless DC motor and its control. (Journal of electronics, 2012).
3. Yin Dai, Research of PID control method of brushless dc motor based on BP neural network(master degree thesis of Hefei university of technology, 2007).
4. Honghua Wang, Permanent magnet brushless DC motor. (series lecture of new type of ac motor and control technology, 2004). 2004.
5. Liqun Han, Artificial neural network [M]. (Bejjing university of posts and telecommunications publishing house, 2006).
6. Umbers I, King, An analysis of human decision-making in cement kiln control and the implication for automation. (Int. J. man-machine Studies,1976).
7. Xianzhi Jiang, The server control of joints on two-way pull off pneumatic muscle and the application on rehabilitation robot. (PHD thesis of Huazhong university of science and technology, 2011).

Brain Activity of Visual Working Memory Predicted from Image Target Numbers — An EEG Study

Juan HUO

Zheng Zhou University
Zhengzhou, Henan Province, China
E-mail: juanhuo@126.com

The Electroencephologram (EEG) experiments were designed in this paper to emulate our daily visual working memory task and demonstrate the effect of image target numbers and background textures on our brains' visual working memory. This paper discovered that there is a possibly of implementing a neural network to predict memory-related brain activity in a visual working memory experiment, where participants were presented with images of different target item numbers and asked to remember as many target objects as possible. Both the Multi-Layer Perceptron (MLP) network and support vector machine (SVM) were used as training methods for the prediction. The prediction results are consistent with the actual EEG power variation observed in the experiment, which demonstrate the effect of target item number and background texture on the level of difficulty in image memorization.

Keywords: EEG; Visual working memory; SVM; Neural network; Prediction.

1. Introduction

In our daily life, the human being's memory process seems to be much slower than the computer can do, but this information storage process is the foundation for knowledge formation. It has been claimed in many papers that the EEG power is closely related to the memory load change. In an early time, the research in [1] studied the memory process by investigating the neural population's oscillation and proved the short term memory demand leads to the EEG power increase in the theta bands. Later study in [2, 3] shows the increased memory load also enhanced the alpha and gamma band EEG power, although there is still argument about the different power variation among the scalp sites. The above studies all have observed the working memory load effects on human EEG power and proved the increase of EEG power with the memory load. Essentially, this is because the EEG power reflects the excitability of the neuron groups, so that event related brain activity level can be observed by estimating the EEG power changes [2, 3, 4, 5]. In addition, several modeling studies have related the brain state of cortex network dynamics to EEG signal [6]. Thus in the following sections of this paper, the value of EEG power is treated as a representation of the state of brain activity.

In this paper, the image target numbers and the image background textures are found to be closely related to the strength of EEG power. Based on the results of regression analysis, two popular neural network models: multilayer perceptron (MLP) and support vector machine (SVM) are used to explore the possibility to predict the brain activity with the target numbers of the image. Results of these neural network models are expected to provide a reference for the estimation of the memorability of visual information and the study of human learning process. Results from the training show the variation of the EEG power can be predicted from the values of image features by both MLP and SVM. This also proves that our memory ability is largely affected by the visual information load, especially the memory target item numbers.

2. Brain Computer Interface Experiments

Data were sampled from 4 male and female young adults (students) with an average age of 23.8, STD 1.45. All attendances of this experiment have signed consent papers which is in agreement with the ethical standards. This task is to remember the numbers attached to the white balls scattered in different image backgrounds as shown in Fig. 1. The stimuli were presented and the subjects' response was recorded by EPrime software. The participants were placed 70cm ahead of a 19 inches LCD screen straight ahead of their eyes horizontally where the visual stimuli were displayed at the center of the subjects' visual field. After the stimuli presentation, the participants then had another 1000ms interval of retention time before the memory recall.

3. Image Measurement

The target numbers were shown in limited digit length(< 4) on different image backgrounds and the length of one number is randomly selected. Each number is an item to be remembered. These numbers were generated by a random process and the repeated ones were eliminated. This is to minimize the perception difference caused by the vocabulary sequence of numbers. We have 4 subjects tried 252 groups of images, namely 252 trials. The image background varies from simple to complex and classified into four levels as shown in Fig. 1.

We measure an image by using a factor vector X,{Xnum, Xback, Xacc, Xpos}. Xnum is the number of items shown per image, whose value varies from

3 to 50 per image. Image background is the second factor considered. This study has used the classical image stimuli. These stimuli are different from previous researches which have used simple shape and color items on a mono-color background, different texture backgrounds were added in the image as noise. The image background noise level (Xback) hereby can be counted as another factor

Fig. 1. Images of visual stimuli. The numbers in the white ball is the target object for the subjects to be remembered.

that influences the memorability and brain activity. The level of Xback is determined according to the complexity of image background. The value of Xback for images in Fig. 1 varies from 1 to 4 in order. The response accuracy is labeled as the third factor Xacc. Another factor is the position distribution of the items which is referred to as factor Xpos. In some images, the items are in random sequence while in the other images, the items were well arranged in arrays. Xpos value is high if the arrangement of the items is random and is low if the arrangement of the items is in array. The number of images played continuously in a special trial is labeled as the last factor X rep. In most of the trials, only one image was shown. In a few special trials, 2 or 3 images were shown one after another. The memory recall process from the subjects were recorded and the subjects' responses were automatically calculated at the end of each trial. To make sure the subject is not aware of the factor level change, all the factors are composed and arranged randomly.

4. Electrophysiological Analysis

A simple MLP network is used for the advantage of low complexity. The input values to the network is defined as: $X_i \in$ {Xnum, Xback, Xacc, Xpos, Xrep}, where i = 1, ..., 5. The first layer output of this MLP thus can be defined as:

$$L_j = \sum_{i=1}^{d} W_{ji} X_i + b_j \qquad j = 1, \ldots M \ . \tag{1}$$

where L_j is associated with each hidden unit. In the initial design, the MLP network has 6 neurons as input and 30 hidden units with logistic sigmoidal activation function and 1 output neuron with linear activation function.

4.1. *Training and validation sets*

Every subject has EEG experiment in different time and their EEG signal baseline were influenced by environmental factors. Thus every subject has its own EEG power value normalized by dividing the maximum power value among all trials. This is to minimize the baseline difference between subjects. Each EEG power value corresponds to one factor vector X_i. EEG power value Y is the output value to be predicted. Leave-one-out-cross-validation (LOOCV) is used for validation. The estimation of each subject was repeated 200 times and the prediction results were statistically analyzed.

4.2. *Network training results*

Since the EEG test is a continuous process, the EEG power amplitude theoretically varies with the change of factor vectors of different trials. The prediction for the four students' record was independent with each other. The quality of its corresponding segment of EEG signal wave was re-checked before the training. Fig. 2 shows the training results from the LOOCV. The wide red line represents the real normalized EEG power value and the blue line represents the predicted mean value from the MLP network. Box plots of the blue line were the anova test result of n = 200 repeated MLP training for one subject. Basically, in all the plots, the blue lines follow the variation of the red lines. The correlation between the averaged blue line and the red line is listed in Table 1. From the Table 1, the Pearson correlation coefficient of all prediction values are positive with four subjects $p < 0.05$. From this result, the correlation between the predicted EEG power value and the real test value is generally significant. This eliminates the possibility that the successful MLP prediction being a result of a random event. This indicates the MLP network prediction is reliable and the prediction result is consistent with the real EEG data. The synchronization between the red and blue lines shows the variance of the EEG power amplitude value is closely related to the difficulty level of the memory task which is defined by the pattern of factor vectors. The decision for whether the value of each subject's *ro* in each subject's 200 sample is random or not, is returned by a Kolmogorov-Smirnov test. The null hypothesis of the test that *ro* comes from a standard normal distribution was rejected at the 5% significant level. The variation of the absolute value of *ro* may due to the other environmental factors, such as the conductive gem between the electrode and the cortex. Test of the weight distribution of the MLP shows the similar result and indicates the weight distribution of the network is not random. By comparison, although the average prediction accuracy of SVM is slightly higher than MLP, MLP performs better than SVM for some specific subjects' data such as (a)(b) and (d).

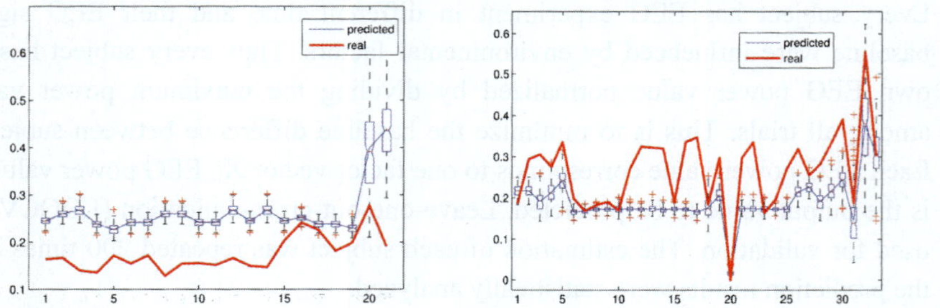

(a) (b)

Fig. 2. Four of the five LOOCV test results. The mean correlation of predicted and real EEG power is listed in (a)(b)(c)(d) shown in Table 1 and 2 model the impact of the information load on brain activity.

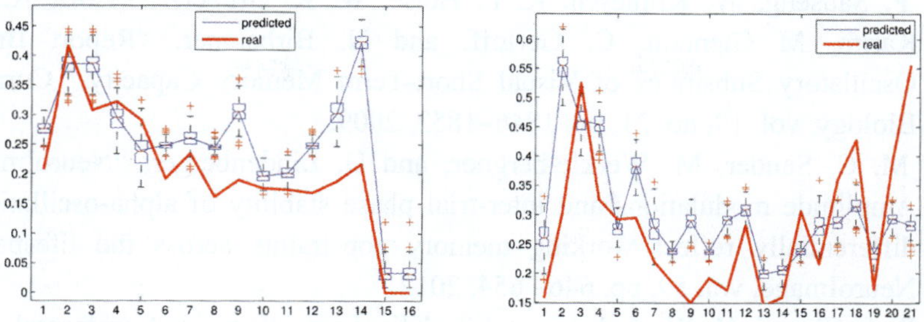

(c) (d)

Fig. 2. (*Continued*)

Table 1. Correlation between the mean predicted results from MLP and the real measured EEG power value in the LOOCV. ** $p < 0.0001$, * $p < 0.05$.

Training set	(a)*	(b)**	(c)**	(d)*
mean *ro*	0.4123	0.7515	0.8202	0.4633

Table 2. Correlation between the mean predicted results from SVM and the real measured EEG power value in the LOOCV. ** $p < 0.0001$, * $p < 0.05$.

Training set	(a)*	(b)**	(c)**	(d)*
mean *ro*	0.3849	0.6769	0.9274	0.4588

5. Conclusion

Most of the previous research for short term memory is for the neuron signature rather than the correlation between the input stimuli and the brain activity. Results of this research show the target item number and the background textures have effect on the visual working memory and this effect is predictable. Successful prediction of the brain activity from the learning of image factors give us a reference to measure the input information that we are going to study and potentially help us to improve the learning process. The current work proved the possibility to model the impact of the information load on brain activity.

References

1. W. Klimesch, “Memory processes, brain oscillations and EEG synchronization,” International Journal of sychophysiology, vol. 24, no. 1-2, pp. 61–100, 1996.

2. P. Sauseng, W. Klimesch, K. F. Heise, W. R. Gruber, E. Holz, A. A. Karim, M Glennon, C. Gerloff, and N. Birbaumer, "Report Brain Oscillatory Substrates of Visual Short-Term Memory Capacity," Current Biology, vol. 19, no. 21, pp. 1846–1852, 2009.
3. M. C. Sander, M. Werkle-bergner, and U. Lindenberger, "NeuroImage Amplitude modulations and inter-trial phase stability of alpha-oscillations differentially reflect working memory constraints across the lifespan," NeuroImage, vol. 59, pp. 646– 654, 2012.
4. P. J. Olesen, H. Westerberg, and T. Klingberg, "Increased prefrontal and parietal activity after training of working memory," Nat Neurosci, vol. 7, pp. 75–79, 2004.
5. K. Cuevas and M. A. Bell, "EEG and ECG from 5 to 10 months of age : Developmental changes in baseline activation and cognitive processing during a working memory task," International Journal of Psychophysiology, vol. 80, pp. 119–128, 2011.
6. R. Meier, A. Kumar, A. Schulze-bonhage, and A. Aertsen, "Comparison of dynamical states of random networks with human EEG," Neurocomputing, vol. 70, pp. 1843–1847, 2007.

A Parallel Algorithm Based On OpenMP + STM for FPGA Timing-Driven Placement

Jia-qi ZHANG*, Hui-juan LV, Li-bo TAN and Tao-tao PAN

National Digital Switching System Engineering and Technological Research Center, Zhengzhou, Henan, China

**E-mail: zhangjqfriend@yahoo.com*

Traditional FPGA placement algorithms based on simulated annealing is time-consuming and thus we have proposed a parallel FPGA timing-driven placement algorithm using OpenMP + STM programming method. In this paper, we distribute swaps to multi-threads by OpenMP and protect the shared memory using software transactional memory. An improved timing optimization algorithm is also added in the transaction. Experimental results on MCNC benchmarks demonstrate that our algorithm achieves a speedup of 1.6x and scales well with the increasing of threads. It also reduces the critical path delay by an average of 4.2%.

Keywords: Parallel; OpenMP; Transactional memory; FPGA; Timing-driven placement.

1. Introduction

FPGAs have been widely used in the current communication, industrial control and many other fields by the advantage of flexibility and usability. However, the growth rate of the FPGA sizes is almost three times faster than the performance improvement of the single-core CPU[1]. With the increasing popularity of multi-core processors, industrial and academic circles have begun to apply parallel methods to SA placement algorithm. A simple attempt is made by distributing each swap to muti-threads [2], but it's lack of parallelism and scales not well. Altera's Quartus II[1] uses one thread monitoring swaps, while the other threads evaluating new placement at the same time. It avoids conflicts by using a "dependency checker". But the acceleration effect is limited, and it's relatively difficult to implement because of the large amount of code lines. TVPR [3] parallel block swaps based on software transactional memory (STM) to detect and resolve conflicts automatically. It's a simple and convenient way to implement and scales well with the increase of threads, with an average of only 1% quality loss. The STM mechanism can greatly simplify the parallelization progress compared with other parallel methods. But the excessive overhead caused by STM affects the acceleration effect seriously. MoveSpec-STM [4] implements fine-grained transaction scope, and achieves better speedup. But all aspects of the placement quality have decreased.

In this paper, we firstly propose a novel timing information updating strategy that can reflect the change of placement more accurately; then we parallelize the timing-driven placement algorithm using STM, and append the timing optimization module into transactions; at last we implement our algorithm based on VPR. After optimization for the paralleled algorithm, We obtain scalable acceleration and better timing result at the same time.

2. Related Work

2.1. *FPGA timing-driven placement*

Among the current FPGA timing-driven placers, the academic authoritative placement and routing tool VPR[5] uses a representative timing-driven simulated annealing algorithm. VPR sets up the cost function as a combination of wiring cost and timing cost, so that both the wire length and critical path delay are taken into account. The key method is a two-layer loop:

In the inner loop, VPR swaps the configurable logic blocks (CLB) randomly within a limited range Rlim, then calculates the delta cost after each swap using Eq. (1):

$$\Delta C = \lambda \frac{\Delta Wiring\_Cost}{Pre\_Wiring\_Cost} + (1-\lambda) \frac{\Delta Timing\_Cost}{Pre\_Timing\_Cost} . \quad (1)$$

λ is used to adjust the weighting of wiring cost and timing cost, with a default value of 0.5. It determines whether to accept a swap using Metropolis criteria shown as Eq. (2):

$$\varepsilon < exp \frac{-\Delta C}{T} . \quad (2)$$

Where ε values in a random number between [0,1). When $\Delta C<0$, the new state will be accepted. When $\Delta C>0$, there is still a certain probability to accept the new state.

The delay cost calculation is realized by static timing analysis. The calculation of the criticality and timing cost are respectively shown as Eq.(3) and Eq. (4):

$$Crit(i,j) = 1 - slack(i,j) / D_{max} . \quad (3)$$

$$Timing\_Cost(i,j) = Delay(i,j) * Crit(i,j)^{Crit\_Exp} . \quad (4)$$

Where Dmax represents the criticality path delay(CPD); Crit_Exp represents the criticality exponent.

Finally, the timing cost of the overall placement is obtained as shown in Eq. (5).

$$Timing\_Cost = \sum Timing\_Cost(i,j) . \quad (5)$$

However, VPR only updates criticality until annealing temperature decreases, thus some error may occur when judging whether a swap should be accepted, affecting the optimization of placement results. By adding in timing optimization module, we can analyze the change of the placement more accurately, further reduce the critical path delay.

In this paper, we intend to use an improved timing optimization strategy to correct the criticality dynamically, aiming to achieve better timing results.

2.2. *Serial program parallelization*

The current multi-processor CPUs are becoming more and more popular. However, most of the single-core serial programs are unable to take advantage of multi-core processors. Parallel programming methods have attracted more and more attention. At present, several parallel methods have been widely used: Message Passing Interface (MPI), OpenMP, Pthreads, etc.

OpenMP [6] is an industrial standard API for shared memory programming, which is designed for parallelization of existing serial programs incrementally[7]. OpenMP provides shared memory API based on a set of instruction clause: it uses #pragma preprocessor directives and a series of control clause. Only a small part of source code needs to be modified to realize parallelization.

However, multi-thread synchronization and access control for shared resources are important problems when developing parallel programs, which directly relates to the algorithm's correctness. The OpenMP compiler does not check the data and loop dependencies. It just provides mechanisms like locks and the critical regions. The lock granularity control, deadlocks etc. bring great limitations to parallel methods. They not only affect the performance of parallel algorithms, but also increase the programming difficulty.

Transactional Memory (TM) indicates a new way for shared memory access control. TM provides ease of use lock mechanism. It divides the program into tasks which would be assigned to multi-threads to execution as a "transaction".

It applies atomic and continuous operation to the code region which accesses the shared memory. Since the independence of tasks is unpredictable, the TM system will monitor memory accesses of all transactions to ensure the correctness of the program. Threads remain visible to each other. When multiple transactions are in conflict with the same block of memory, "ABORT" and "ROLL BACK" will be triggered. Transactions will be "COMMIT" until the main memory could be changed without conflicts.

TM can be divided into hardware transactional memory (HTM) and software transactional memory (STM) depending on ways of implementation. All functions of STM are achieved through pure code, which can be used to trace the memory access automatically by just adding some instructions in the program. STM is much easier to implement, and has no capacity limit compared with HTM, which is more convenient for academic research; But it has a higher overhead and the promotion efficiency will be limited.

In this paper, we intend to use OpenMP + STM to achieve FPGA placement algorithm parallelization.

3. Parallel Timing-Driven Placement Algorithm

3.1. *Timing optimization*

By default, VPR does not update criticalities in the inner loop, at the expense of precision to save time. So it is possible to calculate the delta timing cost in error.

For this purpose, we firstly put forward a new timing information updating strategy:

(1) Keep the value of D_{max} at the same temperature until the temperature decreases;

(2) Allow the critical values greater than 1.

By this means, it is more encouraged to abandon placement with a higher CPD, and accept a reduced CPD placement.

However, real-time timing analysis has a high complexity, so we adopt the method of updating criticalities dynamically. With a relatively lower run-time cost, we achieve as close as full timing analysis results. Whenever two blocks swap positions, the criticality information on the whole changed path will be updated. Assuming that when temperature was t and path (k, l)'s timing delay was changed after the mth swap, the criticality of each connection (i, j) on path (k, l) would be corrected according to Eq. (6) and Eq. (7):

$$\Delta Crit(k,l,t,m) = [Delay(k,l,t,m) - Delay(k,l,t,m-1)] / D_{max} \quad . \qquad (6)$$

$$Crit(i,j,t,m) = Crit(i,j,t,m) + \Delta Crit(k,l,t,m) \quad . \qquad (7)$$

The calculation of timing cost and delta timing cost are also changed as shown in Eq. (8) and Eq. (9):

$$Timing\_Cost(i,j,t,m) = Delay(i,j,t,m) * Crit(i,j,t,m)^{Crit\_Exp} \quad . \tag{8}$$

$$\begin{aligned}\Delta Timing\_Cost(i,j,t,m) &= [Delay(i,j,t,m) * Crit(i,j,t,m)^{Crit\_Exp}] \\ &-[Delay(i,j,t,m-1) * Crit(i,j,t,m-1)^{Crit\_Exp}]\end{aligned} \quad . \tag{9}$$

Compared with the timing correction method described in [8-9], this algorithm has higher accuracy when calculating timing cost. Thus it can better reflect how the circuit changes after one swap and achieve better placement results.

3.2. *VPR parallelization*

The simulated annealing algorithm processes a large number of block swaps in the inner loop, which is very time-consuming and will become even worse after timing optimization. In order to improve the efficiency, we distribute swaps to multi-threads using OpenMP. As threads are unable to predict the positions of one swap, the parallel movement may lead to conflicts. Conflicts can be divided into hard and soft conflicts: Hard conflict occurs when the swaps by multiple threads involve in the same module or location, resulting in swap failures, as shown in Fig. 1a; Soft conflict occurs when the swapped blocks are in the same netlist. Because the cost function is calculated according to the changed placement, uncertain locations of blocks within the same netlist will bring in unpredictable errors, as shown in Fig. 1b.

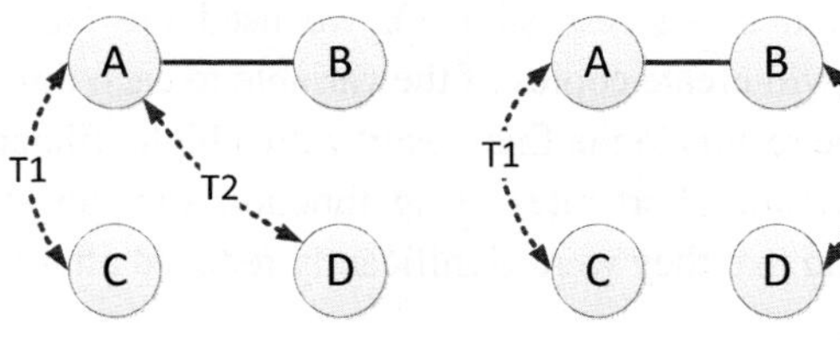

a. Hard conflict b. Soft conflict

Fig. 1. Conflicts in parallelization.

In order to avoid possible conflicts, we add in the STM mechanism. There are some mature STM software available. TinySTM [10-11] is a C software library, by which developers only needs to specify the transaction boundaries and implement read and write operations by adding macros to shared data.

Firstly, We defined function try_swap together with the timing optimization module as a transaction, marking it using TM_START and TM_COMMIT macro. Then used TM_STORE, TM_LOAD such macros annotating read and write operations to shared memory. Whenever read and write operations with annotation appears, the corresponding STM libraries will be called automatically. This ensures that no multiple swaps will simultaneously access the same data structure.

To improve the parallel efficiency and reduce possible conflicts, we optimized the parallel algorithm as follows:

(1) Since VPR selects blocks to swap by generating random numbers, we firstly used the omp_get_thread_num function provided by OpenMP to obtain the initial random seeds for each thread. Then we used linear congruence random number generator to generate independent random number sequence for each thread. Each group of random number queue is equivalent to a set of different swap schemes, so that the choice of blocks to swap will have some degree of independence, which reduces the conflict.

(2) Big nets have higher possibility to raise conflicts, so we delivered them only to the master thread (the main thread in OpenMP standard). This helps avoid some multiple threads to swap blocks in the same nets at the same time. We made the judgment of "big nets" the referring to TVPR[3]: nets containing more than 10% of total number of blocks were regarded as big nets.

(3) For some global variables (such as block), we used OpenMP's first private clause to make a copy of data to each thread. For some reduction operations (such as success_sum++), we used the OpenMP's reduction clause, which will create copies of the variable to each thread automatically and overlay the results to the final result with a high efficiency.

We got the average abort rates using function stm_get_stats provided by TinySTM, and found that they were significantly reduced after optimization.

4. Testing

We implemented our algorithm based on the open source VPR 7.0[12]. We selected 20 largest MCNC simulated circuits provided by VPR. Our algorithm was simulated on the Intel Core i7 3.6GHz quad-core processor, 8GB memory, Ubuntu operating system. The timing cost weight parameter λ was set to 0.5, and the Crit_Exp was used as its default value, from 1 to 8 increasing gradually.

Compared to VPR, the total wire length has increased by 2.1%, while the critical path delay has decreased by 4.2%. The overall results are acceptable. we have also reduced the run-time by 41.3% in average (1.7x faster). Comparison with other similar algorithms is shown in Table 1. We can see that although the total wire length has a slightly increase, the critical path delay is much better than the other algorithms. The speedup is also restricted by the overhead of software transactional memory. In contrast, the hardware transactional memory HTM achieves the best speedup.

Table 1. Placement performance test.

Algorithm	Threads	Speedup	Total wire length	Critical path delay
VPR	1	1.0	1.0	1.0
TVPR[3]	8	0.9x	+1.6%	+1%
MoveSpec-STM[4]	16	3.6x	+8.5%	+2.3%
MoveSpec-HTM[4]	4	8.1x	+19%	+1.7%
Our Algorithm	8	1.7x	+2.1%	-4.2%

Then we tested the scalability of our parallel algorithm. We set the number of threads to 1, 2, 4, 8 respectively to test the relative speedup to a single thread, as shown in Fig. 2. It shows that, with the increase of threads, the acceleration effect is almost raising linearly. This indicates that our algorithm has a good scalability.

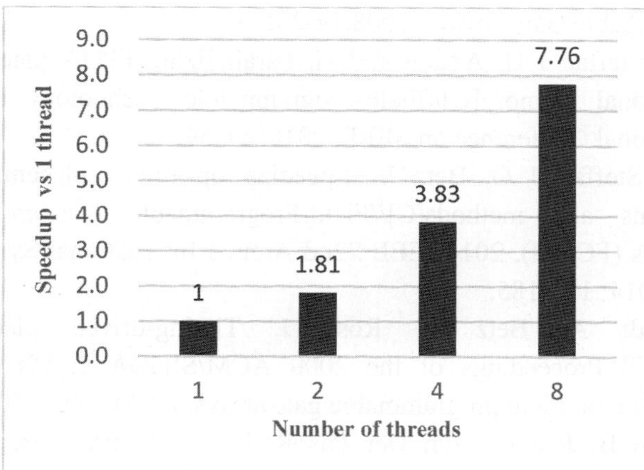

Fig. 2. Scalability test.

5. Conclusion

In this paper, we have presented a parallel FPGA timing-driven placement algorithm using OpenMP + STM programming method. We parallelized block swaps and added in an improved timing optimization algorithm. Test results show that the proposed algorithm can achieve good scalability and can effectively reduce the critical path delay. However, the additional overhead of STM has a great effect on the acceleration. With the popularization of HTM supports and the continuous improvement of the GPU programming interfaces, parallel methods using HTM and GPU will be important research directions in the future.

Acknowledgments

This work is supported by grant 61309020, 61521003 of The National Natural Science Foundation of China.

References

1. Ludwin A, Betz V. Efficient and Deterministic Parallel Placement for FPGAs[J]. Acm Transactions on Design Automation of Electronic Systems, 2011, 16(3):233-250.
2. Ludwin A, Betz V, Padalia K. High-quality, deterministic parallel placement for FPGAs on commodity hardware.[C]// Symposium on Field Programmable Gate Arrays. 2008:14-23.
3. Birk S, Steffan J G, Anderson J H. Parallelizing FPGA placement using transactional memory[C]//Field-Programmable Technology (FPT), 2010 International Conference on. IEEE, 2010: 61-69.
4. An M, Steffan J G, Betz V. Speeding up FPGA placement: Parallel algorithms and methods[C]//Field-Programmable Custom Computing Machines (FCCM), 2014 IEEE 22nd Annual International Symposium on. IEEE, 2014: 178-185.
5. Marquardt A, Betz V, Rose J. Timing-driven placement for FPGAs[C]//Proceedings of the 2000 ACM/SIGDA eighth international symposium on Field programmable gate arrays. ACM, 2000: 203-213.
6. Chapman B, Jost G, Van Der Pas R. Using OpenMP: portable shared memory parallel programming[M]. MIT press, 2008.
7. Pacheco P. An introduction to parallel programming[M]. Elsevier, 2011.

8. Eguro K, Hauck S. Enhancing timing-driven FPGA placement for pipelined netlists[C]// Design Automation Conference, 2008. DAC 2008. 45th ACM/IEEE. IEEE, 2008:34-37.
9. REN Xiaoxi, WU Chu, DING Yu. Time Delay Improvement of FPGA Placement Algorithm Based on VPR[J]. Computer Engineering, 2014, 40(12): 302-305. (In Chinese)
10. Felber P, Fetzer C, Marlier P, et al. Time-Based Software Transactional Memory[J]. IEEE Transactions on Parallel & Distributed Systems, 2010, 21(12):1793-1807.
11. Felber P, Fetzer C, Riegel T. Dynamic performance tuning of word-based software transactional memory[J]. Ppopp Proceedings of Acm Sigplan Symposium on Principles & Practice of Parallel Progr, 2008:237-246.
12. Luu J, Tim L, Betz V, et al. VPR 7.0 Full Release [EB/OL]. `http://www.eecg.toronto.edu/~vaughn/vpr/vpr.html`, 2013-05-18.

Teaching Reform Based on Curricular Integration of *C Programming Language & Data Structure* for Cultivation of Practical Programming Skills

Lian-jun CHEN

School of Information Technology, Shanghai Jianqiao University,
Shanghai,201319, China
E-mail: lianjunchen@gench.edu.cn

Hong-bo ZHOU

Department of Computer Science, Slippery Rock University,
Slippery Rock ,PA16057, USA
E-mail: hongbo.zhou@sru.edu

The cultivation of programming skills is the essential goal of professional education in application-oriented universities. To address the problems in the professional education of computer science undergraduate students in the two courses, C Programming Language and Data Structure, the paper introduces the current knowledge structure of the two courses. It then reconstructs the modularized education content focused on the data object, and proposes the curricular structure of Teach after Study. It can improve the practical teaching system that is currently driven by assignments and projects, optimize the assessment system, and eventually lead to the curriculum integration of C Programming Language & Data Structure and pedagogy based on the cultivation of programming skills.

Keywords: Application-oriented university; Curricular structure; Practical teaching; Assessment system; Curriculum integration.

1. Introduction

In June 2014, the State Department published the Decision of State Department to Accelerate Development of Modern Professional Education, aiming to promote the professional education to undergraduate level. There are increasing numbers of local undergraduate colleges that redirect their objective of talent cultivation into the application-oriented education according to the local economy and the demands of the society. Their faculty and administration follow the career demands and professional skills development, discuss the innovative education methods, establish the education ideas to improve students' practical and creative ability , which becomes the key of the educational reform.

There are three elements in the integrated professional ability: core ability based on general standard, professional ability based on practical application, and continuous creative ability. As a typical engineering major, computer science undergraduate major requires a lot on practical application ability. As a result, the development of professional ability of computer science students in application-oriented university is a key issue.

The program design ability is an essential capability of the computer undergraduate major university students. In order to let the students establish the way of problem solving with computer and have the basic ability to design programs using tools. In most of the application-oriented university, C programming, Data Structure and related course design are arranged as the first stage of program design ability cultivation in computer majors, Traditional teaching mode set these two courses separately, The understanding between the knowledge and technology are missed， and negative practice effects. Therefore， to discuss the educational mode of C programming & Data Structure integration, to strengthen energetically the practice and application of the program design foundation course, to improve the teaching quality, it is significant beneficial to reform teaching, education innovation, and it is beneficial to cultivate creative talents of computer undergraduate major.

2. The Cultivation Methods of Practical Software Developing Ability in Computer Science Undergraduate Major

Take the major of Computer Science and Technology as an example. According to the surveys of companies and analysis of job-hunting websites, the practical software developing ability is the crucial competence of computer science and technology students. Fig.1 presents the methods to cultivate this kind of ability in the students of computer science and technology.

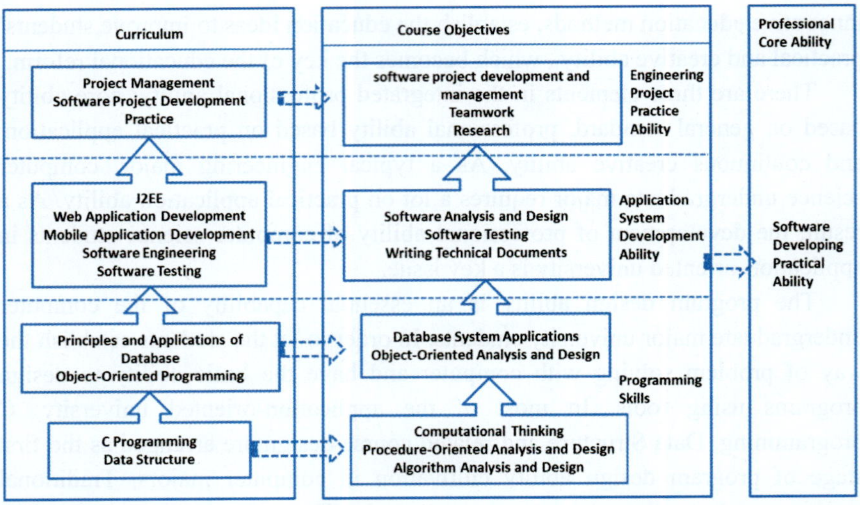

Fig. 1. The cultivation methods of practical software developing ability.

Practical software developing ability is a core ability of computer science undergraduate major. It takes more than several courses to cultivate and improve. This ability has to be built up gradually. The programming ability is the base, which requires the whole curriculum of the cultivation of practical software programming ability. It starts with the procedure-oriented program design, followed by two fundamental courses, *C Programming Language* and *Data Structure*. Thus, the students will develop their abilities of logical thinking, data abstraction, and computational thinking [1], so to solve real application problems with programming languages.

3. Modularization and Exploration of Pedagogical Methods on *C Programming Language & Data Structure* Courses

3.1. *The status quo and the problems of fundamental programming courses*

In most of the application-oriented universities, *C Programming Language*, *Data Structure,* and related courses are arranged as the first stage in the cultivation of programming skills in computer majors, as the experts of ACM/IEEE-CS stated in CS2013. Traditional teaching sets these two courses separately, and makes the courses loosely connected. They are taught in two semesters and by different teachers, first *C Programming Language*, then *Data Structure.* Thus, it makes the theme of knowledge structure less clear.

3.1.1. *The integration of the knowledge and technology is absent*

In the conventional curriculum of *C Programming Language* course, students spend plenty of time on the usage of syntax, but neglect the application of programming cases. Meanwhile in *Data Structure*, they focus too much on the logical and storage structure of data. Students' understanding of Data Structure stays on the basic level. They do not fully master the complex concepts and modularized functions such as arrays, structures and pointers in C, the implementation of algorithms, the storage and processing of chained lists, and so on. Thus, the students eventually get a negative education experience.

3.1.2. *Negative practice effects*

Lecture is the main form of pedagogy, with programming exercise as an aid in the traditional curriculum. As a result, there is not enough practice time. Most of programming assignments are simply based on imitation or proof. They are loosely connected to practical projects. Thus, the students are not motivated. All these factors lead to poor programming skills in the students [2].

3.1.3. *Isolated exam method*

It is common that the students are always assessed by the final exam for the whole semester, which apparently contradicts the purpose of cultivation of one's abilities.

3.2. *Modularized programming skills-oriented curricular design*

Curricular design refers to the process of choosing, organizing, and arranging course elements. Course elements usually include the objectives, contents, activities, and methods. The fundamental of practice and research has five stages, as illustrated in Fig 2[3].

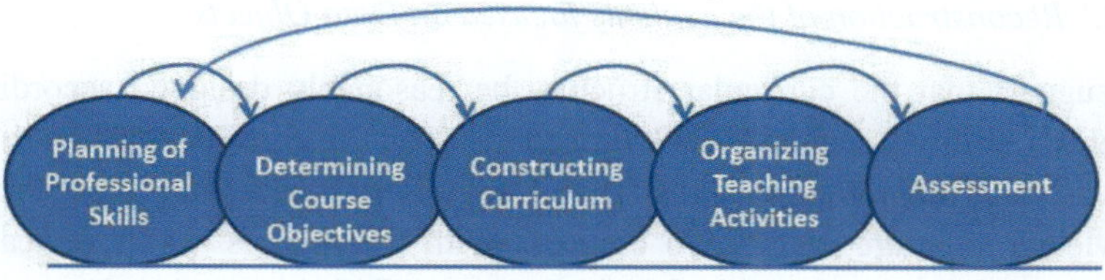

Fig. 2. Fundamental course design mode.

The most basic professional ability of a computer science underground student is programming skills. The educational objectives driven by the curricular integration of *C Programming Language* and *Data Structure* are:

- Approach the problem from the computer's point of view;
- Develop computational thinking ability and procedure-oriented design method;
- Be able to choose a reasonable computer storage structure and to design efficient algorithm for non-numerical calculation problems;
- Accomplish the project with readable and clear C programs, testing examples, and technical report to develop independent design and procedure-oriented ability;
- Develop creative thinking ability.

3.2.1. *Modularized curricular plan*

We propose to create an independent curriculum that combines *C Programming Language* and *Data Structure*, as illustrated in Fig 3. It consists of multiple modules focused on the students' programming skills, to provide students gradual training on knowledge and practice.

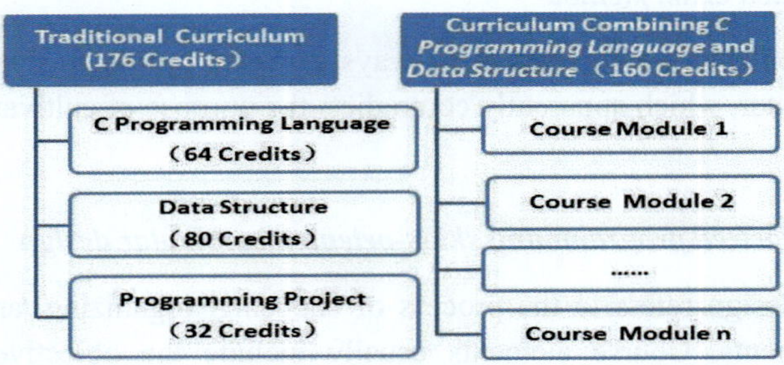

Fig. 3. Modularized course constructing plan.

3.2.2. *Reconstruction of the contents focused on Data Objects*

We suggest that the curricular structure be reasonably designed according to students' ability, standards of procedure, and features to achieve ideal cultivation of programming skills. Therefore, it is very necessary to organize the knowledge structure in the two courses. With the authors' years of teaching experience, we propose a modularized course *C Programming Language & Data Structure* to be constructed driven by Data Objects. It is scheduled to be in one semester. With modules being presented gradually, it can achieve the objectives of cultivating students' programming skills. Meanwhile, these two separate courses are merged into one, as in Fig. 4.

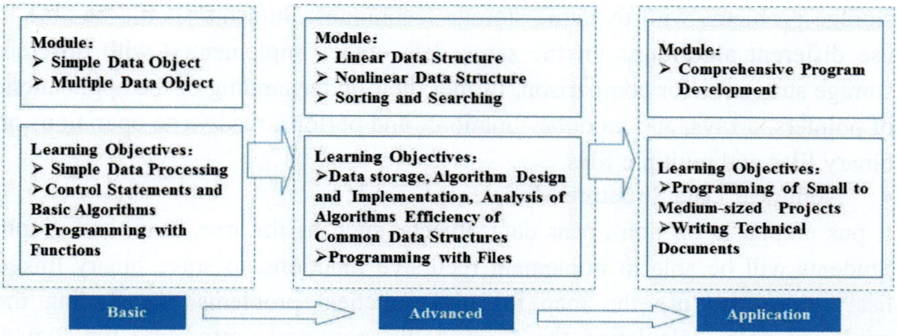

Fig. 4. The modularized course structure driven by data object.

The basic rules of building this structure is to reorganize the contents of two original courses. On the one hand, the new course introduces data structures and algorithms gradually based on the main theme of Data Objects, and placing the difficult topics from two courses into different modules. On the other hand, it sets separate learning objectives of the modules, and forms cultivation methods to improve students' practical programming skills. The contents of all the modules are as follows:

- Simple Data Module

It starts from the basic data types of integer, real number, and character, and lets the students use four basic control statements – sequential statements, conditional statements, loops, and self-defined functions- to write programs with correct grammar and logic. The students will learn to use pointers to pass the data between functions, to write code to read from and write to data files, and to deal with simple data processing and storage problem.

- Multiple Data Module

It deals with single and multiple dimension arrays consisting of basic data types. It lets students implement typical algorithms such as input, output, data access, counting, search, insertion, deletion, and sorting operations. The students will be able to access the array element with pointers, pass array data between functions, to further improve the use of pointers, modular design with functions, and read/write procedures of text file. They can solve the problem of batch processing and storage.

- Linear Data Structure Module

It focuses on linear data structure like lists, stacks, queues, and linked lists. It enables students to solve sequential storage problems with arrays and chained storage problems with dynamic storage techniques. Students should be able to use different algorithms on the same data object implemented with different storage structures for comparison, further their understanding of the applications of pointers, arrays, and modular functions, and perform read/write operations on binary files and multiple files.

- Nonlinear Data Structure Module

It pus emphasis on non-linear data objects, such as the tree, map, and graph. Students will be able to implement recursive functions, to solve binary linked list problem, to use the map to solve practical problems like finding the minimum path, calculating the shortest distance, and performing topological sorting. It further improves students' ability to create algorithms for complex datatype in complex storage scheme.

- Sorting and Searching Module

It covers the data object of sequential list structures. After this module, students can design and analyze some classic sorting or search algorithms, choose and implement the most efficient algorithm when it comes to some practical problem.

- Comprehensive Program Development Module

Its topic is on general practical application problems. The module trains students to choose the reasonable data storage structures, build efficient algorithms, write a complete program, design testing examples, do the program testing, and write a technical report.

In the construction of the modules mentioned above, the topics will be focused on the data object designed in C. *C Programming Language* and *Data Structure* will be merged into the educational objective of cultivating students' programming skills. The contents are organized in a nested loop structure, to teach students in a gradual and effective way.

3.3. *The exploration of ability cultivation oriented pedagogical methods*

There are four components in programming skills: computational thinking, algorithm analysis and design, programming, and system analysis and implementation. The key to improve the skills is to improve the pedagogical methods.

3.3.1. *Cultivate computational thinking from beginning to end*

To improve students' computational thinking ability is the goal of *C programming & Data Structure*. Basically, a program is the implementation of algorithms plus data structures. Therefore, the grammar-oriented education has to be transformed to problem-oriented by choosing the right data structure for the problem, translating it into algorithms, and solving the problem in C programming language. As a result, the learning experience switches from being exposed to separate topics to computational thinking methods and problem solving procedures, in order to train the students' thinking [4].

3.3.2. *The student-centered pedagogy*

The traditional pedagogy is driven by the instructors, which makes the students passive receivers and less motivated [5].They simply recite the answers or programs, but are not able to solve unseen problems on themselves. In the student-centered pedagogy, students become proactive, while the instructor is merely a coach. The active participation of students in the class will intrigue their interest in programming. So it is necessary to transform the pedagogy from Teaching First to Teach After Study. The difference of two pedagogies are presented in Fig 5.

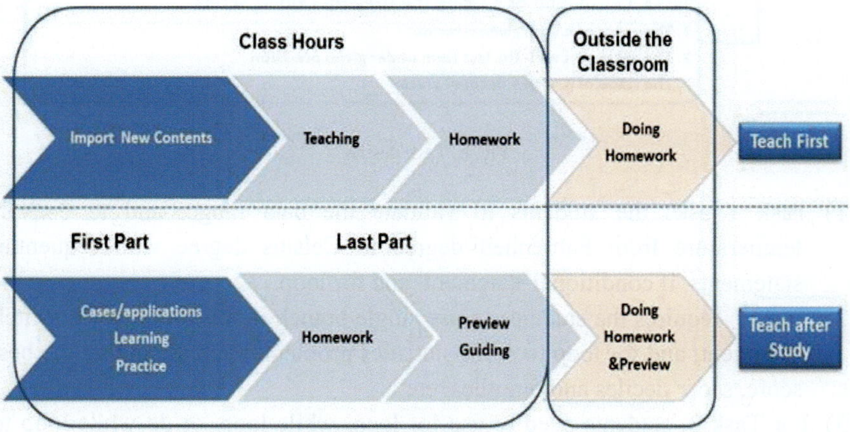

Fig. 5. The comparison of class teaching structure.

In the learning process of Teach After Study, the instructor functions as a coach to let the students study while programming. The first step is to move the class from a multi-media classroom to a computer lab. The class session is then divided into three parts. They are Cases/Applications, Learning, and Practice. We can use the teaching process of Simple Data module as an example.

- Cases/Applications

Fig 6 shows 3 teaching tasks combined with the problems in the daily life. The contents of tasks follow the rule of "simple to difficult, specific to abstract, individual to general". Students will be trained to recognize the connection between the program code and its running results, visualize the code, and intrigue their interest on programming[6]. The students will have the ability to use the three basic control statements: sequential statements, conditionals, and loops.

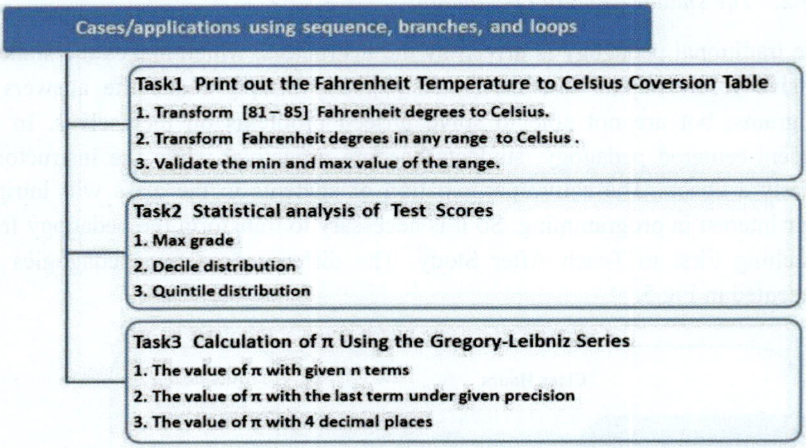

Fig. 6. Task design.

(1) Task 1 asks the students to validate the data range, and to convert temperature from Fahrenheit degree to Celsius degree with sequential statements, if conditional statement, and for loop.

(2) Task 2 requires the students to use single branch if, multi-branch if, switch statement, and for loop to solve statistics problems such as finding the best score, score deciles and quintiles, etc.

(3) For Task 3, students need to use for loop, while loop, or do-while loop to solve problems like calculating π's value to get the specified precision [6].

All these tasks are practical problems.

When picking the tasks, the instructor needs to know the students' interests. With divide and conquer methodology, the solving process can inspires their exploratory nature, and broaden their horizon. If the instructor always follow the three stages of task analysis, algorithm design, and coding, the students will get used to approaching the problem from computer's point of view, analyzing the problem, and describing the solution with pseudo-code[7].

- Learning

The pedagogy of Cases/Applications avoids the one-way teaching. The problem solving process is combined with new ways and knowledge of real-life problems, in order to inspire their critical thinking. Meanwhile, the instructor can deliberately give them the codes with errors, so that they get a chance to strengthen the knowledge by running and debugging the program.

- Practice

The best way to know if the students can apply their knowledge into practice is to test them with separate program design. Since they have been guided by their critical thinking ability in previous examples, now they will develop their problem analysis and solving ability, and will follow the same procedure to solve similar new problems.

3.3.3. *The cultivation of project-oriented practical application ability*

The teaching method driven by projects will be in the advanced stage of programming. For instance, students are working on the Student Basic Information Management System project. This project integrates data structures, data file processing, graphical user interface design, multi-module multi-file program design, linear data structure sequential storage and chained storage, classic sort and search algorithms, etc. The project not only inspires their interest, it also improves their ability of applying the knowledge in practice.

It is the goal of the course that the students can finish the course design independently. Class projects are in parallel to the development of practical application. With the teaching method focused on practical problem solving in the first stage, students will not fear the difficulty in programming. Instead, they should have already gained experience in software project analysis, design and implementation, and been adept at writing well-formed code. The curricular design will dramatically improve their ability in computational thinking, program debugging, problem solving, and creative thinking.

3.4. *The practice of diversified and procedure-based test method*

The university of one of authors working at has started to adopt the new assessment system for all the courses since 2013. It is based on procedure-based "1 + X" test method, in which "X" stands for the at least three procedure-based exam throughout a semester, and 1 is for the final exam. The test method of *C Programming Language & Data Structure* is driven by "Skill Test" combined with the features of modularized curriculum. It is based on the platform of distance education to put emphasis on the procedure-based "X" exams. Thus, it establishes a diversified test method to examine students' skills, knowledge, and creative thinking. The System is presented in Table 1.

Table 1. Course assessment system.

Assessment Format	Assessment Objectives	Assessment Standard	Percent	Stages		
				Basic	Advanced	Application
Online Discussion	Participation of students after class	Time spent in forum and number of posts	5%	√	√	√
Online Test	Understanding of fundamental knowledge	Correct answers to multiple choice questions, True/False question, fill-in-the blank questions	10%	√	√	
In-class assignments	Knowledge application based on in-class exploratory assignments	The quality and completeness of solutions	10%	√	√	
Programming test	Programming and debugging	Program grading rubric	30%	√		
Written test of analysis and application	Classic data structures, storage, and algorithms	Written test results	30%		√	
Comprehensive programming test	Project implementation, documentation, presentation, and innovation	Efficiency and results	15%			√

The assessment of teaching effectiveness is as important as assessment of the students. The assessment in each stage can expose the problems during the teaching by providing feedback, so that the contents and pedagogy can be revised. Since Fall semester in 2014, the author used the exams mentioned above in *C Programming Language & Data Structure* with computer science undergraduate majors, and the results are presented in Fig 7.

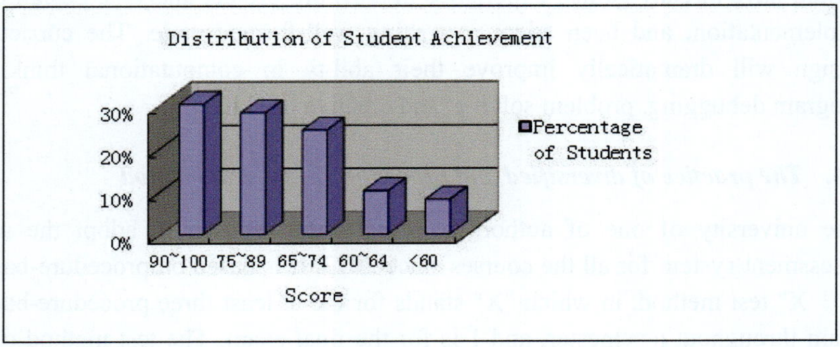

Fig. 7. Score distribution of procedured-based exams.

As Fig 7 shows, the percentage of students with good programming skills is near 59%. Nearly 92% of students passed the course. It aligns with Mr. Benjamin Bloom's observation, who was a famous educator. He noticed that given optimal pedagogical methods and enough learning time, the distribution of student's grades should not be normal distribution. Instead, most of them will accomplish learning task and earn good grades. He believed at least 90% of students should have solid understanding of the contents with appropriate methods.

4. Conclusion

Programming skills are the key factor of marketability in computer science undergraduate. With the authors' years of teaching experience, the reform of modularized curricular design, pedagogical method innovation, and assessment system based on merging *C Programming language* and *Data Structure*, along with the interactive course website on campus courseware center, has already made achievements on teaching of the new course *C Programming Language & Data Structure*.

References

1. Dan Jia. The research of education thought and teaching method of object-oriented data structure [J]. Changchun Normal College Paper: Nature Science Part, 2006(4): 130-132.
2. Yupenghu, Rui Li, LijunCai, etc. Implementation and research of data structure course education mode of model software college [J]. Education teaching forum, 2011(29): 195-197.
3. Zemin Deng, Qinghe Chen. Career Education Course Design [M]. China Railway Publication. 2006: 80-81.
4. Xiaohong Su, WanxaingChe, Tiantian Wang, etc. How to cultivate computational thinking in the program design courses [J]. Computer Education. 2011(14): 102-105.
5. Lianjun Chen, Qingting Zhu. The C programming Teaching Research driven by ability cultivation. Computer Education [J]. 2011(14): 102-105.
6. Huayou Si, Yun Zhao, Xiangui Luo. Program Design Ability Cultivation Explore based on C programming [J]. Computer Time, 2008(3): 68-69.
7. Xu Huang. Student Program Design Ability Cultivation Mode of Application Undergraduate University [J]. Computer Education, 2015(4): 8-10.

Construction of a Campus Cloud Platform to Improve Students' Course Selection

Ying ZHANG*, Shu-yuan SHANG and Hai-bo ZHANG

Computer information center, Beijing Institute Of Fashion Technology, Beijing, China

**jsjzhy@bift.edeu.cn*

Currently, there is an increasing dependence on the educational administration system in colleges and universities. As the educational administration system supports the school teaching resources, the massive access pressure during course selection is a problem that is becoming increasingly prominent. We propose the construction of a cloud platform to pool all physical servers and the setting up of virtual machines. During course selection, the cloud platform can increase or decrease the number of virtual machines automatically through the load elastic flexible configuration and the monitoring of parameters such as the number of requests and CPU usage. This greatly improves the efficiency of course selection and student satisfaction while significantly reducing server hardware expenditure and raising the efficiency of maintenance and operations.

Keywords: Cloud platform; Course selection; Load balancing; Elastic group; Virtualization.

1. Introduction

Educational administration management is the core management of the school. The development of the educational administration system represents the development of university informatization [1]. Since our school's educational administration management system was put into use, it has effectively supported the school daily teaching. However, with the continuous development of network information technology, the course selection problem is becoming more and more prominent, and student course selection has become the school periodically thorny issues. At the selection course time of each semester, students begin to constantly refresh the page day and night. Whether students can login the system all by luck. The access pressure often leads the system into crashing, so even some students login into the course system, they may not be able to select course successfully. At the same time, in order to disperse course selection pressure, system administrator needs to build several application servers in advance, to know the number of the students for each department group, and then according to the distribution of students, provides a url for each group, and then departments inform their students to login with the different course selection url. In the process of course selection, system administrator needs to keep watch of each server in the state of the CPU, memory, and so on, constantly to restart the application server. The system administrator keeps busy still unable to provide satisfactory services.

Above the cause of the problem is due to the infrastructure architecture does not have the flexible callable and extensibility. In the early days of the construction of campus informatization, the educational administration system is deployed in one to several servers, the server hardware resources is not easy to extend. During the course once application load beyond the server load, the server will be to restart, then the student course selection will not be successful.

If we can unify all server resources to the resource pool, use the load balancing, dynamically extend resources to meet the needs of application, then will be able to solve the problem easily. Colleges need an IT infrastructure which can automatically extend resources according to the business needs [2]. Through constructing a cloud platform, flexibly deploy the pooling of physical resources, not only can easily solve the problem of students' course selection, also can free the system administrator from tedious work, this will be greatly improve the work efficiency, reduce the maintenance cost.

2. Cloud Platform

2.1. *Introduction*

Our cloud platform functions cover all kinds of technology which are needed to implement the strategy of cloud computing. Such as server virtualization, distributed storage, load balance simulator, database deployment automation, cloud management platform, DevOps, large data processing, SDN, operational billing and so on.

At the bottom of the cloud platform is the core part of the platform, it is responsible for scheduling, management and monitoring of the resources on the cloud platform, including processor, memory, computational resources and virtual logical volume management, volume snapshots storage management, network resource management and monitoring tasks[3].

The second is the platform service layer, it is the open layer of the core layer, and it is the soul of the cloud platform. Service layer provides various types of services through using the ability of computing, storage, and network which are provided by core layer. These services include some basic services such as EC2 service which can provide the server on demand, EBS service which can add disk for the server, LB service which can do load balancing for application services and so on, also include some cross services such as AutoScale service which can automatically adjust the server’s scale on demand, monitoring CloudWatch service for various resources, MapReduce service which can provide parallel and distributed computation for huge amounts of data[4].

3. Platform Construction

Cloud platform has been built by 9 HuaWei 2285 servers. Each server configuration is as follows: CPU is Intel Xeon (R) (R) E5-2420 v2 @ 2.20 GHz, memory is 128 g, hard disk 300 g * 6, the 9 units (NC01 - NC09) roles are shown in figure 1.

Roles
CLC+CC1+MysqlHA+Bfs+NC
CLC+CC1+MysqlHA+BfsM1+NC
BfsHA+Bfs+NC
BfsHA+Bfs+NC
Bfs+NC
Bfs+NC
Bfs+NC
Bfs+NC
Bfs+NC

Fig. 1. Server role function.

The NC01 and NC02 two serve as the cloud controller, cluster controller, MySQL database, and metadata backup of distributed storage, etc.

The NC03 and NC04 two serve as distributed storage metadata HA role.

The NC01 - NC09 nine servers are served for the distributed storage section (provide distributed storage disk space) and the compute nodes.

After the platform construction is completed, the formal tree diagram is shown in figure 2[5] .

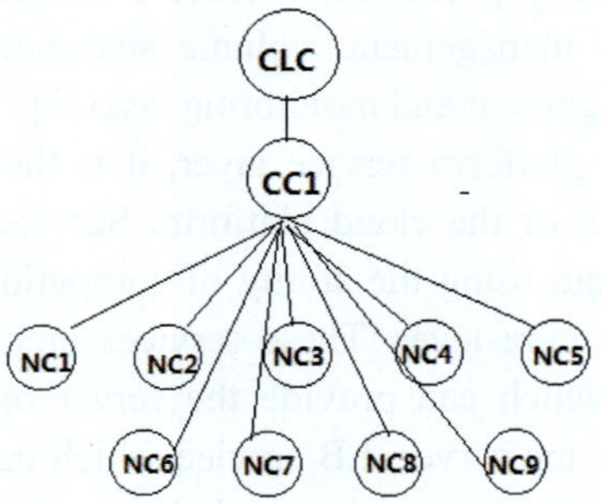

Fig. 2. The formal tree diagram.

4. Instance Deployment

4.1. *Migration of Educational administration system*

In the cloud platform choose RedHat5.5 mirror to build a new virtual machine, instance scale is defined as the CPU: 6, memory: 16g, extend the disk: 40 GB. After packaged the educational administration system on the physical server, we redeploy it in the new virtual machine, and define the educational security group to isolate it from the other application systems on network firewall. Through the above approach to ensure that each application runs alone in their own group, avoids unnecessary network attack. Thus, network security will be greatly improved. Deployment instance is shown in figure 3.

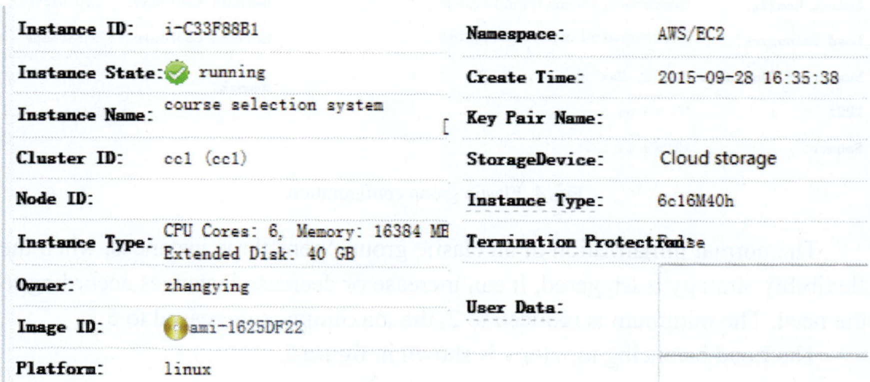

Fig. 3. Educational administration system instance.

4.2. *Elastic load balancing*

Because the undergraduate educational administration system undertakes the task of course selection, its characteristic is that in course selection stageitneeds more server service, in the non-course selection stage, only needs a small amount of server support. After moved to the cloud platform, the system can be applied with load and elastic cloud platform strategy, it will automatically increase virtual machine instances to meet the needs of students' course selection according to the dimensional parameters such as CPU utilization, the number of requests, etc., and at the end of the course it will release the virtual service resources automatically.

4.2.1. *Deployment*

First, we create a new load balancer for the educational administration system, and then create a new startup configuration which is specified in the use of system mirror and security group. And then create a new Elastic group for the educational administration system, assign the above load balancer to the elastic group, and initialize the maximum, minimum, and the required number of the instance, and configure the strategy for the group to increase and decrease instances. Elastic group configuration is shown in figure 4.

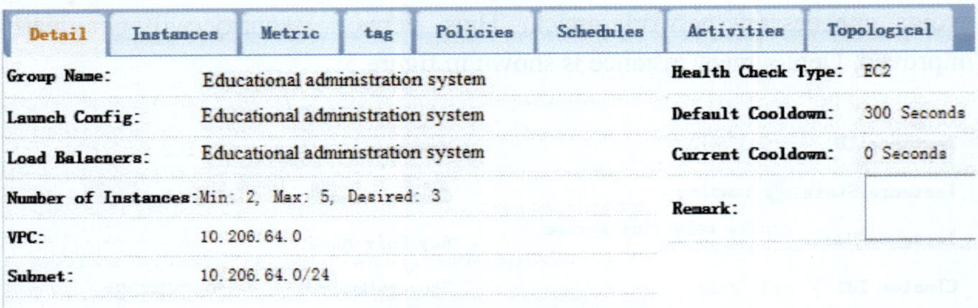

Fig. 4. Elastic group configuration.

The normal initialization of an elastic group opens three instances, when the flexibility strategy is triggered, it can increase or decrease instances according to the need. The minimum is reduced to 2, the maximum is increased to 5.

The Load balancing topology is shown in figure 5.

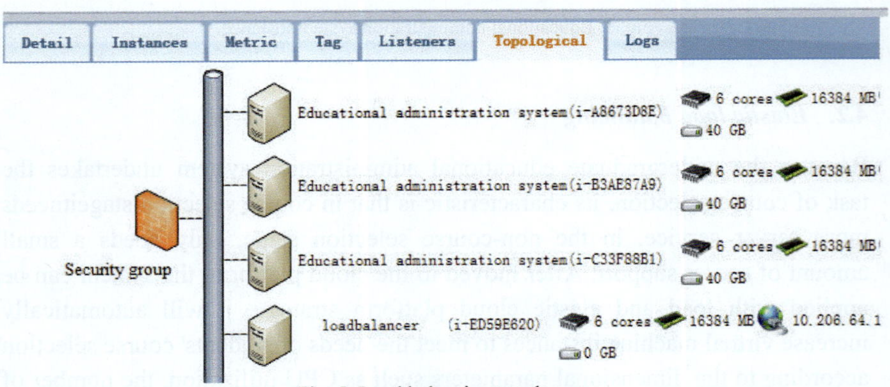

Fig. 5. Load balancing topology.

4.2.2. *Course selection*

On the day of the course selection around 3200 students are expected, and the actual number is 3072. During the peak of the two hours of the course selection, the monitoring data of the elastic group is shown in Figure 6. From the picture we can see that the reading and writing numbers on disk has reached the peak.

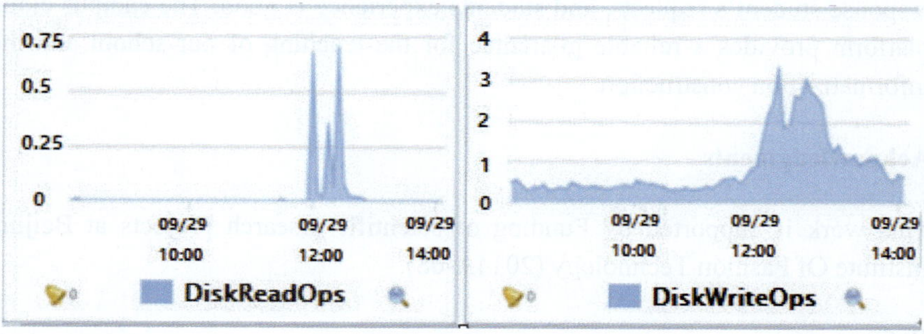

Fig. 6. Elastic group monitoring.

Figure 7 is the peak of load balance monitoring, from the graph we can see that the peak number of the request has exceeded 400.

Fig. 7. Load balancing monitoring.

5. Conclusion

After educational administration system has migrated to the cloud platform, its performance is greatly enhanced. In the selection stage, with the increase of the number of course selection, the system which equipped with a load balancing will automatically increase or decrease the number of virtual machines by monitoring the number of requests and the usage of CPU, in this way to ensure the success rate of the students. The platform automatically increases or decreases virtual machines' number without human intervention. During the peak of course selection, system equipped with five virtual machines can hold 100 students per second to visit at the same time, the cloud platform automatically expands and recycles resources, thus to improve the utilization of resources. In the whole process of course selection, the platform can quickly response student's requests, and students experience is good. The campus cloud platform provides a reliable guarantee for the teaching of our school and the informatization construction.

Acknowledgments

This work is supported by Funding of scientific research projects at Beijing Institute Of Fashion Technology (2014A-08).

References

1. Xiaolong. Fu, Hua. Xuan, Fang. Yuan, Qixin. Liu, The design and implementation of a new generation of comprehensive educational administration system, *Experimental Technology and Management, 04*, 2011, 95-100. In Chinese
2. Shuang. Dai, H3C:Bring cloud change for college course, *China Education informationization*, *14*, 2015, 91-92. In Chinese
3. Wanyun. Lei, *Cloud computing — the technology, platform and application cases* (Beijing, China: Tsinghua University press, 2011). In Chinese
4. Thomas ERL, *Cloud Computing Concepts, Technology& Architecture* (Beijing, China: China Machine press, 2014).
5. Liang. Zhang, Bingbing. Fan, Weiping. Zheng, Research on the migration method of cloud platform application system, *Computer Science*, *S1*, 2013, 271-275. In Chinese

Robust PID Controller for AR Drone

Jin-hong SUN
Department of Electronic Engineering, City University of Hong Kong
HKSAR, China
E-mail: jhsun3-c@my.cityu.edu.hk

L.L. CHENG
Department of Electronic Engineering, City University of Hong Kong
HKSAR, China
E-mail: itacheng@cityu.edu.hk

This paper proposes an integral predictive control strategy, a hierarchical scheme consisting of the Runge-kutta controller and PID controller to stabilize the rotational movements of the AR Drone. The Runge-kutta algorithm can predict states in advance and hence we utilize this robust algorithm to build the Runge-kutta controller. The control strategy combining both the Runge-kutta controller and PID controller can be considered as a Robust PID controller, which improves the drone's robust performance especially when flying at high speed. The controller reduces the positioning error in conditions of continuous disturbances in the operation environment. The experimental results demonstrate that the Robust PID controller possess good accuracy and robustness in drone control for both indoor and outdoor environments.

Keywords: Integral predictive; Runge-Kutta controller; PID controller; Robust PID controller; AR Drone.

1. Introduction

Till now, The drone's path following problem was settled by many different methods, for instance, the exact linearization and non-interacting control in a dynamic modeling of the quadrotor[1], the IMC position controller and PID controller[2].However, these controllers do not consider the influence of external interferences. The FLC was proposed and implemented on AR Drone to solve the drone's motion problems[3]. However, the above controllers are still not able to solve the lagging problem especially when the drone's following path has one turn or more.

In order to solve these problems, this paper puts forward a hierarchical controller, and defines the Runge-kutta controller as the forward controller, the PID controller as the backward controller.

2. Control Strategy

This controller is designed as a hierarchical scheme: the forward controller is build based on the fourth order Runge-kutta algorithm; the backward controller can calculate the data output by the forward controller.

The attitude parameters can be calculated and considered as the forward controller's input values. After under the fourth order Runge-kutta calculation, these parameters can be output. Then they are continue considered as the backward controller's input values.

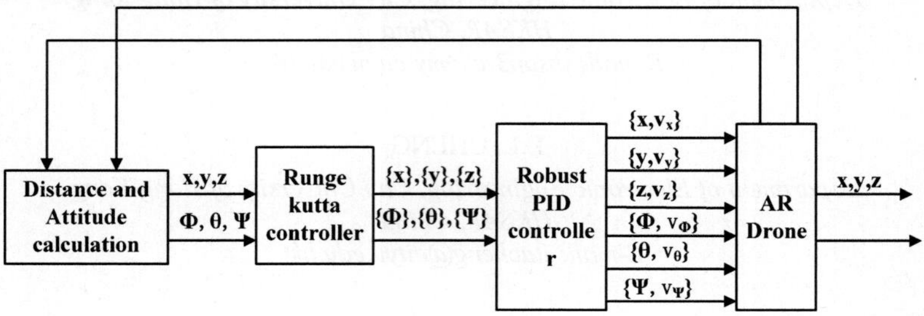

Fig. 1. The block diagram of this controller.

2.1. *Runge–Kutta controller*

This controller is built based on fourth order Runge-Kutta algorithm, which main principle is to do interpolation in the integrating range [x, x + d] and predict the update results $\hat{y}(x+d)$ through using the current one y(x). It can get a more accuracy result than directly do the integral calculation.

$$\hat{y}(x+d) = y(x) + \frac{d(K_1+2K_2+2K_3+K_4)}{6}. \tag{1}$$

$$K_1 = y(x),\quad K_2 = y(x) + \frac{K_1}{2},\quad K_3 = y(x) + \frac{K_2}{2},\quad K_4 = y(x) + \frac{K_3}{2}. \tag{2}$$

First of all, the parameters of AR Drone based on the drone's dynamic and kinematic equation sets should be calculated.

$$K = \frac{\Delta t \times U_1 \times (\sin\Psi\sin\Phi + \cos\Psi\sin\theta\cos\Phi) - f_x}{m}$$

$$L = \frac{\Delta t \times U_1 \times (\sin\Psi\sin\theta\cos\Phi - \cos\Psi\sin\Phi) - f_y}{m}$$

$$M = \frac{\Delta t \times U_1 \times (\cos\Psi\cos\Phi) - f_z}{m}$$

$$N = \Delta t \times \frac{dx}{dt} O = \Delta t \times \frac{dy}{dt} P = \Delta t \times \frac{dz}{dt}$$

$$Q = \frac{\Delta t \times [U_2 \times l - \frac{d\theta}{dt}\frac{d\Psi}{dt}(I_Z - I_Y)]}{I_X}$$

$$R = \frac{\Delta t \times [U_3 \times l - \frac{d\Phi}{dt}\frac{d\Psi}{dt}(I_X - I_Z)]}{I_Y}$$

$$S = \frac{\Delta t \times [U_4 \times l - \frac{d\theta}{dt}\frac{d\theta}{dt}(I_Y - I_X)]}{I_Z}$$

$$T = \Delta t \times \frac{d\Phi}{dt} U = \Delta t \times \frac{d\theta}{dt} V = \Delta t \times \frac{d\Psi}{dt}. \quad (3)$$

$$K = v_x, L = v_y, M = v_z, N = x, O = y, P = z$$

$$Q = v_\Phi, R = v_\theta, S = v_\Psi, T = \Phi, U = \theta, V = \Psi$$

2.2. *Robust PID controller*

After calculating the drone's parameters under the forward controller, {K…V} are output and continue used as the input values of the backward controller.

The first step is to calculate the drone's parameters based on equation (3), then get values like $\{K_1 \ldots V_1\}$; The second step is to update the drone's current parameters based on equation (2), then update values of $\{K_2 \ldots V_2\}$:

$$v_{x_2} = v_{x_1} + \frac{K_1}{2} v_{y_2} = v_{y_1} + \frac{L_1}{2} v_{z_2} = v_{z_1} + \frac{M_1}{2}$$

$$x_2 = x_1 + \frac{N_1}{2} y_2 = y_1 + \frac{O_1}{2} z_2 = z_1 + \frac{P_1}{2}$$

$$\frac{d\Phi_2}{dt} = \frac{d\Phi_1}{dt} + \frac{Q_1}{2} \frac{d\theta_2}{dt} = \frac{d\theta_1}{dt} + \frac{R_1}{2} \frac{d\Psi_2}{dt} = \frac{d\Psi_1}{dt} + \frac{S_1}{2}$$

$$\Phi_2 = \Phi_1 + \frac{T_1}{2} \theta_2 = \theta_1 + \frac{U_1}{2} \Psi_2 = \Psi_1 + \frac{V_1}{2}$$

The third and fourth steps are similar to step two. Besides, in the fourth step, the drone's next time parameter values can be predicted through equation (1):

$$v_x = v_{x_4} + \frac{(K_1 + 2K_2 + 2K_3 + K_4)}{6}$$

$$v_y = v_{y_4} + \frac{(L_1 + 2L_2 + 2L_3 + L_4)}{6}$$

.

.

.

$$\Psi = \Psi_4 + \frac{(V_1 + 2V_2 + 2V_3 + V_4)}{6}$$

$$a = \frac{(v_Z - v_{Z_4})}{\Delta t}$$

$$F_1 = F_2 = F_3 = F_4 = \frac{m(a+g)}{4}$$

$$T_{c_X} = (I_Y - I_X - I_Z) \times d\Psi - K_{P_1} \times \Phi - K_{D_1} \times d\Phi - K_{I_1} \times \Phi_0$$

$$T_{c_y} = -K_{P_2} \times \theta - K_{D_2} \times d\theta - K_{I_2} \times \Phi_0$$

$$T_{c_Z} = (I_X - I_Y + I_Z) \times d\Psi - K_{P_3} \times \Psi - K_{D_3} \times d\Psi - K_{I_3} \times \Psi_0$$

These parameters are finally computed under the PID algorithm, then the drone's attitude can be adjusted and used to control the drone fly steadily.

3. The Simulation Result

3.1. *Selected reason*

Compared to the general PID controller, the PID controller that combined with Runge-kutta method can quickly let the system achieve the steady state. Using a classical lag system model to verify this:

$G(s) = \frac{e^{-10s}}{1.5s+1}$ Where: sampling period T=0.15s; input r(t)=1; step d=3

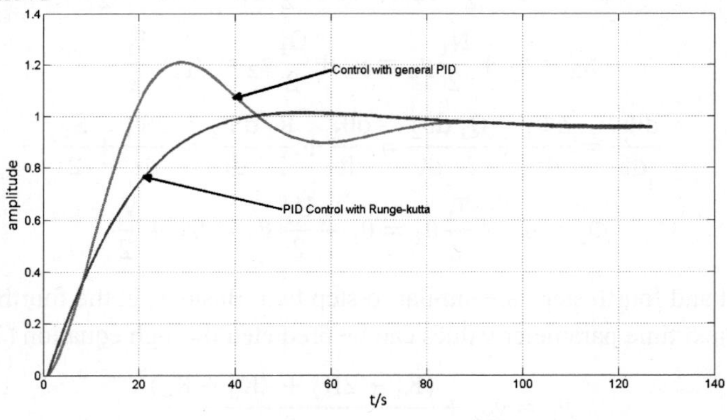

Fig. 2. The response of the control algorithm.

This PID controller can let the system quickly let the lag system achieve flat, almost at 40 second. However, this lag system controlled by the general PID controller has a large overshoot and can't achieve stable until 80 second.

This paper also demonstrates some simulation experiments. First of all, the drone's following path is designed by Gen_Trajectory.m. Then AR Drone can follow this path in the indoor and outdoor environment.

3.2. *Indoor path following*

The following path is designed with four big turns, separately in time 100s, 125s, 150s and 175s. The controller's control performance is mainly reflected in these time quantum. Some results in the indoor environment as following:

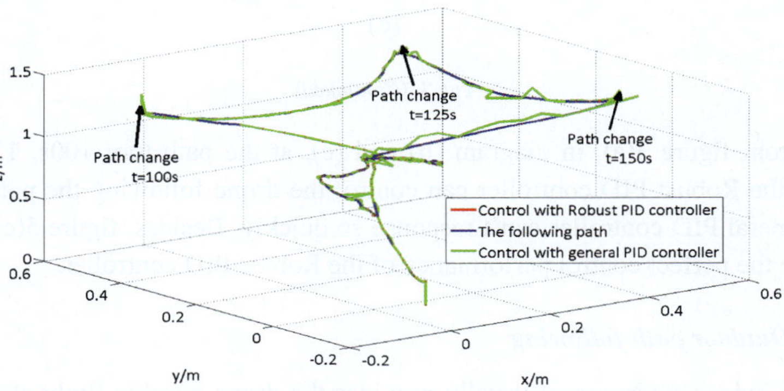

(a)

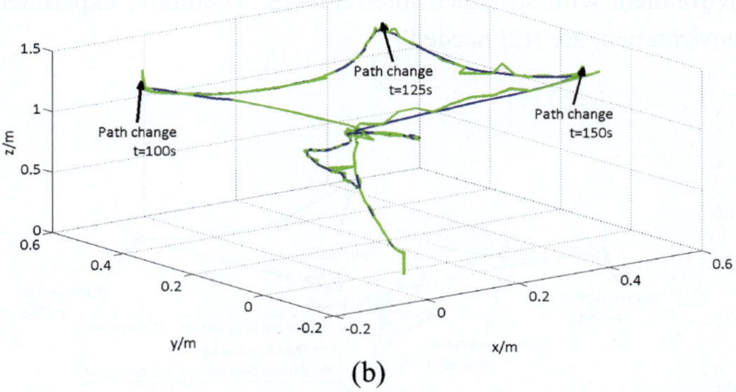

(b)

Fig. 3. Diagram (a) contains the general PID controller's control effect and the Robust PID controller's control effect; diagram(b) only has the general PID controller's control performance; diagram (c)shows the Robust PID controller's control performance.

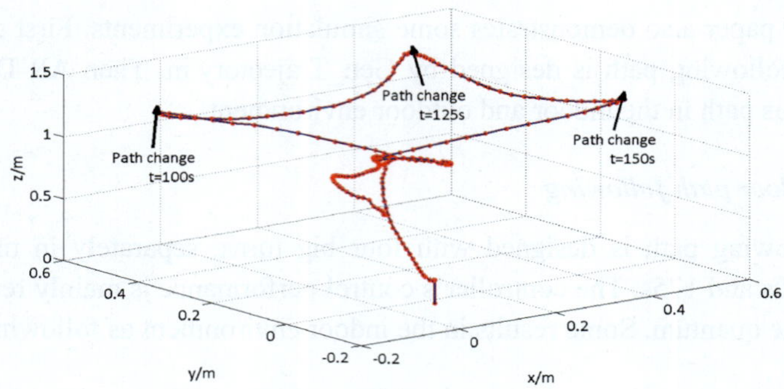

(c)

Fig. 3. (*Continued*)

From figure 3(a), in diagram (b) and (c), at the path turn 100s, 125s and 150s, the Robust PID controller can control the drone following the path while the general PID controller can't response so quickly. Besides, figure 5(c) shows people the perfect control performance of the Robust PID controller.

3.3. *Outdoor path following*

As the indoor environment usually provides the drone a stable flight state, so it can't verify whether the Robust PID controller has a good control performance in the environment with sustained interferences. Therefore, experiments in the outdoor environment are still needed.

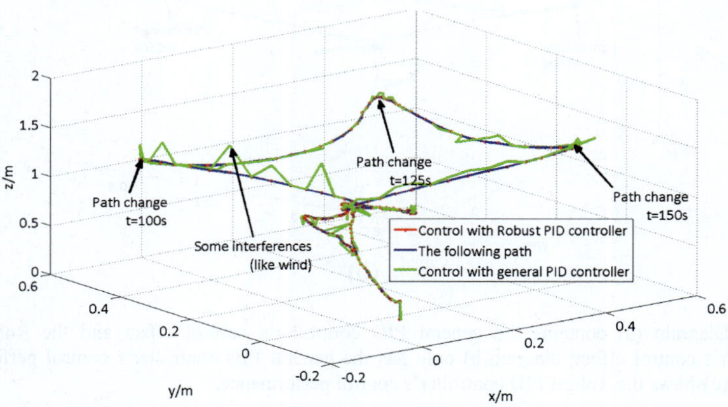

(a)

Fig. 4. Diagram(a) contains the general PID controller's control effect and the Robust PID controller's control effect both in the outdoor environment; diagram (b)only has the general PID controller's control performance; diagram (c)shows the Robust PID controller's control performance.

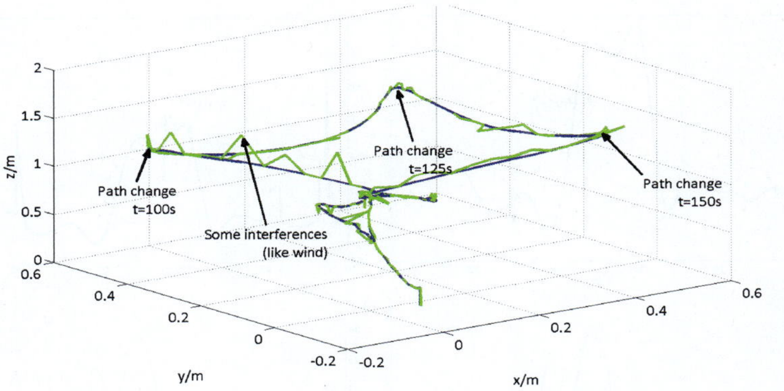

(b)

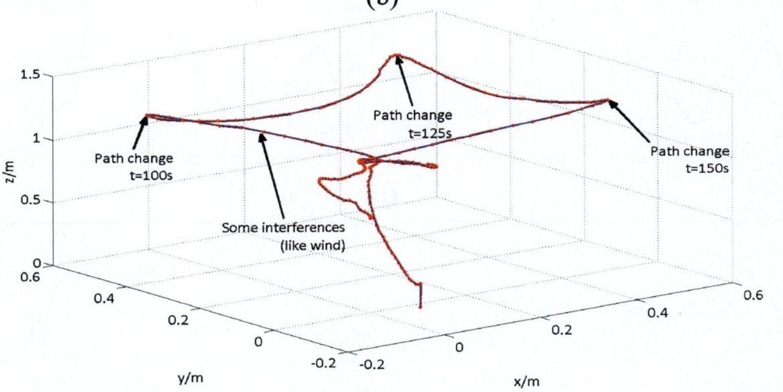

(c)

Fig. 4. (*Continued*)

The control performance in path turns of outdoor is similar to the control performance in the indoor environment. The outdoor experiments mainly contribute to verify whether the Robust PID controller is able to control the drone fly stable in the environment with sustained interferences or not.

During the time period 75s-100s, the sustained interference happened in outdoor environment. Figure 4 (c) demonstrates that the Robust PID controller can control the drone preciously follow the path. While in figure 4 (b), the general PID controller do not has the capability to control the drone fly stable.

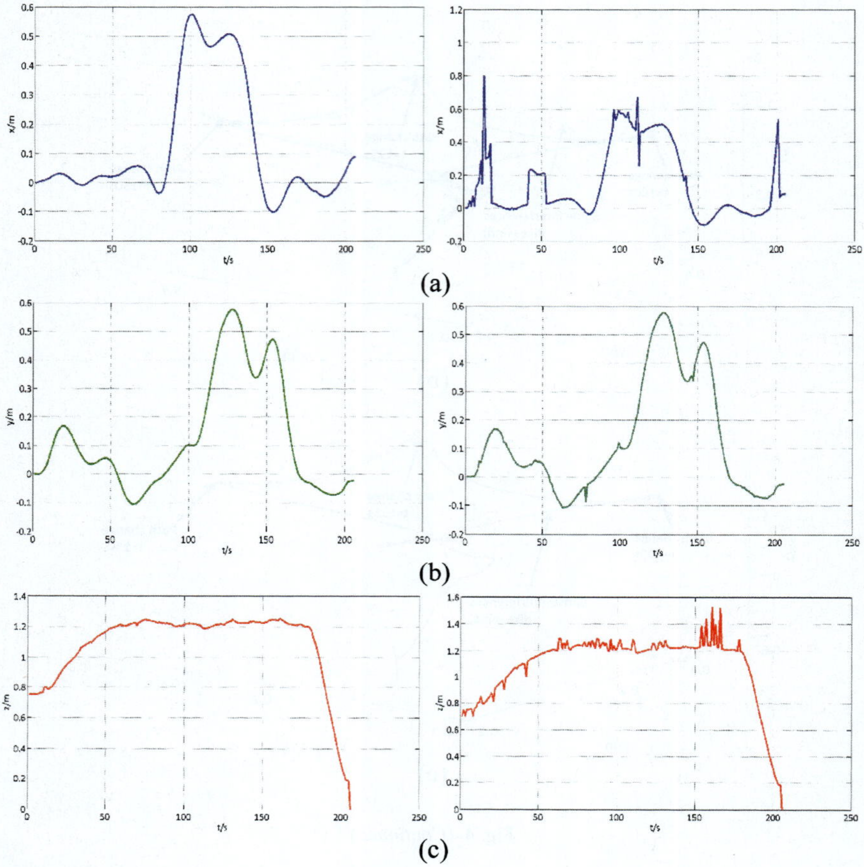

Fig. 5. Diagrams (a) express the x position under the control of general PID controller (right) and the Robust PID controller (left); diagrams(b) express the y position under the control of general PID controller (right) and the Robust PID controller (left); diagrams (c) express the x position under the control of general PID controller (right) and the Robust PID controller (left).

The above figures have shown two advantages of the Robust PID controller: the first one is that when the drone fly to the path turn (in 100s, 125s,150s),this controller can control the drone do a wonderful path following. While the drone that under the general PID controller's control may fly in a big deviation; the second one is that during the sustained interference time (75s-100s), this controller can control the drone fly stable. However, the drone under the general PID controller's control will produce huge shaking.

4. Conclusion

Usually, PID controller can't preciously control the drone fly in high speed, so this paper puts forward a Robust PID controller which has the ability to integral predict the drone's next flight state and do robust calculation. As the Robust PID controller is built based on fourth order Runge-kutta algorithm, it can predict the next flight state vector and let the drone easily reject the extern sustained disturbances.

The performances of this proposed controller are verified in the simulation results. During this simulation part, many uncertainties of AR Drone's parameters in dynamic and kinematic are considered. The results have presented that the ability of prediction can largely reduce the controller's control error, especially when the uncertain disturbance happened and the drone can act on all freedom degrees since controlled under this controller.

This Robust PID controller can let the system quickly achieve the target value, which is very significant in drone's flight control especially in path turns and sustained disturbances environment. In the future, some details of this algorithm will be improved to better control other quadrotors not only AR Drone.

References

1. V. Mistier, a. Benallegue, and N. K. M'Sirdi, *"Exact linearization and noninteracting control of a 4 rotors helicopter via dynamic feedback,"* Proc. - IEEE Int. Work. Robot Hum. Interact. Commun., pp. 586–593, 2001.
2. A. Hernandez, C. Copot, R. De Keyser, T. Vlas, and I. Nascu, *"Identification and path following control of an AR.Drone quadrotor,"*2013 17th Int. Conf. Syst. Theory, Control Comput. ICSTCC 2013; Jt. Conf. SINTES 2013, SACCS 2013, SIMSIS 2013 - Proc., pp. 583–588, 2013.
3. A. Prayitno, V. Indrawati, and G. Utomo, *"Trajectory Tracking of AR.Drone Quadrotor Using Fuzzy Logic Controller,"* TELKOMNIKA (Telecommunication Comput. Electron. Control., vol. 12, no. 4, p. 819, 2014.
4. Yang Shengyi, *"Exploration and Maneuver Control Methods in Unknown Indoor Environment for Agile Aircraft,"* Beijing Institute of Technology, 2015.

CRW: A Method for Identifying Essential Proteins Based on Random Walks

Li-ping YANG[1,2], Song-feng LU[2†] and Cheng ZHANG[1]

[1]College of Informatics, Huazhong Agricultural University, Wuhan 430070, China
[2]College of Computer Science and Technology, Huazhong University of Science and Technology, Wuhan 430074, China
[†]E-mail: teresa@mail.hzau.edu.cn

Current methods for identifying essential proteins based on protein-protein interaction network do not provide sufficient information about the biological functions of proteins. In order to solve this problem, we introduce the use of protein complex information and propose an algorithm named CRW. CRW is based on the random walks model and integrates edge clustering coefficients in protein-protein interaction network in order to predict essential proteins. The experiment results demonstrate that the number of essential proteins identified by CRW exceeds the number identified by the five centrality measure methods.

Keywords: Essential protein; Protein-protein interaction network; Random walks; Protein complex.

1. Introduction

Essential proteins are the necessary proteins for organisms' living and propagating. They play an important part in vital activity. Identifying essential proteins is very important for studying the bioscience and it also has significant application role in treating diseases, designing drugs and so on.

Currently there is research proving that criticality of proteins has close relationship with the centrality of proteins in protein-protein interaction (PPI) network. So, some centrality methods based on the topological characteristics of network are proposed for predicting the essential proteins. For example, Degree Centrality (DC)[1], Betweenness Centrality (BC)[2], Closeness Centrality (CC)[3], Subgraph Centrality (SC)[4], Eigenvector Centrality (EC)[5], and so on. But these centrality methods also have limitation. Because most of the centrality methods seldom analyze inherent biological features, but only score for the proteins making use of their topological characteristics in PPI network. Thus it will influence the accuracy of identifying essential proteins.

Moreover, researchers prove that there is close relationship between the protein complex and the essential proteins. Hart et al.[6] has verified by experiment that essential proteins usually are concentrated in the certain protein complex with special function. Therefore, this paper introduces the protein complex information, and then designs a method named CRW for identifying essential proteins based on random walk model. This method combines the degree of participation in protein complex with its topological characteristics in PPI network, in order to improve its performance of predicting essential proteins. CRW will provide new ideas for identifying essential proteins.

2. Materials and Methods

2.1. *Data sources*

The essential proteins data and PPI data of Saccharomyces cerevisiae is most reliable and complete in all species, so this paper chooses PPI of Saccharomyces cerevisiae as the research subjects. The PPI data of Saccharomyces cerevisiae chosen by our experiment come from the database DIP[11]. There are 5093 proteins and 24743 PPI edges in total. The number of the essential proteins of Saccharomyces cerevisiae is 1285. These essential proteins data is obtained by integrating the criticality information of proteins from the four databases: MIPS, SGD, DEG, SGDP.

2.2. *Random walks model*

The main idea of the random walks model is that a particle traverses a graph with beginning from one or several vertexes. When beginning from any one of vertexes on the graph, the particle random walks to the neighbor vertex of this beginning vertex with the probability p^t. After this time of walk, the probability distribution $p^{t+1}$is obtained. When the next time of random walk, the probability distribution p^{t+1} is assigned to p^t as the input, and the process is iterated and so on. On condition that a certain prerequisite is satisfied, the convergence occurs when p^{t+1} and p^t changes. This moment a stationary probability distribution is obtained.

Based on the random walks model, there are many algorithms to solve the problems such as network nodes sorting, computing the similarity of nodes, specially the famous PageRank algorithm. When identifying the essential proteins and virulence genes, PageRank algorithm is used to score and sort the nodes in PPI network. The proteins with higher score are believed to be essential proteins or virulence genes. This paper improves the traditional PageRank algorithm, and proposes a random walks algorithm named CRW which considers not only protein complex information but also module information in PPI network.

2.3. *Scores of participation degree in complexes*

The protein complexes are blocks of proteins with polymolecule which are composed by interaction at the same time and space. Currently much research already shows that protein complex has close relationship with the essential proteins. So in this paper, when CRW algorithm marks the proteins in PPI network, firstly each protein is given an initial score, i.e. the score of participation degree in complexes.

This paper chooses the excellent MCODE algorithm[8] which was proposed by Bader etc. to find protein complex. The algorithm classifies all the protein nodes into two types, one is protein node inside of complex, the other is protein node outside of complex. The inside degree of complex inner node i is defined to be the number of neighbor nodes which are inside the same complex C with node i. The inside degree of node i which is denoted by $k_{in}(i,C)$, is expressed by the following Eq. (1):

$$k_{in}(i,C) = |E(i,j)|, i, j \in V(C). \tag{1}$$

where $E(i,j)$ represents the edge whose endpoints are node i and node j. $V(C)$ is a set of all the protein nodes in the protein complex C. Because one protein maybe belongs to several different complexes, the participation degree in complexes of the node inside of complexes is defined to be the sum of its inside degrees among all the complexes with respective weight. This weight $w(C_i)$ which is no less than 1, is each complex C_i's value which is evaluated by *MCODE* algorithm. This value is equal to the ratio of the edges of PPI to the protein nodes in the complex C_i. The participation degree in complexes of the node outside of complexes is defined to be the number of its neighbor nodes which are inside of protein complexes[9]. In a summary, the equation of the participation degree in complexes of the protein node I is defined as following:

$$FD(i) = \begin{cases} \sum_{i \in C_i} k_{in}(i, C_i) \times w(C_i), i \in V(|C|) \\ \sum_{j \in V(|C|)} |E(i,j)|, i \notin V(|C|) \end{cases} . \tag{2}$$

where $V(|C|)$ denotes the set of all the protein nodes which form protein complexes. C_i denotes all the protein complexes which include the protein node i. The weight $w(C_i)$ is each complex C_i's value evaluated by *MCODE* algorithm.

2.4. *Edge clustering coefficients*

The concept of the edge clustering coefficients derives from the complex network. The edge clustering coefficient describes the compactness of the relationship between the two nodes of the edge and their neighbor nodes. Hart et al.[6] has discovered that the criticality of one protein has close relationship with the compactness between this protein and its neighbors. So this paper introduces edge clustering coefficients to the PPI network as the weight of each edge for identifying essential proteins.

The edge clustering coefficient is defined as following. The PPI network is considered as an undirected graph$G=(V,E)$.Z_{ij} denotes the number of the triangles which base on *edge*(v_i, v_j). The k_i and k_j denote the degree of the nodes v_i and v_j. The expression $min(k_i-1, k_j-1)$ denotes the possible and maximum number of the triangles which base on *edge*(v_i, v_j). Thus the edge clustering coefficient of *edge*(v_i, v_j) is as following[10]:

$$ECC(i,j)=\frac{Z_{ij}}{\min(k_i-1,k_j-1)}. \tag{3}$$

2.5. *Algorithm CRW*

After the edges in PPI network are weighted by edge clustering coefficients, the incidence matrix of the PPI network can be built to denote the connected relation between the proteins. Here the symbol H is used to denote the $N\times N$ incidence matrix of the graph $G=(V,E)$. The element $h(i, j)$ of this matrix is defined as following[7]:

$$h(i,j)=\begin{cases} Norm_i(ECC(i,j))=\dfrac{ECC(i,j)}{\sum_{w\in Ne(i)} ECC(i,w)}, if \sum_{w\in Ne(i)} ECC(i,w)>0 \\ 0, otherwise \end{cases}. \tag{4}$$

where $Ne(i)$ denotes the set of the neighbors of the node v_i. $Norm_i(ECC(i,j))$ denotes any one edge's clustering coefficient value which has been normalized.

Let $rw(i)$ denote the sorting score of the protein node v_i. The expression $\sum_{j\in Ne(i)} h(i,j)rw(j)$ denotes the derived score of its neighbor node. By means of the random walk model, for the each protein in the PPI network, its sorting score can be calculated as following:

$$rw(i)=(1-\alpha)FD(i)+\alpha\sum_{j\in Ne(i)} h(i,j)rw(j). \tag{5}$$

The sorting score of a protein can be considered to be linear combination of this protein's score of participation degree in complexes and its neighbor's sorting score. The parameter $\alpha(0\leq\alpha<1)$ is used to adjust the proportion of these two scores. Because the number of proteins in the PPI network is so many that the complexity of calculation is too great. Hence this paper rewrites the Eq. (5) to the form of matrix vector, and then rewrites it to the following equation by means of *Jacobi* iteration method:

$$rw^{t+1}=(1-\alpha)FD+\alpha H * rw^{t}. \tag{6}$$

where the vector $rw=(rw(1),\ldots,rw(N))$, the vector $FD=(FD(1),\ldots, FD(N))$, and $t=0,1,2,\ldots$, it denotes the frequency of the iteration.

In summary, the steps of the algorithm CRW is as following:

(1) Calculate each protein's score of participation degree in complexes using the Eq. (2).

(2) Calculate the edge clustering coefficient of each edge in PPI network using the Eq. (3).

(3) Build the matrix H using the Eq. (4).

(4) Initialize the value of rw:rw^0=FD .

(5) Calculate the value of rw^{t-1}using the Eq. (6), and then iterate: $t=t+1$.

(6) Repeat the step (5) until

$$\|rw^t - rw^{t-1}\|_1 \leq \varepsilon$$

whereε is the termination error.

(7) All the proteins are sorted in descending order according to their value of rw.

(8) Output the top K% proteins as the identified essential proteins.

3. Results

3.1. *Evaluation indicators*

In order to evaluate CRW's performance about predicting the essential proteins, in this research the following classical evaluation indicators are utilized to evaluate CRW and the five centrality measures. Specificity (*SP*): it denotes the proportion of the correctly eliminated non-essential proteins. Sensitivity (*SN*): it denotes the proportion of the correctly identified essential proteins. Accuracy (*ACC*): it denotes the proportion of the true results in all the prediction results. Positive Predictive Value (*PPV*): it denotes the proportion of the true essential proteins in the selected proteins. Negative Predictive Value (*NPV*): it denotes the proportion of the correctly predicted non-essential proteins in the eliminated proteins. The equations of the above evaluation indicators are shown below in Eq. (7) to Eq. (11). Among them, *TP* (true positive) represents the quantity of the essential proteins which are correctly predicted as essential proteins. *FN* (false negative) represents the quantity of the essential proteins which are falsely predicted as non-essential proteins. *TN* (true negatives) represents the quantity of the non-essential proteins which are correctly predicted as non-essential proteins. *FP* (false positives) represents the quantity of the non-essential proteins which are falsely predicted as essential proteins[9].

$$SN = \frac{TP}{TP + FN} \,. \tag{7}$$

$$SP = \frac{TN}{TN + FP} \,. \tag{8}$$

$$ACC = \frac{TP + TN}{P + N} \,. \tag{9}$$

$$PPV = \frac{TP}{TP + FP} \,. \tag{10}$$

$$NPV = \frac{TN}{TN + FN} \,. \tag{11}$$

3.2. *Experimental results and analysis*

The centrality measures have become the popular research methods for identifying essential proteins. The *Degree Centrality* (*DC*), *Betweenness Centrality* (*BC*), *Eigenvector Centrality* (*EC*), *Subgraph Centrality* (*SC*) and *Closeness Centrality* (*CC*) are all utilized to predict the essential proteins in biological network. And experiments have proved that these methods are effective. So this paper compares the prediction results of CRW with those of the mentioned above five centrality measures in order to evaluate the prediction performance of CRW, according to the principle "sorting-selecting".

The specific method in the experiment is that sorting the experimental results of CRW and other five centrality measures descending. And then we select the top 1%, 5%, 10% and 15% proteins as the identified essential proteins. Then we compare the number of the true essential proteins in the prediction result of each measure. The experimental results are shown in Fig. 1.

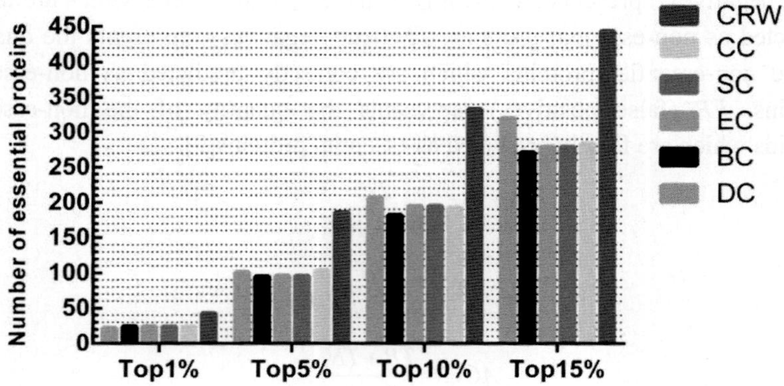

Fig. 1. Comparing CRW with the five centrality measures.

The Fig. 1 shows that the number of the identified essential proteins of CRW is generally more than those of other five centrality measures. At any one of the sample levels (top 1%, top 5%, top 10%, top 15%), the identification hit rate of CRW is higher 20% than those of *BC* and *CC*. The centrality measure *DC* is a widely used identification method. However, CRW is also obviously superior to *DC*. Especially, when selecting the top 1% proteins, the identified essential proteins accuracy of CRW is 1.7 times that of *DC*. When selecting the top 5% and top 10% proteins, CRW's accuracy of identifying essential proteins is respectively higher 34% and 24% than *DC*.

In order to further evaluate CRW's performance about predicting essential proteins, this research also compares CRW with other five centrality measures about the five statistical indicators (SP, SN, etc.). The comparison results are shown in the Table 1.

The Table 1 shows that all the indicator values of CRW are higher than those of other five centrality measures. It proves that CRW possesses better performance about predicting essential proteins.

Table 1. CompareCRW with other five centrality measure on SP, SN, PPV, NPV, ACC.

Identification methods	SP values	SN values	PPV values	NPV values	ACC values
DC	0.812	0.442	0.446	0.814	0.718
BC	0.797	0.387	0.396	0.794	0.695
EC	0.812	0.417	0.428	0.803	0.710
SC	0.810	0.415	0.426	0.802	0.711
CC	0.802	0.387	0.396	0.792	0.697
CRW	0.822	0.468	0.475	0.821	0.733

4. Conclusion

This research introduces protein complex information and proposes the algorithm CRW which is based on random walks model and combines with the edge clustering coefficients in PPI network to identify essential proteins. Comparing with other supervised machine learning methods, CRW doesn't need to know some essential proteins in advance. Comparing with present centrality measures, when CRW identifies essential proteins, it depends on not only protein complex information but also its neighbors' characteristics. The experimental results show that all the numbers of the essential proteins identified by CRW are more than those of centrality measures at any one of the sample levels.CRW also provides researchers with a framework to identify essential proteins combining other biological information with the PPI information. In the current experiment of this research, the parameter α is assigned the constant value 0.5 when the algorithm CRW calculates. However, we find that the sorting scores of proteins may change after the value of α is changed. In the further research, we can assign α various values ranging from 0 to 0.99, and then study how the different values of α influence CRW's accuracy of identifying essential proteins.

Acknowledgments

This work is supported by the Fundamental Research Funds for the Central Universities under Grant No. 2662015QC040.

References

1. M.W. Hahn and A.D. Kern, Mol Biol Evol, vol. 22 (2005), pp. 803-806.
2. M.P. Joy, A. Brock, D.E. Ingber and S. Huang, Journal of Biomedicine and Biotechnology (2005), pp. 96-103.
3. S. Wuchty and P.F. Stadler, Journal of Theoretical Biology, vol. 223 (2003), pp. 45-53.
4. E. Estrada and J.A. Rodriguez, Physical Review E, vol. 71 (2005).
5. P. Bonacich, American journal of sociology, vol. 92, (1987).
6. G.T. Hart, I. Lee and E.M. Marcotte, BMC Bioinformatics, vol. 8 (2007).
7. W. Peng, Research of Protein Network Based on Random Walk Model, PhD thesis, College of Information Science and Engineering, Central South University, (Changsha, China) 2013 (In Chinese).
8. G.D. Bader and C.W. Hogue, BMC Bioinformatics, vol. 4 (2003).
9. M.M. Li, B.C. Qiu, H. Wang and K. Liu, Natural Science Journal of Xiangtan University, vol. 36 (2014) (In Chinese).

10. H. Wang, Identifying Essential Proteins Based on Protein Interaction Networks, Master thesis, College of Information Science and Engineering, Central South University, (Changsha, China) 2011 (In Chinese).
11. I. Xenarios, L. Salwinski, X. J. Duan, P. Higney, S. M. Kim and D. Eisenberg, Nucleic Acids Res, vol. 30 (2002): pp. 303-305.

SD Rat Liver 9-dehydro-17-hydro-andrographolide Concentration Control Based on Calculative Optimization PID

Jian-yang LIN[1*], Jin-rui GAO[2] and Yu-shuai BU[2]

1.Department of Pharmacy, the First Hospital of China Medical University, Shenyang City, 110001, China

2.School of Automobile and Transportation, Shenyang Ligong University, Shenyang City, 110159, China

[*]E-mail address: linjianyangcmu@126.com

In this paper, we use the PID control algorithm based on the calculative optimization method to control the concentration of the 9-dehydro-17-hydro-andrographolide administered to the liver of SD rats. Through data processing and with the assistance of the polynomial fitting function in MATLAB, we obtained a fitting analysis by using the 9-dehydro-17-hydro-andrographolide distribution data in SD rats' liver tissues and achieving a close fitting effect. Based on the fitting function obtained, we can not only design the PID control system and calculate the PID controller parameters that content of the sensitivity index, but also utilize the PID algorithm to attain the effect of the expected model. The mathematical model that we developed is clear and accurate, it can reflect the dynamic changes law of the drug in the body, from which, we can observe and analyzes the input-output curves to draw accurate conclusions. Simulation results demonstrate that the control algorithm has relatively high adaptability and robustness, and we can obtain better control effects.

Keywords: SD rat; Liver tissue distribution; Polynomial fitting; PID control algorithm.

1. Introduction

Andrographolide is extracted from whole leaves of the Andrographis, which is the main ingredient of Xiyanping injection. Andrographolide has a significant curative effect on antipyretic, anti-inflammatory, anti-viral, and it is frequently used for treating acute viral upper respiratory infection, bacterial pneumonia, acute and chronic bronchitis, the therapeutic effect of which is obvious[1,2]. Investigation on the in vitro metabolism rate of Andrographolide, the metabolism rate of the drugs were quite rapid. With the in-depth study of its pharmacological effects and its mechanism, it not only greatly promote the research and development of the new drugs of andrographolides, but also facilitate its clinical application[3,4]. PID controller is a common feedback loops in industrial control applications and consists of proportion element, integral

[*] Corresponding author.

element, differential element. Designing a PID controller appears to be conceptually intuitive, but it can be hard in practice, if a high stability of objective is to be achieved[5,6]. The PID control algorithm based on the method of calculative optimization can improve the control precision, which can make the control law occurred within a reasonable range.

2. Date[7]

Concentration of 9-dehydro-17-hydro-andrographolide in Liver of SD rats after intravenous administration are as following Table 1.

Table 1. The data of drug distribution in liver tissue.

Time(min)	Liver tissue concentration (mean±SD, ng/g)
5	301.94±50.39
10	228.75±34.94
20	156.93±43.77
30	69.82±12.29
40	43.35±10.66
60	27.53±5.76
90	2.77±1.73

3. Acquisition Method about Fitting Function

3.1. *Polynomial fitting method*

In this paper, we fit a function through the polynomial fitting method. According to simulation methods, we give different segments and the precision of the polynomial fitting with different degree[8]. The method of curve fitting problems is that when given a set of data, there exist n points (x_i, y_i) in the plane, which satisfy I = 1, 2,... , n, and to seek a function y = f (x) what makes the f (x) under certain standards with all data points is the most close to the curve fitting of the best.

If you take $\{r_1(x), ..., r_{m+1}(x)\} = \{1, x, ..., x^m\}$, which uses m-order polynomial fitting given data. There are existing the ready-made functions in the Matlab: a=ployfit(x_0, y_0, m).

In this formula, input parameters x_0, $y_0$are data to fitting and m is the times offitting polynomial. Output parameter is a fitting polynomial $y = a_0 + a_1x + a_2x^2 + a_3x^3 + ... + a_mx^m$, which satisfy $a = [a_0, a_1, ..., a_m]$. The following functions y = polyval (a, x) can be used to calculate the polynomial value of y about x.

3.2. *The fitting and obtaining transfer function*

According to settings program, we respectively adopted two, three, four inferior high polynomial to fitting a function. Through comparing, we find that the cubic function has the best effect. The fitting results are shown in Figure 1.

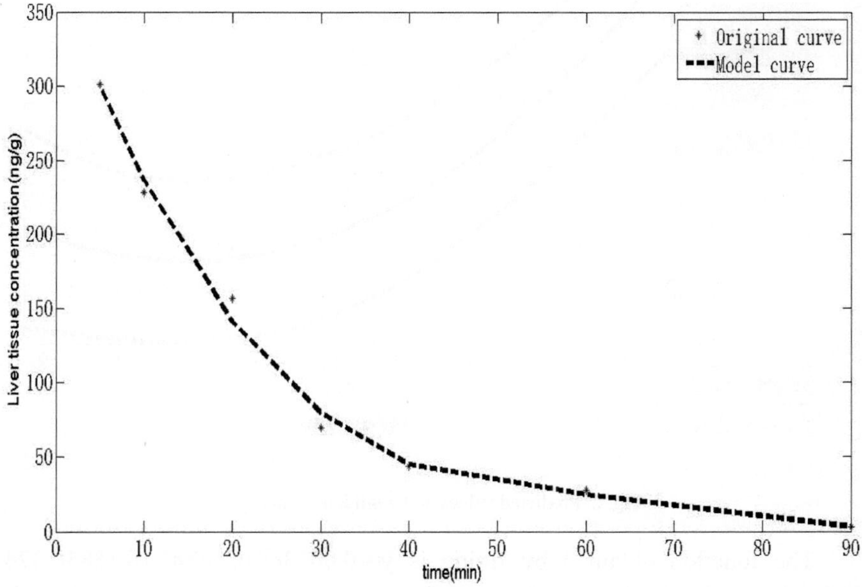

Fig. 1. Polynomial fitting curve.

The expression of cubic function $y = a_1t^3 + a_2t^2 + a_3t + a_4$, which is include the numerical of parameters:

(1) a_1=-0.0013 a_2=0.2490 a_3=-16.1585 a_4=374.9556,

(2) b= 236.7437 -3.2397,

(3) bint = 135.8146 337.6728 -5.4403 -1.0391,

(4) stats = 0.7 14.3 0.0 3983.5.

In other words, the confidence interval of β_0 is [135.8146, 337.6728] and β_1 is [-5.4403, -1.0391], β_0=236.7437, β_1=-3.2397, R^2=0.7, F=14.3, P=0.0000, S^2=3983.5.

The polytool(t, y, 2) can be used to get an interactive screen in Matlab, and the green curve is the fitting curve in the picture. The red line on both sides of the green curve is the confidence interval of y , and we can move the reticle by using the mouse to change the figure t in the graph. The left side of the graph is the predicted value of y and confidence intervals, it is shown in Figure 2.

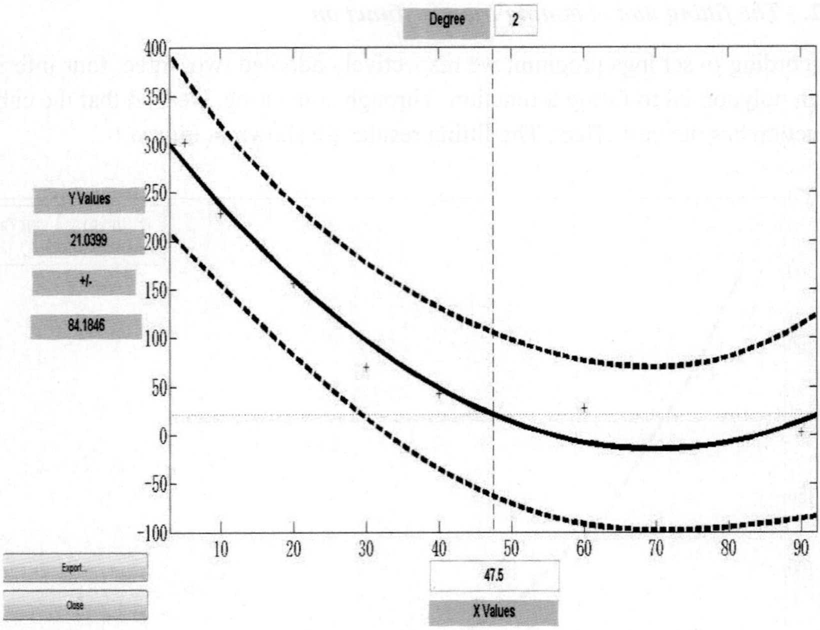

Fig. 2. Predicted values and confidence intervals.

The function obtained by fitting is $y=-0.0013t^3+0.2490t^2-16.1585t+374.9556$. Using Laplace transforming function y(t), we can obtain the transfer function of fitting function, the figure 3 is the run results:

```
>> syms t
>> laplace(-0.0013*t.^3+0.2490*t.^2-16.1585*t+374.9556)

ans =

1649072168398907/(4398046511104*s) - 32317/(2000*s^2) + 249/(500*s^3) - 39/(5000*s^4)
```

Fig. 3. Output the transfer function.

The transfer function can be obtained as formula(1):

$$G(s)=\frac{374.9556}{s}-\frac{16.1585}{s^2}+\frac{249}{500\,s^3}-\frac{39}{5000\,s^4}. \quad (1)$$

4. PID Control System Design

Through controlling the algorithm to design a system what makes it control the transfer function to get a satisfactory outcome. As a classical control method, PID control is widely used in industrial control, and it is the basic guarantee of normal operation of the actual industrial process[9]. The principle block diagram of PID control system is shown in figure 4.

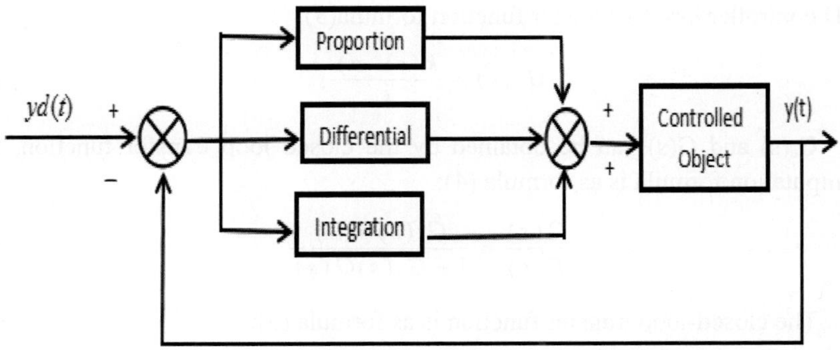

Fig. 4. The principle diagram of the PID control system.

PID control law is as formula (2) (written in the form of transfer function)[10]:

$$G(s) = \frac{U(s)}{E(s)} = k_p(1 + \frac{1}{T_i s} + T_d s). \qquad (2)$$

In this formula(2): T_P for the proportional coefficient, T_i for the integral time constant, T_d for the differential time constant.

Simplicity, robustness, a wide range of applicability and near-optimal performance are some of the reasons that have made PID control so popular in the academic and industry sectors. However, there are still some problems to be solved. The traditional PID control system parameter setting bad will influence the control accuracy[11,12]. In this paper, the PID control algorithm based on the method of calculative optimization can make to improve control precision, make the control law occurred within a reasonable range.

The root locus diagrams of the system are shown in figure 5.

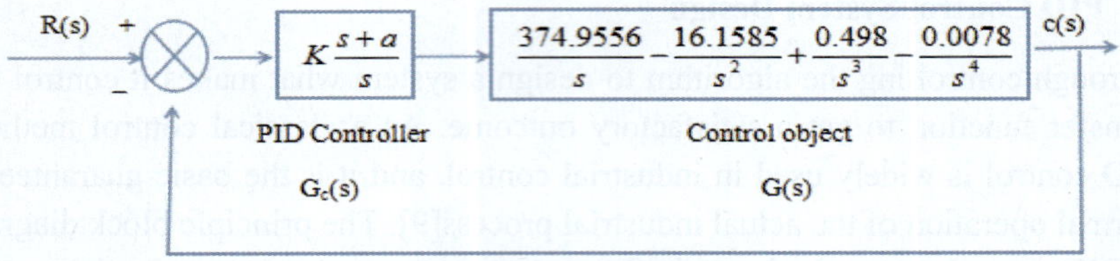

Fig. 5. The root locus diagram of PID control system.

PID controller has the transfer function formula(3):

$$G_c(s) = \frac{k(s+a)}{s}. \tag{3}$$

$G_c(s)$ and $G(s)$ can be obtained by the closed loop transfer function, the computation formula is as formula (4):

$$\frac{C(s)}{R(s)} = \frac{G_c(s)G(s)}{1+G_c(s)G(s)}. \tag{4}$$

The closed-loop transfer function is as formula (5):

$$\frac{C(s)}{R(s)} = \frac{K\left[b_1 s^4 + (ab_1 - b_2)s^3 + (b_3 - ab_2)s^2 + (ab_3 - b_4)s - ab_4\right]}{s^5 + K\left[b_1 s^4 + (ab_1 - b_2)s^3 + (b_3 - ab_2)s^2 + (ab_3 - b_4)s - ab_4\right]}. \tag{5}$$

In this formula, which is include the numerical of parameters: b_1=374.9556, b_2=16.1585, b_3=0.498, b_4=0.0078. We use the PID control algorithm based on the method of calculative optimization, it is obtained the best collection of parameter values to meet the response indicators. In the design process, we need to turn the step is small enough and K value should not be too large. We choose K step length 0.0005 and a step length of 0.05. By writing the MATLAB program[10], we can find out more set of values for K and a. According to requirements of performance indicators, the reasonable value are: K= 0.001, a= 0.5. According to the Step program command in MATLAB, the generated unit step response curve are shown in figure 6.

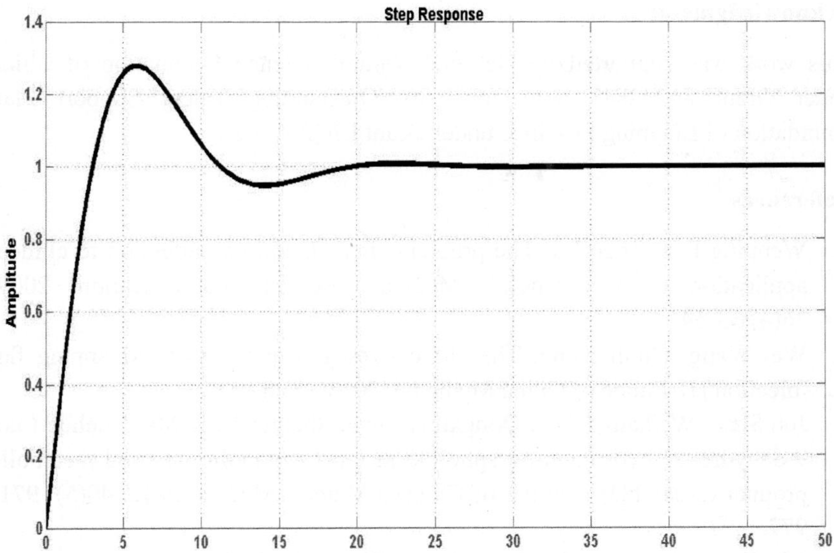

Fig. 6. Unit step response curve.

5. Conclusion

(1) Simulation results show that the PID control algorithm based on the method of calculative optimization have certain robustness and can achieve a good result to the external disturbance and parameter uncertainty. It is an effective control method for the concentration of the 9-dehydro-17-hydro-andrographolidein the liver of SD rats. This shows that the data fitting method is suitable for this drug.

(2) According to the response results, the control law and jitter error occurred within a reasonable range, and has greatly reduced the jitter of the control amount. Data fitting and control have achieved the desired effects, it expresses that the control method is applicable to this drug.

(3) The mathematical model that we made is clear and accurate, it can reflect the dynamic change law of the drug in the body. It is easy to observe and analyze the input-output curves, and it is suitable for the development of new drugs.

(4) This method not only can make the results more accurate, save the SD rats and equipment, but also save the cost. It is also applicable to similar situations, we can estimate the results of tests carried out.

Acknowledgments

This work was supported by National Natural Science Foundation of China under Grant 81302841 and University Outstanding Talent Support Plan Foundation of Liaoning Province under Grant LJQ2014086.

References

1. Wenping Fan, Zhen Lu. The problems that should pay attention to clinical application of xiyanping[J]. Medical research and education, 2009, 26(4):53-54.
2. Wei Wang, Guoli Dong. The clinical research progress of xiyanping flat injection [J]. Guide of China Medicine, 2013(18):87-88.
3. Jun Shao, Weikang Chen, Dongkun Zheng, Shuangcheng Ma, Yuehua Luo. 9-dehydro-17-hydro-andrographolide in vitro metabolic rate and metabolic product research[J]. Journal of Chinese Materia Medica, 2015, 40(5): 971-977.
4. Qiaoli Lv, Guogang Tu, Jiaqi Wang, Shaohua Li. Research progress and clinical application of andrographolide[J]. Journal of nanchang university: medicine, 2013, 53(01): 83-86.
5. KH Ang, G Chong, Y Li. PID control system analysis, design, and technology[J]. Control Systems Technology IEEE Transactions on, 2005, 13(4): 559-576.
6. Michael A. Johnson, Mohammad H.Moradi.PID Control: New Identification and Design Methods-[Book Review][J]. IEEE Control Systems Magazine, 2006, 26(1): 95-97.
7. Lan Chong. Effective ingredients in xiyanping injection in rats in vivo pharmacokinetics and tissue distribution study [D]. Nanchang: Nanchang University College of Pharmacy, 2013:1-30.
8. Jianqiang Wang, Jiancheng Li, Guoqiang Zhao, etc. Polynomial fitting fast calculating gravity disturbance method[J]. Geodesy and geodynamics, 2013, 4(4):52-55.
9. Yiqing Huang. The PID controller parameter setting and its application research [D]. Anhui: Anhui university of science and technology, 2009: 1-3.
10. Boying Lu, Mingan Tong. Modern control engineering [M]. Beijing: electronic industry press, 2011: 431-447.

11. Shuyun Qiao, Yueming Dai. Mine hoist speed regulation system of the PID controller parameters optimization[J]. Mining Machinery, 2014, 12 (12): 146-148.
12. P. Cominos, N. Munro. PID controllers: recent tuning methods and design to specification.IEE Proceedings - Control Theory and Applications,2002, 149(1): 46-53.

Study on Evaluation Model of Internet Social Networking Applications Based on Humanology Research

Guang-hui SHI[1,2,*] and San-yuan ZHANG [1]
[1]*Computer Science Institute, Zhejiang University,*
[2]*Zhejiang Wanli University*
[1]*Hangzhou, 310027, China*
[2]*Ningbo, 315100, China*
[*]*E-mail: netsgh@163.com*

This paper discusses the evaluation method of mobile internet social apps through a humanist perspective. We analyzed classic humanlogy theories such as Marxist practical human thought and demand theory, Freud's sub consciousness theory, Sartre's freedom to pursue ideas, Fromm's interpersonal and social demand, Marcuse creative lust theory and Maslow's hierarchy of needs in the growth of the existing research achievements, etc. By integrating the interaction design theory with related digital art design theory, we carried out a series of experiments to explore this new evaluation method for social applications. Research conducted in this paper based on the study of Social applications DPCF (Demand Production Consume Feeling) model and the SFT (Social Feeling Tools) Social application evaluation model, provides new methods to optimize the design of social applications.

Keywords: Social Apps; Evaluation model; Interactive design.

1. Introduction

With the arrival of the mobile Internet Era, Interactive design needs to solve many new problems, including design issues, market issues, product evaluation, and so on. In this paper, we mainly discuss the product evaluation problem of mobile social applications, proposed a theory of SFT evaluation model based on humanology learning. We try to verify the validity and effectiveness of the model by comparing the experiments.

Mobile communication and Internet has become the fastest growing, the most attractive prospects of two fields in the world today. The market potential is also the biggest. As of April 2014, China mobile's population has exceeded

848 million[12]. The mobile Internet user population has reached 500 million, This data is more than eighty percent of the total number of Internet users. Mobile phones became the first Internet terminals equipment. China mobile Internet development into an era of universal.

Mobile Internet includes three parts, respectively Mobile Terminals, Software, and Application. The mobile terminal is referring to the mobile Phone, tablet, etc., software refers to the operating system (IOS, Android, Windows mobile, Symbian, etc.), database, and security software, Application refers to Apps such as Tools Apps, Entertainment Apps, Reading Apps. In this paper, we study the social application belongs to the category of mobile Internet applications. In the PC era, the Internet field of interaction design, designers and developers have made a consistent view in three aspects including Utility, Usability and Pleasurablity. As we entered the mobile Internet era, interactive scene changed, Interaction design in terms of ease of use and usefulness of research need to be rethinking.

The advent of the Mobile Internet Era also means that the digital survival become an integral part of life, it essentially changed people's quality of life and lifestyle, people's survival state changed to digital survial from the simple real survival. Digital survival is essentially the virtualization of social relations in reality. It reflects the real life, people and society, man and nature, all kinds of relations between people. In digital survival environment[1], people exhibited more purely spiritual needs and spiritual pursuit, reflects the human research should have reached level. Social applications are the main scene of virtual survival, better social application design will not only affect the user experience, and even affect the person's survival and development. Application based on the study of social evaluation model can help designers and developers to evaluate social applications of validity, intuitive evaluation "Humanology Experience Level" of products, provides the Humanology Angle of view for product design and development for social application.

2. Design Survey Questionnaire

We begin with comb common problems in the research of humanology and mature conclusion, We integrated the theory of classic Marxist humanology, Freud, Sartre, Frome, Marcuse representative humanology theory, From the results of their study especially selected research element of demand theory as observation points in the design of the questionnaire. In addition, we integrated the experience of Emotional Design[2] and User-centered Design, Starting from the Cognitive theory of Interaction Design, Social network Model, such as research foundation, to extract the common characteristic and humanology research can docking elements as the observation point. Questionnaire designed a total of 79 items in question, contain True-False questions, Single or Multiple choice questions, Subjective questions, etc. We chose China Ningbo city, Zhejiang province arts undergraduate, ranging in age from 20 to 23 between college students as the object of investigation. Survey form to fill out a form is given priority to, face to face interview questions and answers, sampling operation experience is complementary.

2.1. *DPCF questionnaire model*

According to the theory research results of Humanology and Research approaches, we put the research questions designed to Measure Dimension Model (Figure 1).

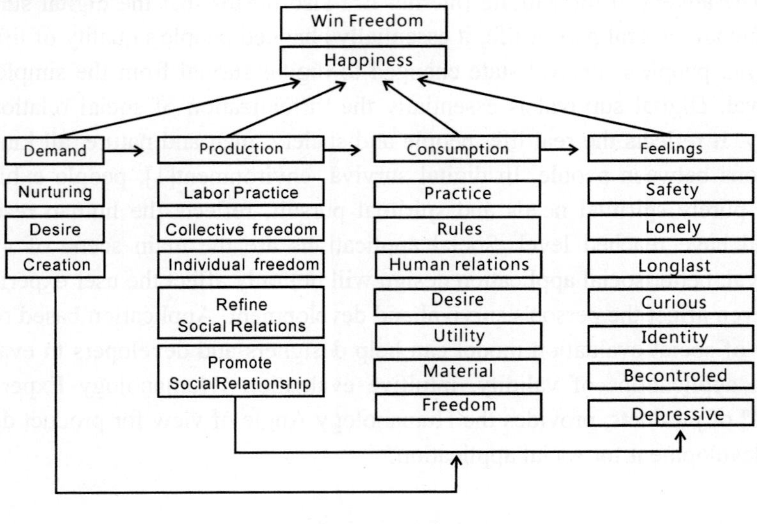

Fig. 1. DPCD questionnaire model.

We divide the content and aim of Humanology research for four categories : Demand, Production, Consumption and Feeling. Among them, the requirements types were divided into Desire (the subconscious mind, consciousness, sex, lust), Nurturing, Creative needs three levels, These three levels do not distinguish between high and low depth. Production types including five levels of production behavior, they are Labor practices (spiritual practice) virtual world, Collective freedom, Individual freedom, Refine social relations, and Promote harmonious social relations, etc. Consumption categories are divided into Consumer freedom, Happiness, Rules of consumption, Consumption ethics, Consumption desire, Consumption utility, Consumption material the seven sub category. Feeling class contains seven sub categories, they are Security, Lasting sense of loneliness, Depression, Anxiety, Identity and The sense of control, etc. All the observation point index finally pointing in the direction of development is the ultimate goal -Happiness and to Win freedom.

DPCF is Demand, Production, Consume, Feeling the abbreviation of four words the first letters. Observation points are divided into four stages include demand, production, consumption and the feelings. Demand phase mainly according to "the physical demand, natural demand"[3] theory put forward by Marx, "people of the original impulse, instincts, acquired the desire"[4] theory proposed by Freud and "Lust"[5] theory proposed by Marcuse.

Marxist humanology believes that "the history of the objective conditions constraints of people's thinking and behavior, so people have demand of liberation by creating activities[6] ", Freud's "seeking" and "displacement" and "sublimation" theory also can be classified as Creation. Create demand also include Sartre "of existence[7]", Fromm's "man does not dare the has been in a passive state[8]", Marcuse "the liberation of eros" theory. "Ehics, Social rule" theory[9] by Confucian, "Strictly avoid excessive faculties stimulation and vent, dispense with the temptation of external monogatari[10]" put forward by The Taoist were classified as Nurturing demand.

The concept of "Production" here is generalized, include Sent message, Post an image on Mobile Social Network etc. The activity of create new content is defined as Labor Practice. "Collective Freedom" means people response the social group of organizers, engaged in the activities of social network, create benefit for some parties, class and the collective. In order to relief, vent, transfers own some negative emotions of social network activity is defined as "Individual Freedom". Behavior of develop interpersonal relationships is defined as "Refine Social Relations". Behavior of Improve interpersonal relationship is defined as "Promote Social Relations".

The concept of "Consumption" here is active behavior make "Production" value. "Like", "Good" and "Share" on Mobile Social Network are defined as Consumption Behaviors. Obey the laws, Civilization, Ethical behavior is defined as "Human relations". "Echo response others negative emotions, Lust, Obedience," such as behavior is defined as "Desire". Engage in profitable as a starting point of social relations activity is defined as "Utility"; Engaged in shopping, electric business, advertising and other promotion activities is defined as "Material"; Such as diving, browse the activities defined as "Freedom".

“Feeling” in this model mainly include Sense of security, loneliness and lasting, anxiety, depression and identity and the sense of control. The sense of happiness and satisfaction are subdivided as observation point of view with other positive and negative emotions.

In this system, the ultimate goal of social activities is to achieve freedom, If you do not have the freedom to experience, but also often accompanied by the pursuit of self perfection. From the demand to the feelings are not necessarily experienced two stages of Production and Consumption, can also from the Demand --Production, Feeling, or from the Demand Consumption -- Feeling. Actually people's Mobile Social Network life is usually complete from the Demand (Production and Consumption of staggered together) -- Feelings in the process.

2.2. *Analysis of DPCF questionnaire survey results*

Research suggests that respondents have seen the offline social activity and online social activity as a whole, People tend to choose Social Acquaintances, Strangers Social exhibit two characteristics including a small number of friends, with low frequency. People tend to choose Voice Communication, but at the same time think that the Text Communication is more efficient. Respondents, mostly using relatively fixed Social Applications, the number of about 1-3 and application of these is used by most of the social circle. Social objects have obvious problems in the generation gap. In social behavior, more people choose to Chat, browse circle of friends to kill time, relax, only about 25% of the people will release information, widen your circle of friends, curiosity or seek help. In the Circle of Friends, respondents by praise, love, comments and other interactive way to maintain social relations. In social applications only a few people will often publish information. People although hope to meet Frank treat friends in social networking applications, but close to half of the respondents Will not show the true self in the virtual society. Nevertheless, 20-40% of the respondents still get a sense of happiness, satisfaction and a sense of security from the social network. The negative effects of design applications are much lower than the positive effects. Social networking applications has become one of the main scene to carry out social activities, more than half of the respondents will be online 1-3 hours for different levels of social activities every day. Respondents have obvious antipathy towards the advertising, social application level charges, the electricity supplier shopping, privacy collection and other content. Although there are half like subscription information, but lower the frequency of use. In terms of payment function of the social applications, envelopes, transfers, taxi become three popular features.

After statistical analysis, we found that: first, most people use the social networking applications to kill time and relax, and it is used to chase the satisfaction of self desire. Second, social applications did not become a tool for most people to active create content, more and more people pursuit of free experience through diving, browsing activity. Third, social applications provides interactive way, such as allowing users to take the initiative by commenting, "praise" way to maintain and promote social relationships. Fourth, social applications are more likely to stimulate utilitarian social behavior, to stimulate red envelopes, consumption and other material pursuits. Fifth, although social applications had not been able to satisfy most people a sense of happiness, satisfaction, the pursuit of a sense of security, but happy is it has not brought more negative influence.

3. SFT Social Application Evaluation Model

According to DPCF Questionnaire Model, we proposed SFT (Social Feeling Tools) social application evaluation model (Figure 2).

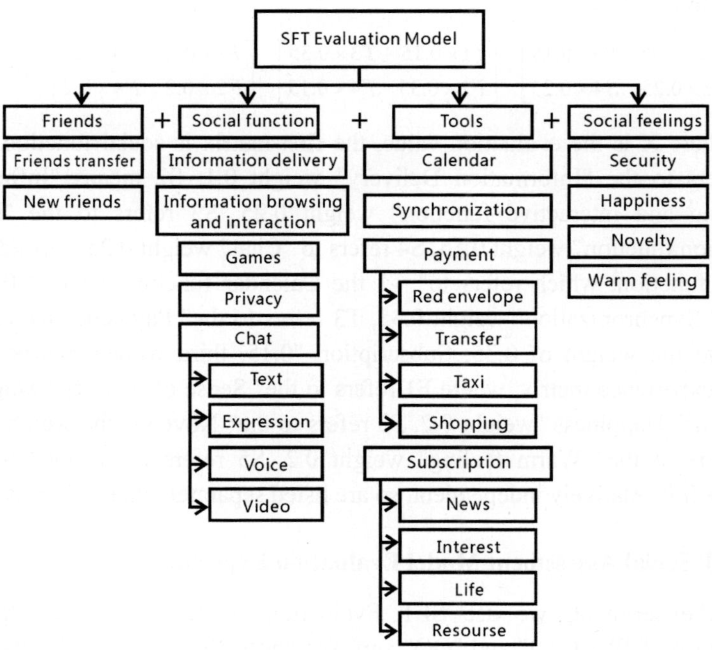

Fig. 2. SFT evaluation model.

Social evaluation model could be divided into "Friends", "Social function" (100 points), "Tools" (100 points), Social feelings "(100 points) four main evaluation factors, The "Social function" is divided into "Information delivery", "Information browsing and interaction", "Games", "Privacy", "Chat" five indicators. Chat feature is subdivided into "Text", "Expression", "Voice", "Video" four second level indicators. The tool is divided into "Calendar", "Synchronization", "Payment", "Subscription" four indicators, Payment function is divided into " Red envelope ", "Transfer", "Taxi", "Shopping" two level indicators; The subscription function is divided into "News", "Interest", "Life" and "Resources subscribe" two level indicators. Social feelings are divided into "Security", "Happiness", "Novelty", "Warm feeling" four indicators. According to DPCF survey of the corresponding statistical data, we designed the weight of each level indicators. Design weights to proportion in the total score of an important indicator of the level of control in the reasonable scope, reduce the impact of non important index to the total score. In order to make the parameter setting more reasonable, we use the cross analysis method for DPCF data analysis.

SFT social application evaluation model can be expressed as a matrix expression:

$$X = \begin{bmatrix} S1\times 0.1 & S3\times 0.15 \\ S2\times 0.25 & S4\times 0.25 \end{bmatrix} + \begin{bmatrix} T1\times 0.15 & T3\times 0.35 \\ T2\times 0.35 & T4\times 0.15 \end{bmatrix} + \begin{bmatrix} F1\times 0.2 & F3\times 0.4 \\ F2\times 0.2 & F4\times 0.2 \end{bmatrix} + S5\times 0.25$$

Where X is the evaluation value, the first matrix is social function, which S1 refers to the "Information Delivery" weight 0.1, S2 means "Information browsing and interactive function" weight 0.25, S3 refers to the "Privacy protection function" weight 0.15, S4 refers to "Chat" weight 0.25. second matrix is tool function, which refers to" T1 the Calendar function "weight 0.15, T2 means" Synchronization "weight 0.35, T3 refers to the" Payment function "T4" refers to the weight of 0.35, Subscription "0.15. third weight matrix for the Social experience matrix, where F1 refers to the" Sense of security "weight 0.2, F2 means" Happiness "weight 0.2, F3 refers to the" Novelty "the weight of 0.4, F4 refers to the" Warm feeling" weight 0.2. S5 refers to "Game" function, because it is relatively independent, so are listed separately, the weight is 0.25.

4. SFT Social Assessment Model Evaluation Experiment

In this experiment, we use SFT Evaluation Model to evaluate the user experience of "We Chat" and "QQ" app. We chose about 40 participants to take part in the experiment. First, we use SFT model to design the corresponding satisfaction questionnaire. Then, we put statistical data set into the matrix formula. At last we obtain the following results.

"We Chat" user satisfaction survey results are as follows. The first matrix value S1=73.69, S2=73.68, S3=36.84, S4=77.63; the second matrix value T1=18.42, T2=39.47, T3=48.42, T4=52.10; the third matrix value F1=55.27, F2=50, F3=55.27, F4=52.63. Finally S5=36.84. We put the data into the statistical formula evaluation results:

$$X=\begin{bmatrix}7.369 & 5.526\\ 18.42 & 19.40\end{bmatrix}+\begin{bmatrix}2.763 & 16.947\\ 13.815 & 7.815\end{bmatrix}+\begin{bmatrix}11.054 & 22.108\\ 10 & 10.526\end{bmatrix}+9.21$$

In QQ evaluation, the first matrix valued S1=52.63, S2=47.37, S3=39.47, S4=63.419; the second matrix value T1=21.05, T2=44.73, T3=18.683, T4=28.945; the third matrix value F1=26.31, F2=36.85, F3=26.31, F4=39.47. Finally S5=55.27. We put the above statistical parameters into the formula that QQ application assessment results:

$$X=\begin{bmatrix}5.263 & 5.921\\ 11.843 & 15.854\end{bmatrix}+\begin{bmatrix}3.158 & 6.539\\ 15.656 & 4.342\end{bmatrix}+\begin{bmatrix}5.262 & 10.524\\ 7.37 & 7.894\end{bmatrix}+13.817$$

By contrast, we can find that: Although the We Chat and QQ app is from the same company, they have hundreds of millions of users, but the We Chat has 9 wins in 13 indicators, QQ has four wins, including S3, T1, T2, S5. Payment function is the lowest evaluation function in QQ app, Calendar function is the lowest evaluation function in We Chat app. In general, QQ can bring the user's sense of security, well-being, novelty and warm feeling below We Chat app more than 20%.

In the interview on groups of respondents, many users of QQ poor rating and dissatisfaction, specific problems and discontent, degree of dissatisfaction are in the survey data in one has been verified, social application experience differences and differences in the extent of from SFT evaluation model has been verified.

5. Conclusion

Social applications are important entrances to the people engaged in social activities. In recent years, mobile Internet social networking applications are emerging in an endless stream, but the quality is quite different from that of. Social application user experience evaluation method is not mature. Traditional black box testing and white box testing method are error correcting code based testing methods. Risk based testing emphasizes the software error problem. And based on the testing method for the model have been gradually recognized. This method can test and design of the software at the same time, the change in software engineering now programming and testing later "way of working[11].

This paper mainly discussed the design of SFT social assessment model. We use the model to complete the QQ app and We Chat app comparative evaluation experiment. Results showed that the application of We Chat more in line with humanology theory and the theory of human needs, so it more popular with the users than QQ app. The validity and reliability of the SFT model were verified by the evaluation experiment. SFT social application evaluation model can be used to carry on the evaluation of social applications, can also be used to improve the design and development of social networking applications. Evaluation of the test effect is obvious, clear hierarchy. The research provides a convenient and effective way for the design and development of social applications.

Acknowledgments

This work is supported by NSFC (No. 61272304). This work is supported by NSFC (No. 61272304). Work partially supported by Ningbo Leading Academic Discipline Project, Project Number: SZ23000580.

References

1. Nicholas Negroponte, *Being Digital,* (Hainan Press, 1997).
2. DONALD. A. NORMAN, *Emotional Design*, (Electronics Industry Publishing House, 2005).
3. Karl Heinrich Marx, Karl Heinrich Marx, *Marx Engels Anthology (second volumes)*, (People's Publishing house, 1995).
4. Sun Shuqiao, Freud's psychoanalytic philosophical implication. Master's thesis, Guangxi Normal University (2007).
5. Hou Zhimei, from the "repression and liberation of Eros" to see Marcuse's humanology, Master's thesis, Shanxi University (2010).
6. Liu Weican, Study on the change of Marx human study, Master's thesis, Hunan Normal University (2014).
7. Yu Tao, Suddenly human carnival -- Interpretations of the people of Marxist Existentialism, Master's thesis, South University of Science and Technology of China (2012).
8. Fromm, *Perfect society*, (International Culture Publishing House, 1999).

9. Chen Ling, Kong Zi's thought research, Master thesis, Sichuan University (2006).
10. Liu Xinli, Lao Tzu thought and its contemporary value, Master's thesis, Zhengzhou University (2004).
11. Qian Zhongsheng, Model-based Appoaches to Generating Test Cases for Web Applications, PhD thesis, Shanghai University, (SH, China, 2008).
12. Data from the Institute of RENMIN Website, "China Mobile Internet development report (2014)" Blue Book.

An Occlusion Method for Approximate Global Illumination

Hua LI* and Hua-min YANG

Department of Computer Science and Technology,
Changchun University of Science and Technology ,
Changchun, 130022, China
**E-mail: lihua@cust.edu.cn*

In this paper, we propose an approximate method for global illumination. We build an occluded estimator based on an algorithm of parallel line sweep for shadow maps. The virtual point lights are classified and a method is proposed to generate irradiance estimator (IE) by azimuthally analysis of normal. For each pixel rendering, we sample the IE around the pixel to fast approximate the percentage of irradiance to the point in the scene. The experiments demonstrate that our algorithm is an effective method of approximate global illumination.

Keywords: Rendering; Global illumination; Reflective shadow maps; Ambient occlusion.

1. Introduction

Global illumination computing is a fundamentally difficult task. It requires solutions to the integral equations that recursively expresses the radiance leaving a surface as a function of the radiance leaving other surfaces. Lots of methods are presented to approximate the global illumination effect. Ambient occlusion (AO)is one of the lighting models that coarse approximates the global illumination from ambient lighting based on its direct visible occluders. In this paper, we present a novel method to compute indirect illumination based on the idea of reflective shadow map using a irradiance estimator. We borrow some ideas from horizon-based ambient occlusion algorithm[1] to generate the irradiance estimator by parallel sweep the virtual point light sources(VPLs).

2. Related Work

Ambient occlusion (AO) has been used in films as an alternative to full-scale global illumination methods. It gives a unique edge by a crude and a simple approximation of global illumination with a significant increase in quality. AO can be seen as an diffuse illumination without directional effect while in indoor environments[2][3]. In outdoor environments AO is done by estimating the amount of visible sky for each point. AO can be rendered with ray tracing by casting rays from the point p and testing the intersections, while the performance is low. A variety of techniques are used to approximate the effects. A multi-pass algorithm was presented to separate the ambient occlusion problem into detailed ambient occlusion with high-frequency and distant ambient occlusion domains with low-frequency[4]. Horizon-based ambient occlusion[1] (HBAO) split the unit sphere by a horizon line defined by the signed horizon angle $h(\theta)$ and found the horizon angle in each direction θ. Height field line sweep[5] methods solve obscruance in discrete azimuthal directions by performing line sweeps across the depth buffer in each direction. Screen-Space Far-Field ambient obscurance[6] generated an intermediate representation of the depth field and samples the points to generate local peaks of the geometry from the point of view of the receiver. Reflective shadow map is another method to approximate global illumination based on Instance Radiosity(IR). This algorithm sampled the points from shadow maps as virtual point lights source to fast compute indirect illumination[7]. These algorithms compute the approximation global illumination from different point of view. Our method borrows the ideas from them to take the shadow map as a height field and computes each point's horizon angle to construct a lighting estimator and compute the final lighting of pixels by an estimator within the sampling sphere.

3. Approximate Global Illumination

3.1. *Line sweep shadow map*

All the texel stored in the shadow map determines the indirect illumination. Our method analysis the normal from N directions, and computes the irradiance using an attenuation coefficient K . In Fig.1, (a) shows the line sweeping on the shadow map with 4 directions along horizontal and vertical dirtection and (b) shows 8 directions adding the diagonal. Our approach sweeps the shadow map in a dense set of parallel lines. The parallel lines are spaced one texel width apart. The lines are traversed one texel width step at one time.

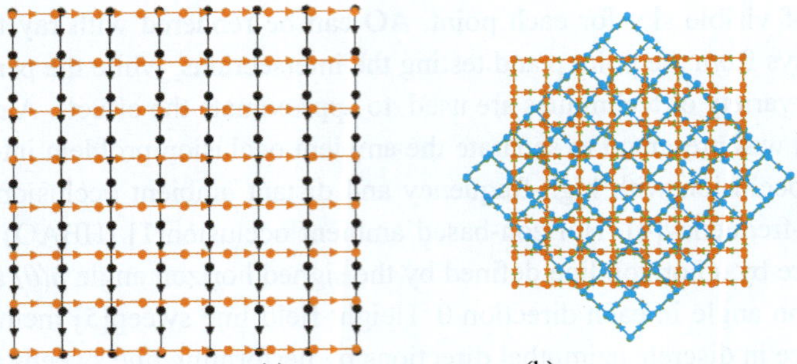

(a) (b)

Fig. 1. Sweep direction with shadow map (a) N=4,(b) N=8.

3.1.1. *Normal analysis*

We generate the IE like a reflective shadow map (RSM). Normal buffer, world space position buffer and flux buffer are needed. For each line sweep direction, our method accumulates the virtual point lights those have the same normal direction along the sweep line and stores it in a lighting estimator map (LEMap). We category the normal into three types by the analysis of horizon angles: has contributions to the indirect illumination, no contributions and undetermined. VPLs will has contributions for the irradiance when the horizon angle is less than 90 degree along the sweep line direction. Otherwise no contributions. We define the flux emitted into direction ω as equation (1)

$$I_{P(\omega)} = \Phi \max\{0, \langle N_i | \omega \rangle\}. \quad (1)$$

where ⟨|⟩is the dot product, N_i is the surface normal , Fig.2 (a)shows normal on one sweep line and different types of normal classified by our method, where ω_1 is less than 90 degree and has contribution to the corresponding sweep direction. The irradiance at a surface point x with normal n is due to the accumulation of radiant intensity emitted into direction of sweep line. We store these corresponding texel information to generate each IE line. Light estimator are enforced by sample the valuable VPLs at the corresponding directions. For the undetermined normal, we estimate them within a sphere space in 3.2.

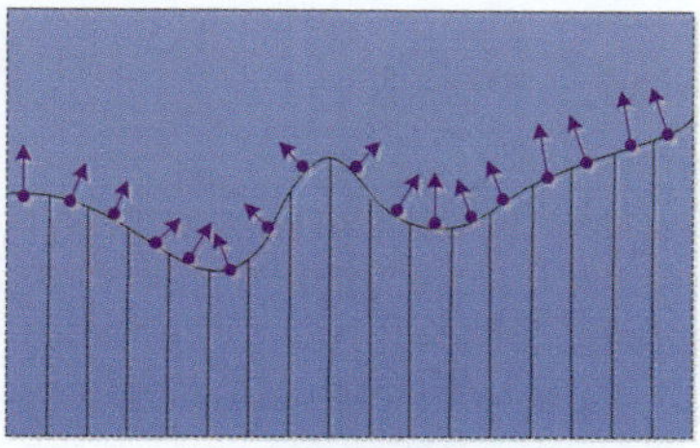

(a) (b)

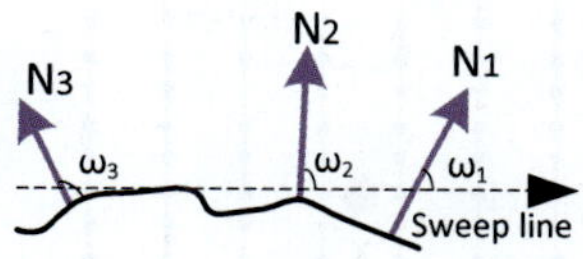

Fig. 2. (a) Normal on one sweep line (b) three types of normal vector.

3.2. *Irradiance estimator*

The ambient occlusion $A_{\bar{p}}$ at a point $\bar{p}$ can be computed by equation (2):

$$A_{\bar{p}} = \frac{1}{\pi}\int_{\Omega} V_{\bar{p},\omega}(\hat{n},\hat{\omega})d\omega \qquad (2)$$

where $\hat{n}$ is the surface normal and $V_{\bar{p},\hat{\omega}}$ is the visibility function at $\bar{p}$. If $\bar{p}$ is occluded in the direction $\hat{\omega}$, then $V_{\bar{p},\hat{\omega}}$ is zero, otherwise is one. Integration variable $\hat{\omega}$ is integrated by an infinitesimal solid angle $d\omega$.

We generate the lighting estimator by computing the irradiance at a surface point x by equation(3) , which is the summing up of illumination due to all pixel lights from a sphere sample space.

$$E_p(x,n) = \sum_{pixelsp} I'_{P(\omega)} \frac{1}{\pi}\int_{\Omega} V_{\bar{p},\hat{\omega}}(\hat{n},\hat{\omega})d\omega \qquad (3)$$

where $I'_{P(\omega)} = K \cdot \Phi\max\{0, \langle N_i|\omega\rangle\}$, K is attenuation coefficient. As shown in Fig. 3. The sample range is restricted by a sphere space from 8 directions within radius of R.

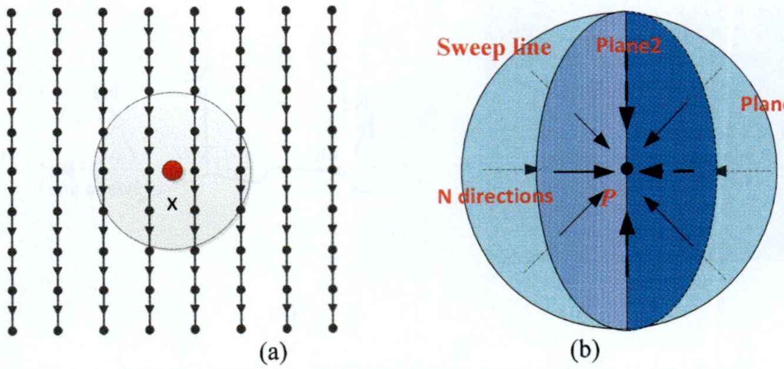

Fig. 3. (a) is one sweep direction on one plane. (b) is 8 sweep direction on one plane and lighting estimator from the sphere sample space.

4. Generation

We implemented our method with CUDA and G3D. An IE was generated just like a reflective shadow map with multiple render targets: depth values dp was stored in a depth buffer, normal N was stored in a normal buffer and world space position xp was stored in a world space position buffer. Also we need a buffer to store the reflected flux of lighting estimation.

Our experiment does not consider occlusion for indirect illumination. All the VPLs those have contributions to the sample point will be gathered by the irradiance estimator from 8 directions within radius of R. Fig. 4 shows a spot light illuminates cubes from the upper, where sample radius of R is 5 and 10 respectively. Early z-culling techniques are used to avoid the recomputation of all pixels. Fig. 6 shows sun illuminates of spheres from the upper, where sample direction of sweep line is 4 and 8 respectively. All timings were captured using a GeForce Quadro K5000.

Fig. 4. Fast approximation global illumination using our method. (a) screen quads is 32×32 with sweep line of 4.(b) screen quads is 32×32 with sweep line of 8. (c)screen quads is 16×16 with sweep line of 8. (d) screen quads is 16×16 with sweep line of 4.(d) screen quads is 16×16 with sweep line of 8.

Fig. 5 shows the indirect illumination by different sample radius of R. The effect of indirect illumination of (a) is brighter than (b) with a greater generated radius. Fig. 6. shows the visualization of raw ambient occluder buffer and the result buffer with resolution of 1408 × 848. We also compare the effect of reflective shadow map(a) and our method(b) as shown in Fig. 7, where the resolution of shadow map is 512×512. Our method is visually acceptable and more faster than RSM method.

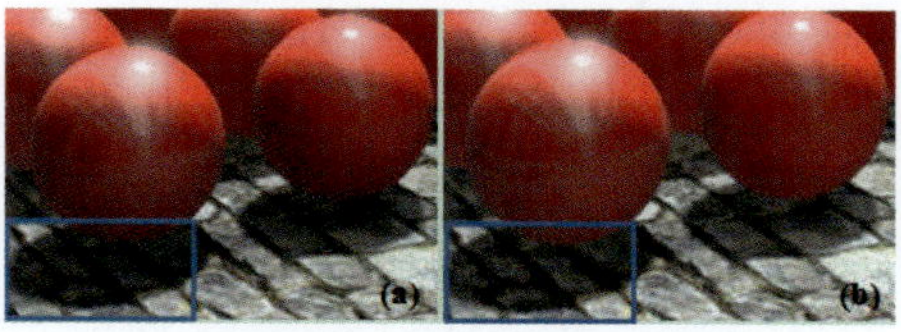

Fig. 5. Comparison of Indirect illumination by different sample radius of R. (a). R= 5 and (b). R= 10.

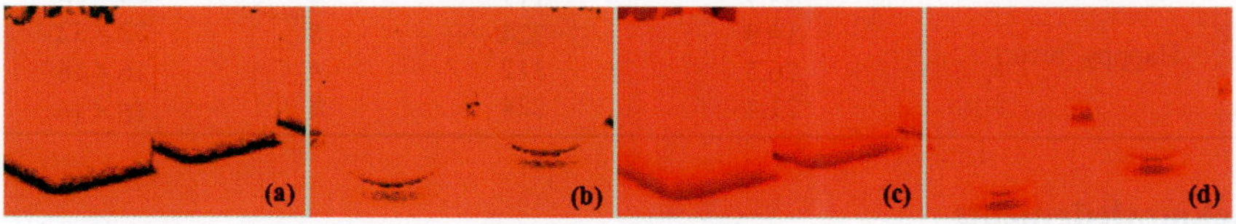

Fig. 6. Visualization of buffer(a) and (b) is raw ambient occluder buffer, (c) and (d) is the result buffer with resolution of 1408*848.

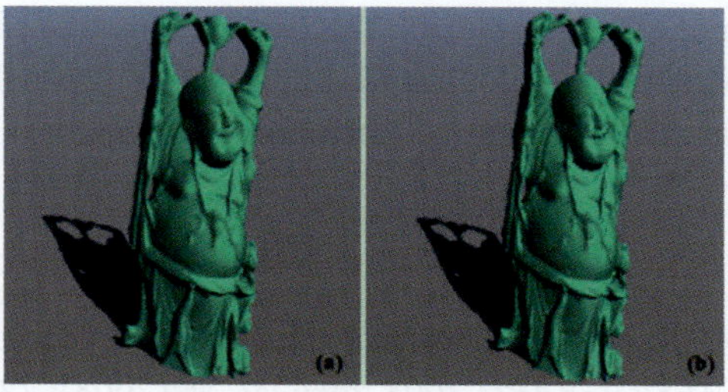

Fig. 7. Global illumination using reflective shadow map and ours. (a) RSM (b) LEMap.

5. Conclusion

Our irradiance estimator is a fast approximation way to simulate the indirect illumination, which is built upon the directional sweeping of the shadow map to classify the normal and real world position. Experiments show that our method is a method for approximate global illumination at interactive frame rate.

Table 1. Frame rate at a resolution of 512×512 with lighting estimated by different number of sweep lines.

Scene	Fps	Samples	Sweep line	Screen quads
Cube	33.4	112	4	32×32
	30.3	224	8	32×32
	37.6	112	4	16×16
	34.2	224	8	16×16
Sphere	33.5	112	4	32×32
	29.9	224	8	32×32
	36.5	112	4	16×16
	32.3	224	8	16×16
Happpy_recon	23.7	112	4	32×32
	19.9	224	8	32×32
	26.5	112	4	16×16
	21.4	224	8	16×16

Acknowledgments

This work was financially supported by development project of Jilin province science and technology (20140204009GX) and major scientific and technological plan of Changchun City(14KG008). This work is supported by the Special Effects Movie Technique and Equipment National and Local Joint Engineering Research Center, Changchun University of Science and Technology.

References

1. L. Bavoil, M. Sainz, R. Dimitrov, Image-space horizon-based ambient occlusion, *ACM SIGGRAPH 2008 talks. ACM*, (2008): 22.
2. H. Landis, Production-ready global illumination. Siggraph course notes, (2002), 6: pp. 11.
3. P.H. Christensen, Global illumination and all that, In ACM SIGGRAPH Course (2003), 9: pp. 31-72.
4. P.Shanmugam, O.Arikan, Hardware accelerated ambient occlusion techniques on GPUs, *Proceedings of the 2007 symposium on Interactive 3D graphics and games. ACM*, (2007), pp. 73-80.
5. V. Timonen, Line‐Sweep Ambient Obscurance, *Computer Graphics Forum. Blackwell Publishing Ltd*, Volume 32, Issue 4 (2013), pp. 97-105.
6. V. Timonen, Screen-space far-field ambient obscurance,*Proceedings of the 5th High-Performance Graphics Conference. ACM*, (2013), pp. 33-43.
7. C.Dachsbacher, M. Stamminger, Reflective shadow maps. *In Symposium on Interactive 3D Graphics* (2005), pp. 203–231.

Author Index